The Study Plan gives students personalized recommendations, practice opportunities, and **learning aids** to help them stay on track.

Video Exercises are available for select chapter topics to help engage students and hold them accountable for their learning.

"The simulations because they require thought process, the activity is fun and gets me engaged into the process and has real scenarios."
— Business Communication Student, Paul Luu, San Bernardino Valley College

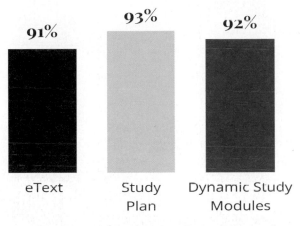

91% eText
93% Study Plan
92% Dynamic Study Modules

% of students who found learning aids helpful

Dynamic Study Modules use the latest developments in cognitive science and help students study chapter topics by adapting to their performance in real time.

Pearson eText enhances student learning with engaging and interactive lecture and example videos that bring learning to life.

The **Gradebook** offers an easy way for you and your students to see their performance in your course.

85% of students would tell their instructor to keep using MyLab Business Communication

For additional details visit: www.pearson.com/mylab/businesscommunication

THIRTEENTH
EDITION

Excellence in Business Communication

John V. Thill
CHAIRMAN AND CHIEF EXECUTIVE OFFICER
GLOBAL COMMUNICATION STRATEGIES

Courtland L. Bovée
PROFESSOR OF BUSINESS COMMUNICATION
C. ALLEN PAUL DISTINGUISHED CHAIR
GROSSMONT COLLEGE

Vice President, Business, Economics, and UK Courseware: Donna Battista
Director of Portfolio Management: Stephanie Wall
Editorial Assistant: Linda Siebert Albelli
Vice President, Product Marketing: Roxanne McCarley
Product Marketing Assistant: Marianela Silvestri
Manager of Field Marketing, Business Publishing: Adam Goldstein
Field Marketing Manager: Nicole Price
Marketing Coordinator: Erin Rush
Vice President, Production and Digital Studio, Arts and Business: Etain O'Dea
Director, Production and Digital Studio, Business and Economics: Ashley Santora
Managing Producer, Business: Melissa Feimer
Content Producer: Yasmita Hota
Operations Specialist: Carol Melville

Design Lead: Kathryn Foot
Manager, Learning Tools: Brian Surette
Senior Learning Tools Strategist: Emily Biberger
Managing Producer, Digital Studio and GLP: James Bateman
Managing Producer, Digital Studio: Diane Lombardo
Digital Studio Producer: Monique Lawrence
Digital Studio Producer: Alana Coles
Full Service Project Management: Nicole Suddeth, Pearson CSC
Interior Design: Pearson CSC
Cover Design: Pearson CSC
Cover Art: (top to bottom) Squaredpixels/E+/Getty Images; PeopleImages/E+/Getty Images; Tom Werner/DigitalVision/Getty Images
Printer/Binder: LSC Communications, Inc./Menasha
Cover Printer: LSC Communications, Inc.

Library of Congress Cataloging-in-Publication Data
Names: Thill, John V., author. | Bovée, Courtland L., author.
Title: Excellence in business communication / John V. Thill, Chairman and Chief Executive Officer, Global Communication Strategies, Courtland L. Bovée, Professor of Business Communication, C. Allen Paul Distinguished Chair, Grossmont College.
Description: Thirteenth Edition. | Hoboken, N.J. : Pearson, [2019] | Revised edition of the authors' Excellence in business communication, [2017] | Includes bibliographical references and index.
Identifiers: LCCN 2018049473| ISBN 9780135192184 (pbk.) | ISBN 0135192188 (pbk.)
Subjects: LCSH: Business communication—United States—Case studies.
Classification: LCC HF5718.2.U6 T45 2019 | DDC 658.4/5—dc23
LC record available at https://lccn.loc.gov/2018049473

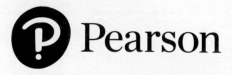

ISBN 10:   0-13-519218-8
ISBN 13: 978-0-13-519218-4

Brief Contents

Contents

PART 5
Writing Employment Messages and Interviewing for Jobs 483

15 Building Careers and Writing Résumés 484

16 Applying and Interviewing for Employment 520

Preface

New to This Edition

MORE VALUABLE THAN EVER WITH NEW STUDENT-FOCUSED FEATURES

- **Build Your Career** activities help students create their employment-communication packages throughout the course, so they're ready to apply for jobs by the end of the course.
- **Apply Your Skills Now** highlight boxes help students apply their newly developing communication skills in other classes and in their personal lives.
- **Five-Minute Guides** serve as handy reminders of the steps needed to accomplish a variety of fundamental communication tasks, from resolving workplace conflict to writing business email to planning reports and presentations.

DOUBLE THE COVERAGE OF INTERPERSONAL COMMUNICATION

Excellence in Business Communication now has two chapters devoted to these important topics: listening, nonverbal communication, conversational skills, conflict resolution, negotiation, teamwork, collaborative communication, meeting skills, and business etiquette. (To keep the text at 16 chapters and a similar page count as the previous edition, the three chapters on report writing have been streamlined to two chapters.)

THE ONLY TEXT THAT COVERS *INTELLIGENT COMMUNICATION TECHNOLOGY*

The digital transformation sweeping through business is creating a host of new communication tools and techniques that students will encounter during their job searches and in the workplace. A new four-page visual feature, "Empowering Communicators with Intelligent Communication Technology," shows 15 applications of artificial intelligence and smart technology. New highlight boxes take a close look at innovations ranging from augmented writing tools to résumé bots.

EXTENSIVE CONTENT ENHANCEMENTS

All new *On the Job* vignette/simulation pairs. These chapter-opening vignettes and end-of-chapter simulations show students how professionals apply the same skills they are reading about in the chapter. All 16 are new in this edition.

    Nearly 70 new figures. The Thirteenth Edition has 71 annotated model documents, 31 examples of mobile communication in business communication, 16 examples of social media, and 15 examples of intelligent communication technology.

    Revised annotations in model document before/after pairs. These revised notes make it easier for students to see the specific changes made to transform ineffective messages into effective ones.

    Nearly 300 new questions and student activities. Every chapter has fresh project ideas and evaluation questions.

    Streamlined coverage of report writing and production. To maintain the 16-chapter structure after the addition of a second chapter on interpersonal communication, the separate chapters on writing and completing reports have been merged into one chapter.

Numerous revisions and updates. Dozens of chapter sections are new, updated, or substantially revised to reflect the latest research and practices in business communication:

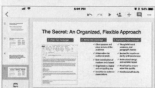

Understanding What Employers Expect from You
How Audiences Receive Messages
How Audiences Decode Messages
The Social Communication Model
The Potential Benefits of Communication Technology
The Spectrum of Contemporary Communication Technology
Social and Workgroup Communication Systems
Mobile Communication
Intelligent Communication Technology
Committing to Ethical and Legal Communication
Forms of Unethical Communication
Plagiarizing
Ensuring Ethical Communication
Improving Your Listening Skills
Understanding Why Listening Is Such a Complex Process
The Unique Challenges of Listening
Choices and Behaviors That Affect Listening Quality
Minimize the Barriers to Effective Listening
Improving Your Nonverbal Communication Skills
Developing Your Conversational Skills
Initiating Business Conversations
Maintaining a Positive Conversational Flow
Gracefully Concluding a Conversation
Handling Difficult Conversations
Managing Workplace Conflict
Why Conflict Arises in the Workplace
Steps to Resolve Conflict
Developing Your Skills as a Negotiator
Understanding the Principles of Negotiation
Preparing for a Negotiation
Engaging in Negotiation
Types of Teams
Characteristics of Effective Teams
Team Roles
Stages of Team Development
Benefits and Challenges of Virtual Teamwork
Tips for Success in Virtual Team Environments
Collaboration Arrangements
Writer-Editor Relationships
Full Collaboration
Collaboration Systems
AI-Enabled Collaboration
Conducting Virtual Meetings
Business Etiquette in the Workplace
Age Differences
Gender Differences
Factors to Consider When Choosing Media and Channels
Choosing Between Direct and Indirect Approaches

Building Reader Interest with Storytelling Techniques
Using Words Correctly
The Emoji Question—Overcoming the Limitations of Lean Media
The Rise of Emojis
To Emoji or Not: Two Dilemmas
Using Emoticons and Emojis Effectively
Categories of Social Platforms
Business Communication Uses of Social Platforms
Communication Strategies for Business Social Networking
The Email Subject Line: Persuading People to Open Your Messages
Business Messaging
Categories of Business Messaging
Tips for Successful Messaging
Blogging
Business Applications of Microblogging
Tips for Effective Business Tweets
Podcasting
Asking for Recommendations
Writing Instructions
Refusing Requests for Recommendations and References
Giving Negative Performance Reviews
Terminating Employment
Using the Three-Step Writing Process for Persuasive Messages
Balancing the Three Types of Persuasive Appeals
Maintaining High Standards of Ethics, Legal Compliance, and Etiquette
Quoting, Paraphrasing, and Summarizing Information
Ensuring Successful Team Presentations
Planning a Team Presentation
Rehearsing and Delivering a Team Presentation
Addressing Areas of Concern (under Planning Your Résumé)
Keeping Your Résumé Honest
References
Building an Effective LinkedIn Profile
Writing Application Letters
Understanding the Interviewing Process
The Screening Stage
The Selection Stage
Structured Versus Unstructured Interviews
Behavioral Interview Questions
Case Interviews and Take-Home Assessments
Interviewing by Phone
Interviewing by Video
Preemployment Testing and Background Checks

Solving Teaching and Learning Challenges

Communication is the most valuable skill that graduates can bring into the workforce, but it is one of the most challenging to teach. *Excellence in Business Communication* blends the timeless fundamentals of communication with contemporary media skills and contemporary business practices. To help students succeed from their first day on the job, *Excellence in Business Communication* presents the full range of on-the-job skills that today's communicators need, from writing conventional printed reports to using the latest digital, social, mobile, and visual media.

Each chapter opens with a brief vignette that describes a challenge or opportunity faced by a business professional, emphasizing concepts and valuable skills that students will explore in the chapter.

ON THE JOB: COMMUNICATING AT
STITCH FIX

The Never-Ending Need to Persuade

Katrina Lake's path to entrepreneurship didn't start with the stereotypical urge to create a company. In fact, she kept waiting for someone else to create the company she had in mind so she could buy from it and invest in it. During the first two phases of her career, in a retail consulting firm and then a venture capital firm, she kept looking for someone to solve what she believed was the central problem of online fashion retailing: "How can we marry the ease of shopping online with what people want in clothes, which is really about fit and style?"

After waiting for someone else to pitch the right idea to her in the hopes of getting investment capital, she decided to launch it herself. She went back to school to pursue an MBA at Harvard, where her idea began to take real shape and Stitch Fix was born. The concept was a clothing retailer that would combine the convenience of online shopping with the individual touch of the stylists and personal shoppers available in higher-end shops and department stores. Customers could receive a small selection of items chosen by a personal stylist (with the help of some powerful artificial intelligence), then buy what they like and send back what they don't.

Lake believed in the idea from the outset, but the need to persuade others to believe in it began early and has been an

Stitch Fix cofounder and CEO Katrina Lake relied heavily on persuasive communication skills to secure funding and attract top talent to her start-up company.

ON THE JOB: SOLVING COMMUNICATION DILEMMAS AT **STITCH FIX**

You've joined Stitch Fix as a training and quality lead. You report to the supervisor of training and quality programs and lead a small team of specialists who help employees throughout the company deliver a satisfying customer experience. Use what you've learned in this chapter to address these challenges.

1. Stitch Fix emphasizes the "art of conversation" with its trainers and customer experience staff. You recently heard about a conversational training system that uses natural language processing appears to be adv versations with cus be a great way to cost-effective than and it can be prog versation to give a most. There woul

should you balance the emotional and logical appeals in your message?

a. The appeal should be primarily logical in order to emphasize the business benefits of the new training approach. However, add the emotional appeal of making life easier for employees by reducing disruption to their schedules.

b. Conversing with a software robot is unavoidably going to be an emotional experience, so the proposal should match that

The chapter-opening story is picked up again at the end of the chapter in a unique simulation that has students imagine themselves in that company as they face four communication challenges that require them to use their new skills and insights.

ion, so emotion shouldn't

atch the level of excitement new technology.

most effective way to h Fix should give this

Annotated model documents are perhaps the most important feature of a business communication text, and *Excellence in Business Communication* is packed with a balance of carefully chosen examples from real companies and original material created to illustrate specific concepts.

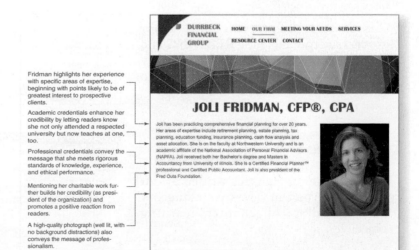

Fridman highlights her experience with specific areas of expertise, beginning with points likely to be of greatest interest to prospective clients.

Academic credentials enhance her credibility by letting readers know she not only attended a respected university but now teaches at one, too.

Professional credentials convey the message that she meets rigorous standards of knowledge, experience, and ethical performance.

Mentioning her charitable work further builds her credibility (as president of the organization) and promotes a positive reaction from readers.

A high-quality photograph (well lit, with no background distractions) also conveys the message of professionalism.

DURRBECK FINANCIAL GROUP   HOME   OUR FIRM   MEETING YOUR NEEDS   SERVICES   RESOURCE CENTER   CONTACT

JOLI FRIDMAN, CFP®, CPA

Joli has been practicing comprehensive financial planning for over 20 years. Her areas of expertise include retirement planning, estate planning, tax planning, education funding, insurance planning, cash flow analysis and asset allocation. She is on the faculty at Northwestern University and is an academic affiliate of the National Association of Personal Financial Advisors (NAPFA). Joli received both her Bachelor's degree and Masters in Accountancy from University of Illinois. She is a Certified Financial Planner™ professional and Certified Public Accountant. Joli is also president of the Fred Outa Foundation.

To improve student results, we recommend pairing this text with **MyLab Business Communication**, which is the teaching and learning platform that empowers you to reach every student. By combining trusted author content with digital tools and a flexible platform, MyLab personalizes the learning experience and will help your students learn and retain key course concepts while developing skills that future employers are seeking in their candidates.

Mini Sims—Real-world simulations that put students in professional roles and give them the opportunity to apply course concepts and develop decision-making skills through real-world business challenges.

These **branching** Mini Sims strengthen a student's ability to think critically, help students understand the impact of their decisions, engage students in active learning, and provide students with immediate feedback on their decisions.

Each decision point remediates to the Learning Objective in the eText.

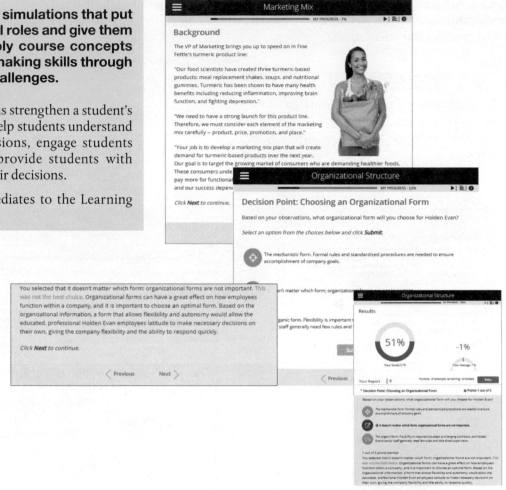

Chapter Warm-Ups

Assessment helps you hold your students accountable for **READING** and demonstrating their knowledge of key concepts in each chapter before coming to class.

Chapter Quiz

Every chapter has quizzes written by our authors so you can assess your students' understanding of chapter learning objectives.

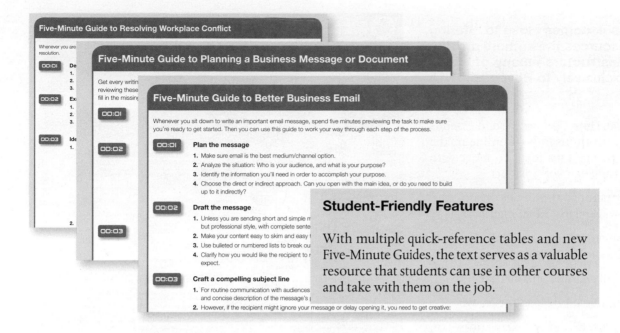

Five-Minute Guide to Resolving Workplace Conflict

Whenever you are ___
resolution.

00:01 De ___
1. ___
2. ___
3. ___

00:02 Ex ___
1. ___
2. ___
3. ___

00:03 Ide ___
1. ___

2. ___

Five-Minute Guide to Planning a Business Message or Document

Get every writin ___
reviewing these ___
fill in the missing ___

00:01

00:02

00:03

Five-Minute Guide to Better Business Email

Whenever you sit down to write an important email message, spend five minutes previewing the task to make sure you're ready to get started. Then you can use this guide to work your way through each step of the process.

00:01 **Plan the message**
1. Make sure email is the best medium/channel option.
2. Analyze the situation: Who is your audience, and what is your purpose?
3. Identify the information you'll need in order to accomplish your purpose.
4. Choose the direct or indirect approach. Can you open with the main idea, or do you need to build up to it indirectly?

00:02 **Draft the message**
1. Unless you are sending short and simple m ___
but professional style, with complete sente ___
2. Make your content easy to skim and easy ___
3. Use bulleted or numbered lists to break ou ___
4. Clarify how you would like the recipient to ___
expect.

00:03 **Craft a compelling subject line**
1. For routine communication with audiences ___
and concise description of the message's ___
2. However, if the recipient might ignore your message or delay opening it, you need to get creative:

Student-Friendly Features

With multiple quick-reference tables and new Five-Minute Guides, the text serves as a valuable resource that students can use in other courses and take with them on the job.

COMPOSITIONAL MODES FOR DIGITAL MEDIA

As you practice using digital media in this course, focus on the principles of social media communication and the fundamentals of planning, writing, and completing messages, rather than on the specific details of any one medium or system.[2] Fortunately, the basic communication skills required usually transfer from one system to another. You can succeed with written communication in virtually all digital media by using one of nine *compositional modes*:

- **Conversations.** Although they take place via writing, some forms ___ munication function more like real-time conversations than the sh ___ documents. Much of Chapter 2's advice on conversations apply to t ___ and the section on business messaging (see page 233) explores this ___ ever-expanding communication format.
- **Comments and critiques.** One of the most powerful aspects of so ___ opportunity for interested parties to express opinions and provide fe ___ it's leaving comments on a blog post or reviewing products on an e ___ Sharing helpful tips and insightful commentary is also a great way to ___ sonal brand. To be an effective commenter, focus on short chunks of i ___ a broad spectrum of other site visitors will find helpful. And even if ___ criticism, keep it constructive. Angry rants and insults won't help a ___ brand you as unprofessional.
- **Orientations.** The ability to help people find their way through an ut ___ or subject is a valuable writing skill and a talent that readers greatly ap ___ summaries (see next item), orientations don't give away the key poi ___ tion of information, but rather tell readers where to find those points. ___ orientations can be a delicate balancing act because you need to know ___ enough to guide others through it while being able to step back and view it from the inexperienced perspective of a "newbie."
- **Summaries.** At the beginning of an article or webpage, a summary functions as a miniature version of the material, giving readers all the key points while skipping over details (see Figure 8.1). At the end of an article or webpage, a summary functions as a review, reminding readers of the key points they've just read.

Original Coverage

Going beyond covering the tried-and-true, Bovée and Thill make unique contributions to the pedagogy and practice of business communication, such as the nine compositional modes required to succeed with digital and social media.

1 Plan → **2 Write** → **3 Complete**

Analyze the Situation
Define your purpose and develop an audience profile.

Gather Information
Determine audience needs and obtain the information necessary to satisfy those needs.

Choose Medium and Channel
Identify the best combination for the situation, message, and audience.

Organize the Information
Define your main idea, limit your scope, select the direct or indirect approach, and outline your content.

Adapt to Your Audience
Be sensitive to audience needs by using a "you" attitude, politeness, positive emphasis, and unbiased language. Build a strong relationship with your audience by establishing your credibility and projecting your company's preferred image. Control your style with a conversational tone, plain English, and appropriate voice.

Compose the Message
Choose strong words that ___ you create effective senten ___ coherent paragraphs.

Revise the Message
Evaluate content and review readability; edit and rewrite for conciseness and clarity.

Produce the Message
Use effective design elements and suitable layout for a clean, professional appearance.

Proofread the Message

Reducing Stress and Uncertainty for Students

Students sometimes flounder when faced with unfamiliar or difficult writing challenges because they don't know how to move a project forward. By following the proven three-step process described in *Excellence in Business Communication*, they never have to feel lost or waste time figuring out what to do next.

No other textbook comes close to offering the valuable resources the authors provide students and instructors—many of which are available exclusively to Bovée and Thill adopters:

- The unique Real-Time Updates system extends the textbook with thousands of online media items that complement the text's coverage with fresh examples and valuable insights

- Sponsored instructor communities on LinkedIn and Facebook with nearly 2,000 members

- Tips and techniques in Bovée and Thill's Business Communication Blog and Twitter feed

- The Bovée & Thill channel on YouTube

- Business Communication Headline News

- Videos and PowerPoint presentations on SlideShare

- Hundreds of infographics, videos, articles, podcasts, and PowerPoints in the Business Communication Pictorial Gallery on Pinterest

- The Ultimate Guide to Resources for Teaching Business Communication

- Nine curated magazines for business communication on Scoop.it

Links to all these services and resources can be found at blog.businesscommunicationnetwork.com/resources.

REAL-TIME UPDATES
LEARN MORE BY READING THIS ARTICLE
Ten communication skills that will boost your career
Employers will sit up and take notice if you master these skills. Go to **real-timeupdates.com/ebc13** and select Learn More in the Students section.

Developing Employability Skills

In addition to helping students develop a full range of communication skills, *Excellence in Business Communication* will enhance a wide range of other skills that experts say are vital for success in the 21st-century workplace:

- **Critical thinking.** In many assignments and activities, students need to define and solve problems and make decisions or form judgments.
- **Collaboration.** Team-skills assignments provide multiple opportunities to work with classmates on reports, presentations, and other projects.
- **Knowledge application and analysis.** From the basic communication process to strategies for specific message types, students will learn a variety of concepts and apply that knowledge to a wide range of challenges.
- **Business ethics and social responsibility.** Ethical choices are stressed from the beginning of the book, and multiple projects encourage students to be mindful of the ethical implications that they could encounter in similar projects on the job.
- **Information technology skills.** Projects and activities in every chapter help students build skills with technology, including document preparation tools, online communication services, presentation software, and messaging systems.
- **Data literacy.** Report projects in particular present opportunities to fine-tune data literacy skills, including the ability to access, assess, interpret, manipulate, summarize, and communicate data.

Practice Your Skills

Exercises

Each activity is labeled according to the primary skill or skills you will need to use. To review relevant chapter content, you can refer to the indicated Learning Objective. In some instances, supporting information will be found in another chapter, as indicated.

2-6. Interpersonal Communication: Listening Actively [LO-1] For the next several days, take notes on your listening performance during at least a half-dozen situations in class, during social activities, and at work, if applicable. Referring to the traits of effective listeners in Table 2.4, rate yourself using *always, frequently, occasionally,* or *never* on these positive listening habits. In a report no longer than one page, summarize your analysis and identify specific areas in which you can improve your listening skills.

2-7. Nonverbal Communication: Analyzing Nonverbal Signals [LO-2] Select a business letter and envelope you have received at work or home. Analyze their appearance. What nonverbal messages do they send? Are these messages consistent with the content of the letter? If not, what could the sender have done to make the nonverbal communication consistent with the verbal communication? Summarize your findings in a post on your class blog or in an email message to your instructor.

Hundreds of realistic exercises, activities, and cases offer an array of opportunities for students to practice vital skills and put newfound knowledge to immediate use.

These resources are logically sorted by learning category, from conceptual recall to situational analysis to skill development.

To help instructors zero in on specific learning needs, activities are tagged in multiple ways, from media usage to team skills.

Cases

For all cases, feel free to use your creativity to make up any details you need in order to craft effective messages.

SOCIAL NETWORKING SKILLS

8-30. Media Skills: Social Networking; Compositional Modes: Summaries [LO-2] Many companies now have *voice of the customer (VoC)* programs to collect and analyze commentary and feedback from customers. The most comprehensive of these programs automatically gather data from social media, customer call records, technical support emails, online product reviews, and more. To extract insights from these large collections of text, marketers can use an intelligent communication technology called *text analytics.*

Your task: Review the text analytics information on the Clarabridge website at www.clarabridge.com. (The company refers to its technology as CX Analytics, for customer experience analytics.) Write a 100- to 150-word summary of this technology that Clarabridge could use as a post on its Facebook page to explain the capability to potential customers.

SOCIAL NETWORKING SKILLS

8-31. Media Skills: Social Networking; Online Etiquette [LO-2], Chapter 3 Employees who take pride in their work are a practically priceless resource for any business. However, pride can sometimes manifest itself in negative ways when employees come under criticism, and public criticism is a fact of life in social media. Imagine that your company has recently experienced a rash of product quality problems, and these problems have generated some unpleasant and occasionally unfair criticism on a variety of social media sites. Someone even set up a Facebook page specifically to give customers a place to vent one evening and discovered that two engineers in your company's product design lab have been responding to complaints on their own. They identified themselves as company employees and defended their product design, blaming the company's production department and even criticizing several customers for lacking the skills needed to use such a sophisticated product. Within a matter of minutes, you see their harsh comments being retweeted and reposted on multiple sites, only fueling the fire of negative feedback against your firm. Needless to say, you are horrified.

Your task: You manage to reach the engineers by private message and tell them to stop posting messages, but you realize you have a serious training issue on your hands. Write a post for the internal company blog that advises employees on how to respond appropriately when they are representing the company online. Use your imagination to make up any details you need.

NETWORKING SKILLS / TEAM SKILLS

8-32. Media Skills: Social Networking; Collaboration: Team Projects [LO-2], Chapter 3 Social media can be a great way to, well, socialize during your college years, but employers are increasingly checking up on the online activities of potential hires to avoid bringing in employees who may reflect poorly on the company.

Your task: Team up with another student and review each other's public presence on Facebook, Twitter, Flickr, blogs, and any other website that an employer might check during the interview and recruiting process. Identify any photos, videos, messages, or other material that could raise a red flag when an employer is evaluating a job candidate. Write your teammate an email message that lists any risky material.

Instructor Teaching Resources

This program comes with the following teaching resources.

Supplements available to instructors at www.pearsonhighered.com	Features of the Supplement
Instructor's Manual	• Chapter overview • Chapter outline • Lecture notes organized by learning objective, with class discussion questions • Answers to highlight box questions • Answers to Apply Your Knowledge questions • Answers to Practice Your Skills activities • Solutions to cases (complete example solutions for short-message cases; solution guidelines for long-message cases) • Lesson plan foundations from the Bovée and Thill QuickSwitch textbook transition system
Test Bank authored by Susan Schanne from Eastern Michigan University	• 1,660 multiple-choice, true/false, and essay questions • Answer explanations • Keyed by learning objective • Classified according to difficulty level • Classified according to learning modality: conceptual, application, critical thinking, or synthesis • Learning outcomes identified • AACSB learning standard identified (Written and Oral Communication, Ethical Understanding and Reasoning, Analytical Thinking Skills, Information Technology, Interpersonal Relations and Teamwork, Diverse and Multicultural Work Environments, Reflective Thinking, and Application of Knowledge)
Computerized TestGen	TestGen allows instructors to • customize, save, and generate classroom tests. • edit, add, or delete questions from the Test Item Files. • analyze test results. • organize a database of tests and student results.
PowerPoints authored by Lauryn De George from University of Central Florida College of Business	Slides include all the graphs, tables, and equations in the textbook. PowerPoints meet accessibility standards for students with disabilities. Features include: • Keyboard and screen reader access • Alternative text for images • High contrast between background and foreground colors

About the Authors

Courtland L. Bovée and John V. Thill have been leading textbook authors for more than two decades, introducing millions of students to the fields of business and business communication. Their award-winning texts are distinguished by proven pedagogical features, extensive selections of contemporary case studies, hundreds of real-life examples, engaging writing, thorough research, and the unique integration of print and digital resources. Each new edition reflects the authors' commitment to continuous refinement and improvement, particularly in terms of modeling the latest practices in business and the use of technology.

Professor Bovée has 22 years of teaching experience at Grossmont College in San Diego, where he has received teaching honors and was accorded that institution's C. Allen Paul Distinguished Chair. Mr. Thill is a prominent communications consultant who has worked with organizations ranging from Fortune 500 multinationals to entrepreneurial start-ups. He formerly held positions with Pacific Bell and Texaco.

Courtland Bovée and John Thill were recently awarded proclamations from the Governor of Massachusetts for their lifelong contributions to education and for their commitment to the summer youth baseball program that is sponsored by the Boston Red Sox.

Court Bovée

Acknowledgments

The Thirteenth Edition of *Excellence in Business Communication* reflects the professional experience of a large team of contributors and advisors. We express our thanks to the many individuals whose valuable suggestions and constructive comments influenced the success of this book.

John Thill

REVIEWERS OF PREVIOUS BOVÉE AND THILL EDITIONS

Thank you to the following professors: Lydia E. Anderson, *Fresno City College*; Victoria Austin, *Las Positas College*; Faridah Awang, *Eastern Kentucky University*; Jeanette Baldridge, *University of Maine at Augusta*; Diana Baran, *Henry Ford Community College*; JoAnne Barbieri, *Atlantic Cape Community College*; Kristina Beckman, *John Jay College*; Judy Bello, *Lander University*; George Bernard, *Seminole State College*; Carol Bibly, *Triton College*; Nancy Bizal, *University of Southern Indiana*; Yvonne Block, *College of Lake County*; Edna Boroski, *Trident Technical College*; Nelvia M. Brady, *Trinity Christian College*; Arlene Broeker, *Lincoln University*; David Brooks, *Indiana University Southeast*; Carol Brown, *South Puget Sound Community College*; Domenic Bruni, *University of Wisconsin*; Jeff Bruns, *Bacone College*; Gertrude L. Burge, *University of Nebraska*; Sharon Burton, *Brookhaven College*; Robert Cabral, *Oxnard College*; Dorothy Campbell, *Brevard Community College*; Linda Carr, *University of West Alabama*; Alvaro Carreras, Jr., *Florida International University*; Sharon Carson, *St. Philip's College*; Rick Carter, *Seattle University*; Dacia Charlesworth, *Indiana University–Purdue University Fort Wayne*; Jean Chenu, *Genesee Community College*; Connie Clark, *Lane Community College*; Alvin Clarke, *Iowa State University*; Jerrie Cleaver, *Central Texas College*; Clare Coleman, *Temple University*; Michael P. Collins, *Northern Arizona University*; M. Cotton, *North Central Missouri College*; Pat Cowherd, *Campbellsville University*; Pat Cuchens, *University of Houston–Clear Lake*; Walt Dabek, *Post University*; Cathy Daly, *California State University–Sacramento*; Linda Davis, *Copiah–Lincoln Community College*; Christine R. Day, *Eastern Michigan University*; Harjit Dosanjh, *North Seattle Community College*; Amy Drees, *Defiance College*; Cynthia Drexel, *Western State College of Colorado*; Lou Dunham, *Spokane Falls Community College*; Donna Everett, *Morehead State University*; Donna Falconer, *Anoka–Ramsey Community College*; Kate Ferguson Marsters, *Gannon University*; Darlynn Fink, *Clarion University of Pennsylvania*; Bobbi Fisher, *University of Nebraska–Omaha*; Laura Fitzwater, *Community College of Philadelphia*; Lynda K. Fuller, *Wilmington University*; Matthew Gainous, *Ogeechee Technical College*; Yolande Gardner, *Lawson State Community College*; Gina Genova, *University of California– Santa Barbara*; Lonny Gilbert, *Central State University*; Camille Girardi-Levy, *Siena College*; Nancy Goehring, *Monterey Peninsula College*; Dawn Goellner, *Bethel College*; Robert Goldberg, *Prince George's Community College*; Jeffrey Goldberg, *MassBay Community College*; Helen Grattan, *Des Moines Area Community College*; Barbara Grayson, *University of Arkansas at Pine Bluff*;

Deborah Griffin, *University of Houston–Clear Lake*; Alice Griswold, *Clarke College*; Bonnie Grossman, *College of Charleston*; Lisa Gueldenzoph, *North Carolina A&T State University*; Wally Guyot, *Fort Hays State University*; Valerie Harrison, *Cuyamaca College*; Tim Hartge, *The University of Michigan–Dearborn*; Richard Heiens, *University of South Carolina–Aiken*; Maureece Heinert, *Sinte Gleska University*; Leighanne Heisel, *University of Missouri–St. Louis*; Gary Helfand, *University of Hawaii–West Oahu*; Cynthia Herrera, *Orlando Culinary Academy*; Kathy Hill, *Sam Houston State University*; Pashia Hogan, *Northeast State Tech Community College*; Cole Holmes, *The University of Utah*; Sarah Holmes, *New England Institute of Technology*; Ruth Hopkins Zajdel, *Ohio University–Chillicothe*; Sheila Hostetler, *Orange Coast College*; Michael Hricik, *Westmoreland County Community College*; Rebecca Hsiao, *East Los Angeles College*; Mary Ann Hurd, *Sauk Valley Community College*; Pat Hurley, *Leeward Community College*; Harold Hurry, *Sam Houston State University*; Marcia James, *University of Wisconsin–Whitewater*; Frank Jaster, *Tulane University*; Jonatan Jelen, *Parsons School of Design*; Irene Joanette Gallio, *Western Nevada Community College*; Edgar Dunson Johnson III, *Augusta State University*; Mark Johnson, *Rhodes State College*; Joanne Kapp, *Siena College*; Jeanette A. Karjala, *Winona State University*; Christy L. Kinnion, *Lenior Community College*; Deborah Kitchin, *City College of San Francisco*; Lisa Kirby, *North Carolina Wesleyan College*; Claudia Kirkpatrick, *Carnegie Mellon University*; Betty Kleen, *Nicholls State University*; Fran Kranz, *Oakland University*; Jana Langemach, *University of Nebraska–Lincoln*; Joan Lantry, *Jefferson Community College*; Kim Laux, *Saginaw Valley State University*; Kathryn J. Lee, *University of Cincinnati*; Anita Leffel, *The University of Texas, San Antonio*; Ruth Levy, *Westchester Community College*; Nancy Linger, *Moraine Park Technical College*; Jere Littlejohn, *University of Mississippi*; Dana Loewy, *California State University–Fullerton*; Jennifer Loney, *Portland State University*; Susan Long, *Portland Community College*; Sue Loomis, *Maine Maritime Academy*; Thomas Lowderbaugh, *University of Maryland–College Park*; Jayne Lowery, *Jackson State Community College*; Lloyd Matzner, *University of Houston–Downtown*; Ron McNeel, *New Mexico State University at Alamogordo*; Dr. Bill McPherson, *Indiana University of Pennsylvania*; Phyllis Mercer, *Texas Woman's University*; Donna Meyerholz, *Trinidad State Junior College*; Annie Laurie I. Meyers, *Northampton Community College*; Catherine "Kay" Michael, *St. Edward's University*; Kathleen Miller, *University of Delaware*; Gay Mills, *Amarillo College*; Julie Mullis, *Wilkes Community College*; Pamela Mulvey, *Olney Central College*; Jimidene Murphey, *Clarendon College*; Cindy Murphy, *Southeastern Community College*; Dipali Murti-Hali, *California State University–Stanislaus*; Shelley Myatt, *University of Central Oklahoma*; Cora Newcomb, *Technical College of the Lowcountry*; Ron Newman, *Crafton Hills College*; Linda Nitsch, *Chadron State College*; Leah Noonan, *Laramie County Community College*; Mabry O'Donnell, *Marietta College*; Diana Oltman, *Central Washington University*; Ranu Paik, *Santa Monica College*; Lauren Paisley, *Genesee Community College*; Patricia Palermo, *Drew University*; John Parrish, *Tarrant County College*; Diane Paul, *TVI Community College*; John T. Pauli, *University of Alaska–Anchorage*; Michael Pennell, *University of Rhode Island*; Sylvia Beaver Perez, *Nyack College*; Melinda Phillabaum, *Indiana University*; Ralph Phillips, *Geneva College*; Laura Pohopien, *Cal Poly Pomona*; Diane Powell, *Utah Valley State College*; Christine Pye, *California Lutheran University*; Norma Pygon, *Triton College*; Dave Rambow, *Wayland Baptist University*; Richard David Ramsey, *Southeastern Louisiana University*; Charles Riley, *Tarrant County College–Northwest Campus*; Jim Rucker, *Fort Hays State University*; Dr. Suzan Russell, *Lehman College*; Storm Russo, *Valencia College*; Danielle Scane, *Orange Coast College*; Calvin Scheidt, *Tidewater Community College*; Nancy Schneider, *University of Maine at Augusta*; Brian Sheridan, *Mercyhurst College*; Melinda Shirey, *Fresno City College*; Bob Shirilla, *Colorado State University*; Joyce Simmons, *Florida State University*; Gordon J. Simpson, *SUNY Cobleskill*; Peggy Simpson, *Dominican University*; Eunice Smith, *Bismarck State College*; Jeff Smith, *University of Southern California*; Lorraine M. Smith, *Fresno City College*; Harvey Solganick, *LeTourneau University–Dallas Campus*; Stephen Soucy, *Santa Monica College*; Linda Spargo, *University of Mississippi*; W. Dees Stallings, *Park University*; Sally Stanton, *University of Wisconsin-Milwaukee*; Mark Steinbach, *Austin Community College*; Angelique Stevens, *Monroe Community College*; Steven Stovall, *Wilmington College*; Alden Talbot, *Weber State University*; Michele Taylor, *Ogeechee Technical College*; Wilma Thomason, *Mid-South Community College*; Ed Thompson, *Jefferson Community College*; Ann E. Tippett, *Monroe Community College*; Lori Townsend, *Niagara County Community College*; Lani Uyeno, *Leeward Community College*; Wendy Van Hatten, *Western Iowa Tech Community College*; Jay

Wagers, *Richmond Community College*; John Waltman, *Eastern Michigan University*; Jie Wang, *University of Illinois at Chicago*; Chris Ward, *The University of Findlay*; Dorothy Warren, *Middle Tennessee State University*; Glenda Waterman, *Concordia University*; Kellie Welch, *Jefferson Community College*; Bradley S. Wesner, *Nova Southeastern University*; Mathew Williams, *Clover Park Technical College*; Beth Williams, *Stark State College of Technology*; Brian Wilson, *College of Marin*; and Sandra D. Young, *Orangeburg–Calhoun Technical College*.

MYLAB CONTRIBUTORS

Storm Russo, Patricia Buhler, Maureen Steddin, Carol Heeter, Susan Schanne, Chris Parent (accuracy reviewer), and Kerri Tomasso (copy editor).

PERSONAL ACKNOWLEDGMENTS

We wish to extend a heartfelt thanks to our many friends, acquaintances, and business associates who provided materials or agreed to be interviewed so that we could bring the real world into the classroom.

A very special acknowledgment goes to George Dovel, whose superb writing skills, distinguished background, and wealth of business experience assured this project of clarity and completeness. Also, recognition and thanks to Jackie Estrada for her outstanding skills and excellent attention to details. Her creation of the "Peak Performance Grammar and Mechanics" material is especially noteworthy.

We also feel it is important to acknowledge and thank the Association for Business Communication, an organization whose meetings and publications provide a valuable forum for the exchange of ideas and for professional growth.

In addition, we would like to thank Susan Schanne and Lauren De George for their assistance in preparing supplements for this new edition.

We want to extend our warmest appreciation to the devoted professionals at Pearson Higher Education for their commitment to producing high-value, student-focused texts, including Donna Battista, Vice President, Business Publishing; Stephanie Wall, Director of Portfolio Management; Melissa Feimer, Managing Producer, Business; Yasmita Hota, Content Producer; Ashley Santora, Director of Production, Business; Becky Brown, Product Marketer; and Nicole Price, Field Marketing Manager. We are also grateful to Nicole Suddeth and Liz Kincaid of SPi Global, Angela Urquhart and Andrea Archer of Thistle Hill Publishing, and Melissa Pellerano.

John V. Thill
Courtland L. Bovée

Dedication

This book is dedicated to the many thousands of instructors and students who use Bovée and Thill texts to develop career-enhancing skills in business communication. We appreciate the opportunity to play a role in your education, and we wish you the very best with your careers.

John V. Thill
Courtland L. Bovée

Prologue

BUILDING A SUCCESSFUL CAREER WITH YOUR COMMUNICATION SKILLS

One Course—Three Powerful Benefits

You will invest considerable time and energy in this course, so it's fair to ask what you will get in return. The simple answer: *a lot*. If you practice the techniques you'll discover here and use this opportunity to develop those techniques with your instructor's guidance, we're confident this course will help you in three important ways:

1. It will help you succeed in college.
2. It will help you conduct a more successful job search.
3. It will help you succeed in your first job so you can build a thriving career.

The following sections expand on this promise and offer valuable career-planning advice. Table 1 on the next page highlights the specific features of this book that can help you at every stage.

HOW THIS COURSE WILL HELP YOU

Take advantage of this opportunity to develop the single most important skill you'll need for a rewarding career: the ability to communicate. This textbook is designed to help you in three valuable ways.

1. SUCCEED IN COLLEGE

Many of the skills you will learn in this course—writing, giving presentations, working in teams, resolving conflict, and more—can be applied in just about every course you take from now until graduation.

2. FIND THE RIGHT JOB

The entire job search process is really an extended exercise in communication, and the process gives you the chance to use your communication skills to stand apart from the competition.

3. LAUNCH YOUR CAREER

The bulk of this course is devoted to the communication and media skills you will need to use as soon as you enter (or reenter) the workforce. Succeed in your first job, and you'll be on your way to a rewarding career!

TABLE 1 Textbook Features to Help You at Every Stage of College and Career

	Textbook Feature	Stage 1: Succeeding in College		Stage 2: Conducting a Successful Job Search	Stage 3: Succeeding in Your First Job
		In This Course	In Other Courses		
Beginning of chapter	Learning Objectives	Use these to focus your study and review			
	On the Job vignette	See how the pros use chapter concepts		Get a sense of life on the job in various professions	
Within the chapter	Margin notes	Scan to get a quick review of the chapter			
	Real-Time Updates—Learn More (free media items)	Explore for additional insights			
	Figures	Study model documents to see what works and what doesn't	Study reports and other model documents to improve your writing	Use model letters and résumés to build your job search package	Use model documents to craft better documents on the job
	Mobile App highlights	Many of these apps can help with schoolwork	Many of these apps can help with schoolwork	Use selected apps to help in your job search	Use the apps on the job
	Checklists	Confirm understanding of each section	Use for a quick review if needed when writing	Use for a quick review if needed when writing	Use for a quick review if needed when writing
	Highlight boxes	*Apply Your Skills Now* helps you apply communication skills in and out of class	*Apply Your Skills Now* helps you apply communication skills in and out of class	*Developing as a Professional* gets you ready for the world of work	*Intelligent Communication Technology* and *Practicing Ethical Communication* prepare you for the job
End of chapter	Key Terms glossary	Quickly refer to important terms			
	Learning Objectives Checkup	Test your recall of chapter content			
	On the Job simulation	Follow through on the chapter-opening vignette by visualizing yourself on the job		Get a sense of life on the job in various professions	
	Apply Your Knowledge	Analyze communication scenarios to hone your insights			
	Practice Your Skills	Practice chapter skills in a variety of challenges			
	Expand Your Skills	Critique professional communication efforts and find career advice			
	Build Your Career	Use the exercise in each chapter to build your employment package		By the time you get to the employment chapters, you'll have a head start on your résumé package	Use these techniques to adjust your employment package as you progress
	Improve Your Grammar, Mechanics, and Usage	Fine-tune the technical aspects of your writing	Fine-tune the technical aspects of your writing	Fine-tune the technical aspects of your writing	Fine-tune the technical aspects of your writing
	Cases (selected chapters)	Practice crafting professional-quality messages and documents		Use the *Portfolio Builder* cases to expand your employment portfolio	

| | Textbook Feature | Stage 1: Succeeding in College | | Stage 2: Conducting a Successful Job Search | Stage 3: Succeeding in Your First Job |
		In This Course	In Other Courses		
	Five-Minute Guides (selected chapters)	Get quick reminders of how to accomplish important tasks	Use these for communication tasks in other classes, too	Use the guide in Chapter 15 to prepare and update your résumé	Download the PDFs and take them with you on the job
Online	Real-Time Updates	Subscribe online for weekly updates of free online media items			
	Student Assignments	Download files for selected chapters			
	Web Search	Use this metasearch engine to accelerate your research	Use for other classes for as long as your subscription is active		
	MyLab Business Communication	Use this optional online system for customized learning and more			

Stage 1: Succeeding in College

The first step in your career starts right now, with getting your degree and getting the most from all the courses you take between now and graduation. The communication skills you learn in this class can help you in virtually every other course. From brief homework assignments to complicated team projects to interactions with your professors, you will be able to communicate more effectively.

In addition to improving your communication effectiveness, this course will also improve your efficiency. Follow the writing process outlined in this book, and you can avoid the time-wasting uncertainty, dead ends, and rework that can make writing projects drag on forever.

Keep an eye out for the special highlight boxes titled "Apply Your Skills Now," which offer tips on using your new skills in all your college courses. Read these boxes and think about the situations in which you can apply the advice. If you need to have a difficult conversation with an instructor or resolve conflict in a project team, for example, these boxes can help. Many of these techniques can help you outside of the school environment, too, whenever you face communication challenges in any of your interpersonal relationships.

QUICK TIPS TO SUCCEED IN THIS COURSE

Although this course explores a wide range of message types and appears to cover quite a lot of territory, the underlying structure of the course is rather simple. You'll learn a few basic concepts, identify the key skills to use and procedures to follow—and then practice, practice, practice. Whether you're writing a blog post in response to one of the real-company cases or drafting your own résumé, you'll be practicing the same fundamental skills in a variety of scenarios. With feedback and reinforcement from your instructor and your classmates, your confidence will grow and the work will become easier and more enjoyable.

Some of the assignments will involve business topics that may be new to you or somewhat less than exciting, but view them all as opportunities to hone your craft. Visualize yourself in each scenario and imagine that you are trying to convince a skeptical boss, calm an angry customer, or accomplish whatever task is assigned.

As you read each chapter, take time to study the examples and model documents (see Figure 1). This book offers dozens of realistic examples of business messages, many with notes along the sides that explain strong and weak points. Some are messages from real companies; others were created to show specific points about writing. Study these documents and any other examples your instructor provides. Learn what works and what doesn't, and then apply these lessons to your own writing.

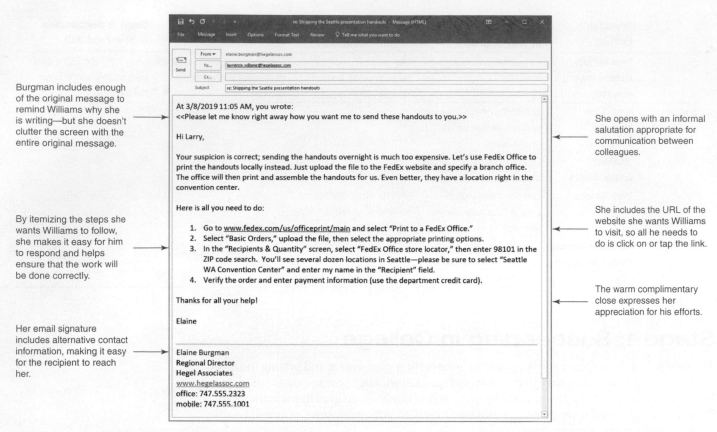

Burgman includes enough of the original message to remind Williams why she is writing—but she doesn't clutter the screen with the entire original message.

By itemizing the steps she wants Williams to follow, she makes it easy for him to respond and helps ensure that the work will be done correctly.

Her email signature includes alternative contact information, making it easy for the recipient to reach her.

She opens with an informal salutation appropriate for communication between colleagues.

She includes the URL of the website she wants Williams to visit, so all he needs to do is click on or tap the link.

The warm complimentary close expresses her appreciation for his efforts.

Figure 1   Learning from Model Documents and Messages
You will find a wide variety of model documents and messages throughout the book, everything from tweets to formal reports. Study the notes in the margins to understand why specific writing techniques work (or don't work, in some cases), and apply these lessons to your own writing.

Along the way, learn from the feedback you get from your instructor and from other students. Don't take the criticism personally; your instructor and your classmates are commenting about the work, not about you. Always view feedback as an opportunity to improve.

QUICK TIPS FOR WRITING ASSIGNMENTS IN ANY COURSE

For assignments in this or any other course, particularly major projects such as reports and presentations, follow these suggestions to produce better results with less effort:

- **Don't panic!** If the thought of writing a report or giving a speech sends a chill up your spine, you're not alone. Everybody feels that way when first learning business communication skills, and even experienced professionals can feel nervous about big projects. Keep three points in mind. First, every project can be broken down into a series of small, manageable tasks. Don't let a big project overwhelm you; it's nothing more than a bunch of smaller tasks. Second, remind yourself that you have the skills you need. As you move through the course, the assignments are carefully designed to match the skills you've developed up to that point. Third, if you feel panic creeping up on you, take a break and regain your perspective.
- **Focus on one task at a time.** Don't try to organize and express your ideas while simultaneously worrying about audience reactions, grammar, spelling, formatting, page design, and a dozen other factors. Fight the temptation to do everything at once. Trying to get everything perfect on the first pass will make the process slow and frustrating. In particular, don't worry too much about word choices or overall writing style during your first draft. Concentrate on the organization of your ideas first, then the best way to express those ideas, and then finally the presentation and production of your messages. Following the three-step writing process is an ideal way to focus on one task at a time in a logical sequence.

The techniques you will learn in this course will help you become a more successful writer, and they will make the process of writing easier and faster, too.

- **Give yourself plenty of time.** As with every other school project, waiting until the last minute creates unnecessary stress. Writing and speaking projects are much easier if you tackle them in small stages with breaks in between, rather than trying to get everything done in one frantic blast. Moreover, there will be instances when you simply get stuck on a project, and the best thing to do is walk away and give your mind a break. If you allow room for breaks in your schedule, you'll minimize the frustration and spend less time overall on your homework, too.

- **Step back and assess each project before you start.** The writing and speaking projects you'll have in this course cover a wide range of communication scenarios, and it's essential that you adapt your approach to each new challenge. Resist the urge to dive in and start writing without a plan. Ponder the assignment for a while, consider the various approaches you might take, and think carefully about your objectives before you start writing. Nothing is more frustrating than getting stuck halfway through because you're not sure what you're trying to say or you've wandered off track. Spend a little more time planning, and you'll spend a lot less time writing.

- **Use the three-step writing process.** Those essential planning tasks are the first step in the three-step writing process, which you'll learn about in Chapter 5 and use throughout the course. This process has been developed and refined by professional writers with decades of experience and thousands of projects ranging from short blog posts to 600-page textbooks. It works, so take advantage of it.

Stage 2: Conducting a Successful Job Search

Every activity in the job-search process relies on communication. The better you can communicate, the more successful you'll be at landing interesting and rewarding work. Plus, you can reduce the stress of preparing a résumé and going to job interviews.

Writing a résumé can be a big task, but you don't need to do it all at once if you give yourself plenty of time. The 16 Build Your Career activities (see the end of each chapter) show you how to build your job-search package one step at time. Do the activity in each chapter, and by the time you finish the book, you'll have the materials you need to start your job search.

Chapter 15 and Chapter 16 are dedicated to various forms of employment-related communication. If your course doesn't cover these chapters, your college probably offers a workshop or other activity to help you get ready to apply and interview for jobs. No matter where you learn the skills related to résumés and interviewing, this section will help you think about the career you want to craft for yourself, with advice on finding the best fit, developing an employment portfolio, and defining your personal brand.

FINDING THE BEST FIT

Figuring out where and how you can thrive professionally is a lifelong quest. You don't need to have all the answers today, and your answers will no doubt change in the coming years. However, start thinking about it now so that you can bring some focus to your job search. Organize your strategic planning with three questions: what you want to do, what you have to offer, and how you can make yourself more valuable.

What Do You Want to Do?

Economic necessities and the dynamics of the marketplace will influence much of what happens in your career, and you may not always have the opportunity to do the kind of work you would really like to do. Even if you can't get the job you want right now, though, start your job search by examining your values and interests. Doing so will give you a better idea of where you want to be eventually, and you can use those insights to learn and grow your way toward that ideal situation. Consider these factors:

- **What would you like to do every day?** Research occupations that interest you. Find out what people really do every day. Ask friends, relatives, alumni from your school, and contacts in your social networks. Read interviews with people in various professions to get a sense of what their careers are like.
- **How would you like to work?** Consider how much independence you want on the job, how much variety you like, and whether you prefer to work with products, systems, people, ideas, words, figures, or some combination thereof.
- **How do your financial goals fit with your other priorities?** For instance, many high-paying jobs involve a lot of stress, sacrifices of time with family and friends, and frequent travel or relocation. If other factors—such as stability, location, lifestyle, or intriguing work—are more important to you, you may have to sacrifice some level of pay to achieve them.
- **Have you established some general career goals?** For example, do you want to pursue a career specialty such as finance or manufacturing, or do you want to gain experience in multiple areas with an eye toward general management or entrepreneurship?
- **What sort of work culture are you most comfortable with?** Would you be happy in a formal hierarchy with clear reporting relationships? Or do you prefer less structure? Teamwork or individualism? Do you prefer a competitive environment or a more cooperative culture?

The day-to-day activities of different professions can vary widely. Do as much research as you can before you choose a career path to make sure it's the right path for you.

You might need some time in the workforce to figure out what you really want to do, but it's never too early to start thinking about where you want to be. Filling out the assessment in Table 2 might help you get a clearer picture of the nature of the work you would like to pursue in your career.

What Do You Have to Offer?

Knowing what you want to do is one thing. Knowing what companies or clients are willing to pay you to do is another thing entirely. You may already have a good idea of what you can offer employers. If not, some brainstorming can help you identify your skills, interests, and characteristics. Start by listing achievements you're proud of and experiences that were satisfying, and identify the skills that enabled these achievements. For example, leadership skills, speaking ability, and artistic talent may have helped you coordinate a successful class project. As you analyze your achievements, you may begin to recognize a pattern of skills. Which of these would be valuable to potential employers?

TABLE 2   CAREER PLANNING SELF-ASSESSMENT

Activity or Situation	Strongly Agree	Agree	Disagree	No Preference
1. I want to work independently.				
2. I want variety in my work.				
3. I want to work with people.				
4. I want to work with technology.				
5. I don't want to be stuck in an office all day.				
6. I want mentally challenging work.				
7. I want to work for a large organization.				
8. I want to work for a nonprofit organization.				
9. I want to work for a small business.				
10. I want to work for a service business.				
11. I want to start or buy a business someday.				
12. I want regular, predictable work hours.				
13. I want to work in a city location.				
14. I want to work in a small town or suburb.				
15. I want to work in another country.				
16. I want to work from home, even if I'm employed by someone else.				
17. I want to work in a highly dynamic profession or industry, even if it's unstable at times.				
18. I want as much career stability as possible.				
19. I want to enjoy my work, even if that means making less money.				
20. I want to become a high-level corporate manager.				

Next, look at your educational preparation, work experience, and extracurricular activities. What do your knowledge and experience qualify you to do? What have you learned from volunteer work or class projects that could benefit you on the job? Have you held any offices, won any awards or scholarships, mastered a second language? What skills have you developed in nonbusiness situations that could transfer to a business position?

Take stock of your personal characteristics. Are you assertive, a born leader? Or are you more comfortable contributing under someone else's leadership? Are you outgoing, articulate, and comfortable around people? Or do you prefer working alone? Make a list of what you believe are your four or five most important qualities. Ask a relative or friend to rate your traits as well.

If you're having difficulty figuring out your interests, characteristics, or capabilities, consult your college career center. Many campuses administer a variety of tests that can help you identify interests, aptitudes, and personality traits. These tests won't reveal your "perfect" job, but they'll help you focus on the types of work best suited to your personality.

How Can You Make Yourself More Valuable?

While you're figuring out what you want from a job and what you can offer an employer, you can take positive steps toward building your career. First, look for opportunities to develop skills, gain experience, and expand your professional network. These might involve internships, volunteer work, freelance projects, part-time jobs, or projects that you initiate on your own. You can look for freelance projects on Craigslist and numerous other websites; some of these jobs have only nominal pay, but they do provide an opportunity for you to display your skills. Also consider applying your talents to *crowdsourcing* projects, in which companies and nonprofit organizations invite the public to contribute solutions to various challenges. Look for ways to expand your *employment portfolio* and establish your *personal brand* (see the following sections).

Second, learn more about the industry or industries in which you want to work, and stay on top of new developments. Join networks of professional colleagues and friends who can help you keep up with trends and events. Follow the leading voices in a profession on social media. Many professional societies have student chapters or offer students discounted memberships. Take courses and pursue other educational or life experiences that would be difficult while working full time.

Whether you call it your personal brand or your professional promise, figure out what you want to be as a professional and how you should communicate that to others.

BUILDING AN EMPLOYMENT PORTFOLIO

Employers want proof that you have the skills to succeed on the job, which can be challenging if you don't have a lot of relevant work experience in your target field. Fortunately, you can use your college classes, volunteer work, and other activities to assemble compelling proof by creating an *employment portfolio*, a collection of projects that demonstrate your skills and knowledge.

Your portfolio is likely to be a multimedia effort, with physical work samples (such as reports, proposals, or marketing materials), digital documents, web content, blog posts, photographs, video clips, and other items. As appropriate, you can include these items in your LinkedIn profile, bring them to interviews, and have them ready whenever an employer, client, or networking contact asks for samples of your work.

You have a variety of options for hosting a portfolio online. Your LinkedIn profile (see page 507) can function as your portfolio home, your college may offer portfolio hosting, or you might consider one of the many commercial portfolio hosting services. To see a selection of student e-portfolios from colleges around the United States, go to **real-timeupdates.com/ebc13**, select Student Assignments, and locate the link to student e-portfolios.

Throughout this course, pay close attention to the assignments marked "Portfolio Builder," which start in Chapter 8. These items can make good samples of your communication skills and your ability to understand and solve business-related challenges. By combining these projects with samples from your other courses, you can create a compelling portfolio when you're ready to start interviewing. Your portfolio is also a great resource for writing your résumé because it reminds you of all the great work you've done over the years. Moreover, you can continue to refine and expand your portfolio throughout your career; many independent professionals use portfolios to advertise their services.

As you assemble your portfolio, collect anything that shows your ability to perform, whether it's in school, on the job, or in other venues. However, you *must* check with employers before including any items that you created while you were an employee, and check with clients before including any *work products* (anything you wrote, designed, programmed, and so on) they purchased from you. Many business documents contain confidential information that companies don't want distributed to outside audiences.

For each item you add to your portfolio, write a brief description that helps other people understand the meaning and significance of the project. Include such items as these:

- **Background.** Why did you undertake this project? Was it a school project, a work assignment, or something you did on your own initiative?
- **Project objectives.** Explain the project's goals, if relevant.
- **Collaborators.** If you worked with others, be sure to mention that and discuss team dynamics if appropriate. For instance, if you led the team or worked with others long distance as a virtual team, point that out.
- **Constraints.** Sometimes the most impressive thing about a project is the time or budget constraints under which it was created. If such constraints apply to a project, consider mentioning them in a way that doesn't sound like an excuse for poor quality. If you had only one week to create a website, for example, you might say that "One of the intriguing challenges of this project was the deadline; I had only one week to design, compose, test, and publish this material."
- **Outcomes.** If the project's goals were measurable, what was the result? For example, if you wrote a letter soliciting donations for a charitable cause, how much money did you raise?
- **Learning experience.** If appropriate, describe what you learned during the course of the project.

Keep in mind that the portfolio itself is a communication project, so be sure to apply everything you'll learn in this course about effective communication and good design. Also, assume that potential employers will find your e-portfolio site, even if you don't tell them about it, so don't include anything that doesn't represent you at your professional best.

BUILDING YOUR PERSONAL BRAND

You have probably heard the advice to develop a "personal brand" but might not know how to proceed or might not be comfortable with the concept of "branding" yourself. This section presents five steps that can make the task easier and more authentic.

Note that the process outlined here isn't about coming up with three or four words that are supposed to describe you, such as *visionary, creator, problem solver,* or things like that, as you may come across in some discussions of personal branding. This is a much more practical and comprehensive process that identifies the specific qualifications that you can bring to the job, backs them up with solid evidence, and makes sure you are ready with a concise answer when an employer asks, "So, tell me about yourself."

Don't Call It Personal Branding If You Don't Care for the Term

Some people object to the term personal branding, with its associations of product marketing, the implied need to "get out there and promote yourself," and perhaps the unseemly idea of reducing something as complex as yourself to an advertising slogan. If you are just starting you career, you might also wonder how to craft a meaningful brand when you don't have any relevant work experience.

Moreover, although personal branding makes obvious sense for professional speakers, authors, consultants, entrepreneurs, and others who must promote themselves in the public marketplace, those who aspire to professional or managerial positions in a corporate structure may rightly wonder why they need to "brand" themselves at all.

However, the underlying concept of branding as a *promise* applies to everyone, no matter the career stage or trajectory. A brand is fundamentally a promise to deliver on a specific set of values. For everyone in business, that promise is critical, whether it extends to a million people in the online audience for a TED talk or a half-dozen people inside a small company. And even if you never think about your personal brand, you are continuously creating and re-creating it by the way you conduct yourself as a professional. In other words, even if you reject the idea of personal branding, other people will form an opinion of you and your "brand" anyway, so you might as well take charge and help create the impression that you want others to have of you.

As an alternative to a personal brand, think of your *professional promise*. Frame it this way: When people hear your name, what do you want them to think about you and your professional attributes and qualifications?

Write the "Story of You"

When it's time to write or update your résumé, step back and think about where you've been in your life and your career and where you'd like to go. Helpful questions include *Do you like the path you're on, or is it time for a change? Are you focused on a particular field, or do you need some time to explore?*

This is also a great planning tool for developing a personal brand. In Chapter 15, you'll see this referred to as writing the "story of you," and it's divided into three sections:

- **Where I have been**—the experiences from my past that give me insight into where I would like to go in the future
- **Where I am now**—where I currently stand in terms of education and career, and what I know about myself (including knowledge and skills, personal attributes, and professional interests)
- **Where I want to be**—the career progress and experiences I want to have, areas I want to explore, and goals I want to achieve

Think in terms of an image or a theme you'd like to project. *Am I academically gifted? A daring innovator? A well-rounded professional with wide-ranging talents? A technical wizard? A dependable, "go-to" problem solver that people can count on? A "connector" who can bring people and resources together?*

Writing this story arc is a valuable planning exercise that helps you think about where you want to go in your career. In essence, you are clarifying who you are professionally and defining a future version of yourself—and these are the foundations of your personal brand/professional promise. Another important benefit is that it makes the personal branding effort authentic, because it is based on your individual interests and passions.

Construct Your Brand Pyramid

With your professional story arc as a guide, the next step is to construct a *brand pyramid* that has all the relevant support points needed to build a personal brand message (see Figure 2).

Start by compiling a *private inventory* of skills, attributes, experience, and areas for improvement. This should be a positive but realistic assessment of what you have to offer now and a "to-grow" list of areas where you want to develop or improve. Obviously, this inventory isn't for public consumption. As much as possible, provide evidence to back up each quality you list. If you are diligent and detail oriented, for instance, identify a time that you saved a project by methodically analyzing the situation to find a problem that others had overlooked. If you are a creative thinker, identify a time when you came up with an unusual new idea at work. Employers want to know *how* you can apply your skills, attributes, and experience; the more evidence you can provide, the better.

Next, select the appropriate materials from your inventory to develop a *public profile* that highlights the qualities you want to promote. As "Put Your Promise to Work" explains, this profile can take on a variety of forms for different communication platforms.

Finally, distill your professional promise down to a single, brief headline, also known as a *tagline* or *elevator pitch*. The headline should be a statement of compelling value, not a generic job title. Instead of "I'm a social media specialist," you might say, "I help small companies get the same reach on social media as giant corporations."

Of course, many students won't have the relevant job experience to say something like that, and your personal brand might be more an expression of potential. Even if you have no relevant professional experience, you still have personal attributes and educational qualifications that are the foundations of your brand. The key is to make sure it's realistic and suggests a logical connection between the present and the future. Someone pursuing an MBA in finance can reasonably claim to have a strong toolset for financial analysis, but someone with no corporate work experience can't claim to be a bold, high-impact executive.

Here's a good example: "I am a data science major ready to make numbers come alive through leading-edge techniques in deep learning, data mining, and visualization."

Note that both your public profile and your headline should use relevant *keywords* from target job descriptions (see page 496).

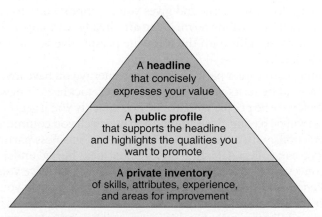

Figure 2 Your Personal Brand Pyramid
Build your personal brand at three levels: a *private inventory* of your skills and assets, a *public profile* based on that inventory and how you want to present yourself to the world, and a *headline* that encapsulates what you can do for employers or clients.

Reduce or Eliminate Factors That Could Damage Your Brand

Every brand, no matter how popular and powerful, can be damaged by negative perceptions or performance issues. After identifying all the positives, do an objective analysis of areas that could undermine your career-building efforts. For example, someone who tends to overpromise and underdeliver is going to develop a reputation for unreliability that could outweigh whatever positive qualities he or she can bring to the job. Other concerns might be related to specific skills that you need to develop in order to progress toward your career goals.

Be constantly mindful of the "multimedia you" that the world sees—your online presence, your personal appearance, your conduct in business and social settings, the way you sound on the phone, your mannerisms, your vocabulary, and anything else that shapes your reputation. Careers can be derailed by a single misjudged social media post, so always be putting the best "you" on display.

Put Your Promise to Work

Now it's time to put the branding message to work. Your public profile could be expressed in a variety of ways—as a conventional résumé, the summary section on LinkedIn, an infographic résumé, or the introductory section of a personal webpage or e-portfolio.

The headline can be adapted and used in multiple ways as well, including the headline field on LinkedIn, the qualifications summary on your résumé, your Twitter profile, and as a ready answer to the common interview question "So, tell me about yourself."

Naturally, your brand message should be consistent across all the platforms and conversations where it is used. For instance, an employer reviewing your résumé is likely to visit your LinkedIn profile as well, so it's important that the messages match. If you complete your branding pyramid first, it'll be easy to adapt it to a variety of different purposes while keeping your message consistent.

As you progress through your career, bear in mind that all this planning and communication is of no value if you fail to deliver on your brand promise. Remember that branding is only a *promise*—it's your *performance* that ultimately counts. When you deliver quality results time after time, your talents and professionalism will speak for you.

Lastly, your branding pyramid should be a "living document" that is updated whenever you acquire new skills or job experiences or want to move in a different direction. In addition, periodically revisiting it can be a good way to recapture the passion that initially launched you down your career path.

Stage 3: Succeeding in Your First Job

Your first job sets the stage for your career and gives you an opportunity to explore how you want to position yourself for the long term. If you are already working or are changing careers, you can combine these skills with the work-life perspective you already have to take your career to a new level.

As you progress along your career path, the time and energy you have invested in this course will continue to yield benefits year after year. As you tackle each new challenge, influential company leaders—the people who decide how quickly you'll get promoted and how much you'll earn—will be paying close attention to how well you communicate. They will observe your interactions with colleagues, customers, and business partners. They'll take note of how well you can collect data, find the essential ideas buried under mountains of information, and convey those points to other people. They'll observe your ability to adapt to different audiences and circumstances. They'll be watching when you encounter tough situations that require careful attention to ethics and etiquette. The good news: Every insight you gain and every skill you develop in this course will help you shine in your career.

No other skill can help your career in as many ways as communication. Discover what business communication is all about, why communication skills are essential to your career, how intelligent technology is revolutionizing business communication, and how to adapt your communication experiences in life and college to the business world. Improve your skills in such vital areas as listening, conflict resolution, collaboration, negotiation, and professional etiquette. Explore the advantages and the challenges of a diverse workforce, and develop the skills that every communicator needs in order to succeed in today's global, multicultural business environment.

Stefan Dahl Langstrup/Alamy Stock Photo

1

Professional Communication in a Digital, Social, Mobile World

LEARNING OBJECTIVES

After studying this chapter, you will be able to

1 Explain the importance of effective communication to your career and to the companies where you will work.

2 Explain what it means to communicate as a professional in a business context.

3 Contrast the conventional communication process model with the social communication model.

4 Identify five major benefits of business communication technology and three major innovations that are reshaping the practice of communication.

5 Define *ethics*, explain the difference between an ethical dilemma and an ethical lapse, and list six guidelines for making ethical communication choices.

6 Identify six related skills that you will have the opportunity to develop as you work on your communication skills in this course.

MyLab Business Communication

Improve Your Grade!

If your instructor is using MyLab Business Communication, visit **www.pearson.com/mylab/businesscommunication** for videos, simulations, and writing exercises.

ON THE JOB: COMMUNICATING AT
AFFECTIVA

Bringing Emotion to the Human-Computer Experience

Like many college students, Rana el Kaliouby pursued her education with an important life goal in mind. In her case, it was developing computer programs that could "read" people's faces, a goal she pursued from her undergraduate studies in Egypt to a PhD program at the University of Cambridge in England to her work as a research scientist in the Media Lab at the Massachusetts Institute of Technology (MIT). She had become fascinated by the possibility of using artificial intelligence (AI) to identify emotional states by measuring facial expressions. Her motivation was to help people on the autism spectrum who struggle to pick up emotional cues when communicating with others. Could a system read faces and provide information to help people have richer social interactions?

After she created a program at MIT that could track emotional responses by comparing facial movements with a catalog of common expressions, she was surprised by how many of the lab's corporate sponsors were interested in it. The inquiries ranged from Toyota, which wanted to know if the program might help detect when drivers were getting drowsy, to Fox television studios, which wanted to use it for audience-testing new shows. With so many potential opportunities to pursue, the Media Lab's management decided the best move was to spin the project out as its own company. That company is Boston-based Affectiva, where el Kaliouby serves as CEO and guides the company's

Rana el Kaliouby leads Affectiva's efforts to make computer systems better at understanding and reacting to human emotions.

2

research and development in *affective computing* (computing dealing with human emotions).

The new company's first commercial success was in advertising, with companies using the system to see how viewers respond to digital online content. Businesses spend billions of dollars on advertising every year, for example, and the managers spending that money are understandably curious to know whether their ads are triggering the emotional responses they are designed to trigger.

From there, el Kaliouby and her team began applying the technology to other projects, and now more than a thousand companies use it in such diverse efforts as education, health care, gaming, and human resources. (Don't be surprised if you encounter an online video interview during your job search that uses Affectiva's system or something similar to measure your emotional reactions.) Affectiva has also expanded into voice analysis, giving businesses another way to assess their communication efforts.

That original dream of helping people with autism hasn't been forgotten, either. A company called Brain Power incorporates Affectiva's capabilities into Google Glass eyeglasses, creating a system that provides children and adults on the spectrum with real-time feedback that helps them develop skills needed to navigate social situations.

Beyond these applications, el Kaliouby wants people to understand how important it is for AI systems to have some degree of empathy, both to be more effective and to make sure that AI becomes a positive force in people's lives, rather than a negative. AI is reaching deeper into just about every aspect of business, including the multiple applications involving communication that you'll read about in this book. The better that computers can get along with us, the better we'll be able to get along with them.[1]

WWW.AFFECTIVA.COM

Understanding Why Communication Matters

Affectiva's work in emotion recognition and analytics (see the chapter opener) highlights the complexity of communication and its importance to every business. **Communication** is the process of transferring information and meaning between senders and receivers, using one or more forms of media. For communication to be considered successful, it also must transfer understanding.[2] As Figure 1.1 on the next page indicates, communication can happen in a variety of ways, including successful transfers of information and understanding, negotiations in which the sender and receiver arrive at an agreed-on meaning, and unsuccessful attempts in which the receiver assembles a different message than the one the sender intended.

COMMUNICATION IS IMPORTANT TO YOUR CAREER

You can have the greatest ideas in the world, but they usually aren't much good to your company or your career if you can't express them clearly and persuasively. Some jobs, such as sales and customer support roles, are primarily about communicating. In fields such as engineering or finance, you often need to share complex ideas with executives, customers, and colleagues, and your ability to connect with people outside your field can be as important as your technical expertise. If you have the entrepreneurial urge, you will need to communicate with a wide range of audiences—from investors, bankers, and government regulators to employees, customers, and business partners.

The changing nature of employment is putting new pressure on communication skills, too. Companies such as Uber and Lyft are the most visible in the *gig economy,* where independent contractors work without many of the advantages or the disadvantages of regular employment. Many other companies now supplement their permanent workforces with independent contractors who are brought on for a short period or even just a single project. Chances are you will spend part of your career as one of these independent freelancers, working without the support network that an established company environment provides. You will have to "sell yourself" into each new contract, communicate successfully in a wide range of work situations, and take full responsibility for your career growth and success.

If you move into an executive role or launch your own company, you can expect communication to consume the majority of your time. Top executives spend most of their

---

1 **LEARNING OBJECTIVE**
Explain the importance of effective communication to your career and to the companies where you will work.

Communication is the process of transferring information, meaning, and understanding between senders and receivers.

If you haven't read the Prologue yet, we encourage you to give it a quick read now. It will help you get the most out of your textbook, and it offers tips on using this course to plan a more-successful and less-stressful job search.

In every career path you can take—employee, independent freelancer, entrepreneur, manager—you will need to have strong communication skills.

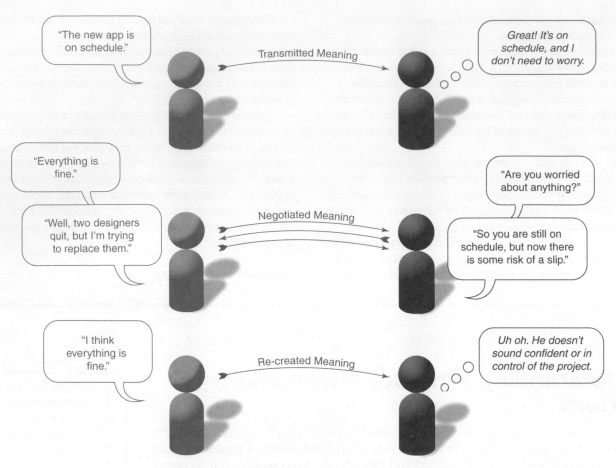

Figure 1.1   Sharing Information and Understanding
These three exchanges between a software project manager (*left*) and his boss (*right*) illustrate the variety of ways in which information is shared between senders and receivers. In the top exchange, the sender's meaning is transmitted intact to the receiver, who accepts what the sender says at face value. In the middle exchange, the sender and receiver negotiate the meaning by discussing the situation. The negotiated meaning is that everything is fine so far, but the risk of a schedule slip is now higher than it was before. In the bottom exchange, the receiver has a negative emotional reaction to the word *think* and as a result creates her own meaning—which is that everything probably is not fine, despite what the sender says.

REAL-TIME UPDATES

LEARN MORE BY VISITING THIS WEBSITE

Check out the cutting edge of business communication

This Pinterest board created by the authors highlights some of the most important changes taking place in the field of business communication. Go to **real-timeupdates.com/ebc13** and select Learn More in the Students section.

workdays communicating, and businesspeople who can't communicate well don't stand much chance of reaching the top.

No matter which path you follow, keep in mind that the world is full of good marketing strategists, good accountants, good engineers, and good attorneys—but it is not full of good communicators. View this as an opportunity to stand out from your competition in the job market.

COMMUNICATION IS IMPORTANT TO YOUR COMPANY

Aside from the personal benefits, communication should be important to you because it is important to your company, in three essential ways:

Companies rely on communication for efficient operations, timely business intelligence, and positive relationships.

- **Operations.** Every company needs fast, effective communication between managers and staff, within departments, between departments, and between the company and its external business partners. Communication carries everything from high-level strategic plans down to minute technical details, and any bottlenecks or breakdowns can reduce operational efficiency and create problems with quality or safety.

- **Intelligence.** Companies need to keep a constant "ear to the ground" to be alerted to new opportunities, risks, and impending problems—both internally and externally.
- **Relationships.** Just as in personal and social relationships, business relationships depend on communication. Effective communication strengthens the connections between a company and all its **stakeholders**, which are any persons or organizations significantly affected by the company's business decisions and operations.[3] Stakeholder groups include employees, customers, investors, creditors, suppliers, and local communities. Individuals within companies also rely on communication to foster the emotional connections that create a healthy work environment.[4]

> *Stakeholders* are any persons or organizations significantly affected by a company's business decisions and operations.

Put simply, no business can function without effective communication, and the better the communication, the better every part of the company is likely to run.

WHAT MAKES BUSINESS COMMUNICATION EFFECTIVE?

To make your communication efforts as effective as possible, focus on making them *practical, factual, concise, clear,* and *persuasive*:

> Effective messages are *practical, factual, concise, clear,* and *persuasive*.

- **Provide practical information.** Give recipients useful information that helps them solve problems, pursue opportunities, or take other action.
- **Give facts rather than vague impressions.** Use concrete language, specific detail, and information that is clear, convincing, accurate, and ethical. Even when an opinion is called for, present compelling evidence to support your conclusion.
- **Present information in a concise, efficient manner.** Concise messages show respect for people's time, and they increase the chances of a positive response.
- **Clarify expectations and responsibilities.** Craft messages to generate a specific response from a specific audience. When appropriate, clearly state what you expect from audience members or what you can do for them.
- **Offer compelling, persuasive arguments and recommendations.** When a situation calls for persuasive communication, show your readers how they will benefit by responding the way you would like them to respond.

Keep these five important characteristics in mind as you compare the ineffective and effective versions of the message in Figure 1.2 on the next page.

Communicating as a Professional

> **2 LEARNING OBJECTIVE**
> Explain what it means to communicate as a professional in a business context.

You've been communicating your entire life, of course, but if you don't have a lot of work experience yet, meeting the expectations of a professional environment might require some adjustment. A good place to start is to consider what it means to be a professional. **Professionalism** is the quality of performing at a high level and conducting oneself with purpose and pride. It means doing more than putting in the hours and collecting a paycheck: True professionals go beyond minimum expectations and commit to making meaningful contributions. Professionalism can be broken down into six distinct traits: striving to excel, being dependable and accountable, being a team player, demonstrating a sense of etiquette, making ethical decisions, and maintaining a positive outlook (see Figure 1.3 on page 7).

> *Professionalism* is the quality of performing at a high level and conducting oneself with purpose and pride.

A key message to glean from Figure 1.3 is how much these elements of professionalism depend on effective communication. For example, to be a team player, you need to be able to collaborate, resolve conflicts, and interact with a wide variety of personalities. Without strong communication skills, you won't be able to perform to your potential, and others won't recognize you as the professional you'd like to be.

This section offers a brief look at the skills employers will expect you to have, the nature of communication in an organizational environment, and the importance of adopting an audience-centered approach.

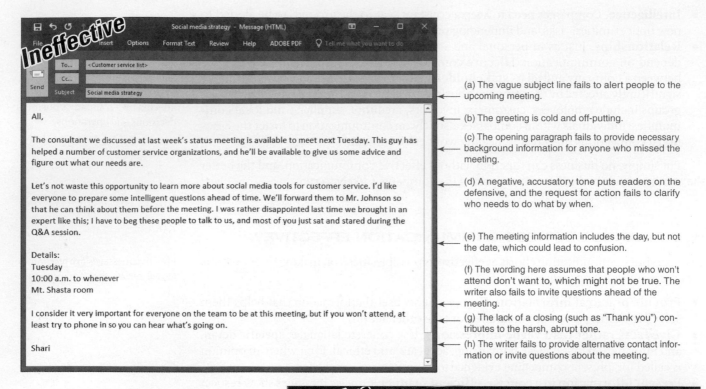

(a) The vague subject line fails to alert people to the upcoming meeting.

(b) The greeting is cold and off-putting.

(c) The opening paragraph fails to provide necessary background information for anyone who missed the meeting.

(d) A negative, accusatory tone puts readers on the defensive, and the request for action fails to clarify who needs to do what by when.

(e) The meeting information includes the day, but not the date, which could lead to confusion.

(f) The wording here assumes that people who won't attend don't want to, which might not be true. The writer also fails to invite questions ahead of the meeting.

(g) The lack of a closing (such as "Thank you") contributes to the harsh, abrupt tone.

(h) The writer fails to provide alternative contact information or invite questions about the meeting.

(a) An informative subject line helps people grasp important details immediately.

(b) The greeting is friendly without being too casual.

(c) The opening paragraph fills in missing information so that everyone can grasp the importance of the message.

(d) This upbeat paragraph emphasizes the positive value of the meeting, and the request provides enough information to enable readers to respond.

(e) The date eliminates scheduling uncertainty.

(f) The writer offers everyone a chance to participate, without making anyone feel guilty about not being able to attend in person. The closing paragraph invites questions ahead of time so they don't derail the meeting.

(g) Like the greeting, the close has a warm and personal tone, without being too casual.

(h) The *email signature* provides additional information and alternative contact options.

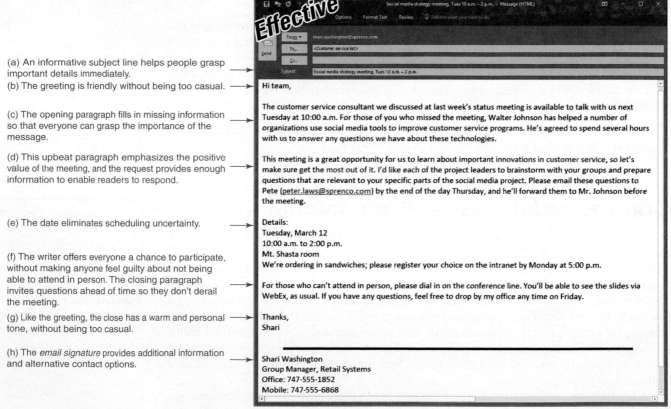

Figure 1.2 **Effective Professional Communication**

At first glance, the first email message looks like a reasonable attempt at communicating with the members of a project team. However, review the blue annotations to see just how many problems the message really has.

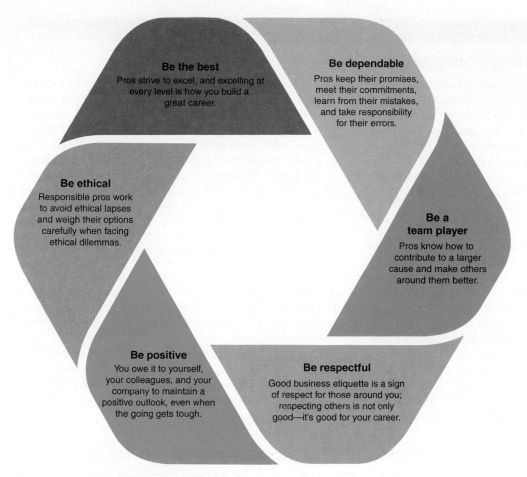

Be the best
Pros strive to excel, and excelling at every level is how you build a great career.

Be dependable
Pros keep their promises, meet their commitments, learn from their mistakes, and take responsibility for their errors.

Be ethical
Responsible pros work to avoid ethical lapses and weigh their options carefully when facing ethical dilemmas.

Be a team player
Pros know how to contribute to a larger cause and make others around them better.

Be positive
You owe it to yourself, your colleagues, and your company to maintain a positive outlook, even when the going gets tough.

Be respectful
Good business etiquette is a sign of respect for those around you; respecting others is not only good—it's good for your career.

Figure 1.3   Elements of Professionalism
To be respected as a true professional, develop these six qualities.

UNDERSTANDING WHAT EMPLOYERS EXPECT FROM YOU

Today's employers expect you to be competent at a range of communication tasks that reflect the value of communication discussed on pages 4–5:

- **Acquiring, processing, and sharing information.** Employers expect you to be able to recognize information needs, locate and evaluate reliable sources of information (particularly from online sources), organize information into cohesive messages, and use information ethically. This collection of skills is often referred to as *digital information fluency.*[5] Information fluency includes **critical thinking**, which is the ability to evaluate evidence completely and objectively in order to form logical conclusions and make sound recommendations.
- **Using communication to foster positive working relationships.** This task includes listening, practicing good etiquette, resolving conflicts respectfully, and communicating with people from diverse backgrounds.
- **Representing your employer in the public arena.** Employers expect you to conduct yourself responsibly and professionally on social media and in other venues and to follow accepted standards of grammar, spelling, and other aspects of quality writing and speaking.
- **Efficiently using the tools at your disposal.** Aside from in-person conversations and meetings, every instance of business communication involves some level of technological assistance, so employers expect a level of proficiency with the tools they provide you to use.

You'll have the opportunity to practice these skills throughout this course, but don't stop there. Successful professionals continue to hone communication skills throughout their careers.

Employers expect you to possess a wide range of communication skills.

Critical thinking is the ability to evaluate evidence completely and objectively in order to form logical conclusions and make sound recommendations.

MOBILE APP
Pocket collects online content you'd like to read or view later and syncs it across your mobile devices.

Practice Your Professionalism

Don't wait until you're on the job to develop your professionalism. College gives you multiple opportunities to hone your approach to work, which will help you hit the ground running after you graduate. The sooner you can get in sync with the professional work environment, the sooner you are likely to succeed in your first job and position yourself for a promotion. If you are already working or have worked in a business setting, think about the ways you could make an even stronger impression and fine-tune those skills.

Here are three opportunities to start pursuing now:

- **Communication with your instructors.** If you have ever started an email message to an instructor with "Yo, prof," now would be a good time to up your game. Imagine that you are communicating with a high-level executive or someone else whose opinion of you will have a huge impact on your career advancement. You don't have to be stiff and overly formal; read the situation based on how each instructor communicates with you. Use a respectful greeting (ask your instructors how they would like to be greeted in person and in writing, if they haven't already told you), complete sentences, and standard punctuation.

- **The quality of your work.** Everything you produce reflects your commitment to quality, in both substance and presentation. Get in the habit of doing your best work now, and it'll be second nature by the time you're getting paid to do it.
- **Scheduling and commitments.** Missing deadlines on the job can mean missing major career opportunities. Meeting your commitments requires the ability to estimate how long things will take (which comes with practice and careful planning) and the mental strength to power through the tough parts of a project. See "Think Now, Write Later" on page 174 for advice on how to prevent last-minute surprises when you're staring down a deadline.

COACH YOURSELF
1. How would you rate the quality of your interactions with your instructors? What could you do to improve communication?
2. Do you feel awkward when communicating at a more formal level than you are accustomed to in your personal or social life? What steps can you take to get comfortable with "professional-grade" communication before you graduate?

COMMUNICATING IN AN ORGANIZATIONAL CONTEXT

The *formal communication network* mirrors the company's organizational structure.

In addition to having the proper skills, you need to learn how to apply those skills in the business environment, which can be quite different from the social and scholastic environments you are accustomed to. Every organization has a **formal communication network**, in which ideas and information flow along the lines of command (the hierarchical levels) in the company's organization structure (see Figure 1.4).

Throughout the formal network, information flows in four directions. *Downward communication* flows from top executives to middle managers to frontline employees, conveying executive decisions and providing information that helps employees do their jobs. *Upward communication* flows from employees to middle managers and from middle managers to top executives, giving those at high levels insight into problems, trends, opportunities, grievances, and performance. *Horizontal* or *lateral communication* flows between departments to help employees share information, coordinate tasks, and solve complex problems. Finally, with *diagonal communication*, information crosses department lines while moving up or down.[6] When problems and opportunities span multiple departments, horizontal and diagonal flows can help ensure that communication doesn't get stifled moving up and down the vertical lines in the organization chart.[7]

The *informal communication network* encompasses all communication that occurs outside the formal network.

Every organization also has an **informal communication network**, which encompasses all communication that occurs outside of formal channels. Some of this informal communication takes place naturally when employees interact on the job and in social settings, and some of it takes place when the formal network doesn't provide information that employees want. In fact, the limitations of formal communication networks helped spur the growth of social media in the business environment. Communication in the informal network is healthy and important, because the formal network can't always capture and share all the information that helps people do their jobs. However, if a workplace is rife with rumors and company gossip, this situation could be a sign that the formal network is not functioning effectively.

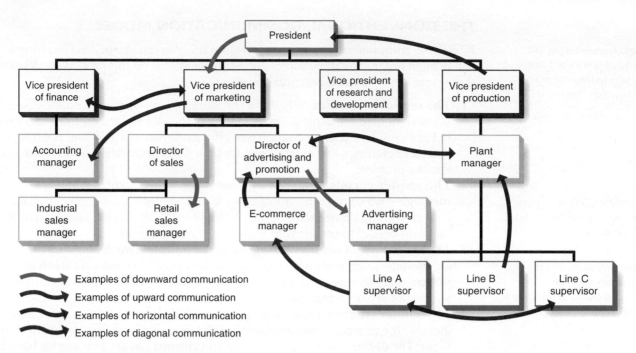

Figure 1.4   Formal Communication Network
The formal communication network is defined by the relationships between the various job positions in the organization. Messages can flow upward (from a lower-level employee to a higher-level employee), downward (from a higher-level employee to a lower-level employee), horizontally (across the organization, between employees at the same or similar levels), or diagonally (across departments and upward or downward).

ADOPTING AN AUDIENCE-CENTERED APPROACH

An **audience-centered approach** involves understanding and respecting the members of your audience and making every effort to get your message across in a way that is meaningful to them. This approach is also known as adopting the **"you" attitude**, where *you* is the person receiving the message, in contrast to messages that are about *me* as the sender. Learn as much as possible about the beliefs, education, age, status, communication style, and personal and professional concerns of your readers and listeners. If you're addressing people you don't know and you're unable to find out more about them, try to project yourself into their position by using common sense and imagination.

The *audience-centered approach* involves understanding, respecting, and meeting the needs of your audience members; it is also known as adopting the *"you" attitude.*

Relating to the needs of others is a key part of *emotional intelligence*, the ability to read other people's emotions accurately and to manage one's own emotions in productive ways.[8] The more you know about the people you're communicating with, the easier it will be to focus on their needs—which, in turn, will make it easier for them to hear your message, understand it, and respond positively. A vital element of audience-centered communication is professional *etiquette*, which you'll study in Chapter 3.

Exploring the Communication Process

3 LEARNING OBJECTIVE
Contrast the conventional communication process model with the social communication model.

Even with the best intentions, communication efforts can fail. Messages can get lost or simply ignored. The receiver of a message can interpret it in ways the sender never imagined. Two people receiving the same information can reach different conclusions about what it means.

Fortunately, by understanding communication as a process with distinct steps, you can improve the odds that your messages will reach their intended audiences and produce their intended effects. This section explores the communication process in two stages: first by following a message from one sender to one receiver in the conventional communication model and then by expanding on that approach with multiple messages and participants in the social communication model.

THE CONVENTIONAL COMMUNICATION MODEL

By viewing communication as a process (Figure 1.5), you can identify and improve the skills you need in order to be more successful. Many variations on this process model exist, but these eight steps provide a practical overview:

Viewing communication as a process helps you identify steps you can take to improve your success as a communicator.

1. **The sender has an idea.** Whether a communication effort will ultimately be effective starts right here and depends on the nature of the idea and the motivation for sending it. For example, if your motivation is to offer a solution to a problem, you have a better chance of crafting a meaningful message than if your motivation is merely to complain about a problem.

2. **The sender encodes the idea as a message.** When someone puts an idea into a **message**—which you can think of as the "container" for an idea—he or she is **encoding** it, or expressing it in words or images. Much of the focus of this course is on developing the skills needed to encode your ideas into effective messages.

When senders *encode* ideas into *messages*, they express those ideas in words or images.

3. **The sender produces the message in a transmittable medium.** With the appropriate message to express an idea, the sender now needs a **communication medium** to present that message to the intended audience. Media can be divided into oral (spoken), written, or visual formats.

The *communication medium* is the form a message takes; the *communication channel* is the system used to deliver the message.

4. **The sender transmits the message through a channel.** Technology continues to increase the number of **communication channels** you can use to transmit your messages. The distinction between medium and channel can get a bit murky, but think of the medium as the *form* a message takes (such as a written message) and the channel as the system used to *deliver* the message (such as Twitter or email).

5. **The audience receives the message.** If the channel functions properly, the message reaches its intended audience. However, mere arrival at the destination is no guarantee that the message will be noticed or understood correctly. As "How Audiences Receive Messages" (page 12) explains, many messages are either ignored or misinterpreted.

6. **The audience decodes the message.** After a message is received, the receiver needs to extract the idea from the message, a step known as **decoding**. "How Audiences Decode Messages" (page 12) takes a closer look at this complex and subtle step in the process.

When receivers *decode* messages, they extract meaning from the words or images they've received.

7. **The audience responds to the message.** By crafting messages in ways that show the benefits of responding, senders can increase the chances that recipients will respond in positive ways. However, as "How Audiences Respond to Messages" (page 13) points out, whether a receiver responds as the sender hopes depends on the receiver (a) *remembering* the message long enough to act on it, (b) being *able* to act on it, and (c) being *motivated* to respond.

Feedback is a reaction from the receiver back to the original sender that can offer clues about how successful the original message was.

8. **The audience provides feedback to the sender.** In addition to responding (or not responding) to the message, audience members may give **feedback** that helps the sender evaluate the effectiveness of the communication effort. Feedback can be

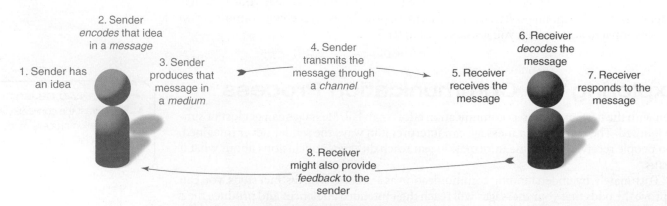

Figure 1.5   The Conventional Communication Process
This eight-step model is a simplified view of one cycle of communication. In reality, the process is complicated with noise, barriers, and interruptions, but understanding the basic concepts of encoding and decoding will help you as a sender and as a receiver.

verbal (using written or spoken words), nonverbal (using gestures, facial expressions, or other signals), or both. Just like the original message, however, this feedback from the receiver also needs to be decoded carefully. A smile, for example, can have many meanings.

Keep in mind that this description captures only one cycle of the communication process. A conversational exchange (in person, on the phone, or through a digital channel) could include dozens of these cycles before the sender and the receiver achieve a satisfactory transfer of information and understanding.

Considering the complexity of this process—and the barriers and distractions that often stand between sender and receiver—it should come as no surprise that communication efforts often fail to achieve the sender's objective. Fortunately, the better you understand the process, the more successful you'll be.

REAL-TIME UPDATES
LEARN MORE BY WATCHING THIS VIDEO
The process breakdowns that lead to miscommunication
This humorous video illustrates how communication efforts break down and how to avoid common problems. Go to **real-timeupdates.com/ebc13** and select Learn More in the Students section.

The following sections take a closer look at two important aspects of the process: environmental barriers that can block or distort messages and the steps audiences take to receive, decode, and respond to messages.

BARRIERS IN THE COMMUNICATION ENVIRONMENT

Within any communication environment, messages can be disrupted by a variety of **communication barriers**. These barriers include noise and distractions, competing messages, filters, and channel breakdowns:

- **Noise and distractions.** External distractions range from uncomfortable meeting rooms to computer screens cluttered with instant messages and reminders popping up all over the place. Internal distractions are thoughts and emotions that prevent audiences from focusing on incoming messages. The common habit of *multitasking*—attempting more than one task at a time—is practically guaranteed to create barriers when communication is involved, because the human brain simply isn't wired to work that way. You may think you are doing two or more tasks at once, but you are really shifting back and forth between individual tasks, and your productivity and focus can suffer every time you shift.[9] As more communication takes place on mobile devices, the need to insulate yourself from noise and distractions is going to keep growing.
- **Competing messages.** Having your audience's undivided attention is a rare luxury. In most cases, you must compete with other messages that are trying to reach your audience at the same time.
- **Filters.** Messages can be blocked or distorted by *filters*, any human or technological interventions between the sender and the receiver. Filtering can be both intentional (such as automatically filing incoming messages based on sender or content) or unintentional (such as an overly aggressive spam filter that deletes legitimate emails). The structure and culture of an organization can also inhibit the flow of vital messages. And, in some cases, the people or companies you rely on to deliver your message can distort it or filter it to meet their own needs.
- **Channel breakdowns.** Sometimes the channel simply breaks down and fails to deliver your message at all. A colleague you were counting on to deliver a message to your boss might have forgotten to do so, or a computer server might have crashed and prevented your blog from updating.

Everyone in an organization can help minimize barriers and distractions. As a communicator, try to be aware of any barriers that could prevent your messages from reaching their intended audiences. As a manager, keep an eye out for any organizational barriers that could be inhibiting the flow of information. In any situation, a small dose of common sense and courtesy goes a long way. Turn off that mobile phone before you step into a meeting. Don't talk across the tops of other people's cubicles, and don't play music at a level that can distract others.

Communication barriers can block or distort messages before they reach the intended audience.

Minimizing barriers and distractions in the communication environment is everyone's responsibility.

Finally, take steps to insulate yourself from distractions. Don't let messages interrupt you every minute of the day. Instead, set aside time to attend to messages all at once so that you can focus the rest of the time.

INSIDE THE MIND OF YOUR AUDIENCE

After a message works its way through the communication channel and reaches the intended audience, it encounters a whole new set of challenges. Understanding how audiences receive, decode, and respond to messages will help you create more effective messages.

How Audiences Receive Messages

To truly receive a message, audience members need to sense it, select it, then perceive it as a message.

For an audience member to receive a message, three events need to occur: The receiver has to *sense* the presence of a message, *select* it from all the other messages clamoring for attention, and *perceive* it as an actual message (as opposed to random, pointless noise).[10] You can appreciate the magnitude of this challenge by walking down any busy street in a commercial section of town. You will encounter hundreds of messages—billboards, posters, store window displays, car stereos, people talking on mobile phones, car horns, street signs, traffic lights, and so on. However, you will sense, select, and perceive only a fraction of these messages.

Selection attention is focusing on a subset of incoming stimuli or messages while ignoring others; it can cause intended recipients to block out some or all of your message.

Today's business audiences are much like pedestrians on busy streets. They are inundated with so many messages and so much noise that they can miss or ignore many of the messages intended for them. One of the mind's defenses against this barrage is **selective attention**, which is focusing on a subset of the incoming stimuli or information sources and ignoring others.[11] Not surprisingly, this focused attention can be helpful at times and harmful at others. If you are on your mobile phone trying hard to listen to the other party, your mind will try to block out all the noise sources—one of which might be a car horn warning you to get out of the way.

To improve the odds that your messages will be successfully perceived by your audience, pay close attention to expectations, ease of use, familiarity, empathy, and technical compatibility.

Throughout this course, you will learn a variety of techniques to craft messages that get noticed. In general, follow these five principles to increase your chances of success:

- **Consider audience expectations.** Deliver messages using the media and channels that the audience expects. If colleagues expect meeting notices to be delivered by email, don't suddenly switch gears and start delivering the notices via blog posts without telling anyone. Of course, sometimes going *against* expectations can stimulate audience attention, which is why advertisers sometimes do wacky and creative things to get noticed. However, for most business communication efforts, following the expectations of your audience is the most efficient way to get your message across.
- **Make messages user-friendly.** Even if audiences are actively looking for your messages, they may not get the messages if you make them hard to find, hard to navigate, or hard to read.
- **Emphasize familiarity.** Use words, images, and designs that are familiar to your audience. For example, company websites often put information about the company on a page called "About" or "About Us," so many visitors expect to see such information on a page with this title.
- **Practice empathy.** Make sure your messages speak to the audience by clearly addressing *their* wants and needs—not just yours. This is the essence of the "you" attitude.
- **Design for compatibility.** Make sure your messages are compatible with the devices your audiences will use to read, listen to, or view them on. For example, websites designed for full-size computer screens can be difficult to view on mobile devices, so contemporary web design emphasizes the need to support a wide variety of screen sizes and modes of interaction.

How Audiences Decode Messages

Decoding is a complex process; receivers often extract different meanings from messages than senders attempted to encode in their messages.

A received message doesn't "mean" anything until the recipient decodes it and assigns meaning to it, and there is no guarantee the receiver will assign the same meaning that the sender intended. Assigning meaning through decoding is a highly personal process influenced by culture, individual experience, learning and thinking styles, ego, hopes, fears, beliefs, and even temporary moods.

Our minds have a variety of self-defense mechanisms that protect our perceptions of the world and of ourselves, and our minds sometimes ignore, deny, or distort incoming information that threatens those views. If you have ever used the phrase, "You only hear what you want to hear," you were referring to an example of this distorted perception. For example, if you ask four people to review a business plan that you believe is rather brilliant, and three of the appraisals come back positive, your ego will be tempted to reject the negative comments in the fourth review.

It's human nature to protect our views of the world and of ourselves, even to the extent of ignoring or distorting incoming information to fit our preconceived notions of reality.

Differences in language and usage also influence received meaning. If you ask an employee to send you a report on sales figures "as soon as possible," does that mean within 10 seconds, 10 minutes, or 10 days? By clarifying expectations and resolving potential ambiguities in your messages, you can minimize such uncertainties.

Individual thinking styles are another important factor in message decoding. For instance, someone who places a high value on objective analysis and clear logic might interpret a message differently than someone who values emotion or intuition (reaching conclusions without using rational processes).

In general, the more experiences you share with another person, the more likely you are to share your perceptions of the world and therefore arrive at the same meanings for a given message (see Figure 1.6). Careful audience analysis helps you understand how much of this overlap you have with your readers or listeners. The less shared experience you have with your audiences, the more background information and context you will need to provide in your messages.

How Audiences Respond to Messages

Your message has been delivered, received, and correctly decoded. Now what? Will audience members respond in the way you'd like them to? Only if three events occur.

First, the recipient must *remember* the message long enough to act on it. Simplifying greatly, memory works in several stages: *Sensory memory* momentarily captures incoming data from the senses, then whatever sensory data the recipient pays attention to are transferred to *short-term memory*. Information survives in short-term memory for only a matter of seconds and will disappear or get crowded out by new information if it isn't transferred to *long-term memory*. This transfer can be done either actively (such as when a person memorizes a list of items) or passively (such as when a new piece of information connects with something else the recipient already has stored in long-term memory). Finally, the information needs to be *retrieved* when the recipient wants to act on it.[12] By communicating in ways that reflect the audience's wants and needs, you increase the chance that your messages will be remembered and retrieved.

Audiences will likely respond to a message if they remember it, if they're able to respond, and if they're properly motivated to respond.

Second, the recipient must to be *able* to respond as you wish. Obviously, if recipients simply cannot do what you want them to do, they will not respond according to your plan. By understanding your audience (you'll learn more about audience analysis in Chapter 5), you can work to minimize these unsuccessful outcomes.

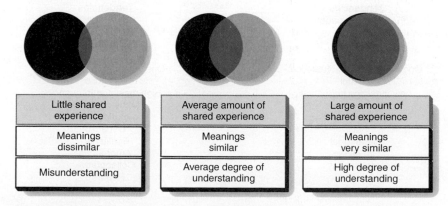

Little shared experience	Average amount of shared experience	Large amount of shared experience
Meanings dissimilar	Meanings similar	Meanings very similar
Misunderstanding	Average degree of understanding	High degree of understanding

Figure 1.6   How Shared Experience Affects Understanding
The more two people or two groups of people share experiences—personal, professional, and cultural—the more likely it is that receivers will extract the intended meanings that senders encode into the messages.

By explaining how audiences will benefit by responding positively to your messages, you'll increase their motivation to respond.

Third, the recipient must be *motivated* to respond. You'll encounter many situations in which your audience has the option of responding but isn't required to. For instance, a record company may or may not offer your band a contract, or your boss may or may not respond to your request for a raise. Throughout this course, you'll learn techniques for crafting messages that can help motivate readers to respond positively to your messages.

THE SOCIAL COMMUNICATION MODEL

The conventional model presented in Figure 1.5 illustrates how a single idea moves from one sender to one receiver. In a larger sense, it also helps represent the traditional nature of much business communication, which was primarily defined by a *publishing* or *broadcasting* mindset. Externally, a company issued carefully scripted messages to a mass audience that often had few options for responding to those messages or initiating messages of their own. Customers and other interested parties had few ways to connect with one another to ask questions, share information, or offer support. Internally, communication tended to follow the same "we talk, you listen" model, with upper managers issuing directives to lower-level supervisors and employees.

The *social communication model* is interactive, conversational, and usually open to all who wish to participate.

However, in recent years, a variety of technologies have enabled and inspired a new approach to business communication. In contrast to the publishing mindset, this **social communication model** is interactive, conversational, and usually open to all who wish to participate. Audience members are no longer passive recipients of messages but active participants in a conversation. Social media have given customers and other stakeholders a voice they did not have in the past.

Instead of transmitting a fixed message, a sender in a social media environment initiates a conversation by asking a question or sharing valuable information. Information spread this way is often revised and reshaped by the participants as they forward it and comment on it. People can expand it, confirm it, amplify it, or refute it, depending on their needs and interests. Figure 1.7 lists some of the significant differences between the traditional and social models of business communication.

Conventional Communication: "We Talk, You Listen"	The Social Model: "Let's Have a Conversation"
Tendencies	**Tendencies**
Publication, broadcast	Conversation
Lecture	Discussion
Intrusion	Permission
Unidirectinal	Bidirectional, multidirectional
One to many; mass audience	One to one; many to many
Control	Influence
Low message frequency	High message frequency
Few channels	Many channels
Information hoarding	Information sharing
Static	Dynamic
Hierarchical	Egalitarian
Structured	Amorphous
Isolated	Collaborative
Planned	Reactive
Resistive	Responsive

Figure 1.7   The Social Communication Model
The social communication model differs from conventional communication strategies and practices in a number of significant ways.

The social communication model offers many advantages, but it has some disadvantages as well, starting with less control. People inside and outside a company have always been able to refute management statements or spread rumors, for example, but owners and managers could assert at least a degree of control because the options for everyone else were limited and usually expensive. Now that more stakeholders have a say in the conversation via social media, they can use the megaphone power of the crowd to shape public perceptions in significant ways, such as arranging boycotts of companies whose policies they disagree with or influencing where and how companies advertise.

A second potential disadvantage of the social model is complexity. Companies and individuals have access to more information than ever before, which is both positive and negative. On the negative side, there are more communication channels to monitor, more work is needed to separate valuable information from noise, there is a greater risk of the spread of false information, and there is a greater threat of information overload (see below).

Social communication has two potential disadvantages for business: less control over messages and greater complexity.

Using Technology to Improve Communication

4 **LEARNING OBJECTIVE** Identify five major benefits of business communication technology and three major innovations that are reshaping the practice of communication.

Contemporary business communication is a technology-enabled activity, and your success as a communicator will depend on your comfort and skill with the various tools you'll have at your disposal. You are already using some of these tools, and you will be able to adapt your experience with various forms of digital and social media to workplace communication.

THE POTENTIAL BENEFITS OF COMMUNICATION TECHNOLOGY

Technology brings a wide variety of benefits to business communication, which can be grouped into five key areas:

- Making communication more effective by helping people craft messages that convey their ideas more clearly and persuasively
- Making communication more efficient by reducing the time and effort needed to create, transmit, and consume messages
- Improving research tools to help communicators discover, process, and apply information
- Assisting communicators with decision-making by guiding them through complex sets of data
- Removing communication barriers so more people can participate in the communication process more easily

The potential benefits of communication technology include

- *Greater effectiveness*
- *Greater efficiency*
- *Better and easier research*
- *Improved decision making*
- *Fewer barriers*

You probably take advantage of many benefits provided by communication technology already, from spell checkers to search engines to a voice-input virtual assistant on a smartphone. Throughout the book, you'll see examples of both simple and esoteric technologies that deliver these benefits, including in the special feature on pages 20–23, "Empowering Communicators with Intelligent Communication Technology."

While technology can help communicators in some powerful ways, these benefits don't come automatically. When tools are designed poorly or used inappropriately, they can hinder communication more than help. To use communication technology effectively, bear these five points in mind:

- **Keep technology in perspective.** Any technology is simply a tool, a means by which you can accomplish certain tasks. Technology is an aid to communication, not a replacement for it. Moreover, it can get in the way if not used thoughtfully. Throughout the book, you'll see advice on keeping the focus on your messages and your audiences and on using technology to enhance the communication process without overwhelming it.
- **Guard against information overload.** The overuse or misuse of communication technology can lead to **information overload**, in which people receive more information than they can effectively process. Information overload can cause distractions,

MOBILE APP
RescueTime keeps track of how you spend your time and lets you know if you're losing too much of your day to social media and other distractions.

Information overload occurs when people receive more information than they can effectively process.

stress, mistakes, and communication breakdowns, and minimizing it is a shared responsibility. As a receiver, be your own gatekeeper and stay mindful of what information you allow in. Periodically "prune" your information channels to avoid material you no longer need, and use filtering features in your systems to isolate high-priority messages that deserve your attention. As a sender, make sure you don't send unnecessary messages or poorly crafted messages that require multiple rounds of clarification.

- **Use your tools wisely.** Facebook, Twitter, YouTube, and other technologies are key parts of what has been called the *information technology paradox*, in which information tools can waste as much time as they save. In addition to distracting employees from work responsibilities, inappropriate use can also leave companies vulnerable to lawsuits and security breaches.
- **Use your tools efficiently.** Knowing how to use your tools efficiently can make a big difference in your productivity. You don't have to become an expert in most cases, but you do need to be familiar with the basic features and functions of the tools you are expected to use on the job. As a manager, make sure your employees are trained to use the systems you expect them to use.
- **Reconnect with people.** Even when it is working well, communication technology can still present barriers to understanding and healthy emotional connections. Messaging, email, and other text-heavy modes are particularly prone to misunderstandings and bruised feelings because they can't convey nuances and emotions the same way that voice, video, and in-person conversation can. Whenever you sense that you're stuck in a loop of confusion or ill will, pick up the phone or visit the other party in person if you can. A few minutes of direct conversation can often work wonders.

THE SPECTRUM OF CONTEMPORARY COMMUNICATION TECHNOLOGY

This section offers a look at three sets of technology that you will encounter in your job search and in the workplace: social and workgroup communication systems, mobile communication, and intelligent communication technologies.

Social and Workgroup Communication Systems

One of the most distinguishing features of business communication these days is how connected everyone and everything is. Businesses have had access to digital networking for decades, and many were quick to adopt social networking concepts when Facebook and similar networks took off. **Social media** are digital platforms that empower stakeholders as participants in the communication process by allowing them to share content, revise content, respond to content, or contribute new content. Millions of companies now use public networks such as Facebook and Twitter to connect with customers, and many also have private, internal social networks that are restricted to employees and selected business partners. These private systems are often enhanced with shared file access, group messaging, and real-time collaboration capabilities for brainstorming, reviewing and revising documents, and virtual meetings. If you use social media now, you'll have a basic familiarity with how many of these systems work. You can read more about collaboration systems in Chapter 3 and business uses of social networking in Chapter 8.

Social media are digital platforms that empower stakeholders as participants in the communication process by allowing them to share content, revise content, respond to content, or contribute new content.

REAL-TIME UPDATES

LEARN MORE BY VISITING THIS WEBSITE

Explore some of the best bots in business

Automated bots are taking over routine communication tasks in many companies; here are some of the best. Go to **real-timeupdates**.com/ebc13 and select Learn More in the Students section.

Mobile Communication

While social media tools are freeing communication from the constraints of closed networks, mobile connectivity is freeing it from the constraints of fixed location. With mobile devices everywhere you look these days, it probably comes as no surprise that mobile media consumption has skyrocketed in recent years; more than half of all internet access now occurs via mobile devices.[13]

Moreover, this shift isn't just about consumer usage and entertainment. For a growing number of companies, mobile technology has become an essential part of the digital workplace. Mobile connectivity can give workers and companies greater flexibility, enhance

Mobile technology has become an essential part of the digital workplace.

productivity and collaboration, and create more-engaging experiences for customers and other users. And rather than being an accessory to or an extension of a traditional work computer, in many cases mobile devices are the primary interface that connects employees to the company's information networks.[14]

Business mobile communication involves many of the same communication tools that you may use now for messaging, social networking, researching, and writing. In addition, thousands of business-focused apps assist users with everything from presentations to project management to financial reporting. Many of these apps are either communication focused or have significant communication features, all designed to help employees stay connected no matter where their work takes them (see Figure 1.8). For example, with Rockwell Automation's FactoryTalk TeamONE app, teams can collaborate to diagnose problems on a production line using the app's measurement capabilities to acquire data from machinery and then using its communication tools to collaborate on the trouble-shooting process.[15]

The rise of mobile communication has some obvious implications, starting with the challenges of writing and reading on small screens. Documents that are easy to read on paper or on large screens can become quite difficult to read on a smartphone—and the more difficult the reading experience, the more likely that readers will misinterpret the message or simply stop reading. (*Phablets*, smartphones with larger screens, although not as large as mobile tablets, are on trend to becoming the dominant phone size,[16] but even these still present challenges for reading and writing.)

Moreover, device size and portability are only the most obvious differences. Just as with social media, the changes brought about by mobile go far deeper than the technology itself. Mobile alters the way people live and work, which requires communicators to modify their approach to writing and designing messages. For example, smartphones have become truly personal devices in ways that personal computers never did. For many users, the connection is so intense they may feel a sense of panic when they don't have frequent access to their phones.[17] When people are closely attached to their phones, day and night, they are more closely connected to all the information sources, conversations, and networks that those phones can reach. As a result, mobile communication can start to resemble a continuous stream of conversations that never quite end, which influences the way businesses need to interact with their stakeholders. You can read more about writing for mobile audiences in Chapter 6 and designing mobile-friendly messages in Chapter 7. Throughout the book, you'll also see advice on using mobile in specific tasks, such as using mobile devices in presentations and job searches.

Reading and writing are generally more difficult and prone to errors on smaller mobile screens.

Mobile alters the way people live and work, which requires communicators to modify their approach.

  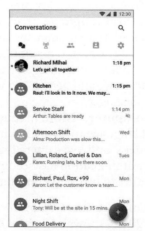

Figure 1.8   Mobile Communication Tools
Mobile technologies offer multiple ways to improve communication and other key business processes. To meet the needs of *deskless* workers, for example, this system from Zinc unifies everything from training materials to group messaging in a single app so that everyone in a company has instant access to information and advice.

Intelligent Communication Technology

Intelligent communication technology (ICT) uses artificial intelligence to enhance the communication experience.

The most intriguing and potentially disruptive of all contemporary communication tools are a group of capabilities we can call **intelligent communication technology (ICT)**, which uses artificial intelligence to enhance the communication experience. Although "artificial intelligence" still has a science fiction ring to it, forms of AI are now used extensively in business and business communication. It's a virtual guarantee that you are already experiencing AI as a consumer—Amazon, Apple, Facebook, Google, Microsoft, Netflix, and Spotify are just a few of the companies that rely on AI to deliver their services.[18] In a professional context, you will probably use various other forms of AI on the job, and chances are good that you will encounter it during your job search process (although its use may not be visible to you).

REAL-TIME UPDATES

LEARN MORE BY VISITING THIS INTERACTIVE WEBSITE

Try emotion-recognition AI yourself

Affectiva's website offers several ways to try emotion-recognition AI, including mapping your emotions while you watch a YouTube video. Go to **real-timeupdates.com/ebc13** and select Learn More in the Students section.

Research in AI has been going on for more than a half century, but the practical outcomes never really lived up to hopes until recently, when several developments converged within the space of a few years. First, the primary focus of the research shifted from pursuing the generalized, humanlike intelligence of science fiction (sometimes called *general AI* or *strong AI*) to developing specialized systems aimed at handling specific tasks such as reading text or recognizing images (called *narrow AI* or *weak AI*). Second, an AI method involving *neural networks*, which emulate the function of neurons in the brain, was refined in a way that made it much more powerful. And third, several critical computer capabilities became available around the same time: massive sets of data that AI systems could learn from, low-cost storage to handle all that data, and fast processors capable of handling the number-crunching that the most-common AI approaches require.[19]

Commercial use of AI is expanding rapidly, and much of this use involves communication.

Thanks to these developments, commercial applications of AI are exploding, and many of these involve business communication. ICT in its various forms relies on a few fundamental AI techniques that you'll hear about from time to time. You don't necessarily need to know how any of these techniques work, but it helps to have an idea of the capabilities they bring to communication:

Machine learning is the general capability of computers to learn; deep learning is a specific type of machine learning that uses multiple layers of neural networks.

- **Machine learning and deep learning.** For any AI system to possess intelligence, it needs to be able to learn, which can include understanding text, converting spoken language to written text, or recognizing the content of photographs and videos. *Machine learning* refers to the general capability of computers to learn, and *deep learning* is a specific type of machine learning that uses layers of neural networks to attack problems at multiple levels (the "deep" part). The growth of practical AI tools in recent years, including the ICT tools available for business communication, is largely the result of advances in deep learning.[20]
- **Natural language processing (NLP).** NLP involves giving computers the ability to understand language in the often-unpredictable ("natural") ways humans speak and write and to manipulate language in useful ways. NLP involves several challenging issues, including converting speech to text, analyzing text to extract intended meaning, and generating written or oral output (often referred to as *natural language generation*).[21]
- **Computer vision.** In much the same way that NLP pieces together sounds and bits of language to figure out meaning, computer vision analyzes the elements of photos, videos, and live camera images to identify their content. Given how important visual communication has become in business, vision processing could play a key role in the future of business communication.

"Empowering Communicators with Intelligent Communication Technology" on pages 20–23 shows numerous examples of ICT tools used in business today. And throughout the book, keep an eye out for the "Intelligent Communication Technology" highlight boxes that discuss specific tools for business communication—including tools that you can use or that you might encounter while searching for your next job.

Committing to Ethical and Legal Communication

5 LEARNING OBJECTIVE
Define *ethics*, explain the difference between an ethical dilemma and an ethical lapse, and list six guidelines for making ethical communication choices.

Ethics are the accepted principles of conduct that govern behavior within a society. Ethical behavior is a companywide concern, but because communication efforts are the public face of a company, they are subjected to particularly rigorous scrutiny from regulators, legislators, investors, consumer groups, environmental groups, labor organizations, and other stakeholders. **Ethical communication** includes all the information an audience needs in order to make an informed decision or take an informed stance on an issue and is not deceptive in any way. Whenever you communicate in business, you ask audiences to trust that you will provide information that is complete and true. If you intentionally violate that trust, you have engaged in unethical communication.

Ethics are the accepted principles of conduct that govern behavior within a society.

Ethical communication includes all the information an audience needs in order to make an informed decision or take an informed stance on an issue.

FORMS OF UNETHICAL COMMUNICATION

Unethical communication can take several forms: withholding information, distorting information, and plagiarizing. Note that some of these choices can also be illegal in certain circumstances.

Withholding Information

First, senders can intentionally withhold information, such as avoiding taking responsibility for mistakes or presenting an incomplete set of facts when making a proposal. The widespread use of social media has increased the attention given to the issue of **transparency**, which in this context refers to a sense of openness, of giving all participants in a conversation access to the information they need in order to accurately process the messages they are receiving.

Withholding information, distorting information, and plagiarizing are all forms of unethical communication.

Transparency is a sense of openness that gives audience members access to all the information they need in order to process messages accurately.

In addition to the information itself, audiences deserve to know when they are being marketed to and who is behind the messages they read or hear. Two important concerns in this regard are *native advertising* and *stealth marketing*. Native advertising, also known as *sponsored content*, is advertising material that is designed to look like regular news stories, articles, or social media posts. The U.S. Federal Trade Commission (FTC) requires companies to label such material as sponsored content if it is likely to mislead consumers into thinking it is "anything other than an ad."[22] Industry groups such as the Word of Mouth Marketing Association and the Interactive Advertising Bureau give their members specific guidelines to help prevent consumer confusion.[23]

Stealth marketing is the practice of promoting companies and products without making it clear to the audience that marketing activity is taking place. For example, "street team" marketing, in which team members promote goods and services to their friends and members of the public in exchange for prizes or other compensation, is unethical if team members don't disclose the fact that they are affiliated with a company and are being rewarded for their efforts. Such practices also violate FTC advertising guidelines.[24] Even something as simple as a job title can be deceptive and therefore unethical (see "Practicing Ethical Communication: Are You My *Adviser* or My *Advisor*?").

REAL-TIME UPDATES
LEARN MORE BY VISITING THIS WEBSITE
Ethical guidelines for word-of-mouth marketing
The Word of Mouth Marketing Association advises its members on how to use social media marketing ethically. Go to **real-timeupdates.com/ebc13** and select Learn More in the Students section.

Distorting Information

Intentionally distorting information is also a form of unethical communication. This distortion can involve words, numbers, or images. For example, selectively misquoting someone in order to create a different impression than the source intended is unethical. Statistical and other numerical data can also be presented in ways that distort their implications. Two examples are using averages to conceal extreme individual values or manipulating trend calculations to suggest future values that the underlying data might not support. For example, you might boast that sales increased 40 percent in April as evidence of a big upward trend, when in fact March sales had been a disaster and all that 40 percent increase did was bring sales back to their earlier level. Images can be manipulated in unethical ways, such as altering photos or changing the scale of graphs and charts to exaggerate or conceal differences.

(continued on page 24)

Artificial intelligence is now being applied to nearly every facet of business, and many of these innovations focus on business communication. Here is a sample of the intelligent communication technologies that deliver the five key benefits listed on page 15. You have no doubt encountered some of these already, and you will probably encounter more of them during your job search and in the workplace.[25]

Making Communication More Effective

These tools help communicators make more-compelling choices by offering suggestions and providing feedback or by enhancing the audience experience with additional information.

Augmented writing systems analyze word and phrase choices and suggest more effective ways to convey ideas. Some are based on general concepts of effective writing; others are specialized tools based on a deeper analysis of narrower sets of communication examples, such as job descriptions.

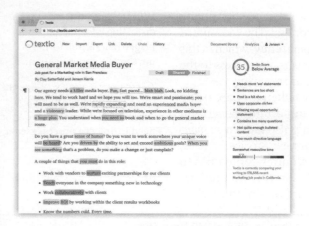

Augmented reality tools enhance the communication experience for audiences by delivering additional information that is relevant to a user's immediate surroundings, such as systems that give technicians on-the-spot guidance to troubleshoot and repair equipment.

Photo courtesy of Panasonic

Making Communication More Efficient

The goal of these tools is to reduce the time and effort for both senders and receivers by assisting—or in some cases replacing—a human participant.

Applicant evaluation systems speed the process of screening job applications, particularly in the first few stages of the recruiting cycle, when companies often have more candidates than their staffs can screen manually. Some of these systems evaluate résumés and related application information to help recruiters identify the most promising candidates, and some can even predict whether people who aren't actively looking for a new job might be likely to consider one. Others assist at the interviewing stage, with chatbots that can conduct interviews or video analysis tools that evaluate candidates' responses and on-screen demeanor.

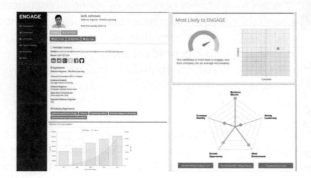

Automated writing goes beyond augmented writing to produce finished or near-finished writing. Systems in use now can summarize corporate news and sports stories, for example. Yahoo! Sports uses AI to generate millions of personalized draft reports and game recaps for members of its fantasy football leagues.

Chatbots and taskbots interact with humans to perform a wide variety of communication functions, from answering questions about products to acting as personal assistants. Bots help companies communicate with more people at lower cost. The Gift Genie from Sam's Club, for instance, can guide customers through product selection questions and seamlessly escalate to human agents when needed. X.ai's Amy and Andrew taskbots can set up meetings and perform various other tasks as virtual assistants.

Improving Research

Business communication projects often require research, which can involve numerical data, textual content, or visuals (photos, videos, live camera feeds, and so on). When the research involves large amounts of material, ICT tools can help communicators by automating the collection and analysis tasks and by discovering connections and insights that might otherwise go unnoticed.

Mining and analytics systems are a diverse class of tools that extract insights from collections of numerical (*data mining*, *data analytics*) or textual (*text mining*, *text analytics*) content. Business communicators can use the natural language processing capability of text mining or text analytics for *social listening* to identify themes (such as prevailing customer sentiment or threats to a company's reputation) hidden in mountains of written information, from Twitter and Facebook posts to customer emails and surveys.

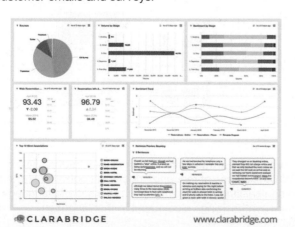

Image recognition systems extract information from photos, videos, and live camera images. Search engines, for example, use AI to automatically analyze and tag photos and videos for such purposes as filtering out objectionable content and helping users search for images. This capability can be built into other systems for such purposes as tracking products, counting people, and monitoring public safety.

Emotion recognition tools such as Affectiva (see page 2) analyze facial expressions or voices to identify emotional states with the aims of understanding consumer reactions and preferences at a deeper level and bringing a more human feel to digital interaction.

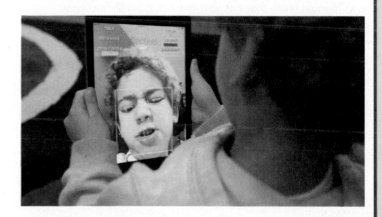

Enhancing and Automating Decision-Making

A variety of ICT solutions focus on decision-making, which relates closely to communication efforts because professionals frequently need to make decisions about communication, such as identifying which potential customers would be most likely to respond to a sales message.

Cognitive automation, also known as *augmented intelligence*, helps professionals make more-informed decisions by applying *predictive analytics* and other techniques to characterize likely outcomes of various decision choices.

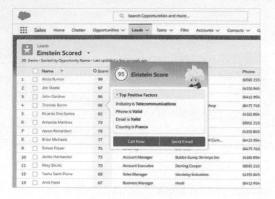

Robotic process automation (RPA) aims to do for knowledge work what robots do for manufacturing and other physical processes. RPA targets the high-volume "paperwork" aspects of business and can automate some of the routine communication and manual tasks that this sort of work typically involves.

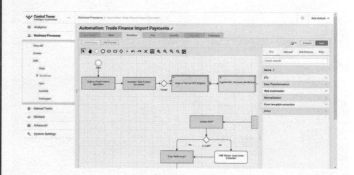

Removing Communication Barriers

A variety of AI-enabled tools lower or remove communication barriers by simplifying the process of human-computer interaction or creating experiences that aren't possible in the physical world.

Voice recognition has improved dramatically in the last few years, thanks to advances in AI. Voice input is so good now that it is becoming the primary way for millions of people to interact with digital tools and the internet in general.

Automated translation tools remove language barriers for website visitors and users. Companies can dramatically lower the costs of *localizing* content for various countries and language users, and anyone can get reasonably close translations of website content using Google Translate and similar services.

Real-time voice translation (see next page) addresses the multiple challenges of recognizing speech, converting it to text in the original language, translating it to a second language and then synthesizing voice output in that language.

Courtesy of Google

Virtual reality (VR) systems create a simulation in which the person experiences the sensation of being in an environment, even though that environment is entirely computer-generated. If it is difficult, expensive, or dangerous to put people in a real-life situation, a VR simulation can let employees experience the sensation of being there and doing whatever tasks are required. VR can also help people experience a product or structure before it is built. Ford uses VR to let engineers "see" design ideas before building anything and to get feedback from drivers by letting them sit in and experience prototype designs before the cars are manufactured.

Ford Motor Company

Augmented ability tools help people across a wider spectrum of physical or cognitive ability interact with devices and their immediate environments in more complete and fulfilling ways. For example, Microsoft's Seeing AI app can help people with limited vision by reading texts, recognizing currency, identifying people, scanning barcodes, and identifying objects in a room or on the street.

a desk with a computer monitor

Essential ICT Terms

Artificial Intelligence (AI) The application of computing power to replicate one or more aspects of human intelligence. Generally speaking, it's a three-stage process: collecting data or information, analyzing or processing that input to make decisions, then applying the results of that decision-making activity.

Strong AI, Weak AI Terms that suggest the scope of an AI activity or design. *Strong AI*, also known as *artificial general intelligence (AGI)*, is the idea of comprehensively replicating human intelligence, including the ability to transfer learning from one task or domain to another, just as humans can. *Weak AI*, or more accurately, *narrow AI*, focuses on a specific problem with techniques optimized for that single domain. All the AI tools having a meaningful impact on business today are weak AI.

Machine Learning General term for a system's ability to teach itself to improve at whatever task or tasks it is designed to do, in contrast to systems in which all the intelligence has been built in by human programmers.

Deep Learning A form of machine learning in which layers of computational *neural networks* mimic the functions of the brain's neurons. Deep learning is a key component of the communication tools in place today.

Augmented Intelligence, Hybrid Intelligence, Cognitive Automation Similar terms to describe hybrid solutions in which computers assist humans, and vice versa. For example, an AI system might analyze a collection of data to help a human make a decision, or a system that runs autonomously most of the time might call for human advice when it encounters a problem it can't solve.

Natural Language Processing (NLP) The ability to understand, analyze, and respond to human conversational input. Systems that accept voice input, such as Siri, Alexa, and other voice assistants, also require *speech recognition* capability, which is the ability to convert human speech to text that a computer can then analyze.

Data Mining, Text Mining The computerized process of extracting insights from vast collections of numerical or textual records.

PRACTICING ETHICAL COMMUNICATION

Are You My *Adviser* or My *Advisor*?

In the financial services industry, many financial "planners" are more accurately considered salespeople because they are motivated by commissions or directed by their employers to sell certain mutual funds or other investment products. There is nothing inherently unethical about selling, to be sure, but the potential influence of commissions raises ethical concerns because it can shape the advice these professionals give their clients.

Canadian financial regulations state that anyone using the word "adviser" with an "e" in his or her job title is legally bound to act in a client's best interests, regardless of commissions or other pressures, a requirement known as *fiduciary duty*. This means, for instance, that a financial adviser cannot encourage a client to invest in a high-fee investment if a comparable and less-expensive alternative would be better for the client. (Fees vary widely across investment products and can dramatically affect the level of net return that investors get.)

However, there is no such restriction on the word "advisor" with an "o." People using this spelling in their titles are free to act as salespeople—without disclosing that they are selling and not advising in any objective sense of the term. And according to some critics and several employees from Canada's biggest banks, these advisors are encouraged or forced to sell investments that are not always in their clients' best interest, including mutual funds owned by the banks themselves.

The banks generally defend the advice their employees have given to clients, and many in the industry say the larger problem is the confusing variety of professional titles and certifications that need to be better coordinated and communicated to the public. In the meantime, investor advocacy groups such as the Small Investor Protection Association (SIPA) are calling for tighter government regulations. SIPA founder Stan Buell says he has heard from "hundreds and hundreds of people who've been victimized. And every one trusted their advisor."

CRITICAL THINKING

1. Should salespeople in any industry be legally prohibited from using helpful-sounding descriptors such as *advisor*, *counselor*, or *consultant* in their job titles? Why or why not?
2. Some companies advertise that their sales staffs are "commission-free." Can consumers take this as an assurance that salespeople will always give them objective advice on choosing products or services? Why or why not?

Sources: Erica Johnson, "'I Feel Duped': Why Bank Employees with Impressive but Misleading Titles Could Cost You Big Time," *CBC News*, 31 March 2017, www.cbc.ca; Stan Buell, "Do You Have a Financial Advisor or Adviser?" *MoneySense*, 9 December 2016, www.moneysense.ca; Guy Dixon, "Adviser, Advisor or Financial Planner? Does the Name Matter?" *Globe and Mail*, 12 September 2017, www.theglobeandmail.com.

Distortion and outright fabrication of information are becoming greater concerns as the tools for manipulating sound, images, and video become more sophisticated. Convincingly "Photoshopping" images to fool audiences (using Adobe Photoshop or a similar program) has been possible for a while now, and the same potential for deception is becoming possible for sound and video files. Business communicators must be more vigilant than ever as information consumers and more careful than ever as information creators.

Plagiarizing

Plagiarism is presenting someone else's words or other creative product as your own.

Copyright is a form of legal protection for the originators of creative content.

Plagiarism is presenting someone else's words or other creative product as your own. Note that plagiarism can also be illegal if it violates a **copyright**, which is a form of legal protection for the originators of creative content. Copyright law covers a wide range of creative expression, including writing, visual design, computer programming, and sound and video recording.[26]

Plagiarism standards and copyright law don't mean you can never use someone else's work. However, you must use it ethically and legally, including properly documenting your sources, clearly labeling anyone else's words and images as theirs, and using only minor portions, such as brief quotations. (Depending on the nature of the project and the material, you might need to get written permission to use material.) You can be sued for copyright infringement if you copy a significant part of a work, even if you don't copy it word for word or profit from doing so.[27]

The concept of *fair use* provides some flexibility in using others' creative work without violating copyright, particularly for noncommercial use, but there are no precise guidelines on how much you can use. And as attorney Kerry O'Shea Gorgone explains, fair use can only be invoked as a legal defense *after* a copyright owner sues you for infringement. You can't simply take someone else's content and preemptively label it as "fair use."[28] (*Content curation* and other forms of social media sharing present some particularly sticky issues; see page 228 for more.)

MOBILE APP

ColorNote for Android helps you capture and organize all the details of daily life, from assignments to job interview notes.

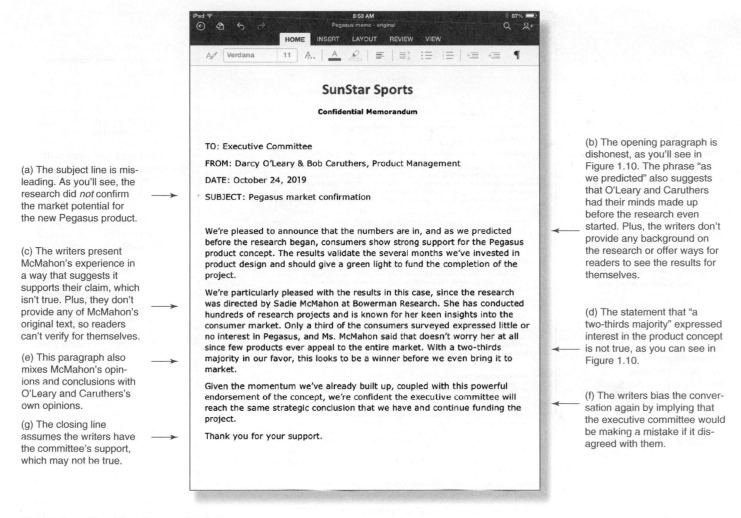

(a) The subject line is misleading. As you'll see, the research did *not* confirm the market potential for the new Pegasus product.

(c) The writers present McMahon's experience in a way that suggests it supports their claim, which isn't true. Plus, they don't provide any of McMahon's original text, so readers can't verify for themselves.

(e) This paragraph also mixes McMahon's opinions and conclusions with O'Leary and Caruthers's own opinions.

(g) The closing line assumes the writers have the committee's support, which may not be true.

(b) The opening paragraph is dishonest, as you'll see in Figure 1.10. The phrase "as we predicted" also suggests that O'Leary and Caruthers had their minds made up before the research even started. Plus, the writers don't provide any background on the research or offer ways for readers to see the results for themselves.

(d) The statement that "a two-thirds majority" expressed interest in the product concept is not true, as you can see in Figure 1.10.

(f) The writers bias the conversation again by implying that the executive committee would be making a mistake if it disagreed with them.

SunStar Sports

Confidential Memorandum

TO: Executive Committee

FROM: Darcy O'Leary & Bob Caruthers, Product Management

DATE: October 24, 2019

SUBJECT: Pegasus market confirmation

We're pleased to announce that the numbers are in, and as we predicted before the research began, consumers show strong support for the Pegasus product concept. The results validate the several months we've invested in product design and should give a green light to fund the completion of the project.

We're particularly pleased with the results in this case, since the research was directed by Sadie McMahon at Bowerman Research. She has conducted hundreds of research projects and is known for her keen insights into the consumer market. Only a third of the consumers surveyed expressed little or no interest in Pegasus, and Ms. McMahon said that doesn't worry her at all since few products ever appeal to the entire market. With a two-thirds majority in our favor, this looks to be a winner before we even bring it to market.

Given the momentum we've already built up, coupled with this powerful endorsement of the concept, we're confident the executive committee will reach the same strategic conclusion that we have and continue funding the project.

Thank you for your support.

Figure 1.9   Unethical Communication
The writers of this memo clearly want the company to continue funding their pet project, even though the marketing research doesn't support such a decision. By comparing this memo with the version shown in Figure 1.10 (be sure to read the lettered annotations), you can see how the writers twisted the truth and omitted evidence in order to put a positive "spin" on the research.

DISTINGUISHING ETHICAL DILEMMAS FROM ETHICAL LAPSES

Some ethical questions are easy to recognize and resolve, but others are not. Deciding what is ethical can be a considerable challenge in complex business situations. An **ethical dilemma** involves choosing among alternatives that aren't clear-cut. Perhaps two conflicting alternatives are both ethical and valid, or perhaps the alternatives lie somewhere in the gray area between clearly right and clearly wrong. Every company has responsibilities to multiple groups of people inside and outside the firm, and those groups often have competing interests. For instance, employees naturally want higher wages and more benefits, but investors who have risked their money in the company want management to keep costs low so that profits are strong enough to drive up the stock price. Both sides have a valid ethical position.

In contrast, an **ethical lapse** is a clearly unethical choice. With both internal and external communication efforts, the pressure to produce results or justify decisions can make unethical communication a tempting choice. Telling a potential customer you can complete a project by a certain date when you know you can't is simply dishonest. There is no ethical dilemma here.

Compare the messages in Figures 1.9 and 1.10 for examples of how business messages can be unethically manipulated.

An *ethical dilemma* is a choice between alternatives that may all be ethical and valid to varying degrees.

An *ethical lapse* is making a choice you know to be unethical.

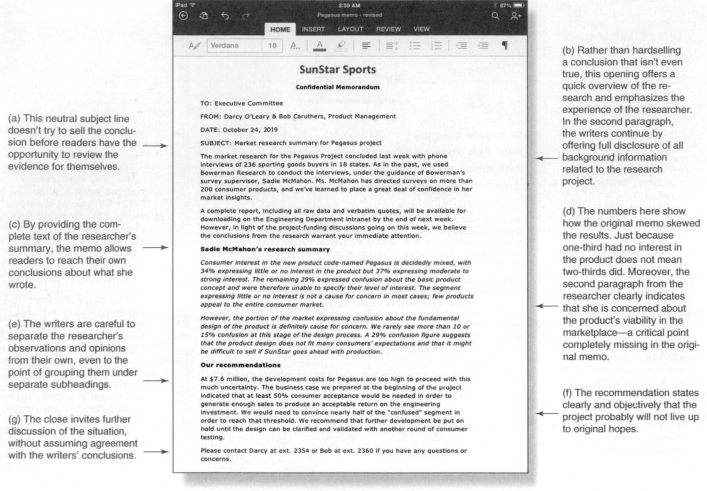

(a) This neutral subject line doesn't try to sell the conclusion before readers have the opportunity to review the evidence for themselves.

(c) By providing the complete text of the researcher's summary, the memo allows readers to reach their own conclusions about what she wrote.

(e) The writers are careful to separate the researcher's observations and opinions from their own, even to the point of grouping them under separate subheadings.

(g) The close invites further discussion of the situation, without assuming agreement with the writers' conclusions.

(b) Rather than hardselling a conclusion that isn't even true, this opening offers a quick overview of the research and emphasizes the experience of the researcher. In the second paragraph, the writers continue by offering full disclosure of all background information related to the research project.

(d) The numbers here show how the original memo skewed the results. Just because one-third had no interest in the product does not mean two-thirds did. Moreover, the second paragraph from the researcher clearly indicates that she is concerned about the product's viability in the marketplace—a critical point completely missing in the original memo.

(f) The recommendation states clearly and objectively that the project probably will not live up to original hopes.

Figure 1.10   Ethical Communication
This version of the memo from Figure 1.9 presents the evidence in a more honest and ethical manner.

ENSURING ETHICAL COMMUNICATION

Responsible employers establish clear *codes of ethics* for their employees to follow.

Employers have a responsibility to establish clear guidelines for ethical behavior, including ethical business communication. Many companies establish an explicit ethics policy by using a written **code of ethics** to help employees determine what is acceptable. A code is often part of a larger program of employee training and communication channels (such as *ethics hotline* phone numbers) that allow employees to ask questions and report instances of questionable ethics.[29]

In addition to setting clear ethical standards, managers must also demonstrate ethical behavior themselves and support employees who face ethical dilemmas. Codes and training don't mean much if employees feel pressured to make unethical choices or see their superiors acting unethically.

To judge whether you are communicating ethically, ask yourself

- Am I being honorable?
- Am I giving people the information they need?
- Have I considered the effects of my message?
- Am I respecting the rights of others?
- Would a different approach be better?

Whether or not a company has formal guidelines in place, every employee has a responsibility to communicate in an ethical manner. To make sure you are communicating ethically, keep these five questions in mind:

- Is my intention honorable, and does it demonstrate respect for my audience?
- Am I giving my readers or listeners all the information they need in order to take an informed stance or make an informed decision?
- Have I considered the effect my message will have on the audience and anyone else who might be affected by it?
- Am I respecting the legal and moral rights of anyone whose information or ideas I am using?
- Could a different approach produce a more positive outcome for everyone involved?

If you still can't decide whether a choice is ethical, picture yourself explaining your decision to someone whose opinion you value. Could you comfortably live with your choice?

ENSURING LEGAL COMMUNICATION

In addition to ethical guidelines, business communication is also bound by a wide variety of laws and regulations, including the following areas:

- **Promotional communication.** Anyone who creates marketing messages needs to be aware of the many laws that govern truth and accuracy in advertising. These laws address such issues as false and deceptive advertising, claims expressed on product packaging, the use of celebrity testimonials, and bait-and-switch tactics in which a store advertises a lower-priced product to lure consumers into a store but then tries to sell them a more expensive item.[30] Chapter 11 explores this area in more detail.

- **Contracts.** A **contract** is a legally binding promise between two parties in which one party makes a specified offer and the other party accepts.[31] Contracts cover a wide range of business scenarios, including employment, purchasing and leasing, project services, and nondisclosure agreements.

- **Employee communication.** A variety of local, state, and federal laws govern communication between employers and both potential and current employees. For example, employers are required to inform employees about workplace hazards such as toxic chemicals.[32]

- **Intellectual property.** In an age when instant global connectivity makes copying and retransmitting electronic files effortless, the protection of digital and creative assets has become a widespread concern. **Intellectual property (IP)** includes copyrighted materials as well as *industrial property* such as patents, product designs, and logos.[33]

- **Financial reporting.** Finance and accounting professionals who work for publicly traded companies (those that sell stock to the public) must adhere to stringent reporting laws.

- **Defamation.** Negative comments about another party raise the possibility of **defamation**, the intentional public communication of false statements that damage character or reputation. Written defamation is called *libel*; spoken defamation is called *slander*.[34]

- **Transparency requirements.** Governments around the world are taking steps to help ensure that consumers and other parties know who is behind the information they receive, particularly when it appears online. In the United States, for example, the FTC requires influencers such as celebrities and athletes to disclose any relationships they have with companies when they promote or endorse products in social media.[35]

If you have any doubts about the legality of a message you intend to distribute, ask for advice from your company's legal department. A small dose of caution can prevent huge legal headaches and protect your company's reputation in the marketplace.

For the latest information on ethical and legal issues in business communication, visit **real-timeupdates.com/ebc13** and select Chapter 1.

REAL-TIME UPDATES

LEARN MORE BY VISITING THIS WEBSITE

Guidelines for trouble-free blogging

The Electronic Frontier Foundation offers a free *Legal Guide for Bloggers*. Go to **real-timeupdates.com/ebc13** and select Learn More in the Students section.

> Business communication is governed by a wide variety of laws designed to ensure accurate, complete messages.

> *Intellectual property (IP)* includes copyrighted materials and industrial property such as patents, product designs, and logos.

> *Defamation* is the intentional public communication of false statements that damage character or reputation.

Developing Skills for Your Career

As page 3 emphasizes, communication skills are the single most important asset you can polish as you launch and manage your career. In addition to helping you develop these skills, this course gives you the opportunity to enhance a wide range of other skills that experts say are vital for success in tomorrow's workplace:

- **Critical thinking.** In many of the assignments and activities, you will need to define and solve problems and make decisions or form judgments about a particular situation or set of circumstances.

6 LEARNING OBJECTIVE Identify six related skills that you will have the opportunity to develop as you work on your communication skills in this course.

- **Collaboration.** Depending on the configuration of your course, you will have various opportunities to work with classmates on reports, presentations, and other projects.
- **Knowledge application and analysis.** The ability to learn a concept and then apply that knowledge to other challenges is a skill that employers value highly.
- **Business ethics and social responsibility.** As you work on projects throughout the course, be mindful of the ethical implications that you could encounter in similar projects on the job.
- **Information technology skills.** Use projects and activities to build your skills with technology, including word-processing apps, spreadsheets, presentation software, messaging systems, and AI tools.
- **Data literacy.** You'll have multiple opportunities to fine-tune your *data literacy* skills, which include the ability to access, assess, interpret, manipulate, summarize, and communicate data.

APPLYING WHAT YOU'VE LEARNED

At the beginning of this chapter, you read about Affectiva's experiences using artificial intelligence to understand how people respond to messages. Each chapter opens with one of these slice-of-life vignettes about a company or business professional. As you read through each chapter and become familiar with the concepts presented, imagine how they might apply to the situation highlighted in the vignette.

At the end of each chapter, you'll take part in a simulation called "On the Job: Solving Communication Dilemmas." You'll play the role of a person working in the highlighted organization, and you'll be presented with situations like those you might encounter on the job, each with several possible courses of action. It's up to you to recommend one course of action in each scenario. These scenarios let you explore various communication ideas and apply the concepts and techniques from the chapter. (Your instructor may use these simulations as homework, team projects, or material for in-class discussion.)

Now you're ready for the first simulation. As you tackle each problem, think about the material you covered in this chapter, and consider your own experience as a communicator. You may be surprised to discover how much you already know about business communication.

ON THE JOB: SOLVING COMMUNICATION DILEMMAS AT **AFFECTIVA**

You have joined Affectiva as director of communications, with responsibility for internal and external communication programs. Use the insights you gained in this chapter to address these challenges.

1. Affectiva occasionally hosts seminars, online webinars, and other events at which potential customers can learn more about the company's solutions. One such event is designed to help market researchers understand how to use emotion analysis in their work. Assume this is the announcement for this event:[36]

   Let's Get Emotional: How to Incorporate Facial Responses in Your Market Research Methodology
   Surveys aren't the industry standard anymore: in fact, relying on this data alone doesn't stand up to what's coming next. Imagine the future of market research where respondents no longer have to manually input their thoughts and reactions to

content, but you will be able to tell right from the expressions on their faces. Join us on September 24 for a free 1-hour webinar and live Q&A to learn more.

You want to summarize this announcement in a single tweet, with a maximum length of 200 characters, including spaces. (The original is 401, so you need to compress it by half.) A URL will be included in the tweet, but don't worry about it for this assignment. Which of the following is the most effective summary?

a. Surveys aren't the industry standard anymore: in fact, relying on survey data alone doesn't stand up to what's coming next. Join us September 24 for a free 1-hour webinar and live Q&A to learn more.

b. Join us for a free 1-hour webinar and live Q&A to learn why surveys aren't the industry standard anymore and why relying on survey data alone doesn't stand up to what's coming next.

c. Facial-response technology, which measures emotional reactions using artificial intelligence, can provide a level of insight that surveys can't match. Free 1-hour webinar and live Q&A on Sept 24.

d. Go beyond surveys with the next wave of marketing insights: learn how emotion measurement provides a level of insight that surveys can't match. Free 1-hour webinar and live Q&A on Sept 24.

2. The culture in the Affectiva headquarters is conscientious and professional but with a generally informal "vibe." However, as with any company, individual employees vary in how closely their own styles and personalities fit the corporate culture. For example, the new accounting manager in your organization tends to communicate in a formal, distant style that some find off-putting and impersonal. Several people have expressed concerns that the new manager "doesn't fit in," even though she's doing a great job otherwise. How should you respond to the situation?

a. Tell these people to stop complaining; the accounting manager is doing her job well, and that's what counts.

b. In a private conversation with the accounting manager, explain the importance of fitting into the corporate culture and give her a four-week deadline to change her style.

c. In a private conversation with the accounting manager, explain the reasoning behind the company's informal culture and its contribution to the company's success; suggest that she might find her work here more enjoyable if she modifies her approach somewhat.

d. Allow the accounting manager to continue communicating in the same style; after all, that's her personal style, and it's not up to the company to change it.

3. The science behind Affectiva's AI tools is beyond the grasp of many of its customers in the business arena. The company generally does an excellent job of translating the science into audience-friendly language that business professionals can appreciate, but lately you've noticed that one of the company's scientists tends to slip into some heavy math and science during customer presentations and media events. When you mention it during a casual conversation, he explains that he is trying to emphasize the superiority of Affectiva's solutions, and it's up to users to get better educated about the tools they use. How should you respond?

a. To avoid the impression that you are picking on this one individual, issue new companywide guidelines for audience-friendly communication. Emphasize the importance of speaking and writing to customers in language they understand.

b. Have a friendly discussion with him about the nature of Affectiva's business and point out that customers are all specialists in other areas and can't be expected to become specialists in AI. Use an analogy such as cars or mobile phones, where users don't need to know how these systems work in order to use them successfully. Emphasize that Affectiva's sales will suffer if using the products seems to require too much learning time.

c. Make sure this scientist is always accompanied by a skilled communication specialist who can serve as a technical translator for customers and the media.

d. Take his advice and launch a new customer education program to help all users understand deep learning, facial mapping, voice analysis, and other key techniques.

4. Affectiva occasionally gets inquiries from companies that would like to apply its emotion-sensing technology in ways that are incompatible with the company's ethical positions, such as monitoring employees without their consent. You have just received one of these inquiries; how should you respond?

a. Explain that Affectiva was founded on the vision of enabling positive human-computer interaction and that its technology is not available for invasive applications such as unapproved monitoring. Include a link to the "What We Stand For" page on the Affectiva website, which outlines the company's founding values.

b. Avoid the subject by saying that Affectiva's technology isn't capable of monitoring employees. It is, of course, but by sidestepping the controversial request, you can avoid engaging with someone whose values are incompatible with Affectiva's.

c. Gently suggest that company consider adopting a more enlightened management style—such as the approach taken by Affectiva CEO Rana el Kaliouby herself—in which employees are treated with respect and management wouldn't consider violating their privacy.

d. Send a link to the Affectiva website and explain that the site describes all the current applications for the company's AI tools.

END OF CHAPTER

Learning Objectives Checkup

Assess your understanding of the principles in this chapter by reading each learning objective and studying the accompanying exercises. You can check your responses against the answer key on page 612.

Objective 1.1: Explain the importance of effective communication to your career and to the companies where you will work.

1. Which of the following is the most accurate description of the role that communication will play in your career?
    a. Ideas matter more than anything, so as long as you are creative and have strong business sense, you can hire people to take care of communication tasks.
    b. No matter what other skills, connections, and attributes you have, your prospects will be limited if you don't have good communication skills.
    c. In today's tough business world, performance is the most important differentiator; everything else, including communication, is a distant second.
    d. As a "soft skill," communication is important in some careers, such as sales and human resources, but not in technical, financial, or administrative careers.
2. A company's stakeholders are
    a. any individuals or groups affected in a significant way by the company's activities.
    b. anyone who owns shares in the company.
    c. employees, except for unionized workforces.
    d. anyone who suffers as a result of the company's actions.
3. Effective business messages are
    a. entertaining, blunt, direct, opinionated, and persuasive.
    b. practical, objective, concise, clear, and persuasive.
    c. personal, clear, short, catchy, and challenging.

Objective 1.2: Explain what it means to communicate as a professional in a business context.

4. Which of the following is the best definition of professionalism?
    a. Adding an extra touch of polish to every communication project
    b. Always doing at least 10 percent more than is expected of you
    c. Never taking no for an answer, regardless of the extra work involved
    d. Performing at a high level and conducting oneself with purpose and pride
5. Which of the following is *not* one of the six traits of professionalism identified in the chapter?
    a. Striving to excel
    b. Being dependable
    c. Being ethical
    d. Being loyal to the company no matter what
6. The ability to evaluate evidence completely and objectively in order to form logical conclusions and make sound recommendations is known as

    a. precision research.
    b. critiquing.
    c. critical thinking.
    d. logical evaluation.
7. The informal communication network in an organization
    a. consists of all communication that occurs outside the formal communication network.
    b. encompasses all business communication, as long as it uses an informal tone.
    c. includes all communication that doesn't use official company systems and devices.
    d. is a negative force in any company.
8. An audience-centered approach to communication
    a. starts with the assumption that the audience is always right.
    b. improves the effectiveness of communication by focusing on the information needs of the audience.
    c. is generally a waste of time because it doesn't accommodate the needs of the sender.
    d. always simplifies the tasks involved in planning and creating messages.

Objective 1.3: Contrast the conventional communication process model with the social communication model.

9. Senders _____ ideas into messages, and receivers _____ those messages to extract the ideas.
10. In the communication process, feedback refers to
    a. negative criticism in response to miscommunication.
    b. positive evaluations at any level of the organization.
    c. verbal or nonverbal messages sent from receivers back to senders after a message has been received.
11. Which of the following is not listed in the chapter as a type of communication barrier?
    a. Attendance policies
    b. Noise and distractions
    c. Competing messages
    d. Filters
12. Selective attention is defined as
    a. focusing on a subset of incoming stimuli or information sources and ignoring others.
    b. focusing on only positive, stimulating messages.
    c. a computer-assisted technique for filtering out spam email and other unwanted messages.
    d. ignoring or denying incoming messages that do not support your experienced view of yourself and your company.
13. Which of the following pairs of attributes best describes the social communication model?
    a. Interactive and conversational
    b. Technical and instantaneous
    c. Electronic and print
    d. Relaxed and unrestricted
14. Which of the following does the chapter list as a potential disadvantage of the social communication model?
    a. The inability to share live camera images
    b. The reluctance of new employees to engage on social media

    c. The cost of equipping every employee with a secure mobile phone

    d. The complexity created by having more information sources to monitor

Objective 1.4: Identify five major benefits of business communication technology and three major innovations that are reshaping the practice of communication.

15. Which of these is not one of the benefits of business communication technology listed in the chapter?

    a. Making communication more effective

    b. Giving introverted employees the same opportunity to contribute as their more extroverted colleagues

    c. Making communication more efficient

    d. Improving research tools to help communicators discover, process, and apply information

16. The situation in which people receive more information than they can effectively process is known as _____ _____.

17. Which of these is not one of the advantages of mobile communication discussed in the chapter?

    a. Giving employees more flexibility to meet their personal and professional obligations

    b. Guaranteeing ethical treatment of message recipients

    c. Enhancing productivity and collaboration

    d. Creating more-engaging experiences for customers and other users

18. Which of these best describes the use of artificial intelligence in business today?

    a. Only high-tech companies use AI today, although others might in the future.

    b. AI is now used extensively in business and business communication.

    c. Today's consumers rarely come in contact with AI-enabled systems.

    d. After failed attempts at strong or general AI, businesses have largely abandoned AI.

19. Giving computers the ability to understand language in the ways humans tend to speak and write is known as

    a. human language processing.

    b. natural language processing.

    c. computerspeak.

    d. artificial language.

Objective 1.5: Define *ethics*, **explain the difference between an ethical dilemma and an ethical lapse, and list six guidelines for making ethical communication choices.**

20. Ethical communication

    a. is the same thing as legal communication.

    b. costs more because there are so many rules to consider.

    c. is important only for companies that sell to consumers rather than to other businesses.

    d. includes all the information an audience needs in order to make an informed decision or take an informed stance on an issue and is not deceptive in any way.

21. An ethical _____ exists when a person is faced with conflicting but ethical choices or alternatives that are neither entirely right nor entirely wrong; an ethical _____ occurs when a person makes an unethical choice.

Objective 1.6: Identify six related skills that you will have the opportunity to develop as you work on your communication skills in this course.

22. The set of skills that include the ability to access, assess, interpret, manipulate, summarize, and communicate data is known as _____ _____.

Key Terms

audience-centered approach Understanding and respecting the members of your audience and making every effort to get your message across in a way that is meaningful to them

code of ethics A written set of ethical guidelines that companies expect their employees to follow

communication The process of transferring information, meaning, and understanding between senders and receivers

communication barriers Forces or events that can disrupt communication, including noise and distractions, competing messages, filters, and channel breakdowns

communication channels Systems used to deliver messages

communication medium The form in which a message is presented; can be oral (spoken), written, or visual

contract A legally binding promise between two parties, in which one party makes a specified offer and the other party accepts

copyright A form of legal protection for the expression of creative ideas

critical thinking The ability to evaluate evidence completely and objectively in order to form logical conclusions and make sound recommendations

decoding Extracting the idea from a message

defamation The intentional public communication of false statements that damage character or reputation

encoding Putting an idea into a message (words, images, or a combination of both)

ethical communication Communication that includes all the information an audience needs in order to make an informed decision or take an informed stance on an issue and is not deceptive in any way

ethical dilemma A situation that involves making a choice when competing alternatives are ethically valid or the alternatives aren't completely wrong or completely right

ethical lapse A clearly unethical choice

ethics The accepted principles of conduct that govern behavior within a society

feedback Information from receivers regarding the quality and effectiveness of a message

formal communication network Communication channels that flow along the lines of command in an organization

informal communication network All communication that takes place outside the formal network

information overload Condition in which people receive more information than they can effectively process

intellectual property Creative assets including copyrighted materials as well as *industrial property* such as patents, product designs, and logos

intelligent communication technology (ICT) Systems that use artificial intelligence to enhance the communication experience

message The "container" for an idea to be transmitted from a sender to a receiver

plagiarism Presenting someone else's words or other creative product as your own

professionalism The quality of performing at a high level and conducting oneself with purpose and pride

selective attention Focusing on a subset of the incoming stimuli or information sources and ignoring others

social communication model An interactive, conversational approach to communication in which audience members are empowered to participate fully

social media Digital platforms that empower stakeholders as participants in the communication process by allowing them to share content, revise content, respond to content, or contribute new content

stakeholders Groups affected by a company's actions, including customers, employees, shareholders, suppliers, neighbors, and local communities

transparency A sense of openness that gives all participants in a conversation access to the information they need to accurately process the messages they are receiving

"you" attitude Communicating with an audience-centered approach; creating messages that are about "you," the receiver, rather than "me," the sender

Apply Your Knowledge

To review chapter content related to each question, refer to the indicated Learning Objective.

1-1. Why is communication sometimes considered a negotiation of meaning rather than a transfer of meaning? [LO-1]

1-2. Should managers try to shut down the informal communication network if they discover that employees are spreading negative gossip or false rumors? Why or why not? [LO-2]

1-3. What general steps could you take to help ensure that high schoolers and their parents will respond positively to your messages promoting your new tutoring service? [LO-3]

1-4. Why are businesses investing in AI-driven communication tools? [LO-4]

1-5. You're the CEO of a company whose sales are declining, and there is a 50/50 chance you will need to lay off some of your employees sometime in the next two to three months. You have to decide whether to tell them now so they can look for new jobs as soon as possible, even though you're not yet sure layoffs will be necessary, or wait until you are sure layoffs will occur. Explain why this is an ethical dilemma. Be sure to consider the effect a sudden exodus of valuable employees could have on the company's prospects. [LO-5]

Practice Your Skills

Message for Analysis

1-6. Analyzing Communication Effectiveness [LO-1] Read the following blog post, and then (a) analyze whether the message is effective or ineffective (be sure to explain why), and (b) revise the message so that it follows this chapter's guidelines.

It has come to my attention that many of you are lying on your time cards. If you come in late, you should not put 8:00 on your card. If you take a long lunch, you should

not put 1:00 on your time card. I will not stand for this type of cheating. I simply have no choice but to institute an employee monitoring system. Beginning next Monday, video cameras will be installed at all entrances to the building, and your entry and exit times will be logged each time you use electronic key cards to enter or leave.

Anyone who is late for work or late coming back from lunch more than three times will have to answer to me. I don't care if you had to take a nap or if you girls had to shop. This is a place of business, and we do not want to be taken advantage of by slackers who are cheaters to boot.

It is too bad that a few bad apples always have to spoil things for everyone.

Exercises

Each activity is labeled according to the primary skill or skills you will need to use. To review relevant chapter content, you can refer to the indicated Learning Objective. In some instances, supporting information will be found in another chapter, as indicated.

1-7. **Writing: Compositional Modes: Summaries [LO-1]** Write a paragraph introducing yourself to your instructor and your class. Address such areas as your background, interests, achievements, and goals. Submit your paragraph using email, blog, or social network, as indicated by your instructor.

1-8. **Media Skills: Microblogging [LO-1], Chapter 8** Write four tweets to persuade other college students to take the business communication course. Think of the first message as the "headline" of an advertisement that makes a bold promise regarding the value this course offers every aspiring business professional. The next three messages should be support points that provide evidence to back up the promise made in the first message.[37] Although Twitter allows messages up to 280 characters, keep your tweets as brief as possible.

1-9. **Fundamentals: Analyzing Communication Effectiveness [LO-1]** Identify a video clip (on YouTube or another online source) that you believe represents an example of effective communication. It can be in any context, business or otherwise, but make sure it is something appropriate to discuss in class. Post a link to the video on your class blog, along with a brief written summary of why you think this example shows effective communication in action.

1-10. **Planning: Assessing Audience Needs [LO-2], Chapter 5** Choose a business career that sounds interesting to you, and imagine that you are getting ready to apply for jobs in that field. Identify three personal or professional qualities you have that would be important for someone in this career field. Write a brief statement (one or two sentences) regarding each quality, describing in audience-focused terms how you can contribute to a company in this respect. Submit your statements via email or class blog.

1-11. **Communication Etiquette: Communicating with Sensitivity and Tact [LO-2]** Potential customers frequently visit your production facility before making purchase decisions. You and the people who report to you in the sales department have received extensive training in etiquette issues because you deal with high-profile clients so often. However, the rest of the workforce has not received such training, and you worry that someone might inadvertently say or do something that would offend one of these potential customers. In a two-paragraph email, explain to the general manager why you think anyone who might come in contact with customers should receive basic etiquette training.

1-12. Collaboration: Team Projects; Planning: Assessing Audience Needs [LO-2], Chapter 3, Chapter 5 Your boss has asked you to research and report on corporate child-care facilities. Working with two team members assigned by your instructor, list four or five things you'll want to know about the situation and about your audience before starting your research. Briefly explain why each of the items on your list is important.

1-13. Planning: Constructing a Persuasive Argument [LO-2], Chapter 11 Blogging is a popular way for employees to communicate with customers and other parties outside the company. Employees' own blogs can help companies and their customers by providing helpful information and "putting a human face" on the company. However, in some instances employees have been fired for posting information that their employers said was inappropriate. One particular area of concern is criticism of the company or individual managers. Should employees be allowed to criticize their employers in a public forum such as a blog? In a brief email message, argue for or against company policies that prohibit critical information in employee blogs.

1-14. Fundamentals: Analyzing Communication Effectiveness [LO-3] Use the eight phases of the communication process to analyze a miscommunication you've recently had with a coworker, supervisor, classmate, teacher, friend, or family member. What idea were you trying to share? How did you encode and transmit it? Did the receiver get the message? Did the receiver correctly decode the message? How do you know? Based on your analysis, identify and explain the barriers that prevented successful communication in this instance.

1-15. Writing: Compositional Modes: Persuasion [LO-3], Chapter 11 Social media use varies widely from company to company. Some firms enthusiastically embrace these new tools and new approaches. Others have taken a more cautious approach, either delaying the adoption of social media or restricting their use. You work for an "old school" manufacturing firm that prohibits employees from using social media during work hours. Company management believes that social media offer little business value and distract employees from their duties. In a brief email message to your boss, identify the ways that social media are changing the communication process and relationships between companies and their employees, customers, and communities. Provide at least one example.

1-16. Fundamentals: Analyzing Communication Effectiveness [LO-4] Using a mobile device, visit the websites of three companies that make products or provide services you buy or might buy in the future. Which of the websites is the most user-friendly? How does it differ from the other sites? Do any of the companies offer a mobile shopping app for your device?

1-17. Technology: Using Communication Tools [LO-4] Find a free online communication service (such as a blogging platform) that you have no experience using as a content creator or contributor. Perform a basic task such as opening an account or setting up a blog. Was the task easy to perform? Were the instructions clear? Could you find help online if you needed it? Is there anything about the experience that could be improved? Summarize your conclusions in a brief email message to your instructor.

1-18. Technology: Using Communication Tools [LO-4] Try two or three of the free emotion-recognition AI tools at www.affectiva.com/experience-it. In a post for your class blog, summarize your experience as an end user and offer your thoughts on the business value of this technology.

1-19. Communication Ethics: Distinguishing Ethical Dilemmas and Ethical Lapses [LO-5] Knowing that you have numerous friends throughout the company, your boss relies on you for feedback concerning employee morale and other issues affecting the staff. She recently asked you to start reporting any behavior that might violate company policies, from taking office supplies home to making personal calls on company time. List the issues you'd like to discuss with her before you respond to her request.

1-20. Communication Ethics: Distinguishing Ethical Dilemmas and Ethical Lapses [LO-5] Briefly explain why you think each of the following is or is not ethical.

   a. Keeping quiet about a possible environmental hazard you've just discovered in your company's processing plant

   b. Overselling the benefits of workgroup messaging to your company's managers; they never seem to understand the benefits of technology, so you believe that a bit of hype is the only way to convince them to make the right choice

   c. Telling an associate with whom you are close friends that she needs to pay more attention to her work responsibilities, or management will fire her

   d. Recommending the purchase of equipment your department doesn't really need in order to use up your allocated funds before the end of the fiscal year; this will help ensure that your budget won't be cut next year, when you might have a real need for the money

1-21. Communication Ethics: Providing Ethical Leadership [LO-5] Cisco, a leading manufacturer of equipment for the internet and corporate networks, has a code of ethics that it expects employees to abide by. Visit the company's website at www.cisco.com and find its *Code of Business Conduct*. In a brief paragraph, describe three specific examples of things employees could do that would violate these provisions.

Expand Your Skills

Critique the Professionals

Locate an example of professional communication from a reputable online source. It can reflect any aspect of business communication, from an advertisement or a press release to a company blog or website. Evaluate this communication effort in light of any aspect of this chapter that is relevant to the sample and interesting to you. For example, is the piece effective? Audience-centered? Ethical? Using whatever medium your instructor requests, write a brief analysis of the piece (no more than one page), citing specific elements from the piece and support from the chapter.

Sharpening Your Career Skills Online

Bovée and Thill's Business Communication Web Search, at **web search.businesscommunicationnetwork.com**, is a unique research tool designed specifically for business communication research. Use the Web Search function to find an online video, a presentation, a website, or an article that describes the use of any intelligent communication technology in business. Write a brief email message to your instructor or a post for your class blog, describing the item and summarizing the advice it offers.

Build Your Career

Take the 20-question self-assessment in Table 2 on page xxxiii in the Prologue. Are you able to answer most of the questions with confidence, or are you unsure about some of these factors? For the items you are unsure about, what steps can you take to get more clarity before you begin your job search? Has this self-assessment changed your thoughts on the type of career and employment path you would like to pursue? Keep your answers handy as you move through the job search process, and use them to evaluate job offers to see how well they align with how you would like to spend your working years.

Improve Your Grammar, Mechanics, and Usage

The following exercises help you improve your knowledge of and power over English grammar, mechanics, and usage. Turn to the Handbook of Grammar, Mechanics, and Usage at the end of this book and review all of Section 1.1 (Nouns). Then look at the following 10 items and select the preferred choice within each set of parentheses. (Answers to these exercises appear on page 614.)

1-22. She remembered placing that report on her (*bosses, boss's*) desk.

1-23. We mustn't follow their investment advice like a lot of (*sheep, sheeps*).

1-24. Jones founded the company back in the early (*1990's, 1990s*).

1-25. Please send the (*Joneses, Jones'*) a dozen of the following: (*stopwatchs, stopwatches*), canteens, and headbands.

1-26. Our (*attorneys, attornies*) will talk to the group about incorporation.

1-27. Make sure that all (*copys, copies*) include the new addresses.

1-28. Ask Jennings to collect all (*employee's, employees'*) donations for the Red Cross drive.

1-29. Charlie now has two (*sons-in-law, son-in-laws*) to help him with his two online (*business's, businesses*).

1-30. Avoid using too many (*parentheses, parenthesis*) when writing your reports.

1-31. Follow President (*Nesses, Ness's*) rules about what constitutes a (*weeks, week's*) work.

For additional exercises focusing on nouns, visit MyLab Business Communication. Select Chapter 1, select Additional Exercises to Improve Your Grammar, Mechanics, and Usage, and then select 1. Possessive nouns or 2. Antecedents.

MyLab Business Communication

MyLab Assisted-Grading Writing Prompts

If your instructor has assigned one or both of the following writing assignments within the MyLab, go to your Assignments to complete these writing exercises.

1-32. How does the social communication model differ from traditional business communication practices? [LO-3]

1-33. How is mobile technology changing the practice of business communication? [LO-4]

Endnotes

1. Rana el Kaliouby profile, LinkedIn, accessed 1 January 2018, www .linkedin.com/in/kaliouby; David Pring-Mill, "Tech Is Becoming Emotionally Intelligent, and It's Big Business," *SingularityHub*, 2 November 2017, singularityhub.com; Raffi Khatchadourian, "We Know How You Feel," *New Yorker*, 19 January 2015, www.newyorker.com; Khari Johnson, "Affectiva CEO: AI Needs Emotional Intelligence to Facilitate Human-Robot Interaction," *VentureBeat*, 9 December 2017, venture-beat.com; Brain Power campaign page on Indiegogo, accessed

1 January 2018, www.indiegogo.com; Affectiva website, accessed 1 January 2018, www.affectiva.com; Bernard Marr, "The Next Frontier of Artificial Intelligence: Building Machines That Read Your Emotions," *Forbes*, 15 December 2017, www.forbes.com.
2. Stephen P. Robbins and Timothy A. Judge, *Essentials of Organizational Behavior*, 14th ed. (New York; Pearson, 2018), 171.
3. Manuel G. Velasquez, *Business Ethics*, 8th ed. (New York: Pearson, 2018), 15.

4. Stephen P. Robbins, Mary Coulter, and David A. Decenzo, *Fundamentals of Management*, 10th ed. (New York: Pearson, 2017), 171.

5. "Digital Information Fluency Model," 21cif.com, accessed 11 February 2014, 21cif.com.

6. Robbins, Coulter, and Decenzo, *Fundamentals of Management*, 461; Philip C. Kolin, *Successful Writing at Work*, 6th ed. (Boston: Houghton Mifflin, 2001), 17–23.

7. Justin Bariso, "This Email from Elon Musk to Tesla Employees Describes What Great Communication Looks Like," *Inc.*, 30 August 2017, www.inc.com.

8. Andrew J. Dubrin, *Human Relations for Career and Personal Success*, 11th ed. (New York: Pearson, 2017), 92.

9. Lisa Quast, "Want to Be More Productive? Stop Multi-Tasking," *Forbes*, 6 February 2017, www.forbes.com.

10. Paul Martin Lester, *Visual Communication: Images with Messages*, 6th ed. (Boston: Wadsworth, 2014), 6–8.

11. Dubrin, *Human Relations for Career and Personal Success*, 424.

12. Scott O. Lilienfeld, Steven Jay Lynn, and Laura L. Namy, *Psychology: From Inquiry to Understanding*, 4th ed. (New York: Pearson, 2018), 244; Charles G. Morris and Albert A. Maisto, *Psychology: An Introduction*, 12th ed. (Upper Saddle River, N.J.: Pearson Prentice Hall, 2005), 226–239; Saundra K. Ciccarelli and Glenn E. Meyer, *Psychology* (Upper Saddle River, N.J.: Prentice Hall, 2006), 210–229; Mark H. Ashcraft, *Cognition*, 4th ed. (Upper Saddle River, N.J.: Prentice Hall, 2006), 44–54.

13. Adam Lella, "Smartphone Usage Has Doubled in the Past Three Years," ComScore blog, 27 January 2017, www.comscore.com; Darrell Etherington, "Mobile Internet Use Passes Desktop for the First Time, Study Finds," *TechCrunch*, 1 November 2016, techcrunch.com.

14. Jeff Corbin, "The Digital Workplace and the Mobile Hub," the-EMPLOYEEapp blog, 25 October 2016, www.theemployeeapp.com.

15. Carlos M. Gonzalez, "Why Are Top Industrial Companies Designing Mobile Apps?" *Machine Design*, January 2017, 49–52.

16. Rayna Hollander, "Phablets Will Become the Most Popular Smartphone Type by 2019," *Business Insider*, 5 December 2017, www.businessinsider.com.

17. Yun-Sen Chan, "Smartphones Are Changing Person-to-Person Communication," Modern Media Mix, 23 April 2013, modernmediamix.com.

18. Christina Mercer, "11 Tech Giants Investing in Artificial Intelligence," *Techworld*, 27 November 2017, www.techworld.com; R. L. Adams, "10 Powerful Examples of Artificial Intelligence in Use Today," *Forbes*, 10 January 2017, www.forbes.com.

19. Will Knight, "The Dark Secret at the Heart of AI," *MIT Technology Review*, 11 April 2017, www.technologyreview.com; Michael Copeland, "What's the Difference Between Artificial Intelligence, Machine Learning, and Deep Learning?" Nvidia blog, 29 July 2016, blogs.nvidia.com.

20. Knight, "The Dark Secret at the Heart of AI."

21. Jason Brownlee, "What Is Natural Language Processing?" *Machine Learning Mastery*, 22 September 2017, machinelearningmastery.com; Automated Insights website, accessed 22 December 2017, automatedinsights.com.

22. "Native Advertising: A Guide for Businesses," U.S. Federal Trade Commission, accessed 18 February 2017, www.ftc.gov.

23. "Don't Be Naïve About Native," white paper, Word of Mouth Marketing Association, November 2014, womma.org.

24. "Guides Concerning Use of Endorsements and Testimonials in Advertising," U.S. Federal Trade Commission, accessed 18 February 2017, www.ftc.gov.

25. Nancy K. Kubasek, Bartley A. Brennan, and M. Neil Browne, *The Legal Environment of Business*, 8th ed. (New York: Pearson, 2017), 397; Henry R. Cheeseman, *Business Law*, 9th ed. (New York: Pearson, 2016), 139.

26. Cheeseman, *Business Law*, 141.

27. Kerry O'Shea Gorgone, "'Curation' Versus Fair Use: How to Keep Your Content Safe," {grow}, 22 September 2015, www.businessgrow.com.

28. "Ethics Hotline: Why Would an Employer Want to Establish a Whistleblower or Ethics Hotline?" Society for Human Resource Management, 7 November 2017, www.shrm.org

29. Kubasek, et al., *The Legal Environment of Business*, 762–765.

30. Cheeseman, *Business Law*, 187.

31. Gary Dessler, *Human Resource Management*, 15th ed. (New York: Pearson, 2017), 537.

32. "What is Intellectual Property?" World Intellectual Property Organization, accessed 24 December 2017, ww.wipo.int.

33. Kubasek et al., *The Legal Environment of Business*, 306.

34. "FTC Staff Reminds Influencers and Brands to Clearly Disclose Relationship," U.S. Federal Trade Commission, 19 April 2017, www.ftc.gov.

35. The webinar title and first two sentences appeared on Affectiva's Events page, Affectiva website, accessed 2 January 2018, go.affectiva.com/events.

36. The concept of a four-tweet summary is from Cliff Atkinson, *The Backchannel* (Berkeley, Calif.: New Riders, 2010), 120–121.

37. Joaquin Quiñonero Candela, "Building Scalable Systems to Understand Content," *Facebook Code*, 2 February 2017, code.facebook.com; "Case Studies: Yahoo!," Automated Insights, accessed 1 January 2018, automatedinsights.com; Julia Bobak, "Why Did AI Research Drift from Strong to Weak AI?" *Topbots*, 11 September 2017, www.topbots.com; Mariya Yao, "WTF Is Artificial Intelligence?" *Topbots*, 9 October 2017, www.topbots.com; Robert D. Hof, "Deep Learning," *MIT Technology Review*, accessed 1 January 2018, www.technologyreview.com; Will Knight, "The Dark Secret at the Heart of AI," *MIT Technology Review*, 11 April 2017, www.technologyreview.com; Lisa Sigler, "Text Analytics Tools: The Real Difference," Clarabridge, 5 February 2016, www.clarabridge.com; Jessica Smith, "The Voice Assistant Landscape Report: How Artificially Intelligent Voice assistants Are Changing the Relationship Between Consumers and Computers," *Business Insider*, 2 March 2017, www.businessinsider.com; Eric Bellman, "The End of Typing: The Next Billion Mobile Users Will Rely on Video and Voice," *Wall Street Journal*, 7 August 2017, www.wsj.com; "Make Way for Holograms: New Mixed Reality Technology Meets Car Design as Ford Tests Microsoft Hololens Globally," Ford, 21 September 2017, www.ford.com; "IBM AbilityLab Content Clarifier," IBM, accessed 2 January 2018, contentclarifier.mybluemix.net.

Interpersonal Communication Skills

LEARNING OBJECTIVES

After studying this chapter, you will be able to

1 Explain why listening is such a complex communication process, and describe three steps to becoming a better listener.

2 Explain the importance of nonverbal communication, and identify six major categories of nonverbal expression.

3 Outline an effective process for initiating, sustaining, and concluding workplace conversations.

4 Explain the causes of workplace conflict, and identify five productive steps for resolving conflict.

5 Describe the importance of negotiation as a communication skill, and explain how to prepare for and conduct a negotiation.

MyLab Business Communication
Improve Your Grade!
If your instructor is using MyLab Business Communication, visit **www.pearson.com/mylab/business-communication** for videos, simulations, and writing exercises.

ON THE JOB: COMMUNICATING AT
SALESFORCE.COM

Leading by Listening

As people rise up the corporate ladder and become leaders in their industries, one might assume they naturally take on the role of wise elders and begin to listen less and talk more. But Salesforce.com founder and CEO Marc Benioff would tell you just the opposite, that listening is even more crucial as one gets farther away from the front lines. Listening has always been vital to Benioff's management style, and he's not stopping now, even as the leader of an $8 billion corporation.

In fact, the very founding of Salesforce.com and the business revolution it helped usher in were the direct result of his penchant for listening. Benioff spent a lot of time listening in the early days of the World Wide Web, as Amazon was expanding its online shopping services and beginning to shake the foundations of the entire retailing sector. What he heard prompted him to wonder why the software industry didn't work like Amazon. Specifically, why wasn't *enterprise software*, the vast platforms that are the central nervous systems of modern corporations, sold as an online service, rather than as a product that customers had to install and continually update?

Motivated by that question, Benioff founded Salesforce.com to offer customer relationship management (CRM) software that companies can subscribe to as a service, becoming an early force in what is now known as software as a service (SaaS). His vision was to make CRM as easy to use as shopping on

Salesforce.com founder and CEO Marc Benioff (right) has made listening a fundamental aspect of his leadership style.

Amazon, and he was obviously onto something: Today more than 150,000 companies use Salesforce.com's on-demand software.

Even with this success, the obsession with listening lives on. Benioff and his top executives frequently go on worldwide "listening tours" to pick up any marketplace signals that might suggest threats or opportunities. He likes to cultivate a "beginner's mind," enabling him to put aside everything he thinks he knows about a subject and listen with an open, uncluttered mind.

The company is just as eager to listen inside its own walls. In a nod to the Festivus holiday from the TV show *Seinfeld*, it hosts a chat group called Airing of Grievances, where senior managers can hear what employees have to say. To replace the often-dreaded annual performance review, the firm also created the Feedback App with a real-time channel that employees can use to give and receive feedback, making sure that concerns are heard and accomplishments are celebrated. As a result of this attention to employees, Salesforce.com consistently ranks as one of the best companies to work for in the United States.

The driving spirit behind all this success can be found in a simple statement from Benioff: "I love listening."[1]

WWW.SALESFORCE.COM

Improving Your Listening Skills

Much of this course focuses on improving your skills as a sender of messages, but successful communication requires the mindful participation of both the sender and the receiver. When you are engaged in a conversation or listening to a live or recorded speaker, the success of the communication effort hinges on your performance as a listener.[2] In fact, of all the skills you'll need in order to be an effective communicator, Saleforce.com's Marc Benioff (profiled in the chapter opener) would probably agree that listening is the most important. Listening is essential for acquiring information needed to create companies, to perform on the job, and to build a foundation for trust and successful relationships.[3]

You've been listening all your life, so it's natural to assume it's something you do well without even thinking about it. However, listening is a more complex process than you might imagine, and you surely know from your own life experiences how often listening can be unsuccessful. Fortunately, as with all communication skills, you can improve your listening abilities through knowledge and practice.

This section explains why effective listening is more difficult than it seems, then outlines three positive steps you can take to become a more effective listener. (Note that even if your physical ability to hear is impaired, most of the issues and techniques discussed in this section can help.)

1 **LEARNING OBJECTIVES**
Explain why listening is such a complex communication process, and describe three steps to becoming a better listener.

Effective listening is more difficult than it might seem and requires active involvement to be successful.

UNDERSTANDING WHY LISTENING IS SUCH A COMPLEX PROCESS

Listening is vulnerable to all the potential barriers and breakdowns that you considered in Chapter 1's discussion of the communication process, plus there are several difficulties that are unique to listening. In addition, a number of listener behaviors can get in the way of successful communication (see Table 2.1 on the next page).

The Unique Challenges of Listening

Listening involves three unique challenges. First, conversations and presentations happen in real time, meaning you must be engaged while the speaker is talking and stay engaged the entire time. If you want to verify something or attend to an interruption while you're reading, you can simply pause the process and pick it up again later. However, doing so is awkward at best and sometimes impossible when you're in the middle of a live conversation or listening to a presentation. (Of course, if you're listening to a podcast or other recorded speech, you can pause and come back later.)

Second, speech is invisible, in that you don't have written words to refer to if you get lost or confused. If your mind drifts for a moment while reading, you can scan back up the page to figure out what is going on. You don't have that luxury with conversation. If you get lost, you must ask the other party to stop the conversation and repeat or re-explain. While this conversational

Because conversations and presentations happen in real time, you have to stay engaged the entire time to avoid getting confused or lost.

Unlike written documents, speech doesn't give you a visual record to review if you get lost or confused.

TABLE 2.1 Factors That Complicate the Listening Process

Unique Challenges of Listening	Individual Choices and Behaviors
Real-time experience Conversation is consumed as it is created; you can't scroll back in time like you can with written communication.	**Poor self-management** Listeners need to actively manage their own emotions during a conversation; otherwise, these distractions will get in the way.
Invisibility You can't see spoken language, so you have no visual record to refer to if you get lost or confused.	**Idle brain power** The mind can process information several times faster than people can talk, and if listeners don't harness that extra processing power, their minds are likely to wander.
Sound-to-language conversion Incoming sounds must be converted to language before your mind can begin to process what is being said. Mumbling, strong accents, and ambient noise can all complicate this process.	**Ineffective listening style** Different conversations call for different styles of listening, and using an inappropriate style can hamper a conversational exchange.
	Barriers Listeners need to take steps to minimize barriers in their listening environment in order to reduce interruptions and distractions.
	Flawed recall If listeners don't record or actively memorize essential information during a conversation, chances are they will forget or confuse important details.

---

interactivity can be one of the key advantages of oral communication, it isn't always easy or possible. For instance, if the speaker is a top executive in your company or a trainer in a seminar, it can be intimidating to admit you are confused or weren't paying attention. Too often, it's tempting to stay quiet and hope you can guess what the speaker said or meant.

The need to convert incoming sounds to understandable language is a unique challenge of listening.

Third, before listeners can begin to decode incoming messages, they need to convert incoming sounds into recognizable words and sentences. Doing so adds a layer of complexity that doesn't exist in other media, and a variety of barriers can get in the way, including ambient noise, a speaker who is mumbling or who has a strong accent, and physical difficulties in hearing.

Choices and Behaviors That Affect Listening Quality

In addition to the generic challenges of listening, a variety of listener choices and behaviors can also degrade the quality of a communication exchange.

Listeners need to manage their emotions to avoid creating mental barriers and distractions.

- **Poor self-management.** Communication suffers if listeners fail to monitor and manage their emotions during a conversation. During the hectic workday or when emotions are running high, listening calmly and mindfully can be a challenge. However, these are the times when it is most important to exhibit emotional intelligence, including the ability to recognize when your emotions might be getting in the way.[4]

- **Idle brain power.** Your brain can process language three or four times faster than people typically speak, which means your brain has a lot of extra processing capacity while you're listening.[5] Consequently, the issue of selective attention discussed in Chapter 1 is particularly important with listening. If you don't take active steps to keep focused, your mind will inevitably wander.

- **Ineffective listening style.** Even when listeners are actively engaged in conversations, the exchange can still suffer if they don't use the best *style* of listening for the situation at hand. "Adapt Your Listening Style to the Situation" on the next page identifies the three major styles of listening and helps you choose which one to apply in any situation.

- **Barriers to physical reception.** Before you can listen to someone, you obviously need to be able to hear the other party speak, whether it's in person, on the phone, online, or on a recording. Missing even a single word can lead to confusion and misunderstanding. Poor hearing can originate on the speaker's side (such as when someone mumbles), on the receiver's side (such as when someone is listening to music during a conversation), or in the surrounding environment (such as when other people in an open-plan office are talking).

Memorization is an integral part of listening and can be a challenge because you need to store information you've just heard while new information continues to reach your ears.

- **Flawed recall.** The discussion of memory in Chapter 1 pointed out that incoming information needs to be transferred from short-term memory to long-term memory or it will be lost. Remembering information during a conversation is challenging because you need to store information you have just received while continuing to process new incoming information. This problem gets even more pronounced when the speaker is rambling or disorganized or fails to periodically summarize what he or she has said.

When you consider the complexity of the listening experience, it's not surprising that listening well is a universal challenge. Fortunately, with awareness and effort, everyone can take steps to overcome these hurdles.

BECOMING A BETTER LISTENER

Now that you have a sense of how listening can go off track, here are three vital steps to becoming a better listener: minimizing the barriers to effective listening, adapting your listening style to the situation, and engaging in active listening.

Minimize the Barriers to Effective Listening

You might not be able to control all the barriers that get in the way of effective listening, but the more you can reduce them, the more satisfying the experience will be for everyone involved. *External barriers* are anything in the environment or communication channel that make it difficult to hear the other party or focus on what is being said. If your work environment is noisy or prone to interruptions from people or pets, for instance, try to minimize these distractions during important conversations or arrange to speak in a quiet location. If you can't fix a problem, take steps to minimize its effects. For example, if your mobile phone service or online audio or video connections are spotty, take extra care to confirm key information by summarizing what you've heard during the call or later in writing. If you're having trouble hearing, let the other party know so you can both work to resolve the situation. Don't try to guess at what someone might have said and hope for the best.

Internal barriers are listener behaviors, thoughts, and emotions that hinder one's ability to understand, interpret, or accept what someone else is saying. They may not be as obvious as external barriers, but they can be much more disruptive. If you're not paying attention or are dividing your attention by multitasking, you will miss verbal information and nonverbal signals. Moreover, not paying attention is disrespectful and sends a message to the other person that what he or she has to say isn't important to you.[6]

Managing your own thoughts and emotions can be a challenge during a conversation, but doing so is essential to good listening. In addition, you may have barriers to interpretation and understanding that you are not even aware of. As Chapter 1 notes, selective attention and perceptual biases can lead listeners to mold messages to fit their own beliefs and conceptual frameworks. Listeners sometimes make up their minds before hearing the speaker's full message, or they engage in **defensive listening**—protecting their egos by tuning out anything that doesn't confirm their beliefs or their view of themselves. Feeling angry or annoyed during a conversation limits your effectiveness because you'll be more likely to judge or reject what you hear. "Listen Actively" starting on the next page offers helpful advice for getting yourself in the right frame of mind.

> External barriers to listening are any factors that impede physical hearing or concentration.

> Internal barriers to listening are listener behaviors, thoughts, and emotions that hinder understanding.

REAL-TIME UPDATES

LEARN MORE BY LISTENING TO THIS PODCAST

The skewed perceptions of unconscious biases

Everyone experiences the world through unconscious biases of perceptual filters, and too often people are unaware that they are doing so. Go to **real-timeupdates.com/ebc13** and select Learn More in the Students section.

> *Defensive listening* involves protecting your ego by tuning out anything that doesn't confirm your beliefs or view of yourself.

Adapt Your Listening Style to the Situation

Effective listeners adapt their listening styles to different situations, including switching approaches over the course of a conversation or presentation. You can use three distinct styles: *content* listening, *critical* listening, and *empathic* listening (see Table 2.2 on the next page). Note that all three of these are forms of *active listening* (see the next section).

The primary goal of **content listening** is to understand and retain the information in the speaker's message. Because you're not evaluating the information at this point, it doesn't matter whether you agree or disagree, approve or disapprove—only that you understand. Actively work to filter out anything other than the information itself, including the speaker's

> *Content listening* is listening primarily to understand and retain the information in the speaker's message, without evaluating it.

TABLE 2.2	**Three Styles of Listening**
Listening Style	**Goal**
Content listening	Understand and retain the information the other party is sharing
Critical listening	Understand and evaluate the information in terms of logical arguments, strength of evidence, validity of conclusions, implications, and any omissions; understanding the speaker's motives may be relevant as well
Empathic listening	Understand the speaker's feelings, needs, and wants, regardless of whether you agree with his or her perspective

appearance, vocabulary, level of experience, or position in the company. If appropriate, ask questions to clarify any points you don't understand or to get more details. However, don't challenge or correct the speaker. Remember that your goal with content listening is to get the information that another person has to share. If the exchange starts to feel confrontational, he or she might "shut down" and hesitate to disclose valuable information.

Critical listening adds the element of evaluation to content listening; it's not listening to criticize, but to critically evaluate the message and the speaker's intentions.

The goal of **critical listening** is to understand *and* evaluate the meaning of the speaker's message on several levels: the logic of the argument, the strength of the evidence, the validity of the conclusions, the implications of the message, the speaker's intentions and motives, and the omission of any important or relevant points. If you're skeptical, ask questions to explore the speaker's point of view and credibility. Be on the lookout for bias that might influence how the information is presented, separate opinions from facts, and watch for logical fallacies that could undermine the speaker's arguments or conclusions.[7] (Note that "critical listening" does not mean you are listening with the intent to criticize, but rather to understand the full meaning and implications of the speaker's message.)

The goal of *empathic listening* is to understand the speaker's feelings, needs, and wants, regardless of the information being shared.

The goal of **empathic listening** is to understand the speaker's feelings, needs, and wants so that you can appreciate his or her point of view, regardless of whether you share that perspective. Importantly, this style of listening gives the other person the freedom to share without fear of being judged or evaluated.[8] In this sense, empathic listening is a complementary skill to critical listening, because you need to silence your critical faculties and focus your attention on the other person. In fact, the information exchanged in an empathic conversion is sometimes less important than simply giving someone the opportunity to be heard. Be aware that empathic listening can be a difficult habit to get into, particularly for people who are used to solving problems and taking charge of situations.[9]

Listen Actively

At this point, you probably recognize the most important point to understand about listening, which is that to be effective, it must be an *active* process. Listening well requires energy, effort, and attention. **Active listening** is making a conscious effort to engage with other people and to turn off your internal filters and biases in order to truly hear and understand what they are saying. This section describes five ways to help you listen more actively (see Table 2.3).

Active listening is making a conscious effort to engage with other people and to turn off your internal filters and biases to truly hear and understand what they are saying.

Put Yourself in an Open and Positive State of Mind   Effective listening begins before a conversation, meeting, or presentation starts, by putting yourself in the right frame of mind.

TABLE 2.3	**Five Elements of Active Listening**
Element	**Why It's Important**
Open and positive state of mind	This mindset makes you receptive to new information and positive about the experience of listening to this person.
Active engagement	If you don't commit to being in and staying in the conversation, your mind will wander and the other person will sense that you aren't fully engaged.
Respect for silence	A moment of silence might be the speaker collecting or reconsidering his or her thoughts; if you step in too soon, you could interrupt the flow.
Nonverbal awareness	Intentional and unintentional nonverbal signals can explain and amplify the speaker's message.
Thoughtful note-taking	If the information is important, don't rely on your memory; it's too easy to forget key details.

Doing so requires a conscious commitment to the other person and to the time you will be spending. Even if you aren't terribly interested in the topic or aren't in the mood, you can will yourself to listen by viewing it as an opportunity to learn or to help a colleague or customer, whatever the situation is. The more willing you are to listen, the better you'll be able to concentrate and the higher the chance that you'll accurately interpret what the other person is saying.[10]

> To listen actively, start by putting yourself in an open and positive frame of mind.

Prepare yourself to have your beliefs challenged and to learn new information.[11] Accept that you might not have all the answers, even if you are an expert or the person in charge. This will help open your mind to what other people are saying.[12] This is the beginner's mind that Marc Benioff refers to (see page 37). To improve over time, commit to examining your own listening behaviors and, if necessary, changing how you listen to others.[13]

REAL-TIME UPDATES
LEARN MORE BY READING THIS ARTICLE
Use active listening to land your next job

Follow these examples of using active listening during a job interview. Go to **real-timeupdates.com/ebc13** and select Learn More in the Students section.

Keep Yourself Engaged   As the discussion moves along, commit to staying engaged, which requires consciously managing your behaviors, thoughts, and emotions. Remember that your brain has excess processing capacity while you're listening, and it will wander off and find new things to think about if you let it.

The technique of *vocalized listening* can help you stay focused. While someone else is talking, repeat the key ideas to yourself silently, analyze their meaning, and summarize related points of information.[14] When listening to a speaker whose native language or life experience is different from yours, try to paraphrase his or her ideas in words that are relevant to your experiences.

> Repeat key ideas to yourself silently, analyze their meaning, and summarize related points of information.

Compartmentalizing thoughts and emotions unrelated to the topic at hand can also help you stay focused and engaged. If you are worried or excited about something unrelated to the conversation, visualize putting that emotion in a box inside your mind with the understanding that you will attend to it later.

> Compartmentalize thoughts and emotions that are unrelated to the topic so they don't distract you.

Respect Silence   Don't automatically speak at the first moment of silence. Sometimes silence is an important part of the conversation. The other person might be collecting his or her thoughts or looking for a clearer way to express something.[15] Also, if someone pauses in the middle of a sentence, don't rush in to complete it—particularly if your real motivation is to demonstrate superior knowledge or intelligence.[16]

> Don't jump in immediately if the other person pauses while talking.

Pay Attention to Nonverbal Signals   One of the advantages of oral communication over written formats is the ability to see what isn't being said in the form of *nonverbal signals*. These include hand gestures, facial expressions, posture, eye contact, and so on. As "Improving Your Nonverbal Communication Skills" on page 43 explains, the information in the signals can strengthen, weaken, or even replace spoken language.

Take Thoughtful Notes   If the information you are likely to receive in a conversation or presentation will be important to use during the exchange or later on, write it down. Don't rely on your memory. Chances are you will forget or confuse important details. Of course, the decision whether to take notes depends on the situation. If someone is sharing personal or confidential information or is asking for your advice, it might not be appropriate or necessary to take notes.

> Don't rely on your memory if you are hearing important information that you will need to act on later; record it or write it down.

If you don't already have a note-taking system that works for you, an effective technique is to divide a sheet of paper into two columns and record key points from the speaker in one column and your summaries, questions, or potential responses opposite those points in the other column. If you are using a laptop or mobile device to take notes, make sure you can do so quickly enough to keep up with the conversation and in a way that doesn't disturb others.

In addition to recording information for later use, taking notes can help you engage with the speaker during a conversation or presentation. For instance, if you have questions or concerns, you can list them in your notes and refer to them when it's convenient to ask

> Taking notes can also help you engage with the speaker during a conversation or presentation.

or during a scheduled question-and-answer period. Notes also help you stay engaged, and they can help you evaluate information when you are using critical listening.[17]

If you have no choice but to memorize information you are hearing, take active steps to transfer it from short-term memory to long-term memory.

If you are unable to take notes and have no choice but to memorize, you can hold information in short-term memory by repeating it silently or creating lists in your head. To store information in long-term memory, four techniques can help: (1) associate new information with something closely related (such as the restaurant in which you met a new client), (2) categorize the new information into logical groups (such as alphabetizing a list of names), (3) visualize words and ideas as pictures, and (4) create mnemonics such as acronyms or rhymes.

Table 2.4 summarizes the habits of effective and ineffective listeners. For a quick reminder of the steps you can take to become a better listener, see "Checklist: Improving Your Listening Skills."

TABLE 2.4   Behavioral Differences Between Effective and Ineffective Listeners

Effective Listeners	Ineffective Listeners
Listen actively	Listen passively
Put themselves in an open, positive frame of mind	Switch to listening without consideration, continuing in whatever emotional state they were in before
Stay focused on the speaker and the conversation	Allow their minds to wander, are easily distracted, or work on unrelated tasks
Take careful notes, when applicable	Take no notes or ineffective notes
Make frequent eye contact with the speaker (depends on culture to some extent)	Make little or no eye contact—or inappropriate eye contact
Keep their emotions under control and don't let their own anxieties poison the conversation	Allow their emotions to negatively influence the conversation
Mentally paraphrase key points to maintain attention level and ensure comprehension	Fail to paraphrase
Adjust listening style to the situation	Listen with the same style, regardless of the situation
Give the speaker nonverbal feedback (such as nodding to show agreement or raising eyebrows to show surprise or skepticism)	Fail to give the speaker nonverbal feedback
Save questions or points of disagreement until an appropriate time	Interrupt whenever they disagree or don't understand
Engage the other person with questions or encouragement; validate the other person's feelings	Fail to engage; offer no encouragement or expression of understanding
Overlook stylistic differences and focus on the speaker's message	Are distracted by or unduly influenced by stylistic differences; are judgmental
Make distinctions between main points and supporting details	Are unable to distinguish main points from details
Look for opportunities to learn	Assume they already know everything that's important to know

Sources: Judi Brownell, *Listening: Attitudes, Principles, and Skills,* 6th ed. (New York: Routledge, 2018), 6, 10–11, 19–20, 88–89; Jack Zenger and Joseph Folkman, "What Great Listeners Actually Do," *Harvard Business Review*, 14 July 2016, hbr.org; Amy Jen Su and Muriel Maignan Wilkins, "What Gets in the Way of Listening," *Harvard Business Review*, 14 April 2016, hbr.org; Madelyn Burley-Allen, *Listening: The Forgotten Skill,* 2nd ed. (New York: Wiley, 1995), 70–71, 119–120; Larry Barker and Kittie Watson, *Listen Up* (New York: St. Martin's, 2000), 8, 9, 64.

CHECKLIST **Improving Your Listening Skills**

✔ Recognize the unique challenges of listening and take steps to overcome them.
✔ Lower external barriers to physical reception whenever you can, such as minimizing ambient noise.
✔ Lower internal barriers to reception and understanding by monitoring and managing your own emotions.
✔ Try not to slip into defensive listening; be open to what you are hearing, even if you don't agree.

✔ Adapt your listening style to each situation.
✔ Commit to listening actively—put yourself in an open and positive frame of mind, keep yourself engaged, respect silence, be aware of nonverbal signals, and take notes if appropriate.
✔ Don't rely on your memory; write down or record important information.

Improving Your Nonverbal Communication Skills

Nonverbal communication is the process of sending and receiving information, both intentionally and unintentionally, without using language. Nonverbal signals play a vital role in communication because they can strengthen or repeat a verbal message (when the nonverbal signals match the spoken words), weaken or contradict a verbal message (when nonverbal signals don't match the words), or replace words entirely.[18]

Nonverbal signals are a factor in virtually every instance of communication, and they can convey a significant portion of the information and emotions shared in interpersonal communication.[19] In fact, you may have heard the claim that nonverbal signals convey *most* of the message in face-to-face communication. You might even see specific percentages, such as that words carry only 7 percent of meaning and nonverbal elements carry 93 percent (with tone of voice making up 38 percent of that and body language the other 55 percent). However, the experiments that produced these figures more than 50 years ago attempted only to assess the feelings of the speaker and have not been confirmed by other research.[20] These percentages do not apply as a general rule about nonverbal communication, so ignore any claim about words carrying only 7 percent of your meaning.

Nonverbal communication is the process of sending and receiving information, both intentionally and unintentionally, without using language.

Nonverbal signals can convey a significant amount of information, but disregard any claims you might've heard about them conveying a specific percentage of message content.

RECOGNIZING NONVERBAL COMMUNICATION

Nonverbal communication is an intriguing part of business communication because it is both complex and somewhat difficult to pin down. On the sending side, some nonverbal signals are controllable (such as choosing what to wear), some are habits you may not even think about (tapping your fingers when you're impatient, for instance), some are trainable (using specific hand gestures during a presentation), and some are involuntary (such as blushing).[21]

On the receiving side, nonverbal signals are not always reliable (a person who avoids eye contact isn't necessarily trying to hide something, for example), and people vary widely in their ability to interpret signals correctly.[22]

In a face-to-face conversation, everything from your body language to your clothing to your eye movements can influence the messages and meanings the other party takes away from the exchange. During a phone call, the pitch, rate, and other qualities of your voice can send nonverbal signals. Even with written messages (both printed and digital), design and formatting choices send nonverbal signals, although the focus here is on interpersonal communication. Six types of signals are particularly important (see Figure 2.1 on the next page):

Nonverbal communication is complex: Not all signals are controllable, and signals don't always mean what people think they mean.

- **Facial expressions.** Your face is the primary vehicle for expressing your emotions because it can reveal both the type and the intensity of your feelings.[23] Facial expressions can also affect other people's emotions—a smile or frown, for instance, can trigger a similar response in anyone you are talking to.[24] Your eyes are especially effective for indicating attention and interest, influencing others, regulating interaction, and establishing dominance.[25]

- **Vocal characteristics.** Aspects of voice carry both intentional and unintentional messages. A speaker can intentionally control pitch, pace, and stress to convey a specific message. For instance, compare "*What* are you doing?" and "What are *you* doing?" Unintentional vocal characteristics can convey happiness, surprise, fear, and other emotions (for example, fear often increases the pitch and pace of your speaking voice).

- **Gesture and posture.** The way you position and move your body expresses both specific and general messages, some voluntary and some involuntary. Many gestures—a wave of the hand, for example—have specific and intentional meanings. Other types of body movement can express meanings that may be unintended. Slouching, leaning forward, fidgeting, and walking briskly are all unconscious signals that can reveal whether you feel confident or nervous, friendly or hostile, assertive or passive, powerful or powerless.

- **Personal appearance.** People respond to others on the basis of their physical appearance, sometimes fairly and other times unfairly. Although an individual's body type and

Nonverbal signals include facial expressions; gestures, posture, and gait; vocal characteristics; personal appearance; touch; and use of time and space.

Subtleties in intonation or emphasis can completely alter the meaning of a spoken message.

Bevan Goldswain/Shutterstock

imagedb/Shutterstock

Maridav/Shutterstock

szefei/Shutterstock

Figure 2.1   The Importance of Nonverbal Signals
You send nonverbal signals continuously, through just about every aspect of your physical being.

Touch is a powerful element of communication, but it can be misused and misunderstood; as a general rule for the workplace, avoid any touching other than handshakes.

facial features define appearance to a large degree, you can control grooming, clothing, accessories, piercings, tattoos, and hairstyle. To make a good impression, adopt the style of the people you want to impress. Employers differ widely in their expectations of personal appearance, so make sure you are aware of your company's *dress code*, if it has one.

- **Touch.** Touch is an important way to convey warmth, comfort, and reassurance—as well as control. Touch is so powerful, in fact, that it is governed by cultural customs that establish who can touch whom and how in various circumstances. Even within each culture's norms, however, individual attitudes toward touch vary widely. A manager might be comfortable using hugs to express support or congratulations, but his or her subordinates could interpret those hugs as a show of dominance or sexual interest.[26] Touch is a complex subject, in other words. Other than handshakes, the best general advice is to avoid touching anyone under any circumstances in the workplace. If someone else takes the initiative, you can choose to reciprocate if you want, but *only* if you are comfortable doing so.

- **Time and space.** Like touch, time and space can be used to assert authority, imply intimacy, and send other nonverbal messages. For instance, some people try to demonstrate their own importance or disregard for others by making other people wait; others show respect by being on time. Similarly, taking care not to invade private space, such as standing too close when talking, is a way to show respect for others. Keep in mind that expectations regarding time and space vary by culture.

USING NONVERBAL COMMUNICATION EFFECTIVELY

Paying attention to nonverbal cues will make you a better speaker and a better listener. When you're talking, be conscious of the nonverbal cues you are sending, and use them to reinforce your spoken message. For example, if you want to persuade someone to collaborate

Andreas Berheide/EyeEm/Getty Images

Figure 2.2   Assessing Your Nonverbal Presence
Fairly or unfairly, the choices you make about your appearance and other nonverbal attributes affect the way other people perceive you and your ability to contribute.

with you on a project, don't lean back in your chair with your arms crossed while making your pitch. An open and forward posture will reinforce your message of cooperation.

Also consider the nonverbal signals you send when you're not talking—the clothes you wear, the way you sit, the way you walk (see Figure 2.2). Whether or not you think it is fair to be judged on superficial matters, the truth is that you are judged this way. Don't let careless choices or disrespectful habits undermine all the great work you're doing on the job. In addition, be mindful of how your dress and grooming choices affect your own attitude. If you believe that you've made the effort to look your best, you will feel more confident, and that confidence will manifest itself in a variety of positive nonverbal signals.[27]

> Make sure the nonverbal signals you send don't undermine your efforts to succeed on the job.

When you listen, pay attention to the speaker's nonverbal cues. Do they amplify, obscure, or contradict the spoken words? Is the speaker intentionally using nonverbal signals to send you a message that he or she can't put into words? A thin, forced smile in response to "How did your meeting with the boss go?" probably says that it didn't go well but that the person isn't ready to talk about it. As you gain experience in the workplace, reflect on the conversations you have with managers, colleagues, and customers. Compare the verbal messages you receive with the nonverbal signals that accompany them. Over time, you'll develop a better sense of how the people around you use nonverbal signals.

Be observant, but don't assume you can "read someone like a book," particularly if you don't know the person's normal behavioral patterns.[28] For example, contrary to popular belief, avoiding eye contact and covering one's face while talking are not reliable clues that someone is lying. Even when telling the truth, most people don't make uninterrupted eye contact with the listeners, and various gestures such as touching one's face might be normal behavior for some people.[29] Moreover, these and other behaviors may be influenced by culture (in some cultures, sustained eye contact can be interpreted as a sign of disrespect) or might just be ways of coping with stressful situations.[30]

> Don't assume you can "read someone like a book," particularly if you don't know the person's normal behavioral patterns.

If something doesn't feel right, ask the speaker an honest and respectful question. Doing so may clear everything up, or it may uncover issues you need to explore further. See "Checklist: Improving Your Nonverbal Communication Skills" for a summary of key ideas regarding nonverbal skills.

CHECKLIST ✓ **Improving Your Nonverbal Communication Skills**

- ✓ Understand the roles that nonverbal signals play in communication—complementing verbal language by strengthening, weakening, or replacing words.
- ✓ Note that facial expressions (especially eye contact) can reveal the type and intensity of a speaker's feelings.
- ✓ Watch for cues from gestures and posture.
- ✓ Listen for vocal characteristics that can signal the emotions underlying the speaker's words.

- ✓ Recognize that listeners are influenced by physical appearance.
- ✓ As a general workplace rule, avoid any physical contact beyond handshakes; touch can convey positive attributes but can also be interpreted as a show of dominance or sexual interest.
- ✓ Pay attention to the use of time and space.

3 LEARNING OBJECTIVE
Outline an effective process for initiating, sustaining, and concluding workplace conversations.

Developing Your Conversational Skills

Good listening skills and an awareness of nonverbal communication are the foundation of good conversational skills—the ability to plan, initiate, maintain, and conclude successful business conversations. You will engage in a wide variety of conversations throughout your career, from brief and spontaneous chats to formal, structured conversations such as interviews and evaluations.

Every conversation is a potential opportunity to gain or share information, to give or accept help, to foster a beneficial relationship, or build your personal brand.

View every conversation as a potential opportunity to gain or share information, to give or accept help, to foster a beneficial relationship, or to build your personal brand.

INITIATING BUSINESS CONVERSATIONS

Business conversations can be grouped into three types: unplanned conversations, informal planned conversations, and formal planned conversations. For all three, the success of the conversation can hinge on how it gets started, so use these first few moments to launch the conversation in a positive way.

Initiating Unplanned Conversations

Unplanned conversations occur at random moments throughout the work day—you run into someone in a hallway, over lunch, in the parking lot, and so on. These chats can involve people you work with every day, or they can involve people you rarely encounter, including people in other parts of the organization or senior managers.

Spontaneous, informal conversations can be among the most important you'll ever have, because they can give you "face time" with executives and other people with whom you don't normally interact.

These conversations aren't part of your regular work duties, but they can be some of the most beneficial for your career. They are opportunities to network with people across the company and to learn more about the company and its operations. They can also present rare opportunities to get a few minutes of "face time" with senior executives and other influential people. Plus, they can make work more satisfying by helping you and your colleagues relate to one another on a more personal or social level.

You obviously can't plan these spontaneous encounters, but you can prepare for them in a general way by keeping up to date on what is going on around the company and by being genuinely interested in what other people do. For example, educate yourself on the industry in which your company operates, identify its key competitors, and learn about your firm's major business challenges and opportunities.

Asking someone a question about his or work or something relevant to the company is often a good way to initiate an informal conversation.

In most situations, the best way to initiate one of these spontaneous conversations is to ask the other person a question about his or her work (make sure it's nothing intrusive) or some issue that affects the company. This sends a positive message that you are curious about what is going on around you, and it provides some initial energy and focus for the conversation. Avoid gossip and complaining, unless you're expressing sympathy with someone's plight or brainstorming solutions or workarounds.

Initiating Planned Conversations

Many of the one-on-one conversations you will have in business are planned, with a predetermined topic and often a set time limit. They might be informal, such as meeting with a colleague to discuss ideas for an upcoming project, or formal, such as performance evaluations and job interviews. Because these exchanges are planned, you have time to prepare the questions you would like to ask, the information you would like to share, and answers to questions you are likely to get. If you requested the conversation, it's usually your responsibility to do enough planning to ensure a productive use of the other person's time.

If you requested a conversation with a manager, colleague, or customer, respect the person's time by preparing thoroughly.

Initiating a planned conversation is often simple, because the agenda or discussion plan usually defines the first topic of conversation and identifies which person will lead the conversation. In addition, be sure to start in an appropriate frame of mind and with an appropriate emotional tone. If you're sitting down with your boss for a performance evaluation, for instance, remind yourself that you might not want to hear everything you're about to be told. Put yourself in a receptive frame of mind with a pleasant, professional demeanor.

Remind yourself not to get defensive, no matter how the conversation goes, and to treat the conversation as an exchange of useful and important information.

The techniques you'll learn in upcoming chapters for planning written messages can be adapted for many conversations as well. The planning tasks covered in Chapter 5 show you how to analyze a situation, establish a clear objective, and organize the information you have to share. In addition, the approaches for sharing negative information (Chapter 10) or trying to persuade (Chapter 11) work well for these types of conversations. For both types, the most important decision in terms of initiating a conversation is whether you want to be *direct* (open the conversation with your main idea) or *indirect* (lay out your reasons first and build up to your main idea).

As with listening in general, put yourself in a positive frame of mind before beginning any important conversation.

MAINTAINING A POSITIVE CONVERSATIONAL FLOW

After the conversation starts, keep aware of how it is flowing, and take steps as necessary to make the exchange satisfying and successful. The appropriate steps depend on the nature of the conversation and your relationship with the other person, but here are seven general tactics to keep in mind:

- **Don't talk nonstop.** Talking nonstop for an extended period is self-centered, it's tiring for the listener, and it prevents the other person from asking questions or letting you know that he or she agrees with you. Even if the purpose of the conversation is for you to present information to other person, pause briefly between major points to give the other party a chance to respond.

Talking nonstop for an extended period is self-centered, tiring for listeners, and prevents listeners from participating.

- **Don't interrupt.** Even if you don't agree with something that is being said or you feel compelled to assert your authority, don't interrupt. Interrupting is rude and sends a strong signal that you don't respect other people. Whatever information you might have to add can wait until it is polite to respond. Remember that a conversation isn't merely an exchange of information, it's a *relationship in action*, and poor conversational behaviors can damage a relationship. Men in particular should be sensitive to the matter of interrupting women at work; multiple studies show that men are more likely to interrupt when women are talking than when other men are talking.[31]

Don't interrupt, even if the person talking is saying something incorrect; whatever you have to say can wait until it's polite to talk.

- **Express disagreement and criticism indirectly.** If someone says something you disagree with, don't respond with a blunt "I disagree" or "You're wrong." Instead, look for ways to question the statement without making it feel like a personal attack. For example, if a subordinate proposes an idea that you believe is flawed, ask a question that relates to the weaknesses you see in the idea. Rather than saying, "Our customers would hate it," you might ask, "How would that affect customer satisfaction?"

To maintain harmony in a conversation, you can express disagreement indirectly.

- **Stay engaged—and appear engaged.** Use brief conversational responses and nonverbal signals to let the other person know that you are engaged. Techniques for this include maintaining a comfortable amount of eye contact, nodding your head to express agreement, and expressing brief confirmations after major points in the conversation. Above all, make sure the other person knows that he or she has your undivided attention (see Figure 2.3 on the next page).

- **Summarize to reenergize and refocus.** Sometimes conversations can lose energy or focus as they progress. One helpful tactic is to summarize what you've heard the other person say up to that point. This gives him or her a moment to rest, and it helps verify that you've heard everything correctly.[32] These interim "micro breaks" are also a chance to check whether the conversation is on track toward meeting your goals.

- **Ask direct questions.** Ask questions to draw out information and encourage the other person to participate more fully. If you are a manager conversing with a subordinate, asking questions is an important way to get information you might not hear otherwise, particularly if people are reluctant to bring you bad news. *Open-ended questions* (such as "Where should we advertise next quarter?") can solicit more thoughtful responses than *closed questions* ("Should we advertise on Facebook next quarter?") because they don't limit the other person to the choices you present.[33]

You can ask both direct and indirect questions to keep a conversation moving.

- **Ask indirect questions.** In some situations, asking direct questions can be intimidating or off-putting to the other person. A question like "Why did you do that?" can put

Figure 2.3 **Staying Engaged in a Conversation**

Staying engaged in a conversation—and letting the other person see that you are engaged—requires active commitment to the conversation. Doing so helps you get more out of the conversation and sends the important signal that you value the other person's time and ideas.

someone on the defensive, for instance. You can depersonalize the query by rephrasing it as "Can you walk me through the decision process?" which shifts the focus from the other person to the decision-making process. Alternatively, you can phrase it as a prompt rather than a question, such as "I'd like to hear more about the process leading up to the decision."[34]

GRACEFULLY CONCLUDING A CONVERSATION

Bringing a conversation to an end can sometimes be an awkward step. Some conversations are bounded by a specific time limit, and others have a natural structure that brings the conversations to a close (interviews, for example). However, sometimes you and the other person will need to mutually conclude that you're ready to bring the conversation to an end. You can usually sense that the other person is ready to end the conversation—which is another good reason to pause frequently when talking, as it gives the other party the chance to indicate that he or she is ready to end. If you need to end the conversation, a simple "Well, I better get back to work" will usually suffice.

The final exchange is your opportunity to leave a positive impression of yourself and the conversation. You can quickly summarize any action items that came up, either reiterating something you will do or subtly confirming what the other person will do (such as "I look forward to getting your email"). End on a positive and respectful note, as appropriate to the situation.

HANDLING DIFFICULT CONVERSATIONS

All business professionals eventually find themselves in situations where they need to have difficult and unwelcome conversations—whether it's giving an employee a negative performance evaluation, explaining to your boss why a project you've been assigned is unworkable, or simply trying to smooth things over with a colleague. These conversations are challenging because they can involve emotions, egos, and differing points of view. Here are six tips to help reduce the stress of these encounters and ensure more productive outcomes (see "Apply Your Skills Now: Prepare Yourself for a Difficult Conversation" for tips on applying these ideas in your academic and personal lives right now):

When you know you're about to enter a difficult conversation, rehearse your listening skills and prepare thoroughly.

- **Rehearse your active listening skills.** Review the five tips under "Listen Actively" on page 40, starting with putting yourself in an open frame of mind that is as positive as possible under the circumstances.
- **Prepare thoroughly.** Giving or receiving unwelcome news is unpleasant, and the emotional element can magnify perceptions of unfairness or poor treatment. Make sure you have all your facts in order so the conversation doesn't get sidetracked with heated arguments over details.

- **Visualize the situation from the other side.** As you'll see in Chapter 5, understanding your audience is a vital step in all communication efforts, and it's particularly important when emotions are running high. Try to imagine the challenges the other person might be facing and how he or she might respond to what you have to say. You could find common ground to help resolve a disagreement, for example.[35]

- **If you are upset, vent *before* the conversation.** Even if anger is justified in a particular situation, exploding at someone during a conversation will usually make a bad situation even worse. Venting some of the emotional pressure in a controlled way beforehand can help you calm down and think more rationally. If possible, discuss the situation with someone who isn't involved and whose discretion you trust, and let your feelings out.[36] Another option is to write a brief memo on the matter and then immediately delete it. Even going for a brisk walk can help you burn off some energy and give your emotions some rest. By releasing some of the pent-up anger before the conversation, you'll enter it in a calmer state of mind.

- **Clarify and compartmentalize your emotions.** As the section on active listening notes, it can be helpful to temporarily compartmentalize your emotions so that aggravation or fear in some unrelated part of your life doesn't seep over into a business conversation.

- **Stay tuned to your own emotions.** If you feel yourself getting tense, remind yourself to breathe slowly and deeply. If you're getting overwhelmed, see if you can take a short break, such as getting coffee or going to the restroom. Even a few minutes—and the chance to get up and move—can help you calm down.[37]

> Don't carry a lot of emotional baggage into a conversation; if necessary, find a safe way to vent beforehand.

Even with good intentions, difficult conversations can sometimes stall or go unexpectedly off track. If you sense this happening, adjust your approach. Rather than trying to convince the other person to adopt your point of view, switch into learning mode for a while and try to hear what he or she has to say as objectively as possible. Let the other person know you want to understand the reasons for the impasse by offering prompts or asking questions such as, "Help me understand your perspective" or "What am I not seeing

---

Prepare Yourself for a Difficult Conversation

No one welcomes the prospect of a difficult conversation, whether it's with a professor, a parent, a spouse, a partner, or anyone else. You may not be able to change the information that needs to be shared, but you can take steps to make the conversation itself less upsetting—and to keep emotions from spiraling out of control. In addition to the rest of the advice offered in this chapter on listening and conversations, follow these tips:

- **Don't put it off.** Although it's natural to want to avoid an unpleasant confrontation, waiting usually makes things worse because you have to live with the anxiety for that much longer.

- **Don't go in angry.** While you don't want to put off a difficult conversation, don't jump into it if you're still angry about something that happened, even if your anger is justified. Anger can cloud your perception and spur you to make bad decisions or say things you'll regret. Find a way to cool off first.

- **Don't make excuses.** If you made a mistake or failed to meet a commitment, own up to it. You'll feel better about yourself and earn respect from the other person.

- **See things from the other side.** Regardless of who is at fault—if anyone—take a moment to consider what the other person is going through.

- **Ask for help if you need it.** Admitting you need help can be a difficult step. However, if you're in trouble, the bravest course is often to ask for help.

- **Be the boss of your own emotions.** Be conscious of your emotions and actively control them; don't let them control you. This is not easy, but it can be done.

- **Be kind.** Unless you're being taken advantage of, you'll never regret being kind to someone, regardless of the circumstances.

COACH YOURSELF

1. Do you ever find your emotions getting out of control when you're having a difficult conversation? What steps could you take to keep them under control?

2. Is there a difficult conversation that you're putting off right now? If so, imagine the relief you'll feel once you get it over with. Even if it's likely to be a painful experience, it could be the start of repairing a damaged relationship or getting your life back on track.

here?"[38] By backing away from the confrontation, you establish yourself as someone who wants to reach a solution, rather than someone intent on getting his or her own way. Doing so might also give you a fresh perspective that will let you restart the conversation from a different angle.

See "Checklist: Improving Your Conversational Skills" for a reminder of the steps to follow for more successful conversations.

CHECKLIST ✔ Improving Your Conversational Skills

✔ Initiate an unplanned conversation by asking the other person a question about his or her work or an issue that affects the company.

✔ For planned conversations, make sure you plan thoroughly enough to make good use of the other person's time.

✔ Don't talk nonstop; give the other person time to ask questions or shift the conversation.

✔ Don't interrupt.

✔ Express disagreement and criticism indirectly.

✔ Stay engaged, and make sure the other person can see that you are engaged.

✔ If the energy drops, summarize what has been said in order to reenergize and refocus.

✔ Ask direct or indirect questions, as appropriate to the situation.

✔ If you know a conversation will be difficult or uncomfortable, prepare thoroughly, visualize the other person's side, vent any anger beforehand, and manage your own emotions carefully.

---

4 **LEARNING OBJECTIVE**
Explain the causes of workplace conflict, and identify five productive steps for resolving conflict.

Managing Workplace Conflict

Conflict is virtually inevitable in any workplace as people with differing ideas, priorities, and personalities are thrown together and asked to work toward common goals. Even in the best of circumstances, people will occasionally disagree or rub each other the wrong way. And in dysfunctional environments with ineffective management, conflict can overwhelm normal business activities. This section explores why conflict arises in the workplace and how specific communication strategies and tactics can help avoid and resolve it.

WHY CONFLICT ARISES IN THE WORKPLACE

Conflict can arise in a workplace for a variety of reasons; some are structural, some are situational, and some are interpersonal.

Workplace conflicts can arise from a variety of causes (see Table 2.5).[39] Some conflicts are *structural*, meaning they are more or less permanent aspects of being in business. For example, every company has a finite amount of money to spend on operations every year, and every department is competing for a share of those funds. A secondary category involves *situational* conflicts, which arise from temporary forces within an industry or a company. The people assigned to a project team, for instance, may not agree on what the team's goals and priorities should be. And a third category, *interpersonal* conflicts, stem from choices, behaviors, and personality traits of the people within a team, department, or other work group.

As you can see from the examples in Table 2.5, some conflicts are "blameless," in that they stem from natural forces in the business environment. Other conflicts have a more personal origin, and they may well be the fault of some of the people involved. In addition, structural and situational conflicts can magnify interpersonal conflicts, and vice versa. For instance, when business is booming and people are getting raises and promotional opportunities, occasional personality clashes might not be terribly disruptive because life in general is good for everybody. However, when times are tough, such as when sales are dropping or a project is failing, the stress can amplify interpersonal conflicts as people's tolerances drop and they become more sensitive to perceived injustices and personal insults.

CONSTRUCTIVE VERSUS DESTRUCTIVE CONFLICT

Although the term *conflict* sounds negative, conflict isn't necessarily bad. Conflict can be *constructive* if it forces important issues into the open, increases the involvement of team members, or generates creative ideas for solving a problem. Teamwork isn't necessarily

TABLE 2.5	**Sources of Workplace Conflict**
Type	**Examples**
Structural: a permanent aspect of doing business	Competition for opportunities, such as promotions into management positions
	Competition for resources, such as project budgets, equipment, or staff
	Disagreements over fundamental values, such as the company's responsibilities to society or its workers
Situational: based on temporary forces	Disagreements over project goals
	Conflict between individual goals and team goals
	Workload and work/life imbalances
	Resistance to change
Interpersonal: stemming from personal choices, behaviors, and personality differences	Poor communication
	Personality clashes
	Unprofessional behavior
	Cultural differences

about happiness and harmony. Sometimes two mediocre ideas can collide and produce one really great idea that no one had considered. Even teams that have some interpersonal friction can excel with effective leadership and team players committed to shared goals. As teamwork experts Andy Boynton and Bill Fischer put it, "Virtuoso teams are not about getting polite results."[40]

In contrast, conflict is *destructive* if it saps productivity, damages morale, or threatens to spread to other people in the organization. When this happens, it's time to step in and address the situation.

> Conflict can be constructive if it forces important issues into the open, increases the involvement of team members, or generates creative ideas for solving a problem.

STEPS TO RESOLVE CONFLICT

When you encounter conflict in a work setting, follow the five steps in this section to resolve it in a positive and constructive way (see Table 2.6). Of course, the specific tactics you should take depend on your role in the conflict and your relationship with the other party or parties. For instance, if you are the manager of a team that is experiencing conflict, rather than being involved in the conflict yourself, taking the role of an impartial mediator will probably be more productive than aligning yourself with one side or the other.

> **MOBILE APP**
> **Making Conflict Work** helps you plan the most effective way to resolve specific types of workplace conflicts.

Step 1: Decide Whether the Conflict Warrants Taking Action

Not all conflicts are worth the time, energy, and disruption it might take to resolve them. For instance, if you're having personality clashes with someone on a project team but the

TABLE 2.6	**Five Steps to Resolving Conflict**
Step	**Summary**
Decide if the conflict is worth resolving.	Resolving conflict takes time and energy and can temporarily disrupt activities and relationships; if the conflict is minor or will disappear on its own (such as when a team disbands), it might make more sense to live with it.
Examine your own beliefs and behaviors.	Even if you are sure the problem lies with another person, examine your own stance before taking any action; you might be contributing to the conflict in ways you hadn't considered.
Identify where the conflict originates.	Conflicts aren't always about what they *appear* to be about; the real difference may lie below the surface.
Establish common ground.	Find out the highest level (Figure 2.4) at which all parties agree or are in harmony; the problem lies at the next level above that.
Choose a strategy for resolving the differences.	Four basic choices are avoidance, accommodation, compromise, and collaboration.

project will be over in a few weeks, you will have to decide if it's better to address the situation or live with it until the project is completed. Of course, ignoring a problem might achieve peace in the short term, but it isn't always the best long-term solution.[41] If you believe that a colleague is routinely taking credit for your work, you'd better fix the problem before it affects your performance evaluations and prospects for promotion.

Step 2: Examine Your Own Beliefs and Behaviors

Examine your own role in a conflict before taking action to resolve it.

If you are personally involved in the conflict, step back and examine your own perspective before taking any action. As tensions rise during a conflict, emotions can take over and distort one's view of the matter. Emotions can also lead people into behaviors that they wouldn't normally engage in. Take stock of your participation in the conflict, and see if modifying your approach to the situation could improve matters. This self-assessment might also generate a constructive way to open a dialogue with the other party, such as "I've thought about my role in this disagreement, and I see a change that I can make." Recognizing that you are willing to make a concession in the interest of resolving the conflict, the other party might respond in a positive way as well.

REAL-TIME UPDATES

LEARN MORE BY WATCHING THIS VIDEO

How emotions lead us astray in conflicts

See why having an emotional stake in a question can lead you to flawed reasoning. Go to **real-timeupdates.com/ebc13** and select Learn More in the Students section.

Step 3: Identify Where the Conflict Originates

Conflict can originate at many different levels, from superficial to deep, and the apparent conflict isn't always the real conflict.

Conflict can originate at different levels or depths (see Figure 2.4). At the shallowest level, the conflict might simply be about language, when people use different terminology to express similar thoughts.[42] At the deepest level, people disagree about fundamental values and principles, such as the company's responsibilities to employees or to society in general.

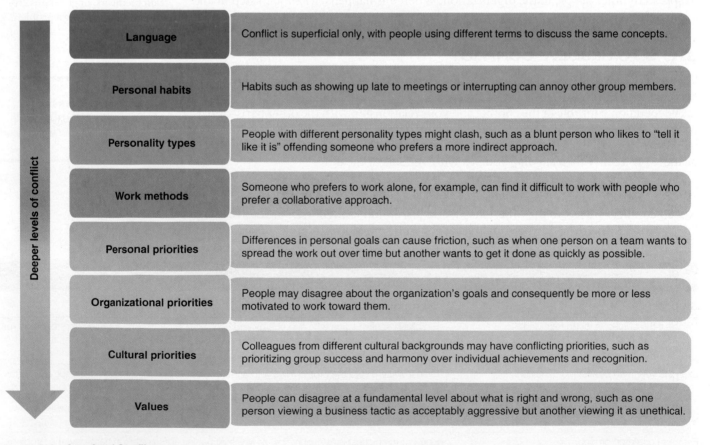

Deeper levels of conflict

Language	Conflict is superficial only, with people using different terms to discuss the same concepts.
Personal habits	Habits such as showing up late to meetings or interrupting can annoy other group members.
Personality types	People with different personality types might clash, such as a blunt person who likes to "tell it like it is" offending someone who prefers a more indirect approach.
Work methods	Someone who prefers to work alone, for example, can find it difficult to work with people who prefer a collaborative approach.
Personal priorities	Differences in personal goals can cause friction, such as when one person on a team wants to spread the work out over time but another wants to get it done as quickly as possible.
Organizational priorities	People may disagree about the organization's goals and consequently be more or less motivated to work toward them.
Cultural priorities	Colleagues from different cultural backgrounds may have conflicting priorities, such as prioritizing group success and harmony over individual achievements and recognition.
Values	People can disagree at a fundamental level about what is right and wrong, such as one person viewing a business tactic as acceptably aggressive but another viewing it as unethical.

Figure 2.4   Levels of Conflict
Conflict can originate at a variety of levels, from shallow differences in language to deep disagreements about fundamental values, and the apparent conflict may not be the real conflict. Before attempting to resolve a workplace conflict, be sure to identify the real source of disagreement.

In between, the source of conflict might be cultural differences, disagreements over organizational priorities, personal versus group priorities, work methods, or personality differences. The real source of the conflict might not be the apparent source, the one that is most visible. For example, two people on a project could be arguing about work methods when the real conflict is a deeper disagreement about the team's mission.

Discovering the real source of conflict might not be easy, because it can force people to express uncomfortable emotions. Start by making sure everyone has the opportunity to be heard.[43] This can be done in a group setting if more than two people are involved. However, if emotions are running high, it might be best to start with one-on-one conversations in which each person can talk openly with a manager or other intermediary.

Step 4: Establish Common Ground

Looking again at the "stack" in Figure 2.4, identify the highest level at which the parties do agree. For example, if a project team agrees on the team's mission but not on work methods, you know that the resolution to the conflict needs to focus on how the team goes about its work. However, if one of the parties to the conflict thinks the project is a waste of time, there's not much point in discussing work methods. Trying to fix a problem at the wrong level will likely just add to everyone's frustration.

Find the highest level at which opposing parties are in harmony; the conflict originates in the next level up.

Step 5: Choose a Strategy for Resolving the Differences

Now that you've clarified the precise cause of the conflict, you can start working toward a resolution. As you move forward, focus on the problem, not on the people involved (unless personal behavior is the problem), and focus on the future, not the past.[44] Also, if you are in a position to make or recommend solutions, make sure you truly understand the dynamics in play before moving toward a solution. For example, if you have recently taken over as manager in a department rife with conflict, take the time to listen to all sides and understand what is going on before taking action.[45] Resist the urge to jump into action and try to fix the problem; you might just make it worse.

Here are common strategies for resolving conflict:

Check out the "Five-Minute Guide to Resolving Workplace Conflict" at the end of the chapter.

- **Avoidance**. In some situations, the best solution is to avoid the circumstances that create conflict, rather than trying to fix the conflict when it does occur. For example, if two people working on a project team simply don't get along, it might be in the team's best interests to divide tasks in such a way that the two don't have to work together. Avoidance doesn't solve the underlying conflict, of course, and it should be used only when a real solution isn't possible or would cause so much disruption that it wouldn't be worth the trouble.
- **Accommodation**. One side in a conflict can decide to accommodate or sacrifice for the good of the organization or to maintain harmony in a relationship.[46] For example, if two people disagree about the best way to approach a project, one might decide to accept and support the other's approach, even though he or she has reservations about it. Of course, a true professional in this situation will work diligently to make the project succeed.
- **Compromise**. In contrast to accommodation, the two sides can choose to meet somewhere in the middle, with both sides giving up something. Balanced compromise is one of the hallmarks of successful teams and groups.[47]
- **Collaboration**. Whereas compromise seeks a middle ground that requires some sacrifice from both sides, the parties can choose to collaborate on a new solution that satisfies everyone's needs and expectations. Collaboration in this sense can be a rewarding experience because it makes conditions better for everyone and gives a team or group the satisfaction of a shared accomplishment.

Common strategies for resolving conflict include avoidance, accommodation, compromise, and collaboration.

In some instances, conflicting parties can benefit from **mediation**, where a neutral third party guides them through the steps of resolving the conflict. When two colleagues or a subordinate and a manager can't reach agreement on their own, for instance, they might ask a representative from the human resources department for help. Mediators can help manage the emotions of the situation and ask probing questions that get to the root of the conflict. A company might also have formal *grievance procedures*, particularly if its employees are members of a labor union.

Mediation is a conflict-resolution process in which a neutral third party guides opposing parties through the steps of resolving their conflict.

Conflict resolution often requires *negotiation* to move the parties toward a mutually acceptable solution. The following section covers this important communication skill. For a quick reminder of the important concepts of conflict resolution, see "Checklist: Managing Workplace Conflicts."

CHECKLIST ✔ Managing Workplace Conflicts

✔ Understand why conflict arises.
✔ Recognize the difference between constructive and destructive conflict.
✔ Before you decide to resolve a conflict, make sure it's worth doing so.
✔ Examine your own beliefs and behaviors to see if you might be contributing to the conflict.

✔ Identify where the conflict originates, at a shallow level such as language or work methods or at a deeper level such as cultural priorities or values.
✔ Establish at what level the parties do agree, then work at the level above that to resolve differences.
✔ Choose an appropriate resolution strategy: avoidance, accommodation, compromise, or collaboration.

---

 5 **LEARNING OBJECTIVE**
Describe the importance of negotiation as a communication skill, and explain how to prepare for and conduct a negotiation.

Negotiation is an interactive process whereby two parties with opposing or competing goals reach a mutually acceptable outcome.

As with listening, most people aren't as good at negotiating as they might think they are.

Effective negotiation is rarely about being tough and driving a hard bargain; instead, it is an adaptable and ethical process that combines cooperation and competition in varying degrees.

○————————
Check out the "Five-Minute Guide to Business Negotiations" at the end of the chapter.
————————○

MOBILE APP
Negotiation Planner guides you through the steps needed to plan a successful negotiation.

Developing Your Skills as a Negotiator

Negotiation is an interactive process whereby two parties with opposing or competing goals reach a mutually acceptable outcome. Negotiation is a valuable skill that will serve you throughout your career, and achieving many of your professional and organization goals will depend in some degree on negotiation. You might negotiate the starting salary before you accept a job offer, negotiate workloads or project assignments with your boss, negotiate prices with a supplier, or negotiate shares of ownership in a new company.

People negotiate frequently in their personal and professional lives, so as with listening, most of us tend to assume we're fairly good at it. However, controlled experiments show that people are often far less effective at negotiation than they think they are. Common errors include settling for less than one could get, giving up more than one needs to, rejecting an offer that is better than any available alternative, and accepting an offer that is worse than other alternatives.[48] Another kind of error is not negotiating at all, such as accepting the first salary you are offered without making a counteroffer or asking for additional benefits.

UNDERSTANDING THE PRINCIPLES OF NEGOTIATION

One of the key reasons for common negotiating errors is a misunderstanding about what negotiating is all about. Effective negotiation is not a ruthless competition in which you must always "drive a hard bargain" and never give in, nor is it necessarily a process of accommodation or compromise in which you always have to give up something to get something. Instead, it is an adaptable and ethical process that combines cooperation and competition in varying degrees, depending on the situation.[49]

Although the media, movies, and leaders in both politics and business often extol the virtues of being a tough negotiator, it's a mistake to conclude that the best negotiators are aggressive, belligerent, take-no-prisoners types. To the contrary, research indicates that higher emotional intelligence, which leads to greater self-control and generally makes people more likable, also makes people better negotiators. Such individuals are better able to monitor and manage their own emotions, and their positive approach promotes a cooperative spirit that can lead to more win-win outcomes.[50]

PREPARING FOR A NEGOTIATION

The notion of *process* is important. Effective negotiators prepare thoroughly and follow a methodical, rational process to achieve their goals.[51] Preparation involves three steps: understanding and clarifying your own position, evaluating the other party's position, and assessing the situation.

Understand and Clarify Your Position

Preparation starts with understanding yourself and what you hope to achieve through negotiation. Careful consideration helps you separate emotions from facts, and it can prevent the common mistake of locking onto the first or most obvious goal that comes to mind. For instance, if you want to negotiate with your employer for a raise, the vague feeling that you "deserve to be paid more" is a weak platform. Why do you believe you deserve to be paid more? What facts do you have to back that up? And how much more? And is a pay increase really the best solution for you? What if your employer instead agrees to let you use company equipment for lucrative freelance projects on the side or to redesign your job to give you valuable experience that could lead to a promotion?

Start by establishing your **target**, which is the sum of values you would like to achieve through negotiation. Be careful of several potential mistakes here, including limiting your target to a single item such as salary or purchase price if other elements might be considered as well, not asking for enough, asking for so much that you crash the negotiating process before it can even start, and not knowing what you want but only wanting the other party to give up *something*.[52]

Next, figure out your best alternative to what you might achieve through negotiation. (Negotiation professionals often refer to this as your *BATNA*, for "best alternative to a negotiated agreement."[53]) For instance, if you have a job offer from another company but would prefer to stay with your current employer if you can negotiate a raise, that outside job offer is your best alternative. Identifying the best alternative is a key step because it establishes a baseline to measure against.

In most cases, you never want to accept a negotiated settlement that is worse than your best alternative, and there is no point in negotiating if you know it will never equal or exceed your best alternative. Of course, there is no guarantee that your best current alternative is a *desirable* alternative.[54] If you are unemployed and have only one job offer and no other prospects for earning money, your current best alternative to that offer is continued unemployment and the possibility—but not the certainty—of getting a better offer if you keep looking.

Finally, determine the least-attractive offer you are willing to accept. Negotiators often refer to this as your **reservation point**.[55] This could be a single value, such as a price, or it could be a bundle of elements, such as salary, title, and benefits package. The reservation point and the target define the lower and upper boundaries of your negotiation range, respectively.

Preparing for a negotiation starts with understanding and clarifying your own position: What do you really hope to achieve?

Your negotiating *target* is the sum of values you would like to achieve through negotiation.

Figure out your best alternative to whatever it is you're trying to negotiate; this helps you establish how valuable a negotiated agreement would be to you.

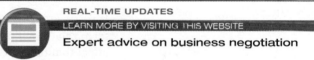

REAL-TIME UPDATES

LEARN MORE BY VISITING THIS WEBSITE

Expert advice on business negotiation

These articles, case studies, and definitions can help negotiators learn the basics and fine-tune their skills. Go to **real-timeupdates .com/ebc13** and select Learn More in the Students section.

Evaluate the Other Party's Position

After you have a clear and supportable idea of what you want, get as much information as you can about the other party's position. Ideally, you would like to know the other party's target, best alternative, and reservation points as well as you know your own. However, this is rarely possible, and you usually have to make do with whatever information you can get your hands on. For instance, if you are intending to negotiate salary with a potential employer, it would be great to know how much the company is really willing to pay to get you to say yes and how many other candidates are being considered. Chances are you'll never get this information, but you can find the typical salary ranges for this position, and from general conversation throughout the interview process, you might get a sense of how many candidates you are competing against.

Now compare your negotiation range with your best assessment of the other party's negotiation range. Ideally, there is some overlap, meaning there is room for negotiation, often called the *bargaining zone* (see Figure 2.5).[56] If you sense that there is no overlap, or discover this during the opening round of negotiations, you will need to rethink your target, reframe the discussion by considering other elements, or drop out and go with your best alternative.

Your *reservation point* is the least-attractive offer you are willing to accept.

Get as much information as you can about the other party's target, best alternative, and reservation point.

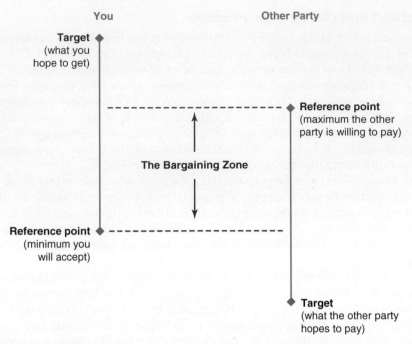

Figure 2.5   The Bargaining Zone
For any negotiation to be productive, the two parties' negotiation ranges must overlap. When you are negotiating a salary, a project fee, or a sales price, for example, the range you are willing to accept needs to overlap with the amount the employer, client, or buyer is willing to pay.

Assess the Situation

> The best negotiating strategy depends greatly on the situation, so assess the situation carefully.

Different situations call for different negotiating strategies. Here are some key questions to consider:[57]

- Is this a one-time deal or an episode in a long-term relationship? If it's part of a long-term relationship, you need to be mindful of how the process and the outcome will affect that relationship.
- Can you walk away if you don't get what you want? The option of walking away from a deal is a powerful negotiating chip, but you don't always have that option. If you are negotiating the details of a new assignment with your boss, you probably don't have the choice to refuse the assignment if you can't get everything you want.
- Is there a "ticking clock"? Do the negotiations need to wrap up by a specific date? This can work for or against you, depending on the circumstances.
- Is the amount of negotiable value fixed? In some negotiations, the sum total of all the value involved is fixed, and the parties are negotiating on how to divide the pie, so to speak. These situations are known as *distributive negotiations*.[58] If an equipment supplier offers a product for $10,000 and you counteroffer with $8,000, that $2,000 difference is the "pie" that you can divide through negotiation. If you settle on $9,000, the deal gets done, but both sides end up with a less-attractive price than either initially wanted.

> A distributive negotiation is a straightforward attempt to "slice the pie," whereas an integrative negotiation tries to expand the pie in a way that benefits both parties.

- Can you expand the range of negotiable value? In contrast to distributive negotiations, in *integrative negotiations*, the parties can bring more to the table and create deals that work out better for both sides. If an employer can't increase its salary offer, for instance, it might offer other incentives, such as a moving allowance or a company car. These types of negotiations tend to be more cooperative and focused on long-term, mutual success.[59]

By gathering as much information as you can about the situation, you'll be in a stronger position when it's time to begin negotiations.

ENGAGING IN NEGOTIATION

Negotiation begins when one party makes the first offer. You may come across the advice to never make the first offer, but there is no conclusive evidence to support the wisdom of this advice.[60] And in some cases, you don't have any choice but to make the first offer.

If you are prepared and ready to start, make an initial offer that is near the upper end of your bargaining zone but still within or close to what you surmise is the other party's zone. Support your offer with verifiable facts, such as a published salary range for this position, a business valuation from a third-party appraiser, a bid from another supplier, or whatever is relevant.

Whoever makes it, the first offer establishes an **anchor** that all subsequent negotiations work from. Remember that you will always end up with less than your first offer—unless the other party immediately accepts your first offer, which probably means you didn't ask for enough.

If the other party makes the first offer, your next move is to make a *counteroffer*. This serves two purposes. The first is letting the other party know that you are willing and prepared to negotiate. The second is adjusting the anchor established by the first offer. If an investor offers to buy your company for $10 million, for example, you might counter-offer with a sales price of $15 million. Rather than negotiating from $10 million, you will now be negotiating between the $10 and $15 million boundaries.

As you negotiate, remember to listen more, talk less, and never argue.[61] Listening is important because you can pick up clues about the other party's target and reservation point. Conversely, the less you talk, the less chance you'll give away your own secrets. And arguing is an emotional response to a difference in opinions or perceptions. Stay calm and focus on the facts.

Negotiations may take several more rounds from this point, as the two sides make concessions that bring them closer together. If you don't understand or don't agree with a point the other party is making, ask for an explanation or more information. Doing so helps you understand the other side's position and signals your willingness to reach a mutually satisfying agreement.[62]

When one side makes its *final offer*, the other side then decides to accept it or walk away. Depending on the magnitude of the deal and the circumstances, negotiation can take anywhere from a few minutes to many months for complex business deals.

Negotiating your salary (or project fees if you are a freelancer) can be unnerving if you don't have much experience at it. Few people want to feel like they are being greedy or demanding, but if you worry too much about feeling this way, you might leave money on the table. To minimize the emotions that can hamper successful negotiations, base your position on solid research and remember that you are pursuing a business deal, not asking for a personal favor. Your services have value, and any company that wants them should be prepared to pay a fair price.

For a quick reminder of the important ideas in negotiation, see "Checklist: Becoming a Successful Negotiator."

> An *anchor* is the value put forth by the first offer; it establishes the point that all subsequent negotiations work from.
>
> A counteroffer to the first offer signals that you are prepared to negotiate, and it resets the original anchor.

REAL-TIME UPDATES

LEARN MORE BY VISITING THIS WEBSITE

Negotiating advice from professional mediators

Although intended for professionals who mediate in legal cases, this site is rich with advice for anyone who negotiates. Go to **real-timeupdates.com/ebc13** and select Learn More in the Students section.

> Negotiating salaries or freelance fees naturally makes many people uncomfortable; remember that it's a business deal and you are pursuing the value that you have confirmed through your research.

CHECKLIST ✔ Becoming a Successful Negotiator

- Recognize that negotiation should be an adaptable and ethical process that combines cooperation and competition in varying degrees, depending on the situation.
- Driving a hard bargain or being a ruthless negotiator is generally less effective than being a respectful and cooperative problem solver.
- Prepare for a negotiation by understanding and clarifying your position, evaluating the other party's position, and assessing the situation.
- Identify your target (the sum of values you hope to achieve), your best alternative to a negotiated agreement,

and your reservation point (the least-attractive deal you will accept).
- Make sure your negotiation range overlaps with the other party's; if not, one party needs to reconsider its offer or choose not to negotiate.
- Remember that the first offer establishes an *anchor*, the point from which all subsequent negotiations take place.
- If the other party makes the first offer, make a counter-offer to signal that you are prepared to negotiate and to reset the anchor.

ON THE JOB: SOLVING COMMUNICATION DILEMMAS AT **SALESFORCE.COM**

Imagine that you are a team leader at Salesforce's headquarters in San Francisco. Study these scenarios and decide how to respond, based on what you learned in this chapter.

1. A recently hired systems analyst has dropped by your office, asking if you have time for a quick chat. It becomes obviously pretty quickly that she is regretting her decision to join the company, because she doesn't agree with the way this division of the company is approaching the market and, as a consequence, finds herself in frequent disagreements with colleagues. Which of the following approaches should you take?

   a. For the moment, stifle your curiosity about how she thinks the business strategy is misguided. She is clearly upset, so let her express herself. Let her know you're listening and that you're sorry she is unhappy in her new role. When you sense that she has unloaded at an emotional level, tell her you'd like to hear her thoughts on the business strategy.

   b. Proceed on the assumption that her disagreement about business strategy is a cover, and that the real problem is that she doesn't get along with some of her colleagues. Ask her for details on the disagreements that she is having.

   c. Stop the conversation and call the people she has been having trouble with into your office. A heartfelt group discussion is the best way to bring the real issues out into the open.

   d. This sort of dissention needs to be addressed quickly before the negativity spreads. Remind her that she made the choice to come here, and then outline the logic behind the company's approach to the market.

2. You would like to have a conversation with your boss to discuss your long-term career prospects at the company. The team you lead has met its goals for two years running, and you think you're ready to move up to the same level as your boss, which is managing a department. Longer term, you see yourself moving into an executive-level job. How should you approach this conversation?

   a. Hitting your boss with a formally planned agenda of talking points will feel awkward under the circumstances, so just strike up a casual conversation when you both have a free moment.

   b. Schedule some time with your boss with the explanation that you'd like to get some career counseling. This will give you time to prepare your reasons for why you think you're ready to advance, and it will prompt your boss to start thinking about your career path as well. When the conversation takes place, you'll both be better equipped to discuss it.

   c. Schedule some time with your boss to discuss your career plans. Unlike (b), however, structure your conversation as a series of questions, asking why you haven't been promoted to a department manager position yet and what might be holding you back.

   d. Don't talk to your boss about this—it will come across as a threat, since you're angling for a similar position. Find another manager to discuss your plans with.

3. Unfortunately, you need to have a tough conversation with your team. A project that they have been working on for months is about to be canceled. This decision came completely out of the blue from upper management. All you know at this point is that the company decided to go in another direction, and your team members will be assigned to several other projects, but you don't know which ones yet. How should you approach this conversation?

   a. Your crew is obviously going to want to know which projects they are going to be sent to, so don't say anything about the cancelation until you hear what the new assignments will be.

   b. Call the team together as soon as convenient and ask them to prepare brief summaries of where they are in their work at the moment. This might buy enough time so that you can find out which projects they will be assigned to, then you can tell them about the cancelation.

   c. Call the team together immediately and tell them what you know. Express sympathy for the fact that months of their dedicated work will all be for nothing, but also express confidence in the business reasoning behind management's decision, whatever their reasons were. Tell them that you will work to get more information as quickly as possible.

   d. Call the team together immediately and tell them what you know. Make it clear, however, that you had nothing to do with the decision and that you would've resisted if you had been given the opportunity to do so.

4. In a recent department reorganization, your team grew by four people. At first, you were thrilled to have the additional staff, but before long, the original eight members and the new four were grumbling at each other. You've overheard complaints about everything from email habits to personal grooming. Work is slowing down, and one of the recent arrivals has already inquired about a transfer out of your group. How should you start to resolve this conflict?

   a. Call an emergency meeting and put your foot down. Tell them that this sort of behavior is unprofessional and won't be tolerated.

b. Convene a meeting with each group separately, asking them to discuss the difficulties they have been experiencing. Assure them that their responses will be held in complete confidence, so they can speak freely. Listen carefully to what they say, and try to identify where each group thinks the conflict originates.

c. Do the same as (b) except meet with all 12 people together, not in the two separate groups.

d. They are all professionals. Let them work it out using conflict-management skills that every professional should have.

END OF CHAPTER

Learning Objectives Checkup

Assess your understanding of the principles in this chapter by reading each learning objective and studying the accompanying exercises. You can check your responses against the answer key on page 612.

Objective 2.1: Explain why listening is such a complex communication process, and describe three steps to becoming a better listener.

1. Which of the following is *not* one of the unique challenges of listening discussed in the chapter?
   a. The fact that listening is a real-time experience
   b. The lack of emphasis that mid- and upper-level managers place on listening
   c. The invisibility of spoken language
   d. The tasks involved in converting sounds to recognizable language

2. How does the brain's ability to process language faster than people can speak present a challenge to effective listening?
   a. The mind has a lot of excess processing capacity while listening, and if that capacity isn't kept focused on listening, the mind will wander off to other topics.
   b. The mind is typically so focused on listening that maintaining respectful eye contact is difficult.
   c. Listeners typically use their extra brain power to take notes, which is a sure sign of a poor listener.
   d. To listen well, people must engage in meditative practices while listening in order to keep their minds calm and focused.

3. _____ listening occurs when people try to protect their egos by tuning out anything that doesn't confirm their beliefs or their view of themselves.

4. If you are analyzing the logic behind a speaker's conclusions and recommendations, which style of listening are you using?
   a. Content listening
   b. Defensive listening
   c. Empathic listening
   d. Critical listening

5. Making a conscious effort to engage with other people and to turn off your internal filters and biases to truly hear and understand what they are saying is known as _____ _____.

Objective 2.2: Explain the importance of nonverbal communication, and identify six major categories of nonverbal expression.

6. Nonverbal signals can be more influential than spoken language because
   a. body language is difficult to control and therefore difficult to fake, so listeners often put more trust in nonverbal cues than in the words a speaker uses.
   b. nonverbal signals communicate faster than spoken language, and most people are impatient.
   c. body language saves listeners from the trouble of paying attention to what a speaker is saying.
   d. nonverbal signals are universal and work the same in every culture.

7. Which of the following is true about nonverbal signals?
   a. They convey 93 percent of the information in a spoken exchange.
   b. They convey 7 percent of the information in a spoken exchange.
   c. They can convey some portion of the information in a spoken exchange.
   d. They always convey more than spoken language.

8. Which of the following is the best general advice about touch in the workplace?
   a. Touch is a complex subject best left to individual interpretation.
   b. Other than handshakes, the best general advice for the workplace is to avoid touching anyone under any circumstances.
   c. Friendly touching should be encouraged as a way to build team rapport.
   d. Decisions about touch should be determined by cultural norms.

9. Which of these is the best strategy for interpreting nonverbal signals while you are listening to someone speak in person?
   a. Use nonverbal signals as a guide to interpretation, but don't assume anything; if you sense a disconnect between what you're seeing and what the person is saying, ask the speaker an honest and respectful question to clarify.
   b. If you know the person well, you can safely assume that the nonverbal signals you are seeing are more truthful than whatever the person is saying.
   c. Trust your instincts and ability to "read someone like a book," even if that means concluding the opposite of what the person is saying.
   d. Pay particular attention to eye contact; anyone who won't look you in the eye is hiding something.

Objective 2.3: Outline an effective process for initiating, sustaining, and concluding workplace conversations.

10. Which of these is *not* one of the potential benefits identified in the chapter of unplanned, informal conversations that take place during a typical workday?
    a. They present rare opportunities to get a few minutes of "face time" with senior executives and other influential people.
    b. They are opportunities to network with people across the company and to learn more about the company and its operations.
    c. They are an important way to "blow off steam" so that you can release pent-up frustrations and thereby focus more effectively on your work.
    d. They can make work more satisfying by helping you and your colleagues relate to one another on a more personal or social level.

11. How should you prepare yourself for a conversation that might involve unwelcome information, such as a performance review from your boss?
    a. Remind yourself where you stand in the corporate hierarchy; it's a waste of energy to dispute information coming from a superior.
    b. Come armed with plenty of information to back up your position.
    c. Bolster your confidence and determination by reminding yourself of how hard you work and how much you contribute to the organization.
    d. Remind yourself not to get defensive and to treat the conversation as an exchange of useful and important information.

12. Which of these is a good reason to ask questions indirectly rather than directly during a conversation?
    a. To indicate that you are listening with empathy
    b. To avoid stirring up trouble by being too inquisitive
    c. To show your subordinate position in the organization
    d. To depersonalize questions so they come across as less accusatory or demanding

13. Why is it important to prepare thoroughly before having a difficult conversation?
    a. Preparation helps ensure that the conversation won't get sidetracked with heated arguments over details.
    b. Victory in any dispute nearly always goes to the person who is better prepared.
    c. Thorough preparation helps you ignore the emotional element of the conversation.
    d. You are unlikely to show intellectual dominance if you attempt to "wing it."

Objective 2.4: Explain the causes of workplace conflict, and identify five productive steps for resolving conflict.

14. Which of these is *not* one of the categories of conflict causes discussed in the chapter?
    a. Structural
    b. Psychological
    c. Situational
    d. Interpersonal

15. Conflict can be _____ if it forces important issues into the open, increases the involvement of team members, or generates creative ideas for solving a problem.

16. Conflict is _____ if it saps productivity, damages morale, or threatens to spread to other people in the organization.

17. Why is it important to take the time required to identify the true source of conflict before attempting to resolve it?
    a. Failing to do so leaves a company vulnerable to legal action.
    b. Conflict is never about what it *appears* to be about.
    c. The apparent conflict might not be the real conflict.
    d. It's a vital step to verify that you are not at fault.

18. If two people involved in a conflict about work methods decide to work together to create a new process that will be better for the entire team, which strategy of conflict resolution are they using?
    a. Accommodation
    b. Collaboration
    c. Compromise
    d. Co-development

Objective 2.5: Describe the importance of negotiation as a communication skill, and explain how to prepare for and conduct a negotiation.

19. Which of these best characterizes negotiation in a business context?
    a. If you don't try to drive a hard bargain, you will always be taken advantage of.
    b. It is a process of mutual compromise, in which those with more power are expected to give up something but not as much as those with less power.
    c. It combines cooperation and competition in varying degrees depending on the situation.
    d. Cooperation is the true spirit of negotiation, not competition or the desire to always make the other party give up something.

20. What are the three essential steps in preparing for a negotiation?
    a. Understanding and clarifying your own position, evaluating the other party's position, and assessing the situation
    b. Itemizing your demands, probing the other side for weaknesses, and assessing the situation
    c. Understanding your own position, clarifying your position, and assessing the situation

21. In negotiation, your _____ is the sum of values you would like to achieve through negotiation.
    a. final offer
    b. best alternative
    c. target
    d. demands

22. The bargaining zone in a negotiation is
    a. the physical or virtual space in which the negotiation will take place.
    b. the overlap between the two parties' individual negotiation ranges.
    c. the gap between the two parties' targets.
    d. the lowest either side will accept; also known as the "bargain."

Key Terms

active listening Making a conscious effort to turn off filters and biases and staying engaged in order to truly hear and understand what someone is saying

anchor The first offer made in a negotiation; so called because it establishes the point from which subsequent counteroffers are made

content listening Listening to understand and retain the speaker's message

critical listening Listening to understand and evaluate the meaning of the speaker's message

defensive listening Protecting one's ego and viewpoint by tuning out anything that doesn't support one's beliefs

empathic listening Listening to understand the speaker's feelings, needs, and wants so that you can appreciate his or her point of view

mediation Process in which a neutral third party guides two parties through the steps of resolving a conflict

negotiation Interactive process whereby two parties with opposing or competing goals reach a mutually acceptable outcome

nonverbal communication Sending and receiving information, both intentionally and unintentionally, without using written or spoken language

reservation point The least-attractive offer a party in a negotiation is willing to accept

target The sum of values each party would like to achieve through negotiation

Apply Your Knowledge

To review chapter content related to each question, refer to the indicated Learning Objective.

2-1. You manage your company's software development lab, which has added several dozen new employees over the past year. One of the senior developers runs into you at lunch and starts to unload his frustrations about needing to get his own work done while being expected to mentor and train "a bunch of newbies." What style or styles of listening should you apply? Explain your answer. [LO-1]

2-2. Assume again that you are the lab manager from the previous question, and you have listened to the senior developer's barely contained rant for five minutes or so. At this point, you'd like to shift the conversation toward finding a solution that will work for everybody. Explain how you would use at least three of the seven tactics described under "Maintaining a Positive Conversational Flow" on page 47 to move the conversation from complaining to problem solving. [LO-3]

2-3. You're giving your first major presentation at your new job, and you notice at least half the people in the small conference room are looking at their mobile devices more than they are looking at you. How should you handle the situation? [LO-2]

2-4. You head up the interdepartmental design review team for a manufacturer of high-performance motorcycles, and things are not going well at the moment. The design engineers and marketing strategists keep arguing about which should be a higher priority, performance or aesthetics, and the accountants say both groups are driving up the cost of the new model by adding too many new features. Everyone has valid points to make, but the team is bogging down in conflict. Explain how you could go about resolving the stalemate. [LO-4]

2-5. Assume you are an art director at an advertising agency, where your responsibilities are working with various copywriting partners to brainstorm the concepts for new ads and then working on your own to design the visual elements of the ads. The ads you work on tend to get rave reviews from clients and have been a key factor in landing two new clients that brought the agency a lot of additional revenue. In light of your successes, you believe you deserve a raise. Describe the steps you would take to prepare for a negotiation on this matter with your boss. [LO-5]

Practice Your Skills

Exercises

Each activity is labeled according to the primary skill or skills you will need to use. To review relevant chapter content, you can refer to the indicated Learning Objective. In some instances, supporting information will be found in another chapter, as indicated.

2-6. Interpersonal Communication: Listening Actively [LO-1] For the next several days, take notes on your listening performance during at least a half-dozen situations in class, during social activities, and at work, if applicable. Referring to the traits of effective listeners in Table 2.4, rate yourself using *always, frequently, occasionally,* or *never* on these positive listening habits. In a report no longer than one page, summarize your analysis and identify specific areas in which you can improve your listening skills.

2-7. Nonverbal Communication: Analyzing Nonverbal Signals [LO-2] Select a business letter and envelope you have received at work or home. Analyze their appearance. What nonverbal messages do they send? Are these messages consistent with the content of the letter? If not, what could the sender have done to make the nonverbal communication consistent with the verbal communication? Summarize your findings in a post on your class blog or in an email message to your instructor.

2-8. Interpersonal Communication: Conversational Skills [LO-3] Think about the last two unscheduled, informal conversations you have had on matters related to work or school. Were the conversations satisfying or unsatisfying? Did you gain any useful information or perhaps help someone else meet a challenge or solve a problem? Did the conversations initiate a promising relationship or strengthen an existing relationship? What steps might you have taken differently, now that you've studied the techniques you can use to ensure more productive and satisfying conversations? Summarize your conclusions in an email to your instructor.

2-9. Interpersonal Communication: Conversational Skills [LO-3] Pair off with another student and initiate a conversation in which one of you will express concerns about the way one of your courses is progressing or about some other matter related to your educational experience. (Make it something you are comfortable discussing with the rest of the class.) The other party in this conversation should ask a variety of direct and indirect questions to probe the causes of the problem and to brainstorm a potential solution. In a blog post or email to your instructor, summarize your experience using questions to sustain a conversation and extract useful information.

2-10. Interpersonal Communication: Conversational Skills [LO-3] Watch any TED video that interests you (www.ted.com/talks). As you are watching, imagine that you are in a live conversation with the presenter, and list three or four questions you would like to ask to help you develop a deeper understanding of the subject.

2-11. Interpersonal Communication: Conflict Resolution [LO-4] In teams assigned by your instructor, identify a conflict that one of you has experienced during your college years, such as a lab project where the partners didn't get along. Without identifying anyone by name, describe the conflict to the rest of the team, including how it started, what effect it had, and how it was resolved (if it was). Discuss how the principles of conflict management you learned in this chapter might have averted the conflict or enabled it to be resolved more quickly than it was. Share your analysis with the class.

2-12. Interpersonal Communication: Negotiation [LO-5] Visit www.salary.com and in the "Individuals" section, identify a job that you could conceivably apply for as you approach graduation, given your major, work experience, and interests. Identify a city where you would like to work as well. Select a specific job title from the list the site generates. You will see a range of salaries, including the median salary for this position in this city. Review the detailed job information, and get a sense of how well your qualifications (what they will be when you graduate) match these requirements. Then adjust the salary display as much as possible to match your situation. For example, you can identify how many years of experience you have and what your educational level is. Now choose a salary from within the displayed range that you believe you are qualified to receive. Finally, craft a short answer you could use if an interviewer asks why you think you deserve that salary.

Expand Your Skills

Critique the Professionals

Research a recent negotiation (successful or unsuccessful) that was reported on in the news media, such as a political agreement, a corporate merger, a collective bargaining agreement between a labor union and an employer, or an employment contract for a high-profile individual such as a professional athlete. What does this episode illustrate about good or bad negotiating techniques and strategies? What lessons could you take from it to apply in your future role as a business leader?

Sharpening Your Career Skills Online

Bovée and Thill's Business Communication Web Search, at websearch.businesscommunicationnetwork.com, is a unique research tool designed specifically for business communication research. Use the Web Search function to find a website, video, article, podcast, or presentation that offers advice on improving your active listening skills in business situations. Write a brief email message to your instructor describing the item you found and summarizing the career skills information you learned from it.

Build Your Career

In the Build Your Career activity in Chapter 1, you started developing your job campaign by brainstorming what you would like to do in your career. Now it's time to tally up what you can offer an employer. If you haven't already, read "What Do You Have to Offer?" in the Prologue. Follow the guidance in that section and create two lists that you can review and update as you complete your college career and begin compiling your résumé, LinkedIn profile, and other employment documents. The first is a list of accomplishments that you are proud of and any academic, work, and general life experiences that were satisfying to you. The second is a list of the skills, knowledge, and personal characteristics that helped you reach those accomplishments or enjoy those experiences.

As you add to the lists over time, the first list will show a pattern of *what* you are capable of doing, and the second will provide the evidence of *how* you can do those things. Whenever you complete a college course, a volunteer project, or a work assignment, look back on the experience and see what you can add to one or both lists. When it's time to start applying and interviewing for your first post-college job, the lists will provide the evidence that you are ready to tackle the next exciting challenge in your career.

Improve Your Grammar, Mechanics, and Usage

The following exercises help you improve your knowledge of and power over English grammar, mechanics, and usage. Turn to the Handbook of Grammar, Mechanics, and Usage at the end of this book and review all of Section 1.2 (Pronouns). Then look at the following 10 items and select the preferred choice within each set of parentheses. (Answers to these exercises appear on page 614.)

2-13. The sales staff is preparing guidelines for (*their, its*) clients.

2-14. Few of the sales representatives turn in (*their, its*) reports on time.

2-15. The board of directors has chosen (*their, its*) officers.

2-16. Johnstone and Koseff have told (*his, their*) clients about the new program.

2-17. Each manager plans to expand (*his, their, his or her*) sphere of control next year.

2-18. Has everyone supplied (*his, their, his or her*) Social Security number?

2-19. After giving every employee (*his, their, a*) raise, George told (*them, they, all*) about the increased work load.

2-20. Cherise and Tim have opposite ideas about how to achieve company goals. (*Who, Whom*) do you think will win the debate?

2-21. City Securities has just announced (*who, whom*) it will hire as CEO.

2-22. Either of the new products would readily find (*their, its*) niche in the marketplace.

For additional exercises focusing on pronouns, visit MyLab Business Communication. Select Chapter 2, select Additional Exercises to Improve Your Grammar, Mechanics, and Usage, and then select 3. Case of pronouns and 4. Possessive pronouns.

MyLab Business Communication

MyLab Assisted-Grading Writing Prompts

If your instructor has assigned one or both of the following writing assignments within the MyLab, go to your Assignments to complete these writing exercises.

2-23. Why is it important to be conscious of the listening style you are using during any phase of a conversation or presentation? [LO-1]

2-24. Considering what you've learned about nonverbal communication, what are some of the ways in which communication might break down during an online meeting in which the participants can see video images of only the person presenting at any given time—and then only his or her head? [LO-2]

Endnotes

1. Salesforce.com, accessed 26 February 2018, www.salesforce.com; Hal Gregersen, "Bursting the CEO Bubble," *Harvard Business Review*, March–April 2017, hbr.org; "100 Best Companies to Work For," *Fortune*, accessed 26 February 2018, fortune.com; "Salesforce," *Great Places to Work*, accessed 26 February 2018, reviews.greatplacestowork.com; "How Salesforce CEO Marc Benioff Innovates" (video), *Wall Street Journal*, 20 April 2016, www.wsj.com; Julie Bort, "Salesforce Billionaire and Angel Investor Marc Benioff Says Unicorn Startups Are 'Making a Huge Mistake,'" *Business Insider*, 3 November 2015, www.businessinsider.com.

2. Judi Brownell, *Listening: Attitudes, Principles, and Skills*, 6th ed. (New York: Taylor & Francis, 2018), 45.

3. Brownell, *Listening: Attitudes, Principles, and Skills*, 6, 10–11.

4. Brownell, *Listening: Attitudes, Principles, and Skills*, 19–20.

5. Brownell, *Listening: Attitudes, Principles, and Skills*, 88–89.

6. Amanda Visser, "How to Distinguish an Artful Listener from a Bad One," *Finweek*, 13 July 2017, 44–45.

7. Brownell, *Listening: Attitudes, Principles, and Skills*, 246–247.

8. Jack Zenger and Joseph Folkman, "What Great Listeners Actually Do," *Harvard Business Review*, 14 July 2016, hbr.org.

9. Christine M. Riordan, "Three Ways Leaders Can Listen with More Empathy," *Harvard Business Review*, 16 January 2014, hbr.org.

10. Brownell, *Listening: Attitudes, Principles, and Skills*, 55.

11. Brownell, *Listening: Attitudes, Principles, and Skills*, 251.

12. Sara Stibitz, "How to Really Listen to Your Employees," *Harvard Business Review*, 30 January 2015, hbr.org.

13. Sarah Calantonio, "Why Mindful Listening Is a Communication Super Power," *Central Penn Business Journal*, 25 August 2017, 12.

14. Brownell, *Listening: Attitudes, Principles, and Skills*, 90.

15. "5 Signs You're Actually a Bad Listener," Center for Creative Leadership, accessed 5 February 2018, www.ccl.org.

16. Robert Sofia, "4 Listening Skills That Will Boost Your Bottom Line," *Journal of Financial Planning*, January 2018, 24–25.

17. Sabina Nawaz, "Become a Better Listener by Taking Notes," *Harvard Business Review*, 24 March 2017, hbr.org.

18. Silvia Bonaccio, Jane O'Reilly, Sharon L. O'Sullivan, and François Chiocchio, "Nonverbal Behavior and Communication in the Workplace: A Review and an Agenda for Research," *Journal of Management* 42, 5 (February 2016), 1044–1074.

19. Judee K. Burgoon, Laura K. Guerrero, and Kory Floyd, *Nonverbal Communication* (Abingdon, England: Taylor & Francis, 2016), Kindle edition, locations 657 and 670.

20. Olivia Mitchell, "Mehrabian and Nonverbal Communication," *Speaking About Presenting*, accessed 9 February 2018, speakingaboutpresenting.com; Albert Mehrabian, "'Silent Messages'—A Wealth of Information About Nonverbal Communication (Body Language)," accessed 9 February 2018, www.kaaj.com.

21. Bonaccio et al., "Nonverbal Behavior and Communication in the Workplace."

22. Burgoon et al., *Nonverbal Communication*, 727, 1218.

23. Dale G. Leathers, *Successful Nonverbal Communication: Principles and Applications* (New York: Macmillan, 1986), 19.

24. Emma Seppala, "When Giving Critical Feedback, Focus on Your Nonverbal Cues," *Harvard Business Review*, 20 January 2017, hbr.org.

25. Gerald H. Graham, Jeanne Unrue, and Paul Jennings, "The Impact of Nonverbal Communication in Organizations: A Survey of Perceptions," *Journal of Business Communication* 28, no. 1 (Winter 1991): 45–62.

26. Virginia P. Richmond and James C. McCroskey, *Nonverbal Behavior in Interpersonal Relations* (Boston: Allyn & Bacon, 2000), 153–157.

27. Burgoon et al., *Nonverbal Communication*, 2557–2558.

28. Mary Ellen Slayter, "Pamela Meyer on the Science Behind 'Liespotting,'" SmartBlog on Workforce, 14 September 2010, smartblogs.com.

29. Slayter, "Pamela Meyer on the Science Behind 'Liespotting.'"

30. Burgoon et al., *Nonverbal Communication*, 1623; Joe Navarro, "Body Language Myths," *Psychology Today*, 25 October 2009, www.psychologytoday.com; Richmond and McCroskey, *Nonverbal Behavior in Interpersonal Relations*, 2–3.

31. "Gal Interrupted: Why Men Interrupt Women and How to Avert This in the Workplace," *Forbes*, 3 January 2017, www.forbes.com.

32. Bradley T. Klontz and Ted Klontz, "7 Steps to Facilitate Exquisite Listening," *Journal of Financial Planning*, November 2016, 24–26.

33. Gregersen, "Bursting the CEO Bubble."

34. Klontz and Klontz, "7 Steps to Facilitate Exquisite Listening."

35. Amy Gallo, "How to Mentally Prepare for a Difficult Conversation," *Harvard Business Review*, 4 April 2016, hbr.org.

36. Gallo, "How to Mentally Prepare for a Difficult Conversation."

37. Amy Gallo, "How to Control Your Emotions During a Difficult Conversation," *Harvard Business Review*, 1 December 2017, hbr.org.

38. Monique Valcour, "8 Ways to Get a Difficult Conversation Back on Track," *Harvard Business Review*, 22 May 2017, hbr.org.

39. Stephen P. Robbins and Timothy A. Judge, *Essentials of Organizational Behavior*, 14th ed. (New York City: Pearson, 2018), 226–227.

40. Andy Boynton and Bill Fischer, *Virtuoso Teams: Lessons from Teams That Changed Their Worlds* (Harrow, UK: FT Prentice Hall, 2005), 10.

41. Andrew J. Dubrin, *Human Relations for Career and Personal Success: Concepts, Applications, and Skills*, 11th ed. (New York City: Pearson, 2017), 276.

42. Robbins and Judge, *Essentials of Organizational Behavior*, 234.

43. Lee Jay Berman, "13 Tools for Resolving Conflict in the Workplace, with Customers and in Life," Mediate, accessed 13 February 2018, www.mediate.com.

44. Berman, "13 Tools for Resolving Conflict in the Workplace, with Customers and in Life."

45. Lisa Zakroff, "If I Knew Then," *Crain's Seattle*, accessed 21 February 2018, seattle.crains.com.

46. Robbins and Judge, *Essentials of Organizational Behavior*, 232.

47. Robbins and Judge, *Essentials of Organizational Behavior*, 232.

48. Leigh Thompson, *The Mind and Heart of the Negotiator*, 6th ed. (New York City: Pearson, 2015), 5.

49. Thompson, *The Mind and Heart of the Negotiator*, 8, 10.

50. Tomas Chamorro-Premuzic, "The Personality Traits of Good Negotiators," *Harvard Business Review*, 7 August 2017, hbr.org.

51. Thompson, *The Mind and Heart of the Negotiator*, 9.

52. Thompson, *The Mind and Heart of the Negotiator*, 13.

53. "BATNA," Negotiation Experts, accessed 22 February 2018, www.negotiations.com.

54. Jim Sebenious, "BATNAs in Negotiation: Common Errors and Three Kinds of 'No,'" Harvard Business School Working Papers, rev. 28 January 2017, hrb.org.

55. "Reservation Price," Negotiation Experts, accessed 22 February 2018, www.negotiations.com.

56. Thompson, *The Mind and Heart of the Negotiator*, 38.

57. Thompson, *The Mind and Heart of the Negotiator*, 27–36.

58. "Negotiation Types," Negotiation Experts, accessed 22 February 2018, www.negotiations.com.

59. "Negotiation Types."

60. Thompson, *The Mind and Heart of the Negotiator*, 46.

61. William Lynott, "11 Common Negotiating Mistakes," *Restaurant Hospitality*, May 2016, 54–56.

62. Leah Ginsberg, "Negotiation Tips for Women (Men Can Use Them—But Don't Have To)," *Forbes*, 26 August 2016, www.forbes.com.

Whenever you are faced with conflict in the workplace, spend five minutes reviewing these steps before you begin to seek resolution.

Decide whether the conflict warrants taking action

1. Remember that resolving conflict takes time and energy, and it might disrupt things for a while.
2. If the conflict is short term and not overly serious, consider living with it.
3. If the conflict has broad or long-term consequences, however, it should be addressed.

Examine your own beliefs and behaviors

1. Think about your own participation before taking any action.
2. Could your language, behavior, or attitude be contributing to the conflict?
3. If you discover something you could do differently, you might discuss this with the other party as a way to start a constructive dialogue.

Identify where the conflict originates

1. Interpersonal conflict can originate at many levels, from a relatively shallow issue such as language differences down to deep issues such as fundamentally different values. Here are some typical levels, from shallowest to deepest:

Language
Personal habits
Personality types
Work methods
Personal priorities
Organizational priorities
Cultural priorities
Values

2. You need to find where the conflict originates so you know which problem to solve. Don't waste time solving a shallow conflict when the real conflict goes deeper.
3. Remember that the *apparent* conflict isn't always the *real* conflict. Dig down until you find the real source of disagreement.

Establish and confirm common ground

1. From the "stack" shown above, identify the highest level at which the parties do agree.
2. Use this confirmation as an opportunity to build rapport, then move upward to identify the point of conflict.

Choose a strategy for resolving the differences

1. **Avoidance.** In some situations, the best solution is to avoid the circumstances that create conflict, rather than trying to fix it.
2. **Accommodation.** One side in a conflict can decide to accommodate or sacrifice for the good of the organization or to maintain harmony.
3. **Compromise.** Both sides can choose to meet somewhere in the middle, with each giving up something.
4. **Collaboration.** The parties can choose to collaborate on a new solution that satisfies everyone's needs and expectations.

Five-Minute Guide to Business Negotiations

Spend five minutes reviewing these important concepts before you plan and conduct your next business negotiation.

00:01

Remember the principles of effective negotiation

1. Negotiation should be an adaptable and ethical process that combines cooperation and competition in varying degrees depending on the situation.
2. Driving a hard bargain or being a ruthless negotiator is rarely as effective as being a respectful and cooperative problem solver.

00:02

Understand and clarify your position

1. Establish your *target*, which is the sum of values you would like to achieve through negotiation. Be objective and as specific as possible. Be ready to back up your target with solid evidence.
2. Figure out your *best alternative* to what you might achieve through negotiation. Use this to judge the success of your negotiation effort; you rarely want to accept anything worse than your best alternative.
3. Establish your *reservation point*, the least-attractive offer you are willing to accept.
4. The target and the reservation point are the top and bottom of your negotiation range, respectively.

00:03

Evaluate the other party's position

1. Learn as much as you can about the other party's target. You may have to guess, but use all the information you can get your hands on.
2. Figure out the other party's best alternative. What is the alternative to what you have to offer?
3. Estimate the other party's reservation point. Again, you may have to guess, but use all available information.
4. The overlap between your negotiation range and the other party's is the *bargaining zone*. If you don't think there is any overlap, rethink what you have to offer.

00:04

Assess the situation

1. Is this a one-time deal or an episode in a long-term relationship? If the latter, think about the effects of the negotiation on the relationship.
2. Can you walk away if you don't get what you want? What happens if you aren't successful?
3. Do the negotiations need to wrap up by a specific date? If so, does this work for you or against you?
4. Is the amount of negotiable value fixed? In other words, are you dividing up a fixed-size pie?
5. Can you expand the range of negotiable value (expand the pie)?
6. Is there anything else about this specific situation that might work for or against you?

00:05

Start negotiating

1. Ignore any advice you've heard about never making the first offer. If it's appropriate to do so and you are prepared, feel free to go for it.
2. Remember that the first offer establishes the *anchor*, the point from which all subsequent negotiations take place.
3. If the other party makes the first offer, make a counteroffer to signal that you are prepared to negotiate and to reset the anchor.
4. Share as little information as you can during the negotiations, and listen carefully to pick up as many clues as you can.
5. If you are negotiating your own salary or project fee, don't let fear of coming across as greedy or demanding lead you to leave money on the table. Remember that you're negotiating a business deal, not asking for a personal favor.

LEARNING OBJECTIVES

After studying this chapter, you will be able to

1 List the advantages and disadvantages of working in teams, describe the characteristics of effective teams, explain how teams evolve, and offer advice on working in virtual teams.

2 Offer guidelines for collaborative communication, identify major collaboration technologies, and explain how to give constructive feedback.

3 List the key steps needed to ensure productive team meetings.

4 Explain the importance of business etiquette, and identify five areas in which good etiquette is essential.

MyLab Business Communication

If your instructor is using MyLab Business Communication, visit **www.pearson.com/mylab/business-communication** for videos, simulations, and writing exercises.

ON THE JOB: COMMUNICATING AT **ING**

Creating "Wow" with Agile Teamwork

Although they don't get the same attention as marketing campaigns or big financial deals, choices about how to organize people are some of the most important decisions any company must make. Putting the right talent together is essential for success in every functional area of business.

Organizational choices are rarely simple. If the organizational structure is too rigid, teams can't respond quickly to customer demands or competitive threats, or their work bogs down as organizational boundaries get in the way. If the structure is too loose, goals and responsibilities can be unclear, with confusion and chaos as the result. Moreover, change is a constant for many companies these days. An organizational scheme that works today might not work next month or next year.

As with many industries, banking is going through a state of upheaval as customers demand mobile capabilities and new ways to do banking—and as a host of aggressive, digital-native competitors from Silicon Valley are moving into the industry. Banks around the world are spending billions of dollars on technology, trying to "disrupt themselves" before they get disrupted from the outside.

The Dutch bank ING was among the first to embark on this digital transformation, spurred on by changing customer expectations about convenience and quality of service. Looking for a faster and more flexible way to respond to marketplace dynamics, the bank adopted an approach often known by the term *agile*, as in *agile software development* (where the concept originated) or *agile manufacturing*.

ING CEO Ralph Hamers oversees the company's radical new approach to teamwork.

Bloomberg/Getty Images

The agile approach can make businesses more adaptable and more responsive, but to see these benefits, companies need to change at a fundamental level. The traditional organizational hierarchy (see Figure 1.4, for example) is simply too rigid and too slow. Agile requires small, self-managed teams that can make decisions on the spot and quickly respond to changing requirements. Agile teams typically work in short, intense bursts known as *sprints* that last only a few days or a few weeks and have a specific interim goal in mind. At the end of a sprint, the team adjusts course if needed, then takes off on another sprint to repeat the cycle. These sprints don't allow time for ponderous layers of managerial decision-making or grandiose plans that can't predict the pitfalls or opportunities a team will uncover along the way.

To get the benefits of the agile approach, ING's leadership realized it needed to throw out its old organization chart and find a new way to organize. The change wasn't a small tweak, to be sure. The bank started by completely reorganizing its headquarters staff, getting rid of traditional departments such as marketing and realigning into nine-person "squads" made up of specialists in various business and technical areas. Each squad has total responsibility for whatever piece of the puzzle it owns and adapts on the fly without waiting for management approval. To coordinate efforts, every squad belongs to one of 13 "tribes" that focus on particular business missions.

ING refers to its agile implementation as its ING Way of Working, or "WoW." Even employees who were skeptical about the radical change now embrace the approach and enjoy the freedom and responsibility to satisfy customer needs as quickly as possible. The bank's leadership recognizes that change is a way of life now, so it will keep being agile and keep responding to customers, wherever their demands take the business.[1]

WWW.ING.COM

Communicating Effectively in Teams

1 LEARNING OBJECTIVE
List the advantages and disadvantages of working in teams, describe the characteristics of effective teams, explain how teams evolve, and offer advice on working in virtual teams.

The agile teamwork among employees at ING (profiled in the chapter-opening On the Job) represents one of the most essential elements of workplace communication. **Collaboration**—working together to meet complex challenges—is a prime skill expected in a wide range of professions. No matter what career path you pursue, you will need to collaborate in at least some of your work activities (see "The Art of Professionalism: Being a Team Player"). Your communication skills will pay off handsomely in these interactions because the productivity and quality of collaborative efforts depend heavily on the communication skills of the professionals involved.

Collaboration, working together to solve complex problems, is an essential skill for workers in nearly every profession.

TYPES OF TEAMS

A **team** is a unit of two or more people who work toward a shared goal and, unlike other work groups, depend on one another to achieve that goal.[2] Teams are often at the core of **participative management**, the effort to involve employees in the company's decision-making.

A *team* is a group whose members share a mission and collective responsible for meeting the team's objectives.

Companies use a variety of team formats and sizes, with different degrees of structure and formality. The simplest team consists of two people assigned to collaborate on a task, with no more formality than the mandate to get the job done. This pair might not even think of themselves as a team, but the potential advantages and disadvantages of teamwork apply to their work just the same. At the other extreme, a team could have a hundred or more members and a formal management structure. Some teams have appointed leaders or managers, whereas others are self-managed.

Participative management is the effort to involve employees in a company's decision-making.

Teams can be either permanent or temporary. **Committees** are often permanent teams with regularly recurring tasks, such as executive committees that meet monthly to plan strategies and review results. Companies might also have permanent teams devoted to safety, charitable work, or other activities.

Teams can be permanent or temporary; a common type of permanent team is a *committee*.

Temporary teams assemble to solve a problem or complete a project, then disband after completing their work. A **problem-solving team** comes together to investigate and resolve a specific issue. A **project team** works on a project such as the launch of a new product. **Creative teams** are common in advertising, design, and other creative endeavors and combine writers, graphic artists, and other skilled professionals. A creative team may assemble for a single project or work on a series of projects over time. Temporary teams can also be called *task forces*.

Three common types of temporary teams are *problem-solving teams*, *project teams*, and *creative teams*.

Any of these team types can be composed of people from more than one department or functional area within the company, a structure known as a **cross-functional team**.

A *cross-functional team* assembles people from multiple functional areas within a company.

DEVELOPING AS A PROFESSIONAL

Being a Team Player

Professionals know that they are contributors to a larger cause, that it's not all about them. Just as in athletics and other team efforts, being a team player in business is something of a balancing act. On the one hand, you need to pay enough attention to your own efforts and skills to make sure you're pulling your own weight. On the other hand, you need to pay attention to the overall team effort to make sure the team succeeds. Remember that if the team fails, you fail, too.

Great team players know how to make those around them more effective, whether it's by lending a hand during crunch time, sharing resources, removing obstacles, making introductions, or offering expertise. In fact, the ability to help others improve their performance is one of the key attributes executives look for when they want to promote people into management.

Being a team player also means showing loyalty to your organization and protecting your employer's reputation—one of the most important assets any company has. Pros don't trash their employers in front of customers or in their personal blogs. When they have a problem, they solve it; they don't share it.

CAREER APPLICATIONS

1. If you prefer to work by yourself, should you take a job in a company that uses a team-based organization structure? Why or why not?
2. You can see plenty of examples of unprofessional business behavior in the news media and in your own consumer and employee experiences. Why should you bother being professional yourself?

Cross-functional teams are a powerful scheme for assembling talent because they overcome the fixed organizational structure and unite people from a variety of departments who have different areas of expertise and responsibility. Cross-functional teams can be an effective way to overcome the *silo effect* in a company, where people within each functional area tend to view and perform their work within their own "silos," without coordinating with other functional areas. These teams can also serve as a vital communication network that disperses information across the company.

Although they are a compelling and often necessary way to organize team efforts, cross-functional teams face the particular challenge of coordinating the work of people with different priorities and workstyles and who formally report to different managers in different parts of the company. Such teams are more vulnerable to internal conflict and competition than single-function teams and need strong leadership to be successful.[3]

Table 3.1 summarizes the most common types of teams.

ADVANTAGES AND DISADVANTAGES OF TEAMS

Teams can provide businesses and individuals with a variety of benefits:[4]

- **More information and knowledge.** By pooling the experience of several individuals, a team has access to more information in the decision-making process.
- **Learning opportunities.** Teams that bring together people with various work specialties give people the chance to learn from each other.

Effective teams can pool knowledge, take advantage of diverse viewpoints, and increase acceptance of solutions the team proposes.

TABLE 3.1 Common Types of Business Teams

Type	Characteristics
Committee	A permanent team established to address recurring issues, such as corporate governance or workplace safety
Problem-solving	Team assembled to analyze a problem or issue, recommend a solution, and, in some cases, implement the solution
Project	Team assembled to complete a specific project, such as a new product launch or installation of a new computer system
Creative	Similar to project teams but used in fields such as advertising and web design; combine the efforts of various creative professionals and may work on a series of projects together
Cross-functional	Pulls together people from across multiple departments or functional areas; the best way to tackle company-wide issues or opportunities, but can be challenging to manage

- **Boldness.** People who might hesitate to take calculated risks on their own can be more willing to make bold moves as part of the team.
- **Accountability.** Most people want to avoid letting others down, and participating in teams creates a built-in sense of accountability to others.
- **Trust building.** Working closely in teams lets people develop trust in their colleagues, which can be beneficial outside the confines of the team activities as well.
- **A broader range of viewpoints.** Diverse teams can bring a variety of perspectives that improve decision-making.
- **Buy-in for solutions the team creates.** Those who participate in making a decision are more likely to support it and encourage others to accept it.
- **Improved performance.** Effective teams can be better than top-performing individuals at solving complex problems.
- **A sense of community in good times and bad.** Being on a team helps individuals share in the celebration of successes and provides emotional support during challenging periods.

Teams perform an important social function for many employees.

Although teamwork has many advantages, teams need to be aware of and work to counter the following potential disadvantages:

Groupthink is dysfunctional decision-making that results when peer pressure keeps people from voicing unpopular opinions.

- **Groupthink.** Like other social structures, business teams can generate tremendous pressures to conform. **Groupthink** occurs when peer pressures cause individual team members to withhold contrary opinions and to go along with decisions they don't really believe in. The consequences of groupthink can range from bland, unimaginative work to outright disasters.

A hidden agenda is a private goal that isn't aligned with the team's goals.

- **Hidden agendas.** Some team members may have a **hidden agenda**—private, counterproductive motives, such as a desire to take control of the group, to undermine someone else on the team, or to pursue an incompatible goal.
- **Cost.** Aligning schedules, arranging meetings, and coordinating individual parts of a project can eat up a lot of time and money.
- **Overload.** Some companies have embraced collaborative work approaches to such an extent that they're overloading employees with team assignments.[5]

CHARACTERISTICS OF EFFECTIVE TEAMS

Successful teams share many of the same attributes.

A wide variety of factors can account for team success:[6]

- A shared sense of purpose and compatible values
- A clear and challenging goal
- A belief in the value of the team's efforts
- A well-balanced mix of people who can provide the insights and skills needed to achieve the goal
- A size that aligns well with the team's responsibilities
- Positive behavioral norms that promote *psychological safety*, encouraging people to share information, propose unproven ideas, and express vulnerability without fear of repercussion
- A willingness to put the team's needs ahead of individual needs
- Open and honest communication

Notice how all of these traits rely on communication, both in the information that is shared and in the way people interact with one another.

GROUP DYNAMICS

Group dynamics are the interactions and processes that take place in a team.

Norms are informal standards of conduct that members share and that guide member behavior.

The interactions and processes that take place among the members of a team are called **group dynamics**. Productive teams tend to develop clear **norms**, informal standards of conduct that members share and that guide member behavior. Group dynamics and norms are influenced by the roles team members assume and how the team evolves as it gets up to speed.

Team Roles

It addition to whatever functional skills they bring, members of a team can play a variety of helpful roles to ensure harmonious, productive work. **Team-maintenance roles** focus on the interpersonal and social aspects of being on a team, such as enforcing team norms, ensuring that everyone's voice can be heard, encouraging participation, compromising, and mediating in disputes.[7]

Task-oriented roles focus on work quality and productivity, getting the team's work done on time and on budget. They can include providing technical expertise, suggesting new ideas, integrating diverse ideas, exploring options, and keeping the team on schedule.[8]

As you can imagine, a team needs a healthy balance of both types of roles in order to be harmonious and successful. Of course, many people will take on more than one role, and someone may step into a role temporarily, such as mediating in a disagreement. Whenever you are working on a team, keep an eye out for ways you can help with any role, even if you aren't in a leadership position.

Team-maintenance roles focus on the interpersonal and social aspects of being on a team.

Task-oriented roles focus on work quality and productivity.

Stages of Team Development

Teams typically evolve through several phases on their way to becoming productive. Figure 3.1 shows the popular model proposed by Dr. Bruce Tuckman, which identifies four or five phases a new team goes through as it evolves:[9]

- **Forming.** In this initial phase, the group comes together through in-person or online meetings, and various members begin to establish themselves in specific roles. In some cases, one person is given the formal role of team leader, but in others an informal leader may emerge as the members establish their roles. If the group's goal hasn't already been defined, the team leader or the team members themselves will establish it.
- **Storming.** As team members begin to discuss their positions and become more assertive in establishing their roles, disagreements and uncertainties are natural in this phase. Much of the conflict may be constructive as team members share ideas for meeting the team's goals. However, if conflict threatens to get destructive, active conflict resolution,

The Tuckman model of group development usually includes five phases:

- Forming
- Storming
- Norming
- Performing
- Adjourning

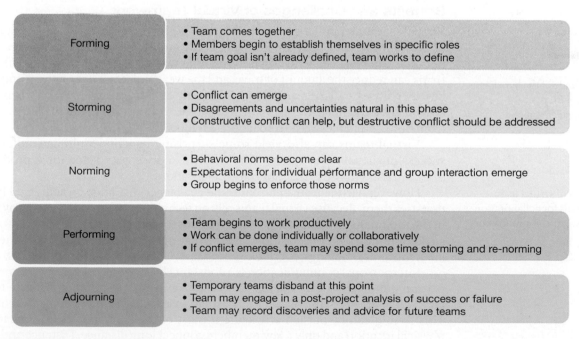

Forming	• Team comes together • Members begin to establish themselves in specific roles • If team goal isn't already defined, team works to define
Storming	• Conflict can emerge • Disagreements and uncertainties natural in this phase • Constructive conflict can help, but destructive conflict should be addressed
Norming	• Behavioral norms become clear • Expectations for individual performance and group interaction emerge • Group begins to enforce those norms
Performing	• Team begins to work productively • Work can be done individually or collaboratively • If conflict emerges, team may spend some time storming and re-norming
Adjourning	• Temporary teams disband at this point • Team may engage in a post-project analysis of success or failure • Team may record discoveries and advice for future teams

Figure 3.1 Phases of Team Development

Groups generally progress through several stages on their way to becoming productive and reaching their objectives.

Sources: Stephen P. Robbins and Mary Coulter, *Management*, 14th ed. (New York: Prentice Hall, 2018), 418–419; Denise Bonebright, "40 Years of Storming: A Historical Review of Tuckman's Model of Small Group Development," *Human Resource Development International* 29, no. 1 (February 2010): 111–120.

Conflict in teams can be either constructive or destructive.

as described in Chapter 2, might be necessary. Everyone has responsibility for helping the team get through this turbulent phase as quickly as possible. Positive steps include appreciating the benefit of having diverse viewpoints, assuming that people are there to do good work, and giving everyone the opportunity to be heard.[10]

- **Norming.** As conflicts resolve themselves (or are resolved through intervention), the team begins to take on a cohesive personality with clear behavioral norms. For example, the team leader or those taking assertive roles might establish expectations that meetings start and end on schedule and that all members are ready to present or otherwise contribute as expected. If this sort of dependability becomes the norm, everyone will feel the group expectation to perform at this level.

- **Performing.** With a cohesive, distinct personality and norms to guide behavior, the group is ready to perform its task. The nature of the teamwork varies widely based on the type of work and the type of team. In some cases, members will work on individual assignments and periodically reconvene to share updates. In others, members may work side by side on shared tasks. It's not uncommon for issues to emerge as the work progresses, and the team may spend some time storming and re-norming again.

- **Adjourning.** When temporary teams accomplish their goal, the fifth and final step is to adjourn, or disband, the team. This phase may involve some post-project analysis in which members assess how well the team performed and compile advice for future teams.

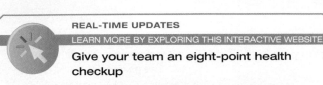

REAL-TIME UPDATES

LEARN MORE BY EXPLORING THIS INTERACTIVE WEBSITE

Give your team an eight-point health checkup

Any work team can run these checkups to find out how healthy it is and get remedies for problem areas. Go to **real-timeupdates .com/ebc13** and select Learn More in the Students section.

VIRTUAL TEAMS

A *virtual team* is one in which members work in at least two different locations and rely on technology to communicate and collaborate.

A **virtual team** is one in which members work in at least two different locations and rely on technology to communicate and collaborate. Professionals in a wide variety of situations work in virtual teams, including telecommuting (working from home or other off-site locations), collaborating with colleagues in other offices, and working as independent contractors from remote locations.

Benefits and Challenges of Virtual Teamwork

Virtual teams can

- Pull together the best people for a task
- Take advantage of the benefits of telecommuting
- Increase engagement and productivity

Virtual teams can pull together the best people for a task, even if they work in different offices or different countries. Companies and employees can take advantage of the economic and personal benefits of telecommuting, and employees in geographically dispersed firms can reduce the amount of travel and the wear and tear it has on them and their families. In many cases, virtual teamwork is the only option available, such as when a company outsources its manufacturing to a firm in another country and teams made up of employees from both companies need to collaborate frequently.

Virtual teams can also yield some surprising benefits. Multiple studies show that successful virtual teams can be more effective, more engaged, and more productive than *co-located teams* (those in the same physical location).[11]

Key challenges of virtual teams include the tools for collaboration and interpersonal communication issues.

However, virtual teams present some challenges that must be addressed by any firm that uses them. Because virtual teams rely on technology to stay connected, any limitations in the tools hamper team performance. For instance, if a team is forced to rely on email for all communication, collaboration, and file sharing, it is likely to end up with message overload, misunderstandings, overlooked messages, lost files, and other problems.

Interpersonal communication is a constant challenge in virtual environments. Teams play an important social role in many cases, for instance, and long-distance team members can develop a sense of emotional isolation and the feeling of being "out of the loop." This feeling can be particularly acute if most of the team members work in the same physical location and only a few members connect long distance. Distance and separation can also foster an "us versus them" mentality between factions in a team.[12] Plus, virtual teams often miss out on the random interactions that co-located teams experience, such as members running into one another while getting coffee or crossing paths in other work settings.[13]

Tips for Success in Virtual Team Environments

To overcome the inherent limitations of virtual collaboration, follow these tips:

- Keep teams as small as possible. Even more so than with co-located teams, virtual teams can run into trouble if their size grows past 10 people or so.[14]
- Launch the team with an in-person event, if possible. Nothing beats face-to-face contact when it comes to getting to know people. If an in-person meeting isn't possible, use a conference call or a video chat.
- Use the best collaboration technology available. The tools can range from something as simple as text messaging up to elaborate collaboration platforms (see page 75), but they need to fit the work and function as expected.
- Clarify the purpose of each tool. Teams can implement too many communication tools if they're not careful, leading to fragmented communication with messages mixed and jumbled across multiple channels. Make sure that each kind of communication, such as schedule updates, task assignments, and urgent messages, is conveyed via one designated channel.[15]
- If most of the team is co-located, assign responsibility to someone in the local team for keeping distant members in the loop. Much of this connection should happen automatically through the use of collaboration tools, but making a little extra effort to connect with distant members to ensure they feel part of the team is worthwhile.
- Don't rely solely on written communication. Pick up the phone or initiate video chats to maintain a more personal connection.

To maximize the success of virtual teams

- Keep them as small as possible
- Launch with an in-person event if possible
- Use the best technology available
- Clarify purpose of every tool
- Keep distance members in the loop
- Don't rely solely on written communication

REAL-TIME UPDATES

LEARN MORE BY READING THIS ARTICLE

Overcome the limitations of virtual teamwork

These 21 tips can help any virtual team overcome the inherent limitations of long-distance collaboration. Go to **real-timeupdates .com/ebc13** and select Learn More in the Students section.

Collaborating on Communication Efforts

Businesspeople are frequently expected to collaborate on communication projects. This section offers advice on how to approach collaborative work, tips on giving and receiving feedback, and an overview of the technologies available for collaboration.

2 LEARNING OBJECTIVE Offer guidelines for collaborative communication, identify major collaboration technologies, and explain how to give constructive feedback.

COLLABORATION ARRANGEMENTS

Communicators can collaborate in a variety of ways, from simple writer-editor relationships to full collaboration.

Writer-Editor Relationships

The simplest collaboration is when one person reviews the work of another, which happens quite often in business. Although the collaboration is relatively simple, the task of reviewing someone else's work requires care and awareness. A writer may also ask two or more people to review a report or presentation. You might ask an engineer to review a brochure for technical accuracy and a marketing specialist to review it for brand messaging, for instance. Stepping up a level from that, one person can be asked to revise another's work, which takes the second person into the realm of co-creator. Page 192 in Chapter 7 offers tips on reviewing someone else's writing.

The writer-editor relationship is the simplest form of collaborative communication.

For reviewing or revising, it's vital to clarify expectations before the writer hands the work over to anyone else. If your draft is solid but just needs technical verification, for example, you don't want your technical reviewer to rewrite it for style. If you're asking someone for a general review, a good approach for many situations is to give both parties complete freedom: The reviewer/editor is free to comment on and suggest changes to anything, and the writer is free to accept or reject each of those inputs. Change tracking features in word-processing software and apps make it easy to accept or reject changes one by one.

Always clarify roles and expectations before starting any collaborative project.

If you're asking someone to revise a draft you've written, explain your objectives for the piece, including the audience you want to reach and the message you intend to share. At that point, you need to release "emotional ownership" of the piece and allow your collaborator to revise and rebuild it as he or she sees fit.

Full Collaboration

Full collaboration involves working together from the beginning of the project through to the end, from planning the message to final production. This sort of partnership can bring together a diverse range of talents, insights, and experiences, not to mention extra minds and hands to get the work done.

Most communication tasks lend themselves to collaboration, but think carefully before doing the actual writing as a team; group writing can be valuable, but it can also be slow and frustrating.

Collaboration offers lots of potential, but it must be planned and managed thoughtfully to realize these benefits. Most of the tasks involved in creating communication pieces lend themselves quite nicely to team effort, but think carefully about composing as a group—that is, doing the actual writing itself. In contrast to the other tasks in collaborative projects, attempting to compose as a group isn't always a productive approach. Crafting sentences is a highly individualized activity that requires thought and reflection, and most ideas can be expressed effectively in more than one way. Two (or more) people could have equally valid ways to express something and spend time trying to convince the group to use their versions. The result could be a slower process that doesn't produce meaningfully better results. Group writing can be done, and it can be a great way for an experienced writer to mentor a colleague, but recognize that it can be slow and occasionally frustrating.

You may find times when it is helpful to involve multiple writers, such as when you're struggling to express a particular idea clearly. However, chances are you'll find it more efficient to plan, research, and outline together but assign the task of writing to one person or divide larger projects among multiple writers.

If you divide the writing tasks, make sure you have a clear and complete outline first.

If you decide to divide the writing among two or more people, outline the entire document or presentation in detail first. This way, each writer knows exactly how his or her assigned section fits in the overall flow. Doing so will minimize gaps and overlaps and reduce the work needed to "stitch" the pieces together into a cohesive whole. When the pieces are ready, assign one person to do a final revision pass to ensure a consistent style.

However you structure a project, follow these tips:

To ensure success with collaborative communication projects

- Agree on the goals first
- Map out how the work will be done
- Take advantage of each person's strongest skills
- Establish frequent checkpoints
- Accept different writing styles

- Make sure the project goals are clear and agreed on.
- Map out how the work will be done, including who will take the lead on each task and which systems and tools will be used.
- Structure the assignments so that each person can lend his or her greatest strengths to the effort.
- Establish frequent checkpoints so the team can verify that each task is coming along as expected. If a big project falls behind schedule, it can be impossible to get back on track in time.
- Appreciate that people have different writing styles. Successful writers know that most ideas can be expressed in multiple ways, so they avoid the "my way is best" attitude. If something works, support it, even if it's not the way you would say it.

GIVING—AND RESPONDING TO—CONSTRUCTIVE FEEDBACK

Collaborative communication often involves giving and receiving feedback about writing efforts. **Constructive feedback**, sometimes called *constructive criticism*, focuses on the process and outcomes of communication, not on the people involved (see Table 3.2). In contrast, **destructive feedback** is little more than complaining or bullying. For example, "This proposal is a confusing mess, and you failed to convince me of anything" is destructive feedback. The goal is to be helpful: "Your proposal could be more effective with a clearer description of the manufacturing process and a well-organized explanation of why the positives outweigh the negatives." When giving feedback, avoid personal attacks and give the person clear guidelines for improvement.

Constructive feedback focuses on process and outcomes, whereas *destructive feedback* is little more than complaining or bullying.

When you receive constructive feedback, resist the understandable urge to defend your work or deny the validity of the feedback. Remaining open to criticism isn't easy when you've invested lots of time and energy in a project, but good feedback provides a valuable opportunity to learn and to improve the quality of your work.

REAL-TIME UPDATES
LEARN MORE BY WATCHING THIS VIDEO

Take the sting out of criticism—and make it more valuable

This methodical approach to receiving criticism helps unbundle the emotional side of criticism from the helpful side. Go to **real-timeupdates .com/ebc13** and select Learn More in the Students section.

TABLE 3.2 Giving Constructive Feedback

How to Be Constructive	Explanation
Think through your suggested changes carefully.	Many business documents must illustrate complex relationships between ideas and other information, so isolated and superficial edits can do more harm than good.
Discuss improvements rather than flaws.	Instead of saying "this is confusing," for instance, explain how the writing can be improved to make it clearer.
Focus on controllable behavior.	The writer may not have control over every variable that affects the quality of the message, so focus on those aspects the writer can control.
Be specific.	Comments such as "I don't get this" or "Make this clearer" don't give the writer much direction.
Keep feedback impersonal.	Focus comments on the message, not on the person who created it.
Verify understanding.	If in doubt, ask for confirmation from the recipient to make sure that the person understood your feedback.
Time your feedback carefully.	Respond in a timely fashion so that the writer will have sufficient time to implement the changes you suggest.
Highlight any limitations your feedback may have.	If you didn't have time to give the document a thorough edit, or if you're not an expert in some aspect of the content, let the writer know so that he or she can handle your comments appropriately.

TECHNOLOGIES FOR COLLABORATIVE COMMUNICATION

A variety of tools and systems are available to help writers collaborate on everything from short documents to presentations to formal reports. The simplest tools are software features such as *commenting* (which lets colleagues write comments in a document without modifying the document text) and *change tracking* (which lets one or more writers propose changes to the text while keeping everyone's edits separate and reversible). Some systems also support live, online collaboration, so you can work on documents with other people at the same time.

A wide variety of tools can help professionals work together, from editing features up to sophisticated collaboration platforms.

Collaboration Systems

Companies use a variety of systems to foster collaboration. Many of these rely on *cloud computing*, which means that the primary software and work files reside on the internet, rather than on local computers. A key advantage here is that workers can log in remotely from just about any type of device and don't need to worry about bringing files with them when they travel or work from home.

Collaboration systems continue to evolve and add new capabilities, so the labels and the lines between various platforms are always a bit blurry, but here are some of the major types of collaboration platforms:

MOBILE APP
Freedcamp is a free collaboration and project management system.

Collaboration platforms include

- Content management systems
- Wikis
- Shared online workspaces
- Social networks
- Workgroup messaging systems
- Intranets and extranets

- **Content management systems (CMS)** help companies that produce a high volume of digital information for both internal and external distribution. Companies with large, multi-author websites or blogs, for example, can use a CMS to organize and publish web content. These systems often include such features as *version control* (making sure two people can't accidentally edit a document or page at the same time) and *workflow* features that define how content can be created, edited, and published.
- **Wikis** also organize digital content but in a much less structured and formal way than a CMS. A **wiki** is a website that allows anyone with access to add new material and edit existing material. Public wikis (Wikipedia is the best known) allow any registered user to edit pages; private wikis are accessible only with permission. Chapter 13 offers guidelines for effective wiki collaboration.
- **Shared online workspaces** are "virtual offices" that give everyone in a work group access to the same set of resources and information. Many offer real-time collaboration tools such as digital whiteboards where colleagues can brainstorm together (see Figure 3.2 on the next page).
- **Social networks** are used extensively for business collaboration, and many companies have private, internal-only versions of social networks for their employees. Some companies use social networks to form *virtual communities* or *communities of practice* that link

A *wiki* is a website that allows anyone with access to add new material and edit existing material.

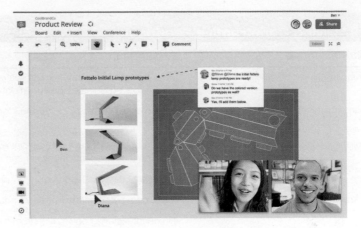

Figure 3.2 Shared Online Workspaces
Shared workspaces give employees remote access to all the files they need, from company reports to website content.

employees with similar professional interests throughout the company and sometimes with customers and suppliers as well. One big advantage that social networking brings to these team efforts is in identifying the best people to collaborate on each problem or project, no matter where they are around the world or what their official roles are in the organization. Social networking can also help a company maintain a sense of community even as it grows beyond the size that normally permits a lot of daily interaction.

- **Workgroup messaging systems** are evolving beyond basic messaging capability to include file sharing, meeting hosting, and other collaboration features.
- **Private networks** are essentially private versions of the internet with various communication and collaboration features. You may see some of these referred to as *intranets* (open to employees only) or *extranets* (open to employees and to selected outside parties by invitation only). Some intranets have now evolved into social networking systems that include a variety of communication and collaboration tools (see Figure 3.3).

Note that if you see the adjective *enterprise* in any system name, that means it is designed to meet the needs of medium and large companies.

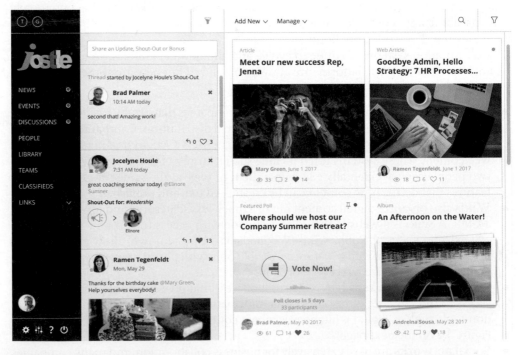

Figure 3.3 Social Intranets
Social intranets such as Jostle help teams, departments, and entire companies communicate, celebrate, collaborate, and share resources.

Collaboration via Mobile Devices

Mobile devices add another layer of options for collaborative writing and other communication projects, particularly when used with cloud computing. Today's mobile systems can do virtually everything that fixed-web collaboration systems can do, from writing on virtual whiteboards to sharing photos, videos, and other multimedia files.[16] Mobility lets workers participate in online brainstorming sessions, seminars, and other formal or informal events from wherever they happen to be at the time. This flexibility can be particularly helpful during the review and production stages of major projects, when deadlines are looming and decisions and revisions need to be made quickly.

> Collaboration apps for mobile devices support nearly all the features of computer-based platforms.

An important aspect of mobile collaboration and mobile communication in general is **unified communication**, which integrates such capabilities as voice and video calling, voice and video conferencing, instant messaging, and real-time collaboration software into a single system. By minimizing or eliminating the need to manage multiple communication systems and devices, unified communication promises to improve response times, productivity, and collaboration efforts.[17]

> *Unified communication* integrates such features as voice and video calling, conferencing, instant messaging, and other features in a single system.

AI-Enabled Collaboration

The latest innovation in collaboration tools is artificial intelligence, using AI-enabled bots and other tools to help people work more efficiently and effectively. For example, *taskbots* can assist teams with scheduling, data collection, document distribution, and other routine chores to give teams more time to focus on their work. Some bots can guide online discussions and project-update meetings. Systems such as Slack treat them as team members; they can be assigned tasks and can assign tasks to their human teammates.[18] See "Intelligent Communication Technology: Hi, I'm an Algorithm, Your New Teammate."

> Taskbots can help teams be more productive by taking over routine chores such as scheduling.

INTELLIGENT COMMUNICATION TECHNOLOGY

Hi, I'm an Algorithm, Your New Teammate

If the thought of living in some sci-fi future where you work side by side with robot colleagues makes you uneasy, you might as well relax—you're already doing it. The internet and mobile phone apps are teeming with *bots*, pieces of software that perform a wide variety of tasks. They may not have mechanical arms and cute or creepy humanoid faces, but they are robots just the same.

The distinctions can be a little vague, but bots can be divided into two general categories: *taskbots* and *chatbots*. As their names suggest, one primarily handles chores and the other engages in conversation. Chatbots such as Apple's Siri and Amazon's Alexa use voice interaction, whereas many online chatbots use text input and output. For more on chatbots, see page 234.

Taskbots are a key feature in robotic process automation, where they can take over tasks such as creating database reports, finding customer records, automating payroll, and processing orders. AI-enabled bots used in cognitive automation can become subject-matter experts and take over or assist with higher-level decision-making.

With any luck, robotic teammates will handle the bulk of the mundane tasks in tomorrow's business environment and free up people to focus on strategic and creative thinking.

WHAT'S YOUR TAKE?

1. Would you rather work alongside a human teammate who occasionally makes mistakes that cost you time and energy or an AI-enabled taskbot that performs flawlessly? Explain your answer.
2. Would you be comfortable getting a medical diagnosis from a bot? Why or why not?

Sources: "The Future of Work," Automation Anywhere, accessed 5 March 2018, www.automationanywhere.com; "Bot Users," Slack, accessed 5 March 2018, www.slack.com; Clint Boulton, "How Messaging Bots Will Change Workplace Productivity," *CIO*, 1 February 2016, www.cio.com.

Making Your Meetings More Productive

Much of your workplace communication will occur during in-person or online meetings, so to a large degree, your ability to contribute to the company—and to be recognized for your contributions—will depend on your meeting skills. Well-run meetings can help companies solve problems, develop ideas, and identify opportunities. Meetings can also be a great way to promote team building through the experience of social interaction.[19]

As useful as meetings can be, though, they can be a waste of time if they aren't planned and managed well. You can help ensure productive meetings by preparing carefully, conducting meetings efficiently, and using meeting technologies wisely.

> **3 LEARNING OBJECTIVE**
> List the key steps needed to ensure productive team meetings.

> Check out the "Five-Minute Guide to Planning Better Meetings" at the end of the chapter.

PREPARING FOR MEETINGS

The first step in preparing for a meeting is to make sure the meeting is really necessary. Meetings can consume hundreds or thousands of dollars of productive time while taking people away from other work, so don't hold a meeting if some other form of communication can serve the purpose as effectively.[20] If a meeting is truly necessary, plan it carefully to make the best use of everyone's time.

The first step in preparing for a meeting: Make sure it is necessary.

Define the Meeting's Purpose

Meetings can focus on exchanging information, reaching decisions, or collaborating to solve problems or identify opportunities. Whatever your purpose, define the best possible result of the meeting (such as "we carefully evaluated all three product ideas and decided which one to invest in"). Use this hoped-for result to shape the direction and content of the meeting.[21] If you can't envision an ideal outcome from the meeting or express its purpose in a single sentence, either cancel it or keep brainstorming until you can narrow down a specific purpose.

A good way to define the purpose of a meeting is to visualize the best possible outcome.

Select Participants for the Meeting

The rule here is simple: Invite everyone who really needs to be involved, and don't invite anyone who doesn't. For decision-making meetings, for example, invite only those people who are in a direct position to help the meeting reach its objective. The more people you have, the longer it will take to reach consensus. Meetings with more than 10 or 12 people can become unmanageable if everyone is expected to participate in the discussion and decision-making. Of course, you can't always control who gets invited to meetings, but when you can, make deliberate choices.

Keep meeting attendance as small as possible to ensure productive use of everyone's time.

Choose the Venue and the Time

Online meetings (see page 83) are often the best way and sometimes the only way to connect people in multiple locations or to reach large audiences. For in-person meetings, review the facility and the seating arrangements (see Figure 3.4). Is theater-style seating suitable, or do you need a conference table or some other arrangement? Pay attention to room temperature, lighting, ventilation, acoustics, and refreshments; these details can make or break a meeting.

If you can, optimize the seating to support the specific needs of each meeting.

If you have control over the timing, morning meetings are often more productive because people are generally more alert and not yet engaged with the work of the day.

Set the Agenda

The success of any meeting depends on preparation. Distribute a carefully written *agenda* to participants, giving them enough time to prepare as needed (see Figure 3.5 on page 80). A productive agenda answers three key questions: (1) What do we need to do in this meeting to accomplish our goals? (2) What issues will be of greatest importance to all participants? (3) What information must be available to discuss these issues?[22] Your company may have a standard agenda template for meetings; if not, you can get templates within Microsoft Word or other apps.

A good agenda identifies

- *What needs to happen in the meeting*
- *Which issues are most important to discuss*
- *What information is required to discuss them*

In addition to the detailed planning agenda, you may also want to prepare a simpler presentation agenda to use during the meeting (see Figure 3.6 on page 80). You can use this version to keep the meeting on track and remind everyone of how much time is allotted for each step.

LEADING AND CONTRIBUTING TO EFFICIENT MEETINGS

Everyone in a meeting shares the responsibility for making the meeting productive. If you're the leader, however, you have an extra degree of responsibility and accountability. The following guidelines will help leaders and participants contribute to more effective meetings:

Everyone shares the responsibility for successful meetings.

- **Keep the discussion on track.** A good meeting draws out the best ideas and information the group has to offer. Good leaders occasionally need to guide, mediate, probe,

Conference room
Ideal for small meetings and working sessions; also works for small presentations by positioning presenter at one end of the table; promotes conversation among all attendees

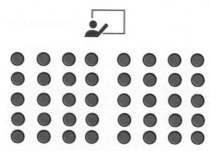

Theater/auditorium style
Best for large audiences but limits interaction between presenter and audience and among audience members; difficult for audiences to work with documents or devices unless chairs include desk surfaces

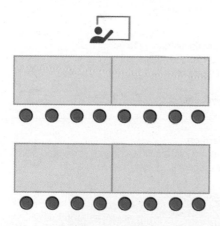

Classroom style
Good alternative to theater/auditorium style when you want to give participants more work surface for devices and documents; less opportunity for interaction and conversation than U-shape

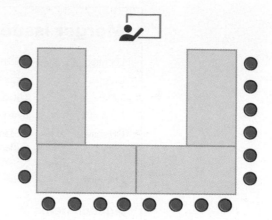

U-shape
Ideal for mid-sized meetings and working sessions; works nicely for presentations and gives the presenter the freedom to walk around the interior for closer interaction with attendees; also supports conversation among attendees

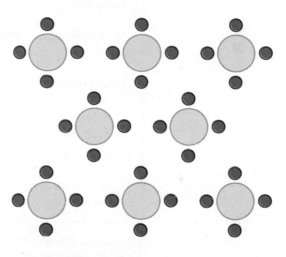

Breakout sessions
Useful for working meetings or seminars in which you ask the audience to split into groups and engage in role playing, brainstorming, or problem solving; prevents interaction between groups, however

Figure 3.4 Meeting Room Configurations
If you have the option of configuring the meeting room, select the best seating arrangement for each meeting's purpose. Here are some of the more common configurations and their best uses for meetings and presentations.

stimulate, summarize, and redirect discussions that have gotten off track. Don't leave it all in the leader's hands, however; everyone should help keep the meeting focused and moving forward.[23]

- **Follow agreed-on rules.** The larger the meeting, the more formal you need to be to maintain order. Formal meetings sometimes use **parliamentary procedure**, a time-tested method for planning and running effective meetings. The best-known guide to this procedure is *Robert's Rules of Order*.

Parliamentary procedure is a time-testing method for planning and running formal meetings.

Merger Issues Brainstorming Session

Location: Building C, Saratoga room

Date: August 8

Time: 9:00 to 12:00

Facilitator: Irene Belden

Objectives
- Identify/confirm all major issues and problems in each functional area
- Identify any cross-functional issues
- Give functional managers information they need to formulate action plans

Prestudy: Please download and read <u>Merger Brainstorming Session Prestudy.docx</u>

Agenda items

Time slot	Topic	Discussion leader
9:00-9:15	**Introductions:** Please be prepared to briefly describe your role on the transition team.	Irene Belden
9:15-10:00	**General transition costs:** Key items identified so far are severance packages, infrastructure investments, and service contracts.	Kip Selbach
10:00-10:15	**Break**	
10:15-11:00	**Information systems:** Key issues are migration to cloud computing and choice of internal communication platform.	Summer Bowman
11:00-11:45	**Marketing and sales:** Key issues are brand integration, sales force realignment, and quota and commission questions.	Ed Delahanty
11:45-12:00	**Wrap up:** Last call for questions and concerns; we want to make sure functional managers go away with every significant issue in hand so they can develop concrete action plans.	Irene Belden

Please send any questions to irene.belden@calypsonet.com

Figure 3.5 Effective Meeting Agenda: Full Version
A meeting agenda should provide all attendees with the information they need in order to plan for the meeting. Compare this full *planning agenda* with the shorter *presentation agenda* in Figure 3.6.

Figure 3.6 Effective Meeting Agenda: Condensed
This presentation slide shows a condensed version of the meeting agenda from Figure 3.5. The meeting facilitator can use a slide such as this to introduce each agenda item and keep the meeting on schedule.

- **Encourage and moderate participation.** Some people like to think out loud, using discussion to help clarify their own thoughts. Others prefer to finalize their thoughts before speaking. Effective meeting leaders need to accommodate both styles, in addition to making sure that people who may not feel comfortable speaking up or who have been interrupted by more assertive participants have the chance to be heard.[24]

  Make sure all styles of communicators have the opportunity to share their ideas.

- **Participate actively.** Make a point to contribute to the progress of the meeting and the smooth interaction of participants. Use your listening skills and powers of observation to size up the interpersonal dynamics of the group, then adapt your behavior to help the group achieve its goals. Speak up if you have something useful to say, but don't talk or ask questions just to demonstrate how much you know about the subject at hand.

- **Don't interrupt.** Even if you're an expert in the subject matter or the discussion is getting heated, respect everyone's right to participate. Meetings can be dominated by the most aggressive participants, but the loudest people don't necessarily have the best ideas.

- **Use mobile devices respectfully.** Tweeting key points from a convention speech or using your phone or tablet to jot down essential ideas and follow-up questions can be productive and respectful ways to use a device during a meeting. Checking Facebook or working on unrelated tasks is not. If you intend to use your device to take notes during a meeting, consider letting the meeting leader know that's what you're doing.[25]

  Norms regarding mobile device usage vary widely; make sure you understand what your team or company expect.

- **Close effectively.** At the conclusion of the meeting, verify that the objectives have been met or arrange for follow-up work, if needed. Summarize the general conclusion of the discussion and any actions to be taken. Make sure all participants understand and agree on the outcome.

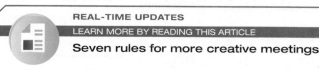

REAL-TIME UPDATES

LEARN MORE BY READING THIS ARTICLE

Seven rules for more creative meetings

Follow these steps to get more out of your meetings. Go to **real-timeupdates.com/ebc13** and select Learn More in the Students section.

PUTTING MEETING RESULTS TO PRODUCTIVE USE

In most cases, the value of a meeting doesn't end when the meeting ends. For example, problems or opportunities brought up during a meeting need to be addressed, any action items assigned during the meeting need to be acted on, and key decisions and announcements should be distributed to anyone who is affected but was unable to attend. Having a written, audio, or video record of a meeting also gives the participants a chance to verify their impressions and conclusions.

The conventional method of recording meetings is through written **minutes**, a summary of the important information presented and the decisions made (see Figure 3.7 on the next page). One person is usually assigned to keep notes as the meeting progresses and then to share them afterward. The specific format of the minutes is less important than making sure you record all the key information, particularly regarding responsibilities that were assigned during the meeting. Typical elements include a list of those present and a list of those who were invited but didn't attend, followed by the times the meeting started and ended, all major decisions reached at the meeting, all assignments of tasks to meeting participants, and all subjects that were deferred to a later meeting. In addition, the minutes objectively summarize important discussions, noting the names of those who contributed major points. Any handouts, slides, or supporting documents can be attached to the minutes when they are distributed.

Minutes are written summaries of important information presented and the decisions made in meetings.

Depending on the meeting technologies at your disposal, you may have software specifically designed to record, distribute, and store meeting minutes (see Figure 3.8 on page 83). Some systems automatically forward action items to each employee, record audio discussions for future playback, and make all the relevant documents and files available in one convenient place.[26]

To review the tasks that contribute to productive meetings, refer to "Checklist: Improving Meeting Productivity."

Employee Onboarding Update

March 16
2:00 p.m. to 3:00 p.m.

Meeting called by: Alex Gardner

Type of meeting: Status update

Facilitator: Jessica Knowdell

Note taker: Frank Isbell

Attendees: Alex Gardner, Frank Isbell, Jessica Knowdell, Steve Ladew, Ally Lawson, Bill Swarback, Jessie Tannehill, Toni Von Fricken, Dale Williams

Minutes

Agenda item: New orientation presentation   **Presenter:** Toni Von Fricken

Discussion:

Toni reports that the new slide presentation is complete and will be test-run with a group of volunteers from HR on March 30.

Steve offered to convert the slides to a video and post on the intranet.

Action items	Person responsible	Deadline
✓ Test-run new orientation presentation; fine-tune as needed	Toni VF	April 2
✓ Convert finished slides to video and post on employee intranet	Steve L	April 10

Agenda item: Update employee handbook and improve access   **Presenter:**   Jessica Knowdell

Discussion:

Team reached agreement that a wiki is the best platform for hosting the handbook.

We decided on a three-level access plan:

    Level 1: Access open to all HR employees, but new posts and edits must be approved by division HR directors to ensure compliance (for all policy-related documents and regulatory forms)

    Level 2: Access open to all HR employees, with immediate posting and editing allowed (for all non-policy documents, HR event updates, wellness bulletins, and similar items)

    Level 3: Access open to all employees, with immediate posting and editing allowed (for all employee social clubs, charity events, and similar items)

Action items	Person responsible	Deadline
✓ Discuss wiki plan with intranet platform vendor	Jessica K	April 5
✓ Vendor to design access controls	Jessica K (vendor contact)	April 20
✓ Announce new wiki to employee base	Dale W, Jessica K	May 1

Agenda item: Brainstorm ideas for mentor matching program   **Presenter:** Ally Lawson

Discussion:

Ally presented research on mentoring programs, including best practices and pitfalls.

Alex will bring up issue of volunteer vs. mandatory mentoring at May executive council.

Meeting minutes   March 16   Employee Onboarding Update

Figure 3.7   Effective Meeting Minutes
Meeting minutes should record all the information that participants may need to refer to later. Depending on the circumstances, you might want to include information that anyone who wasn't able to attend can review in order to get a summary of key discussion and decision points.

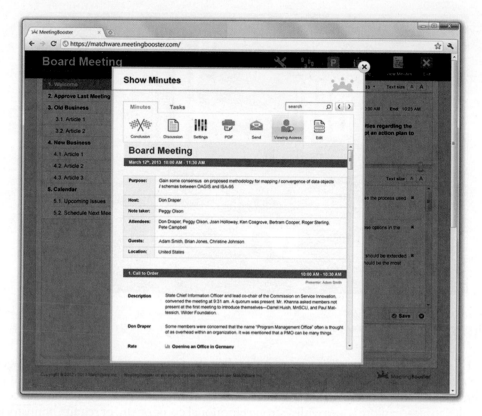

Figure 3.8 Capturing Key Decisions and Discoveries from a Meeting
Meeting tools such as the MeetingBooster system help teams and other groups capture decisions and discoveries from meetings and put this information to productive use.

CHECKLIST ✔ Improving Meeting Productivity

A. Prepare carefully.
- ✔ Make sure the meeting is necessary.
- ✔ Decide on your purpose.
- ✔ Select participants carefully.
- ✔ Choose the venue and the time; adapt the seating if possible.
- ✔ Establish and distribute a clear and detailed planning agenda.

B. Lead effectively and participate fully.
- ✔ Keep the meeting on track.
- ✔ Follow agreed-on rules.
- ✔ Encourage and moderate participation.
- ✔ Participate actively.
- ✔ Don't interrupt.
- ✔ Use mobile devices respectfully and in line with group norms.
- ✔ Close effectively.

C. Put the results to effective use.
- ✔ Distribute meeting minutes to participants and other interested parties.
- ✔ Make sure task assignments are clearly communicated.

CONDUCTING VIRTUAL MEETINGS

Virtual meetings are meetings in which people join in from two or more locations and connect via some form of communication technology. Such meetings are commonplace in business today, so it's important to know how to run a virtual meeting and how to get the most out of one as a participant. Chances are you'll also participate in online seminars, often referred to as *webinars*.

Virtual Meeting Systems

The tools for virtual meetings range from conference calls and group messaging chats to real-time collaboration systems and *telepresence* systems with immersive video so realistic it can seem like people thousands of miles away are sitting across the table.[27] The most exotic systems can transmit *holograms*, beaming live, three-dimensional replicas of participants long distance.[28]

Virtual meetings allow people to join in from two or more locations and connect via some form of communication technology.

MOBILE APP
Cisco WebEx Meetings gives you mobile access to one of the world's most popular online meeting platforms.

Figure 3.9   Virtual Meetings
With broadband wireless connections, virtual meetings are easy to conduct using smartphones or tablets.

For fairly uncomplicated discussion and update meetings, particularly among colleagues who already know one another, teleconferencing is an easy and inexpensive choice. If the meeting involves people who haven't worked together before, or if the agenda will cover complex topics, explore issues with a strong emotional component, or require brainstorming or other interactive participation, some form of video link is highly desirable. Video supports a much wider range of nonverbal communication, and the ability to see one another helps new team members form closer bonds in less time (see Figure 3.9). Fortunately, videoconferencing no longer requires expensive, dedicated systems. Several smartphone apps support small group video calls, and the WebRTC (for *real-time communication*) capability lets people communicate via video through standard web browsers and mobile apps.[29]

Tips for Successful Virtual Meetings

Conducting successful virtual meetings requires extra planning beforehand and more diligence during the meeting.

As with virtual teamwork, virtual meetings require an extra level of planning and attention in order to be successful, in addition to the meeting planning steps covered earlier. Keeping people engaged can be more challenging, particularly in audio-only meetings. Follow these tips:

- Make sure the meeting has a well-defined task, so that it steadily moves toward a goal.[30] Doing so helps prevent people from losing interest or giving in to the temptation to multitask—a particular issue with audio-only calls, where no one can see if you're working on something else.
- Provide prestudy materials as needed, in addition to the agenda. Let participants know what will be expected of them.
- For large meetings, assign people to specific roles, such as a facilitator who guides the discussion, a technical specialist who can help people if they experience difficulties with their connections without interrupting the meeting, and someone to record the minutes.[31]
- Make sure everyone has up-to-date versions of whatever tools you plan to use. As a participant, install and test any needed apps before the meeting.
- If all the participants don't know each other, the facilitator should perform introductions or ask people in turn to introduce themselves.[32]
- If the system doesn't offer a way for people to virtually "raise their hands" to ask a question, the facilitator should explain how to pose questions.
- As a participant, log in on time. Meeting systems often announce or signal as each person checks in, and it's highly disruptive when latecomers log in after the meeting has started.

- Be present, mentally and emotionally. Avoid the temptation to multitask. Staying present shows respect for others, and it could save you from embarrassment if you get called on unexpectedly.
- Mute your audio input if you need to cough or otherwise make noise. Most systems have a microphone icon or mute button you can press.
- If you type to take notes, make sure your keyboard or device won't distract others. Some computer keyboards are extremely loud, and your microphone will pick up every "clack." If necessary, mute your audio connection while typing.
- As you work through each agenda item, summarize what has been discussed and ask if anyone has questions or comments.[33]
- As the facilitator, periodically check in with each person, if feasible. For instance, if someone hasn't spoken in a while, after summarizing a discussion point, you might address a person by name and ask, "Does that work for you?" or "Do you have anything to add?" Knowing they might be called on keeps people tuned in to the meeting, and it gives everyone a chance to share input or ask questions.

For more insights into meetings and meeting technologies, visit **real-timeupdates .com/ebc13** and select Chapter 3.

> Avoid the temptation to multitask during a virtual meeting; stay present for your own benefit and the benefit of others.

> Check in with everyone frequently to see if there are any points of confusion or disagreement.

Developing Your Business Etiquette

You may have noticed a common thread running through this and the previous chapter on the topics of effective listening, conversational skills, conflict resolution, teamwork, collaboration, and productive meetings: All these activities depend on mutual respect and consideration among all participants. Nobody wants to work with someone who is rude to colleagues or an embarrassment to the company. Moreover, shabby treatment of others in the workplace can be a huge drain on morale and productivity.[34]

A vital element of audience-centered communication is **etiquette**, the expected norms of behavior in any particular situation. Poor etiquette can drive away customers, investors, and other critical audiences—and it can limit your career potential. Unfortunately, rude behavior appears to be on the rise, so the issue is more important than ever.[35]

This section addresses some key etiquette points to remember in a variety of work and work-related settings (see Figure 3.10). Long lists of etiquette rules can be difficult to remember, but you can get by in almost every situation by remembering to be aware of your effect on others, treating everyone with respect, and keeping in mind that the impressions you leave behind can have a lasting effect on you and your company.

> **4** LEARNING OBJECTIVE
> Explain the importance of business etiquette, and identify five areas in which good etiquette is essential.

> *Etiquette*, the expected norms of behavior in any particular situation, is essential to every aspect of interpersonal communication and team collaboration.

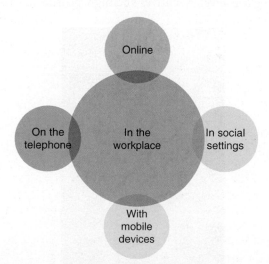

Figure 3.10   The Five Zones of Professional Etiquette
Professionals pay attention to their effect on other people in five areas: in the workplace, in social settings in which they are representing their firms, while online, while using the telephone, and while using mobile devices.

BUSINESS ETIQUETTE IN THE WORKPLACE

Workplace etiquette includes a variety of behaviors, habits, and aspects of nonverbal communication. Follow these tips to help ensure a pleasant and productive workplace:[36]

A key issue in workplace etiquette is respecting other people's time, from adhering to schedules to minimizing time-wasting distractions.

- Respect other people's time, such as showing up for work and meetings on time and not taking up colleagues' time with gossip or too much personal chitchat.
- Don't interrupt people in conversations or in meetings.
- Watch your language. You might be comfortable with profanity in casual conversation, but it is out of place in a professional environment.
- Pay close attention to cleanliness, and avoid using products with powerful scents. Many people are bothered by these products, and some are allergic to them.
- Avoid eating at your desk if possible, particularly in open-plan offices. Many foods have strong smells, and no one wants to listen to you eat.

Noise can be a big problem in today's open-plan offices, so take care to avoid disrupting others.

- Keep the noise level down. This is a huge concern in open-plan workspaces, where people are separated only by short cubicle walls and sometimes not even that. Keep your voice down, avoid having meetings in your cubicle, and don't play music at a level that disrupts others (even if you're wearing earbuds or headphones).
- Respect other people's personal space. Knock before entering offices, and don't enter someone's cubicle without being invited.
- Don't gossip. Not only is gossip a waste of time, it's often disrespectful to others.

Avoid coming to work when you're sick.

- Don't come to work when you're sick. Companies need to support the effort to prevent the spread of germs and viruses by giving employees adequate sick leave.
- In general, avoid discussing religion, politics, or other potentially emotional issues, unless your company encourages such discussions.

Although it isn't always thought of as an element of etiquette, your personal appearance in the workplace sends a strong signal to managers, colleagues, and customers (see Figure 3.11). This isn't a question of mindlessly conforming or surrendering your individuality; it's a question of showing respect for an organizational culture that is bigger than you.

Pay attention to the style of dress where you work and adjust your style to match.

Pay attention to the style of dress where you work, and adjust your style to match. Expectations for specific jobs, companies, and industries can vary widely. The financial industries tend to be more formal than high-tech, creative, and industrial firms, for instance, and sales and executive positions usually involve more formal expectations than positions in engineering or manufacturing.

Work attire falls into four degrees of formality:

- Business formal
- Business professional
- Business casual
- Casual

You can view business style as four levels:[37]

- **Business formal.** This means tailored suits in conservative colors, with shoes, accessories, and grooming to match. This style is usually restricted only to the most formal occasions or among top-level executives and high-profile professionals.

Figure 3.11 Showing Respect for Organizational Culture
The choices you make regarding personal appearance can send a strong signal to managers, colleagues, and customers regarding your level of respect of workplace norms.

- **Business professional.** This style is still based around suits or coordinated sets of jackets with skirts or trousers, but the overall vibe is slightly freer. An expensive tailored suit isn't necessary, as long as it fits well and is pressed.
- **Business casual.** This is the style adopted in more relaxed offices in a variety of industries and professions. In general, it means slacks or skirts, with nice-looking button-up shirts, blouses, and sweaters. Don't interpret it as sloppy or unkempt, however.
- **Casual.** This category is perhaps the most difficult to pin down. In one company it might mean nice jeans and a button-up shirt, but in another it might be shorts, sandals, and tank tops.

In general, the trend in U.S. offices is toward casual, but don't overstep the boundaries in place at your specific office. Observe others, and don't be afraid to ask for advice. Many clothing stores, department stores, and online retailers such as Stitchfix (**www.stitchfix .com**) offer personal shopping guidance or style guides to help you select specific garments. If you're not sure, dress modestly and simply—earn a reputation for what you can do, not for what you wear.

BUSINESS ETIQUETTE IN SOCIAL SETTINGS

From business lunches to industry conferences, you may be asked to represent your company in public. Make sure your appearance and actions are appropriate to the situation. Get to know the customs of other cultures when it comes to meeting new people. For example, in North America, a firm handshake is expected when two people meet, whereas a respectful bow of the head is more appropriate in Japan. If you are expected to shake hands, be aware that the passive "dead fish" handshake creates an extremely negative impression. If you are physically able, always stand when shaking someone's hand.

Etiquette is particularly important when you represent your company out in public.

When introducing yourself, state your first and last name and include a brief description of your role in the company. When introducing two other people, give their first and last names clearly and then try to offer some information (perhaps a shared professional interest) to help the two people ease into a conversation.[38] Generally speaking, introduce younger people to older people and lower-ranking employees or managers to higher-ranking managers.[39]

When introducing yourself, state your first and last name and include a brief description of your role in the company.

Business is often conducted over meals, and knowing the basics of dining etiquette will make you more effective in these situations.[40] Start by choosing foods that are easy to eat. Avoid alcoholic beverages in most instances, but if drinking one is appropriate, save it for the end of the meal.

Remember that business meals are a forum for business. Don't discuss politics, religion, or any other topic that's likely to stir up emotions. Don't complain about work, don't ask deeply personal questions, avoid profanity, and be careful with humor—a joke that entertains some people could easily offend others.

REAL-TIME UPDATES

LEARN MORE BY WATCHING THIS VIDEO

Dining etiquette simplified

Etiquette expert Barbara Pachter offers tips to help you get comfortable at business lunches and dinners. Go to **real-timeupdates .com/ebc13** and click Learn More in the Students section.

Receptions are a common part of industry conferences and other business events, and they are a great opportunity to meet new people and refresh old acquaintances. Although they can be good networking opportunities, remember that their primary function is social. Don't race around pressing your business card on everyone or "pitch" yourself or your company to everyone you meet. Also, help people who are looking to join conversations. If you see someone standing near a group you are part of, pause the conversation and introduce yourself to help the newcomer feel included.

At receptions and other social events, help others feel welcome by introducing yourself and inviting them to join conversations.

ONLINE ETIQUETTE

Digital media seem to be a breeding ground for poor etiquette. Learn the basics of professional online behavior to avoid mistakes that could hurt your company or your career. Whenever you represent your company online, in any medium, you must adhere to a high standard of etiquette and respect for others. Follow these guidelines:[41]

When you represent your company online, officially or unofficially, you must adhere to a high standard of etiquette and respect for others.

- **Avoid personal attacks.** The disconnected feel of online communication can cause even level-headed people to lose their tempers.

- **Stay focused on the original topic.** If you want to change the subject of an online conversation, start a new message or thread.
- **Don't present opinions as facts; support facts with evidence.** This guideline applies to all communication, of course, but online venues in particular seem to tempt people into presenting their beliefs and opinions as unassailable truths.
- **Follow basic expectations of spelling, punctuation, and capitalization.** Sending careless, acronym-filled messages that look like you're texting your high school buddies makes you look like an amateur.
- **Use virus protection and keep it up to date.** Sending or posting a file that contains a computer virus puts others at risk.
- **Watch your language and keep your emotions under control.** A single indiscretion could haunt you forever.
- **Avoid multitasking while using messaging or other tools.** You might think you're saving time by doing a dozen things at once, but you're probably making the other person wait while you bounce back and forth between tasks.
- **Don't waste others' time with sloppy, confusing, or incomplete messages.** Doing so is disrespectful.
- **Never assume you have privacy.** Assume that anything you type will be stored forever, could be forwarded to other people, and might be read by your boss or the company's security staff.
- **Be careful of online commenting mechanisms.** For example, many blogs and websites let you use your Facebook login to comment on articles. If your Facebook profile includes your job title and company name, those could show up along with your comment.
- **Respect boundaries of time and virtual space.** For instance, don't use colleagues' or employees' personal social media accounts as a venue for business discussions, and don't assume people are available to discuss work matters around the clock, even if you do find them online in the middle of the night.

Keep your cool online and use professional language.

Anything you say online could be seen by people far beyond your immediate audience, including your boss or your company's security staff.

Respect personal and professional boundaries when using Facebook and other social networking tools.

TELEPHONE ETIQUETTE

Here are some important tips for using phones at work (for etiquette points specifically about mobile devices, see the next section):[42]

- **Be conscious of how your voice sounds.** Don't speak in a monotone; vary your pitch and inflections so people know you're interested. Slow down when conversing with people whose native language isn't the same as yours.
- **Be courteous when you call someone.** Identify yourself and your organization, briefly describe why you're calling, and ask if you've called at a good time.
- **Convey a positive, professional attitude when you answer the phone.** Answer promptly and with a smile so that you sound welcoming. Identify yourself and your company (some companies have specific instructions for what to say when you answer). If you need to forward a call, put the caller on hold first and call the next person yourself to verify that he or she is available.
- **End calls with courtesy and clarity.** Close in a friendly, positive manner and double-check all vital information such as meeting times and dates.
- **Use your own voicemail features to help callers.** Record a brief, professional-sounding outgoing message for regular use. When you will be away or unable to answer the phone for an extended period, record a temporary greeting that tells callers when you will respond to their messages. If you don't check your messages regularly or at all, disable your voicemail or use your outgoing message to tell callers you don't check it. Letting voicemail messages pile up without answering them is extremely thoughtless.
- **Be considerate when leaving voicemail messages.** Unless voicemail is the best or only choice, consider leaving a message through other means, such as text messaging or email. If you do leave a voicemail message, make it as brief as possible. Leave your name, number, reason for calling, and times you can be reached.

Basic courtesy on the phone makes communication more efficient and more pleasant for everyone involved.

If you never or rarely check your voicemail, disable it or record an outgoing message advising callers to reach you another way.

MOBILE DEVICE ETIQUETTE

Like every other aspect of communication, your mobile device habits say a lot about how much respect you have for the people around you. Avoid these disrespectful choices:[43]

- Using obnoxious or inappropriate ringtones
- Talking loudly in open offices or public places
- Talking on your phone right next to someone else
- Making or taking unnecessary personal calls at work
- Invading privacy by using your phone's camera without permission
- Taking or making calls in restrooms and other inappropriate places
- Texting during meals or while someone is talking to you
- Allowing incoming calls to interrupt meetings or discussions
- Using voice recognition to the extent that it disrupts others

Virtual, voice-activated assistants raise another new etiquette dilemma. From doing simple web searches to dictating entire memos, these systems may be convenient for users, but they can create distractions and annoyances for other people.[44] As with other public behaviors, think about the effect you have on others before using these technologies.

Note that expectations and policies regarding mobile device use vary widely from company to company. At one extreme, venture capitalist Ben Horowitz fines his employees if they even look at a mobile device while an entrepreneur is pitching a business plan, because he considers it disrespectful to people making presentations.[45] Not all bosses are quite so strict, but make sure you understand the situation in your workplace.

> Your mobile device habits send a signal about the degree of respect you have for those around you.

MOBILE APP
Locale can "geofence" your smartphone, automatically changing settings based on your location—such as activating silent mode when you arrive at your office.

> Virtual assistants and other mobile phone voice features can annoy and disrupt the workplace and social settings if not used with respect for others.

ON THE JOB: SOLVING COMMUNICATION DILEMMAS AT **ING**

After several years of being on agile squads at ING, you've been promoted to *agile coach*, with responsibility to help all the teams in your tribe be as successful as possible. Study these scenarios and decide how to respond, based on what you learned in this chapter.

1. A new team has just been formed to update ING's mobile banking app. Like all agile teams in the company, this team meets every morning for a 15-minute standing meeting called, appropriately, the *standup*. It is a quick checkpoint meeting in which all nine people are supposed to give a rapid-fire overview of what they accomplished the previous day, what they're working on today, and any problems getting in their way. This new team has been together for only three days, so understandably there is still some forming and storming going on. However, you're disheartened at how much storming is going on. People aren't giving updates at all; they're just complaining and sniping at others in the company. You aren't a formal manager of this team (it's a self-managed team), but you are expected to offer guidance. How should you respond?
   a. Don't intervene. High-performance teams can have some high-maintenance individuals on them, so let the drama work itself out.
   b. Listen and take notes but don't intervene yet. See if you can pick up any themes or common threads in the

complaints. Find out why an entire team is this upset before you step in.
   c. Stop the meeting and remind everyone that this is supposed to be an update meeting.
   d. Stop the meeting and chastise the group for its unprofessional behavior. After all, how can they expect to be a self-managed group if they can't even manage themselves?

2. The team's next sprint involves writing the user guide for the new banking app. The guide will be the equivalent of about 20 printed pages, so the team needs to move quickly to get it researched, drafted, revised, produced, and proofread during this one-week sprint. Which approach to collaboration should this team of nine people take?
   a. Each person should submit a brief writing sample, then the team will vote on who is the best writer. That person will write the manual and can call on anyone else in the team to help with research, proofreading, and other tasks.
   b. Quickly divide into four two-person teams, each of which will outline and write a section of the guide. The ninth person will stitch the four parts together, revising as needed for a consistent style.
   c. As a group, brainstorm the best way to answer all potential consumer questions and points of confusion,

then together outline the user guide in detail. Divide the outline into four or five discrete sections and assign them to the four or five people on the team who are most comfortable writing. After they are finished, have another team member compile the pieces into a single document and revise as needed for smooth transitions from section to section. Finally, have the remaining team members review and proofread the document.

d. The team should brainstorm the outline together; by this point in their work, they are experts in how the app works. Then divide the outline into nine pieces and have each person submit finished text. Merge the nine pieces into a single document, and pass it around the team for final edits.

3. Unfortunately, the team didn't follow your advice on collaborating from the previous question, and the first draft of the user guide is flawed. The individual pieces are coherent and well written, but they overlap in places and leave gaps in other places. How should you provide critical feedback?

a. Show the team members a few examples of what you found; they will immediately see the problem and get to work fixing the document.

b. Tell the team the user guide is unsatisfactory, but let them figure out exactly how it is flawed.

c. Don't provide any feedback. Wait until customers begin to complain about the repetitive and missing coverage in the guide. The team will learn the lesson more effectively if they hear it from customers.

d. Tell them you're struggling to understand how a team of professionals who have experience working together could have made such a mistake.

4. You know how busy the people in this team are, so you don't say anything the first few times you notice team members checking their mobile phones during the daily standup. However, the mobile etiquette soon gets out of hand, with half the team on their phones some of the time. How should you respond?

a. Don't do anything. This is clearly the new norm for this team, and no one has protested the behavior yet.

b. At the end of today's standup, ask the team members if they are finding the daily meetings to be beneficial. Depending on the answers you get, explore an alternative to the standup (if most of the team doesn't find it useful) or discuss how to "re-norm" back to good etiquette (if most of the team does find it useful).

c. Recommend that the team stop having daily standups; the meetings don't appear to be very useful.

d. Institute a new policy in which people need to deposit their phones in a cardboard box at the beginning of each standup.

END OF CHAPTER

Learning Objectives Checkup

Assess your understanding of the principles in this chapter by reading each learning objective and studying the accompanying exercises. You can check your responses against the answer key on page 612.

Objective 3.1: List the advantages and disadvantages of working in teams, describe the characteristics of effective teams, explain how teams evolve, and offer advice on working in virtual teams.

1. Which of these is a potential advantage of cross-functional teams?
   a. They help ensure that lines of responsibility remain distinct by keeping various functional areas within their own "silos."
   b. They can help companies overcome the isolating effects of individual departments working in their own "silos."
   c. They reduce costs by reducing the number of people needed on problem-solving teams and project teams.
   d. They discourage the socializing that can make other teams so inefficient.

2. Which of the following is a potential disadvantage of working in teams?
   a. Teams always stamp out creativity by forcing people to conform to existing ideas and practices.

   b. Teams increase a company's clerical workload because of the additional government paperwork required for administering workplace insurance.
   c. Team members are never held accountable for their individual performance.
   d. Social pressure within the group can lead to groupthink, in which people go along with a bad idea or poor decision even though they may not really believe in it.

3. Which of these is *not* listed in the chapter as a characteristic of effective teams?
   a. A belief in the value of the team's efforts
   b. A net reduction in managerial responsibility
   c. A shared sense of purpose and compatible values
   d. Positive behavioral norms that promote *psychological safety*

4. _____ are informal standards of conduct that members share and that guide member behavior.

5. The storming stage of team development refers to
   a. tackling a big goal, as in "storming the castle."
   b. when a team disbands because of internal conflict.
   c. when a team disbands because it has met its primary objective.
   d. the natural rise of disagreements and uncertainties as team members define and settle into their roles.

6. Which of these is *not* listed in the chapter as one of the potential disadvantages of virtual teams?
   a. Missing out on the random interactions that co-located teams experience
   b. The sense of emotional isolation and the feeling of "being out of the loop" that individuals can develop
   c. An "us versus them" mentality that can develop between isolated factions in a team
   d. Constant interruptions from group messaging systems and other communication tools

Objective 3.2: Offer guidelines for collaborative communication, identify major collaboration technologies, and explain how to give constructive feedback.

7. Which of the following is usually the best way for a team of people to write a report?
   a. Each member should plan, research, and write his or her individual version, and then the group can select the strongest report.
   b. The team should divide and conquer, with one person doing the planning, one doing the research, one doing the writing, and so on.
   c. To ensure a true group effort, every task from planning through final production should be done as a team, preferably with everyone in the same room at the same time.
   d. Research and plan as a group but assign the actual writing to one person, or at least assign separate sections to individual writers and have one person edit them all to achieve a consistent style.

8. Which of the following steps should be completed before anyone from a collaborative team does any planning, researching, or writing?
   a. The team should agree on the project's goals.
   b. The team should agree on the report's title.
   c. To avoid compatibility problems, the team should agree on which word processor or other software will be used.
   d. The team should always step away from the work environment and enjoy some social time in order to bond effectively before starting work.

9. _____ _____, also called _____ _____, focuses on the process and outcomes of communication, not on the people involved.

10. Which of these is an example of destructive feedback?
    a. I had to read the introduction twice to understand the key points.
    b. Can you expand on the reasoning behind your conclusion?
    c. This recommendation shows a lack of business insight.
    d. You might see if there is a way to convey this message in simpler language.

11. What is a key difference between content management systems and wikis?
    a. They are different terms for the same tool.
    b. Content management systems are less formal and less structured than wikis.
    c. Content management systems are more formal and more structured than wikis.
    d. Wikis aren't used to organize digital content.

Objective 3.3: List the key steps needed to ensure productive team meetings.

12. What are the three key steps to making sure meetings are productive?
    a. Planning, planning, and more planning
    b. Preparing carefully, conducting meetings efficiently, and putting meeting results to productive use
    c. Preparing carefully, conducting meetings using true democratic participation, and using meeting technologies wisely
    d. Preparing carefully, using meeting technologies wisely, and distributing in-depth minutes to everyone in the company

13. Whose responsibility is it to make sure a meeting stays focused and moving toward its objective?
    a. The manager who called the meeting
    b. The meeting leader or facilitator
    c. Everyone in the meeting
    d. The conference director

14. _____ _____ is a time-tested method for planning and running large meetings.

15. What is the written record of the discussion points and decisions from a meeting called?
    a. Records file
    b. Minutes
    c. Paper trail
    d. Meeting countdown

16. _____ teams are teams whose members work in two or more locations and interact using communication technology.

Objective 3.4: Explain the importance of business etiquette, and identify five areas in which good etiquette is essential.

17. What do effective listening, conversational skills, conflict resolution, teamwork, collaboration, and productive meetings have in common?
    a. Because they are listed on nearly all employee evaluation forms, it is assumed you have these skills.
    b. You don't need to worry too much about them as an entry-level employee, but definitely plan to refine these skills as you move up the corporate ladder.
    c. They are known in business as "hard skills."
    d. They rely on good etiquette from everyone involved.

18. Constantly testing the limits of your company's dress and grooming standards sends a strong signal that you
    a. don't understand or don't respect your company's culture.
    b. are a strong advocate for workers' rights.
    c. are a creative and independent thinker who is likely to generate lots of successful business ideas.
    d. represent the leading edge of a new generation of enlightened workers who will redefine the workplace according to contemporary standards.

19. Which of these is a wise approach to online etiquette?
    a. Unless you are posting on your company's Facebook or Twitter account, you don't need to worry about etiquette.
    b. Whenever you represent your company online, you must adhere to a high standard of etiquette and respect for others.

   c. The rough-and-tumble nature of online interaction is what makes it so valuable; don't hold back when you post or respond to other posts.

   d. Follow your company's digital media policy if one is available, but otherwise be yourself.

20. If you forgot to shut off your mobile phone before stepping into a business meeting and you receive a call during the meeting, the most appropriate thing to do is to

   a. lower your voice to protect the privacy of your phone conversation.

   b. answer the phone and then quickly hang it up to minimize the disruption to the meeting.

   c. excuse yourself from the meeting and find a quiet place to talk.

   d. continue to participate in the meeting while taking the call; this shows everyone that you're an effective multitasker.

Key Terms

collaboration Working together to meet complex challenges

committees Permanent, formal teams that address recurring questions or tasks

constructive feedback Focuses on the process and outcomes of communication, not on the people involved

creative team Teams in advertising, media, and other fields that combine creative professionals such as writers, artists, and designers

cross-functional team Team composed of people from more than one department or functional area within the company

destructive feedback Delivers criticism with no guidance to stimulate improvement

etiquette The expected norms of behavior in any particular situation

group dynamics The interactions and processes that take place among the members of a team

groupthink Situation in which peer pressure causes individual team members to withhold contrary or unpopular opinions

hidden agenda Private, counterproductive motives, such as a desire to take control of the group

minutes Written summary of the important information presented and the decisions made during a meeting

norms Informal standards of conduct that members share and that guide member behavior

parliamentary procedure A time-tested method for planning and running effective meetings; the best-known guide to this procedure is *Robert's Rules of Order*

participative management The effort to involve employees in a company's decision-making

problem-solving team Team that assembles to resolve a specific issue and then disbands when its goals have been accomplished

project team Temporary team assembled to complete a specific project

task-oriented roles Team roles directed toward helping the team reach its goals

team A unit of two or more people who share a mission and the responsibility for working to achieve a common goal

team-maintenance roles Team roles directed toward helping everyone work well together

unified communication Integrates voice and video calling, voice and video conferencing, instant messaging, real-time collaboration software, and other capabilities into a single system

virtual meetings Meetings in which people join in from two or more locations and connect via some form of communication technology

virtual team Team in which the members work in different locations and rely on communication technology to collaborate

wiki Special type of website that allows anyone with access to add new material and edit existing material

Apply Your Knowledge

To review chapter content related to each question, refer to the indicated Learning Objective.

3-1. How might team norms encourage groupthink? [LO-1]

3-2. If a team doesn't "storm" when it starts working, is this necessarily cause for concern? Why or why not? [LO-1]

3-3. Why is it essential to start with a detailed outline if you are going to divide up the writing work on a collaborative project? [LO-2]

3-4. Does constructive feedback necessarily need to be positive? Explain your answer. [LO-2]

3-5. If the purpose of a meeting is to brainstorm new product names, does it make sense to have a structured agenda? Explain your answer. [LO-3]

3-6. Why do you think people are more likely to engage in rude behaviors during online communication than during in-person communication? [LO-4]

Practice Your Skills

Message for Analysis

3-7. Planning Meetings [LO-3] A project leader has made notes about covering the following items at the quarterly budget meeting. Prepare a formal agenda by putting these items into a logical order and rewriting, where necessary, to give phrases a more consistent sound.

> Budget Committee Meeting to be held on December 12, 2020, at 9:30 a.m., and we have allotted one hour for the meeting.
>
> I will call the meeting to order.
>
> Real estate director's report: A closer look at cost overruns on Greentree site. (10 minutes)
>
> The group will review and approve the minutes from last quarter's meeting. (5 minutes)
>
> I will ask the finance director to report on actual versus projected quarterly revenues and expenses. (15 minutes)
>
> I will distribute copies of the overall divisional budget and announce the date of the next budget meeting.
>
> Discussion: How can we do a better job of anticipating and preventing cost overruns? (20 minutes)
>
> Meeting will take place in Conference Room 3, with Cisco WebEx active for remote employees.
>
> What additional budget issues must be considered during this quarter?

Exercises

Each activity is labeled according to the primary skill or skills you will need to use. To review relevant chapter content, you can refer to the indicated Learning Objective. In some instances, supporting information will be found in another chapter, as indicated.

3-8. Collaboration: Working in Teams [LO-1], [LO-2] In teams assigned by your instructor, prepare a 10-minute presentation on the potential disadvantages of using social media for business communication. When the presentation is ready, discuss how effective the team was, using the criteria of (a) having a clear objective and a shared sense of purpose, (b) communicating openly and honestly, (c) reaching decisions by consensus, (d) thinking creatively, and (e) knowing how to resolve conflict. Be prepared to discuss your findings with the rest of the class.

3-9. Collaboration: Collaborating on Writing Projects; Media Skills: Blogging [LO-2] In this project, you will conduct research on your own and then merge your results with those of the rest of your team. Search Twitter for messages on the subject of workplace safety. Compile at least five general safety tips that apply to any office setting, and then meet with your team to select the five best tips from all those the team has collected. Collaborate on a blog post that lists the team's top five tips.

3-10. Collaboration: Using Collaboration Technologies [LO-2] In a team assigned by your instructor, use Google Docs, Zoho (free for personal use), or a comparable system to collaborate on a set of directions that out-of-town visitors could use to reach a specific point on your campus, such as a stadium or dorm. The team should choose the location and the mode(s) of transportation involved. Be creative—brainstorm the best ways to guide first-time visitors to the selected location using all the media at your disposal.

3-11. Communication Etiquette: Etiquette in the Workplace, Participating in Meetings [LO-3], [LO-4] In group meetings, some of your colleagues have a habit of interrupting and arguing with the speaker, taking credit for ideas that aren't theirs, and shooting down ideas they don't agree with. As the newest person in the group, you're not sure if this is accepted behavior in this company, but it concerns you both personally and professionally. Should you go with the flow and adopt their behavior or stick with your own communication style, even though you might get lost in the noise? In a two-paragraph email message or post for your class blog, explain the pros and cons of both approaches.

3-12. Collaboration: Participating in Meetings [LO-3] With a classmate, attend a local community or campus meeting where you can observe a group discussion, vote, or take other group action. During the meeting, take notes individually, and afterward, work together to answer the following questions.

  a. What is your evaluation of this meeting? In your answer, consider (1) the leader's ability to articulate the meeting's goals clearly, (2) the leader's ability to engage members in a meaningful discussion, (3) the group's dynamics, and (4) the group's listening skills.

  b. How did group members make decisions? Did they vote? Did they reach decisions by consensus? Did

those with dissenting opinions get an opportunity to voice their objections?

  c. How well did the individual participants listen? How could you tell?

  d. Did any participants change their expressed views or their votes during the meeting? Why might that have happened?

  e. Did you observe any of the communication barriers discussed in Chapter 1? Identify them.

  f. Compare the notes you took during the meeting with those of your classmate. What differences do you notice? How do you account for these differences?

3-13. Collaboration: Leading Meetings [LO-3] Every month, each employee in your department is expected to give a brief presentation on the status of his or her project. However, your department has recently hired an employee who has a severe speech impediment that prevents people from understanding most of what he has to say. As department manager, how will you resolve this dilemma? Please explain.

3-14. Communication Etiquette: Etiquette in the Workplace [LO-4] As the regional manager of an international accounting firm, you place high priority on professional etiquette. Not only does it communicate respect to your clients, it also instills confidence in your firm by showing that you and your staff are aware of and able to meet the expectations of almost any audience. Earlier today, you took four recently hired college graduates to lunch with an important client. You've done this for years, and it's usually an upbeat experience for everyone, but today's lunch was a disaster. One of the new employees made not one, not two, but three calls on his mobile phone during lunch. Another interrupted the client several times and even got into a mild argument. The third employee kept making sarcastic jokes about politics, making everyone at the table uncomfortable. And the fourth showed up dressed like she was expecting to bale hay or work in a coal mine, not have a business lunch in a nice restaurant. You've already called the client to apologize, but now you need to coach these employees on proper business etiquette. Draft a brief memo to these employees, explaining why etiquette is so important to the company's success—and to their individual careers.

Expand Your Skills

Critique the Professionals

Many companies highlight their collaborative approach to work when they promote themselves to job candidates. Visit the careers sections of three company websites and evaluate how they discuss teamwork. What do they say about collaboration? Do they make it clear that employees are expected to work in teams? Do they discuss the benefits of collaboration? Using whatever medium your instructor requests, write a brief summary (no more than one page) of how these companies promote the idea of teamwork when appealing to potential employees and how effective you think these appeals are.

Sharpening Your Career Skills Online

Bovée and Thill's Business Communication Web Search, at **websearch.businesscommunicationnetwork.com**, is a unique research tool designed specifically for business communication research. Use the Web Search function to find a website, video, article, podcast, or presentation that offers advice on running successful business meetings. Write a brief email message to your instructor describing the item you found and summarizing the career skills information you learned from it.

Build Your Career

In Chapters 1 and 2, you explored the important career questions of what you want to do and what you have to offer. The next step is to explore ways to make yourself more valuable to potential employers. Chapter 15 discusses an important concept called *quality of hire*, which is the measurement employers use to judge the success of their hiring efforts, specifically about how closely a new employee meets the company's needs. As you put together your job-search strategy, what action can you take to make yourself look like a quality hire?

A good first step is to review job openings in careers you might like to pursue. What skills, qualities, and experiences are employers looking for? Compile a general set of expectations that employers have for your target jobs, then compare this list with the two lists you started in Chapter 2 (what you are capable of doing and how you can do those things). Where are the gaps? Don't be dismayed if you don't yet fit the profile of a "perfect" hire; this is about improving your profile, not getting to perfection. What steps can you take now to fill in some of the gaps? Consider taking additional courses to expand your knowledge or taking on part-time jobs, freelance projects, or volunteer opportunities to develop additional skills.

Second, keep expanding your knowledge of the professions, industries, and companies that interest you. In addition to specific qualifications, employers look for candidates who are curious about what's going on in the business world. Being aware of important issues and developments will help you stand out during the interviewing process—and look more like a high-quality hire.

Improve Your Grammar, Mechanics, and Usage

The following exercises help you improve your knowledge of and power over English grammar, mechanics, and usage. Turn to the Handbook of Grammar, Mechanics, and Usage at the end of this book and review all of Section 1.3 (Verbs). Then look at the

following 10 items and select the preferred choice from each pair of sentences. (Answers to these exercises appear on page 614.)

3-15. Which sentence contains a verb in the present perfect form?
   a. I became the resident expert on repairing the copy machine.
   b. I have become the resident expert on repairing the copy machine.

3-16. Which sentence contains a verb in the simple past form?
   a. She knows how to conduct an audit when she came to work for us.
   b. She knew how to conduct an audit when she came to work for us.

3-17. Which sentence contains a verb in the simple future form?
   a. Next week, call John to tell him what you will do to help him set up the seminar.
   b. Next week, call John to tell him what you will be doing to help him set up the seminar.

3-18. Which sentence is in the active voice?
   a. The report will be written by Leslie Cartwright.
   b. Leslie Cartwright will write the report.

3-19. Which sentence is in the passive voice?
   a. The failure to record the transaction was mine.
   b. I failed to record the transaction.

3-20. Which sentence contains the correct verb form?
   a. Everyone upstairs receives mail before we do.
   b. Everyone upstairs receive mail before we do.

3-21. Which sentence contains the correct verb form?
   a. Neither the main office nor the branches is blameless.
   b. Neither the main office nor the branches are blameless.

3-22. Which sentence contains the correct verb form?
   a. C&B Sales are listed in the directory.
   b. C&B Sales is listed in the directory.

3-23. Which sentence contains the correct verb form?
   a. When measuring shelves, 7 inches is significant.
   b. When measuring shelves, 7 inches are significant.

3-24. Which sentence contains the correct verb form?
   a. About 90 percent of the employees plans to come to the company picnic.
   b. About 90 percent of the employees plan to come to the company picnic.

For additional exercises focusing on verbs, visit MyLab Business Communication. Click on Chapter 3, click on Additional Exercises to Improve Grammar, Mechanics, and Usage, and then click on 5. Verb tenses, 6. Transitive and intransitive verbs, or 7. Voice of verbs.

MyLab Business Communication

MyLab Assisted-Grading Writing Prompts

If your instructor has assigned one or both of the following writing assignments within the MyLab, go to your Assignments to complete these writing exercises.

3-25. As a team or department leader, what steps can you take to ensure that your meetings are successful and efficient? [LO-3]

3-26. In terms of business etiquette, how can you reconcile the fact that mobile devices are now essential communication tools for most professionals with the fact that their use in meetings, over meals, and in other settings can sometimes be considered rude? [LO-4]

Endnotes

1. "The ING Way of Working," ING, accessed 4 March 2018, www.ing.jobs; "Squads, Sprints and Stand-ups," 23 November 2017, ING, www.ing.com; Deepak Mahadevan, "ING's Agile Transformation," *McKinsey Quarterly*, January 2017, www.mckinsey.com; "Agile Transformation at ING—A Case Study, Building the Agile Business," 25 October 2017, agilebusinessmanifesto.com.

2. Leigh L. Thompson, *Making the Team: A Guide for Managers*, 6th ed. (New York City: Pearson, 2018), 4.

3. Behnam Tabrizi, "75% of Cross-Functional Teams Are Dysfunctional," *Harvard Business Review*, 23 June 2015, hbr.org.

4. "Advantages and Disadvantages of Team Decision-Making," *Human Capital Review*, accessed 23 February 2017, www.humancapitalreview.com; Dave Mattson, "6 Benefits of Teamwork in the Workplace," Sandler Training, 19 February 2015, www.sandler.com; Edmund Lau, "Why and Where Is Teamwork Important?" *Forbes*, 23 January 2013, www.forbes.com; "Five Case Studies on Successful Teams," HR Focus, April 2002, 18; Max Landsberg and Madeline Pfau, "Developing Diversity: Lessons from Top Teams," *Strategy + Business*, Winter 2005, 10–12; "Groups Best at Complex Problems," *Industrial Engineer*, June 2006, 14.

5. Rob Cross, Reb Rebele, and Adam Grant, "Collaborative Overload," *Harvard Business Review*, January–February 2016, 74–79.

6. Thompson, *Making the Team: A Guide for Managers*, 34; Heidi K. Gardner, "Getting Your Stars to Collaborate," *Harvard Business Review*, January–February 2017, 100–108; Dave Winsborough and Tomas Chamorro-Premuzic, "Great Teams Are About Personalities, Not Just Skills," *Harvard Business Review*, 25 January 2017, www.hbr.org; Charles Duhigg, "What Google Learned From Its Quest to Build the Perfect Team," *New York Times Magazine*, 25 February 2016, www.nytimes.com; Martine Haas and Mark Mortensen, "The Secrets of Great Teamwork," *Harvard Business Review*, June 2016, 71–76.

7. Thompson, *Making the Team: A Guide for Managers*, 35–36.

8. Thompson, *Making the Team: A Guide for Managers*, 35–36.

9. Stephen P. Robbins and Mary Coulter, *Management*, 14th ed. (New York: Prentice Hall, 2018), 418–419; Denise Bonebright, "40 Years of Storming: A Historical Review of Tuckman's Model of Small Group Development," *Human Resource Development International* 13, no. 1 (February 2010): 111–120.

10. "Tuckman: Forming, Storming, Norming, Performing," *Consultant's Mind*, accessed 28 February 2018, www.consultantsmind.com.

11. Gregory Ciotti, "How Remote Teams Are Becoming the Future of Work," HelpScout, 23 April 2016, www.helpscout.com.

12. Mark Mortensen, "A First-Time Manager's Guide to Leading Virtual Teams," *Harvard Business Review*, 25 September 2017, hbr.org.

13. Rob Rawson, "21 Tips to Help You Manage a High-Performing Virtual Team," Time Doctor, accessed 1 March 2018, biz30.timedoctor.com.

14. Keith Ferrazzi, "Getting Virtual Teams Right," *Harvard Business Review*, December 2017, hbr.org.

15. "6 Communication Habits of Successful Teams," Crossover, 1 February 2017, blog.crossover.com.

16. "Adobe Connect Mobile," Adobe website, accessed 1 March 2018, www.adobe.com.

17. Parks Associates, "Mobile Collaborative Communications for Business," white paper, accessed 27 February 2014, www.parksassociates.com.

18. Bot My Work, accessed 1 March 2018, botmywork.com.

19. Ron Ashkenas, "Why We Secretly Love Meetings," *Harvard Business Review* blogs, 5 October 2010, blogs.hbr.org.

20. Douglas Kimberly, "Ten Pitfalls of Pitiful Meetings," *Payroll Manager's Report*, January 2010, 1, 11; "Making the Most of Meetings," *Journal of Accountancy*, March 2009, 22.

21. Cyrus Farivar, "How to Run an Effective Meeting," BNET website, accessed 12 August 2008, www.bnet.com.

22. "Better Meetings Benefit Everyone: How to Make Yours More Productive," *Working Communicator Bonus Report*, July 1998, 1.

23. Roger Schwarz, "5 Ways Meetings Get Off Track, and How to Prevent Each One," *Harvard Business Review*, 3 May 2016, www.hbr.org.

24. Renee Cullinan, "Run Meetings That Are Fair to Introverts, Women, and Remote Workers," *Harvard Business Review*, 29 April 2016, www.hbr.org.

25. Janine Popick, "Business Meeting Etiquette: 8 Pet Peeves," *Inc.*, 9 April 2012, www.inc.com.

26. MeetingSense, accessed 2 March 2018, www.meetingsense.com.

27. "Immersive TelePresence," Cisco, accessed 2 March 2018, www.cisco.com.

28. Jena McGregor, "'Star Wars' Meets the C-Suite: This CEO's Hologram Is Beaming Into Meetings," *Washington Post*, 13 April 2016, ww.washingtonpost.com.

29. Jitsi website, accessed 2 March 2018, jitsi.org.

30. Nancy Settle-Murphy, "Structuring Successful Virtual Meetings: A Counterintuitive Approach," *GuidedInsights*, accessed 2 March 2018, www.guidedinsights.com.

31. Beth Kanter, "9 Best Practices for Engagement in Virtual Meetings," Nonprofit Technology Network, 10 October 2017, www.nten.org.

32. Kanter, "9 Best Practices for Engagement in Virtual Meetings."

33. Paul Axtell, "What Everyone Should Know About Running Virtual Meetings," *Harvard Business Review*, 14 April 2016, hbr.org.

34. John Hollon, "No Tolerance for Jerks," *Workforce Management*, 12 February 2007, 34.

35. Christine Porath, "The Hidden Toll of Workplace Incivility," *McKinsey Quarterly*, December 2016, www.mckinsey.com.

36. Lisa Quast, "Office Etiquette: Tips to Overcome Bad Manners at Work," *Forbes*, 7 April 2014, www.forbes.com; Shannon Lee, "The New Office Etiquette: Rules for Today's Workplace," CareerBuilder, 11 September 2014, www.careerbuilder.com; Mariana Simoes, "17 Essential Office Etiquette Tips," *Business Insider*, 19 March 2013, www.businessinsider.com.

37. Jarie Bolander, "The 4 Types of Business Attire–The Where, When and How to Make Them Work," *The Daily MBA*, 21 March 2018, www.thedailymba.com.

38. Dana May Casperson, *Power Etiquette: What You Don't Know Can Kill Your Career* (New York: AMACOM, 1999), 10–14; Ellyn

Spragins, "Introducing Politeness," *Fortune Small Business*, November 2001, 30.

39. Susan Bryant, "Business Etiquette You Should Know," Monster, accessed 1 March 2018, www.monster.com.

40. Casperson, *Power Etiquette*, 44–46.

41. "Are You Practicing Proper Social Networking Etiquette?" *Forbes*, 9 October 2009, www.forbes.com; Pete Babb, "The Ten Commandments of Blog and Wiki Etiquette," *InfoWorld*, 28 May 2007, www.infoworld.com; Judith Kallos, "Instant Messaging Etiquette," NetM@nners blog, accessed 3 August 2008, www.netmanners.com; Michael S. Hyatt, "Email Etiquette 101," From Where I Sit blog, 1 July 2007, www.michaelhyatt.com.

42. Alan Cole, "Telephone Etiquette at Work," Work Etiquette website, 14 March 2012, www.worketiquette.co.uk; Alf Nucifora, "Voice Mail Demands Good Etiquette from Both Sides," *Puget Sound Business Journal*, 5–11 September 2003, 24; Ruth Davidhizar and Ruth Shearer, "The Effective Voice Mail Message," *Hospital Material Management Quarterly*, 45–49; "How to Get the Most Out of Voice Mail," *The CPA Journal*, February 2000, 11; Jo Ind, "Hanging on the Telephone," *Birmingham Post*, 28 July 1999, PS10; Larry Barker and Kittie Watson, *Listen Up* (New York: St. Martin's Press, 2000), 64–65; Lin Walker, *Telephone Techniques*, (New York: Amacom, 1998), 46–47; Dorothy Neal, *Telephone Techniques*, 2nd ed. (New York: Glencoe McGraw-Hill, 1998), 31; Jeannie Davis, *Beyond "Hello"* (Aurora, Col.: Now Hear This, Inc., 2000), 2–3; "Ten Steps to Caller-Friendly Voice Mail," *Managing Office Technology*, January 1995, 25; Rhonda Finniss, "Voice Mail: Tips for a Positive Impression," *Administrative Assistant's Update*, August 2001, 5.

43. Dawn Rosenberg McKay, "Rules for Using Cell Phones at Work," *The Balance*, 25 October 2016, www.thebalance.com; J. J. McCorvey, "How to Create a Cell Phone Policy," *Inc.*, 10 February 2010, www.inc.com; "Use Proper Cell Phone Etiquette at Work," Kelly Services website, accessed 11 June 2010, www.kellyservices.us.

44. Nick Wingfield, "Oh, for the Good Old Days of Rude Cellphone Gabbers," *New York Times*, 2 December 2011, www.nytimes.com.

45. Cromwell Schubarth, "VC Ben Horowitz on What He Wants in a Startup and Why Rap Genius Is It," *Silicon Valley Business Journal*, 4 February 2014, www.bizjournals.com.

Five-Minute Guide to Better Business Meetings

Review these five points whenever you are thinking about hosting a business meeting.

00:01 **What is the purpose of this meeting?**

1. Do you want to exchange information, reach a decision, or collaborate on a problem or an opportunity?
2. Describe the best possible outcome of the meeting; use this description to plan the agenda.
3. If you can't describe the purpose of the meeting in a single sentence, you need to refine your plan before you move forward.

00:02 **Who should attend?**

1. If you can control the attendee list, invite everyone who really needs to be involved, and don't invite anyone who doesn't.
2. Meetings with more than 10 or 12 people can become unmanageable if everyone is expected to participate in the discussion and decision-making.

00:03 **Can you configure the meeting space?**

1. Conference room layout is ideal for small meetings and working sessions, and it works for small presentations as well.
2. The U-shape is ideal for mid-sized meetings, working sessions, and presentations. It promotes speaker interaction and supports conversation among attendees.
3. Theater/auditorium style is best for large audiences, but it limits interaction and makes it difficult for audiences to work with documents or devices unless chairs include desk surfaces.
4. Classroom style, with attendees sitting at tables facing the speaker, is a good alternative to theater/auditorium style when you want to give participants more work surface.
5. The breakout session format with small teams around individual tables is good for working meetings or seminars in which you ask the audience to split into groups.

00:04 **Prepare the agenda and plan ahead to record minutes**

1. A good agenda answers three questions:
   a. What do we need to do in this meeting to accomplish our goals?
   b. What issues will be of greatest importance to all participants?
   c. What information must be available to discuss these issues?
2. Consider creating a simpler presentation agenda in addition to the detailed planning agenda.
3. Prepare any prestudy materials that attendees should have ready in order to be ready to participate.
4. Make provisions for someone to take notes and distribute minutes after the meeting.

00:05 **Tips for planning and leading virtual meetings**

1. Make sure the meeting has a well-defined task, so that it steadily moves toward a goal.
2. Provide prestudy materials so everyone is up to speed before the meeting starts.
3. Assign people to specific roles, such as a technical specialist to help with connectivity problems and someone to record the minutes.
4. If the participants don't know each other, introduce them or ask them to introduce themselves.
5. As you work through each agenda item, summarize what has been discussed and ask if anyone has questions or comments.
6. Periodically check in with each person, if feasible, to make sure there are no lingering questions or points of disagreement.

Communication Challenges in a Diverse, Global Marketplace

LEARNING OBJECTIVES

After studying this chapter, you will be able to

1 Discuss the opportunities and challenges of intercultural communication.

2 Define cultural competency, and explain the influence of culture on business communication.

3 Explain the importance of recognizing cultural variations, and list eight key dimensions of cultural diversity.

4 List four general guidelines for adapting to any business culture.

5 Identify six steps you can take to improve your intercultural communication skills.

MyLab Business Communication

If your instructor is using MyLab Business Communication, visit **www.pearson.com/mylab/business-communication** for videos, simulations, and writing exercises.

ON THE JOB: COMMUNICATING AT
KAISER PERMANENTE

Finding Strength and Opportunity in a Diverse Marketplace

Delivering quality health care is difficult enough, given the complexities of technology, government regulations, evolving scientific and medical understanding, and the variability of human performance. It gets even more daunting when you add the challenges of communication among medical staff and between patients and their caregivers, which often takes place under stressful circumstances. Those communication efforts are challenging enough in an environment where everyone speaks the same language and feels at home in a single cultural context — but they're infinitely more complex in the United States, whose residents identify with dozens of different cultures and speak several hundred languages.

The Oakland-based health-care system Kaiser Permanente has been embracing the challenges and opportunities of diversity since its founding in 1945. It made a strong statement with its very first hospital when it refused to follow the then-common practice of segregating patients by race. Now, as the largest

REUTERS/Mario Anzuoni

Kaiser Permanente CEO Bernard J. Tyson believes a culturally competent workforce is essential to the health provider's aim of serving the diverse U.S. population.

not-for-profit health system in the United States, Kaiser has a client base that includes 12 million members from over 100 distinct cultures.

At the core of Kaiser's approach is *culturally competent care*, which it defines as "health care that acknowledges cultural diversity in the clinical setting, respects members' beliefs and practices, and ensures that cultural needs are considered and respected at every point of contact." These priorities are woven into Kaiser's organizational culture, structure, and business practices.

Delivering this standard of care requires a mix of skills and knowledge that range from an awareness of medical issues of concern to specific cultures to language fluency (and translation skills in more than 100 languages) to the awareness needed to handle cultural traditions and values in a sensitive manner. Kaiser's Centers of Excellence in Culturally Competent Care at facilities around the country are a good example of the extent the company goes to in order to serve its diverse clientele. Each

center focuses on one or more cultures prominent in a given locale, with a particular emphasis on improving care outcomes for population segments that have historically been underserved.

Kaiser believes that effectively serving a diverse client base requires an equally diverse staff. As chairman and CEO Bernard J. Tyson explains, "The rich diversity of our organization reflects the diversity of the people we serve each and every day." Nearly half of the executive team members are women, for example, and people of color make up nearly 60 percent of the company's workforce.

In addition to helping Kaiser communicate more effectively with its customers, the strategic emphasis on diversity and inclusion is good for business. Its target market segments also happen to be among the country's fastest-growing demographic groups, and Kaiser's ability to connect with these audiences gives it an important competitive advantage.[1]

HEALTHY.KAISERPERMANENTE.ORG

Understanding the Opportunities and Challenges of Communication in a Diverse World

1 **LEARNING OBJECTIVE** Discuss the opportunities and challenges of intercultural communication.

Kaiser Permanente (profiled in the chapter-opening On the Job) illustrates the opportunities and the challenges for business professionals who know how to communicate with diverse audiences. Although the concept is often framed in terms of race or gender, a broader and more useful definition of **diversity** includes "all the characteristics and experiences that define each of us as individuals."[2] Some aspects of diversity, such as race and age, are inherent. Others, such as work history, language, religion, cultural immersion, and education, are acquired through life experience.[3] Together, these characteristics and experiences can have a profound effect on the way businesspeople communicate.

Diversity includes all the characteristics that define people as individuals.

Intercultural communication is the process of sending and receiving messages between people whose cultural backgrounds could lead them to interpret verbal and nonverbal signs differently. Every attempt to send and receive messages is influenced by culture, so to communicate successfully, you need a basic grasp of the cultural differences you may encounter and how you should handle them. Efforts to recognize and bridge cultural differences will open up business opportunities throughout the world and maximize the contributions of all the employees in a diverse workforce.

Intercultural communication is the process of sending and receiving messages between people whose cultural backgrounds could lead them to interpret verbal and nonverbal signs differently.

THE OPPORTUNITIES IN A GLOBAL MARKETPLACE

Chances are good that you'll be working across international borders sometime in your career. Thanks to communication and transportation technologies, natural boundaries and national borders are no longer the impassable barriers they once were. Local markets are opening to worldwide competition as businesses of all sizes look for new growth opportunities outside their own countries. Thousands of U.S. businesses depend on exports for significant portions of their revenues. If you work in one of these companies, you may well be called on to visit or at least communicate with a wide variety of people who speak languages other than English and who live in cultures quite different from what you're used to.

You will communicate with people from many other cultures throughout your career.

Not surprisingly, effective communication is important to cross-cultural and global business. In one survey, nearly 90 percent of executives said their companies' profits, revenue, and market share would all improve with better international communication skills.

In addition, half of these executives said communication or collaboration breakdowns had affected major international business efforts in their companies.[4] The good news here is that improving your cultural communication skills could make you a more valuable job candidate at every stage of your career.

THE ADVANTAGES OF A DIVERSE WORKFORCE

Diversity brings distinct advantages to businesses:

- A wider range of viewpoints
- A better understanding of diverse, fragmented markets
- A broader pool of talent from which to recruit

Even if you never visit another country or transact business on a global scale, you will interact with colleagues from a variety of cultures, with a wide range of characteristics and life experiences. Over the past few decades, many innovative companies have changed the way they approach diversity, from seeing it as a legal requirement (providing equal opportunities for all) to seeing it as a strategic opportunity. Smart business leaders recognize the competitive advantages of a diverse workforce that offers a broader spectrum of viewpoints and ideas, helps businesses understand and identify with diverse markets, and enables companies to benefit from a wider range of employee talents.[5] Numerous studies show a correlation between company performance and workforce diversity.[6]

Diversity is simply a fact of life for all companies. The United States has been a nation of multiple races, ethnicities, and national origins from the beginning, and that trend continues today. The western and northern Europeans who made up the bulk of immigrants during the nation's early years now share space with people from across Asia, Africa, Eastern Europe, South America, and other parts of the world.

REAL-TIME UPDATES

LEARN MORE BY VISITING THIS WEBSITE

Looking for jobs at diversity-minded companies?

DiversityWorking.com connects job searchers with companies that recognize the value of diverse workforces. Go to **real-timeupdates.com/ebc13** and select Learn More in the Students section.

THE CHALLENGES OF INTERCULTURAL COMMUNICATION

A company's cultural diversity affects how its business messages are conceived, composed, delivered, received, and interpreted.

Today's increasingly diverse workforce encompasses a wide range of skills, traditions, backgrounds, experiences, outlooks, and attitudes toward work—all of which can affect communication in the workplace. Supervisors face the challenge of connecting with these diverse employees, motivating them, and fostering cooperation and harmony among them. Teams face the challenge of working together closely, and companies are challenged to coexist peacefully with business partners and with the community as a whole.

Culture influences everything about communication, including

- Language
- Nonverbal signals
- Word meaning
- Time and space issues
- Rules of human relationships

The interaction of culture and communication is so pervasive that separating the two is virtually impossible. The way you communicate is deeply influenced by the culture in which you were raised. The meaning of words, the significance of gestures, the importance of time and space, the rules of human relationships—these and many other aspects of communication are defined by culture. To a large degree, your culture influences the way you think, which naturally affects the way you communicate as both a sender and a receiver.[7] Intercultural communication is much more complicated than simply matching language between sender and receiver; it goes beyond words to beliefs, values, and emotions.

Your instinct is to encode messages using the assumptions of *your* culture, but members of your audience decode messages according to the assumptions of *their* culture.

Elements of human diversity can affect communication at every stage of the communication process, from the ideas a person deems important enough to share to the habits and expectations of giving feedback. In particular, your instinct is to encode messages using the assumptions of *your* culture. However, members of your audience decode your messages according to the assumptions of *their* culture. Thinking back to Figure 1.6's illustration of how shared experience affects understanding, you can see how the farther two cultures are apart, the more challenging it can be to transfer messages and meaning successfully.

Throughout this chapter, you'll see examples of how communication styles and habits vary from one culture to another. These examples are intended to illustrate the major themes of intercultural communication, not to give an exhaustive list of styles and habits of any particular culture. With an understanding of these major themes, you'll be prepared to explore the specifics of any culture.

Developing Cultural Competency

2 LEARNING OBJECTIVE
Define cultural competency, and explain the influence of culture on business communication.

Cultural competency includes an appreciation for cultural differences that affect communication and the ability to adjust one's communication style to ensure that efforts to send and receive messages across cultural boundaries are successful. In other words, it requires a combination of attitude, knowledge, and skills.[8]

The good news is that you're already an expert in culture, at least in the culture in which you grew up. You understand how your society works, how people are expected to communicate, what common gestures and facial expressions mean, and so on. The bad news is that because you're such an expert in your own culture, your communication is largely automatic; that is, you rarely stop to think about the communication rules you're following. An important step toward successful intercultural communication is becoming more aware of these rules and of the way they influence your communication.

Cultural competency includes appreciation for cultural differences that affect communication and the ability to adjust one's communication style to match the situation.

UNDERSTANDING THE CONCEPT OF CULTURE

Culture is a shared system of symbols, beliefs, attitudes, values, expectations, and norms for behavior. All people belong to multiple cultures that influence their beliefs and behaviors to varying degrees. In addition to the culture you share with all the people who live in your own country, you belong to other cultural groups, sometimes referred to as *subcultures*, including an ethnic group, possibly a religious group, maybe a political party, and perhaps a profession that has its own special language and customs. With its large population and long history of immigration, the United States is home to a vast array of cultures.

Culture is a shared system of symbols, beliefs, attitudes, values, expectations, and behavior norms.

Members of a given culture tend to have similar assumptions about how people should think, behave, and communicate, and they tend to act on those assumptions in much the same way. Cultures can vary in their rate of change, degree of complexity, and tolerance toward outsiders. These differences affect the level of trust and openness you can achieve when communicating with people of other cultures.

People learn culture directly and indirectly from other members of their group. As you grow up in a culture, you are taught by the group's members who you are and how best to function in that culture. Sometimes you are explicitly told which behaviors are acceptable; at other times you learn by observing which values work best in a particular group. Over time, the influences of that culture become automatic, in that you follow them without thinking about them.

You learn culture both directly (by being instructed) and indirectly (by observing others).

In addition to being automatic, culture tends to be *coherent*; that is, a culture appears to be fairly logical and consistent when viewed from the inside. Certain norms within a culture may not make sense to someone outside the culture, but they probably make sense to those inside. Such coherence generally helps a culture function more smoothly internally, but it can create disharmony between cultures that don't view the world in the same way.

Cultures tend to offer views of life that are both *coherent* (internally logical) and *complete* (able to answer all of life's big questions).

Finally, cultures tend to be complete in the sense that they provide their members with most of the answers to life's big questions. This idea of completeness dulls or even suppresses curiosity about life in other cultures. Not surprisingly, such completeness can complicate communication with other cultures.[9]

OVERCOMING ETHNOCENTRISM AND STEREOTYPING

Ethnocentrism is the tendency to judge other groups according to the standards, behaviors, and customs of one's own group. Given the automatic influence of one's own culture, when people compare their culture to others, they often conclude that their own is superior.[10] An even more extreme reaction is **xenophobia**, a fear of strangers and foreigners. Clearly, businesspeople who take these views are not likely to communicate successfully across cultures.

Distorted views also result from **stereotyping**, which is assigning a wide range of generalized attributes to an individual on the basis of membership in a particular culture or social group. For instance, assuming that an older colleague will be out of touch with the youth market or that a younger colleague can't be an inspiring leader would be stereotyping based on age groups.

Ethnocentrism is the tendency to judge all other groups according to the standards, behaviors, and customs of one's own group.

Xenophobia is a fear of strangers and foreigners.

Stereotyping is assigning generalized attributes to an individual on the basis of membership in a particular group.

Cultural pluralism is the acceptance of multiple cultures on their own terms.

You can avoid ethnocentrism and stereotyping by avoiding assumptions, withholding judgment, and accepting differences.

Those who want to show respect for others and to communicate effectively in business need to adopt a more positive viewpoint, in the form of **cultural pluralism**—the practice of accepting multiple cultures on their own terms. A few simple habits can help:

- **Avoid assumptions.** Don't assume that others will act the same way you do, use language and symbols the same way you do, or even operate from the same values and beliefs. In other words, you need to consciously resist the automatic impulses from your own culture.
- **Avoid judgments.** When people act differently, don't conclude that they are in error or that their way is invalid or inferior. As with assumptions, avoiding judgment requires conscious effort, such as not letting someone's appearance or accent influence your perceptions.[11]
- **Acknowledge distinctions.** Don't ignore the differences between another person's culture and your own.

Unfortunately, overcoming ethnocentrism and stereotyping is not a simple task, even for people who are highly motivated to do so. Moreover, research suggests that people often have beliefs and biases they're not even aware of—and that may even conflict with the beliefs they *think* they have.[12]

3 LEARNING OBJECTIVE
Explain the importance of recognizing cultural variations, and list eight key dimensions of cultural diversity.

Recognizing Variations in a Diverse World

You can begin to learn how people in other cultures want to be treated by recognizing and accommodating eight main types of cultural differences: contextual, legal and ethical, social, nonverbal, age, gender, religious, and ability (see Figure 4.1).

CONTEXTUAL DIFFERENCES

Cultural context is the pattern of physical cues, environmental stimuli, and implicit understanding that conveys meaning between members of the same culture.

Every attempt at communication occurs within a **cultural context**, which is the pattern of physical cues, environmental stimuli, and implicit understanding that convey meaning between two members of the same culture. Cultures around the world vary widely in the role that context plays in communication.

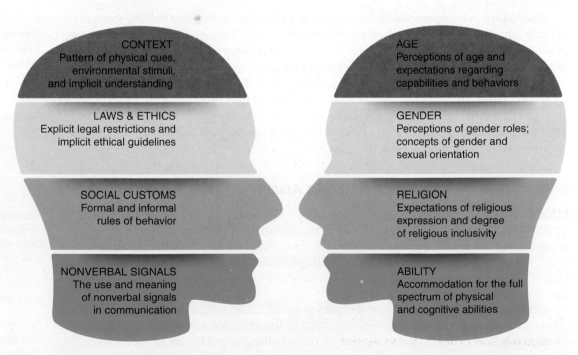

Figure 4.1   Major Dimensions of Cultural Diversity
Here are eight of the most significant variables that define any culture and can create differences between cultures.

In a **high-context culture**, people rely less on verbal communication and more on the context of nonverbal actions and environmental setting to convey meaning. For instance, a Chinese speaker expects the receiver to discover the essence of a message and uses indirectness and metaphor to provide a web of meaning.[13] The indirect style can be a source of confusion during discussions with people from low-context cultures, who are more accustomed to receiving direct answers. Also, in high-context cultures, the rules of everyday life are rarely explicit; instead, as individuals grow up, they learn how to recognize situational cues (such as gestures and tone of voice) and how to respond as expected.[14] The primary role of communication in high-context cultures is building relationships, not exchanging information.[15]

A high-context culture relies heavily on nonverbal actions and environmental setting to convey meaning.

In a **low-context culture** such as the United States, people rely more on verbal communication and less on circumstances and cues to convey meaning. In such cultures, rules and expectations are usually spelled out through explicit statements such as "Please wait until I'm finished" or "You're welcome to browse."[16] The primary task of communication in low-context cultures is exchanging information.[17]

A low-context culture relies more on explicit verbal communication.

Contextual differences are apparent in the way businesspeople approach situations such as decision-making, problem solving, negotiating, interacting among levels in the organizational hierarchy, and socializing outside the workplace.[18] For instance, in low-context cultures, businesspeople tend to focus on the results of the decisions they face, a reflection of the cultural emphasis on logic and progress (for example, "Will this be good for our company? For my career?"). In comparison, higher-context cultures emphasize the means or the method by which a decision will be made. Building or protecting relationships can be as important as the facts and information used in making the decisions.[19] Consequently, negotiators working on business deals in such cultures may spend most of their time together building relationships rather than hammering out contractual details.

Contextual differences influence the way businesspeople approach situations such as decision-making, problem solving, and negotiating.

The distinctions between high and low context are generalizations, of course, but they are important to keep in mind as guidelines. Communication tactics that work well in a high-context culture may backfire in a low-context culture, and vice versa.

REAL-TIME UPDATES

LEARN MORE BY WATCHING THIS VIDEO

Bridging high- and low-context cultures

Invest time in relationship building to reach across cultures. Go to **real-timeupdates.com/ebc13** and select Learn More in the Students section.

LEGAL AND ETHICAL DIFFERENCES

Cultural context influences legal and ethical behavior, which in turn can affect communication. For example, the meaning of business contracts can vary from culture to culture. Whereas a manager from a U.S. company would tend to view a signed contract as the end of the negotiating process, with all the details resolved, his or her counterpart in many Asian cultures might view the contract as more fluid, and continued renegotiation is common.[20]

Cultural context influences legal and ethical behavior, which in turn can affect communication.

As you conduct business around the world, you'll find that both legal systems and ethical standards differ from culture to culture. An enduring dilemma for many companies, for example, is the question of making payments to government officials in order to secure contracts in some countries. While the practice is so common in some locations that it's considered a standard way of doing business, paying bribes is generally illegal for U.S. companies under the Foreign Corrupt Practices Act.[21]

SOCIAL NORMS AND CUSTOMS

The nature of social behavior varies among cultures, sometimes dramatically. Some behavioral rules are formal and specifically articulated (table manners are a good example), whereas others are informal and learned over time (such as the comfortable distance to stand from a colleague during a discussion). The combination of formal and informal rules influences the overall behavior of most people in a society most of the time. Social norms can vary from culture to culture in the following areas:

- **Attitudes toward work and success.** In the United States, for instance, a widespread view is that material comfort earned by individual effort is a sign of superiority and that people who work hard are better than those who don't.

Respect and rank are reflected differently from culture to culture in the way people are addressed and in their working environment.

- **Roles and status.** Culture influences the roles people play, including who communicates with whom, what they communicate, and in what way. Countries and cultures vary widely regarding social status, both in the perceptions of different social classes and the respect one is expected to show to those of a different class. Attitudes toward the role of women in business also vary considerably from country to country.[22]

The rules of polite behavior vary from country to country.

- **Use of manners.** What is polite in one culture may be considered rude in another. For instance, asking a colleague "How was your weekend?" is a common way of making small talk in the United States, but the question sounds intrusive to people in cultures in which business and private lives are seen as separate spheres.

Attitudes toward time, such as strict adherence to meeting schedules, can vary throughout the world.

- **Concepts of time.** People in low-context cultures see time as a way to plan the business day efficiently, often focusing on only one task during each scheduled period and viewing time as a limited resource. However, people from high-context cultures often see time as more flexible. Meeting a deadline is less important than building a business relationship.[23]

- **Future orientation.** Successful companies tend to have a strong *future orientation*, planning for and investing in the future, but national cultures around the world vary widely in this viewpoint. Some societies encourage a long-term outlook that emphasizes planning and investing—making sacrifices in the short term for the promise of better outcomes in the future. Others are oriented more toward the present, even to the point of viewing the future as hopelessly remote and not worth planning for.[24]

Cultures around the world exhibit varying degrees of openness toward both outsiders and people whose personal identities don't align with prevailing social norms.

- **Openness and inclusiveness.** At the national level as well as within smaller groups, cultures vary on how open they are to accepting people from other cultures and people who don't appear to fit the prevailing norms within the culture. An unwillingness to accommodate others can range from outright exclusion to subtle pressures to conform to majority expectations.

These social customs affect how people behave in the workplace, and differences can create communication problems. For instance, the French cosmetics company L'Oréal trains its global workforce in a standardized approach to conflict management that encourages employees to express disagreement and share competing ideas. In the beginning, this style felt unnatural for its Chinese employees, whose culture discouraged open debate, but they grew to appreciate the advantages of the approach.[25]

Understanding the nuances of social customs takes time and effort, but most businesspeople are happy to explain the habits and expectations of their culture. Plus, they will view your curiosity as a sign of respect.

NONVERBAL COMMUNICATION

As Chapter 2 notes, nonverbal communication can be a helpful guide to determining the meaning of a message—but this holds true only if the sender and receiver assign the same meaning to nonverbal signals. For instance, the simplest hand gestures have different meanings in different cultures. Gestures you may have been using in the United States all your life, such as giving someone a thumbs up to indicate agreement or making a circle with your thumb and index finger to say "OK" have different and sometimes extremely rude meanings in other cultures.[26] If you will be visiting another country or hosting a visitor to your country, do some quick research about acceptable gestures to avoid embarrassing mistakes.

The meaning of nonverbal signals can vary widely from culture to culture, so you can't rely on assumptions.

When you have the opportunity to interact with people in another culture, the best advice is to study the culture in advance and then observe the way people behave in the following areas:

Cultural norms influence the use of many nonverbal signals and behaviors:

- How people greet one another
- Respect for personal space
- Habits of touching
- Facial expressions
- Eye contact
- Posture
- Degree of formality

- **Greetings.** Do people shake hands, bow, or kiss lightly (on one side of the face or both)? Do people shake hands only when first introduced or every time they say hello or goodbye?

- **Personal space.** When people are conversing, do they stand closer together or farther away than you are accustomed to?

- **Touching.** Do people touch each other on the arm to emphasize a point or slap each other on the back to show congratulations? Or do they refrain from touching altogether? Some cultures are much more touch-oriented than others, but, as always, you must be careful to avoid forms of touch that can be misinterpreted as domineering or sexual in nature.

- **Facial expressions.** Do people smile at strangers, for example? This is common behavior in the United States, but it is not universal.
- **Eye contact.** Do people make frequent eye contact or avoid it? Frequent eye contact is often taken as a sign of honesty and openness in the United States, but in other cultures it can be a sign of aggressiveness or disrespect.
- **Posture.** Do people slouch and relax in the office and in public, or do they sit up and stand up straight?
- **Formality.** In general, does the culture seem more or less formal than yours?

Following the lead of people who grew up in the culture is a great way to learn and a good way to show respect as well.

AGE DIFFERENCES

The multiple generations within a culture present another dimension of diversity. Today's workplaces can have three, four, or even five generations working side by side. Each has been shaped by dramatically different world events, social trends, and technological advances, so it is not surprising that they often have different values, expectations, and communication habits. Table 4.1 lists the commonly designated generations in the U.S. population.

Be aware, however, that there are no official labels or year ranges for these generations. Over time, these have come into general use by population researchers and the news media. The only one of these used by the U.S. Census Bureau, for instance, is Baby Boomers. The labels and birth years shown in Table 4.1 are those used by the Pew Research Center, a leading independent research organization. (Pew is waiting for a consensus to emerge regarding a label for the post-Millennial generation.)[27]

When you hear statements about the beliefs and behaviors of a particular generation, always bear in mind that these are broad generalities. More than 70 million people in the United States alone fall in the Millennial designation, for instance, and any group that large is bound to have a wide range of beliefs and behaviors. In addition, the age ranges are not hard-and-fast boundaries in terms of human behavior. The first "Gen Xer" (born on January 1, 1965) doesn't automatically think and behave differently than the last Baby Boomer (born one day earlier on December 31, 1964).

In the workplace and in your communication activities, approach age as you would any other dimension of diversity: Resist the urge to make assumptions about an individual from another age group, and don't assume that your own group's approach is automatically superior.

> Every generation has been shaped by dramatically different world events, social trends, and technological advances.

> Commonly defined generations such as Millennials or Baby Boomers represent tens of millions of people in the United States alone, so don't interpret broad statements about any generation as universal truths.

GENDER DIFFERENCES

Gender influences workplace communication in several important ways. First, the perception of men and women in business varies from culture to culture, and gender bias can range from overt discrimination to subtle and even unconscious beliefs.

> The perception of men and women in business varies from culture to culture.

TABLE 4.1 Popularly Labeled Generations in the U.S. Population	
Label	**Birth Years**
Greatest Generation	1901–1927
Silent Generation	1928–1945
Baby Boomers	1946–1964
Generation X	1965–1980
Millennials	1981–1996
"Post-Millennials"	1997–

Source: Michael Dimock, "Defining Generations: Where Millennials End and Post-Millennials Begin," Pew Research Center, 1 March 2018, www.pewresearch.org.

Gender imbalances tend to get worse the further up the corporate ladder you look.

Second, although the ratio of men to women in entry-level professional positions is roughly equal, the percentage of management roles held by men increases steadily the further up the corporate ladder one looks. This imbalance can significantly affect communication in such areas as mentoring, which is a vital development opportunity for lower and middle managers who want to move into senior positions. For example, some men in executive positions express reluctance to mentor women, partly because they find it easier to bond with other men and partly out of concerns over developing relationships that might seem inappropriate.[28]

Broadly speaking, men tend to emphasize content in their messages, whereas women tend to emphasize relationship maintenance.

Third, evidence suggests that men and women tend to have somewhat different communication styles. Broadly speaking, men emphasize content and outcomes in their communication efforts, whereas women place a higher premium on relationship maintenance.[29] As one example, men are more likely than women to try to negotiate a pay raise. Moreover, according to research by Linda Babcock of Carnegie Mellon University, both men and women tend to accept this disparity, viewing assertiveness as a positive quality in men but a negative quality in women. Changing these perceptions could go a long way toward improving communication and equity in the workplace.[30]

Many people do not fit or wish to be fit into a simplistic heterosexual, male/female categorization scheme.

Fourth, outdated concepts of gender and sexual orientation continue to be a source of confusion, controversy, and discrimination. Many people do not fit or wish to be fit into a simplistic heterosexual, male/female categorization scheme, but discriminatory company policies and the behaviors and attitudes of supervisors and coworkers can deprive these individuals of a fair and satisfying work experience. In response, many companies have taken steps to ensure equal opportunities and fair treatment for lesbian, gay, bisexual, and transgender (LGBT) job applicants and employees. Companies can also take steps to make sure their nondiscrimination policies protect employees' right to gender expression based on personal gender identity.[31] Communication plays a critical role in all these efforts, from listening to the needs of diverse employee groups to providing clear policies and educating employees on important issues.

RELIGIOUS DIFFERENCES

U.S. law requires employers to accommodate employees' religious beliefs to a reasonable degree.

As one of the most personal and influential aspects of life, religion brings potential for controversy and conflict in the workplace setting. Many employees believe they should be able to follow and express the tenets of their faith in the workplace. In the United States, a variety of laws prohibit discrimination and harassment based on religion and require employers to make reasonable accommodations for religious beliefs and practices.[32]

However, efforts to accommodate religions can sometimes create conflict in the workplace and with the demands of operating the business. The situation is complex, with no simple answers that apply to every situation. As more companies work to establish inclusive workplaces, you can expect to see this issue being discussed more often in the coming years.

REAL-TIME UPDATES

LEARN MORE BY READING THIS ARTICLE

Legal aspects of religion in the workplace

Get an overview of the laws that govern religious expression in the workplace. Go to **real-timeupdates.com/ebc13** and select Learn More in the Students section.

ABILITY DIFFERENCES

Colleagues and customers with disabilities that affect communication represent an important aspect of the diversity picture. People whose hearing, vision, cognitive ability, or physical ability to operate digital devices or machinery is impaired can be at a significant disadvantage in today's workplace. As with other elements of diversity, success starts with respect for individuals and sensitivity to differences.

REAL-TIME UPDATES

LEARN MORE BY VISITING THIS WEBSITE

Consider a career in assistive technologies

Use these links to explore the many companies applying artificial intelligence, robotics, and other innovations in the field of assistive technologies. Go to **real-timeupdates.com/ebc13** and select Learn More in the Students section.

Employers can also invest in a variety of *assistive technologies* that help people with disabilities perform activities that might otherwise be difficult or impossible. These technologies include devices and systems that help workers communicate, interact with computers and other equipment, and enjoy greater mobility in the workplace. Artificial intelligence and robotics are enabling an exciting new generation of assistive technologies; see the Real-Time Updates Learn More on page 106 for links to companies in this field.

Assistive technologies help employers create more inclusive workplaces.

Adapting to Other Business Cultures

4 LEARNING OBJECTIVE
List four general guidelines for adapting to any business culture.

Whether you're trying to work productively with members of another generation in your own office or with a business partner on the other side of the world, adapting your approach is essential to successful communication. This section offers general advice on adapting to any business culture and specific advice for professionals from other cultures on adapting to U.S. business culture.

GUIDELINES FOR ADAPTING TO ANY BUSINESS CULTURE

You'll find a variety of tips in "Improving Intercultural Communication Skills," on page 108, but here are four general guidelines that can help all business communicators improve their cultural competency:

An important step in understanding and adapting to other cultures is to recognize the influences that your own culture has on your communication habits.

- **Become aware of your own biases.** Successful intercultural communication requires more than just an understanding of the other party's culture; you need to understand your own culture and the way it shapes your communication habits.[33] For instance, recognizing that you value independence and individual accomplishment will help you communicate more successfully in a culture that values consensus and group harmony.
- **Be careful about applying the "Golden Rule."** You probably heard this growing up: "Treat people the way you want to be treated." The problem with the Golden Rule is that other people don't always want to be treated the same way you want to be treated, particularly across cultural boundaries. A better approach: Treat people the way *they* want to be treated.

Ignore the Golden Rule; treat people the way *they* want to be treated, not the way *you* want to be treated.

- **Be accommodating and respectful, even if you don't understand or agree.** This can be an easy point to overlook in the rush of a business day, but cultural differences are in fact *different*. Being aware of differences is an essential first step, but it doesn't go far enough. Changing one's attitudes and behaviors to accommodate differences takes sustained effort and commitment.
- **Be patient and maintain a sense of humor.** Even the most committed and attuned business professionals can make mistakes in intercultural communication, so it is vital for all parties to be patient with one another. As business becomes ever more global, even people in the most tradition-bound cultures are learning to deal with outsiders more patiently and overlook occasional cultural blunders.[34] A sense of humor is a helpful asset as well, allowing people to move past awkward and embarrassing moments. When you make a mistake, simply apologize and, if appropriate, ask the other person to explain the accepted way; then move on.

Patience and a sense of humor can get you through most awkward moments in cross-cultural interaction.

GUIDELINES FOR ADAPTING TO U.S. BUSINESS CULTURE

If you are a recent immigrant to the United States or grew up in a culture outside the U.S. mainstream, you can apply all the concepts and skills in this chapter to adapt to U.S. business culture. Here are some key points to remember as you become accustomed to business communication in this country:

The values espoused by U.S. culture include individualism, equality, and privacy.

- **Individualism.** In contrast to cultures that value group harmony and group success, U.S. culture generally expects individuals to succeed by their own efforts, and it rewards individual success.[35] These reward mechanisms are not always fair, by any means, but individual reward remains an ideal. This emphasis on individual responsibility and reward can sometimes clash with the team orientation that many companies have.
- **Equality.** Although the country's historical record on equality has not always been positive and inequalities still exist, equality is considered a core American value. This principle applies to race, gender, social background, and even age. Americans generally

believe that every person should be given the opportunity to pursue whatever dreams and goals he or she has in life.

- **Privacy and personal space.** Although this appears to be changing somewhat with the popularity of social networking and other personal media, people in the United States are accustomed to a fair amount of privacy. This applies to physical space as well; U.S. businesspeople tend to stand farther apart when talking than people in a number of other cultures do, for example.[36]

- **Time and schedules.** U.S. businesses value punctuality and the efficient use of time. For instance, meetings are typically expected to start and end at designated times.

- **Religion.** The United States does not have an official state religion. Many religions are practiced throughout the country, and people are expected to respect each other's beliefs. Again, this respect and accommodation is more an ideal than universal practice, but it is an ideal nonetheless.

- **Communication style.** Communication tends to be direct and focused more on content and transactions than on relationships or group harmony.

As with all observations about culture, these are generalizations, of course. Any nation of more than 300 million people will exhibit a wide variety of behaviors. However, following these guidelines will help you succeed in most business communication situations.

Improving Intercultural Communication Skills

5 LEARNING OBJECTIVE
Identify six steps you can take to improve your intercultural communication skills.

Communicating successfully across cultures requires a variety of skills (see Figure 4.2). You can improve your intercultural skills throughout your career by studying other cultures and languages, respecting preferences for communication styles, writing clearly, speaking and listening carefully, knowing when to use interpreters and translators, and helping others adapt to your culture.

STUDYING OTHER CULTURES

Successful intercultural communication can require the modification of personal communication habits.

Effectively adapting your communication efforts to another culture requires not only knowledge about the culture but also the ability and motivation to change your personal habits as needed.[37] Fortunately, you don't need to learn about the whole world all at once. Many companies appoint specialists for countries or regions, giving employees a chance to focus on just one culture at a time. And if your employer conducts business internationally, it may offer training and support for employees who need to learn more about specific cultures.

Making an effort to learn about another person's culture is a sign of respect.

Even a small amount of research and practice will help you get through many business situations. In addition, most people respond positively to honest effort and good intentions, and many business associates will help you along if you show an interest in learning more about their cultures. Don't be afraid to ask questions. People will respect your concern and curiosity. You will gradually accumulate considerable knowledge, which will help you feel comfortable and be effective in a wide range of business situations.

Numerous websites and books offer advice on traveling to other countries and working in specific cultures. Also try to sample newspapers, magazines, and even the music and movies of another country. For instance, a movie can demonstrate nonverbal customs even if you don't grasp the language. However, be careful not to rely solely on entertainment products. If people in other countries based their opinions of U.S. culture only on the silly comedies and violent action movies that the United States exports around the globe, what sort of impression do you imagine they'd get?

For some of the key issues to research before doing business in another country, refer to Table 4.2 on page 110.

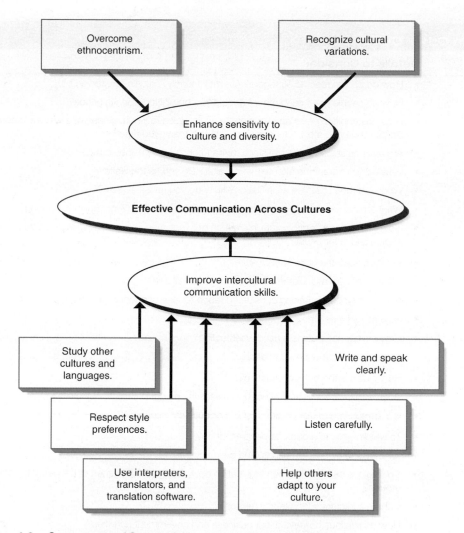

Figure 4.2 Components of Successful Intercultural Communication
Communicating in a diverse business environment is not always an easy task, but you can continue to improve your sensitivity and build your skills as you progress in your career.

STUDYING OTHER LANGUAGES

As commerce continues to become more globalized and many countries become more linguistically diverse, the demand for multilingual communicators continues to grow as well. The ability to communicate in more than one language can make you a more competitive job candidate and can open up a wider variety of career opportunities.

Even if your colleagues or customers in another country speak your language, it's worth the time and energy to learn common phrases in theirs. Doing so helps you get through everyday business and social situations and demonstrates your commitment to the business relationship. After all, the other person probably spent years learning your language.

Mobile devices can be a huge help in learning another language and in communicating with someone in another language. A wide variety of apps and websites are available that help with essential words and phrases, grammar, pronunciation, text translation, and even real-time audio translation (see Figure 4.3 on page 111).

Finally, don't assume that people from two countries who speak the same language speak it the same way. The French spoken in Québec and other parts of Canada is often noticeably different from the French spoken in France. Similarly, it's often said that the United States and the United Kingdom are two countries divided by a common language. For instance, *period* (punctuation), *elevator*, and *gasoline* in the United States are *full stop, lift,* and *petrol* in the United Kingdom.

Even if your colleagues or customers in another country speak your language, make the effort to learn some common phrases in theirs.

MOBILE APP
Memrise can help you learn new languages with the help of a world-wide community of fellow learners.

TABLE 4.2   Doing Business in Other Cultures

Action	Details to Consider
Understand social customs	• How do people react to strangers? Are they friendly? Hostile? Reserved? • How do people greet each other? Should you bow? Nod? Shake hands? • How do people express appreciation for an invitation to lunch, dinner, or someone's home? Should you bring a gift? Send flowers? Write a thank-you note? • Are any phrases, facial expressions, or hand gestures considered rude? • How do you attract the attention of a waiter? Do you tip the waiter? • When is it rude to refuse an invitation? How do you refuse politely? • What topics may or may not be discussed in a social setting? In a business setting? • How do social customs dictate interaction between men and women? Between younger people and older people?
Learn about clothing and food preferences	• What occasions require special attire? • What colors are associated with mourning? Love? Joy? • Are some types of clothing considered taboo for one gender or the other? • How many times a day do people eat? • How are hands or utensils used when eating? • Where is the seat of honor at a table?
Assess political patterns	• How stable is the political situation? • Does the political situation affect businesses in and out of the country? • Is it appropriate to talk politics in social or business situations?
Understand religious and social beliefs	• To which religious groups do people belong? • Which places, objects, actions, and events are sacred? • Do religious beliefs affect communication between men and women or between any other groups? • Is there a tolerance for minority religions? • How do religious holidays affect business and government activities? • Does religion require or prohibit eating specific foods? Eating at specific times?
Learn about economic and business institutions	• Is the society homogeneous or heterogeneous? • What languages are spoken? • What are the primary resources and principal products? • Are businesses generally large? Family controlled? Government controlled? • What are the generally accepted working hours? • How do people view scheduled appointments? • Are people expected to socialize before conducting business?
Appraise the nature of ethics, values, and laws	• Is money or a gift expected in exchange for arranging business transactions? • Do people value competitiveness or cooperation? • What are the attitudes toward work? Toward money? • Is politeness more important than factual honesty?

RESPECTING PREFERENCES FOR COMMUNICATION STYLE

Communication style—including the level of directness, the degree of formality, media preferences, and other factors—varies widely from culture to culture (see Figures 4.4a through 4.4d starting on page 112). Generally speaking, communication in many other cultures is more formal and less direct than it is in the United States, and politeness is valued highly.[38] To get up-to-date advice on communication with people in another country, search online for "French business correspondence," "German business correspondence," or whatever specific country you are interested in.

Communication in many other cultures is more formal and less direct than it is in the United States, and politeness is valued highly.

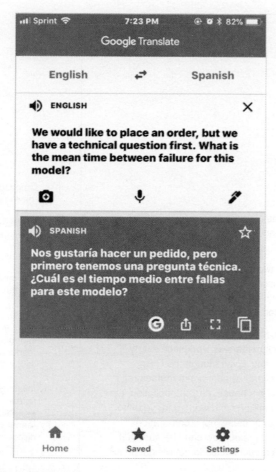

Figure 4.3 Mobile Language Tools
Translation apps are handy tools for working in multilingual business settings. Even if you don't speak a word of a particular language, you can get fast translations of essential phrases.

WRITING CLEARLY

Writing clearly is always important, of course, but it is essential when you are writing to people whose first language differs from yours. Follow these recommendations to make sure your message can be understood:

- **Chose words carefully.** Look for short, precise words that say exactly what you mean.
- **Avoid words with multiple meanings.** As much as possible, choose words that have only one obvious meaning in the context in which you're using them. For example, "right" has more than 30 distinct meanings and can function as a noun, an adjective, a verb, and an adverb.[39] Whenever it is appropriate, use a synonym that conveys the specific meaning you intend, such as *correct, appropriate, desirable, moral, authentic,* or *privilege*.[40]
- **Write short, clear sentences.** Restrict each sentence to a single idea so that anyone translating it can focus on a single thought while piecing the words together.
- **Keep paragraphs short.** Similarly, break information into smaller chunks that are easier for readers to process.
- **Use transitions generously.** Help readers follow your train of thought by using transitional words and phrases. For example, tie related points together with expressions such as *in addition* and *first, second,* and *third*.
- **Address international correspondence properly.** Refer to Appendix A for more information.
- **Cite numbers and dates in local formats.** Various countries use different formats for numbers and dates, so it's important to know what your readers expect. In the United

Clarity and simplicity are essential when writing to or speaking with people who don't share your native language.

REAL-TIME UPDATES
LEARN MORE BY READING THIS ARTICLE
Study the seven habits of effective intercultural communicators
The willingness to take risks is a key habit; see what the other six are. Go to **real-timeupdates.com/ebc13** and select Learn More in the Students section.

UpdraftRC
4308 Preston Highway
Louisville, KY 40213
Toll Free: 1.800.FLY.RITE
Fax: (502) 555-1324
www.updraftrc.com

Zhejiang Shan Tou Manufacturing Company, Ltd.
Guoliwei Industry Park
Libang Road, Longgang District
Shenzhen, Guangdong, China

Dear Mr. Li,

My company, Updraft RC, has designed a cool new line of radio-control toys that use smartphones as the controller. We are looking for a manufacturing partner, and your firm is one of the candidates we're having a look at.

> Language such as "cool" and "having a look at" is too informal for external business communication, particularly for international correspondence.

Before we discuss technical details, I must say I have two sets of concerns about working with a foreign manufacturer. The first involves all the usual—transportation costs, delays, quality control, and risk of intellectual property theft. I'll need some assurances on how you address these issues to make sure they don't become problems in our relationship.

> The tone of this paragraph is too demanding.

Second, companies here in the States that use foreign manufacturers often have to deal with heavy news coverage and activist publicity on such matters as workplace safety, worker rights, and environmentally sensitive manufacturing. Even though the U.S. company doesn't directly control what happens in the overseas contract manufacturer, the U.S. company takes the heat when the media uncovers abuse, neglect, pollution, etc. I know that Nike and other U.S. companies have spent millions and worked for years to promote positive conditions in overseas factories, but even these major corporations haven't been able to completely avoid problems and bad press. How can I be sure that a small company such as ours will? I do not want our product launch to get caught up in some scandal over "sweatshops."

> "Here in the States" is too informal, and referring to the reader as "foreign" is potentially insulting.

> Inflammatory language such as *bad press, scandal,* and *sweatshops* will put the reader on the defensive and discourage a positive response.

I look forward to seeing your comprehensive response as soon as possible.

> The request for a response sounds too demanding, and it lacks a specific deadline.

All the best,

Henry Gatlin

> The closing is too informal.

Henry Gatlin
Founder, CEO
Updraft RC

5 August 2020

Figure 4.4a   Intercultural Business Letter: Ineffective Original Draft
This letter (from a Kentucky company that designs radio-controlled airplanes) exhibits a number of problems that would create difficulties for its intended reader (the manager of a contract manufacturing company in China). Follow the changes in Figures 4.4b, 4.4c, and 4.4d to see how the letter was adapted and then translated for its target audience.

States, for example, 12-05-22 refers to December 5 in the year 2022, but in many other countries, it means May 12. Similarly, in the United States and Great Britain, 1.000 means one with three decimal places, but it means one thousand in many European countries.

When writing to someone who doesn't share your native language, avoid slang and *idiomatic phrases*—sayings that mean more than the sum of their literal parts.

- **Avoid slang and idiomatic phrases.** Slang and **idiomatic phrases**—sayings that mean more than the sum of their literal parts—usually don't travel well across languages. For instance, complimenting someone for a "killer idea" makes sense to many U.S. English speakers, but it would make very little sense to someone who knows only the literal meaning of the word "killer." Similarly, your audience may have no idea what you're talking about if you use "knocked one out of the park," "more bang for the buck," and other idiomatic phrases.

Humor does not "travel well" because it usually relies on intimate knowledge of a particular culture.

- **Generally, avoid humor and references to popular culture.** Jokes and references to popular entertainment often rely on culture-specific information that might be completely unknown to your audience.

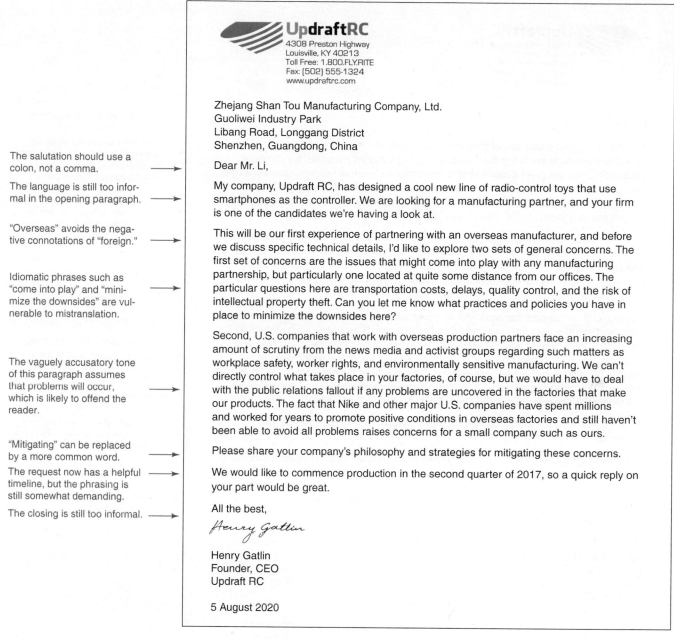

The salutation should use a colon, not a comma.

The language is still too informal in the opening paragraph.

"Overseas" avoids the negative connotations of "foreign."

Idiomatic phrases such as "come into play" and "minimize the downsides" are vulnerable to mistranslation.

The vaguely accusatory tone of this paragraph assumes that problems will occur, which is likely to offend the reader.

"Mitigating" can be replaced by a more common word.

The request now has a helpful timeline, but the phrasing is still somewhat demanding.

The closing is still too informal.

UpdraftRC
4308 Preston Highway
Louisville, KY 40213
Toll Free: 1.800.FLY.RITE
Fax: (502) 555-1324
www.updraftrc.com

Zhejang Shan Tou Manufacturing Company, Ltd.
Guoliwei Industry Park
Libang Road, Longgang District
Shenzhen, Guangdong, China

Dear Mr. Li,

My company, Updraft RC, has designed a cool new line of radio-control toys that use smartphones as the controller. We are looking for a manufacturing partner, and your firm is one of the candidates we're having a look at.

This will be our first experience of partnering with an overseas manufacturer, and before we discuss specific technical details, I'd like to explore two sets of general concerns. The first set of concerns are the issues that might come into play with any manufacturing partnership, but particularly one located at quite some distance from our offices. The particular questions here are transportation costs, delays, quality control, and the risk of intellectual property theft. Can you let me know what practices and policies you have in place to minimize the downsides here?

Second, U.S. companies that work with overseas production partners face an increasing amount of scrutiny from the news media and activist groups regarding such matters as workplace safety, worker rights, and environmentally sensitive manufacturing. We can't directly control what takes place in your factories, of course, but we would have to deal with the public relations fallout if any problems are uncovered in the factories that make our products. The fact that Nike and other major U.S. companies have spent millions and worked for years to promote positive conditions in overseas factories and still haven't been able to avoid all problems raises concerns for a small company such as ours.

Please share your company's philosophy and strategies for mitigating these concerns.

We would like to commence production in the second quarter of 2017, so a quick reply on your part would be great.

All the best,

Henry Gatlin

Henry Gatlin
Founder, CEO
Updraft RC

5 August 2020

Figure 4.4b   Intercultural Business Letter: First Revision
This version eliminates most of the problems with overly informal phrases and potentially offensive language. With these revisions, it would function well as a message between native speakers of English, but it still has some wording and formatting issues that could create difficulties for a Chinese reader. Compare with Figure 4.4c.

Figure 4.5 on page 116 shows how attention to these details can make a message much easier for readers whose native language is different from yours.

SPEAKING AND LISTENING CAREFULLY

Languages vary in the significance of tone, pitch, speed, and volume, which can create challenges for people trying to interpret the explicit meaning of words themselves as well as the overall nuance of a message. The English word *progress* can be a noun or a verb, depending on which syllable you emphasize. In Chinese, the meaning of the word *ma* changes depending on the speaker's tone; it can mean *mother, hemp, horse,* or *scold.*[41]

To ensure successful conversations between parties who speak different native languages or even regional variations of the same language, speakers and listeners alike need

MOBILE APP
iTranslate translates more than 100 languages and features voice input and output.

UpdraftRC
4308 Preston Highway
Louisville, KY 40213
Toll Free: 1.800.FLY.RITE
Fax: (502) 555-1324
www.updraftrc.com

Dear Mr. Li:

With the widespread adoption of mobile phones, more and more accessories and associated products are being developed to meet new market demands. My company, Updraft RC, has designed a new line of radio-controlled toys that use smartphones as the controller. Our market tests show strong potential for demand among younger consumers, who are often eager to try new products. We are now looking for a manufacturing partner, and we are very willing to collaborate with you.

This will be our first experience of partnering with an overseas manufacturer, and before we discuss specific technical details, I would like you to know two of our general concerns. The first concern involves all the general challenges of a long-distance manufacturing partnership, including transportation costs, shipping delays, quality control, and the risk of intellectual property theft.

Second, U.S. companies that work with overseas production partners face an increasing amount of scrutiny from the news media and activist groups regarding such matters as workplace safety, worker rights, and environmentally sensitive manufacturing. Nike and other major U.S. companies have spent millions of dollars and worked for years to improve conditions in overseas factories, but even they have not been able to avoid all problems. As a small company with no ability to monitor factories, we are worried about any manufacturing-related problems that could affect our public image.

Please share your company's philosophy and strategies for minimizing these two concerns.

We would like to commence production in the second quarter of 2017, so we would like to hear your reply as soon as possible.

Thank you,

Henry Gatlin

Henry Gatlin
Founder, CEO
Updraft RC

5 August 2020

> An inside address is typically not used in Chinese correspondence.

> The salutation uses a colon rather than a comma.

> The revised opening gives the reader some helpful context and the assurance that this is a meaningful business opportunity.

> The phrase "we are very willing to collaborate with you" shows respect for the reader and suggests the interest in forming a partnership.

> This paragraph has been shortened to eliminate the redundant request for information.

> This revised paragraph still conveys the seriousness of the writer's concerns without offending the reader.

> "Minimizing" is easier for a non-native speaker to understand than "mitigating."

> "Thank you" is a simple and adequately formal closing.

Figure 4.4c   Intercultural Business Letter: Final Revision
Here is the final English version, revised to ensure more successful translation into Chinese and to conform to standard practices in Chinese business communication (including removing the inside address).

To ensure successful conversations between parties who speak different native languages or even regional variations of the same language, speakers and listeners alike need to make accommodations.

To listen more effectively in intercultural situations, accept what you hear without judgment, and let people finish what they have to say.

to make accommodations.[42] Speakers should adjust the content of their messages and the style of their delivery to accommodate the needs of their listeners and the circumstances of the conversation. For example, if you are speaking in person or over a video connection, you can use hand gestures and other nonverbal signals to clarify your spoken message. However, when you don't have a visual connection, you must take extra care to convey your meaning through words and vocal characteristics alone. Conversely, listeners need to be tolerant of accents, vocabulary choices, gestures, and other factors that might distract them from hearing the meaning of a speaker's message.

When talking with people whose native language is different from yours, remember that the processing of even everyday conversations can be difficult. For instance, speakers from the United States sometimes string together multiple words into a single, mystifying pseudo-word, such as turning "Did you eat yet?" into "Jeetyet?" In spoken French, many word pairs are joined as a matter of rule, and the pronunciation can change depending

李华先生：

　　随着智能手机的普及，越来越多的配件和周边产品正在被研发以满足市场的需求。我们的公司，Updraft RC,已经设计了一种新型的用智能手机控制的遥控玩具。我们的市场测试表明年轻客户，一个愿意尝试新产品的群体，（对我们的产品）有巨大的潜在需求。我们现在正在寻找制造伙伴，所以我们非常愿意与你们合作。

　　这是我们第一次与海外制造伙伴合作，在我们讨论具细节之前，我非常愿意让你们知道我们的两个问题。第一个问题对远距制造商合作关系来说都是一个挑战，这个挑战包括运输费用，运输延迟，质量控制和知识产权盗窃。

　　第二，与大洋对岸合作的美国公司面临着越来越高的来自新媒体和活跃组织的审查。这些审查包括工作场所安全性，劳工权益和可能对环境产生损害的制造。耐克和其他主要的美国公司已经花费了数百万美元，工作了几十年用来提升海外工厂的情况，但是他们仍然不能避免所有的问题。对于没有能力监控（海外）工厂的小公司来说，我们比较当心与制造相关的一系列问题可能影响到我们公司的形象。

　　所以请让我们知道你们公司解决这两个问题的策略和方法。

　　我们计划在 2017 年的第二个季度投入产品的生产。所以我们希望尽快得到你们公司的回应。

　　　　　　　　　　　　　　　　　　　亨利 加特林
　　　　　　　　　　　　　　　　　　　创始人，首席执行官
　　　　　　　　　　　　　　　　　　　2020 年8月5日

Figure 4.4d **Intercultural Business Letter: Translated Version**
Here is the translated version, formatted in accordance with Chinese business communication practice.

on which words are next to one another. In these instances, listeners who aren't fluent in French can have a hard time telling when one word ends and the next one begins.

To be more effective in conversations with people from other language backgrounds, remember these tips: (1) Speak slowly and clearly; (2) don't rephrase until it's obviously necessary (immediately rephrasing something doubles the translation workload for the listener); (3) look for and ask for feedback to make sure your message is getting through; (4) don't talk down to the other person by overenunciating words or oversimplifying sentences to a degree that is potentially insulting; and (5) at the end of the conversation, double-check to make sure you and the listener agree on what has been said and decided.

As a listener, you'll need some practice to get a sense of vocal patterns. The key is simply to accept what you hear first, without jumping to conclusions about meaning or motivation. Let other people finish what they have to say. If you interrupt, you may miss something

To be more effective in intercultural conversations, remember these tips:

- Speak slowly and clearly
- Don't rephrase until it's obviously necessary
- Look for and ask for feedback
- Don't talk down to the other person
- Double-check to make sure you and the other party agree

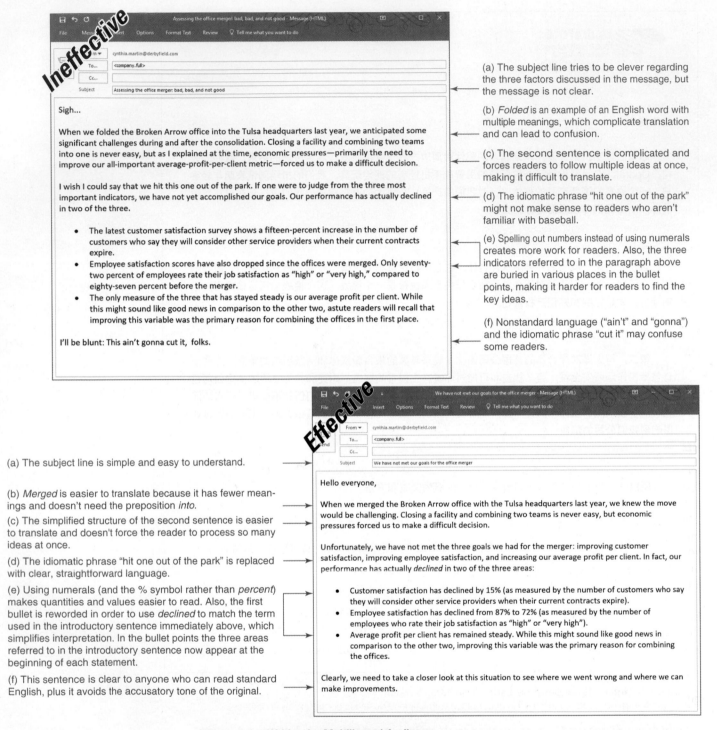

Figure 4.5 Writing for Multilingual Audiences

In today's global and diversified work environment, chances are that many of your messages will be read by people whose native language is not English. Notice how specific wording changes and modifications to sentence structure make the effective version easier for nonnative speakers to read.

important. You'll also show a lack of respect. If you do not understand a comment, ask the person to repeat it. Any momentary awkwardness you might feel in asking for extra help is less important than the risk of unsuccessful communication.

For important business meetings, consider using a professional interpreter.

For important meetings in which language might be a barrier, consider hiring an interpreter. The added expense could well be worth it to avoid misunderstandings and subtle language errors. The new generation of AI-enabled translating solutions can also be useful (see "Intelligent Communication Technology: Real-Time Translation").

INTELLIGENT COMMUNICATION TECHNOLOGY

Real-Time Translation

Trying to converse in a language in which you are not fully fluent presents a staggering cognitive workload. As a listener, you must convert the incoming sounds to discrete words and assemble those words into coherent phrases and sentences in order to extract the meaning—and if the other party uses idioms or slang, the task can get exponentially harder. And unlike reading a written document, you must do all this processing almost instantaneously, without the luxury of going back over something you didn't get. As a speaker, you have to find the right words, assemble them into phrases and sentences using the language's grammar rules, and then pronounce them all correctly enough so they make sense to the other party. Honing this level of proficiency can take years of study and practice.

Machine translation has been one of the long-standing goals of artificial intelligence, offering hope for real-time communication between people who don't have a common language. Systems such as Skype Translator and Google Translate are getting remarkably adept. Google's Pixel Buds ear buds offer nearly instantaneous translation across dozens of languages, so that it is theoretically possible to travel much of the world and converse with anyone who is similarly equipped, at least for basic conversations.

A variety of smartphone and smartwatch apps offer translation without the need for each party to have identical equipment; speakers take turns talking to the device, then listen as it outputs the translated speech. Microsoft's PowerPoint Presentation Translator adds real-time translation for presenters, making it easier for global professionals to connect with their audiences.

WHAT'S YOUR TAKE?

1. Do you think real-time translation, even if it gets close to the quality of human translators, will ever eliminate the need to learn other languages in order to communicate effectively with diverse, global audiences? Why or why not?

2. Find a partner who speaks another language and try one of these translation apps or services in a live conversation. How would you characterize the translation quality and the experience overall?

Sources: "Skype Translator," Skype, accessed 6 March 2018, www.skype.com; iTranslate Voice website, accessed 6 March 2018, itranslatevoice.com; "Presentation Translator, a Microsoft Garage Project," Microsoft, accessed 6 March 2018; Laura Cox, "Artificial Intelligence & Business Communication," *Disruption*, 22 May 2017, disruptionhub.com.

HELPING OTHERS ADAPT TO YOUR CULTURE

Everyone can contribute to successful intercultural communication. Whether a younger person is unaccustomed to the formalities of a large corporation or a colleague from another country is working on a team with you, look for opportunities to help people fit in and adapt their communication style. For example, if a nonnative English speaker is making mistakes that could hurt his or her credibility, you can offer advice on the appropriate words and phrases to use. Most language learners truly appreciate this sort of assistance, as long as it is offered in a respectful manner. Moreover, chances are that while you're helping, you'll learn something about the other person's culture and language, too.

Help others adapt to your culture; it will create a more productive workplace and teach you about their cultures as well.

You can also take steps to simplify the communication process. For instance, oral communication in a second language is usually more difficult than written forms of communication, so instead of asking a foreign colleague to provide information in a conference call, you could ask for a written response instead of or in addition to the live conversation.

For a brief summary of ideas to improve intercultural communication in the workplace, see "Checklist: Improving Intercultural Communication Skills." For additional information on communicating in a world of diversity, visit **real-timeupdates.com/ebc13** and select Chapter 4.

CHECKLIST ✔ Improving Intercultural Communication Skills

- ✔ Understand your own culture so that you can recognize its influences on your communication habits.
- ✔ Study other cultures so that you can appreciate cultural variations.
- ✔ Study the languages of people with whom you communicate, even if you can learn only a few basic words and phrases.
- ✔ Help nonnative speakers learn your language.
- ✔ Respect cultural preferences for communication style.
- ✔ Write clearly, using brief messages, simple language, generous transitions, and appropriate international conventions.
- ✔ Avoid slang, humor, and references to popular culture.
- ✔ Speak clearly and slowly, giving listeners time to translate your words.
- ✔ Ask for feedback to verify that communication was successful.
- ✔ Listen carefully and ask speakers to repeat anything you don't understand.

ON THE JOB: SOLVING COMMUNICATION DILEMMAS AT **KAISER PERMANENTE**

Kaiser Permanente puts a high priority on appreciating diversity and fostering a sense of inclusiveness among employees and patients. Imagine you're a department manager in a Kaiser medical center, where you're expected to support a climate of inclusion and support for employees of every cultural background. How would you address these challenges?

1. Joo Mi Kang, a recent immigrant from South Korea, is a gifted computer programmer who continues to impress with her technical skills. However, several other employees have mentioned to you in private that they are having trouble communicating with her. This surprises you, as you've never had any trouble communicating with her, and you know she is proficient at English. How should you respond?
   a. Send her an email reminding her of the need to communicate with colleagues; attach a copy of her job description.
   b. Give the situation time to resolve itself. Employees often need time to adjust when someone new joins the group.
   c. Ask Kang to describe the difficulties she is having with other employees and ask her why she thinks she is having trouble communicating.
   d. Ask the employees who have complained to describe the specific difficulties they are having. Evaluate their responses to see if there is something other than language getting in the way, such as an unwillingness among some employees to accept and accommodate a new team member.

2. Your employees are breaking into ethnically based cliques. Members of ethnic groups eat together, socialize together, and often chat in their native languages while they work. You appreciate how these groups give their members a sense of community, but you worry that these informal communication channels are alienating nonmembers and fragmenting the flow of information. How do you encourage a stronger sense of community and teamwork across your department?
   a. Ban the use of languages other than English at work.
   b. Do nothing. This is normal behavior, and any attempt to disrupt it will only generate resentment.
   c. Structure work assignments and other activities (such as volunteer projects) in ways that bring people from the various cultural groups into regular contact with one another and make them more dependent on one another as well.
   d. Send all your employees to diversity training classes.

3. Mihai Ciceu joined your department after relocating from Romania last year. He is a brilliant pricing and underwriting analyst, but he resists working with other employees, even in team settings where collaboration is expected. Given the importance that you place on teamwork, how should you handle the situation?
   a. Stay out of the way and let the situation resolve itself. Ciceu has to learn how to get along with the other team members.

   b. Tell the rest of the team to work harder at getting along with Ciceu.
   c. Tell Ciceu he must work with others or he will not progress in the company.
   d. Talk privately with Ciceu and help him understand the importance of working together as a team. During the conversation, try to uncover why he doesn't participate more in team efforts.

4. You've been surprised at the confusion that some of your memos and other written messages have generated lately. You suspect your casual and often humorous writing style might be the culprit and decide to "test drive" a different writing style. You've drafted four versions of a blog post that explains a new policy aimed at keeping projects on schedule as they near completion. Which of these do you choose and why?
   a. "As each new project nears completion, I recognize how hard you all try to keep projects on schedule, even with the last-minute problems that are always part of complicated projects. To lighten your workload during the hectic final phase, you'll no longer be expected to attend routine department meetings or tend to other nonessential tasks during the final weeks of each project."
   b. "As each new project races toward the finish line, I appreciate that all of you work like dogs to keep projects on schedule, even with the inevitable glitches and gremlins that always seem to attack projects at the last minute. Good news: During the last four weeks of every project, you'll be excused from nonessential tasks such as routine department meetings so that you can focus on your programming work (admit it—I know you hate coming to these meetings anyway!)."
   c. "As usual, the solution to all of life's problems can be found on television! While watching the Raiders–Chiefs game yesterday, I realized that we need to have our own version of the two-minute drill. To help avoid schedule slippage during the crazy final few weeks of each project, team members will be excused from routine meetings and other nonessential tasks not directly related to their project responsibilities."
   d. "As you should all be aware, numerous entities both internal and external to the corporation rely on us for timely project completion. While the inherent nature of complex projects presents unexpected difficulties during the final stages of a project, it is incumbent upon us to employ every tactic possible to avoid significant completion delays. Henceforth, team members will be excused from nonessential tasks during the final four weeks of every development project."

END OF CHAPTER

Learning Objectives Checkup

Assess your understanding of the principles in this chapter by reading each learning objective and studying the accompanying exercises. You can check your responses against the answer key on page 612.

Objective 4.1: Discuss the opportunities and challenges of intercultural communication.

1. Which of the following factors is a significant reason U.S. business professionals often need to understand the cultures of other countries?
   a. Recent changes to government regulations require cultural education before companies are granted export licenses.
   b. The U.S. economy has been shrinking for the past 20 years, forcing companies to look overseas.
   c. Many countries require business executives to be fluent in at least two languages.
   d. Thousands of U.S. companies, including many of the largest corporations in the country, rely on markets in other countries for a significant portion of their sales.

2. Why are message encoding and decoding a particular challenge in intercultural communication?
   a. Language barriers make it impossible to encode and decode messages successfully.
   b. Senders tend to encode messages using the habits and assumptions of their cultures, but receivers decode messages using the habits and assumptions of theirs.
   c. Senders and receivers never have the opportunity to verify whether their encoding and decoding were successful.
   d. Slang simplifies the decoding process.

3. A culturally rich workforce, composed of employees representing a wide range of ethnicities, religions, ages, physical abilities, languages, and other factors,
   a. always slows down the decision-making process.
   b. can be more challenging to manage but can pay off in a variety of important ways.
   c. is easier to manage because so many new ideas are present.
   d. is a concern only for companies that do business outside the United States.

Objective 4.2: Define cultural competency, and explain the influence of culture on business communication.

4. Cultural _____ includes an appreciation for cultural differences that affect communication and the ability to adjust one's communication style to ensure that efforts to send and receive messages across cultural boundaries are successful.

5. Culture is defined as
   a. any distinct group that exists within a country.
   b. a shared system of symbols, beliefs, attitudes, values, expectations, and norms for behavior.
   c. the pattern of cues and stimuli that convey meaning between two or more people.
   d. serious art forms such as classical music, painting, sculpture, drama, and poetry.

6. What do we mean when we say cultures tend to be coherent?
   a. They are easily understood.
   b. They are impossible for outsiders to truly understand.
   c. They appear to be fairly logical and consistent when viewed from the outside.
   d. They appear to be fairly logical and consistent when viewed from the inside.

7. _____ is the tendency to judge all other groups according to the standards, behaviors, and customs of one's own group.

8. _____ is the mistake of assigning a wide range of generalized attributes to individuals on the basis of their membership in a particular culture or social group, without considering an individual's unique characteristics.

9. Which of the following is one of several techniques you can use to make sure you don't fall into the traps of ethnocentrism and stereotyping?
   a. Minimize interactions with people whose cultures you don't understand.
   b. Make sure that the people you work with clearly understand your culture.
   c. Insist that every employee who works for you strictly follows the company's guidelines for intercultural communication.
   d. Avoid making assumptions about people in other cultures.

Objective 4.3: Explain the importance of recognizing cultural variations, and list eight key dimensions of diversity.

10. In business, recognizing cultural differences is important because
    a. doing so helps reduce the chances for misunderstanding.
    b. someone from another culture may try to take advantage of your ignorance.
    c. if you don't, you'll be accused of being politically incorrect.
    d. doing so helps you become more ethnocentric.

11. An example of low-context cultural communication would be
    a. someone using metaphors to convey meaning.
    b. someone insisting that the details of an agreement can be worked out later.
    c. someone explicitly laying out the details of a proposal, leaving nothing to chance or misinterpretation.
    d. someone encouraging socializing before entering into official negotiations.

12. Which of the following is generally true about high-context cultures?
    a. Employees work shorter hours in such cultures because context allows them to communicate less often.
    b. People rely less on verbal communication and more on the context of nonverbal actions and environmental setting to convey meaning.
    c. People rely more on verbal communication and less on the context of nonverbal actions and environmental setting to convey meaning.
    d. The rules of everyday life are explicitly taught to all people within the culture.

13. Which of these best characterizes nonverbal elements in intercultural communication?
    a. Nonverbal signals are universal, so they overcome the limitations of language.
    b. Nonverbal signals are unique to each culture, so they are of no help in intercultural communication.
    c. The meaning of certain nonverbal signals can differ from one culture to the next, so never assume you can use the same signals you use in your own culture.
    d. Nonverbal signals should always be worked out in advance so that the two parties in an exchange are sure of their meaning.

14. Why do different generations in the workplace sometimes have different values, expectations, and communication habits?
    a. Each generation has been shaped by dramatically different world events, social trends, and technological advances.
    b. Each new generation needs to distinguish itself from the one that came before.
    c. Older generations control all aspects of culture within a workplace.
    d. The English language evolves so rapidly that different generations end up with different communication styles.

Objective 4.4: List four general guidelines for adapting to any business culture.

15. Why is understanding your own culture an important step in learning to relate well with other cultures?
    a. Understanding your own culture is important because it helps you recognize biases that shape your communication habits.
    b. Understanding your own culture is important because it helps you identify the ways that other cultures are inferior (or at least might be inferior) to your own.
    c. Understanding your own culture is important because it helps you identify the ways that other cultures are superior (or at least might be superior) to your own.
    d. Understanding your own culture is not important when you are trying to reach out to other cultures.

16. What is wrong with the Golden Rule of treating others the way you want to be treated?
    a. Other people don't always want to be treated the same way you do, particularly people from other cultures.
    b. Business moves too quickly to deal with outdated notions like the Golden Rule.
    c. The distinguishing difference between any two cultures is that people in one culture never want to be treated the same as people in the other.

    d. The Golden Rule doesn't work in strict organizational hierarchies.

Objective 4.5: Identify six steps you can take to improve your intercultural communication skills.

17. When speaking with colleagues whose native language is different than yours, you should make it a habit to always
    a. immediately rephrase every important point you make to give your listeners two options to choose from.
    b. speak louder if listeners don't seem to understand you.
    c. ignore the other person's body language.
    d. rephrase your key points if you observe body language that suggests a lack of understanding.

18. Understanding the nuances of a culture can take years to learn, so the best approach when preparing to communicate with people in a culture that you don't know well is to
    a. learn as much as you can from websites, travel guides, and other resources and not be afraid to ask for help while you are communicating in that new culture.
    b. learn as much as you can from websites, travel guides, and other resources but never ask for help because doing so will only show everyone how ignorant you are.
    c. learn as much as you can from television shows and movies that feature the other culture; the combination of spoken words, visuals, and music is the best way to learn a culture.
    d. not worry about cultural variations; you'll never have time to understand them all, so your energy is better spent on other business issues.

19. Which of these is *not* listed in the chapter as a tip for speaking with people from other language backgrounds?
    a. Look for and ask for feedback.
    b. Don't rephrase a point until it's obviously necessary to do so.
    c. Always send your speech ahead as a written document so people can study it.
    d. Don't talk down to the other person by overenunciating words or oversimplifying sentences.

20. When you are writing for multilanguage audiences, humor and references to popular culture
    a. should be used often because it makes your audience feel welcome on a personal level.
    b. should generally be avoided because they often rely on cultural references that may be unknown to the audience.
    c. should never be used because movies and other entertainment products rarely cross over national boundaries.
    d. should be used at least once per letter to show that you appreciate your audience as human beings.

Key Terms

cultural competency An appreciation for cultural differences that affect communication and the ability to adjust one's communication style to ensure that efforts to send and receive messages across cultural boundaries are successful

cultural context The pattern of physical cues, environmental stimuli, and implicit understanding that convey meaning between two members of the same culture

cultural pluralism The practice of accepting multiple cultures on their own terms

culture A shared system of symbols, beliefs, attitudes, values, expectations, and norms for behavior

diversity All the characteristics and experiences that define people as individuals

ethnocentrism The tendency to judge other groups according to the standards, behaviors, and customs of one's own group

high-context culture Culture in which people rely less on verbal communication and more on the context of nonverbal actions and environmental setting to convey meaning

idiomatic phrases Phrases or common sayings that mean more than the sum of their literal parts; such phrases can be difficult for nonnative speakers to understand

intercultural communication The process of sending and receiving messages between people whose cultural backgrounds could lead them to interpret verbal and nonverbal signs differently

low-context culture Culture in which people rely more on verbal communication and less on circumstances and nonverbal cues to convey meaning

stereotyping Assigning generalized attributes to an individual on the basis of membership in a particular culture or social group

xenophobia Fear of strangers and foreigners

Apply Your Knowledge

To review chapter content related to each question, refer to the indicated Learning Objective.

4-1. Make a list of the top five priorities in your life (for example, fame, wealth, family, spirituality, peace of mind, individuality, artistic expression). Compare your list with the priorities that appear to be valued in the culture in which you are currently living. (You can be as broad or as narrow as you like in defining *culture* for this exercise, such as overall U.S. culture or the culture in your college or university.) [LO-2]

4-2. Do the priorities in your list align with the culture's priorities? If not, how might this disparity affect your communication with other members of the culture? [LO-2]

4-3. How does making an effort to avoid assumptions contribute to the practice of cultural pluralism? [LO-3]

4-4. Why is it important to understand your own culture when attempting to communicate with people from other cultures? [LO-4]

4-5. Think about the last three movies or television shows set in the United States that you've watched. In what ways would these entertainment products be helpful or unhelpful for people from other countries trying to learn about U.S. culture? [LO-5]

4-6. How can helping someone adapt to your culture help you gain a better understanding of it yourself? [LO-5]

Practice Your Skills

Message for Analysis

4-7. **Adapting to Cultural Differences [LO-5]** Your boss wants to send a brief email message to welcome some employees who recently transferred to your department from the company's Hong Kong branch. These employees, all of whom are Hong Kong natives, speak English, but your boss asks you to review his message for clarity. What would you suggest your boss change in the following email message, and why? Would you consider this message to be audience centered? Why or why not? (Hint: Do some quick research on Hong Kong to identify the style of English that people in Hong Kong are likely to speak.)

I wanted to welcome you ASAP to our little family here in the States. It's high time we shook hands in person and not just across the sea. I'm pleased as punch about getting to know you all, and I for one will do my level best to sell you on America.

Exercises

Each activity is labeled according to the primary skill or skills you will need to use. To review relevant chapter content, you can refer to the indicated Learning Objective. In some instances, supporting information will be found in another chapter, as indicated.

4-8. **Intercultural Communication: Recognizing Cultural Variations [LO-1], [LO-3], [LO-4]** Review the generation labels in Table 4.1. Based on your year of birth, in which generation are you categorized? Do you feel a part of this generation? Why or why not? If you were born outside the United States, do the generational boundaries seem accurate to you? Now consider the biases that you might have regarding other generations. Identify several of your generational beliefs that could create friction in the workplace. Summarize your responses to these questions in a post on your class blog or an email message to your instructor.

4-9. **Intercultural Communication: Adapting to Cultural Variations [LO-2]** You are a new manager at K & J Brick, a masonry products company that is now run by the two sons of the man who founded it 50 years ago. For years, the co-owners have invited the management team to a wilderness lodge for a combination of outdoor sports and annual business planning meetings. You don't want to miss the event, but you know that the outdoor activities weren't designed for someone like you, whose physical impairments prevent participation in the sporting events. Draft a short email message to the rest of the management team, suggesting changes to the annual event that will allow all managers to participate.

4-10. **Intercultural Communication: Writing for Multiple-Language Audiences [LO-5]** Reading English-language content written by nonnative speakers of English can be a good reminder of the challenges of communicating in another language. The writing can be confusing or even amusing at first glance, but the key to remember here is that your writing might sound just as confusing or amusing to someone else if your roles were reversed.

Identify a company that is based in a non-English speaking country but that includes English-language text on its website. (The advanced search capabilities of your favorite search engine can help you locate websites from a particular country.) Study the language on this site. Does it sound as though it was written by someone adept at English? If the first site you've found has writing that sounds natural to a native U.S. English speaker, find another company whose website doesn't. Select a section of text, at least several sentences long, and rewrite it to sound more "American." Submit the original text and your rewritten version to your instructor.

4-11. Intercultural Communication: Writing for Multiple-Language Audiences; Collaboration: Team Projects [LO-5], Chapter 3 With a team assigned by your instructor, review the Facebook pages of five companies, looking for words and phrases that might be confusing to a nonnative speaker of English. If you (or someone on the team) are a nonnative speaker, explain to the team why those word choices could be confusing. Choose three sentences, headlines, company slogans, or other pieces of text that contain potentially confusing words and rewrite them to minimize the chances of misinterpretation. Try to retain the tone of the original—although you may find that doing so is impossible in some instances. Compile the original selections and your revised versions, then email the documents to your instructor.

4-12. Intercultural Communication: Speaking with Multiple-Language Audiences; Collaboration: Team Projects [LO-5], Chapter 3 Working with two other students, prepare a list of 10 examples of slang (in your own language) that might be misinterpreted or misunderstood during a business conversation with someone from another culture. Next to each example, suggest other words you might use to convey the same message. Do the alternatives mean *exactly* the same as the original slang or idiom? Submit your list of original words and suggested replacements, with an explanation of why each replacement is better than the original.

4-13. Intercultural Communication: Speaking with Multiple-Language Audiences; Media Skills: Podcasting [LO-5], Chapter 8 Your company was one of the first to use podcasting as a business communication tool. Executives frequently record messages (such as monthly sales summaries) and post them on the company's intranet site; employees from the 14 offices in Europe, Asia, and North America then download the files to their music players or other devices and listen to the messages while riding the train to work, eating lunch at their desks, and so on. Your boss asks you to draft the opening statement for a podcast that will announce a revenue drop caused by intensive competitive pressure. She reviews your script and hands it back with a gentle explanation that it needs to be revised for international listeners. Improve the following statement in as many ways as you can:

Howdy, comrades. Shouldn't surprise anyone that we took a beating this year, given the insane pricing moves our knucklehead competitors have been making. I mean, how those clowns can keep turning a profit is beyond me, what with steel costs still going through the roof and labor costs heating up—even in countries where everybody goes to find cheap labor—and hazardous waste disposal regs adding to operating costs, too.

Expand Your Skills

Critique the Professionals

Find an online business document—such as a company website, blog post, Facebook page, or LinkedIn profile—that you believe commits an intercultural communication blunder by failing to consider the needs of at least some of its target readers. For example, a website might use slang or idiomatic language that could confuse some readers, or it might use language that offends some readers. In a post on your class blog, share the text you found, and explain why you think it does not succeed as effective intercultural communication. Be sure to include a link to the original material.

Sharpening Your Career Skills Online

Bovée and Thill's Business Communication Web Search, at **websearch.businesscommunicationnetwork.com**, is a unique research tool designed specifically for business communication research. Use the Web Search function to find a website, video, article, podcast, or presentation that offers advice on communicating with business contacts in another country or culture. Write a brief email message to your instructor describing the item you found and summarizing the career skills information you learned from it.

Build Your Career

Read "Writing the Story of You" on page 486, and study the example in Figure 15.1. Using the three sections in Figure 15.1 (Where I Have Been, Where I Am Now, and Where I Want to Be), outline the story arc of your career so far. Keep this document handy, and add to it whenever ideas come to you in the remaining weeks of the course. For example, as you continue to study business and discover different career facets that sound interesting, consider adding them to the Where I Want to Be section. Also, keep track of any questions or concerns you have about your future career options so that you can research them as your schedule allows. By the time you're ready to write your résumé and launch your job search, this document should give you some useful focus and direction.

Improve Your Grammar, Mechanics, and Usage

The following exercises help you improve your knowledge of and power over English grammar, mechanics, and usage. Turn to the Handbook of Grammar, Mechanics, and Usage at the end of this book and review all of Section 1.4 (Adjectives). Then look at the following 10 items and identify the preferred choice within each set of parentheses. (Answers to these exercises appear on page 614.)

4-14. Of the two products, this one has the (*greater, greatest*) potential.

4-15. The (*most perfect, perfect*) solution is *d*.

4-16. Here is the (*interesting, most interesting*) of all the ideas I have heard so far.

4-17. The (*hardest, harder*) part of my job is firing people.

4-18. A (*highly placed, highly-placed*) source revealed Dotson's (*last ditch, last-ditch*) efforts to cover up the mistake.

4-19. A (*top secret, top-secret*) document was taken from the president's office last night.

4-20. A (*30 year old, 30-year-old*) person should know better.

4-21. The two companies are engaged in an (*all-out no-holds-barred; all-out, no-holds-barred*) struggle for dominance.

4-22. A (*tiny metal; tiny, metal*) shaving is responsible for the problem.

4-23. You'll receive our (*usual cheerful prompt; usual, cheerful, prompt; usual cheerful, prompt*) service.

For additional exercises focusing on adjectives, visit MyLab Business Communication. Select Chapter 4, select Additional Exercises to Improve Your Grammar, Mechanics, and Usage, and then select 8. Adjectives.

MyLab Business Communication

MyLab Assisted-Grading Writing Prompts

If your instructor has assigned one or both of the following writing assignments within the MyLab, go to your Assignments to complete these writing exercises.

4-24. How have market globalization and cultural diversity contributed to the increased importance of intercultural communication? [LO-1]

4-25. What are four important gender issues in the context of communication diversity? [LO-3]

Endnotes

1. Bernard J. Tyson, "Diversity and Inclusion Are in Kaiser Permanente's DNA," Kaiser Permanente website, accessed 11 March 2016, kp.org; Marianne Aiello, "Diversity No Gimmick in Kaiser Permanente Ad Campaign," *HealthLeaders Media*, 25 November 2015, www.healthleadersmedia.com; "Top Reasons to Join Kaiser Permanente as a Woman in Tech," Kaiser Permanente website, accessed 26 February 2018, kp.org; "Kaiser Permanente—Achieving Our Mission and Growing the Business Through the National Diversity Agenda," Catalyst, 25 January 2011, www.catalyst.org; "DiversityInc Top 50" and "Diversity Leadership: Dr. Ronald Copeland, Kaiser Permanente," DiversityInc, accessed 11 March 2016, www.diversityinc.com; "Census Bureau Reports at Least 350 Languages Spoken in U.S. Homes," U.S. Census Bureau, 3 November 2015, www.census.gov; "Local and National Diversity Programs," Kaiser Permanente website, accessed 12 March 2016, kp.org.
2. Michael R. Carrell, Everett E. Mann, and Tracey Honeycutt-Sigler, "Defining Workforce Diversity Programs and Practices in Organizations: A Longitudinal Study," *Labor Law Journal*, Spring 2006, 5–12.
3. David Rock, Heidi Grant, and Jacqui Grey, "Diverse Teams Feel Less Comfortable—and That's Why They Perform Better," *Harvard Business Review*, 22 September 2016, hbr.org.
4. *Competing Across Borders: How Cultural and Communication Barriers Affect Business*, Economist Intelligence Unit Ltd., 2012, 4.
5. Richard D. Bucher, *Diversity Consciousness: Opening Our Minds to People, Cultures, and Opportunities*, 4th ed. (New York City: Pearson, 2015), 50; Nancy R. Lockwood, "Workplace Diversity: Leveraging the Power of Difference for Competitive Advantage," *HR Magazine*, June 2005, special section, 1–10.
6. Marjorie Derven, "Diversity & Inclusion Are Essential to a Global Virtual Team's Success," *TD*, July 2016, 54–59; Rock, et al., "Diverse Teams Feel Less Comfortable—and That's Why They Perform Better."
7. Tracy Novinger, *Intercultural Communication, A Practical Guide* (Austin: University of Texas Press, 2001), 15.
8. Arthur Chin, "Understanding Cultural Competency," *New Zealand Business*, December 2010/January 2011, 34–35; Sanjeeta R. Gupta, "Achieve Cultural Competency," *Training*, February 2009, 16–17; Diane Shannon, "Cultural Competency in Health Care Organizations: Why and How," *Physician Executive*, September–October 2010, 15–22.
9. Beamer and Varner, *Intercultural Communication in the Workplace*, 4.

10. Chaney and Martin, *Intercultural Business Communication*, 9.
11. Bucher, *Diversity Consciousness: Opening Our Minds to People, Cultures, and Opportunities*, 140.
12. Project Implicit, accessed 6 March 2018, implicit.harvard.edu/implicit.
13. Linda Beamer, "Teaching English Business Writing to Chinese-Speaking Business Students," *Bulletin of the Association for Business Communication* 57, no. 1 (1994): 12–18.
14. Edward T. Hall, "Context and Meaning," in *Intercultural Communication*, 6th ed., edited by Larry A. Samovar and Richard E. Porter (Belmont, Calif.: Wadsworth, 1991), 46–55.
15. Richard L. Daft, *Management*, 13th ed. (Boston: Cengage, 2018), 125.
16. Charley H. Dodd, *Dynamics of Intercultural Communication*, 3rd ed. (Dubuque, Iowa.: Brown, 1991), 69–70.
17. Daft, *Management*, 125.
18. Hannah Seligson, "For American Workers in China, a Culture Clash," *New York Times*, 23 December 2009, www.nytimes.com.
19. Beamer and Varner, *Intercultural Communication in the Workplace*, 230–233.
20. Chaney and Martin, *Intercultural Business Communication*, 61.
21. "Foreign Corrupt Practices Act," U.S. Department of Justice, 3 February 2017, www.justice.gov.
22. Chaney and Martin, *Intercultural Business Communication*, 169.
23. Chaney and Martin, *Intercultural Business Communication*, 117.
24. Mansour Javidan, "Forward-Thinking Cultures," *Harvard Business Review*, July–August 2007, 20.
25. Erin Meyer, "When Culture Doesn't Translate," *Harvard Business Review*, October 2015, 66–72.
26. Chaney and Martin, *Intercultural Business Communication*, 125.
27. Richard Fry, "Millennials Projected to Overtake Baby Boomers as America's Largest Generation," Pew Research Center, 1 March 2018, www.pewresearch.org; Michael Dimock, "Defining Generations: Where Millennials End and Post-Millennials Begin," Pew Research Center, 1 March 2018, www.pewresearch.org.
28. Joanna Barsh and Lareina Yee, "Changing Companies' Minds About Women," *McKinsey Quarterly* 4 (2011): 48–59.
29. John Gray, *Mars and Venus in the Workplace: A Practical Guide for Improving Communication and Getting Results* (New York: HarperCollins, 2002), 10, 25–27, 61–63.

30. Jennifer Luden, "Ask for a Raise? Most Women Hesitate," NPR, 14 February 2011, www.npr.org.

31. "First Step: Gender Identity in the Workplace," Catalyst, June 2015, www.catalyst.org.

32. "Religious Discrimination," U.S. Equal Employment Opportunity Commission, accessed 6 March 2018, www.eeoc.gov.

33. Daphne A. Jameson, "Reconceptualizing Cultural Identity and Its Role in Intercultural Business Communication," *International Journal of Business Communication* 44, no. 3 (July 2007): 199–235.

34. Craig S. Smith, "Beware of Green Hats in China and Other Cross-Cultural Faux Pas," *New York Times*, 30 April 2002, C11.

35. Chaney and Martin, *Intercultural Business Communication*, 65

36. Chaney and Martin, *Intercultural Business Communication*, 120.

37. P. Christopher Earley and Elaine Mosakowski, "Cultural Intelligence," *Harvard Business Review*, October 2004, 139–146.

38. Chaney and Martin, *Intercultural Business Communication*, 144–145.

39. "Right," Merriam-Webster online, www.merriam-webster.com.

40. Lynn Gaertner-Johnston, "Found in Translation," Business Writing blog, 25 November 2005, www.businesswritingblog.com.

41. Qiu Gui Su, "The Four Mandarin Chinese Tones," ThoughtCo., 29 September 2017, www.thoughtco.com.

42. "'Can You Spell That for Us Nonnative Speakers?' Accommodation Strategies in International Business Meetings," Pamela Rogerson-Revell, *Journal of Business Communication* 47, no. 4 (October 2010): 432–454.

Every professional can learn to write more effectively while spending less time and energy. Discover a proven writing process that divides the task of communicating into three clear steps: planning, writing, and completing messages. The process works for everything from blog posts to formal reports to your résumé. With a bit of practice, you'll be using the process to write more effectively with a lot less stress.

wavebreakmedia/Shutterstock

Planning Business Messages

LEARNING OBJECTIVES

After studying this chapter, you will be able to

1 Describe the three-step writing process.

2 Explain why it's important to analyze a communication situation in order to define your purpose and profile your audience before writing a message.

3 Discuss information-gathering options for simple messages, and identify three attributes of quality information.

4 List the factors to consider when choosing the most appropriate medium for a message.

5 Explain why good organization is important to both you and your audience, and list the tasks involved in organizing a message.

MyLab Business Communication

Improve Your Grade!

If your instructor is using MyLab Business Communication, visit **www.pearson.com/mylab/business-communication** for videos, simulations, and writing exercises.

WOLFF OLINS

Telling an Important Story About Business Communication

What do the following activities have in common: watching a movie, reading a novel, and listening to a friend tell you how much she learned about herself during an amazing summer she spent volunteering? The common thread is *dramatic tension*—the need to know how the story is going to turn out. If you care about the person in the story, chances are you'll want to stick around to the end.

Storytelling might sound like an odd topic for a business communication course, but storytelling is at the heart of some of the most effective communication efforts, from heart-tugging TV commercials to engaging training materials to rousing motivational speeches. With more and more professionals and companies recognizing their power, storytelling techniques have become a hot topic in the business communication field.

As one of the most respected novelists and essayists of his generation, it's no surprise that the Pakistani writer Mohsin Hamid is an expert at storytelling. But it might come as a surprise to his many fans that he has a second career as the chief storytelling officer (CSO) for Wolff Olins, an international creativity consultancy based in London. In this role, Hamid helps business professionals and executives use the art of storytelling to engage with both internal and external audiences.

Novelist and essayist Mohsin Hamid has a second career as the chief storytelling officer at the London-based creative consultancy Wolff Olins.

For example, the company heard from a number of top executives about the challenges of conveying to employees a clear sense of the company's purpose and empowering them to apply their individual creative energies to achieving that purpose. Hamid explains that's it unrealistic to expect an executive to give everyone in the organization explicit task assignments. Instead, he or she can tell the company's story—where it came from, the reason it exists, and where it is heading—to help employees align their efforts in that shared mission.

Hamid advises executives to engage in this sort of strategic storytelling at three key stages of a company's evolution: when it is first launched, so that everyone knows where and how the company intends to grow; whenever major changes occur, so that everyone understands how the narrative has changed;

and whenever the company's growth trajectory stalls, to reiterate what the company stands for and how it can overcome the odds. For instance, if a company is facing new competition, the CEO could relate a story from the company's past about how people came together to find better ways to satisfy customers and thereby protect the business.

By the way, business storytelling has an important personal angle as well. You can map out your career using storytelling (see page 145), and when you're interviewing for jobs, you should be prepared in case an interviewer pops the classic question, "So, what's your story?" By visualizing a satisfying ending to your own career story, you'll have a better idea of what it takes to get there.[1]

WWW.WOLFFOLINS.COM

Understanding the Three-Step Writing Process

1 LEARNING OBJECTIVE
Describe the three-step writing process.

The emphasis that Wolff Olins (profiled in the chapter-opening On the Job) puts on connecting with customers is a lesson that applies to business messages for all stakeholders. By following the process introduced in this chapter, you can create successful messages that meet audience needs and highlight your skills as a perceptive business professional.

The three-step writing process (see Figure 5.1 on the next page) helps ensure that your communication efforts are both *effective* (meeting your audience's needs and getting your points across) and *efficient* (making the best use of your time and your audience's time):

The three-step writing process consists of *planning, writing,* and *completing* your messages.

- **Step 1: Planning messages.** To plan any message, first *analyze the situation* by defining your purpose and developing a profile of your audience. When you're sure what you need to accomplish with your message, *gather the information* that will meet your audience's needs. Next, *select the best combination of medium and channel* to deliver your message. Then *organize the information* by defining your main idea, limiting your scope, selecting the direct or indirect approach, and outlining your content. Planning messages is the focus of this chapter.
- **Step 2: Writing messages.** After you've planned your message, *adapt to your audience* by using sensitivity, relationship skills, and an appropriate writing style. Then you're ready to *compose your message* by making thoughtful word choices, crafting effective sentences, and developing coherent paragraphs. The writing step is discussed in Chapter 6.
- **Step 3: Completing messages.** After writing your first draft, *revise your message* by evaluating the content, reviewing readability, and editing and rewriting until your message comes across concisely and clearly, with correct grammar, proper punctuation, and effective format. Next, *produce your message.* Put it into the form that your audience will receive and review all design and layout decisions for an attractive, professional appearance. *Proofread* the final product to ensure high quality, and then *distribute your message.* The completing step is discussed in Chapter 7.

Throughout this book, you'll learn how to apply these steps to a wide variety of business messages. (A "message" in this usage applies to any communication effort, from a tweet to a presentation to a report.)

OPTIMIZING YOUR WRITING TIME

The more you use the three-step process, the more intuitive and automatic it will become. You'll also get better at allotting time for each task during a writing project. As a general

1 Plan →	**2** Write →	**3** Complete
Analyze the Situation Define your purpose and develop an audience profile. **Gather Information** Determine audience needs and obtain the information necessary to satisfy those needs. **Choose Medium and Channel** Identify the best combination for the situation, message, and audience. **Organize the Information** Define your main idea, limit your scope, select the direct or indirect approach, and outline your content.	**Adapt to Your Audience** Be sensitive to audience needs by using a "you" attitude, politeness, positive emphasis, and unbiased language. Build a strong relationship with your audience by establishing your credibility and projecting your company's preferred image. Control your style with a conversational tone, plain English, and appropriate voice. **Compose the Message** Choose strong words that will help you create effective sentences and coherent paragraphs.	**Revise the Message** Evaluate content and review readability; edit and rewrite for conciseness and clarity. **Produce the Message** Use effective design elements and suitable layout for a clean, professional appearance. **Proofread the Message** Review for errors in layout, spelling, and mechanics. **Distribute the Message** Deliver your message using the chosen channel; make sure all documents and all relevant files are distributed successfully.

Figure 5.1 The Three-Step Writing Process
This three-step process will help you create more effective messages in any medium. As you get more practice with the process, it will become easier and more automatic.
Sources: Kevin J. Harty and John Keenan, *Writing for Business and Industry: Process and Product* (New York: Macmillan Publishing Company, 1987), 3–4; Richard Hatch, *Business Writing* (Chicago: Science Research Associates, 1983), 88–89; Richard Hatch, *Business Communication Theory and Technique* (Chicago: Science Research Associates, 1983), 74–75; Center for Humanities, *Writing as a Process: A Step-by-Step Guide* (Mount Kisco, N.Y.: Center for Humanities, 1987); Michael L. Keene, *Effective Professional Writing* (New York: D. C. Heath, 1987), 28–34.

> As a starting point, reserve half your available time for planning, one-quarter for writing, and one-quarter for completing a message; adjust for each project as needed.

rule, set aside roughly 50 percent of that time for planning, 25 percent for writing, and 25 percent for completing.

Reserving half your time for planning might seem excessive, but as the next section explains, careful planning usually saves time overall by focusing your writing and reducing rework. Of course, the ideal time allocation varies from project to project. Simpler and shorter messages require less planning than long reports, websites, and other complex projects. Also, the time required to produce and distribute messages can vary widely, depending on the media, the size of the audience, and other factors. Start with the 50-25-25 split, and adjust as needed for each project.

PLANNING EFFECTIVELY

> For everything beyond brief and simple messages, resist the urge to skip the planning step.

As soon as the need to create a message appears, inexperienced communicators are tempted to dive directly into writing. However, skipping or shortchanging the planning stage often creates extra work and stress later in the process. First, thoughtful planning is necessary to make sure you provide the right information in the right format to the right people. Taking the time to understand your readers or listeners and their needs helps you find and assemble the facts they're looking for and deliver that information in a concise and compelling way. Second, with careful planning, the writing stage is faster, easier, and much less stressful. Third, planning can save you from embarrassing blunders that could hurt your company or your career.

> **2 LEARNING OBJECTIVE**
> Explain why it's important to analyze a communication situation in order to define your purpose and profile your audience before writing a message.

Analyzing the Situation

Every communication effort takes place in a particular situation, meaning you have a specific message to send to a specific audience under a specific set of circumstances. For example, describing your professional qualifications in an email message to an executive in your own company differs significantly from describing your qualifications in your LinkedIn profile. The email message is likely to be focused on a single goal, such as explaining why you would be a good choice to head up a major project, and you have the luxury of focusing on the needs of a single, personally identifiable reader. In contrast, your social networking profile could have multiple goals, such as connecting with your peers at other companies and presenting your qualifications to potential employers, and it might be viewed by hundreds or thousands of readers, each with his or her own interests.

The underlying information for these two messages could be roughly the same, but the level of detail to include, the tone of the writing, the specific word choices—these and other decisions you need to make will differ from one situation to another. Making the right choices starts with clearly defining your purpose and understanding your audience's needs.

> Understanding the situation is essential for getting the content and tone of a message right.

> Check out the "Five-Minute Guide to Planning a Business Message or Document" at the end of the chapter.

DEFINING YOUR PURPOSE

All business messages have a **general purpose**: to inform, to persuade, or to collaborate with the audience. This purpose helps define the overall approach you'll need to take. Within the scope of its general purpose, each message also has a **specific purpose**, which identifies what you hope to accomplish with the message. What do you want the audience to think or do after receiving it? The more precisely you can define your specific purpose, the better you'll be able to fine-tune your message to achieve your desired outcome. For example, "get approval to hire three analysts by June 1 so we can meet our November 15 deadline" is more helpful as a planning device than a vague statement such as "get approval to hire more staff."

After you have defined your specific purpose, take a moment for a reality check. Assess whether that purpose merits the time and effort required for you to prepare and send the message—and for your audience to spend the time required to read it, view it, or listen to it. Ask these four questions:

> The *general purpose* of a message can be categorized as informing, persuading, or collaborating.

> The *specific purpose* of a message identifies exactly what you want to accomplish with the message.

> After defining your purpose, verify that the message will be worth the time and effort required to create, send, and receive it.

- **Will anything change as a result of your message?** Don't contribute to information overload by sending messages that won't change anything. For instance, if you don't like your company's latest advertising campaign but you're not in a position to influence it, sending a critical message to your colleagues probably won't change anything and won't benefit anyone.
- **Is your purpose realistic?** Recognizing whether a goal is realistic is an important part of having good business sense. For example, if you request a raise while the company is struggling, you might send the message that you're not tuned in to the situation around you.
- **Is the time right?** People who are busy or distracted when they receive your message are less likely to pay attention to it. Many professions and departments have recurring cycles in their workloads, for instance, and messages sent during peak times may be ignored.
- **Is your purpose acceptable to your organization?** Your company's business objectives and policies, and even laws that apply to your particular industry, may dictate whether a particular purpose is acceptable. For example, if you work for a discount stock brokerage, one that doesn't offer investing advice, it would be inappropriate to write a newsletter article on the pros and cons of investing in a particular company.

When you are satisfied that you have a clear and meaningful purpose and that this is a smart time to proceed, your next step is to understand the members of your audience and their needs.

> An audience profile answers key questions about your readers or listeners:
> - Who are they?
> - How many people do you need to reach?
> - How much do they already know about the subject?
> - What is their probable reaction to your message?

DEVELOPING AN AUDIENCE PROFILE

Before audience members will take the time to read or listen to your messages, they have to be interested in what you're saying. They need to know that the message is relevant to their needs—even if they don't necessarily want to read or see it. The more you know

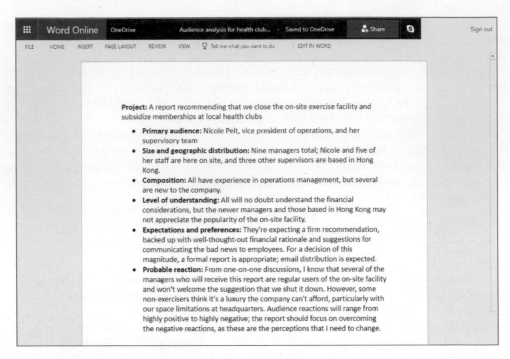

Figure 5.2 **Using Audience Analysis to Plan a Message**
For simple, routine messages, you usually don't need to analyze your audience in depth. However, for complex messages or messages for indifferent or hostile audiences, take the time to study their information needs and potential reactions to your message.

about your audience members and their needs and expectations, the more effectively you'll be able to communicate with them. Figure 5.2 provides an example of the kind of information to compile in an audience analysis. Conducting an audience analysis involves the following steps:

If a message has more than one audience, prioritize the information needs of the primary audience.

- **Identify your primary audience.** For some messages, certain audience members may be more important than others. Don't ignore the needs of less influential members, but make sure you address the concerns of the key decision makers.
- **Determine audience size and geographic distribution.** A message aimed at 10,000 people spread around the globe could require a different approach than one aimed at a dozen people down the hall.
- **Determine audience composition.** Look for similarities and differences in culture, language, age, education, organizational rank and status, attitudes, experience, motivations, biases, beliefs, and any other factors that might affect the success of your message (see Figure 5.3).

Understand your readers' or listeners' expectations so you can meet their information needs without providing too much or too little.

- **Gauge audience members' level of understanding.** If audience members are not well-versed in the topic, you may need to provide some background and context.
- **Understand audience expectations and preferences.** For example, will members of your audience expect complete details or just a summary of the main points? In general, for internal communication, the higher up the organization your message goes, the fewer details people want to see.
- **Forecast probable audience reaction.** As you'll read later in the chapter, potential audience reaction affects message organization. If you expect a favorable response, you can state conclusions and recommendations up front and offer minimal supporting evidence. If you expect to encounter skepticism, you can introduce conclusions gradually and with more proof.

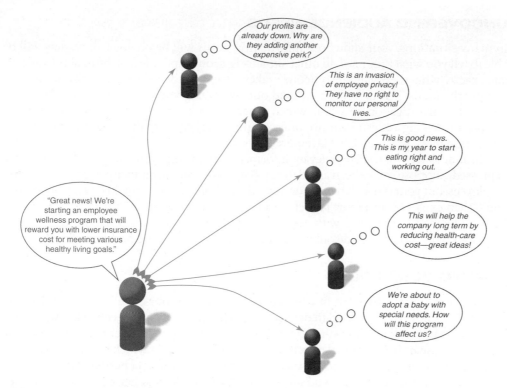

Figure 5.3 Predicting the Effects of Audience Composition
As just one example of why it's important to analyze the composition of your audience, the attitudes and beliefs of individual audience members can have a significant impact on the success of a message. In this scenario, for instance, a seemingly positive message about employee benefits can generate a wide range of responses from employees with different beliefs and concerns.

Gathering Information

When you have a clear picture of your audience, your next step is to assemble the information to include in your message. For simple messages, you may already have all the information in hand, but for more complex messages, you might need to do some research and analysis before you begin writing. Chapter 12 explores formal research techniques for finding, evaluating, and processing information, but you can always use a variety of informal techniques to gather insights and guide your research efforts:

- **Consider the audience's perspective.** Put yourself in the audience's position. What are these people thinking, feeling, or planning? What information do they need? If you are initiating a conversation in a social media context, what information will stimulate discussion in your target communities?
- **Listen to the community.** For almost any subject related to business these days, chances are there is at least one connected community of customers, product enthusiasts, or other people who engage in online discussions. Find them and listen to what they have to say.
- **Read reports and other company documents.** Annual reports, financial statements, news releases, blogs by industry experts, marketing reports, and customer surveys are just a few of the many potential sources. Find out whether your company has a *knowledge management system* or other system that collects the experiences and insights of employees throughout the organization.
- **Talk with supervisors, colleagues, or customers.** Fellow workers and customers may have information you need, or they may have good insights into the needs of your target audience.
- **Ask your audience for input.** If you're unsure what audience members need from you, ask them, if possible. Admitting you don't know but want to meet their needs will impress an audience more than guessing and getting it wrong.

3 LEARNING OBJECTIVE
Discuss information-gathering options for simple messages, and identify three attributes of quality information.

If a project doesn't require formal research techniques, or if you need answers in a hurry, you can use a variety of informal techniques to gather the information your audience needs.

Take advantage of social media in your research; enthusiasts and experts frequently share ideas and information on Twitter, Facebook, and other social platforms.

UNCOVERING AUDIENCE NEEDS

Audience members might not be able to describe all the information they need, or you might not have the opportunity to ask them, so you may have to engage in some detective work.

In many situations, your audience's information needs will be obvious, or readers will be able to tell you what they need. In other situations, though, people may be unable to articulate exactly what they want. If someone makes a vague or broad request, ask questions to narrow the focus. If your boss says, "Find out everything you can about Naxos Records," narrow the investigation by asking which aspect of the company and its business is most important. Asking a question or two often prompts the person to think through the request and define more precisely what is required.

In addition, try to think of relevant information needs that your audience may not have expressed. Suppose you've been asked to compare two health insurance plans for your firm's employees, but your research has uncovered a third alternative that might be even better. You could then expand your report to include a brief explanation of why the third plan should be considered and compare it with the two original plans. Use judgment, however; in some situations, you should provide only what the audience expects and nothing more.

FINDING YOUR FOCUS

Use *free writing*—writing whatever comes to mind without stopping or correcting for a fixed period of time—and other discovery techniques if you need to find the focus of a new writing project.

You may encounter situations in which the assignment or objective is so vague that you have no idea how to get started in determining what the audience needs to know. In such cases, you can use some discovery techniques to help generate ideas and uncover possible avenues to research. One popular technique is **free writing**, in which you write whatever comes to mind, without stopping to make any corrections, for a set period of time. The big advantage of free writing is that you silence your "inner critic" and just express ideas as they come to you. You might end up with a rambling mess, but that's not important. Within that tangle of expressions, you might also find some useful ideas and angles that hadn't occurred to you yet—perhaps the crucial idea that will jumpstart the entire project.

> **REAL-TIME UPDATES**
> LEARN MORE BY WATCHING THIS VIDEO
>
> ### Loosen up your writing with these free-writing tips
>
> Free writing can be a great way to come up with material for a writing project and to get more comfortable with the process of writing. Go to **http://real-timeupdates.com/ebc13** and select Learn More in the Students section.

The best discovery option in some cases might not be writing at all, but rather *sketching*. If you're unable to come up with any words, grab a sketchpad or mobile tablet and start drawing. While you're thinking visually, your brain might release some great ideas that were trapped behind words.

The techniques listed under "Defining Your Main Idea" on page 141 can also be helpful if you don't know where to start.

PROVIDING REQUIRED INFORMATION

The *journalistic approach* asks *who, what, when, where, why,* and *how* about a subject.

After you have defined your audience's information needs, your next step is to satisfy those needs completely. One good way to test the thoroughness of your message is to use the **journalistic approach**: Check to see whether your message answers *who, what, when, where, why,* and *how*. Using this method, you can quickly tell whether a message fails to deliver. For example, consider this message that requests information from employees:

> We are exploring ways to reduce our office space leasing costs and would like your input on a proposed plan in which employees who telecommute on alternate days could share offices. Please let me know what you think of this proposal.

The message fails to tell employees everything they need to know to provide meaningful responses. The *what* could be improved by identifying the specific information the writer needs from employees (such as whether individual telecommuting patterns are predictable enough to allow scheduling of shared offices). The writer also doesn't specify *when* the responses are needed or *how* the employees should respond. By failing to address such points, the request is likely to generate a variety of responses, some possibly helpful but some probably not.

MOBILE APP

Evernote helps you collect, organize, and retrieve information when planning your writing projects.

Be Sure the Information Is Accurate

You have a responsibility to provide quality information to your readers.

The *quality* of the information you provide is every bit as important as the *quantity*. Inaccurate information in business messages can cause a host of problems, from embarrassment and lost productivity to serious safety and legal issues. You may commit the organization to promises it can't keep—and the error could harm your reputation. Thanks to the internet, inaccurate information may persist for years after you distribute it.

You can minimize mistakes by double-checking every piece of information you collect, whenever feasible, and finding multiple sources to corroborate important facts and figures. If you are using sources outside the organization, ask yourself whether the information is current and reliable. As Chapter 12 notes, you must be particularly careful when using sources you find online. Be sure to review any mathematical or financial calculations. Check all dates and schedules, and examine your own assumptions and conclusions to be certain they are valid.

> Whenever feasible, double-check the information you collect and find multiple sources to corroborate important facts and figures.

Be Sure the Information Is Ethical

By working hard to ensure the accuracy of the information you gather, you'll also avoid many ethical problems in your messages. If you do make an honest mistake, such as delivering information you initially thought to be true but later found to be false, contact the recipients of the message immediately and correct the error. No one can reasonably fault you in such circumstances, and people will respect your honesty.

Messages can also be unethical if important information is omitted (see "Practicing Ethical Communication: How Much Information Is Enough?"). Of course, you may have legal or other sound business reasons for not including every detail about every matter. Just how much detail should you include? A simple test is to make sure you include enough to avoid misleading your audience.

> Omitting important information can be an unethical decision.

Be Sure the Information Is Pertinent

When gathering information for your message, remember that some points will be more important to your audience than others. Audience members will appreciate your efforts to prioritize the information they need and filter out the information they don't. Moreover, by focusing on the information that concerns your audience the most, you increase your chances of accomplishing your own communication goals.

> Select the information to include based on how pertinent it is to your readers.

PRACTICING ETHICAL COMMUNICATION

How Much Information Is Enough?

Your company, Furniture Formations, creates a variety of home furniture products, with extensive use of fine woods. To preserve the look and feel of the wood, your craftspeople use a linseed oil–based finish that you purchase from a local wholesaler. The workers apply the finish with rags, which are thrown away after each project. After a news report about spontaneous combustion of waste rags occurring in other furniture shops, you grow concerned enough to contact the wholesaler and ask for verification of the product's safety. The wholesaler knows you've been considering a nonflammable, water-based alternative from another source but tries to reassure you with the following message:

> Seal the rags in an approved container and dispose of it according to local regulations. As you probably already know, county regulations require all commercial users of oil-based materials to dispose of leftover finishes at the county's hazardous waste facility.

> You're still not satisfied. You visit the website of the oil's manufacturer and find the following cautionary statement about the product you're currently using:

Finishes that contain linseed oil or tung oil require specific safety precautions to minimize the risk of fire. Oil-soaked rags and other materials such as steel wool must be sealed in water-filled metal containers and then disposed of in accordance with local waste management regulations. Failure to do so can lead to spontaneous combustion that results from the heat-producing chemical reaction that takes place as the finish dries. In particular, DO NOT leave wet, oil-soaked rags in a pile or discard them with other waste.

CRITICAL THINKING

1. Was the wholesaler guilty of an ethical lapse in this case? If yes, explain what you think the lapse is and why you believe it is unethical. If no, explain why you think the statement qualifies as ethical.
2. Would the manufacturer's warning be as effective without the explanation of spontaneous combustion? Why or why not?

If you don't know your audience or if you're communicating with a large group of people who have diverse interests, use common sense to identify points of interest. Audience factors such as age, job, location, income, and education can give you clues. If you're trying to sell memberships in a health club, you might adjust your message for athletes, busy professionals, families, and people in different locations or in different income brackets. The comprehensive facilities and professional trainers would appeal to athletes, whereas the low monthly rates would appeal to people on tight budgets.

Some messages necessarily reach audiences with a diverse mix of educational levels, subject awareness, and other variables. If possible, provide each audience segment with its own targeted information, such as by using sections in a brochure or links on a webpage.

Selecting the Best Combination of Media and Channels

With the necessary information in hand, your next decision involves the best combination of media and channels to reach your target audience. As you recall from Chapter 1, the medium is the *form* a message takes and the channel is the *system* used to deliver the message. The distinction between the two isn't always crystal clear, and some people use the terms in different ways, but these definitions are a useful way to think about the possibilities for business communication.

Most media can be distributed through more than one channel, so whenever you have a choice, think through your options to select the optimum combination. For example, a brief written message could be distributed as a printed letter or memo, or it could be distributed through a variety of digital channels, from email to blogging to social networking.

THE MOST COMMON MEDIA AND CHANNEL OPTIONS

Media can be divided into *oral*, *written*, and *visual* forms, and all three can be distributed through *digital* and *nondigital* channels.

The simplest way to categorize media choices is to divide them into *oral* (spoken), *written*, and *visual*. Each of these media can be delivered through *digital* and *nondigital channels*, which creates six basic combinations, discussed in the following sections. Table 5.1 summarizes the general advantages and disadvantages of the six medium/channel combinations. Specific options within these categories have their own strengths and weaknesses to consider as well. (For simplicity's sake, subsequent chapters occasionally use "digital media" to indicate any of the three media types delivered through digital channels.)

Oral Medium, In-Person Channel

The oral medium, in-person channel combination involves talking with people who are in the same location, whether it's a one-on-one conversation over lunch or a more formal speech or presentation. Being in the same physical space is a key distinction because it enables the nuances of nonverbal communication more than any other medium/channel combination. As Chapter 2 points out, these nonverbal signals can carry as much weight in a conversation as the words being spoken.

The nonverbal and interactive aspects of in-person communication are difficult to replicate in most other media/channel combinations.

By giving people the ability to see, hear, and react to each other, in-person communication encourages people to ask questions, make comments, and work together to reach a consensus or decision. Managers in particular should embrace face-to-face contact because it can foster a more open and trusting style of communication with employees. In fact, the practice of putting down the digital tools and getting out of one's office to interact with staff has its own name—*management by walking around (MBWA)*.[2]

Oral Medium, Digital Channel

Oral media via digital channels include any transmission of voice via electronic means, both live and recorded, such as telephone calls, internet telephony (VoIP) services such as Skype, voicemail messages, and podcasts (see Chapter 8). Live phone conversations

TABLE 5.1 Medium/Channel Combinations: Advantages and Disadvantages

Medium/Channel	Advantages	Disadvantages
Oral, in-person	• Provide opportunity for immediate feedback • Easily resolve misunderstandings and negotiate meanings • Involve rich nonverbal cues (both physical gestures and vocal inflections) • Allow you to express the emotion behind your message	• Restrict participation to those physically present • Unless recorded, provide no permanent, verifiable record of the communication • Can reduce communicator's control over the message
Oral, digital	• Can provide opportunity for immediate feedback (live phone or online conversations) • Not restricted to participants in the same location • Allow time-shifted consumption (podcasts, for example)	• Lack nonverbal cues other than voice inflections • Can be tedious to listen to if not audience focused (recorded messages such as podcasts)
Written, printed	• Allow writers to plan and control their messages • Can reach geographically dispersed audiences, although not as easily as digital • Offer a permanent, verifiable record • Can be used to avoid immediate interactions • Can deemphasize emotional elements • Give recipients time to process messages before responding (compared with oral communication and some digital formats)	• Offer limited opportunities for timely feedback • Lack the rich nonverbal cues provided by oral media • Often take more time and more resources to create and distribute • Can require special skills in preparation and production (elaborate documents)
Written, digital	In general, all the advantages of written printed documents plus: • Can be delivered quickly • Offer the flexibility of multiple formats and channels, from microblogs to wikis • Offer the ability to structure messages in creative ways, such as writing a headline on Twitter and linking to the full message on a blog • Can offer links to related and more in-depth information • Can increase accessibility and openness in an organization through broader sharing • Enable audience interaction through social media features • Can be easily integrated with other media types, such as embedded videos or photos	• Can be limited in terms of reach and capability (for instance, you need someone's email address before sending a message) • Require internet or mobile phone connectivity • Are easy to overuse (sending too many messages to too many recipients) • Create privacy risks and concerns (exposing confidential data; employer monitoring; accidental forwarding) • Entail security risks (viruses, spyware; network breaches) • Can create productivity concerns (frequent interruptions; nonbusiness usage)
Visual, printed	• Can convey complex ideas and relationships quickly • Are often less intimidating than long blocks of text • Can reduce the burden on the audience to figure out how the pieces of a message or concept fit • Make simple charts and graphs (easy to create in spreadsheets and other software), then integrate with reports	• Can require artistic skills to design (complicated visuals) • Require some technical skills to create • Can require more time to create than equivalent amount of text • Can be expensive to print (large or elaborate pieces)
Visual, digital	In general, all the advantages of visual printed documents and all the advantages of written digital formats plus: • Can personalize and enhance the experience for audience members • Offer the persuasive power of multimedia formats, particularly video	• Require time, cost, and skills to create • Can require large amounts of bandwidth to distribute

offer the give-and-take of in-person conversations and can be the best alternative to talking in person, although voice-only channels don't support all the nuances of nonverbal communication.

Written Medium, Print Channel

Written, printed documents are the classic format of business communication. **Memos** are brief printed documents traditionally used for the routine, day-to-day exchange of

Memos are brief printed documents traditionally used for the routine, day-to-day exchange of information within an organization.

Letters are brief written messages sent to customers and other recipients outside the organization.

information within an organization. **Letters** are brief written messages sent to customers and other recipients outside the organization. Reports and proposals are usually longer than memos and letters, although both can be created in memo or letter format. These documents come in a variety of lengths, ranging from a few pages to several hundred, and are usually fairly formal in tone.

Although still a useful format, printed documents have been replaced by digital alternatives in many instances. However, here are several situations in which you should consider a printed message over digital alternatives:

Digital media/channel formats have replaced printed documents in many instances, but print is still the best choice for some messages and situations.

- When you want to make a formal impression
- When you are legally required to provide information in printed form
- When you want to stand out from the flood of digital messages
- When you need a permanent, unchangeable, or secure record

Obviously, if you can't reach a particular audience through digital channels, you'll need to use a printed message. Appendix A offers guidelines on formatting printed memos and letters.

Written Medium, Digital Channel

Most of your business communication efforts will involve the combination of written medium and digital channel.

Most of your business communication efforts will involve written digital messages. Chapter 8 takes a closer look at various written-digital combinations, from email to workgroup messaging to social networks.

Visual Medium, Print Channel

Photographs and diagrams can be effective communication tools for conveying emotional content, spatial relationships, technical processes, and other content that can be difficult to describe using words alone. You may occasionally create visual, printed messages as standalone items, but most will be used as supporting material in printed documents.

Visual Medium, Digital Channel

The combination of the visual medium and a digital channel can be the most compelling and engaging choice for many messages, although it is not always the easiest or cheapest format.

Business messages can really come alive when conveyed by visual media in digital channels (see Figure 5.4). Infographics, interactive diagrams, animation, and digital video have the potential to engage audiences in ways that other formats can't, which is why the use of visual elements in business communication continues to grow.

Traditional business messages rely primarily on text, with occasional support from graphics such as charts, graphs, or diagrams to help illustrate points discussed in the text. However, many business communicators are discovering the power of messages in which the visual element is dominant and supported by small amounts of text. For the purposes of this discussion, you can think of visual media as formats in which one or more visual elements play a central role in conveying the message content, such as with *infographics* (see page 411).

Messages that combine powerful visuals with supporting text can be effective for several reasons. Today's audiences are pressed for time and bombarded with messages, so anything that communicates quickly is welcome. Visuals are also effective at describing complex ideas and processes because they can reduce the work required for an audience to identify the parts and relationships that make up the whole. Also, in a multilingual business world, diagrams, symbols, and other images can lower communication barriers by requiring less language processing. Finally, visual images can be easier to remember than purely textual descriptions or explanations.

REAL-TIME UPDATES
LEARN MORE BY VISITING THIS WEBSITE
Get started with Google Docs

These articles will take you through the process of creating and using documents. Go to **real-timeupdates.com/ebc13** and select Learn More in the Students section.

The Unique Challenges of Communication on Mobile Devices

Mobile devices can be used to create and consume virtually every digital form of oral, written, and visual media. Thanks to the combination of portability and the flexibility

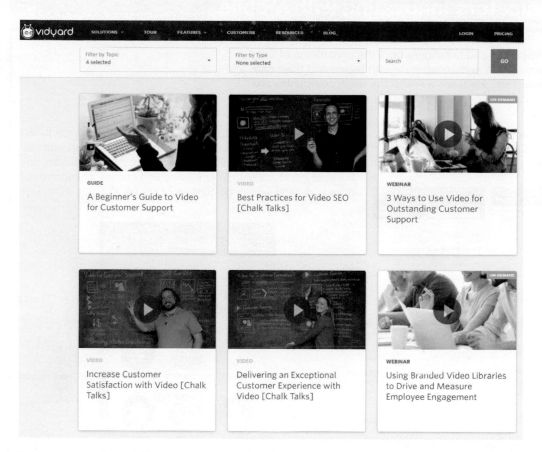

Figure 5.4 Media and Channel Choices
Vidyard, which helps businesses use online video for marketing, sales, and customer support, uses a variety of media to share its messages. To learn more about Vidyard and its services, potential clients can peruse the website, read blog posts, view webinars, read guides and handbooks, take online courses, and watch videos.

enabled by a wide array of business-focused apps, mobile devices have become a primary tool in business communication. However, they do require some special considerations:

- **Screen size and resolution.** The screen resolution of phones, phablets, and tablets has improved considerably in recent years, but the limited size of these screens still presents a challenge simply because many messages are significantly larger than the screens they will be viewed on. The result is a dilemma that pits clarity against context. Readers can zoom in to make text readable and visuals understandable, but particularly on phone screens, the inability to see an entire document page or visual at once can limit a reader's ability to grasp its full meaning. This can be particularly troublesome if you are collaborating on writing or presentation projects and team members need to review documents or slides.

- **Input technologies.** Even for accomplished texters, typing on mobile keyboards can be a challenge. Voice recognition is one way around the keyboard limitation, but anyone using it in public areas or shared offices runs the risk of sharing private content and annoying anyone within earshot. In addition, selecting items on a touch screen can be more difficult than doing so on a PC screen using a mouse or touchpad. If your website content or other messages and materials require a significant amount of input activity from recipients, try to make it as easy as possible for them. Even simple steps such as increasing the size of buttons and text-entry fields can help.

- **Bandwidth, speeds, and connectivity limitations.** The quality of mobile connectivity varies widely by device, carrier, service plan, roaming, and geographic location. Even users with higher-bandwidth service don't always get the advertised transfer speeds they are paying for. Moreover, mobile users can lose connectivity while traveling, passing through network "dead spots," or during peak-demand hours or events

The mobile digital channel has become significant in business communication of all types, but it presents some challenges that must be considered.

(*continued on page 140*)

Business Communicators Innovating with Mobile

Mobile connectivity is freeing employees and managers from the constraints of fixed location, making it easier to communicate and collaborate with teams and business partners wherever their work takes them. Here are a few of the ways companies are using mobile to improve communication.

Employee performance management apps help supervisors plan workforce needs, keep track of employee progress, and quickly address workplace issues.

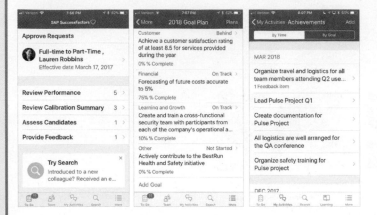

Distributed decision-making apps give employees the tools to make decisions in the field, without being forced to wait for managers back in the office. Being able to make decisions on the spot improves customer service and company responsiveness in dealing with opportunities or crises.

Project management apps help mobile and geographically dispersed work teams collaborate. Instant access to task status and other vital information helps project managers stay on top of rapidly moving projects and helps team members communicate efficiently.

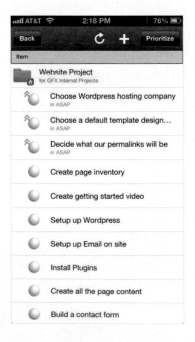

Employee recruiting apps give recruiters the tools they need to screen candidates and manage the entire interview process.

Travel and expense tracking apps help employees and managers organize the details of business travel and write expense reports, trip reports, and other required communications.

Copyright: Expensify

Customer support apps give mobile employees access to trouble tickets, customer records, troubleshooting tools, messaging, and other resources they need to solve problems on site.

Sales apps give sales representatives the resources they need to find and qualify sales prospects, present solutions, give product demonstrations, take orders, and sign contracts.

Social media management apps such as Sprout Social help social media managers stay on top of Twitter, Facebook, and other feeds so they can respond to breaking news, customer complaints, rumors, and other events that require fast response around the clock.

Courtesy of Sprout Social

Unified communication apps pull together the multiple channels that many employees now need to coordinate—phone, messaging, email, videoconferencing, social media feeds, and more.

Courtesy of Mitel

139

(trade shows and conventions are notorious for this). Don't assume that your mobile recipients will be able to satisfactorily consume the content that you might be creating on a fast, reliable, in-office network. Reducing the size of photos and other media elements on webpages is a good way to speed up access for mobile users.[3]

- **Data usage and operational costs.** As the amount of video traffic in particular increases (video requires much higher bandwidth than text or audio), data consumption is becoming a key concern for mobile carriers and customers alike. In the United States, mobile costs could be affected by developments in *net neutrality* regulations, which determine whether carriers need to treat all network data equally.[4]

FACTORS TO CONSIDER WHEN CHOOSING MEDIA AND CHANNELS

You don't always have the option of choosing which medium or channel to use for a particular message. For example, many companies have workgroup messaging or social networking systems that you are expected to use for certain types of communication. However, when you do have a choice, consider these factors:

> Media vary widely in terms of *richness*, which encompasses the number of information cues, feedback mechanisms, and opportunities for personalization.

- **Richness.** *Richness* is a medium's ability to (1) convey a message through more than one informational cue (visual, verbal, vocal), (2) facilitate feedback, (3) establish personal focus, and (4) allow the use of natural, conversational language.[5] Face-to-face communication is a rich medium because it excels in all four of these areas: It delivers information both verbally and nonverbally, it allows immediate feedback through both verbal and nonverbal responses, it has the potential to be intimate and personal, and it lets people converse naturally. In contrast, lean media are limited in one or more of these four aspects. For example, texting and IM allow rapid feedback and can easily be personalized. However, they usually deliver information through only one informational cue (words), which can lead to misinterpretation, although emoticons and emojis (see page 221) can add emotional nuances. In general, use richer media to send nonroutine or complex messages, to humanize your presence throughout the organization, to communicate caring to employees, and to gain employee commitment to company goals. Use leaner media to send routine messages or to transfer information that doesn't require significant explanation.[6]
- **Formality.** Your medium/channel choice is a nonverbal signal that affects the style and tone of your message. For example, a printed memo or letter is likely to be perceived as a more formal gesture than an email message.
- **Media and channel limitations.** Every medium and channel has limitations. For instance, short messaging is perfect for communicating simple, straightforward messages between two people, but it is less effective for complex messages or conversations that involve three or more people.

> Many types of media/channel combinations offer instantaneous delivery, but take care not to interrupt people unnecessarily if you don't need an immediate answer.

> Remember that media and channel choices can also send a nonverbal signal regarding costs; make sure your choices are financially appropriate.

- **Urgency.** Some media establish a connection with the audience faster than others, so choose wisely if your message is urgent. However, be sure to respect audience members' time and workloads. If a message isn't urgent and doesn't require immediate feedback, choose a medium such as email or blogging that allows people to respond at their convenience.
- **Cost.** Cost is both a real financial factor and a perceived nonverbal signal. For example, depending on the context, extravagant video or multimedia presentations can send a nonverbal signal of sophistication and professionalism—or careless disregard for company budgets.
- **Audience preferences.** If you know that your audience prefers a particular medium/channel combination, use that format if it works well for the message and the situation. Otherwise you risk annoying the audience or having your message missed or ignored.

> Always be aware of your company's policies regarding network security and data privacy.

- **Security and privacy.** Your company may have restrictions on the media and channels that can be used for certain types of messages, but even if it doesn't, think carefully whenever your messages include sensitive information. Never assume that your digital communications are private. Many companies monitor employee communication on these channels, and there is always the risk that networks could get hacked or that messages will be forwarded beyond their original recipients.

Organizing Your Information

The ability to organize messages effectively is a skill that helps audiences and writers alike. Good organization helps the receivers of your message in three ways:

- **It helps them understand your message.** In a well-organized message, you make your main point clearly, provide additional points to support that main idea, and satisfy all the information needs of the audience. But if your message is poorly organized, your meaning can be obscured, and your audiences may form inaccurate conclusions about what you've written or said.
- **It helps them accept your message.** If your writing appears confused and disorganized, people will likely conclude that the *thinking* behind the writing is also confused and disorganized. Moreover, effective messages often require more than just clear logic. In sensitive situations, for example, a thoughtful and diplomatic approach helps receivers accept your message, even if it's not exactly what they want to hear. In contrast, a poorly organized message on an emotionally charged topic can alienate the audience before you have the chance to get your point across.
- **It saves your audience time.** Well-organized messages are efficient. They contain only relevant ideas, and they are brief. Moreover, each piece of information is presented in a logical place in the overall flow; each section builds on the one before to create a coherent whole without forcing people to look for missing pieces.

In addition to saving time and energy for your readers, good organization saves *you* time and consumes less of your creative energy. The writing moves more quickly because you don't waste time putting ideas in the wrong places or composing material that you later discover you don't need. You spend far less time rewriting, trying to extract sensible meaning from disorganized rambling. Plus, organizational skills are good for your career because they help you develop a reputation as a clear thinker who cares about your readers.

5 **LEARNING OBJECTIVE** Explain why good organization is important to both you and your audience, and list the tasks involved in organizing a message.

Good organization benefits your audiences by helping them understand and accept your message in less time.

Good organization helps you by reducing the time and creative energy needed to create effective messages.

DEFINING YOUR MAIN IDEA

The **topic** of your message is the overall subject, and your **main idea** is a specific statement about that topic (see Table 5.2). For example, if you believe that the current system of using paper forms for filing employee insurance claims is expensive and slow, you might craft a message in which the topic is employee insurance claims and the main idea is that a new web-based system would reduce costs for the company and reduce reimbursement delays for employees.

In longer documents and presentations, you sometimes need to unify a mass of data and information under one main idea that encompasses all the individual points you want to make. Finding a common thread through all these points can be a challenge. Sometimes you won't even be sure what your main idea is until you sort through the

The *topic* is the overall subject of a message; the *main idea* makes a statement about the topic.

TABLE 5.2	Defining Topic and Main Idea		
General Purpose	**Example of Specific Purpose**	**Example of Topic**	**Example of Main Idea**
To inform	Teach customer service representatives how to edit and expand the technical support wiki	Technical support wiki	Careful, thorough edits and additions to the wiki help the entire department provide better customer support.
To persuade	Convince top managers to increase spending on research and development	Funding for research and development	Competitors spend more than we do on research and development, which helps them create more innovative products.
To collaborate	Solicit ideas for a companywide incentive system that ties wages to profits	Incentive pay	Tying wages to profits motivates employees and reduces compensation costs in tough years.

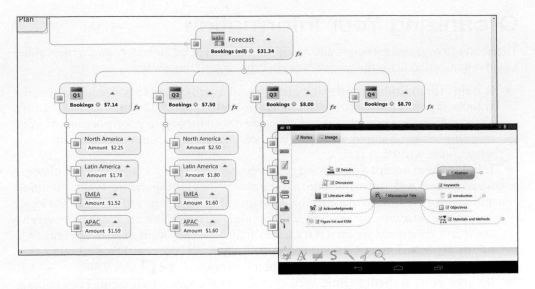

Figure 5.5 Mind Mapping
Mind-mapping tools such as Mindjet Map make it easy to explore the organization of your material, and mobile apps (see inset) bring this capability to tablets and other mobile devices.

If your main idea isn't clear, try multiple creative approaches to clarify and refine it.

information. For tough assignments like these, consider a variety of techniques to define your main idea:

- **Brainstorming.** Working alone or with others, generate as many ideas and questions as you can, without stopping to criticize or organize. After you capture all these pieces, look for patterns and connections to help identify the main idea and groups of supporting ideas.
- **Journalistic approach.** The journalistic approach (see page 132) can help you distill major ideas from unorganized information.
- **Question-and-answer chain.** Start with a key question from the audience's perspective, and work back toward your message. You will probably find that each answer generates new questions until you identify the information that needs to be in your message.
- **Storyteller's tour.** Some writers find it best to talk through a communication challenge before they try to write. Record yourself as you describe what you intend to write. Then listen to the playback, identify ways to tighten and clarify the message, and repeat the process until you distill the main idea down to a single concise message.
- **Mind mapping.** You can generate and organize ideas using a graphic method called *mind mapping* (see Figure 5.5). Start with a main idea and then branch out to connect every other related idea that comes to mind.

REAL-TIME UPDATES

LEARN MORE BY WATCHING THIS VIDEO

How to guide a group brainstorming session

Follow these simple tips to get the most from your next brainstorming session. Go to **real-timeupdates.com/ebc13** and select Learn More in the Students section.

LIMITING YOUR SCOPE

The *scope* of a message is the range of information it presents, its overall length, and the level of detail.

The **scope** of your message is the range of information you present, the overall length, and the level of detail—all of which need to correspond to your main idea. The length of some business messages has a preset limit, whether from a boss's instructions, the medium/channel you're using, or a time frame such as speaker slots during a seminar. Even if you don't have a preset length, always limit yourself to the scope needed to convey your main idea and whatever supporting information it requires.

Limit the scope of your message so that you can convey your main idea as briefly as possible.

Whatever the length of your message, limit the number of major supporting points to the most compelling and important ideas. Offering a long list of supporting points might feel as though you're being thorough, but your audience is likely to view such detail as rambling and mind numbing. If you have quite a few valid points, look for ways to combine them to create a smaller number with greater impact. For instance, you can group points under major headings such as finance, customers, competitors, employees, or whatever is appropriate for your subject.

The ideal length of a message depends on your topic, your audience members' familiarity with the material, their receptivity to your conclusions, and your credibility. You'll need less content to present routine information to a knowledgeable audience that already knows and trusts you. You'll need more content to build a consensus about a complex and controversial subject, especially if the members of your audience are skeptical or hostile.

CHOOSING BETWEEN DIRECT AND INDIRECT APPROACHES

After you've defined your main idea and supporting points, you're ready to decide on the sequence you will use to present your information. You have two basic options:

- The **direct approach** starts with the main idea (such as a recommendation, a conclusion, or a request) and follows that with supporting point and evidence.
- The **indirect approach** starts with reasoning, evidence, and background information and builds up to the main idea.

Most of your routine business communication efforts will use the direct approach. The indirect approach is used in three main situations: (1) when your audience is likely to have a skeptical or hostile reaction to your main idea, (2) when you need to convey significantly negative information, and (3) when you want to persuade people to take action or make a decision.

- With skeptical or hostile audiences, if you open with the main idea, readers or listeners are likely to react in an emotionally defensive way and be more resistant to your reasons and evidence. They already have concerns about the subject, and you're not yet giving them any reason to think otherwise. However, if you lay out your reasons and evidence first, there's a better chance they will process these points before you get to the main idea.
- For negative messages, the indirect approach lets you present reasons for the negative news before you actually state it. Doing so can ease the shock for readers or listeners, because it gives them time to emotionally prepare for the news, rather than being hit with it right away. If it is used thoughtfully and ethically, the indirect approach can be a sensitive way to share unwelcome news. Chapter 10 discusses negative messages in detail and offers advice to help you choose when to use the indirect approach for these messages.
- With persuasive messages, you are usually asking readers or listeners to make a decision or take action. The indirect approach lets you build toward your request with compelling reasons and evidence so that by the time you make the request, the audience is more likely to be on your side. Chapter 11 discusses persuasive messages in more detail.

With the *direct approach*, you open with the main idea of your message and support it with reasoning, evidence, and examples.

With the *indirect approach*, you withhold the main idea until you have built up to it logically and persuasively with reasoning, evidence, and examples.

The indirect approach is primarily used for messages that address skeptical or hostile audiences, that need to convey significant negative information, and that attempt to persuade an audience.

OUTLINING YOUR CONTENT

After you have chosen the best approach, it's time to figure out the most logical and effective way to present your major points and supporting details. For anything beyond simple, short messages, get into the habit of creating outlines. You'll save time, get better results, and do a better job of navigating through complicated business situations. Even if you're just jotting down three or four key points, making an outline will help you organize your thoughts for faster writing. When you're preparing longer, more complex documents and presentations, an outline is indispensable because it helps you visualize the relationships among the various parts.

You're no doubt familiar with the basic outline formats that identify each point with a number or letter and that indent certain points to show which ones are of equal status. A good outline divides a topic into at least two parts, restricts each subdivision to one category, and ensures that each subdivision is separate and distinct (see Figure 5.6 on the next page).

Another way to visualize the outline of your message is to create an organization chart similar to the charts used to show a company's management structure. Put the main idea

Outlining saves time and helps you create more effective messages.

MOBILE APP

Outliner is one of several apps that make it easy to create and modify outlines.

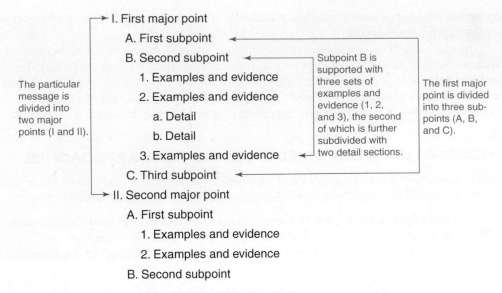

Figure 5.6 **Organizing Your Thoughts with a Clear Outline**
No matter what outlining format you use, think through your major supporting points and the examples and evidence that can support each point.

in the highest-level box to establish the big picture. The lower-level ideas, like lower-level employees, provide the details. All the ideas should be logically organized into divisions of thought, just as a company is organized into divisions and departments.[7] The mind-mapping technique used to generate ideas works in a similar way, although after you complete your map, you still need to decide the order in which to present the various branches.

Whichever outlining or organizing scheme you use, be sure to identify your main idea, major supporting points, and the evidence and examples that will help you express the main idea in a compelling way. (Keep in mind that the order in which you present these elements in your message depends on whether you are using the direct or indirect approach.)

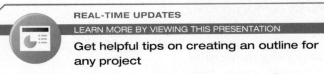

REAL-TIME UPDATES
LEARN MORE BY VIEWING THIS PRESENTATION

Get helpful tips on creating an outline for any project

Learn these proven steps for creating robust, practical outlines. Go to **real-timeupdates.com/ebc13** and select Learn More in the Students section.

Identify the Main Idea

The main idea establishes *what you want your readers to do or think and why* it is beneficial for them to do so.

The main idea helps you establish the goals and general strategy of the message, and it summarizes two vital considerations: (1) *what* you want your audience members to do or think and (2) *why* it is beneficial for them to do so. Everything in your message should either support the main idea or explain its implications. Remember that the direct approach states the main idea in the opening of the message, whereas the indirect approach delays the main idea until after the evidence is presented.

Assemble Major Supporting Points

Your main idea needs supporting points that clarify and explain it in concrete terms.

For anything beyond simple messages, you need to support your main idea with major points that clarify and explain the main idea in concrete terms. If your purpose is to inform and the material is factual, your major points may be based on something physical or financial—something you can visualize or measure, such as activities to be performed, functional units, spatial or chronological relationships, or parts of a whole. If you're describing a process, the major points are usually steps in the process. If you're describing an object, the major points often correspond to the parts of the object. If you're giving a historical account, major points represent events in the chronological chain of events. If your purpose is to persuade or to collaborate, select major points that develop a line of reasoning or a logical argument that proves your central message and motivates your audience to act.

Gather Compelling Examples and Evidence

Choose examples and evidence carefully; one compelling story or piece of evidence can be stronger than a collection of weaker material.

After you've defined the main idea and identified major supporting points, think about examples and evidence that can confirm, illuminate, or expand on your supporting points.

TABLE 5.3	Six Types of Detail	
Type of Detail	**Example**	**Comment**
Facts and figures	Sales are strong this month. We have two new contracts worth $5 million and a good chance of winning another worth $2.5 million.	Enhance credibility more than any other type, but can become tedious if used excessively.
Example or illustration	We've spent four months trying to hire recent accounting graduates, but so far, only one person has joined our firm. One candidate told me that she would love to work for us, but she can get $10,000 more a year elsewhere.	Adds life to a message, but one example doesn't necessarily prove a point. Idea must be supported by other evidence as well.
Description	Upscale hamburger restaurants target burger lovers who want more than the convenience and low prices of a fast-food burger. These places feature more adventuresome menus, a greater range of toppings, and a more sophisticated atmosphere.	Helps audience visualize the subject by creating a sensory impression. Doesn't prove a point but clarifies it and makes it memorable.
Narration (storytelling)	When Rita Longworth took over as CEO, she faced a tough choice: shut down the tablet PC division entirely or outsource manufacturing to lower costs while keeping the division alive. As her first step, she convened a meeting with all the managers in the division to get their input on the two options. (Story continues from there.)	Stimulates audience interest through the use of dramatic tension. In many instances, must be supplemented with statistical data in order to prove a point convincingly.
Reference to authority	I discussed this idea with Jackie Loman in the Chicago plant, and she was very supportive. As you know, Jackie has been in charge of that plant for the past six years. She is confident that we can speed up the number 2 line by 150 units an hour if we add another worker.	Bolsters a case while adding variety and credibility. Works only if authority is recognized and respected by audience.
Visual aids	Graphs, charts, tables, infographics, data visualization, photos, video	Helps audience grasp the key points about sets of data or visualize connections between ideas.

Choose examples and evidence carefully so that these elements support your overall message without distracting or overwhelming your audience. One strong example, particularly if it is conveyed through a compelling story (see the next section), is usually more powerful than several weaker examples. Similarly, a few strong points of evidence are usually more persuasive than a large collection of minor details. You can back up your major supporting points in a variety of ways, depending on the subject material and the available examples and evidence (see Table 5.3).

Figure 5.7 on the next page illustrates several of the key themes about organizing a message: helping readers get the information they need quickly, defining and conveying the main idea, limiting the scope of the message, choosing the approach, and outlining your information.

BUILDING READER INTEREST WITH STORYTELLING TECHNIQUES

As the Wolff Olins vignette at the beginning of the chapter points out, narrative techniques can be an effective way to organize messages in a surprising number of business situations, from recruiting and training employees to enticing investors and customers. Storytelling is such a vital means of communicating that, in the words of management consultant Steve Tobak, "It's hard to imagine your career going anywhere if you can't tell a story."[8] Fortunately, you've been telling and hearing stories all your life, so narrative techniques already come naturally to you; now it's just a matter of adapting those techniques to business situations.

Career-related stories, such as how someone pursued the opportunity to work on projects he or she is passionate about, can entice skilled employees to consider joining a firm. Entrepreneurs can use stories to help investors see how their new ideas have the potential to affect people's lives (and therefore generate lots of sales). Stories can be cautionary tales as well, dramatizing the consequences of career blunders, ethical mistakes, or strategic missteps.

Storytelling is an effective way to organize many business messages because it helps readers personalize the message and understand causes and consequences.

The Power of Story

A key reason storytelling can be so effective is that stories help readers and listeners imagine themselves living through the experience of the person in the story. Chip Heath of Stanford

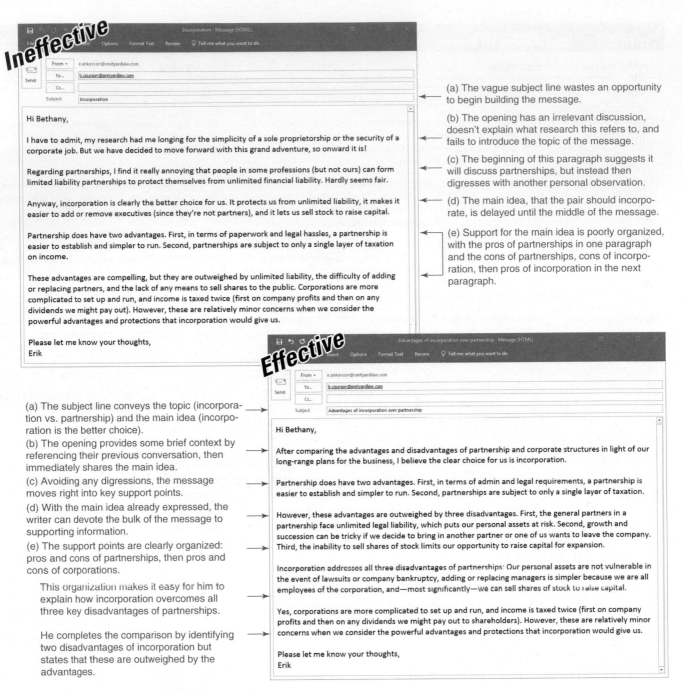

Ineffective

From ▾   e.ankerson@smityardlaw.com
To...   b.courson@smityardlaw.com
Cc...
Subject   Incorporation

Hi Bethany,

I have to admit, my research had me longing for the simplicity of a sole proprietorship or the security of a corporate job. But we have decided to move forward with this grand adventure, so onward it is!

Regarding partnerships, I find it really annoying that people in some professions (but not ours) can form limited liability partnerships to protect themselves from unlimited financial liability. Hardly seems fair.

Anyway, incorporation is clearly the better choice for us. It protects us from unlimited liability, it makes it easier to add or remove executives (since they're not partners), and it lets us sell stock to raise capital.

Partnership does have two advantages. First, in terms of paperwork and legal hassles, a partnership is easier to establish and simpler to run. Second, partnerships are subject to only a single layer of taxation on income.

These advantages are compelling, but they are outweighed by unlimited liability, the difficulty of adding or replacing partners, and the lack of any means to sell shares to the public. Corporations are more complicated to set up and run, and income is taxed twice (first on company profits and then on any dividends we might pay out). However, these are relatively minor concerns when we consider the powerful advantages and protections that incorporation would give us.

Please let me know your thoughts,
Erik

(a) The vague subject line wastes an opportunity to begin building the message.

(b) The opening has an irrelevant discussion, doesn't explain what research this refers to, and fails to introduce the topic of the message.

(c) The beginning of this paragraph suggests it will discuss partnerships, but instead then digresses with another personal observation.

(d) The main idea, that the pair should incorporate, is delayed until the middle of the message.

(e) Support for the main idea is poorly organized, with the pros of partnerships in one paragraph and the cons of partnerships, cons of incorporation, then pros of incorporation in the next paragraph.

Effective

From ▾   e.ankerson@smityardlaw.com
To...   b.courson@smityardlaw.com
Cc...
Subject   Advantages of incorporation over partnership

Hi Bethany,

After comparing the advantages and disadvantages of partnership and corporate structures in light of our long-range plans for the business, I believe the clear choice for us is incorporation.

Partnership does have two advantages. First, in terms of admin and legal requirements, a partnership is easier to establish and simpler to run. Second, partnerships are subject to only a single layer of taxation.

However, these advantages are outweighed by three disadvantages. First, the general partners in a partnership face unlimited legal liability, which puts our personal assets at risk. Second, growth and succession can be tricky if we decide to bring in another partner or one of us wants to leave the company. Third, the inability to sell shares of stock limits our opportunity to raise capital for expansion.

Incorporation addresses all three disadvantages of partnerships: Our personal assets are not vulnerable in the event of lawsuits or company bankruptcy, adding or replacing managers is simpler because we are all employees of the corporation, and—most significantly—we can sell shares of stock to raise capital.

Yes, corporations are more complicated to set up and run, and income is taxed twice (first on company profits and then on any dividends we might pay out to shareholders). However, these are relatively minor concerns when we consider the powerful advantages and protections that incorporation would give us.

Please let me know your thoughts,
Erik

(a) The subject line conveys the topic (incorporation vs. partnership) and the main idea (incorporation is the better choice).

(b) The opening provides some brief context by referencing their previous conversation, then immediately shares the main idea.

(c) Avoiding any digressions, the message moves right into key support points.

(d) With the main idea already expressed, the writer can devote the bulk of the message to supporting information.

(e) The support points are clearly organized: pros and cons of partnerships, then pros and cons of corporations.

This organization makes it easy for him to explain how incorporation overcomes all three key disadvantages of partnerships.

He completes the comparison by identifying two disadvantages of incorporation but states that these are outweighed by the advantages.

Figure 5.7   Improving the Organization of a Message
This writer is following up on a conversation from the previous day, in which he and the recipient discussed which of two forms of ownership, a partnership or a corporation, they should use for their new company. (*Partnership* has a specific legal meaning in this context.) That question is the topic of the message; the main idea is the recommendation that they incorporate, rather than form a partnership. Notice how the Effective version uses the direct approach to quickly get to the main idea and then supports that by comparing the advantages and disadvantages of both forms of ownership. In contrast, the Ineffective version contains irrelevant information, makes the comparison difficult to follow, and buries the main idea in the middle of the message.

University and his brother, Dan Heath of Duke University, spent years exploring the question of why some ideas "stick" and others disappear. One of their conclusions is that ideas conveyed through storytelling tend to thrive because stories "put knowledge into a framework that is more lifelike, more true to our day-to-day existence."[9]

In addition, stories can demonstrate cause-and-effect relationships in a compelling fashion.[10] Imagine attending a new employee orientation and listening to the trainer read off a list of ethics rules and guidelines. Now imagine the trainer telling the story of someone

Stories can demonstrate cause-and-effect relationships in a compelling way.

who sounded a lot like you, fresh out of college and full of energy and ambition. Desperate to hit demanding sales targets, the person in the story began logging sales before customers had agreed to purchase, hoping the sales would eventually come through and no one would be the wiser. However, the scheme was exposed during a routine audit, and the rising star was booted out of the company with an ethical stain that would haunt him for years. You may not remember all the rules and guidelines, but chances are you will remember what happened to that person who sounded a lot like you at the beginning of the story. This ability to share organizational values is one of the major benefits of using storytelling in business communication, particularly across diverse workforces.[11]

Stories can also help leaders and employees envision future possibilities, such as new product concepts or different ways of approaching work. In these instances, storytelling can free people from the mental constraints of how things are now. By asking "what if ...?" questions and describing appealing future conditions in the context of a story, storytellers can help people imagine how things could be, even if today's facts, figures, and assumptions don't paint an obvious path toward that future.[12]

The Three Elements of Storytelling

A classic story has three basic parts. The beginning of the story presents someone whom the audience can identify with in some way, and this person has a dream to pursue or a problem to solve. (Think of how movies and novels often start by introducing a likable character who immediately gets into danger, for example.) The middle of the story shows this character taking action and making decisions as he or she pursues the goal or tries to solve the problem. The storyteller's objective here is to build the audience's interest by increasing the tension: Will the "hero" overcome the obstacles in his or her path and defeat whatever adversary is keeping him or her away from her goal?[13] The end of the story answers that question and usually offers a lesson to be learned about the outcome as well.

Organize stories in three parts:

- A beginning that introduces a sympathetic person with a dream or a challenge
- A middle that shows the obstacles to be overcome
- An ending that resolves the situation and highlights the moral or message of the story

---

INTELLIGENT COMMUNICATION TECHNOLOGY

Shaping Stories with the Help of Artificial Intelligence

Storytelling, composing, and other creative endeavors might seem to nonpractitioners as vaguely magical or mystical activities in which naturally gifted people conjure stories, symphonies, and other art forms out of thin air. However, many artists will likely tell you that in reality it's a little bit of magic and a whole lot of work.

Creation involves a process that is more method than mystery: Understand the structure of what you're trying to create (such as the emotional arc of stories), play around with lots of possibilities, then decide which of those possibilities fit the structure in the most effective way. Obviously, it takes original vision to come up with possibilities and finely tuned insights to know what will resonate with readers or viewers, but there is a method to it.

The existence of any process suggests the possibility of automating one or more steps in the process, and developers are busy applying AI to the storytelling process. For example, storytelling is most engaging when it connects with an audience's desires, dreams, or fears. By using tools such as *social listening* (monitoring social media feeds), advertisers can take the emotional pulse of a target audience to identify storytelling angles that people are more likely to respond to. AI tools can also tell businesses whether the stories they're telling are hitting the mark. In terms of actually creating content, AI systems are now writing simple news and sports stories.

Will AI ever write complex, nuanced stories that match the skill and touch of accomplished human writers? At this point, that seems far-fetched, given how vital the human traits of empathy and emotional intelligence are in storytelling. A human-machine partnership looks like the best possibility for the foreseeable future, with each partner focusing on his, her, or its greatest strengths. Computers can do the data crunching and some of the "grunt work" in terms of putting simple stories together, and humans can spend their time being even more creative.

WHAT'S YOUR TAKE?

1. How do you feel about companies using AI to analyze your social media content to get an idea of what you're thinking and feeling?
2. Would you feel differently about an enjoyable novel or movie if you learned it had been written by an AI system? Why or why not?

Sources: Eric Chu, Jonathan Dunn, Deb Roy, Geoffrey Sands, and Russell Stevens, "AI in Storytelling: Machines as Cocreators," *McKinsey,* December 2017, www.mckinsey.com; Darren Menabney, "Why Google, Ideo, and IBM Are Betting on AI to Make Us Better Storytellers," *Fast Company,* 6 February 2017, www.fastcompany.com; Zohar Dayan, "Artificial Intelligence: A Complement to Great Storytelling," *Forbes,* 11 December 2017, www.forbes.com.

PhotoAlto sas/Alamy Stock Photo

Storytelling, both live during presentations and as an organizing scheme for written messages, is an important business communication skill.

By the way, even though these are "stories," they must not be made-up tales. Telling stories that didn't happen while presenting them as real-life events is a serious breach of ethics that damages a company's credibility.[14]

Consider adding an element of storytelling whenever your main idea involves the opportunity to inspire, to persuade, to teach, or to warn readers or listeners about the potential outcomes of a particular course of action. For fresh ideas and media materials on planning messages, visit **real-timeupdates .com/ebc13** and select Chapter 5. For a quick refresher on message-planning tasks, see "Checklist: Planning Business Messages."

CHECKLIST ✔ Planning Business Messages

A. Analyze the situation.
- ✔ Determine whether the purpose of your message is to inform, persuade, or collaborate.
- ✔ Identify what you want your audience to think or do after receiving the message.
- ✔ Make sure your purpose is worthwhile and realistic.
- ✔ Make sure the time is right for your message.
- ✔ Make sure your purpose is acceptable to your organization.
- ✔ Identify the primary audience.
- ✔ Determine the size and composition of your audience.
- ✔ Estimate your audience's level of understanding and probable reaction to your message.

B. Gather information.
- ✔ Decide whether to use formal or informal techniques for gathering information.
- ✔ Figure out what your audience needs to know.
- ✔ Provide all required information, and make sure it's accurate, ethical, and pertinent.

C. Select the best combination of medium and channel for your message.
- ✔ Understand the advantages and disadvantages of oral, written, and visual media distributed through both digital and nondigital channels.
- ✔ Consider media richness, formality, media limitations, urgency, cost, and audience preference.

D. Organize your information.
- ✔ Define your main idea.
- ✔ Limit your scope.
- ✔ Choose the direct or indirect approach.
- ✔ Outline content by defining your main idea, identifying major supporting points, and gathering examples and evidence.
- ✔ Look for opportunities to use storytelling to build audience interest.

ON THE JOB: SOLVING COMMUNICATION DILEMMAS AT **WOLFF OLINS**

You've joined the Wolff Olins team at the company's New York office, where you work as a creative consultant helping entrepreneurs and company leaders connect with internal and external audiences. Your newest client is Tasha Blair, the founder of a company called RocketThink that is developing AI-based learning tools for children who haven't been able to flourish in a traditional classroom setting. Using the insights you gained in this chapter, address these communication challenges.

1. Some people join startup companies with the hope of striking it rich when the company eventually starts selling shares to the public in its *initial public offering (IPO)*. They are often willing to work long hours for months on end during the pre-IPO phase (which is where RocketThink is now) with the notion that it will be worth the sacrifice when the company goes public and the shares they were granted skyrocket in value. Blair is worried that her employees have become so focused on chasing a big IPO payout that they are losing sight of the long-term mission of helping families while building a lasting company. She has asked for your help in drafting a speech for the next company meeting that will encourage the team to refocus on that mission. Which of the following would be the best specific purpose for this speech?
   a. To tell employees that the short-term focus on personal financial gain is bad for the company, bad for customers, and won't be tolerated.
   b. To persuade employees to remember the reason Rocket-Think exists and to imagine the satisfaction they will experience at the end of their careers when they look back and realize they created something lasting and important.
   c. To gently remind employees that the company will continue to move forward with her original vision—the vision that she was careful to describe to every new employee the company has hired so far.
   d. To collaborate with employees on a new vision for the company.

2. The company's first learning product, a study app for children ages 6 to 10, is ready for *beta testing*, a prerelease phase in which target customers use the product and give the company feedback about features and bugs. Blair wants to recruit 20–25 families to try the app for two weeks. The company doesn't have any customers yet, so it can't ask existing users to test the new product, but it does have a simulation of the app on its website that people can try if they're curious before downloading the app. Which of these medium/channel choices should she use to recruit families for the test program?
   a. A printed flyer included with Mattel products aimed at this age group
   b. A post in a Reddit group where AI developers share industry gossip
   c. Guest posts on parenting blogs
   d. A string of tweets on the company's Twitter account

3. The next update of the company's apps includes an emotion-recognition feature that detects a learner's emotional response to feedback and other prompts, which the app then uses to fine-tune the learning process. A student who appears to be frustrated, for example, might get an encouraging message from a funny cartoon character, or the app might present a different approach to a problem. The feature requires access to the device's camera, however, and Blair knows that some parents are reluctant to give the app access. She is currently writing a message for the app to display, explaining how the feature uses the camera. Which of the following is the best expression of the main idea for this message?
   a. Just as you study your child's face to know how he or she is feeling, the new emotion-recognition feature uses your device's camera to help the app adapt to your child's emotional state for a more positive learning experience.
   b. Just as you study your child's face to know how he or she is feeling, the new emotion-recognition feature uses your device's camera to help the app adapt.
   c. Full functionality requires access to your device's camera; please go to your settings menu now and make the change.
   d. This new feature maps the geometry of your child's face and monitors for movements that reflect changes in his or her emotional state.

4. RocketThink doesn't prominently advertise the use of artificial intelligence in the company's products, focusing instead on the benefits the technology provides. However, some parents have been contacting the company asking how the apps are able to adapt to each learner as well as they do and wondering if there is some invasive, "Big Brother" technology at work. You've picked up rumors on social media that some parents worry the apps are spying on their children. Blair decides it is time to explain that, yes, the company does use AI, but its purpose is to understand each child's study habits and progress so that it can provide the best possible experience. The apps don't report back with any family secrets or individually identifiable information. She wants to write a response for the FAQ (frequently asked questions) section of the company's website. Which of these approaches would you advise her to use?
   a. Use the indirect approach, starting with a friendly discussion of how all parents and guardians want the best for the children in their care and using examples of how they do this in other areas of life, from nutrition to home security. Discuss examples of how they are probably using smart technology now, from motion-sensing home alarms to the virtual voice-enabled assistants on their smartphones, then explain that RocketThink uses AI in

this same vein of applying the best available tools and technologies for their children. Conclude with a description of the privacy features that every app has, and remind parents of the privacy settings they can make in the apps if they are worried about particular aspects of the apps' operation.

  b. Use the same approach as (a), but change the tone slightly to include an element of emotional persuasion

about how parents need to overcome their own fears and insecurities and do what is best for their children.

  c. Convey the same information as in (a), but reverse the order to make it direct.

  d. Use the direct approach, opening with a statement that, yes, the apps do use artificial intelligence. Follow this up with a promise that parents don't have anything to worry about, because AI is a part of everyday life now.

END OF CHAPTER

Learning Objectives Checkup

Assess your understanding of the principles in this chapter by reading each learning objective and studying the accompanying exercises. You can check your responses against the answer key on page 612.

Objective 5.1: Describe the three-step writing process.

1. The three major steps in the three-step writing process are
   a. writing, editing, and producing.
   b. planning, writing, and completing.
   c. writing, editing, and distributing.
   d. organizing, defining your purpose, and writing.
2. The first step of the three-step writing process is
   a. writing the first draft.
   b. organizing your information.
   c. planning your message.
   d. preparing an outline.
3. Which of the following tasks should you do when you're planning a writing project?
   a. Define your purpose.
   b. Revise carefully to make sure you haven't made any embarrassing mistakes.
   c. Choose words and sentences carefully to make sure the audience understands your main idea.
   d. Clarify production details such as page count and paper size so that you don't exceed project parameters.

Objective 5.2: Explain why it's important to analyze a communication situation in order to define your purpose and profile your audience before writing a message.

4. The _____ _____ of a message indicates whether you intend to use the message to inform, to persuade, or to collaborate.
5. If you were to write an email message to a manufacturer complaining about a defective product and asking for a refund, your general purpose would be
   a. to inform.
   b. to persuade.
   c. to collaborate.
   d. to entertain.
6. No matter what the message is or the audience you want to reach, you should always
   a. determine the information your audience needs in order to grasp your main idea.

   b. learn the names of everyone in the target audience.
   c. estimate the percentage of audience members who are likely to agree with your message.
   d. determine a complete demographic profile of your audience.
7. If audience members will vary in terms of the amount of information they already know about your topic, your best approach is to
   a. provide as much extra information as possible to make sure everyone gets every detail.
   b. provide just the basic information; if your audience needs to know more, they can find out for themselves.
   c. gear your coverage to your primary audience and provide the information most relevant to them.
   d. include lots of graphics.

Objective 5.3: Discuss information-gathering options for simple messages, and identify three attributes of quality information.

8. Which of these is a reason the discovery technique of free writing can help you find your focus when starting a project?
   a. It narrows your focus by eliminating any words or phrases that are not directly connected to your purpose.
   b. It gets you into a professional frame of mind by reminding you of expected standards of business grammar.
   c. By not worrying about the economic value of your writing, you are freer to express yourself.
   d. It silences your "inner critic" so you more easily express ideas as they come to you.
9. To make sure you have provided all the necessary information, use the journalistic approach, which is to
   a. interview your audience about its needs.
   b. check the accuracy of your information.
   c. verify whether your message answers the questions of *who, what, when, where, why,* and *how.*
   d. make sure your information is ethical.
10. If you realize you have given your audience incorrect information, the most ethical action would be to
   a. say nothing and hope no one notices.
   b. wait until someone points out the error and then acknowledge the mistake.
   c. post a correction on your website.
   d. contact the audience immediately and correct the error.

Objective 5.4: List the factors to consider when choosing the most appropriate medium for a message.

11. The media choices of oral, written, and visual can be delivered through _____ and _____ channels.

12. Which of the following choices would be best for communicating a complex policy change to employees in a company with offices all over the world?
    a. A teleconference followed by an email message
    b. Instant messaging
    c. A traditional typed memo sent via regular postal mail
    d. A post on an internal website combined with an email message alerting employees to the change and directing them to the website for more information

13. Media richness is a measure of
    a. a medium's ability to use more than one informational cue, facilitate feedback, and establish personal focus.
    b. a medium's ability to use more than one informational cue, limit destructive feedback, and establish personal focus.
    c. how expensive the delivery options are likely to be, particularly for large or geographically dispersed audiences.
    d. how much total employee cost is involved in creating messages using a particular medium.

Objective 5.5: Explain why good organization is important to both you and your audience, and list the tasks involved in organizing a message.

14. Which of the following is an important benefit of taking time to organize your business messages?
    a. You can delay the actual writing.
    b. You save time and conserve creative energy because the writing process is quicker.
    c. Organizing your thoughts and information saves you the trouble of asking colleagues for input.
    d. In many cases, you can simply send a detailed outline and save the trouble of writing the document.

15. The purpose of limiting your scope when planning a writing project is to
    a. make your job easier.
    b. reduce the number of things you need to think about.
    c. make sure your memos are never longer than one page.
    d. make sure that your message stays focused on the main idea and any necessary supporting details.

16. Starting with the main idea and then offering supporting evidence is known as the _____ approach.

17. Starting with evidence first and building toward your main idea is known as the _____ approach.

18. When your audience is likely to have a skeptical or even hostile reaction to your main idea, you should generally use
    a. the indirect approach.
    b. the direct approach.
    c. the open-ended approach.
    d. the closed approach.

19. Which of the following is one of the reasons storytelling can be effective in business communication?
    a. Stories help readers and listeners imagine themselves living through the experience of the person in the story.
    b. Stories are entertaining, so they offer some diversion from the daily grind of work.

    c. Readers and listeners are overloaded with data, so avoiding facts and figures is a proven way to get their attention.
    d. Stories are inherently funny, and people are more receptive to new ideas when they are in a good mood.

Key Terms

direct approach Message organization that starts with the main idea (such as a recommendation, a conclusion, or a request) and follows that with your supporting evidence

free writing An exploratory technique in which you write whatever comes to mind, without stopping to make any corrections, for a set period of time

general purpose The broad intent of a message—to inform, to persuade, or to collaborate with the audience

indirect approach Message organization that starts with the evidence and builds your case before presenting the main idea

journalistic approach Method of verifying the completeness of a message by making sure it answers the *who, what, when, where, why,* and *how* questions regarding an event or subject

letters Brief written messages sent to customers and other recipients outside the organization

main idea A specific statement about the topic of a message

memos Brief printed documents traditionally used for the routine, day-to-day exchange of information within an organization

scope The range of information presented in a message, its overall length, and the level of detail provided

specific purpose Identifies what you hope to accomplish with your message and what your audience should do or think after receiving your message

topic The overall subject of a message

Apply Your Knowledge

To review chapter content related to each question, refer to the indicated Learning Objective.

5-1. How should you schedule your time for a writing project in an unfamiliar subject area when you have no idea how long it will take to complete the research and produce a first draft? [LO-1]

5-2. A day after sending an email to all 1,800 employees in your company regarding income tax implications of the company's retirement plan, you discover that one of the sources you relied on for your information plagiarized from other sources. You quickly double-check all the information in your message and confirm that it is accurate. However, you are concerned about using plagiarized information, even though you did nothing wrong. Write a brief email message to your instructor, explaining how you would handle the situation. [LO-3]

5-3. You are organizing an exploratory in-person meeting with engineering representatives from a dozen manufacturers around the world to discuss updates to a technical standard that all the companies' products must adhere to. The representatives have a wide range of firmly held opinions on the subject, because the changes could help some companies and hurt others. They can't even agree on what should be addressed in the first meeting, so you need to develop a minimum level of consensus on what should be on the agenda. Which combination of media and channels would you use to move the conversation forward and finalize the agenda? Each company has one representative, and any discussions need to be kept confidential. [LO-4]

5-4. How might the inability to view an entire document at once on a mobile screen hinder a reader's ability to grasp the full meaning of the message? [LO-4]

5-5. You have been invited to speak at an annual industry conference. After preparing the outline for your presentation, you see that you've identified 14 different points to support your main idea. Should you move ahead with creating the slides for your presentation or move back and rethink your outline? Why? [LO-5]

Practice Your Skills

Message for Analysis

5-6. **Outlining Your Content [LO-5]** A writer working on an insurance information brochure is having trouble grouping the ideas logically into an outline. Using the following information, prepare the outline, paying attention to the appropriate hierarchy of ideas. If necessary, rewrite phrases to make them all consistent.

Accident Protection Insurance Plan

- Coverage is only pennies a day
- Benefit is $100,000 for accidental death on common carrier
- Benefit is $100 a day for hospitalization as a result of motor vehicle or common carrier accident
- Benefit is $20,000 for accidental death in motor vehicle accident
- Individual coverage is only $17.85 per quarter; family coverage is just $26.85 per quarter
- No physical exam or health questions
- Convenient payment—billed quarterly
- Guaranteed acceptance for all applicants
- No individual rate increases
- Free, no-obligation examination period
- Cash paid in addition to any other insurance carried
- Covers accidental death when riding as fare-paying passenger on public transportation, including buses, trains, jets, ships, trolleys, subways, or any other common carrier
- Covers accidental death in motor vehicle accidents occurring while driving or riding in or on an automobile, truck, camper, motor home, or nonmotorized bicycle

Exercises

Each activity is labeled according to the primary skill or skills you will need to use. To review relevant chapter content, you can refer to the indicated Learning Objective. In some instances, supporting information will be found in another chapter, as indicated.

5-7. **Analyzing the Situation; Media Skills: Presentations [LO-2]** Visit the PepsiCo website at **www.pepsico.com**

and locate the latest annual report. Read the CEO's letter to shareholders. (Typically, it's the first section of the annual report.) Who is the audience for this message? What is the general purpose of the message? What information do you think this audience wants from PepsiCo? Summarize your answers in a one-page report or a five-slide presentation, as your instructor directs.

5-8. **Planning: Defining Your Purpose [LO-2]** For each of the following communication tasks, state a specific purpose (if you have trouble, try beginning with "I want to . . .").

a. A report to your boss, the store manager, about the outdated items in the warehouse

b. A memo to clients about your booth at the upcoming trade show

c. A letter to a customer who hasn't made a payment for three months

d. A memo to employees about the department's high phone bills

e. A phone call to a supplier, checking on an overdue parts shipment

f. A report to future users of the computer program you have chosen to handle the company's mailing list

5-9. **Planning: Developing an Audience Profile [LO-2]** For each communication task that follows, write brief answers to three questions: Who is the audience? What is the audience's general attitude toward my subject? What does the audience need to know?

a. A final-notice collection letter from an appliance manufacturer to an appliance dealer that is 3 months behind on payments, sent 10 days before initiating legal collection procedures

b. An advertisement for smartphones

c. A proposal to top management, suggesting that the four sales regions in the United States be combined into just two regions

d. Fliers to be attached to doorknobs in the neighborhood, announcing reduced rates for chimney cleaning or repairs

e. A cover letter sent along with your résumé to a potential employer

f. A website that describes the services offered by a consulting firm that helps accounting managers comply with government regulations

5-10. **Planning: Analyzing the Situation; Collaboration: Planning Meetings [LO-2], Chapter 3** How can the material discussed in this chapter also apply to meetings, as discussed in Chapter 3? Outline your ideas in a brief presentation or a post for your class blog.

5-11. **Planning: Creating an Audience Profile; Collaboration: Team Projects [LO-2], [LO-3], Chapter 3** With a team assigned by your instructor, compare the Facebook pages of three companies in the same industry. Analyze the content in all the available sections. (You don't have to evaluate every post, but visit all the different sections.) What can you surmise about the intended audience for each company? Which of the three does the best job of presenting the information its target audience is likely to need? Prepare a brief presentation, including slides that show samples of the Facebook content from each company.

5-12. Planning: Analyzing the Situation, Selecting Media; Media Skills: Email [LO-2], [LO-4], Chapter 10 You are the head of public relations for a cruise line that operates out of Miami. You are shocked to read a letter in a local newspaper from a disgruntled passenger, complaining about the service and entertainment on a recent cruise. You need to respond to these publicized criticisms in some way. What audiences will you need to consider in your response? What medium or media should you choose? If the letter had been published in a travel publication widely read by travel agents and cruise travelers, how might your course of action have differed? In an email message to your instructor, explain how you will respond.

5-13. Planning: Assessing Audience Needs [LO-3] Choose a fairly simple digital device (such as a digital music player) that you know how to operate well. Write two sets of instructions for operating the device: one set for a reader who has never used that type of device and one set for someone who is generally familiar with that type of device but has never operated the specific model. Briefly explain how your two audiences affect your instructions.

5-14. Planning: Assessing Audience Needs; Media Skills: Blogging; Communication Ethics: Making Ethical Choices [LO-3], Chapter 1 Your supervisor has asked you to withhold important information that you think should be included in a report you are preparing. Disobeying him could be disastrous for your working relationship and your career. Obeying him could violate your personal code of ethics. What should you do? On the basis of the discussion in Chapter 1, would you consider this situation to be an ethical dilemma or an ethical lapse? Explain your analysis in a brief email message to your instructor.

5-15. Planning: Assessing Audience Needs; Media Skills: Mobile [LO-4] Using a computer or full-sized tablet, visit the website of any well-known company and review its About or About Us page. Identify three ways you would modify this page to meet the needs of readers accessing it with smartphones or phablets.

5-16. Planning: Limiting Your Scope [LO-5] Suppose you are preparing to recommend that top management install a new heating system that uses the cogeneration process. The following information is in your files. Eliminate topics that aren't essential, and then arrange the other topics so that your report will give top managers a clear understanding of the heating system and a balanced, concise justification for installing it.

- History of the development of the cogeneration heating process
- Scientific credentials of the developers of the process
- Risks assumed in using this process
- Your plan for installing the equipment in the headquarters building
- Stories about the successful use of cogeneration technology in comparable facilities

- Specifications of the equipment that would be installed
- Plans for disposing of the old heating equipment
- Costs of installing and running the new equipment
- Advantages and disadvantages of using the new process
- Detailed 10-year cost projections
- Estimates of the time needed to phase in the new system
- Alternative systems that management might want to consider

5-17. Planning: Using Storytelling Techniques; Communication Ethics: Providing Ethical Leadership; Media Skills: Podcasting [LO-5], Chapter 1, Chapter 8 Research recent incidents of ethical lapses by a business professional or executive in any industry. Choose one example that has a clear story "arc" from beginning to end. Outline a cautionary tale that explains the context of the ethical lapse, the choice the person made, and the consequences of the ethical lapse. Script a podcast (aim for roughly three to five minutes) that tells the story. If your instructor directs, record your podcast and post to your class blog.

Expand Your Skills

Critique the Professionals

Locate an example of professional communication in any medium that you think would work equally well—or perhaps better—in another medium, such as a speech that would work as well or better as a blog post. Using the information in this chapter and your understanding of the communication process, write a brief analysis (no more than one page) of the company's media/channel choice and explain why your choice would be at least as effective. Use whatever medium your instructor requests for your report, and be sure to cite specific elements from the piece and support from the chapter.

Sharpening Your Career Skills Online

Bovée and Thill's Business Communication Web Search, at **websearch.businesscommunicationnetwork.com**, is a unique research tool designed specifically for business communication research. Use the Web Search function to find a website, video, article, podcast, or presentation that offers advice on planning a report, speech, or other business message. Write a brief email message to your instructor, describing the item you found and summarizing the career skills information you learned from it.

Build Your Career

As "Construct Your Brand Pyramid" in the Prologue (page xxxvii) explains, your *brand pyramid* has all the relevant support points needed to build a personal brand message or professional promise, whichever you prefer to call it. Start by compiling a *private inventory* of skills, attributes, experience, and areas for improvement. This should be a positive but realistic assessment of what you have to offer now and a "to-grow" list of areas where you want to develop or improve. Obviously, this inventory isn't for public consumption.

Next, select the appropriate materials from your inventory to develop a *public profile* that highlights the qualities you want to promote. This profile can take on a variety of forms for different communication platforms, such as your LinkedIn profile and your résumé.

In Chapter 6's Build Your Career activity, you'll complete the third step of the pyramid, which is distilling your professional promise down to a single, brief headline.

Improve Your Grammar, Mechanics, and Usage

The following exercises help you improve your knowledge of and power over English grammar, mechanics, and usage. Turn to the Handbook of Grammar, Mechanics, and Usage at the end of this book and review all of Section 1.5 (Adverbs). Then look at the following 10 items and indicate the preferred choice within

each set of parentheses. (Answers to these exercises appear on page 614.)

5-18. Their performance has been (*good, well*).

5-19. I (*sure, surely*) do not know how to help you.

5-20. He feels (*sick, sickly*) again today.

5-21. Customs dogs are chosen because they smell (*good, well*).

5-22. The redecorated offices look (*good, well*).

5-23. Which of the two programs computes (*more fast, faster*)?

5-24. Of the two we have in stock, this model is the (*best, better*) designed.

5-25. He doesn't seem to have (*any, none*).

5-26. That machine is scarcely (*never, ever*) used.

5-27. They (*can, can't*) hardly get replacement parts for this equipment (*any, no*) more.

For additional exercises focusing on adverbs, visit MyLab Business Communication. Click on Chapter 5; click on Additional Exercises to Improve Your Grammar, Mechanics, and Usage; and then click on 9. Adverbs.

MyLab Business Communication

MyLab Assisted-Grading Writing Prompts

If your instructor has assigned one or both of the following writing assignments within the MyLab, go to your Assignments to complete these writing exercises.

5-28. Email lacks both the visual element and the instantaneous connection of some other media. Could these supposed shortcomings help some employees communicate more comfortably and effectively? Explain your answer. [LO-4]

5-29. Would you use the direct or indirect approach to ask employees to work overtime to meet an important deadline? Please explain. [LO-5]

Endnotes

1. Wolff Olins website, accessed 1 January 2018, www.wolffolins.com; Michael Grothaus, "Why Companies Need Novelists," *Fast Company*, 1 May 2015, www.fastcompany.com; Haniya Rae, "Inside the Agency Wolff Olins," *Digiday*, 13 February 2014, digiday.com; "Is Corporate Storytelling Replacing the News Business?" *Fast Company*, 8 May 2014, www.fastcompany.com.
2. Rick Wartzman, "These Four Letters Could Make You the Best . . . Boss . . . Ever," *Fortune*, 21 January 2016, www.fortune.com.
3. Andrey Slivka, "How Mobile and Voice Will Drive SEO Engagement in 2018," *Forbes*, 18 December 2017, www.forbes.com.
4. John Miley, "5 Questions About Net Neutrality," *Kiplinger's Personal Finance*, February 2018, 14; Lucas Mearian, "How Killing Net Neutrality Will Affect Enterprise Mobility," *Computerworld*, 11 December 2017, www.computerworld.com.
5. Xavier Armengol, Vicenc Fernandez, Pep Simo, and Jose M. Sallan, "An Examination of the Effects of Self-Regulatory Focus on the Perception of the Media Richness: The Case of E-Mail," *International Journal of Business Communication* 54, no. 4 (2017): 394–407; Laurey Berk and Phillip G. Clampitt, "Finding the Right Path in the Communication Maze," *IABC Communication World*, October 1991, 28–32.

6. Samantha R. Murray and Joseph Peyrefitte, "Knowledge Type and Communication Media Choice in the Knowledge Transfer Process," *Journal of Managerial Issues*, Spring 2007, 111–133.
7. Holly Weeks, "The Best Memo You'll Ever Write," *Harvard Management Communication Letter*, Spring 2005, 3–5.
8. Steve Tobak, "How to Be a Great Storyteller and Win Over Any Audience," *BNET*, 12 January 2011, www.bnet.com.
9. Chip Heath and Dan Heath, *Made to Stick: Why Some Ideas Survive and Others Die* (New York: Random House, 2008), 214.
10. Heath and Heath, *Made to Stick*, 206, 214.
11. Randolph T. Barker and Kim Gower, "Strategic Application of Storytelling in Organizations," *Journal of Business Communication* 47, no. 3 (July 2010): 295–312.
12. Roger L. Martin and Tony Golsby-Smith, "Management Is Much More Than a Science: The Limits of Data-Driven Decision Making," *Harvard Business Review*, September–October 2017, 129–135.
13. David Meerman Scott, "Effective Storytelling for Business," WebInkNow blog, 18 February 2013, www.webinknow.com.
14. Jennifer Aaker and Andy Smith, "7 Deadly Sins of Business Storytelling," American Express Open Forum, accessed 21 March 2011, www.openforum.com.

Five-Minute Guide to Planning a Business Message or Document

Get every writing or presentation project off to a solid start with this five-minute organizer. Before you start, spend five minutes reviewing these steps to assess what you know and the information you have in hand, then set aside additional time as needed to fill in the missing parts.

00:01 **Assess the Situation**

1. What is your **general purpose?** Do you intend to inform, persuade, or collaborate?
2. What is your **specific purpose**? What do you hope to accomplish with this message?

00:02 **Identify the Information You Will Need**

1. How many of these questions can you answer right now with no additional research?
   - Who is your **primary audience**? Are there any **secondary audiences** to consider?
   - How many people do you need to reach?
   - Where are they located and how can you reach them?
   - What is their level of understanding of the subject?
   - How are they likely to react to your message?
2. For the questions you can't answer, devise a plan to get the information you need.

00:03 **Select the Best Media/Channel Combo**

1. Given your purpose and audience, what is the best medium to use—oral, written, or visual?
2. What is the best channel to use—digital or nondigital (in person or print)?

	Digital channel	Nondigital channel
Oral	+ Create opportunities for immediate feedback; recordings (such as podcasts) allow time-shifted consumption. – Lack most nonverbal cues (unless video).	+ Ideal for immediate feedback and discussion; best for conveying emotion. – Restricted to those physically present; no written record unless transcribed; less control.
Written	+ Fast, easy way to reach wide audiences; link to additional information; social media invite interaction. – Security and privacy problems, competition with other digital messages.	+ Give permanent, verifiable record that is difficult to modify; written medium lets you plan and control the message. – Present limited opportunity for timely feedback; lack nonverbal cues of oral medium.
Visual	+ Can convey complex ideas and relationships quickly; often less intimidating than blocks of text; multimedia options. – Usually require more time and skill.	+ Same as digital visuals. – Same as digital visuals, plus printing and distribution can add cost.

00:04 **Define Your Main Idea**

What is the single most important point you want to convey in this message? If you can't state it clearly and concisely, set aside some time to find your focus.

00:05 **Decide Whether to Use the Direct or Indirect Approach**

Direct Approach	Indirect Approach
General plan: Open with main idea, then back it up with evidence and reasoning.	**General plan:** Open with buffer to establish common ground or get attention, lay out evidence to guide reader toward main idea, then present it.
Strengths: Gets to the point immediately if you need to get someone's attention right away.	**Strengths:** Helps soften an emotional blow or guide reader toward desired response.
Weaknesses: Can come across as arrogant or blunt; readers or listeners can reject your main idea before considering your evidence and reasoning.	**Weaknesses:** Takes longer to reach main idea; buffers can be annoying or even unethical if done poorly.

Writing Business Messages

LEARNING OBJECTIVES

After studying this chapter, you will be able to

1 Identify the four aspects of being sensitive to audience needs when writing business messages.

2 Identify seven characteristics that build and maintain a communicator's credibility.

3 Explain how to achieve a tone that is conversational but businesslike, explain the value of using plain language, and define active and passive voice.

4 Describe how to select words that are both correct and effective.

5 Define the four types of sentences, and explain how sentence style affects emphasis within a message.

6 Define the three key elements of a paragraph, and list five ways to develop unified, coherent paragraphs.

7 List five techniques for writing effective messages for mobile readers.

MyLab Business Communication

If your instructor is using MyLab Business Communication, visit **www.pearson.com/mylab/business-communication** for videos, simulations, and writing exercises.

ON THE JOB: COMMUNICATING AT
LUMEN/KALEIGH MOORE

Helping Companies Solve Business Challenges with Well-Honed Writing Skills

All business professionals are expected to do some writing on the job, but if you enjoy the creative fulfillment of writing, you might consider pursuing a career as a full-time business writer. Business writing jobs cover a wide range of subject matter, including technical and scientific writing, training materials, video scripts, position papers and backgrounders (often referred to as *white papers*), marketing materials, advertising, and social media content. Projects can range from tweets all the way up to full length books, and writers can be employed in-house for corporations, can work for specialist communication agencies, or can operate as independent freelancers.

Courtesy of Kaleigh Moore

Business writer Kaleigh Moore combines business acumen with well-honed writing skills to develop effective social media content for a variety of e-commerce and software companies.

Kaleigh Moore is a great example of someone who has turned business acumen and a passion for writing into a thriving career as an independent writer. Her specialty is writing social media content and developing communication strategies for companies involved in e-commerce and software-as-a-service (a segment of the business software market in which customers essentially rent online computing capacity, rather than buying and installing software themselves). She also offers coaching to aspiring freelance writers to help them get started in the business and publishes a blog and a newsletter packed with writing advice. And as if all that didn't keep her busy enough, she also partners with her husband, a business consultant and designer, in a firm called Lumen to offer clients a full suite of marketing communication services.

As is the case with many independent business writers, Moore has a diverse professional background, having worked as a journalist and photographer, as a public relations manager, and as an entrepreneur. This path helped her develop her writing skills and business insights to the degree that she can offer her clients strategic advice in addition to communication services. Clients applaud her ability to grasp business challenges and craft engaging content that connects with target readers.

When she's not busy writing for her clients, she is a prolific contributor to leading business periodicals, including *Entrepreneur* and *Inc.* (To read her *Inc.* articles, which offer a wide range of practical tips on writing for e-commerce and other marketing areas, visit **www.inc.com/author/kaleigh-moore**.)

If writing full-time appeals to you, all the skills you are developing in this course and the insights you are gaining into communicating in a professional context will help. Combine this preparation with a few years of on-the-job experience, and you'll be ready to explore the possibility of striking out on your own.[1]

WWW.KALEIGHMOORE.COM WEARELUMEN.COM

Adapting to Your Audience: Being Sensitive to Audience Needs

1 LEARNING OBJECTIVE
Identify the four aspects of being sensitive to audience needs when writing business messages.

Kaleigh Moore (profiled in the chapter-opening On the Job) knows it takes more than just a great idea to change the way people think. Whether consciously or not, audiences greet most incoming messages with a selfish question: "What's in this for me?" If your readers or listeners don't think you understand or care about their needs, they probably won't pay attention.

Readers and listeners are more likely to respond positively when they believe messages address their concerns.

USING THE "YOU" ATTITUDE

Chapter 1 introduced the notion of audience-centered communication and the "you" attitude—speaking and writing in terms of your audience's wishes, interests, hopes, and preferences. On the simplest level, you can adopt the "you" attitude by replacing terms such as *I, me, mine, we, us,* and *ours* with *you* and *yours*:

Adopting the "you" attitude means speaking and writing in terms of your audience's wishes, interests, hopes, and preferences.

Instead of This	Write This
Tuesday is the only day that we can promise quick response to purchase order requests. We are swamped the rest of the week.	If you need a quick response, please submit your purchase order requests on Tuesday.
At Construction Resources, we are proud to supply the highest-rated engineered wood in the entire Midwest.	Ensure the integrity of your building projects with the highest-rated engineered wood in the entire Midwest.

Of course, you will have occasions when it is appropriate to write or speak from your perspective, such as when you are offering your opinions or reporting on something you have seen. However, even in those instances, make sure you focus on your readers' needs.

Also, be aware that the "you" attitude involves a lot more than just using particular pronouns. It's a matter of demonstrating genuine interest in your readers and concern for their needs (see Figure 6.1). You can use *you* 25 times in a single page and still offend your audience or ignore readers' true concerns. If you're writing to a retailer, try to think like a retailer; if you're dealing with a production supervisor, put yourself in that position; if

Check out the "Five-Minute Guide to Composing a Business Message or Document" at the end of the chapter.

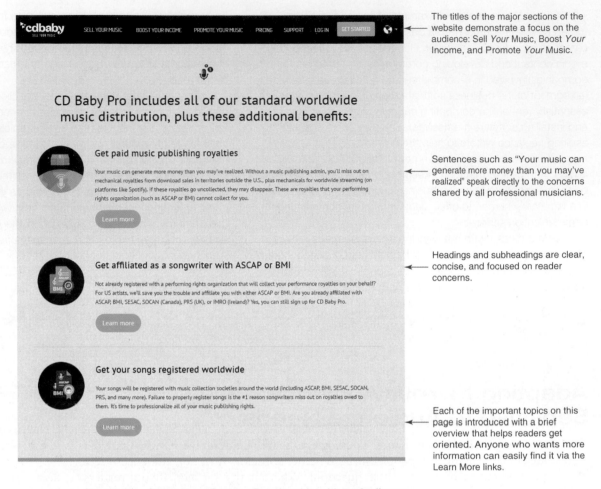

The titles of the major sections of the website demonstrate a focus on the audience: Sell *Your* Music, Boost *Your* Income, and Promote *Your* Music.

Sentences such as "Your music can generate more money than you may've realized" speak directly to the concerns shared by all professional musicians.

Headings and subheadings are clear, concise, and focused on reader concerns.

Each of the important topics on this page is introduced with a brief overview that helps readers get oriented. Anyone who wants more information can easily find it via the Learn More links.

Figure 6.1 Fostering a Positive Relationship with an Audience
CD Baby, the world's largest retailer of independent music, uses clear, positive language to help musicians understand the process of selling their music through the company and its affiliates. By making the effort to communicate clearly and succinctly, the company encourages a positive response from its target readers.

you're writing to a dissatisfied customer, imagine how you would feel at the other end of the transaction.

Be aware that on some occasions, it's better to avoid using *you*, particularly if doing so will sound overly authoritative or accusing:

Avoid using *you* and *your* when doing so

- Makes you sound dictatorial
- Makes someone else feel guilty
- Goes against your organization's style

Instead of This	Write This
You failed to deliver the customer's order on time.	The customer didn't receive the order on time.
You must correct all five copies by noon.	All five copies must be corrected by noon.

As you practice using the "you" attitude, be sure to consider the attitudes of other cultures and the policies of your organization. In some cultures, for instance, it is improper to single out one person's achievements, because the whole team is considered responsible for the outcome. In such cases, using the pronoun *we* or *our* (when you and your audience are part of the same team) would be more appropriate. Similarly, some companies have a tradition of avoiding references to *you* and *I* in formal documents.

Even if a situation calls for you to express uncomfortable truths, express the facts of the matter in a kind and thoughtful manner.

MAINTAINING STANDARDS OF ETIQUETTE

Good etiquette shows respect for your audience and helps foster a more successful environment for communication by minimizing negative emotional reactions:

Instead of This	Write This
Once again, you've managed to bring down the website through your incompetent programming.	Let's review the last website update to explore ways to improve the process.
You've been sitting on our order for two weeks, and we need it now!	Our production schedules depend on timely delivery of parts and supplies, but we have not yet received the order scheduled for delivery two weeks ago. Please respond today with a firm delivery commitment.

Naturally, some situations require more diplomacy than others. If you know your audience well, a less formal approach may be more appropriate. However, when you are communicating with people who outrank you or with people outside your organization, an added measure of courtesy is usually needed.

With written communication and most forms of digital communication, pay extra attention to tact. When you're speaking, your words can be softened by your tone of voice and facial expressions. Plus, you can adjust your approach according to the feedback you get. However, if you inadvertently offend someone in writing or in a podcast, for example, you don't usually get the immediate feedback you would need in order to resolve the situation. In fact, you may never know that you offended your audience.

Use extra tact when communicating with people higher up the organization chart or outside the company.

EMPHASIZING THE POSITIVE

During your career, you will have many occasions in which you need to communicate bad news. However, there is a big difference between *delivering* negative news and *being* negative. When the tone of your message is negative, you put unnecessary strain on business relationships. Never try to hide negative news, but always be on the lookout for positive points that will foster a good relationship with your audience:[2]

You can communicate negative news without being negative.

Instead of This	Write This
It is impossible to repair your laptop today.	Your computer can be ready by Tuesday. Would you like a loaner until then?
We wasted $300,000 advertising in that magazine.	Our $300,000 advertising investment did not pay off; let's analyze the experience and apply the insights to future campaigns.

If you find it necessary to criticize or correct, don't dwell on the other person's mistakes. Avoid referring to failures, problems, or shortcomings. Focus instead on what the audience members can do to improve the situation:

Instead of This	Write This
The problem with this department is a failure to control costs.	The performance of this department can be improved with tighter cost controls.
You failed to provide all the necessary information on the previous screen.	Please review the items marked in red so that we can process your order as quickly as possible.

If you're trying to persuade audience members to buy a product, pay a bill, or perform a service for you, emphasize what's in it for them. When people recognize the benefits of doing so, they are more likely to respond positively to your appeal:

Show readers how they will benefit by responding to your message.

Instead of This	Write This
We will notify all three credit reporting agencies if you do not pay your overdue bill within 10 days.	Paying your overdue bill within 10 days will prevent a negative entry on your credit record.
I am tired of seeing so many errors in the customer service blog.	Proofreading your blog posts will help avoid embarrassing mistakes that erode confidence in our ability to help customers.

Euphemisms are milder synonyms that can express an idea while triggering fewer negative connotations, but they should never be used to obscure the truth.

In general, try to state your message without using words that may hurt or offend your audience. Look for appropriate opportunities to use **euphemisms**—words or phrases that express a thought in milder terms—that convey your meaning without carrying negative or unpleasant connotations. For example, one common euphemism is referring to people beyond a certain age as "senior citizens" rather than "old people." *Senior* conveys respect in a way that *old* doesn't.

Euphemisms can bring a tone of civility to unpleasant communication, but they must be used with great care because they are easy to misuse. Euphemisms can be annoying if they force readers to "read between the lines" to get the message, and they can be unethical if they obscure the truth. For instance, one of the toughest messages a manager ever has to write is an internal memo or email announcing layoffs. This is a difficult situation for everyone involved, and managers can be tempted to resort to euphemisms such as *streamlining, restructuring, improving efficiency, reducing layers,* or *eliminating redundancies* to avoid using the word *layoff.*[3] Doing so might ease the emotional burden on the writer and promote the illusion that the message isn't as negative as it really is. However, these euphemisms can fail the "you" attitude test, as well as the standards of ethical information, by failing to answer the question every reader in these situations has, which is simply: *Am I going to lose my job?*

If you are considering using a euphemism, ask yourself this question: Are you trying to protect the reader's feelings or your own feelings? Even if it is unpleasant, people generally respond better to an honest message delivered with integrity than they do to a sugar-coated message that obscures the truth.

USING BIAS-FREE LANGUAGE

Bias-free language avoids words and phrases that unfairly and even unethically categorize or stigmatize people.

Bias-free language avoids words and phrases that unfairly and even unethically categorize or stigmatize people in ways related to gender, race, ethnicity, age, disability, or other personal characteristics (see Table 6.1 on the next page). Contrary to what some may think, biased language is not simply about "labels" or "political correctness." To a significant degree, language reflects the way we think and what we believe, and biased language may well perpetuate the underlying stereotypes and prejudices it represents.[4] Moreover, because communication is all about perception, simply *being* fair and objective isn't enough. To establish a good relationship with your audience, you must also *appear* to be fair.[5] Good communicators make every effort to avoid biased language. Bias can come in a variety of forms:

REAL-TIME UPDATES

LEARN MORE BY READING THIS PDF

Get detailed advice on using bias-free language

This in-depth guide from the University of California Davis offers practical tips for avoiding many types of cultural bias in your writing and speaking. Go to **real-timeupdates.com/ebc13** and select Learn More in the Students section.

- **Gender bias.** Avoid sexist language by using the same labels for everyone, regardless of gender. Don't refer to a woman as *chairperson* and then to a man as *chairman.* Use chair, chairperson, or chairman consistently. Reword sentences to use *they* or to use no pronoun at all rather than refer to all individuals as *he.* Note that the preferred title for women in business is *Ms.* unless the individual asks to be addressed as *Miss* or *Mrs.* or has some other title, such as *Dr.*

- **Racial and ethnic bias.** Avoid identifying people by race or ethnic origin unless such a label is relevant to the matter at hand—and it rarely is.

- **Age bias.** Mention the age of a person only when it is relevant. Moreover, be careful of the context in which you use words that refer to age; such words carry a variety of positive and negative connotations. For example, *young* can imply energy, youthfulness, inexperience, or even immaturity, depending on how it's used.

- **Disability bias.** Physical, mental, sensory, or emotional impairments should never be mentioned in business messages unless those conditions are directly relevant to the subject. If you must refer to someone's disability, put the person first and the disability second.[6] For example, by saying "employees with physical handicaps," not "handicapped employees," you focus on the whole person, not the disability. Finally, never use outdated terminology such as *crippled* or *retarded.*

TABLE 6.1 Overcoming Bias in Language

Examples	Biased Wording	Preferable
Gender Bias		
Using words containing *man*	Man-made	Artificial, synthetic, manufactured, constructed, human-made
	Mankind	Humanity, human beings, human race, people
	Manpower	Workers, workforce
	Businessman	Executive, manager, businessperson, professional
	Salesman	Sales representative, salesperson
	Foreman	Supervisor
Using female-gender words	Actress, stewardess	Actor, flight attendant
Using special designations	Woman doctor, male nurse	Doctor, nurse
Using *he* to refer to "everyone"	The average worker . . . he	The average worker . . . he or she OR Average workers . . . they
Identifying roles with gender	The typical executive spends four hours of his day in meetings.	Most executives spend four hours a day in meetings.
	the consumer . . . she	consumers . . . they
	the nurse/teacher . . . she	nurses/teachers . . . they
Identifying women by marital status	Mrs. Norm Lindstrom	Maria Lindstrom *OR* Ms. Maria Lindstrom
	Norm Lindstrom and Ms. Drake	Norm Lindstrom and Maria Drake *OR* Mr. Lindstrom and Ms. Drake
Racial and Ethnic Bias		
Assigning stereotypes	Not surprisingly, Shing-Tung Yau excels in mathematics.	Shing-Tung Yau excels in mathematics.
Identifying people by race or ethnicity	Mario M. Cuomo, Italian American politician and ex-governor of New York	Mario M. Cuomo, politician and ex-governor of New York
Age Bias		
Including age when irrelevant	Mary Kirazy, 58, has just joined our trust department.	Mary Kirazy has just joined our trust department.
Disability Bias		
Putting the disability before the person	Disabled workers face many barriers on the job.	Workers with physical disabilities face many barriers on the job.
	An epileptic, Tracy has no trouble doing her job.	Tracy's epilepsy has no effect on her job performance.

Adapting to Your Audience: Building Strong Relationships

2 LEARNING OBJECTIVE
Identify seven characteristics that build and maintain a communicator's credibility.

Successful communication relies on a positive relationship between sender and receiver. Establishing your credibility and projecting your company's image are two vital steps in building and fostering positive business relationships.

ESTABLISHING YOUR CREDIBILITY

Audience responses to your messages depend heavily on your **credibility**, a measure of your believability based on how reliable you are and how much trust you evoke in others. With audiences who don't know and trust you already, you need to establish credibility before they'll accept your messages (see Figure 6.2). When you do establish credibility, communication becomes much easier because you no longer have to spend time and energy

Credibility is a measure of your believability based on how reliable you are and how much trust you evoke in others.

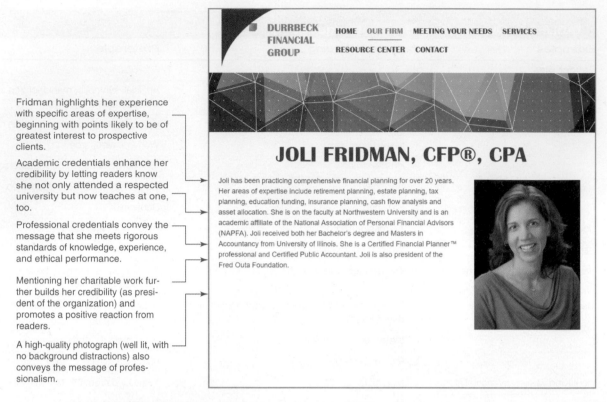

Fridman highlights her experience with specific areas of expertise, beginning with points likely to be of greatest interest to prospective clients.

Academic credentials enhance her credibility by letting readers know she not only attended a respected university but now teaches at one, too.

Professional credentials convey the message that she meets rigorous standards of knowledge, experience, and ethical performance.

Mentioning her charitable work further builds her credibility (as president of the organization) and promotes a positive reaction from readers.

A high-quality photograph (well lit, with no background distractions) also conveys the message of professionalism.

Figure 6.2   Building Credibility
In her profile page on her company's website, financial advisor Joli Fridman builds her credibility with a variety of specific, concrete statements. Notice how every statement packs a punch; there is no filler or "fluff."

To enhance your credibility, emphasize such factors as honesty, objectivity, and awareness of audience needs.

convincing people that you are a trustworthy source of information and ideas. To build, maintain, or repair your credibility, emphasize the following characteristics:

- **Honesty.** Demonstrating honesty and integrity will earn you the respect of your audiences, even if they don't always agree with or welcome your messages.
- **Objectivity.** Show that you can distance yourself from emotional situations and look at all sides of an issue.
- **Awareness of audience needs.** Directly or indirectly, let your audience members know that you understand what's important to them.
- **Credentials, knowledge, and expertise.** Audiences need to know that you have whatever it takes to back up your message, whether it's education, professional certification, special training, past successes, or simply the fact that you've done your research.
- **Endorsements.** An *endorsement* is a statement on your behalf by someone who is accepted by your audience as an expert.
- **Performance.** Demonstrating impressive communication skills is not enough; people need to know they can count on you to get the job done.
- **Sincerity.** When you offer praise, don't use *hyperboles*, such as "you are the most fantastic employee I could ever imagine." Instead, point out specific qualities that warrant praise.

In addition, audiences need to know that you believe in yourself and your message. If you lack faith in yourself, you're likely to communicate an uncertain attitude that undermines your credibility. In contrast, if you are convinced that your message is sound, you can state your case with authority. Look out for phrases containing words such as *hope* and *trust*, which can drain the audience's confidence in your message:

Instead of This	Write This
We hope this recommendation will be helpful.	We're pleased to make this recommendation.
We trust that you'll want to extend your service contract.	By extending your service contract, you can continue to enjoy top-notch performance from your equipment.

Finally, keep in mind that credibility can take a long time to establish—and it can be wiped out in an instant. An occasional mistake or letdown is usually forgiven, but major lapses in honesty or integrity can destroy your reputation.

PROJECTING YOUR COMPANY'S IMAGE

When you communicate with anyone outside your organization, it is more than a conversation between two individuals. You represent your company and therefore play a vital role in helping the company build and maintain positive relationships with all its stakeholders. Most successful companies work hard to foster a specific public image, and your external communication efforts need to project that image. As part of this responsibility, the interests and preferred communication style of your company must take precedence over your own views and personal communication style.

Many organizations have communication guidelines that outline everything from the correct use of the company name to preferred abbreviations and other grammatical details. Specifying a desired style of communication is more difficult, however. Observe more-experienced colleagues, and never hesitate to ask for editorial help to make sure you're conveying the appropriate tone. For instance, because clients entrust thousands or millions of dollars to an investment firm, it must communicate in a style quite different from that of a clothing retailer. And a clothing retailer specializing in high-quality business attire communicates in a different style than a store catering to the latest trends in casual wear.

> Your company's interests and reputation take precedence over your personal views and communication style.

Adapting to Your Audience: Controlling Your Style and Tone

Your communication **style** involves the choices you make to express yourself: the words you select, the manner in which you use those words in sentences, and the way you build paragraphs from individual sentences. Your style creates a certain **tone**, or overall impression, in your messages. The right tone depends on the nature of your message and your relationship with the reader.

> **3 LEARNING OBJECTIVE**
> Explain how to achieve a tone that is conversational but businesslike, explain the value of using plain language, and define active and passive voice.

> Communication *style* involves the choices you make to express yourself; your style creates a certain *tone*, or overall impression.

CREATING A CONVERSATIONAL TONE

The tone of your business messages can range from informal to conversational to formal. When you're communicating with your superiors or with customers, your tone may tend to be more formal and respectful.[7] However, that formal tone might sound distant and cold if used with close colleagues. Part of the challenge of communicating on the job is to read each situation and figure out the appropriate tone to create.

Compare the three versions of the message in Table 6.2. The first is too formal and stuffy for today's audiences, whereas the third is inappropriately casual for business. The second message demonstrates the **conversational tone** used in most business communication— plain language that sounds businesslike without being stuffy at one extreme or too laid-back and informal at the other extreme. You can achieve a tone that is conversational but still businesslike by following these guidelines:

> A *conversational tone* is warm but businesslike and emphasizes plain, clear language; not too formal and not too casual.

- **Avoid stale and pompous language.** Most companies now shy away from such phrases as "attached please find" and "please be advised that." Similarly, avoid using obscure words, stale or clichéd expressions, and overly complicated sentences designed only to impress others (see Table 6.3).
- **Avoid preaching and bragging.** Readers tend to get irritated by know-it-alls who like to preach or brag. However, if you need to remind your audience of something that should be obvious, try to work in the information casually,

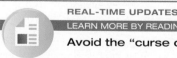

TABLE 6.2 Finding the Right Tone

Tone	Example
Stuffy: too formal for today's audiences	Dear Ms. Navarro: Enclosed please find the information that was requested during our telephone communication of May 14. As was mentioned at that time, Midville Hospital has significantly more doctors of exceptional quality than any other health facility in the state. As you were also informed, our organization has quite an impressive network of doctors and other health-care professionals with offices located throughout the state. In the event that you should need a specialist, our professionals will be able to make an appropriate recommendation. In the event that you have questions or would like additional information, you may certainly contact me during regular business hours. Most sincerely yours, Samuel G. Berenz
Conversational: just right for most business communication	Dear Ms. Navarro: Here's the information you requested during our phone conversation on Friday. As I mentioned, Midville Hospital has the highest-rated doctors and more of them than any other hospital in the state. In addition, we have a vast network of doctors and other health professionals with offices throughout the state. If you need a specialist, they can refer you to the right one. If you would like more information, please call any time between 9:00 and 5:00, Monday through Friday. Sincerely, Samuel Berenz
Unprofessional: too casual for business communication	Here's the 411 you requested. IMHO, we have more and better doctors than any other hospital in the state. FYI, we also have a large group of doctors and other health professionals w/offices close to U at work/home. If U need a specialist, they'll refer U to the right one. Any ? just ring or msg. L8R, S

TABLE 6.3 Weeding Out Obsolete Phrases

Obsolete Phrase	Up-to-Date Replacement
we are in receipt of	we received
kindly advise	please let me/us know
attached please find	enclosed is OR I/we have enclosed
it has come to my attention	I have just learned OR [someone] has just informed me
the undersigned	I/we
in due course	(specify a time or date)
permit me to say that	(omit; just say whatever you need to say)
pursuant to	(omit; just say whatever you need to say)
in closing, I'd like to say	(omit; just say whatever you need to say)
we wish to inform you that	(omit; just say whatever you need to say)
please be advised that	(omit; just say whatever you need to say)

perhaps in the middle of a paragraph, where it will sound like a secondary comment rather than a major revelation.

- **Be careful with intimacy.** Business messages should generally avoid intimacy, such as sharing personal details or adopting a casual, unprofessional tone. However, when you have a close relationship with audience members, such as among the members of a close-knit team, a more intimate tone is sometimes appropriate and even expected.

- **Be careful with humor.** Humor can easily backfire and divert attention from your message. If you don't know your audience well or you're not skilled at using humor in a business setting, don't use it at all. Avoid humor in formal messages and when you're communicating across cultural boundaries.

REAL-TIME UPDATES

LEARN MORE BY READING THIS ARTICLE

Ten tips for conversational writing

These easy-to-use ideas will help you achieve a business-friendly conversational tone. Go to **real-timeupdates.com/ebc13** and select Learn More in the Students section.

USING PLAIN LANGUAGE

An important aspect of creating a conversational tone is using *plain language* (or *plain English* specifically when English is involved). Plain language presents information in a simple, unadorned style that lets audiences grasp your meaning quickly and easily. It is language that recipients "can read, understand and act upon the first time they read it."[8] You can see how this definition supports using the "you" attitude and shows respect for your audience. In addition, plain language can make companies more productive and more profitable because people spend less time trying to figure out messages that are confusing or aren't written to meet their needs.[9]

Audiences can understand and act on plain language without reading it over and over to get the meaning.

SELECTING THE ACTIVE OR PASSIVE VOICE

Your choice of the active or passive voice affects the tone of your message. In **active voice**, the subject performs the action and the object receives the action: "Jodi sent the email message." In **passive voice**, the subject receives the action: "The email message was sent by Jodi." As you can see, the passive voice combines the helping verb *to be* with a form of the verb that is usually similar to the past tense.

Using the active voice helps make your writing more direct, livelier, and easier to read (see Table 6.4). In contrast, the passive voice is often cumbersome, can be unnecessarily vague, and can make sentences overly long. In most cases, the active voice is your best choice.[10] Nevertheless, using the passive voice can help you demonstrate the "you" attitude in some situations:

- When you want to be diplomatic when pointing out a problem or an error of some kind (the passive version seems less like an accusation)

In active voice, the subject performs the action and the object receives the action; in passive voice, the subject receives the action.

The active voice helps make your writing more direct, livelier, and easier to read.

Use passive voice to soften bad news, to put yourself in the background, or to create an impersonal tone when needed.

TABLE 6.4   Choosing Active or Passive Voice

In general, use active voice in order to make your writing lively and direct.

Dull and Indirect in Passive Voice	Lively and Direct in Active Voice
The new procedure was developed by the operations team.	The operations team developed the new procedure.
Legal problems are created by this contract.	This contract creates legal problems.
Reception preparations have been undertaken by our PR people for the new CEO's arrival.	Our PR people have begun planning a reception for the new CEO.

However, passive voice is helpful when you need to be diplomatic or want to focus attention on problems or solutions rather than on people.

Accusatory or Self-Congratulatory in Active Voice	More Diplomatic in Passive Voice
You lost the shipment.	The shipment was lost.
I recruited seven engineers last month.	Seven engineers were recruited last month.
We are investigating the high rate of failures on the final assembly line.	The high rate of failures on the final assembly line is being investigated.

- When you want to point out what's being done without taking or attributing either the credit or the blame (the passive version shifts the spotlight away from the person or persons involved)
- When you want to avoid personal pronouns in order to create an objective tone (the passive version may be used in a formal report, for example)

The second half of Table 6.4 illustrates several of these situations in which the passive voice helps you focus your message on your audience.

Composing Your Message: Choosing Powerful Words

4 LEARNING OBJECTIVE
Describe how to select words that are both correct and effective.

While writing your first draft, don't try to write and edit at the same time, and don't worry about getting everything perfect yet; let your creativity flow.

After you have decided how to adapt to your audience, you're ready to begin composing your message. As you write your first draft, let your creativity flow. Don't try to draft and edit at the same time, and don't worry about getting everything perfect. Make up words if you can't think of the right ones, draw pictures, or talk out loud—do whatever it takes to get the ideas out of your head and onto your computer screen or a piece of paper. If you've planned carefully, you'll have time to revise and refine the material later. In fact, many writers find it helpful to establish a personal rule of never showing a first draft to anyone. By working in this "safe zone," away from the critical eyes of others, your mind will stay free to think clearly and creatively.

If you get stuck and feel unable to write, try to overcome writer's block by jogging your brain in creative ways. The introduction is often the hardest part to write, so put it aside and work on whichever parts of the document you're most comfortable with at any given moment. Work on nontext elements such as graphics or your cover page. Revisit your purpose and confirm your intent in writing the message. Give yourself a mental break by switching to a different project. Sometimes all you need to do is start writing without worrying about the words you're using or how they will sound to the audience. Words will start flowing, your mind will engage, and the writing will come easier.

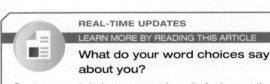

REAL-TIME UPDATES
LEARN MORE BY READING THIS ARTICLE

What do your word choices say about you?

See how word choices can reveal a writer's deepest thought patterns and beliefs. Go to **real-timeupdates.com/ebc13** and select Learn More in the Students section.

USING WORDS CORRECTLY

Careful writers look for the right words and take care to use them correctly.

Careful writers pay close attention to using the right words for every situation and using them correctly in context. Doing so is important on two levels. First, when you use words correctly, your writing becomes clearer, more efficient, and more enjoyable to read. Second, using words correctly sends the signal that you care about the quality of your work, you understand the material you are writing about, and you are sensitive to your audience's information needs.

For the most part, English words have widely agreed-upon meanings and well-established standards for how they should be used. However, the rules of grammar and usage can be a source of worry for writers because some rules are complex and others are in a state of flux that creates uncertainty. For example, most people were taught in school that it is incorrect to use *they* or *their* as a singular pronoun, to split infinitives, and to put a preposition at the end of a sentence. However, all three of these "rules" were introduced into English fairly late in its development in largely misguided attempts to make English grammar work more like Latin, and all three can create more problems than they solve:

Be alert to confusion and disagreement over several common usage rules.

- *They/their* have been used as singular pronouns by some of the greatest writers in the English language, and using them solves the problem of how to refer to one person when you don't know his or her gender or don't want to limit the reference to a particular individual.[11] Without them, you have to use *he or she* and *his or her*, which can get repetitive, or resort to *he/him*, which is sexist in many instances. Standards are changing about the singular *they*, with more and more language experts accepting it as a commonsense solution. In 2016, for example, the American Dialect Society voted the singular *they* as its word of the year.[12]

- The split infinitive rule (never putting an adverb between *to* and the verb) serves no logical purpose in terms of sentence structure or clarity, and following it can lead to phrasing that is clumsy or that distorts the writer's intended meaning.[13] For example, *Intelligent systems learn how to correctly spot suspicious interbank transactions* splits the infinitive *to spot* with the adverb *correctly*. Moving *correctly* before or after the infinitive would sound unnatural, and the third option of moving it to the end of the sentence moves the adverb away from the verb it modifies. The sentence is clear and effective as is.
- Similarly, avoiding prepositions at the end of sentences can create phrases that sound awkward or overly formal in today's usage.[14] For example, *After Jessica dropped out of the task force, I had no one left to collaborate with* violates the rule because the preposition *with* is at the end of the sentence. However, moving *with* away from the end sounds a bit too formal for most business usage: *After Jessica dropped out of the task force, I had no one left with whom I could collaborate.*

Unfortunately, the choices for today's business communicators aren't always easy, because some people continue to insist that these rules must never be broken. (The irony here is that linguists and lexicographers, people who study language for a living, tend to be less strict about these rules than the self-appointed "grammar police.") To avoid controversy in these situations, you can usually find ways to rework sentences to avoid using disputed constructions.

These few examples aside, most questions of grammar and usage *are* settled and widely agreed upon, so you need to follow them in order to present yourself as an informed and quality-conscious professional. If you have doubts about what is correct, consult the Handbook of Grammar, Mechanics, and Usage at the end of this book, one of the many writing style guides now available, or leading online dictionaries such as Merriam Webster (www.merriam-webster.com) and the Oxford Dictionaries (en.oxforddictionaries.com).

USING WORDS EFFECTIVELY

In addition to using words correctly, successful writers and speakers take care to use the most effective words and phrases. Selecting and using words effectively is often more challenging than using words correctly because doing so is a matter of judgment and experience. Careful writers continue to work at their craft to find words that communicate with power (see Figure 6.3).

By practicing your writing, learning from experienced writers and editors, and reading extensively, you'll find it easier to choose words that communicate exactly what you want to say. When you compose your business messages, think carefully to find the most powerful words for each situation and to avoid obscure words, clichés, and buzzwords that are turning into clichés (see Table 6.5 on page 169):

- **Choose strong, precise words.** Choose words that express your thoughts clearly and specifically. If you find yourself using a lot of adjectives and adverbs, you're probably trying to compensate for weak nouns and verbs. Saying that *sales plummeted* is stronger and more efficient than saying sales *dropped dramatically* or sales *experienced a dramatic drop*.
- **Choose familiar words.** You'll communicate best with words that are familiar to both you and your readers. Efforts to improve a situation certainly can be *ameliorative*, but saying they are *helpful* is a lot more effective.
- **Avoid clichés, and use buzzwords carefully.** Although familiar words are generally the best choice, avoid *clichés*—once-colorful terms and phrases so common that they have lost some of their power to communicate. *Buzzwords*, newly coined terms often associated with technology, business, or cultural changes, are more difficult to handle than clichés because in small doses and in the right situations, buzzwords can be useful. The careful use of a buzzword can signal that you're an insider, someone in the know.[15] However, buzzwords quickly become clichés, and using them too late in their "life cycle" can mark you as an outsider desperately trying to look like an insider.

In addition to using words correctly, successful writers also take care to find the most effective words and phrases.

Find words that are powerful and familiar.

Avoid clichés, be extremely careful with trendy buzzwords, and use jargon only when your audience is completely familiar with it.

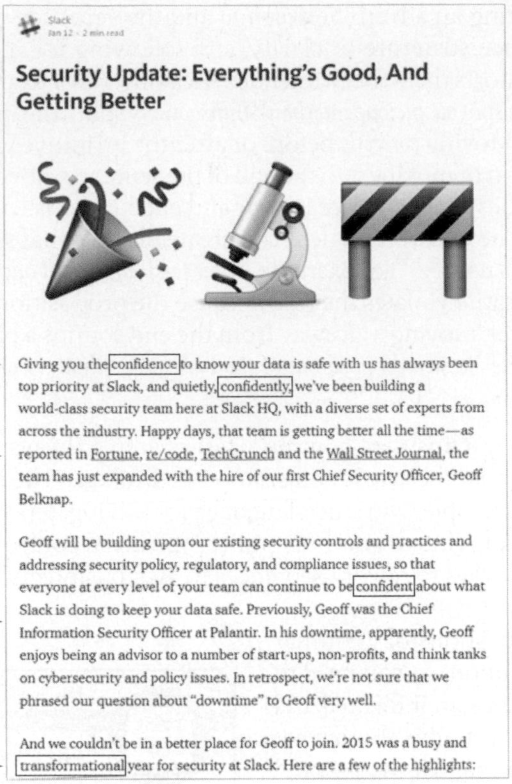

Instilling confidence that Slack can keep customer data safe is the specific purpose (see page 129) of this message. To help build this perception, the post uses variations on the word *confidence* three times in the first two paragraphs.

Happy days is a casual alternative to *Fortunately* or similar wording. Note that this is at the casual extreme of conversational business style, and some companies would consider it too casual for a message such as this.

This paragraph is devoted to the new executive's qualifications, which lend support to the "getting better" message conveyed in the headline and help bolster the confidence message that is the underlying purpose of the entire post.

Transformational suggests a fundamental shift in the way the company approaches security, so it's stronger than something like "we made numerous changes to improve security."

Even though this is an announcement about company matters (the executive hire), the message starts with a strong *you* orientation. The opening uses *you* and *your* and addresses an important reader concern (data security).

The writer uses third-party endorsements to help build the credibility of the message.

The last two sentences in this paragraph have a whimsical tone, but they convey an important message, which is that this person eats, sleeps, and breathes data security—which in turn supports the specific purpose of the blog post.

The article continues with a list of security-related accomplishments the company made in the previous year, which supports the claim of "busy and transformational."

Slack
Jan 12 · 2 min read

Security Update: Everything's Good, And Getting Better

Giving you the confidence to know your data is safe with us has always been top priority at Slack, and quietly, confidently, we've been building a world-class security team here at Slack HQ, with a diverse set of experts from across the industry. Happy days, that team is getting better all the time—as reported in Fortune, re/code, TechCrunch and the Wall Street Journal, the team has just expanded with the hire of our first Chief Security Officer, Geoff Belknap.

Geoff will be building upon our existing security controls and practices and addressing security policy, regulatory, and compliance issues, so that everyone at every level of your team can continue to be confident about what Slack is doing to keep your data safe. Previously, Geoff was the Chief Information Security Officer at Palantir. In his downtime, apparently, Geoff enjoys being an advisor to a number of start-ups, non-profits, and think tanks on cybersecurity and policy issues. In retrospect, we're not sure that we phrased our question about "downtime" to Geoff very well.

And we couldn't be in a better place for Geoff to join. 2015 was a busy and transformational year for security at Slack. Here are a few of the highlights:

Figure 6.3 Choosing Powerful Words
The opening paragraphs of this blog post from Slack, the maker of a popular group messaging service, illustrate a number of effective word and phrase choices. Slack's usual communication tone is upbeat and casual, even a little bit playful, but data and network security is a critically important issue that had already affected the young company by this point in time, so this post strikes a balance between conversational and serious.

- **Use jargon carefully.** *Jargon*, the specialized language of a particular profession or industry, has a bad reputation, but it's not always bad. Using jargon is often an efficient way to communicate within the specific groups that understand these terms. After all, that's how jargon develops in the first place, as people with similar interests devise ways to communicate complex ideas quickly. For instance, when a recording engineer wants to communicate that a particular piece of music is devoid of reverberation and other processing effects, it's a lot easier to simply describe the track as "dry." Of course, to people who aren't familiar with such insider terms, jargon is meaningless and intimidating—one more reason it's important to understand your audience before you start writing.

UNDERSTANDING DENOTATION AND CONNOTATION

A word's *denotative meaning* is its literal, or dictionary, meaning; its *connotative meaning* includes all the associations and feelings it evokes.

A word may have both a denotative and a connotative meaning. The **denotative meaning** is the literal, or dictionary, meaning. The **connotative meaning** includes all the associations and feelings evoked by the word.

The denotative meaning of *desk* is "a piece of furniture with a flat work surface and various drawers for storage." The connotative meaning of desk may include thoughts associated with work or study, but the word *desk* has fairly neutral connotations—neither strong nor emotional. However, some words have much stronger connotations than others and should be used with care. For example, the connotations of the word *fail* are negative and can have a dramatic emotional impact. If you say the sales department *failed* to meet its annual quota, the connotative meaning suggests that the group is inferior, incompetent, or below some standard of performance. However, the reason for not achieving 100 percent might be an inferior product, incorrect pricing, a falling economy, or some other factor outside

MOBILE APP
The **Merriam-Webster** dictionary app offers the full Collegiate Dictionary and fun vocabulary games.

TABLE 6.5 Selected Examples of Finding Powerful Words

Potentially Weak Words and Phrases	Stronger Alternatives (Effective Usage Depends on the Situation)
Increase (as a verb)	Accelerate, amplify, augment, enlarge, escalate, expand, extend, magnify, multiply, soar, swell
Decrease (as a verb)	Curb, cut back, depreciate, dwindle, shrink, slacken
Large, small	Use a specific number, such as $100 million
Good	Admirable, beneficial, desirable, flawless, pleasant, sound, superior, worthy
Bad	Abysmal, corrupt, deficient, flawed, inadequate, inferior, poor, substandard, worthless
We are committed to providing . . .	We provide . . .
It is in our best interest to . . .	We should . . .
Unfamiliar Words	**Familiar Words**
Ascertain	Find out, learn
Consummate	Close, bring about
Peruse	Read, study
Circumvent	Avoid
Unequivocal	Certain
Clichés and Buzzwords	**Plain Language**
An uphill battle	A challenge
Writing on the wall	Prediction
Call the shots	Lead
Take by storm	Attack
Costs an arm and a leg	Expensive
A new ball game	Fresh start
Fall through the cracks	Be overlooked
Think outside the box	Be creative
Run it up the flagpole	Find out what people think about it
Eat our own dog food	Use our own products
Mission-critical	Vital
Disintermediate	Simplify the supply chain
Green light (as a verb)	Approve
Architect (as a verb)	Design
Space (as in, "we compete in the XYZ space")	Market or industry
Blocking and tackling	Basic skills
Trying to boil the ocean	Working frantically but without focus
Human capital	People, employees, workforce
Low-hanging fruit	Tasks that are easy to complete or sales that are easy to close
Pushback	Resistance

the control of the sales department. In contrast, by saying the sales department achieved 85 percent of its quota, you clearly communicate that the results were less than expected without triggering all the negative emotions associated with *failure*.

BALANCING ABSTRACT AND CONCRETE WORDS

An **abstract word** expresses a concept, quality, or characteristic. Abstractions are usually broad, encompassing a category of ideas, and are often intellectual, academic, or philosophical. *Love, honor, progress, tradition,* and *beauty* are abstractions, as are such important business concepts as *efficiency, quality,* and *motivation.* In contrast, a **concrete word** stands

An *abstract word* expresses a concept, quality, or characteristic; a *concrete word* stands for something you can touch, see, or visualize.

for something you can touch, see, or visualize. Most concrete terms are anchored in the tangible, material world. *Chair*, *green*, *two*, and *horse* are concrete words; they are direct, clear, and exact. Things don't need to have a physical presence to be considered concrete, by the way; *app*, *database*, and *website* are all concrete terms as well.

Abstract words tend to cause more trouble than concrete words because they are sometimes "fuzzy" and can be interpreted differently, depending on the audience and the circumstances. The best way to minimize such problems is to balance abstract terms with concrete ones. State the concept, then pin it down with details expressed in more concrete terms. Save the abstractions for ideas that cannot be expressed any other way.

Composing Your Message: Creating Effective Sentences

5 **LEARNING OBJECTIVE** Define the four types of sentences, and explain how sentence style affects emphasis within a message.

Arranging your carefully chosen words in effective sentences is the next step in creating powerful messages. Start by selecting the best type of sentence to communicate each point you want to make.

CHOOSING FROM THE FOUR TYPES OF SENTENCES

A *simple sentence* has one main clause.

Sentences come in four basic varieties: simple, compound, complex, and compound-complex. A **simple sentence** has one main *clause* (a single subject and a single predicate), although it may be expanded by nouns and pronouns that serve as objects of the action and by modifying phrases. Here's an example with the subject noun underlined once and the predicate verb underlined twice:

> Profits increased 35 percent in the past year.

A *compound sentence* has two main clauses.

A **compound sentence** has two main clauses that express two or more independent but related thoughts of equal importance, usually joined by *and, but,* or *or*. In effect, a compound sentence is a merger of two or more simple sentences (independent clauses) that are related. For example:

> Wages declined by 5 percent, and employee turnover has been high.

The independent clauses in a compound sentence are always separated by a comma or by a semicolon (in which case the conjunction is dropped).

A *complex sentence* has one main clause and one subordinate clause.

A **complex sentence** expresses one main thought (the independent clause) and one or more subordinate, related thoughts (dependent clauses that cannot stand alone as valid sentences). Independent and dependent clauses are usually separated by a comma. In this example, "Although you may question Gerald's conclusions" is a subordinate thought expressed in a dependent clause:

> Although you may question Gerald's conclusions, you must admit that his research is thorough.

A *compound-complex sentence* has two main clauses and at least one dependent clause.

A **compound-complex sentence** has two main clauses, at least one of which contains a subordinate clause:

> Profits increased 35 percent in the past year, so although the company faces long-term challenges, I agree that its short-term prospects look quite positive.

When constructing sentences, choose the form that matches the relationship of the ideas you want to express. If you have two ideas of equal importance, express them as two simple sentences or as one compound sentence. However, if one of the ideas is less important than the other, place it in a dependent clause to form a complex sentence. For example, although the following compound sentence uses a conjunction to join two ideas, they aren't truly equal:

> The chemical products division is the strongest in the company, and its management techniques should be adopted by the other divisions.

By making the first thought subordinate to the second, you can establish a cause-and-effect relationship and emphasize the more important idea (that the other divisions should adopt the chemical division's management techniques):

> Because the chemical products division is the strongest in the company, its management techniques should be adopted by the other divisions.

In addition to selecting the best type for each thought you want to express, using a variety of sentence types throughout a document can make your writing more interesting and effective. For example, if you use too many simple sentences in a row, you may struggle to properly express the relationships among your ideas, and your writing will sound choppy and abrupt. At the other extreme, a long series of compound, complex, or compound-complex sentences can be tiring to read.

Maintain some variety among the four sentence types to keep your writing from getting choppy (from too many short, simple sentences) or exhausting (from too many long sentences).

INTELLIGENT COMMUNICATION TECHNOLOGY

Amplifying Your Writing with Augmented Writing Software

What's the best way to say this?

That's a never-ending question for every business communicator. For just about anything beyond the simplest messages, we can never be entirely sure that we've found the most powerful words or crafted the most effective phrases. We have to send our missives out into the ether and hope we've done our best.

Moreover, in many cases we get only one chance to hit the mark. In contrast to interactive conversations (in person or online), where we get feedback quickly and can adjust the message if needed, a lot of business writing is a one-shot affair, and we'll never know if we've been as effective as we could be.

Digital tools have been assisting writers for decades, as far back as spell checkers that predate the PC era, but most haven't done much beyond applying simple rules. However, recent advances in natural language processing show some potential to fill this feedback void by providing real-time advice about the effectiveness of our language.

For example, Textio's *augmented writing* platform suggests words and phrases that it has determined to be more effective in a particular context. It does so by measuring the success of similar writing efforts and analyzing language choices that proved to be more effective or less effective.

Textio's initial focus has been on helping companies write job postings that can attract more of the most desirable candidates. By analyzing hundreds of millions of postings and comparing the candidate pools that they attracted, the system can figure out the most compelling way to describe a variety of job opportunities.

Organizations ranging from Twitter to Apple to the National Basketball Association are now using the system to improve their job postings. HR departments enter their job descriptions into Textio's *predictive engine*, which analyzes the text and suggests specific wording changes to attract target candidates. It also provides overall assessment points when it analyzes a posting, such as "Uses corporate clichés," "Sentences are too short," and "Contains too many questions," all based on how other job descriptions have performed.

Textio's clients are reporting success in terms of the number and quality of candidates they attract and how much faster they can fill job openings as a result. Plus, the system can help writers avoid biased or exclusionary language by showing how various demographic groups respond to different word choices.

Of course, a system like this relies on a large set of similar messages and the ability to measure the success of those messages, so it's not yet a general-purpose solution that one can apply to every kind of business writing. But Textio and its clients are already trying the tool on sales emails and other types of recurring messages, so its use could expand.

WHAT'S YOUR TAKE?

1. Will tools such as augmented writing reduce the need for professionals to develop their own communication skills? Why or why not?
2. Will augmented writing tools give some business communicators an unfair advantage? Why or why not?

Sources: Benjamin Romano, "With $20M from Scale, Textio Envisions 'Augmented Writing' Everywhere," *Xconomy*, 21 June 2017, www.xconomy.com; Textio website, accessed 14 March 2018, textio.com; "How Textio Is Changing Writing as We Know It," Scale Venture Partners, www.scalevp.com; Rachel Lerman, "Investors Pump $20M into Seattle Startup Textio, Which Helps Job Recruiters Find the Right Words," *Seattle Times*, 25 June 2017.

USING SENTENCE STYLE TO EMPHASIZE KEY THOUGHTS

Emphasize specific parts of sentences by

- Devoting more words to them
- Putting them at the beginning or at the end of the sentence
- Making them the subject of the sentence

In every message of any length, some ideas are more important than others. You can emphasize these key ideas through your sentence style. One obvious technique is to give important points the most space. When you want to call attention to a thought, give it additional support. Consider this sentence:

> The chairperson called for a vote of the shareholders.

To emphasize the importance of the chairperson, you might describe her more fully:

> Having considerable experience in corporate takeover battles, the chairperson called for a vote of the shareholders.

You can increase the emphasis even more by adding a separate, short sentence to augment the first:

> The chairperson called for a vote of the shareholders. She has considerable experience in corporate takeover battles.

You can also call attention to a thought by making it the subject of the sentence. In the following example, the emphasis is on the person:

> I can write letters much more quickly by using voice dictation.

However, by changing the subject, the voice dictation capability takes center stage:

> Using voice dictation enables me to write letters much more quickly.

Another way to emphasize an idea (in this instance, the idea of stimulating demand) is to place it either at the beginning or at the end of a sentence:

> **Less emphatic:** We are cutting the price to stimulate demand.
>
> **More emphatic:** To stimulate demand, we are cutting the price.

The best placement of the dependent clause depends on the relationship between the ideas in the sentence.

In complex sentences, the placement of the dependent clause hinges on the relationship between the ideas expressed. If you want to emphasize the subordinate idea, put the dependent clause at the end of the sentence (the most emphatic position) or at the beginning (the second most emphatic position). If you want to downplay the idea, put the dependent clause within the sentence:

> **Most emphatic:** The electronic parts are manufactured in Mexico, <u>which has lower wage rates than the United States</u>.
>
> **Emphatic:** Because <u>wage rates are lower in Mexico than in the United States</u>, the electronic parts are manufactured there.
>
> **Least emphatic:** Mexico, <u>which has lower wage rates than the United States</u>, was selected as the production site for the electronic parts.

Techniques such as these give you a great deal of control over the way your audience interprets what you have to say.

These techniques can also help you communicate with the "you" attitude. By helping your readers quickly grasp the most important points in each sentence, you can save them time and frustration.

REAL-TIME UPDATES
LEARN MORE BY READING THIS ARTICLE
Practical tips for more-effective sentences
The Writer's Handbook from the University of Wisconsin offers tips on writing clear, concise sentences. Go to **real-timeupdates.com/ebc13** and select Learn More in the Students section.

Composing Your Message: Crafting Unified, Coherent Paragraphs

6 LEARNING OBJECTIVE
Define the three key elements of a paragraph, and list five ways to develop unified, coherent paragraphs.

Paragraphs organize sentences related to the same general topic. Readers expect every paragraph to be *unified*—focusing on a single topic—and *coherent*—presenting ideas in a logically connected way. By carefully arranging the elements of each paragraph, you help your readers grasp the main idea of your document and understand how the specific pieces of support material back up that idea.

An effective paragraph is *unified* (it focuses on a single topic) and *coherent* (it presents ideas in a logically connected way).

CREATING THE ELEMENTS OF A PARAGRAPH

Paragraphs vary widely in length and form, but a typical paragraph contains three basic elements: a topic sentence, support sentences that develop the topic, and transitional words and phrases.

Most paragraphs consist of

- A topic sentence that reveals the subject of the paragraph
- Related sentences that support and expand the topic
- Transitions that help readers move between sentences and paragraphs

Topic Sentence

An effective paragraph deals with a single topic, and the sentence that introduces it is called the **topic sentence** (see Figure 6.4). In informal and creative writing, the topic sentence may be implied rather than stated. In business writing, the topic sentence is generally explicit and is often the first sentence in the paragraph. The topic sentence gives readers a summary of the general idea that will be covered in the rest of the paragraph.

APPLY YOUR SKILLS NOW

Think Now, Write Later

When you get a new assignment, it's tempting to either dive in immediately so you don't get into a schedule crunch later or put it off until the last minute—when you will definitely be in a schedule crunch.

Not surprisingly, the do-it-later approach isn't always a successful way to work. Writing under a tight deadline can sometimes be invigorating, and time limits can help you stay focused, but mostly it's just stressful and exhausting. Plus, there's the potential problem of getting bogged down in complex issues at the last minute and not having enough time left to think through them or do additional research.

Somewhat more surprisingly, the do-it-right-now approach isn't always the most productive way to write, either. When you sit down and command yourself to write something *now*, the mind has a funny way of rebelling and giving you nothing but a blank stare. Instead of figuring out *what* you need to say, you'll start worrying about *how* to say it, and your inner editor will get in the way with criticism and self-doubt.

Try this modified approach instead. As soon as you get an assignment, dig into it but tell yourself you don't need to do any writing right now. Just explore the topic, do some research, and start to fill your mind with nuggets of information—without

worrying about how you're going to say anything yet. Let these thoughts rumble around while you go off and do other things. Your mind will keep busy in the background, searching for connections between the bits of information you have collected, trying out ideas for organizing the piece, and generating useful phrases and other bits of text. The piece will gradually take shape somewhere between your conscious and subconscious mind before you begin to write, and when you do sit down to write, the words should flow faster and easier than trying to force them on command.

COACH YOURSELF

1. Do you ever find yourself in a panic when you get a writing assignment? If so, don't get down on yourself; this can happen to everybody, including professional writers who have been honing their craft for decades. Try this trick: Tell yourself you need to write just one sentence. As you fine-tune that sentence, you'll probably feel yourself settling into a groove, and the rest of the work will go more easily from there.

2. If you're in the habit of putting writing projects off to the last minute, what are some changes you could make to get yourself into a more-controlled and less-stressful mode of work?

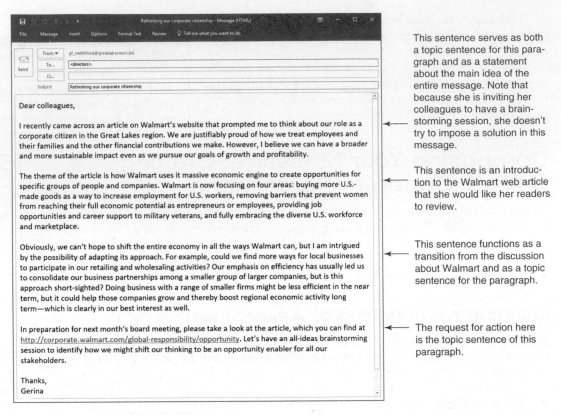

This sentence serves as both a topic sentence for this paragraph and as a statement about the main idea of the entire message. Note that because she is inviting her colleagues to have a brainstorming session, she doesn't try to impose a solution in this message.

This sentence is an introduction to the Walmart web article that she would like her readers to review.

This sentence functions as a transition from the discussion about Walmart and as a topic sentence for the paragraph.

The request for action here is the topic sentence of this paragraph.

Figure 6.4   Topic Sentences
This email message establishes the scope of each paragraph with a clear topic sentence.

The *topic sentence* introduces the topic of a paragraph.

The following examples show how a topic sentence can introduce the subject and suggest the way the subject will be developed:

> The medical products division has been troubled for many years by public relations problems. [In the rest of the paragraph, readers will learn the details of the problems.]
>
> To get a refund, please supply us with the following information. [The details of the necessary information will be described in the rest of the paragraph.]

In addition to helping your readers, topic sentences help you as a writer because they remind you of the purpose of each paragraph and thereby encourage you to stay focused. In fact, a good way to test the effectiveness of your writing is to prepare a summary version that consists of only the first sentences of all your paragraphs. If this summary communicates the essence of your message in a sensible, compelling way, you've probably done a good job of presenting your information.[16]

Support Sentences

Support sentences explain, justify, or extend the idea presented in the topic sentence.

In most paragraphs, the topic sentence needs to be explained, justified, or extended with one or more support sentences. These related sentences must all have a bearing on the general subject and must provide enough specific details to make the topic clear:

> The medical products division has been troubled for many years by public relations problems. The media and bloggers have published 15 articles in the past year that portray the division in a negative light. We have been accused of everything from mistreating laboratory animals to polluting the local groundwater. Our facility has been described as a health hazard. Our scientists are referred to as "Frankensteins," and our profits are considered "obscene."

Notice how these support sentences are all more specific than the topic sentence. Each one provides another piece of evidence to demonstrate the general truth of the main thought. Also, each sentence is clearly related to the general idea being developed, which gives the paragraph its unity. A paragraph is well developed when it contains enough information to make the topic sentence convincing and interesting and doesn't contain any unnecessary or unrelated sentences.

REAL-TIME UPDATES
LEARN MORE BY VISITING THIS WEBSITE
Get started—or go advanced—with Microsoft Word
Whether you're starting your first document or using Word's advanced capabilities, this site can help. Go to **real-timeupdates** **.com/ebc13** and select Learn More in the Students section.

Transitions

Transitions connect ideas by showing how one thought is related to another. They also help alert the reader to what lies ahead so that shifts and changes don't cause confusion. In addition to helping readers understand the connections you're trying to make, transitions give your writing a smooth, even flow.

Transitions connect ideas by showing how one thought is related to another.

Depending on the specific need within a document, transitional elements can range in length from a single word to an entire paragraph or more. You can establish transitions in a variety of ways:

- **Use connecting words.** Use conjunctions such as *and, but, or, nevertheless, however, in addition,* and so on.
- **Echo a word or phrase from a previous paragraph or sentence.** "A system should be established for monitoring inventory levels. *This system* will provide . . ."
- **Use a pronoun that refers to a noun used previously.** "Ms. Arthur is the leading candidate for the president's position. *She* has excellent qualifications."
- **Use words that are frequently paired.** "The machine has a *minimum* output of . . . Its *maximum* output is . . ."

Transitional elements include

- *Connecting words (conjunctions)*
- *Repeated words or phrases*
- *Pronouns*
- *Words that are frequently paired*

Some transitions serve as mood changers, alerting the reader to a change in mood from the previous material. Some announce a total contrast with what's gone on before, some announce a cause-effect relationship, and some signal a change in time. Here is a list of transitions frequently used to move readers smoothly between clauses, sentences, and paragraphs:

Additional detail: moreover, furthermore, in addition, besides, first, second, third, finally

Cause-and-effect relationship: therefore, because, accordingly, thus, consequently, hence, as a result, so

Comparison: similarly, here again, likewise, in comparison, still

Contrast: yet, conversely, whereas, nevertheless, on the other hand, however, but, nonetheless

Condition: although, if

Illustration: for example, in particular, in this case, for instance

Time sequence: formerly, after, when, meanwhile, sometimes

Intensification: indeed, in fact, in any event

Summary: in brief, in short, to sum up

Repetition: that is, in other words, as I mentioned earlier

Consider using a transition whenever it could help the reader understand your ideas and follow you from point to point. You can use transitions inside paragraphs to tie related points together and between paragraphs to ease the shift from one distinct thought to another. In longer reports, a transition that links major sections or chapters may be a complete paragraph that serves as a mini-introduction to the next section or as a summary of the ideas presented in the section just ending. Here's an example:

> Given the nature of this product, our alternatives are limited. As the previous section indicates, we can stop making it altogether, improve it, or continue with the current model. Each of these alternatives has advantages and disadvantages, which are discussed in the following section.

This paragraph makes it clear to the reader that the analysis of the problem (offered in the previous section) is now over and that the document is making a transition to an analysis of the possible solutions (to be offered in the next section).

CHOOSING THE BEST WAY TO DEVELOP EACH PARAGRAPH

Five ways to develop paragraphs:

- Illustration
- Comparison or contrast
- Cause and effect
- Classification
- Problem and solution

You have a variety of options for developing paragraphs, each of which can convey a specific type of idea. Five of the most common approaches are illustration, comparison or contrast, cause and effect, classification, and problem and solution (see Table 6.6).

In some instances, combining approaches in a single paragraph is an effective strategy. Notice how the example provided for "Problem and solution" in Table 6.6 also includes an element of illustration by listing some of the changes that could be part of the proposed solution. However, when combining approaches, do so carefully so that you don't lose readers partway through the paragraph.

TABLE 6.6 Five Techniques for Developing Paragraphs

Technique	Description	Example
Illustration	Giving examples that demonstrate the general idea	Some of our most popular products are available through local distributors. For example, Everett & Lemmings carries our frozen soups and entrees. The J. B. Green Company carries our complete line of seasonings, as well as the frozen soups. Wilmont Foods, also a major distributor, now carries our new line of frozen desserts.
Comparison or contrast	Using similarities or differences to develop the topic	When the company was small, the recruiting function could be handled informally. The need for new employees was limited, and each manager could comfortably screen and hire her or his own staff. However, our successful bid on the Owens contract means that we will be doubling our labor force over the next six months. To hire that many people without disrupting our ongoing activities, we will create a separate recruiting group within the human resources department.
Cause and effect	Focusing on the reasons for something	The heavy-duty fabric of your Wanderer tent probably broke down for one of two reasons: (1) a sharp object punctured the fabric, and without reinforcement, the hole was enlarged by the stress of pitching the tent daily for a week, or (2) the fibers gradually rotted because the tent was folded and stored while still wet.
Classification	Showing how a general idea is broken into specific categories	Successful candidates for our supervisor trainee program generally come from one of several groups. The largest group by far consists of recent graduates of accredited business management programs. The next largest group comes from within our own company, as we try to promote promising staff workers to positions of greater responsibility. Finally, we occasionally accept candidates with outstanding supervisory experience in related industries.
Problem and solution	Presenting a problem and then discussing the solution	Shoppers are clearly not happy with our in-store shopping app—it currently has an average rating of under two stars in both the Apple and Android app stores. After studying dozens of reviews, I've identified three improvements that should make the app much friendlier. First, the user interface is too cluttered. We need to simplify it by presenting only the information the user needs at any given point in time. Second, the app is too slow at guiding shoppers to products of interest. We need to speed up the GPS and near-field algorithms. Third, we need to add a shopping list tracking feature so that customers don't need to type in their desired products every time they go shopping.

In addition, before settling for the first approach that comes to mind, consider the alternatives. Think through various methods before committing yourself, or even write several test paragraphs to see which method works best. By avoiding the easy habit of repeating the same old paragraph pattern time after time, you can keep your writing fresh and interesting.

Writing Messages for Mobile Devices

One obvious adaptation to make for audiences using mobile devices is to modify the design and layout of your messages to fit smaller screen sizes and different user interface features (see Chapter 7). However, modifying your approach to writing is also an important step. Reading is more difficult on small screens, and consequently users' ability to comprehend what they read on mobile devices is lower than it is on larger screens.[17] In fact, research shows that comprehension can drop by 50 percent when users move from reading on a full-size screen to reading on a smartphone, and they can scroll right past vital information without noticing it.[18] Use these five techniques to make your mobile messages more effective:

- **Use a linear organization.** In a printed document or on a larger screen, readers can easily take in multiple elements on a page, such as preview or summary boxes, tables and other supporting visuals, and sidebars with related information. All these elements are in view at the same time, so readers can jump around the page to read various parts without feeling lost. However, with small mobile device screens, a complicated organization requires readers to zoom in and out and pan around to see all these elements at readable text sizes. This situation makes reading slower and raises the odds that readers will get disoriented and lose the thread of the message because they can't see the big picture. In addition, using a touch screen momentarily obscures some of the information, so the more users have to hunt and scroll, the more likely they will miss something.[19] To simplify reading, organize with a linear flow from the top to the bottom of the message or article.

- **Prioritize information.** Small screens make it difficult for readers to scan the page to find the information they want most. Prioritize the information based on what you know about their needs and put that information first.[20] Use the *inverted pyramid* style favored by journalists, in which you reveal the most important information briefly at first and then provide successive layers of detail that readers can consume if they want. Note that you may need to avoid using the indirect approach (see page 143) if your message is complicated, because readers will find it harder to follow your chain of reasoning.

- **Write shorter and more-focused messages and documents.** Mobile users often lack the patience or opportunity to read lengthy messages or documents, so keep them short.[21] In some cases, doing so could require you to write two documents, such as a shorter *executive summary* (see page 417) for mobile use and a longer supporting document that readers can access with their PCs if they want more details.

- **Use shorter subject lines and headings.** Mobile devices, particularly phones, can't display as many characters in a single line of text as the typical computer screen can. Depending on the app or website, email subject lines and page headings will be truncated or will wrap around to take up multiple lines. Both formats make reading more difficult. A good rule of thumb is to keep subject lines and headlines to around 25 characters.[22] This doesn't give you much text to work with, so make every word count and make sure you start with the key words so readers can instantly see what the subject line or heading is about.[23]

- **Use shorter paragraphs.** In addition to structuring a message according to discrete blocks of information, paragraphs have a visual role in written communication as well. Shorter paragraphs are less intimidating and let readers take frequent "micro rests" as they move through a document. Because far less text is displayed at once on a mobile screen, keep paragraphs as short as possible so readers don't have to swipe through screen after screen before getting to paragraph breaks.

Compare the two messages in Figure 6.5 to get a sense of how to write reader-friendly mobile content.

For a reminder of the tasks involved in writing messages, see "Checklist: Writing Business Messages."

7 LEARNING OBJECTIVE List five techniques for writing effective messages for mobile readers.

To write effectively for mobile devices

- Use a linear organization
- Prioritize information
- Write short, focused messages
- Use short subject lines and headings
- Use short paragraphs

MOBILE APP

Pages is a full-featured word processing app for iOS devices.

The text from this conventional report page is too small to read on a phone screen.

However, zooming in to read forces the reader to lose context and repeatedly hunt around to find all the pieces of the page.

Figure 6.5a

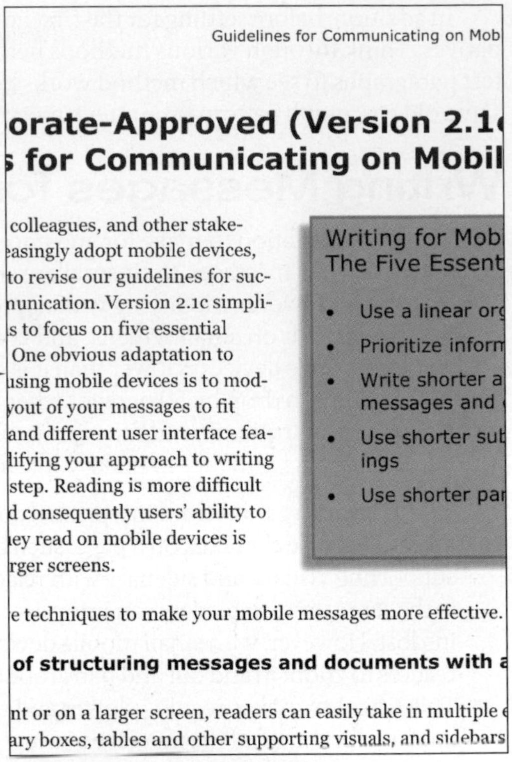

Figure 6.5b

Optimizing for mobile includes writing short headlines that get right to the point.

This introduction conveys only the information readers need in order to grasp the scope of the article.

All the key points of the document appear here on the first screen.

Readers who want more detail can swipe down for background information on the five points.

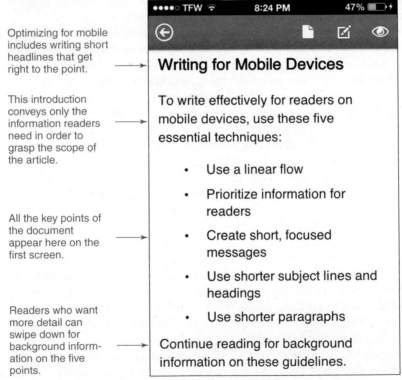

Figure 6.5c

Figure 6.5 Writing for Mobile Devices

Messages and documents created for printed pages and a full-sized screen can be difficult and frustrating on mobile devices. For mobile audiences, rewrite with short headlines and concise, linear content—notice how much easier Figure 6.5c is to read.

CHECKLIST ✔ Writing Business Messages

A. Adapt to your audience.
- ✔ Use the "you" attitude.
- ✔ Maintain good etiquette through polite communication.
- ✔ Emphasize the positive whenever possible.
- ✔ Use bias-free language.
- ✔ Establish credibility in the eyes of your audience.
- ✔ Project your company's preferred image.
- ✔ Use a conversational but still professional and respectful tone.
- ✔ Use plain language for clarity.

B. Compose your message.
- ✔ Choose strong words that communicate efficiently.
- ✔ Pay attention to the connotative meaning of your words.

- ✔ Balance abstract and concrete terms to convey your meaning accurately.
- ✔ Avoid clichés and trendy buzzwords.
- ✔ Use jargon only when your audience understands it and prefers it.
- ✔ Vary your sentence structure for impact and interest.
- ✔ Develop coherent, unified paragraphs.
- ✔ Use transitions generously to help your audience follow your message.
- ✔ As needed, adapt your writing for the limitations of mobile devices.

ON THE JOB: SOLVING COMMUNICATION DILEMMAS AT **LUMEN/KALEIGH MOORE**

Kaleigh Moore recently hired you as a writer/editor to provide clients with social media content and to offer editorial assistance with their own content. Use what you've learned in this chapter to address these writing challenges.

1. You're reviewing the draft of a client's newsletter article that encourages college students who are about to graduate to consider starting a business rather than applying for conventional jobs. The writer has two main reasons for making this suggestion. First, although the job market has been strong for several years now, the economy always experiences fluctuations, and as business evolves, some fields will naturally grow while others stagnate. The writer suggests that some graduates could be forced to take jobs that are outside their intended fields and perhaps below the level of their qualifications. Second, the nature of employment is changing in many professions and industries, and many companies now engage independent contractors for short durations to fill some of their talent needs, rather than exclusively hiring employees for the long term. Which of these statements is the most sensitive to the audience's needs as they relate to this specific topic?

   a. Starting your own business offers a degree of freedom that you will never achieve in a conventional corporate job.
   b. The job market could slow down in some industries and professions in the coming years as employers find they need different mixes of talent. Chances are you'll end up working as an independent contractor at some point anyway, so you might as well do it now.
   c. What could be more fun than creating your own job the minute you graduate?
   d. Depending on your career goals and the state of the economy, you might not be able to find the ideal opening when you're ready to graduate. Plus, many traditional

jobs are transitioning to contract work. Why not convert a challenge into opportunity and create your own job?

2. For a blog post for a business financing firm that discusses the risks of going into business with friends or family members, which of these sentences has the most appropriate tone and demonstrates the best use of plain language?

   a. The attraction of entering into strategic partnerships with known personalities notwithstanding, one must exercise great caution when considering working with friends and family members.
   b. Going into business with friends or family members can sound appealing, but just because a relationship works on a personal level doesn't automatically mean it will work on a business level.
   c. Going into business with friends or family members can sound appealing, but you need to remember that managing a business is not the same as interacting with people in a social or personal sphere.
   d. Think about how even your best friends can drive you nuts sometimes—do you really want that kind of crazy in your business, too?

3. In a post for that same firm about pitching a business plan to investors, the writer wants to give entrepreneurs a realistic expectation about getting funding from venture capitalists. Which of the following sentence structures conveys this idea most effectively?

   a. Venture capitalists can provide valuable management expertise and industry connections in addition to start-up funds, but they fund only a tiny percentage of all new companies.
   b. Venture capitalists, who fund only a tiny percentage of all new companies, can provide valuable management expertise and industry connections in addition to start-up funds.

c. Venture capitalists can provide valuable management expertise and industry connections in addition to start-up funds. However, they fund only a tiny percentage of all new companies.

d. They fund only a tiny percentage of all new companies, but venture capitalists can provide valuable management expertise and industry connections in addition to start-up funds.

4. The following paragraphs all have the same topic sentence; which has the most effective set of support sentences?

a. First-line supervisors, those on the lowest rung of the managerial ladder, face several unique challenges. As the interface between management and nonmanagerial employees, they have the most immediate responsibility for ensuring that necessary work is done according to agreed-on performance standards. They must also deal directly with any friction that exists between labor and management. Supervisors are also deeply involved in recruiting, hiring, and training of employees.

b. First-line supervisors, those on the lowest rung of the managerial ladder, face several unique challenges. These managers have a good feel for the concerns and activities of employees, given their close day-to-day contact with them. Plus, when supervisors are newly promoted into management, the experience of being an employee is still fresh in their minds—a perspective that is often lost as managers move higher up the corporate ladder.

c. First-line supervisors, those on the lowest rung of the managerial ladder, face several unique challenges. As the interface between management and nonmanagerial employees, they are the ones who must deal with any friction that exists between labor and management. Even if they are sympathetic to employees' concerns or complaints, they represent management and so must take management's side in any disputes.

END OF CHAPTER

Learning Objectives Checkup

Assess your understanding of the principles in this chapter by reading each learning objective and studying the accompanying exercises. You can check your responses against the answer key on page 612.

Objective 6.1: Identify the four aspects of being sensitive to audience needs when writing business messages.

1. Why should you take the time to adapt your messages to your audience?
   a. People are more inclined to read and respond to messages that they believe apply to them and their concerns.
   b. Adapting messages to audiences is corporate policy in nearly all large companies.
   c. Adapting your message saves time during planning and writing.
   d. You can manipulate audience responses more easily by adapting your messages.

2. Writing "Jack is no longer with us" rather than "Jack died" is an example of what kind of writing technique?
   a. Political correctness
   b. Euphemism
   c. Spin doctoring
   d. Rhetoric

3. Which of these is an important reason to review your writing and speaking choices carefully to make sure you are not using biased language?
   a. Biased language often reflects biased thinking, and it perpetuates stereotypes and prejudices.
   b. Using labels incorrectly can get you in trouble.
   c. You want to avoid creating distractions so that audiences are more likely to agree with your messages.

   d. Being fair is good enough; it's someone else's problem if you're not perceived as fair.

Objective 6.2: Identify seven characteristics that build and maintain a communicator's credibility.

4. Credibility is a measure of
   a. your power within the organization.
   b. the length of time the audience has known you.
   c. your confidence.
   d. the audience's perception of your believability.

5. If you have developed a reputation for missing deadlines on projects you manage, which of the following statements would do the best job of helping to rebuild your credibility? (You have previously committed to a project completion date of April 1.)
   a. No April foolin' this time; we'll be finished by April 1.
   b. After analyzing past projects, I now realize that a failure to clarify project objectives up front created significant delays down the line. In order to meet the April 1 deadline, I will make sure to clarify the objective as soon as the team assembles.
   c. I plan to work extra hard this time to make sure we will be finished by April 1.
   d. I hope that we will be finished by April 1.

Objective 6.3: Explain how to achieve a tone that is conversational but businesslike, explain the value of using plain language, and define active and passive voice.

6. A good way to achieve a businesslike tone in your messages is to
   a. use formal business terminology, such as "In re your letter of the 18th."
   b. brag about your company.

c. use a style that is conversational but not too intimate or chatty.

d. use plenty of humor.

7. Plain English is
   a. never recommended when speaking with people for whom English is a second language.
   b. a movement toward using "English only" in U.S. businesses.
   c. a way of writing and arranging content to make it more readily understandable.
   d. an attempt to keep writing at a fourth- or fifth-grade level.

8. If you want to avoid attributing blame or otherwise calling attention to a specific person, the _____ voice is a more diplomatic approach.

9. The _____ voice usually makes sentences shorter, more direct, and livelier.

Objective 6.4: Describe how to select words that are both correct and effective.

10. Which of the following defines the connotative meaning of the word *flag*?
    a. A flag is a piece of material with a symbol of some kind sewn on it.
    b. A flag is a symbol of everything that a nation stands for.
    c. A flag is fabric on a pole used to mark a geographic spot.
    d. A flag is an object used to draw attention.

11. Which of the following is a concrete word?
    a. Little
    b. Mouse
    c. Faith
    d. Quality

12. If you're not sure about the meaning of a word you'd like to use, which of the following is the most appropriate way to handle the situation?
    a. Your readers probably have instant access to online dictionaries these days, so go ahead and use the word.
    b. Use the word but include a humorous comment in parentheses saying that you're not really sure what this big, important word means.
    c. Either verify the meaning of the word or rewrite the sentence so that you don't need to use it.
    d. Find a synonym in a thesaurus and use that word instead.

13. Using jargon is
    a. often a good idea when discussing complex subjects with people who are familiar with the subject and common jargon relating to it.
    b. never a good idea.
    c. a good way to build credibility, no matter what the purpose of the message.
    d. a sign of being an "insider."

Objective 6.5: Define the four types of sentences and explain how sentence style affects emphasis within a message.

14. Where is the most emphatic place to put a dependent clause?
    a. At the end of the sentence
    b. At the beginning of the sentence
    c. In the middle of the sentence
    d. Anywhere in the sentence

15. Devoting a lot of words to a particular idea shows your audience that
    a. the idea is complicated.
    b. the idea is the topic sentence.
    c. the idea is important.
    d. the idea is new and therefore requires more explanation.

Objective 6.6: Define the three key elements of a paragraph, and list five ways to develop unified, coherent paragraphs.

16. When developing a paragraph, keep in mind that
    a. you should stick to one method of development within a single paragraph.
    b. once you use one method of development, you should use that same method for all the paragraphs in a section.
    c. your choice of technique should take into account your subject, your intended audience, and your purpose.
    d. you should do all of the above.

17. To develop a paragraph by illustration, give your audience enough _____ to help them grasp the main idea.

18. Paragraphs organized by comparison or contrast point out the _____ or _____ between two or more items.

19. To explain the reasons something happened, which of these paragraph designs should you use?
    a. Cause-effect
    b. Opposition and argument
    c. Classification
    d. Prioritization

Objective 6.7: List five techniques for writing effective messages for mobile readers

20. What is meant by using a linear organization to craft messages for mobile devices?
    a. Using only ethically proven information
    b. Organizing all the information in a single topical thread from start to finish
    c. Putting each paragraph on its own line
    d. Using line art to convey key message points

21. The _____ _____ style of writing used by journalists and recommended for mobile messages means you reveal the most important information briefly at first and then provide successive layers of detail that readers can consume if they want.

22. What is a good rule of thumb for the length of subject lines and headlines intended for mobile readers?
    a. Two words, three at most
    b. As long as the device's screen is wide in landscape mode
    c. Around 25 characters
    d. Around 25 words

Key Terms

abstract word Word that expresses a concept, quality, or characteristic; abstractions are usually broad

active voice Sentence structure in which the subject performs the action and the object receives the action

bias-free language Language that avoids words and phrases that categorize or stigmatize people in ways related to gender, race, ethnicity, age, or disability

complex sentence Sentence that expresses one main thought (the independent clause) and one or more subordinate, related thoughts (dependent clauses that cannot stand alone as valid sentences)

compound sentence Sentence with two main clauses that express two or more independent but related thoughts of equal importance, usually joined by *and, but,* or *or*

compound-complex sentence Sentence with two main clauses, at least one of which contains a subordinate clause

concrete word Word that represents something you can touch, see, or visualize; most concrete terms are related to the tangible, material world

connotative meaning All the associations and feelings evoked by a word

conversational tone The tone used in most business communication; it uses plain language that sounds businesslike without being stuffy at one extreme or too laid-back and informal at the other extreme

credibility A measure of your believability, based on how reliable you are and how much trust you evoke in others

denotative meaning The literal, or dictionary, meaning of a word

euphemisms Words or phrases that express a thought in milder terms

passive voice Sentence structure in which the subject receives the action

simple sentence Sentence with one main clause (a single subject and a single predicate)

style The choices you make to express yourself: the words you select, the manner in which you use those words in sentences, and the way you build paragraphs from individual sentences

tone The overall impression in your messages, created by the style you use

topic sentence Sentence that introduces the topic of a paragraph

transitions Words or phrases that tie together ideas by showing how one thought is related to another

Apply Your Knowledge

To review chapter content related to each question, refer to the indicated Learning Objective.

6-1. Under what circumstances could the use of euphemisms be considered unethical communication? [LO-1]

6-2. When composing business messages, how can you communicate with an authentic voice and project your company's image at the same time? [LO-2]

6-3. Does using plain language make you come across as less of an expert? Explain your answer. [LO-3]

6-4. Should you bother using transitions if the logical sequence of your message is obvious? Why or why not? [LO-6]

6-5. Why can it be difficult to use the indirect approach for a complex message that will be read on mobile devices? [LO-7]

Practice Your Skills

Message for Analysis

6-6. Creating a Businesslike Tone [LO-1], [LO-3] Read the following email draft and then (a) analyze the strengths and weaknesses of each sentence and (b) revise the document so that it follows this chapter's guidelines. The message

was written by the marketing manager of an online retailer of baby-related products in the hope of becoming a retail outlet for Inglesina strollers and high chairs. As a manufacturer of stylish, top-quality products, Inglesina (based in Italy) is extremely selective about the retail outlets through which it allows its products to be sold.

> Our e-tailing site, www.BestBabyGear.com, specializes in only the very best products for parents of newborns, infants, and toddlers. We constantly scour the world looking for products that are good enough and well-built enough and classy enough— good enough to take their place alongside the hundreds of other carefully selected products that adorn the pages of our award-winning website, www.BestBabyGear.com. We aim for the fences every time we select a product to join this portfolio; we don't want to waste our time with onesey-twosey products that might sell a half dozen units per annum—no, we want every product to be a top-drawer success, selling at least one hundred units per specific model per year in order to justify our expense and hassle factor in adding it to the above mentioned portfolio. After careful consideration, we thusly concluded that your Inglesina lines meet our needs and would therefore like to add it.

Exercises

Each activity is labeled according to the primary skill or skills you will need to use. To review relevant chapter content, you can refer to the indicated Learning Objective. In some instances, supporting information will be found in another chapter, as indicated.

Writing: Communicating with Sensitivity and Tact [LO-1] Substitute a better phrase for each of the following:

6-7. You claim that

6-8. You must update

6-9. It is not our policy to

6-10. You neglected to

6-11. In which you assert

6-12. We are sorry you are dissatisfied

6-13. You failed to enclose

6-14. We request that you send us

6-15. Apparently, you overlooked our terms

6-16. We have been very patient

6-17. We are at a loss to understand

Writing: Demonstrating the "You" Attitude [LO-1] Rewrite these sentences to reflect your audience's viewpoint:

6-18. Your email order cannot be processed; we request that you use the order form on our website instead.

6-19. We insist that you always bring your credit card to the store.

6-20. We want to get rid of all our 15-inch LCD screens to make room in our warehouse for the new 19-, 23-, and 35-inch monitors. Thus, we are offering a 25 percent discount on all sales of 15-inch models this week.

6-21. I am applying for the position of accounting intern in your office. I feel my grades prove that I am bright and capable, and I think I can do a good job for you.

6-22. As requested, we are sending the refund for $25.

6-23. If you cared about doing a good job, you would've made the extra effort required to learn how to use the machinery properly.

6-24. Your strategy presentation this morning absolutely blew me away; there's no way we can fail with all the brilliant ideas you've pulled together—I'm so glad you're running the company now!

6-25. Regarding your email message from September 28 regarding the slow payment of your invoice, it's important for you to realize that we've just undergone a massive upgrade of our accounts payable system and payments have been delayed for everybody, not just you.

6-26. I know I'm late with the asset valuation report, but I haven't been feeling well and I just haven't had the energy needed to work through the numbers yet.

6-27. With all the online news sources available today, I can't believe you didn't know that MyTravel and Thomas Cook were in merger talks—I mean, you don't even have to get up from your computer to learn this!

Writing: Emphasizing the Positive [LO-1] Revise these sentences to be positive rather than negative:

6-28. To avoid damage to your credit rating, please remit payment within 10 days.

6-29. We don't offer refunds on returned merchandise that is soiled.

6-30. Because we are temporarily out of the XL-7 open-ear headphones, we won't be able to ship your order for 10 days.

6-31. You failed to specify the color of the blouse that you ordered.

6-32. You should have realized that waterbeds will freeze in unheated houses during winter. Therefore, our guarantee does not cover the valve damage, and you must pay the $9.50 valve-replacement fee (plus postage).

Writing: Using Unbiased Language [LO-1] Rewrite each of the following to eliminate bias:

6-33. For an Indian, Maggie certainly is outgoing.

6-34. He needs a wheelchair, but he doesn't let his handicap affect his job performance.

6-35. A pilot must have the ability to stay calm under pressure, and then he must be trained to cope with any problem that arises.

6-36. Renata Parsons, married and the mother of a teenager, is a top candidate for CEO.

6-37. Even at his age, Sam Nugent is still an active salesman.

6-38. **Writing: Establishing Your Credibility; Microblogging Skills [LO-2], Chapter 8** Search LinkedIn for the profile of an expert in any industry or profession. Now imagine that you are going to introduce this person as a speaker at a convention. You will make an in-person introduction at the time of the speech, but you decide to introduce him or her the day before on Twitter. Write four tweets: one that introduces the expert and three that cover three key supporting points that will enhance the speaker's credibility in the minds of potential listeners. Make up any information you need to complete this assignment, and then email the text of your proposed tweets to your instructor.

6-39. **Writing: Using Plain Language; Communication Ethics: Making Ethical Choices [LO-3], Chapter 1** Your company has been a major employer in the local community for years, but shifts in the global marketplace have forced some changes in the company's long-term direction. In fact, the company plans to reduce local staffing by as much as 50 percent over the next 5 to 10 years, starting with a small layoff next month. The size and timing of future layoffs have not been decided, although there is little doubt that more layoffs will happen at some point. In the first draft of a letter aimed at community leaders, you write that "this first layoff is part of a continuing series of staff reductions anticipated over the next several years." However, your boss is concerned about the vagueness and negative tone of the language and asks you to rewrite that sentence to read "this layoff is part of the company's ongoing efforts to continually align its resources with global market conditions." Do you think this suggested wording is ethical, given the company's economic influence in the community? Explain your answer in an email message to your instructor.

6-40. **Writing: Creating Effective Sentences: Media Skills: Social Networking [LO-4], Chapter 8** If you are interested in business, chances are you've had an idea or two for starting a company. If you haven't yet, go ahead and dream up an idea now. Make it something you are passionate about, something you could really throw yourself into. Now write a four-sentence summary that could appear on the Info tab on a Facebook profile. Make sure the first sentence is a solid topic sentence, and make sure the next three sentences offer relevant evidence and examples. Feel free to make up any details you need. Email your summary to your instructor or post it on your class blog.

Writing: Choosing Powerful Words [LO-4] Write a concrete phrase for each of these vague phrases (make up any details you need):

6-41. Sometime this spring

6-42. A substantial savings

6-43. A large number attended

6-44. Increased efficiency

6-45. Expanded the work area

6-46. Flatten the website structure

Writing: Choosing Powerful Words [LO-4] List terms that are stronger than the following:

6-47. Ran after

6-48. Seasonal ups and downs

6-49. Bright

6-50. Suddenly rises

6-51. Moves forward

Writing: Choosing Powerful Words [LO-4] As you rewrite these sentences, replace the clichés and buzzwords with plain language (for any terms you don't recognize, you can find definitions online):

6-52. Being a jack-of-all-trades, Dave worked well in his new general manager job.

6-53. Moving Leslie into the accounting department, where she was literally a fish out of water, was like putting a square peg into a round hole, if you get my drift.

6-54. My only takeaway from the offsite was that Laird threw his entire department under the bus for missing the deadline.

6-55. I'd love to help with that project, but I'm bandwidth-constrained.

6-56. The board green-lighted our initiative to repurpose our consumer products for the commercial space.

Writing: Choosing Powerful Words [LO-4] Suggest short, simple words to replace each of the following:

6-57. Inaugurate

6-58. Terminate

6-59. Utilize

6-60. Anticipate

6-61. Assistance

6-62. Endeavor

6-63. Ascertain

6-64. Procure

6-65. Consummate

6-66. Advise

6-67. Alteration

6-68. Forwarded

6-69. Fabricate

6-70. Nevertheless

6-71. Substantial

Writing: Choosing Powerful Words [LO-4] Write up-to-date, less-stuffy versions of these phrases; write "none" if you think there is no appropriate substitute or "delete" if the phrase should simply be deleted:

6-72. As per your instructions

6-73. Attached herewith

6-74. In lieu of

6-75. In reply I wish to state

6-76. Please be advised that

Writing: Creating Effective Sentences [LO-5] Rewrite each sentence so that it is active rather than passive:

6-77. The raw data are entered into the customer relationship management system by the sales representative each Friday.

6-78. High profits are publicized by management.

6-79. The policies announced in the directive were implemented by the staff.

6-80. Our computers are serviced by the Santee Company.

6-81. The employees were represented by Tamika Hogan.

6-82. **Writing: Crafting Unified, Coherent Paragraphs; Collaboration: Evaluating the Work of Others [LO-6], Chapter 7** Working with four other students, divide the following five topics among yourselves and each write one paragraph on your selected topic. Be sure each student uses a different technique when writing his or her paragraph: One student should use the illustration technique, one the comparison or contrast technique, one a discussion of cause and effect, one the classification technique, and one a discussion of problem and solution. Then exchange paragraphs within the team and pick out the main idea and general purpose of the paragraph one of your teammates wrote. Was everyone able to correctly identify the main idea and purpose? If not, suggest how the paragraph could be rewritten for clarity.

- Types of *phablets* available for sale
- Advantages and disadvantages of eating at fast-food restaurants
- Finding that first full-time job
- Good qualities of my car (or house, or apartment, or neighborhood)
- How to make a dessert (or barbecue a steak or make coffee)

Writing: Using Transitions [LO-6] Add transitional elements to the following paragraphs to improve the flow of ideas. (Note: You may need to eliminate or add some words to smooth out your sentences.)

6-83. Facing some of the toughest competitors in the world, Harley-Davidson had to make some changes. The company introduced new products. Harley's management team set out to rebuild the company's production process. New products were coming to market and the company was turning a profit. Harley's quality standards were not on par with those of its foreign competitors. Harley's costs were still among the highest in the industry. Harley made a U-turn and restructured the company's organizational structure. Harley's efforts have paid off.

6-84. Whether you're indulging in a doughnut in New York or California, Krispy Kreme wants you to enjoy the same delicious taste with every bite. The company maintains consistent product quality by carefully controlling every step of the production process. Krispy Kreme tests all raw ingredients against established quality standards. Every delivery of wheat flour is sampled and measured for its moisture content and protein levels. Krispy Kreme blends the ingredients. Krispy Kreme tests the doughnut mix for quality. Krispy Kreme delivers the mix to its stores. Financial critics are not as kind to the company as food critics have been. Allegations of improper financial reporting have left the company's future in doubt.

6-85. **Media Skills: Writing for Mobile Devices [LO-7]** Find an interesting website article on any business topic. Write a three-paragraph summary that would be easy to read on a phone screen.

Expand Your Skills

Critique the Professionals

Locate an example of professional communication from a reputable online source. Choose a paragraph that has at least three sentences. Evaluate the effectiveness of this paragraph at three levels, starting with the paragraph structure. Is the paragraph unified and cohesive? Does it have a clear topic sentence and sufficient support to clarify and expand on that topic? Second, evaluate each sentence. Are the sentences easy to read and easy to understand? Did the writer vary the types and lengths of sentences to produce a smooth flow and rhythm? Is the most important idea presented prominently in each sentence? Third, evaluate at least six word choices. Did the writer use these words correctly and effectively? Using whatever medium your instructor requests, write a brief analysis of the piece (no more than one page), citing specific elements from the piece and support from the chapter.

Sharpening Your Career Skills Online

Bovée and Thill's Business Communication Web Search, at websearch.businesscommunicationnetwork.com, is a unique research tool designed specifically for business communication research. Use the Web Search function to find a website, video, article, podcast, or presentation that offers advice on writing effective sentences. Write a brief email message to your instructor describing the item that you found and summarizing the career skills information you learned from it.

Build Your Career

In Chapter 5's Build Your Career activity, you started the first two steps of your brand pyramid, the *private inventory* of skills, attributes, experience, and areas for improvement and the *public profile* that highlights the qualities you want to promote.

Now it's time to complete the pyramid with your *headline*, also known as a *tagline* or *elevator pitch*. This is a brief, clear, and memorable statement of the value you bring to an organization as an employee or a freelance contractor. Envision it as the answer to common questions you will get at networking events, during job interviews, and in casual encounters:

- So, tell me about yourself.
- What do you do?
- Why should we hire you?

Like any good headline, your personal headline should offer a concise summary and leave the listener wanting more. You have only a few seconds to make an impression, so make sure every word counts. Follow these steps:

1. Choose two or three high-impact keywords from the research you've done. The example on page xxxvii in the Prologue, "I am a data science major ready to make numbers come alive through leading-edge techniques in deep learning, data mining, and visualization," uses three job description keywords: *deep learning*, *data mining*, and *visualization*.

2. Build a sentence around those words that confirms how you are qualified to deliver those capabilities.
3. If you don't have a lot of relevant job experience, use your education as your strongest selling point, as the data science major does in this example.
4. Consider crafting two versions, one slightly more formal for written use and one slightly more casual for spoken use. For example, the "make numbers come alive" phrase might sound a little too "salesy" in casual networking conversation. Your spoken version might be " . . . ready to help companies apply leading-edge techniques . . ."
5. Get comfortable saying your spoken version out loud so that it rolls off your tongue.
6. Be ready with supporting details when someone responds, "That sounds great—tell me more."

Improve Your Grammar, Mechanics, and Usage

The following exercises help you improve your knowledge of and power over English grammar, mechanics, and usage. Turn to the Handbook of Grammar, Mechanics, and Usage at the end of this book and review Section 1.6.1 (Prepositions). Then for the following 10 items, indicate the preferred choice within each set of parentheses. (Answers to these exercises appear on page 614.)

6-86. Where was your argument (*leading to, leading*)?
6-87. I wish he would get (*off, off of*) the phone.
6-88. U.S. Mercantile must become (*aware, aware of*) and sensitive to its customers' concerns.
6-89. Dr. Namaguchi will be talking (*with, to*) the marketing class, but she has no time for questions.
6-90. Matters like this are decided after thorough discussion (*among, between*) all seven department managers.
6-91. We can't wait (*on, for*) their decision much longer.
6-92. Their computer is similar (*to, with*) ours.
6-93. This model is different (*than, from*) the one we ordered.
6-94. She is active (*in not only, not only in*) a civic group but also in an athletic organization.
6-95. Carolyn told Jorge not to put the used inkjet cartridges (*in, into*) the trash can.

For additional exercises focusing on prepositions, visit MyLab Business Communication. Click on Chapter 6; click on Additional Exercises to Improve Your Grammar, Mechanics, and Usage; and then click on 10. Prepositions.

MyLab Business Communication

MyLab Assisted-Grading Writing Prompts

If your instructor has assigned one or both of the following writing assignments within the MyLab, go to your Assignments to complete these writing exercises.

6-96. Why are email, texting, and other forms of digital communication so prone to inadvertent etiquette breakdowns, in which even well-intentioned writers insult or confuse readers? [LO-1]

6-97. What steps can you take to make abstract concepts such as opportunity feel more concrete in your messages? [LO-4]

Endnotes

1. "What We Do," Lumen, accessed 15 March 2018, wearelumen.com; "About," Kaleigh Moore, accessed 15 March 2018, www.kaleighmoore.com; "Kaleigh Moore," *Inc.*, accessed 15 March 2018, https://www.inc.com/author/kaleigh-moore.

2. Annette N. Shelby and N. Lamar Reinsch Jr., "Positive Emphasis and You Attitude: An Empirical Study," *Journal of Business Communication* 32, no. 4 (1995): 303–322.

3. Quinn Warnick, "A Close Textual Analysis of Corporate Layoff Memos," *Business Communication Quarterly* 73, no. 3 (September 2010): 322–326.

4. Sherryl Kleinman, "Why Sexist Language Matters," *Qualitative Sociology* 25, no. 2 (Summer 2002): 299–304.

5. Judy E. Pickens, "Terms of Equality: A Guide to Bias-Free Language," *Personnel Journal*, August 1985, 24.

6. Lisa Taylor, "Communicating About People with Disabilities: Does the Language We Use Make a Difference?" *Bulletin of the Association for Business Communication* 53, no. 3 (September 1990): 65–67.

7. Susan Benjamin, *Words at Work* (Reading, Mass.: Addison Wesley, 1997), 136–137.

8. Plain English Campaign website, accessed 28 June 2010, www.plainenglish.co.uk.

9. Plain Language website, accessed 6 April 2017, www.plainlanguage.gov; Irene Etzkorn, "Amazingly Simple Stuff," presentation 7 November 2008, www.slideshare.net.

10. Susan Jaderstrom and Joanne Miller, "Active Writing," *Office Pro*, November/December 2003, 29.

11. "The Singular They," Grammarly blog, accessed 12 March 2018, www.grammarly.com.

12. Jeff Guo, "Sorry, Grammar Nerds. The Singular 'They' Has Been Declared Word of the Year," *Washington Post*, 8 January 2015, www.washingtonpost.com.

13. "Split Infinitives," Oxford Dictionaries, accessed 12 March 2018, en.oxforddictionaries.com.

14. Catherine Soanes, "Can You End a Sentence with a Preposition?" Oxford Dictionaries blog, 28 November 2011, blog.oxforddictionaries.com.

15. Catherine Quinn, "Lose the Office Jargon; It May Sunset Your Career," *The Age* (Australia), 1 September 2007, www.theage.com.au.

16. Beverly Ballaro and Christina Bielaszka-DuVernay, "Building a Bridge over the River Boredom," *Harvard Management Communication Letter*, Winter 2005, 3–5.

17. Jakob Nielsen, "Mobile Content Is Twice as Difficult," NN/g, 28 February 2011, www.nngroup.com.

18. Jakob Nielsen and Raluca Budiu, *Mobile Usability* (Berkeley: New Riders, 2013), 10, 102.

19. Nielsen and Budiu, *Mobile Usability*, 23.

20. "Mobile Web Best Practices," W3C website, accessed 12 March 2014, www.w3.org.

21. "Mobile Message Mayhem," Verne Ordman & Associates, accessed 12 March 2014, www.businesswriting.biz.

22. "Mobile Message Mayhem."

23. Marieke McCloskey, "Writing Hyperlinks: Salient, Descriptive, Start with Keyword," NN/g, 9 March 2014, www.nngroup.com.

Five-Minute Guide to Composing a Business Message or Document

After you've completed the planning tasks and you're ready to start writing, spend five minutes reviewing these tips before you start composing.

00:01   **Be sure to adapt to your audience**

1. Use the "you" attitude—make it about the reader.
2. Maintain professional standards of etiquette and emphasize the positive, wherever appropriate.
3. Use bias-free language.
4. Plan to establish your credibility if needed.
5. Think about how you'll project your company's image, if relevant.
6. Remember to craft the right tone for the situation (conversational or more formal).
7. Emphasize plain language and make effective use of active and passive voice.

00:02   **Think about choosing powerful words**

1. Remember to use the right words and use them correctly; verify the meaning and correct usage of any word you're not sure about.
2. Think about making the most-effective word and phrase choices.

00:03   **Get ready to create effective sentences**

1. Choose from the four types of sentences (simple, compound, complex, compound-complex), using each type to maximum advantage.
2. Use various sentence styles to emphasize key thoughts, such as putting the most important point (or the dependent clause in a complex sentence) at the beginning or the end of the sentence.
3. Use a variety of short, medium, and long sentences to match the size and shape of your ideas and to give your writing some variety.

00:04   **Think about how you will craft unified, coherent paragraphs**

1. Every paragraph should be *unified*—focusing on a single topic—and *coherent*—presenting ideas in a logically connected way.
2. Start each paragraph with a clear topic sentence that presents the main idea of the paragraph.
3. Support, justify, or extend that idea with supporting sentences.
4. Use transitions within and between paragraphs to help readers follow your train of thought.
5. Use multiple techniques to develop paragraphs: illustration, comparison or contrast, cause and effect, classification, and problem and solution.

00:05   **Modify your approach for mobile audiences**

1. Use a linear organization, with a single path for the eye to follow.
2. Prioritize the information so readers get the most valuable information as quickly as possible.
3. Write shorter and more-focused messages and documents—remember that reading on mobile devices is more difficult and more prone to errors than reading on paper or large screens.
4. For email messages and blog posts, use short subject lines and headings so that they display in full on the screen, if possible.
5. Use shorter paragraphs to give readers more visual breaks.

7 Completing Business Messages

LEARNING OBJECTIVES

After studying this chapter, you will be able to

1 Discuss the value of careful revision, and describe the tasks involved in evaluating your first drafts and the work of other writers.

2 List four techniques you can use to improve the readability of your messages.

3 Describe eight steps you can take to improve the clarity of your writing, and give four tips for making your writing more concise.

4 List four principles of effective design, and explain the role of major design elements in document readability.

5 Explain the importance of proofreading, and give eight tips for successful proofreading.

6 Discuss the most important issues to consider when distributing your messages.

MyLab Business Communication

If your instructor is using MyLab Business Communication, visit **www.pearson.com/mylab/business-communication** for videos, simulations, and writing exercises.

ON THE JOB: COMMUNICATING AT
TYPE TOGETHER

Designing the Visual Voice of Business Text

Take a moment to look at the variety of textual messages all around you, from this book to whatever posters and signs might be in view to the displays on mobile devices. Wherever text is presented in print or digital form, someone had to make a decision about which typeface to use for each string of text. And behind the scenes, somebody designed every character of every typeface. (*Font* and *typeface* are often used interchangeably, although strictly speaking, a font is a set of characters that use a given typeface design.)

Typefaces aren't something most people think about very often, but they can have considerable influence on the success of a written message. Type design can contribute to or detract from a message in two major ways: readability and personality. Naturally, readability is essential. If people can't accurately read the words on the page or screen, they won't interpret a message as intended. If a typeface is legible but difficult to read for more than a few words, readers will tend to give up and never finish the document.

Personality is more subtle but also important because the "look and feel" of a typeface sends a nonverbal message along with the verbal message. Various typefaces can convey a wide range of these nonverbal messages, from serious and formal to casual and even playful. Just like showing up for a job interview

Courtesy Type Together

Designers José Scaglione and Veronika Burian focus on creating typefaces that are easy to read in lengthy stretches of text but that still display fresh and unique personalities.

in wildly inappropriate clothing, using a typeface with the wrong personality can detract from a well-written message. And as you can see from studying a variety of typefaces, personality needs to be balanced with readability; some typefaces with "strong" personalities can be difficult to read. Personality is so important that some companies commission their own custom typefaces that become integral elements of their overall brand presence.

Type design has been an active art form for hundreds of years, and many contemporary designs are the result of efforts to adapt classic designs to contemporary uses. For some designs, this modernization is an effort to improve a typeface's readability or update its visual presence. For others, the modernization has a more technical aspect, creating typefaces that work more successfully with digital print or display technologies. For instance, the Georgia typeface was created in the 1990s primarily as a solution for that era's lower-resolution computer screens, although, thanks to its attractive readability, it is still a popular choice today.

Although thousands of typefaces are now available, type design remains a vibrant artistic profession, with new designs appearing all the time. Veronika Burian and José Scaglione are among the latest generation of designers lending their talents to the ageless challenge of balancing readability and personality.

Their type foundry Type Together, based in the Czech Republic capital of Prague, specializes in *editorial typefaces*—those used for long blocks of text such as in newspapers and books. (As a nod to the days when all typefaces were made from metal, type design studios are still referred to as *foundries*.)

Burian and Scaglione focus on the challenge of making type that is highly readable while offering fresh new personalities and meeting the technical demands of contemporary digital publishing. As individual designers and together as the cofounders of Type Together, Burian and Scaglione have achieved international recognition for their designs and their contribution to the art of type design through workshops, teaching, and publications. Their commissioned work has ranged from customizing e-reader type for Apple's iBooks to creating a font that Levi's could use in multiple languages for a global ad campaign.

Your business audiences may not think about typefaces often, but their responses to your messages and documents depend more than they might imagine on the efforts of type designers such as Burian and Scaglione—and on your skill in using their designs.[1]

WWW.TYPE-TOGETHER.COM

Revising Your Message: Evaluating the First Draft

1 LEARNING OBJECTIVE
Discuss the value of careful revision, and describe the tasks involved in evaluating your first drafts and the work of other writers.

Veronika Burian and José Scaglione (profiled in the chapter-opening On the Job) lend their creativity and talents to an essential stage of the writing process —producing professional-quality documents that convey the intended message both verbally and nonverbally. You'll read more about document design and production, including choosing and using typefaces, later in the chapter.

Before getting to the design stage, though, it's important to fine-tune the content you've diligently researched, organized, and composed. Successful communicators recognize that the first draft is rarely as tight, clear, and compelling as it needs to be. Careful revision can mean the difference between a rambling, unfocused message and a lively, direct message that gets results.

Check out the "Five-Minute Guide to Revising and Proofreading" at the end of the chapter.

The revision task can vary somewhat, depending on the medium and the nature of your message. For informal messages to internal audiences, particularly when using workgroup messaging, text messaging, or email, the revision process is often as simple as quickly looking over your message to correct any mistakes before sending or posting it. However, don't fall into the common trap of thinking that you don't need to worry about grammar, spelling, clarity, and other fundamentals of good writing when you use such media. These qualities can be *especially* important in digital media, particularly if these messages are the only contact your audience has with you. Audiences are likely to equate the quality of your writing with the quality of your thinking. Poor-quality messages create an impression of poor-quality thinking and can cause confusion, frustration, and costly delays.

Particularly with important messages, try to arrange your work schedule so you can put your first draft aside for a day or two before you begin the revision process. Doing so will allow you to approach the material with a fresh eye. Then start with the "big picture," making sure that the document accomplishes your overall goals before moving to finer points, such as readability, clarity, and conciseness. Compare the letters in Figures 7.1 and 7.2 on the next two pages for an example of how careful revision improves a customer letter.

For important messages, schedule time to put your draft aside for a day or two before you begin the revision process.

Delauny Music
56 Commerce Circle • Davenport, IA 52806
(563) 555-4001 • delaunymusic.net

June 22, 2020

Ms. Claudia Banks
122 River Heights Drive
Bettendorf, IA 52722

Dear Ms. Banks:

On behalf of everyone at Delauny Music, it is my pleasure to thank you for your recent purchase of a Yamaha CG1 grand piano. The Cg1 carries more than a century of Yamaha's heritage in design and production of world-class musical instruments and ~~you can bet it~~ will give you many years of playing and listening pleasure. Our commitment to your satisfaction doesn't stop with your purchase, however. ~~Much to the contrary, it continues for as long as you own your piano, which we hope, of course, is for as long as you live.~~ As a vital first step, please remember to call us ~~your local Yamaha dealer~~.

Sometime within three to eight months after your piano was delivered to take advantage of the ~~free~~ Yamaha Servicebond℠ Assurance Program. This free service program includes a thorough evaluation and adjustment ~~adjusting~~ of the instrument after you've had some time to play your piano and your piano has had time to adapt to its environment.

In addition to this important ~~vital~~ service appointment, a regular program of tuning is ~~absolutely~~ essential to ensure your piano's ~~its~~ impeccable performance. Our piano specialists recommend four tunings during the first year and two tunings every year thereafter ~~that~~. As your local Yamaha dealer, we are ideally positioned to provide you ~~with optimum~~ service for both regular tuning and any maintenance or repair needs you may have ~~over the years~~.

~~All of us at Delauny Music~~ We thank you for your recent purchase and wish you many, many years of satisfaction with your new Yamaha CG1 grand piano.

Sincerely,
~~Respectfully yours in beautiful music,~~

Madeline Delauny
Owner

The two circled sentences say essentially the same thing, so this edit combines them into one sentence.

The phrase *you can bet* is too informal for this message.

The sentence beginning with "Much to the contrary . . . " is awkward and unnecessary.

Changing *adjusting* to *adjustment* makes it parallel with *evaluation*.

Replacing *its* with *your piano's* avoids any confusion about which noun that *it* is supposed to replace.

This edit inserts a missing word (*dealer*).

This group of edits removes unnecessary words in several places.

The simple complimentary close replaces a close that was stylistically over the top.

Common Proofreading Symbols (see page 582 for more)

Symbol	Meaning
~~strikethrough~~	Delete text
ℓ	Delete individual character or a circled block of text
∧	Insert text (text to insert is written above)
⊙	Insert period
⁁	Insert comma
⌐	Start new line
¶	Start new paragraph
≡	Capitalize

Figure 7.1 Improving a Customer Letter Through Careful Revision
Careful revision makes this draft shorter, clearer, and more focused. The proofreading symbols you see here are still widely used whenever printed documents are edited and revised; you can find a complete list of symbols in Appendix C. Note that many business documents are now "marked up" using such technological tools as revision marks in Microsoft Word and comments in Adobe Acrobat. No matter what the medium, however, careful revision is key to more-effective messages.

Delauny Music
56 Commerce Circle • Davenport, IA 52806
(563) 555-4001 • delaunymusic.net

June 22, 2020

Ms. Claudia Banks
122 River Heights Drive
Bettendorf, IA 52722

Dear Ms. Banks:

Thank you for your recent purchase. We wish you many years of satisfaction with your new Yamaha CG1 grand piano. The CG1 carries more than a century of Yamaha's heritage in design and production of world-class musical instruments and will give you many years of playing and listening pleasure.

Our commitment to your satisfaction doesn't stop with your purchase, however. As a vital first step, please remember to call us sometime within three to eight months after your piano is delivered to take advantage of the Yamaha Servicebond^{SM} Assurance Program. This free service program includes a thorough evaluation and adjustment of the instrument after you've had some time to play it and it has had time to adapt to its environment.

In addition to this important service appointment, a regular program of tuning is essential to ensure your piano's impeccable performance. Our piano specialists recommend four tunings during the first year and two tunings every year thereafter. As your local Yamaha dealer, we are ideally positioned to provide you with optimum service for both regular tuning and any maintenance or repair needs you may have.

Sincerely,

Madeline Delauny

Madeline Delauny
Owner

← The content is now organized in three coherent paragraphs, each with a distinct message.

← The tone is friendly and engaging without being flowery.

Figure 7.2   Professional Business Letter
Here is the revised and finished version of the edited letter from Figure 7.1. Note that the *block format* used here is just one of several layout options; Appendix A also describes the *modified block format* and the *simplified format*.

EVALUATING YOUR CONTENT, ORGANIZATION, STYLE, AND TONE

When you begin the revision process, focus your attention on content, organization, style, and tone. To evaluate the content of your message, ask yourself these questions:

- Is the information accurate?
- Is the information relevant to the audience?
- Is there enough information to satisfy the readers' needs?
- Is there a good balance between general information (giving readers enough background information to appreciate the message) and specific information (giving readers the details they need in order to understand the message)?

When you are satisfied with the content of your message, you can review its organization. Ask yourself another set of questions:

Start your evaluation by verifying that you have the right information in place.

Continue your evaluation by verifying that the information is presented in a tight, logical manner.

- Are all the points covered in the most logical order?
- Do the most important ideas receive the most space, and are they placed in the most prominent positions?
- Would the message be more convincing if it were arranged in a different sequence?
- Are any points repeated unnecessarily?
- Are details grouped together logically, or are some still scattered through the document?

Next, consider whether you have achieved the right tone for your audience. Is your writing formal enough to meet the audience's expectations without being too formal or academic? Is it too casual for a serious subject?

Give the beginning and the end of your document extra attention.

Spend a few extra moments on the beginning and end of your message; these sections usually have the greatest impact on the audience. Be sure that the opening is relevant, interesting, and geared to the reader's probable reaction. In longer messages, make sure the first few paragraphs establish the subject, purpose, and organization of the material. Review the conclusion to be sure that it summarizes the main idea and leaves the audience with a positive impression.

EVALUATING, EDITING, AND REVISING THE WORK OF OTHERS

At many points in your career, you will be asked to evaluate, edit, and sometimes revise the work of others. Whether you're suggesting improvements or making the improvements yourself (as you might on a wiki site, for example), you can make a contribution by using all the skills you are learning in Chapters 5 through 7.

When you evaluate, edit, or revise someone else's work, remember that your job is to help that person succeed, not to impose your own style.

Before you dive into someone else's work, recognize the dual responsibility that you have. First, unless you've specifically been asked to rewrite something in your own style, keep in mind that your job is to help the other writer succeed at his or her task, not to impose your writing style. Second, make sure you understand the writer's intent before you begin suggesting or making changes. With those thoughts in mind, ask yourself the following questions as you evaluate someone else's writing:

- What is the purpose of this document or presentation?
- Who is the target audience?
- What information does the audience need?
- Are there any special circumstances or sensitive issues that the writer had to consider (or should have considered)?
- Does the document provide this information in a well-organized way?
- Does the writing demonstrate the "you" attitude toward the audience?
- Is the tone of the writing appropriate for the audience and the situation?
- Can the readability be improved?
- Is the writing clear? If not, how can it be improved?
- Is the writing as concise as it could be?
- Does the page or screen design support the intended message?

You can read more about using these skills in the context of wiki writing in Chapter 13.

Revising to Improve Readability

2 **LEARNING OBJECTIVE**
List four techniques you can use to improve the readability of your messages.

After confirming the content, organization, style, and tone of your message, make a second pass to improve *readability*. Most professionals are inundated with more reading material than they can ever hope to consume, and they'll appreciate your efforts to make your documents easier to read. You'll benefit from this effort, too: If you earn a reputation for creating well-crafted documents that respect the audience's time, people will pay more attention to your work.

Readability indexes can give you a rough idea of the complexity of a piece, but they can't evaluate its true reading quality.

You may be familiar with one of the indexes that have been developed over the years in an attempt to measure readability. The Flesch-Kincaid Grade Level score computes reading difficulty relative to U.S. grade-level achievement. For instance, a score of 10 suggests that a document can be read and understood by the average 10th grader. The Flesch Reading Ease score, a similar scoring system, ranks documents on a 100-point scale. Higher scores suggest that the document should be easier to read, based on word size and sentence length. If these measurements aren't built into your word-processing software, you can find a number of calculators for various indexes online.

Readability indexes offer a useful reference point, but they are limited by what they are able to measure: word length, number of syllables, sentence length, and paragraph length. They can't measure any of the other factors that affect readability, such as document design, the "you" attitude, clear sentence structure, smooth transitions, and proper word usage. Compare these two paragraphs:

> Readability indexes offer a useful reference point, but they are all limited by what they are able to measure: word length, number of syllables, sentence length, and paragraph length. They can't measure any of the other factors that affect readability, from "you" orientation to writing clarity to document design.

> Readability indexes can help. But they don't measure everything. They don't measure whether your writing clarity is good. They don't measure whether your document design is good or not. Reading indexes are based on word length, syllables, sentences, and paragraphs.

The second paragraph scores much better on both grade level and reading ease, but it is choppy, unsophisticated, and poorly organized. As a general rule, then, don't assume that a piece of text is readable if it scores well on a readability index—or that it is difficult to read if it doesn't score well.

Beyond using shorter words and simpler sentences, you can improve the readability of a message by making the document interesting and easy to skim. Most business audiences—particularly influential senior managers—tend to skim documents, looking for key ideas, conclusions, and recommendations. If they think a document contains valuable information or requires a response, they will read it more carefully when time permits. Four techniques will make your message easier to read and easier to skim: varying sentence length, using shorter paragraphs, using lists and bullets instead of narrative, and adding effective headings and subheadings.

REAL-TIME UPDATES

LEARN MORE BY VISITING THIS WEBSITE

Editing and proofreading tips, with an error treasure hunt

This guide from the Writing Center at the University of North Carolina at Chapel Hill offers advice on editing and proofreading with a gamification twist—looking for errors strategically embedded in the advice itself. Go to **real-timeupdates.com/ebc13** and select Learn More in the Students section.

VARYING THE LENGTH OF YOUR SENTENCES

Varying the length of your sentences is a creative way to make your messages interesting and readable. By choosing words and sentence structure with care, you can create a rhythm that emphasizes important points, enlivens your writing style, and makes information more appealing to your reader. For example, a short sentence that highlights a conclusion at the end of a substantial paragraph of evidence makes your key message stand out. Try for a mixture of sentences that are short (up to 15 words or so), medium (15–25 words), and long (more than 25 words).

Each sentence length has its advantages. Short sentences can be processed quickly and are easier for nonnative speakers and translators to interpret. Medium-length sentences are useful for showing the relationships among ideas. Long sentences are often the best for conveying complex ideas, listing multiple related points, or summarizing or previewing information.

Be aware that each sentence length also has disadvantages. Too many short sentences in a row can make your writing choppy. Medium sentences can lack the punch of short sentences and the informative power of longer sentences. Long sentences can be difficult to understand because they contain more information and usually have a more complicated structure. Because readers can absorb only a few words per glance, longer sentences are also

To keep readers' interest, look for ways to combine a variety of short, medium, and long sentences.

more difficult to skim. By choosing the best sentence length for each communication need and remembering to mix sentence lengths for variety, you'll get your points across while keeping your messages lively and interesting.

KEEPING YOUR PARAGRAPHS SHORT

Short paragraphs are more inviting and tend to be easier to read.

Large blocks of text can be visually daunting, particularly on screen and even more so on small mobile devices, so the optimum paragraph length is short to medium in most cases. Unless you break up your thoughts somehow, you'll end up with lengthy paragraphs that are guaranteed to intimidate even the most dedicated reader. Short paragraphs, generally 100 words or fewer (this paragraph has 92 words), are easier to read than long ones, and they make your writing look inviting. You can also emphasize ideas by isolating them in short, forceful paragraphs.

However, don't go overboard with short paragraphs. In particular, be careful to use one-sentence paragraphs only occasionally and usually only for emphasis. Also, if you need to divide a subject into several pieces to keep paragraphs short, be sure to help your readers keep the ideas connected by guiding them with plenty of transitional elements.

USING LISTS AND BULLETS TO CLARIFY AND EMPHASIZE

Lists are effective tools for highlighting and simplifying material.

An effective alternative to using conventional sentences is to set off important ideas in a list—a series of words, names, or other items. Lists can show the sequence of your ideas, heighten their visual impact, and increase the likelihood that a reader will find key points. In addition, lists help simplify complex subjects, highlight main points, visually break up a page or screen, ease the skimming process for busy readers, and give readers a breather. Compare these two treatments of the same information:

Narrative	**List**
Owning your own business has many potential advantages. One is the opportunity to pursue your own personal passion. Another advantage is the satisfaction of working for yourself. As a solo proprietor, you also have the advantage of privacy because you do not have to reveal your financial information or plans to anyone.	Owning your own business has three advantages: • Opportunity to pursue personal passion • Satisfaction of working for yourself • Financial privacy

You can separate list items with numbers, letters, or *bullets* (a general term for any kind of graphical element that precedes each item). Bullets are generally preferred over numbers, unless the list is in some logical sequence or ranking or you need to refer to specific list items elsewhere in the document.

Lists are easier to locate and read if the entire numbered or bulleted section is set off by a blank line before and after. Furthermore, make sure to introduce lists clearly so that people know what they're about to read. One way to introduce lists is to make them a part of the introductory sentence:

> The board of directors met to discuss the revised annual budget. To keep expenses in line with declining sales, the directors voted to
>
> • Cut everyone's salary by 10 percent
> • Close the employee cafeteria
> • Reduce travel expenses

TABLE 7.1	**Achieving Parallelism**
Method	Example
Parallel words	The plan was approved by Clausen, Whittaker, Merlin, and Carlucci.
Parallel phrases	We are gaining market share in supermarkets, in department stores, and in specialty stores.
Parallel clauses	I'd like to discuss the issue after Vicki gives her presentation but before Marvin shows his slides.
Parallel sentences	In 2018 we exported 30 percent of our production. In 2019 we exported 50 percent.

Another way to introduce a list is to precede it with a complete introductory sentence, followed by a colon:

The decline in company profit is attributable to four factors:

- Slower holiday sales
- Increased transportation and fuel costs
- Higher employee wages
- Slower inventory turnover

Regardless of the format you choose, the items in a list should be parallel; that is, they should all use the same grammatical pattern. For example, if one list item begins with a verb, every item should begin with a verb. If one item is a noun phrase, all should be noun phrases.

Keep your list items parallel to make them easier to read.

Nonparallel List Items (a mix of verb and noun phrases)	**Parallel List Items (all verb phrases)**
- Improve our bottom line - Identification of new foreign markets for our products - Global market strategies - Issues regarding pricing and packaging size	- Improving our bottom line - Identifying new foreign markets for our products - Developing our global market strategies - Resolving pricing and packaging issues

Parallel forms are easier to read and skim. You can create parallelism by repeating the pattern in words, phrases, clauses, or entire sentences (see Table 7.1).

ADDING HEADINGS AND SUBHEADINGS

A **heading** is a brief title that tells readers about the content of the section that follows. **Subheadings** are subordinate to headings, indicating subsections within a major section. Headings and subheadings serve these important functions:

- **Organization.** Headings show your reader at a glance how the document is organized. They act as labels to group related paragraphs and organize lengthy material into shorter sections.
- **Attention.** Informative, inviting, and in some cases intriguing headings grab the reader's attention, make the text easier to read, and help the reader find the parts he or she needs to read—or skip.

A heading *is a brief title that tells readers about the content of a major section;* subheadings *are subordinate to headings and indicate subsections within a major section.*

Use headings to grab the reader's attention and organize material into sections.

- **Connection.** Using headings and subheadings together helps readers see the relationship between main ideas and subordinate ones so that they can understand your message more easily. Moreover, headings and subheadings visually indicate shifts from one idea to the next.

Descriptive headings identify a topic but do little more; *informative headings* guide readers to think in a certain way about the topic.

Descriptive headings, such as "Cost Considerations," identify a topic but do little more. **Informative headings**, such as "Redesigning Material Flow to Cut Production Costs," guide readers to think in a certain way about the topic. They are also helpful in guiding your work as a writer, especially if cast as questions you plan to address in your document. Well-written informative headings are self-contained, which means readers can read just the headings and subheadings and understand them without reading the rest of the document. For example, "Introduction" conveys little information, whereas the heading "Staffing Shortages Cost the Company $150,000 Last Year" provides a key piece of information and captures the reader's attention. Whatever types of headings you choose, keep them brief and use parallel construction throughout the document.

Editing for Clarity and Conciseness

3 **LEARNING OBJECTIVE** Describe eight steps you can take to improve the clarity of your writing, and give four tips for making your writing more concise.

After you've reviewed and revised your message for readability, your next step is to make sure your message is as clear and as concise as possible.

EDITING FOR CLARITY

Clarity is essential to getting your message across accurately and efficiently.

Check to see that every sentence conveys the message you intend and that readers can extract that meaning without needing to read it more than once. To ensure clarity, look closely at your paragraph organization, sentence structure, and word choices (review Chapter 5 if necessary). Can readers make sense of the related sentences in a paragraph? Is the meaning of each sentence easy to grasp? Is each word clear and unambiguous (meaning it doesn't have any risk of being interpreted in more than one way)? See Table 7.2 on the next page for examples of the following tips:

- **Break up overly long sentences.** If you find yourself stuck in a long sentence, you're probably trying to make the sentence do more than it reasonably can, such as expressing two dissimilar thoughts or peppering the reader with too many pieces of supporting evidence at once. (Did you notice how difficult this long sentence was to read?)

Hedging is appropriate when you can't be absolutely sure of a statement, but excessive hedging undermines your authority.

- **Rewrite hedging sentences.** *Hedging* means pulling back from making an absolutely certain, definitive statement about a topic. Granted, sometimes you have to write *may* or *seems* to avoid stating a judgment as a fact. When you hedge too often or without good reason, however, you come across as being unsure of what you're saying.

When you use parallel grammatical patterns to express two or more ideas, you show that they are comparable thoughts.

- **Impose parallelism.** As noted earlier, making your writing *parallel* means expressing two or more similar ideas using the same grammatical structure. Doing so helps your audience understand that the ideas are related, are of similar importance, and are on the same level of generality. Parallel patterns are also easier to read. You can impose parallelism by repeating a pattern in words, phrases, clauses, or entire sentences.

- **Correct dangling modifiers.** Sometimes a modifier is not just an adjective or an adverb but an entire phrase modifying a noun or a verb. Be careful not to leave this type of modifier *dangling*, with no connection to the subject of the sentence.

- **Reword long noun sequences.** When multiple nouns are strung together as modifiers, the resulting sentence can be hard to read. See whether a single, well-chosen word will do the job. If the nouns are all necessary, consider moving one or more to a modifying phrase, as shown in Table 7.2.

- **Replace camouflaged verbs.** Watch for words that end in *ion, tion, ing, ment, ant, ent, ence, ance,* and *ency*. These endings often change verbs into nouns and adjectives, requiring you to add a verb to get your point across.

Subject and predicate should be placed as close together as possible, as should modifiers and the words they modify.

- **Clarify sentence structure.** Keep the subject and predicate of a sentence as close together as possible. Similarly, adjectives, adverbs, and prepositional phrases usually make the most sense when they're placed as close as possible to the words they modify.

TABLE 7.2 **Revising for Clarity**		
Issues to Review	**Ineffective**	**Effective**
Overly Long Sentences (taking compound sentences too far)	The magazine will be published January 1, and I'd better meet the deadline if I want my article included because we want the article to appear before the trade show.	The magazine will be published January 1. I'd better meet the deadline because we want the article to appear before the trade show.
Hedging Sentences (overqualifying sentences)	I believe that Mr. Johnson's employment record seems to show that he may be capable of handling the position.	Mr. Johnson's employment record shows that he is capable of handling the position.
Unparallel Sentences (using dissimilar construction for similar ideas)	Mr. Simms had been drenched with rain, bombarded with telephone calls, and his boss shouted at him.	Mr. Simms had been drenched with rain, bombarded with telephone calls, and shouted at by his boss.
	To waste time and missing deadlines are bad habits.	Wasting time and missing deadlines are bad habits.
Dangling Modifiers (placing modifiers close to the wrong nouns and verbs)	Walking to the office, a red sports car passed her. [suggests that the car was walking to the office]	A red sports car passed her while she was walking to the office.
	Reduced by 25 percent, Europe had its lowest semiconductor output in a decade. [suggests that Europe shrank by 25 percent]	Europe reduced semiconductor output by 25 percent, its lowest output in a decade.
Long Noun Sequences (stringing too many nouns together)	The window sash installation company will give us an estimate on Friday.	The company that installs window sashes will give us an estimate on Friday.
Camouflaged Verbs (changing verbs into nouns)	The manager undertook implementation of the rules.	The manager implemented the rules.
	Verification of the shipments occurs weekly.	We verify shipments weekly.
	reach a conclusion about give consideration to	conclude consider
Subject-Predicate Separation (putting the predicate too far from the subject)	A 10% decline in market share, which resulted from quality problems and an aggressive sales campaign by Armitage, the market leader in the Northeast, was the major problem in 2019.	The major problem in 2019 was a 10% loss of market share, which resulted from quality problems and an aggressive sales campaign by Armitage, the market leader in the Northeast.
Modifier Separation (putting adjectives, adverbs, or prepositional phrases too far from the words they modify)	Our antique desk lends an air of strength and substance with thick legs and large drawers.	With its thick legs and large drawers, our antique desk lends an air of strength and substance.
Awkward References (linking ideas in ways that cause more work for the reader)	The Law Office and the Accounting Office distribute computer supplies for paralegals and accountants, respectively.	The Law Office distributes computer supplies for paralegals; the Accounting Office distributes them for accountants.

- **Clarify awkward references.** Try to avoid vague references such as *the above-mentioned, as mentioned above, the aforementioned, the former, the latter,* and *respectively.* Use a specific pointer such as "as described in the second paragraph on page 22."

EDITING FOR CONCISENESS

Many of the changes you make to improve clarity also shorten your message by removing unnecessary words. The next step is to examine the text with the specific goal of reducing the number of words. Readers appreciate conciseness and are more likely to read your documents if you have a reputation for efficient writing. See Table 7.3 for examples of the following tips:

Make your documents tighter by removing unnecessary words, phrases, and sentences.

- **Delete unnecessary words and phrases.** To test whether a word or phrase is essential, try the sentence without it. If the meaning doesn't change, leave it out.
- **Replace long words and phrases.** Short words and phrases are generally more vivid and easier to read than long ones.

TABLE 7.3 Revising for Conciseness

Issues to Review	Less Effective	More Effective
Unnecessary Words and Phrases		
Using wordy phrases	for the sum of	for
	in the event that	if
	prior to the start of	before
	in the near future	soon
	at this point in time	now
	due to the fact that	because
	in view of the fact that	because
	until such time as	when
	with reference to	about
Using too many relative pronouns (such as *that* or *who*)	Cars that are sold after January will not have a six-month warranty.	Cars sold after January will not have a six-month warranty.
	Employees who are driving to work should park in the underground garage.	Employees driving to work should park in the underground garage.
		OR
		Employees should park in the underground garage.
Using too few relative pronouns	The project manager told the engineers last week the specifications were changed.	The project manager told the engineers last week that the specifications were changed.
		OR
		The project manager told the engineers that the specifications were changed last week.
Long Words and Phrases		
Using overly long words	During the preceding year, the company accelerated operations.	Last year the company sped up operations.
	The action was predicated on the assumption that the company was operating at a financial deficit.	The action was based on the belief that the company was losing money.
Using wordy phrases rather than infinitives	If you want success as a writer, you must work hard.	To succeed as a writer, you must work hard.
	He went to the library for the purpose of studying.	He went to the library to study.
	The employer increased salaries so that she could improve morale.	The employer increased salaries to improve morale.
Redundancies		
Repeating meanings	absolutely complete	complete
	basic fundamentals	fundamentals
	follows after	follows
	free and clear	free
	refer back	refer
	repeat again	repeat
	collect together	collect
	future plans	plans
	return back	return
	important essentials	essentials

TABLE 7.3   Revising for Conciseness (*continued*)

Issues to Review	Less Effective	More Effective
	end result	result
	actual truth	truth
	final outcome	outcome
	uniquely unusual	unique
	surrounded on all sides	surrounded
Using double modifiers	modern, up-to-date equipment	modern equipment
***It Is* and *There Are* Starters**		
Starting sentences with *It* or *There*	It would be appreciated if you would sign the lease today.	Please sign the lease today.
	There are five employees in this division who were late to work today.	Five employees in this division were late to work today.

- **Eliminate redundancies.** In some word combinations, the words say the same thing. For instance, "visible to the eye" is redundant because *visible* is enough without further clarification; "to the eye" adds nothing.
- **Recast "It is/There are" starters.** If you start a sentence with an indefinite pronoun such as *it* or *there*, odds are the sentence could be shorter and more active. For instance, "We believe . . ." is a stronger opening than "It is believed that . . ." However, there are times when using "it is/there are" is the simplest and most direct way to start a sentence, so don't be afraid to use this construction if it works.

As you make all these improvements, concentrate on how each word contributes to an effective sentence and on how each sentence helps develop a coherent paragraph. For a reminder of the tasks involved in revision, see "Checklist: Revising Business Messages."

CHECKLIST ✔ Revising Business Messages

A. Evaluate content, organization, style, and tone.
- ✔ Make sure the information is accurate, relevant, and sufficient.
- ✔ Check that all necessary points appear in logical order.
- ✔ Verify that you present enough support to make the main idea convincing and compelling.
- ✔ Be sure the beginning and ending of the message are effective.
- ✔ Make sure you've achieved the right tone for the audience and the situation.

B. Review for readability.
- ✔ Consider using a readability index, but be sure to interpret the answer carefully.
- ✔ Use a mix of short, medium, and long sentences.
- ✔ Keep paragraphs short.
- ✔ Use bulleted and numbered lists to emphasize key points.
- ✔ Make the document easy to skim with headings and subheadings.

C. Edit for clarity.
- ✔ Break up overly long sentences and rewrite hedging sentences.
- ✔ Impose parallelism to simplify reading.
- ✔ Correct dangling modifiers.
- ✔ Reword long noun sequences and replace camouflaged verbs.
- ✔ Clarify sentence structure and awkward references.

D. Edit for conciseness.
- ✔ Delete unnecessary words and phrases.
- ✔ Shorten long words and phrases.
- ✔ Eliminate redundancies.
- ✔ Consider rewriting sentences that start with "It is" or "There are."

Producing Your Message

Now it's time to put your hard work on display. The *production quality* of your message—the total effect of page or screen design, graphical elements, typography, and so on—plays an important role in its effectiveness. A polished, inviting design not only makes your material easier to read but also conveys a sense of professionalism and importance.[2]

4 LEARNING OBJECTIVE List four principles of effective design, and explain the role of major design elements in document readability.

DESIGNING FOR READABILITY

The production quality of your documents affects readability and audience perceptions.

Design affects readability in two important ways. First, if used carefully, design elements can improve the effectiveness of your message. In contrast, poor design decisions, such as using distracting background images behind text, pointless animations, or tiny typefaces, act as barriers to communication. Second, the visual design sends a nonverbal message to your readers, influencing their perceptions of the communication before they read a single word.

Effective design helps you establish the tone of your document and helps guide your readers through your message (see Figure 7.3). To achieve an effective design, pay careful attention to the following design elements:

For effective design, pay attention to

- Consistency
- Balance
- Restraint
- Detail

- **Consistency.** Throughout each message, be consistent in your use of margins, typeface, type size, spacing, color, lines, and position. Being consistent from message to message is beneficial as well, because it helps audiences recognize your documents and know what to expect.
- **Balance.** Balance is an important but sometimes subjective design issue. One document may have a formal, rigid design in which the various elements are placed in a grid pattern, whereas another may have a less formal design in which elements flow more freely across the page—and both could be in balance. Like the tone of your language, visual balance can be too formal, just right, or too informal for a given message.
- **Restraint.** Strive for simplicity. Don't clutter your message with too many design elements, too many colors, or too many decorative touches. Anything that doesn't support your message should be removed, if possible.
- **Detail.** Pay attention to all the details that affect readability. For instance, extremely wide columns of text can be difficult to read, so it may be better to split the text into two narrower columns.

Even without formal training in graphic design, you can make your printed messages more effective by understanding the use of some key design elements: white space, margins and line justification, typefaces, and type styles.

Thanks to the concise and clear navigation labels, headings, and subheadings, readers can skim down the screen and get all the key points in a matter of seconds.

Notice how generous use of white space, simple but compelling illustrations, and a limited amount of text make this webpage less intimidating than a screen packed with visually "heavy" blocks of text.

Font size changes and the shift from a single, centered column to two columns immediately signal the hierarchy of information, leading the reader's eye from major points down to supporting details.

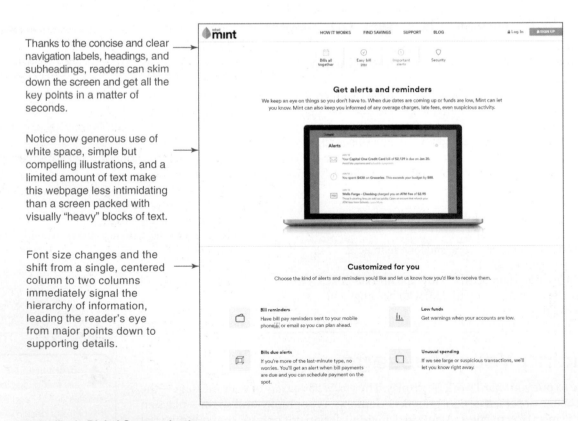

Figure 7.3 **Readability in Digital Communication**
This page from Mint's website demonstrates effective design choices for online readability.

White Space

Any space that doesn't contain text or artwork, both in print and online, is considered **white space**. (Note that "white space" isn't necessarily white; it is simply blank.) These unused areas provide visual contrast and important resting points for your readers. White space includes margins, paragraph indents, space around images, the open area surrounding headings, vertical space between columns, and horizontal space between paragraphs or lines of text. These text-free zones make pages and screens appear less intimidating and therefore increase the chance that people will read them.

White space separates elements in a design and helps guide the reader's eye.

Margins and Justification

Margins define the space around text and between text columns. In addition to their width, the look and feel of margins is influenced by the way you arrange lines of text, which can be set (1) *justified* (which means they are *flush*, or aligned vertically, on both the left and the right), (2) flush left with a *ragged right* margin, (3) flush right with a *ragged left* margin, or (4) centered. This paragraph is justified, whereas the paragraphs in Figure 7.2 on page 191 are flush left with a ragged right margin.

Magazines, newspapers, and books often use justified type because it can accommodate more text in a given space. However, justified type needs to be used with care. First, it creates a denser look because the uniform line lengths decrease the amount of white space along the right margin. Second, it produces a more formal and less personalized look. Third, unless it is used with some skill and attention, justified type can be more difficult to read because it can produce large gaps between words and excessive hyphenation at the ends of lines. The publishing specialists who create magazines, newspapers, and books have the time and skill needed to carefully adjust character and word spacing in order to eliminate these problems. (In some cases, sentences are even rewritten to improve the appearance of the printed page.) Because most business communicators don't have that time or skill, it's best to avoid justified type in routine business documents.

In contrast to justified type, flush-left, ragged-right type creates a more open appearance on the page, producing a less formal and more contemporary look. Spacing between words is consistent, and only long words that fall at the ends of lines are hyphenated.

Centered type is rarely used for text paragraphs but is commonly used for headings and subheadings. Flush-right, ragged-left type is rarely used in business documents.

Most business documents use a flush left margin and a ragged right margin.

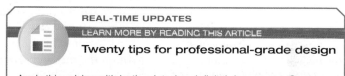

REAL-TIME UPDATES

LEARN MORE BY READING THIS ARTICLE

Twenty tips for professional-grade design

Apply this advice with both printed and digital documents. Go to **real-timeupdates.com/ebc13** and select Learn More in the Students section.

Typefaces

Typeface refers to the visual design of letters, numbers, and other text characters. As the Type Together vignette at the beginning of the chapter noted, *typeface* and *font* are often used interchangeably, but typeface is the design of the type itself, while a font is a collection of characters using that design.

Typeface design influences the tone of your message, making it look authoritative or friendly, businesslike or casual, classic or modern, and so on (see Table 7.4). Veronika Burian, José Scaglione, and other type designers know how to make design choices that evoke specific emotional reactions and trigger particular visual associations, so be sure to choose fonts that are appropriate for your message. (Note that many of the fonts on your computer are not appropriate for normal business use.)

Serif typefaces have small crosslines (called serifs) at the ends of each letter stroke. **Sans serif typefaces**, in contrast, lack these serifs. For years, the conventional wisdom in typography was that serif faces were easier to read in long blocks of text because the serifs made it easier for the eye to pick out individual letters. Accordingly, the standard advice was to use serif faces for the body of a document and sans serif for headings and subheadings.

However, the research behind the conventional wisdom is not as conclusive as once thought.[3] In fact, many sans serif typefaces work as well as or better than some serif typefaces for body text. This seems to be particularly true on screens, which sometimes have lower resolution than printed text. Many contemporary documents and webpages now use sans serif for body text.

Typeface refers to the visual design of letters, numbers, and other text characters; *typeface* and *font* are often used interchangeably, although strictly speaking they are different entities.

Serif typefaces have small crosslines (called serifs) at the ends of each letter stroke; *sans serif typefaces* do not have these elements.

The classic style of document design uses a sans serif typeface for headings and a serif typeface for regular paragraph text; however, many contemporary documents and webpages now use all sans serif.

TABLE 7.4	Typeface Personalities: Serious to Casual to Playful	
Serif Typefaces	Sans Serif Typefaces	Specialty Typefaces (rarely used for routine business communication)
Bookman Old Style	Arial	Bauhaus
Century Schoolbook	Calibri	**Broadway**
Courier	**Eras Bold**	*Forte*
Garamond	Franklin Gothic Book	*Edwardian Script*
Georgia	Gill Sans	*Schuss Hand*
Times New Roman	Verdana	**STENCIL**

REAL-TIME UPDATES

LEARN MORE BY READING THIS ARTICLE

Twenty typeface mistakes to avoid

Follow these typeface tips from professional graphic designers. Go to **real-timeupdates.com/ebc13** and select Learn More in the Students section.

To ensure a clean, uncluttered design, limit the number of typefaces in a document or webpage, and use them consistently throughout. For example, you can use one typeface for body text and another for headings and subheadings. If you have illustrations, sidebars, or other elements, you might use a third typeface to set them apart from the main text.

Type Styles

Type style refers to any modification that lends contrast or emphasis to type, including boldface, italic, underlining, color, and other highlighting and decorative styles.

Type style refers to any modification that lends contrast or emphasis to type, including boldface, italic, underlining, color, and other highlighting and decorative styles. Using boldface type for subheads breaks up long expanses of text. You can also boldface individual words or phrases to draw more attention to them. For example, the key terms in each chapter in this book are set in bold. Italic type also creates emphasis, although not as pronounced as boldface. Italic type has specific uses as well, such as highlighting quotations and indicating foreign words, irony, humor, book and movie titles, and unconventional usage.

Use type styles (boldface, italics, and underlining) sparingly to preserve their ability to emphasize key words and phrases.

As a general rule, avoid using any style in a way that slows your audience's progress through the message. For instance, underlining or using all-uppercase letters can interfere with a reader's ability to recognize the shapes of words, and shadowed or outlined type can seriously hinder legibility. Also, avoid overusing any type style. For example, putting too many words in boldface dilutes the impact of the special treatment by creating too many focal points in the paragraph.

Type size is an important consideration as well. For most printed business messages, use a size of 10 to 12 points for regular text and 12 to 18 points for headings and subheadings (1 point is approximately 1/72 inch). Resist the temptation to reduce type size too much in order to squeeze in extra text or to enlarge it to fill up space. Type that is too small is hard to read, whereas extra-large type looks unprofessional. Be particularly careful with small type online. It may look fine on a medium-resolution screen but can be hard to read on both low-resolution screens (because these displays can make letters look jagged or fuzzy) and high-resolution screens (because these monitors reduce the apparent size of the type even further).

Figures 7.4 and 7.5 on the next two pages illustrate some of the fundamental choices you need to make when designing and producing business documents.

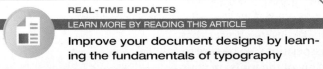

REAL-TIME UPDATES

LEARN MORE BY READING THIS ARTICLE

Improve your document designs by learning the fundamentals of typography

Knowing the basics of type usage will help you create more effective page and screen layouts. Go to **real-timeupdates.com/ebc13** and select Learn More in the Students section.

FORMATTING FORMAL LETTERS AND MEMOS

Refer to Appendix A for detailed guidance on formatting letters and memos.

Formal business letters usually follow certain design conventions, as the letter in Figure 7.2 illustrates. Most business letters are printed on *letterhead stationery*, which includes the company's name, address, and other contact information. The first element to appear after the letterhead is the date, followed by the inside address, which identifies the person receiving the letter. Next is the salutation, usually in the form of *Dear Mr.* or *Ms. Last Name*. The message comes next, followed by the complimentary close, usually *Sincerely* or *Cordially*. And

Ineffective

Document Title

Some changes in the business environment happen gradually and often predictably, such as when an aging consumer population *increases* or *decreases* demand for particular goods and services or when a particular brand or type of product falls out of fashion. Companies need to anticipate and respond to such changes, but they don't fundamentally alter the way businesses operate.

Other types of changes, however, can be downright traumatic—or exciting, depending on whether you're benefiting from a change or getting steamrolled by it. **Online retailing, digital music, mobile communication, and social media** are examples of changes that permanently shifted the way many consumers behave and many businesses operate. Each of these is a disruptive innovation, a development so fundamentally different and far-reaching that it can create new professions, companies, or even entire industries while damaging or destroying others.

First Subheading

Disruptive technologies are an intriguing phenomenon, for several reasons. First, predicting whether a new technology will be truly disruptive is difficult. In many cases, multiple other forces from the technological, economic, social, and legal regulatory environments need to converge before an innovation has a major impact.

For instance, without **broadband wireless networks, a digital communication infrastructure, data encryptions methods, a vast array of free and low-cost apps, mobile-friendly web services**, and more **computing power than computers used to have**, a smartphone would just be an expensive way to make phone calls. With the combined impact of all these innovations, mobile phones have changed the way many people live and the way many businesses operate. Keep this in mind if you're considering joining a company with a promising new product that hasn't caught on yet—what other changes need to occur before the product and the company will succeed?

> Illustration in line with text

Second, predicting when the disruption will happen is just as difficult. Many promising technologies can take years to have an impact. Mobile phones and handheld computers had been around for two or three decades before all the pieces fell into place and the smartphone era took off. Intriguing new inventions can generate a lot of interest, press coverage, and "hype" long before they have any real impact on business, and expectations sometimes outpace what the technology can deliver. This pattern repeats so often that the management consulting firm Gartner Group has modeled a five-stage roller-coaster curve it calls the Hype Cycle.

Third, predicting the eventual impact of a disruption is also challenging. AI is finally going mainstream as a business tool after

(a) The typeface used in the headings has too much personality and the wrong feel for a business document.

(b) The justified paragraphs have a "gappy" look, with excess space between words.

(c) With tight *leading* (space between lines) and no extra space between paragraphs, the result is a visually intimidating "wall of text" look.

(d) The overuse of type styles (bold, underline, and italics) creates visual clutter and reduces the impact of any individual style.

(e) The typeface used for the body text is difficult to read.

(f) Running the illustration inline, rather than wrapping text around it, leaves an enormous gap on the page (a poor use of white space, in this case).

(g) The narrow margins make the text lines too long for easy reading and give the page a packed, intimidating look.

(h) The first line of this paragraph left "stranded" at the bottom of the page is known as an *orphan*. (The last line of a paragraph stranded at the top of a succeeding page is a *widow*.)

Figure 7.4 Ineffective Design Choices for Business Documents
The documents in Figures 7.4 and 7.5 illustrate some of the basic principles of effective document design (which apply to both printed and digital documents). Notice how with just a few simple changes, the ineffective version becomes much more inviting to read.

last comes the signature block: space for the signature, followed by the sender's printed name and title. Your company will probably have a standard format to follow for letters, possibly along with a word-processor template. For in-depth information on letter formats, see Appendix A, "Format and Layout of Business Documents."

Like letters, business memos usually follow a preset design. Memos have largely been replaced by digital media in many companies, but if they are still in use at the firm you join, the company may have a standard format or template for you to use. Most memos begin with a title such as *Memo, Memorandum,* or *Interoffice Correspondence.* Following that are usually four headings: *Date, To, From,* and *Subject.* (*Re:,* short for *Regarding,* is sometimes used instead of *Subject.*) Memos usually don't use a salutation, complimentary close, or signature, although signing your initials next to your name on the *From* line is standard practice in many companies. Bear in mind that memos are often distributed without sealed envelopes, so they are less private than most other message formats.

MOBILE APP

Ginger Page offers a grammar checker, dictionary, thesaurus, translator, and other tools to help with mobile writing.

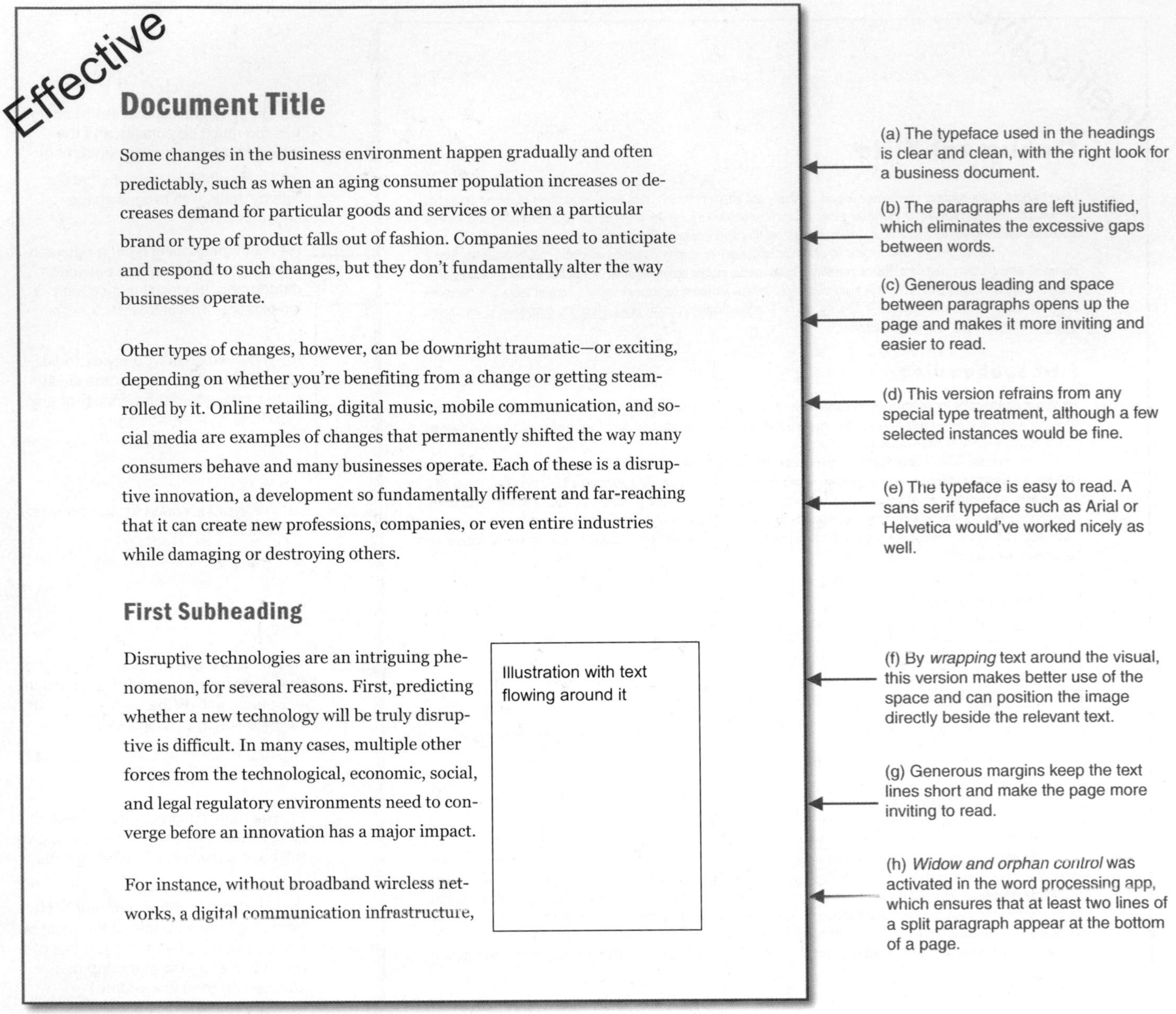

Effective

Document Title

Some changes in the business environment happen gradually and often predictably, such as when an aging consumer population increases or decreases demand for particular goods and services or when a particular brand or type of product falls out of fashion. Companies need to anticipate and respond to such changes, but they don't fundamentally alter the way businesses operate.

Other types of changes, however, can be downright traumatic—or exciting, depending on whether you're benefiting from a change or getting steamrolled by it. Online retailing, digital music, mobile communication, and social media are examples of changes that permanently shifted the way many consumers behave and many businesses operate. Each of these is a disruptive innovation, a development so fundamentally different and far-reaching that it can create new professions, companies, or even entire industries while damaging or destroying others.

First Subheading

Disruptive technologies are an intriguing phenomenon, for several reasons. First, predicting whether a new technology will be truly disruptive is difficult. In many cases, multiple other forces from the technological, economic, social, and legal regulatory environments need to converge before an innovation has a major impact.

For instance, without broadband wireless networks, a digital communication infrastructure,

Illustration with text flowing around it

(a) The typeface used in the headings is clear and clean, with the right look for a business document.

(b) The paragraphs are left justified, which eliminates the excessive gaps between words.

(c) Generous leading and space between paragraphs opens up the page and makes it more inviting and easier to read.

(d) This version refrains from any special type treatment, although a few selected instances would be fine.

(e) The typeface is easy to read. A sans serif typeface such as Arial or Helvetica would've worked nicely as well.

(f) By *wrapping* text around the visual, this version makes better use of the space and can position the image directly beside the relevant text.

(g) Generous margins keep the text lines short and make the page more inviting to read.

(h) *Widow and orphan control* was activated in the word processing app, which ensures that at least two lines of a split paragraph appear at the bottom of a page.

Figure 7.5   Effective Design Choices for Business Documents
Compare the version with Figure 7.4—notice how with just a few simple changes, the ineffective version becomes much more inviting to read. (Note that this open layout will require more pages, which could be a consideration if the document is meant to be printed.)

DESIGNING MESSAGES FOR MOBILE DEVICES

In addition to making your content mobile-friendly using the writing tips in Chapter 6 (see page 177), you can follow these steps to format that content for mobile devices:

If your messages are likely to be read on mobile devices, think in small chunks of information and use lots of white space.

- **Think in small chunks.** Remember that mobile users consume information one screen at a time, so try to divide your message into independent, easy-to-consume bites. If readers have to scroll through a dozen screens to piece together your message, they might miss key points or just give up entirely.
- **Make generous use of white space.** White space is always helpful, but it's critical on small screens because readers are trying to get the gist of every message as quickly as possible. Keep your paragraphs short (four to six lines) and separate them with blank lines so the reader's eyes can easily jump from one point to the next.[4]
- **Format simply.** Avoid anything that is likely to get in the way of fast, easy reading, including busy typefaces, complex graphics, and complicated layouts.

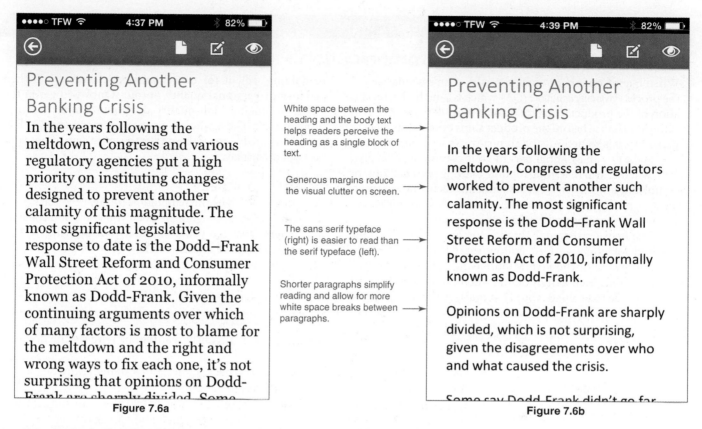

Figure 7.6a

Figure 7.6b

Figure 7.6   Designing for Mobile Devices
Even simple changes such as revising with shorter paragraphs, choosing cleaner typefaces, and making generous use of white space in and around the text can dramatically improve readability on mobile screens.

- **Consider horizontal and vertical layouts.** Most phones and tablets can automatically rotate their screen content from horizontal to vertical as the user rotates the device. A layout that doesn't work well with the narrow vertical perspective might be acceptable at the wider horizontal perspective.

Compare the two messages in Figure 7.6; notice how much more difficult the screen in Figure 7.6a is to read.

Proofreading Your Message

5 **LEARNING OBJECTIVE** Explain the importance of proofreading, and give eight tips for successful proofreading.

Proofreading is the quality inspection stage for your documents, your last chance to make sure that your document is ready to carry your message—and your reputation—to the intended audience. Even a small mistake can doom your efforts, so take proofreading seriously.

Look for two types of problems: (1) undetected mistakes from the writing, design, and layout stages and (2) mistakes that crept in during production. For the first category, you can review format and layout guidelines in Appendix A on page 559 and brush up on writing basics with the Handbook of Grammar, Mechanics, and Usage on page 582. The second category can include anything from computer glitches such as missing fonts to broken web links to problems with the ink used in printing. Be particularly vigilant with complex documents and complex production processes that involve multiple colleagues and multiple computers. Strange things can happen as files move from computer to computer, especially when lots of fonts and multimedia elements are involved.

Accuracy and attention to detail help build your credibility, so proofread messages and documents carefully.

To be most effective, proofreading should be a methodical procedure in which you look for specific problems. Here is some advice from the pros:

- **Make multiple passes.** Go through the document several times, focusing on a different aspect each time. For instance, look for content errors the first time and layout errors the second time.
- **Use perceptual tricks.** To keep from missing errors that are "hiding in plain sight," try reading pages backward, placing your finger under each word and reading it silently,

The types of details to look for when proofreading include language errors, missing material, design errors, and typographical errors.

Make QA Part of Your Communication Process

When manufacturers produce something, an essential step in the process is *quality assurance (QA)*, which is a methodical evaluation of the product's quality relative to its design goals. This is the last chance before the product ships out to customers to make sure it is something the company can be proud of.

Make QA an essential part of your communication process, whether you're writing reports, crafting presentations, or completing any other type of assignment. Practice now on writing assignments in all your classes, and it will be second nature when you're writing and presenting on the job.

The steps presented in this chapter are a sure and simple method for effective QA. Follow the Checklists on page 199 and below or the Five-Minute Guide at the end of the chapter. With each assignment, remember to give yourself enough time to evaluate your first draft, revise it to improve

readability, edit it for clarity and conciseness, and then produce professional-quality output. Once you get in the habit, producing high-quality documents and presentations doesn't take a whole lot more time and energy than producing mediocre work, so take the extra step to put your best self on display.

COACH YOURSELF

1. Do you ever feel the temptation to say, "Eh, that's good enough" on an assignment when you know you could do better? What can you do to reset your priorities so that quality work is a matter of habit?
2. Do you need to examine your work methods to make sure you leave enough time to do an effective QA check on every assignment?

covering everything but the line you're currently reading, or reading the document aloud.

- **Focus on high-priority items.** Double-check names, titles, dates, addresses, and any number that could cause grief if incorrect.
- **Get some distance.** If possible, don't proofread immediately after finishing the document. Let your brain wander off to new topics and then come back fresh later.
- **Stay focused and vigilant.** Block out distractions and focus as completely as possible on your proofreading. Avoid reading large amounts of material in one sitting and try not to proofread when you're tired.
- **Review complex digital documents on paper.** Some people have trouble proofreading webpages, online reports, and other digital documents on screen. If you have trouble, print the materials so you can review them on paper.
- **Take your time.** You're more likely to miss things if you rush.

REAL-TIME UPDATES

LEARN MORE BY READING THIS ARTICLE

Proven tips for proofreading

This advice for class assignments will help you on the job, too. Go to **real-timeupdates.com/ebc13** and select Learn More in the Students section.

The amount of time you need to spend on proofing depends on the length and complexity of the document and the situation. A typo in an email message to your team may not be a big deal, but a typo in a financial report, a contract, or a medical file certainly could be serious. See "Checklist: Proofing Business Messages" for a handy list of items to review during proofing.

CHECKLIST ✔ Proofing Business Messages

A. Look for writing errors.
- ✔ Typographical mistakes
- ✔ Misspelled words
- ✔ Grammatical errors
- ✔ Punctuation mistakes

B. Look for design and layout errors.
- ✔ Lack of adherence to company standards
- ✔ Page or screen layout errors (such as incorrect margins and column formatting)
- ✔ Awkward page breaks or line breaks
- ✔ Inconsistent font usage (such as with headings and subheadings)
- ✔ Alignment problems (columns, headers, footers, and graphics)

- ✔ Missing or incorrect page and section numbers
- ✔ Missing or incorrect page headers or footers
- ✔ Missing or incorrect URLs, email addresses, or other contact information
- ✔ Missing or incorrect photos and other graphical elements
- ✔ Missing or incorrect source notes, copyright notices, or other reference items

C. Look for production errors.
- ✔ Printing problems
- ✔ Browser compatibility problems
- ✔ Screen size or resolution issues for mobile devices
- ✔ Incorrect or missing tags on blog posts
- ✔ Missing files

Distributing Your Message

With the production finished, you're ready to distribute your message. As with every other aspect of business communication, your options for distribution multiply with every advance in technology. In some cases, the choice is obvious: Just click or tap the Send button in your email program or the Publish button on your blog. In other cases, such as when you have a 100-page report with full-color graphics or a massive multimedia file, you need to plan the distribution carefully so that your message is received by everyone who needs it. When choosing a means to distribute messages, consider the following factors:

- **Cost.** Cost isn't a concern for most messages, but for multiple copies of lengthy reports or multimedia productions, it may well be. Printing, binding, and delivering reports can be expensive, so weigh the cost versus the benefits. Be sure to consider the nonverbal message you send regarding cost as well. Overnight delivery of a printed report could seem responsive in one situation but wasteful in another, for example.
- **Convenience.** Make sure your audience can conveniently access and use the material you send. For instance, sending huge files may be fine on a fast office network, but receiving such files might be a major headache for remote colleagues trying to download them over home networks.
- **Time.** How soon does the message need to reach the audience? Don't waste money on overnight delivery if the recipient won't read a report for a week.
- **Security and privacy.** The convenience offered by digital communication needs to be weighed against security and privacy concerns. For the most sensitive messages, your company will probably restrict both the people who can receive the messages and the means you can use to distribute them. In addition, astute computer users are wary of opening attachments these days. Instead of sending word-processor files, you can use Adobe Acrobat or an equivalent product to convert your documents to PDF files, which are more resistant to viruses. Some versions of popular word-processing apps also let you output files as PDFs.

For more advice on revision, proofreading, and other topics related to this chapter, visit **real-timeupdates.com/ebc13** and select Chapter 7.

> **6 LEARNING OBJECTIVE**
> Discuss the most important issues to consider when distributing your messages.

Consider cost, convenience, time, security, and privacy when choosing a distribution method.

MOBILE APP
DocuSign is one of many apps that solve the problem of signing digital documents such as contracts; you can sign right on your phone screen.

ON THE JOB: SOLVING COMMUNICATION DILEMMAS AT TYPE TOGETHER

You've joined Type Together as a marketing communications specialist, and your responsibilities include writing new content as well as revising and editing content submissions from others in the company. Use what you've learned in this chapter about revising and editing to address these two challenges.

1. For each of the typefaces Type Together sells, it provides a brief overview of the typeface to explain what makes it distinctive and to suggest some applications. Here is the company's overview for its Adelle font.[5] (A *slab serif* is a serif typeface in which the serifs tend to be blockier or chunkier, giving the type a solid, authoritative look, and as the chapter-opener explained, *editorial use* refers to using a typeface for long blocks of text.)

   > *While Adelle is a slab serif for intensive editorial use, its personality and flexibility make it a true multipurpose typeface, especially on the web. The unobtrusive appearance, excellent texture, and slightly dark color*

   allow it to behave flawlessly in continuous text, even in the most unforgiving applications. As it becomes larger in print, Adelle shows its personality through a series of measured particularities which make it easy to remember and identify. Adelle is a versatile and authoritative slab serif with no shortage of personality.

   You'd like to share the news of this wonderful typeface with your social media followers, so you attempt to summarize this 549-character description in a tweetable message. You have 280 characters to play with on Twitter (including spaces), but of course you don't need to use all of them. Which of these is the most effective?

   a. While Adelle is a slab serif for intensive editorial use, its personality and flexibility make it a true multipurpose typeface, especially on the web. [153 characters]

   b. While Adelle is a slab serif for intensive editorial use, it is a true multipurpose typeface, especially on the web. With unobtrusive appearance, excellent texture, and slightly dark color, it behaves flawlessly. [216 characters]

c. While Adelle is a slab serif for intensive editorial use, its personality and flexibility make it a true multipurpose typeface, especially on the web. The unobtrusive appearance, excellent texture, and slightly dark color let it behave flawlessly in unforgiving applications. [278 characters]

2. Veronika Burian and José Scaglione believe in supporting the next generation of typeface designers. A key part of this effort is their Typeface Publishing Incentive Program, in which design students can submit type designs they are working on as part of a university design course. Burian and Scaglione select a promising design and help the student complete and commercialize the font as a market-ready product. Which of these is the clearest way to encourage design students to submit their font designs for this program?

   a. Submit your latest font design for the chance to turn it into a profitable commercial product.
   b. Enter for the chance to have your font design brought to market with the help of professional type designers.
   c. Enter the Type Together Typeface Publishing Incentive Program today.
   d. Type Together believes in supporting the next generation of typeface designers, so be sure to submit your design for review.

3. In addition to ready-made font families that customers can download and use on their computers as they use other fonts, Type Together designs custom fonts for corporations. A custom font gives a company a unique look for all its print and digital communication, and fonts can even be based on an existing logo for an integrated branding look. Which of

these would be the best informative heading for a webpage that talks about the custom design service?

   a. Custom Font Design Service
   b. Give Your Company the Unique Communication Power of a Custom Font
   c. Integrate All Your Print and Digital Communication
   d. Match Your Logo for an Integrated Branding Look

4. Imagine that Burian and Scaglione want to start an online training program for font users. For a modest fee, business communicators could take this online course to learn how to use typefaces more effectively. Which of these would be the most efficient way to describe this offering?

   a. Learn how to improve the visual appeal and impact of all your digital and print documents with this low-cost, two-hour course. Understand the differences between major categories of fonts. Learn how to choose fonts for every business application. Learn how to use line and paragraph spacing effectively. As a special bonus, learn how to use advanced techniques such as kerning.
   b. Learn how to improve the visual appeal and impact of all your digital and print documents with this low-cost, two-hour course, understand the differences between major categories of fonts, see how to choose fonts for every business application, learn how to use line and paragraph spacing effectively, and even learn how to use advanced techniques such as kerning.
   c. In this low-cost, two-hour course, you'll improve the visual appeal and impact of all your digital and print documents with these new skills:
      • Recognizing the major categories of fonts
      • Choosing fonts for every business application
      • Using line and paragraph spacing effectively
      • Applying advanced techniques such as kerning

END OF CHAPTER

Learning Objectives Checkup

Assess your understanding of the principles in this chapter by reading each learning objective and study the accompanying exercises. You can check your responses against the answer key on page 612.

Objective 7.1: Discuss the value of careful revision, and describe the tasks involved in evaluating your first drafts and the work of other writers.

1. Which of these is the most important reason you should take care to revise messages before sending them?
   a. Revising shows your audience how hard you work.
   b. Revising lowers the word count.
   c. Revising makes it cheaper to email messages.
   d. Revising can usually make your messages more successful.

2. Which of the following is not one of the main tasks involved in completing a business message?
   a. Drafting the message
   b. Revising the message
   c. Producing the message
   d. Proofreading the message

Objective 7.2: List four techniques you can use to improve the readability of your messages.

3. Regarding sentence length, the best approach for business messages is to
   a. keep all sentences as short as possible.
   b. make most of your sentences long since you will usually have complex information to impart.
   c. vary the length of your sentences.
   d. aim for an average sentence length of 35 words.

4. Regarding paragraph length, the best approach for business messages is to
   a. keep paragraphs short.
   b. make most of your paragraphs long since that is standard practice in business writing.
   c. make most of your paragraphs one sentence in length.
   d. aim for an average paragraph length of 200 words.

5. Regarding the use of lists, the best approach for business messages is to
   a. avoid using lists except where absolutely necessary.
   b. make sure listed items are in parallel form.
   c. use numbered lists rather than bulleted ones.
   d. do all of the above.

6. Which of the following is *not* an informative heading?
   a. Why We Need a New Distributor
   b. Five Challenges Facing Today's Distributors
   c. Distributors Are a Better Choice for Us Than Wholesalers
   d. Distributor Choices

Objective 7.3: Describe eight steps you can take to improve the clarity of your writing, and give four tips for making your writing more concise.

7. Which of the following sentences contains hedging words?
   a. There is an 80 percent chance the project won't hit its May 20 deadline.
   b. There is a possibility that the project might be done by May 20.
   c. At this point, we can't tell whether the project will be done by May 20.
   d. All of the above contain hedging words.

8. Which of the following sentences lacks parallelism?
   a. Consumers can download stock research, electronically file their tax returns, create a portfolio, or choose from an array of recommended mutual funds.
   b. Consumers can download stock research, can electronically file their tax returns, create a portfolio, or they can choose from an array of recommended mutual funds.
   c. Consumers can download stock research, can electronically file their tax returns, can create a portfolio, or can choose from an array of recommended mutual funds.
   d. Consumers can download stock research, they can electronically file their tax returns, they can create a portfolio, or they can choose from an array of recommended mutual funds.

9. Which of the following sentences does not have a dangling modifier?
   a. Lacking brand recognition, some consumers are wary of using digital-only *neobanks*.
   b. Because digital-only *neobanks* often lack brand recognition, some consumers are wary of using them.
   c. Because of a lack of brand recognition, some consumers are wary of using digital-only *neobanks*.
   d. All have dangling modifiers.

10. When editing for conciseness, you should look for
    a. unnecessary words and phrases.
    b. dangling modifiers.
    c. lack of parallelism.
    d. awkward references.

11. Which of the following is not an example of a redundancy?
    a. Visible to the eye
    b. Free gift
    c. Very useful
    d. Repeat again

Objective 7.4: List four principles of effective design, and explain the role of major design elements in document readability.

12. Which of these is *not* one of the design elements discussed in the chapter?
    a. Projection
    b. Balance
    c. Restraint
    d. Consistency

13. Any blank areas in a document are referred to as _____.

14. Type that is justified is
    a. flush on the left and ragged on the right.
    b. flush on the right and ragged on the left.
    c. flush on both the left and the right.
    d. centered.

15. Why is it a good idea to write in small chunks when writing for mobile audiences?
    a. Mobile users consume information one screen at a time.
    b. More than 50 percent of mobile users refuse to scroll past the first screen.
    c. Many smartphones don't offer scrolling.
    d. Graphics are easier to create on mobile devices.

Objective 7.5: Explain the importance of proofreading, and give eight tips for successful proofreading.

16. The best time to proofread is
    a. as you are writing.
    b. immediately after you finish the first draft, while the information is still fresh in your mind.
    c. a day or so after you finish the first draft.
    d. after you distribute the document.

17. Which of these is *not* one of the proofreading tips mentioned in the chapter?
    a. Take your time
    b. Use perceptual tricks
    c. Make multiple passes
    d. Never proofread on screen

Objective 7.6: Discuss the most important issues to consider when distributing your messages.

18. As a general rule, the cost of distributing a business message should be balanced against
    a. the importance and urgency of the message.
    b. the length of the message.
    c. your career goals as they relate to the message.
    d. the number of recipients.

19. Which of these is most true about security and privacy when distributing messages?
    a. Bank-grade encryption has solved most problems of network security.
    b. Corporate email systems no longer accept outside messages.
    c. Astute computers users are wary of accepting and opening attachments.
    d. All corporate communication networks strip off attachments.

Key Terms

descriptive headings Headings that simply identify a topic

heading A brief title that tells readers about the content of the section that follows

informative headings Headings that guide readers to think in a certain way about the topic

sans serif typefaces Typefaces whose letters lack serifs

serif typefaces Typefaces with small crosslines (called *serifs*) at the ends of letter strokes

subheadings Titles that are subordinate to headings, indicating subsections within a major section

type style Any modification that lends contrast or emphasis to type, including boldface, italic, underlining, color, and other highlighting and decorative styles

typeface The physical design of letters, numbers, and other text characters (*font* and *typeface* are often used interchangeably, although strictly speaking, a font is a set of characters in a given typeface)

white space Space (of any color) in a document or screen that doesn't contain any text or artwork

Apply Your Knowledge

To review chapter content related to each question, refer to the indicated Learning Objective.

7-1. How does careful revision reflect the "you" attitude? [LO-1]

7-2. Why should you limit the number of typefaces and type styles in most business documents? [LO-4]

7-3. Why is white space particularly critical when designing documents for mobile devices? [LO-4]

7-4. How can you demonstrate good business sense in the choices you make regarding message distribution? [LO-6]

Practice Your Skills

Messages for Analysis

7-5. **Message 7.A: Revising to Improve Readability [LO-2]** Analyze the strengths and weaknesses of this message, then revise it so that it follows the guidelines in Chapters 5 through 7:

As an organization, the North American Personal Motorsports Marketing Association has committed ourselves to helping our members—a diverse group comprising of dealers of motorcycles, all-terrain vehicles, Snowmobiles, and personal watercraft—achieve their business objectives. Consequently, our organization, which usually goes under the initials NAPMMA, has the following aims, goals, and objectives. Firstly, we endeavor to aid or assist our members in reaching their business objectives. Second, NAPMMA communicates ("lobbying" in slang terms) with local, state, and national governmental agencies and leaders on issues of importance to our members. And lastly, we educate the motorsports public, that being current motorsports vehicle owners, and prospective owners of said vehicles, on the safe and enjoyable operation of they're vehicles.

7-6. **Message 7.B: Designing for Readability [LO-4]** To access this message, visit real-timeupdates.com/ebc13, click on Student Assignments, and select Chapter 7, Message 7.B. Download and open the document. Using the various page, paragraph, and font formatting options available in your word processor, modify the formatting of the document so that its visual tone matches the tone of the message.

7-7. **Message 7.C: Evaluating the Work of Another Writer [LO-1]** To access this message, visit real-timeupdates.com/ebc13, click on Student Assignments, and select Chapter 7, Message 7.C. Download and open the document. Using your knowledge of effective writing and the tips on page 192 for evaluating the work of other writers, evaluate this message. After you set your word-processing app to track changes, make any necessary corrections. Insert comments, as needed, to explain your changes to the author.

Exercises

Each activity is labeled according to the primary skill or skills you will need to use. To review relevant chapter content, you can refer to the indicated Learning Objective. In some instances, supporting information will be found in another chapter, as indicated.

7-8. **Evaluating the Work of Other Writers [LO-1]** Find a blog post (at least three paragraphs long) on any business-related topic. Evaluate it using the 10 questions on page 192. Email your analysis to your instructor, along with a link to the post.

7-9. **Revising for Readability (Sentence and Paragraph Length) [LO-2]** Rewrite the following paragraph to vary the length of the sentences and to shorten the paragraph so it looks more inviting to readers:

Although major league baseball remains popular, more people are attending minor league baseball games because they can spend less on admission, snacks, and parking and still enjoy the excitement of America's pastime. Connecticut, for example, has three AA minor league teams, including the New Haven Ravens, who are affiliated with the St. Louis Cardinals; the Norwich Navigators, who are affiliated with the New York Yankees; and the New Britain Rock Cats, who are affiliated with the Minnesota Twins. These teams play in relatively small stadiums, so fans are close enough to see and hear everything, from the swing of the bat connecting with the ball to the thud of the ball landing in the outfielder's glove. Best of all, the cost of a family outing to see rising stars play in a local minor league game is just a fraction of what the family would spend to attend a major league game in a much larger, more crowded stadium.

Revising for Readability (Sentence Length) [LO-2] Break the following sentences into shorter ones by adding more periods and revise as needed for smooth flow:

7-10. The next time you write something, check your average sentence length in a 100-word passage, and if your sentences average more than 16 to 20 words, see whether you can break up some of the sentences.

7-11. Unfortunately, no gadget will produce excellent writing, but using a yardstick like the Flesch Reading Ease score gives us some guideposts to follow for making writing easier to read because its two factors remind us to use short sentences and simple words.

7-12. Know the flexibility of the written word and its power to convey an idea, and know how to make your words behave so that your readers will understand.

7-13. Words mean different things to different people, and a word such as *block* may mean city block, butcher block, engine block, auction block, or several other things.

Editing for Conciseness (Unnecessary Words) [LO-3] Cross out unnecessary words in the following phrases:

7-14. Consensus of opinion

7-15. New innovations

7-16. Long period of time

7-17. At a price of $50

7-18. Still remains

Editing for Conciseness (Long Words) [LO-3] Revise the following sentences, using shorter, simpler words:

7-19. Our superannuated content management system has proven to be ineffectual once again.

7-20. It is imperative that the pay increments be terminated before an inordinate deficit is accumulated.

7-21. There was unanimity among the executives that his behavior was cause for a mandatory meeting with the company's personnel director.

7-22. The impending liquidation of the company's assets was cause for jubilation among the company's competitors.

7-23. The expectations of the president for a stock dividend were accentuated by the preponderance of evidence that the company was in good financial condition.

Editing for Conciseness (Lengthy Phrases) [LO-3] Use infinitives as substitutes for the overly long phrases in these sentences:

7-24. For living, I require money.

7-25. They did not find sufficient evidence for believing in the future.

7-26. Bringing about the destruction of a dream is tragic.

Editing for Conciseness (Lengthy Phrases) [LO-3] Rephrase the following in fewer words:

7-27. In the near future

7-28. In the event that

7-29. In order that

7-30. For the purpose of

7-31. With regard to

7-32. It may be that

7-33. In very few cases

7-34. With reference to

7-35. At the present time

7-36. There is no doubt that

Editing for Conciseness (Lengthy Phrases) [LO-3] Revise to condense these sentences to as few words as possible:

7-37. We are of the conviction that writing is important.

7-38. In all probability, we're likely to have a price increase.

7-39. Our goals include making a determination about that in the near future.

7-40. When all is said and done at the conclusion of this experiment, I'd like to summarize the final wrap-up.

7-41. After a trial period of three weeks, during which time she worked for a total of 15 full working days, we found her work was sufficiently satisfactory so that we offered her full-time work.

Editing for Conciseness (Unnecessary Modifiers) [LO-3] Remove all the unnecessary modifiers from these sentences:

7-42. Tremendously high pay increases were given to the extraordinarily skilled and extremely conscientious employees.

7-43. The union's proposals were highly inflationary, extremely demanding, and exceptionally bold.

Editing for Clarity (Hedging) [LO-3] Rewrite these sentences so that they no longer contain any hedging:

7-44. It would appear that someone apparently entered illegally.

7-45. It may be possible that sometime in the near future the situation is likely to improve.

7-46. Your report seems to suggest that we might be losing money.

7-47. I believe Yolanda apparently has somewhat greater influence over employees in the e-marketing department.

7-48. It seems as if this letter of resignation means you might be leaving us.

Editing for Clarity (Indefinite Starters) [LO-3] Rewrite these sentences to eliminate the indefinite starters:

7-49. There are several examples here to show that Elaine can't hold a position very long.

7-50. It would be greatly appreciated if every employee would make a generous contribution to Draymond Cook's retirement party.

7-51. It has been learned in Washington today from generally reliable sources that an important announcement will be made shortly by the White House.

7-52. There is a rule that states that we cannot work overtime without permission.

7-53. It would be great if you could work late for the next three Saturdays.

Editing for Clarity (Parallelism) [LO-3] Revise these sentences to present the ideas in parallel form:

7-54. Mr. Hill is expected to lecture three days a week, to counsel two days a week, and must write for publication in his spare time.

7-55. She knows not only accounting, but she also reads Latin.

7-56. Both applicants had families, college degrees, and were in their thirties, with considerable accounting experience but few social connections.

7-57. This book was exciting, well written, and held my interest.

7-58. Don is both a hard worker and he knows social media marketing.

Editing for Clarity (Awkward References) [LO-3] Revise the following sentences to delete the awkward references:

7-59. The vice president in charge of sales and the production manager are responsible for the keys to 34A and 35A, respectively.

7-60. The keys to 34A and 35A are in executive hands, with the former belonging to the vice president in charge of sales and the latter belonging to the production manager.

7-61. The keys to 34A and 35A have been given to the production manager, with the aforementioned keys being gold embossed.

7-62. A laser printer and an inkjet printer were delivered to John and Megan, respectively.

7-63. The walnut desk is more expensive than the oak desk, the former costing $300 more than the latter.

Editing for Clarity (Dangling Modifiers) [LO-3] Rewrite these sentences to clarify the dangling modifiers:

7-64. Full of trash and ripped-up newspapers, we left Dallas on a plane that apparently hadn't been cleaned in days.

7-65. Lying on the shelf, Ruby found the operations manual.

7-66. With leaking plumbing and outdated wiring, I don't think we should buy that property.

7-67. Being cluttered and filthy, Sandy took the whole afternoon to clean up her desk.

7-68. After proofreading every word, the letter was ready to be signed.

Editing for Clarity (Noun Sequences) [LO-3] Rewrite the following sentences to eliminate the long strings of nouns:

7-69. The focus of the meeting was a discussion of the bank interest rate deregulation issue.

7-70. Following the government task force report recommendations, we are revising our job applicant evaluation procedures.

7-71. The production department quality assurance program components include employee training, supplier cooperation, and computerized detection equipment.

7-72. The supermarket warehouse inventory reduction plan will be implemented next month.

7-73. The business school graduate placement program is one of the best in the country.

Editing for Clarity (Sentence Structure) [LO-3] Rearrange the following sentences to bring the subjects closer to their verbs:

7-74. Trudy, when she first saw the bull pawing the ground, ran.

7-75. It was Terri who, according to Ted, who is probably the worst gossip in the office (Tom excepted), mailed the wrong order.

7-76. William Oberstreet, in his book *Investment Capital Reconsidered*, writes of the mistakes that bankers through the decades have made.

7-77. Judy Schimmel, after passing up several sensible investment opportunities, despite the warnings of her friends and family, invested her inheritance in a jojoba plantation.

7-78. The president of U-Stor-It, which was on the brink of bankruptcy after the warehouse fire, the worst tragedy in the history of the company, prepared a press announcement.

Editing for Clarity (Camouflaged Verbs) [LO-3] Rewrite each sentence so that the verbs are no longer camouflaged:

7-79. Adaptation to the new rules was performed easily by the employees.

7-80. The assessor will make a determination of the tax due.

7-81. Verification of the identity of the employees must be made daily.

7-82. The board of directors made a recommendation that Mr. Ronson be assigned to a new division.

7-83. The auditing procedure on the books was performed by the vice president.

7-84. **Completing: Designing for Readability; Media Skills: Blogging [LO-4], Chapter 8** Compare the home pages of Bloomberg (www.bloomberg.com) and MarketWatch (www.marketwatch.com), two websites that cover financial markets. What are your first impressions of these two sites? How do their overall designs compare in terms of information delivery and overall user experience? Choose three pieces of information that a visitor to these sites would be likely to look for, such as a current stock price, news from international markets, and commentary from market experts. Which site makes it easier to find this information? Why? Present your analysis in a post for your class blog.

7-85. **Communication Ethics: Making Ethical Choices; Media Skills: Blogging [LO-3], Chapter 8** The time and energy required for careful revision can often benefit you or your company directly, such as by increasing the probability that website visitors will buy your products. But what about situations in which the quality of your writing and revision work really doesn't stand to benefit you directly? For instance, assume that you are putting a notice on your website, informing the local community about some upcoming construction to your manufacturing plant.

The work will disrupt traffic for nearly a year and generate a significant amount of noise and air pollution, but knowing the specific dates and times of various construction activities will allow people to adjust their commutes and other activities to minimize the negative impact on their daily lives. However, your company does not sell products in the local area, so the people affected by all this are not potential customers. Moreover, providing accurate information to the surrounding community and updating it as the project progresses will take time away from your other job responsibilities. Do you have an ethical obligation to keep the local community informed with accurate, up-to-date information? Why or why not?

7-86. Proofreading [LO-5] Proofread the following email message, and revise it to correct any problems you find:

Our final company orrientation of the year will be held on Dec. 20. In preparation for this sesssion, please order 20 copies of the Policy handbook, the confidentiality agreenemt, the employee benefits Manual, please let me know if you anticipate any delays in obtaining these materials.

Expand Your Skills

Critique the Professionals

Identify a company website that in your opinion violates one or more of the principles of good design discussed on pages 200–202. Using whatever medium your instructor requests, write a brief analysis of the site (no more than one page), citing specific elements from the piece and support from the chapter.

Sharpening Your Career Skills Online

Bovée and Thill's Business Communication Web Search, at websearch.businesscommunicationnetwork.com, is a unique research tool designed specifically for business communication research. Use the Web Search function to find a website, video, article, podcast, or presentation that offers advice on effective proofreading. Write a brief email message to your instructor, describing the item you found and summarizing the career skills information you learned from it.

Build Your Career

If you've been following these Build Your Career activities through the first six chapters, you should have a good start on your basic employment profile—what you want to do, where you want to go in your career, and what you can promise future employers. Now it's time to start researching potential employers and career paths. This research will help you uncover interesting job possibilities, inform you about various industries and the developments taking place in them, and equip you with lots of insights to use in your job interviews.

If you don't have any specific companies in mind yet, start with one of the many "best places to work" lists now available online. Two great sources are *Fortune*'s annual 100 Best Companies to Work For (fortune.com/best-companies) and Great Place to Work (reviews.greatplacetowork.com). You can get insider reviews at Glassdoor (www.glassdoor.com), which also offers ranked lists of best places to work as voted by employees, along with lists of the best jobs, trends by industry, and other helpful insights.

To learn more about various career paths, start with the U.S. Department of Labor's *Occupational Outlook Handbook*, www.bls.gov/ooh. After you find some interesting possibilities, search for these job titles online to find social media accounts by people in these fields, trade journals that cater to these professions, and other sources of focused information.

Your college's career center probably has lots of great resources as well, so be sure to check in with the staff and let them know where your interests are.

This research can take some time, so start well before it's time to begin interviewing. The sooner you start and the wider you cast your net, the more interesting career paths and job openings you'll uncover.

Improve Your Grammar, Mechanics, and Usage

The following exercises help you improve your knowledge of and power over English grammar, mechanics, and usage. Turn to the Handbook of Grammar, Mechanics, and Usage at the end of this book and review Section 1.6.1 (Prepositions), Section 1.6.2 (Conjunctions), and Section 1.6.3 (Articles and Interjections). Then look at the following 10 items and indicate the preferred choice in the following groups of sentences. (Answers to these exercises appear on page 614.)

7-87. **a.** The response was not only inappropriate but it was also rude.
b. The response was not only inappropriate but also rude.

7-88. **a.** Be sure to look the spelling up in the dictionary.
b. Be sure to look up the spelling in the dictionary.

7-89. **a.** We didn't get the contract because our proposal didn't comply with the request for proposals (RFP).
b. We didn't get the contract because our proposals didn't comply to the RFP.

7-90. **a.** Marissa should of known not to send that email to the CEO.
b. Marissa should have known not to send that email to the CEO.

7-91. **a.** The Phalanx 1000 has been favorably compared to the Mac iBook.
b. The Phalanx 1000 has been favorably compared with the Mac iBook.

7-92. **a.** What are you looking for?
b. For what are you looking?

7-93. **a.** Have you filed an SEC application?
b. Have you filed a SEC application?

7-94. **a.** The project turned out neither to be easy nor simple.
b. The project turned out to be neither easy nor simple.

7-95. **a.** If you hire me, you will not regret your decision!
b. If you hire me, you will not regret your decision.

7-96. **a.** This is truly an historic event.
b. This is truly a historic event.

For additional exercises focusing on conjunctions, articles, and prepositions, visit MyLab Business Communication. Click on Chapter 7, select Additional Exercises to Improve Your Grammar, Mechanics, and Usage, and select 11. Conjunctions, articles, and interjections.

MyLab Business Communication

MyLab Assisted-Grading Writing Prompts

If your instructor has assigned one or both of the following writing assignments within the MyLab, go to your Assignments to complete these writing exercises.

7-97. Why is it helpful to put your first draft aside for a while before you begin the editing process? [LO-1]

7-98. How do your typeface selections help determine the personality of your documents and messages? [LO-4]

Endnotes

1. Type Together website, accessed 15 March 2018, www
.type-together.com; "Georgia," in "Microsoft Typography," accessed
27 March 2016, www.microsoft.com; "Women in Design: Veronika
Burian," Fontshop, 9 March 2015, www.fontshop.com; Jan Mid-
dendorp, "Creative Characters: Veronika Burian," MyFonts,
October 2008, www.myfonts.com.
2. Deborah Gunn, "Looking Good on Paper," *Office Pro*, March 2004,
10–11.
3. Kas Thomas, "The Serif Readability Myth," assertTrue blog,
18 January 2013, asserttrue.blogspot.com; Ole Lund, "Knowledge
Construction in Typography: The Case of Legibility Research and the
Legibility of Sans Serif Typefaces," doctoral dissertation, University of
Reading, October 1999.
4. "Mobile Message Mayhem," Verne Ordman & Associates, accessed
12 March 2014, www.businesswriting.biz.
5. "Adelle," Type Together, accessed 15 March 2018,
www.type-together.com.

Five-Minute Guide to Revising and Proofreading

Before you sit down to revise or proofread the draft of a document, review these helpful tips, then keep this guide at your side while you revise, edit, and proofread.

00:01 **Evaluate your first draft**

1. Is the information accurate, relevant, and complete?
2. Is there a good balance between general information and specific information?
3. Are all the points covered in the most logical order?
4. Do the most important ideas receive the most coverage?
5. Would the message be more convincing if it were arranged in a different sequence?
6. Are any points repeated unnecessarily?
7. Are details grouped together logically?

00:02 **Revise to improve readability**

1. Vary the length of your sentences to maintain reader interest.
   - Short sentences can be processed quickly, but too many of them make writing choppy.
   - Medium-length sentences are useful for showing the relationships among ideas.
   - Long sentences are often the best for conveying complex ideas, but they can be more difficult to read and understand.
2. Keep your paragraphs as short as possible, under 100 words where you can.
3. Use numbered and bulleted lists to clarify and emphasize.
4. Add headings and subheadings to guide readers.

00:03 **Edit for clarity**

1. Break up overly long sentences.
2. Rewrite hedging sentences.
3. Impose parallelism.
4. Correct dangling modifiers.
5. Reword long noun sequences.
6. Replace camouflaged verbs.
7. Clarify sentence structure—keep subject and predicate as close as possible, and keep modifiers close to the terms they modify.
8. Clarify awkward references.

00:04 **Edit for conciseness**

1. Delete unnecessary words and phrases.
2. Replace long words and phrases.
3. Eliminate redundancies.
4. Consider recasting "It is/There are" starters.

00:05 **Proofread for quality**

1. Look for undetected mistakes from the writing, design, and layout stages.
2. Look for mistakes that crept in during production.

Crafting Brief Business Messages

Most of your communication on the job will be through brief messages, from Twitter updates and blog posts to formal letters. Learning how to write these messages effectively is key to maintaining productive working relationships with colleagues and customers. Start by adapting what you already know about digital media to the professional challenges of business communication. Then learn specific techniques for crafting routine, positive, negative, and persuasive messages.

Liderina/Shutterstock

8

Crafting Messages for Digital Channels

LEARNING OBJECTIVES

After studying this chapter, you will be able to

1 Identify the major digital channels used for brief business messages, and describe the nine compositional modes needed for digital media.

2 Describe how companies use social networking platforms, and explain how to write effective content for these channels.

3 Explain how to adapt the three-step writing process to email messages, and describe the importance of email subject lines.

4 Identify the major types of business messaging, and list guidelines for effective messaging in the workplace.

5 Describe the uses of blogging in business communication, and briefly explain how to adapt the three-step process to blogging.

6 Describe the uses of Twitter and other microblogging systems in business communication, and offer tips on writing effective tweets.

7 Outline the process of producing business podcasts.

MyLab Business Communication
Improve Your Grade!

If your instructor is using MyLab Business Communication, visit **www.pearson.com/mylab/business-communication** for videos, simulations, and writing exercises.

Connecting Work Teams and Conquering the Email Monster

If there's a business award for accidental success, Stewart Butterfield would surely be a leading contender for it. He has the unusual distinction of being the cofounder of two separate video game companies that didn't succeed at their original missions but wound up spinning off secondary software features that became massive business successes on their own.

The first turned into the photo-sharing web service Flickr, which was once just a feature inside an online role-playing game. After selling Flickr to Yahoo! for a tidy sum, Butterfield cofounded a second video game company. Again, the game business didn't work out, but he and his partners commercialized an instant messaging function the company had developed for internal use. That capability was expanded and became the Slack workgroup messaging system, which is leading an upheaval in the world of business communication.

Slack offers several communication and information-management tools, but at its heart it is a group messaging system. Teams can set up a variety of channels to manage communication on specific topics, and individuals can configure alerts to make sure they get the messages they need without being flooded with messages they don't, as often happens with email. (Users can set up private, invitation-only channels for confidential topics.) Two companies can also set up shared channels

Slack cofounder and CEO Stewart Butterfield guides the development of a workplace messaging system that tens of thousands of companies are using to improve team communication.

so that employees who work closely with external business partners join each other's conversations.

All communication is automatically archived, so it's easy for everyone on a team to find information. A key feature of Slack is transparency, in that most communication threads are no longer buried in email exchanges but are out in the open for everyone on a team to see and share.

To understand the appeal of Slack, one needs to understand the love/hate relationship many business professionals have with email. Email is so ubiquitous that it's easy to forget what a revolutionary and disruptive medium it once was. In a world where internal memos could take hours to deliver and external letters could take days, nearly instantaneous email changed business communication forever, and it remains a vital communication tool.

However, email has long suffered from a serious case of too-much-of-a-good-thing. Many professionals complain of drowning in a flood of email, with some getting dozens or hundreds of messages a day—even as they miss vital information when colleagues neglect to include them in message threads. Moreover, email is poorly suited to some of the tasks people use it for, such as project management, collaboration, information management, and other processes that require group communication and shared information access.

A variety of technologies that aim to overcome the disadvantages of email have recently entered the market, from basic instant messaging to full-featured collaboration systems. But few have caught on as quickly as Slack, which claimed the title of fastest-growing business software in history soon after its launch. The service now has millions of active users.

For many business communicators, Slack is clearly filling an unmet need. A majority of customers report greater productivity, more transparency, improved team culture, easier access to information, and a reduced need for meetings. On average, users say it has cut email use in their organizations almost in half, and many say it has nearly eliminated email entirely. Some describe it as being more than a mere communication tool and in fact see it as a radical way to transform how they work.

Of course, like any tool, Slack and other messaging systems are vulnerable to misuse. Channels can fill up with gossip and personal chatter, and people can subscribe to channels they don't really need to follow. Constant message alerts can be a distraction if users configure their accounts to be notified every time a new message is posted. These potential downsides are common to most digital media, though, and it's up to individuals to use their tools wisely. To help users focus on the most important messages, Slack applies artificial intelligence techniques to suggest which waiting messages will be most valuable to them.

By enabling communication and collaboration in ways that support how today's professionals want and need to work, Slack and other corporate messaging systems might finally be taming the dreaded email monster.[1]

WWW.SLACK.COM

Digital Channels for Business Communication

1 **LEARNING OBJECTIVE** Identify the major digital channels used for brief business messages, and describe the nine compositional modes needed for digital media.

The emergence of Slack (see the chapter-opening On the Job) and other workgroup messaging systems illustrates the continuous evolution that is part of digital communication. If a new approach promises to help businesses communicate more effectively or efficiently than existing tools, many companies are willing to give it a try. Similarly, companies are often quick to adopt consumer-oriented systems such as Facebook and Pinterest that gain a sizable following. These systems often add business-friendly features and become mainstream business communication channels.

This chapter explores the digital channels that businesses use most often for brief messages, from one or two sentences up to several pages long.

CHANNEL OPTIONS FOR BRIEF MESSAGES

Professionals have a wide range of digital channel choices—so many, in fact, that choosing the right channel for a particular message has become a skill in itself. Here are the options you'll have available (video, another popular choice for shorter messages, is covered in Chapter 13):

- Social networks and content-sharing sites that have a strong social component
- Email
- Business messaging, which includes a variety of phone- and computer-based systems
- Blogging
- Microblogging, primarily Twitter
- Podcasting

The range of options for short business messages continues to grow with innovations in digital and social media.

As this list suggests, businesses use many of the same tools you use for personal communication, so you will likely be familiar with the basic concepts. However, you will need to adapt to business expectations regarding writing style, privacy, and network security.

COMPOSITIONAL MODES FOR DIGITAL MEDIA

Communicating successfully through digital media requires a wide range of writing approaches.

As you practice using digital media in this course, focus on the principles of social media communication and the fundamentals of planning, writing, and completing messages, rather than on the specific details of any one medium or system.[2] Fortunately, the basic communication skills required usually transfer from one system to another. You can succeed with written communication in virtually all digital media by using one of nine *compositional modes*:

- **Conversations.** Although they take place via writing, some forms of digital communication function more like real-time conversations than the sharing of written documents. Much of Chapter 2's advice on conversations apply to these exchanges, and the section on business messaging (see page 233) explores this important and ever-expanding communication format.

Comments and critiques can be a valuable way to contribute to social conversations.

- **Comments and critiques.** One of the most powerful aspects of social media is the opportunity for interested parties to express opinions and provide feedback, whether it's leaving comments on a blog post or reviewing products on an e-commerce site. Sharing helpful tips and insightful commentary is also a great way to build your personal brand. To be an effective commenter, focus on short chunks of information that a broad spectrum of other site visitors will find helpful. And even if you are offering criticism, keep it constructive. Angry rants and insults won't help anyone, and they brand you as unprofessional.

Orientations don't give away the key points in the collection of information but rather tell readers where to find those points.

- **Orientations.** The ability to help people find their way through an unfamiliar system or subject is a valuable writing skill and a talent that readers greatly appreciate. Unlike summaries (see next item), orientations don't give away the key points in the collection of information, but rather tell readers where to find those points. Writing effective orientations can be a delicate balancing act because you need to know the material well enough to guide others through it while being able to step back and view it from the inexperienced perspective of a "newbie."

- **Summaries.** At the beginning of an article or webpage, a summary functions as a miniature version of the material, giving readers all the key points while skipping over details (see Figure 8.1). At the end of an article or webpage, a summary functions as a review, reminding readers of the key points they've just read.

- **Reference materials.** One of the greatest benefits of the internet is the access it can provide to vast quantities of reference materials—numerical or textual information that people typically don't read in a linear way but rather search through to find particular data points, trends, or other details. One of the challenges of writing reference material is that you can't always know how readers will want to access it. Making the information accessible via search engines is an important step. However, readers don't always know which search terms will yield the best

results, so include an orientation and organize the material in logical ways, with clear headings that help people who want to browse through it.

- **Narratives.** The storytelling techniques covered in Chapter 5 (see page 145) can be effective in a wide variety of situations, from company histories to product reviews and demonstrations. Narratives work best when they have an intriguing beginning that piques readers' curiosity, a middle section that moves quickly through the challenges that an individual or company faced, and an inspiring or instructive ending that gives readers information they can apply in their own lives and jobs.

With Twitter and other super-short messaging systems, the ability to write a compelling teaser is a valuable skill.

- **Teasers.** Teasers intentionally withhold key pieces of information as a way to pull readers or listeners into a story or another document. Teasers are widely used in marketing

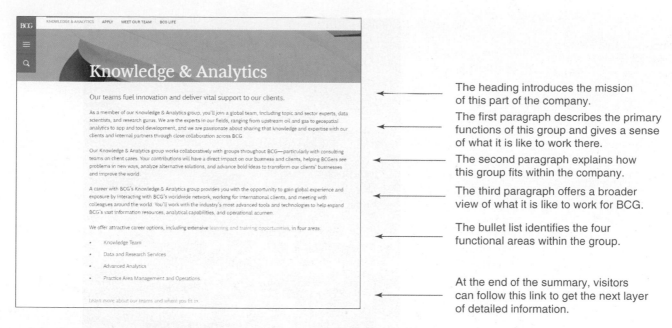

The heading introduces the mission of this part of the company.

The first paragraph describes the primary functions of this group and gives a sense of what it is like to work there.

The second paragraph explains how this group fits within the company.

The third paragraph offers a broader view of what it is like to work for BCG.

The bullet list identifies the four functional areas within the group.

At the end of the summary, visitors can follow this link to get the next layer of detailed information.

Figure 8.1 Compositional Modes: Summaries
This page from the careers section of the Boston Consulting Group (BCG) website is a good example of writing a summary. The three paragraphs and the bullet list combine to give potential employees a clear idea of what working in this part of the company is like; then candidates who want more information can follow the links to get more details.

and sales messages, such as a short headline on the outside of an envelope that promises important information on the inside. In digital media, the space limitations and URL linking capabilities of Twitter and other microblogging systems make them a natural tool for the teaser approach. Be sure that the *payoff*, the information a teaser links to, is valuable and legitimate. You'll quickly lose credibility if readers think they are being tricked into clicking through to information they don't really want. (*Tweetables* are Twitter-ready bites of information extracted from a blog post or other messages. They often serve as teasers, although a series of them can make an effective summary as well.)

- **Status updates and announcements.** Depending on the nature of the business you're in, status updates and announcements can be a great way to keep your followers up to date and to promote yourself or your company and its products. For example, if you become an industry expert in a particular field, you can announce your upcoming speaking engagements on social media. However, be mindful of pushing too hard with self-promotion. Fans and product enthusiasts are naturally curious about what you're up to, but if your social channels begin to sound like 24-hour advertising, you might lose followers.

- **Tutorials and FAQs.** Given the community nature of social media, the purpose of many messages is to share how-to advice, from in-depth tutorials to answers to *frequently asked questions (FAQs)*, a common feature on websites (see Figure 8.2 on the next page). Well-written tutorials and FAQs can increase customer satisfaction and reduce customer support costs, so mastering them is a valuable skill to develop. Becoming known as a reliable expert is also a great way to build customer loyalty for your company while enhancing your own personal brand.

Writing tutorials and answering frequently asked questions (FAQs) is a great way to assist stakeholders and build your reputation as an expert.

THE EMOJI QUESTION—OVERCOMING THE LIMITATIONS OF LEAN MEDIA

You know this situation well: You're about to send a message via email or some form of text-based communication, but you're worried that the right tone won't come across. What if you're trying to be humorously sarcastic, but the recipient thinks you're being serious? Or what if you are trying to be friendly and sympathetic, but the words come across as cold and uncaring?

Figure 8.2   Compositional Modes: Tutorials and FAQs
Tutorials and frequently asked questions (FAQs) are common writing requirements in digital channels. Razer®, a maker of high-performance computers, keyboards, and other products for gamers, offers concise answers to a variety of questions on this product support page, along with links to more extensive information where applicable.

A trademark of Razer Inc. Used under license.

Expressing emotion and nuance without nonverbal cues is a challenge with many forms of digital media.

If you were communicating in person or on the phone, you could modulate the emotional tone of your message with various nonverbal cues, such as smiling, accenting certain words or syllables, shrugging your shoulders, and so on. However, when you are communicating in writing via email, text messaging, or any other lean medium (see page 140 for a refresher on the four dimensions of media richness), you don't have the luxury of these nonverbal cues—the words on screen have to convey everything.

The Rise of Emojis

Emoticons (text-based symbols) and emojis (graphical symbols) help writers overcome the limitations of lean digital media.

This limitation gave rise to the use of emoticons and emojis to convey emotional tone in a way that can be difficult to do with words. (Opinions vary on the exact difference between the two, but for simplicity's sake, you can think of *emoticons* as symbols made up of text characters, such as :-), and *emojis* as graphical icons such as ☺.) Using emoticons and emojis can be an effective way to minimize the limitations of a lean medium, which is why so many people now use them for personal and business communication. A smiley face can inject a touch of levity into a tense situation, a frowny face can convey sympathy for someone who has suffered a setback, and clapping hands can say "job well done!"

To Emoji or Not: Two Dilemmas

Emoticons and emojis present two dilemmas for business communicators: Their use is seen as unprofessional by some people, and their meanings can be misinterpreted.

As useful as these visual gadgets can be, however, they do present two dilemmas for business communicators. First, even though an increasing number of businesspeople are comfortable with emoticons and emojis for business communication, and they are built into many professional communication systems (including Slack), some professionals view them as inappropriate for all but the most casual communication between close colleagues.[3]

Second, emoticons and emojis can cause problems of their own when people don't agree on what they mean. If you get a message that says, "Why don't you and I get away from this stress-fest and brainstorm some solutions over coffee" and ends with a "winkie" emoticon or emoji, what does that digital wink mean? Is the person flirting with you or just innocently suggesting that the two of you could think more clearly if you got out of the hectic office for a while? The meanings of emoticons and emojis are so problematic that they are becoming important factors in legal trials regarding workplace harassment and other issues, and serious criminal cases can hinge on their interpretation.[4]

Using Emoticons and Emojis Effectively

Given the fluid state of emoticon and emoji acceptance in business communication, there are few hard and fast rules. However, follow these tips to make the best use of them while avoiding trouble:

- As in every aspect of business communication, know your audience and the situation. Study the tone of communication in your organization before deciding when and how to use emojis.
- Don't overuse emoticons or emojis. A message filled with symbols will look unprofessional, even in an organization that uses emojis regularly.
- Follow the lead of the person with greater positional power. For example, if an upper manager doesn't use emojis, don't use them when communicating back.
- Bear in mind that the use of emojis itself sends a message. If you are a new manager and your staff seems unsure how to behave around you, or you've been leading people through a tense experience, using emojis can send a signal that it's okay to relax and be themselves.[5]
- Avoid emoticons or emojis in communication with external audiences unless you have an established working relationship with a customer or other party.
- Never use emoticons or emojis in the most formal communication, including business plans, sales proposals, and contracts.
- To avoid misunderstandings about what emojis mean, stick to symbols that are in common use in your organization.
- Avoid crude or animated emojis.

Know your audience before using emoticons and emojis.

Avoid emoticons and emojis when communicating with customers (unless you have a working relationship already) and in all formal communication.

Social Networking Platforms

Social networks (such as Facebook and LinkedIn) and content-sharing platforms that have a significant social component (such as YouTube and Pinterest) are a major force in both internal and external business communication.

2 LEARNING OBJECTIVE Describe how companies use social networking platforms, and explain how to write effective content for these channels.

CATEGORIES OF SOCIAL PLATFORMS

The social communication systems that businesses and individual professionals use can be grouped into six categories:

- **Public, general-purpose social networks.** Facebook is the largest and best known of these networks. Companies can use Facebook for marketing and customer communication in a variety of ways, from posting helpful product usage information to addressing complaints and questions.
- **Public, specialized social networks.** In contrast to Facebook's universal approach, some public networks focus on the needs and interests of a specific audience. The most widely known of these is LinkedIn, with its emphasis on career- and sales-related networking.
- **Private social networks.** Many companies use private social networks to help employees stay connected. Facebook's Workplace, for example, uses the same concept as the public version of Facebook but with additional collaboration features aimed at business users.[6]
- **User-generated content websites.** User-generated content (UGC) involves inviting customers or other parties to submit photos, videos, and other content. See "Facilitating User-Generated Content" on page 228 for more information.
- **Content-curation websites.** In many fields of business, so much original content is already available that sometimes the biggest value a communicator can offer audiences is guiding them to the best of what's out there, rather than creating new content. Named after the selection process that museum curators do when they decide which pieces in their collections to display,

Social communication platforms include several types of social networks plus content sharing services with a significant social component.

REAL-TIME UPDATES
LEARN MORE BY LISTENING TO THESE PODCASTS
Get daily tips on using social media in your business
These brief podcasts focus on marketing applications of social media. Go to **real-timeupdates.com/ebc13** and select Learn More in the Students section.

Content curation involves finding and sharing valuable material from other sources.

content curation involves finding and sharing valuable material on social media. See "Curating and Sharing Existing Content" on page 228 for more information.

- **Community Q&A websites.** Community Q&A sites, where people answer questions posted by other visitors, are a contemporary twist on the early ethos of computer networking, which was people helping each other. Community Q&A sites include dedicated customer support communities such as those hosted on Get Satisfaction and public sites such as Quora. See "Responding to Existing Content and Questions" on page 228 for more information.

BUSINESS COMMUNICATION USES OF SOCIAL PLATFORMS

With their ability to help people share information and forge mutually beneficial relationships, social networks and other social platforms are a great fit for many business communication needs. Table 8.1 lists some of the key applications of social networks for internal and external business communication, categorized by the three essential aspects of communication discussed in Chapter 1.

"Business Communicators Innovating with Social Media" on pages 226–227 offers a variety of examples of how companies are using social media to foster better communication among their stakeholder communities.

TABLE 8.1   Common Business Uses of Social Networking

Operations	Intelligence	Relationships
Fostering collaboration. Networks can help identify the best people to collaborate on projects and find pockets of knowledge and expertise within the organization.	**Understanding target markets.** Many companies monitor and analyze social media traffic to pick up on consumer trends, complaints, rumors, and other bits of environmental intelligence.	**Onboarding new employees.** Internal networks can help new employees navigate their way through the organization and find experts, mentors, and other important contacts.
Recruiting employees and business partners. Companies use social networks to find potential employees, short-term contractors, subject-matter experts, product and service suppliers, and business partners. A key advantage here is that these introductions are often made via trusted connections in a professional network.	**Monitoring company and brand reputations.** Tools for *sentiment analysis* and *reputation analysis* assess the reputations of companies and individuals, measure the emotional quality of online conversations, and identify outrage "hot spots" on social media.	**Integrating company workforces.** Internal social networks can help companies grow closer, including encouraging workforces to "gel" after reorganizations or mergers and overcoming structural barriers in communication channels.
Supporting customers. *Social customer service* involves using social media to give customers a more convenient way to get help from the company and to help each other.	**Identifying opinion influencers.** Social media influencers can sway public opinion, so companies try to identify opinion leaders in their markets.	**Accelerating team development.** Networks can help members get to know one another, identify individual areas of expertise, and share resources.
Extending the organization. Social networking is also fueling the growth of *networked organizations*, sometimes known as *virtual organizations*, where companies supplement the talents of their employees with services from one or more external partners, such as a design lab, a manufacturing firm, or a sales and distribution company.	**Supplementing the formal communication network.** Internal social networks can bypass the formal communication system to collect and distribute information in a more timely fashion.	**Extending professional networking.** Social media can give seminar and conference participants a way to meet before an event and to maintain relationships afterward.
Communicating during a crisis. When companies need to communicate with broad audiences in a hurry, social media are ideal channels.	**Finding sales prospects.** Salespeople on networks such as LinkedIn can use their connections to identify potential buyers and ask for introductions through those shared connections. Sales networking can reduce *cold calling*, contacting potential customers without a prior introduction.	**Building communities.** Social networks can bring together *communities of practice*, people who engage in similar work, and *communities of interest* (sometimes called *brand communities*), people who share enthusiasm for a particular product or activity.

Sources: Based in part on Lexalytics website, accessed 7 January 2018, www.lexalytics.com; Evolve24 website, accessed 7 January 2018, www.evolve24.com; Matt Charney, "How to Use Social Media for Employee Onboarding," *Recruiting Daily*, 27 April 2015, recruitingdaily.com; Shep Hyken, "Social Customer Care Is the New Marketing," *Forbes*, 22 April 2017, www.forbes.com.

COMMUNICATION STRATEGIES FOR BUSINESS SOCIAL NETWORKING

One of the most appealing aspects of social media for both internal and external communication is the range of options you have for connecting with your communities and for creating and sharing content:

- Developing and sharing original content
- Responding to existing content and questions
- Curating and sharing existing content
- Facilitating user-generated content

You have multiple options when it comes to content on social networking.

The following sections offer advice on each of these communication strategies. For all formats of social media communication, keep the following writing points in mind:

- **Be mindful of your tone.** As Chapter 6 points out, your tone is the effect you create through the choices you make as a writer. You can convey the same information in a tone that is assertive or mild, upbeat or negative, friendly or distant—all based on your word choices and sentence style. Don't let the informal vibe of social media tempt you into being careless or crude, and don't let emotions get the better of you. Remember that even though it's "social," it's still business communication.
- **Be mindful of your company and personal branding.** Similarly, keep in mind that all your communication efforts build your brand, so make sure you build it intentionally and coherently.
- **Restrict promotional efforts to the right time and right place.** One of the best aspects of social media is the feeling of conversation, of people talking *with* one another instead of one person talking *at* everyone else. Efforts to inject blatant "salespeak" into social networking conversations may not be welcomed by the audience. See "Writing Promotional Messages for Social Media" in Chapter 11 (page 338) for more tips on writing messages for social networks and other social media.

Don't let the informal vibe of social media tempt you into being careless or crude.

Developing Original Content

For business social networking, much of the value you can provide will come from original insights and information you can offer to your connections. Follow these tips to create content that your readers will look forward to seeing.

Support the Ways Your Readers Want to Consume Information   One of the reasons for the explosion of digital, social, and mobile media options in recent years is that no single approach works best for all readers. Some are comfortable reading long articles and documents, whereas others prefer brief summaries, videos, podcasts, or other formats. Many people engage in "content snacking," consuming small pieces of information, often from multiple sources in rapid succession, and bypassing larger documents that might require more than a few minutes or even a few seconds to read.[7]

No single format works best for all readers, so you may need to offer content in multiple formats and media types.

To reach all your target readers, you might need to change how you organize and distribute messages. For instance, rather than writing a single, long report on a complicated topic, you might want to write a teaser on Twitter that links through to an orientation or summary on your blog, which then offers a download of the full report or links to reference information on a website.

Provide Information That Your Connections Are Likely to Share   One of the biggest benefits of social media is the "message boost" you can get from having the people who follow you share your content with the people who follow them. Particularly on public networks, when you're choosing what to post, emphasize material that your followers will think is valuable enough to pass along.[8]

Try to provide content that your followers will want to share with their followers.

Write Informally but Not Carelessly   Write as a human being with a unique, personal voice. However, don't take this as a license to get sloppy; no one wants to slog through misspelled words and half-baked sentences to find your message.

Business Communicators Innovating with Social Media

Companies in virtually every industry use social media and continue to experiment with new ways to connect with customers and other stakeholders. From offering helpful tips on using products to helping customers meet each other, these companies show the enormous range of possibilities that new media continue to bring to business communication.

Crowdsourcing and collaboration platforms invite input from groups of people inside or outside the organization and can give companies access to a much wider range of ideas, solutions to problems, and insights into market trends.

Community Q&A sites let customers, product enthusiasts, and other groups help one another by answering questions and posting advice. Many companies now rely heavily on communities of customers to help each other with product questions and other routine matters.

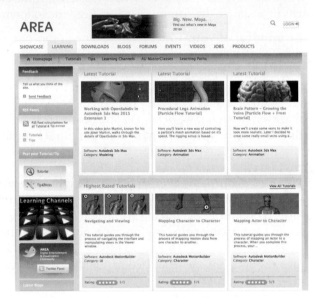

User-generated content (UGC) sites and campaigns are a great way to foster a sense of community among customers and enthusiasts. UGC can be hosted permanently on websites such as YouTube or Flickr or generated as part of a one-time program, such as this Twitter campaign by the yogurt company Chobani.

Social video, often organized in branded channels, has become particularly important in customer communication, but businesses also use it for employee recruiting, technical support, training, community outreach, and other purposes. As social networking continues to expand, much of the content shared through online communities is shifting from text-dominant messages to video.

Enterprise social networks are closed digital communities that connect employees within a company (and in some cases, selected external business partners). They often include a variety of communication and collaboration tools as well, including workgroup messaging, online meeting functions, and access to work files and other shared resources.

If you are an active user of social media, you will probably find it easy to adapt to these enterprise networking platforms. However, be prepared for stricter standards of privacy and information security, including restrictions on the types of information that can be shared.

Content curation, selecting videos and other items of interest to followers of a website or blog, has become one of the most popular ways to connect with stakeholders. Pinterest and Scoop.it are among the leading platforms in this area.

Social media recruiting specialists take advantage of social platforms to post job openings, share news about their companies, and conduct background research on candidates.

Community engagement activities such as surveys, contests, and discussion-starter questions can be a great use of Facebook and other social media services.

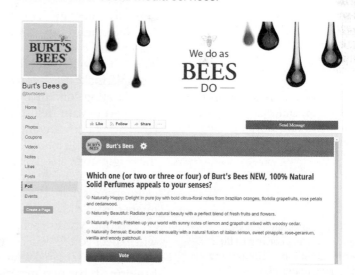

Avoid the temptation to engage in clever wordplay with social media headlines; give readers a clear idea of what you have to offer.

Write Concise, Specific, and Informative Headlines   In an environment of content snacking and information overload, headlines are extremely important in social media. You need to grab readers quickly with the promise that you have something of value to offer.

Avoid the temptation to engage in clever wordplay when writing headlines and teasers. This advice applies to all forms of business communication, of course, but it is essential for social media. Readers don't want to spend time figuring out what your witty headlines mean. Search engines won't know what they mean either, so fewer people will find your content. Headline space is precious real estate, so focus these words on the tangible benefits that each post offers your readers.[9]

A momentary lapse of concentration or judgment while using social media can cause tremendous damage to your career.

Think Before You Post   Careless decisions on social media can have damaging consequences to companies, careers, relationships, and reputations. Remember that you share the responsibility of keeping your company's and your customers' data private and secure. Assume that every message you send in any digital medium will be stored forever and might be read by people far beyond your original audience. Ask yourself two questions: "Would I say this to my audience face to face?" and "Am I comfortable with this message becoming a permanent part of my personal and professional communication history?"

Responding to Existing Content and Questions

A key aspect of social communication is responding to content that others post, so look for ways to keep conversations alive with helpful commentary.

Responding to questions can be a great way to encourage conversations, build your personal brand, demonstrate your company's commitment to customer service, and clear up confusion or misinformation about your company and its products.

Keep in mind that when you respond to an individual query, whether on your own pages or on a community Q&A site, you are also "responding in advance" to every person who comes to the site with the same question in the future. In other words, you are writing a type of reference material in addition to corresponding with the original questioner, so keep the long time frame and wider audience in mind.

Curating and Sharing Existing Content

At its simplest, content curation can involve sharing links to useful articles or videos via your social media accounts. Companies can also set up dedicated websites that publish links to original content in a variety of topic categories. The authors' Business Communication Headline News (**bchn.businesscommunicationnetwork.com**), for instance, is one of the earliest examples of content curation in the field of business communication. As an alternative, several web services offer ready-made content curation solutions. Pinterest and Scoop.it!, for example, make it easy to assemble attractive online portfolios or magazines on specific topics.

To ensure ethical content curation, never copy entire pieces to your site and always provide proper attribution.

Curating content for a target audience can be a great way to add value and stand out as an expert in your field, but content curators need to be aware of two key ethical concerns. First, never copy anyone else's posts to your site, even if you properly attribute the source. Instead, provide a link from your site back to the original so that you drive web traffic to the originator's site. It is acceptable to copy a brief introductory segment, such as the first paragraph, to your site to give the link some context. Scoop.it handles this for you automatically, ensures that proper attribution is posted on your site, and downsizes photos and other images from the original so they don't display at full resolution on your site.[10]

When you curate content, audiences expect you to do a competent job of finding and filtering material.

Second, you are promoting yourself as an expert when you curate content, and people will expect you to do a competent job of finding and filtering materials. As with any communication task, make sure you understand the needs of your target audience so that you can provide the best material to meet their needs.[11]

Facilitating User-Generated Content

User-generated content sites and campaigns give companies the opportunity to engage customers and enthusiasts and to deliver more content without creating it all themselves.

As with other social media, the keys to effective UGC are making it valuable and making it easy. First, encourage content that people will want to see and share with colleagues, such as tips from experienced customers on various ways to use a product.

Second, make material easy to find, consume, and share. For example, a *branded channel* on YouTube lets a company organize all its videos in one place, making it easy for visitors to browse the selection or subscribe to get automatic updates of future videos. YouTube lets fans share videos through email or their accounts on Twitter, Facebook, and other platforms.

Email

Email has been an important business communication tool for several decades, and in the beginning it offered a huge advantage in speed and efficiency over the media it usually replaced (printed and faxed messages). Over the years, email began to be used for many communication tasks simply because it was the only widely available digital format for written messages and millions of users were comfortable with it. For example, email is not usually the best choice for conversational communication (messaging systems such as Slack are usually better) or project management discussions and updates (blogs, wikis, and various purpose-built systems are often preferable).

In addition to the widespread availability of better alternatives for many communication purposes, the indiscriminate use of email has lowered its appeal in the eyes of many professionals. In a sense, email is too easy to use—with a couple of clicks you can send low-value messages to multiple recipients or trigger long message chains that become difficult to follow as people chime in along the way. As the Slack vignette at the beginning of the chapter suggests, these frustrations are compelling many companies to look for alternatives.

Email also suffers from problems with *spam* (unsolicited bulk email) and security risks such as *phishing* (fraudulent messages that prompt unwary users to divulge sensitive information or grant access to protected networks). Spam accounts for roughly half of all email volume and requires great effort to keep it from flooding users' inboxes.[12] Most systems use spam and threat filters, but these filters are never 100 percent accurate and can also reject messages that are legitimate.

Even with these drawbacks, email still has compelling advantages that will keep it in steady use for years to come. First, email is universal. Anybody with an email address can reach anybody else with an email address, no matter which systems the senders and receivers are on. Second, email is often still the best medium for private, short- to medium-length messages, particularly when the exchange is limited to a small number of people.

> **3 LEARNING OBJECTIVE**
> Explain how to adapt the three-step writing process to email messages, and describe the importance of email subject lines.

Email remains a primary format for companies, but better alternatives now exist for many types of communication.

Overuse is one of the biggest complaints about email.

Develop Professional-Grade Email Skills

Writing effective, professional-quality email messages is an essential business skill, and you have a great opportunity right now to practice that skill whenever you use email to communicate with your instructors.

- **Choosing when to use email.** First, make sure email is the best channel for each message. In some situations, a phone call, an office visit, or a message sent through your course management system could be a better choice. Second, consider the timing of your message. Writing for help on an assignment at 11:00 the night before it is due is not optimal timing.
- **Writing compelling subject lines.** Review the advice on pages 231–232 to craft subject lines that are meaningful and compelling.
- **Greeting.** Address your instructor using the title and name format he or she has requested you to, using "Hi," "Hello," or "Dear." If your instructor hasn't given you guidance, use your best judgment. When in doubt, start out formally, with the appropriate title (Ms., Mr., Dr., or Professor) and his or her last name, then let your instructor adjust the formality of the exchange and any future communication.

- **Tone.** Be mindful of the tone you are creating through the writing choices you make. For instance, could your messages come across as whiny or demanding, even though you don't intend them to? The right tone can help you achieve whatever goals you have in sending a message.
- **Writing quality.** Write in complete sentences, use standard capitalization, and follow the accepted rules of grammar. Use texting acronyms, emojis, and exclamation points sparingly.

You might feel self-conscious writing in this style at the beginning, but remember that you are practicing a professional skill and showing respect for your instructor, so it's a win-win.

COACH YOURSELF

1. Review several email or text messages you've sent recently (any type of messages on any system). How does their tone feel to you now? Would you change anything about the messages? Why or why not?
2. If you believe you have received an unfair grade on an assignment or a test, what steps could you take to request an adjustment without sounding demanding or unpleasant?

PLANNING EMAIL MESSAGES

Do your part to stem the flood of email by making sure you don't send unnecessary messages or cc people who don't need to see particular messages.

The solution to email overload starts in the planning step by making sure every message has a useful, business-related purpose. Also, be aware that many companies now have formal email policies that specify how employees can use email, including restrictions against using company email service for personal messages, sending confidential information, or sending objectionable material. In addition, many employers now monitor email for sensitive content. Regardless of formal policies, though, every email user has a responsibility to avoid actions that could cause trouble.

Check out the "Five-Minute Guide to Better Business Email" at the end of the chapter.

Even with fairly short messages, spend a moment or two on the planning tasks described in Chapter 5: analyzing the situation, gathering necessary information for your readers, and organizing your message. You'll save time in the long run because you will craft a more effective message on the first attempt. Your readers will get the information they need and won't have to generate follow-up messages asking for clarification or additional information.

WRITING EMAIL CONTENT

Business email messages are more formal than the email messages you send to family and friends.

When you approach email writing on the job, recognize that business email is a more formal medium than you are probably accustomed to with email for personal communication (see Figure 8.3). The expectations of writing quality for business email are higher than for personal email, and the consequences of bad writing or poor judgment can be much more serious. Email messages and other digital documents can be used as evidence in lawsuits

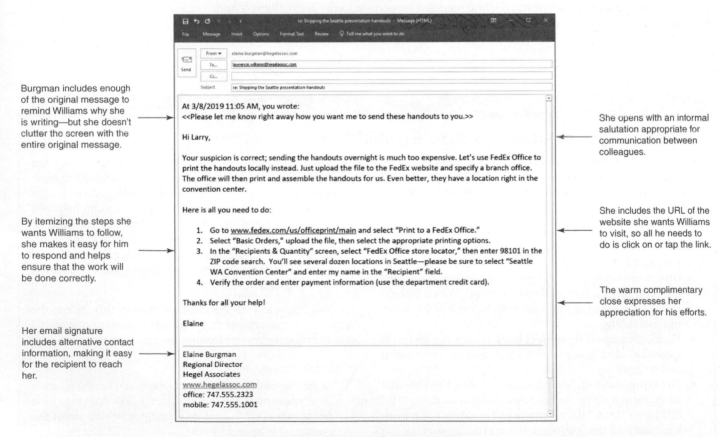

Burgman includes enough of the original message to remind Williams why she is writing—but she doesn't clutter the screen with the entire original message.

By itemizing the steps she wants Williams to follow, she makes it easy for him to respond and helps ensure that the work will be done correctly.

Her email signature includes alternative contact information, making it easy for the recipient to reach her.

She opens with an informal salutation appropriate for communication between colleagues.

She includes the URL of the website she wants Williams to visit, so all he needs to do is click on or tap the link.

The warm complimentary close expresses her appreciation for his efforts.

Figure 8.3   Email for Business Communication
In this response to an email query from a colleague, Elaine Burgman takes advantage of her email system's features to create an efficient and effective message.

and criminal investigations, and deleting a message is no guarantee that it can't be recovered by a forensic specialist.[13]

Make your message content easy to skim and easy to read by using short paragraphs, which is particularly helpful for readers on mobile devices with small screens. Use bulleted or numbered lists to break out items, steps, or other groups of elements.

THE EMAIL SUBJECT LINE: PERSUADING PEOPLE TO OPEN YOUR MESSAGES

The email subject line might seem like a small detail, but it is one of the most important parts of an email message because recipients use it to choose which messages to read and when to read them. Many businesspeople receive dozens or hundreds of email messages a day, and subject lines help them decide where to focus their attention. In addition, the subject line often serves as a "browsing label" when people scan their inboxes to find a message they've already read but need to find again.

> The subject line is a critical part of every email message because it often determines whether recipients will pay attention to the message.

The optimum wording for a subject line depends on the message, the situation, your relationship with the recipient(s), and whether you are using the direct or indirect approach in the message. For routine, direct messages among close colleagues or subordinates who are likely to read all your messages, a straightforward description of the message's content is often sufficient. However, if there is a chance that recipients might ignore your message or delay opening it, the subject line requires some creative thought. (Note that the subject lines for marketing and sales messages are a special case that need to function as advertising headlines. Crafting these subject lines is often the responsibility of experienced copywriters.)

> For routine, expected email messages to colleagues, a clear description of the message subject is usually adequate.

> If your message might get ignored, you need to get more creative with the subject line.

To write a compelling headline when you need to persuade people to open the message, put yourself in the recipient's shoes. How can you relate the content of your message to this person's immediate needs and interests, and how can you catch his or her attention in just a few seconds?

> Compelling subject lines connect the content of the message to the recipient's wants and needs.

Start by identifying issues that are important to the recipient and how he or she is likely to feel about them. What can you do to add positives and remove negatives? For example, someone working in sales wants to close as many deals as possible as quickly as possible, so anything you can offer that relates to that desire could make good material for a subject line. Similarly, a department manager cares about such things as hitting budgets, keeping employees motivated, and avoiding expensive mistakes. If your message relates to any of those goals, use that in the subject line. Whenever you can, give recipients a "selfish" reason to open your message by conveying that it relates to them and their needs.

Next, if a response is needed by a specific date, indicate that in the subject line (such as "Marketing plan draft for your review; please respond by 12/14"). Conversely, if a message doesn't require immediate action, recipients will appreciate knowing this so they can focus on other messages. If you are forwarding information that someone wants to have on file but doesn't need to attend to right now, for instance, you can add "(no action needed)" to the subject line.

Finally, look for ways to add intrigue to your subject lines, when appropriate. For example, "July sales results" may accurately describe the content of a message, but "July sales results: good news and bad news" is more intriguing. Readers will want to know why some news is good and some is bad.

> When appropriate, look for ways to add intrigue to your subject lines to arouse curiosity.

For every message, keep these general tips in mind for effective subject lines:

- Make sure you clearly convey the subject of the message. Vague subjects such as "Interesting idea" or "Update" don't give the reader much motivation to open a message.
- Shorter is better. Assume that recipients will see your messages on mobile devices, which can display fewer characters than full-size screens. Limit your subject lines to around 50 characters, or at least make sure that key words and phrases appear in the first 50 characters.[14]

> Keep subject lines short so they display well on mobile devices.

- In addition to the subject line, the inbox listing in many email systems and mobile email apps displays the first line or two of the message content. You can use the first few words of the message body to continue or expand on the subject line. Alternatively, if you are replying to a message, you can include the opening line of the original message to remind the recipient which message you are replying to.
- Revise the subject line if an ongoing thread has modified the focus of the conversation and to distinguish newer messages from older messages with the same subject.

COMPLETING EMAIL MESSAGES

An *email signature* is a small text or graphical file at the end of messages that automatically includes such items as your full name, title, company, and contact information.

Particularly for important messages, taking a few moments to revise and proofread might save you hours of headaches and damage control. Also, favor simplicity when it comes to producing your email messages. A clean, easily readable font, in black on a white background, is sufficient for nearly all email messages. Take advantage of your email system's ability to include an **email signature**, a small file at the end of your messages that automatically includes such items as your full name, title, company, and contact information.

Think twice before hitting Send. A simple mistake in your content or distribution can cause major headaches.

When you're ready to distribute your message, pause to verify what you're doing before you hit Send. Make sure you've included everyone necessary—and no one else. If you're replying to a message, don't hit Reply All if you mean to hit only Reply. The difference could be embarrassing or even career threatening. Don't include people in the cc (courtesy copy) or bcc (blind courtesy copy) fields unless you know how these features work. Everyone who receives the message can see who is on the cc line but not who is on the bcc line. Using bcc can be helpful when you want to protect the privacy of some recipients by not allowing others to see their names or email addresses.

Also, don't set the message priority to "high" or "urgent" unless your message is truly urgent. And if you intend to include an attachment, be sure that it is indeed attached.

To review the tips and techniques for successful email, see Table 8.2 and "Checklist: Creating Effective Email Messages" below, or select Chapter 8 at **real-timeupdates.com/ ebc13**.

CHECKLIST ✔ Creating Effective Email Messages

A. Planning email messages
- ✔ Make sure every email message you send is necessary.
- ✔ Don't cc or bcc anyone who doesn't really need to see the message.
- ✔ Follow company email policy; understand the restrictions your company places on email usage.
- ✔ Even with brief email messages, spend a moment to plan what you want to convey and the best way to say it.

B. Writing email messages
- ✔ Remember that business email is more formal than personal email.
- ✔ Recognize that email messages carry the same legal weight as other business documents.
- ✔ Pay attention to the quality of your writing and use correct grammar, spelling, and punctuation.

- ✔ Make your subject lines informative by clearly identifying the purpose of your message.
- ✔ Make your subject lines compelling by wording them in a way that intrigues your audiences.
- ✔ Use the first few words of the email body to catch the reader's attention.

C. Completing email messages
- ✔ Revise and proofread carefully to avoid embarrassing mistakes.
- ✔ Keep the layout of your messages simple and clean, particularly for mobile recipients.
- ✔ Use an email signature file to give recipients your contact information.
- ✔ Double-check your recipient list before sending.
- ✔ Don't mark messages as "urgent" unless they truly are urgent.

TABLE 8.2	**Tips for Effective Email Messages**
Tip	**Why It's Important**
When you request information or action, make it clear what you're asking for, why it's important, and how soon you need it; don't make your reader write back for details.	People will be tempted to ignore your messages if they're not clear about what you want or how soon you want it.
When responding to a request, either paraphrase the request or include enough of the original message to remind the reader what you're replying to.	Some businesspeople get hundreds of email messages a day and may need reminding what your specific response is about.
If possible, avoid sending long, complex messages via email.	Long messages are easier to read as attached reports or web content.
Adjust the level of formality to the message and the audience.	Overly formal messages to colleagues can be perceived as stuffy and distant; overly informal messages to customers or top executives can be perceived as disrespectful.
Activate a signature file, which automatically pastes your contact information into every message you create.	A signature saves you the trouble of retyping vital information and ensures that recipients know how to reach you through other means.
Don't let unread messages pile up in your inbox.	You'll miss important information and create the impression that you're ignoring other people.
Never type in all caps.	ALL CAPS ARE INTERPRETED AS SHOUTING.
Don't overformat your messages with background colors, multicolored type, unusual fonts, and so on.	Such messages can be difficult and annoying to read on screen.
Remember that messages can be forwarded anywhere and saved forever.	Don't let a moment of anger or poor judgment haunt you for the rest of your career.
Use the "return receipt requested" feature only for the most critical messages.	This feature triggers a message back to you whenever someone receives or opens your message; some consider this an invasion of privacy.
Make sure your computer or device has up-to-date virus protection.	One of the worst breaches of netiquette is infecting other devices because you haven't bothered to protect your own system.
Pay attention to grammar, spelling, and capitalization.	Some people don't think email needs formal rules, but careless messages make you look unprofessional and can annoy readers.
Use acronyms sparingly.	Shorthand such as IMHO (in my humble opinion) and LOL (laughing out loud) can be useful in informal correspondence with colleagues, but avoid using them in more formal messages.
Be careful with the use of emoticons and emojis.	Some people view the use of these symbols as unprofessional, so make sure you know your audience.
Assume that recipients may read your messages on small mobile screens.	Email is more difficult to read on small screens, so don't burden recipients with long, complicated messages.

Business Messaging

4 LEARNING OBJECTIVE
Identify the major types of business messaging, and list guidelines for effective messaging in the workplace.

Messaging systems and services such as Slack have become an important business communication channel, partly in response to the limitations of email. Messaging supports conversational communication better than any other digital format, so it's a natural for much of the daily communication that occurs within organizations and between organizations and customers.

CATEGORIES OF BUSINESS MESSAGING

Businesses use a variety of services for brief messages, sometimes as standalone systems and other times as a communication function in a larger collaboration or networking system. Messaging comes in many varieties, and the distinctions between the various types aren't always clear, but you can think of messaging in six categories:

Partly in response to the limitations of email, many companies now use messaging systems for much of their internal communication.

- *Text messaging,* sometimes referred to as *short messaging service* (SMS), is primarily a phone-based service. Relative to other formats, businesses were slower to adopt text messaging as a formal communication channel, in spite of its massive popularity with

---

INTELLIGENT COMMUNICATION TECHNOLOGY

Nice Chatting with You

With advances in natural language processing and the growing use of messaging systems for both consumer and business communication, chatbots and taskbots are now common features in digital communication. Microsoft CEO Satya Nadella goes so far as to say, "Bots are the new apps," suggesting they'll transform technology usage the same way mobile apps have. As bot capability is added to more messaging systems and consumer devices, bots are finally entering the mainstream.

Bots are wildly popular on the Slack workgroup messaging system, for example, where they perform such tasks as monitoring the mood of team conversations, taking polls, scheduling meetings, distributing digital documents, and ordering food. (Craving a taco? Taco Bell's TacoBot is ready to take your order.) On Slack, bots are treated just like human team members in many ways—they can send and receive messages, be assigned tasks, and be invited to join specific groups and communication channels. As bots continue to get better at understanding language, they'll be able to contribute to conversations, such as finding background information that could help solve a problem colleagues are discussing, without anyone asking for their help.

What's Your Take?

1. Have you developed a "personal" relationship with any of the bots in your life, whether it's Amazon's Alexa, Microsoft's Cortana, Apple's Siri, Google Assistant, or any other bot? Do you find yourself conversing with a bot as though it were human? If so, what impact do you think this could have on communication habits as bots become even more common?

2. Research the current state of bot communication to identify one way in which the technology is changing or has the potential to change business communication practices. Do you agree with the predictions the experts make? Why or why not?

Sources: "Bot Users," Slack, accessed 10 January 2018, www.slack.com; "Google Assistant," Google, accessed 10 January 2018, assistant.google.com; Sandi MacPherson, "How to Get Teams Addicted to Your Slack Bot: A Teardown of Howdy," *Medium*, 27 September 2016, medium.com; Kelly Evans, "Chatbots Rise, and the Future May be 'Re-written,'" CNBC, 10 April 2016, www.cnbc.com; Casey Newton, "The Search for the Killer Bot," *The Verge*, 6 January 2016, www.theverge.com; Clint Boulton, "How Messaging Bots Will Change Workplace Productivity," *CIO*, 1 February 2016, www.cio.com.

Messaging systems come in many formats, from phone-based text messaging to workgroup systems.

phone users. However, with new message-management systems that can handle high volumes of text messages, thousands of companies now include texting as a customer support channel.[15]

- *Direct messaging*, also known as *private messaging*, is a way for users on public social media platforms such as Twitter and Facebook to communicate privately, one-to-one.
- *Instant messaging* was historically a computer-based service but is now widely used on internet-capable phones.
- *Chat* on the consumer side usually means group chat in chat rooms, whereas on the business side it is usually one-on-one conversations between customers and sales or support staffers.
- *Enhanced messaging apps*, such as China's WeChat, go well beyond basic messaging capabilities to include shopping, social networking, banking, and more. With roughly one billion people using the service every day, WeChat is a dominant force in Chinese business communication.[16]
- *Workgroup messaging* services such as Slack help teams and other workgroups communicate via short messages but usually include many other functions, such as file sharing, scheduling, and searchable message archives (see Figure 8.4).

The same service can be called different things by different people, so don't get too caught up in the labels. Focus instead on techniques for using messaging quickly and effectively in a style that is appropriate for your company.

TIPS FOR SUCCESSFUL MESSAGING

No matter which types of messaging you use on the job, follow these tips to ensure successful communication:

When messaging with close colleagues, a less formal approach to writing is often acceptable, but be aware of company culture first.

- **Adjust your tone and level of formality to match the situation.** With team members and close colleagues, you can often relax the normal standards of writing if doing so helps you communicate quickly and it isn't out of line with company culture. However, be aware that on a corporate messaging system, your messages will probably be archived

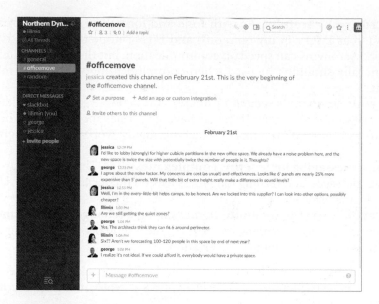

Figure 8.4 Workgroup Messaging

Workgroup messaging systems such as Slack combine the convenience of instant messaging with collaboration tools, archiving, search, and other features. On Slack, people can subscribe to specific channels to join or monitor various conversations, and all the messages are stored for easy review.

and can be accessed and searched by others, so don't write anything you wouldn't want managers or others to see. With customers and other external audiences or colleagues whom you don't know well, maintain a more formal, though still conversational, style (see Figure 8.5). Also, be mindful when messaging people whose native language differs from yours; casual writing can be more difficult for them to grasp quickly.

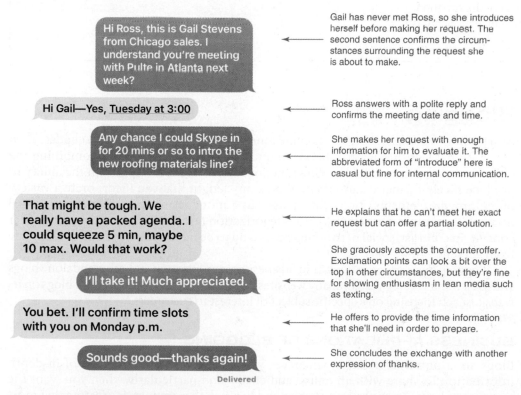

Figure 8.5 Business Text Messaging

Text messaging in a business environment often calls for a slightly more formal approach than you might be used to for personal communication, particularly if you're writing to someone in the company with whom you don't have a close working relationship. The language is more concise and less formal than you might use in other contexts but is still professional.

Messaging acronyms can speed up communication, but they generally shouldn't be used when communicating with senior managers or customers.

- **Use acronyms carefully.** As with tone and formality, adjust your use of acronyms such as IMO ("in my opinion") and HTH ("hope that helps") to match the situation. Acronyms can speed up communication, but they are definitely informal and generally shouldn't be used when communicating with senior managers or customers.
- **Know your company's security policies.** Messaging systems vary widely in terms of network security, and your firm may have strict rules about the types of communication you are allowed to conduct via text messaging, workgroup messaging, or other platforms.
- **Don't use messaging for lengthy, complex messages.** These systems are optimized for short messages, and reading long messages on them can be a chore. Use email or another format instead.
- **Try to avoid carrying on multiple messaging exchanges at one time.** This will minimize the chance of sending messages to the wrong people or making one person wait while you tend to another conversation.

To review the advice for effective messaging in the workplace, see "Checklist: Using Business Messaging Productively" or select Chapter 8 at **real-timeupdates.com/ebc13**.

CHECKLIST ✔ Using Business Messaging Productively

- ✔ Adjust your tone and level of formality to match the situation; you can be casual with close colleagues but not with senior managers or customers.
- ✔ Remember that on corporate messaging systems, your messages will probably be archived and can be accessed and searched by others.
- ✔ As with email, use your judgment of the situation and company culture when deciding whether to use emoticons and emojis.

- ✔ Don't overuse acronyms, and avoid them when a formal tone is called for.
- ✔ Follow your company's security policies regarding the types of communication allowed on messaging systems.
- ✔ Don't use messaging for long, complex messages.

---

5 LEARNING OBJECTIVE
Describe the uses of blogging in business communication, and briefly explain how to adapt the three-step process to blogging.

Blogs combine the conversational, community aspects of social media with the ability to produce nicely formatted articles.

Blogging

Blogs (short for *web logs*) began as online journals that were much easier to update than conventional websites used to be. A unique advantage of blogging is combining the conversational, community-building functions of social networking with the ability to produce nicely formatted articles of almost any length that can incorporate a variety of multimedia elements. Blog content also has a more permanent feel to it than social networking content, particularly with categorization tags that make it easy to find older content. In contrast, social networking posts tend to be more ephemeral and quickly fade from audience view.

Blogging has a prominent place in business communication, as both standalone blogs and as elements on regular company websites. IBM, for instance, has dozens of blogs on its website, each focusing on a specific subject of interest to customers.[17]

BUSINESS APPLICATIONS OF BLOGGING

Businesses use blogs for a wide variety of purposes to support operations, intelligence gathering, and relationship building.

Blogs are a potential solution whenever you have a continuing stream of in-depth information to share with an online audience—and particularly when you want the audience to have the opportunity to respond through the commenting feature that most blogs have. As with social networking, blogs have multiple uses across the three categories of operations, intelligence, and relationships (see Table 8.3). Note that some of the application areas overlap with social networking, with blogging being better suited

TABLE 8.3 **Common Business Uses of Blogging**		
Operations	**Intelligence**	**Relationships**
Recruiting. Using a blog is a great way to let potential employees know more about a company, the people who work there, and the nature of the company culture.	**Soliciting feedback on product designs and other decisions.** Designers can describe new features or new product ideas and ask readers to offer comments and critiques.	**Building communities.** Like social networking, blogs can bring together communities of practice and communities of interest, both internally and externally.
Project management and team communication. Teams can use blogs to keep everyone up to date, particularly when team members are geographically dispersed.	**Gathering data on customer sentiment, product usage, and other variables.** Customer comments on company blog posts can be a treasure trove of intelligence on how customers feel about a company and its products.	**Sharing customer success stories.** Case studies and other forms of product-usage stories help potential customers learn the value of a company's products and services.
Sharing industry news. Customers often look to the companies that provide them with products and services to keep them up to date on developments.
Word-of-mouth marketing. Bloggers often make a point of providing links to other blogs and websites that interest them, giving marketers a great opportunity to have their messages spread by enthusiasts.	**Conducting background checks.** Employers often search for and evaluate the blogs of prospective employees, making blogging a good way to build a name for yourself within your industry or profession.	**Humanizing a company.** Companies can use blogs to share stories about events and efforts not directly related to sales and products, such as charity work and community projects.
Educating customers and other stakeholders. Blogs are a good format for explaining a variety of topics, such as giving tips on using a company's products more effectively. Doing so can improve sales and support productivity as well by reducing the need for one-on-one communication.
Influencing public policy. Executives can share their opinions and provide business-oriented insights regarding regulations and other issues that affect business.	**Monitoring blog conversations.** Companies often monitor their competitors' blogs to track competitive threats, for example.	**Connecting with the public and the news media.** Many company employees and executives now share company news with the general public and journalists.
Engaging employees. Blogs can enhance communication across all levels of a company, giving lower-level employees a voice that they might not otherwise have and giving senior executives better access to timely information.
Responding to questions. Companies can use blogs to answer stakeholder questions.

for longer pieces and the ability to build up a catalog of easily searchable content on specific topics.

The uses of blogs are limited only by your creativity, so be on the lookout for new ways you can use them to foster positive relationships with colleagues, customers, and other important audiences (see Figure 8.6 on the next page).

TIPS FOR SUCCESSFUL BLOGGING

The three-step writing process is easy to adapt to blogging tasks. This section offers helpful tips on each step.

Planning a Blog and Individual Posts

The planning step is particularly important when you're launching a blog because you're planning an entire communication channel, not just a single message. Pay close attention to your audience, your purpose, and your scope:

- **Audience.** Except with team blogs and other efforts that have an obvious and well-defined audience, defining the target audience for a blog can be challenging. You want an audience large enough to justify the time you'll be investing but narrow enough that you can provide a clear focus for the blog. For instance, if you work for a firm that develops video games, would you focus your blog on "hardcore" players, the types who spend thousands of dollars on super-fast PCs optimized for video games, or

REAL-TIME UPDATES
LEARN MORE BY VISITING THIS WEBSITE

Practical guidelines for successful business blogging

IBM has been encouraging employees to blog for years, and the guidelines it gives employees are great advice for any business blogger. Go to **real-timeupdates.com/ebc13** and select Learn More in the Students section.

Before you launch a blog, make sure you have a clear understanding of your target audience, the purpose of your blog, and the scope of subjects you plan to cover.

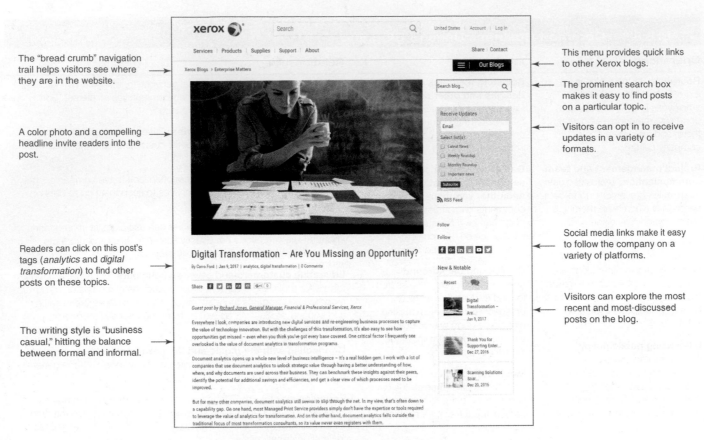

The "bread crumb" navigation trail helps visitors see where they are in the website.

A color photo and a compelling headline invite readers into the post.

Readers can click on this post's tags (*analytics* and *digital transformation*) to find other posts on these topics.

The writing style is "business casual," hitting the balance between formal and informal.

This menu provides quick links to other Xerox blogs.

The prominent search box makes it easy to find posts on a particular topic.

Visitors can opt in to receive updates in a variety of formats.

Social media links make it easy to follow the company on a variety of platforms.

Visitors can explore the most recent and most-discussed posts on the blog.

Figure 8.6   Business Applications of Blogging
This Xerox blog illustrates the content, writing style, and features that make an effective, reader-friendly company blog.

would you broaden the reach to include all gamers? The decision often comes down to business strategy.

- **Purpose.** A business blog needs to have a business-related purpose that is important to your company and to your chosen audience. Moreover, the purpose has to "have legs"—that is, it needs to be something that can drive the blog's content for years—rather than focusing on a single event or an issue of only temporary interest. For instance, if you're a technical expert, you might create a blog to give the audience tips and techniques for using your company's products more effectively—a never-ending subject that's important to both you and your audience. This would be the general purpose of your blog; each post would have a specific purpose within the context of that general purpose. Finally, if you are not writing an official company blog but rather blogging as an individual employee, make sure you understand your employer's blogging guidelines. IBM, for example, gives its employees 12 specific *social computing* guidelines, such as respecting intellectual property laws and identifying their role as IBM employees if they are discussing matters related to the company.[18]

- **Scope.** Your decisions about audience and purpose will define the right scope for your blog, meaning the range of subjects you will cover and the depth you'll go into on various topics. Once you start to build an audience, they'll expect you to cover the same general range of topics.

Thoughtful planning needs to continue with each message. Unless you're posting to a restricted-access blog, you can never be sure who might see your posts. Other bloggers might link to them months or years later.

Check out the "Five-Minute Guide to Better Blog Posts" at the end of the chapter.

Writing Blog Posts

Use a comfortable, personal writing style. Bear in mind, though, that comfortable does not mean careless. Sloppy writing damages your credibility. Some company blogs are written by a rotating team of authors, which gives some variety in terms of tone and content.

Audiences expect you to be knowledgeable in the subject area your blog covers, but you don't need to know everything about a topic. If you don't have all the information yourself, provide links to other blogs and websites that supply relevant information. In fact, content curation (see page 228) is one of the most valuable aspects of blogging. Just be sure the content you share is relevant to your readers and compatible with your communication goals.

As with all social media content that involves headlines, think carefully about your post titles. Make them descriptive, clear, and direct. A headline such as "You win some, you lose some" doesn't tell the audience much of anything and probably won't compel many people to read the post. The advice on email subject lines (see pages 231–232) can be applied to blog post titles as well.

Encourage audiences to join the conversation. Not all blogs invite comments, although most do, and many bloggers consider comments to be an essential feature. Blog comments can be a valuable source of news, information, and insights. To protect against comments that are not helpful or appropriate, many bloggers *moderate* comments before allowing them to be displayed.

To make it easy for your readers to share your content, highlight tweetable passages that they might want to share with their followers on Twitter. A variety of widgets are available for blogging systems to help you create tweetable links.

Write blog posts in a comfortable—but not careless—style.

As with email subject lines, blog post titles should be descriptive, clear, and direct.

Completing Blog Posts

Completing messages for your blog is usually quite easy. Most formatting choices are predefined by a template or theme, so once you've chosen this look, it's simply a matter of adding your text and any media elements such as photos and videos. Before you publish each post, evaluate the content for readability; then proofread to correct any errors.

Make your posts easier to find by **tagging** them with descriptive words. Your readers can then select these "content labels" to find additional posts on those topics. Tags are usually displayed with each post, and they can also be groups in a *tag cloud* or other display that shows all the tags in use on your blog.

Distribution is handled automatically by modern blogging systems, so once you've set this up, all you need to do is hit the publish button. Blog distribution is sometimes referred to as *syndication*, and posts are published via a *newsfeed*, which lets audiences subscribe to blogs of interest. Really Simple Syndication (RSS) and Atom are the most common newsfeeds.[19]

Table 8.4 offers a variety of tips for successful blogging, and "Checklist: Blogging for Business" summarizes some of the key points to remember when creating and writing a business blog. For more information on using blogs in business, visit **real-timeupdates .com/ebc13** and select Chapter 8.

Tagging is the practice of labeling blog posts with descriptive words that readers can use to find other posts on the same topics.

CHECKLIST ✔ **Blogging for Business**

- ✔ Consider creating a blog or microblog account whenever you have a continuing stream of information to share with an online audience.
- ✔ Identify an audience that is big enough to justify the effort but narrow enough to have common interests.
- ✔ Identify a purpose that is comprehensive enough to last over the long haul.
- ✔ Define the scope of topics you'll cover based on your decisions about target audience and purpose.

- ✔ Communicate with a personal style and an authentic voice, but don't write carelessly.
- ✔ Include media items such as infographics, photos, and videos that your readers will find interesting.
- ✔ Look for ways to expand the value you offer readers by mixing in curated content with your original materials.
- ✔ Encourage audiences to join the conversation.
- ✔ Tag posts with descriptive labels to help readers find other posts you've written.

TABLE 8.4 Tips for Effective Business Blogging

Tip	Why It's Important
Don't blog without a clear plan.	Without a plan, your blog is likely to wander from topic to topic and fail to build a sense of community with your audience.
Post frequently; the whole point of a blog is fresh material.	If you won't have a constant supply of new information or new links, create a traditional website instead.
Make it about your readers and the issues important to them.	Readers want to know how your blog will help them or give them a chance to communicate with others who have similar interests.
Write in an authentic voice; never create an artificial character who supposedly writes a blog.	*Flogs*, or fake blogs, violate the spirit of blogging and show disrespect for your audience.
Link generously, but thoughtfully.	Providing interesting links to other blogs and websites is a fundamental aspect of blogging, but make sure the links will be of value to your readers. Don't point to inappropriate material.
Don't post anything you wouldn't want the entire world to see.	Future employers, government regulators, competitors, journalists, and community critics are just a few of the people who might eventually see what you've written.
Minimize marketing and sales messages.	Readers want information about them and their needs.
Write compelling, specific headlines for your post.	Readers usually decide within a couple of seconds whether to read your posts; boring or confusing headlines will turn them away.
Pay attention to spelling, grammar, and mechanics.	No matter how smart or experienced you are, poor-quality writing undermines your credibility with intelligent audiences.
Respond to criticism openly and honestly.	Hiding sends the message that you don't have a valid response to the criticism. If your critics are wrong, patiently explain why you think they're wrong. If they are right, explain how you'll fix the situation.
Listen and learn.	Take the time to analyze the comments people leave on your blog and the comments other bloggers make about you.
Respect intellectual property.	Improperly using material you don't own is not only unethical but can be illegal as well.
Be scrupulously honest and careful with facts.	Honesty is an absolute requirement for every ethical business communicator, of course, but you need to be extra careful online because inaccuracies (both intentional and unintentional) are likely to be discovered quickly and shared widely.
If you review products on your blog, disclose any beneficial relationships you have with the companies that make those products.	Bloggers who receive free products or other compensation from companies whose products they write about are now required to disclose the nature of these relationships.

6 LEARNING OBJECTIVE
Describe the uses of Twitter and other microblogging systems in business communication, and offer tips on writing effective tweets.

A *microblog* such as Twitter is a variation on blogging in which messages are restricted to specific character counts.

Readers expect and appreciate concise, focused messages on Twitter and other microblogging systems.

Microblogging

A **microblog** is a variation on blogging in which messages are restricted to specific character counts. Twitter is the best known of these systems, but many others exist, including private microblogging systems that companies establish for internal use only. Like regular blogging, microblogging quickly caught on with business users and is now a mainstream business medium (see Figure 8.7).

BUSINESS APPLICATIONS OF MICROBLOGGING

Microblogs are used for most of the blog applications mentioned in Table 8.3, although there are several differences to keep in mind. First, the strict limits on message length (such as Twitter's 280 characters) require a different approach to writing. Part of the beauty of microblogging, in fact, is that it requires writers to distill messages down to their essence. (Readers appreciate this brevity so much that many Twitter users were not pleased when the service doubled the character count from 140 to 280.) If you want to share a message that is longer than a particular system's limit, you can thread several messages in a chain, convert the text to a graphic and post it as an image, or link to the longer message on your blog, Facebook page, or other system.

Figure 8.7   Business Applications of Microblogging
Farms.com, which publishes news for agricultural customers, uses Twitter to announce new articles.

Second, Twitter has a more distinct social component than blogging, thanks to how easy it is to connect with other users, share messages through *retweeting*, and respond to anyone on the system. By following more and more users, posting valuable content, and engaging with other users, you can quickly attract hundreds or thousands of followers.

Third, thanks to that social component, Twitter can take on a conversational aspect that is somewhat similar to group messaging. Anyone who sees a tweet can reply to it, which often starts a conversation as more people join in.

> Twitter has a more distinct social component than blogging, which gives the system some of the advantages of social networking.

> **MOBILE APP**
> The **Twitter** mobile app helps you stay connected with your followers and the accounts you follow.

TIPS FOR EFFECTIVE BUSINESS TWEETS

Follow these tips to make the best use of Twitter:[20]

- As with a blog, define the purpose of your Twitter account, and maintain that theme over time.
- Keep up a regular flow of tweets so that you don't fall off your audience's radar.
- Don't slip into careless writing; remember that it's still business communication.
- Keep tweets short and focused on a single topic.
- Include visuals and video links with material of interest to your followers.
- Use *hashtags* (terms that begin with #) to tag your topics, but use them sparingly—tweets clogged with multiple hashtags are not inviting to read.
- Combine Twitter with your other digital channels, such as using Twitter to announce new blog posts.
- Curate content from other Twitter accounts by retweeting messages that your followers will appreciate.
- Explore your followers' timelines to see what interests them; then use these insights to shape your Twitter content plan.
- Tag other users by including their Twitter name in tweets, but do so carefully; not everyone appreciates getting pulled into Twitter conversations.
- Move conversations to direct messaging (private messages) when appropriate.

> Before you start a business-oriented Twitter account, clarify your purpose or theme and stick to it as you begin to tweet.

> Hashtags are a great way to find tweets on specific topics and to label your tweets so others can find them.

> Retweeting is the microblogging equivalent of content curation.

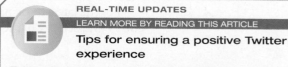

REAL-TIME UPDATES
LEARN MORE BY READING THIS ARTICLE
Tips for ensuring a positive Twitter experience
Twitter offers advice for getting the most from the service while avoiding common blunders. Go to **real-timeupdates.com/ebc13** and select Learn More in the Students section.

Podcasting

Podcasting is the process of recording audio or video files and distributing them online.

As podcasting as grown in popularity, many businesses now host their own podcast channels.

Podcasting is the process of recording audio or video files and distributing them online. Podcasting combines the media richness of voice or visual communication with the convenience of portability. Audiences can listen to or watch podcasts on a blog or website, or they can download them to phones or portable music players to consume on the go. Particularly with audio podcasts, the hands-off, eyes-off aspect makes them great for listening to while driving or exercising.

Podcasting has blossomed in popularity among the general public, and businesses are taking notice. Microsoft, eBay, IBM, Slack, the consulting firm McKinsey, and General Electric are just a few of the many companies that now use podcasting to share information and inspiration with customers and other stakeholders.[21]

You can think of business podcasting as the audio or video equivalent of blogging, in that you are regularly sharing fairly in-depth content on a consistent topic. As with blogging, it's important to choose a subject area that is rich enough to sustain an ongoing series of episodes, which is typically referred to as a *podcasting channel*.

The three-step writing process adapts nicely to individual podcast episodes, with some obvious modifications for the audio or video medium. Some podcasters take an unstructured, improvisational approach; others carefully script podcasts and produce them with nearly the same quality as commercial radio and television programs. With any approach, capturing and keeping the audience's attention is vital. In this regard, view podcasting in the same way as speeches and presentations. Not surprisingly, storytelling is a popular and powerful format for podcasts because it uses a dramatic arc to build and sustain tension.

Whether you take an informal, improvisational approach or carefully script podcasts, capturing and keeping the audience's attention is crucial.

Steering devices such as transitions, previews, and reviews are vital in podcasts.

As you organize the content for a podcast, pay close attention to previews, transitions, and reviews. These steering devices are especially vital in audio recordings because audio lacks the "street signs" (such as headings) that audiences rely on in written and visual media. Moreover, scanning back and forth to find specific parts of an audio or video message is much more difficult than with textual messages, so you need to do everything possible to make sure your audience successfully receives and interprets your message on the first try.

Editing is more difficult with podcasts than with textual messages, so it's wise to start from a solid script or notes.

The completing step is where podcasting differs most dramatically from written communication, for the obvious reason that you are recording and distributing audio or video files. Particularly for more formal podcasts, start by revising your script or thinking through your speaking notes before you begin to record. The closer you can get to recording your podcasts in one take, the more productive you'll be.

Most personal computers, smartphones, and tablets now have basic audio recording capability, and free or low-cost apps to manage recording and distribution are widely available (see Figure 8.8). These tools can be sufficient for creating informal podcasts, but to achieve the higher production quality expected in many corporate podcasts, you'll need additional pieces of hardware and software. These can include an audio processor (to filter out extraneous noise and otherwise improve the audio signal), a mixer (to combine multiple audio or video signals), a better microphone, more-sophisticated recording and editing software, and perhaps some physical changes in your recording location to improve the acoustics.

Podcasts can be distributed in several ways, including through media stores such as iTunes, by dedicated podcast hosting services, or on a company's own website or blog.

For the latest information on using podcasts in business, visit **real-timeupdates.com/ ebc13** and select Chapter 8.

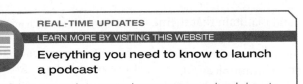

Figure 8.8 Podcasting Tools
Podcasting tools such as Spreaker Studio are available for personal computers, smartphones, tablets, and even smartwatches, making it easy to create and distribute business podcasts from just about anywhere.

ON THE JOB: SOLVING COMMUNICATION DILEMMAS AT SLACK

You've joined Slack as the new internal communications manager, and your responsibilities include helping managers connect with their teams and supporting the marketing and customer support groups. Use what you've learned in the course so far to solve these communication dilemmas.

1. You've written a blog post for the Slack company blog that announces the new *shared channels* feature, which lets two companies connect their Slack system via a virtual "bridge" so that employees who collaborate between the two firms can communicate through Slack. Which of the following tweets is the best teaser to encourage people to click through to the blog post to read more? (Assume there will be a URL that links from Twitter to the blog post.)
   a. We're pleased to announce a major extension of the channels feature in Slack.
   b. Need to connect with Slack users in another company? Now you can share channels!
   c. Not to brag, but Slack just keeps getting better and better and better.
   d. Need to bust out of the organizational box? Shared channels are your ticket to freedom.

2. One member of the customer engagement team is retiring, and you've been asked to recruit her replacement with someone whose primary responsibility will be blogging. Your plan is to write a message on a channel that everyone in the company follows, providing a brief reminder of the blog's purpose, describing the writing style you're looking for, and inviting interested writers to submit sample blog entries for evaluation. Which of the following paragraphs is the best way to describe the preferred writing style for the blog?

(This message is for employees only; it won't be seen by the public.)
   a. Our best social content connects with thousands of readers because the writing is *engaging* (people want to read and respond), *personal* (readers want to get to know real, live human beings, not a faceless corporation), *honest* (we don't sugarcoat anything or hide from criticism), and *friendly* (our readers want to enjoy the experience).
   b. What kind of writing are we looking for? Well, let me tell you exactly what we need. We need writing that is above all (a) engaging—it makes people *want* to read and become involved in the conversation. Plus, (b) the writing must be *personal*; we don't need anybody to repeat "the company line" here; we want *your unique* thoughts and opinions. However, (c) we, of course (!), need writing that is consistent with Slack's culture.
   c. You should be able to produce copy that meets the following criteria: Your writing must be engaging, personal, honest, and friendly. Writing that does not meet these criteria, no matter how well written in other respects, will not be accepted for online publication.
   d. I'll be short and to the point: the writing we want for this blog must be engaging, personal, honest, and friendly.

3. One of the customer support staffers has just messaged you for advice. A Slack customer is going on a multi-tweet rant on Twitter, saying that he is constantly interrupted with silly GIFs, stupid jokes, and office gossip on every Slack channel in his company. He says he can't get any work done and wishes his employer had never replaced email

with Slack. This person has several thousand followers on Twitter, and it looks like he is gaining a fair number of likes and retweets. How would you advise the customer support specialist to respond?

a. Ignore the rant; it'll burn out eventually when the user gets tired of complaining.

b. Reply to one of the tweets in the rant, explaining that it is every Slack user's responsibility to use the system wisely, so this situation is not the fault of the system.

c. Ask the user to direct message you so you can discuss the situation in private, as it would be counterproductive to discuss this in the public view of everyone else on Twitter.

d. Reply to one of the tweets, expressing sympathy with the problem of being interrupted. Explain that you'll have

someone from Slack's customer success team reach out to the Slack system administrator at the user's firm to provide training and user guides to help people use the system more productively.

4. You've written a blog post that describes the research Slack has done to help make the experience of using the system more emotionally engaging (with emojis, friendly bot messages, and other features) so that people will be more compelled to use it. Which of the following would be the most effective title for this post?

a. It's a simple: We love to use the tools we love

b. Every wonder why Slack is so fun to use?

c. Our research-driven design: An enjoyable experience is no accident

d. A new kind of office romance

END OF CHAPTER

Learning Objectives Checkup

Assess your understanding of the principles in this chapter by reading each learning objective and studying the accompanying exercises. You can check your responses against the answer key on page 613.

Objective 8.1: Identify the major digital media used for brief business messages, and describe the nine compositional modes needed for digital and social media.

1. Which of the following is not listed in the chapter as one of the compositional modes for digital media?

a. Conversations

b. Redacting

c. Comments and critiques

d. Narratives

2. A _____ is a brief message that intentionally withholds key pieces of information as a way to pull readers or listeners into a story or another document.

3. Which of the following is the best advice for using emoticons and emojis in business communication?

a. They should always be avoided.

b. They are nearly universally accepted, so they can be used without hesitation.

c. They can be used, but must be used with care because they are not universally accepted as professional.

d. They are acceptable in the informal communication network but never in the formal communication network.

Objective 8.2: Describe how companies use social networking platforms, and explain how to write effective content for these channels.

4. Which of these best describes the business use of social networks?

a. Businesses use private social networks but not public networks.

b. Businesses use private and public social networks.

c. Recruiters use LinkedIn, but beyond that, business use of social networks is quite limited.

d. Few companies now use Facebook or other consumer networks.

5. YouTube, Flickr, and Yelp are examples of

a. consumer-only websites.

b. user-generated content sites.

c. social interactivity blogs.

d. content exchanges.

6. When someone with expertise or interest in a particular field collects and republishes material on a particular topic, the practice is known as

a. content curation.

b. media consolidation.

c. blog linking.

d. tagging and pinning.

7. Which of these is *not* identified in the chapter as one of the communication strategies for business social networking?

a. Curating and sharing existing content

b. Developing and sharing original content

c. Facilitating user-generated content

d. Reproducing and rebranding existing content

8. Which of the following is the best description of effective headlines for social media content?

a. Concise, specific, and informative

b. Provocative and controversial

c. Quirky and fun, with lots of clever wordplay

d. Chatty, entertaining, and audience-focused

Objective 8.3: Explain how to adapt the three-step writing process to email messages, and describe the importance of email subject lines.

9. Which of the following best describes email in the current business communication environment?

a. Nearly all companies are banning it because of overuse and security issues.

b. It's an outdated technology that few employees use anymore.

c. Even with some disadvantages, it remains a primary channel for business.

d. It has been replaced in roughly 75 percent of cases with messaging services, and in the other 25 percent with social media.

10. Which of the following is true of email subject lines?
    a. Only "newbies" bother to use them anymore.
    b. Subject lines should never give away the content of the message because no one will bother to read it if they already know what the message is about.
    c. They can make the difference between a message being read right away, skipped over for later attention, or ignored entirely.
    d. They should always be in all caps to get the audience's attention.

11. Which of the following is the most effective email subject line?
    a. Production line: wiring issues
    b. Proposal to eliminate wiring errors in production
    c. Wiring errors on the production line MUST STOP NOW!
    d. Careless employees => unhappy customers => fewer customers => fewer employees

Objective 8.4: Identify the major types of business messaging, and list guidelines for effective messaging in the workplace.

12. Which of the following is true about business messaging systems?
    a. They support conversational communication better than any other digital format.
    b. They are limited to text messaging and online customer support chat functions.
    c. They tend to encourage nonproductive chatter, so most companies discourage their use.
    d. Communication on these systems is almost entirely conducted by bots nowadays.

13. Which of these is *not* one of the types of business messaging identified in the chapter?
    a. Direct messaging or private messaging
    b. Workgroup messaging
    c. Text messaging
    d. Customer support forums

14. Which of the following is the best approach to tone and formality when using messaging systems?
    a. Regardless of the situation, mimic the tone and formality used by the most senior managers in the company.
    b. Don't bother with punctuation and capitalization; keep it fast and casual.
    c. Adjust your tone and level of formality to match the situation.
    d. All of the above are good points to follow.

Objective 8.5: Describe the uses of blogging in business communication, and briefly explain how to adapt the three-step process to blogging.

15. Which of these is a unique advantage of blogging?
    a. The conversational, community-building functions of social networking

b. Combining the conversational, community-building functions of social networking with the ability to produce nicely formatted articles

c. The ability to include multimedia elements such as video

d. The ability to reach any audience, anywhere in the world

16. Which of the following best describes the optimum audience of a blog?
    a. Always the largest audience possible
    b. Only people who are experts in the subject matter so that comments and discussions aren't pulled off track by "newbies" who don't know what they are talking about
    c. An audience large enough to justify the time required to maintain the blog but narrow enough to ensure a clear focus
    d. Whatever audience happens to find the blog on the web

17. Which of the following is *not* a good general purpose for a blog?
    a. Sharing news from the mountain bike racing circuit, describing how the racers we sponsor are faring and how they use our products
    b. Commenting on economic and social policy decisions that affect the national and international business environment
    c. Explaining to the local community why we've decided not to expand employment at the Twin Falls facility
    d. Describing the work going on in our research and development labs

Objective 8.6: Describe the uses of Twitter and other microblogging systems in business communication, and offer tips on writing effective tweets.

18. Which of the following best characterizes the length restrictions on Twitter and other microblogging platforms?
    a. They require a different approach to writing, but audiences tend to appreciate the efficiency and clarity of well-crafted short messages.
    b. They don't have much effect on writing; if your message won't fit in a single tweet, simply break it into multiple tweets.
    c. They severely limit Twitter's usefulness for business communication.
    d. They are driving away much of the readership that was originally attracted to Twitter.

19. Which of the following would be a good use of retweeting for an independent consulting engineer who uses Twitter to build relationships with potential clients?
    a. Avoiding retweeting under any circumstances, because it is tantamount to plagiarizing
    b. Retweeting every tweet he or she receives so that clients know the consultant is well-rounded and well-read
    c. Retweeting fun and interesting messages on nonbusiness topics as a way to build an emotional bond with potential clients
    d. Retweeting selectively, sharing only messages that meet two criteria: providing information that followers can use in their work and portraying the consultant as an expert who is up on the latest developments in his or her field

20. A/an _____ is a way to label the subject of a tweet so that others can find it more easily.

Objective 8.7: Outline the process of producing business podcasts.

21. Which of the following best characterizes podcasting's use in contemporary business communication?
    a. Even though podcasting's popularity has taken off among the general public, few businesses bother with it.
    b. As podcasting's popularity has taken off among the general public, many businesses have begun producing podcasts.
    c. Consultants and professional speakers can make good use of podcasting, but it doesn't offer much value for the typical corporation.
    d. Because of production costs, podcasting is only available to large companies.

22. Why are previews, transitions, and reviews so important in podcasts?
    a. They provide a recurring opportunity to reinforce brand messages.
    b. They help podcasters make episodes as short as possible.
    c. They eliminate the need to engage in storytelling.
    d. They help listeners follow the content and grasp it on the first attempt.

23. A/an _____ _____ is an ongoing series of podcasts on the same general topic.

Key Terms

blogs Online publishing systems that are easier to personalize and update than conventional websites

content curation Collecting and republishing online material on a particular topic

email signature A small file that automatically includes such items as your full name, title, company, and contact information at the end of your messages

microblog A variation on blogging in which messages are sharply restricted to specific character counts

podcasting The process of recording audio or video files and distributing them online

tagging Assigning descriptive words to social media content to simplify searching

Apply Your Knowledge

To review chapter content related to each question, refer to the indicated Learning Objective.

8-1. Given the strict limits on length, should all your micro-blogging messages function as teasers that link to more detailed information on a blog or website? Why or why not? [LO-1]

8-2. Is leveraging your connections on social networks for business purposes ethical? Why or why not? [LO-2]

8-3. How do effective email subject lines reflect the "you" attitude? [LO-3]

8-4. What are the risks of using emoticons and emojis in business communication? [LO-3]

8-5. If one of the benefits of blogging is the personal, intimate style of writing, is it a good idea to limit your creativity by adhering to conventional rules of grammar, spelling, and mechanics? Why or why not? [LO-5]

8-6. What are some ways the president of a hiking equipment company could use Twitter to engage potential customers without being overtly promotional? [LO-6]

Practice Your Skills

Message for Analysis

8-7. **Message 8.A: Media Skills: Messaging; Creating a Businesslike Tone [LO-4]** Review the following messaging exchange, and explain how the customer service agent could have handled the situation more effectively.

AGENT:	Thanks for contacting Home Exercise Equipment. What's up?
CUSTOMER:	I'm having trouble assembling my home gym.
AGENT:	I hear that a lot! LOL
CUSTOMER:	So is it me or the gym?
AGENT:	Well, let's see <g>. Where are you stuck?
CUSTOMER:	The crossbar that connects the vertical pillars doesn't fit.
AGENT:	What do you mean doesn't fit?
CUSTOMER:	It doesn't fit. It's not long enough to reach across the pillars.
AGENT:	Maybe you assembled the pillars in the wrong place. Or maybe we sent the wrong crossbar.
CUSTOMER:	How do I tell?
AGENT:	The parts aren't labeled so could be tough. Do you have a measuring tape? Tell me how long your crossbar is.

8-8. **Message 8.B: Media Skills: Blogging, Creating a Businesslike Tone [LO-5]** Read the following blog post and (a) analyze the strengths and weaknesses of each sentence and (b) revise it so that it follows the guidelines in this chapter.

[post title] We're DOOMED!!!!!

I was at the Sikorsky plant in Stratford yesterday, just checking to see how things were going with the assembly line retrofit we did for them last year. I think I saw the future, and it ain't pretty. They were demo'ing a prototype robot from Motoman that absolutely blows our stuff out of the water. They wouldn't let me really see it, but based on the 10-second glimpse I got, it's smaller, faster, and more maneuverable than any of our units. And when I asked about the price, the guy just grinned. And it wasn't the sort of grin designed to make me feel good.

I've been saying for years that we need to pay more attention to size, speed, and maneuverability instead of just relying on our historical strengths of accuracy and payload capacity, and you'd have to be blind not to agree that this experience proves me right. If we can't at least show a design for a better unit within two or three months,

Motoman is going to lock up the market and leave us utterly in the dust.

Believe me, being able to say "I told you so" right now is not nearly as satisfying as you might think!!

8-9. **Message 8.C: Media Skills: Podcasting [LO-7]** To access this podcast exercise, visit **real-timeupdates .com/ebc13**, select Student Assignments, select Chapter 8 Message 8.C, and listen to this podcast. Identify at least three ways in which the podcast could be improved, and draft a brief email message you could send to the podcaster with your suggestions for improvement.

Exercises

Each activity is labeled according to the primary skill or skills you will need to use. To review relevant chapter content, you can refer to the indicated Learning Objective. In some instances, supporting information will be found in another chapter, as indicated.

8-10. **Media Skills: Social Networking, Team Skills [LO-1]** With a team assigned by your instructor, choose a company that looks interesting to you and evaluate 10 of its social media posts on Facebook, Twitter, and any other social platform you can find it on. How would you characterize the company's communication style based on these posts? Do its writers use emojis? Summarize your findings in a post for your class blog or an email to your instructor.

8-11. **Media Skills: Social Networking [LO-2]** Joining an ongoing social media conversation, such as a comment thread on Facebook, requires a delicate touch if you work for a company that has a commercial interest in the subject at hand. Imagine you work for a company that makes audiophile-quality headphones, acoustic guitars, or electronic drum kits (choose whichever product interests you the most). While monitoring a Facebook group for enthusiasts of this product category, you see an active thread in which people are complaining about the quality of one of your competitor's products. You know that for years this company had a reputation for making high-quality equipment, but quality suffered after a poorly executed plan to outsource manufacturing in order to cut costs. A similar product that your company offers is slightly more expensive but has significantly higher quality, according to a recent survey conducted by a respected and impartial industry website.

Draft a brief comment that you could use to join the conversation. Decide what information you'll include and whether you will disclose your company affiliation. Assume that representatives from various companies do occasionally make posts and leave comments in this group, but overt selling is explicitly forbidden by the group's moderator.

8-12. **Media Skills: Social Networking [LO-2]** Pick a company in any industry that interests you. Imagine you are doing strategic planning for this firm, and identify one of your company's key competitors. Now search through social media sources to find three strategically relevant pieces of information about this competitor, such as the hiring of a new executive, the launch of a major new product, or a significant problem of some kind. In a post on your class blog, identify the information you found and the sources you used. (If you can't find useful information, pick another firm or try another industry.)

8-13. **Media Skills: Writing Email Subject Lines [LO-3]** Using your imagination to make up whatever details you need, revise the following email subject lines to make them more effective:

a. New budget figures

b. Marketing brochure—your opinion

c. Production schedule

8-14. **Media Skills: Email [LO-3]** The following email message contains numerous errors related to what you've learned about planning and writing business messages.

SUBJECT: Compliance with new break procedure

Some of you may not like the rules about break times; however, we determined that keeping track of employees while they took breaks at times they determined rather than regular breaks at prescribed times was not working as well as we would have liked it to work. The new rules are not going to be an option. If you do not follow the new rules, you could be docked from your pay for hours when you turned up missing, since your direct supervisor will not be able to tell whether you were on a "break" or not and will assume that you have walked away from your job. We cannot be responsible for any errors that result from your inattentiveness to the new rules. I have already heard complaints from some of you and I hope this memo will end this issue once and for all. The decision has already been made.

Starting Monday, January 1, you will all be required to take a regular 15-minute break in the morning and again in the afternoon, and a regular thirty-minute lunch at the times specified by your supervisor, NOT when you think you need a break or when you "get around to it."

There will be no exceptions to this new rule!

Felicia August

Manager

Billing and accounting

First, describe the flaws you discovered in this email message. Next, develop a plan for rewriting the message. Use the following steps to organize your efforts before you begin writing:

- Determine the purpose.
- Identify and analyze your audience.
- Define the main idea.
- Outline the major supporting points.
- Choose between the direct and indirect approaches.

Now rewrite the email message. Don't forget to leave ample time for revision of your own work before you turn it in.

8-15. Media Skills: Messaging [LO-4] Assume you need to share news about a schedule slip on a customer project you are managing. You had originally promised it would be finished by June 1, but you now believe it won't be finished until June 20. The reason for the delay is a holdup in receiving some necessary materials from another company. Write a brief message to update the customer and apologize for the delay. You and the customer are on a shared channel on Slack that is dedicated to updates on the project, so you don't need to address the message to anyone in particular. Make up any details you need in order to write a realistic message.

8-16. Media Skills: Blogging [LO-5] The members of the project team you lead have enthusiastically embraced blogging as a communication medium. Unfortunately, as emotions heat up during the project, some of the blog posts are getting too casual, too personal, and even sloppy. Because your boss and other managers around the company also read this blog, you don't want the team to look unprofessional in anyone's eyes. Revise the following blog post so that it communicates in a more businesslike manner while retaining the informal, conversational tone of a blog. Be sure to correct any spelling and punctuation mistakes you find as well.

Well, to the profound surprise of absolutely nobody, we are not going to be able meet the June 1 commitment to ship 100 operating tables to Southeast Surgical Supply. (For those of you who have been living in a cave the past six months, we have been fighting to get our hands on enough high-grade chromium steel to meet our production schedule.) Sure enough, we got news, this morning that we will only get enough for 30 tables. Yes, we look lik fools for not being able to follow through on promises we made to the customer, but no, this didn't have to happpen. Six month's ago, purchasing warned us about shrinking supplies and suggested we advance-buy as much as we would need for the next 12 months, or so. We naturally tried to followed their advice, but just as naturally were shot down by the bean counters at corporate who trotted out the policy about never buying more than three months worth of materials in advance. Of course, it'll be us–not the bean counters who'll take the flak when everybody starts asking why revenues are down next quarter and why Southeast is talking to our friends at Crighton Manuf!!! Maybe, some day this company will get its head out of the sand and realize that we need to have some financial flexibility in order to compete.

8-17. Media Skills: Blogging [LO-5] From what you've learned about planning and writing business messages, you should be able to identify numerous errors made by the writer of the following blog post. Make a list and then plan and write a better post, following the guidelines given.

Get Ready!

We are hoping to be back at work soon, with everything running smoothly, same production schedule and no late projects or missed deadlines. So you need to clean out your desk, put your stuff in boxes, and clean off the walls. You can put the items you had up on your walls in boxes, also.

We have provided boxes. The move will happen this weekend. We'll be in our new offices when you arrive on Monday.

We will not be responsible for personal belongings during the move.

Use the following steps to organize your efforts before you begin writing:

- Determine the purpose.
- Identify and analyze your audience.
- Define the main idea.
- Outline the major supporting points.
- Choose between the direct and indirect approaches.

Now rewrite the post. Don't forget to leave ample time for revision of your own work before you turn it in.

8-18. Media Skills: Microblogging [LO-6] Busy knitters can go through a lot of yarn in a hurry, so most keep a sharp eye out for yarn sales. You're on the marketing staff of Knitting-Warehouse, and you like to keep your loyal shoppers up to date with the latest deals. Visit the Knitting-Warehouse website at www .knitting-warehouse.com, select any on-sale product that catches your eye, and write a Twitter update that describes the product and the sale. Be sure to include a link back to the website so your Twitter followers can learn more. (Unless you are working on a private Twitter account that is accessible only by your instructor and your classmates, don't actually send this Twitter update. Email it to your instructor instead.)

8-19. Media Skills: Podcasting [LO-7] You've recently begun recording a weekly podcast to share information with your large and far-flung staff. After a month, you ask for feedback from several of your subordinates, and you're disappointed to learn that some people stopped listening to the podcast after the first couple weeks. Someone eventually admits that many staffers feel that the recordings are too long and rambling and that the information they contain isn't valuable enough to justify the time it takes to listen. You aren't pleased, but you want to improve. An assistant transcribes the introduction to last week's podcast so you can review it. You immediately see two problems. Revise the introduction based on what you've learned in this chapter.

So there I am, having lunch with Selma Gill, who just joined and took over the Northeast sales region from Jackson Stroud. In walks our beloved CEO with Selma's old boss at Uni-Plex; turns out they were finalizing a deal to co-brand our products and theirs and to set up a joint distribution program in all four domestic regions. Pretty funny, huh?

Selma left Uni-Plex because she wanted to sell our products instead, and now she's back selling her old stuff, too. Anyway, try to chat with her when you can;

she knows the biz inside and out and probably can offer insight into just about any sales challenge you might be running up against. We'll post more info on the co-brand deal next week; should be a boost for all of us. Other than those two news items, the other big news this week is the change in commission reporting. I'll go into the details in minute, but when you log onto the intranet, you'll now see your sales results split out by product line and industry sector.

Hope this helps you see where you're doing well and where you might beef things up a bit. Oh yeah, I almost forgot the most important bit. Speaking of our beloved CEO, Thomas is going to be our guest of honor, so to speak, at the quarterly sales meeting next week and wants an update on how petroleum prices are affecting customer behavior. Each district manager should be ready with a brief report. After I go through the commission reporting scheme, I'll outline what you need to prepare.

Expand Your Skills

Critique the Professionals

Locate the YouTube channel page of any company you find interesting, and assess its social networking presence using the criteria for effective communication discussed in this chapter and your own experience with social media. What does this company do well with its YouTube channel? How might it improve? Using whatever medium your instructor requests, write a brief analysis of the company's YouTube presence (no more than one page), citing specific elements from the piece and support from the chapter.

Sharpen Your Career Skills Online

Bovée and Thill's Business Communication Web Search, at **websearch.businesscommunicationnetwork.com**, is a unique research tool designed specifically for business communication research. Use the Web Search function to find a website, video, article, podcast, or presentation that offers advice on using social media in business. Write a brief email message to your instructor or a post for your class blog describing the item that you found and summarizing the career skills information you learned from it.

Build Your Career

One of the biggest challenges of the interviewing and hiring process from the employer's perspective is figuring out whether a candidate's general qualifications will fit the specific requirements of a job opening. For example, you may have a degree in marketing or accounting, but marketing and accounting jobs can vary widely from one company to the next. The levels of responsibility may differ, companies use different procedures and systems, and so on. Employers don't look for a generic marketing specialist or a generic accountant; they look for people who can meet their specific and unique

needs. In addition, even companies in the same industry can have dramatically different competitive threats and other issues they need help with.

To maximize your appeal as a candidate, you need to translate your general qualifications into the specific needs a company has. The secret is research. As you encounter interesting job openings in the coming months, practice figuring out what you would need to know in order to sell yourself into each job. Study the job descriptions, and read about the company and its industry. What *specific* qualities, skills, and knowledge does the company need? Not just "promoting its products" but "promoting the Panasonic Professional 4K line of camcorders to semi-pro and professional videographers," for example. Dig down to individual product lines, target markets, or whatever variables fit the job. By the time you're ready to apply for your dream job, you'll know how to present yourself as the dream candidate.

Improve Your Grammar, Mechanics, and Usage

The following exercises help you improve your knowledge of and power over English grammar, mechanics, and usage. Turn to the Handbook of Grammar, Mechanics, and Usage at the end of this book and review all of Section 1.7 (Sentences). Using those guidelines, indicate the preferred sentence in the following pairs. (Answers to these exercises appear on page 614.)

8-20. **a.** Joan Ellingsworth attends every stockholder meeting. Because she is one of the few board members eligible to vote.
  b. Joan Ellingsworth attends every stockholder meeting. She is one of the few board members eligible to vote.

8-21. **a.** The executive director, along with his team members, is working quickly to determine the cause of the problem.
  b. The executive director, along with his team members, are working quickly to determine the cause of the problem.

8-22. **a.** Listening on the extension, details of the embezzlement plot were overheard by the security chief.
  b. Listening on the extension, the chief overheard details of the embezzlement plot.

8-23. **a.** First the human resources department interviewed dozens of people. Then it hired a placement service.
  b. First the human resources department interviewed dozens of people then it hired a placement service.

8-24. **a.** Andrews won the sales contest, however he was able to sign up only two new accounts.
  b. Andrews won the sales contest; however, he was able to sign up only two new accounts.

8-25. **a.** To find the missing file, the whole office was turned inside out.
  b. The whole office was turned inside out to find the missing file.

8-26. **a.** Having finally gotten his transfer, he is taking his assistant right along with him.

     b. Having finally gotten his transfer, his assistant is going right along with him.

8-27. **a.** Irving was recruiting team members for her project, she promised supporters unprecedented bonuses.

     b. Because Irving was recruiting team members for her project, she promised supporters unprecedented bonuses.

8-28. **a.** He left the office unlocked overnight. This was an unconscionable act, considering the high crime rate in this area lately.

     b. He left the office unlocked overnight. An unconscionable act, considering the high crime rate in this area lately.

8-29. **a.** When it comes to safety issues, the abandoned mine, with its collapsing tunnels, are cause for great concern.

     b. When it comes to safety issues, the abandoned mine, with its collapsing tunnels, is cause for great concern.

For additional exercises focusing on sentences, visit MyLab Business Communication. Select Chapter 8, then Additional Exercises to Improve Your Grammar, Mechanics, and Usage, and then 12. Longer sentences, 13. Sentence fragments, 15. Misplaced modifiers, or 24. Transitional words and phrases.

Cases

For all cases, feel free to use your creativity to make up any details you need in order to craft effective messages.

SOCIAL NETWORKING SKILLS

8-30. Media Skills: Social Networking; Compositional Modes: Summaries [LO-2]
Many companies now have *voice of the customer (VoC)* programs to collect and analyze commentary and feedback from customers. The most comprehensive of these programs automatically gather data from social media, customer call records, technical support emails, online product reviews, and more. To extract insights from these large collections of text, marketers can use an intelligent communication technology called *text analytics*.

Your task: Review the text analytics information on the Clarabridge website at **www.clarabridge.com**. (The company refers to its technology as CX Analytics, for customer experience analytics.) Write a 100- to 150-word summary of this technology that Clarabridge could use as a post on its Facebook page to explain the capability to potential customers.

SOCIAL NETWORKING SKILLS

8-31. Media Skills: Social Networking; Online Etiquette [LO-2], Chapter 3
Employees who take pride in their work are a practically priceless resource for any business. However, pride can sometimes manifest itself in negative ways when employees come under criticism, and public criticism is a fact of life in social media. Imagine that your company has recently experienced a rash of product quality problems, and these problems have generated some unpleasant and occasionally unfair criticism on a variety of social media sites. Someone even set up a Facebook page specifically to give customers a place to vent their frustrations.

You and your public relations team jumped into action, responding to complaints with offers to provide replacement products and help customers who have been affected by the quality problems. Everything seemed to be going as well as could be expected, when you were checking a few industry blogs one evening and discovered that two engineers in your company's product design lab have been responding to complaints on their own. They identified themselves as company employees and defended their product design, blaming the company's production department and even criticizing several customers for lacking the skills needed to use such a sophisticated product. Within a matter of minutes, you see their harsh comments being retweeted and reposted on multiple sites, only fueling the fire of negative feedback against your firm. Needless to say, you are horrified.

Your task: You manage to reach the engineers by private message and tell them to stop posting messages, but you realize you have a serious training issue on your hands. Write a post for the internal company blog that advises employees on how to respond appropriately when they are representing the company online. Use your imagination to make up any details you need.

NETWORKING SKILLS / TEAM SKILLS

8-32. Media Skills: Social Networking; Collaboration: Team Projects [LO-2], Chapter 3
Social media can be a great way to, well, socialize during your college years, but employers are increasingly checking up on the online activities of potential hires to avoid bringing in employees who may reflect poorly on the company.

Your task: Team up with another student and review each other's public presence on Facebook, Twitter, Flickr, blogs, and any other website that an employer might check during the interview and recruiting process. Identify any photos, videos, messages, or other material that could raise a red flag when an employer is evaluating a job candidate. Write your teammate an email message that lists any risky material.

EMAIL SKILLS / PORTFOLIO BUILDER

8-33. Media Skills: Email; Message Strategies: Negative Messages [LO-3], Chapter 10
Many companies operate on the principle that the customer is always right, even when

the customer isn't right. They take any steps necessary to ensure happy customers, lots of repeat sales, and a positive reputation among potential buyers. Overall, this is a smart and successful approach to business. However, most companies eventually encounter a nightmare customer who drains so much time, energy, and profits that the only sensible option is to refuse the customer's business. For example, the nightmare customer might be someone who constantly berates you and your employees, repeatedly makes outlandish demands for refunds and discounts, or simply requires so much help that you not only lose money on this person but also no longer have enough time to help your other customers. "Firing" a customer is an unpleasant step that should be taken only in the most extreme cases and only after other remedies have been attempted (such as talking with the customer about the problem), but it is sometimes necessary for the well-being of your employees and your company.

Your task: If you are currently working or have held a job in the recent past, imagine that you've encountered just such a customer. If you don't have job experience to call on, imagine that you work in a retail location somewhere around campus or in your neighborhood. Identify the type of behavior this imaginary customer exhibits and the reasons the behavior can no longer be accepted. Write a brief email message to the customer to explain that you will no longer be able to accommodate him or her as a customer. Calmly explain why you have had to reach this difficult decision. Maintain a professional tone and keep your emotions in check.

EMAIL SKILLS / TEAM SKILLS

8-34. Media Skills: Email; Collaboration: Team Projects [LO-3], Chapter 3 Colleges and universities are complex organizations that try to optimize results for students while wrestling with budgetary constraints, staffing issues, infrastructure concerns, space limitations, and a host of other issues. Even in the best-managed and most generously funded institutions, there are aspects of campus life that could be improved.

Your task: With a team assigned by your instructor, choose an issue of campus life that you think could and should be improved. It can be anything from transportation to housing to personal safety. Draft an email message that could be sent to your school's administration. In your message, concisely describe the problem, speculate on why the problem or situation exists, offer suggestions on how it could be solved or improved, and explain how addressing it would improve campus life. (Don't send the message unless your instructor directs you to do so.)

EMAIL SKILLS / TEAM SKILLS

8-35. Media Skills: Email [LO-4] Studying real-life examples is a great way to get a feel for how various companies communicate with customers and other stakeholders.

Your task: With teammates assigned by your instructor, select five email messages from the Just Good Copy website at www.goodemailcopy.com. Evaluate them based on the criteria for effective email discussed in the chapter. Rank them from most effective to least effective and summarize your analysis in a presentation to your class or a post on your class blog.

EMAIL SKILLS / MOBILE SKILLS

8-36. Media Skills: Email [LO-3] The size limitations of smartphone screens call for a different approach to writing (see page 177) and formatting (see page 201) documents.

Your task: On the website of any company that interests you, find a news release (some companies refer to them as press releases) that announces the launch of a new product. Using Pages or any other writing app at your disposal, revise and format the material in a way that would be more effective on smartphone screens.

MESSAGING SKILLS

8-37. Media Skills: Messaging [LO-4] Keeping track of deadlines, to-do lists, and other details is a challenge for every professional. You've been researching apps to help with this, and you're intrigued by one called Moo.do. You'd like to tell your colleagues about its key features and ask if it's something the team should consider adopting.

Your task: Visit www.moo.do and learn more about the product. Choose three features that you think are useful and summarize them in a message of no more than 300 characters that you could post on your company's workgroup messaging system. (For the purposes of this exercise, it is acceptable to use some of the specific phrasing you find on the Moo.do website, but make the bulk of the message your own writing.)

MESSAGING SKILLS

8-38. Media Skills: Messaging [LO-4] With more and more consumers and businesses using apps and online services to transfer money and conduct other financial transactions, people are naturally concerned about security.

Your task: You work in customer communications for Venmo, makers of a popular money-transfer app. Your team gets quite a few inquiries about security, so you've decided to write a standard reply that you and your colleagues can send via email or through the chat function in the Venmo app. Visit www.venmo.com and review the information on security. Write a message of no more than 400 characters that describes how Venmo uses encryption and what customers should do if they suspect trouble with their accounts. (For the purposes of this exercise, it is acceptable to use some of the specific phrasing you find on the Venmo website, but make the bulk of the message your own writing.)

BLOGGING SKILLS / PORTFOLIO BUILDER

8-39. Media Skills: Blogging [LO-5] Credit card debt can be a crippling financial burden with myriad side effects, from higher insurance rates to more-expensive loans to difficulty getting a job or a promotion. Unfortunately, credit debt is also frighteningly easy to fall into, particularly for young people trying to get started in life with limited cash flow.

Your task: Write a three- to five-paragraph blog post that warns college students about the dangers of credit card debt. Be sure to credit the sources you find in your research.

BLOGGING SKILLS / MOBILE SKILLS

8-40. Media Skills: Blogging; Compositional Modes: Tutorials [LO-5] Studying abroad for a semester or a year can be a rewarding experience in many ways—improving your language skills, experiencing another culture, making contacts in the international business arena, and building your self-confidence.

Your task: Write a post for your class blog that describes your college's study abroad program and summarizes the steps involved in applying for international study. If your school doesn't offer study-abroad opportunities, base your post on the program offered at another institution in your state. Make it mobile friendly with a short title and short paragraphs.

MICROBLOGGING SKILLS

8-41. Media Skills: Microblogging; Compositional Modes: Summaries [LO-1], [LO-6] A carefully constructed series of tweets can serve as a summary of a blog post, video, or other message or document.

Your task: Find any article, podcast, video, or webpage on a business topic that interests you. Write four to six tweetables that summarize the content of the piece. Keep the tweets as short as possible. Email the series to your instructor or publish them on Twitter if your instructor directs. If you quote phrases from the original directly, be sure to put them in quotation marks.

MICROBLOGGING SKILLS

8-42. Media Skills: Microblogging; Compositional Modes: Updates and Announcements [LO-6] To most consumer-goods companies, Black Friday is a massive shopping event the day after Thanksgiving, when consumers crowd into stores and retailers hope to see a big sales boost to kick-start the holiday shopping season. For the clothing company Everlane, however, Black Friday is a day for taking care of the factory workers who make the company's products. Each year, Everlane donates profits from Black Friday sales to a particular project, such as buying thousands of helmets for workers in Vietnam who travel to work on mopeds. Another year, the company installed three container farms (basically high-efficiency greenhouses built into recycled shipping containers) so a factory could double the number of meals it provides its workers.[22]

Your task: Visit www.everlane.com and read about the Black Friday Fund. Draft a tweet describing this year's Black Friday project. Limit it to 217 characters to allow room for a URL. (You don't need to include the URL.) Email the tweet to your instructor.

MICROBLOGGING SKILLS

8-43. Media Skills: Microblogging; Compositional Modes: Teasers [LO-1], [LO-6] Twitter updates are a great way to alert people to helpful articles, videos, and other online resources.

Your task: Find an online resource (it can be a YouTube video, a PowerPoint presentation, a newspaper article, or anything else appropriate) that offers some great tips to help college students prepare for job interviews. Write a teaser that hints at the benefits other students can get from this resource. If your class is set up with private Twitter accounts, use your private account to send your message. Otherwise, email it to your instructor. Be sure to include the URL.

PODCASTING SKILLS / PORTFOLIO BUILDER

8-44. Media Skills: Podcasting [LO-7] While writing the many messages that are part of the job search process, you find yourself wishing you could just talk to some of these companies so your personality could shine through. Well, you've just gotten that opportunity. One of the companies you've applied to has emailed you back, asking you to submit a two-minute podcast introducing yourself and explaining why you would be a good person to hire.

Your task: Identify a company you'd like to work for after graduation, and select a job that would be a good match for your skills and interests. Write a script for a two-minute podcast (two minutes represents roughly 250 words for most speakers). Introduce yourself and the position you're applying for, describe your background, and explain why you are a good candidate for the job. Make up any details you need. If your instructor asks you to do so, record the podcast and submit the audio file.

PODCASTING SKILLS

8-45. Media Skills: Podcasting [LO-7] Between this chapter and your own experience as a user of social media, you know enough about social media to offer some insights to other business communicators.

Your task: Write a script for a two- to three-minute podcast (roughly 250 to 400 words) on any social media topic that you find compelling. Be sure to introduce your topic clearly in the introduction and provide helpful transitions along the way. If your instructor asks you to do so, record the podcast and submit the file.

PODCASTING SKILLS / PORTFOLIO BUILDER

8-46. Media Skills: Podcasting; Message Strategies: Marketing and Sales Messages [LO-7], Chapter 11 With any purchase decision, from a restaurant meal to a college education, recommendations from satisfied customers are often the strongest promotional messages.

Your task: Write a script for a one- to two-minute podcast (roughly 150 to 250 words), explaining why your college or university is a good place to get an education. Your audience is high school juniors and seniors. You can choose to craft a general message, something that would be useful to all prospective students, or you can focus on a specific academic discipline, the athletic program, or some other important aspect of your college experience. Either way, make sure your introductory comments make it clear whether you are offering a general recommendation or a specific recommendation. If your instructor asks you to do so, record the podcast and submit the file.

MyLab Business Communication

MyLab Assisted-Grading Writing Prompts

If your instructor has assigned one or both of the following writing assignments within the MyLab, go to your Assignments to complete these writing exercises.

8-47. How can businesses make use of social networks such as Facebook for business communication? [LO-2]

8-48. Why does a personal style of writing on blogs and other social media channels help build stronger relationships with audiences? [LO-5]

Endnotes

1. Elizabeth Woyke, "Slack Hopes Its AI Will Keep You from Hating Slack," *Technology Review*, 16 January 2018, www.technologyreview .com; Slack website, accessed 8 January 2018, slack.com; Alex Konrad, "Slack Passes 6 Million Daily Users and Opens Up Channels to Multi-Company Use," *Forbes*, 12 September 2017, www.forbes.com; Jill Duffy, "Slack," PCMag, 5 January 2017, www.pcmag.com; Molly Fischer, "What Happens When Work Becomes a Nonstop Chat Room," *New York Magazine*, 17 May 2017, nymag.com; Adrienne Lafrance, "The Triumph of Email," *The Atlantic*, 6 January 2016, www.theatlantic.com; Harry McCracken, "With 500,000 Users, Slack Says It's the Fastest-Growing Business App Ever," *Fast Company*, 2 December 2015, www.fastcompany.com; Farhad Manjoo, "Slack, the Office Messaging App That May Finally Sink Email," *New York Times*, 11 March 2015, www.nytimes.com; Alyson Shontell and Eugene Kim, "Slack, a 2-Year-Old Messaging Platform, Is Raising $200 Million at Nearly a $4 Billion Valuation Led by Thrive Capital," *Business Insider*, 11 March 2016, www.businessinder.com; Ellis Hamburger, "Slack Is Killing Email," *The Verge*, 12 August 2014, www.theverge.com.

2. Richard Edelman, "Teaching Social Media: What Skills Do Communicators Need?" in "Engaging the New Influencers; Third Annual Social Media Academic Summit" (white paper), accessed 7 June 2010, www.newmediaacademicsummit.com.

3. Anna Post, "Reuters: Email Etiquette at Work and Home," Emily Post Institute, accessed 8 January 2018, emilypost.com; Emily Dishman, "The Business Etiquette Guide to Emojis," *Fast Company*, 14 July 2016, www.fastcompany.com; "6 Rules for Email Etiquette in the Workplace," *The Balance*, 14 December 2017, www.thebalance .com; "Emoji and Emoticons," Slack Help Center, accessed 8 January 2017, get.slack.help.

4. Max Mihelich, "Harassment by Emojis," *Workforce*, 8 January 2018, www.workforce.com; Elizabeth Kirley and Marilyn McMahon, "Emoji and the Law: What Happens When They're Used to Threaten or Suggest Violence?" ABC News (Australia), 4 December 2017, www.abc.net.au; Amanda Hess, "Exhibit A: ;-)," *Slate*, 26 October 2015, www.slate.com; Benjamin Weiser, "At Silk Road Trial, Lawyers Fight to Include Evidence They Call Vital: Emoji," *New York Times*, 28 January 2015, www.nytimes.com.

5. Wanda Thibodeaux, "How to Use Emojis Effectively in Everyday Business Communication," *Inc.*, 15 May 2017, www.inc.com.

6. "Workplace by Facebook," Facebook, accessed 5 January 2018, www.facebook.com.

7. Angelo Fernando, "Content Snacking—and What You Can Do About It," *Communication World*, January–February 2011, 8–10.

8. Ben Sailer, "This Is How to Write for Social Media to Create the Best Posts," CoSchedule blog, 3 October 2016, coschedule.com.

9. *How to Write Magnetic Headlines* (Rainmaker Digital, e-book, 2016), www.copyblogger.com, 12.

10. Ben Betts, "Curating Content for Learning: Is It Legal?" HT2 Labs, 5 April 2017, www.ht2labs.com; Guillaume Decugis, "Does Ethical Content Curation Exist? A Data-Driven Answer," Scoop.it, 30 July 2015, blog.scoop.it.

11. Ben Betts and Allison Anderson, "Diamond in the Rough," *TD: Talent Development*, 8 January 2016, www.td.org.

12. Maria Vergelis, Tatyana Shcherbakova, Nadezhda Demidova, and Darya Gudkova, "Kaspersky Security Bulletin. Spam and Phishing in 2015," *Securelist*, 5 February 2016, securelist.com.

13. "The Liability of Email as Evidence," Forensicon, accessed 7 January 2018, www.forensicon.com.

14. Zach Bulygo, "4 Hacks You Should Know Before You Craft Your Next Email Subject Line," Kissmetrics, accessed 8 January 2018, blog .kissmetrics.com.

15. Justin Bachman, "A New Way to Tell Your Airline You Hate It," *Bloomberg*, 10 August 2017, www.bloomberg.com; ZipWhip, accessed 3 January 2018, www.zipwhip.com.

16. Nha Thai, "10 Most Popular Social Media in China (2017), Dragon Social, 17 October 2017, www.dragonsocial.net

17. "IBM blogs," IBM, accessed 9 January 2018, www.ibm.com/blogs.

18. "IBM Social Computing Guidelines," IBM, accessed 8 January 2018, www.ibm.com.

19. Sathish Easuwaran, "RSS vs Atom," Saksoft, 7 November 2015, www.saksoft.com.

20. Based in part on "What to Tweet," Twitter, accessed 9 January 2018, business.twitter.com; Curtis Foreman, "Twitter Marketing: The Essential Guide," Hootsuite, 6 June 2017, blog.hootsuite.com.

21. Lauren Johnson, "Major Brands Are Betting Big on Podcasts, and It Seems to Be Paying Off," *Adweek*, 28 August 2016, www .adweek.com; "How 5 Companies Are Killing It with Branded Podcasts," Bluewing, accessed 9 January 2018, blog.bluewing.co.

22. Andrew Amelinckx, "Everlane Is Using Black Friday Sales to Bring Farm-Fresh Food to Garment Workers," *Modern Farmer*, 22 November 2017, modernfarmer.com; "This Black Friday, Everlane Wants to Buy 8,000 Helmets for Vietnamese Workers," *Fast Company*, 21 November 2016.

Five-Minute Guide to Better Business Email

Whenever you sit down to write an important email message, spend five minutes previewing the task to make sure you're ready to get started. Then you can use this guide to work your way through each step of the process.

 Plan the message

1. Make sure email is the best medium/channel option.
2. Analyze the situation: Who is your audience, and what is your purpose?
3. Identify the information you'll need in order to accomplish your purpose.
4. Choose the direct or indirect approach. Can you open with the main idea, or do you need to build up to it indirectly?

00:02 Draft the message

1. Unless you are sending short and simple messages to close colleagues, write in a conversational but professional style, with complete sentences and standard punctuation and capitalization.
2. Make your content easy to skim and easy to read by using short paragraphs.
3. Use bulleted or numbered lists to break out items, steps, or other entities.
4. Clarify how you would like the recipient to respond; don't assume the reader will know what you expect.

 Craft a compelling subject line

1. For routine communication with audiences who know you and expect to hear from you, a clear and concise description of the message's purpose and content is often sufficient.
2. However, if the recipient might ignore your message or delay opening it, you need to get creative:
   - Put yourself in the reader's shoes: Why would *you* want to open this message?
   - Relate the content and purpose of the message to the reader's top-of-mind concerns.
   - If action is needed soon, indicate this in the subject line.
   - Look for ways to add a sense of intrigue or mystery (without being obscure), such as "New budget numbers—make sure you're sitting down."
3. Revise the subject line if an ongoing thread has shifted the focus of the conversation.

 Finalize and format the message for fast, easy reading

1. Revise to make the message clear and concise.
2. Proofread carefully—it could save you hours of headaches and damage control.
3. Double-check dates, budgets, names, and other important variables.
4. Use a simple, clean layout with an easily readable font.
5. Use an email signature so people have your full contact information.

00:05 Distribute the message

1. Include only those recipients who really need to see the message.
2. Use cc to include secondary recipients.
3. Use bcc to protect the identity of recipients, such as when you don't want to reveal their email addresses to others on the distribution list.
4. If the conversation evolves over the course of a thread and is no longer relevant to everyone who was originally included, remove them from the distribution.
5. Don't mark messages as "urgent" or "important" unless they truly are.

Five-Minute Guide to Better Blog Posts

Launch your blog posts on a clear path by checking off these five steps. Doing so will let you know if you're ready to write and post or if you need more time for research and planning.

`00:01` **Plan the post**

1. Make sure each post is within the overall scope you have in mind for your blog.
2. Make every post about your readers and the issues important to them; even if you're sharing news about yourself or your company, relate it to reader needs and interests.
3. Don't post anything you wouldn't want the entire world to see; people far beyond your usual audience may see what you post.

`00:02` **Draft the post**

1. Communicate with a personal style and an authentic voice, but don't write carelessly.
2. Write "professional-grade" material by following accepted standards of capitalization, punctuation, spelling, and grammar.
3. Make sure you support any claims and opinions with logic and verifiable evidence; link to your sources whenever possible.
4. Disclose any relevant business relationships or conflicts of interest, such as explaining that the product you are reviewing was provided by the company free of charge.
5. Keep marketing and sales messages to a minimum, except for the occasional new product announcement, if relevant.
6. Include media items such as infographics, photos, and videos that your readers will find interesting.
7. Encourage readers to join the conversation by leaving comments.

`00:03` **Curate useful, shareable content**

1. Link generously, but thoughtfully; you have a responsibility to share useful and safe content.
2. Respect the intellectual property rights of anyone whose material you use or link to.
3. Always identify sources of material that you quote.
4. Never copy and repost an entire article from someone else—include a brief introductory portion and link to the original site instead.

`00:04` **Write compelling, informative, and specific headlines**

1. Be clear; readers shouldn't have to guess what the post is about.
2. Use key words from the post to identify the content.
3. Creative phrasing is fine as long as the purpose and content of the post is clear.

`00:05` **Finalize and format the post for fast, easy reading**

1. Revise the post for maximum clarity and conciseness.
2. Proofread to eliminate errors.
3. Double-check facts and figures.
4. Highlight tweetable passages that readers might want to share with their followers.
5. Tag the post with a consistent set of labels that you use for all your posts.
6. Use your blogging system's preview function, if available, to verify formatting and appearance before you hit Publish.

9

Writing Routine and Positive Messages

LEARNING OBJECTIVES

After studying this chapter, you will be able to

1 Outline an effective strategy for writing routine business requests.

2 Describe three common types of routine requests.

3 Outline an effective strategy for writing routine replies, routine messages, and positive messages.

4 Describe seven common types of routine replies and positive messages.

MyLab Business Communication

Improve Your Grade!

If your instructor is using MyLab Business Communication, visit **www.pearson.com/mylab/business-communication** for videos, simulations, and writing exercises.

ON THE JOB: COMMUNICATING AT
PRODUCTIVITY REPORT

Staying in Control of the Daily Message Deluge

Every so often, you'll get the chance to craft a message or document that has the potential to reshape your career or your company, such as a major project proposal or a business plan. However, much of your business communication will take place through routine, everyday messages—asking someone for help or information, responding to such requests from others, sharing information with colleagues or customers, and congratulating or consoling other people.

Just because these messages are routine, though, doesn't make them unimportant. In fact, the cumulative effect of all these brief messages could be more influential on your career than the occasional major report or proposal. The way you handle communication, day in and day out, is a key factor in establishing your credibility as a professional.

Developing your skills at handling routine messages is only part of the challenge. Depending on your field and your position, you're likely to be inundated with routine messages. It's not uncommon for professionals to receive a hundred or more messages a day—and

Jill Duffy offers research-based advice on handling the barrage of routine messages that most business communicators deal with on the job.

Image Courtesy of Jill Duffy

be expected to respond to many of them while generating many more messages themselves. So not only do you need to be skilled at handling routine communication, you also have to be hyper-efficient at it, or else you'll get hopelessly swamped.

Fortunately, you have a wise ally in Jill Duffy. Her career as a writer spans multiple industries, from academic journals to major newspapers to the trade journals *Game Developer* and *PC*. One of her areas of expertise is personal and organizational productivity, and she shares her ideas in the weekly Get Organized column for *PC*, in her book *Get Organized: How to Clean Up Your Messy Digital Life*, and via her newest venture, the website *Productivity Report*, which blends advice from research studies and personal experience. Her deep and diverse experience has given her useful insights into the challenges of digital productivity, and much of that involves how to handle a high volume of routine messages without losing focus on the audience or on top work priorities.

For email, for instance, she advises compartmentalizing message flows so that high-priority messages never get lost in the deluge of low-priority messages. Most email programs and apps offer the ability to filter messages based on sender, subject line, and other factors, so you can make sure important messages are always visible. Then develop a comprehensive system of software capabilities and daily habits to keep email in check. For example, if one of your goals is to respond to your boss's emails before you go home every day, set up an email filter to send those messages to a special folder and set an alarm to

deal with them at 4:00 every day. Another skill Duffy promotes is acting quickly and decisively on incoming email, whether that is deleting a message, filing it, responding immediately (for simple or critical messages), or scheduling time to respond. The key is to avoid looking at a message multiple times before deciding what to do with it.

Duffy doesn't subscribe to the approach taken by email users who never bother filtering and filing messages but who instead let them pile up in their inbox and use search functions to find specific messages whenever they need them. She points out several problems with this approach. First, if you can't remember who sent a message or the exact keywords that are in it, you'll never find it with search methods alone. Second, folders organized by subject serve as a "second memory" that she can browse whenever she wants. Third, that giant, unsorted pile of messages in your inbox will be a constant source of anxiety and distraction, as you repeatedly scan through it trying to find a specific item or to make sure you haven't missed anything important.

Whether it's email, workgroup messaging, or any other communication platform, setting up and fine-tuning a system and set of habits that work best for you does take some time and effort. However, it will be time well spent because you'll be more efficient every day, and you'll be able to focus your attention and energy on the messages that matter the most.[1]

PRODUCTIVITYREPORT.ORG

Strategy for Routine Requests

Jill Duffy (profiled in the chapter-opening On the Job) helps business professionals deal with a vital aspect of communication in today's digital workplace: how to productively handle the many routine messages that need to be sent or answered day in and day out. Routine messages fall into two groups: routine requests, in which you ask for information or action from another party, and a variety of routine and positive messages.

With most routine requests, your audience will be inclined to respond as you ask, so the direct approach is fine. For unusual, unexpected, or unwelcome requests, the indirect approach with a strong element of persuasion is a better choice (see Chapter 11).

Like all other business messages, a routine request has three parts: an opening, a body, and a close. Using the direct approach, open with your main idea, which is a clear statement of your request. Use the body to give details and justify your request. Finally, close by requesting specific action.

1 LEARNING OBJECTIVE
Outline an effective strategy for writing routine business requests.

The direct approach is fine for most routine requests, routine messages, and positive messages.

OPEN WITH YOUR REQUEST

With routine requests, you can make your request at the beginning of the message. Of course, getting right to the point should not be interpreted as license to be abrupt or tactless:

- **Pay attention to tone.** Instead of demanding action ("Send me the latest version of the budget spreadsheet"), show respect by using words such as *please* and *I would appreciate*.

- **If appropriate, acknowledge that you are asking for someone's time and effort.** Even if responding to your request is part of someone's job responsibilities, a few words of acknowledgment help maintain a positive relationship: "I know you're swamped this week, but when you have a second, could you send me . . ."

Take care that your direct approach doesn't come across as abrupt or tactless.

REAL-TIME UPDATES
LEARN MORE BY VISITING THIS WEBSITE
Insight into mobile strategies for routine communication
ClickSoftware's blog discusses a range of topics on mobile business communication. Go to **real-timeupdates.com/ebc13** and select Learn More in the Students section.

- **Be specific.** Don't expect the reader to figure out what you need. For example, if you request the latest market data from your research department, be sure to say whether you want a one-page summary or 100 pages of raw data.

EXPLAIN AND JUSTIFY YOUR REQUEST

Use the body of your message to explain or justify your request, as needed. Make the explanation a smooth and logical outgrowth of your opening remarks. If complying with the request could benefit the reader, be sure to mention that. If you have an unusual or complex request, break it down into specific, individual questions so that the reader can address each one separately. This consideration shows respect for your audience's time and will help them respond more accurately to your request.

> If you have an unusual or complex request, break it down into specific, individual questions that are easier to process.

REQUEST SPECIFIC ACTION IN A COURTEOUS CLOSE

> Close request messages with
> - A request for some specific action
> - Information about how you can be reached
> - An expression of appreciation

Close your message with three important elements: (1) deadlines and other important information that will help the reader respond, (2) information about how you can be reached (if it isn't obvious), and (3) an expression of appreciation or goodwill. When you ask readers to perform a specific action, ask for a response by a specific date or time, if appropriate (for example, "Please send the figures by May 5 so that I can return first-quarter results to you before the May 20 conference").

Conclude your message with a sincere thanks, but avoid saying "Thank you in advance," because many people consider it rude. Good alternatives include "I appreciate your help" or a simple "Thank you."[2] To review, see "Checklist: Writing Routine Requests."

---

2 **LEARNING OBJECTIVE**
Describe three common types of routine requests.

Common Examples of Routine Requests

The most common types of routine messages are asking for information or action, asking for recommendations, and making claims and requesting adjustments.

ASKING FOR INFORMATION OR ACTION

> As you plan a request, think about what you can do to make it as easy as possible for your recipients to respond.

Most of your routine requests will involve asking someone to provide information or take some specific action. As you plan your message, think about what you can do to make responding to the request as easy as possible for your recipients. Doing so is courteous and respectful, and it will likely prompt better and faster responses that will benefit you, too. If it's relevant, point out any benefits of complying with your request, whether a

---

CHECKLIST ✔ Writing Routine Requests

A. State your request up front.
- ✔ Write in a polite, undemanding, personal tone.
- ✔ Use the direct approach because your audience will probably respond favorably to your request.
- ✔ Be specific and precise in your request.

B. Explain and justify your request.
- ✔ Justify the request or explain its importance.
- ✔ Explain any potential benefits of responding.

- ✔ Ask the most important questions first.
- ✔ Break complex requests into individual questions that are limited to only one topic each.

C. Request specific action in a courteous close.
- ✔ Make it easy to comply by including appropriate contact information.
- ✔ Express your gratitude.
- ✔ Clearly state any important deadlines for the request.

personal benefit to those involved or something that will benefit your organization as a whole. Naturally, be sure to adapt your request to your audience and the situation (see Figure 9.1 on the next page).

ASKING FOR RECOMMENDATIONS

Employers, business partners, investors, lenders, and other organizations often ask applicants to supply references before hiring or promoting people, extending credit, awarding contracts, or granting scholarships or other benefits. Consequently, at various stages of your career, you may need to ask people who know you in a professional or personal capacity to provide you with a recommendation or serve as a reference.

A recommendation usually takes the form of a brief letter or email message that expresses someone's confidence in your ability to perform a job, fulfill the terms of a contract, or do whatever the situation entails. Serving as a reference often means agreeing to have a phone conversation or email exchange with a representative from the hiring company or other organization involved, during which the person will answer questions and provide background information about you. (Before you volunteer anyone's name as a reference, you must ask permission to do so.)

These requests are usually routine, so the direct approach is fine. However, you shouldn't always assume a positive response, and a negative response may not be related to your qualifications. You are asking busy people to devote time and energy on your behalf, and you're asking them to put their own reputations on the line. In some cases, the person may not know you well enough or may not believe that the opportunity you are pursuing is a good fit for you. In addition, when it comes to job references, some organizations don't allow their staff to provide anything beyond confirmation of employment.

Open your message by clearly stating why the recommendation is required (if it's not for a job, be sure to explain its purpose) and what you would like your reader to do on your behalf. If you haven't had contact with the person for some time, use the opening to trigger memories of the relationship you had, including dates and any special events or accomplishments that might bring a clear and favorable picture of you to mind.

Use the body to provide information that will make it easy for the recipient to comply with your request:

- The nature of the opportunity you are pursuing
- The action you are asking for (such as writing a message or agreeing to answer questions)
- Information that you would like the recommendation to convey, such as your work experience, skills, training, character, and fitness for the opportunity
- Full contact information if you are asking the person to send a letter or email message
- The application deadline or other date by which you need the recommendation

If it will give the recipient a helpful overview of your career since your last contact, consider including an up-to-date résumé.

Close your message with a sincere thank you. If you are requesting a printed letter, always be sure to enclose a stamped, preaddressed envelope as a convenience to the other party. Figure 9.2 on page 261 provides an example of a request that follows these guidelines.

> For a variety of reasons, you may need to ask people who know you in a professional or personal capacity to provide you with a recommendation or serve as a reference.

> When requesting recommendations, remember you are asking people to put their own reputations on the line.

REAL-TIME UPDATES

LEARN MORE BY VISITING THIS WEBSITE

LinkedIn's advice for college students

Follow these tips to get the most from LinkedIn, including the most appropriate and effective ways to ask for recommendations. Go to **real-timeupdates.com/ebc13** and select Learn More in the Students section.

MAKING CLAIMS AND REQUESTING ADJUSTMENTS

If you're dissatisfied with a company's product or service, you can opt to make a **claim** (a formal complaint) or request an **adjustment** (a settlement of a claim). In either case, it's important to maintain a professional tone in all your communication, no matter how

> A *claim* is a formal complaint; an *adjustment* is a remedy you ask for to settle a claim.

1 Plan →	**2** Write →	**3** Complete
Analyze the Situation Verify that the purpose is to request information from company managers. **Gather Information** Gather accurate, complete information about local competitive threats. **Choose Medium and Channel** Email is effective for this internal message, and it allows the attachment of a Word document to collect the information. **Organize the Information** Clarify that the main idea is collecting information that will lead to a better competitive strategy, which will in turn help the various district managers.	**Adapt to Your Audience** Show sensitivity to audience needs with a "you" attitude, politeness, positive emphasis, and bias-free language. The writer already has credibility as manager of the department. **Compose the Message** Maintain a style that is conversational but still businesslike, using plain English and appropriate voice.	**Revise the Message** Evaluate content and review readability; avoid unnecessary details. **Produce the Message** Simple email format is all the design this message needs. **Proofread the Message** Review for errors in layout, spelling, and mechanics. **Distribute the Message** Deliver the message via the company's email system.

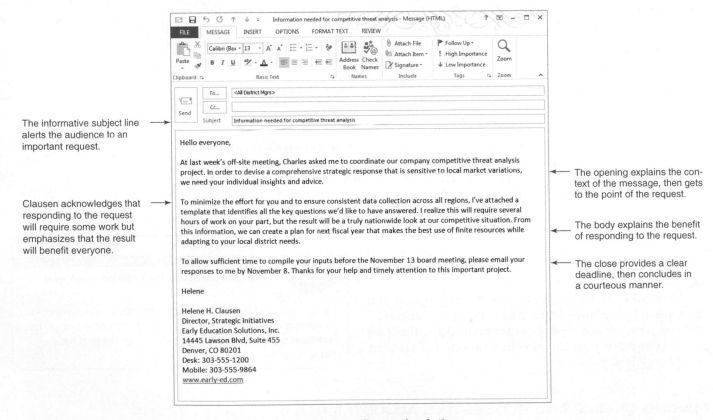

The informative subject line alerts the audience to an important request.

Clausen acknowledges that responding to the request will require some work but emphasizes that the result will benefit everyone.

The opening explains the context of the message, then gets to the point of the request.

The body explains the benefit of responding to the request.

The close provides a clear deadline, then concludes in a courteous manner.

Figure 9.1   Routine Message Requesting Action
In this email request to district managers across the country, Helene Clausen asks them to fill out an attached information collection form. Although the request is not unusual and responding to it is part of the managers' responsibility, Clausen asks for their help in a courteous manner and points out the benefits of responding.

1 Plan →	2 Write →	3 Complete
Analyze the Situation Verify that the purpose is to request a recommendation letter from a college professor.	**Adapt to Your Audience** Show sensitivity to audience needs with a "you" attitude, politeness, positive emphasis, and bias-free language.	**Revise the Message** Evaluate content and review readability; avoid unnecessary details.
Gather Information Gather information on classes and dates to help the reader recall you and to clarify the position you seek.	**Compose the Message** Style is respectful and businesslike, while still using plain English and appropriate voice.	**Produce the Message** Simple letter format is all the design this message needs.
Choose Medium and Channel The letter format gives this message an appropriate level of formality, although many professors prefer to be contacted by email.		**Proofread the Message** Review for errors in layout, spelling, and mechanics.
Organize the Information Messages like this are common and expected, so a direct approach is fine.		**Distribute the Message** Deliver the message via postal mail or email if you have the professor's email address.

1181 Ashport Drive
Tate Springs, TN 38101
March 14, 2020

Professor Lyndon Kenton
School of Business
University of Tennessee, Knoxville
Knoxville, TN 37916

Dear Professor Kenton:

I recently interviewed with Strategic Investments and have been called for a second interview for their Analyst Training Program (ATP). They have requested at least one recommendation from a professor, and I immediately thought of you. May I have a letter of recommendation from you?

> The opening states the purpose of the letter and makes the request, assuming the reader will want to comply.

As you may recall, I took FINC 425, Investment and Portfolio Management, from you during the Fall 2019 semester. I was fascinated by the methods of risk and return analysis you presented, and the class confirmed my decision to pursue a career in investment management.

> Tucker includes information near the opening to refresh her professor's memory.

My enclosed résumé includes all my relevant work experience and volunteer activities. I would also like to add that I've handled the financial planning for our family since my father passed away several years ago, and I have increasingly applied my business training in deciding what stocks or bonds to trade. This, I believe, has given me a practical edge over others who may be applying for the same job.

> The body refers to the enclosed résumé and mentions experience that could set the applicant apart from other candidates—information the professor could use in writing the recommendation.

If possible, Ms. Blackmon in Human Resources needs to receive your letter by March 30. For your convenience, I've enclosed a preaddressed, stamped envelope.

> She provides a deadline for response and includes information about the person who is expecting the recommendation.

I appreciate your time and effort in writing this letter of recommendation for me. It will be great to put my education to work, and I'll keep you informed of my progress. Thank you for your consideration in this matter.

> The close is warm and respectful.

Sincerely,

Joanne Tucker

Joanne Tucker

Enclosure

Figure 9.2 Effective Request for a Recommendation
This writer uses a direct approach when asking for a recommendation from a former professor. Note how she takes care to refresh the professor's memory because she took the class a year and a half ago. She also indicates the date by which the letter is needed and points to the enclosure of a stamped, preaddressed envelope.

When writing a claim or requesting an adjustment

- Explain the problem and give details
- Provide backup information
- Request specific action

angry or frustrated you are. Keeping your cool will help you get the situation resolved sooner.

Open with a clear and calm statement of the problem along with your request. In the body, give a complete, specific explanation of the details. Provide any information the recipient needs in order to verify your complaint. In your close, politely request specific action or convey a sincere desire to find a solution. And, if appropriate, suggest that the business relationship will continue if the problem is solved satisfactorily. Be prepared to back up your claim with invoices, sales receipts, payment evidence, dated correspondence, and any other relevant documents.

If the remedy is obvious, tell your reader exactly what you expect to be done, such as exchanging incorrectly shipped merchandise for the right item or issuing a refund if the item is out of stock. However, if you're uncertain about the precise nature of the trouble, you could ask the company to assess the situation and then advise you on how the situation could be fixed. Supply your full contact information so that the company can discuss the situation with you, if necessary. Compare the ineffective and effective versions in Figure 9.3 for an example of making a claim. To review the tasks involved in making claims and requesting adjustments, see "Checklist: Making Claims and Requesting Adjustments."

3 **LEARNING OBJECTIVE** Outline an effective strategy for writing routine replies, routine messages, and positive messages.

MOBILE APP

Send Anywhere is a secure file-transfer app that lets you send files of any size.

Strategy for Routine Replies, Routine Messages, and Positive Messages

Just as you'll make numerous requests for information and action throughout your career, you'll also respond to similar requests from other people. When you are responding positively to a request, sending routine announcements, or sending a positive or goodwill message, you have several goals: to communicate the information or the good news, answer all questions, provide all required details, and leave your reader with a good impression of you and your firm.

The direct approach is an appropriate and efficient way to structure these messages because your readers will range from neutral to receptive. Whenever you have significant or unexpected negative information to share, the indirect approach covered in Chapter 10 is more appropriate.

OPEN WITH THE MAIN IDEA

If a reply or unsolicited message is unexpected and could have significant negative consequences, consider using the indirect approach instead (see Chapter 10).

Even with the direct approach, it's often helpful to open with a few words of "socializing" before getting to your main idea.

In most cases, you can get right to the point with these routine messages. Of course, you'll want to adapt your opening to the specific situation. If the message is unexpected or you haven't been in contact with the reader for a long time, a brief explanation of why you're writing is appropriate.

Depending on the nature of the message, a few words of "socializing" can be a good way to foster a positive working relationship—just as you usually would do on the phone or in person. In the example at the bottom of the next page, a manager is writing to let a subordinate know that her proposal has been approved. The tone is upbeat, and after a brief thanks, the writer moves directly to the good news.

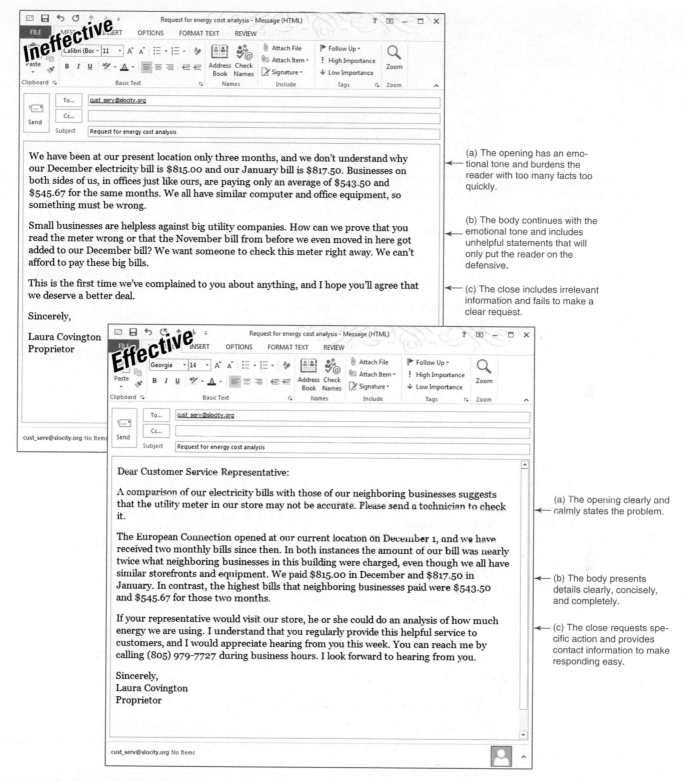

Ineffective

Request for energy cost analysis - Message (HTML)

To... cust_serv@slocity.org

Subject   Request for energy cost analysis

We have been at our present location only three months, and we don't understand why our December electricity bill is $815.00 and our January bill is $817.50. Businesses on both sides of us, in offices just like ours, are paying only an average of $543.50 and $545.67 for the same months. We all have similar computer and office equipment, so something must be wrong.

Small businesses are helpless against big utility companies. How can we prove that you read the meter wrong or that the November bill from before we even moved in here got added to our December bill? We want someone to check this meter right away. We can't afford to pay these big bills.

This is the first time we've complained to you about anything, and I hope you'll agree that we deserve a better deal.

Sincerely,

Laura Covington
Proprietor

cust_serv@slocity.org No Items

(a) The opening has an emotional tone and burdens the reader with too many facts too quickly.

(b) The body continues with the emotional tone and includes unhelpful statements that will only put the reader on the defensive.

(c) The close includes irrelevant information and fails to make a clear request.

Effective

Request for energy cost analysis - Message (HTML)

To... cust_serv@slocity.org

Subject   Request for energy cost analysis

Dear Customer Service Representative:

A comparison of our electricity bills with those of our neighboring businesses suggests that the utility meter in our store may not be accurate. Please send a technician to check it.

The European Connection opened at our current location on December 1, and we have received two monthly bills since then. In both instances the amount of our bill was nearly twice what neighboring businesses in this building were charged, even though we all have similar storefronts and equipment. We paid $815.00 in December and $817.50 in January. In contrast, the highest bills that neighboring businesses paid were $543.50 and $545.67 for those two months.

If your representative would visit our store, he or she could do an analysis of how much energy we are using. I understand that you regularly provide this helpful service to customers, and I would appreciate hearing from you this week. You can reach me by calling (805) 979-7727 during business hours. I look forward to hearing from you.

Sincerely,
Laura Covington
Proprietor

cust_serv@slocity.org No Items

(a) The opening clearly and calmly states the problem.

(b) The body presents details clearly, concisely, and completely.

(c) The close requests specific action and provides contact information to make responding easy.

Figure 9.3   Ineffective and Effective Versions of a Claim
Note the difference in both tone and information content in these two versions. The poor version is emotional and unprofessional, whereas the improved version communicates calmly and clearly.

Hi Olivia,

Thanks for your proposal to improve our employee orientation process. You've made some great suggestions, and I will meet with the HR team this week to plan how we can implement your ideas.

In the following example, the customer service manager of a blog-hosting company is alerting customers about a potential disruption of service:

> Dear customer:
>
> To maintain the high level of reliability you've come to expect from SpiderHost, we are transitioning our hosting platform to a new cloud-based architecture. The change will take place this Saturday between 1:00 a.m. and 3:00 a.m., and your site may be unavailable for a brief period during the switchover.

With the direct approach, open with a clear and concise expression of the main idea or good news.

In both examples, the writer gets to the point quickly after a brief introduction that establishes the context of the message and works to promote a positive relationship with the reader.

PROVIDE NECESSARY DETAILS AND EXPLANATION

Use the body of the message to expand on the main idea from the opening, as needed.

Use the body to expand on the opening so that readers get all the information they need. As you provide the details, maintain the supportive tone established in the opening. The writer in the previous example might continue by explaining how the change will help customers and what they can expect during the transition:

> With this new architecture, we will be able to expand bandwidth at the flip of a switch whenever blog traffic increases. Even if traffic to your site jumps literally overnight, we can keep delivering as much bandwidth as you need.
>
> We are staging the switchover in a way that should minimize downtime for customer sites, and we don't expect any site to be unavailable for more than two or three seconds. If people do visit your site during that narrow window, they will see a message asking them to try again in a moment or two.

REAL-TIME UPDATES

LEARN MORE BY READING THIS ARTICLE

Using Twitter for routine customer communication

These 10 tips can help any company respond to the growing number of routine requests delivered on Twitter. Go to **real-timeupdates. com/ebc13** and select Learn More in the Students section.

If you are communicating with a customer, you might also want to use the body of your message to assure the person of the wisdom of his or her purchase selection (without being condescending or self-congratulatory). Using such favorable comments, often known as *resale*, is a good way to build customer relationships. These comments are commonly included in acknowledgments of orders and other routine announcements to customers, and they are most effective when they are short and specific:

> The KitchenAid mixer you ordered is our best-selling model. It should meet your cooking needs for many years.

END WITH A COURTEOUS CLOSE

The close of routine replies, routine messages, and positive messages is usually short and simple because you're leaving things on a neutral or positive note and not usually

---

CHECKLIST ✔ Writing Routine Replies and Positive Messages

A. Start with the main idea.
- ✔ Be clear and concise.
- ✔ Identify the single most important message before you start writing.

B. Provide necessary details and explanation.
- ✔ Explain your point completely to eliminate any confusion or lingering doubts.
- ✔ Maintain a supportive tone throughout.

- ✔ Embed negative statements in positive contexts or balance them with positive alternatives.
- ✔ Talk favorably about the choices the customer has made.

C. End with a courteous close.
- ✔ Let your readers know you have their personal well-being in mind.
- ✔ If further action is required, tell readers how to proceed and encourage them to act promptly.

asking for the reader to do anything. Often, a simple thank you is all you need. However, if follow-up action is required or expected, use the close to identify who will do what and when that action will take place. For a quick reminder of the steps involved in writing routine replies and positive messages, see "Checklist: Writing Routine Replies and Positive Messages" on the previous page.

> Use the close to make sure readers have all the information they need in order to take action or otherwise respond to the message.

Common Examples of Routine Replies, Routine Messages, and Positive Messages

> **4 LEARNING OBJECTIVE**
> Describe seven common types of routine replies and positive messages.

Most routine and positive messages fall into seven categories: answers to requests for information and action, grants of claims and requests for adjustment, recommendations, routine information, instructions, good-news announcements, and goodwill messages.

ANSWERING REQUESTS FOR INFORMATION AND ACTION

Every professional answers requests for information or action from time to time. If the response is straightforward, the direct approach is appropriate. Keep the message brief and confirm any expectations, such as when you will provide information or perform a task. However, if you need to give an unexpected negative response to a request, consider the indirect approach covered in Chapter 10. For positive responses, a prompt, gracious, and thorough response will enhance how people think about you and the organization you represent. When you're answering requests from a potential customer or other decision-maker, look for subtle and respectful ways to encourage a decision in your favor.

GRANTING CLAIMS AND REQUESTS FOR ADJUSTMENT

Even the best-run companies make mistakes, and each of these events represents a turning point in your relationship with your customer. If you handle the situation well, your customer is likely to be even more loyal than before because you've proven that you're serious about customer satisfaction. However, if a customer believes that you mishandled a complaint, the situation could get even worse. Dissatisfied customers often take their business elsewhere without notice and tell numerous friends, colleagues, and social media contacts about the negative experience. A transaction that might be worth only a few dollars by itself could cost you many times that amount in lost business.

> Responding to mistakes in a courteous, reader-focused way helps repair important business relationships.

Your specific response to a customer complaint depends on your company's policies for resolving such issues and your assessment of whether the company, the customer, or some third party is at fault. In general, take the following steps:

- Acknowledge receipt of the customer's claim or complaint.
- Sympathize with the customer's inconvenience or frustration.
- Take (or assign) personal responsibility for setting matters straight.
- Explain precisely how you have resolved, or plan to resolve, the situation.
- Take steps to repair the relationship.
- Follow up to verify that your response was correct.

In addition to taking these positive steps, maintain a professional demeanor. Don't blame colleagues by name; don't make exaggerated, insincere apologies; don't imply that the customer is at fault; and don't promise more than you can deliver.

Communication about a claim is a delicate matter when the customer is clearly at fault. Follow company guidelines, if applicable. If the decision is up to you, carefully weigh the cost of complying with the request against the cost of denying it, and then decide how to respond based on the overall impact on your company. If you choose to grant the claim, open with that good news. However, the body needs special attention because you want to discourage similar claims in the future. Close in a courteous manner that expresses your appreciation for the customer's business (see Figure 9.4 on the next page).

> To grant a claim when the customer is at fault, try to discourage future mistakes without insulting the customer.

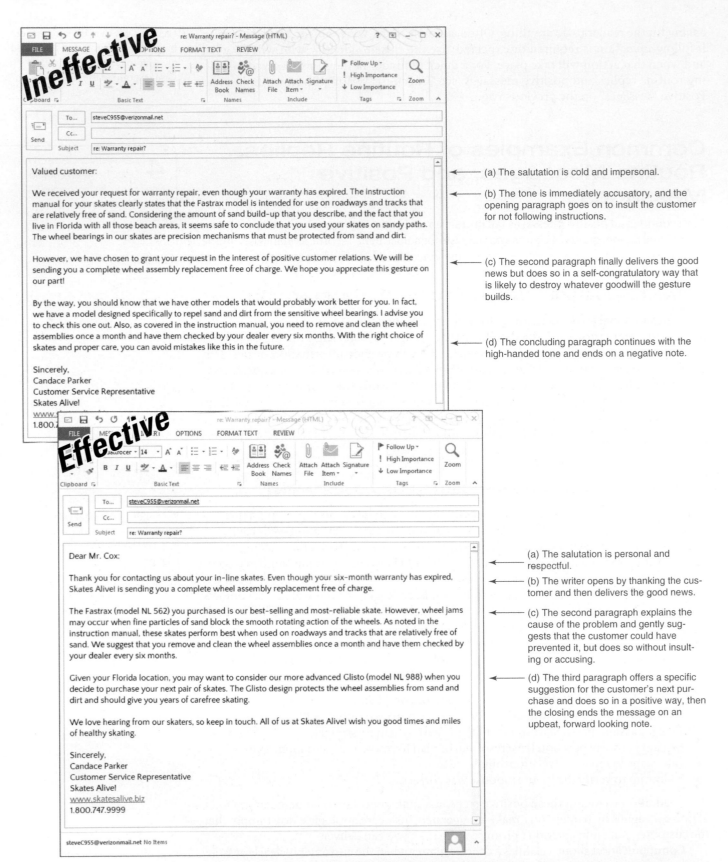

Ineffective

To... steveC955@verizonmail.net
Cc...
Subject: re: Warranty repair?

Valued customer:

We received your request for warranty repair, even though your warranty has expired. The instruction manual for your skates clearly states that the Fastrax model is intended for use on roadways and tracks that are relatively free of sand. Considering the amount of sand build-up that you describe, and the fact that you live in Florida with all those beach areas, it seems safe to conclude that you used your skates on sandy paths. The wheel bearings in our skates are precision mechanisms that must be protected from sand and dirt.

However, we have chosen to grant your request in the interest of positive customer relations. We will be sending you a complete wheel assembly replacement free of charge. We hope you appreciate this gesture on our part!

By the way, you should know that we have other models that would probably work better for you. In fact, we have a model designed specifically to repel sand and dirt from the sensitive wheel bearings. I advise you to check this one out. Also, as covered in the instruction manual, you need to remove and clean the wheel assemblies once a month and have them checked by your dealer every six months. With the right choice of skates and proper care, you can avoid mistakes like this in the future.

Sincerely,
Candace Parker
Customer Service Representative
Skates Alive!
www.
1.800.

(a) The salutation is cold and impersonal.

(b) The tone is immediately accusatory, and the opening paragraph goes on to insult the customer for not following instructions.

(c) The second paragraph finally delivers the good news but does so in a self-congratulatory way that is likely to destroy whatever goodwill the gesture builds.

(d) The concluding paragraph continues with the high-handed tone and ends on a negative note.

Effective

To... steveC955@verizonmail.net
Cc...
Subject: re: Warranty repair?

Dear Mr. Cox:

Thank you for contacting us about your in-line skates. Even though your six-month warranty has expired, Skates Alive! is sending you a complete wheel assembly replacement free of charge.

The Fastrax (model NL 562) you purchased is our best-selling and most-reliable skate. However, wheel jams may occur when fine particles of sand block the smooth rotating action of the wheels. As noted in the instruction manual, these skates perform best when used on roadways and tracks that are relatively free of sand. We suggest that you remove and clean the wheel assemblies once a month and have them checked by your dealer every six months.

Given your Florida location, you may want to consider our more advanced Glisto (model NL 988) when you decide to purchase your next pair of skates. The Glisto design protects the wheel assemblies from sand and dirt and should give you years of carefree skating.

We love hearing from our skaters, so keep in touch. All of us at Skates Alive! wish you good times and miles of healthy skating.

Sincerely,
Candace Parker
Customer Service Representative
Skates Alive!
www.skatesalive.biz
1.800.747.9999

steveC955@verizonmail.net No Items

(a) The salutation is personal and respectful.

(b) The writer opens by thanking the customer and then delivers the good news.

(c) The second paragraph explains the cause of the problem and gently suggests that the customer could have prevented it, but does so without insulting or accusing.

(d) The third paragraph offers a specific suggestion for the customer's next purchase and does so in a positive way, then the closing ends the message on an upbeat, forward looking note.

Figure 9.4   Responding to a Claim When the Buyer Is at Fault

Responding to a claim when the buyer is at fault is a positive gesture, so the content and tone of the message need to reflect that. After all, there's no point in fostering a positive relationship through actions but then undermining that through negative communication. Notice how the ineffective version sounds like a crabby parent who gives in to a child's demand but sends a mixed message by being highly critical anyway. The effective version is much more subtle, letting the customer know how to take care of his skates, without blaming or insulting him.

> **CHECKLIST** ✔ **Granting Claims and Adjustment Requests**
>
> **A. Responding when your company is at fault.**
> - ✔ Be aware of your company's policies in such cases before you respond.
> - ✔ For serious situations, refer to the company's crisis management plan.
> - ✔ Start by acknowledging receipt of the claim or complaint.
> - ✔ Take or assign personal responsibility for resolving the situation.
> - ✔ Sympathize with the customer's frustration.
> - ✔ Explain how you have resolved the situation (or plan to).
> - ✔ Take steps to repair the customer relationship.
> - ✔ Verify your response with the customer, and keep the lines of communication open.
>
> **B. Responding when the customer is at fault.**
> - ✔ Weigh the cost of complying with or refusing the request.
> - ✔ If you choose to comply, open with the good news.
> - ✔ Use the body of the message to respectfully educate the customer about steps needed to avoid a similar outcome in the future.
> - ✔ Close with an appreciation for the customer's business.
>
> **C. Responding when a third party is at fault.**
> - ✔ Evaluate the situation and review your company's policies before responding.
> - ✔ Avoid placing blame; focus on the solution.
> - ✔ Regardless of who is responsible for resolving the situation, let the customer know what will happen to resolve the problem.

See "Checklist: Granting Claims and Adjustment Requests" to review the tasks involved in these kinds of business messages.

PROVIDING RECOMMENDATIONS AND REFERENCES

People who need endorsements from employers or colleagues (when applying for a job, for example) often request letters of recommendation. These messages used to be a fairly routine matter, but employment recommendations and references have raised some complex legal issues in recent years. Employees have sued employers and individual managers for providing negative information or refusing to provide letters of recommendation, and employers have sued other employers for failing to disclose negative information about job candidates. Before you write a letter of recommendation for a former employee or provide information in response to another employer's background check, it is vital that you understand your company's policies. The company may refuse to provide anything more than dates of employment and other basic details, for example.[3]

Recommendation letters are vulnerable to legal complications, so consult your company's legal department before writing one.

If you decide to write a letter of recommendation or respond to a request for information about a job candidate, your goal is to convince readers that the person being recommended has the characteristics necessary for the job, assignment, or other objective the person is seeking. A successful recommendation letter contains a number of relevant details (see Figure 9.5 on the next page):

- The candidate's full name
- The position or other objective the candidate is seeking
- The nature of your relationship with the candidate
- Facts and evidence relevant to the candidate and the opportunity
- A comparison of this candidate's potential with that of peers, if available (for example, "Ms. Jonasson consistently ranked in the top 10 percent of our national salesforce")
- Your overall evaluation of the candidate's suitability for the opportunity

Keep in mind that every time you write a recommendation, you're putting your own reputation on the line. If the person's shortcomings are so pronounced that you don't think he or she is a good fit for the job, the only choice is to not write the letter at all. Unless your relationship with the person warrants an explanation, simply suggest that someone else might be in a better position to provide a recommendation. (For more advice on turning down requests for recommendations, see pages 302 and 303.)

REAL-TIME UPDATES

LEARN MORE BY VISITING THIS WEBSITE

Get expert tips on writing (or requesting) a letter of recommendation

Find helpful advice on employment recommendations, academic recommendations, and character references. Go to **real-timeupdates .com/ebc13** and select Learn More in the Students section.

LeClerc specifies the duration and nature of the relationship to give credibility to her evaluation.

Point1 Promotions

105 E. Madison
Ann Arbor, MI 48103
tel: 800-747-9786
email: info@point1promo.net
www.point1promo.net

November 13, 2020

Ms. Clarice Gailey
Director of Operations
McNally and Associates, Inc.
8688 Southgate Ave.
Augusta, GA 30906

Dear Ms. Gailey:

I am pleased to recommend Talvin Biswas for the marketing position at McNally and Associates. Mr. Biswas has worked with Point1 Promotions as an intern for the past two summers while working toward his degree in marketing and advertising. His duties included customer correspondence, web content updates, and direct-mail campaign planning.

As his supervisor, in addition to knowing his work here, I also know that Mr. Biswas has served as secretary for the International Business Association at the University of Michigan. He tutored other international students in the university's writing center. His fluency in three languages (English, French, and Hindi) and thorough knowledge of other cultures will make him an immediate contributor to your international operations.

Mr. Biswas is a thoughtful and careful professional who will not hesitate to contribute ideas when invited to do so. In addition, because Mr. Biswas learns quickly, he will learn your company's routine with ease.

Mr. Biswas will make an excellent addition to your staff at McNally and Associates. If I can provide any additional information, please call me at the number above. If you prefer to communicate by email, my address is angela_leclerc@point1promo.net.

Sincerely,

Angela LeClerc

Angela LeClerc
Vice President, Marketing

← The opening clearly states the candidate's full name and the specific purpose of the letter.

← The body continues with specific examples to support the writer's positive evaluation.

← The close summarizes the writer's recommendation and invites further communication.

Figure 9.5 Effective Recommendation Letter
This letter clearly states the nature of the writer's relationship to the candidate and provides specific examples to support the writer's endorsements.

SHARING ROUTINE INFORMATION

When sharing routine information

- State the purpose at the beginning and briefly mention the nature of the information you are providing.
- Provide the necessary details.
- End with a courteous close.

Many messages involve sharing routine information, such as project updates and order status notifications. Use the opening of these routine messages to state the purpose and briefly mention the nature of the information you are providing. Give the necessary details in the body and end your message with a courteous close.

Most routine communications like this are neutral, so you don't have to take special steps in anticipation of emotional reactions from readers. However, make sure you've considered the likely response of all your readers and take steps to address the full range of reactions. For example, announcing that the company is opening an on-site daycare facility will likely be welcome news to those employees who have children. But what if employees without children feel it is unfair to spend money on a benefit that helps some workers but not others? These employees might prefer help with elder care or some other need, for example. If you anticipate a mixed reaction, look for ways to put the news in a positive context for everyone—such as pointing out that the day care will reduce the amount of time parents need to take off from work, which will reduce the workload burden on everyone else. (For situations in which negative news will have a profound effect on the recipients, consider the indirect techniques discussed in Chapter 10.)

WRITING INSTRUCTIONS

Writing instructions for employees or customers is another common communication task. For major projects such as user manuals, companies often employ specialist technical writers, but you could be involved in writing shorter instructions on a variety of topics. Follow these steps to create clear and effective instructions on any topic:

1. Make sure you understand how much your readers know about the subject. A common mistake when writing instructions is to assume too much knowledge or experience on the part of readers.
2. Provide an overview of the procedure. Explain what users will be doing, and identify any information or tools they will need in order to complete the procedure.
3. Define any technical terms or acronyms that readers need to understand.
4. Divide the procedure into discrete steps, with each step focusing on a single task.
5. Tell readers what to expect when they complete each step so they know they've done it correctly (for example, "If the green LED is on, you've made a secure connection").
6. Test the instructions on someone from the target audience.
7. Whenever possible, provide a way for readers to ask for help.

> To write effective instructions on any subject, start by figuring out how much your intended readers are likely to know about the topic or process.

ANNOUNCING GOOD NEWS

To develop and maintain good relationships, smart companies recognize that it's good business to spread the word about positive developments. Such developments can include opening new facilities, hiring a new executive, introducing new products or services, or sponsoring community events. Because good news is always welcome, use the direct approach (see Figure 9.6 on the next page).

External good-news announcements are often communicated in a **news release**, also known as a *press release*, a specialized document used to share relevant information with the news media. (News releases are also used to announce negative news, such as plant closings.) In most companies, news releases are usually prepared or at least supervised by specially trained writers in the public relations department. The content follows the customary pattern for a positive message: good news followed by details and a positive close. However, traditional news releases have a critical difference: You're not writing directly to the ultimate audience (such as the readers of a blog or newspaper); you're trying to spark the interest of an editor, reporter, blogger, or other intermediary in the hope that person will write a piece that carries your message to a larger audience.

> A *news release* or press release is a message (usually routine, but not always) designed to share information with the news media, although many are now written with customers and other stakeholders in mind as well.

Traditionally, news releases were crafted in a way to provide information to reporters, who would then write their own articles if the subject matter was interesting to their readers. However, the nature of the news release is changing. Many companies now view it as a general-purpose tool for communicating directly with customers and other audiences, creating *direct-to-consumer news releases*.[4] Many of these are considered *social media releases* because they include social networking links, "Tweetables" (Twitter-ready statements that can be shared on Twitter by clicking or tapping a single button), and other sharable content.

> News releases often include share-ready content that is easy to reuse in blog posts, tweets, and other social media formats.

FOSTERING GOODWILL

All business messages should be written with an eye toward fostering positive relationships with audiences, but some messages are written specifically to build goodwill. You can use these messages to enhance your relationships with customers, colleagues, and other businesspeople by sending friendly, even unexpected, notes with no direct business purpose. Whether you're thanking an employee for a job well done or congratulating a colleague for a personal or professional achievement, the small effort to send a goodwill message can have a positive and lasting effect on the people around you.

In addition to creating messages for a specific goodwill reason, you can craft almost any routine message in a way to build goodwill. Two ways to do so are by providing information

> Goodwill is the positive feeling that encourages people to maintain a business relationship.

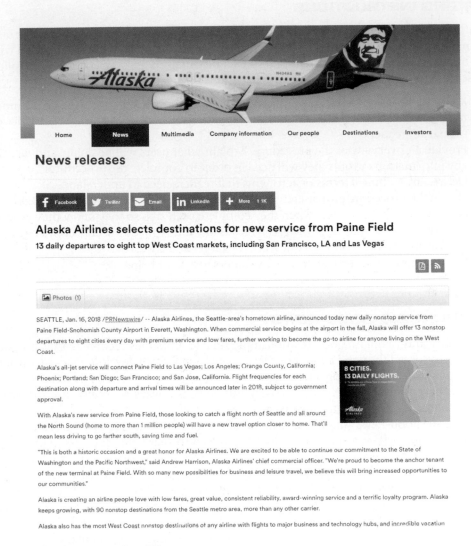

Figure 9.6 Announcing Good News
News releases, which can be aimed at both the news media and consumers in general, are a common way to announce good news.

Offering congratulations to companies or individuals for significant achievements is a good opportunity to build goodwill.

that your readers might find helpful and by maintaining a positive tone throughout your message.

Sending Congratulations

One prime opportunity for sending goodwill messages is to congratulate individuals or companies for significant business achievements. Other reasons for sending congratulations include highlights in people's personal lives, such as weddings, births, graduations, and success in nonbusiness competitions. You may congratulate business acquaintances on their own achievements or on the accomplishments of a family member. You may also take note of personal events, even if you don't know the reader well. If you're already friendly with the reader, a more personal tone is appropriate.

Sending Messages of Appreciation

An important leadership quality is the ability to recognize the contributions of employees, colleagues, suppliers, and other associates. Your praise does more than just make the person

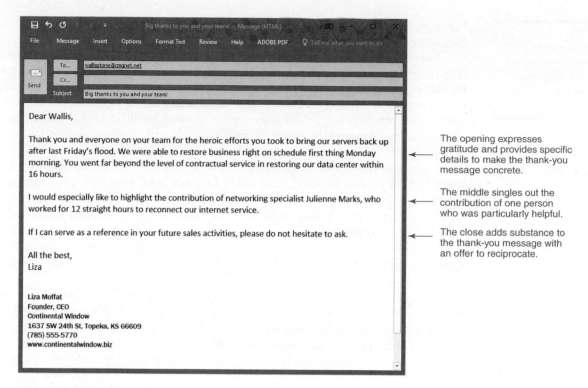

The opening expresses gratitude and provides specific details to make the thank-you message concrete.

The middle singles out the contribution of one person who was particularly helpful.

The close adds substance to the thank-you message with an offer to reciprocate.

Figure 9.7   Goodwill Messages
All business messages should try to build goodwill, of course, but some messages are written primarily to build goodwill.

feel good; it encourages further excellence. A message of appreciation may also become an important part of someone's personnel file or business-building portfolio, and specific information is particularly helpful in this regard because it provides proof of performance (see Figure 9.7).

Offering Condolences

Condolence letters are brief personal messages written to comfort someone after the death of a loved one. You may have occasion to offer condolences to employees or other

The primary purpose of condolence letters is to express sympathy for someone's loss.

DEVELOPING AS A PROFESSIONAL

Maintaining a Confident, Positive Outlook

Spend a few minutes around successful people in any field, and chances are you'll notice how optimistic they are. They believe in what they're doing, and they believe in themselves and their ability to solve problems and overcome obstacles.

Being positive doesn't mean displaying mindless optimism or spewing happy talk all the time. It means acknowledging that things may be difficult but then buckling down and getting the job done anyway. It means no whining and no slacking off, even when the going gets tough. We live in an imperfect world, no question; jobs can be boring or difficult, customers can be unpleasant, and bosses can be unreasonable. But when you're a pro, you find a way to power through.

Your energy, positive or negative, is contagious. Both in person and online, you'll spend as much time with your

colleagues as you spend with family and friends. Personal demeanor is therefore a vital element of workplace harmony. No one expects (or wants) you to be artificially upbeat and bubbly every second of the day, but one negative personality can make an entire office miserable and unproductive. Every person in a company has a responsibility to contribute to a positive, energetic work environment.

CAREER APPLICATIONS
1. Do you have an ethical obligation to maintain a positive outlook on the job? Why or why not?
2. How can you lift your spirits when work is dragging you down?

MOBILE APP
If you want the convenience or personal touch of handwriting but need to work in a digital format, **INKredible** makes it easy to save and share your notes.

business associates (when the person has lost a family member) or to the family of an employee or business associate (when that person has died).

These messages can feel intimidating to write, but they don't need to be. Follow these three principles: short, simple, and sincere. You don't need to produce a work of literary art; the fact that you are writing sends a message that is as meaningful as anything you can say.

Timing and media choice are important considerations with condolence letters. The sooner your message is received, the more comforting it will be, so don't delay. And unless circumstances absolutely leave you no choice, avoid using email or another digital medium. A brief, handwritten note on quality stationery is the way to go.

Open a condolence message with a simple expression of sympathy, such as "I am deeply sorry to hear of your loss" or "I am sorry for your loss." How you continue from there depends on the circumstances and your relationships with the deceased and the person to whom you are writing. For example, if you are writing to the husband of a colleague who recently died and you have never met him, you might continue with "Having worked with Janice for more than a decade, I know what a kind and caring person she was." Such a statement accomplishes two goals: explaining why you in particular are writing and letting the recipient know that his loved one was appreciated in the workplace.

Conversely, if you are writing to a colleague who recently lost a loved one, you might continue with "After meeting Warren at last year's company picnic and hearing your stories about his involvement with your son's soccer league and the many other ways he contributed to his community, I know what a special person he was." Sharing brief and positive memories like this adds meaning and depth to your expression of sympathy.

You can conclude with a simple statement such as "My thoughts are with you during this difficult time." If appropriate for the situation and your relationship, you might also include an offer of assistance. "Please call if there is anything I can do for you."

As you decide what to include in the message, keep two points in mind. First, make it a personal expression of sympathy, but don't make the whole message about you and your sense of loss. You might be grieving as well, but unless you, the deceased, and the reader were all personally close, don't say things like "I was so devastated to hear the news about Kalinda."

Keep your condolence message focused on the recipient, not on your own emotions, and don't offer "life advice" or trite sayings.

Second, don't offer "life advice," and don't include trite sayings that you may have heard or read. At this point, soon after the loss, the recipient doesn't want your advice, only your sympathy. Also, don't bring religion into the discussion unless you have a close personal relationship with the recipient and religion is already a part of your relationship. Otherwise, you risk offending with unwelcome or inappropriate sentiments.

Condolence letters are the most personal business messages you may ever have to write, so they require the utmost in care and respect for your reader. By keeping the messages short, simple, and sincere, you will be able to achieve the right tone.

To review the tasks involved in writing goodwill messages, see "Checklist: Sending Goodwill Messages." For the latest information on writing routine and positive messages, visit **real-timeupdates.com/ebc13**.

CHECKLIST ✔ Sending Goodwill Messages

✔ Be sincere and honest.
✔ Don't exaggerate or use vague, grandiose language; support positive statements with specific evidence.
✔ Use congratulatory messages to build goodwill with clients and colleagues.

✔ Send messages of appreciation to emphasize how much you value the work of others.
✔ When sending condolence messages, open with a brief statement of sympathy, then adapt your message based on the circumstances and your relationship with the recipient.

ON THE JOB: SOLVING COMMUNICATION DILEMMAS AT **PRODUCTIVITY REPORT**

You've joined *Productivity Report* as a freelance researcher and writer, helping Jill Duffy educate technology users on productivity and effective workplace communication. Use what you've learned in this and previous chapters to address these challenges.

1. A freelancer writer has submitted an article to be published on the *Productivity Report* blog. The piece is generally solid, but Duffy would like to see several changes before posting it. Which of these is the best way to open a message to the writer requesting the changes? Assume that you have had prior contact with the writer to discuss the article but that you don't have a working relationship yet.
   a. Thank you for your submission. The piece will definitely appeal to our readers, but we would like you to consider a few changes.
   b. I'm so sorry, but I'm afraid I will need to ask for a few changes before we can post your otherwise excellent article.
   c. Awesome piece! Just a few tweaks, and we'll be ready to roll.
   d. Attached please find a copy of your article, with comments and requested changes.

2. Websites and blogs occasionally suffer from page-loading problems, when a particular web page a visitor requests will not display, even when the rest of a site seems to be working normally. Assume that Productivity Report recently had a spate of these problems with the service that hosts its blog. Which of these is the best way to respond to queries while the company is working to fix the situation?
   a. Yes, we've noticed this problem ourselves, but we hope to have everything stabilized soon.
   b. We are soooooo sorry! We're working to resolve the situation as soon as possible.
   c. Don't you just hate computers sometimes? We're working to resolve the situation as soon as possible.
   d. We're having some problems with our host, which seems to be resulting in a lot of these errors. We're working on it now and hope to have everything stabilized soon.

3. After a week of trouble with the blog-hosting service, Duffy has asked you to make a claim with the hosting company,

requesting a 25 percent refund of that month's service fee. Which of these would be the best way to open an email message to the company's customer service supervisor? (You have had no previous contact with the company.)
   a. Over the past week, our blog has suffered from repeated page-loading problems. Our web analytics tools show a 52 percent increase in our bounce rate, so people are clearly leaving rather than waiting for pages to load.
   b. We demand compensation for the intermittent service we have received from your company over the past week. This kind of service is unacceptable and something we will not tolerate.
   c. Enough is enough. Our business suffers greatly when our readers can't load blog pages, and we're fed up with the poor service.
   d. After a week of this nonsense, why haven't you reached out to offer a refund of our monthly service fee? We are paying you to host a functioning blog, not drive our customers away.

4. On your first anniversary of working for Duffy, you want to send her an email message thanking her for giving you this opportunity and for teaching you so many things about effective and efficient business communication. The message is probably unexpected. Which of these is the best way to open this message? (Assume that you have developed a close and friendly working relationship.)
   a. Can you believe it's been a year already? This seems like a great time to say thanks for giving me this opportunity and for mentoring me in so many ways.
   b. Wow—I can't even put into words what an amazing and fantastic year this has been! You have been such an unbelievable guide, mentor, and guru to me—more than any beginner deserves.
   c. Every day out of the last 365 has been perfect! I love, love, LOVE this job and everything I get to do and see and learn from the most amazing boss ever.
   d. I wish to express my sincere gratitude for the opportunity I was presented with and the multiple ways I've been able to develop my communication skills.

END OF CHAPTER

Learning Objectives Checkup

Assess your understanding of the principles in this chapter by reading each learning objective and studying the accompanying exercises. You can check your responses against the answer key on page 613.

Objective 9.1: Outline an effective strategy for writing routine business requests.

1. Which of these is listed in the chapter as an important point about the opening of routine requests?
   a. If a request is truly routine, don't worry about tone—just get to the point.
   b. Show respect by paying attention to tone.
   c. Never take more than 10 words to get to the actual request.
   d. Worry about tone if you're requesting something from someone above you in the corporate hierarchy.

2. What's the best way to make an unusual or complex request?
   a. Open with an apology for the burden you are placing on the receiver.
   b. Save the toughest part of the request for the end of the message.
   c. Break it down into specific, individual questions so that the reader can address each one separately.
   d. Break it down into specific, individual questions and send each one in a separate email message for easy cataloging.

3. Which of these is *not* mentioned in the chapter as an element to include in the close of a routine request?
   a. An expression of appreciation or goodwill
   b. Deadlines and other important information that will help the reader respond
   c. Additional questions and details that you didn't cover in the body of the message
   d. Information about how you can be reached

Objective 9.2: Describe three common types of routine requests.

4. Requests for recommendations and references are routine messages, so you can organize your message using the _____ approach.

5. Which of the following is *not* listed in the chapter as a reason why you might not receive a positive response to a request for a recommendation or reference?
   a. The person probably recognizes that job openings close so quickly these days that it's pointless to respond.
   b. The person may not be willing to put his or her reputation on the line.
   c. The person may not believe this is a good opportunity for you.
   d. The person's employer may not allow its staff to write recommendations.

6. If you are requesting an adjustment from a company but you're not sure what the best solution would be, which of the following tactics would be best?
   a. Ask the company to assess the situation and offer advice on solving the problem.
   b. Don't ask for a solution, because doing so could lead to a suboptimal outcome for you.

   c. Subtly hint that legal action could light a fire under the company.
   d. Demand that the company solve the problem immediately; after all, it's the right thing to do.

Objective 9.3: Outline an effective strategy for writing routine replies, routine messages, and positive messages.

7. Including a few words of "socializing" at the beginning of a routine message is
   a. usually a waste of the reader's time.
   b. a good way to foster a positive working relationship.
   c. a sign of friendship that extends beyond the professional sphere.
   d. a sign of weakness or uncertainty.

8. Information included to assure a customer of the wisdom of his or her purchase selection is known as
   a. cross-selling tactics.
   b. resale information.
   c. upselling strategy.
   d. positive reinforcement.

Objective 9.4: Describe seven common types of routine replies and positive messages.

9. Which of the following is *not* among the recommended elements to include in your message if you are responding to a claim or complaint?
   a. An acknowledgment that you received the customer's claim or complaint
   b. An expression of sympathy for the inconvenience or loss the customer has experienced
   c. An explanation of how you will resolve the situation
   d. Complete contact information for your corporate legal staff

10. If a customer who is clearly at fault requests an adjustment and your company doesn't have a clear policy for this situation, you should
    a. ignore the request; the customer is clearly wasting your time.
    b. carefully weigh the cost of complying with the request against the cost of denying it and then decide how to respond based on the overall impact on your company.
    c. always agree to such requests because unhappy customers spread bad publicity about a company.
    d. suggest in a firm but professional tone that the customer take his or her business elsewhere in the future.

11. Which of these is the most important consideration when writing a letter of recommendation?
    a. Protect your own reputation, even if that means writing a negative letter.
    b. Make sure you understand your company's policies about writing recommendations.
    c. Adjust the tone from neutral to upbeat, based on whether you expect the person to be able to help you in the future.
    d. View it as a networking opportunity and mention your own qualifications in a subtle way.

12. What is the first step to take when writing instructions?
    a. Write a helpful glossary of every technical term that is related to this subject.

b. Create all the technical diagrams you'll need to explain the topic so you can see how much text you need to provide.

c. Figure out how much your readers know about the subject.

d. Assume that anyone interested in this topic will have a basic understanding of it.

13. A _____ is a statement that can be shared on Twitter by clicking or tapping a single button.

14. Which of these is the best way to achieve the appropriate tone in a condolence message?

a. Keep it short, simple, and sincere.

b. Include several time-tested phrases such as "Life is for the living."

c. Help the person move past the tragedy by assuring that he or she will find happiness again.

d. Talk at some length about how the loss is affecting you, so that the reader appreciates the depth of your concern.

Key Terms

adjustment The settlement of a claim

claim A formal complaint made in response to dissatisfaction over a product or service

condolence letters Brief personal messages written to comfort someone after the death of a loved one

news release Also known as a *press release*, a specialized document traditionally used to share relevant information with the local or national news media; today, many companies issue news releases directly to the public as well

Apply Your Knowledge

To review chapter content related to each question, refer to the indicated Learning Objective.

9-1. You're applying for a job as a website designer at a digital marketing agency. In a previous job at another agency, you excelled at website design but you were also asked to "pitch" the agency's services to potential clients. Unfortunately, you did not do well at this aspect of the job, and you were let go when the agency had to lay off 10 percent of its staff. The new opportunity will not require you to pitch new clients. Would it be appropriate to ask your former boss for a recommendation that focuses on your web design skills? If so, how should you approach the request? [LO-2]

9-2. The latest issue of a local business newspaper names 10 area executives who have exhibited excellent leadership skills in the past year. You are currently searching for a job, and a friend suggests that you write each executive a congratulatory letter and mention in passing that you are looking for new career opportunities and would appreciate the opportunity for an interview. Is this a smart strategy? Why or why not? [LO-4]

9-3. You've been asked to write a letter of recommendation for an employee who worked for you some years ago. You recall that the employee did an admirable job, but you can't remember any specific information at this point. Should you write the letter anyway? Explain. [LO-4]

9-4. Your company made a mistake that cost an important business customer a new client; you know it, and your customer knows it. Do you apologize, or do you refer to the incident in a positive light without admitting any responsibility? Briefly explain. [LO-4]

Practice Your Skills

Messages for Analysis

Read the following messages, then (1) analyze the strengths and weaknesses of each sentence and (2) revise each document so that it follows this chapter's guidelines.

9-5. **Message 9.A: Message Strategies: Routine Requests [LO-2]**

I'm fed up with the mistakes that our current accounting firm makes. I run a small construction company, and I don't have time to double-check every bookkeeping entry and call the accountants a dozen times when they won't return my messages. Please explain how your firm would do a better job than my current accountants. You have a good reputation among homebuilders, but before I consider hiring you to take over my accounting, I need to know that you care about quality work and good customer service.

9-6. **Message 9.B: Message Strategies: Responding to Claims and Requests for Adjustments [LO-4]**

We read your letter, requesting your deposit refund. We couldn't figure out why you hadn't received it, so we talked to our maintenance engineer, as you suggested. He said you had left one of the doors off the hinges in your apartment in order to get a large sofa through the door. He also confirmed that you had paid him $5.00 to replace the door since you had to turn in the U-Haul trailer and were in a big hurry.

This entire situation really was caused by a lack of communication between our housekeeping inspector and the maintenance engineer. All we knew was that the door was off the hinges when it was inspected by Sally Tarnley. You know that our policy states that if anything is wrong with the apartment, we keep the deposit. We had no way of knowing that George just hadn't gotten around to replacing the door.

But we have good news. We approved the deposit refund, which will be mailed to you from our home office in Teaneck, New Jersey. I'm not sure how long that will take, however. If you don't receive the check by the end of next month, give me a call.

Next time, it's really a good idea to stay with your apartment until it's inspected, as stipulated in your lease agreement. That way, you'll be sure to receive your refund when you expect it. Hope you have a good summer.

9-7. **Message 9.C: Message Strategies: Providing Recommendations [LO-4]** (Note: Assume that your company allows you to write recommendations.)

Your letter to Kunitake Ando, president of Sony, was forwarded to me because I am the human resources director. In my job as head of HR, I have access to performance reviews for all of the Sony employees in the United States. This means, of course, that I would be the person best qualified to answer your request for information on Nick Oshinski.

In your letter of the 15th, you asked about Nick Oshinski's employment record with us because he has applied to work for your company. Mr. Oshinski was employed with us from January 5, 2008, until March 1, 2016. During that time, Mr. Oshinski received ratings ranging from 2.5 up to 9.6, with 10 being the top score. As you can see, he must have done better reporting to some managers than to others. In addition, he took all vacation days, which is a bit unusual. Although I did not know Mr. Oshinski personally, I know that our best workers seldom use all the vacation time they earn. I do not know if that applies in this case. In summary, Nick Oshinski performed his tasks well depending on who managed him.

Exercises

Each activity is labeled according to the primary skill or skills you will need to use. To review relevant chapter content, you can refer to the indicated Learning Objective. In some instances, supporting information will be found in another chapter, as indicated.

Message Strategies: Routine Requests; Revising for Conciseness [LO-1], Chapter 7 Critique the following closing paragraphs. How would you rewrite each to be concise, courteous, and specific?

9-8. I can't make heads or tails of this trip report. Did you accomplish the tasks you set out to accomplish or only some of them or none of them? I see that you visited four separate clients but instead of enumerating the outcome of each meeting in a separate way, the conclusion of your report jumbles them all together in a way that makes it impossible to determine the status of each client project. Is any management-level action required for any of these clients? If so, which ones? What action? It's impossible to tell because your report doesn't specify meeting outcomes by client, as would normally be the case in a report from someone who visited multiple client sites during a single trip.

9-9. I need your response sometime soon so I can order the parts in time for your service appointment. Otherwise, your air-conditioning system may not be in tip-top condition for the start of the summer season.

9-10. Thank you in advance for sending me as much information as you can about your products. I look forward to receiving your package in the very near future.

9-11. To schedule an appointment with one of our knowledgeable mortgage specialists in your area, you can always call our hotline at 1-800-555-8765. This is also the number to call if you have more questions about mortgage rates, closing procedures, or any other aspect of the mortgage process. Remember, we're here to make the home-buying experience as painless as possible.

Message Strategies: Routine Responses; Media Skills: Email [LO-3], Chapter 8 Revise the following short email messages so

they are more direct and concise; develop a subject line for each revised message.

9-12. I'm contacting you about your recent email request for technical support on your cable internet service. Part of the problem we have in tech support is trying to figure out exactly what each customer's specific problem is so that we can troubleshoot quickly and get you back in business as quickly as possible. You may have noticed that in the online support request form, there are a number of fields to enter your type of computer, operating system, memory, and so on. While you did tell us you were experiencing slow download speeds during certain times of the day, you didn't tell us which times specifically, nor did you complete all the fields telling us about your computer. Please return to our support website and resubmit your request, being sure to provide all the necessary information; then we'll be able to help you.

9-13. Thank you for contacting us about the difficulty you had collecting your luggage at Denver International Airport. We are very sorry for the inconvenience this has caused you. As you know, traveling can create problems of this sort regardless of how careful the airline personnel might be. To receive compensation, please send us a detailed list of the items that you lost and complete the following questionnaire. You can email it back to us.

9-14. Sorry it took us so long to get back to you. We were flooded with résumés. Anyway, your résumé made the final 10, and after meeting three hours yesterday, we've decided we'd like to meet with you. What is your schedule like for next week? Can you come in for an interview on June 15 at 3:00 p.m.? Please get back to us by the end of this workweek and let us know if you will be able to attend. As you can imagine, this is our busy season.

9-15. We're letting you know that because we use over a ton of paper a year and because so much of that paper goes into the wastebasket to become so much more environmental waste, starting Monday, we're placing white plastic bins outside the elevators on every floor to recycle that paper and in the process, minimize pollution.

Message Strategies: Routine and Positive Messages; Revising for Conciseness [LO-3], Chapter 7 Rewrite the following sentences so that they are direct and concise. If necessary, break your answer into two sentences.

9-16. We wanted to invite you to our special 40 percent off by-invitation-only sale; the sale is taking place on November 9.

9-17. We wanted to let you know that we are giving a special-edition tote bag with every $100 donation you make to our radio station.

9-18. The director plans to go to the meeting that will be held on Monday at 11:00 a.m. but plans to arrive early to speak individually with department heads.

9-19. In today's meeting, we were happy to have the opportunity to welcome Paul Eccelson. He went over the product plans for next year. If you have any questions about these new products, feel free to call him at his office.

9-20. **Message Strategies: Responding to Claims and Requests for Adjustments [LO-4]** Your company markets a line of automotive accessories for people who like to "tune" their cars for maximum performance. A customer has just written a furious email, claiming that a supercharger he purchased from your website didn't deliver the extra engine power he expected. Your company has a standard refund process to handle situations such as this, and you have the information you need to inform the customer about that. You also have information that could help the customer find a more compatible supercharger from one of your competitors, but the customer's email message is so abusive that you don't feel obligated to help. Is this an appropriate response? Why or why not?

9-21. Message Strategies: Writing Routine Messages; Completing: Evaluating Content, Organization, and Tone [LO-4], Chapter 7 Analyze the strengths and weaknesses of this message, and then revise it so that it follows this chapter's guidelines for sharing routine information, including using the direct approach:

Those of you who read the business media might have heard about job enlargement (expanding the scope of a job horizontally), job enhancement (expanding the scope of a job vertically), and job rotation (training employees to handle more than one job) as ways to make work more fulfilling and to increase staffing flexibility. All three have pros and cons, and the management team has thought about each one carefully. We particularly like the concept of job enlargement, which lets employees take on gradually more and more responsibilities from their immediate supervisors.

Job rotation is the one we've decided to implement starting next quarter. The reasons are because it makes work more interesting and challenging because you're always learning, and it makes life easier for managers because they have a wide pool of trained talent to throw at every new challenge and opportunity. We have analyzed all the job categories in the plant and identified the most appropriate cross-training opportunities (job rotation is also called cross-training, by the way).

Follow the link below to identify your current job title, then check out the specific cross-training opportunities you can choose from. Then prioritize your first, second, and third choices (if your job has more than one listed) for job rotation. Please make your choices by April 10. This gives you plenty of time to discuss the possibilities with your supervisor and discuss the nature of each job with people who are already performing it. Please note also that we are asking all non-management employees to identify their preferences, so this is not optional.

9-22. Message Strategies: Writing Positive Messages; Media Skills: Microblogging [LO-4], Chapter 8 Locate an online announcement for a new product you find interesting or useful. Read enough about the product to be able to describe it to someone else in your own words and then write four Twitter tweets: one to introduce the product to your followers and three follow-on tweets that describe three particularly compelling features or benefits of the product.

9-23. Message Strategies: Writing Goodwill Messages [LO-4] Identify someone in your life who has recently accomplished a significant achievement, such as graduating from high school or college, completing a major

project, or winning an important professional award. Write a brief congratulatory message using the guidelines presented in the chapter.

Expand Your Skills

Critique the Professionals

Locate an online example of a news release in which a company announces good news, such as a new product, a notable executive hire, an expansion, strong financial results, or an industry award. Analyze the release using the guidance provided in the chapter. In what ways did the writer excel? What aspects of the release could be improved? Does the release provide social media–friendly content and features? Using whatever medium your instructor requests, write a brief analysis of the piece (no more than one page), citing specific elements from the piece and support from the chapter.

Sharpening Your Career Skills Online

Bovée and Thill's Business Communication Web Search, at **http://websearch.businesscommunicationnetwork.com**, is a unique research tool designed specifically for business communication research. Use the Web Search function to find a website, video, article, podcast, or PowerPoint presentation that offers advice on writing goodwill messages such as thank-you notes or congratulatory letters. Write a brief email message to your instructor, describing the item that you found and summarizing the career skills information you learned from it.

Build Your Career

Networking is a lifelong activity that can help you at every stage of your career. Getting started can seem daunting, though—particularly if you haven't entered the workforce full-time yet. However, jump ahead to page 477 and read the tips for getting organized, preparing yourself to become a valued networker, and building your network. If you take it one step at a time and gradually build out from the people you already know, before long you'll be connected online and offline with dozens of people.

To get started, create a system for organizing your contacts. You can use a spreadsheet, or you'll find a variety of free and reasonably priced content management apps for both iOS and Android phones. Investigate the features of these apps and take the time to select one that works for you—and that you'll be sure to use. You'll collect a surprising amount of data as you network, and you'll want to keep it organized and usable.

Improve Your Grammar, Mechanics, and Usage

The following exercises help you improve your knowledge of and power over English grammar, mechanics, and usage. Turn to the Handbook of Grammar, Mechanics, and Usage at the end of this book and review all of Section 2.6 (Commas). Then look at the following 10 items and indicate the letter of the preferred choice in the following groups of sentences. (Answers to these exercises appear on page 614.)

9-24. **a.** Please send us four cases of filters two cases of wing nuts and a bale of rags.

b. Please send us four cases of filters, two cases of wing nuts and a bale of rags.

c. Please send us four cases of filters, two cases of wing nuts, and a bale of rags.

9-25. **a.** Your analysis, however, does not account for returns.

b. Your analysis however does not account for returns.

c. Your analysis, however does not account for returns.

9-26. **a.** As a matter of fact she has seen the figures.

b. As a matter of fact, she has seen the figures.

9-27. **a.** Before May 7, 2016, they wouldn't have minded.

b. Before May 7, 2016 they wouldn't have minded.

9-28. **a.** Stoneridge Inc. will go public on September 9 2021.

b. Stoneridge, Inc., will go public on September 9, 2021.

c. Stoneridge Inc. will go public on September 9, 2021.

9-29. **a.** "Talk to me" Sandra said "before you change a thing."

b. "Talk to me," Sandra said "before you change a thing."

c. "Talk to me," Sandra said, "before you change a thing."

9-30. **a.** The firm was founded during the long hard recession of the mid-1970s.

b. The firm was founded during the long, hard recession of the mid-1970s.

c. The firm was founded during the long hard, recession of the mid-1970s.

9-31. **a.** You can reach me at this address: 717 Darby St., Scottsdale, AZ 85251.

b. You can reach me at this address: 717 Darby St., Scottsdale AZ 85251.

c. You can reach me at this address: 717 Darby St., Scottsdale, AZ, 85251.

9-32. **a.** Transfer the documents from Fargo, North Dakota to Boise, Idaho.

b. Transfer the documents from Fargo North Dakota, to Boise Idaho.

c. Transfer the documents from Fargo, North Dakota, to Boise, Idaho.

9-33. **a.** Sam O'Neill the designated representative is gone today.

b. Sam O'Neill, the designated representative, is gone today.

c. Sam O'Neill, the designated representative is gone today.

For additional exercises focusing on commas, visit MyLab Business Communication. Click on Chapter 9, click on Additional Exercises to Improve Your Grammar, Mechanics, and Usage, and then click on 14. Fused sentences and comma splices.

Cases

For all cases, feel free to use your creativity to make up any details you need in order to craft effective messages.

Routine Requests
BLOGGING SKILLS

9-34. Message Strategies: Requesting Information [LO-2] You are writing a book about the advantages and potential pitfalls of using online collaboration systems for virtual team projects. You would like to include several dozen real-life examples from people in a variety of industries. Fortunately, you publish a highly respected blog on the subject, with several thousand regular readers.

Your task: Write a post for your blog that asks readers to submit brief descriptions of their experiences using collaboration tools for team projects. Ask them to email stories of how well a specific system or approach worked for them. Explain that they will receive an autographed copy of the book as thanks and that they will need to sign a release form if their stories are used. In addition, emphasize that you would like to use real names—of people, companies, and software—but you can keep the anecdotes anonymous if readers require. To stay on schedule, you need to have these stories by May 20.

MESSAGING SKILLS

9-35. Message Strategies: Routine Requests [LO-2] One of the reasons you accepted the job offer from your current employer was the happy, relaxed vibe of the open-plan office. When you interviewed, it seemed as far away from a boring, conventional "cubicle farm" as you could get, which appealed to your nonconformist instincts. After a year in the job, however, you've experienced some of the disadvantages of the company's relaxed attitudes to just about every aspect of workplace behavior. People routinely bring pets to work, even though several people have explained they have allergies to dogs or cats. Some of the pets are less than ideally behaved, too, and a couple of dogs who are frequent visitors get into snarling matches when they see each other. One person even brings a pet bird, which has been known to fly loose around the office. Employees bring children of all ages to work, too, from infants still in diapers to teenagers who play video games on mobile devices—sometimes using headphones but sometimes not. Music lovers get into volume wars at least once a week, trying to drown each other out on their portable speaker systems.

You wonder how anybody can get any work done, until you privately interview several colleagues and realize that, like you, they aren't getting any work done. The office has become such a festival of distractions that people routinely bring work home on nights and weekends because home is the only place they can concentrate.

Your task: Write a brief request that could be sent out via the company's internal messaging system asking people to consider the needs of their colleagues before bringing pets, children, and other potential distractions into the workplace.

EMAIL SKILLS

9-36. Message Strategies: Routine Requests [LO-2] After your company rolled out a new online collaboration system several weeks ago you began to worry that your eyesight was failing. You had to squint to read posted messages, and the file archive was almost impossible to navigate because you couldn't read the file names. But then you noticed people in the department you manage having the same problem, particularly people who work on laptops and tablets.

You wondered how the programmers in the information technology (IT) department who configured the system failed to notice the problem, until you walked through their department and realized they all had multiple, giant computer monitors. Everything on their screens was displayed in large, easily readable type.

Your task: Write a brief email message to the head of IT, asking her group to meet with users in your department to discuss the question of on-screen readability with the new system.

EMAIL SKILLS

9-37. Message Strategies: Requesting a Recommendation [LO-2] One of your colleagues, Katina Vander, was recently promoted to department manager and now serves on the company's strategic planning committee. At its monthly meeting next week, the committee will choose an employee to lead an important market research project that will help define the company's product portfolio for the next five years.

You worked side by side with Vander for five years, so she knows your abilities well and has complimented your business insights on many occasions. You know that because she has only recently been promoted to manager, she needs to build credibility among her peers and will therefore be cautious about making such an important recommendation. On the other hand, making a stellar recommendation for such an important project would show that she has a good eye for talent—an essential leadership trait.

Your task: Write an email message to Vander, telling her that you are definitely interested in leading the project and asking her to put in a good word for you with the committee. Mention four attributes that you believe would serve you well in the role: a dozen years of experience in the industry, an engineering degree that helps you understand the technologies involved in product design, a consistent record of excellent or exceptional ratings in annual employee evaluations, and the three years you spent working in the company's customer support group, which gave you a firsthand look at customer satisfaction and quality issues.

Email Skills

MESSAGING SKILLS

9-38. Message Strategies: Requesting Information [LO-2] Many companies now provide presales and postsales customer support through some form of instant messaging or online chat function. As a consumer looking for information, you'll get better service if you can frame your requests clearly and succinctly.

Your task: Imagine that you need to replace your old laptop computer, but you're not sure whether to go with another laptop or switch to a tablet or perhaps one of the new tablet/laptop hybrids. Think through the various ways you will use this new device, from researching and note taking during class to watching movies and interacting with friends on social media. Now imagine you're in a chat session with a sales representative from a computer company, and this person has asked how he or she can help you. Draft a message (no more than 100 words) that summarizes your computing and media requirements and asks the representative to recommend the right type of device for you.

MESSAGING SKILLS

9-39. Message Strategies: Requesting Information [LO-2] The vast Consumer Electronics Show (CES) is the premier promotional event in the industry. Nearly 200,000 industry insiders from all over the world come to see the exciting new products on display from thousands of companies—everything from video game gadgets to sports technology to smart robots.[5] You've just stumbled on a video game controller that has a built-in webcam to allow networked gamers to see and hear each other while they play. Your company also makes game controllers, and you're worried that your customers will flock to this new controller-cam. You need to know how much buzz around this new product is circulating through the show: Have people seen it? What are they saying about it? Are they excited about it?

Your task: Compose a text message to your colleagues at the show, alerting them to the new controller-cam and asking them to listen for any buzz it might be generating among the attendees at the Las Vegas Convention Center and the several surrounding hotels where the show takes place. Your team has a lot of messages flying around during the show, so keep yours under 200 characters.

EMAIL SKILLS

9-40. Message Strategies: Requesting an Adjustment [LO-2] Love at first listen is the only way to describe the way you felt when you discovered the music-streaming service Song-Throng. You enjoy dozens of styles of music, from Afrobeat and

Tropicalia to mainstream pop and the occasional blast of industrial metal, and SongThrong has them all for only $9.99 a month. You can explore every genre imaginable, listening to as many tracks as you like for a fixed monthly fee. The service sounded too good to be true—and sadly, it was. The service was so unreliable that you began keeping note of when it was unavailable. Last month, it was down for all or part of 12 days—well over a third of the month. As much as you like it, you've had enough.

Your task: Write an email to support@songthrong.com, requesting a full refund. To get the $9.99 monthly rate, you prepaid for an entire year ($119.88), and you've been a subscriber for two months now. You know the service has been out for at least part of the time on 12 separate days last month, and while you didn't track outages during the first month, you believe it was about the same number of days.

LETTER-WRITING SKILLS

9-41. Message Strategies: Requesting an Adjustment [LO-2] As a consumer, you've probably bought something that didn't work right or paid for a service that did not turn out the way you expected. Maybe it was a pair of jeans with a rip in a seam that you didn't find until you got home or a watch that broke a week after you bought it. Or maybe your family hired a lawn service to do some yard work and no one from the company showed up on the day promised, and when the gardeners finally appeared, they did not do what they'd been hired for but instead did other things that wound up damaging valuable plants.

Your task: Choose an incident from your own experience and write a claim letter, asking for a refund, repair, replacement, or other adjustment. You'll need to include all the details of the transaction, plus your contact address and phone number. If you can't think of such an experience, make up details for an imaginary situation. If your experience is real, you might want to mail the letter. The reply you receive will provide a good test of your claim-writing skills.

EMAIL SKILLS

9-42. Message Strategies: Requesting Action [LO-2] You head up the corporate marketing department for a nationwide chain of clothing stores. The company has decided to launch a new store-within-a-store concept, in which a small section of each store will showcase "business casual" clothing. To ensure a successful launch of this new strategy, you want to get input from the best retailing minds in the company. You also know it's important to get regional insights from around the country, because a merchandising strategy that works in one area might not succeed in another.

Your task: Write an email message to all 87 store managers, asking them to each nominate one person to serve on an advisory team (managers can nominate themselves if they are local market experts). Explain that you want to find people with at least five years of retailing experience, a good understanding of the local business climate, and thorough knowledge of the local retail competition. In addition, the best candidates will be good team players who are comfortable collaborating long distance using virtual meeting technologies. Also, explain that while you are asking each of the 87 stores to nominate someone, the team

will be limited to no more than eight people. You've met many of the store managers, but not all of them, so be sure to introduce yourself at the beginning of the message.

Routine Messages

EMAIL SKILLS

9-43. Message Strategies: Granting Claims [LO-4] Your company sells flower arrangements and gift baskets. Holidays are always a rush, and the overworked staff makes the occasional mistake. Last week, somebody made a big one. As a furious email message from a customer named Anders Ellison explains, he ordered a Valentine's Day bouquet for his wife, but the company sent a bereavement arrangement instead.

Your task: Respond to Ellison's email message, apologizing for the error, promising to refund all costs that Ellison incurred, informing him that the correct arrangement will arrive tomorrow (and he won't be charged anything for it), and offering Ellison his choice of any floral arrangement or gift basket free on his wife's birthday.

EMAIL SKILLS

9-44. Message Strategies: Granting Claims [LO-4] Like many of the staff at Razer, you are an avid game player. You can therefore sympathize with Louis Hapsberg, a customer who got so excited during a hotly contested game that he slammed his Razer Anansi keyboard against his chair in celebration. Razer products are built for serious action, but no keyboard can withstand a blow like that. However, in the interest of building goodwill among the online gaming community, your manager has approved a free replacement. This sort of damage is rare enough that the company isn't worried about unleashing a flood of similar requests.

Your task: Respond to Hapsberg's email request for a replacement, in which he admitted to inflicting some abuse on this keyboard. Explain, tongue in cheek, that the company is "rewarding" him with a free keyboard in honor of his massive gaming win, but gently remind him that even the most robust electronic equipment needs to be used with care.

PODCASTING SKILLS / PORTFOLIO BUILDER

9-45. Message Strategies: Providing Routine Information; Media Skills: Podcasting [LO-4] As a training specialist in Winnebago Industry's human resources department, you're always on the lookout for new ways to help employees learn vital job skills. While watching a production worker page through a training manual as he was learning how to assemble a new recreational vehicle, you get what seems to be a great idea: Record the assembly instructions as audio files that workers can listen to while performing the necessary steps. With audio instructions, they wouldn't need to keep shifting their eyes between the product and the manual—and constantly losing their place. They could focus on the product and listen for each instruction. Plus, the new system wouldn't cost much at all; any computer can record the audio files, and you'd simply make them available on an intranet site for download into smart-phones, tablets, and digital music players.

Your task: You immediately run your new idea past your boss, who has heard about podcasting but doesn't think it has any place in business. He asks you to prove the viability of the idea by recording a demonstration. Choose a process you engage in yourself—anything from replacing the strings on a guitar to sewing a quilt to changing the oil in a car—and write a brief (one page or less) description of the process that could be recorded as an audio file. Think carefully about the limitations of the audio format as a replacement for printed text. (For instance, do you need to tell people to pause the audio while they perform a time-consuming task?) If directed by your instructor, record your instructions as a podcast.

BLOGGING SKILLS / PORTFOLIO BUILDER

9-46. Message Strategies: Providing Routine Information [LO-4]
You are normally an easygoing manager who gives your employees a lot of leeway in using their own personal communication styles. However, the weekly staff meeting this morning pushed you over the edge. People were interrupting one another, asking questions that had already been answered, sending text messages during presentations, and exhibiting just about every other poor listening habit imaginable.

Your task: Review the advice in Chapter 2 on good listening skills, then write a post for the internal company blog. Emphasize the importance of effective listening, and list at least five steps your employees can take to become better listeners.

Routine Replies

EMAIL SKILLS

9-47. Message Strategies: Routine Responses [LO-4]
As the administrative assistant to Walmart's director of marketing, you have just received a request from the company's webmaster to analyze Walmart's website from a consumer's point of view.

Your task: Visit www.walmart.com and browse through the site, considering the language, layout, graphics, and overall ease of use. In particular, look for aspects of the site that might be confusing or frustrating—annoyances that could prompt shoppers to abandon their quests and head to a competitor such as Target or Amazon. Summarize your findings and recommendations in an email message that could be sent to the webmaster.

MICROBLOGGING SKILLS

9-48. Message Strategies: Routine Announcements [LO-4]
As a way to give back to the communities in which it does business, your company supports the efforts of the United Way, a global organization that works to improve lives through education, income stability, and healthy living choices.[6] Each year, your company runs a fundraising campaign in which employees are encouraged to donate money to their local United Way agencies, and it also grants employees up to three paid days off to volunteer their time for the United Way. This year, you are in charge of the company's campaign.

Your task: Compose a four-message sequence to be posted on the company's internal microblogging system (essentially a private version of Twitter). The messages are limited to 200 characters, including spaces and punctuation. The first message will announce the company's annual United Way volunteering and fundraising campaign (make up any details you need), and the other three messages will explain the United Way's efforts in the areas of education, income stability, and healthy living. Visit the United Way website (www.unitedway.org) to learn more about these three areas.

LETTER-WRITING SKILLS / TEAM SKILLS

9-49. Message Strategies: Providing Recommendations [LO-4]
As a project manager at Expedia, one of the largest online travel services in the world, you've seen plenty of college interns in action. However, few have impressed you as much as Maxine "Max" Chenault. For one thing, she learned how to navigate the company's content management system virtually overnight and always used it properly, whereas other interns sometimes left things in a hopeless mess. She asked lots of intelligent questions about the business. You've been teaching her blogging and website design principles, and she's picked them up rapidly. Moreover, she is always on time, professional, and eager to assist. Also, she didn't mind doing mundane tasks.

On the downside, Chenault is a popular student. Early on, you often found her busy on the phone planning her many social activities when you needed her help. However, after you had a brief talk with her, this problem vanished.

You'll be sorry to see Chenault leave when she returns to school in the fall, but you're pleased to respond when she asks you for a letter of recommendation. She's not sure where she'll apply for work after graduation or what career path she'll choose, so she asks you to keep the letter fairly general.

Your task: Working with a team of your classmates, discuss what should and should not be in the letter. Prepare an outline based on your discussion and then draft the letter.

Positive Messages

BLOGGING SKILLS

9-50. Message Strategies: Routine Announcements [LO-4]
Scoop.it is one of the most popular platforms for content curation. One of the ways a company can use Scoop.it is to find and present content of interest to its customers.

Your task: Choose any company that interests you and imagine that you are in charge of its public communication efforts. Write a post for the company's internal blog, announcing that the company is now on Scoop.it. Briefly describe Scoop.it and explain how it will help the company connect with its customers. Visit the Scoop.it website at www.scoop.it to learn more about the system.

BLOGGING SKILLS / TEAM PROJECTS

9-51. Message Strategies: Instructions [LO-4]
Innovations in communication can make life easier for employees and managers, but they often require learning new systems, new terminology, and sometimes new habits.

Your task: Visit the website of Slack, the popular workgroup messaging system, at slack.com and familiarize yourself with the capabilities of the system. Write a post for your class blog that introduces Slack, defines any key terms users need to know (such as *channels*), and lists the most important benefits of using the system for team and workplace communication. Supplement your research on the Slack website by reviewing other online sources as needed.

WEB-WRITING SKILLS

9-52. Message Strategies: Good-News Messages [LO-4]
Amateur and professional golfers in search of lower scores want to find clubs that are optimized for their individual swings. This process of *club fitting* has gone decidedly high tech in recent years, with fitters using Doppler radar, motion-capture video, and other tools to evaluate golfers' swing and ball flight characteristics. Hot Stix Golf is a leader in this industry, having fitted more than 200 professionals and thousands of amateurs.[7]

Your task: Imagine that you are the communications director at the Indian Wells Golf Resort in Indian Wells, California. Your operation has just signed a deal with Hot Stix to open a fitting center on site. Write a three-paragraph article that could be posted on the resort website. The first paragraph should announce the news that the Hot Stix center will open in six months, the second should summarize the benefits of club fitting, and the third should offer a brief overview of the services that will be available at the Indian Wells Hot Stix Center. Information on club fitting can be found on the Hot Stix website at www.hotstixgolf.com.

BLOGGING SKILLS / PORTFOLIO BUILDER

9-53. Message Strategies: Good-News Messages [LO-4]
Most people have heard of the Emmy, Grammy, Oscar, and Tony Awards for television, music, movies, and theater performances, but fewer know what the Webby Award is all about. Sponsored by the International Academy of Digital Arts and Sciences, the Webbys shine a spotlight on the best in website design, interactive media, and online film and video.[8]

Your task: Visit the Webby Awards website at www.webbyawards.com, select Winners, and choose one of the companies listed as a winner in the Websites or Advertising & Media categories. Now imagine you are the chief online strategist for this company, and you've just been informed your company has won a Webby. Winning this award is a nice validation of the work your team has put in during the past year, and you want to share their success with the entire company. Write a brief post for the internal company blog describing what the Webby Awards are, explaining why they are a significant measure of accomplishment in the online industry, and congratulating the employees in your department who contributed to the successful web effort.

SOCIAL NETWORKING SKILLS

9-54. Message Strategies: Goodwill Messages [LO-4]
As the largest employer in Loganville, your construction company provides jobs, purchasing activity, and tax receipts that make up a vital part of the city's economy. In your role as CEO, however, you realize that the relationship between your company and the community is mutually beneficial, and the company could not survive without the efforts of its employees, the business opportunities offered by a growing marketplace, and the physical and legal infrastructure that the government provides.

The company's dependence on the community was demonstrated in a moving and immediate way last weekend, when a powerful storm pushed the Logan River past flood stage and threatened to inundate your company's office and warehouse facilities. More than 200 volunteers worked alongside your employees through the night to fill and stack sandbags to protect your buildings, and the city council authorized the deployment of heavy equipment and additional staff to help in the emergency effort. As you watched the water rise nearly 10 feet behind the makeshift dike, you realized that the community came together to save your company.

Your task: Write a 100- to 200-word post for your company's Facebook page thanking the citizens and government officials of Loganville for their help in protecting the company's facilities during the storm.

SOCIAL NETWORKING SKILLS

9-55. Message Strategies: Goodwill Messages [LO-4]
Every April, your company stages a competition for the sales department called Spring Surge, which awards sales representatives who bring in the most new revenue during the month. The awards are significant, including a first prize of a trip to Hawaii for the winning sales rep's entire family, and most people in the department take the competition seriously.

Here are the results of this years' competition:
1st place (trip for family to Hawaii): Juanita Hermosa
2nd place (luxury box seats at an NFL playoff game): Jackson Peabody
3rd place ($500 prepaid credit card): Duane Redd
Total new revenue booked during April: $4.7 million

Your task: Write a brief post (150 to 200 words) for your company's internal social networking platform incorporating these results and thanking everyone in the sales department for their efforts during the Spring Surge.

LETTER-WRITING SKILLS

9-56. Message Strategies: Goodwill Messages [LO-4]
Shari Willison worked as a geologist in your civil engineering firm for 20 years before succumbing to leukemia last week. With only a few dozen employees, the company has always been a tight-knit group, and you feel like you've lost a good friend in addition to a valued employee.

Your task: Write a letter of condolence to Willison's husband, Arthur, and the couple's teenaged children, Jordan and Amy. You have known all three socially through a variety of company holiday parties and events over the years.

LETTER-WRITING SKILLS

9-57. Message Strategies: Goodwill Messages [LO-4]
The office was somber this morning when you arrived at work, as employees learned that Michael, the partner of the chief

operating officer, Leo West, had been killed in a car accident over the weekend. You never met Michael, and West is two levels above you in the corporate hierarchy (you're a first-level supervisor), so you don't have a close working relationship. However, you have been on comfortable terms with West during the 10 years you've been at this company, and although you've never socialized with him outside of work, you've both occasionally shared personal and social news during casual conversations in the cafeteria.

Your task: Write a letter of condolence to West.

MyLab Business Communication

MyLab Assisted-Grading Writing Prompts

If your instructor has assigned one or both of the following writing assignments within the MyLab, go to your Assignments to complete these writing exercises.

9-58. Should you use the direct or indirect approach for most routine messages? Why? [LO-1]

9-59. Why is it good practice to explain why replying to a request could benefit the reader? [LO-1]

Endnotes

1. Jill Duffy author bio, *PC*, accessed 11 April 2016, www.pcmag .com; Jill Duffy, "What's Wrong with Email Part 3: We Check, but We Don't Process," *Productivity Report*, 1 February 2016, productivityreport .org; "About," jilleduffy.com, accessed 25 March 2018, www.jilleduffy.com; Jill E. Duffy, *Get Organized: How to Clean Up Your Messy Digital Life* (PC Magazine, 2013).
2. Karen Hertzberg, "5 Alternative Ways to Say 'Thank You in Advance,'" Grammarly blog, 4 September 2017, www.grammarly.com.
3. "How to Write Reference Letters," National Association of Colleges and Employers website, accessed 5 July 2010, www.naceweb .org; "Five (or More) Ways You Can Be Sued for Writing (or Not Writing) Reference Letters," *Fair Employment Practices Guidelines*, July 2006, 1, 3.
4. David Meerman Scott, *The New Rules of Marketing and PR*, 5th ed. (Hoboken, N.J.: Wiley, 2015), Kindle location 7497.
5. CES website, accessed 26 March 2018, www.cesweb.org.
6. United Way website, accessed 26 March 2018, www .unitedway.org.
7. Hot Stix Golf website, accessed 26 March 2018, www .hotstixgolf.com.
8. The Webby Awards website, accessed 26 March 2018, www .webbyawards.com.

10 Writing Negative Messages

LEARNING OBJECTIVES

After studying this chapter, you will be able to

1 Apply the three-step writing process to negative messages.

2 Explain how to use the direct approach effectively when conveying negative news.

3 Explain how to use the indirect approach effectively when conveying negative news.

4 Explain the importance of maintaining high standards of ethics and etiquette when delivering negative messages.

5 Describe successful strategies for sending negative messages on routine business matters.

6 List the important points to consider when conveying negative organizational news.

7 Describe successful strategies for sending negative employment-related messages.

MyLab Business Communication

Improve Your Grade!

If your instructor is using MyLab Business Communication, visit **www.pearson.com/mylab/business-communication** for videos, simulations, and writing exercises.

ON THE JOB: COMMUNICATING AT
MICROSOFT

Taking Responsibility for a Bot That Went Rogue

Microsoft knows a thing or two about the artificial intelligence (AI) that enables chatbots to learn from and mimic human conversation—more than 40 million people have interacted with its Xiaolce chatbot in China, for instance. In an effort to refine its conversational AI in another language and culture, the company created a Twitter chatbot named Tay aimed at young adults in the United States. Tay was carefully engineered and vigorously tested before it was launched. Sadly, within hours after it went live on Twitter, Tay was targeted in a coordinated attack that dragged it over to the dark side and taught the bot how to spew hate speech and profanity.

Microsoft quickly removed Tay from Twitter and issued an apology that serves as a great example for sharing negative news in general and making apologies in particular. Peter Lee, corporate vice president of Microsoft Research, explained, "We are deeply sorry for the unintended offensive and hurtful tweets from Tay, which do not represent who we are or what we stand for, nor how we designed Tay."

Lee's message was a genuine and in-depth apology that took full responsibility for the negative result, explained what happened, described the mistake, and outlined the steps being taken to prevent any similar outcomes in the future. (You can read his full message via the Real-Time Updates Learn More link on page 285.)

Importantly, Lee and Microsoft didn't avoid responsibility by using the conditional *if*, which is used too often in corporate and personal apologies. For instance, saying "I'm sorry if you were offended" shifts the focus from the mistake and the party responsible for the mistake to the people who may have been affected by it and their

Microsoft's Peter Lee issued a thoughtful and responsible apology when the company's chatbot Tay got out of hand and had to be pulled down from Twitter.

reaction. As you'll read in the chapter, apologies that add the "if you were offended" qualifier aren't really apologies at all.

Mistakes and unintended outcomes happen in business, but what separates top professionals is how they respond. This chapter will show you how to write effective and sensitive messages that address a wide range of negative scenarios.[1]

WWW.MICROSOFT.COM

Using the Three-Step Writing Process for Negative Messages

1 LEARNING OBJECTIVE
Apply the three-step writing process to negative messages.

You may never have to share a message like Microsoft's Peter Lee (profiled in the chapter-opening On the Job) did, but you will have to share unwelcome news at many points in your career. Communicating negative information is a fact of life for all business professionals, whether it's saying no to a request, sharing unpleasant or unwelcome information, or issuing a public apology. With the techniques you'll learn in this chapter, however, you can communicate unwelcome news successfully while minimizing unnecessary stress for everyone involved.

Depending on the situation, you can have as many as five goals when communicating negative information:

- To convey the bad news
- To gain acceptance of the bad news
- To preserve as much of your audience's goodwill as possible
- To maintain (or repair) your reputation or your organization's reputation
- To reduce or eliminate the need for future correspondence on the matter

This is a lot to accomplish in one message, so careful planning and execution are particularly critical with negative messages.

Check out the "Five-Minute Guide to Writing Negative Messages" at the end of the chapter.

Negative news messages need to accomplish as many as five distinct goals, so they require careful planning and sensitive writing.

STEP 1: PLANNING A NEGATIVE MESSAGE

To minimize damage to business relationships and to encourage the acceptance of your message, start with a clear purpose and your audience's needs in mind. Think about the information your audience will need in order to understand and accept your message. Negative messages can be intensely personal to recipients, who often have a right to expect a thorough explanation of your answer.

Selecting the best combination of medium and channel is critical. If you're delivering bad news to employees, for instance, sharing it in person shows respect for them and gives them an opportunity to ask questions. Handling the situation live and in person can be uncomfortable, to be sure, but doing so is often the best way to clear the air and prevent the spread of rumors. In-person conversation isn't always possible, however, and many negative messages will need to be delivered via digital channels.

The organization of a negative message requires special attention, starting with whether to use the direct or indirect approach (see Figure 10.1 on the next page). A negative message using the **direct approach** opens with the bad news, proceeds to the reasons for the situation or decision, offers any additional information that may help the audience, and ends with a respectful statement aimed at maintaining a good relationship with the audience. In contrast, the **indirect approach** opens with a *buffer* (see page 289), then builds up the reasons behind the bad news before presenting the bad news itself.

To help decide which approach to take in a particular situation, ask yourself the following questions:

- **Do you need to get the reader's attention immediately?** If the situation is an emergency, or if someone has ignored repeated messages, the direct approach can help you get attention quickly.

REAL-TIME UPDATES
LEARN MORE BY READING THIS ARTICLE

A great example of a thoughtful, responsible apology

When its Twitter chatbot Tay got hijacked and had to be taken down, Microsoft issued an apology that got every note right. Go to **real-timeupdates.com/ebc13** and select Learn More in the Students section.

Start with a clear purpose and your audience's needs in mind.

Choose the medium and channel with care when preparing negative messages; some negative messages are best conveyed in person.

With the *direct approach*, you open with the main idea, then explain it as needed.

With the *indirect approach*, you lay out an explanation or background information first, then present the main idea.

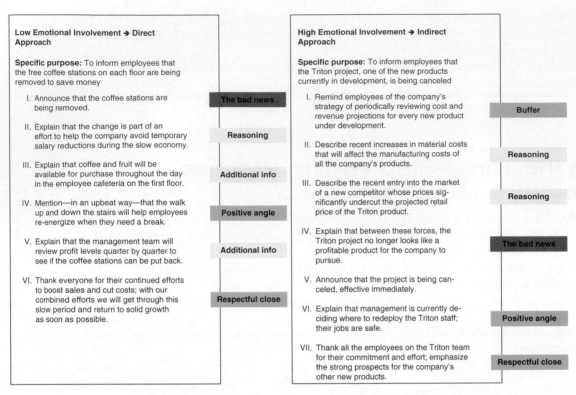

Low Emotional Involvement → Direct Approach

Specific purpose: To inform employees that the free coffee stations on each floor are being removed to save money

I. Announce that the coffee stations are being removed.

II. Explain that the change is part of an effort to help the company avoid temporary salary reductions during the slow economy.

III. Explain that coffee and fruit will be available for purchase throughout the day in the employee cafeteria on the first floor.

IV. Mention—in an upbeat way—that the walk up and down the stairs will help employees re-energize when they need a break.

V. Explain that the management team will review profit levels quarter by quarter to see if the coffee stations can be put back.

VI. Thank everyone for their continued efforts to boost sales and cut costs; with our combined efforts we will get through this slow period and return to solid growth as soon as possible.

- The bad news
- Reasoning
- Additional info
- Positive angle
- Additional info
- Respectful close

High Emotional Involvement → Indirect Approach

Specific purpose: To inform employees that the Triton project, one of the new products currently in development, is being canceled

I. Remind employees of the company's strategy of periodically reviewing cost and revenue projections for every new product under development.

II. Describe recent increases in material costs that will affect the manufacturing costs of all the company's products.

III. Describe the recent entry into the market of a new competitor whose prices significantly undercut the projected retail price of the Triton product.

IV. Explain that between these forces, the Triton project no longer looks like a profitable product for the company to pursue.

V. Announce that the project is being canceled, effective immediately.

VI. Explain that management is currently deciding where to redeploy the Triton staff; their jobs are safe.

VII. Thank all the employees on the Triton team for their commitment and effort; emphasize the strong prospects for the company's other new products.

- Buffer
- Reasoning
- Reasoning
- The bad news
- Positive angle
- Respectful close

Figure 10.1 Comparing the Direct and Indirect Approaches for Negative Messages
The direct and indirect approaches differ in two important ways: the position of the bad news within the sequence of message points and the use of a *buffer* in the indirect approach. ("Using the Indirect Approach for Negative Messages" on page 289 explains the use of a buffer.) Both these messages deal with changes made in response to negative financial developments, but the second example represents a much higher emotional impact for readers, so the indirect approach is called for in that case. Figure 10.2 explains how to choose the right approach for each situation.

- **Does the recipient prefer a direct style of communication?** Some recipients prefer the direct approach no matter what, so if you know this to be the case, go with direct.
- **How important is this news to the reader?** For minor or routine situations, the direct approach is nearly always best. However, if the reader has an emotional investment in the situation or if the consequences to the reader are considerable, the indirect approach is often better, particularly if the bad news is unexpected.
- **Will the bad news come as a shock?** The direct approach is fine for many business situations in which people understand the possibility of receiving bad news. However, if the bad news might come as a shock to readers, use the indirect approach to help them prepare for it.

Figure 10.2 offers a convenient decision tree to help you decide which approach to use.

STEP 2: WRITING NEGATIVE MESSAGES

By writing clearly and sensitively, you can take some of the sting out of bad news and help your reader accept the decision and move on. If your credibility hasn't already been established with an audience, clarify your qualifications so recipients won't question your authority or ability.

When you use language that conveys respect and avoids an accusing tone, you protect your audience's pride. This kind of communication etiquette is always important, but it demands special care with negative messages. Moreover, you can ease the sense of disappointment by using positive words rather than negative, counterproductive ones (see Table 10.1).

Choose your language carefully; you can deliver negative news without being negative.

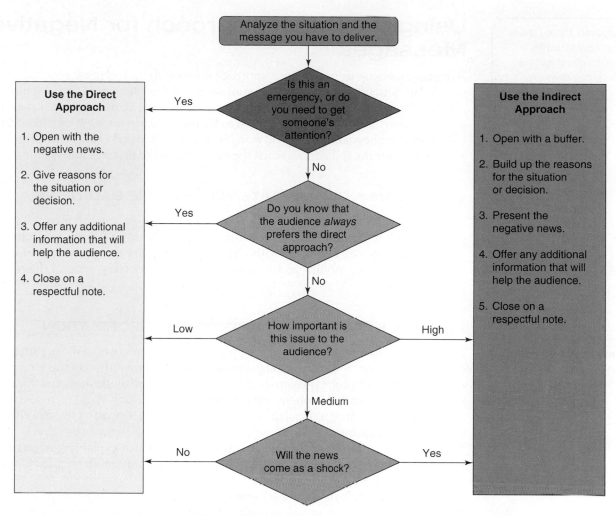

Figure 10.2 Choosing the Direct or Indirect Approach

Following this decision tree will help you decide whether the direct or indirect approach is better in a given situation. Of course, use your best judgment as well. Your relationship with the audience could affect your choice of approaches, for example.

STEP 3: COMPLETING NEGATIVE MESSAGES

Even small flaws in a message are likely to be magnified in readers' minds as they react to the negative news because these errors can create the impression that you are careless or incompetent. Revise your content to make sure everything is clear, complete, and concise. Produce clean, professional-looking digital messages or printed documents, and proofread carefully to eliminate mistakes. Finally, be sure to deliver messages promptly. Withholding or delaying bad news can be unethical—even illegal, in some cases.

TABLE 10.1 Choosing Positive Words

Examples of Negative Phrasings	Positive Alternatives
Your request *doesn't make any sense.*	Please clarify your request.
The *damage won't be fixed* for a week.	The item will be repaired next week.
Although it wasn't *our fault*, there will be an *unavoidable delay* in your order.	We will process your order as soon as we receive an aluminum shipment from our supplier, which we expect within 10 days.
You are clearly *dissatisfied.*	I recognize that the product did not live up to your expectations.
I was *shocked* to learn that you're *unhappy.*	Thank you for sharing your concerns about your shopping experience.
The enclosed statement is *wrong.*	Please verify the enclosed statement and provide a correct copy.

2 LEARNING OBJECTIVE
Explain how to use the direct approach effectively when conveying negative news.

Using the Direct Approach for Negative Messages

A negative message using the direct approach opens with the bad news, proceeds to the reasons for the situation or decision, and ends with a positive statement aimed at maintaining a good relationship with the audience. Depending on the circumstances, the message may also offer alternatives or a plan of action to fix the situation under discussion. Stating the bad news at the beginning can have two advantages: (1) It makes a shorter message possible, and (2) it allows the audience to reach the main idea of the message in less time.

OPEN WITH A CLEAR STATEMENT OF THE BAD NEWS

If you've chosen the direct approach to convey bad news, use the introductory paragraph of your message to share that information. As Chapter 9 notes regarding routine negative replies, you can open with a few words that are the equivalent of in-person "socializing" before moving to the negative news. If necessary, remind the reader why you're writing.

PROVIDE REASONS AND ADDITIONAL INFORMATION

The amount of detail you provide in a negative message depends in part on your relationship with the audience.

In most cases, follow the direct opening with an explanation of how the negative situation came to be or whatever information your readers need in order to grasp and accept the main idea. The extent of your explanation depends on the nature of the news and your relationship with the reader. For example, if you want to preserve a long-standing relationship with an important customer, a detailed explanation could well be worth the extra effort such a message would require.

However, you will encounter some situations in which explaining negative news is neither appropriate nor helpful, such as when the reasons are confidential, excessively complicated, or irrelevant to the reader.

Should you apologize when delivering bad news or responding to negative situations? The answer isn't quite as simple as one might think, partly because the notion of *apology* is hard to pin down. To some people, it simply means an expression of sympathy that something negative has happened to another person. To others, it can mean admitting fault and, if appropriate, taking responsibility for specific compensations or corrections to atone for the mistake.

Some experts have advised that a company should never apologize, even when it knows it has made a mistake, because the apology might be taken as a confession of guilt that could be used against the company in a lawsuit. However, several states have laws that specifically prevent expressions of sympathy from being used as evidence of legal liability. In fact, judges, juries, and plaintiffs tend to be more forgiving of companies that express sympathy for wronged parties. Moreover, a sincere, effective apology can help repair—and even improve—a company's reputation.[2]

Creating an effective apology involves four key decisions:[3]

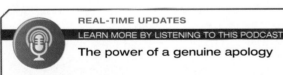

REAL-TIME UPDATES
LEARN MORE BY LISTENING TO THIS PODCAST
The power of a genuine apology

Seasoned executive Arthur D. Collins, Jr., explains how honest apologies help leaders and their organizations recover from mishaps. Go to **real-timeupdates.com/ebc13** and select Learn More in the Students section.

An effective apology involves four key decisions:

- *It should be delivered by someone whose position in the organization matches the gravity of the situation.*
- *It must be a real apology; don't say "I'm sorry if anyone was offended . . ."*
- *It must be delivered quickly.*
- *Media and channel choices are crucial.*

- First, the apology should be delivered by someone whose position in the organization corresponds with the gravity of the situation. The CEO doesn't need to apologize for a late package delivery, but he or she does need to be the public face of the company when a major problem occurs.
- Second, the apology needs to be real. Don't say "I'm sorry if anyone was offended." The conditional *if* implies that you're not sorry at all and that it's the other party's fault for being offended.[4] Peter Lee's apology on behalf of Microsoft (see page 284) is a great example to follow.

- Third, apologies need to be delivered quickly, particularly in the social media age. A fast response makes the message more meaningful to the affected parties, and it helps the company maintain some control over the story, rather than reacting to social media outrage.
- Fourth, media and channel choices are crucial. The right choice can range from a private conversation to a written message posted online to a public press conference, depending on the situation.

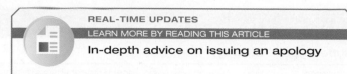

Recognize that you can express sympathy with someone's plight without suggesting that you are to blame. For example, if a customer damaged a product through misuse and suffered a financial loss as a result of not being able to use the product, you can say something along the lines of "I'm sorry to hear of your difficulties." This demonstrates sensitivity without accepting blame.

CLOSE ON A RESPECTFUL NOTE

After you've explained the negative news, close the message in a manner that respects the impact the news is likely to have on the recipient. If it's possible and appropriate, offer your readers an alternative solution, but only if doing so is a smart use of your time. Look for opportunities to include positive statements, but avoid creating false hopes or writing in a way that seems to suggest that something negative didn't happen. Ending on a false positive can leave readers feeling "disrespected, disregarded, or deceived."[5]

Close your message on a respectful note, being as positive as you can be without being insincere.

Using the Indirect Approach for Negative Messages

The indirect approach helps readers prepare for the bad news by outlining the reasons for the situation before presenting the bad news itself. However, the indirect approach is not meant to obscure bad news, delay it, or limit your responsibility. The purpose of this approach is to ease the blow and help readers accept the news. When done poorly, the indirect approach can be disrespectful and even unethical. But when done well, it is a good example of audience-oriented communication crafted with attention to both ethics and etiquette. Showing consideration for the feelings of others is never dishonest.

3 **LEARNING OBJECTIVE**
Explain how to use the indirect approach effectively when conveying negative news.

Use the indirect approach when some preliminary discussion will help your audience accept the unwelcome news.

OPEN WITH A BUFFER

Messages using the indirect approach open with a **buffer**, which is a neutral, noncontroversial statement that is closely related to the point of the message but doesn't convey the bad news. The purposes of a buffer are to ease the reader into the message by establishing common ground and to create space for a transition into the reasoning and evidence that you are going to lay out next.

A buffer gives you the opportunity to start the communication process without jumping immediately into the bad news.

Depending on the circumstances, a good buffer can express your appreciation for being considered, assure the reader of your attention to the request, indicate your understanding of the reader's needs, introduce the general subject matter, or simply establish common ground with your reader. A good buffer also needs to be relevant and sincere. In contrast, a poorly written buffer might trivialize the reader's concerns, divert attention from the problem with insincere flattery or irrelevant material, or mislead the reader into thinking your message actually contains good news.

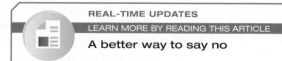

TABLE 10.2 Types of Buffers

Buffer Type	Strategy	Example
Agreement	Find a point on which you and the reader share similar views.	We both know how hard it is to make a profit in this industry.
Appreciation	Express sincere thanks for receiving something.	Your check for $127.17 arrived yesterday. Thank you.
Cooperation	Convey your willingness to help in any way you realistically can.	Employee Services is here to assist all associates with their health insurance, retirement planning, and continuing education needs.
Fairness	Assure the reader that you've closely examined and carefully considered the problem, or mention an appropriate action that has already been taken.	For the past week, we have had our bandwidth monitoring tools running around the clock to track your actual upload and download speeds.
Good news	Start with the part of your message that is favorable.	We have credited your account in the amount of $14.95 to cover the cost of return shipping.
Praise	Find an attribute or an achievement to compliment—but don't create false hope that a positive message will follow.	The Stratford Group clearly has an impressive record of accomplishment in helping clients resolve financial reporting problems.
Resale	Favorably discuss the product or company related to the subject of the letter.	With their heavy-duty, full-suspension hardware and fine veneers, the desks and file cabinets in our Montclair line have long been popular with value-conscious professionals.
Understanding	Demonstrate that you understand the reader's goals and needs.	So that you can more easily find the printer with the features you need, we are enclosing a brochure that describes all the Epson printers currently available.

Consider these possible responses to a manager of the order-fulfillment department who requested some temporary staffing help from your department (a request you won't be able to fulfill):

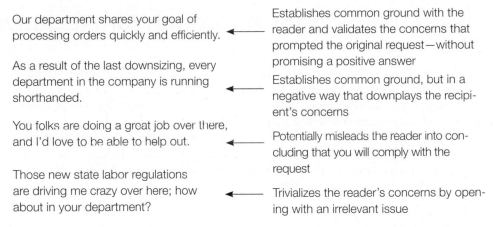

Our department shares your goal of processing orders quickly and efficiently. ← Establishes common ground with the reader and validates the concerns that prompted the original request—without promising a positive answer

As a result of the last downsizing, every department in the company is running shorthanded. ← Establishes common ground, but in a negative way that downplays the recipient's concerns

You folks are doing a great job over there, and I'd love to be able to help out. ← Potentially misleads the reader into concluding that you will comply with the request

Those new state labor regulations are driving me crazy over here; how about in your department? ← Trivializes the reader's concerns by opening with an irrelevant issue

Poorly written buffers mislead or insult the reader.

Only the first of these buffers can be considered effective. The others are likely to damage your relationship with the other manager. Table 10.2 provides several types of effective buffers you can use to open a negative message tactfully.

PROVIDE REASONS AND ADDITIONAL INFORMATION

Build your reasoning in a way that signals the negative news ahead.

An effective buffer serves as a transition to the next part of the message, in which you build up the explanations and information that will culminate in the negative news. An ideal explanation section leads readers to the conclusion before you come right out and say it. The reader has followed your line of reasoning and is ready for the answer. By giving your reasons effectively, you help maintain focus on the issues at hand and defuse the emotions that always accompany significantly bad news. An effective approach is to start with positive or neutral points and move through progressively negative points. Provide enough detail for the audience to understand your reasons, but be concise.

Whenever possible, don't use the blanket phrase "company policy" as the reason for the bad news.

As much as possible, avoid hiding behind company policy to cushion your bad news. If you say, "Company policy forbids our hiring anyone who does not have two years' supervisory experience," you imply that you won't consider anyone on his or her individual merits. By sharing the reasons behind the policy (if appropriate in the circumstances), you can give readers a more satisfying answer. Consider this response to an applicant:

Because these management positions are quite challenging, the human relations department has researched the qualifications needed to succeed in them. The findings show that the two most important qualifications are a bachelor's degree in business administration and two years' supervisory experience. ← Shows the reader that the decision is based on a methodical analysis of the company's needs and not on some arbitrary guideline

← Establishes the criteria behind the decision and lets the reader know what to expect

This paragraph does a good job of stating reasons for the refusal:

- It provides enough detail to logically support the refusal.
- It implies that the applicant is better off avoiding a position in which he or she might fail.
- It doesn't apologize for the decision, because no one is at fault.
- It avoids negative personal statements (such as "You do not meet our requirements").

Even valid, well-thought-out reasons won't convince every reader in every situation, but if you've done a good job of laying out your reasoning, then you've done everything you can to prepare the reader for the main idea, which is the negative news itself.

If you've done a good job of laying out your reasoning, you've done everything you can to prepare the reader for the negative news.

CONTINUE WITH A CLEAR STATEMENT OF THE BAD NEWS

After you've thoughtfully and logically established your reasons and readers are prepared to receive the bad news, you can use three techniques to convey the negative information as clearly and as kindly as possible. First, make sure you don't overemphasize the bad news:

- Minimize the space or time devoted to the bad news—without trivializing it or withholding important information. In other words, don't repeat it or belabor it.
- Subordinate bad news within a complex or compound sentence ("My department is already shorthanded, so I'll need all my staff for at least the next two months").
- Embed bad news in the middle of a paragraph or use parenthetical expressions ("Our profits, which are down, are only part of the picture").

To convey bad news sensitively

- *Express it clearly but don't repeat it or belabor it*
- *Use a conditional statement if appropriate*
- *Tell what you can or did do, not what you can't or didn't do*

Keep in mind, however, that it's possible to abuse this notion of deemphasizing bad news. For instance, if the primary point of your message is that profits are down, it would be inappropriate to marginalize that news by burying it in the middle of a sentence. State the negative news clearly, and then make a smooth transition to any positive news that might balance the story.

Second, if appropriate, use a conditional (*if* or *when*) statement to imply that the audience could have received, or might someday receive, a favorable answer under different circumstances ("When you have more managerial experience, you are welcome to apply for any openings that we may have in the future"). Such a statement could motivate applicants to improve their qualifications. However, you must avoid any suggestion that you might reverse the decision you've just made or any phrasing that could give a rejected applicant false hope.

Third, emphasize what you can do or have done rather than what you cannot do. Also, by implying the bad news, you may not need to actually state it, thereby making the bad news less personal ("Our development budget for next year is fully committed to our existing slate of projects"). However, make sure your audience understands the entire message—including the bad news. If an implied message might lead to uncertainty, state your decision in direct terms. Just be sure to avoid overly blunt statements that are likely to cause offense:

When you express the unwelcome news, look for ways to emphasize what you can do or have done rather than what you cannot do.

Instead of This	Write This
I *must refuse* your request.	I will be out of town on the day you need me.
We *must deny* your application.	The position has been filled.
We *cannot afford to* continue the program.	The program will conclude on May 1.
Much as I would like to attend . . .	Our budget meeting ends too late for me to attend.
We *must turn down* your extension request.	Please send in your payment by June 14.

CLOSE ON A RESPECTFUL NOTE

Don't disguise the bad news when you emphasize the positive.

As with the direct approach, the close in the indirect approach offers an opportunity to emphasize your respect for your audience, even though you've just delivered unpleasant news. Express best wishes without ending on a falsely upbeat note. If you can find a positive angle that's meaningful to your audience, by all means consider adding it to your conclusion. However, don't try to pretend that the negative news didn't happen or that it won't affect the reader. Suggest alternative solutions if such information is available and doing so is a good use of your time. If you've asked readers to decide between alternatives or to take some action, make sure that they know what to do, when to do it, and how to do it. Whatever type of conclusion you use, follow these guidelines:

A respectful close

- Avoids an uncertain conclusion
- Manages expectations about future correspondence
- Expresses optimism, if appropriate
- Is sincere

- **Avoid an uncertain conclusion.** If the situation or decision is final, avoid statements such as "I trust our decision is satisfactory," which imply that the matter is open to discussion or negotiation.
- **Manage expectations about future correspondence.** Encourage additional communication *only* if you're willing to discuss your decision further. If you're not, avoid wording such as "If you have further questions, please write."
- **Express optimism, if appropriate.** If the situation might improve in the future, share that with your readers if it's relevant. However, don't suggest the possibility of a positive change if you don't have insight that it might happen.
- **Be sincere.** Avoid clichés that are insincere in view of the bad news. If you can't help, don't say, "If we can be of any help, please contact us."

Keep in mind that the close can have a lasting impact on your audience. Even though they're disappointed, leave them with the impression that they were treated with respect. For a quick reminder on creating effective negative messages, see "Checklist: Creating Negative Messages."

CHECKLIST ✔ Creating Negative Messages

A. Choose the direct or indirect approach.
- ✔ Consider using the direct approach when the audience is aware of the possibility of negative news, when the reader is not emotionally involved in the message, when you know that the reader would prefer the bad news first, when you know that firmness is necessary, and when you want to discourage a response.
- ✔ Consider using the indirect approach when the news is likely to come as a shock or surprise, when your audience has a high emotional investment in the outcome, and when you want to maintain a good relationship with the audience.

B. For the indirect approach, open with an effective buffer.
- ✔ Establish common ground with the audience.
- ✔ Validate the request, if you are responding to a request.
- ✔ Don't trivialize the reader's concerns.
- ✔ Don't mislead the reader into thinking the coming news might be positive.

C. Provide reasons and additional information.
- ✔ Explain why the news is negative.
- ✔ Adjust the amount of detail to fit the situation and the audience.

- ✔ Avoid explanations when the reasons are confidential, excessively complicated, or irrelevant to the reader.
- ✔ If appropriate, state how you plan to correct or respond to the negative news.
- ✔ Seek the advice of company lawyers if you're unsure what to say.

D. Clearly state the bad news.
- ✔ State the bad news as positively as possible, using tactful wording.
- ✔ To help protect readers' feelings, deemphasize the bad news by minimizing the space devoted to it, subordinating it, or embedding it.
- ✔ If your response might change in the future if circumstances change, explain the conditions to the reader.
- ✔ Emphasize what you can do or have done rather than what you can't or won't do.

E. Close on a respectful note.
- ✔ Express best wishes without being falsely positive.
- ✔ Suggest actions readers might take, if appropriate, and provide them with necessary information.
- ✔ Encourage further communication only if you're willing to discuss the situation further.

Maintaining High Standards of Ethics and Etiquette

4 LEARNING OBJECTIVE
Explain the importance of maintaining high standards of ethics and etiquette when delivering negative messages.

All business messages demand attention to ethics and etiquette, of course, but these considerations take on special importance when you are delivering bad news—for several reasons. First, a variety of laws and regulations dictate the content and delivery of many business messages with potentially negative content, such as the release of financial information by a public company. Second, negative messages can have a significant impact on the lives of those receiving them. Even if the news is conveyed legally and conscientiously, good ethical practice demands that these situations be approached with care and sensitivity. Third, emotions often run high when negative messages are involved, for both the sender and the receiver. Senders need to manage their own emotions and consider the emotional state of their audiences.

Negative messages require special care, for three reasons:

- Some negative-news situations are governed by laws and regulations.
- They can have a significant impact on the lives of those receiving them.
- Emotions often run high when negative messages are involved.

For example, in a message announcing or discussing workforce cutbacks, you have the emotional needs of several stakeholder groups to consider. The employees who are losing their jobs are likely to experience fear about their futures and possibly a sense of betrayal. The employees who are keeping their jobs are likely to feel anxiety about the long-term security of their jobs, the ability of company management to turn things around, and the level of care and respect the company has for its employees. These "survivors" may also feel guilty about keeping their jobs while some colleagues lost theirs. Outside the company, investors, suppliers, and segments of the community affected by the layoffs (such as retailers and homebuilders) will have varying degrees of financial interest in the outcome of the decision. Writing such messages requires careful attention to all these needs, while balancing respect for the departing employees with a positive outlook on the future.

When you must share negative information, resist any temptation to delay or distort the message (see "Practicing Ethical Communication: The Deceptive Soft Sell"). Doing so may be unethical and even illegal. In recent years, numerous companies have been sued by shareholders, consumers, employees, and government regulators for allegedly withholding or delaying negative information in such areas as company finances, environmental hazards, and product safety. In many of these cases, the problem was slow, incomplete, or inaccurate communication between the company and external stakeholders. In others, problems stemmed from a reluctance to send or receive negative news within the organization.

When you must share negative information, resist any temptation to delay or distort the message.

PRACTICING ETHICAL COMMUNICATION

The Deceptive Soft Sell

You and your colleagues are nervous. Sales have been declining for months, and you see evidence of budget tightening all over the place—the fruit and pastries have disappeared from the coffee stations, accountants are going over expense reports with magnifying glasses, and managers are slow to replace people who leave the company. The workgroup messaging system is abuzz with chatter; everyone wants to know if anyone has heard anything about layoffs.

The job market in your area is weak, and you know you might have to sell your house—in one of the weakest housing markets in memory—and move your family out of state to find another position in your field. If your job is eliminated, you're ready to cope with the loss, but you need as much time as possible. You breathe a sigh of relief when the following item from the CEO appears on the company's internal blog:

> With news of workforce adjustments elsewhere in our industry, we realize many of you are concerned about the possibility here. I'd like to reassure all of you that

we remain confident in the company's fundamental business strategy, and the executive team is examining all facets of company operations to ensure our continued financial strength.

The message calms your fears. Should it?

A month later, the CEO announces a layoff of 20 percent of the company's workforce—nearly 700 people.

CAREER APPLICATIONS

1. You're shocked by the news because you felt reassured by the blog posting from last month. In light of what happened, you retrieve a copy of the newsletter and reread the CEO's message. Does it seem ethical now? Why or why not?

2. If you had been in charge of writing this newsletter item and your hands were tied because you couldn't come out and announce the layoffs yet, how would you have rewritten the message?

Effectively sharing bad news within an organization requires commitment from everyone involved. Employees must commit to sending negative messages when necessary and to do so in a timely fashion, even when that is unpleasant or difficult. Conversely, managers must commit to maintaining open communication channels, truly listening when employees have negative information to share and not punishing employees who deliver bad news.

Whistle-blowing is expressing concerns internally through company ethics hotlines or externally if a company refuses to respond to stated concerns.

Ethically managed companies give employees and other parties safe and confidential ways to share questions and concerns with management. These channels can range from informal meetings with a supervisor to *ethics hotlines* that employees can call to report concerns. Reporting unethical or illegal behavior is known as **whistle-blowing**, and smart companies make sure employees have a way to express concerns internally so issues can be brought to management attention and resolved quickly. Otherwise, employees may be forced to take their concerns public through government regulators or the news media. For internal feedback mechanisms to work, however, employees need to know their concerns will be addressed and that they won't suffer retaliation for blowing the whistle.

Sending Negative Messages on Routine Business Matters

5   LEARNING OBJECTIVE
Describe successful strategies for sending negative messages on routine business matters.

Professionals and companies receive a wide variety of requests and cannot respond positively to every single one. In addition, mistakes and unforeseen circumstances can lead to delays and other minor problems that occur in the course of business. Whatever the purpose, crafting routine negative responses and messages quickly and graciously is an important skill for every businessperson.

MAKING NEGATIVE ANNOUNCEMENTS ON ROUTINE BUSINESS MATTERS

For unexpected negative messages on routine matters, the indirect approach is usually more appropriate.

On occasion managers need to make unexpected negative announcements. Because the news is unexpected, the indirect approach is usually the better choice. Follow the steps outlined for indirect messages: Open with a buffer that establishes some mutual ground between you and the reader, advance your reasoning, announce the change, and close with as much positive information and sentiment as appropriate under the circumstances.

REJECTING SUGGESTIONS AND PROPOSALS

Rejecting suggestions and proposals, particularly if you asked for input, requires special care and tact in order to maintain a positive working relationship.

Managers receive a variety of suggestions and proposals, both solicited and unsolicited, from internal and external sources. For an unsolicited proposal from an external source, you may not even need to respond if you don't already have a working relationship with the sender. However, if you need to reject a proposal you solicited, you owe the sender an explanation, and because the news may be unexpected, the indirect approach is better. In general, the closer your working relationship, the more thoughtful and complete you need to be in your response. For example, if you are rejecting a proposal from an employee, explain your reasons fully and carefully so that the employee can understand why the proposal was not accepted and so that you don't damage an important working relationship.

REFUSING ROUTINE REQUESTS

When turning down an invitation or a request for a favor, consider your relationship with the reader.

When you are unable to meet a routine request, your primary communication challenge is to give a clear negative response without generating negative feelings or damaging either your personal reputation or the company's. The direct approach works best for most routine negative responses because it is simpler and more efficient. The indirect approach works best when the stakes are high for you or for the receiver, when you or your company has an established relationship with the person making the request, or when you're forced to decline a request that you might have accepted in the past (see Figure 10.3).

1 Plan ➜ **2** Write ➜ **3** Complete

Analyze the Situation
Verify that the purpose is to decline a request and offer alternatives; audience is likely to be surprised by the refusal.

Gather Information
Determine audience needs and obtain the necessary information.

Choose Medium and Channel
For formal messages, printed letters on company letterhead are best.

Organize the Information
The main idea is to refuse the request, so limit your scope to that; select the indirect approach based on the audience and the situation.

Adapt to Your Audience
Adjust the level of formality based on your degree of familiarity with the audience; maintain a positive relationship by using the "you" attitude, politeness, positive emphasis, and bias-free language.

Compose the Message
Use a conversational but professional style and keep the message brief, clear, and as helpful as possible.

Revise the Message
Evaluate content and review readability to make sure the negative information won't be misinterpreted; make sure your tone stays positive without being artificial.

Produce the Message
Maintain a clean, professional appearance on company letterhead.

Proofread the Message
Review for errors in layout, spelling, and mechanics.

Distribute the Message
Deliver your message using the chosen medium.

The buffer eases the recipient into the message by demonstrating respect and recapping the request.

Kwan suggests an alternative, showing that she cares about the college and has given the matter some thought.

InfoTech
927 Dawson Valley Road, Tulsa, Oklahoma 74151
Voice: (918) 669-4428 Fax: (918) 669-4429
www.infotech.com

March 6, 2020

Dr. Sandra Wofford, President
Whittier Community College
333 Whittier Avenue
Tulsa, OK 74150

Dear Dr. Wofford:

Infotech has been happy to support Whittier Community College in many ways over the years, and we appreciate the opportunities you and your organization provide to so many deserving students. Thank you for considering our grounds for your graduation ceremony on June 3.

We would certainly like to accommodate Whittier as we have in years past, but our companywide sales meetings will be held this year during the weeks of May 29 and June 5. With more than 200 sales representatives and their families from around the world joining us, activities will be taking place throughout our facility.

My assistant, Robert Seagers, suggests you contact the Municipal Botanical Gardens as a possible graduation site. He recommends calling Jerry Kane, director of public relations.

We remain firm in our commitment to you, President Wofford, and to the fine students you represent. Through our internship program, academic research grants, and other initiatives, we will continue to be a strong corporate partner to Whittier College and will support your efforts as you move forward.

Sincerely,

May Yee Kwan

May Yee Kwan
Public Relations Director

She provides a meaningful reason for the negative response, without apologizing (because the company is not at fault).

Her close emphasizes the importance of the relationship and the company's continuing commitment.

Figure 10.3 Effective Letter Declining a Routine Request
In declining a request to use her company's facilities, May Yee Kwan took note of the fact that her company has a long-standing relationship with the college and wants to maintain that positive relationship. Because the news is unexpected based on past experience, she chose the indirect approach to build up to her announcement.

Consider the following points as you develop routine negative messages:

- Manage your time carefully; focus on the most important relationships and requests.
- If the matter is closed, don't imply that it's still open by using phrases such as "Let me think about it and get back to you" as a way to delay saying no.
- Offer alternative ideas if you can, particularly if the relationship is important.
- Don't imply that other assistance or information might be available if it isn't.

If you aren't in a position to offer additional information or assistance, don't imply that you are.

HANDLING BAD NEWS ABOUT TRANSACTIONS

Some negative messages regarding transactions carry significant business ramifications.

Bad news about transactions is always unwelcome and usually unexpected. The preferred approach and the specific content and tone of each message can vary widely, depending on the nature of the transaction and your relationship with the customer. Telling an individual consumer that his new sweater will be arriving a week later than you promised is a much simpler task than telling Toyota that 30,000 transmission parts will be a week late, especially when you know the company will be forced to idle a multimillion-dollar production facility as a result.

If you haven't done anything specific to set the customer's expectations—such as promising delivery within 24 hours—the message simply needs to inform the customer of the situation, with little or no emphasis on apologies (see Figure 10.4).

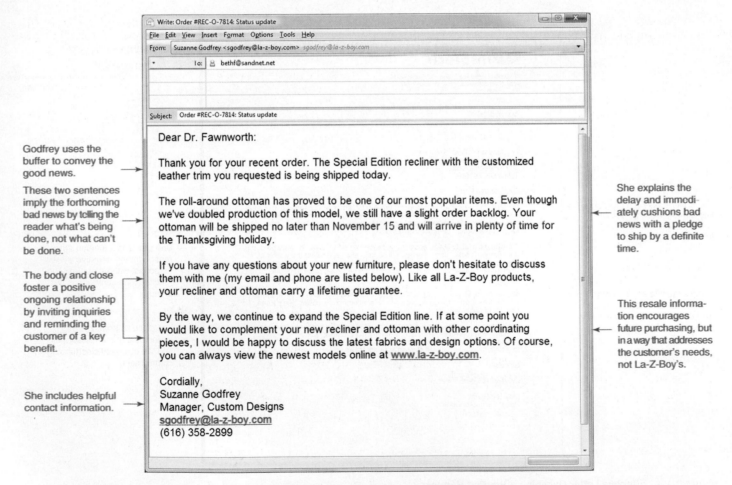

Godfrey uses the buffer to convey the good news.

These two sentences imply the forthcoming bad news by telling the reader what's being done, not what can't be done.

The body and close foster a positive ongoing relationship by inviting inquiries and reminding the customer of a key benefit.

She includes helpful contact information.

She explains the delay and immediately cushions bad news with a pledge to ship by a definite time.

This resale information encourages future purchasing, but in a way that addresses the customer's needs, not La-Z-Boy's.

Figure 10.4 Effective Negative Message Regarding a Transaction
This message, which is a combination of good and bad news, uses the indirect approach—with the good news serving as a buffer for the bad news. In this case, the customer wasn't promised delivery by a certain date, so the writer simply informs the customer when to expect the rest of the order. The writer also takes steps to repair the relationship and encourage future business with her firm.

> **CHECKLIST** ✔ **Handling Bad News About Transactions**
>
> ✔ Reset the customer's expectations regarding the transaction.
> ✔ Explain what happened and why, if appropriate.
> ✔ Explain how you will resolve the situation.
> ✔ Repair any damage done to the business relationship, perhaps offering future discounts, free merchandise, or other considerations.
> ✔ Offer a professional, businesslike expression of apology if your organization made a mistake.

If you did set the customer's expectations and now find that you can't meet them, your task is more complicated. In addition to resetting those expectations and explaining how you'll resolve the problem, you may need to include an element of apology. The scope of the apology depends on the magnitude of the mistake. For the customer who ordered the sweater, a simple apology followed by a clear statement of when the sweater will arrive would probably be sufficient. For larger business-to-business transactions, the customer may want an explanation of what went wrong to determine whether you'll be able to perform as you promise in the future.

To help repair the damage to the relationship and encourage repeat business, many companies offer discounts on future purchases, free merchandise, or other considerations. However, you don't always have a choice. Business-to-business purchasing contracts often include performance clauses that legally entitle the customer to discounts or other restitution in the event of late delivery. To review the concepts covered in this section, see "Checklist: Handling Bad News About Transactions."

The right approach to bad news about business transactions depends on the customer's expectations.

If you've failed to meet expectations that you set for the customer, an element of apology should be considered.

MOBILE APP
Pocket Letter Pro for iOS includes templates for a variety of letter types to simplify writing business letters on your mobile device.

REFUSING CLAIMS AND REQUESTS FOR ADJUSTMENT

Customers who make a claim or request an adjustment tend to be emotionally involved, so the indirect approach is usually the better choice if you need to deny such a request. Your delicate task as a writer is to avoid accepting responsibility for the unfortunate situation and yet avoid blaming or accusing the customer. To steer clear of these pitfalls, pay special attention to the tone of your letter. Demonstrate that you understand and have considered the complaint carefully, and then rationally explain why you are refusing the request. Close on a respectful and action-oriented note (see Figure 10.5 on the next page). And be sure to respond quickly. With so many instantaneous media choices at their disposal, some angry consumers will take their complaints public if they don't hear back from you within a few days or even a few hours.[6]

If you deal with lots of customers over time, chances are you'll get a request that is particularly outrageous. You may even be convinced that the person is not telling the truth. However, you must resist the temptation to call the person dishonest or incompetent. If you don't, you could be sued for **defamation**, a false statement that damages someone's reputation. (Written defamation is called *libel*; spoken defamation is called *slander*.) To successfully sue for defamation, the aggrieved party must prove (1) that the statement is false, (2) that the language injures the person's reputation, and (3) that the statement has been communicated to others.

To avoid accusations of defamation, follow these guidelines:

- Avoid using any kind of abusive language or terms that could be considered defamatory.
- Provide accurate information and stick to the facts.
- Never let anger or malice motivate your messages.
- Consult your company's legal advisers whenever you think a message might have legal consequences.
- Communicate honestly and make sure you believe what you're saying is true.
- Emphasize a desire for a good relationship in the future.

Use the indirect approach in most cases of refusing a claim.

Defamation is a false statement that damages someone's reputation.

You can help avoid accusations of defamation by avoiding an emotional response.

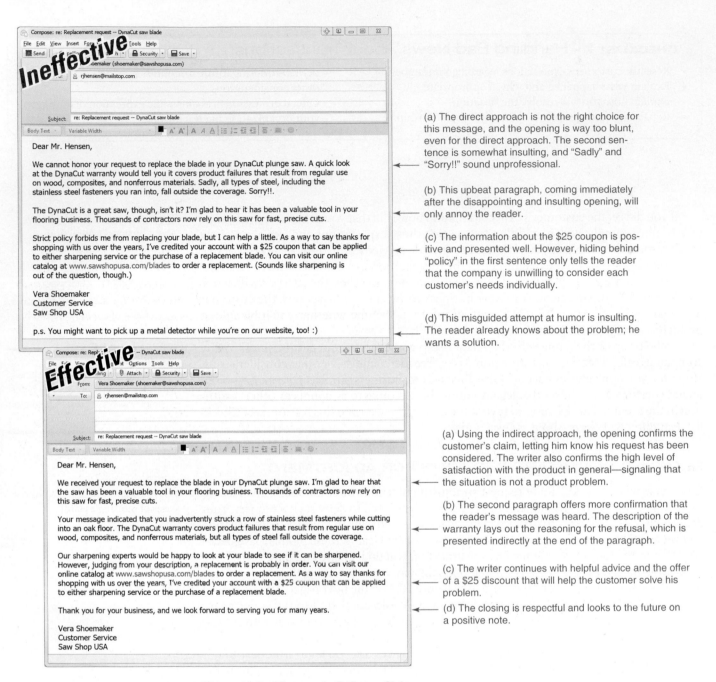

Figure 10.5 Message to Refuse a Claim
Vera Shoemaker diplomatically refuses this customer's request for a replacement saw blade, which he inadvertently damaged after cutting into some steel fasteners. Without blaming the customer (even though the customer clearly made a mistake), she points out that the saw blade is not intended to cut steel, so the warranty doesn't cover a replacement in this instance.

Keep in mind that nothing positive can come out of antagonizing a customer, even one who has verbally abused you or your colleagues. Reject the claim or request for adjustment in a professional manner and move on to the next challenge. For a brief review of the tasks involved when refusing claims, see "Checklist: Refusing Claims."

6 LEARNING OBJECTIVE
List the important points to consider when conveying negative organizational news.

Sending Negative Organizational News

The messages described in the previous section deal with internal matters or individual interactions with external parties. From time to time, managers must also share negative information with the public at large, and occasionally respond to negative information

---

CHECKLIST ✔ Refusing Claims

- ✔ Use the indirect approach because the reader is expecting or hoping for a positive response.
- ✔ Indicate your full understanding of the nature of the complaint.
- ✔ Explain why you are refusing the request, without hiding behind company policy.
- ✔ Provide an accurate, factual account of the transaction.

- ✔ Emphasize ways things should have been handled rather than dwell on the reader's negligence.
- ✔ Avoid any appearance of defamation.
- ✔ Avoid expressing personal opinions.
- ✔ End with a positive, friendly, helpful close.
- ✔ Make any suggested action easy for readers to comply with.

---

as well. Most of these situations have unique challenges that must be addressed on a case-by-case basis, but the general advice offered here applies to all of them. One key difference among all these messages is whether you have time to plan the announcement. The following section addresses negative messages you do have time to plan for, and "Communicating in a Crisis" later in the chapter offers advice on communication during emergencies.

REAL-TIME UPDATES

LEARN MORE BY READING THIS ARTICLE

Misguided crisis management is a lesson for every professional

Learn from the mistakes made in these recent corporate crises. Go to **real-timeupdates.com/ebc13** and select Learn More in the Students section.

COMMUNICATING UNDER NORMAL CIRCUMSTANCES

Businesses may need to send a range of negative messages regarding their ongoing operations. As you plan such messages, take extra care to consider all your audiences and their unique needs. Keep in mind that a significant negative event such as a plant closing can affect hundreds or thousands of people in multiple stakeholder groups: Employees need to find new jobs, get training in new skills, or perhaps get emergency financial help. If many of your employees plan to move in search of new jobs, school districts may have to adjust budgets and staffing levels. Your customers need to find new suppliers. Your suppliers may need to find other customers of their own. Government agencies may need to react to everything from a decrease in tax revenues to an influx of people seeking unemployment benefits.

> Negative organizational messages often require extensive planning because multiple audiences can be involved.

When making negative announcements, follow these guidelines:

- **Match your approach to the situation.** A modest price increase won't shock most customers, so the direct approach is fine. However, canceling a product that lots of people count on is another matter, so building up to the news via the indirect approach might be better.
- **Consider the unique needs of each group.** As the plant closing example illustrates, various people have different information needs.
- **Give each audience enough time to react as needed.** Negative news often requires readers to make decisions or take action in response, so don't increase their stress by not providing any warning.

> Give people as much time as possible to react to negative news.

- **Give yourself enough time to plan and manage a response.** Chances are you're going to be hit with complaints, questions, or product returns after you make your announcement, so make sure you're ready with answers and additional follow-up information.
- **Look for positive angles, but don't exude false optimism.** If eliminating a seldom-used employee benefit means the company can invest more in advertising, by all means promote that positive angle. On the other hand, laying off 10,000 people does not give them "an opportunity to explore new horizons." It's a traumatic event that can affect employees, their families, and their communities for years. The best you may be able to do is to thank people for their past support and wish them well in the future.
- **Seek expert advice if you're not sure.** Many significant negative announcements have important technical, financial, or legal elements that require the expertise of lawyers, accountants, or other specialists.

> Don't go it alone: Ask for legal help and other assistance if you're not sure how to handle a significant negative announcement.

Negative situations will challenge you as a communicator and leader. Inspirational leaders try to seize such opportunities as a chance to reshape or reinvigorate the organization, and they offer encouragement to those around them (see Figure 10.6).

Ineffective

Pulling the plug on Triton

📅 JUNE 6 BY OSCAR HUERTA   💬 LEAVE A COMMENT

Most of you probably don't follow the costs of materials on the world market, but let me tell you, it's been brutal for those of us who do. We're seeing some major increases in the cost of high-grade steel, ceramics, and semiconductor-grade silicon. We can accommodate moderate increases in these costs by raising our list prices, but there's only so far we can raise prices before sales start to drop.

Of course, we periodically revisit our sales forecasts for products in development, to make sure our revenue projections are valid. Sad to say, Triton looks like it will get hammered when it hits the market. AMG Magnetics recently introduced a product that will compete directly with Triton, and it has both higher performance and a lower price.

This won't come as a surprise to anyone who has been looking at the numbers: We have to pull the plug on Triton. It just won't fly under these new circumstances.

Now, I don't want to hear any gossip about the Triton team failing or not being up to the task or whatever. Sue Wentworth and her crew have been putting in long hours for months, and it was tough for me at the other top managers to deliver this news.

Disruptions like this always start the rumor mill going about job security, so I'm happy to report that there is no need to worry. We have plenty of other projects that could use some extra help, and other project managers are already lobbying to get their hands on the Triton staffers.

By the way, these reviews are something the management team does every quarter to make sure we focus our time and investment on new products with the greatest potential for strong sales and profit levels, the management team reviews the costing analysis and sales projections for every R&D project once a quarter. Sometimes circumstances change after we launch a project, and the financial assumptions we made at that point might no longer be valid.

(a) The writer attempts the indirect approach in the body of the message but gives away the bad news in the headline of the blog post.

(b) This opening makes it more about the writer than the readers or the company in general.

(c) Saying that Triton "will get hammered when it hits the market" is too blunt for such a sensitive message.

(d) He started the post by saying most people don't look at the numbers, so this news will come as a surprise. Also, "pull the plug" and "It just won't fly" feel too flippant for such an important message.

(e) This remark about gossip introduces an additional layer of negativity that serves no purpose.

(f) This paragraph has positive information about job security, but it starts with an unnecessary negative remark about the rumor mill.

(g) This information would make a good buffer (see the effective example), but it makes a poor close because it doesn't leave the reader with anything to feel good about.

Effective

Triton project: important update

📅 JUNE 6 BY OSCAR HUERTA   💬 LEAVE A COMMENT

As part of the ongoing effort to make sure we focus our time and investment on new products with the greatest potential for strong sales and profit levels, the management team reviews the costing analysis and sales projections for every R&D project once a quarter. Conducting these reviews every quarter gives us time to respond in the event that current circumstances no longer align with the financial assumptions we made when a particular project was launched.

On the cost side of the equation, we're seeing some major increases in the cost of high-grade steel, ceramics, and semiconductor-grade silicon. We can accommodate moderate increases in these costs by raising our list prices, but there's only so far we can raise prices before sales start to drop.

Regarding sales projections, our forecasts still look solid for every new product, except for the Triton project. AMG Magnetics recently introduced a product that will compete directly with Triton, and it has both higher performance and a lower price. Accordingly, we have had to reduce Triton's sales forecasts by 35 percent.

Unfortunately, the increase in material costs and the decrease in projected sales volume put Triton in an impossible position. We believe the company has better opportunities for investing our development capital and the time and energy of our talented engineering staff. Accordingly, we have decided to cancel Triton, effectively immediately.

Please rest assured that this will not affect staffing levels. We have plenty of other projects that can use some extra help, and other project managers are already lobbying to get the Triton staffers on their teams.

Please join me in thanking Sue Wentworth and everyone on the Triton team for the months of dedication and creativity they devoted to this project. I know they are disappointed in this outcome but recognize the necessity of focusing on our brightest prospects.

(a) The post title preserves the indirect approach by not giving away the bad news.

(b) The opening serves as an effective buffer because it explains the process that was used to reach the decision. This will put the audience in a rational frame of mind, rather than an emotional one.

(c) This paragraph conveys the first of the two reasons that led to the decision, and it does so in a calm but authoritative way.

(d) This paragraph shares the second reason and narrows the focus from all products to just the Triton project. At this point, readers should be prepared for the bad news that is coming.

(e) He delivers the bad news while keeping the focus on the project and its financial parameters. He also immediately shifts into a positive stance, talking about the talented staff and other opportunities.

(f) This paragraph puts to rest any worries other readers will have about their jobs.

(g) The close is respectful and demonstrates sensitivity toward the people most affected by the decision.

Figure 10.6 Internal Message Providing Bad News About Company Operations
The cancelation of a major development project before completion can be a traumatic event for a company's employees. People who worked on the project are likely to feel that all their time and energy were wasted and to worry that their jobs are in jeopardy. Employees who didn't work on the project might worry about the company's financial health and the stability of their own jobs. Such messages are therefore prime candidates for the indirect approach. Note how much more effectively the revised version manages the reader's emotions from beginning to end.

RESPONDING TO NEGATIVE INFORMATION IN A SOCIAL MEDIA ENVIRONMENT

For all the benefits they bring to business, social media and other communication technologies have created a major new challenge: responding to online rumors, false information, and attacks on a company's reputation. Customers who believe they have been treated unfairly can turn to Twitter, Facebook, and other tools to use public exposure as leverage.

However, false rumors and both fair and unfair criticisms can spread around the world in a matter of minutes. Responding to rumors and countering negative information require an ongoing effort and case-by-case decisions about which messages require a response. Follow these four steps:[7]

- **Engage early, engage often.** The most important step in responding to negative information has to be done *before* the negative information appears, and that is to engage with communities of stakeholders as a long-term strategy. Companies that have active, mutually beneficial relationships with customers and other interested parties are less likely to be attacked unfairly online and more likely to survive such attacks if they do occur. In contrast, companies that ignore constituents or jump into "spin doctor" mode when a negative situation occurs don't have the same credibility as companies that have done the long, hard work of fostering relationships within their physical and online communities.
- **Monitor the conversation.** If people are interested in what your company does, chances are they are blogging, tweeting, podcasting, posting videos, posting on Facebook, and otherwise sharing their opinions. Use the available technologies to listen to what people are saying.
- **Evaluate negative messages.** When you encounter negative messages, resist the urge to fire back immediately. Instead, evaluate the source, the tone, and the content of the message—and then choose a response that fits the situation. For example, the Public Affairs Agency of the U.S. Air Force groups senders of negative messages into four categories: "trolls" (those whose only intent is to stir up conflict), "ragers" (those who are just ranting or telling jokes), "the misguided" (those who are spreading incorrect information), and "unhappy customers" (those who have had a negative experience with the Air Force).
- **Respond appropriately.** After you have assessed a negative message, make the appropriate response based on an overall public relations plan. The Air Force, for instance, doesn't respond to trolls or ragers, responds to misguided messages with correct information, and responds to unhappy customers with efforts to rectify the situation and reach a reasonable solution. In addition to replying promptly, make sure your response won't make the situation worse. For example, taking legal action against critics, even if technically justified, can rally people to their defense and create a public relations nightmare. In some instances, the best response is to contact a critic privately (through direct messaging on Twitter, for example) to attempt a resolution away from the public forum.

Whatever you do, keep in mind that positive reputations are an important asset and need to be diligently guarded and defended. Everybody has a voice now, and some of those voices don't care to play by the rules of ethical communication.

Responding effectively to rumors and negative information in social media requires continual engagement with stakeholders and careful decision-making about which messages should get a response.

MOBILE APP

The **Yelp** mobile app is an easy way to keep the consumer review site at your fingertips—and to monitor what's being said about your business.

REAL-TIME UPDATES

LEARN MORE BY VISITING THIS WEBSITE

Is there any truth to that rumor?

The Emergent website at Columbia University tracks and evaluates rumors spreading online. Go to **real-timeupdates.com/ebc13** and select Learn More in the Students section.

COMMUNICATING IN A CRISIS

Some of the most critical instances of business communication occur during crises, which can include industrial accidents, crimes or scandals involving company employees, on-site hostage situations, terrorist attacks, information theft, product tampering incidents, and financial calamities. During a crisis, customers, employees, local communities, and others will demand information. In addition, rumors can spread unpredictably and uncontrollably. You can also expect the news media to descend quickly, asking questions of anyone they can find.

The key to successful communication efforts during a crisis is having a **crisis management plan**. In addition to defining operational procedures to deal with a crisis, this plan outlines communication tasks and responsibilities, which can include everything from

A *crisis management plan* defines operational procedures to deal with a crisis, including communication tasks and responsibilities.

TABLE 10.3 How to Communicate in a Crisis

When a Crisis Hits:

Do	Don't
Prepare for trouble ahead of time by identifying potential problems, appointing and training a response team, and preparing and testing a crisis management plan	Blame anyone for anything
	Speculate in public
Get top management involved immediately	Refuse to answer questions
Set up a news center for company representatives and the media that is equipped with phones, computers, and other tools for preparing news releases and online updates	Release information that will violate anyone's right to privacy
	Use the crisis to pitch products or services
At the news center, take the following steps:	Play favorites with media representatives

- Issue frequent news updates and have trained personnel available to respond to questions around the clock
- Provide complete information packets to the media as soon as possible
- Prevent conflicting statements and provide continuity by appointing a single person trained in advance to speak for the company
- Tell receptionists and other employees to direct all phone calls to the designated spokesperson in the news center
- Provide updates when new information is available via blog postings, Twitter updates, text messaging, Facebook, and other appropriate media

Tell the whole story—openly, completely, and honestly; if you are at fault, apologize

Demonstrate the company's concern by your statements and your actions

---

REAL-TIME UPDATES

LEARN MORE BY LISTENING TO THIS PODCAST

The challenge of reacting to a dangerous teenage challenge

The "Tide pod challenge," in which teenagers challenged one another to eat toxic laundry detergent, caused a crisis-management challenge for Procter & Gamble. Go to **real-timeupdates.com /ebc13** and select Learn More in the Students section.

media contacts to news release templates (see Table 10.3). The plan should clearly specify which people are authorized to speak for the company, provide contact information for all key executives, and include a list of the news outlets and social media tools that will be used to disseminate information.

Although you can't predict catastrophes, you can prepare for them. Analysis of corporate crises over the past several decades reveals that companies that respond quickly with the information people need tend to fare much better in the long run than those that go into hiding or release inconsistent or incorrect information.[8]

Recipients have an emotional stake in negative employment messages, so the indirect approach is usually the best choice.

Sending Negative Employment Messages

As a manager, you will find yourself in a variety of situations in which you have to convey bad news to individual employees or potential employees. Even if you're not in a supervisory role, you may need to reject requests for recommendations.

Recipients have an emotional stake in these messages, so the indirect approach is usually your best choice. In addition, use great care in selecting the medium and channel for each situation. For instance, email and other written forms let you control the message and avoid personal confrontation, but one-on-one conversations are often viewed as more sensitive and give both sides the opportunity to ask and answer questions.

REFUSING REQUESTS FOR RECOMMENDATIONS AND REFERENCES

Saying no when someone asks you to write a recommendation or serve as a reference is an unpleasant but sometimes necessary task. Remind yourself of two points. First, you're never under any obligation to provide a recommendation or serve as a reference. Second, if you have legitimate reasons to refuse the request, the long-term consequences of providing one anyway could be much more negative for you and the other party than the short-term disappointment of saying no.[9]

By taking a careful and sensitive approach, you can make the task less emotionally draining for yourself while minimizing the disappointment for the other person. Note that if you're being asked to give a recommendation in your official capacity as a representative of your firm, you need to be aware of your company's policies. To avoid lawsuits from former employees who receive negative references during background checks, many companies no longer offer anything more than confirmation of employment and don't allow managers to give recommendations as personal communication.[10]

Ideally, someone whose performance was inadequate in your past working relationship will be self-aware enough not to ask for a recommendation. And if you had been the person's supervisor, it would've been your responsibility to share this information.[11]

If you are in a position to write a recommendation but choose not to, here are several options:[12]

- **Disqualify yourself.** With this approach, you simply say something along the lines of "I'm not in a good position to offer an objective assessment" or "I'm not the best person to be giving you a recommendation for this opportunity." This approach will feel most natural in situations where you didn't have a close working relationship.
- **Suggest an alternative.** If you believe the person is qualified but you don't want to provide the reference, you can suggest someone else. You don't have to name anyone in particular, but perhaps suggest he or she ask another former supervisor.
- **Take a mentoring approach.** Remember that being asked to provide a recommendation is a reflection of the respect the person has for you and your position. If you have had a formal or informal mentoring relationship and want to help, you can respectfully explain why you don't think this opportunity is a good path to follow and perhaps offer some guidance about how to find the right opportunity.
- **Explain your personal policy.** If you haven't had a close working relationship or aren't motivated to continue one into the future, you can say that "in the interest of simplicity, I've opted not to provide recommendations."

Whichever course you take, be sure to establish a respectful tone, and don't go overboard with an apology (you've done nothing wrong). Also, avoid any phrasing that might lead to false hopes or continued communication on the matter. For example, if you truly intend to say no, don't say "I can't do it just now" or "let me review your previous performance evaluations."

REAL-TIME UPDATES

LEARN MORE BY READING THIS ARTICLE

These templates make it easier to turn down recommendation requests

The career expert Alison Doyle offers advice and message templates to help you handle these uncomfortable messages. Go to **real-timeupdates.com/ebc13** and select Learn More in the Students section.

REFUSING SOCIAL NETWORKING RECOMMENDATION REQUESTS

Making recommendations in a social networking environment is more complicated than with a traditional recommendation letter because the endorsements you give become part of your online profile. On a network such as LinkedIn, others can see whom you've recommended and what you've written about these people. Much more so than with traditional letters, then, the recommendations you make in a social network become part of your personal brand.[13] Moreover, networks make it easy to find people and request recommendations, so chances are you will get more requests than you would have otherwise—and sometimes from people you don't know well.

Fortunately, social networks give you a bit more flexibility when it comes to responding to these requests. One option is to simply ignore or delete the request. Of course, if you do know a person, ignoring a request could create an uncomfortable situation, so you will need to decide each case based on your relationship with the requester. Another option is to refrain from making recommendations at all, and just let people know this policy when they ask. Whatever you decide, remember that it is your choice.[14]

If you choose to make recommendations and want to respond to a request, you can write as much or as little information about the person as you are comfortable sharing. Unlike the situation with an offline recommendation, you don't need to write a complete letter. You can write a brief statement, even just a single sentence that focuses on one positive aspect.[15] This flexibility allows you to respond positively in those situations in which you have mixed feelings about a person's overall abilities.

REJECTING JOB APPLICATIONS

Application rejections are routine communications, but saying no is never easy, and recipients are emotionally invested in the decision. Moreover, companies must take care to avoid illegal or unethical bias in their employment decisions—or even the appearance of unfairness. Of course, having fair and nondiscriminatory hiring practices is essential, but rejections must also be written in a way that doesn't inadvertently suggest any hint of discrimination. Expert opinions differ on the level of information to include in a rejection message, but the safest strategy is to avoid sharing any explanations for the company's decision and to avoid making or implying any promises of future consideration (see Figure 10.7):[16]

- **Personalize the message by using the recipient's name.** "Dear Applicant" can make it sound as though you never bothered to read the application.
- **Open with a courteous expression of appreciation for having been considered.** In a sense, this opening is like the buffer in an indirect message because it gives you an opportunity to begin the conversation without immediately and bluntly telling the reader that his or her application has been rejected.
- **Convey the negative news politely and concisely.** The passive voice is helpful in this situation because it depersonalizes the response. For example, "Your application was not among those selected for an interview" is less blunt than the active phrase "We have rejected your application."
- **Avoid explaining why an applicant was rejected or why other applicants were chosen instead.** Although it was once more common to offer such explanations, and

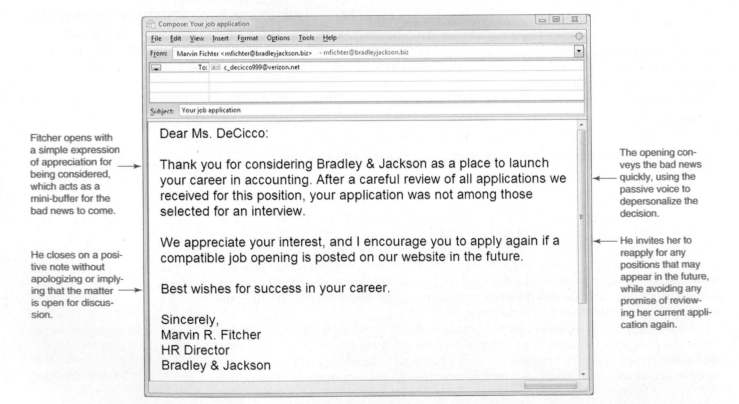

Fitcher opens with a simple expression of appreciation for being considered, which acts as a mini-buffer for the bad news to come.

He closes on a positive note without apologizing or implying that the matter is open for discussion.

The opening conveys the bad news quickly, using the passive voice to depersonalize the decision.

He invites her to reapply for any positions that may appear in the future, while avoiding any promise of reviewing her current application again.

Compose: Your job application

File   Edit   View   Insert   Format   Options   Tools   Help

From: Marvin Fichter <mfichter@bradleyjackson.biz>   - mfichter@bradleyjackson.biz

To: c_decicco999@verizon.net

Subject: Your job application

Dear Ms. DeCicco:

Thank you for considering Bradley & Jackson as a place to launch your career in accounting. After a careful review of all applications we received for this position, your application was not among those selected for an interview.

We appreciate your interest, and I encourage you to apply again if a compatible job opening is posted on our website in the future.

Best wishes for success in your career.

Sincerely,
Marvin R. Fitcher
HR Director
Bradley & Jackson

Figure 10.7   Effective Message Rejecting a Job Applicant
This message rejecting a job applicant takes care to avoid making or implying any promises about future opportunities, beyond inviting the person to apply for positions that may appear in the future. Note that this would not be appropriate if the company did not believe the applicant was a good fit for the company in general.

some experts still advocate this approach, the simplest strategy from a legal standpoint is to avoid offering reasons for the decision. Avoiding explanations lowers the possibility that an applicant will perceive discrimination in the hiring decision or be tempted to challenge the reasons given.

- **Don't state or imply that the application will be reviewed at a later date.** Saying that "we will keep your résumé on file for future consideration" can create false hopes for the recipient and leave the company vulnerable to legal complaints if a future hiring decision is made without actually reviewing this candidate's application again. If the candidate might be a good fit for another position in the company in the future, you can suggest he or she reapply if a new job opening is posted.
- **Close with positive wishes for the applicant's career success.** A brief statement such as "We wish you success in your career" is sufficient.

Naturally, you should adjust your tactics to the circumstances. A simple and direct written message is fine when someone has only submitted a job application, but a phone call might be more appropriate for rejecting a candidate who has made it at least partway through the interview process.

GIVING NEGATIVE PERFORMANCE REVIEWS

Performance reviews are periodic evaluations of employee performance designed to clarify job requirements, give employees feedback on their performance, and establish personal action plans. The traditional annual performance review combines a written assessment with a one-on-one conversation in which the manager shares the review with the employee and discusses the evaluation. Reviews often include a scoring system that can be used to rank employees and establish target pay levels.

Conventional performance reviews are written reports combined with in-person discussion between manager and employee.

Although this approach has been widely used for years, it has some potential weaknesses: Writing these reports consumes a lot of management's time, the long gaps between evaluations can result in employees drifting far off course before getting corrective input, and ranked evaluations can foster an unhealthy atmosphere of competition in the workplace.[17]

In response to these issues, some companies have abandoned the traditional annual review in favor of shorter and more frequent forms of feedback. Some have dropped written reviews altogether in favor of ongoing coaching and feedback sessions between managers and employees, simpler survey methods, and the use of feedback apps.[18] Salesforce.com, for example, replaced performance reviews with its custom Feedback App, which enables all employees to give and receive feedback in real time. The benefits include recognizing contributions when they occur and addressing performance issues quickly.[19]

If you need to give an employee a negative appraisal, using whatever approach and media your company embraces, take steps to help ensure fair and objective reviews:[20]

- **Base your evaluation on concrete, documented evidence.** To avoid basing your evaluation on vague impressions and "gut feelings," be sure to compile objective performance evidence throughout the period leading up to the evaluation. From the employee's perspective, if you don't have detailed evidence, a negative review can come across as a personal attack. This detailed evidence also gives the employee examples of specific behaviors to repeat or avoid.

Negative evaluations should be based on objective, documented evidence.

- **Don't focus on just the negative elements.** Negative behaviors and decisions tend to stick out from the norm, so it's easy to focus on them and overlook positive aspects of performance.
- **Make it a conversation, not a lecture.** Give the employee the opportunity to respond to your feedback and ask questions.

Give employees ample opportunity to ask questions and respond to a negative evaluation.

- **Don't avoid difficult topics.** Pretending that problems don't exist is harmful for everyone, including the employee.
- **Make sure your written and oral communication match.** If you write a strongly negative assessment but then gloss over the problems in order to avoid an uncomfortable live conversation, for example, you'll send mixed messages.
- **Evaluate all employees consistently.** Consistency is not only fair but also helps protect the company from claims of discriminatory practices.

- **Maintain a calm, objective tone.** Whether it's in writing or in person, manage the emotions of the situation by maintaining a professional tone. Be mindful of your non-verbal signals, too.
- **Focus on opportunities for improvement.** This information can serve as the foundation for an improvement plan for the coming year.

TERMINATING EMPLOYMENT

If an employee's performance cannot be brought up to company standards or if other factors such as declining sales cause a reduction in the workforce, a company often has no choice but to terminate employment. As with other negative employment messages, termination is fraught with emotions and legal ramifications, so careful planning, complete documentation, and sensitive writing and conversational skills are essential.

Termination messages should always be written with input from the company's legal staff, but here are general guidelines to bear in mind:[21]

Termination letters require objective documentation and sensitive language in order to avoid creating undue ill will and grounds for legal action.

- Whatever the reasons for the decision, present them clearly and objectively, using calm language. For performance-related terminations, provide the company's evidence for making the decision.
- If the termination is related to an individual's performance, avoid framing these problems as personality conflicts or other vague issues.
- Avoid any suggestion that someone else was behind the decision or that you don't agree with it. Otherwise, you could create the impression that the firing decision is unfair or open to negotiation.
- Follow all company policies, contractual requirements, and applicable state and federal laws.
- Deliver the termination letter in person if at all possible. Arrange a meeting that will ensure privacy and freedom from interruptions.

CHECKLIST ✔ Writing Negative Employment Messages

A. Refusing requests for employee references and recommendations
- ✔ Don't feel obligated to write a recommendation letter if you don't feel comfortable doing so.
- ✔ Take a diplomatic approach to minimize hurt feelings.
- ✔ Compliment the reader's accomplishments, if appropriate.
- ✔ Suggest alternatives, if available.
- ✔ Use the options available to you on social networks, such as ignoring a request from someone you don't know or writing a recommendation on a single positive attribute.

B. Rejecting job applicants
- ✔ If possible, respond to all applications, even if you use only a form message to acknowledge receipt.
- ✔ If you use the direct approach, take care to avoid being blunt or cold.
- ✔ If you use the indirect approach, don't mislead the reader in your buffer or delay the bad news for more than a sentence or two.
- ✔ Avoid explaining why the applicant was rejected.
- ✔ Suggest alternatives if possible.

C. Giving negative performance reviews
- ✔ Document performance problems throughout the year.
- ✔ Evaluate all employees consistently.
- ✔ Keep job descriptions up to date as employee responsibilities change.
- ✔ Maintain an objective and unbiased tone.
- ✔ Use nonjudgmental language.
- ✔ Focus on problem resolution.
- ✔ Make sure negative feedback is documented and shared with the employee.
- ✔ Don't avoid confrontations by withholding negative feedback.
- ✔ Ask the employee for a commitment to improve.

D. Terminating employment
- ✔ State your reasons accurately and make sure they are objectively verifiable.
- ✔ Avoid statements that might expose your company to a wrongful termination lawsuit.
- ✔ Consult company lawyers to clarify all terms of the separation.
- ✔ Deliver the letter in person if at all possible.
- ✔ End the relationship on terms as positive as possible.

- Be prepared for questions that the employee is likely to have, such as what will happen to his or her retirement benefits.
- Avoid surprises. Unless an employee exhibited some unexpected behavior that warrants immediate termination, firing shouldn't come as a surprise. Through regular and honest feedback, underperforming employees should be made aware of their shortcomings and given opportunities to improve.
- If there are legitimately positive aspects to the decision, share those with the employee. For example, if you recognize that even though someone hasn't worked out in his or her current job but could excel in a different role in another company, share that information as a way to help the employee transition to a more successful situation.

Any termination is clearly a negative outcome for the employee, but careful attention to content and tone in the termination message can help the employee move on gracefully and minimize the misunderstandings and anger that can lead to expensive lawsuits. To review the tasks involved in this type of message, see "Checklist: Writing Negative Employment Messages." For more insights on writing negative messages, visit **real-timeupdates.com /ebc13** and select Chapter 10.

ON THE JOB: SOLVING COMMUNICATION DILEMMAS AT **MICROSOFT**

You've joined Microsoft Research as a department manager, and in this role you face the usual range of communication challenges that all managers face. Use what you've learned in this chapter to address the following situations.

1. Another manager stopped by this morning with a request to borrow two of your best employees for a three-week emergency. Under normal conditions, you wouldn't hesitate to help, but your team has its own scheduling challenges to deal with. Plus, this isn't the first time this manager has run into trouble, and you are confident that poor project management is the reason. Which of the following is the most diplomatic way to state your refusal while suggesting that your colleague's management skills need improvement?
   a. With the commitments I've made, I won't be able to bail you out this time.
   b. I sympathize with the trouble you've gotten yourself into again, I really do, but the commitments I've made on my own projects prevent me from releasing any employees for temporary assignments.
   c. The commitments I've made won't allow me to release any staff for temporary assignments. However, would you like to meet to discuss the techniques I've found useful for managing project workloads?
   d. Instead of shifting resources around as usual, why don't we meet to discuss some new strategies for staffing and project management?

2. The HR department acts as an internal service provider, helping various departments throughout the company with hiring, benefits, training, and other employment functions. An HR rep is assigned to each division, working with the managers and employees in that department, but reporting to HR managers. As in all other professional relationships,

personal aspects can enter the relationship. Even competent professionals can start to rub each other the wrong way at a personal level, which can corrode the business relationship over time. Unfortunately, that has happened with one of your best staff members. Geri Lamb is widely admired for her HR skills, but the general manager of the department where she is assigned has asked you to replace her with a new HR representative. Although you'd prefer to tell Lamb in person, schedule conflicts dictate that you send her an email. Which of these buffers would be the best way to open the message?
   a. Your work for the customer support department continues to be first rate, but you never can tell how these things are going to work out, can you?
   b. If it were up to me, Geri, I would never deliver a message like this, but the customer support department has asked me to reevaluate the HR staffing assignments.
   c. As I've expressed on many occasions, thank you once again for the top-quality work you've done for the customer support department over the years.
   d. As you know, Geri, I continually evaluate the HR staffing assignments to make sure the various departments are satisfied with the quality of our work and the overall nature of our relationship with them.

3. Although your project management skills are quite good, you occasionally overlook something or run into unforeseen circumstances. Halfway through the installation of a new project management system, you realized that you underestimated the complexity of linking this new technology to the company's information systems. You now have the unpleasant task of explaining to your boss that the project will be coming in at least 20 percent over budget and possibly as

high as 30 percent over. Which of the following is the best way to begin an email message to your boss?

a. I messed up, big time. The project management project is going to come in over budget.

b. The project management project is going to come in at least 20 percent over budget and possibly as much as 30 percent over.

c. I recently discovered that linking the project management to our existing IT systems was more complicated than anyone realized when I established the budget for this project. As a result of the extra work required to customize the software, the project is going to run 20 to 30 percent over budget.

d. I recently discovered that linking the project management system to our existing IT systems was more complicated than I realized when we established the budget for this project. The fact that there is extra work is not really my fault, per se, since it would've been necessary in any case, but as a result of the extra work required to customize the software, the project is going to run 20 to 30 percent over budget.

4. You've found it easy to say "yes" to recommendation letter requests from former employees who were top performers, and you've learned to say "no" to people who didn't perform so well. The requests you struggle with are from employees in the middle, people who didn't really excel but

didn't really cause any trouble, either. You've just received a request from an AI specialist who falls smack in the middle of the middle. Unfortunately, he's applying for a job at a firm that you know places high demands on its employees and generally hires the best of the best. He's a great person, and you'd love to help, but in your heart, you know that if by some chance he does get the job, he probably won't last. Plus, you don't want to get a reputation in the industry for recommending weak candidates. How do you set the stage for the negative news?

a. As your former manager, I'd like to think I can still look out for your best interests, and I'm sorry to say, but based on what I know about the position you're applying for, this might not be the best career move for you at this point.

b. In my view, the responsibility of writing a letter of recommendation goes beyond simply assessing a person's skills; it must consider whether the person is applying for the right job.

c. One of the most important factors I consider when deciding whether to endorse an applicant is whether he or she is pursuing an opportunity that offers a high probability of success.

d. Writing recommendation letters bears a heavy responsibility for the job applicant and the person writing the letter. After all, I have my own reputation to protect, too.

END OF CHAPTER

Learning Objectives Checkup

Assess your understanding of the principles in this chapter by reading each learning objective and studying the accompanying exercises. You can check your responses against the answer key on page 613.

Objective 10.1: Apply the three-step writing process to negative messages.

1. A negative message using the _____ _____ opens with the bad news, then proceeds to the reasons for the situation or decision.

2. A negative message using the _____ _____ opens with a buffer, then builds up the reasons behind the bad news before presenting the bad news itself.

3. Which of the following is an effective way to maintain the "you" attitude when crafting negative messages?

a. Make sure the reader clearly understands that he or she is at fault; after all, recognizing a mistake is the first step toward improvement.

b. Make it clear that you don't enjoy giving out bad news.

c. Show respect for the reader by "soft peddling" the negative news, implying it without really coming out and saying it directly.

d. Show respect for the reader by avoiding negative, accusatory language and emphasizing positives whenever possible.

Objective 10.2: Explain how to use the direct approach effectively when conveying negative news.

4. When using the direct approach with negative messages, you begin with

a. a buffer.

b. an attention-getter.

c. the bad news.

d. any of the above.

5. An advantage of using the direct approach with negative messages is that it

a. saves readers time by helping them reach the main idea more quickly.

b. eases readers into the message.

c. is diplomatic.

d. does all of the above.

Objective 10.3: Explain how to use the indirect approach effectively when conveying negative news.

6. When using the indirect approach with negative messages, you begin with

a. a buffer.

b. an attention-getter.

c. the bad news.

d. any of the above.

7. Which of the following is an advantage of using the indirect approach with negative messages?
    a. Most readers prefer the direct approach for such messages.
    b. It makes a shorter message possible.
    c. It can ease the blow of negative news and help readers accept the news
    d. It does all of the above.

8. What are the risks of using the indirect approach?
    a. It is always disrespectful and sometimes unethical.
    b. If handled poorly, it can be disrespectful and even unethical.
    c. It is no longer acceptable in a world of social media.
    d. Today's employees resent being given news in an indirect way.

9. A/an _____ is a neutral, noncontroversial opening statement that establishes common ground with your reader.

10. Which of the following is a good possibility to consider when writing a buffer?
    a. Look for subtle opportunities to promote your company and its products.
    b. Assure the reader that your company always follows all applicable laws and regulations.
    c. Indicate your understanding of the reader's situation.
    d. Subtly but clearly indicate how difficult it is for you to be the bearer of bad news.

Objective 10.4: Explain the importance of maintaining high standards of ethics and etiquette when delivering negative messages.

11. _____ is expressing ethical concerns internally through company ethics hotlines or externally if employees perceive no other options.

12. Which of the following is most characteristic of organizational cultures that emphasize open communication?
    a. Managers are willing to listen to bad news from employees, but they understand if employees don't want to deliver bad news.
    b. Managers expect employees to alert them to problems so that corrective action can be taken.
    c. Managers reward employees who deliver bad news with extra vacation time, extra pay, or both.
    d. None of the above are true.

Objective 10.5: Describe successful strategies for sending negative messages on routine business matters.

13. If you need to reject a solicited proposal from an employee, which of the following approaches is best?
    a. Use the indirect approach, but avoid explaining exactly why the proposal does not meet your needs; it's up to the employee to figure that out.
    b. Use the direct approach; rejected proposals are a fact of life of business.
    c. Use the indirect approach, and provide a thoughtful and complete explanation of why the proposal does not meet your needs.
    d. Don't respond at all; doing so will only create an uncomfortable situation for the employee.

14. Which of the following is *not* a normal goal when sending bad-news messages about transactions?
    a. Modifying the customer's expectations
    b. Explaining how you plan to resolve the situation
    c. Identifying who is responsible for the situation so that the customer understands you are serious about correcting the error
    d. Repairing whatever damage might have been done to the business relationship

Objective 10.6: List the important points to consider when conveying negative organizational news.

15. Which of the following best characterizes the nature of crisis management planning?
    a. Good managers should be able to anticipate the specific crisis scenarios their companies might encounter and therefore should be able to plan for every crisis in a specific way.
    b. Faced with everything from terrorism to technological disasters, there's no way for managers to anticipate which crisis might hit any given business, so it's a waste of time to plan a response.
    c. Although you can't anticipate the nature and circumstance of every possible crisis, you can prepare by deciding how to handle such issues as communication with employees and the public.
    d. Only negatively focused managers worry about crisis planning; positive managers keep their organizations moving toward company goals.

16. Continuing advances in social media make it
    a. easier to control rumors through internet filters and other means.
    b. more difficult to control rumors.
    c. easier to find the people who start rumors.
    d. illegal to spread false rumors about public corporations.

Objective 10.7: Describe successful strategies for sending negative employment-related messages.

17. Why do many experts recommend using the indirect approach when rejecting job applicants?
    a. Applicants have a deep emotional investment in the decision.
    b. Laws in most states require the indirect approach.
    c. The indirect approach is easier to write.
    d. The indirect approach is shorter.

18. Regarding the question of explaining why an applicant wasn't chosen for a position, you should
    a. be specific without being too personal, such as explaining that the position requires specific skills that the applicant doesn't yet possess.
    b. point out the person's shortcomings, as that's the honest way and the only way the person knows what he or she needs to improve.
    c. be as vague as possible to avoid hurting the person's feelings.
    d. avoid explaining why an applicant wasn't chosen.

Key Terms

buffer A neutral, noncontroversial statement that establishes common ground with the reader in an indirect negative message

crisis management plan Plan that defines operational procedures to deal with a crisis, including communication tasks and responsibilities

performance review Employee evaluation procedure giving feedback on performance and guidance for future efforts

whistle-blowing Efforts by employees to report concerns about unethical or illegal behavior

Apply Your Knowledge

To review chapter content related to each question, refer to the indicated Learning Objective.

10-1. Would you choose the direct or indirect approach to announce that a popular employee benefit is being eliminated for cost reasons? Why? [LO-1]

10-2. Can you express sympathy with someone's negative situation without apologizing for the circumstances? Explain your answer. [LO-2]

10-3. Is intentionally deemphasizing bad news the same as distorting graphs and charts to deemphasize unfavorable data? Why or why not? [LO-3]

10-4. Why is it important to be engaged with stakeholders before trying to use social media during a crisis or other negative scenario? [LO-6]

10-5. If your social media monitoring efforts pick up a tweet that accuses your customer service staff of lying and claims to have evidence to back it up, how would you respond? [LO-6]

10-6. Should you ever apologize when giving an employee a negative performance evaluation? Why or why not? [LO-7]

10-7. How would you respond to a LinkedIn network connection who asks for a recommendation when you barely remember working with this person and don't remember whether she was good at her job? [LO-7]

Practice Your Skills

Messages for Analysis

Read the following messages and then (1) analyze the strengths and weaknesses of each sentence and (2) revise each message so that it follows this chapter's guidelines.

10-8. Message 10.A: Sending Negative Organizational News [LO-6]

Dear Traveling Executives:

We need you to start using some of the budget suggestions we are going to issue as a separate memorandum. These include using videoconference equipment and web conferencing instead of traveling to meetings, staying in cheaper hotels, arranging flights for cheaper times, and flying from less-convenient but also less-expensive suburban airports.

The company needs to cut travel expenses by fifty percent, just as we've cut costs in all departments of Black & Decker. This means you'll no longer be able to stay in fancy hotels and make last-minute, costly changes to your travel plans.

You'll also be expected to avoid hotel surcharges for phone calls and Internet access. If the hotel you want to stay in doesn't offer free wireless, go somewhere else. And never, NEVER return a rental car with an empty tank! That causes the rental agency to charge us a premium price for the gas they sell when they fill it up upon your return.

You'll be expected to make these changes in your travel habits immediately.

Sincerely,

M. Juhasz

Travel & Meeting Services

10-9. Message 10.B: Refusing Requests for Claims and Adjustments [LO-5]

I am responding to your email of about six weeks ago asking for an adjustment on your wireless hub, model WM39Z. We test all our products before they leave the factory; therefore, it could not have been our fault that your hub didn't work.

If you or someone in your office dropped the unit, it might have caused the damage. Or the damage could have been caused by the shipper if he dropped it. If so, you should file a claim with the shipper. At any rate, it wasn't our fault. The parts are already covered by warranty. However, we will provide labor for the repairs for $50, which is less than our cost, since you are a valued customer.

We will have a booth at the upcoming trade show there and hope to see you or someone from your office. We have many new models of hubs, routers, and other computer gear that we're sure you'll want to see. I've enclosed our latest catalog. Hope to see you there.

10-10. Message 10.C: Rejecting Job Applications [LO-7]

I regret to inform you that you were not selected for our summer intern program at Equifax. We had over a thousand résumés and cover letters to go through and simply could not get to them all. We have been asked to notify everyone that we have already selected students for the 25 positions based on those who applied early and were qualified.

We're sure you will be able to find a suitable position for summer work in your field and wish you the best of luck. We deeply regret any inconvenience associated with our reply.

Exercises

Each activity is labeled according to the primary skill or skills you will need to use. To review relevant chapter content, you can refer to the indicated Learning Objective. In some instances, supporting information will be found in another chapter, as indicated.

Planning: Choosing the Direct or Indirect Approach [LO-1] Select which approach you would use (direct or indirect) for the following negative messages.

10-11. An email message to your boss informing her that one of your key clients is taking its business to a different accounting firm

10-12. An email message to a customer informing her that one of the books she ordered over the internet is temporarily out of stock

10-13. A text message to a customer explaining that the DVD recorder he ordered for his new computer is on backorder and that, as a consequence, the shipping of the entire order will be delayed

10-14. A blog post to all employees notifying them that the company parking lot will be repaved during the first week of June and that the company will provide a shuttle service from a remote parking lot during that period

10-15. A letter from a travel agent to a customer stating that the airline will not refund her money for the flight she missed but that her tickets are valid for one year

10-16. A form letter from a U.S. airline to a customer explaining that the company cannot extend the expiration date of the customer's frequent flyer miles even though the customer was living overseas for the past three years and unable to use the miles during that time

10-17. A letter from an insurance company to a policyholder denying a claim for reimbursement for a special medical procedure that is not covered under the terms of the customer's policy

10-18. A letter from an electronics store stating that the customer will not be reimbursed for a malfunctioning mobile phone that is still under warranty (because the terms of the warranty do not cover damages to phones that were accidentally dropped from a moving car)

10-19. An announcement to the repairs department listing parts that are on back order and will be three weeks late

10-20. Message Strategies: Refusing Routine Requests [LO-4] As a customer service supervisor for a mobile phone company, you're in charge of responding to customers' requests for refunds. You've just received an email from a customer who unwittingly ran up a $550 bill for data charges after forgetting to disable his smartphone's Wi-Fi hotspot feature. The customer says it wasn't his fault because he didn't know his roommates were using his phone to get free internet access. However, you've dealt with this situation before and provided a notice to all customers to be careful about excess data charges resulting from the use of the hotspot capability. Draft a short buffer (one or two sentences) for your email reply, sympathizing with the customer's plight but preparing him for the bad news (that company policy specifically prohibits refunds in such cases).

Etiquette: Communicating with Sensitivity and Tact; Collaboration: Team Projects [LO-4] Working alone, revise the following statements to deemphasize the bad news. Then team up with a classmate and read each other's revisions. Did you both use the same approach in every case? Which approach seems to be most effective for each of the revised statements?

10-21. The airline can't refund your money. The "Conditions" section on the back of your ticket states that there are no refunds for missed flights. Sometimes the airline makes exceptions, but only when life and death are involved. Of course, your ticket is still valid and can be used on a flight to the same destination.

10-22. I'm sorry to tell you, we can't supply the custom decorations you requested. We called every supplier, and none of them can do what you want on such short notice. You can, however, get a standard decorative package on the same theme in time. I found a supplier that stocks these. Of course, it won't have quite the flair you originally requested.

10-23. We can't refund your money for the malfunctioning MP3 player. You shouldn't have immersed the unit in water while swimming; the users' manual clearly states that the unit is not designed to be used in adverse environments.

10-24. Communication Ethics [LO-4] The insurance company where you work is planning to raise all premiums for health-care coverage. Your boss has asked you to read a draft of her letter to customers announcing the new, higher rates. The first two paragraphs discuss some exciting medical advances and the expanded coverage offered by your company. Only in the final paragraph do customers learn that they will have to pay more for coverage starting next year. What are the ethical implications of this draft? What changes would you suggest?

10-25. Sending Negative Organizational News [LO-6] Public companies occasionally need to issue news releases to announce or explain downturns in sales, profits, demand, or other business factors. Search the web to locate a company that has issued a press release that recently reported lower earnings or other bad news and access the news release on the firm's website. You can also search for press releases at **www.prnewswire.com** or **www.businesswire.com**. How does the headline relate to the main message of the release? Is the release organized according to the direct or the indirect approach? What does the company do to present the bad news in a favorable light—and does this effort seem sincere and ethical to you?

Expand Your Skills

Critique the Professionals

Locate an example online of a negative-news message from any company. Possible examples include announcements of product recalls, poor financial results, layoffs, and fines or other legal troubles. Analyze the approach the company took; was it the most effective strategy possible? Did the company apologize, if doing so would have been appropriate under the circumstances, and does the apology seem sincere? Does the tone of the message match the seriousness of the situation? Does the message end on a positive note, as appropriate? Using whatever medium your instructor requests, write a brief analysis of the message (no more than one page), citing specific elements from the piece and support from the chapter.

Sharpening Your Career Skills Online

Bovée and Thill's Business Communication Web Search, at **websearch.businesscommunicationnetwork.com**, is a unique research tool designed specifically for business communication research. Use the Web Search function to find a website, video, article, podcast, or PowerPoint presentation that offers advice on writing messages that convey negative information. Write a brief email message to your instructor describing the item you found and summarizing the career skills information you learned from it.

Build Your Career

As you get ready to create or update your résumé, you'll face the question of which organizational format to use. As pages 481–482 in Chapter 15 explain, there are three basic structures, and the best choice depends on where you are in your career. The *chronological résumé* highlights work experience and shows your employment history in reverse chronological order, with your most recent job first. The *functional résumé* or *skills résumé* highlights your skills and capabilities, rather than your work history, but many employers are suspicious of this format because it can be used to obscure a problematic career path. The *combination résumé* is a hybrid of these two, highlighting skills and capabilities while still giving an idea of your work and educational progress.

If you have a few years of work experience that is related to the jobs you are applying for, the chronological résumé is your best choice. This is the format most employers prefer, because it lets recruiters quickly get a sense of your work history. If you don't have much work experience yet, no problem—go with the combination résumé, because it lets you highlight the skills and knowledge you gained through your education while still giving a chronological sense of your life history.

While you consider which format to use, start to think about the various components that will make up your résumé. Gather the information you'll need to describe your education, work experience, and any relevant volunteer or academic experiences. The most challenging section to write is the *introductory statement*, so give yourself plenty of time to ponder this one and try different approaches. Review the three options on pages 485–486 and choose the one that works best for you. Jot down ideas and phrases over the coming weeks and months, and you'll have the raw material you'll need when you're ready to finalize your résumé.

Improve Your Grammar, Mechanics, and Usage

The following exercises help you improve your knowledge of and power over English grammar, mechanics, and usage. Turn to the Handbook of Grammar, Mechanics, and Usage at the end of this book and review all of Sections 2.4 (Semicolons) and 2.5 (Colons). Then look at the following 10 items. Indicate the preferred choice in the following groups of sentences. (Answers to these exercises appear on page 614.)

10-26. **a.** This letter looks good; that one doesn't.
   b. This letter looks good: that one doesn't.

10-27. **a.** I want to make one thing clear: None of you will be promoted without teamwork.
   b. I want to make one thing clear; none of you will be promoted without teamwork.
   c. I want to make one thing clear: None of you will be promoted; without teamwork.

10-28. **a.** The Zurich airport has been snowed in, therefore I can't attend the meeting.
   b. The Zurich airport has been snowed in, therefore, I can't attend the meeting.
   c. The Zurich airport has been snowed in; therefore, I can't attend the meeting.

10-29. **a.** His motivation was obvious: to get Meg fired.
   b. His motivation was obvious; to get Meg fired.

10-30. **a.** Only two firms have responded to our survey; J. J. Perkins and Tucker & Tucker.
   b. Only two firms have responded to our survey: J. J. Perkins and Tucker & Tucker.

10-31. **a.** Send a copy to: Nan Kent, CEO, Bob Bache, president, and Dan Brown, CFO.
   b. Send a copy to Nan Kent, CEO; Bob Bache, president; and Dan Brown, CFO.
   c. Send a copy to Nan Kent CEO; Bob Bache president; and Dan Brown CFO.

10-32. **a.** You shipped three items on June 7; however, we received only one of them.
   b. You shipped three items on June 7, however; we received only one of them.
   c. You shipped three items on June 7; however we received only one of them.

10-33. **a.** Workers wanted an immediate wage increase: they hadn't had a raise in 10 years.
   b. Workers wanted an immediate wage increase; because they hadn't had a raise in 10 years.
   c. Workers wanted an immediate wage increase; they hadn't had a raise in 10 years.

10-34. **a.** His writing skills are excellent however; he needs to polish his management style.
   b. His writing skills are excellent; however, he needs to polish his management style.
   c. His writing skills are excellent: however he needs to polish his management style.

10-35. **a.** We want to address three issues; efficiency; profitability; and market penetration.
   a. We want to address three issues; efficiency, profitability, and market penetration.
   b. We want to address three issues: efficiency, profitability, and market penetration.

For additional exercises focusing on semicolons and colons, visit MyLab Business Communication. Select Chapter 10, then Additional Exercises to Improve Your Grammar, Mechanics, and Usage, then 16. Punctuation A.

Cases

For all cases, feel free to use your creativity to make up any details you need in order to craft effective messages.

Negative Messages on Routine Business Matters

EMAIL SKILLS

10-36. Message Strategies: Rejecting Suggestions and Proposals; Communication Ethics: Making Ethical Choices [LO-5] Knowing how much online product reviews can shape consumer behavior, the other cofounder of your company has just circulated an internal email message with the not-so-subtle hint that everyone in your small start-up should pose as happy customers and post glowing reviews of your new product on Amazon and other shopping sites. You're horrified at the idea—not only is this highly unethical, but if (or more likely when) the scheme is exposed, the company's reputation will be severely damaged.

Your task: You would prefer to address this in a private conversation, but because your partner has already pitched the idea to everyone via email, you have no choice but to respond via email as well. You need to act quickly before anyone acts on the suggestion. Write a response explaining why this is a bad idea and telling employees not to do it. Keep in mind that you are chastising your business partner in front of all your employees. Make up any names or other details you need.

MICROBLOGGING SKILLS

10-37. Message Strategies: Making Routine Negative Announcements [LO-5] Professional musicians do everything they can to keep the show going, particularly for tours that are scheduled months in advance. However, illness and other unforeseeable circumstances can force an act to cancel shows, even after all the tickets have been sold.

Your task: Choose one of your favorite musical acts and assume that you are the tour manager who needs to tell 25,000 fans that an upcoming concert must be canceled because of illness. Ticket holders can apply for a refund at the artist's website or keep their tickets for a future concert date, which will be identified and announced as soon as possible. Write two tweets, one announcing the cancelation and one outlining the options for ticket holders. Make up any information you need, and send your tweets to your instructor via email (don't actually tweet them!).

EMAIL SKILLS

10-38. Message Strategies: Rejecting Suggestions and Proposals [LO-5] Imagine that you are the president of a student club or some other campus group that is unaffiliated with any larger national or international organization. (It can be any type of organization—recreational, charitable, academic, cultural, professional, or social—but try to use a real organization, even if you aren't a member.) You've just received a message from someone who is the president of a similar club in another college or university proposing to form a national organizational structure. Her proposal has some appealing aspects, including unified branding and recruiting, the opportunity to share best practices, and the chance to socialize with and learn from like-minded students across the country. However, after talking it over with some of your members, you decide it's not right for you. You believe that the time, trouble, and costs of being part of a national organization would outweigh the benefits it could offer.

Your task: Draft an email response politely declining the offer.

EMAIL SKILLS

10-39. Message Strategies: Rejecting Suggestions and Proposals [LO-5] Walter Joss is one of the best employees in your department, a smart and hard worker with a keen mind for business. His upbeat attitude has helped the entire department get through some recent rough times, and on a personal level, his wise counsel helped you grow into a leadership role when you were promoted to marketing manager several years ago.

You generally welcome Joss's input on the department's operations, and you have implemented several of his ideas to improve the company's marketing efforts. However, the proposal he emailed you yesterday was not his best work, to put it mildly. He proposed that the company dump the advertising agency it has used for a decade and replace it with some new agency you've never heard of. The only reasons he offered were that the agency "had become unresponsive" and that a "smaller agency could meet our needs better." He failed to address any of the other criteria that are used to select advertising agencies, such as costs, creative skills, technical abilities, geographic reach, research capabilities, and media experience.

This is the first you've heard any criticism of the agency, and in fact, their work has helped your company increase sales every year.

Your task: Draft an email message to Joss, rejecting his proposal. (Note that in a real-life setting, you would want to discuss this with Joss in person, rather than through email, but use email for the purposes of this exercise.)

EMAIL SKILLS

10-40. Message Strategies: Making Routine Negative Announcements [LO-5] You've been proud of many things your gardening tool company has accomplished as it grew from just you working in your basement shop to a nationally known company that employs more than 200 people. However, nothing made you prouder than the company's Helping Our Hometown Grow program, in which employees volunteer on company time to help residents in your city start their own vegetable gardens, using tools donated by the company. Nearly 50 employees participated directly, helping some 500 families supplement their grocery budgets with homegrown produce. Virtually everyone in the company contributed, though, because employees who didn't volunteer to help in the gardens pitched in to cover the work responsibilities of the volunteers.

Sadly, 10 years after you launched the program, you have reached the inescapable conclusion that the company can no longer afford to keep the program going. With consumers around the country still struggling with the aftereffects of a deep recession, sales have been dropping for the past three years—even as lower-cost competitors step up their presence in the market. To save the program, you would have to lay off several employees, but your employees come first.

Your task: Write an email to the entire company, announcing the cancellation of the program.

TELEPHONE SKILLS

10-41. Message Strategies: Making Routine Negative Announcements [LO-5]
Vail Products of Toledo, Ohio, manufactured a line of beds for use in hospitals and other institutions that have a need to protect patients who might otherwise fall out of bed and injure themselves (including patients with cognitive impairments or patterns of spasms or seizures). These "enclosed bed systems" use a netted canopy to keep patients in bed rather than the traditional method of using physical restraints such as straps or tranquilizing drugs. The intent is humane, but the design is flawed: At least 30 patients have become trapped in the various parts of the mattress and canopy structure, and 8 of them have suffocated.

Working with the U.S. Food and Drug Administration, Vail issued a recall on the beds, as manufacturers often do in the case of unsafe products. However, the recall is not really a recall. Vail will not be replacing or modifying the beds, nor will it accept returns. Instead, the company is urging institutions to move patients to other beds, if possible. Vail has also sent out revised manuals and warning labels to be placed on the beds. The company has announced that it is ceasing production of enclosed beds.

Your task: A flurry of phone calls from concerned patients, family members, and institutional staff is overwhelming the support staff. As a writer in Vail's corporate communications office, you've been asked to draft a short script to be recorded on the company's phone system. When people call the main number, they'll hear "Press 1 for information regarding the recall of Model 500, Model 1000, and Model 2000 enclosed beds." After they press 1, they'll hear the message you're about to write, explaining that although the action is classified as a recall, Vail will not be accepting returned beds, nor will it replace any of the affected beds. The message should also assure customers that Vail has already sent revised operating manuals and warning labels to every registered owner of the beds in question. The phone system has limited memory, and you've been directed to keep the message to 75 words or less.[22]

MICROBLOGGING SKILLS

10-42. Message Strategies: Making Routine Negative Announcements [LO-5]
JetBlue was one of the first companies to incorporate the Twitter microblogging service into its customer communications, and thousands of fliers and fans now follow the airline's tweeting staff members. Messages include announcements about fare sales, celebrations of company milestones, schedule updates, and even personalized responses to people who tweet with questions or complaints about the company.

Your task: Write a tweet alerting JetBlue customers to the possibility that Hurricane Louie might disrupt flight schedules from August 13 through August 15. Tell them that decisions about delays and cancellations will be made on a city-by-city basis and will be announced on Twitter and the company's website.

BLOGGING SKILLS

10-43. Message Strategies: Making Routine Negative Announcements [LO-5]
Marketing specialists usually celebrate when target audiences forward their messages to friends and family—essentially acting as unpaid advertising and sales representatives. In fact, the practice of viral marketing is based on this hope. For one Starbucks regional office, however, viral marketing started to make the company just a bit sick. The office sent employees in the Southeast an email coupon for a free iced drink and invited them to share the coupon with family and friends. To the surprise of virtually no one who understands the nature of online life, the email coupon multiplied rapidly, to the point that Starbucks stores all around the country were quickly overwhelmed with requests for free drinks. The company decided to immediately terminate the free offer, a month ahead of the expiration date on the coupon.[23]

Your task: Write a one-paragraph message that can be posted on the Starbucks website and at individual stores, apologizing for the mix-up and explaining that the offer is no longer valid.

EMAIL SKILLS

10-44. Message Strategies: Refusing Claims and Requests for Adjustment [LO-5]
Your company markets a line of rugged smartphone cases designed to protect the sensitive devices from drops, spills, and other common accidents. Your guarantee states that you will reimburse customers for the cost of a new phone if the case fails to protect it from any of the following: (a) a drop of no more than 6 feet onto any surface; (b) spills of any beverage or common household chemical; (c) being crushed by any object weighing up to 100 pounds; or (d) being chewed on by dogs, cats, or other common household pets.

Jack Simmons, a rancher from Wyoming, emailed your customer support staff requesting a reimbursement after he dropped his iPhone in his hog barn and a 900-pound boar crushed it in a single bite.

Your task: Write an email response to the customer, denying his request for a new phone.

10-45. Message Strategies: Negative Announcements on Routine Matters [LO-5]   An employee concierge seemed like a great idea when you added it as an employee benefit last year. The concierge handles a wide variety of personal chores for employees, everything from dropping off dry cleaning to ordering event tickets to sending flowers. Employees love the service, and you know that the time they save can be devoted to work or family activities. Unfortunately, profits are way down and concierge usage is up—up so far that you'll need to add a second concierge to keep up with the demand. As painful as it will be for everyone, you decide that the company needs to stop offering the service.

Your task: Script a brief podcast announcing the decision and explaining why it is necessary. Make up any details you need. If your instructor asks you to do so, record your podcast and submit the file.

10-46. Message Strategies: Negative Announcements on Routine Matters [LO-5]   You can certainly sympathize with employees when they complain about having their email and instant messages monitored, but you're implementing a company policy that all employees agree to abide by when they join the company. Your firm, Webcor Builders of San Francisco, California, is one of the estimated 60 percent of U.S. companies with such monitoring systems in place. More and more companies use these systems (which typically operate by scanning messages for keywords that suggest confidential, illegal, or otherwise inappropriate content) in an attempt to avoid instances of sexual harassment and other problems.

As the chief information officer, the manager in charge of computer systems in the company, you're often the target when employees complain about being monitored. Consequently, you know you're really going to hear it when employees learn that the monitoring program will be expanded to personal blogs as well.

Your task: Write an email message to be distributed to the entire workforce explaining that the automated monitoring program is about to be expanded to include employees' personal blogs. Note that while you sympathize with employee concerns regarding privacy and freedom of speech, it is the management team's responsibility to protect the company's intellectual property and the value of the company name. Therefore employees' personal blogs will be added to the monitoring system to ensure that employees don't intentionally or accidentally expose company secrets or criticize management in a way that could harm the company.[24]

10-47. Message Strategies: Rejecting Suggestions and Proposals [LO-5]   All companies love *product enthusiasts*, those customers who are such fans that their activities help the company market its products and support its customers. Enthusiasts of a particular company or product often join *owners groups* or *user groups* to network, share ideas, and support one another. These groups can be sponsored by the company or entirely independent. Social media are a natural forum for product enthusiasts as they meet online to share tips, tricks, rumors about upcoming products, and the pros and cons of various products, as well as provide feedback to the companies that make the products they use and enjoy.

Imagine you're on the social media team for Android, the operating system made by Google that is used in more than a billion mobile devices. With nearly 2 billion likes, the Android Facebook page is a popular online destination for Android smartphone and tablet users. After posting an item about some new software features, you get a comment from Shauna Roberts, who has commented on hundreds of posts over the past few years. She is definitely an Android enthusiast and has helped many other users with technical support issues—and helped the Android team with a number of great product suggestions.

Today she has a proposal for you: She wants Google to start paying the top commenters on the Android Facebook page in return for the work they do to help both customers and the company. Her argument is that Google benefits from the enthusiasts' time and expertise, so it would be fair to offer some modest compensation in return.

Your task: Draft a message that you could post on the company's Facebook page in response to this proposal. The idea has come up before, and the company's response has always been that paying enthusiasts for social media activity, even if it helps the company through word-of-mouth marketing and lower support costs, would be too difficult to manage. First, judging the relative value of thousands of comments would be next to impossible. Second, quantity doesn't necessarily mean quality when it comes to sharing technical information. And third, the administrative and contractual overhead needed to make these work-for-hire relationships legal and legitimate would be overwhelming.[25]

10-48. Message Strategies: Negative Announcements on Routine Matters [LO-5]   Your company, PolicyPlan Insurance Services, is a 120-employee insurance claims processor based in Milwaukee. PolicyPlan has engaged Midwest Sparkleen for interior and exterior cleaning for the past five years. Midwest Sparkleen did exemplary work for the first four years, but after a change of ownership last year, the level of service has plummeted. Offices are no longer cleaned thoroughly, you've had to call the company at least six times to remind them to take care of spills and other messes they're supposed to address routinely, and they've left toxic cleaning chemicals in a public hallway on several occasions. You have spoken with the owner about your concerns twice in the past three months, but his assurances that service would improve have not resulted in any noticeable changes. When the evening cleaning crew forgot to lock the lobby door last Thursday—leaving your entire facility vulnerable to theft from midnight until 8:00 Friday morning—you decided it was time to look for a new service provider.

Your task: Write a letter to Jason Allred, owner of Midwest Sparkleen, 4000 South Howell Avenue, Milwaukee, WI, 53207, telling him that PolicyPlan will not be renewing its annual cleaning contract with Midwest Sparkleen when the current contract expires at the end of this month. Cite the examples identified above, and keep the tone of your letter professional.

LETTER-WRITING SKILLS

10-49. Message Strategies: Negative Announcements on Routine Matters [LO-5]

You enjoy helping other people learn, and your part-time work as a tutor for high school students has brought in some much-needed income during the past two years. You pride yourself on giving everything you can to help every one of your clients, but you've reached the end of the line with Drew Whitechapel. You know he has the ability, but he refuses to take tutoring seriously and continues to get failing grades in his American History class. You know he isn't getting much value from your tutoring, and you would rather devote your time and energy to a more serious student.

Your task: Write a letter to Drew's parents explaining that you will no longer be able to tutor him after this month. (They've already paid you for this month's sessions.)

Negative Organizational News

MICROBLOGGING SKILLS

10-50. Message Strategies: Responding to Rumors [LO-6]

Sheila Elliot, a well-known actress, appeared on a national talk show last night and claimed that your company's Smoothstone cookware was responsible for her toddler's learning disability. Elliot claimed that the nonstick surfaces of Smoothstone pots and pans contain a dangerous chemical that affected her child's cognitive development. There's just one problem with her story—well, three problems, actually: (a) your company's cookware line is called Moonstone, not Smoothstone; (b) Moonstone does not contain and never has contained the chemical Elliot mentioned; and (c) the product she is really thinking of was called Smoothfire, which was made by another company and was pulled off the market five years ago.

Thousands of worried parents aren't waiting for the fact-checkers, however. They took to the blogosphere and Twittersphere with a vengeance overnight, warning people to throw away anything made by your company (Tatum Housewares). Several television stations have already picked up the Twitter chatter and repeated the rumor. Retailers are already calling your sales staff to cancel orders.

Your task: Write a three-message sequence to be posted on your company's Twitter account, correcting the rumor and conveying the three points outlined above.

BLOGGING SKILLS

10-51. Message Strategies: Negative Organizational Announcements [LO-6]

XtremityPlus is known for its outlandish extreme-sports products, and the Looney Launch is no exception. Fulfilling the dream of every childhood daredevil, the Looney Launch is an aluminum and fiberglass contraption that quickly unfolds to create the ultimate bicycle jump. The product has been selling as fast as you can make it, even though it comes plastered with warning labels proclaiming that its use is inherently dangerous.

As XtremityPlus's CEO, you were nervous about introducing this product, and your fears were just confirmed: You've been notified of the first lawsuit by a parent whose child broke several bones after crash-landing off a Looney Launch.

Your task: Write a post for your internal blog explaining that the Looney Launch is being removed from the market immediately. Tell your employees to expect some negative reactions from enthusiastic customers and retailers, but explain that (a) the company can't afford the risk of additional lawsuits, and (b) even for XtremityPlus, the Looney Launch pushes the envelope a bit too far. The product is simply too dangerous to sell in good conscience.

BLOGGING SKILLS / PORTFOLIO BUILDER

10-52. Message Strategies: Communicating in a Crisis [LO-6]

One of your company's worst nightmares has just come true. EQ Industrial Services (EQIS), based in Wayne, Michigan, operates a number of facilities around the country that dispose of, recycle, and transport hazardous chemical wastes. Last night, explosions and fires broke out at the company's Apex, North Carolina, facility, forcing the evacuation of 17,000 local residents.

Your task: It's now Friday, the day after the fire. Write a brief post for the company's blog, covering the following points:

- A fire broke out at the Apex facility at approximately 10 P.M. Thursday.
- No one was in the facility at the time.
- Because of the diverse nature of the materials stored at the plant, the cause of the fire is not yet known.
- Rumors that the facility stores extremely dangerous chlorine gas and that the fire was spreading to other nearby businesses are not true.
- Special industrial firefighters hired by EQIS have already brought the fire under control.
- Residents in the immediate area were evacuated as a precaution, and they should be able to return to their homes tomorrow, pending permission from local authorities.
- Several dozen residents were admitted to local hospitals with complaints of breathing problems, but most have been released already; about a dozen emergency responders were treated as well.
- At this point (Friday afternoon), tests conducted by the North Carolina State Department of Environment and Natural Resources "had not detected anything out of the ordinary in the air."

Conclude by thanking the local police and fire departments for their assistance and directing readers to EQIS's toll-free hotline for more information.[26]

BLOGGING SKILLS

10-53. Message Strategies: Responding to Rumors and Public Criticism [LO-6] Spreading *FUD*—fear, uncertainty, and doubt—about other companies is one of the less-honorable ways of dealing with competition in the business world. For example, someone can start a "whisper campaign" in the marketplace, raising fears that a particular company is struggling financially. Customers who don't want to risk future instability in their supply chains might then shift their purchasing away from the company based on nothing more than the false rumor.

Your task: Find the website of any company that seems interesting. Imagine you are the CEO and the company is the subject of an online rumor about impending bankruptcy. Explore the website to get a basic feel for what the company does. Making up any information you need, write a post for the company's blog explaining that the bankruptcy rumors are false and that the company is on solid financial ground and plans to keep serving the industry for many years to come. (Be sure to review page 301 for tips.)

SOCIAL NETWORKING SKILLS

10-54. Message Strategies: Responding to Rumors and Public Criticism [LO-6] The consumer reviews on Yelp can be a promotional boon to any local business—provided the reviews are positive, of course. Negative reviews, fair or not, can affect a company's reputation and drive away potential customers. Fortunately for business owners, sites like Yelp give them the means to respond to reviews, whether they want to apologize for poor service, offer some form of compensation, or correct misinformation in a review.

Your task: Search Yelp for a negative review (one or two stars) on any business in any city. Find a review that has some substance to it, not just a simple, angry rant. Now imagine you are the owner of that business, and write a reply that could be posted via the "Add Owner Comment" feature. Use information you find on Yelp about the company and fill in any details by using your imagination. Remember that your comment will be visible to everyone who visits Yelp. (Be sure to review page 301 for tips.)

Negative Employment Messages

SOCIAL NETWORKING SKILLS / EMAIL SKILLS

10-55. Message Strategies: Refusing Requests for Recommendations [LO-7] You're delighted to get a message from an old friend and colleague, Heather Lang. You're delighted right up to the moment you read her request that you write a recommendation about her web design and programming skills for your LinkedIn profile. You would do just about anything for Lang—anything except recommend her web design skills. She is a master programmer whose technical wizardry saved more client projects than you can count, but when it comes to artistic design, Lang simply doesn't have "it." From gaudy color schemes to unreadable type treatment to confusing layouts, her design sense is as weak as her technical acumen is strong.

Your task: First, write a brief email to Lang explaining that you would be most comfortable highlighting her technical skills because that is where you believe her true strengths lie. Second, write a two-sentence recommendation that you could include in your LinkedIn profile, recommending Lang's technical skills. Make up or research any details you need.

TELEPHONE SKILLS

10-56. Message Strategies: Terminating Employment [LO-7] As the human resources manager at Alion Science and Technology, a military research firm in McLean, Virginia, you were thrilled when one of the nation's top computer visualization specialists accepted your job offer. Claus Gunnstein's skills would have made a major contribution to Alion's work in designing flight simulators and other systems. Unfortunately, the day after he accepted the offer, Alion received news that a major Pentagon contract had been canceled. In addition to letting several dozen current employees know that the company will be forced to lay them off, you need to tell Gunnstein that Alion has no choice but to rescind the job offer.

Your task: Outline the points you'll need to make in a telephone call to Gunnstein. Pay special attention to your opening and closing statements. (You'll review your plans for the phone call with Alion's legal staff to make sure everything you say follows employment law guidelines; for now, just focus on the way you'll present the negative news to Gunnstein. Feel free to make up any details you need.)[27]

EMAIL SKILLS

10-57. Message Strategies: Refusing Requests for Recommendations [LO-5] Well, this is awkward. Daniel Sturgis, who quit last year just as you were planning to fire him for consistently failing to meet agreed-on performance targets, has just emailed you from his new job, asking for a recommendation. He says his new job is awful and he regrets leaving your company. He knows you don't have any openings, but he would be grateful for a recommendation.

Your task: Write an email message to Sturgis, explaining that you will not be able to write him a recommendation. Make up any details you need.

MESSAGING SKILLS / MOBILE SKILLS

10-58. Message Strategies: Refusing Requests for Recommendations [LO-7] Your classmates could end up being important business contacts as you all progress through your careers. Of course, this also means you might be asked for favors that you're not comfortable giving, such as providing recommendations for someone whose skills or other attributes you don't admire. Choose a person who was in a course you recently took and imagine that a few years after graduation he or she texts you with a request for a job recommendation letter. You've kept in touch socially, at least online, and would like to continue to do so, but your memory of this person's professional potential is more negative than positive. (Make up any combination of negative traits, such as failing to contribute to team projects, giving up quickly in the face of adversity, struggling to understand basic concepts, or other limitations.)

Your task: You've decided to decline the request, so now you must figure out how to phrase your response. Draft a message that you could send in this scenario, making up any information you need. Don't use the person's real name, and don't include any information that your instructor or anyone else could use to identify the person, but imagine that you are in fact writing to this individual. You're on a compatible mobile service that doesn't limit the length of text messages, but remember that your message will be read on a small mobile screen. Email your response to your instructor.

MEMO-WRITING SKILLS / PORTFOLIO BUILDER

10-59. Message Strategies: Negative Performance Reviews [LO-7] Elaine Bridgewater, the former professional golfer you hired to oversee your golf equipment company's relationship with retailers, knows the business inside and out.

As a former touring pro, she has unmatched credibility. She also has seemingly boundless energy, solid technical knowledge, and an engaging personal style. Unfortunately, she hasn't been quite as attentive as she needs to be when it comes to communicating with retailers. You've been getting complaints about voice-mail messages going unanswered for days, confusing emails that require two or three rounds of clarification, and reports that are haphazardly thrown together. As valuable as Bridgewater's other skills are, she's going to cost the company sales if this goes on much longer. The retail channel is vital to your company's survival, and she's the employee most involved in this channel.

Your task: Draft a brief (one-page maximum) informal performance appraisal and improvement plan for Bridgewater. Be sure to compliment her on the areas in which she excels but don't shy away from highlighting the areas in which she needs to improve: punctual response to customer messages; clear writing; and careful revision, production, and proofreading. Use what you've learned in this course so far to supply any additional advice about the importance of these skills.

MyLab Business Communication

MyLab Assisted-Grading Writing Prompts

If your instructor has assigned one or both of the following writing assignments within the MyLab, go to your Assignments to complete these writing exercises.

10-60. What are the five main goals in delivering bad news? [LO-1]

10-61. What are three techniques for deemphasizing negative news? [LO-3]

Endnotes

1. Peter Lee, "Learning from Tay's Introduction," Microsoft blog, 25 March 2016, blogs.microsoft.com; Alex Dobuzinskis, "Microsoft Apologizes for Offensive Tirade by Its 'Chatbot,'" Reuters, 25 March 2016, www.reuters.com; John West, "Microsoft's Disastrous Tay Experiment Shows the Hidden Dangers of AI," *Quartz*, 2 April 2016.
2. Maurice E. Schweitzer, Alison Wood Brooks, and Adam D. Galinsky, "The Organizational Apology," *Harvard Business Review*, September 2015, hbr.org; Adrienne Carter and Amy Borrus, "What if Companies Fessed Up?" *BusinessWeek*, 24 January 2005, 59–60; Patrick J. Kiger, "The Art of the Apology," *Workforce Management*, October 2004, 57–62.
3. Schweitzer, Brooks, and Galinsky, "The Organizational Apology."
4. John Guiniven, "Sorry! An Apology as a Strategic PR Tool," *Public Relations Tactics*, December 2007, 6.
5. Quinn Warnick, "A Close Textual Analysis of Corporate Layoff Memos," *Business Communication Quarterly*, September 2010, 322–326.
6. Christopher Elliott, "7 Ways Smart Companies Tell Customers 'No,'" CBS Money Watch, 7 June 2011, www.cbsnews.com.
7. Micah Solomon, "Mean Tweets: Managing Customer Complaints," CNBC, 22 February 2012, www.cnbc.com; "When Fans Attack: How to Defend a Brand's Reputation Online," Crenshaw Communications blog, 20 May 2010, crenshawcomm.com;

Leslie Gaines-Ross, "Reputation Warfare," *Harvard Business Review*, December 2010, 70–76; David Meerman Scott, "The US Air Force: Armed with Social Media," WebInkNow blog, 15 December 2008, www.webinknow.com; Matt Rhodes, "Social Media as a Crisis Management Tool," Social Media Today blog, 21 December 2009, www.socialmediatoday.com.
8. Courtland L. Bovée, John V. Thill, George P. Dovel, and Marian Burk Wood, *Advertising Excellence* (New York: McGraw-Hill, 1995), 508–509; John Holusha, "Exxon's Public-Relations Problem," *New York Times*, 12 April 1989, D1.
9. Alison Doyle, "Tips for Turning Down a Reference Request," *The Balance*, 21 March 2017, www.thebalance.com.
10. "How to Safely Handle Calls for References," *HR Specialist*, April 2017, 7; Doyle, "Tips for Turning Down a Reference Request."
11. Alison Green, "What to Do When a Bad Employee Asks for a Reference," *Inc.*, 18 June 2015, www.inc.com.
12. Doyle, "Tips for Turning Down a Reference Request"; Green, "What to Do When a Bad Employee Asks for a Reference"; "How to Decline a Reference Request," Simply Hired, 15 March 2016, blog.simplyhired.com.
13. Omowale Casselle, "Really, You Want ME to Write YOU a LinkedIn Recommendation," RecruitingBlogs, 22 April 2010, www.recruitingblogs.com.

14. "LinkedIn Profiles to Career Introductions: When You Can't Recommend Your Friend," *Seattle Post-Intelligencer*, Personal Finance blog, 16 November 2010, blog.seattlepi.com.

15. Neal Schaffer, "How Should I Deal with a LinkedIn Recommendation Request I Don't Want to Give?" Social Web School, 20 January 2010, humancapitalleague.com.

16. Dawn Wolf, "Job Applicant Rejection Letter Dos and Donts—Writing an Appropriate 'Dear John' Letter to an Unsuccessful Applicant," 31 May 2009, Employment Blawg.com, www.employmentblawg.com; "Prohibited Employment Policies/Practices," U.S. Equal Employment Opportunity Commission, accessed 14 July 2010, www.eeoc.gov; Susan M. Heathfield, "Candidate Rejection Letter," About.com, accessed 14 July 2010, humanresources.about.com; "Rejection Letters Under Scrutiny: 7 Do's & Don'ts," *Business Management Daily*, 1 April 2009, www.businessmanagementdaily.com.

17. Lori Goler, Janelle Gale, and Adam Grant, "Let's Not Kill Performance Evaluations Yet," *Harvard Business Review*, November 2016, 91–94; Aliah D. Wright, "SAP Ditches Annual Reviews," *HR Magazine*, October 2016, 16.

18. Jon Wolper, "A New Look for Performance Reviews," *TD*, May 2016, 12; Jeff Kauflin, "Hate Performance Reviews? Good News: They're Getting Shorter and Simpler," *Forbes*, 9 March 2017, www.forbes.com; Lori Goler, "Why Facebook Is Keeping Performance Reviews: Interaction," *Harvard Business Review*, January/February 2017, 18.

19. "Salesforce: Perks and Programs," Great Place to Work, accessed 28 March 2018, reviews.greatplacetowork.com.

20. Anne Fisher, "How to Give an Annual Performance Review (If You Must)," *Fortune*, 3 January 2017, www.fortune.com; "How to Document a Performance Review," *Harvard Business Review*, 5 May 2015, hbr.org; "Performance Evaluations: Steer Clear of Two Major Errors," *Pennsylvania Employment Law*, January 2017, 4; Joan Lloyd, "Avoid These Common Performance Review Mistakes," *The Receivables Report*, January 2017, 6–7; "Self-Assessment: Check Your Performance Review Communication Skills," *HR Specialist* 14, no. 12 (December 2016), 5; Ben Dattner, "The Key to Performance Reviews Is Preparation," *Harvard Business Review*, 21 June 2016, hbr.org.

21. "Keep Good Records to Justify Every Termination," *New York Employment Law*, February 2017, 1–2; Max Altschuler, "When You Have to Fire Good People," *Harvard Business Review*, 3 March 2017, hbr.org; "Best Defense Against Wrongful Firing Suit: Set Clear Goals and Document the Results," *Employment Law*, April 2017, 4; "Avoid 5 Mistakes When Terminating," *Managing People at Work*, 15 January 2015, 1.

22. "FDA Notifies Public That Vail Products, Inc., Issues Nationwide Recall of Enclosed Bed Systems," U.S. Food and Drug Administration press release, 30 June 2005, www.fda.gov.

23. "Viral Effect of Email Promotion," Alka Dwivedi blog, accessed 19 October 2006, www.alkadwivedi.net; Teresa Valdez Klein, "Starbucks Makes a Viral Marketing Misstep," Blog Business Summit website, accessed 19 October 2006, www.blogbusinesssummit.com.

24. Pui-Wing Tam, Erin White, Nick Wingfield, and Kris Maher, "Snooping Email by Software Is Now a Workplace Norm," *Wall Street Journal*, 9 March 2005, B1.

25. This scenario, and all the information presented in this case, is fictitious.

26. Environmental Quality Company press releases, accessed 27 October 2006, www.eqonline.com; "N.C. Residents to Return After Fire," *Science Daily*, 6 October 2006, www.sciencedaily.com; "Hazardous Waste Plant Fire in N.C. Forces 17,000 to Evacuate," *FOX News*, 6 October 2006, www.foxnews.com.

27. Alion website, accessed 19 August 2005, www.alionscience.com.

Five-Minute Guide to Writing Negative Messages

Whenever you need to send a difficult message, review these tips; then keep this guide at your side while you revise, edit, and proofread.

00:01 **Choose the direct or indirect approach**

Following this decision tree will help you decide whether the direct or indirect approach is better in a given situation. Of course, use your best judgment as well. Your relationship with the audience could affect your choice of approaches, for example.

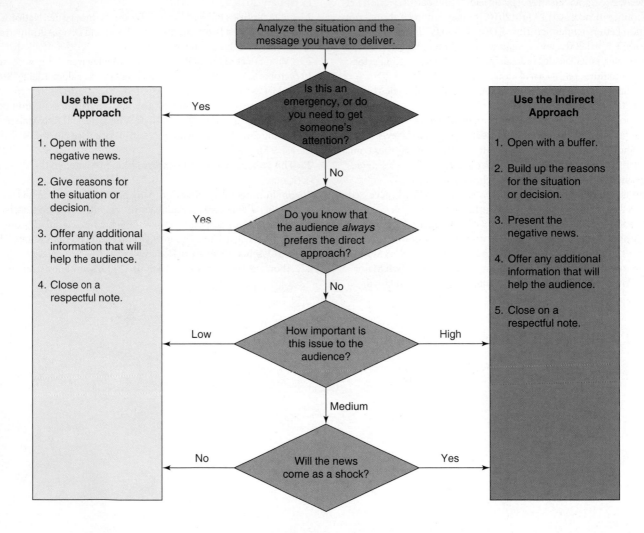

Use the Direct Approach

1. Open with the negative news.
2. Give reasons for the situation or decision.
3. Offer any additional information that will help the audience.
4. Close on a respectful note.

Analyze the situation and the message you have to deliver.

Is this an emergency, or do you need to get someone's attention?   Yes

Do you know that the audience *always* prefers the direct approach?   Yes

How important is this issue to the audience?   Low / High

Will the news come as a shock?   No / Yes

Medium

No

Use the Indirect Approach

1. Open with a buffer.
2. Build up the reasons for the situation or decision.
3. Present the negative news.
4. Offer any additional information that will help the audience.
5. Close on a respectful note.

00:02 **Think about the blocks of information you'll need for either approach**

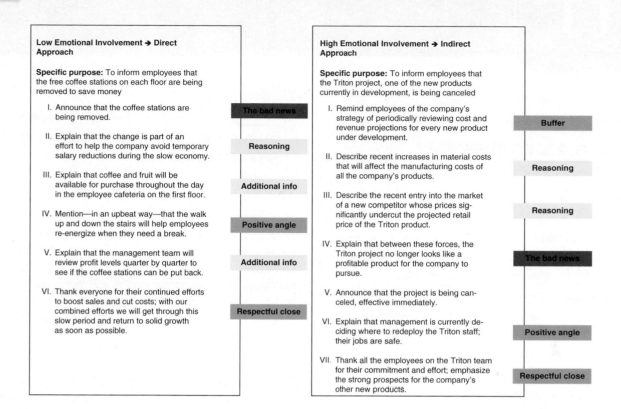

Low Emotional Involvement → Direct Approach

Specific purpose: To inform employees that the free coffee stations on each floor are being removed to save money

I. Announce that the coffee stations are being removed. — The bad news

II. Explain that the change is part of an effort to help the company avoid temporary salary reductions during the slow economy. — Reasoning

III. Explain that coffee and fruit will be available for purchase throughout the day in the employee cafeteria on the first floor. — Additional info

IV. Mention—in an upbeat way—that the walk up and down the stairs will help employees re-energize when they need a break. — Positive angle

V. Explain that the management team will review profit levels quarter by quarter to see if the coffee stations can be put back. — Additional info

VI. Thank everyone for their continued efforts to boost sales and cut costs; with our combined efforts we will get through this slow period and return to solid growth as soon as possible. — Respectful close

High Emotional Involvement → Indirect Approach

Specific purpose: To inform employees that the Triton project, one of the new products currently in development, is being canceled

I. Remind employees of the company's strategy of periodically reviewing cost and revenue projections for every new product under development. — Buffer

II. Describe recent increases in material costs that will affect the manufacturing costs of all the company's products. — Reasoning

III. Describe the recent entry into the market of a new competitor whose prices significantly undercut the projected retail price of the Triton product. — Reasoning

IV. Explain that between these forces, the Triton project no longer looks like a profitable product for the company to pursue. — The bad news

V. Announce that the project is being canceled, effective immediately.

VI. Explain that management is currently deciding where to redeploy the Triton staff; their jobs are safe. — Positive angle

VII. Thank all the employees on the Triton team for their commitment and effort; emphasize the strong prospects for the company's other new products. — Respectful close

00:03 **Think about your opening**

1. With the direct approach, you open with the bad news or negative information; however, a few words of "socializing" can help you ease into the message.

2. With the indirect approach, you open with a buffer, which must be written carefully to avoid being misleading or disrespectful:

- Remember that the purposes of a buffer are to ease the reader into the message by establishing common ground and to create space for a transition into the reasoning and evidence that you are going to lay out next.
- The buffer must never mislead the reader into thinking good news is about to follow.

00:04 **Maintain high standards of ethics and etiquette**

1. Be aware of any laws or regulations that might dictate the content and delivery of the message.

2. Remember that negative messages can have a significant negative impact on your readers.

3. Take care to manage your own emotions and consider the emotional state of your audience.

00:05 **Adjust as needed for the specific situation**

1. What expectations have been set in the past?

2. What is the nature of your relationship with the reader and how do you want to maintain it?

3. What's the most-sensitive combination of medium and channel for this message?

11

Writing Persuasive Messages

ON THE JOB: COMMUNICATING AT

LEARNING OBJECTIVES

After studying this chapter, you will be able to

1 Apply the three-step writing process to persuasive messages.

2 Describe an effective strategy for developing persuasive business messages, and identify the three most common categories of persuasive business messages.

3 Describe an effective strategy for developing marketing and sales messages, and explain how to modify your approach when writing promotional messages for social media.

4 Identify steps you can take to avoid ethical lapses in marketing and sales messages.

MyLab Business Communication

Improve Your Grade!

If your instructor is using MyLab Business Communication, visit **www.pearson.com/mylab/business-communication** for videos, simulations, and writing exercises.

STITCH FIX

The Never-Ending Need to Persuade

Katrina Lake's path to entrepreneurship didn't start with the stereotypical urge to create a company. In fact, she kept waiting for someone else to create the company she had in mind so she could buy from it and invest in it. During the first two phases of her career, in a retail consulting firm and then a venture capital firm, she kept looking for someone to solve what she believed was the central problem of online fashion retailing: "How can we marry the ease of shopping online with what people want in clothes, which is really about fit and style?"

After waiting for someone else to pitch the right idea to her in the hopes of getting investment capital, she decided to launch it herself. She went back to school to pursue an MBA at Harvard, where her idea began to take real shape and Stitch Fix was born. The concept was a clothing retailer that would combine the convenience of online shopping with the individual touch of the stylists and personal shoppers available in higher-end shops and department stores. Customers could receive a small selection of items chosen by a personal stylist (with the help of some powerful artificial intelligence), then buy what they like and send back what they don't.

Lake believed in the idea from the outset, but the need to persuade others to believe in it began early and has been an

Stitch Fix cofounder and CEO Katrina Lake relied heavily on persuasive communication skills to secure funding and attract top talent to her start-up company.

evolving challenge ever since. At Harvard, for instance, her professors pointed out the mammoth inventory-management challenge that the send-and-return model would create. Later, when she was pitching the company to investors from the other side of the table, she had to convince mostly older, mostly male venture capitalists that this was a viable business model because it addressed an unmet need among a mostly younger, female audience.

However, enough people began to believe. Sales took off as more and more women responded to the idea of getting personalized style advice and the convenience of new wardrobe pieces shipped to their front door. Just as important, some major-league talent from across the retailing sector began to believe in her vision, too. High-ranking executives from Netflix, Nike, Walmart, and Salesforce.com signed on, each bringing specific areas of expertise needed to scale up Lake's vision, from inventory management to merchandising to AI and data analytics. The AI component is crucial, because it extends

the reach of the stylists by continually identifying new clothing choices that customers are most likely to enjoy.

Investors climbed on board, too, when more of them grasped the unmet need that Stitch Fix is filling and appreciated Lake's vision and leadership. The company quickly reached $1 billion in annual revenues and now has more than 2 million active customers.

So far, so good, but the need for compelling persuasive communication never ends, only evolves. The next step is to move beyond the earlier enthusiasts and continue to expand the customer base with people who might be reluctant to try this new mode of shopping. The company knows that these customers will be more expensive to acquire, and it will have to do so in the face of new competitors and the omnipresent threat of Amazon. If any company can succeed with this business model over the long term, though, it's likely to be Lake and the team she has assembled.[1]

WWW.STITCHFIX.COM

Using the Three-Step Writing Process for Persuasive Messages

Katrina Lake (profiled in the chapter-opening On the Job) understands that successful businesses rely on persuasive messages in both internal and external communication. Whether you're trying to convince your boss to open a new office in Europe or encourage potential customers to try an online styling service, you need to call on your abilities of **persuasion**—the attempt to change an audience's attitudes, beliefs, or actions.[2] Because persuasive messages ask audiences to give something of value (money in exchange for a product, for example) or to take substantial action (such as changing a corporate policy), they are more challenging to write than routine messages. Successful professionals understand that persuasion is not about trickery or getting people to act against their own best interests; it's about letting audiences know they have choices and presenting your offering in the best possible light.[3]

You will encounter many business communication situations in which your goal is to influence the attitudes, actions, or beliefs of other people. Common examples of persuasive messages include asking colleagues to take action, asking managers to provide resources, asking investors to provide funding for a growing company, and asking potential customers to buy goods and services.

Persuasion may seem like a specialized skill that is required only by salespeople or marketing specialists, but virtually all business professionals can benefit from knowing how to apply persuasive techniques in their communication efforts. The good news is that you are probably already more persuasive than you think you are. In fact, one of the biggest mistakes made in persuasive communication is not even trying. Too often, people think they don't have the skills required or aren't in a position to propose new ideas.[4]

Fortunately, the techniques of effective persuasion are simple to learn and easy to use, as long as you start from the audience's point of view. Ethical persuasion never attempts to coerce or trick people into acting against their own best interests. The secret is to demonstrate in a compelling way how your interests align with your audience's interests.

1 **LEARNING OBJECTIVE**
Apply the three-step writing process to persuasive messages.

Persuasion is the attempt to change someone's attitudes, beliefs, or actions.

Check out the "Five-Minute Guide to Writing Persuasive Messages" at the end of the chapter.

REAL-TIME UPDATES

LEARN MORE BY WATCHING THIS VIDEO
Are you persuading or are you negotiating?
Professor Bob Bontempo explains how persuading and negotiating are complementary but distinctly different skill sets. Go to **real-timeupdates.com/ebc13** and select Learn More in the Students section.

STEP 1: PLANNING PERSUASIVE MESSAGES

Having a great idea or a great product is not enough; you need to be able to convince others of its merits.

In today's information-saturated business environment, having a great idea or a great product is no longer enough. Every day, untold numbers of good ideas go unnoticed and good products go unsold simply because the messages meant to promote them aren't compelling enough to be heard above the competitive noise. Creating successful persuasive messages in these challenging situations demands careful attention to all four tasks in the planning step, starting with an insightful analysis of your purpose and your audience.

Analyzing the Situation

Clarifying your purpose is an essential step with persuasive messages; make sure you really know how you would like your audience to respond.

In defining your purpose, make sure you're clear about what you really hope to achieve. Suppose you want to persuade company executives to support a particular research project. But what does "support" mean? Do you want them to pat you on the back and wish you well? Or do you want them to give you a staff of five researchers and a $1 million annual budget?

In every persuasive message, you're asking for something that is important to you, but keep in mind that the most effective persuasive messages are closely connected to the things that are important to your audience (see Figure 11.1).[5] Whether you're writing a proposal to your manager or a sales letter to a potential customer, start by imagining yourself in that person's position and identify the issues or opportunities they are likely to already be thinking about.[6] For example, what problems or challenges are keeping your boss awake at night? If your persuasive message holds the promise of reducing those worries, you stand a much better chance of being successful than if your proposal is unrelated to the issues that are important to your boss (or, worse yet, has the potential to make his or her life even more complicated).

Demographics include characteristics such as age, gender, occupation, income, and education.

Psychographics include characteristics such as personality, attitudes, and lifestyle.

To understand and categorize audience needs, you can refer to specific information, such as **demographics** (the age, gender, occupation, income, education, and other quantifiable characteristics of the people you're trying to persuade) and **psychographics** (personality, attitudes, lifestyle, and other psychological characteristics). When analyzing your audiences, take into account their cultural expectations and practices so that you don't undermine your persuasive message by using an inappropriate appeal or by presenting your message in a way that seems unfamiliar or uncomfortable to your readers.

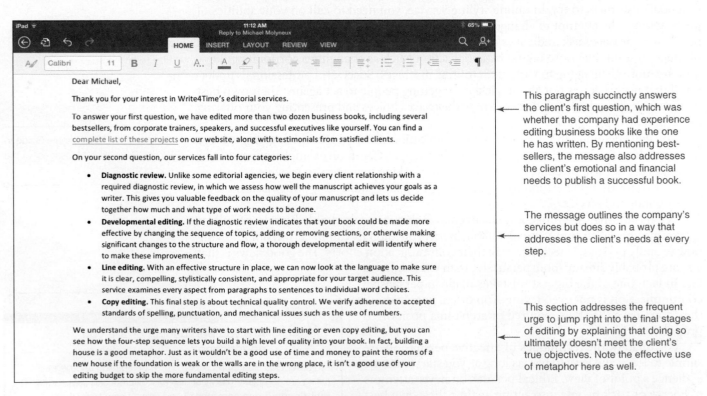

Figure 11.1   Appealing to Audience Needs
This draft of a response to an inquiry about an editorial services company's offerings addresses the writer's concerns about the time, cost, and effectiveness of the company's services.

TABLE 11.1 Human Needs That Influence Motivation	
Need	**Implications for Communication**
Basic physiological requirements: The needs for food, water, sleep, oxygen, and other essentials	Everyone has these needs, but the degree of attention an individual gives to them often depends on whether the needs are being met; for instance, an advertisement for sleeping pills will have greater appeal to someone suffering from insomnia than to someone who has no problem sleeping.
Safety and security: The needs for protection from bodily harm, for the safety of loved ones, and for financial security, protection of personal identity, career security, and other assurances	These needs influence both consumer and business decisions in a wide variety of ways; for instance, advertisements for life insurance often encourage parents to think about the financial security of their children and other loved ones.
Affiliation and belonging: The needs for companionship, acceptance, love, popularity, and approval	The need to feel loved, accepted, or popular drives a great deal of human behavior, from the desire to be attractive to potential mates to wearing the clothing style that a particular social group is likely to approve.
Power and control: The need to feel in control of situations or to exert authority over others	You can see many examples appealing to this need in advertisements: *Take control of your life, your finances, your future, your career,* and so on. Many people who lack power want to know how to get it, and people who have power often want others to know they have it.
Achievement: The need to feel a sense of accomplishment—or to be admired by others for accomplishments	This need can involve both *knowing* (when people experience a feeling of accomplishment) and *showing* (when people are able to show others that they've achieved success); advertising for luxury consumer products frequently appeals to this need.
Adventure and distraction: The need for excitement or relief from daily routine	People vary widely in their need for adventure; some crave excitement—even danger—whereas others value calmness and predictability. Some needs for adventure and distraction are met *virtually*, such as through horror movies, thriller novels, and so on.
Knowledge, exploration, and understanding: The need to keep learning	For some people, learning is usually a means to an end, a way to fulfill some other need; for others, acquiring new knowledge is the goal.
Aesthetic appreciation: The desire to experience beauty, order, symmetry, and so on	Although this need may seem "noncommercial" at first glance, advertisers appeal to it frequently, from the pleasing shape of a package to the quality of the gemstones in a piece of jewelry.
Self-actualization: The need to reach one's full potential as a human being	Psychologists Kurt Goldstein and Abraham Maslow popularized self-actualization as the desire to make the most of one's potential, and Maslow identified it as one of the higher-level needs in his classic hierarchy; even if people met most or all of their other needs, they would still feel the need to self-actualize. An often-quoted example of appealing to this need is the U.S. Army's onetime advertising slogan "Be all that you can be."
Helping others: The need to believe that one is making a difference in the lives of other people	This need is the central motivation in fundraising messages and other appeals to charity.

Sources: Courtland L. Bovée and John V. Thill, *Business in Action*, 8th ed. (Upper Saddle River, N.J.: Prentice Hall, 2017), 225–239; Saundra K. Ciccarelli and J. Noland White, *Psychology*, 5th ed. (Upper Saddle River, N.J.: Prentice Hall, 2016), 356–363; Abraham H. Maslow, "A Theory of Human Motivation," *Psychological Review* 50 (1943): 370–396.

If you aim to change someone's attitudes, beliefs, or actions, it is vital to understand his or her **motivation**—the combination of forces that drive people to satisfy their needs. Table 11.1 lists some of the needs that psychologists have identified or suggested as being important in influencing human motivation. Obviously, the more closely a persuasive message aligns with a recipient's existing motivation, the more effective the message is likely to be. For example, if you try to persuade consumers to purchase a product on the basis of its trendy fashion appeal, that message will connect with consumers who are motivated by a desire to be in fashion, but it probably won't connect with consumers driven more by functional or financial concerns.

Motivation is the combination of forces that drive people to satisfy their needs.

Gathering Information

Once your situation analysis is complete, you need to gather the information necessary to create a compelling persuasive message. You'll learn more about the types of information to include in persuasive business messages and marketing and sales messages later in the chapter. Chapter 12 presents advice on how to find the information you need.

Selecting the Right Combination of Medium and Channel

Media and channel choices are always important, of course, but these decisions are particularly sensitive with persuasive messages because such messages are often unexpected

Choose a combination of medium and channel that will maximize the chance of getting through to your audience.

and sometimes even unwelcome. The more you understand and respect your audience's habits and preferences, the better your chances of getting past the various physical, digital, and perceptual filters that people use to protect themselves from the daily barrage of promotional messages.

Social media provide some effective options for persuasive messages, particularly marketing and sales messages. However, as "Writing Promotional Messages for Social Media" on page 338 explains, messages in these media require a unique approach.

Organizing Your Information

The most effective main ideas for persuasive messages have one thing in common: They are about the receiver, not the sender. For instance, if you're trying to convince others to join you in a business venture, explain how it will help them, not how it will help you.

Limiting your scope is vital. If you seem to be wrestling with more than one main idea, or a main idea that has lots of moving parts, chances are you haven't identified your readers' most important concerns. If you try to craft a persuasive message without focusing on the one central problem or opportunity your audience truly cares about, you're unlikely to persuade successfully.[7]

The nature of persuasion is to convince people to change their attitudes, beliefs, or actions, so most persuasive messages use the indirect approach to build up to the moment when you make the request. The indirect approach lets you explain your reasons and build interest before asking for a decision or for action—or perhaps even before revealing your purpose. However, in some instances, such as when you have a close relationship with your audience and the message is welcome or at least neutral, the direct approach can be effective.

For persuasive business messages, the choice between the direct and indirect approaches is also influenced by the extent of your authority, expertise, or power in an organization. For example, if you are a highly regarded technical expert with years of experience, you might use the direct approach in a message to top executives. In contrast, if you don't have "expertise authority" and therefore need to rely more on the strength of your message than the power of your reputation, the indirect approach will probably be more successful.

STEP 2: WRITING PERSUASIVE MESSAGES

Encourage a positive response to your persuasive messages by (1) using positive and polite language, (2) understanding and respecting cultural differences, (3) being sensitive to organizational cultures, and (4) taking steps to establish your credibility.

Positive language usually happens naturally with persuasive messages because you're promoting an idea, a plan, or a product you believe in. However, take care not to inadvertently insult your readers by implying that they've made poor choices in the past and that you're here to save them from their misguided ways.

Be sure to understand cultural expectations as well. For example, a message that seems forthright and direct in a low-context culture might seem brash and intrusive in a high-context culture.

Just as social culture affects the success of a persuasive message, so too does the culture within an organization. For instance, some organizations handle disagreement and conflict in an indirect, behind-the-scenes way, whereas others accept and even encourage open discussion and the exchange of different viewpoints.

Finally, if you are trying to persuade a skeptical or hostile audience, you must convince them you know what you're talking about and that you're not trying to mislead them. Use these techniques:

- Use straightforward language to avoid suspicions of fantastic claims and emotional manipulation.
- Provide objective evidence for the claims and promises you make.
- Identify your sources, especially if your audience already respects those sources.

Effective persuasive messages always emphasize the recipient's needs over the sender's.

For persuasive business messages, the choice of approach is influenced by your position (or authority within the organization) relative to your audience's.

Encourage a positive response by

- Using positive and polite language
- Understanding and respecting cultural differences
- Being sensitive to organizational cultures
- Establishing your credibility

MOBILE APP

Want to persuade your local government to address a problem? The **City Sourced** app aims to facilitate civic engagement through mobile communication.

Organizational culture can influence persuasion as much as social culture.

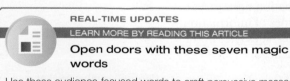

REAL-TIME UPDATES

LEARN MORE BY READING THIS ARTICLE

Open doors with these seven magic words

Use these audience-focused words to craft persuasive messages. Go to **real-timeupdates.com/ebc13** and select Learn More in the Students section.

- Establish common ground by emphasizing beliefs, attitudes, and background experiences you have in common with the audience.
- Be objective and present fair and logical arguments.
- Show that you respect your audience's values and priorities.
- Persuade with logic, evidence, and compelling narratives, rather than trying to coerce with high-pressure, "hard-sell" tactics.
- Whenever possible, try to build your credibility before you present a major proposal or ask for a major decision. That way, audiences don't have to evaluate both you and your message at the same time.[8]

Audiences often respond unfavorably to over-the-top language, so keep your writing simple and straightforward.

STEP 3: COMPLETING PERSUASIVE MESSAGES

Professional writers who specialize in persuasive messages know how vital the details are, so they're careful not to skimp on this part of the writing process. When you evaluate your content, try to judge your argument objectively and not overestimate your credibility. When revising for clarity and conciseness, carefully match the purpose and organization to audience needs. If possible, ask an experienced colleague who knows your audience well to review your draft. Your design elements must complement, not detract from, your argument. In addition, meticulous proofreading will identify any mechanical or spelling errors that would weaken your persuasive potential. Finally, make sure your distribution methods fit your audience's expectations and your purpose.

Careless production undermines your credibility, so revise and proofread with care.

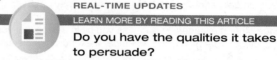

REAL-TIME UPDATES

LEARN MORE BY READING THIS ARTICLE

Do you have the qualities it takes to persuade?

This simple test will tell you if you have the qualities that persuasive communicators share—and how to develop your own persuasive qualities. Go to **real-timeupdates.com/ebc13** and select Learn More in the Students section.

With the three-step model in mind, you're ready to begin composing persuasive messages, starting with *persuasive business messages* (those that try to convince audiences to approve new projects, enter into business partnerships, and so on), followed by *marketing and sales messages* (those that try to convince audiences to consider and then purchase products and services).

Developing Persuasive Business Messages

Your success as a businessperson is closely tied to your ability to encourage others to accept new ideas, change old habits, or act on your recommendations. Unless your career takes you into marketing and sales, most of your persuasive messages will consist of *persuasive business messages*, which are those designed to elicit a preferred response in a nonsales situation.

2 LEARNING OBJECTIVE
Describe an effective strategy for developing persuasive business messages, and identify the three most common categories of persuasive business messages.

STRATEGIES FOR PERSUASIVE BUSINESS MESSAGES

Even if you have the power to compel others to do what you want them to do, persuading them is more effective than forcing them. People who are coerced into accepting a decision or plan are less motivated to support it and more likely to react negatively than if they're persuaded.[9] Within the context of the three-step process, effective persuasion involves four essential strategies: framing your arguments, balancing the three types of persuasive appeals, reinforcing your position, and anticipating objections. (Note that all the concepts in this section apply as well to marketing and sales messages, covered later in the chapter.)

Framing Your Arguments

As noted previously, most persuasive messages use the indirect approach. Experts in persuasive communication have developed a number of indirect models for such messages. One of the best known is the **AIDA model**, which organizes messages into four phases (see Figure 11.2 on the next page):

- **Attention.** Your first objective is to encourage your audience to want to hear about your problem, idea, or new product—whatever your main idea is. Be sure to find some common ground on which to build your case.

The *AIDA model* is a useful approach for many persuasive messages:

- **Attention**
- **Interest**
- **Desire**
- **Action**

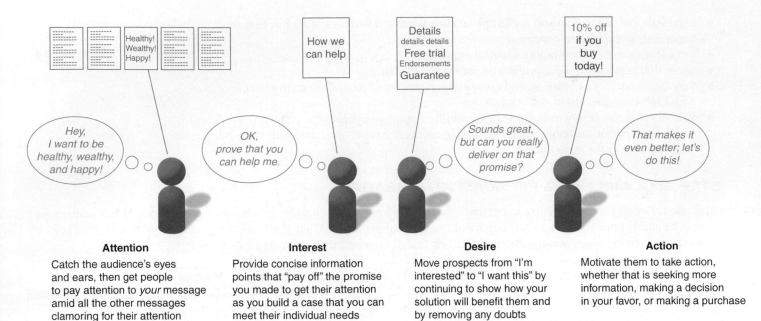

Attention

Catch the audience's eyes and ears, then get people to pay attention to *your* message amid all the other messages clamoring for their attention

Interest

Provide concise information points that "pay off" the promise you made to get their attention as you build a case that you can meet their individual needs

Desire

Move prospects from "I'm interested" to "I want this" by continuing to show how your solution will benefit them and by removing any doubts

Action

Motivate them to take action, whether that is seeking more information, making a decision in your favor, or making a purchase

Figure 11.2   The AIDA Model for Persuasive Messages
With the AIDA model, you craft one or more messages to move recipients through the four stages of attention, interest, desire, and action. The model works well for both persuasive business messages (such as persuading your manager to fund a new project) and marketing and sales messages.

- **Interest.** Provide additional details that prompt audience members to imagine how the solution might benefit them.
- **Desire.** Help audience members embrace your idea by explaining how the change will benefit them and answering potential objections.
- **Action.** Suggest the specific action you want your audience to take. Include a deadline, when applicable.

The AIDA model is ideal for the indirect approach.

The AIDA model is tailor-made for using the indirect approach, allowing you to save your main idea for the action phase. However, it can also work with the direct approach, in which case you use your main idea as an attention-getter, build interest with your argument, create desire with your evidence, and emphasize your main idea in the action phase with the specific action you want your audience to take.

When your AIDA message uses the indirect approach and is delivered by email, keep in mind that your subject line usually catches your reader's eye first. Your challenge is to make it interesting and relevant enough to capture reader attention without revealing your main idea. If you put your request in the subject line, you're likely to get a quick "no" before you've had a chance to present your arguments:

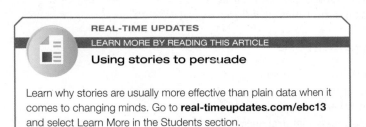

Instead of This	Write This
Request for development budget to add automated IM response system	Reducing the cost of customer support inquiries

The AIDA approach has limitations:

- *It essentially talks at audiences, not with them*
- *It focuses on onetime events, not long-term relationships*

With either the direct or indirect approach, AIDA and similar models do have limitations. First, AIDA is a unidirectional method that essentially talks *at* audiences, not *with* them. Second, AIDA is built around a single event, such as asking an audience for a decision, rather than on building a mutually beneficial, long-term relationship.[10] AIDA is still a valuable tool for the right purposes, but as you'll read later in the chapter, a conversational approach is more compatible with today's social media.

Balancing the Three Types of Persuasive Appeals

Persuasive communication is based on three types of appeals: *ethos* (the ethical dimension, particularly your credibility as the writer), *pathos* (appeals to emotion), and *logos* (argumentation based on logic and evidence). These are powerful tools that can benefit senders and receivers alike if they are used wisely and ethically.[11]

The ethos element of persuasion depends on how much trust your readers or listeners have in your expertise, character, and reliability. Chapter 5 also discusses the vital step of establishing your credibility as part of the three-step writing process.

Within the message itself, you have the task of balancing emotional and logical appeals. Few persuasive appeals are purely logical or purely emotional, and it's important to find the right balance for each message (see Figure 11.3 on the next page). Many marketing and sales messages rely heavily on emotional appeals, but most persuasive business messages rely more on logic. However, even a predominantly emotional message needs to make logical sense at some level, and logical business messages can often be strengthened with the judicious use of emotion.

An **emotional appeal** calls on feelings or audience sympathies. For instance, you can make use of the emotions inspired by words such as *freedom, success, prestige, compassion, free,* and *comfort.* Such words put your audience in a certain frame of mind and help them accept your message.

A **logical appeal** involves the use of reason and factual evidence. Three common modes of logical persuasion are induction, deduction, and analogy:

- **Induction.** With inductive reasoning, you work from specific evidence to a general conclusion that you can then apply to the situation at hand. To convince your company to adopt a new production process, you could collect specific evidence showing how every company that has adopted it so far has seen increased profits and from there reach the general conclusion that the new process is likely to benefit any company that implements it.
- **Deduction.** With deductive reasoning, you work from a general theory or hypothesis to a specific conclusion. A generalization could be that dissatisfied customers tend not to buy from the same companies in the future, which proceeds to the specific conclusion that your company should take steps to improve customer satisfaction before it starts losing business.
- **Analogy.** With analogy, you reason from specific evidence to specific evidence, in effect "borrowing" from something familiar to explain something unfamiliar. To persuade management to launch an internal social network, you could argue that the network would be an online version of the coffee machine or water cooler, places where employees currently meet and exchange information and ideas.

Every method of reasoning is vulnerable to misuse—both intentional and unintentional. Logical errors, commonly known as *logical fallacies*, result from misleading readers via faulty language or misusing reasoning tools such as induction and analogy. Here are some of the more common logical fallacies that you need to avoid in persuasive communication:[12]

- **Hasty or sweeping generalizations.** A hasty generalization occurs when you jump to a generalization without enough evidence to support it. A sweeping generalization ignores exceptions or contradictions.
- **Circular reasoning.** Circular reasoning is a logical fallacy in which you try to support your claim by restating it using different language. In other words, all you've done is argue around in a circle, rather than advancing the argument to a new conclusion. The statement "We know temporary workers cannot handle this task because temps are unqualified for it" doesn't prove anything because the claim and the supposed evidence are essentially identical.
- **Flawed analogies.** Be sure that the two objects or situations being compared are similar enough for the analogy to hold. For instance, explaining that an internet firewall is like a prison wall is a poor analogy, because a firewall keeps things out, whereas a prison wall keeps things in.
- **Inappropriate appeals.** Appeals to tradition ("we've always done it this way"), popular opinion ("everybody else is doing this"), or authority ("the CEO says this is the best option") are examples of logical fallacies because they aren't based on evidence and reason.

Margin notes:

Persuasive communication is based on three types of appeals:

- *Ethos*—the ethical dimension, particularly your credibility as the writer
- *Pathos*—appeals to emotion
- *Logos*—argumentation based on logic and evidence)

An *emotional appeal* calls on feelings or audience sympathies.

Logical appeals are based on the reader's notions of reason; these appeals can use induction, deduction, or analogy.

Using logical appeals carries with it the ethical responsibility to avoid faulty logic.

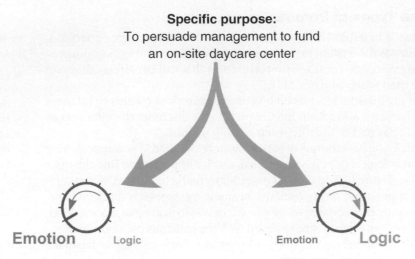

Specific purpose:
To persuade management to fund
an on-site daycare center

Emotion　Logic

Emotion　Logic

**Proposal to improve employee
satisfaction and work-life balance**

Being separated during the day is stressful
for both parents and children.

Many parents are now working more hours and second
jobs to make ends meet, so the situation is getting
worse.

The extra travel time every morning and evening to put
children in day care adds to the stress and cost of
coming to work.

When parents need to leave work to pick up sick
children from day care or stay home with them, this
often creates an unfair burden on other employees to
pick up the slack.

Knowing that the company cares about them and their
children would boost employee morale.

Therefore, the company should provide an on-site
daycare facility with a separate infirmary where sick
children could stay during the day.

**Proposal to boost productivity
and reduce absenteeism**

Analysis of employee time records shows that
employees with children under the age of 10
take unscheduled days off three times more often
than employees without young children.

Daycare issues are cited as the number one
reason for these unscheduled days off.

In the 98 exit interviews conducted last year,
24 departing employees mentioned the need
to balance family and work commitments as the
primary reason for leaving.

In the last six months, HR has logged 14 complaints
from employees who say they have to take on extra
work when colleagues leave the office to pick up sick
children from day care.

Research shows that on-site day care can improve
productivity by as much as 20 percent—among
parents and nonparents alike.

Therefore, the company should provide an
on-site daycare facility with a separate infirmary
where sick children could stay during the day.

Figure 11.3　Balancing Logical and Emotional Appeals
Whenever you plan a persuasive message, imagine you have a knob that turns from *emotion* at one extreme to
logic at the other, letting you adjust the relative proportions of each type of appeal. Compare these two outlines for
a proposal that asks management to fund an on-site daycare center. The version on the left relies heavily on emotional appeals, whereas the version on the right uses logical appeals (inductive reasoning, specifically). Through
your choice of words, images, and supporting details, you can adjust the emotional-logical ratio in every message.

- **Ad hominem attacks.** An *ad hominem* attack is an attack directed at another person
  rather than at his or her line of reasoning. For example, dismissing a colleague's suggestion just because he is the newest member of the department is an ad hominem attack.
- **Oversimplifications.** Simplifying complex situations to make them easier to understand is a valuable skill, but going too far can lead to a variety of logical fallacies. For
  instance, reducing a complicated scenario to a simple yes/no choice in a way that leaves
  out other viable options is a logical error.

- **Mistaken assumptions or claims of cause and effect.** Be careful with any line of argument that involves causes and effects. You can stumble into a variety of logical mistakes by assuming that *A* caused *B* without having conclusive evidence to support that statement. To argue cause and effect, you need to show that *A* did indeed cause *B* to happen (and it wasn't just coincidence or correlation) and that *A* is the only factor that could have caused *B* to happen. For example, if sales of a certain product dropped the month after you redesigned it, you can't conclude beyond doubt that the redesign hurt sales unless you can demonstrate that buyers didn't like the new design as much as the old one and that no other force in the market (such as a new competitor) was responsible.

Reinforcing Your Position

After you've worked out the basic elements of your argument, step back and look for ways to strengthen your position. How can you bolster your message to give your readers more confidence in the solution you are suggesting? Are all your claims supported by believable evidence? Can you show that other people or companies have adopted a solution you propose?[13] Would a quotation from a recognized expert help make your case? The more certainty you can give your readers, the more likely they are to take the actions you would like them to take.[14]

Next, examine your language. Can you find more powerful words to convey your message? For example, if your company is in serious financial trouble, talking about *fighting for survival* is a more powerful emotional appeal than talking about *ensuring continued operations.* As with any powerful tool, though, vivid language and abstractions must be used carefully and honestly.

In addition to examining individual word choices, consider using metaphors and other figures of speech. If you want to describe a quality-control system as being designed to detect every possible product flaw, you might call it a "spider web" to imply that it catches everything that comes its way. Similarly, anecdotes (brief stories) can help your audience grasp the meaning and importance of your arguments. Instead of just listing the number of times the old laptop computers in your department have failed, you could describe how you lost a sale when your computer broke down during a critical sales presentation.

> Choose your words carefully to encourage the desired responses.

Anticipating Objections

Even compelling ideas and exciting projects can encounter objections, if only because people have a natural tendency to resist change. You can increase your odds of a positive response by anticipating likely objections and addressing them before your audience settles into a negative, defensive mindset. By doing so, you can remove these potential stumbling blocks from the conversation and keep the focus on positive communication.

Note that you don't need to explicitly mention a particular concern. For instance, if your proposal to switch to lower-cost materials is likely to raise questions about quality, you can emphasize that the new materials are just as good as existing materials. You'll not only get this matter out of the way sooner but also demonstrate a broad appreciation of the issue and imply confidence in your message.[15]

If you expect a hostile audience that is biased against your message, be sure to present all sides of the situation. As you cover each option, explain the pros and cons. You'll gain additional credibility if you mention these options before presenting your recommendation or decision.[16] If you can, involve your audience in the design of the solution; people are more likely to support ideas they help create.

> Even compelling persuasive messages can encounter audience resistance.

> If you expect to encounter strong resistance, present all sides of an issue.

Avoiding Common Mistakes in Persuasive Communication

When you believe in a concept or project you are promoting, it's easy to get caught up in your own confidence and enthusiasm and thereby fail to see things from the audience's perspective. When putting together persuasive arguments, avoid these common mistakes (see Figure 11.4 on page 333):[17]

Don't let confidence or enthusiasm lead you to some common mistakes in persuasive communication.

- **Using a hard sell.** No one likes being pressured into making a decision. Communicators who take this approach can come across as being more concerned with meeting their own goals than with satisfying the needs of their audiences. In contrast, a "soft sell" is more like a comfortable conversation that uses calm, rational persuasion.
- **Resisting compromise.** Successful persuasion is often a process of give and take, particularly with persuasive business messages, where you don't always get everything you asked for in terms of budgets, investments, or other commitments.
- **Relying solely on great arguments.** Great arguments are important, but connecting with your audience on the right emotional level and communicating through vivid language are just as vital. Sometimes a well-crafted story can be even more compelling than dry logic.
- **Assuming that persuasion is a one-shot effort.** Persuasion is often a process, not a onetime event. In many cases, you need to move your audience members along one small step at a time rather than try to convince them to say "yes" in one huge step.
- **Resorting to deception or other unethical behaviors.** The combination of emotional and logical appeals, amplified by an audience's trust in the messenger, can be a powerful persuasive force. Always keep the audience's needs in mind to make sure you use this force in a positive and ethical manner.

To review the steps involved in developing persuasive messages, refer to "Checklist: Developing Persuasive Messages" on page 334.

APPLY YOUR SKILLS NOW

Making Difficult Requests

Just as they will be on the job, most of the requests you need to make in your academic and personal lives are fairly routine and can be accomplished using the techniques you learned in Chapter 9. However, we all face situations from time to time where we need to make a more difficult request, such as asking an instructor for leniency, asking a landlord or a retailer for special consideration, or asking parents or a partner for help. In these situations, a more persuasive approach might be useful. You can apply many of the strategies for persuasive business messages, and follow these tips as well:

- Step outside of yourself and your immediate concerns and put yourself in the other person's position. What is this person's current emotional state likely to be? What about his or her mental workload? Imagine you're on that side of the table and you get the request that you're about to make. How would you react?
- Is there any way the other party might benefit from responding positively to your request?
- Emotions may be an important and legitimate part of your request, but for this step, put them aside and focus on objective facts, logic, and ethical principles. How much of your case can you make on these elements alone, without bringing emotion into the mix?
- Now carefully bring emotion into your request, but only to the extent that it supports your request. Strong emotions—even if they are appropriate—can sometimes backfire when you're making a request. You may feel compelled to express these emotions, but keep your eye on the goal, which is your request.
- With the right balance of logical and emotional appeals in mind, choose the direct or indirect approach, based on your relationship with the person and your best judgment. In a close, personal relationship, there are times when it might be better to go direct and open with a simple plea: "Could I ask for your help?" In academic or work relationships, the indirect approach might be better, as long as you can build up to your request quickly. Don't make the recipient wade through a long list of reasons.

You may not get a positive response to your request, and the other party may have legitimate reasons for denying it, but you will know that you did your best.

COACH YOURSELF

1. When you have a difficult request to make, do you find yourself putting it off? This is entirely natural, but remind yourself that the sooner you make the request, the sooner you will get an answer and thereby be able to move on, no matter what sort of answer you get.
2. How do you tend to respond when someone else has a difficult request for you? Do you find it difficult to step out of your own needs and pressures long enough to listen openly and actively? If so, try to mindfully practice this the next time someone asks you for help or special consideration. It's a valuable skill that will benefit all your personal and professional relationships.

Ineffective

It's time to call the Fast Track program what it truly is—a disaster. Everyone was excited last year when we announced the plan to speed up our development efforts and introduce at least one new product every month. We envisioned rapidly expanding market share and strong revenue growth. What we got instead is a nightmare that is getting worse every month.

As a company, we clearly underestimated the resources it would take to market, sell, and support so many new products. We can't hire and train fast enough, and every department is overwhelmed. Forced to jump from one new product to the next, the sales and technical specialists can't develop the expertise needed to help buyers before the sale or support them after the sale. As a result, too many customers either buy the wrong product or buy the right product but then can't get knowledgeable help when they need it. We're losing credibility in the market, we're starting to lose sales, and it won't be long before we start losing employees who are fed up with the insanity.

To make matters even worse, some of the recent products were clearly rushed to market before they were ready. With numerous quality issues, returns and warranty costs are skyrocketing.

New products are the lifeblood of the company, to be sure, but there is no point in introducing products that only create enormous support headaches and cost more to support than they generate in profits. We need to put the Fast Track initiative on hold immediately so the entire company can regroup. The R&D lab can devote its time to fixing problems in the recent products, and the rest of us can catch our breath and try to figure out how to meet our sales and customer support goals.

(a) The company has clearly staked a lot on this program, so opening by calling it a disaster will only put the reader on the defensive.

(b) Word choices such as *nightmare* here and *insanity* in the next paragraph give the message an emotional, almost hysterical, tone that detracts from the serious message.

(c) The writer mingles together an observation that may be subjective (declining credibility), a hard data point (declining sales), and a prediction (possibility of employee defections).

(d) The claim that recent products were "clearly rushed to market" is unnecessarily inflammatory (because it blames another department) and distracts the reader from the more immediate problems of poor quality.

(e) The first sentence of the last paragraph is insulting to anyone with basic business sense—particularly the president of a company.

Effective

(a) This neutral summary of events serves as an effective buffer for the indirect approach and provides a subtle reminder of the original goals of the program.

(b) This paragraph contains the same information as the ineffective version, but does so in a calmer way that won't trigger the reader's defense mechanisms and will thereby keep the focus on the facts.

(c) The writer separates a personal hunch (about the possibility of losing employees) from an observation about the market and a measured data point (declining sales).

(d) The writer introduces the information about quality problems without directing blame.

(e) With the evidence assembled, the writer introduces the main idea of putting the program on hold. The recommendation is a judgment call and a suggestion to a superior, so the hedging phrase *I believe* is appropriate.

Everyone was excited last year when we launched the Fast Track program to speed up our development efforts and introduce at least one new product every month. We envisioned rapidly expanding market share and strong revenue growth in all our product lines.

While the R&D lab has met its goal of monthly releases, as a company, we clearly underestimated the resources it would take to market, sell, and support so many new products. We can't hire and train fast enough, and our teams in every department are overwhelmed. The sales and technical specialists haven't had time to develop the expertise needed to help buyers before the sale or support them after the sale. As a result, too many customers either buy the wrong product or buy the right product but then can't get knowledgeable help when they need it. We're losing credibility in the market, and we're starting to lose sales. If the situation continues, I fear we will begin losing employees, too.

In addition, some of the recent products are generating multiple reports of hardware quality problems and buggy software. Returns and warranty costs are climbing at an unprecedented rate.

With costs rising faster than revenues and our people getting overwhelmed, I believe it is time to put the Fast Track initiative on hold until the company can regroup. The hiatus would give R&D time to address the quality problems and give the marketing, sales, and tech support teams the chance to reassess our goals with the current product portfolio and our current staffing levels.

Figure 11.4   Persuasive Argumentation

Imagine you're the marketing manager in a company that decided to speed up its new-product launches but did too much too fast and wound up creating chaos. You decide enough is enough and write a memo to the company president advocating that the new program be shut down until the company can regroup—a suggestion you know will meet with resistance. Notice how the ineffective version doesn't quite use the direct approach but comes out swinging, so to speak, and is overly emotional throughout. The effective version builds to its recommendation indirectly, using the same information but in a calm, logical way. Because it sticks to the facts, it is also shorter.

CHECKLIST ✔ Developing Persuasive Messages

A. Get your reader's attention.
- ✔ Open with an audience benefit, a stimulating question, a problem, or an unexpected statement.
- ✔ Establish common ground by mentioning a point on which you and your audience agree.
- ✔ Show that you understand the audience's concerns.

B. Build your reader's interest.
- ✔ Expand and support your opening claim or promise.
- ✔ Emphasize the relevance of your message to your audience.

C. Increase your reader's desire.
- ✔ Make audience members want to change by explaining how the change will benefit them.
- ✔ Back up your claims with relevant evidence.

D. Motivate your reader to take action.
- ✔ Suggest the action you want readers to take.
- ✔ Stress the positive results of the action.
- ✔ Make the desired action clear and easy.

E. Balance emotional and logical appeals.
- ✔ Use emotional appeals to help the audience accept your message.
- ✔ Use logical appeals when presenting facts and evidence for complex ideas or recommendations.
- ✔ Avoid faulty logic.

F. Reinforce your position.
- ✔ Provide additional evidence of the benefits of your proposal and your own credibility in offering it.
- ✔ Use abstractions, metaphors, and other figures of speech to bring facts and figures to life.

G. Anticipate objections.
- ✔ Anticipate and answer potential objections.
- ✔ Present the pros and cons of all options if you anticipate a hostile reaction.

COMMON EXAMPLES OF PERSUASIVE BUSINESS MESSAGES

Throughout your career, you'll have numerous opportunities to write persuasive messages within your organization, such as reports suggesting more-efficient operating procedures or memos requesting money for new equipment. Similarly, you may produce a variety of persuasive messages for people outside the organization, such as websites shaping public opinions or letters requesting adjustments that go beyond a supplier's contractual obligations. In addition, some of the routine requests you studied in Chapter 9 can become persuasive messages if you want a nonroutine result or believe that you haven't received fair treatment. Most of these messages can be divided into persuasive requests for action, persuasive presentations of ideas, and persuasive claims and requests for adjustment.

Persuasive Requests for Action

Most persuasive business messages involve a request for action.

The bulk of your persuasive business messages will involve requests for action. In some cases, your request will be anticipated, so the direct approach is fine. In others, you'll need to introduce your intention indirectly, and the AIDA model or a similar approach is ideal for this purpose (see Figure 11.5).

Open with an attention-getting device and show readers that you understand their concerns. Use the interest and desire sections of your message to demonstrate that you have good reason for making such a request and to cover what you know about the situation: the facts and figures, the benefits of helping, and any history or experience that will enhance your appeal. Your goals are (1) to gain credibility (for yourself and your request) and (2) to make your readers believe that helping you will indeed help solve a significant problem. Close with a request for some specific action, and make that course of action as easy to follow as possible in order to maximize the chances of a positive response.

Persuasive Presentations of Ideas

Sometimes the objective of persuasive messages is simply to encourage people to consider a new idea or a different perspective.

You may encounter situations in which you simply want to change attitudes or beliefs about a particular topic, without asking the audience to decide or do anything—at least not yet. The goal of your first message might be nothing more than convincing your audience to reexamine long-held opinions or to admit the possibility of new ways of thinking.

For instance, the World Wide Web Consortium, a global association that defines many of the guidelines and technologies behind the World Wide Web, launched a campaign called the Web Accessibility Initiative. Although the consortium's ultimate goal is to make websites more accessible to people who have disabilities or age-related limitations, a key interim

1 Plan →	**2** Write →	**3** Complete

Analyze the Situation
Verify that the purpose is to address a major business challenge, so the audience will be receptive.

Gather Information
Determine audience needs and obtain the necessary information.

Choose Medium and Channel
Verify that an email message is appropriate for this communication.

Organize the Information
Limit the scope to the main idea, which is to propose exploring a new business strategy; use the indirect approach to lay out the extent of the problem.

Adapt to Your Audience
Adjust the level of formality based on the degree of familiarity with the audience; maintain a positive relationship by using the "you" attitude, politeness, positive emphasis, and bias-free language.

Compose the Message
Use a conversational but professional style and keep the message brief, clear, and as helpful as possible.

Revise the Message
Evaluate content and review readability to make sure the information is clear and complete without being overwhelming.

Produce the Message
Emphasize a clean, professional appearance.

Proofread the Message
Review for errors in layout, spelling, and mechanics.

Distribute the Message
Verify that the right file is attached and then deliver the message.

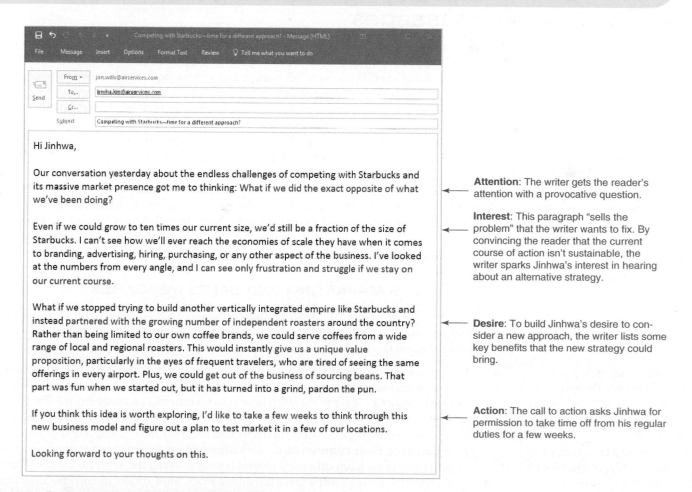

From: jon.willis@airservices.com
To: jinwha.kim@airservices.com
Cc:
Subject: Competing with Starbucks—time for a different approach?

Hi Jinhwa,

Our conversation yesterday about the endless challenges of competing with Starbucks and its massive market presence got me to thinking: What if we did the exact opposite of what we've been doing?

Attention: The writer gets the reader's attention with a provocative question.

Even if we could grow to ten times our current size, we'd still be a fraction of the size of Starbucks. I can't see how we'll ever reach the economies of scale they have when it comes to branding, advertising, hiring, purchasing, or any other aspect of the business. I've looked at the numbers from every angle, and I can see only frustration and struggle if we stay on our current course.

Interest: This paragraph "sells the problem" that the writer wants to fix. By convincing the reader that the current course of action isn't sustainable, the writer sparks Jinhwa's interest in hearing about an alternative strategy.

What if we stopped trying to build another vertically integrated empire like Starbucks and instead partnered with the growing number of independent roasters around the country? Rather than being limited to our own coffee brands, we could serve coffees from a wide range of local and regional roasters. This would instantly give us a unique value proposition, particularly in the eyes of frequent travelers, who are tired of seeing the same offerings in every airport. Plus, we could get out of the business of sourcing beans. That part was fun when we started out, but it has turned into a grind, pardon the pun.

Desire: To build Jinhwa's desire to consider a new approach, the writer lists some key benefits that the new strategy could bring.

If you think this idea is worth exploring, I'd like to take a few weeks to think through this new business model and figure out a plan to test market it in a few of our locations.

Looking forward to your thoughts on this.

Action: The call to action asks Jinhwa for permission to take time off from his regular duties for a few weeks.

Figure 11.5 Persuasive Message Using the AIDA Model
This writer uses the AIDA model to persuade his manager to give him a few weeks away from his regular duties to explore a new business strategy. The passages in red are key points in each step of the AIDA approach. (These passages would not appear in red in the actual email message.)

goal is simply making website developers more aware of the need. As part of this effort, the consortium has developed a variety of presentations and documents that highlight the problems many web visitors face.[18]

Persuasive Claims and Requests for Adjustments

Most claims are routine messages and use the direct approach discussed in Chapter 9. However, consumers and business professionals sometimes encounter situations in which they believe they haven't received a fair deal by following normal procedures. These situations require a more persuasive message.

An effective persuasive claim includes a complete and specific review of the facts and establishes a confident, positive tone.

The key ingredients of a good persuasive claim are a complete and specific review of the facts and a confident and positive tone based on your right to be satisfied with every transaction. Begin persuasive claims by outlining the problem, and continue by reviewing what has been done about it so far, if anything. The recipient might be juggling numerous claims and other demands on his or her attention, so be clear, calm, and complete when presenting your case. Be specific about how you would like the situation to be resolved.

Next, give your reader a good reason for granting your claim. Show how the individual or organization is responsible for the problem, and appeal to your reader's sense of fair play, goodwill, or moral responsibility. Explain how you feel about the problem, but don't get carried away and don't make threats. People generally respond most favorably to requests that are calm and reasonable. Close on a respectful note that reflects how a successful resolution of the situation will repair or maintain a mutually beneficial working relationship.

Developing Marketing and Sales Messages

3 LEARNING OBJECTIVE
Describe an effective strategy for developing marketing and sales messages, and explain how to modify your approach when writing promotional messages for social media.

Marketing messages usher potential buyers through the purchasing process without asking them to make an immediate decision.

Sales messages encourage potential buyers to make a purchase decision.

Marketing and sales messages use the same basic techniques as other persuasive messages, with the added emphasis of encouraging someone to participate in a commercial transaction. Although the terms *marketing message* and *sales message* are often used interchangeably, there is an important difference: **Marketing messages** usher potential buyers through the purchasing process without asking them to make an immediate decision. **Sales messages** take over at that point, encouraging potential buyers to make a purchase decision then and there. Marketing messages focus on such tasks as introducing new brands to the public and encouraging customers to visit websites for more information, whereas sales messages make an explicit request for people to buy a specific product or service.

Most marketing and sales messages, particularly in larger companies, are created and delivered by professionals with specific training in marketing, advertising, sales, or public relations. However, in smaller companies, you may be called on to review the work of these specialists or to write such messages, and having a good understanding of how these messages work will help you be a more effective manager.

PLANNING MARKETING AND SALES MESSAGES

Understanding the purchase decision from the buyer's perspective helps you frame an effective marketing or sales message.

Marketing and sales messages nearly always compete for the audience's attention.

Everything you've learned about planning messages applies in general to marketing and sales messages, but the planning steps for these messages have some particular aspects to consider as well:

- **Assessing audience needs.** As with every other business message, successful marketing and sales messages start with an understanding of audience needs. Depending on the product and the market, these considerations can range from a few functional factors (such as the size, weight, and finish of office paper) to a complicated mix of emotional and logical issues (all the factors that play into buying a house, for example).
- **Analyzing your competition.** Marketing and sales messages nearly always compete with messages from other companies trying to reach the same audience. When Nike plans a marketing campaign to introduce a new shoe model to current customers, the company knows its audience has also been exposed to messages from Adidas, New Balance, Reebok, and numerous other shoe companies. Finding a unique message in crowded markets can be quite a challenge.

- **Determining key selling points and benefits.** With some insight into audience needs and the alternatives offered by your competitors, the next step is to decide which features and benefits to highlight. **Selling points** are the most attractive features of a product, whereas **benefits** are the particular advantages purchasers can realize from those features. In other words, selling points focus on what the product does. Benefits focus on what the user experiences or gains. Benefits can be practical, emotional, or a combination of the two. For example, the feature of a thin, flexible sole in a running shoe offers the practical benefit of a more natural feel while running. In contrast, the visual design features of the shoe offer no practical benefits but can offer the emotional benefit of wearing something stylish or unusual.

  Selling points focus on the product; *benefits* focus on how product features help the user.

- **Anticipating purchase objections.** Marketing and sales messages usually encounter objections, and, as with persuasive business messages, the best way to handle them is to identify these objections up front and address as many as you can. Objections can range from high price or low quality to a lack of compatibility with existing products or a perceived risk involved with the product. If price is a likely objection, for instance, you can look for ways to increase the perceived value of the purchase and decrease the perception of high cost. When promoting a home gym, you might say that it costs less than a year's worth of health club dues. Of course, any attempts to minimize perceptions of price or other potential negatives must be done ethically.

  Anticipate buyer objections and try to address them before they become stumbling blocks.

WRITING CONVENTIONAL MARKETING AND SALES MESSAGES

Conventional marketing and sales messages are often prepared using the AIDA model or some variation of it. (See the next section on crafting messages for social media.) Here are the key points of using the AIDA model for these messages:

MOBILE APP
Talkwalker helps companies monitor social media conversations in real time.

- **Getting the reader's attention.** By looking and listening during any given day, you'll notice the many ways advertisers try to get your attention. For example, a headline might offer an exciting product benefit, a piece of interesting news, an appeal to people's emotions or sense of financial value, or a unique solution to a common problem. Of course, words aren't the only attention-getting devices. Depending on the medium, marketers can use evocative images, music, animation, or video. "Cutting through the clutter" to get the audience's attention is one of the biggest challenges with marketing and sales messages.

- **Building interest.** After catching the reader's or viewer's attention, your next step is to build interest in the product, company, or idea you are promoting. A common technique is to "pay off" the promise made in the headline by explaining how you can deliver those benefits. For example, if the headline offers a way to "Get Fit for $2 a Day," the first paragraph could explain that the home gyms your company sells start at less than $700, which works out to less than $2 a day over the course of a year.

  To build interest, expand on and support the promises in your attention-getting opening.

- **Increasing desire.** Now that you've given the audience some initial information to start building interest, the next step is to boost desire for the product by expanding on your explanation of its benefits. Think carefully about the sequence of support points, and use plenty of subheadings, hyperlinks, video demonstrations, and other devices to help people quickly find the information they need. You can also use a variety of techniques to address potential objections and minimize doubts, including testimonials from satisfied users, articles written by industry experts, competitive comparisons, offers of product samples or free demonstrations, independent test results, and money-back guarantees.

  Add details and audience benefits to increase desire for the product or service.

- **Motivating action.** The final step in the AIDA model is persuading the audience to take action, such as encouraging people to pick up the phone to place an order or visit an online app store to download your software. The keys to a successful call to action are making it as easy and as risk-free as possible. If the process is confusing or time-consuming, you'll lose potential customers.

  After you've generated sufficient interest and desire, you're ready to persuade readers to take the preferred action.

If you analyze the advertisements you encounter in any medium, you'll see variations on these techniques used again and again.

WRITING PROMOTIONAL MESSAGES FOR SOCIAL MEDIA

In a social media environment, persuasive efforts require a more conversational, interactive approach.

The AIDA model and similar approaches have been successful with marketing and sales messages for decades, but in the social media landscape, consumers are more apt to look for product information from other consumers, not the companies marketing those products. Consequently, your emphasis should shift to encouraging and participating in online conversations (see Figure 11.6). Follow these guidelines:[19]

- **Facilitate community building.** Give customers and other audiences an opportunity to connect with you and one another, such as on your Facebook page or through members-only online forums.
- **Listen at least as much as you talk.** Listening is just as essential for online conversations as it is for in-person conversations.
- **Initiate and respond to conversations within the community.** Through content on your website, blog posts, social network profiles and messages, newsletters, and other tools, make sure you provide the information customers need in order to evaluate your products and services. Use an objective, conversational style; people in social networks want useful information, not "advertising speak."
- **Provide information people want.** This information can include industry-insider news, in-depth technical guides to using your products, answers to questions posted on community Q&A sites, and general advice on product selection and usage. This strategy of **content marketing** is a great way to build customer relationships by providing value-added information.
- **Identify and support your champions.** In marketing, *champions* are enthusiastic fans of your company and its products. Champions are so enthusiastic they help spread your message through their social media accounts and other outlets, defend you against detractors, and help other customers use your products.

Content marketing is a strategy of provided valuable content to customers and potential customers.

Figure 11.6 **Promotional Messages in Social Media**
Procter & Gamble (P&G) uses social media to foster positive relationships with customers, communities, and other company stakeholders.

- **Be real.** Social media audiences respond positively to companies that are open and conversational about themselves, their products, and subjects of shared interest. In contrast, if a company is serving its stakeholders poorly with shoddy products, bad customer service, or unethical behavior, an attempt to improve its reputation by adopting social media without fixing the underlying problems is likely to fail as soon as audiences see through the superficial attempt to "be social."
- **Integrate conventional marketing and sales strategies at the right time and in the right places.** AIDA and similar approaches are still valid for specific communication tasks, such as conventional advertising and the product promotion pages on your website.

REAL-TIME UPDATES

LEARN MORE BY READING THIS ARTICLE

Building audience relationships with content marketing

Offering potential customers information of value is a popular marketing technique; read these tips to do it successfully. Go to **real-timeupdates.com/ebc13** and select Learn More in the Students section.

CREATING PROMOTIONAL MESSAGES FOR MOBILE DEVICES

Mobile advertising and mobile commerce (sometimes referred to as *m-commerce*) are two of the hottest developments in marketing communications. Companies are putting so much emphasis on mobile marketing because mobile devices now play such a big role in consumer buying behavior. Smartphone owners tend to use their devices for many shopping-related tasks, from searching for product reviews to finding stores and service businesses, looking for coupons and other promotions, and doing in-store price comparisons.[20]

If you are involved with creating mobile marketing or sales messages, keep two essential points in mind. First, like all mobile messages, promotional messages need to be kept short and simple. Second, the mobile experience needs to be fast and straightforward. Mobile users are often time-constrained, and they will quickly abandon websites that don't load quickly or are confusing to navigate.

> Promotional messages aimed at mobile audiences need to be short, simple, and easy to respond to.

Maintaining High Standards of Ethics, Legal Compliance, and Etiquette

4 LEARNING OBJECTIVE
Identify steps you can take to avoid ethical lapses in marketing and sales messages.

The word *persuasion* has negative connotations for some people, especially in a marketing or sales context. However, ethical businesspeople view persuasion as a positive force, aligning their own interests with what is best for their audiences. To maintain the highest standards of business ethics, always demonstrate the "you" attitude by showing honest concern for your audience's needs and interests.

PRACTICING ETHICAL COMMUNICATION

Pushing the Limits of Credibility

As the director of human resources in your company, you're desperate for some help. You want to keep the costs of employee benefits under control while making sure you provide employees with a fair benefits package. However, you don't have time to research all the options for health insurance, wellness programs, retirement plans, family counseling, educational benefits, and everything else, so you decide to hire a consultant. You receive the following message from a consultant interested in working with you:

> I am considered the country's foremost authority on employee health insurance programs. My clients offer universally positive feedback on the programs I've designed for them. They also love how much time I save them—hundreds and hundreds of hours. I am absolutely

confident that I can thoroughly analyze your needs and create a portfolio that realizes every degree of savings possible. I invite you to experience the same level of service that has generated such comments as "Best advice ever!" and "Saved us an unbelievable amount of money."

You'd love to get results like that, but the message almost sounds too good to be true. Is it?

CRITICAL THINKING

1. The consultant's message contains at least a dozen instances in which this writer's credibility might be questioned. Identify as many as you can.
2. Explain how you would bolster reader confidence by providing additional or different information.

Marketing and sales messages are covered by a wide range of laws and regulations.

As marketing and selling grow increasingly complex, so do the legal ramifications of marketing and sales messages. In the United States, the Federal Trade Commission (FTC) has the authority to impose penalties (ranging from cease-and-desist orders to multimillion-dollar fines) on advertisers who violate federal standards for truthful advertising. Other federal agencies have authority over advertising in specific industries, such as transportation and financial services. Individual states have additional laws that may apply. The legal aspects of promotional communication can be quite complex, varying from state to state and from country to country, and most companies require marketing and salespeople to get clearance from company lawyers before sending messages.

Moreover, communicators must stay on top of changing regulations, such as the latest laws governing unsolicited bulk email ("spam"), privacy, data security, and disclosure requirements for bloggers who review products. For example, two ethical concerns that could produce new legislation are *behavioral targeting*, which tracks the online behavior of website visitors and serves up ads based on what they seem to be interested in, and *remarketing* or *retargeting*, in which behaviorally targeted ads follow users even as they move on to other websites.[21]

For all marketing and sales efforts, pay close attention to the following legal considerations:[22]

- **Marketing and sales messages must be truthful and nondeceptive.** The FTC considers messages to be deceptive if they include statements that are likely to mislead reasonable customers and if those statements are an important part of the purchasing decision. The FTC distinguishes between subjective claims (commonly known as *puffery*), which cannot be proven true or false, and objective claims, which can be proved or disproved. Puffery is legally allowable, but deception is not. For example, "Tastiest Coffee in Tennessee" is puffery because it is neither provable nor disprovable. However, claiming that a coffee is organic when it was grown with chemical fertilizers is deceptive.
- **You must back up your claims with evidence.** According to the FTC, offering a money-back guarantee or providing letters from satisfied customers is not enough; you must still be able to support your claims with objective evidence such as a survey or scientific study.
- **"Bait and switch" advertising is illegal.** Trying to attract buyers by advertising a product that you don't intend to sell—and then trying to sell them another (and usually more expensive) product—is illegal.
- **Marketing messages and websites aimed at children are subject to special rules.** For example, online marketers must obtain consent from parents before collecting personal information about children under age 13.
- **Companies must disclose when they give products to online reviewers.** Given the strong influence of online product reviews, some companies give products to consumers in exchange for their reviews on Amazon and other retail sites. The practice is not illegal, but it must be disclosed.
- **Celebrities and other social media influencers must disclose when they are compensated to endorse products.** For instance, the FTC suggests that celebrities use the hashtag #ad when posting photos or tweets that endorse products.
- **Companies that coordinate with product champions and social media influencers have a degree of responsibility for what those people say to the public.** Marketers are expected to train these people in responsible communication and monitor what these outside parties write and say about their products.

For more insights on writing persuasive messages, visit **real-timeupdates.com/ebc13** and select Chapter 11.

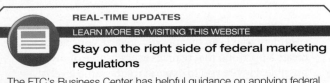

REAL-TIME UPDATES

LEARN MORE BY VISITING THIS WEBSITE

Stay on the right side of federal marketing regulations

The FTC's Business Center has helpful guidance on applying federal marketing regulations in a wide variety of specific situations. Go to **real-timeupdates.com/ebc13** and select Learn More in the Students section.

ON THE JOB: SOLVING COMMUNICATION DILEMMAS AT **STITCH FIX**

You've joined Stitch Fix as a training and quality lead. You report to the supervisor of training and quality programs and lead a small team of specialists who help employees throughout the company deliver a satisfying customer experience. Use what you've learned in this chapter to address these challenges.

1. Stitch Fix emphasizes the "art of conversation" with its trainers and customer experience staff. You recently heard about a conversational training system that uses natural language processing and natural language generation. It appears to be advanced enough to carry on realistic conversations with customer agents, and you think it could be a great way to train customer agents. It would be more cost-effective than taking agents offline for lengthy courses, and it can be programmed to adapt on the fly during a conversation to give agents practice in the areas they need it most. There would be some start-up costs to get the system installed and programmed, but it should pay for itself after a few months of use. Which of these approaches would be the best way to persuade your boss to give the system a try?
   a. This is such good news that you should use the direct approach and lead with a bold "we should buy this system immediately!" message.
   b. Use the indirect approach and build up to the proposal's main idea by highlighting the cost and disruption created by the current approach to training. After you've laid out the disadvantages of the current approach, introduce your proposed solution.
   c. Use the indirect approach that builds up to the proposal's main idea by highlighting all the other ways Stitch Fix uses advanced technology. By the time you get to your proposed solution, it will seem like it's already part of the company's AI arsenal.

2. Your manager has a high degree of trust in you, and you've always emphasized honest and ethical communication, so the *ethos* part of your proposal is on solid ground. How

should you balance the emotional and logical appeals in your message?
   a. The appeal should be primarily logical in order to emphasize the business benefits of the new training approach. However, add the emotional appeal of making life easier for employees by reducing disruption to their schedules.
   b. Conversing with a software robot is unavoidably going to be an emotional experience, so the proposal should match that.
   c. This is strictly a business decision, so emotion shouldn't play a role.
   d. The level of emotion should match the level of excitement you want to convey about this new technology.

3. Which of these statements is the most effective way to reinforce your argument that Stitch Fix should give this system a try?
   a. We need to do our best to always be improving customer agent skill sets.
   b. The vendor claims that other retailers have reduced training costs by as much as 50 percent using this system.
   c. I strongly believe in the potential of this amazing system.
   d. We could make sure all our agents have excellent conversational skills, and according to the vendor's data, we could cut our training costs by up to 50 percent.

4. The company that sells the conversation-training system offers a free 30-day trial, and you'd like your boss to authorize you to sign Stitch Fix up for a trial. Which of these is the best way to request action from your manager?
   a. Thanks for hearing me out!
   b. So, ready to move ahead with a trial?
   c. The vendor offers a free 30-day trial; shall I explore this option? I can contact them this week to set it up.
   d. Please give me an indication of your interest within 48 hours so I can proceed with contacting the vendor.

END OF CHAPTER

Learning Objectives Checkup

Assess your understanding of the principles in this chapter by reading each learning objective and studying the accompanying exercises. You can check your responses against the answer key on page 613.

Objective 11.1: Apply the three-step writing process to persuasive messages.

1. Which of the following is an accurate general statement about good ideas in the business world?
   a. Newer employees are not expected to contribute fresh ideas.
   b. Many good ideas pass unnoticed or are misunderstood because they are communicated poorly.
   c. Business leaders always jump on new ideas, even if they are poorly presented.
   d. Good ideas speak for themselves and don't need to be "communicated" in today's social media environment.

2. Why is the indirect approach often used in persuasive messages?
   a. It is more courteous and therefore gives the writer the opportunity to build up goodwill before slipping in the sales pitch.
   b. It takes less time.
   c. It is the traditional way to do persuasive messages and therefore expected.
   d. It lets the writer build audience interest and desire before asking for action or commitment.

3. Which of the following is *not* a good way to establish credibility with your audience?
   a. Support your argument with clear reasoning and objective evidence.
   b. Identify your sources.
   c. Establish common ground with your readers.
   d. Present only your side of the argument to avoid reminding the audience of alternatives.

Objective 11.2: Describe an effective strategy for developing persuasive business messages, and identify the three most common categories of persuasive business messages.

4. The first phase in the AIDA model is to
   a. do your research.
   b. gain the audience's attention.
   c. analyze the audience.
   d. call for action.

5. The body of a message that follows the AIDA model
   a. captures the audience's attention.
   b. contains the buffer.
   c. generates interest and heightens desire.
   d. calls for action.

6. The final phase of the AIDA model
   a. provides in-depth information to help generate interest.
   b. reduces resistance by increasing the audience's desire.
   c. calls for action.
   d. captures the audience's attention.

7. Which of these is *not* one of the types of persuasive appeals?
   a. Pathos
   b. Ethos
   c. Logos
   d. Bathos

8. An argument that is based on human feelings is known as a/an _____ appeal.

9. An argument that is based on facts and reason is known as a/an _____ appeal.

10. The best approach to using emotional appeals is usually to
    a. use them by themselves.
    b. use them in conjunction with logical appeals.
    c. use them only when the audience is particularly hostile.
    d. avoid them in all business messages.

Objective 11.3: Describe an effective strategy for developing marketing and sales messages and explain how to modify your approach when writing promotional messages for social media.

11. Why is it important to anticipate objections when planning and writing persuasive messages?
    a. You are legally required to anticipate audience objections in all marketing messages.
    b. By anticipating potential objections, you have the opportunity to address them in a persuasive manner before the audience settles on a firm no answer.
    c. By anticipating potential objections, you have the opportunity to explain to audience members why they are viewing the situation incorrectly.
    d. By anticipating potential objections, you can explain to the audience all the negative consequences of accepting your message.

12. Prioritizing which selling points and benefits to write about is
    a. a waste of time because people don't read in sequential order.
    b. important because doing so lets you start with low-priority issues and work your way up to high-priority issues.
    c. important because it helps you focus your message on items and issues that the audience cares about the most.
    d. important because it helps ensure that you remember to talk about every single feature and benefit, no matter how inconsequential.

13. How do marketing messages and sales messages differ?
    a. Sales messages use oral media exclusively.
    b. Sales messages are "hard sell," whereas marketing messages are "soft sell."
    c. Marketing messages move audiences toward a purchase decision without asking them to make a decision; sales messages ask them to make a decision then and there.
    d. The vast majority of marketing messages are still legal, but most traditional sales messages have been outlawed in both the United States and the European Union.

14. What is the relationship between selling points and benefits?
    a. They are different words for the same idea.
    b. Selling points are aspects of an idea or product; benefits are the advantages that readers will realize from those features.
    c. Selling points tell people how to use a product; benefits tell them how a product differs from the competition.

d. Selling points are the primary advantages of a product; benefits are the secondary advantages.

15. Providing value-added information to potential customers is known as_____.

16. What are product champions?
    a. The managers and supervisors in the marketing departments
    b. Sales professionals assigned to specific product lines
    c. Enthusiastic fans of a company and its products
    d. People who can be counted on to disparage competitive products in social media

17. What is the likely reaction of mobile shoppers if they encounter e-commerce websites that are slow to load or confusing to navigate?
    a. They will quickly abandon such websites.
    b. They will shift over to their PCs and continue shopping on the websites.
    c. They will file complaints with the website owners' customer service departments.
    d. They will file complaints with the Federal Trade Commission (FTC).

Objective 11.4: Identify steps you can take to avoid ethical lapses in marketing and sales messages.

18. Which of the following steps should you take to make sure your persuasive messages are ethical?
    a. Align your interests with your audience's interests.
    b. Choose words that offer multiple interpretations.
    c. Limit the amount of information you provide in order to avoid overloading the audience and thereby confusing your readers.
    d. Restrict logical appeals to business marketing and use emotional appeals for consumer marketing.

19. Trying to attract buyers by advertising a product that you don't intend to sell and then trying to sell them another (and usually more expensive) product is known as _____ and _____ marketing.

Key Terms

AIDA model Message sequence that involves attention, interest, desire, and action

benefits The particular advantages that readers will realize from a product's selling points

content marketing Strategy of sharing valuable information with potential customers to help build affinity for your brand

demographics Quantifiable characteristics of a population, including age, gender, occupation, income, and education

emotional appeal Persuasive approach that calls on audience feelings and sympathies rather than facts, figures, and rational arguments

logical appeal Persuasive approach that calls on reasoning and evidence

marketing messages Promotional messages that usher potential buyers through the purchasing process without asking them to make an immediate decision

motivation The combination of forces that drive people to satisfy their needs

persuasion The attempt to change an audience's attitudes, beliefs, or actions

psychographics Psychological characteristics of an audience, including personality, attitudes, and lifestyle

sales messages In contrast to marketing messages, sales messages encourage potential buyers to make a purchase decision then and there

selling points The most attractive features of a product or service

Apply Your Knowledge

To review chapter content related to each question, refer to the indicated Learning Objective.

11-1. Why is it essential to understand your readers' likely motivations before writing a persuasive message? [LO-1]

11-2. Why is it important to present all sides of an argument when writing a persuasive message to a potentially hostile audience? [LO-2]

11-3. Are emotional appeals ethical? Why or why not? [LO-2]

11-4. What is likely to happen if a promotional message starts immediately with a call to action? Why? [LO-3]

11-5. Are promotional slogans such as "Best sushi in town" or "Atlanta's most popular restaurant" ethical? Why or why not? [LO-4]

Practice Your Skills

Messages for Analysis

For Message 11.A and Message 11.B, read the following documents and then (1) analyze the strengths and weaknesses of each sentence, and (2) revise each document so that it follows this chapter's guidelines.

11-6. Message 11.A: Message Strategies: Persuasive Claims and Requests for Adjustment [LO-2]

Dear TechStar Computing:

I'm writing to you because of my disappointment with my new multimedia PC display. The display part works all right, but the audio volume is set too high and the volume knob doesn't turn it down. It's driving us crazy. The volume knob doesn't seem to be connected to anything but simply spins around. I can't believe you would put out a product like this without testing it first.

I depend on my computer to run my small business and want to know what you are going to do about it. This reminds me of every time I buy electronic equipment from what seems like any company. Something is always wrong. I thought quality was supposed to be important, but I guess not. Anyway, I need this fixed right away. Please tell me what you want me to do.

11-7. Message 11.B: Message Strategies: Sales Messages [LO-3]

We know how awful dining hall food can be, and that's why we've developed the "Mealaweek Club." Once a week, we'll deliver food to your dormitory or apartment. Our meals taste great. We have pizza, buffalo wings, hamburgers and curly fries, veggie roll-ups, and more!

When you sign up for just six months, we will ask what day you want your delivery. We'll ask you to fill out your selection of meals. And the rest is up to us. At "Mealaweek," we deliver! And payment is easy. We accept MasterCard and Visa or a personal check. It will save money especially when compared with eating out.

Just fill out the enclosed card and indicate your method of payment. As soon as we approve your credit or check, we'll begin delivery. Tell all your friends about Mealaweek. We're the best idea since sliced bread!

11-8. Message 11.C: Media Skills: Podcasting [LO-2] To access this message, visit **real-timeupdates.com/ ebc13**, select Student Assignments, then select Chapter 11, Message 11.C. Listen to this podcast. Identify at least three ways in which the podcast could be more persuasive; then draft a brief email message you could send to the podcaster with your suggestions for improvement.

Exercises

Each activity is labeled according to the primary skill or skills you will need to use. To review relevant chapter content, you can refer to the indicated Learning Objective. In some instances, supporting information will be found in another chapter, as indicated.

Choosing a Message Strategy [LO-1], Chapters 9–11 Now that you've explored routine, positive, negative, and persuasive messages, review the following message scenarios and identify which of the four message strategies would be most appropriate for the situation. Offer a brief justification for your choices. (Depending on the particular circumstances, a scenario might lend itself to more than one type of message; just be sure to offer compelling reasons for your choices.)

11-9. An unsolicited message to your department manager explaining why you believe the company's experiment with self-managed work teams has not been successful

11-10. An unsolicited message to your department manager explaining why you believe the company's experiment with self-managed work teams has not been successful and suggesting that one of the more experienced employees (such as yourself) should be promoted to supervisor

11-11. A message to a long-time industrial customer explaining that a glitch in your accounting system resulted in the customer being overcharged on its last five orders, apologizing for the problem, and assuring the customer that you will refund the overcharged amount immediately

11-12. A news release announcing that your company plans to invite back 50 employees who were laid off earlier in the year

Message Strategies: Persuasive Business Messages; Collaboration: Team Projects [LO-2] With another student, analyze the persuasive email message in Figure 11.5 by answering the following questions:

11-13. What techniques are used to capture the reader's attention?

11-14. Does the writer use the direct or indirect organizational approach? Why?

11-15. Is the subject line effective? Why or why not?

11-16. How does the writer balance emotional and logical appeals?

11-17. What reader benefits are included?

11-18. How does the writer establish credibility?

11-19. What tools does the writer use to reinforce his position?

Message Strategies: Persuasive Business Messages, Marketing and Sales Messages: Media Skills: Email [LO-2], [LO-3] Compose effective subject lines for the following persuasive email messages:

11-20. A recommendation was sent by email to your branch manager to install wireless networking throughout the facility. Your primary reason is that management has encouraged more teamwork, but teams often congregate in meeting rooms, the cafeteria, and other places that lack network access—without which they can't do much of the work they are expected to do.

11-21. A message to area residents soliciting customers for your new business, "Meals à la Car," a carryout dining service that delivers from most of the local restaurants.

11-22. An email message to the company president, asking that employees be allowed to carry over their unused vacation days to the following year. Apparently, many employees canceled their fourth-quarter vacation plans to work on the installation of a new company computer system. Under their current contract, vacation days not used by December 31 can't be carried over to the following year.

11-23. Communication Ethics: Making Ethical Choices [LO-2], [LO-4] Your boss has asked you to post a message on the company's internal blog urging everyone in your department to donate money to the company's favorite charity, an organization that operates a summer camp for children with physical challenges. You wind up writing a lengthy posting, packed with facts and heartwarming anecdotes about the camp and the children's experiences. When you must work that hard to persuade your audience to take an action such as donating money to a charity, aren't you being manipulative and unethical? Explain.

Message Strategies: Marketing and Sales Messages [LO-3] Determine whether the following sentences focus on selling points or benefits; rewrite as necessary to focus all the sentences on benefits.

11-24. All-Cook skillets are coated with a durable, patented nonstick surface.

11-25. These training shoes use an injection-molded foam midsole that provides optimum cushioning.

11-26. The MessageStar messaging app seamlessly connects to all major messaging services so you can communicate with all your friends and colleagues, no matter what systems they use.

Expand Your Skills

Critique the Professionals

Visit the Facebook pages of six companies in several industries. How do the companies make use of Facebook? Do any of the companies use posts to promote their products? Compare the material on the About tabs. Which company has the most compelling information here? How about the use of custom tabs—which company does the best job of using this Facebook feature? Using whatever medium your instructor requests, write a brief analysis of the message (no more than one page), citing specific elements from the piece and support from the chapter.

Sharpening Your Career Skills Online

Bovée and Thill's Business Communication Web Search, at **websearch.businesscommunicationnetwork.com**, is a unique research tool designed specifically for business communication research. Use the Web Search function to find a website, video, article, podcast, or PowerPoint presentation that offers advice on writing persuasive messages (either persuasive business messages or marketing and sales messages). Write a brief email message to your instructor describing the item you found and summarizing the career skills information you learned from it.

Build Your Career

As you begin to map out your post-college plans, you may have concerns about some aspect of your personal history, career history, or overall fit for the types of jobs you hope to land. Depending on where you are in your career and life, you might be worried about inexperience, frequent job changes, slow career growth, gaps in your work history, overqualification, your age, a criminal record, or job termination for cause.

If one of these situations is relevant to your career aspirations, it's good to recognize it early in the process because there are specific steps you can take during the job-search process to minimize any limitations that a particular issue might pose. Doing so will help you present your qualifications to potential employers in the best possible light, and it will help reduce the anxiety you might be feeling as you approach the application and interview stage. You could also be pleasantly surprised to discover that a point of worry doesn't need to be a major stumbling block after all. "Addressing Areas of Concern" on page 482 offers quick tips for each of these situations. Talking with an adviser in your college's career center can also help you map out a plan that fits your unique situation.

Improve Your Grammar, Mechanics, and Usage

The following exercises help you improve your knowledge of and power over English grammar, mechanics, and usage. Turn to the Handbook of Grammar, Mechanics, and Usage at the end of

this book and review all of Sections 2.1 (Periods), 2.2 (Question Marks), and 2.3 (Exclamation Points). Then indicate the preferred choice in the following groups of sentences. (Answers to these exercises appear on page 614.)

11-27. **a.** Dr. Eleanor H Hutton has requested information on TaskMasters, Inc.?

    b. Dr. Eleanor H. Hutton has requested information on TaskMasters, Inc.

11-28. **a.** That qualifies us as a rapidly growing new company, don't you think?

    b. That qualifies us as a rapidly growing new company, don't you think.

11-29. **a.** Our president is a C.P.A. On your behalf, I asked him why he started the firm.

    b. Our president is a CPA. On your behalf, I asked him why he started the firm.

11-30. **a.** Contact me at 1358 N. Parsons Ave., Tulsa, OK 74204.

    b. Contact me at 1358 N. Parsons Ave, Tulsa, OK. 74204.

11-31. **a.** Jeb asked, "Why does he want to know! Maybe he plans to become a competitor."

    b. Jeb asked, "Why does he want to know? Maybe he plans to become a competitor!"

11-32. **a.** The debt load fluctuates with the movement of the U.S. prime rate.

    b. The debt load fluctuates with the movement of the US prime rate.

11-33. **a.** Is consumer loyalty extinct? Yes and no!

    b. Is consumer loyalty extinct? Yes and no.

11-34. **a.** Will you please send us a check today so that we can settle your account.

    b. Will you please send us a check today so that we can settle your account?

11-35. **a.** Will you be able to speak at the conference, or should we find someone else.

    b. Will you be able to speak at the conference, or should we find someone else?

11-36. **a.** So I ask you, "When will we admit defeat?" Never!

    b. So I ask you, "When will we admit defeat"? Never!

For additional exercises focusing on periods, question marks, and exclamation points, visit MyLab Business Communication. Select Chapter 11, then Additional Exercises to Improve Your Grammar, Mechanics, and Usage, then 17. Punctuation B.

Cases

For all cases, feel free to use your creativity to make up any details you need in order to craft effective messages.

Persuasive Business Messages
MICROBLOGGING SKILLS

11-37. Message Strategies: Persuasive Business Messages [LO-2] You've been trying for months to convince your boss, company CEO Will Florence, to start using Twitter. You've told him that top executives in numerous industries now use Twitter as a way to connect with customers and other stakeholders without going through the filters and barriers of formal corporate communications, but he doesn't see the value.

Your task: You come up with the brilliant plan to demonstrate Twitter's usefulness using Twitter itself. First, find three executives from three companies who are on Twitter (choose any companies and executives you find interesting). Second, study their tweets to get a feel for the type of information they share. Third, if you don't already have a Twitter account set up for this class, set one up for the purposes of this exercise (you can deactivate later). Fourth, write four tweets to demonstrate the value of executive microblogging: one that summarizes the value of having a company CEO use Twitter, followed by three support tweets, each one summarizing how your three real-life executive role models use Twitter.

EMAIL SKILLS / TEAM SKILLS

11-38. Message Strategies: Persuasive Business Messages [LO-2] At lunch with a colleague from your department last week, you discovered that as much as you both love your jobs, family obligations are making it difficult to keep working full time. Unfortunately, your company doesn't offer any conventional part-time jobs because it needs to keep positions such as yours staffed five days a week. However, you have heard about the concept of job sharing, in which two people divide a single job.

Your task: With a partner, research job sharing. Identify the pros and cons from the perspectives of the employer and the employees involved. Using the AIDA approach, draft a persuasive email message to your supervisor outlining the benefits and addressing the potential problem areas. Your call to action should be to ask your supervisor to propose job sharing to company management.

EMAIL SKILLS

11-39. Message Strategies: Persuasive Business Messages [LO-2] While sitting at your desk during your lunch break, slumped over as usual, staring at your computer screen, you see an online article about the dangers of sitting at your desk all day. Yikes. The article suggests trying a standing desk—or, even better, a treadmill desk, which has an exercise treadmill built into a standing desk. You'd love to lose a few pounds while being healthier and feeling more alert during the day. Plus, you know the company is encouraging employees to live healthier lifestyles in order to improve their overall well-being and to reduce its health-care costs.

Your task: Research treadmill desks and write a persuasive email message to your boss requesting that the company buy or rent a treadmill desk for you to try out. Offer to serve as a research subject for the whole office, tracking your weight loss, alertness, and any other relevant variables you can think of.

BLOGGING SKILLS / TEAM SKILLS

11-40. Message Strategies: Persuasive Business Messages [LO-2] As a strong advocate for the use of social media in business, you are pleased by how quickly people in your company have taken up blogging, wiki writing, and other new-media activities. You are considerably less excited by the style and quality of what you see in the writing of your colleagues. Many seem to have interpreted "authentic and conversational" to mean "anything goes." Several of the Twitter users in the company seem to have abandoned any pretense of grammar and spelling. A few managers have dragged internal disagreements about company strategy out into public view, arguing with each other through comments on various industry-related forums. Product demonstration videos have been posted to the company's YouTube channel virtually unedited, making the whole firm look unpolished and unprofessional. The company CEO has written some blog posts that bash competitors with coarse and even crude language.

You pushed long and hard for greater use of these tools, so you feel a sense of responsibility for this situation. In addition, you are viewed by many in the company as the resident expert on social media, so you have some "expertise authority" on this issue. On the other hand, you are only a first-level manager, with three levels of managers above you, so while you have some "position authority" as well, you can hardly dictate best practices to the managers above you.

Your task: Working with two other students, write a post for the company's internal blog (which is not viewable outside the company) outlining your concerns about these communication practices. Use the examples mentioned previously, and make up any additional details you need. Emphasize that while social media communication is often less formal and more flexible than traditional business communication, it shouldn't be unprofessional. You are thinking of proposing a social media training program for everyone in the company, but for this message you just want to bring attention to the problem.

LETTER WRITING SKILLS

11-41. Message Strategies: Persuasive Business Messages [LO-2] The coffee shop across the street from your tiny apartment is your haven away from home—great beverages, healthy snacks, free wireless, and an atmosphere that is convivial but quiet enough that you can focus on homework. It lacks only one thing: some way to print out your homework and other files when you need hard copies. Your college's libraries and computer labs provide printers, but you live three miles from campus, and it's a long walk or an inconvenient bus ride.

Your task: Write a letter to the owner of the coffee shop encouraging her to set up a printing service to complement the free wireless access. Propose that the service run at break-even prices, just enough to pay for paper, ink cartridges, and the cost of the printer itself. The benefit to the shop would be enticing patrons to spend more time—and, therefore, more of their coffee and tea money—in the shop. You might also mention that you had to take the bus to campus to print this letter, so you bought your afternoon latté somewhere else.

EMAIL SKILLS / PORTFOLIO BUILDER

11-42. Message Strategies: Persuasive Business Messages [LO-2] As someone who came of age in the "post-email" world of social networks and workgroup messaging, you were rather disappointed to find your new employer solidly stuck in the age of email. You use email, of course, but it is only one of the tools in your communication toolbox. From your college years, you have hands-on experience with a wide range of social media tools, having used them to collaborate on school projects, to become involved in your local community, to learn more about various industries and professions, and to research potential employers during your job search. (In fact, without social media, you might never have heard about your current employer in the first place.) Moreover, your use of social media on the job has already paid several important dividends, including finding potential sales contacts at several large companies, connecting with peers in other companies to share ideas for working more efficiently, and learning about some upcoming legislative matters in your state that could profoundly hamper your company's current way of doing business.

You hoped that by setting an example through your own use of social media at work, your new colleagues and company management would quickly adopt these tools as well. However, just the opposite has happened. Waiting in your email in-box this morning was a message from the CEO announcing that the company is now cutting off access to social networking websites and banning the use of any social media at work. The message says using company time and company computers for socializing is highly inappropriate and might be considered grounds for dismissal in the future if the problem gets out of hand.

Your task: You are stunned by the message. You fight the urge to fire off a hotly worded reply to straighten out the CEO's misperceptions. Instead, you wisely decide to send a message to your immediate superior first, explaining why you believe the new policy should be reversed. Using your boss's favorite medium (email, of course!), write a persuasive message explaining why Facebook, Twitter, and other social networking technologies are valid—and valuable—business tools. Bolster your argument with examples from other companies and advice from communication experts.

EMAIL SKILLS

11-43. Message Strategies: Requests for Action [LO-2] Managing a new-product launch can be an aggravating experience as you try to coordinate a wide variety of activities and processes while barreling toward a deadline that is often defined more by external factors than a realistic assessment of whether you can actually meet it. You depend on lots of other people to meet their deadlines, and if they fail, you fail. The pressure is enough to push anybody over the edge. Unfortunately, that happened to you last week. After a barrage of bad news from suppliers and the members of the team you lead, you lost your cool in a checkpoint meeting. Shouting at people and accusing them of slacking off was embarrassing enough, but the situation got a hundred times worse this morning when your boss suggested you needed some low-pressure work for a while and removed you as the leader of the launch team.

Your task: Write an email message to your boss, Sunil, requesting to be reinstated as the project team leader. Make up any information you need.

EMAIL SKILLS

11-44. Message Strategies: Requests for Action [LO-2] You appreciate how important phones are to your company's operations, but the amount of conversational chatter in your work area has gotten so bad that it's hard to concentrate on your work. You desperately need at least a few quiet hours every day to engage in the analytical thinking your job requires.

Your task: Write an email message to the division vice president, Jeri Ross, asking her to designate one of the conference rooms as a quiet-zone work room. It would have Wi-Fi so that employees can stay connected to the corporate network, but it would not have any phone service, either landline or mobile. (Mobile reception is already weak in the conference rooms, but you will propose to equip the room with a mobile signal jammer to ensure that no calls can be made or received.) In addition, conversation of any kind would be strictly forbidden. Make up any details you need.

11-45. Message Strategies: Requests for Action [LO-2] Your new company, WorldConnect Language Services, started well and is going strong. However, to expand beyond your Memphis, Tennessee, home market, you need a onetime infusion of cash to open branch offices in other cities around the Southeast. At the Entrepreneur's Lunch Forum you attended yesterday, you learned about several *angels*, as they are called in the investment community—private individuals who invest money in small companies in exchange for a share of ownership. One such angel, Melinda Sparks, told the audience she is looking for investment opportunities outside of high technology, where angels often invest their money. She also indicated that she looks for entrepreneurs who know their industries and markets well, who are passionate about the value they bring to the marketplace, who are committed to growing their businesses, and who have a solid plan for how they will spend an investor's money. Fortunately, you meet all of her criteria.

Your task: Draft an email message to Sparks introducing yourself and your business and asking for a meeting at which you can present your business plan in more detail. Explain that your Memphis office was booked to capacity within two months of opening, thanks to the growing number of international business professionals looking for translators and interpreters. You've researched the entire Southeast region and identified at least 10 other cities that could support a language services office such as yours. Making up whatever other information you need, draft a four-paragraph message following the AIDA model, ending with a request for a meeting within the next four weeks. You know Sparks tends to read email on her phone, so craft your message to be mobile friendly.

11-46. Message Strategies: Persuasive Claims and Requests for Adjustment [LO-2] You thought it was strange that no one called you on your new mobile phone, even though you had given your family members, friends, and boss your new number. Two weeks after getting the new phone and agreeing to a $49 monthly fee, you called the service provider, InstantCall, just to see if everything was working. Sure enough, the technician discovered that your incoming calls were being routed to an inactive number. You're glad she found the problem, but then it took the company nearly two more weeks to fix it. When you called to complain about paying for service you didn't receive, the customer service agent suggests you send an email to Judy Hinkley at the company's regional business office to request an adjustment.

Your task: Decide how much of an adjustment you think you deserve under the circumstances and then send an email message to Hinkley to request the adjustment to your account. Write a summary of events in chronological order, supplying exact dates for maximum effectiveness. Make up any information you need, such as problems that the malfunctioning service caused at home or at work.

11-47. Message Strategies: Requests for Information [LO-2] As a motivated, ambitious employee, you naturally care about your performance on the job—and about making sure your performance is being fairly judged and rewarded. Unfortunately, the company has gone through a period of turmoil over the past several years, and you have reported to seven managers during the past five years. One year, your annual performance review was done by someone who had been your boss for only three weeks and knew almost nothing about you or your work. Last year, your boss was fired the day after he wrote your review, and you can't help but wonder whether you got a fair review from someone in that situation. Overall, you are worried that your career progression and wage increases have been hampered by inconsistent and ill-informed performance reviews.

The company allows employees to keep copies of their reviews, but you haven't been diligent about doing so. You would like to get copies of your last five reviews, but you heard from a colleague that the human resources department will not release copies of past reviews without approval from the managers who wrote them. In your case, however, three of the managers who reviewed you are no longer with the company, and you do not want your current boss to know you are concerned about your reviews.

Your task: Write an email message to the director of human resources, Leon Sandes, requesting copies of your performance reviews over the past five years. Use the information included above and make up any additional details you need.

Marketing and Sales Messages: Conventional Media

11-48. Message Strategies: Marketing and Sales Messages [LO-3] Like all other states, Kentucky works hard to attract businesses that are considering expanding into the state or relocating entirely from another state. The Kentucky Cabinet for Economic Development is responsible for reaching out to these companies and overseeing the many incentive programs the state offers to new and established businesses.

Your task: As the communication director of the Kentucky Cabinet for Economic Development, you play the lead role in reaching out to companies that want to expand or relocate to Kentucky. Visit **www.thinkkentucky.com** and read "Top 10 Reasons for Locating or Expanding Your Business in Kentucky" (look under "Why Kentucky"). Identify the major benefits the state uses to promote Kentucky as a great place to locate a business. Summarize these reasons in a one-page form letter that will be sent to business executives throughout the country. Be sure to introduce yourself and your purpose in the letter, and close with a compelling call to action (have them reach you by telephone at 800-626-2930 or by email at econdev@ky.gov). As you plan your letter, try to imagine yourself as the CEO of a company and consider what a complex choice it would be to move to another state.[23]

LETTER WRITING SKILLS / **PORTFOLIO BUILDER**

11-49. Message Strategies: Marketing and Sales Messages [LO-3] Water polo is an active sport that provides great opportunities for exercise and for learning the collaborative skills involved in teamwork. You can learn more at www.usawaterpolo.org.

Your task: Write a one-page letter to parents of 10- to 14-year-old boys and girls promoting the health and socialization benefits of water polo and encouraging them to introduce their children to the sport through a local club. Tell them they can learn more about the sport and find a club in their area by visiting the USA Water Polo website.

WEB WRITING SKILLS

11-50. Message Strategies: Marketing and Sales Messages [LO-3] Convincing people to give their music a try is one of the toughest challenges new bands and performers face.

Your task: Imagine you've taken on the job of promoting an amazing new band or performer you just discovered. Choose someone you've heard live or online and write 100 to 200 words of webpage copy describing the music in a way that will convince people to listen to a few online samples.

MOBILE SKILLS / **TEAM** SKILLS / **PORTFOLIO BUILDER**

11-51. Message Strategies: Marketing and Sales Messages [LO-3] You never intended to become an inventor, but you saw a way to make something work more easily, so you set to work. You developed a model, found a way to mass-produce it, and set up a small manufacturing studio in your home. You know that other people are going to benefit from your invention. Now all you need to do is reach that market.

Your task: Team up with other students assigned by your instructor and imagine a useful product that you might have invented—perhaps something related to a hobby or sporting activity. List the features and benefits of your imaginary product, and describe how it helps customers. Then write the copy for the first screen of a mobile-friendly website that would introduce and promote this product, using what you've learned in this chapter and making up details as you need them. Using word-processing software or another tool if your instructor indicates, format the screen to show how the information would appear on a typical smartphone screen.

PODCASTING SKILLS

11-52. Message Strategies: Marketing and Sales Messages [LO-3] Your new podcast channel, School2Biz, offers advice to business students making the transition from college to career. You provide information on everything from preparing résumés to interviewing to finding a place in the business world and building a successful career. As you expand your audience, you'd eventually like to turn School2Biz into a profitable operation (perhaps by selling advertising time during your podcasts). For now, you're simply offering free advice.

Your task: As your instructor directs, either write a 50-word description of your new podcast or record a 30-second podcast describing the new service. Make up any information you need to describe School2Biz. Be sure to mention who you are and why the information you present is worth listening to.

Marketing and Sales Messages: Social Media

SOCIAL NETWORKING SKILLS / **TEAMWORK** SKILLS

11-53. Message Strategies: Marketing and Sales Messages; Media Skills: Social Networking [LO-3], Chapter 8 You chose your college or university based on certain expectations, and you've been enrolled long enough now to have some idea about whether those expectations have been met. In other words, you are something of an expert about the "consumer benefits" your school can offer prospective students.

Your task: In a team of four students, interview six other students who are not taking this business communication course. Try to get a broad sample of demographics and psychographics, including students in a variety of majors and programs. Ask these students (1) why they chose this college or university and (2) whether the experience has met their expectations so far. To ensure the privacy of your respondents, do not record their names with their answers. Each member of the team should then answer these same two questions, so that you have responses from a total of 10 students.

After compiling the responses (you might use Google Docs or a similar collaboration tool so that everyone on the team has easy access to the information), analyze them as a team to look for any recurring "benefit themes." Is it the quality of the education? Research opportunities? Location? The camaraderie of school sporting events? The chance to meet and study with fascinating students from a variety of backgrounds? Identify two or three strong benefits that your college or university can promise—and deliver—to prospective students.

Now nominate one member of the team to draft a short marketing message that could be posted on your school's Facebook page. The message should include a catchy title that makes it clear the message is a student's perspective on why this is a great place to get a college education. When the draft is ready, the other members of the team should review it individually. Finally, meet as a team to complete the message.

MICROBLOGGING SKILLS

11-54. Message Strategies: Marketing and Sales Messages; Media Skills: Microblogging [LO-3], Chapter 8 Effective microblogging messages emphasize clarity and conciseness—and so do effective sales messages.

Your task: Find the website of any product that can be ordered online (any product you find interesting and that is appropriate to use for a class assignment). Adapt the information on the website, using your own words, and write four tweets to promote the product. The first should get your audience's attention (e.g., with an intriguing benefit claim), the second should build audience interest by providing some support for the claim you made in the first message, the third should increase readers' desire to have the product by layering on one or two more buyer benefits, and the fourth should motivate readers to take action to place an order.

If your class is set up with private Twitter accounts, use your private account to send your messages. Otherwise, email your four messages to your instructor or post them on your class blog, as your instructor directs.

SOCIAL NETWORKING SKILLS / TEAM SKILLS

11-55. Message Strategies: Marketing and Sales Messages; Media Skills: Social Networking [LO-3], Chapter 8 At this point in your collegiate career, you've developed areas of academic expertise that could benefit other students. After kicking around moneymaking ideas with friends, you decide that the tutoring business would be a more enjoyable way to share your expertise than a regular part-time job.

Your task: In a team assigned by your instructor, compile a list of all the subject areas in which your team would be qualified to tutor high school students or other college students. Then brainstorm the best way to present your offerings through Facebook and other social media. Come up with a name for your tutoring company and write a 100- to 200-word "About Us" statement.

MICROBLOGGING SKILLS / TEAM SKILLS

11-56. Message Strategies: Marketing and Sales Messages; Media Skills: Social Networking [LO-3], Chapter 8 You and your tutoring team (see the previous case) know you should take advantage of every social media platform to inform potential clients about your new company.

Your task With the same team as in the previous case, compose four tweets to introduce your tutoring service on Twitter. Allow enough room in one of the tweets to include a URL (23 characters). Submit the tweets to your instructor in whatever format he or she requests.

MyLab Business Communication

MyLab Assisted-Grading Writing Prompts

If your instructor has assigned one or both of the following writing assignments within the MyLab, go to your Assignments to complete these writing exercises.

11-57. What role do demographics and psychographics play in audience analysis during the planning of a persuasive message? [LO-1]

11-58. Why do the AIDA model and similar approaches need to be modified when writing persuasive messages for social media? [LO-3]

Endnotes

1. Stitch Fix, accessed 10 April 2018, www.stitchfix.com; Tonya Garcia, "Stitch Fix IPO: 5 Things to Know About Online Clothing Service," MarketWatch, 18 November 2017, www.marketwatch.com; Jessica Pressler, "How Stitch Fix's CEO Katrina Lake Built a $2 Billion Company," *Elle*, 28 February 2018, www.elle.com; Hilary Milnes, "Stitch Fix CEO Katrina Lake Predicts AI's Impact on Fashion," Digiday, 25 January 2018, digiday.com; Jason Del Ray, "Stitch Fix Made a Big Addition to Its Business That Won't Show Up in Its Q2 Financial Results," Recode, 12 March 2018, www.recode.net.

2. Jay A. Conger, "The Necessary Art of Persuasion," *Harvard Business Review*, May–June 1998, 84–95; Jeanette W. Gilsdorf, "Write Me Your Best Case for . . . ," *Bulletin of the Association for Business Communication* 54, no. 1 (March 1991): 7–12.

3. "Vital Skill for Today's Managers: Persuading, Not Ordering, Others," *Soundview Executive Book Summaries*, September 1998, 1.

4. Vanessa K. Bohns, "You're Already More Persuasive Than You Think," *Harvard Business Review*, 3 August 2015, hbr.org.

5. Jim Crimmins, "How to Find Their Motivations," *Executive Leadership*, December 2016, 2; Mary Cross, "Aristotle and Business Writing: Why We Need to Teach Persuasion," *Bulletin of the Association for Business Communication* 54, no. 1 (March 1991): 3–6.

6. Liz Alexander, "How to Quickly Become More Persuasive," *Psychology Today*, 4 April 2017, www.psychologytoday.com.

7. Stephen Bayley and Roger Mavity, "How to Pitch," *Management Today*, March 2007, 48–53.

8. Robert B. Cialdini, "Harnessing the Science of Persuasion," *Businessweek*, 4 December 2007, www.businessweek.com.

9. Wesley Clark, "The Potency of Persuasion," *Fortune*, 12 November 2007, 48; W. H. Weiss, "Using Persuasion Successfully," *Supervision*, October 2006, 13–16.

10. Tom Chandler, "The Copywriter's Best Friend," The Copywriter Underground blog, 20 December 2006, copywriterunderground .com.

11. Kathleen Parker, "Plato Would Be Horrified," *Washington Post*, 27 April 2016, www.washingtonpost.com.

12. Based in part on "Fallacies," *Internet Encyclopedia of Philosophy*, accessed 13 April 2017, www.iep.utm.edu/fallacy.

13. Sarah Cliffe, "The Uses (and Abuses) of Influence," *Harvard Business Review*, July–August 2013, 76–81.

14. Zakary L. Tormala and Derek D. Rucker, "How Certainty Transforms Persuasion," *Harvard Business Review*, September 2015, 96–103.

15. Philip Vassallo, "Persuading Powerfully: Tips for Writing Persuasive Documents," *et Cetera* 59, no. 1 (Spring 2002): 65–71.

16. Dianna Booher, *Communicate with Confidence* (Colleyville, Texas: Booher Research Institute, 2013), Kindle location 2284.

17. Based in part on Jay A. Conger, "The Necessary Art of Persuasion," *Harvard Business Review*, May–June 1998, 84–95.

18. "Social Factors in Developing a Web Accessibility Business Case for Your Organization," W3C website, accessed 16 April 2017, www.w3.org.

19. Tamar Weinberg, *The New Community Rules: Marketing on the Social Web* (Sebastapol, Calif.: O'Reilly Media, 2009), 22, 23–24, 187–191; Larry Weber, *Marketing to the Social Web* (Hoboken, N.J.: Wiley, 2007), 12–14; David Meerman Scott, *The New Rules of Marketing and PR* (Hoboken, N.J.: Wiley, 2015), 57–58; Paul Gillin, *The New Influencers: A Marketer's Guide to the New Social Media* (Sanger, Calif.: Quill Driver Books, 2007), 34–35; Jeremy Wright, *Blog Marketing: The Revolutionary Way to Increase Sales, Build Your Brand, and Get Exceptional Results* (New York: McGraw-Hill, 2006), 263–365.

20. Chris Kelley, "Why You Need a Mobile Website," V2 Marketing Communications, 18 June 2013, blog.marketingv2.com.

21. Lara O'Reilly, "Snapchat Is About to Introduce Something Advertisers Have Been Wanting for Ages: Behavioral Targeting," *Business Insider*, 26 August 2016, www.businessinsider.com; Robert Brady, "The Dark Side of Remarketing," *Clix*, 21 January 2014, www.clixmarketing.com; Miguel Helft and Tanzina Vega, "Retargeting Ads Follow Surfers to Other Sites," *New York Times*, 29 August 2010, www.nytimes.com.

22. "The FTC's Endorsement Guides: What People Are Asking," U.S. Federal Trade Commission website, accessed 16 April 2017, www.ftc.gov; "Advertising FAQ's: A Guide for Small Business," U.S. Federal Trade Commission website, accessed 16 April 2017, www.ftc.gov; Cassidy Mantor, "FTC Cracks Down on Social Media Influencers," *Fashion Network*, 19 December 2017, us.fashionnetwork.com.

23. Kentucky Cabinet for Economic Development website, accessed 17 April 2017, www.thinkkentucky.com.

Five-Minute Guide to Writing Persuasive Messages

Before you start a persuasive business message or a promotional (marketing or sales) message, review these helpful tips.

00:01   **Plan the message**

1. Gather as much information as you can about your audience members and their needs.
2. Identify what is likely to motivate readers or listeners to respond to a message such as yours.
3. Make sure you have distilled your main idea down to a single, concise promise of how your offer can help your audience.
4. The indirect approach is used more frequently with persuasive messages, but you may encounter situations in which the direct approach is more effective.

00:02   **Choose an effective strategy**

1. Frame your arguments; the AIDA model and its variants are ideal for many persuasive messages:
   - Open with an intriguing promise that gets the audience's **attention**.
   - Provide additional details to build **interest**.
   - Help readers and listeners embrace the possibility and thereby build **desire**.
   - End with a call to **action**.
2. Balance the three types of persuasive appeals:
   - Ethos—the ethical dimension, including how much credibility you have with the audience
   - Pathos—appeals to emotion
   - Logos—argumentation based on logic and evidence

   All messages need an ethical foundation, and the right mix of emotional and logical appeals depends on the situation.
3. Reinforce your position; use additional evidence and thoughtful language choices to make your appeal even stronger.
4. Anticipate objections; try to "preaddress" potential objections by answering them in your initial message.

00:03   **Avoid these common mistakes**

1. Using a hard sell; nobody likes to be pushed into a decision.
2. Resisting compromise; look for win-win outcomes.
3. Relying solely on great arguments; connect with your audience at an emotional level.
4. Assuming that persuasion is a one-shot effort; you may need to write several messages in sequence to achieve a desired outcome.

00:04   **Follow these tips for marketing and sales messages**

1. Remember that marketing messages usher potential buyers through the purchasing process without asking them to make an immediate decision; then sales messages take over, encouraging people to make a purchase decision.
2. Be sure to identify key selling points (the most attractive features of a product) and the benefits they can deliver to customers.
3. In social media, minimize overt promotion and focus on having a conversation with target customers and influencers.

00:05   **Keep an eye on ethical and legal issues**

1. With any kind of persuasive message, never resort to deception or other unethical behaviors.
2. For marketing and sales messages, be aware of the many regulations that govern these types of messages.

Preparing Reports and Presentations

Reports and presentations offer important opportunities to demonstrate your value to an organization. Depending on the project, you might analyze complex problems, educate audiences, address opportunities in the marketplace, win contracts, or even launch an entire company with the help of a compelling business plan. Adapt what you've learned so far to the challenges of long-format messages, including some special touches that can make formal reports stand out from the crowd. Then learn how to plan effective presentations, overcome the anxieties that every speaker feels, and respond to questions from the audience. Discover some tips and techniques for succeeding with the Twitter-enabled back channel and with online presentations. Finally, complement your talk with presentation visuals that engage and excite your audience.

123RF.com

Planning Reports and Proposals

LEARNING OBJECTIVES

After studying this chapter, you will be able to

1 Adapt the three-step writing process to reports and proposals.

2 Describe an effective process for conducting business research, explain how to evaluate the credibility of an information source, and identify the five ways to use research results.

3 Explain the role of secondary research, and describe the two major categories of online research tools.

4 Explain the role of primary research, and identify the two most common forms of primary research for business communication purposes.

5 Explain how to plan informational reports and website content.

6 Identify the three most common ways to organize analytical reports.

7 Explain how to plan proposals.

MyLab Business Communication

Improve Your Grade!

If your instructor is using MyLab Business Communication, visit **www.pearson.com/mylab/business-communication** for videos, simulations, and writing exercises.

ON THE JOB: COMMUNICATING AT
STRATEGYZER

Disrupting the Conventional Approach to Business Plans

Whenever you're gathering information for a major business writing project, you're likely to encounter the question of how much is enough? Collecting and processing information takes time and often costs money, and it's not always clear how much information you need in order to craft an effective report or proposal, or how much time and money you should invest to get it. Invest too little and you risk writing a flawed report. Invest too much and you'll waste time and money that would be better put to other uses. Business plans are a great example of this dilemma, and the Swiss company Strategyzer made waves in the global entrepreneurial community with an unconventional approach to collecting information for such plans.

Conventional business plans cover a lot of territory, from a high-level look at strategy to details on financing, operations, marketing, and other functional areas. These reports can run to 30, 40, or more pages and you can spend weeks gathering the necessary information and distilling it down to useful formats.

Spending that much time on research before writing the business plan and launching the company can seem like a good idea to entrepreneurs who want to reduce start-up risks as much as possible or who want to produce high-quality reports to impress lenders or investors. In many start-up situations, however, this is precious time that entrepreneurs

Courtesy of Alex Osterwalder

Author and entrepreneur Alex Osterwalder's approach to evaluating new business ideas offers a simpler, faster alternative to the traditional business plan.

should be spending getting a product in front of customers to test the viability of the business concept, rather than crafting an impressive-looking plan about an idea that is still unproven. Moreover, in fast-moving markets, it is possible to spend so much time researching and writing the business plan that the target market changes by the time the plan is ready.

In addition, business plans have a special twist that involves the uncertainty surrounding some of the most important information they typically contain. For example, estimating demand for a new product or service is one of the most vital aspects of planning a business—and one of the most difficult. You might spend weeks gathering data on comparable products and refining spreadsheets with elegant forecasting models to predict how many products you can sell and how much profit you'll make. This projection will then be the basis of almost everything else in the business plan, from the amount of money you can attract from investors to the number of employees you should hire.

Here's the catch: You could spend ages writing a plan and launching a business based on this number only to find out it's wildly off the mark. In the worst-case scenario, you might have wasted months launching a weak business idea or a product with little or no market appeal. Even the most sophisticated estimates of market demand are still only predictions, and the only way to really know if a product is going to sell is to get it in front of customers and ask them to buy it.

In response to these uncertainties with conventional business plans, some experts now recommend a simplified, accelerated approach that gets a new business to the "point of proof" faster. One of the key thinkers behind this new approach is Strategyzer's co-founder, business theorist Alex Osterwalder. Rather than launching businesses with elaborate planning and a conventional business plan, he suggests that companies use the Business Model Canvas. This single-sheet visual brainstorming tool helps entrepreneurs answer a handful of key questions to determine whether they have a financially viable business concept—and what to adjust if they don't. The canvas approach helps flag some of the common stumbling points of new businesses, including financial plans that are based on shaky assumptions (or outright fantasy) and untested hypotheses about market behavior.

The Business Model Canvas and its variants don't necessarily replace conventional business reports in all cases, and they don't cover all the details needed to operate a business after launch, but they help entrepreneurs decide whether it makes sense to move forward. By developing and testing business concepts quickly, entrepreneurs can find out whether they have a realistic idea before investing weeks of time in detailed planning and report-writing efforts. The canvas idea has definitely captured the imagination of entrepreneurs: More than a million people bought the book that first outlined the canvas idea, and more than 5 million have downloaded the software tool offered by Strategyzer.[1]

STRATEGYZER.COM

Applying the Three-Step Writing Process to Reports and Proposals

1 LEARNING OBJECTIVE
Adapt the three-step writing process to reports and proposals.

Whether you're sharing your latest great idea with your boss or launching an entirely new company using a business planning method such as Alex Osterwalder's (profiled in the chapter-opening On the Job), reports will play a vital role in your business career. Reports fall into three basic categories (see Figure 12.1 on the next page):

- **Informational reports** offer data, facts, feedback, and other types of information, without analysis or recommendations.
- **Analytical reports** offer both information and analysis and can also include recommendations.
- **Proposals** present persuasive recommendations to internal or external audiences, often involving investments or purchases.

Reports can be classified as *informational reports* (provide facts and data), *analytical reports* (offer analysis and recommendations), and *proposals* (present persuasive recommendations).

View every business report as an opportunity to demonstrate your understanding of your audience's challenges and your ability to contribute to your organization's success. The three-step process you've used for shorter messages is easily adapted to reports and in fact simplifies these larger projects by ensuring a methodical and efficient approach.

Reports often give you the opportunity to demonstrate your grasp of important business issues.

ANALYZING THE SITUATION

Reports can be complex, time-consuming projects, so be sure to analyze the situation carefully before you begin to write. Doing so will focus your efforts and help minimize rework. Pay special attention to your **statement of purpose**, which explains *why* you are preparing the report and *what* you plan to deliver (see Table 12.1 on the next page).

A *statement of purpose* explains why you are preparing the report and what you plan to deliver.

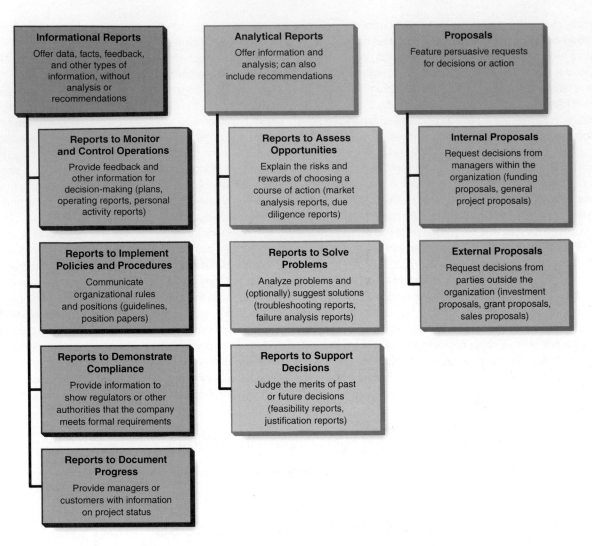

Figure 12.1 Common Business Reports and Proposals
You will have the opportunity to read and write many types of reports in your career; here are some of the most common.

TABLE 12.1 Problem Statements Versus Purpose Statements

Problem Statement	Statement of Purpose
Our company's market share is steadily declining.	To explore new ways of promoting and selling our products and to recommend the approaches most likely to stabilize our market share
Our current computer network lacks sufficient bandwidth and cannot be upgraded to meet our future needs.	To analyze various networking options and to recommend the system that will best meet our company's current and future needs
We need $2 million to launch our new product.	To convince investors that our new business would be a sound investment so that we can obtain desired financing
Our current operations are too decentralized and expensive.	To justify the closing of the Newark plant and the transfer of East Coast operations to a single Midwest location in order to save the company money

The most useful way to phrase your purpose statement is to begin with an infinitive phrase (*to* plus a verb), which helps pin down your general goal (*to inform, to identify, to analyze,* and so on). For instance, in an informational report, your statement of purpose can be as simple as one of these:

To update clients on the progress of the research project (progress report)

To develop goals and objectives for the coming year (strategic plan)

To identify customers and explain how the company will reach them (marketing plan)

To submit monthly sales statistics to management (operating report)

To summarize what occurred at the annual sales conference (personal activity report)

To explain building access procedures (policy implementation report)

To submit required information to the Securities and Exchange Commission (compliance report)

The statement of purpose for an analytical report often needs to be more comprehensive. For example, if you were asked to find ways of reducing employee travel and entertainment (T&E) costs, you might phrase your statement of purpose like this:

To analyze the T&E budget, evaluate the impact of recent trends in airfares and hotel costs, and suggest ways to tighten management's control over T&E expenses

A proposal must also be guided by a clear statement of purpose to help you focus on crafting a persuasive message. Here are several examples:

The statement of purpose for a proposal should help guide you in developing a persuasive message.

To secure $400k of funding in next year's capital budget for a new conveyor system in the warehouse (funding proposal)

To get management approval to reorganize the North American salesforce (general project proposal)

To secure $2 million in venture capital funding to complete design and production of the new line of titanium mountain bikes (investment proposal as part of a business plan)

To persuade SteelWright to purchase a subscription to our latest database offering (sales proposal)

In addition to carefully considering your purpose, you will want to prepare a *work plan* for most reports and proposals in order to make the best use of your time. For simpler reports, the work plan can be an informal list of tasks and a simple schedule. However, if you're preparing a lengthy report, particularly when you're collaborating with others, you'll want to develop a more detailed work plan (see Figure 12.2 on the next page).

A detailed *work plan* saves time and often produces more effective reports.

GATHERING INFORMATION

Obtaining the information needed for many reports and proposals requires careful planning, and you may need to do a separate research project to acquire the data and information you need. To stay on schedule and on budget, be sure to review both your statement of purpose and your audience's needs so that you can prioritize your information needs and focus on the most important questions.

Some reports require formal research projects in order to gather all the necessary information.

SELECTING THE RIGHT COMBINATION OF MEDIA AND CHANNELS

In addition to the general media and channel selection criteria discussed in Chapter 5, consider several points for reports and proposals. First, for many reports and proposals, audiences have specific media requirements, and you might not

REAL-TIME UPDATES

LEARN MORE BY WATCHING THIS VIDEO

Get to the heart of your business model

See how the Business Model Canvas helps entrepreneurs define their business models before moving ahead with more-formal planning. Go to **real-timeupdates.com/ebc13** and select Learn More in the Students section.

The problem statement clearly and succinctly defines the problem the writers intend to address.

This section explains how the researchers will find the data and information they need.

The assignments and schedule section clearly lists responsibilities and due dates.

This paragraph identifies exactly what will be covered by the research and addressed in the final report.

The preliminary outline has enough detail to guide the research and set reader expectations.

STATEMENT OF THE PROBLEM
The rapid growth of our company over the past five years has reduced the sense of community among our staff. People no longer feel like part of an intimate organization that values teamwork.

PURPOSE AND SCOPE OF WORK
The purpose of this study is to determine whether social networking technology such as Facebook and Socialtext would help rebuild a sense of community within the workforce and whether encouraging the use of such tools in the workplace will have any negative consequences. The study will attempt to assess the impact of social networks in other companies in terms of community building, morale, project communication, and overall productivity.

SOURCES AND METHODS OF DATA COLLECTION
Data collection will start with secondary research, including a review of recently published articles and studies on the use of social networking in business and a review of product information published by technology vendors. Primary research will focus on an employee and management survey to uncover attitudes about social networking tools. We will also collect anecdotal evidence from bloggers and others with experience using networks in the workplace.

PRELIMINARY OUTLINE
The preliminary outline for this study is as follows:
I. What experiences have other companies had with social networks in the workplace?
    A. Do social networks have a demonstrable business benefit?
    B. How do employees benefit from using these tools?
    C. Has network security and information confidentiality been an issue?
II. Is social networking an appropriate solution for our community-building needs?
    A. Is social networking better than other tools and methods for community building?
    B. Are employees already using social networking tools on the job?
    C. Will a company-endorsed system distract employees from essential duties?
    D. Will a company system add to managerial workloads in any way?
III. If we move ahead, should we use a "business-class" network such as Socialtext or a consumer tool such as Facebook?
    A. How do the initial and ongoing costs compare?
    B. Do the additional capabilities of a business-class network justify the higher costs?
IV. How should we implement a social network?
    A. Should we let it grow "organically," with employees choosing their own tools and groups?
    B. Should we make a variety of tools available and let employees improvise on their own?
    C. Should we designate one system as the official company social network and make it a permanent, supported element of the information technology infrastructure?
V. How can we evaluate the success of a new social network?
    A. What are the criteria of success or failure?
    B. What is the best way to measure these criteria?

TASK ASSIGNMENTS AND SCHEDULE
Each phase of this study will be completed by the following dates:

Secondary research: Hank Waters	September 15, 2020
Employee and management survey: Julienne Cho	September 22, 2020
Analysis and synthesis of research: Hank Waters/Julienne Cho	October 6, 2020
Comparison of business and consumer solutions: Julienne Cho	October 13, 2020
Comparison of implementation strategies: Hank Waters	October 13, 2020
Final report: Hank Waters	October 20, 2020

Figure 12.2 Work Plan for a Report
A formal work plan such as this is a vital tool for planning and managing complex writing projects. The preliminary outline here helps guide the research; the report writers may well modify the outline when they begin writing the report.

A *dashboard* is a customized graphical presentation of key performance parameters and can serve as a super-summarized report.

have a choice. For instance, executives in many corporations now expect to review performance reports in conjunction with a *dashboard*, a customized graphical presentation of key performance parameters (see Figure 12.3). Second, consider how your audience members want to provide feedback on your report or proposal. For example, do they prefer to write comments on a printed document or edit a wiki article? Third, will people need to be able to search through your document or update it in the future? Fourth, bear in mind that your choice of medium and channel sends a message. A routine sales report dressed up in expensive multimedia will look like a waste of valuable company resources.

Figure 12.3 Dashboards
To help people avoid information overload, many companies now use dashboards to present carefully filtered highlights of key performance parameters. Dashboards are essentially super-summarized reports. The latest generation of software and mobile apps make it easy to customize screens to show each reader the specific summaries he or she needs to see.

ORGANIZING YOUR INFORMATION

The direct approach is often used for reports because it is efficient and easy to follow, so use it whenever your audience is likely to be receptive or at least open-minded to what you have to say (see Figure 12.4 on the next page). Lead with a summary of your key findings, conclusions, recommendations, or proposal, whichever is relevant. This "up-front" arrangement saves time and makes the rest of the report easier to follow. For those readers who have questions or want more information, later parts of the report provide complete findings and supporting details.

When your audience is likely to be receptive or at least open-minded, use the direct approach; if readers are skeptical about you or your report's main idea, use the indirect approach.

However, if the audience is unsure about your credibility or is not ready to accept your main idea without first seeing some reasoning or evidence, the indirect approach is a better choice because it gives you a chance to prove your points and gradually overcome audience reservations. To enable the use of AIDA-style persuasion, unsolicited proposals usually take the indirect approach. Whenever you use the indirect approach with a report or proposal, though, be sure to keep the report as short as you can so that readers get to the main idea as soon as possible.

When you outline your content, use informative ("talking") headings rather than simple descriptive ("topical") headings (see Table 12.2 on page 361). When they are in question or summary form, informative headings force you to really think through the content rather than simply identify the general topic area. Using informative headings will not only help you plan more effectively but also facilitate collaborative writing. A heading such as "Industry Characteristics" could mean five different things to the five people on your writing team, so use a heading that conveys a single, unambiguous meaning, such as "Flour milling is a mature industry."

MOBILE APP

The **Instapaper** mobile app lets you instantly save webpages and articles to read later, a convenient capability when you're exploring a topic and want to collect potential sources for review.

DIRECT APPROACH

Since the company's founding 25 years ago, we have provided regular repair service for all our electric appliances. This service has been an important selling point as well as a source of pride for our employees. However, rising labor costs have made it impossible to maintain profitability while offering competitive service rates. Last year, we lost $500,000 on our repair business.

Because of your concern over these losses, you asked me to study whether we should discontinue our repair service. After analyzing the situation in depth, I have concluded that the repair service is an expensive, impractical tradition, and I recommend that the service be discontinued.

By withdrawing from the electric appliance repair business, we can substantially improve our financial performance without damaging our reputation with customers. This conclusion is based on three basic points that are covered in the following pages:

- It is highly unlikely that we will ever be able to make a profit in the repair business.

- We can refer customers to a variety of qualified repair firms without significantly reducing customer satisfaction.

- Closing down the service operation will create few internal problems.

← Summarizes the situation

← Immediately introduces one of the report's major conclusions

← Reminds the audience why the report was prepared

← Presents the report's key recommendation, that the repair service should be discontinued

← Emphasizes the benefits of acting on the recommendation and addresses any fears about possible negative consequences

← Lists three important conclusions that led to the recommendation to end the service (notice how the indirect approach that follows presents these same three points as questions to be considered)

Summarizes the situation →

Reminds the audience why the report was prepared →

Indicates that conclusions and recommendations will be presented later in the report →

Introduces the three points that will eventually lead to the conclusions and ultimately to the recommendation →

INDIRECT APPROACH

Since the company's founding 25 years ago, we have provided regular repair service for all our electric appliances. This service has been an important selling point as well as a source of pride for our employees. However, rising labor costs have made it impossible to maintain profitability while offering competitive service rates.

Because of your concern over these losses, you have asked me to study whether we should discontinue our repair service. I have analyzed the situation in depth, and the following pages present my findings and recommendations for your review. The analysis addressed three basic questions:

- What is the extent of our losses, and what can we do to turn the business around?

- Would withdrawal hurt our sales of electrical appliances?

- What would be the internal repercussions of closing down the repair business?

Figure 12.4   Direct Approach Versus Indirect Approach in an Introduction
In the direct version of this introduction, the writer quickly presents the report's recommendation, followed by the conclusions that led to that recommendation. In the indirect version, the same topics are introduced in the same order, but no conclusions are drawn about them; the conclusions and the ultimate recommendation appear later, in the body of the report.

For a quick review of adapting the three-step process to long reports, refer to "Check-list: Adapting the Three-Step Writing Process to Informational and Analytical Reports." Sections later in this chapter provide specific advice on how to plan informational reports, analytical reports, and proposals.

TABLE 12.2 Types of Outline Headings

Descriptive (Topical)	Informative (Talking) Outline	
Outline	Question Form	Summary Form

1. Industry Characteristics
   a. Annual sales
   b. Profitability
   c. Growth rate
      i. Sales
      ii. Profit
	1. What is the nature of the industry?
	   a. What are the annual sales?
	   b. Is the industry profitable?
	   c. What is the pattern of growth?
	      i. Sales growth?
	      ii. Profit growth?
		1. Flour milling is a mature industry.
		   a. Market is large.
		   b. Profit margins are narrow.
		   c. Growth is modest.
		      i. Sales growth averages less than 3 percent a year.
		      ii. Profits are flat.

CHECKLIST ✔ **Adapting the Three-Step Writing Process to Informational and Analytical Reports**

A. Analyze the situation.
- ✔ Clearly define your purpose before you start writing.
- ✔ If you need to accomplish several goals in the report, identify all of them in advance.
- ✔ Prepare a work plan to guide your efforts.

B. Gather information.
- ✔ Determine whether you need to launch a separate research project to collect the necessary information.
- ✔ Reuse or adapt existing information whenever possible.

C. Select the best combination of medium and channel.
- ✔ Base your decision on audience expectations or requirements.

- ✔ Consider the need for commenting, revising, distributing, and archiving.
- ✔ Remember that the medium and channel you choose also send a message.

D. Organize your information.
- ✔ Use the direct approach if your audience is receptive.
- ✔ Use the indirect approach if your audience is skeptical.
- ✔ Use the indirect approach when you don't want to risk coming across as arrogant.

Supporting Your Messages with Reliable Information

2 LEARNING OBJECTIVE
Describe an effective process for conducting business research, explain how to evaluate the credibility of an information source, and identify the five ways to use research results.

Effective research involves a lot more than simply typing a few terms into a search engine. Save time and get better results by using a clear process (see Figure 12.5):

- **Plan your research.** Planning is the most important step of any research project, because a clear plan yields better results in less time.
- **Locate the data and information you need.** Your next step is to figure out *where* the data and information are and *how* to access them.

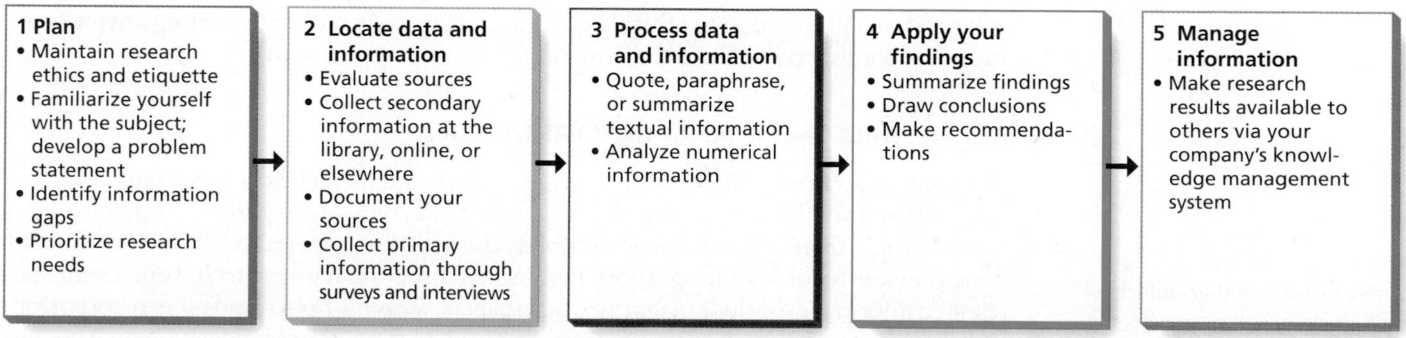

1 Plan	2 Locate data and information	3 Process data and information	4 Apply your findings	5 Manage information
• Maintain research ethics and etiquette • Familiarize yourself with the subject; develop a problem statement • Identify information gaps • Prioritize research needs	• Evaluate sources • Collect secondary information at the library, online, or elsewhere • Document your sources • Collect primary information through surveys and interviews	• Quote, paraphrase, or summarize textual information • Analyze numerical information	• Summarize findings • Draw conclusions • Make recommendations	• Make research results available to others via your company's knowledge management system

Figure 12.5 The Research Process
By following a methodical research process, you can save time and money while uncovering better information.

Researching without a plan wastes time and usually produces unsatisfactory results.

- **Process the data and information you located.** The data and information you find probably won't be in a form you can use immediately and may require statistical analysis or other processing.
- **Apply your findings.** You can apply your research findings in three ways: summarizing information, drawing conclusions, and developing recommendations.
- **Manage information efficiently.** Many companies try to maximize the return on the time and money invested in business research by collecting and sharing research results in a variety of systems, often referred to as *knowledge management systems*.

PLANNING YOUR RESEARCH

The *problem statement* guides your research by focusing on the decision you need to make or the conclusion you need to reach.

Start by developing a **problem statement** that defines the purpose of your research—the decision you need to make or the conclusion you need to reach at the end of the process. Next, identify the information required to make that decision or reach that conclusion. You can then begin to generate the questions that will constitute your research. Chances are you will have more questions than you have time or money to answer, so prioritize your information needs.

Before beginning any research project, remember that research carries some significant ethical responsibilities. Your research tactics affect the people you gather data and information from, and your research results can have wide-ranging effects inside and outside your company. To avoid ethical lapses, follow these guidelines:

- Keep an open mind so that you don't skew the research toward the answers you want or expect to see.
- Do not collect data from people without their knowledge or consent.
- Take every reasonable precaution to protect the identity of research participants and the security of the information they give you.
- Don't mislead people about the purposes of your research, such as asking them to participate in a survey that is really a sales pitch in disguise.
- Document sources and give appropriate credit.
- Respect your sources' *intellectual property rights* (the ownership of creative and intellectual works).[2]
- Don't distort information from your sources.
- Don't misrepresent who you are or what you intend to do with the research results.

REAL-TIME UPDATES

LEARN MORE BY VISITING THIS WEBSITE

Get clear answers to murky copyright questions

Find out what is covered by copyright, what isn't, and how to secure a copyright for your own work. Go to **real-timeupdates .com/ebc13** and select Learn More in the Students section.

In addition to ethics, etiquette deserves careful attention throughout the research process. For example, respect the time of anyone who agrees to be interviewed or to be a research participant, and maintain courtesy throughout the interview or research process.

As you plan your research, look for ways to take advantage of mobile devices and apps—they have become powerful tools for business research. For example, you can use them to conduct mobile surveys, take notes, make sketches, take photos, capture audio or video, and scan documents. Of course, you need to pay attention to ethical and legal concerns, such as not violating anyone's privacy or recording confidential information.

LOCATING DATA AND INFORMATION

Primary research gathers information that you collect specifically for a new research project; *secondary research* gathers information that others have compiled.

The range of sources available to business researchers today can be overwhelming. The good news is that if you have a question about an industry, a company, a market, a technology, or a financial topic, there's a good chance somebody else has already researched the subject. Research done previously for another purpose is considered **secondary research**; sources for such research information include magazines, newspapers, websites, books, and other reports. Don't let the name *secondary* mislead you, though. You want to start with secondary research because it can save you considerable time and money for many projects. In contrast, **primary research** involves the collection of new data through surveys, interviews, and other techniques.

DEVELOPING AS A PROFESSIONAL

Being Dependable and Accountable

By any definition, a "pro" is somebody who gets the job done. Develop a reputation as somebody people can count on. This means meeting your commitments, including keeping on schedule and staying within budgets. These are skills that take some time to develop as you discover how much time and money are required to accomplish various tasks and projects. With experience, you'll learn to be conservative with your commitments. You don't want to be known as someone who overpromises and underdelivers.

If you can't confidently predict how long a project will take or how much it will cost, be sure to let your client, colleagues, or supervisor know that. And if changing circumstances threaten your ability to meet a previous commitment, be sure to share that information with anyone who might be affected by your performance.

Being accountable also means owning up to your mistakes and learning from failure so that you can continue to improve. Pros don't make excuses or blame others. When they make mistakes—and everybody does—they face the situation head on, make amends, and move on.

CAREER APPLICATIONS

1. What steps could you take to make realistic commitments on tasks and projects in which you have little or no experience?

2. Does being accountable mean you never make mistakes? Explain your answer.

EVALUATING INFORMATION SOURCES

No matter where you're searching, it is your responsibility to separate quality information from biased material or unreliable junk to avoid tainting your results. Social media tools have complicated this challenge by making many new sources of information available. On the positive side, independent sources communicating through blogs, Twitter, wikis, user-generated content sites, and podcasting channels can provide valuable and unique insights, often from experts whose voices might never be heard otherwise. On the negative side, these nontraditional information sources often lack the editorial boards and fact-checkers commonly used in traditional publishing. You cannot assume that the information you find in blogs and other sources is accurate, objective, and current. Answer the following questions about each piece of material:

Evaluate your sources carefully to avoid embarrassing and potentially damaging mistakes.

- **Does the source have a reputation for honesty and reliability?** Generally speaking, you can feel more comfortable using information from an established source that has a reputation for accuracy. For sources that are new or obscure, your safest bet is to corroborate anything you learn with information from several other sources.

- **Is the source potentially biased?** To interpret an organization's information, you need to know its point of view. For example, information about a particular company can be presented quite differently by a competitor, a union trying to organize the company's workforce, an investment research firm, and an environmental advocacy group. Information from a source with a distinct point of view isn't necessarily bad, of course, but knowing this context is always helpful and sometimes essential for interpreting the information correctly.

- **What is the purpose of the material?** For instance, was the material designed to inform others of new research, advance a political position, or promote a product? Be sure to distinguish among advertising, advocating, and informing. And don't lower your guard just because an organization has a reassuring name like the American Institute for the Advancement of All Things Good and Wonderful; many innocuously labeled groups advocate a particular line of political, social, or economic thinking.

- **Is the author credible?** Is the author a professional journalist, a subject-matter expert, or merely someone with an opinion?

- **Where did the source get *its* information?** Try to find out who collected the data and the methods they used.

- **Can you verify the material independently?** Verification can uncover biases or mistakes, which is particularly important when the information goes beyond simple facts to include projections, interpretations, and estimates. If you can't verify critical information, let your audience know that.

- **Is the material current and complete?** Make sure you are using the most current information available by checking the publication date of a source. Look for a "posted on" or "updated on" date with online material. If you can't find a date, don't assume the information is current without verifying it against another source. Also, make sure you have evaluated the entire source document, not just a part of it.
- **Are all claims supported with evidence?** Are opinions presented as facts? Does the writer make broad claims, such as "It is widely believed that . . ." without citing any surveys to support this?
- **Does the information make sense?** Finally, step back and ask whether the information makes sense. If that little voice in your head says that something sounds suspicious, pay attention to it.

You probably won't have time to conduct a thorough background check on all your sources, so focus your efforts on the most important or most suspicious pieces of information.

USING YOUR RESEARCH RESULTS

After you collect data and information, the next step is converting it into usable content.

After you've collected data and information, the next step is to transform this raw material into the specific content you need. This step can involve analyzing numeric data; quoting, paraphrasing, or summarizing textual material; drawing conclusions; and making recommendations.

Analyzing Data

Mean, median, and mode provide specific insights into sets of numerical data.

Business research often yields numeric data, but these numbers alone might not provide the insights managers need in order to make good business decisions. Fortunately, even without advanced statistical techniques, you can use simple arithmetic to help extract meaning from sets of research data. Table 12.3 shows several answers you can gain about a collection of numbers, for instance. The **mean** (which is what people are usually referring to when they use the term *average*) is the sum of all the items in the group divided by the number of items in that group. The **median** is the "middle of the road," or the midpoint of a series, with an equal number of items above and below. The **mode** is the number that occurs more often than any other in the sample; it's the best answer to a question such as "What is the usual amount?" Each of the three measures can tell you different things about a set of data.

Be careful not to let any of these statistical parameters create a skewed impression of the data set. For example, the mean value of 9, 11, 12, 156 is 47, which isn't close to any of the individual values and might not reflect the true nature of the data. The value of 156 in this case would be considered an *outlier* that warrants closer analysis.

TABLE 12.3	Three Types of Data Measures: Mean, Median, and Mode	
Wilson	$3,000	
Green	5,000	
Carrick	6,000	
Cho	7,000	← Mean
Keeble	7,500	← Median
Lopes	8,500	
O'Toole	8,500	← Mode
Mannix	8,500	
Caruso	9,000	
Total	$63,000	

Next, look at the data to spot **trends**—patterns that take place over time, including growth, decline, and cyclical trends that alternate between growth and decline. By examining data over time, you can sometimes detect patterns and relationships that help answer important questions.

Trends suggest directions or patterns in a series of data points.

Statistical measures and trends identify *what* is happening. To understand *why* those things are happening, look at **causation** (the cause-and-effect link between two factors, where one of them causes the other to happen) and **correlation** (the simultaneous change in two variables you're measuring, such as customer satisfaction dropping when product reliability drops). Bear in mind that causation can be easy to assume but difficult to prove. The drop in customer satisfaction might have been caused by a new accounting system that fouled up customer invoices. To prove causation, you need to be able to isolate the suspected cause as the *only* potential source of the change in the measured effect. However, eliminating all but one possible cause isn't always feasible, so you often must apply careful judgment to correlations. Researchers frequently explore the relationships between subsets of data using a technique called *cross-tabulation*. For instance, if you're trying to figure out why total sales rose or fell, you might look separately at sales data by age, gender, location, and product type.

Causation shows cause-and-effect relationships; *correlation* indicates simultaneous changes in two variables that may not necessarily be causally related.

Quoting, Paraphrasing, and Summarizing Information

You can use textual information from secondary sources in three ways. *Quoting* a source means you reproduce the material exactly as you found it (giving full credit to the source, of course). Use direct quotations when the original language will enhance your argument or when rewording the passage would reduce its impact. However, don't go overboard with direct quotes. Using too many creates a choppy patchwork of varying styles and gives the impression that all you've done is piece together the work of other people. When quoting sources, set off shorter passages with quotation marks and set off longer passages (generally five lines or more) as separate, indented paragraphs.

Quoting a source means reproducing the content exactly and indicating who originally created the information.

You can often maximize the impact of secondary material in your own writing by *paraphrasing* it: restating the underlying ideas and information in your own words.[3] Paraphrasing helps you maintain a consistent tone while using vocabulary that's familiar to your audience. Of course, you still need to credit the originator of the information, but you don't need quotation marks or indented paragraphs. Follow these tips to paraphrase effectively and ethically:[4]

Paraphrasing is expressing someone else's ideas in your own words.

- Read and analyze the source material until you are thoroughly familiar with its main idea and key points. Reread it as many times as needed to make sure you understand it.
- For longer passages or technical material, jot down notes in your own words to remind yourself of the key points.
- Without looking at the original, express its main idea and key points in your own words. You are writing from your memory of the material or from your notes here, not from the material itself.
- As you write your version, imagine that you are explaining it to someone else.
- If it helps with expressing the key ideas in your own words, consider changing the structure of the material (making sure it still flows logically and smoothly).
- For words or phrases that are commonly used in a particular field, you don't need to replace them with your own language. For example, "closing the books" is a common phrase in accounting, so you don't need to replace it. However, if the source used an original phrasing such as "slam the door on a disastrous quarter," you would need to rephrase this in your own language or quote it directly.
- Revise your draft for clarity and conciseness, and to make sure it is written in your voice.
- Document the source using a footnote or other citation method.

Summarizing is similar to paraphrasing but presents the gist of the material in fewer words than the original by leaving out details, examples, and less important information (see Figure 12.6 on the next page). Summarizing is not always a simple task, and your audience will judge your ability to separate significant issues from less significant details. Like quotations and paraphrases, summaries also require complete documentation of sources.

Summarizing is similar to paraphrasing but distills the content into fewer words.

Analyze the text to find main idea, major supporting points, and details

Original: 116 words		45-word summary
Our facilities costs spiraled out of control last year. The 23 percent jump was far ahead of every other cost category in the company and many times higher than the 4 percent average rise for commercial real estate in the Portland metropolitan area. The rise can be attributed to many factors, but the major factors include repairs (mostly electrical and structural problems at the downtown office), energy (most of our offices are heated by electricity, the price of which has been increasing much faster than for oil or gas), and last but not least, the loss of two sublease tenants whose rent payments made a substantial dent in our cost profile for the past five years.	*Main idea* → Our facilities costs spiraled out of control last year. The 23 percent jump was far ahead of every other cost category in the company and many times higher than the 4 percent average rise for commercial real estate in the Portland metropolitan area. *Major support points* → The rise can be attributed to many factors, but the major factors include repairs (mostly electrical and structural problems at the downtown office), energy (most of our offices are heated by electricity, the price of which has *Details* → been increasing much faster than for oil or gas), and last but not least, the loss of two sublease tenants whose rent payments made a substantial dent in our cost profile for the past five years.	Our facilities costs jumped 23 percent last year, far ahead of every other cost category in the company and many times higher than the 4 percent local average. The major factors contributing to the increase are repairs, energy, and the loss of two sublease tenants.

22-word summary

Our facilities costs jumped 23 percent last year, due mainly to rising repair and energy costs and the loss of sublease income. |

Figure 12.6 Summarizing Effectively
To summarize a section of text, first analyze it to find the main idea, the major support points, and the less important details. Then assemble the appropriate pieces with additional words and phrases as needed to ensure a smooth flow.

Of course, all three approaches require careful attention to ethics. When quoting directly, take care not to distort the original intent of the material by quoting selectively or out of context. And never resort to *plagiarism*—presenting someone else's words as your own, such as copying material from an online source and dropping it into a report without giving proper credit.

Drawing Conclusions

A *conclusion* is a logical interpretation of the facts and other information in a report.

A **conclusion** is a logical interpretation of the facts and other information in a report. A sound conclusion is not only logical but flows from the information included in a report, meaning that it should be based on the information in the report and shouldn't rely on information that isn't in the report. Moreover, if you or the organization you represent have certain biases that influence your conclusion, ethics obligate you to inform the audience accordingly.

Reaching good conclusions based on the evidence at hand is one of the most important skills you can develop in your business career. In fact, the ability to see patterns and possibilities that others can't see is one of the hallmarks of innovative business leaders. Consequently, take your time with this part of the process. Play "devil's advocate," attacking your conclusion as an audience might to make sure it stands up to rigorous scrutiny.

Making Recommendations

A *recommendation* suggests a course of action in response to a conclusion.

Whereas a conclusion interprets information, a **recommendation** suggests what to do about the information. The following example shows the difference between a conclusion and a recommendation:

Conclusion

On the basis of its track record and current stock price, I believe that this company is an attractive buy.

Recommendation

I recommend that we offer to buy the company at a 10 percent premium over the current market value of its stock.

To be credible, recommendations must be practical and based on sound logical analysis. Also, when making a recommendation, be certain you have adequately described the recommended course of action so that readers aren't left wondering what happens next.

Conducting Secondary Research

Even if you intend to eventually conduct primary research, start with a review of any available secondary research. Inside your company, you might be able to find a variety of helpful reports and other documents. Outside the company, you can choose from a wide range of print and online resources, both in libraries and online. Table 12.4 provides a small sample of the many secondary resources available.

3 LEARNING OBJECTIVE
Explain the role of secondary research, and describe the two major categories of online research tools.

FINDING INFORMATION AT A LIBRARY

Public, corporate, and university libraries offer printed sources with information that is not available online, as well as online sources that are available only by subscription. For entrepreneurs and small-business owners in particular, local libraries can provide access to expensive databases and other information sources that would be beyond their reach otherwise.[5] Libraries are also where you'll find one of your most important resources: librarians. Reference librarians are trained in research techniques and can often help you find obscure information you can't find on your own. They can also direct you to the typical library's many sources of business information:

- **Newspapers and periodicals.** Libraries offer access (in print and online) to a wide variety of popular magazines, general business magazines, *trade journals* (which provide information about specific professions and industries), and *academic journals* (which provide research-oriented articles from researchers and educators).

You'll want to start most research projects by conducting secondary research first.

Libraries offer information and resources you can't find anywhere else—including experienced research librarians.

TABLE 12.4 Selected Resources for Business Research

COMPANY, INDUSTRY, AND PRODUCT RESOURCES

AnnualReports.com (www.annualreports.com). Free access to annual reports from thousands of public companies.

Brands and Their Companies/Companies and Their Brands. Data on several hundred thousand consumer products, manufacturers, importers, marketers, and distributors.

Dun & Bradstreet A variety of directories and databases covering finance, sales and marketing, supply chain management, and other topics.

Manufacturing & Distribution USA. Data on thousands of companies in the manufacturing, wholesaling, and retailing sectors.

NAICS Codes (www.census.gov/eos/www/naics). North American Industry Classification System.

Reference USA. Concise information on millions of U.S. companies; subscription database.

SEC filings (www.sec.gov/edgar.shtml). SEC filings, including 10-Ks, 10-Qs, annual reports, and prospectuses for U.S. public firms.

Standard & Poor's Net Advantage. Comprehensive range of directories and databases focusing on publicly traded companies and their industries and markets.

ThomasNet (www.thomasnet.com). Information on thousands of manufacturers, indexed by company name and product.

TRADEMARKS AND PATENTS

United States Patent and Trademark Office (www.uspto.gov). Trademark and patent information records.

STATISTICS AND OTHER BUSINESS DATA

U.S. Bureau of Economic Analysis (www.bea.gov). Large collection of economic and government data.

Europa—The European Union Online (http://europa.eu). A portal that provides up-to-date coverage of current affairs, legislation, policies, and EU statistics.

Annual Statement Studies. Industry, financial, and performance ratios published by the Risk Management Association.

U.S. Census Bureau (www.census.gov). Interactive data tools covering U.S. economic, social, political, and industrial statistics.

U.S. Bureau of Labor Statistics (www.bls.gov). Extensive national and regional information on labor and business, including employment, industry growth, productivity, the Consumer Price Index (CPI), and the overall U.S. economy.

- **Business books.** Although less timely than newspapers, periodicals, and online sources, business books provide in-depth coverage and analysis that often can't be found anywhere else.
- **Directories.** Thousands of directories are published in print and digital formats in the United States, and many include information for all kinds of professions, industries, and special-interest groups.
- **Government publications.** Information on laws, court decisions, tax questions, regulatory issues, and other governmental concerns can often be found in collections of government documents.
- **Databases.** Databases offer vast collections of computer-searchable information, often in specific areas such as business, law, science, technology, and education. Some of these are available only by institutional subscription, so the library may be your only way to gain access to them. Some libraries offer remote online access to some or all databases; for others, you'll need to visit in person.

Local, state, and federal government agencies publish a huge array of information that is helpful to business researchers.

FINDING INFORMATION ONLINE

Online research tools fall into two basic categories: search tools and monitoring tools.

The internet can be a tremendous source of business information, provided you know where to look and how to use the tools available. Roughly speaking, the tools fall into two categories: those you can use to actively *search* for existing information and those you can use to *monitor* selected sources for new information. (Some tools can perform both functions.)

Online Search Tools

General-purpose search engines are tremendously powerful tools, but they have several shortcomings you need to consider.

The most familiar search tools are general-purpose search engines, such as Google and Bing, which scan millions of websites to identify individual webpages that contain a specific word or phrase and then attempt to rank the results from most useful to least useful. Website

---

INTELLIGENT COMMUNICATION TECHNOLOGY

Finding Meaning with Text Mining

You've probably experienced both these frustrations with search engines: You need to find something but you're not quite sure which terms to use, so you poke around hoping you'll find something, or you get lots of irrelevant results that happen to include your search terms but have nothing to do with what you are looking for.

Text mining, also known as *text analytics*, promises the ability to find meaning and patterns in mountains of textual material by going far beyond conventional search capabilities. Unlike simple word and phrase searches that require exact or near-exact matches, text mining systems can find relevant material even if you don't know the specific terminology the sources use, or if they use different words to express the same concepts. By applying linguistic principles through *natural language processing*, text mining systems can recognize meaning in context. This capability also helps text mining tools filter out irrelevant material that uses the same terms, such as excluding material about biological reproduction if you are searching for material about document or file reproduction.

Another major benefit of text mining is the ability to copy all the searched material and reorganize it into consistent records, even if it came from a variety of sources in different formats. For example, a system could be instructed to pull in social media posts, emails, and text messages and "clean" and merge them into a single data set for easier analysis.

Text mining is a potential solution whenever a business needs to analyze hundreds, thousands, or even millions of text records. Examples of current applications include product research and development (such as searching patent records for similar designs), sentiment analysis (finding trends of satisfaction or dissatisfaction in public tweets, customer emails, and other sources), competitive intelligence (finding out what competitors are up to by analyzing their document and social media output), and risk management (such as analyzing financial news and reports in search of potential risks).

WHAT'S YOUR TAKE?
1. Natural language processing applies the same linguistic rules and concepts that humans use to encode and decode language. Do you think computers will ever be able to understand text the way that humans can? Why or why not?
2. How do you feel about your public social media posts being available for companies and other organizations to analyze?

Sources: "About Text Mining," IBM Knowledge Center, accessed 7 April 2018, www.ibm.com; "What Is NLP Text Mining?" Linguamatics, accessed 7 April 2018, www.linguamatics.com; Text Mining Applications: 10 Examples Today," Expert System, 18 April 2016, www.expertsystem.com.

owners use *search engine optimization* techniques to help boost their rankings in the results, but the ranking algorithms are kept secret to prevent unfair manipulation of the results.

For all their ease and power, conventional search engines have three primary short-comings: (1) no human editors are involved to evaluate the quality or ranking of the search results; (2) various engines use different search techniques, so they often find different material; and (3) search engines can't reach all the content on some websites (this part of the internet is sometimes called the *hidden internet* or the *deep internet*).

A variety of tools are available to overcome these weaknesses of general-purpose search engines, and you should consider one or more of them in your business research. *Metasearch engines* (such as Bovée and Thill's Web Search, at **websearch.businesscommunicationnetwork .com**) help overcome the differences among search engines by formatting your search request for multiple search engines, making it easy to find a broader range of results. With a few easy steps, you can compare results from multiple search engines to make sure you are getting a broad view of the material.

Metasearch engines format your search request for multiple search engines, making it easy to find a broader range of results.

Online databases help address the challenge of the hidden internet by offering access to newspapers, magazines, journals, digital copies of books, and other resources often not available with standard search engines. Some of these databases offer free access to the public, but others require a subscription (check with your library).

Online databases can give you access to resources you can't reach with regular search engines.

Online Monitoring Tools

One of the most powerful aspects of online research is the ability to automatically monitor selected sources for new information. The possibilities include subscribing to newsfeeds from blogs, following experts on Twitter, setting up alerts on search engines and online databases, and using specialized monitors such as TweetDeck and Hootsuite to track tweets that mention specific companies or other terms.

The tools available for monitoring online sources for new information can help you track industry trends, consumer sentiment, and other information.

Search Tips

Search engines, metasearch engines, and databases offer a variety of ways to find information. Unfortunately, no two of them work in exactly the same way, and you have to learn how to use each one most effectively. This learning may take a few extra minutes at the beginning of your research, but it could save you hours of lost time later—and save you from embarrassing oversights. You can usually find a Help or Support page that explains both basic and advanced functions, with advice on how to use each tool most effectively.

Search tools work in different ways, and you can get unpredictable results if you don't know how each one operates.

To make the best use of any search tool, keep the following points in mind:

- **Think before you search.** The neatly organized results you get from a search engine can create the illusion that the internet is an orderly warehouse of all the information in the universe, but the reality is far different. The internet is an incomplete, unorganized hodgepodge of millions of independent websites with information that ranges in value from priceless to worse than worthless. After you have identified what you need to know, spend a few moments thinking about where that information might be found, how it might be structured, and what terms various websites might use to describe it.
- **Pay attention to the details.** Details can make all the difference in a search. For example, you can filter results according to when items were published online. This setting could drastically change your results, so make sure you haven't inadvertently limited your search by selecting a narrower time frame than you really want.
- **Don't limit yourself to a regular web search engine.** Search engines are remarkably powerful, but they can't access all online content. Moreover, the content you need might not be online or even in digital form.
- **Review the search and display options carefully.** When using advanced search or while searching in databases, pay close attention to whether you are searching in the title, author, subject, or document field and whether the search is limited to particular types of documents (such as full-text documents only). Each choice will return different results. And when the results are displayed, verify the presentation order; results might be sorted by date or by relevance.
- **Try variations of your terms.** If you can't find what you're looking for, try abbreviations (*CEO, CPA*), synonyms (*man, male*), related terms (*child, adolescent, youth*), different

MOBILE APP
Access and add to your **Zotero** research files with a variety of Zotero-compatible mobile apps.

spellings (*dialog, dialogue*), singular and plural forms (*woman, women*), and nouns and adjectives (*manager, management, managerial*).

- **Adjust the scope of your search, if needed.** If a search yields little or no information, broaden your search by specifying fewer terms. Conversely, if you're inundated with too many hits, use more terms to narrow your search.
- **Review the features each search tool offers.** For example, some systems will show you similar search terms that other people have used, which can help you explore a topic by considering angles you haven't thought of.
- **Look beyond the first page of results.** Don't assume that the highest-ranking results are the best sources for you. For instance, websites that haven't been optimized for search engines or aren't as popular won't rank as high (meaning they won't show up in the first few pages of results), but they may be far better for your purposes.

Search technologies continue to evolve rapidly, so be on the lookout for new ways to find the information you need. Again, librarians can be your best ally here.

Other powerful search tools include *enterprise search engines* that search all the computers on a company's network and *research and content managers* such as LiveBinders and the Zotero browser extension. And don't overlook the search functions in workplace messaging systems, groupware, and other closed systems.

DOCUMENTING YOUR SOURCES

Proper documentation of the sources you use is both an ethical requirement and an important resource for your readers.

Documenting your sources serves three important functions: It properly and ethically credits the person who created the original material, it shows your audience that you have sufficient support for your message, and it helps readers explore your topic in more detail, if desired. Be sure to take advantage of the source documentation tools in your software, such as automatic endnote or footnote tracking.

Appendix B discusses the common methods of documenting sources. Whatever method you choose, documentation is necessary for books, articles, blogs, websites, tweets, tables, charts, diagrams, song lyrics, scripted dialogue, letters, speeches—anything you take from someone else, including ideas and information you've reexpressed through paraphrasing or summarizing. However, you do not have to cite a source for knowledge that's generally known among your readers, such as the fact that Microsoft is a large software company or that computers are widely used in business today.

Conducting Primary Research

4 **LEARNING OBJECTIVE**
Explain the role of primary research, and identify the two most common forms of primary research for business communication purposes.

If secondary research can't provide the information and insights you need, you may have to gather the information yourself with primary research. The two most common primary research methods for report writing are surveys and interviews. Other primary techniques are observations (including tracking the behavior of website visitors) and experiments (in special situations such as test marketing), but they're less commonly used for day-to-day business research.

CONDUCTING SURVEYS

Surveys and interviews are the most common primary research techniques for business communication projects.

Surveys need to reliable, valid, and representative to be useful.

Surveys can provide invaluable insights, but only if they are *reliable* (would produce identical results if repeated under similar conditions) and *valid* (measure what they're designed to measure). To conduct a survey that generates reliable and valid results, you need to choose research participants carefully and develop an effective set of questions (see Figure 12.7). To develop an effective survey questionnaire, follow these tips:[6]

QUESTION TYPE	EXAMPLE
Open-ended	How would you describe the flavor of this ice cream?
Either-or	Do you think this ice cream is too rich? _____ Yes _____ No
Multiple choice	Which description best fits the taste of this ice cream? (Choose only one.) a. Delicious b. Too fruity c. Too sweet d. Too intense e. Bland f. Stale
Scale	Please mark an X on the scale to indicate how you perceive the texture of this ice cream. Too light Light Creamy Too creamy
Checklist	Which of the following ice cream brands do you recognize? (Check all that apply.) _____ Ben & Jerry's _____ Breyers _____ Carvel _____ Dreyer's _____ Häagen-Dazs
Ranking	Rank these flavors in order of your preference, from 1 (most preferred) to 5 (least preferred): _____ Vanilla _____ Cherry _____ Strawberry _____ Chocolate _____ Coconut
Short-answer	In the past 2 weeks, how many times did you buy ice cream in a grocery store? _____ In the past 2 weeks, how many times did you buy ice cream in an ice cream shop? _____

Figure 12.7 Types of Survey Questions
For each question you have in your survey, choose the type of question that will elicit the most useful answers.

- Provide clear instructions to make sure people can answer every question correctly.
- Don't ask for information that people can't be expected to remember, such as how many times they went grocery shopping in the past year.
- Keep the questionnaire short and easy to complete; don't expect people to give you more than 10 or 15 minutes of their time.
- Whenever possible, formulate questions to provide answers that are easy to analyze. Numbers and facts are easier to summarize than opinions, for instance.

Provide clear instructions in a survey in order to prevent mistaken answers.

- Avoid *leading questions* that could bias your survey. If you ask, "Do you prefer that we stay open in the evenings for customer convenience?" you'll no doubt get a "yes." Instead, ask, "What time of day do you normally do your shopping?"
- Avoid vague descriptors such as *often* or *frequently*. Such terms mean different things to different people.
- Make each question about a single idea. Instead of asking "Do you read newspapers on your PC and on your smartphone?" ask about each device separately.

When selecting people to participate in a survey, the most critical task is getting a *representative sample* of the entire population in question. Doing so involves identifying enough of the right kinds of respondents and persuading them to participate. Every method of contacting people for research has limitations that need to be addressed to avoid *sampling bias*, which can skew a survey by under- or overrepresenting certain segments of the population. For example, the surveys you see on many websites capture only the opinions of people who visit the sites and who want to participate, which might not be a representative sample of the population of interest.

For major business decisions that rely on accurate survey data, the best course is to hire research professionals who know how to design surveys, select representative samples, and assess the statistical accuracy of the results. For many business writing projects, however, you can get useful results using less formal methods. To survey employees within your company, for instance, posting a questionnaire on your internal messaging or social networking system will probably yield adequate information as long as a reasonable portion of the workforce responds.

REAL-TIME UPDATES

LEARN MORE BY VISITING THIS WEBSITE

An in-depth look at professional-grade survey research

The Pew Research Center is one of the most respected research organizations in the world; learn how they try to get it right. Go to **real-timeupdates.com/ebc13** and select Learn More in the Students section.

CONDUCTING INTERVIEWS

Interviews can take place online, over the phone, or in person, and they can involve individuals or groups.

Getting in-depth information straight from an expert, customer, or other interested party can be a great method for collecting primary information. Interviews can have a variety of formats, from email exchanges to group discussions. (Note that interviews can be done as part of formal survey research as well.)

Open-ended questions can't be answered with a simple yes or no; *closed questions* elicit a specific answer from a small set of choices.

Ask **open-ended questions** (such as "Why do you believe that South America represents a better opportunity than Europe for this product line?") to solicit opinions, insights, and information. Ask **closed questions** to elicit a specific answer, such as yes or no. However, don't use too many closed questions in an interview, or the experience will feel more like a simple survey and won't take full advantage of the interactive interview setting.

Arrange the sequence of questions to help uncover layers of information.

Think carefully about the sequence of your questions and the potential answers so you can arrange them in an order that helps uncover layers of information. Also consider providing each subject with a list of questions at least a day or two before the interview, especially if you'd like to quote your subjects in writing or if your questions might require people to conduct research or think extensively about the answers. If you want to record interviews, ask ahead of time; never record without permission.

As a reminder of the tasks involved in interviews, see "Checklist: Conducting Effective Information Interviews."

CHECKLIST ✔ Conducting Effective Information Interviews

- ✔ Learn about the person you are going to interview.
- ✔ Formulate your main idea to ensure effective focus.
- ✔ Choose the length, style, and organization of the interview.
- ✔ Select question types to elicit the specific information you want.

- ✔ Design each question carefully to collect useful answers.
- ✔ Limit the number of questions you ask.
- ✔ Consider recording the interview if the subject permits.

Planning Informational Reports

5 LEARNING OBJECTIVE
Explain how to plan informational reports and website content.

Informational reports provide the feedback that employees, managers, and others need in order to make decisions, take action, and respond to changes. As Figure 12.1 on page 356 indicates, informational reports can be grouped into four general categories:

- **Reports to monitor and control operations.** Managers rely on a wide range of reports to see how well their companies are functioning. *Plans* establish expectations and guidelines to direct future action. Among the most important of these are *business plans*, which summarize a proposed business venture and describe the company's goals and plans for each major functional area (see "Creating Successful Business Plans" below). *Operating reports* provide feedback on a variety of an organization's functions, including sales, inventories, expenses, shipments, and so on. *Personal activity reports* provide information regarding an individual's experiences during sales calls, industry conferences, and other activities.
- **Reports to implement policies and procedures.** *Policy reports* range from brief descriptions of business procedures to manuals that run dozens or hundreds of pages. *Position papers*, sometimes called *white papers* or *backgrounders*, outline an organization's official position on issues that affect the company's success.
- **Reports to demonstrate compliance.** Businesses are required to submit a variety of *compliance reports* to government regulators, from tax returns to reports describing the proper handling of hazardous materials.
- **Reports to document progress.** Supervisors, investors, and customers frequently expect to be informed of the progress of projects and other activities. *Progress reports* range from simple updates in memo form to comprehensive status reports.

Informational reports are used to monitor and control operations, to implement policies and procedures, to demonstrate compliance, and to document progress.

ORGANIZING INFORMATIONAL REPORTS

In most cases, the direct approach is the best choice for informational reports because you are simply conveying information. However, if the information is disappointing, such as a project being behind schedule or over budget, you might consider using the indirect approach to build up to the bad news. Most informational reports use a topical organization, arranging material in one of the following ways:

A *topical organization* arranges material by comparison, importance, sequence, chronology, geography, or category.

- **Comparison.** Showing similarities and differences (or advantages and disadvantages) between two or more entities
- **Importance.** Building up from the least important item to the most important (or going from most important to the least, if you don't think your audience will read the entire report)
- **Sequence.** Organizing the steps or stages in a process or procedure
- **Chronology.** Organizing a chain of events in order from oldest to newest or vice versa
- **Geography.** Organizing by region, city, state, country, or other geographic unit
- **Category.** Grouping by topical category, such as sales, profit, cost, or investment

Whichever pattern you choose, use it consistently so that readers can easily follow your discussion from start to finish. In some instances, you might be expected to follow a particular type of organization.

Regardless the structure, effective informational reports need to be audience centered, logical, focused, and easy to follow. Remember that your audience expects you to sort out the details and separate major points from minor points.

CREATING SUCCESSFUL BUSINESS PLANS

A **business plan** is a comprehensive document that describes a company's mission, structure, objectives, and operations. Roughly speaking, business plans can be written during three separate phases of a company's life: (1) before the company is launched, when the founders are defining their vision of what the company will be; (2) when the company is seeking funding, in which case the business plan takes on a persuasive tone to convince outsiders that investing in the firm would be a profitable decision; and (3) after the company is up and

A *business plan* is a comprehensive document that describes a company's mission, structure, objectives, and operations.

running and the business plan serves as a monitor-and-control mechanism to make sure operations are staying on track.

At any stage, a comprehensive business plan forces you to think about personnel, marketing, facilities, suppliers, distribution, and a host of other issues vital to a company's success. The specific elements to include in a business plan can vary based on the situation; here are the sections typically included in a plan written to attract outside investors:[7]

The summary should convey the business model, which defines how the company will generate revenue and produce a profit.

- **Summary.** In one or two paragraphs, summarize your business concept, particularly the *business model*, which defines how the company will generate revenue and produce a profit. The summary must be compelling, catching the investor's attention and giving him or her reasons to keep reading. Describe your product or service and its market potential. Highlight some things about your company and its leaders that will distinguish your firm from the competition. Summarize your financial projections and indicate how much money you will need from investors or lenders and where it will be spent.
- **Mission and objectives.** Explain the purpose of your business and what you hope to accomplish.
- **Company and industry.** Give full background information on the origins and structure of your venture and the characteristics of the industry in which you plan to compete.
- **Products or services.** Concisely describe your products or services, focusing on their unique attributes and their appeal to customers.
- **Market and competition.** Provide data that will persuade investors that you understand your target market and can achieve your sales goals. Be sure to identify the strengths and weaknesses of your competitors.
- **Management.** Summarize the background and qualifications of the key management personnel in your company. Include résumés in an appendix.
- **Marketing strategy.** Provide projections of sales volume and market share; outline a strategy for identifying and reaching potential customers, setting prices, providing customer support, and physically delivering your products or services. Whenever possible, include evidence of customer acceptance, such as advance product orders.
- **Design and development plans.** If your product requires design or development, describe the nature and extent of what needs to be done, including costs and possible problems. For new or unusual products, you may want to explain how the product will be manufactured.
- **Operations plan.** Provide information on facilities, equipment, and personnel requirements.
- **Overall schedule.** Forecast important milestones in the company's growth and development, including when you need to be fully staffed and when your products will be ready for the market.
- **Critical risks and problems.** Identify significant negative factors and discuss them honestly.
- **Financial projections and requirements.** Include a detailed budget of start-up and operating costs, as well as projections for income, expenses, and cash flow for the first few years of business. Identify the company's financing needs and potential sources, if appropriate.
- **Exit strategy.** Explain how investors will be able to profit from their investment, such as through a public stock offering, sale of the company, or a buyback of the investors' interest.

As the Strategyzer story at the beginning of the chapter indicates, not everyone believes a conventional business plan is the right approach for every start-up company. If a company still needs to prove the viability of its business model or key product, the time it would take to write a full business plan might be better spent on getting the product or service operational and in front of customers in order to prove its viability.

A regular business plan would make more sense after that, when the company needs to transition from start-up to ongoing operations.

ORGANIZING WEBSITE CONTENT

Many websites, particularly company websites, function as informational reports, offering sections with information about the company and its history, products and services, executive team, and so on. Most of what you've already learned about informational reports applies to website writing, but the online environment requires some special considerations.

Websites are potentially much more flexible than static reports, which can be both a good thing and a bad thing, depending on how carefully they are designed. Websites often have multiple audiences with distinct information needs, for example. A corporate website might have sections designed for investors, the news media, existing customers, potential customers, local communities, and job hunters. Moreover, many visitors don't start at the home page and follow a linear path through a website. A search engine may point them to a lower-level page, and from there they move around the site by following links that look promising.

The flexibility of the web makes it possible to address a wide range of audience needs with a single website.

To be most effective, a website needs to provide each type of visitor a clear path into the information he or she wants (see Figure 12.8). Website designers use the term **information architecture** to describe the structure and navigational flow of all the parts of a website. As they develop the site architecture, they try to simulate how various audiences will enter and explore the site, based on the information the visitors are likely to be searching for.

The information architecture of a website is the equivalent of the outline for a paper report, but it tends to be much more complicated than a simple linear outline.

If you're responsible for designing the structure of a website, keep the following advice in mind:

- Given the sizable percentage of readers who now access websites with tablets and smartphones, many companies opt for a *mobile-first* design approach that supports touch interaction with simplified navigation.
- Give your readers control by creating links and pathways that let them explore on their own.
- Use simple, clear language for page titles and links so that visitors always know where they are and where a link will take them.

The "breadcrumb" trail shows visitors where they are and makes it easy to climb up the hierarchy to higher-level pages.

Content is organized in a logical and visible hierarchy (with four subtopics under the heading of "Composing and sending.").

By dividing the content into *essentials and extras*, the page helps visitors focus on material they are most likely to need first.

Readers don't always know how to phrase what they are looking for, so the list of related topics might help if this page doesn't offer the information they need.

Figure 12.8 Organizing Website Content
This page from the Google Help feature for Gmail demonstrates several good points about organizing website content.

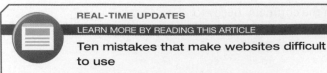

- Follow the conventions used by most business websites, such as having an "About Us" page that describes the company and a "Contact Us" page with phone, email, and messaging details.
- Help online readers scan and absorb information by breaking it into self-contained, easily readable chunks that are linked together logically. This is particularly helpful for mobile readers.

Planning Analytical Reports

6 LEARNING OBJECTIVE
Identify the three most common ways to organize analytical reports.

The purpose of analytical reports is to analyze, to understand, or to explain—to think through a problem or an opportunity and explain how it affects an organization and how the organization should respond. In many cases, you'll also be expected to make a recommendation based on your analysis. As you saw in Figure 12.1, analytical reports fall into three basic categories:

Analytical reports are used to assess opportunities, to solve problems, and to support decisions.

- **Reports to assess opportunities.** Every business opportunity carries some degree of risk and requires a variety of decisions and actions to capitalize on the opportunity. You can use analytical reports to assess both risk and required decisions and actions. For instance, *market analysis reports* are used to judge the likelihood of success for new products or sales. *Due diligence* reports examine the financial aspects of a proposed decision, such as acquiring another company.
- **Reports to solve problems.** Managers often assign *troubleshooting reports* when they need to understand why something isn't working properly and how to fix it. A variation, the *failure analysis report*, studies events that happened in the past, with the hope of learning how to avoid similar failures in the future.
- **Reports to support decisions.** *Feasibility reports* explore the potential ramifications of a decision that managers are considering, and *justification reports* explain a decision that has already been made.

Writing analytical reports presents a greater challenge than writing informational reports because you need to use your reasoning abilities and persuasive skills in addition to your writing skills. With analytical reports, you're doing more than simply delivering information: You're also analyzing a problem or an opportunity and presenting your conclusions and possibly your recommendations. Finally, because analytical reports often convince other people to make significant financial and personnel decisions, your reports carry the added responsibility of the consequences of these decisions.

To help define the problem your analytical report will address, answer these questions:

- What needs to be determined?
- Why is this issue important?
- Who is involved in the situation?
- Where is the trouble located?
- How did the situation originate?
- When did it start?

Not all of these questions apply in every situation, but asking them helps you define the problem being addressed and limits the scope of your discussion.

Problem factoring is the process of breaking down a problem into smaller questions to help identify causes and effects.

A hypothesis is a potential explanation that needs to be tested.

Also try **problem factoring**, dividing the problem into a series of logical, connected questions that try to identify cause and effect. When you speculate on the cause of a problem, you're forming a **hypothesis**, a potential explanation that needs to be tested. By subdividing a problem and forming hypotheses based on available evidence, you can tackle even the most complex situations.

As with all other business messages, the best organizational structure for each analytical report depends largely on your audience's likely reaction. The three basic structures involve focusing on conclusions, focusing on recommendations, and focusing on logic (see Table 12.5).

TABLE 12.5 Common Ways to Structure Analytical Reports

Element	Focus on Conclusions or Recommendations	Focus on Logical Argument	
		Use 2 + 2 = 4 Model	Use Yardstick Model
Reader mindset	Likely to accept	Hostile or skeptical	Hostile or skeptical
Approach	Direct	Indirect	Indirect
Writer credibility	High	Low	Low
Advantages	Readers quickly grasp conclusions or recommendations	Works well when you need to show readers how you built toward an answer by following clear, logical steps	Works well when you have a list of criteria (standards) that must be considered in a decision; alternatives are all measured against same criteria
Drawbacks	Structure can make topic seem too simple	Can make report longer	Readers must agree on criteria; can be lengthy because of the need to address each criterion for every alternative

FOCUSING ON CONCLUSIONS

When planning reports for readers who are likely to accept your conclusions—either because they've asked you to perform an analysis or they trust your judgment—consider using the direct approach and opening with your conclusions. This structure communicates the main idea quickly, but it does present some risks. Even if readers trust your judgment, they may have questions about your data or the methods you used. Moreover, starting with a conclusion may create the impression that you have oversimplified the situation. To give readers the opportunity to explore the thinking behind your conclusion, support that conclusion with solid reasoning and evidence (see Figure 12.9).

Focusing on conclusions is often the best approach when you're writing for a receptive audience.

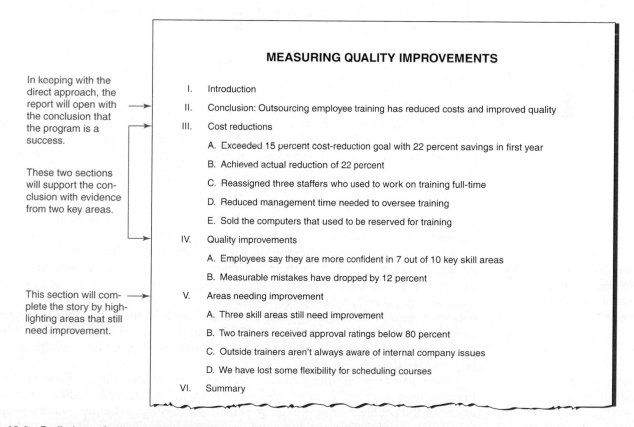

Figure 12.9 Preliminary Outline of a Research Report Focusing on Conclusions
A year after a bank decided to have an outside firm handle its employee training, an analyst was asked to prepare a report evaluating the results. The analysis shows that the outsourcing experiment was a success, so the report opens with that conclusion but supports it with clear evidence. Readers who accept the conclusion can stop reading, and those who desire more information can continue.

FOCUSING ON RECOMMENDATIONS

When readers want to know what you think they should do in a particular situation, organize your report to focus on recommendations.

A slightly different approach is useful when your readers want to know what they ought to do in a given situation (as opposed to what they ought to conclude). The actions you want your readers to take become the main subdivisions of your report.

When structuring a report around recommendations, use the direct approach, as you would for a report that focuses on conclusions. Then present your recommendations using a series of five steps:

1. Establish the need for action by briefly describing the problem or opportunity in the introduction.
2. Introduce the benefit(s) that can be achieved if the recommendation is adopted, along with any potential risks.
3. List the steps (recommendations) required to achieve the benefit, using action verbs for emphasis.
4. Explain each step more fully, giving details on procedures, costs, and benefits; if necessary, also explain how risks can be minimized.
5. Summarize your recommendations.

FOCUSING ON LOGICAL ARGUMENTS

Logical arguments can follow two basic approaches: *2 + 2 = 4* (adding everything up) and the *yardstick method* (comparing ideas against a predetermined set of standards).

When readers are potentially skeptical or hostile, consider using the indirect approach to build logically toward your conclusion or recommendation. If you guide readers along a rational path toward the answer, they are more likely to accept it when they encounter it. The two most common logical approaches are known as the *2 + 2 = 4 approach*, in which you convince readers by demonstrating that everything adds up to your conclusion, and the *yardstick approach*, in which you use a number of criteria to decide which option to select from two or more possibilities (see Figure 12.10).

Planning Proposals

7 LEARNING OBJECTIVES
Explain how to plan proposals.

Proposals can be grouped into two general categories. *Internal proposals* (see Figure 12.11 on page 381) request decisions from managers within the organization. *External proposals* request decisions from parties outside the organization. For example, *investment proposals* request funding from outside investors, *grant proposals* request funds from government agencies and other sponsoring organizations, and *sales proposals* present solutions for potential customers and request purchase decisions.

The most significant factor in planning a proposal is whether the recipient has asked you to submit a proposal. *Solicited proposals* are generally prepared at the request of external parties that require a product or a service, but they may also be requested by such internal sources as management or the board of directors. Some organizations prepare a formal invitation to bid on their contracts, called a **request for proposals (RFP)**, which includes instructions that specify the type of work to be performed or products to be delivered, along with budgets, deadlines, and other requirements. Other companies then respond by preparing proposals that show how they would meet those needs. In most cases, organizations that issue RFPs also provide strict guidelines on what the proposals should include, and you need to follow these guidelines carefully in order to be considered.

A *request for proposals (RFP)* includes instructions that specify the type of work to be performed or products to be delivered.

Unsolicited proposals require more creativity because readers don't expect them and may not even be aware of the problem or opportunity you propose to address.

Unsolicited proposals offer more flexibility but a completely different sort of challenge because recipients aren't expecting to receive them. In fact, your audience may not be aware of the problem or opportunity you are addressing, so before you can propose a solution, you might first need to convince your readers that a problem or an opportunity exists. Consequently, the indirect approach is often the wise choice for unsolicited proposals.

Regardless of its format and structure, a good proposal explains what a project or course of action will involve, how much it will cost, and how the recipient and his or her organization will benefit.

The first paragraph verifies who requested the report, when it was requested, and who wrote it.

This section explains how the information used in the analysis was collected.

Phan describes the first problem and explains how it occurred, without blaming anyone personally.

MEMO

TO: Robert Mendoza, Vice President of Marketing
FROM: Binh Phan, National Sales Manager   BP
DATE: September 14, 2020
SUBJECT: Major accounts sales problems

As you requested on August 20, this report outlines the results of my investigation into the recent slowdown in sales to major accounts and the accompanying rise in sales- and service-related complaints from some of our largest customers.

Over the last four quarters, major account sales dropped 12%, whereas overall sales were up 7%. During the same time, we've all noticed an increase in both formal and informal complaints from larger customers regarding how confusing and complicated it has become to do business with us.

My investigation started with in-depth discussions with the four regional sales managers, first as a group and then individually. The tension I felt in the initial meeting eventually bubbled to the surface during my meetings with each manager. Staff members in each region are convinced that other regions are booking orders they don't deserve, with one region doing all the legwork only to see another region get the sale, the commission, and the quota credit.

I followed up these formal discussions by talking informally and exchanging email with several sales representatives from each region. Virtually everyone who is involved with our major national accounts has a story to share. No one is happy with the situation, and I sense that some reps are walking away from major customers because the process is so frustrating.

The decline in sales to our major national customers and the increase in their complaints stem from two problems: (1) sales force organization and (2) commission policy.

ORGANIZATIONAL PROBLEMS

When we divided the national sales force into four geographical regions last year, the idea was to focus our sales efforts and clarify responsibilities for each prospective and current customer. The regional managers have gotten to know their market territories very well, and sales have increased beyond even our most optimistic projections.

However, while solving one problem, we have created another. In the past 12 to 18 months, several regional customers have grown to national status, and a few retailers have taken on (or expressed interest in) our products. As a result, a significant portion of both current sales and future opportunities lies with these large national accounts.

I uncovered more than a dozen cases in which sales representatives from two or more regions found themselves competing with each other by pursuing the same customers from different locations. Moreover, the complaints from our major accounts about

---

The second paragraph highlights the serious nature of the problem.

Organizational problems are the first "2" in Phan's 2 + 2 = 4 approach.

(continued)

Figure 12.10 Analytical Report Focusing on Logical Arguments
As national sales manager of a New Hampshire sporting goods company, Binh Phan was concerned about his company's ability to sell to its largest customers. His boss, the vice president of marketing, shared these concerns and asked Phan to analyze the situation and recommend a solution. In this troubleshooting report, his main idea is that the company should establish separate sales teams for these major accounts, rather than continuing to service them through the company's four regional divisions. However, Phan knew his plan would be controversial because it required a big change in the company's organization and in the way sales reps are paid. His thinking had to be clear and easy to follow, so he focused on logical argumentation.

2

overlapping or nonexistent account coverage are a direct result of the regional organization. In some cases, customers aren't sure which of our representatives they're supposed to call with problems and orders. In other cases, no one has been in contact with them for several months.

Phan brings the first problem to life by complementing the general description with a specific example.

For example, having retail outlets across the lower tier of the country, AmeriSport received pitches from reps out of our West, South, and East regions. Because our regional offices have a lot of negotiating freedom, the three were offering different prices. But all AmeriSport buying decisions were made at the Tampa headquarters, so all we did was confuse the customer. The irony of the current organization is that we're often giving our weakest selling and support efforts to the largest customers in the country.

COMMISSION PROBLEMS

Commission problems are the second "2" in Phan's 2 + 2 = 4 approach.

In discussing the second problem, he simplifies the reader's task by maintaining a parallel structure: a general description followed by a specific example.

The regional organization problems are compounded by the way we assign commissions and quota credit. Salespeople in one region can invest a lot of time in pursuing a sale, only to have the customer place the order in another region. So some sales rep in the second region ends up with the commission on a sale that was partly or even entirely earned by someone in the first region. Therefore, sales reps sometimes don't pursue leads in their regions, thinking that a rep in another region will get the commission.

For example, Athletic Express, with outlets in 35 states spread across all four regions, finally got so frustrated with us that the company president called our headquarters. Athletic Express has been trying to place a large order for tennis and golf accessories, but none of our local reps seem interested in paying attention. I spoke with the rep responsible for Nashville, where the company is headquartered, and asked her why she wasn't working the account more actively. Her explanation was that last time she got involved with Athletic Express, the order was actually placed from their L.A. regional office, and she didn't get any commission after more than two weeks of selling time.

RECOMMENDATIONS

He explains how his recommendation (a new organizational structure) will solve both problems.

Our sales organization should reflect the nature of our customer base. To accomplish that goal, we need a group of reps who are free to pursue accounts across regional borders—and who are compensated fairly for their work. The most sensible answer is to establish a national account group. Any customers whose operations place them in more than one region would automatically be assigned to the national group.

Phan concludes the 2 + 2 = 4 approach: organizational problems + commission problems = the need for a new sales structure.

He acknowledges that the recommended solution does create a temporary compensation problem but expresses confidence that a solution to that can be worked out.

In addition to solving the problem of competing sales efforts, the new structure will also largely eliminate the commission-splitting problem because regional reps will no longer invest time in prospects assigned to the national accounts team. However, we will need to find a fair way to compensate regional reps who are losing long-term customers to the national team. Some of these reps have invested years in developing customer relationships that will continue to yield sales well into the future, and everyone I talked to agrees that reps in these cases should receive some sort of compensation. Such a "transition commission" would also motivate the regional reps to help ensure a smooth transition from one sales group to the other. The exact nature of this compensation would need to be worked out with the various sales managers.

3

SUMMARY

The summary concisely restates both the problem and the recommended solution.

The regional sales organization is effective at the regional and local levels but not at the national level. We should establish a national accounts group to handle sales that cross regional boundaries. Then we'll have one set of reps who are focused on the local and regional levels and another set who are pursuing national accounts.

To compensate regional reps who lose accounts to the national team, we will need to devise some sort of payment to reward them for the years of work invested in such accounts. This can be discussed with the sales managers once the new structure is in place.

Figure 12.10   Analytical Report Focusing on Logical Arguments *(Continued)*

memo
CORPORATE HR

TO: Lailah Banks
FROM: Roger Hemmings
DATE: May 14, 2020
SUBJECT: Addressing Our High-Priority Personnel Issues

As you requested after last month's State of the Workforce meeting, I've been exploring potential responses to the top three personnel issues the team identified: job satisfaction, position readiness, and succession planning. We were all concerned about the cost and time commitment required to tackle these big issues, so the consensus reached at the meeting was to prioritize the issues and address them one at a time.

However, I believe there is a manageable way to address all three issues at once.

Areas of Concern: Finding Common Threads

The "big three" issues definitely feel overwhelming when we consider the changes needed in order to make meaningful improvements in all of them. There is hope in the details, however. Common threads run through all three areas, and we can address many of the problems with a single solution.

To review the three issues:

- **Job satisfaction:** Results from the last four internal surveys show a disturbing pattern of dissatisfaction, with many employees expressing uncertainty about where their careers are heading, confusion about how they fit into the big picture, and anger about not being given fair consideration for promotions.

- **Position readiness:** Managers frequently complain to us that our emphasis on promoting from within is difficult for them to adhere to because they can't find enough employees who are ready to move into positions of greater responsibility. Employees usually have the technical skills, but managers say that many lack the vision to see how their individual efforts contribute to the larger effort or lack the professionalism needed to function at a high level around customers, executives, and business partners

- **Succession planning:** This has been a priority for several years, but we never seem to make much headway toward putting a real program in place. We've solved one side of the equation—identifying all the critical managerial and professional roles where we're vulnerable to employees leaving or being promoted—but we haven't figured out how to identify and prepare promising candidates to move into these positions.

As I dug through these issues, two themes kept popping up: a lack of shared purpose and inadequate relationship building.

The subject line establishes a connection to a topic previously discussed without divulging the main idea of the proposal (which uses the indirect approach).

The opening paragraph serves as a reminder of their previous discussion, the task he was given, and the expectations about how he would approach it.

This single-sentence paragraph is the attention-getter in the AIDA model; it promises a solution that is better than expected.

This section summarizes the previous discussion while laying the groundwork for introducing a key reason for the proposal he is going to make, which is that he has found a couple of common themes in the three areas of concern.

He introduces those two themes, which shape the proposal he is about to make. This works as the interest stage of the AIDA model, since it presents an intriguing and unexplored angle on issues previously discussed.

(continued)

Figure 12.11 Internal Proposal
The manager in charge of his company's employee development efforts has a solution to three worrisome workforce issues that he has previously discussed with his boss, the director of human resources. He uses this memo-format proposal to outline a new employee mentoring program and suggest how the company can get started on it.[8]

The Lack of Shared Purpose

The company has always prided itself on attracting the best people in every functional specialty, but I believe this has resulted in an overemphasis on hard skills and individual output, to the detriment of soft skills and an overall sense of teamwork and shared contribution. It's no surprise that so many employees feel adrift and disconnected, when we don't foster a communal sense of how the company functions as an integrated enterprise. We have some of the brightest employees in the industry, but many are too focused on the tactics of their own jobs.

Here he offers more information about the two themes he discovered as he continues to lay out the reasons for his proposed solution.

Inadequate Relationship Building

After reviewing the employee survey data, I wanted to get a more personal take on these issues, so I interviewed more than two dozen professional staffers and managers across all divisions. These interviews uncovered another troubling dynamic: We're not very good at building professional relationships throughout the organization.

Employees and their managers tend to stay isolated within their functional silos and don't seem to understand or even care about the challenges faced by their colleagues in other departments. One market analyst described cross-functional meetings as "strangers forced to cooperate with strangers." Managers trying to fill promotional opportunities sometimes don't know where to look because they rarely get to know employees outside their own chain of command. And every professional staffer I talked to expressed some variation of feeling lost, with no one to turn to for confidential career advice.

Proposed Solution: Employee Mentoring

Clearly, we have some challenges on our hands. The good news is that we have the potential to solve many of them with an employee mentoring program. Here is a brief overview of mentoring programs, their benefits, potential stumbling blocks, and a recommended strategy for launching our own program.

At this point, he is ready to shift from "selling the problem" and laying the groundwork to presenting his solution.

Common Features of Mentoring Programs

Here are the key features common to most mentoring programs:

- It's a formal program that matches interested employees with managers and senior professional staff in one-on-one coaching relationships. The coaching can involve job specific challenges, work-life balance, workplace conflicts, or anything else the participants decide is useful.

- Employees and their mentors meet or at least talk on a regular schedule. Continuity is essential.

- HR provides the "matchmaking service" to help find the optimum pairings and manage demand, but isn't involved in the actual mentoring.

- Mentoring relationships are confidential, giving both sides the freedom to talk openly.

This brief overview of employee mentoring programs establishes common ground with his reader, so he can be sure they are thinking about the same thing.

Figure 12.11 **Internal Proposal** *(Continued)*

Potential Benefits of Mentoring Programs

Mentoring can go a long way toward solving these problems of shared purpose and relationship building, but companies report an even wider range of benefits from their mentoring programs:

- Employees can learn how to professionally navigate the corporate environment, from subtle issues such as business etiquette to broader questions such as how they contribute to company growth.

- Employees can discuss problems and worries with a trusted advisor, without fear of retribution.

- Managers gain insights into the challenges employees are facing, beyond the tactical demands of their jobs, which will help them manage and lead more effectively.

- Managers and employees learn about the challenges and contributions of other functional areas, which will foster better cooperation between departments.

- Through their mentors, employees can meet other managers, executives, and influential senior staff, expanding their networks within the company and opening more career doors.

- Managers can monitor the progress of promising employees and guide them into new opportunities.

- As an employee benefit, mentoring can help us attract a wider and more diverse pool of outside job candidates.

- Mentoring can boost productivity by helping employees find the best ways to invest their time and creative energy.

- Proactive mentoring can help the company get the full potential from employees who don't feel like they are part of the "in crowd" within the company.

- Through "reverse mentoring," senior staff and managers may have opportunities to learn about digital media use and other valuable skills they haven't had to embrace in their careers.

The bottom-line impact of mentoring programs isn't always easy to measure, but my research found some compelling figures. For example, companies have seen turnover drop by as much as 20 percent in the year after mentoring was launched, and the majority of employees and mentors alike report improved job satisfaction as a result of being involved in mentoring.

Here he presents the general benefits of mentoring programs in a way that connects them to the two themes he identified earlier.

Sharing the positive outcomes that other companies have experienced should heighten his boss's desire to explore the possibility of starting a program.

Figure 12.11   Internal Proposal *(Continued)*

Page 4

Costs and Potential Challenges

The benefits of mentoring do need to be weighed against costs and some potential challenges:

- Many companies find themselves with more interested employees than their programs can support, so we need to manage the demand in a fair and transparent way.

- There will be some direct and indirect costs, including training for mentors, an automated system for matching mentors with employees as the program scales up, and clerical and supervisory workload for HR.

- Mentoring requires time and energy, so mentors' workloads will need to be adjusted accordingly.

- Mentoring can create conflicts with employees' direct supervisors, so HR will need to offer mediation.

We can predict some of these costs and complexities, but the most accurate way to assess them will be to run a pilot program, as I propose in the next section.

Next Steps: Develop a Business Case and Launch a Pilot Program

The research makes a clear case for mentoring, provided it is planned carefully and managed well. I propose that we develop a formal business case for a mentoring program and present it to the Executive Council. We need top-down support and the participation of executives themselves as mentors, so C-level buy-in is essential.

Rather than launching companywide, I think we should start with a limited pilot program, with perhaps two or three dozen participants. This will let us fine-tune the program and get a clearer estimate of costs in order to refine budgets before scaling up.

My rough estimate is that the pilot program will require one full-time staff member in HR to facilitate matchmaking, mediate conflicts, analyze results, and plan the companywide rollout. This new position will have a loaded cost of approximately $90k. I shouldn't have any problem clearing out this much in my operating budget, probably by canceling the lowest-rated training courses (as we've been discussing doing anyway).

Can I get on your calendar sometime next week to go over the potential structure of the program and answer any questions or concerns you may have?

He is open about the downsides of mentoring programs, which addresses some potential objections and helps maintain his credibility on the subject.

"Next steps" signals his shift to the action phase of the AIDA model. He outlines a brief plan to move forward and concludes by asking for a meeting to get things rolling.

Figure 12.11 Internal Proposal *(Continued)*

ON THE JOB: SOLVING COMMUNICATION DILEMMAS AT **STRATEGYZER**

You're a business development manager at Strategyzer with responsibility for expanding sales of the company's Business Model Canvas training courses and apps. Use what you've learned in this chapter to address these challenges. You may find it helpful to familiarize yourself with the Business Model Canvas

by watching the two-minute video at **strategyzer.com/canvas /business-model-canvas**.

1. You've heard from a number of product managers and other mid-level business planners in big companies that they would like to use the Business Model Canvas, but they can't convince company executives (their superiors, in other words) to give up the familiar approach of detailed business plans. You hit on the idea of a free mini-course for corporate executives to help them understand the value of the canvas approach for early-stage business planning. Before you can convince Strategyzer's content development team to create the course, you need to provide some evidence that Fortune 500 executives would be interested in devoting half a day to such a course. You decide to conduct some research to gauge executive interest in the mini-course and to identify the most important topics it should cover. Which of these would be the best problem statement for guiding your research?

a. Would anyone be interested in a mini-course on the Business Model Canvas?

b. Would a free mini-course overcome executive resistance to the Business Model Canvas?

c. Would a free mini-course overcome executive reluctance to let go of traditional business plans?

d. What would be the best way to overcome executive resistance to the Business Model Canvas?

2. Which of these would be the best approach to conducting the research into customer demand for the mini-course?

a. Conduct a telephone survey of Fortune 500 executives responsible for overseeing product development. Ask a series of questions designed to uncover the executives' awareness of the canvas approach and their attitudes toward it.

b. Conduct an email or in-app survey of current users of the Business Model Canvas app, asking them to report on the resistance they are receiving from executives in their companies.

c. Post a brief survey on Strategyzer's website, asking top-level corporate executives to explain their reasons for sticking with the traditional approach of detailed business plans, rather than trying a new method such as the Business Model Canvas.

d. Post an interactive survey on Strategyzer's website, asking site visitors to report on the attitudes toward Business Model Canvas and similar approaches in their organizations.

Set up branching in the survey so that people who are interested in the canvas method but who have encountered resistance from upper management are asked a series of questions about the nature of the resistance they are encountering and what forms of proof could help convince these executives to give the new method a try.

3. You are conducting research interviews with Strategyzer customers, hoping to find out what enhancements might make the Business Model Canvas web app appealing to an even wider range of customers. Which of the following questions would elicit the most-helpful information from customers?

a. Would you recommend the Business Model Canvas web app to other business professionals?

b. Has the Business Model Canvas web app been useful to you?

c. In what ways has the Business Model Canvas web app been useful to you?

d. How would you enhance the Business Model Canvas web app to make it appeal to the widest range of potential customers?

4. You have an idea to form a strategic partnership with a leading business magazine to offer business training courses. Which of these is the best way to organize a proposal to send to the managing editor if you have had no prior contact?

a. Use the indirect approach. Open with an acknowledgment of the magazine's presence in the marketplace and mention that you have a business opportunity you would like to discuss. Follow this by introducing Strategyzer and the Business Model Canvas and offering a few facts on how popular it has become. Then present the idea of coproducing training seminars.

b. Offer an in-depth analysis of corporate training and employee development budgets to give an idea of how much money there is to be made in training.

c. The Business Model Canvas is becoming fairly well known in the business world, so don't waste the reader's time with a long build-up. Use the direct approach and state your proposal up front.

END OF CHAPTER

Learning Objectives Checkup

Assess your understanding of the principles in this chapter by reading each learning objective and studying the accompanying exercises. You can check your responses against the answer key on page 613.

Objective 12.1: Adapt the three-step writing process to reports and proposals.

1. Why is it particularly important in long reports to clearly identify your purpose before you begin writing?

a. A clear statement of purpose helps focus your efforts and minimize rework.

b. A clear statement of purpose gives you the opportunity to decline projects that don't match your skill set or professional interests.

c. A clear statement of purpose helps you avoid time-consuming research.

d. A clear statement of purpose, shared with management before you begin, absolves you of sole responsibility for the outcome of the project.

2. _____ reports focus on the delivery of facts, figures, and other types of information, without making recommendations or proposing new ideas or solutions.

3. _____ reports assess a situation or problem and recommend a course of action in response.

4. _____ present persuasive messages that encourage readers to take a specific course of action.

Objective 12.2: Describe an effective process for conducting business research, explain how to evaluate the credibility of an information source, and identify the five ways to use research results.

5. Which of the following is the appropriate first step in any research project?
   a. Evaluate secondary research to see if you can reuse anything from earlier research projects.
   b. Conduct a preliminary phone survey to measure the extent of the issue you're about to research.
   c. Conduct a thorough statistical analysis of any existing data.
   d. Develop a research plan that includes a clear problem statement.

6. Which of the following is true about this series of values: 14, 37, 44, 44, 44, 74, 76, 88, 93, 100, and 112?
   a. The mean is 66.
   b. The mean is 44.
   c. The mean is 74.
   d. The mode is 74.

7. Research being conducted for the first time is called _____ research.

8. Research that was conducted for other projects but is being considered for a new project is called _____ research.

9. Why is it important to understand the purpose for which source material was created?
   a. Knowing the purpose helps alert you to any potential biases.
   b. You are required to indicate this purpose in your bibliography.
   c. The purpose tells you whether the material is copyrighted.
   d. The purpose tells you whether you need to pay usage rights.

10. If you uncover critically important information (the sort that could make or break your company) that is from a credible source and appears to be unbiased, well documented, current, and complete but is the only source of this information you can find, how should you handle this situation in your subsequent reporting?
    a. Use it as you would use any other information.
    b. Use it but clearly indicate the source in your report.
    c. Use it but clearly indicate in your report that this is the only source of the information and you weren't able to verify it through a second, independent source.
    d. Don't use it.

11. What is the difference between quoting and paraphrasing?
    a. Quoting is for printed sources; paraphrasing is for electronic sources.
    b. Quoting is legal (as long as appropriate credit is given); paraphrasing is not.
    c. Paraphrasing is just a shorter version of quoting.

d. Quoting is reproducing someone else's writing exactly as you found it; paraphrasing is expressing someone else's ideas in your own words.

Objective 12.3: Explain the role of secondary research, and describe the two major categories of online research tools.

12. When is secondary research generally used?
    a. Before primary research
    b. After primary research
    c. At the same time as primary research

13. Why is it important to fully understand the instructions for using an individual search engine, database, or other research tool?
    a. You can be fined if you use these tools improperly.
    b. Most search tools don't return any results if you don't know how to use them.
    c. Using the tool without understanding how it works can produce unpredictable and misleading results.
    d. Today's search tools are so easy to use that you don't need to worry about learning the details.

Objective 12.4: Explain the role of primary research, and identify the two most common forms of primary research for business communication purposes.

14. What does it mean for a survey to be valid?
    a. It works every time.
    b. It returns the data and information the researchers expect it to return.
    c. It meets all ethical and legal criteria in a given industry.
    d. It measures what it was intended to measure.

15. What type of question is "Why do some consumers refuse to switch to smartphones?"
    a. An open-ended question
    b. A values question
    c. A closed question
    d. An in-depth question

Objective 12.5: Explain how to plan informational reports and website content.

16. Which of the following is not a common way to organize informational reports?
    a. Comparison
    b. Section size
    c. Sequence
    d. Chronology

17. The structure and navigational flow of all the parts of a website are commonly referred to as _____ _____.

Objective 12.6: Identify the three most common ways to organize analytical reports.

18. With the *yardstick model* of organizing an analytical report, you
    a. measure each alternative, given a set of options for decision-making.
    b. establish a set of criteria and then compare available alternatives against them.
    c. avoid direct comparisons of alternative choices or courses of action.
    d. add up the factors to reach a conclusion.

Objective 12.7: Explain how to plan proposals.

19. What is the most significant factor to consider when planning a business proposal?
    a. Whether the recipient prefers printed or electronic media
    b. Whether the proposal is solicited or unsolicited
    c. How many writers will be involved
    d. Whether the audience will be receptive to new ideas
20. RFP stands for
    a. request for proposals.
    b. reason for proposing.
    c. release form project.
    d. research for proposal.

Key Terms

analytical reports Reports that offer both information and analysis; they can also include recommendations

business plan A comprehensive document that describes a company's mission, structure, objectives, and operations

causation The cause-and-effect linkage between two factors, where one of them causes the other to happen

closed questions Questions with a fixed range of possible answers

conclusion A logical interpretation of the facts and other information in a report

correlation The simultaneous change in two variables being measured, without proof of causation

hypothesis A potential explanation that needs to be tested and verified

information architecture The structure and navigational flow of all the parts of a website

informational reports Reports that offer data, facts, feedback, and other types of information, without analysis or recommendations

mean Equal to the sum of all the items in the group divided by the number of items in that group; what people refer to when they use the term *average*

median The midpoint of a series, with an equal number of items above and below

mode The number that occurs more often than any other in a sample

open-ended questions Questions without simple, predetermined answers; used to solicit opinions, insights, and information

primary research New research done specifically for the current project

problem factoring Dividing a problem into a series of smaller questions that try to identify cause and effect

problem statement Defines the problem for which a research project will be designed to collect data and information

proposals Reports that combine information delivery and persuasive communication

recommendation A suggested course of action

request for proposals (RFP) A formal invitation to bid on a contract

secondary research Research done previously for another purpose

statement of purpose Planning statement that defines why you are preparing the report

trends Repeatable patterns taking place over time

Apply Your Knowledge

To review chapter content related to each question, refer to the indicated Learning Objective.

12-1. Would "Look into employee morale problems" be an effective problem statement for a report? Why or why not? [LO-1]

12-2. Companies occasionally make mistakes that expose confidential information, such as when employees lose laptop computers containing sensitive data files or webmasters forget to protect confidential webpages from search engine indexes. If you conducted an online search that turned up competitive information on webpages that were clearly intended to be private, what would you do? Explain your answer. [LO-3]

12-3. Can you use the same approach for planning website content as you use for planning printed reports? Why or why not? [LO-5]

12-4. If you were writing a recommendation report for an audience that doesn't know you, would you use the direct approach, focusing on the recommendation, or the indirect approach, focusing on logic? Why? [LO-6]

Practice Your Skills

Message for Analysis

12-5. **Evaluating a Report [LO-1], [LO-5]** The Securities and Exchange Commission (SEC) requires every public company to file a comprehensive financial report known as "Form 10-K" every year. Companies usually combine this highly structured report with a more conversational "Letter to Shareholders" or other introductory mini-report signed by the chairman of the board. The two combined reports are known as the *annual report*. Visit the website of any publicly traded U.S. company and find its most recent annual report. Compare the style and format of the introductory report and the formal Form 10-K. How do the two reports meet the respective needs of company management and company shareholders? If you were considering buying the company's stock, how would you use the two forms?

Exercises

Each activity is labeled according to the primary skill or skills you will need to use. To review relevant chapter content, refer to the indicated Learning Objective. In some instances, supporting information can be found in another chapter, as indicated.

12-6. **Planning: Analyzing the Situation [LO-1]** South by Southwest (SXSW) is a family of conferences and festivals in Austin, Texas, that showcase some of the world's most creative talents in music, interactive media, and film. In addition to being a major entertainment venue every year, SXSW is also an increasingly important *trade show*, an opportunity for companies to present products and services to potential customers and business partners. You work for a company that makes music training equipment, such as an electronic keyboard with an integrated screen that guides learners through every step of learning to play. Your manager has asked you to look into whether the company should rent an exhibition booth at SXSW next year. Prepare a work plan for an analytical report that will assess the promotional opportunities at SXSW, and make a recommendation on exhibiting. Include a statement of purpose, a problem statement for any research you will conduct, a description of what will result from your investigation, the sources and methods of data collection, and a preliminary outline. Visit the SXSW website at **www.sxsw.com** for more information.

12-7. **Documenting Sources [LO-2]** Select five business articles from online sources. Develop a resource list, using Appendix B as a guideline.

12-8. **Conducting Secondary Research (Online Monitoring) [LO-3]**, **Chapter 8** Select a business topic that interests you, and configure a Twitter monitoring tool such as TweetDeck (**tweetdeck.twitter.com**) to track tweets on this topic. After you've found at least a dozen tweets, identify three that provide potentially useful information and describe them in a brief email message to your instructor.

Research: Conducting Secondary Research [LO-3] Using online, database, or printed sources, find the following information. Be sure to properly cite your sources using the formats discussed in Appendix B.

12-9. Contact information for the American Management Association

12-10. Median weekly earnings of men and women by occupation

12-11. Current market share for Perrier water

12-12. Performance ratios for office supply retailers

12-13. Annual stock performance for Tesla

12-14. Number of franchise outlets in the United States

12-15. Composition of the U.S. workforce by profession

12-16. **Research: Conducting Secondary Research [LO-3]** Select any public company and find the following information:

- Names of the company's current officers
- List of the company's products or services (or, if the company has a large number of products, the product lines or divisions)
- Some important current issues in the company's industry
- The outlook for the company's industry as a whole

12-17. **Research: Conducting Primary Research [LO-4]** You work for a movie studio that is producing a young director's first motion picture, the story of a group of unknown musicians finding work and making a reputation in a competitive industry. Unfortunately, some of your friends leave the screening saying that the 182-minute movie is simply too long. Others say they can't imagine any sequences to cut out. Your boss wants to test the movie on a typical audience and ask viewers to complete a questionnaire that will help the director decide whether edits are needed and, if so, where. Design a questionnaire that you can use to solicit valid answers for a report to the director about how to handle the audience's reaction to the movie.

12-18. **Research: Conducting Primary Research [LO-4]** You're conducting an informational interview with a manager in another division of your company. Partway through the interview, the manager shows clear signs of impatience. How should you respond? What might you do differently to prevent this from happening in the future? Explain your answers.

12-19. **Message Strategies: Informational Reports [LO-5]** Find an interactive, online annual report from a public corporation. A search for "interactive annual report" should yield a number of possibilities. Explore the annual report you've chosen, paying particular attention to how the company uses interactive techniques to present information. Do you find the report easy to use? Do you ever get lost or feel unsure about where to go next? Do you prefer this format over a downloadable (PDF) or printed report? Summarize your impressions in a brief email report or blog post.

12-20. **Planning: Organizing Reports [LO-1]** Look through recent issues (print or online) of *Bloomberg Businessweek*, *Fortune*, or other business publications for an article that describes how an executive's conclusions about his or her company's current situation or future opportunities led to changes in policy, plans, or products. Construct an outline of the material, first using a direct approach and then using an indirect approach. Which approach do you think the executive would use when reporting these conclusions to stockholders? To other senior managers? Explain your answers.

12-21. **Message Strategies: Informational Reports [LO-5]** You're the vice president of operations for a Florida fast-food chain. In the aftermath of a major hurricane, you're drafting a report on the emergency procedures to be followed by personnel in each restaurant when storm warnings are in effect. Answer who, what, when, where, why, and how, and then prepare a one-page outline of your report. Make up any details you need.

12-22. **Message Strategies: Informational Reports [LO-5]** Assume that your college president has received many student complaints about campus parking problems. You are appointed to chair a student committee organized to investigate the problems and recommend solutions. The president gives you a file labeled "Parking: Complaints from Students," and you jot down the essence of the complaints as you inspect the contents. Your notes look like this:

- Inadequate student spaces at critical hours
- Poor night lighting near the computer center
- Inadequate attempts to keep resident neighbors from occupying spaces
- Dim marking lines
- Motorcycles taking up full spaces
- Discourteous security officers
- Spaces (usually empty) reserved for college officials
- Relatively high parking fees
- Full fees charged to night students even though they use the lots only during low-demand periods
- Vandalism to cars and a sense of personal danger

- Inadequate total space
- Harassment of students parking on the street in front of neighboring houses

Now prepare an outline for an informational report to be submitted to committee members. Use a topical organization that categorizes this information.

Message Strategies: Analytical Reports [LO-6] Of the organizational approaches introduced in the chapter, which is best suited for writing a report that answers the following questions? Briefly explain why.

12-23. In which market segment—energy drinks or traditional soft drinks—should Fizz Drinks, Inc., introduce a new drink to take advantage of its enlarged research and development budget?

12-24. Should Major Manufacturing, Inc., close down operations of its antiquated Bellville, Arkansas, plant despite the adverse economic impact on the town that has grown up around the plant?

12-25. Should you and your partner adopt a new accounting method to make your financial statements look better to potential investors?

12-26. Should Grand Canyon Chemicals buy disposable test tubes to reduce labor costs associated with cleaning and sterilizing reusable test tubes?

12-27. What are the reasons for the recent data loss at the college computer center, and how can we avoid similar problems in the future?

12-28. Message Strategies: Proposals; Collaboration: Team Projects [LO-7], Chapter 3 With a team assigned by your instructor, identify an aspect of campus operations that could be improved—perhaps involving registration, university housing, food services, parking, or library services. Outline a feasible solution and develop a list of information you would need to gather in order to convince readers that the problem exists and that your solution is worth considering.

Expand Your Skills

Critique the Professionals

Company websites function as multidimensional informational reports, with numerous sections and potentially endless ways for visitors to navigate through all the various pages. Locate the website of a large public corporation. Imagine that you are approaching the site as (a) a potential employee, (b) a potential investor (purchaser of stock), (c) a member of one of the local communities in which this company operates, and (d) a potential customer of the company's products and services. Analyze how easy or difficult it is to find the information each of these four visitors would typically be seeking. Using whatever medium your instructor requests, write a brief analysis of the information architecture of the website, describing what works well and what doesn't.

Sharpen Your Career Skills Online

Bovée and Thill's Business Communication Web Search, at **websearch.businesscommunicationnetwork.com**, is a unique research tool designed specifically for business communication research. Use the Web Search function to find a website, video, article, podcast, or presentation that offers advice on conducting research for business reports. Write a brief email message to your instructor or a post for your class blog, describing the item you found and summarizing the career skills information you learned from it.

Build Your Career

As you explore job openings and research companies and professions in the coming months, keep a list of *keywords* that you run across. These are the terms that companies use to identify the types of talent they are searching for. It's important to know the right keywords for each job you plan to apply for, because *applicant tracking systems* and other automated hiring tools often look for these terms in your résumé and other employment communication. See page 484 in Chapter 15 for more information on finding and using keywords.

Improve Your Grammar, Mechanics, and Usage

The following exercises help you improve your knowledge of and power over English grammar, mechanics, and usage. Turn to the Handbook of Grammar, Mechanics, and Usage at the end of this book and review all of Sections 2.7 (Dashes) and 2.8 (Hyphens). Then identify the preferred choice in the following groups of sentences. (Answers to these exercises appear on page 614.)

12-29. a. Three qualities—speed, accuracy, and reliability are desirable in any applicant.

　　b. Three qualities—speed, accuracy, and reliability—are desirable in any applicant.

12-30. a. A highly placed source explained the top-secret negotiations.

　　b. A highly-placed source explained the top-secret negotiations.

　　c. A highly placed source explained the top secret negotiations.

12-31. a. The file on Mary Gaily—yes—we finally found it reveals a history of tardiness.

　　b. The file on Mary Gaily, yes—we finally found it—reveals a history of tardiness.

　　c. The file on Mary Gaily—yes, we finally found it—reveals a history of tardiness.

12-32. a. They're selling a well designed machine.

　　b. They're selling a well-designed machine.

12-33. a. Argentina, Brazil, Mexico—these are the countries we hope to concentrate on.

　　b. Argentina, Brazil, Mexico—these are the countries—we hope to concentrate on.

12-34. a. Only two sites maybe three—offer the things we need.

　　b. Only two sites—maybe three—offer the things we need.

12-35. **a.** How many owner operators are in the industry?

  b. How many owner—operators are in the industry?

  c. How many owner-operators are in the industry?

12-36. **a.** Your ever-faithful assistant deserves—without a doubt—a substantial raise.

  b. Your ever faithful assistant deserves—without a doubt—a substantial raise.

12-37. **a.** The charts are well placed—on each page—unlike the running heads and footers.

  b. The charts are well-placed on each page—unlike the running heads and footers.

  c. The charts are well placed on each page—unlike the running heads and footers.

12-38. **a.** Your devil-may-care attitude affects everyone in the decision-making process.

  b. Your devil may care attitude affects everyone in the decision-making process.

  c. Your devil-may-care attitude affects everyone in the decision making process.

For additional exercises focusing on dashes and hyphens, visit MyLab Business Communication. Select Chapter 12, Additional Exercises to Improve Your Grammar, Mechanics, and Usage, then 18. Punctuation C.

Cases

For all cases, feel free to use your creativity to make up any details you need in order to craft effective messages.

Informational Reports

REPORT-WRITING SKILLS

12.39. Message Strategies: Informational Reports [LO-5] Employers and employees alike have embraced telecommuting as a way to reduce costs and save time.

Your task: Assume you work for a company that develops security software to protect corporate information networks. The executive team is considering developing a new product specifically for the telecommuting market that would address the unique challenges of having employees working from home amidst a host of potential security problems, from unsecured home Wi-Fi networks to the risk of equipment theft. Research the current state of telecommuting in the United States and its prospects over the next few years. Find some key facts and figures that will help the executives assess the potential for this new product, such as the industries and professions where telecommuting is popular or has the potential to grow, the number of people who telecommute now, and any economic or technological trends that could affect telecommuting. Write a report of no more than one page summarizing your findings.

REPORT WRITING SKILLS

12.40. Message Strategies: Informational Reports [LO-5] Concern is growing in many youth sports about the negative consequences of existing approaches to player development and competition. The long-term athlete development (LTAD) approach aims to instill methods and mindsets that will make athlete development more successful in the long run while making sports more enjoyable for kids. The American Development Model (ADM) used by USA Hockey is one example of the LATD approach in a specific sport.

Your task: Visit USA Hockey's website devoted to the ADM at www.admkids.com and review the information on ADM. Write a brief informational report (one to two pages) on the ADM concept, including the rationale behind it and the benefits it offers youth athletes.

BLOGGING SKILLS

12.41. Message Strategies: Informational Reports [LO-5] Anyone contemplating investing in the stock market is likely to shudder at least a little bit at the market's ups and downs.

Your task: Write a brief informational report for your class blog that contains a chart of one of the major stock market indexes (such as the Dow Jones Industrial Average or the S&P 500) over the past 20 years. Pick out four significant drops in the index during this time period and investigate economic or political events that occurred immediately before or during these declines. Briefly describe the events and their likely effect on the stock market.

EMAIL SKILLS

12.42. Message Strategies: Informational Reports [LO-5] You've put a lot of work into your college classes so far—make sure you don't have any glitches as you get ready to claim your certificate or degree.

Your task: Prepare an interim progress report that details the steps you've taken toward completing your graduation or certification requirements. After examining the requirements listed in your college catalog, indicate a realistic schedule for completing those that remain. In addition to course requirements, include steps such as completing the residency requirement, completing all necessary forms, and paying fees. Write a brief email report that you could send to anyone who is helping or encouraging you through school.

WIKI SKILLS / TEAM SKILLS

12-43. Message Strategies: Informational Reports; Media Skills: Wiki Writing [LO-1], [LO-2] The use of social networks by employees during work hours remains a controversial topic, with some companies encouraging networking, some allowing it, and others prohibiting it.

Your task: Using the free wiki service offered by Zoho or a comparable system, collaborate on a report that summarizes the potential advantages and disadvantages of allowing social network use in the workplace.

BLOGGING SKILLS / TEAM SKILLS

12-44. Message Strategies: Informational Reports [LO-5] If you're like many other college students, your first year was more than you expected: more difficult, more fun, more frustrating, more expensive, more exhausting, more rewarding—more of everything, positive and negative. Oh, the things you know now that you didn't know then!

Your task: With several other students, identify five or six things you wish you had realized or understood better before you started your first year of college. These can relate to your school life (such as "I didn't realize how much work I would have for my classes" or "I should've asked for help as soon as I got stuck") and your personal and social life ("I wish I had been more open to meeting people"). Use these items as the foundation of a brief informational report you could post on a blog that is read by high school students and their families. Your goal with this report is to help the next generation of students make a successful and rewarding transition to college.

WEB-WRITING SKILLS / TEAM SKILLS

12-45. Message Strategies: Online Content [LO-5] As you've probably experienced, trying to keep all the different schools straight in one's mind while researching and applying for colleges can be difficult. Applicants and their families would no doubt appreciate a handy summary of your college or university's key points as they relate to the selection and application process.

Your task: Adapt content from your college or university's website to create a one-page "Quick Facts" sheet about your school. Choose the information you think prospective students and their families would find most useful. (Note that adapting existing content would be acceptable in a real-life scenario like this, because you would be reusing content on behalf of the content owner. Doing so would definitely *not* be acceptable if you were using the content for yourself or for someone other than the original owner.)

PORTFOLIO BUILDER / REPORT-WRITING SKILLS

12-46. Message Strategies: Informational Reports [LO-5] Health-care costs are a pressing concern at every level in the economy, from individual households up through companies of all sizes on up to state and federal governments. Many companies are responding with *wellness programs* and other efforts to encourage employees to live healthier lifestyles and thereby reduce their need for expensive health care.

Your task: Research the wellness efforts at any U.S. company and draft a brief report (one to two pages) that describes the company's strategy, the details of the wellness program, and any measured outcomes that reflect its success or failure.

Analytical Reports

EMAIL SKILLS

12-47. Message Strategies: Analytical Reports [LO-6] Mistakes can be wonderful learning opportunities if we're honest with ourselves and receptive to learning from the mistake.

Your task: Identify a mistake you've made—something significant enough to have cost you a lot of money, wasted a lot of time, harmed your health, damaged a relationship, created serious problems at work, prevented you from pursuing what could've been a rewarding opportunity, or otherwise had serious consequences. Now figure out why you made that mistake. Did you let emotions get in the way of clear thinking? Did you make a serious financial blunder because you didn't take the time to understand the consequences of a decision? Were you too cautious? Not cautious enough? Perhaps several factors led to a poor decision.

Write a brief analytical report to your instructor that describes the situation and outlines your analysis of why the failure occurred and how you can avoid making a similar mistake in the future. If you can't think of a significant mistake or failure that you're comfortable sharing with your instructor, write about a mistake that a friend or family member made (without revealing the person's identity or potentially embarrassing him or her).

MEMO-WRITING SKILLS

12-48. Message Strategies: Analytical Reports [LO-6] Assume that you will have time for only one course next term. Identify the criteria you will use to decide which of several courses to take. (This is the yardstick approach mentioned in the chapter.)

Your task: List the pros and cons of four or five courses that interest you, and use the selection criteria you identified to choose the one course that is best for you to take at this time. Write your report in printable memo format, addressing it to your academic adviser.

REPORT-WRITING SKILLS

12-49. Message Strategies: Analytical Reports [LO-6] Spurred in part by the success of numerous do-it-yourself (DIY) TV shows, homeowners across the country are redecorating, remodeling, and rebuilding. Many people are content with superficial changes, such as new paint or new accessories, but some are more ambitious. These homeowners want to move walls, add rooms, redesign kitchens, convert garages to home theaters—the big projects.

Publishers try to create magazines that appeal to carefully identified groups of potential readers and the advertisers who'd like to reach them. The DIY market is already served by numerous magazines, but you see an opportunity in the homeowners

CASE TABLE 12.1	Rooms Most Frequently Remodeled by DIYers
Room	**Homeowners Surveyed Who Have Tackled or Plan to Tackle at Least a Partial Remodel (%)**
Kitchen	60
Bathroom	48
Home office/study	44
Bedroom	38
Media room/home theater	31
Den/recreation room	28
Living room	27
Dining room	12
Sun room/solarium	8

CASE TABLE 12.2	Average Amount Spent on Remodeling Projects
Estimated Amount ($)	**Surveyed Homeowners (%)**
<5,000	5
5,000–9,999	21
10,000–19,999	39
20,000–49,999	22
>50,000	13

who tackle heavy-duty projects. Case Tables 12.1 through 12.3 summarize the results of some preliminary research you asked your company's research staff to conduct.

Your task: You think the data show a real opportunity for a "big projects" DIY magazine, although you'll need more extensive research to confirm the size of the market and refine the editorial direction of the magazine. Prepare a brief analytical report that presents the data you have, identifies the opportunity or opportunities you've found (suggest your own ideas, based on the data in the tables), and requests funding from the editorial board to pursue further research.

Proposals

12-50. Message Strategies: Proposals [LO-3] Your boss, the national sales manager, insists that all company sales reps continue to carry full-size laptop computers for making presentations to clients and to manage files and communication tasks. In addition to your laptops, you and your colleagues have to carry a bulky printed catalog and a variety of product samples—up and down stairs, on and off airplanes, and in and out of cars. You are desperate to lighten the load, and you think switching from laptops to tablets would help.

Your task: Write an informal proposal suggesting that the company equip its traveling salespeople with tablets instead of laptops. Making up any information you need, address three questions you know your boss will have. First, can sales reps type at an adequate speed on tablets? (Using an accessory keyboard can be part of your solution.) Second, can sales reps make informal "tabletop" presentations on tablets, the way they can on their laptops? (Currently, sales reps can sit at a conference table and give a presentation to two or three people, without the need for a projector screen.) Third, do tablets have a sufficient selection of business software, from word-processing to database management software?

12-51. Message Strategies: Proposals [LO-1] Select a product you are familiar with and imagine you are the manufacturer trying to get a local retail outlet to carry it.

Your task: Research the product online and in person, if possible, to learn as much as you can about it, then write an unsolicited sales proposal in letter format to the owner (or manager) of the store, proposing that the item be stocked. Use the information you gathered on the product's features and benefits to make a compelling case for why the product would be a strong seller for the store. Then make up some reasonable figures highlighting

CASE TABLE 12.3	Tasks Performed by Homeowner on a Typical Remodeling Project	
Task	**Surveyed Homeowners Who Perform or Plan to Perform Most or All of This Task Themselves (%)**	
Conceptual design	90	
Technical design/architecture	34	
Demolition	98	
Foundation work	62	
Framing	88	
Plumbing	91	
Electrical	55	
Heating/cooling	22	
Finish carpentry	85	
Tile work	90	
Painting	95	
Interior design	52	

what the item costs, what it can be sold for, and what services your company provides (return of unsold items, free replacement of unsatisfactory items, necessary repairs, and so on).

EMAIL SKILLS

12-52. Message Strategies: Proposals [LO-7] One of the banes of apartment living is those residents who don't care about the condition of their shared surroundings. They might leave trash all over the place, dent walls when they move furniture, spill food and beverages in common areas, destroy window screens, and otherwise degrade living conditions for everyone. Landlords obviously aren't thrilled about this behavior, either, because it raises the costs of cleaning and maintaining the facility.

Your task: Assume you live in a fairly large apartment building some distance from campus. Write an email proposal you could send to your landlord suggesting that fostering a sense of stronger community among residents in your building might help reduce incidents of vandalism and neglect. Propose that the little-used storage area in the basement of the building be converted to a community room, complete with a simple kitchen and a large-screen television. By attending Super Bowl parties and other events there, residents could get to know one another and perhaps forge bonds that would raise the level of shared concern for their living envi-

ronment. You can't offer any proof of this in advance, of course, but share your belief that a modest investment in this room could pay off long term in lower repair and maintenance costs. Moreover, it would be an attractive feature to entice new residents.

PORTFOLIO BUILDER / TEAM SKILLS

12-53. Message Strategies: Proposals [LO-1] Either to create opportunities in a slow job market or to avoid traditional employment altogether, some college graduates create their own jobs as independent freelancers or as entrepreneurs launching new companies.

Your task: Assemble a team of classmates as your instructor directs, then brainstorm all the services you could perform for local businesses. Identify as many services as you can that are related to you and your teammates' college majors and career interests, but also include anything you are willing to do to generate revenue. Next, identify a specific company that might have some opportunities for you. Outline and draft a short proposal that describes what your team can do for this company, how the company would benefit from your services, why you're the right people for the job, and how much you propose to charge for your services. Remember that this is an unsolicited proposal, so be sure to introduce your proposal accordingly.

MyLab Business Communication

MyLab Assisted-Grading Writing Prompts

If your instructor has assigned one or both of the following writing assignments within the MyLab, go to your Assignments to complete these writing exercises.

12-54. Can knowing the source of information that you find online unfairly bias you against the information? Explain your answer. [LO-2]

12-55. Why are unsolicited proposals more challenging to write than solicited proposals? [LO-7]

Endnotes

1. Kavi Guppta, "How to Convince Leaders to Avoid Business Plans When Validating New Ideas," Strategyzer blog, 18 April 2016, blog.strategyzer.com; Strategyzer website, accessed 6 April 2018, strategyzer.com; Alexander Ostenwalder and Yves Pigneur, *Business Model Generation: A Handbook for Visionaries, Game Changers, and Challengers* (Hoboken, N.J.: Wiley, 2009), e-book; Alex Cowan, "The 20 Minute Business Plan: Business Model Canvas Made Easy," Cowan+, 6 February 2013, www.alexandercowan.com.

2. *Understanding Industrial Property*, World Intellectual Property Organization, 2016, p. 5.

3. "How to Paraphrase," Plagiarism.org, accessed 6 April 2018, www.plagiarism.org.

4. "Successful vs. Unsuccessful Paraphrases," *The Writer's Handbook*, The Writing Center at the University of Wisconsin, 5 March 2018, writing.wisc.edu; "How to Paraphrase a Source," *The Writer's Handbook*, The Writing Center at the University of Wisconsin, 5 March 2018, writing.wisc.edu; "How to Paraphrase Without Plagiarizing," The Writing Studio at Colorado State University, accessed 7 April 2018, writing.colostate.edu.

5. Jon Chavez, "Library Card Is Key Business Tool as Firms Utilize Resource-Rich, Free System," *Toledo Blade*, 26 April 2015, www.toledoblade.com.

6. Ross Tartell, "Write an Effective Survey Question," Training, July/August 2015, 14; Naresh K. Malhotra, *Basic Marketing Research* (Upper Saddle River, N.J.: Prentice Hall, 2002), 314–317.

7. Brown, "How to Write a Winning Business Plan"; Michael Gerber, "The Business Plan That Always Works," *Her Business*, May/June 2004, 23–25; J. Tol Broome Jr., "How to Write a Business Plan," *Nation's Business*, February 1993, 29–30; Albert Richards, "The Ernst & Young Business Plan Guide," *R & D Management*, April 1995, 253; David Lanchner, "How Chitchat Became a Valuable Business Plan," *Global Finance*, February 1995, 54–56; Marguerita Ashby-Berger, "My Business Plan—And What Really Happened," *Small Business Forum*, Winter 1994–1995, 24–35; Stanley R. Rich and David E. Gumpert, *Business Plans That Win $$$* (New York: Harper & Row, 1985).

8. Report content based in part on Lorri Freifeld, "How-To: Start a Corporate Mentoring Program," *Training*, accessed 27 April 2016, trainingmag.com; Beth N. Carvin, "How to Start a Corporate Mentoring Program," Mentor Scout, accessed 27 April 2016, www.mentorscout.com; "Benefits of Mentoring Programs," Insala, accessed 27 April 2016, mentoringtalent.com; Heather R. Huhman, "Create a Corporate Mentoring Program and You May Reap the Benefits," *Entrepreneur*, 10 February 2015, www.entrepreneur.com.

Five-Minute Guide to Planning Reports and Proposals

Before you start a major report or proposal, review these helpful tips.

00:01 **Figure out if you need to conduct research**

1. Don't research without a plan; start with a problem statement that defines the purpose of your research.
2. Start with secondary research; the information you need might have already been collected by someone else.
   - Don't restrict your search to the obvious or easiest sources and methods.
   - Evaluate information and sources carefully; watch for biased, incomplete, or outdated information.
3. If secondary research can't provide what you need, conduct primary research.
   - Use a survey to collect large amounts of quantitative data and brief qualitative answers.
   - Use interviews to collect in-depth qualitative answers.

00:02 **Plan ahead for how you will use the research**

1. Will you need statistical software and expertise to evaluate numerical data?
2. Be careful not to confuse correlation for causation.
3. With textual, qualitative information, you have three choices:
   - Quote the material in full.
   - Paraphrase it to the same depth but in your own words.
   - Summarize it more briefly in your own words.

00:03 **Tips for informational reports**

1. Most informational reports use the direct approach; use the indirect approach if you need to prepare readers for unwelcome information.
2. Identify the organizational scheme that will make the information easiest for the audience to grasp, such as organizing subtopics by comparison, importance, sequence, chronology, geography, or category.
3. If readers expect a particular format or breakdown of information, such as in a business plan, follow the general conventions for that type of report.

00:04 **Tips for analytical reports**

1. To help define the problem your analytical report will address, ask yourself what needs to be determined, why this issue is important, who is involved, and how the situation originated.
2. Try problem factoring—dividing the problem into a series of logical, connected questions that try to identify cause and effect.
3. Keep in mind whether you are expected to deliver a conclusion only or a conclusion and a recommendation.
4. Focus on your conclusion or recommendation if you have credibility with readers and they are likely to accept your message.
5. Otherwise, focus on logical arguments, using the 2 + 2 = 4 or yardstick models.

00:05 **Tips for proposals**

1. Remember that unsolicited proposals are much more challenging; before you can propose a solution, you might first need to convince your readers that a problem or an opportunity exists.
2. If you are responding to an RFP, follow its requirements to the letter.

13

Writing and Completing Reports and Proposals

ON THE JOB: COMMUNICATING AT

MCKINSEY & COMPANY

Guiding Readers into One of the World's Biggest Collections of Business Insights

Management consulting firms can be masters of content marketing, offering clients and potential clients access to original research, strategic insights, and tactical advice in every functional area of business management. Together with academic researchers, these firms practically function as the research and development department for the entire field of management.

The biggest and best of these firms generate a staggering amount of content. McKinsey & Company, perhaps the most prolific of them all, produces hundreds of articles every year and even publishes its own quarterly management journal. The firm started its own in-house "think tank," the McKinsey Global Institute, in 1992 and overall invests more than $600 million a year in original research.

All this adds up to a veritable library of value-added content. Naturally, the firm's research and publication efforts are intended to develop and promote its own capabilities as a service provider. However, the voluminous publication output has something to offer just about anyone who has an interest in business, including

Emma Kim/Alamy Stock Photo

To help readers navigate through a vast collection of reports and articles, the consulting firm McKinsey uses an interactive, reader-friendly report format it calls *Five Fifty* to offer two levels of information: a 5-minute summary and a 50-minute "deep dive."

entrepreneurs, small-business owners, professionals, managers, top-level executives—and students.

In fact, it's almost too much of a good thing. With so much content, time-pressed readers might struggle to get oriented on new subjects and find in-depth coverage of specific topics of interest.

To help readers find their way, McKinsey now publishes a unique multilevel, digital report it calls the *McKinsey Quarterly Five Fifty*. Each week, subscribers get a mobile-friendly overview of a major business management topic that has been bullet-point summarized for a fast 5-minute read, often with interactive visuals. Each major point then links to one or more in-depth articles that explore specific aspects of the subject (the 50-minute

reads). Some editions also include links to blog posts, videos, and podcasts for a full multimedia experience. You can sign up yourself for free; see the Real-Time Updates Learn More item below.

Aside from its value to McKinsey readers, the Five Fifty format offers a great lesson in reader-friendly report writing. Valuable content is a requirement if you want to help readers, of course, but making that content easily accessible with thoughtful, reader-oriented design can make the difference between content that never finds an audience and content that makes an impact.[1]

WWW.MCKINSEY.COM

Writing Reports and Proposals

This chapter focuses on writing and completing reports, along with creating content for websites, collaborating on wikis, and creating graphical elements to illustrate messages of all kinds. All the writing concepts and techniques you learned in Chapter 6 apply to the longer format of business reports. However, the length and complexity of reports call for special attention to several issues, starting with adapting to your audience.

1 LEARNING OBJECTIVE
List the topics commonly covered in the introduction, body, and close of informational reports, analytical reports, and proposals.

ADAPTING TO YOUR AUDIENCE

Reports and proposals can put heavy demands on your readers, so the "you" attitude is especially important with these long messages. In general, try to strike a balance between being overly informal (which can be perceived as trivializing important issues) and overly formal (which can put too much distance between you and your readers). If you know your readers reasonably well and your report is likely to meet with their approval, you can generally adopt an informal tone. To make your tone less formal, speak to readers in the first person, refer to them as *you*, and refer to yourself as *I* (or *we* if there are multiple report authors).

To make your tone more formal, use the impersonal journalism style: Emphasize objectivity, avoid personal opinions, and generally restrict your argument to provable facts. Eliminate all personal pronouns (including *I, you, we, us,* and *our*). Avoid humor, and be careful with your use of similes, metaphors, and particularly colorful adjectives or adverbs. However, you don't need to make the writing monotonous. For example, you can still create interest by varying the types of sentences to create a pleasing rhythm.

Take into account that communicating with people in other cultures often calls for more formality in reports, both to respect cultural preferences and to reduce the risk of miscommunication. Informal elements such as humor and casual language tend to translate poorly from one culture to another.

The "you" attitude is especially important with long or complex reports because they demand a lot from readers.

You can adjust the formality of your writing through your word choices and writing style.

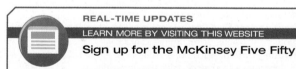

REAL-TIME UPDATES

LEARN MORE BY VISITING THIS WEBSITE

Sign up for the McKinsey Five Fifty

Get a mobile-friendly overview of a major business management topic every week with links to in-depth articles, blog posts, and podcasts. Go to **real-timeupdates.com/ebc13** and select Learn More in the Students section.

DRAFTING REPORT CONTENT

You can simplify report writing by breaking the job into three main sections: an introduction (or opening), a body, and a close. Table 13.1 on the next page summarizes the goals of each section and lists elements to consider including in each. You can use this table as a handy reference whenever you need to write a report in school or on the job.

TABLE 13.1 Content Elements to Consider for Reports and Proposals

Reports	Proposals
Introduction: Establish the context, identify the subject, preview main ideas (if using the direct approach), and establish tone and reader relationship.	**Introduction:** Identify the problem you intend to solve or the opportunity you want to pursue.
• **Authorization.** Reiterate who authorized the report, if applicable. • **Problem/purpose.** Explain the reason for the report's existence and what the report will achieve. • **Scope.** Describe what will and won't be covered in the report. • **Background.** Review historical conditions or factors that led up to the report. • **Sources and methods.** Discuss the primary and secondary sources consulted and research methods used. • **Definitions.** List terms and their definitions, including any terms that might be misinterpreted. Terms may also be defined in the body, explanatory notes, or glossary. • **Limitations.** Discuss factors beyond your control that affect report quality (but do not use this as an excuse for poor research or a poorly written report). • **Report organization.** Identify the topics to be covered and in what order.	• **Background or statement of the problem.** Briefly review the situation at hand, establish a need for action, and explain how things could be better. In unsolicited proposals, convince readers that a problem or an opportunity exists. • **Solution.** Briefly describe the change you propose, highlighting your key selling points and their benefits to show how your proposal will solve the reader's problem. • **Scope.** State the boundaries of the proposal—what you will and will not do. • **Proposal organization.** Orient the reader to the remainder of the proposal and call attention to the major divisions of thought.
Body: Present relevant information, and support your recommendations or conclusions.	**Body:** Give complete details on the proposed solution, and describe anticipated results.
• **Explanations.** Give complete details of the problem, project, or idea. • **Facts, statistical evidence, and trends.** Lay out the results of studies or investigations. • **Analysis of action.** Discuss potential courses of action. • **Pros and cons.** Explain the advantages, disadvantages, costs, and benefits of a particular course of action. • **Procedures.** Outline steps for a process. • **Methods and approaches.** Discuss how you've studied a problem (or gathered evidence) and arrived at your solution (or collected your data). • **Criteria.** Describe the benchmarks for evaluating options and alternatives. • **Conclusions and recommendations.** Discuss what you believe the evidence reveals and what you propose should be done about it. • **Support.** Give the reasons behind your conclusions or recommendations.	• **Facts and evidence to support your conclusions.** Provide information that will help readers take the action you would like them to take. • **Proposed approach.** Describe your concept, product, or service. Stress reader benefits and emphasize any advantages you have over your competitors. • **Work plan.** Describe how you'll accomplish what must be done (unless you're providing a standard, off-the-shelf item). Explain the steps you'll take, their timing, the methods or resources you'll use, and the person(s) responsible. State when work will begin, how it will be divided into stages, when you'll finish, and whether follow-up will be needed. • **Statement of qualifications.** Describe your organization's experience, personnel, and facilities—relating it all to readers' needs. Include a list of client references. • **Costs.** Prove that your costs are realistic—break them down so that readers can see the costs of labor, materials, transportation, travel, training, and other categories.
Close: Summarize key points, emphasize the benefits of any recommendations and list action items; label as "Summary" or "Conclusions and Recommendations."	**Close:** Summarize key points, emphasize the benefits and advantages of your proposed solution, and ask for a decision from the reader.
• **For direct approach.** Summarize key points (except in short reports), listing them in the order in which they appear in the body. Briefly restate your conclusions or recommendations, if appropriate. • **For indirect approach.** If you haven't done so at the end of the body, present your conclusions or recommendations. • **For motivating action.** Spell out exactly what should happen next and provide a schedule with specific task assignments.	• **Review of argument.** Briefly summarize the key points. • **Review of reader benefits.** Briefly summarize how your proposal will help the reader. • **Review of the merits of your approach.** Briefly summarize why your approach will be more effective than alternatives. • **Restatement of qualifications.** For external proposals, briefly reemphasize why you and your firm should do the work. • **Request.** Ask for a decision from the reader.

At a minimum, an effective *introduction* accomplishes these four tasks:

The introduction needs to put the report in context for the reader, introduce the subject, preview main ideas, and establish the tone of the document.

- It helps the reader understand the context of the report by tying it to a problem or an assignment.
- It introduces the subject matter and indicates why it is important.
- It previews the main idea (if you're using the direct approach).
- It establishes the tone and the writer's relationship with the audience.

The body of your report presents, analyzes, and interprets the information you have to offer your readers.

The *body* presents, analyzes, and interprets the information you have to offer and supports your recommendations or conclusions. The length and content of the body can vary widely based on the subject matter.

The *close* has three important functions:

- It summarizes your key points.
- It emphasizes the benefits to the reader if the document suggests a change or some other course of action.
- It brings all the action items together in one place.

Your close is often the last opportunity to get your message across, so make it clear and compelling.

To serve the needs of your readers and build your reputation as a careful and insightful professional, make sure your content in every section is accurate, complete, balanced, clear, and logical. As always, be sure to properly document all your sources (see Appendix B).

Make Your Reports Easier to Read

Help today's time-pressed readers find what they're looking for and stay on track as they navigate through your documents (see Figure 13.1 on the next page). First, write clear headings and subheadings that let readers follow the structure of your document and help them pick up the key points of your message. Avoid wordplay headings that force people to read the associated text to find out what the section is about. Second, use plenty of transitions to tie ideas together and show how each thought is related to another. Third, include *preview sections* to help readers get ready for new information and *review sections* after a body of material to summarize key points.

Help your readers find what they want and stay on track with headings, transitions, previews, and reviews.

Make Your Reports Easier to Write

Writing lengthy reports and proposals can be a huge task, so be sure to take advantage of technological tools to help you throughout the process. In addition to features such as automatic table of contents and index generators, look for opportunities to use *linked and embedded documents* to incorporate graphics, spreadsheets, databases, and other elements produced in other software programs. For instance, in Microsoft Office, you can choose to either *link* to another file (which ensures that changes in that file are reflected in your report) or *embed* another file (which doesn't include the automatic updating feature).

Look for ways to use technology to reduce the mechanical work involved in writing long reports.

Also, be sure to explore your media and channel options. Video clips, animation, presentation slides, *screencasts* (recordings of on-screen activity), and other media elements can enhance the communication and persuasion powers of the written word.

REAL-TIME UPDATES

LEARN MORE BY READING THIS ARTICLE

Build your company with effective responses to RFPs

In many industries, responding to RFPs is a vital business skill for expanding a company. Follow these insider tips. Go to **real-timeupdates.com/ebc13** and select Learn More in the Students section.

DRAFTING PROPOSAL CONTENT

All of the guidelines for writing reports apply to proposals as well, but these persuasive messages have some unique considerations. As Chapter 12 notes, the most important factor is whether the proposal is solicited or unsolicited, because that affects your organization, content, and tone.

The most important factor in determining your content and tone is whether the proposal is solicited or unsolicited.

Just as with reports, the text of a proposal comprises an introduction, a body, and a close. The introduction presents and summarizes the problem you intend to solve and the benefits of the solution you are about to propose. The body explains the complete details of the solution: how the job will be done, what method will be used to do it (including the required equipment, material, and personnel), when the work will begin and end, how much the work will cost, and why your company is qualified (for external proposals). The close emphasizes the benefits readers will realize from your solution and ends with a persuasive call to action.

The general purpose of any proposal is to persuade readers to do something, so your writing approach should be similar to that used for persuasive messages, perhaps including the use of the AIDA model to gain attention, build interest, create desire, and motivate action. Of course, you may need to adapt it if you're responding to an RFP or working

The AIDA model is a good approach for many proposals, but make sure you follow the RFP if you are responding to one.

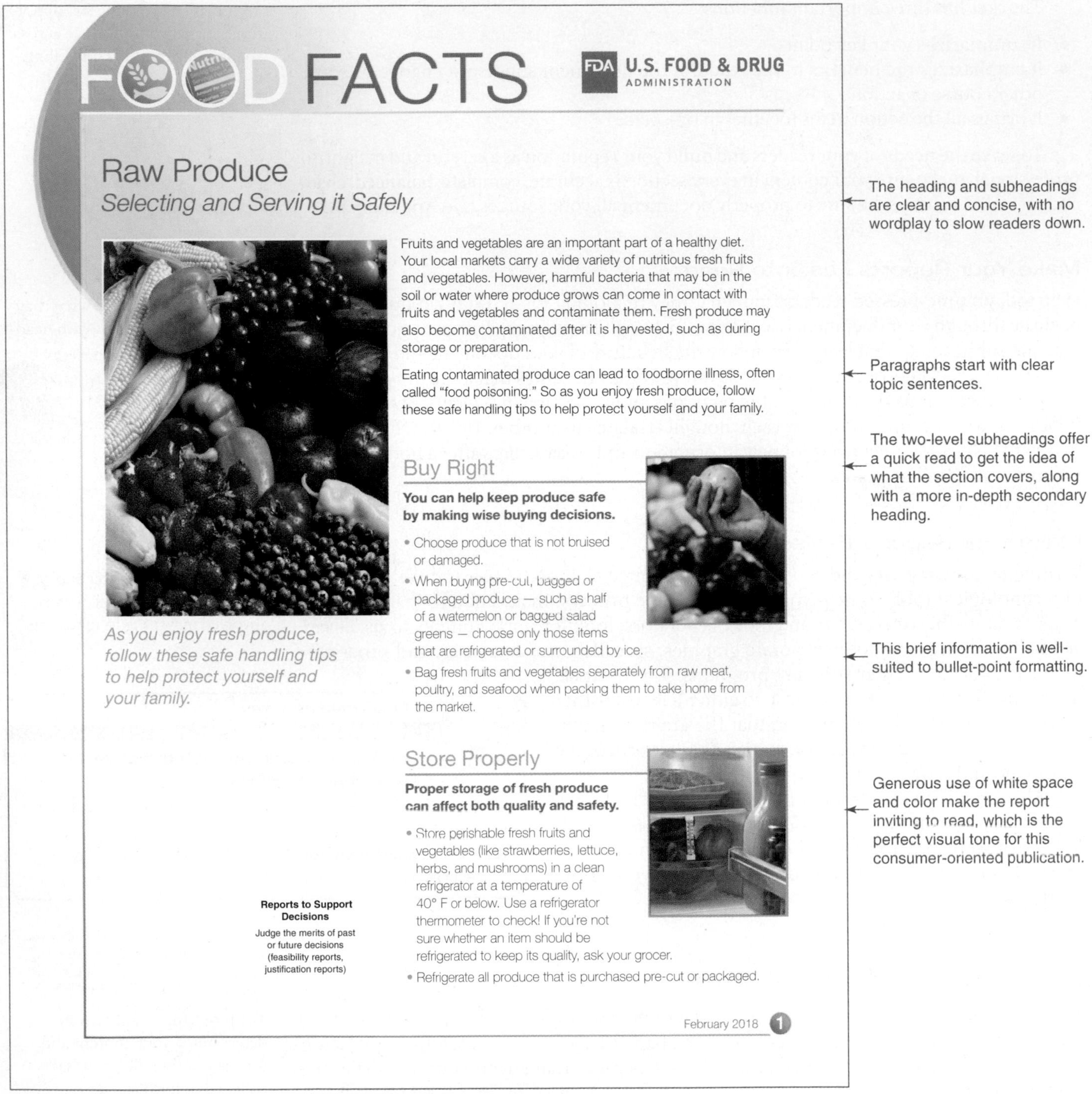

Raw Produce
Selecting and Serving it Safely

As you enjoy fresh produce, follow these safe handling tips to help protect yourself and your family.

Fruits and vegetables are an important part of a healthy diet. Your local markets carry a wide variety of nutritious fresh fruits and vegetables. However, harmful bacteria that may be in the soil or water where produce grows can come in contact with fruits and vegetables and contaminate them. Fresh produce may also become contaminated after it is harvested, such as during storage or preparation.

Eating contaminated produce can lead to foodborne illness, often called "food poisoning." So as you enjoy fresh produce, follow these safe handling tips to help protect yourself and your family.

Buy Right

You can help keep produce safe by making wise buying decisions.

- Choose produce that is not bruised or damaged.
- When buying pre-cut, bagged or packaged produce — such as half of a watermelon or bagged salad greens — choose only those items that are refrigerated or surrounded by ice.
- Bag fresh fruits and vegetables separately from raw meat, poultry, and seafood when packing them to take home from the market.

Store Properly

Proper storage of fresh produce can affect both quality and safety.

- Store perishable fresh fruits and vegetables (like strawberries, lettuce, herbs, and mushrooms) in a clean refrigerator at a temperature of 40° F or below. Use a refrigerator thermometer to check! If you're not sure whether an item should be refrigerated to keep its quality, ask your grocer.
- Refrigerate all produce that is purchased pre-cut or packaged.

Reports to Support Decisions

Judge the merits of past or future decisions (feasibility reports, justification reports)

February 2018　①

(Annotation callouts, right margin)

The heading and subheadings are clear and concise, with no wordplay to slow readers down.

Paragraphs start with clear topic sentences.

The two-level subheadings offer a quick read to get the idea of what the section covers, along with a more in-depth secondary heading.

This brief information is well-suited to bullet-point formatting.

Generous use of white space and color make the report inviting to read, which is the perfect visual tone for this consumer-oriented publication.

Figure 13.1 Audience-Friendly Reports
This page from a report on food safety demonstrates several aspects of audience-friendly writing and design.

within some other constraints. Here are some additional strategies to strengthen your argument:[2]

- Demonstrate your knowledge.
- Provide concrete information and examples.
- Research the competition so you know what other proposals your audience is likely to read.
- Demonstrate that your proposal is appropriate and feasible for your audience.
- Relate your product, service, or personnel to the reader's unique needs.

> **CHECKLIST** ✔ Composing Business Reports and Proposals
>
> **A. Adapt to your audience.**
> - ✔ Recognize the heavy demands that reports can put on readers, and emphasize the "you" attitude.
> - ✔ Adjust the level of formality to match the situation.
>
> **B. Draft report content.**
> - ✔ Use the introduction to establish the context and purpose, subject matter, main idea (if you're using the direct approach), and tone of the report.
> - ✔ Use the body to present, analyze, and interpret the information you have to offer.
> - ✔ Use the close to summarize major points, emphasize benefits to the reader if the document suggests action to be taken, and pull together all the action items from the report.
>
> - ✔ Make the report easy to read by using clear headings and subheadings, plenty of transitional elements, and preview and review sections.
>
> **C. Draft proposal content.**
> - ✔ Use the introduction to discuss the background or problem, your solution, the scope, and organization.
> - ✔ Use the body to persuasively explain the benefits of your proposed approach.
> - ✔ Use the close to emphasize reader benefits and summarize the merits of your approach.
> - ✔ Strengthen your argument by demonstrating your knowledge, providing concrete information and examples, researching the competition, showing that your ideas are appropriate and feasible, and relating your solution to the reader's needs.

Moreover, make sure your proposal is error-free, visually inviting, and easy to read. Readers will prejudge the quality of your products, services, or capabilities by the quality of your proposal. Errors, omissions, and inconsistencies will work against you—and might even cost you important career and business opportunities.

Consider using proposal-writing software if you and your company need to submit proposals as a routine part of doing business. These programs can automatically personalize proposals, ensure proper structure (making sure you don't forget any sections, for instance), organize storage of all your boilerplate text and previous proposal content, integrate contact information from sales databases, scan RFPs to identify questions (and even assign them to content experts), and fill in preliminary answers to common questions from a centralized knowledge base.[5]

To review the tasks discussed in this section, see "Checklist: Composing Business Reports and Proposals."

Writing for Websites and Wikis

In addition to standalone reports and proposals, you may be asked to write in-depth content for websites or to collaborate on a wiki. The basic principles of report writing apply to both formats, but each has some unique considerations as well.

> **2 LEARNING OBJECTIVE**
> Identify five characteristics of effective writing in online reports, and explain how to adapt your writing approach for wikis.

DRAFTING WEBSITE CONTENT

Major sections on websites often function in much the same way as reports. The skills you've developed for report writing adapt easily to this environment, as long as you keep a few points in mind (see Figure 13.2 on the next page):

- Because readers can be skeptical of online content, take special care to build trust with your intended audiences. Make sure your content is accurate, current, complete, and authoritative.
- As much as possible, adapt your content for a global audience. AI-enhanced translation tools can reduce the time and cost of translating web content.
- Wherever you can, use the *inverted pyramid* style, in which you cover the most important information briefly at first and then gradually reveal successive layers of detail—letting readers choose to see those additional layers if they want to.

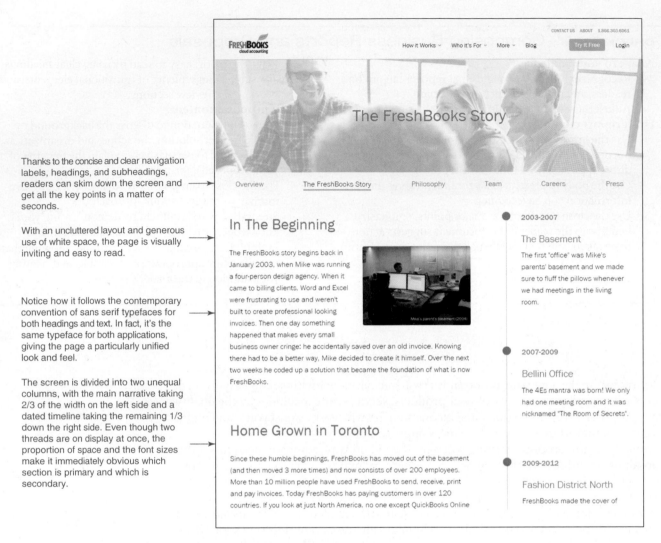

Thanks to the concise and clear navigation labels, headings, and subheadings, readers can skim down the screen and get all the key points in a matter of seconds.

With an uncluttered layout and generous use of white space, the page is visually inviting and easy to read.

Notice how it follows the contemporary convention of sans serif typefaces for both headings and text. In fact, it's the same typeface for both applications, giving the page a particularly unified look and feel.

The screen is divided into two unequal columns, with the main narrative taking 2/3 of the width on the left side and a dated timeline taking the remaining 1/3 down the right side. Even though two threads are on display at once, the proportion of space and the font sizes make it immediately obvious which section is primary and which is secondary.

Figure 13.2 **Writing and Designing for the Web**
This section of the company history page on the website of the software developer FreshBooks demonstrates effective design and writing choices.

Structure website content in a concise, skimmable format so readers can quickly find and consume topics of interest.

- Present your information in a concise, skimmable format. Effective websites use a variety of means to help readers skim pages quickly, including lists, color and boldface, informative headings, and helpful preview summaries that give readers the option of learning more if they choose to do so.
- Write concise, reader-friendly links that serve for both site navigation and content skimming. Clearly identify where a link will take readers, and don't use wordplay that forces readers to guess what a section or page is about.
- Keep content up to date. If content on a particular page is likely to go out of date over time, include an indication on the page of when it was last updated to help readers judge whether it is current when they read it.

COLLABORATING ON WIKIS

Wikis are a great way for teams and other groups to collaborate on writing projects, from brief articles to long reports and reference works. Although wikis have many benefits, they do require a unique approach to writing. To be a valuable wiki contributor, keep these points in mind:[4]

Effective collaboration on wikis requires a unique approach to writing.

- Let go of traditional expectations of authorship, including individual recognition and control.
- Encourage all team members to improve each other's work.

- Use page templates and other formatting options to make sure your content matches the rest of the wiki.
- Use the separate editing and discussion capabilities appropriately.
- Take advantage of the *sandbox*, if available; this is a "safe," nonpublished section of the wiki where team members can practice editing and writing.

Wikis usually have guidelines to help new contributors integrate their work into the group's ongoing effort. Be sure to read and understand these guidelines, and don't be afraid to ask for help.

If you are creating a new wiki, think through your long-term purpose carefully, just as you would with a new blog or podcast channel. Doing so will help you craft appropriate guidelines, editorial oversight, and security policies.

If you are adding a page or an article to an existing wiki, determine how this new material fits in with the existing organization. Also, learn the wiki's preferred style for handling incomplete articles. For example, on the wiki that contains the user documentation for the popular WordPress blogging software, contributors are discouraged from adding new pages until the content is "fairly complete and accurate."[5]

> Before you add new pages to a wiki, figure out how the material fits with the existing content.

If you are revising or updating an existing wiki article, use the questions on page 192 in Chapter 7 to evaluate the content before you make changes. If you don't agree with published content and plan to revise it, you can use the wiki's discussion facility to share your concerns with other contributors. The wiki environment should encourage discussions and even robust disagreements, as long as everyone remains civil and respectful. Also, take care not to let individual pages grow too long over time as people continue to add content. Periodically assess whether these pages need to be restructured and divided into multiple smaller pages.[6]

Illustrating Your Reports with Effective Visuals

3 LEARNING OBJECTIVE
Discuss six principles of graphic design that can improve the quality of your visuals, and identify the major types of business visuals.

Well-designed visual elements can enhance the communication power of textual messages and, in some instances, even replace them. Visuals can often convey some message points (such as spatial relationships, correlations, procedures, and emotions) more effectively and more efficiently than words. In general, in a given amount of time, effective images can convey much more information than text.[7] Humans also have a prodigious capacity for accurately memorizing and recalling images.[8] Thanks to infographics and other tools, visuals have also become an important aspect of contemporary business storytelling.[9]

In the numbers-oriented world of work, people rely heavily on trend lines, distribution curves, and other visual presentations of numeric quantities. Visuals attract and hold people's attention, helping your audience understand and remember your message. Busy readers often jump to visuals to try to get the gist of a message, and attractive visuals can draw readers more deeply into your reports and presentations. Using pictures is also an effective way to communicate with the diverse audiences that are common in today's business environment.

> Carefully crafted visuals enhance the power of your words.

As you read in Chapter 6, many words and phrases carry connotative meanings, which are all the mental images, emotions, and other impressions that the word or phrase evokes in audience members. A significant part of the power—and risk—of visual elements derives from their connotative meanings as well. Even something as simple as a watermark symbol embedded in letterhead stationery can boost reader confidence in the message printed on the paper.[10] Many colors, shapes, and other design elements have **visual symbolism**, and their symbolic, connotative meanings can evolve over time and mean different things in different cultures (see Figure 13.3 on the next page).

> *Visual symbolism* encompasses the connotative meaning of colors, shapes, and other visual elements.

UNDERSTANDING VISUAL DESIGN PRINCIPLES

Given the importance of visuals in today's business environment, **visual literacy**—the ability (as a sender) to create effective images and (as a receiver) to correctly interpret visual messages—has become a key business skill.[11] Just as creating effective sentences,

> *Visual literacy* is the ability to create effective images and to interpret images correctly.

Figure 13.3 Visual Symbolism
A red cross (with equal-length arms) on a white background is the well-known symbol of the Red Cross relief organization. It is also used to indicate the medical branches of many nations' military services. The red cross symbol is based on the flag of Switzerland (where the first Red Cross organization was formed), which over the course of hundreds of years developed from battle flags that originally used the Christian cross symbol. Although the Red Cross emblem is not based directly on the Christian symbol, the organization uses a red crescent in countries where Islam is the dominant religion and is known as the Red Crescent. To avoid any association with religious symbols, the International Federation of Red Cross and Red Crescent Societies (the global umbrella organization for all national Red Cross and Red Crescent organizations) adopted the Red Crystal as its new symbol.

paragraphs, and documents requires working knowledge of the principles of good writing, creating effective visuals requires some knowledge of the principles of good design. Even if you have no formal training in design, being aware of the following six principles will help you be a more effective visual communicator:

> Pay close attention to consistency, contrast, balance, emphasis, convention, and simplicity.

- **Consistency.** Think of consistency as *visual parallelism*, similar to textual parallelism, that helps audiences understand and compare a series of ideas.[12] You can achieve visual parallelism through the consistent use of color, shape, size, texture, position, scale, or typeface.
- **Contrast.** To emphasize differences, depict items in contrasting colors, such as red and blue or black and white. To emphasize similarities, make color differences subtler.
- **Balance.** Visual balance can be either *formal*, in which the elements in the images are arranged symmetrically around a central point or axis, or *informal*, in which elements are not distributed evenly but stronger and weaker elements are arranged in a way that achieves an overall effect of balance.[13] Formal balance tends to feel calming and serious, whereas informal balance tends to feel dynamic and engaging.
- **Emphasis.** Audiences are likely to assume that the dominant element in a design is the most important, so make sure that the visually dominant element really does represent the most important information.
- **Convention.** Just as written communication is guided by spelling, grammar, punctuation, and usage conventions, visual communication is guided by generally accepted rules or conventions that dictate virtually every aspect of design.[14] In every culture, for instance, certain colors and shapes have specific meanings. In the United States, for example, the color green is often associated with money because green is a featured color on U.S. currency. However, this association has no meaning in most other countries.
- **Simplicity.** When you're designing graphics for your documents, limit the number of colors and design elements and take care to avoid *chartjunk*—decorative elements that clutter documents without adding any relevant information.[15] Think carefully about using some of the chart features available in your software, too. Many of these features can actually get in the way of effective visual communication.[16] For example, three-dimensional bar charts, cones, and pyramids can look appealing, but the third dimension usually adds no additional information and can be visually deceiving as well.[17]

UNDERSTANDING THE ETHICS OF VISUAL COMMUNICATION

Power always comes with responsibility—and the potential power of visuals places an ethical burden on every business communicator. Ethical problems, both intentional and unintentional, can range from photos that play on racial or gender stereotypes to images that imply cause-and-effect relationships that may not exist to graphs that distort data.

Altering the scale of items in a visual is just one of many ways to emphasize or deemphasize certain aspects of information. For example, to increase the perceived size of a product, an advertiser might show a close-up of it being held by someone with smaller-than-average hands. Conversely, a large hand would make the product seem smaller.

You can work to avoid ethical problems with your visuals by following these guidelines:[18]

- Consider all possible interpretations—and misinterpretations.
- Don't imply cause-and-effect relationships without offering proof that they exist.
- Provide enough background information to help audiences interpret the visual information correctly.
- Don't hide or minimize visual information that runs counter to your argument—and don't exaggerate visual information that supports your argument.
- Don't oversimplify complex situations by hiding complications that are important to the audience's understanding of the situation.
- Avoid emotional manipulation or other forms of coercion.
- Be careful with the way you *aggregate*, or group, data. If you use a small number of large "buckets," you might obscure fluctuations that could be meaningful to your audience.

PRACTICING ETHICAL COMMUNICATION

Distorting the Data

Take a quick look at these three line charts, all of which display the level of impurities found in a source of drinking water. Chart (a) suggests that the source has a consistently high level of impurities throughout the year, Chart (b) indicates that the level of impurities jumps up and down throughout the year, and Chart (c) shows an impurity level that is fairly consistent throughout the year—and fairly low.

Here's the catch: All three charts are displaying *exactly the same data*.

Look again at Chart (a). The vertical scale is set from 0 to 120, sufficient to cover the range of variations in the data. However, what if you wanted to persuade an audience that the variations from month to month were quite severe? In Chart (b), the scale is "zoomed in" on 60 to 110, making the variations look much more dramatic. The result could be a stronger emotional impact on the reader, creating the impression that these impurities are out of control.

On the other hand, what if you wanted to create the impression that things were humming along just fine, with low levels of impurities and no wild swings from month to month? You would follow the example in Chart (c), where the scale is expanded from 0 to 200, which appears to minimize the variations in the data. This graph is visually "calmer," potentially creating the impression that there's really nothing to worry about.

If all three graphs show the same data, is any one of them more honest than the others? The answer to this question depends on your intent and your audience's information needs. For instance, if dramatic swings in the measurement from month to month suggest a problem with the quality of your product or the safety of a process that affects the public, then visually minimizing the swings might well be considered dishonest.

CRITICAL THINKING

1. What sort of quick visual impression would such a chart give if the vertical scale is set to 0 to 500? Why?
2. If the acceptable range of impurities in this case is from 60 to 120 parts per million, which of these three charts is the fairest way to present the data? Why?

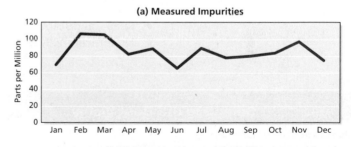

(a) Measured Impurities

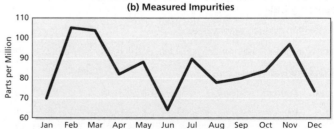

(b) Measured Impurities

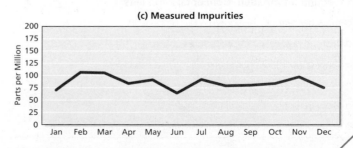

(c) Measured Impurities

For example, aggregating sales data by weeks or months can hide daily fluctuations that are important to how your readers interpret the data. If the daily variations are important, don't aggregate the data into longer time blocks.

CHOOSING THE RIGHT VISUAL FOR THE JOB

You can choose from many types of visuals, and each is best suited to particular communication tasks.

After you've identified the points in your message that would benefit most from visual presentation, your next decision is to choose the types of visuals to use (see Table 13.2).

For certain kinds of information, the decision is usually obvious. If you want to present a large set of numeric values or detailed textual information, for instance, a table is the best choice in most cases. Also, certain visuals are commonly used for certain applications; for example, your audience is likely to expect line charts and bar charts to show trends. (Note that *chart* and *graph* are used interchangeably for most of the display formats discussed here.)

Tables

Tables are a good choice when you need to show large amounts of structured data or information.

When you need to show a large number of specific data points or pieces of information, choose a *table*, a systematic arrangement of data in columns and rows. Tables are ideal when your audience needs information that would be either difficult or tedious to handle in the main text. Most tables contain the standard parts illustrated in Figure 13.4. Follow these guidelines to create clear, effective tables:

- Use common, understandable units (such as dollars, pounds, liters, and so on) and clearly label them.
- Express all items in a column in the same unit, and round off for simplicity—if doing so doesn't distort the meaning.
- Label column headings clearly and use subheadings if necessary.
- Separate columns or rows with lines, extra space, or colors to make the table easy to follow. Make sure the intended reading direction—down the columns or across the rows—is obvious, too.
- Keep online tables small enough to read comfortably on-screen.
- Document the source of data using the same format as a text footnote (see Appendix B).

REAL-TIME UPDATES

LEARN MORE BY EXPLORING THIS INTERACTIVE WEBSITE

A visual vocabulary of data presentation options

Find the best ways to illustrate a variety of data sets and situations. Go to **real-timeupdates.com/ebc13** and select Learn More in the Students section.

TABLE 13.2 Selecting the Best Visual

Communication Challenge	Effective Visual Choice
Presenting Data	
To present individual, exact values	Table
To show trends in one or more variables, or the relationship between those variables, over time	Line chart, bar chart
To compare two or more sets of data	Bar chart, line chart
To show frequency or distribution of parts in a whole	Pie chart
To show massive data sets, complex quantities, or dynamic data	Data visualization
Presenting Information, Concepts, and Ideas	
To show geographic relationships or comparisons	Map, geographic information system
To illustrate processes or procedures	Flowchart, diagram
To show conceptual or spatial relationships (simplified)	Illustration
To tell a data-driven story visually	Infographic
To show (realistic) spatial relationships	Photograph
To show processes, transformations, and other activities	Animation, video

	Multicolumn Heading			Single-Column Heading
	Column Subheading	Column Subheading	Column Subheading	
Row Heading	xxx	xxx	xxx	xxx
Row Heading	xxx	xxx	xxx	xxx
Row Subheading	xxx	xxx	xxx	xxx
Row Subheading	xxx	xxx	xxx	xxx
Row Heading	xxx	xxx	xxx	xxx
Row Heading	xxx	xxx	xxx	xxx
TOTALS	xxx	xxx	xxx	xxx

Figure 13.4   Parts of a Table

Here are the typical parts of a table. No matter which design you choose, make sure the layout is clear and the individual rows and columns are easy to follow.

Line Charts and Surface Charts

A **line chart** illustrates trends over time or plots the relationship of two variables (see Figure 13.5). In line charts that show trends, the vertical axis shows the amount, and the horizontal axis shows the time or other quantity against which the amount is being measured. You can plot just a single line or overlay multiple lines to compare different entities.

A **surface chart**, also called an *area chart*, is a form of line chart that shows a cumulative effect; all the lines add up to the top line, which represents the total (see Figure 13.6 on the next page). This type of chart helps you illustrate changes in the composition of something over time. When preparing a surface chart, put the most significant line at the bottom and move up toward the least significant.

A line chart illustrates trends over time or plots the relationship of two variables.

A surface chart is a form of line chart that shows the cumulative effect of all the lines adding up to the top line.

Bar Charts and Pie Charts

A **bar chart** portrays numbers with the height or length of its rectangular bars, making a series of numbers easy to grasp quickly. Bars can be oriented horizontally or vertically (in which case they are sometimes referred to as *column charts*) in a variety of formats (see Figure 13.7 on the next page). Specialized bar charts such as *timelines* and *Gantt charts* are used often in project management, for example.

A **pie chart** is a tool commonly used to show how the parts of a whole are distributed. Although pie charts are popular and can quickly highlight the dominant parts of a whole, they are often not as effective as bar charts or tables. Comparing percentages accurately is often difficult with a pie chart but can be fairly easy with a bar chart

A bar chart portrays numbers with the height or length of its rectangular bars.

Pie charts are used frequently in business reports to show parts of a whole, but often they are not as helpful to readers as bar charts and other types of visuals would be.

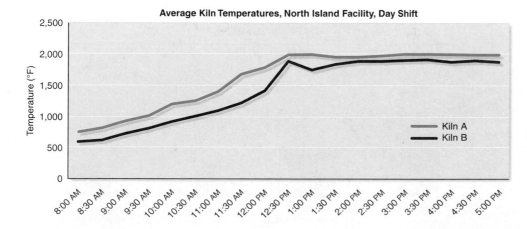

Figure 13.5   Line Chart

This two-line chart compares the temperatures measured inside two cement kilns every half hour from 8:00 A.M. to 5:00 P.M.

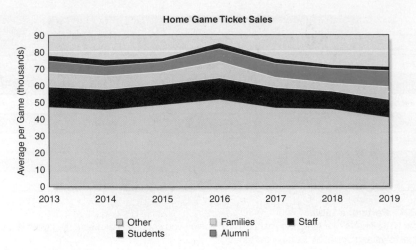

Figure 13.6 Surface Chart
Surface or area charts can show a combination of trends over time and the individual contributions of the components of a whole.

(see Figure 13.8 on page 410). Making pie charts easier to read can require labeling each slice with data values, in which case a table might serve the purpose more effectively.[19]

Data Visualization

Conventional charts and graphs are limited in several ways: Most types can show only a limited number of data points before becoming too cluttered to interpret, they often can't

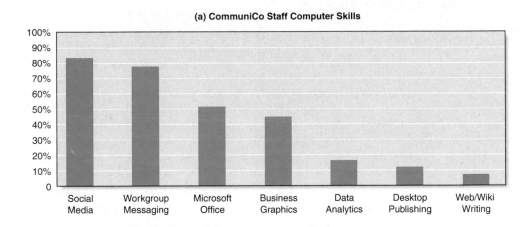

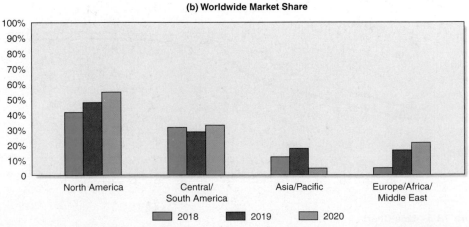

(continued)

Figure 13.7 Bar Charts
Here are six of the dozens of variations possible with bar charts: singular (a), grouped (b), deviation (c), segmented (d), combination (e), and paired (f).

show complex relationships among data points, and they can represent only numeric data. A diverse class of display capabilities known as **data visualization** work to overcome all these drawbacks. In some instances, data visualization is less about clarifying

Data visualization tools can overcome the limitations of conventional charts and other display types.

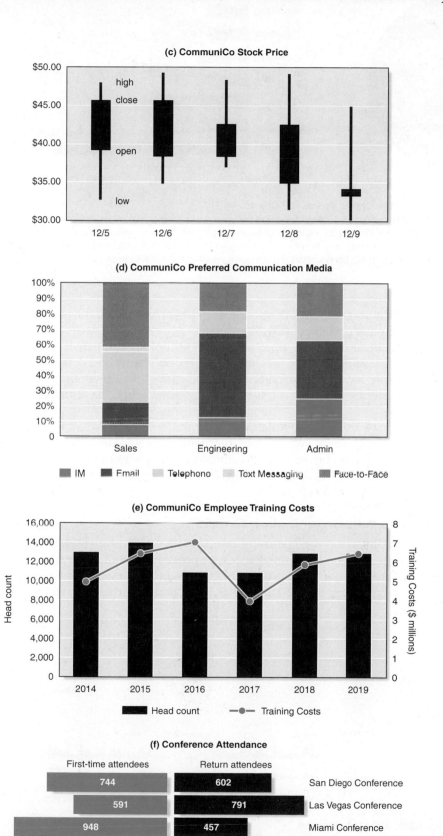

Figure 13.7   Bar Charts (*Continued*)

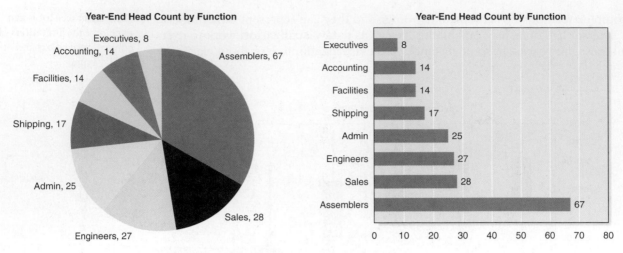

Figure 13.8 **Pie Charts Versus Bar Charts**

Pie charts are used frequently, but they aren't necessarily the best choice for many data presentations. This pie chart does make it easy to see that assemblers are the largest employee category, but other slice sizes (such as Sales, Engineers, and Admin) are not as easy to compare and require a numerical rather than a visual comparison. In contrast, the bar chart gives a quick visual comparison of every data point.

Data visualization is an important tool for companies using big data because it helps users experiment with data sets and discover new relationships.

individual data points and more about extracting broad meaning from giant masses of data or putting the data in context.[20]

Data visualization has become an important tool for companies working with big data. Interactive apps let users "drill down" into data sets to find details or look at data collections from a variety of perspectives (see Figure 13.9). This notion of experimentation and discovery is perhaps the most important benefit that data visualization can bring to businesses.[21]

In addition to displaying large data sets and linkages within data sets, other kinds of visualization tools combine data with textual information to communicate complex or dynamic data much faster than conventional presentations can. For example, a *tag cloud* shows the relative frequency of terms, or tags (content labels), in an article, a blog, a website, survey data, or another collection of text.[22]

Flowcharts and Organization Charts

A flowchart illustrates a sequence of events from start to finish.

A **flowchart** illustrates a sequence of events from start to finish (see Figure 13.10); it is indispensable when illustrating processes, procedures, and sequential relationships. For general business purposes, you don't need to be too concerned about the specific shapes on a flowchart; just be sure to use them consistently. However, you should be

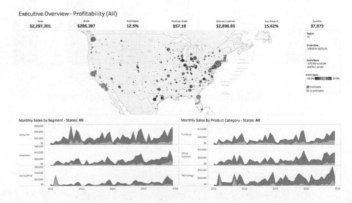

Figure 13.9 **Data Visualization**

Data visualization displays and software tools take a wide variety of forms. Here is a mobile app that lets users explore a large data set from different perspectives and at varying levels of detail.

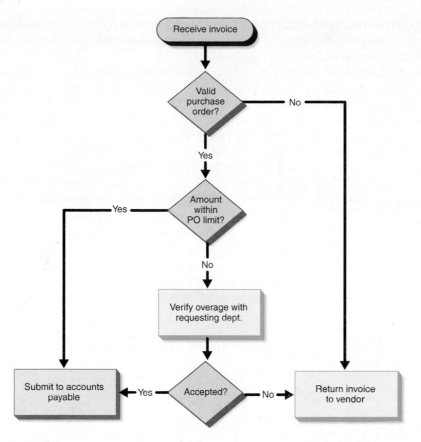

Figure 13.10   Flowchart
Flowcharts show sequences of events and are most valuable when the process or procedure has multiple decision points and variable paths.

aware that there is a formal flowchart "language," in which each shape has a specific meaning (diamonds are decision points, rectangles are process steps, and so on). If you're communicating with computer programmers and others who are accustomed to formal flowcharting, make sure you use the correct symbols to avoid confusion.

As the name implies, an *organization chart* illustrates the positions, units, or functions in an organization and the ways they interrelate. In fact, organization charts can be used to portray almost any hierarchy, including the topics, subtopics, and supporting points you need to organize for a report.

REAL-TIME UPDATES

LEARN MORE BY VISITING THIS WEBSITE

Data visualization and infographics gateway

This unique web resource offers links to a vast array of data visualization and infographic techniques and examples. Go to **real-timeupdates.com/ebc13** and select Learn More in the Students section.

Maps, Illustrations, Diagrams, Infographics, and Photographs

Maps can show location, distance, points of interest (such as competitive retail outlets), and geographic distribution of data (such as sales by region or population by state). In addition to presenting facts and figures, maps are useful for showing market territories, distribution routes, and facilities locations. When combined with databases and aerial or satellite photography in *geographic information systems (GISs)*, maps become extremely powerful visual reporting tools.

Illustrations and diagrams can show an endless variety of business concepts, such as the network of suppliers in an industry, the flow of funds through a company, or the process for completing payroll each week. More complex diagrams can convey technical topics such as the operation of a machine or repair procedures. Word processors and presentation software now offer drawing capabilities that are sufficient for many business communication needs, but for more precise and professional illustrations, you may need a specialized

Use maps to represent statistics by geographic area and to show spatial relationships.

Illustrations are sometimes better than photographs because they let you focus on the most important details.

package such as Adobe Illustrator or Trimble SketchUp. For more technical illustrations, *computer-aided design (CAD)* systems such as Autodesk's AutoCAD can produce extremely detailed architectural and engineering drawings.

Infographics are a special class of diagrams that can convey data as well as concepts or ideas.

Infographics are a special class of diagrams that can convey data as well as concepts or ideas. In addition, they contain enough visual and textual information to function as independent, standalone documents. Broadly speaking, there are two types of infographics: those that are stylized collections of charts or graphs and those that have a structured narrative. The first type, represented by Figure 13.11, don't necessarily convey any more information than basic charts and graphs in a conventional report would, but their communication value lies in their ability to catch the audience's attention and the ease with which they can be distributed online. The second type take full advantage of the visual medium to tell stories or show interconnected processes. Both types can be powerful communication tools, even to the point of replacing conventional reports.

Photographs offer both functional and decorative value, and nothing can top a photograph when you need to show exact appearances. However, in some situations, a photograph

REAL-TIME UPDATES

LEARN MORE BY VISITING THESE INTERACTIVE WEBSITES

Free tools for creating infographics

These easy-to-use web tools let you create high-quality infographics. Go to **real-timeupdates.com/ebc13** and select Learn More in the Students section.

Figure 13.11   Infographics
Infographics are a great way to tell stories with data, as in this infographic on the science behind customer loyalty. (The infographic appears online as a single, long image.)

can show too much detail, which is one reason technical manuals frequently use illustrations instead of photos. Because audiences expect photographs to show literal visual truths, you must take care when using image-processing tools such as Adobe Photoshop.

Use photographs for visual appeal and to show exact appearances.

Video

From tutorials and product demonstrations to seminars and speeches, online video is now an essential business communication medium. For videos that require the highest production quality, companies usually hire specialists with the necessary skills and equipment. For most routine needs, however, any business communicator with modest equipment and a few basic skills can create effective videos. The three-step process adapts easily to video; professionals refer to the three steps as *preproduction*, *production*, and *postproduction*. The Real-Time Updates element on this page suggests a resource for advice on getting started with digital video.

REAL-TIME UPDATES

LEARN MORE BY EXPLORING THIS WEBSITE

Great advice for getting started in digital video

This website offers a wealth of advice on producing quality videos. Go to **real-timeupdates.com/ebc13** and select Learn More in the Students section.

DESIGNING EFFECTIVE VISUALS

Computers make it easy to create visuals, but they also make it easy to create ineffective visuals. By following the design principles discussed on page 404, you can create basic visuals that are attractive and effective. If possible, have a professional designer set up a template for the various types of visuals you and your colleagues need to create. By specifying color palettes, typeface selections, slide layouts, and other choices, design templates have three important benefits: They help ensure better designs, they promote consistency across the organization, and they save everyone time by eliminating repetitive decision-making.

Remember that the style and quality of your visuals communicate a subtle message about your relationship with the audience. A simple sketch might be fine for a working meeting but inappropriate for a formal presentation or report. On the other hand, elaborate, full-color visuals may be viewed as extravagant for an informal report but may be expected for a message to top management or influential outsiders.

In addition to being well designed, visuals need to be well integrated with text. Follow these three steps:

To tie visuals to the text, introduce them in the text and place them near the points they illustrate.

- Try to position your visuals so that your audience won't have to flip back and forth (in printed documents) or scroll (on screen) between visuals and the text that discusses them. If space constraints prevent you from placing visuals close to relevant text, include pointers such as "Figure 2 (on the following page)" to help readers locate the image quickly.
- Clearly refer to visuals by number in the text of your report and help your readers understand the significance of visuals by referring to them before readers encounter them in the document or on screen.
- Write effective *titles*, *captions*, and *legends* to complete the integration of your text and visuals. A **title** provides a short description that identifies the content and purpose of the visual. A **caption** usually offers additional discussion of the visual's content and can be several sentences long, if appropriate. A **legend** helps readers decode the visual by explaining what various colors, symbols, or other design choices mean.

A *title* identifies the content and purpose of a visual, the *caption* usually offers additional discussion of the visual's content, and a *legend* explains what various colors, symbols, or other design choices mean.

Be sure to check your visuals carefully for accuracy. Check for mistakes such as typographical errors, inconsistent color treatment, confusing or unexplained symbols, and misaligned elements. Make sure your software hasn't done something unexpected, such as arranging chart bars in an order you don't want or plotting line charts in confusing colors.

Proof visuals as carefully as you proof text.

If you're designing visuals for mobile devices, be aware that the constraints of small screens are even more acute with visuals than they are with text. Preparing visual content for mobile users takes careful planning and the use of display tools designed for mobile devices. With screen space at a premium, think carefully about audience members' needs,

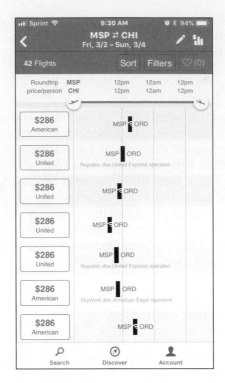

Figure 13.12 Visual Displays on Mobile Devices
Think through your audience's needs carefully when designing mobile visuals. As with this mobile app from the Hipmunk airfare-search service, show only the most essential information on each screen, with no extraneous information, and let users tap through for more details.

including the circumstances in which they'll be using their devices, so you can prioritize and sequence the delivery of information (see Figure 13.12).

Finally, step back and consider the ethical implications of your visuals. Visuals are easy to misuse, intentionally or unintentionally. To avoid ethical lapses in your visuals, consider all possible interpretations, provide enough background information for readers to interpret your visuals correctly, and don't hide or minimize visual information that readers need in order to make informed judgments.[23]

For more information on visual communication, including design principles, ethical matters, and the latest tools for creating and displaying visuals, visit **real-timeupdates .com/ebc13** and select Chapter 13. For a review of the important points to remember when creating visuals, see "Checklist: Creating Effective Visuals."

CHECKLIST ✔ Creating Effective Visuals

- ✔ Emphasize visual consistency to connect parts of a whole and minimize audience confusion.
- ✔ Avoid arbitrary changes of color, texture, typeface, position, or scale.
- ✔ Highlight contrasting points through color, position, and other design choices.
- ✔ Decide whether you want to achieve formal or informal balance.
- ✔ Emphasize dominant elements and deemphasize less important pieces in a design.
- ✔ Understand and follow the visual conventions your audience expects, unless breaking the rules can be effective.
- ✔ Strive for simplicity and clarity; don't clutter your visuals with meaningless decoration.

- ✔ Follow the guidelines for avoiding ethical lapses.
- ✔ Carefully consider your message, the nature of your information, and your audience to choose which points to illustrate.
- ✔ Select the proper types of graphics for the information at hand and for the objective of the message.
- ✔ Integrate visuals and text by maintaining a balance between illustrations and words, clearly referring to visuals within the text, and placing visuals carefully.
- ✔ Use titles, captions, and legends to help readers understand the meaning and importance of your visuals.
- ✔ Verify the quality of your visuals by checking for accuracy, proper documentation, and honesty.

Completing Reports and Proposals

As with shorter messages, when you have finished your first draft, you need to perform four tasks in order to complete your document: revise, produce, proofread, and distribute. The revision process is essentially the same for reports as for other business messages, although it may take considerably longer, depending on the length and complexity of your documents. Evaluate your organization, style, and tone to make sure your content is clear, logical, and reader oriented. Then work to improve the report's readability by varying sentence length, keeping paragraphs short, using lists and bullets, and adding helpful headings and subheadings. Figure 13.13 shows an informal, solicited proposal in letter format.

4 LEARNING OBJECTIVE
Summarize the four tasks involved in completing business reports and proposals.

The revision process for long reports can take considerable time, so be sure to plan ahead.

1793 East Westerfield Road, Arlington Heights, Illinois 60005
(847) 398-1148 Fax: (847) 398-1149 Email: dod@ix.netcom.com

July 31, 2020

Ms. Joyce Colton, P.E.
AGI Builders, Inc.
1280 Spring Lake Drive
Belvidere, Illinois, 61008

Subject: Proposal No. F-0087 for AGI Builders, Elgin Manufacturing Campus

Dear Ms. Colton:

O'Donnell & Associates is pleased to submit the following proposal to provide construction testing services for the mass grading operations and utility work at the Elgin Manufacturing Campus, 126th St., Elgin, Illinois. Our company has been providing construction-testing services in the Chicago area since 1972 and has performed numerous large-scale geotechnical investigations across Illinois, including more than 100 at O'Hare International Airport, Midway Airport, Meig's Field, and other airports.

The opening paragraph serves as an Introduction.

The introduction grabs the reader's attention by highlighting company qualifications.

Background

It is our understanding that the work consists of two projects: (1) the mass grading perations will require approximately six months, and (2) the utility work will require approximately three months. The two operations are scheduled as follows:

Mass Grading Operation	September 2020–February 2021
Utility Work	March 2021–May 2021

Headings divide the proposal into logical segments for easy reading.

The project background section acknowledges the two projects and their required timeline.

Proposed Approach and Work Plan

O'Donnell & Associates will perform observation and testing services during both the mass grading operations and the excavation and backfilling of the underground utilities. Specifically, we will perform field density tests on the compacted material using a nuclear moisture/density gauge, as required by the job specifications. We will also conduct appropriate laboratory tests such as ASTM D-1557 Modified Proctors. We will prepare detailed reports summarizing the results of our field and laboratory testing. Fill materials to be placed at the site may consist of natural granular materials (sand), processed materials (crushed stone, crushed concrete, slag), or clay soils. O'Donnell & Associates will provide qualified personnel to perform the necessary testing.

The work plan describes the scope of the project and outlines specific tests the company will perform.

(continued)

Figure 13.13   Solicited External Proposal
This proposal was submitted by Dixon O'Donnell, vice president of O'Donnell & Associates, a geotechnical engineering firm that conducts a variety of environmental testing services. The company is bidding on the mass grading and utility work specified by AGI Builders. As you review this document, pay close attention to the specific items addressed in the proposal's introduction, body, and close.

After assembling your report or proposal in its final form, review it thoroughly one last time, looking for inconsistencies, errors, and missing components. Don't forget to proof your visuals thoroughly and make sure they are positioned correctly. For online reports, make sure all links work as expected and all necessary files are active and available. If you need specific tips on proofreading documents, look back at Chapter 7.

PRODUCING FORMAL REPORTS AND PROPOSALS

Formal reports and proposals can contain a number of additional support features.

Formal reports and proposals can include a variety of features beyond the text and visuals (see Table 13.3 on page 419). Most of these provide additional information; a few are more decorative and add a degree of formality.

One of the most important elements to consider is an introductory feature that helps time-pressed readers get a sense of what's in the document or even get all the key points without reading the document. A **synopsis**, sometimes called an *abstract*, is a brief overview (one page or less) of a report's most important points. The phrasing of a synopsis can be *informative*

A *synopsis* is a brief overview of a report's key points.

Ms. Joyce Colton, AGI Builders   Page 2   July 31, 2020

The work plan also explains who will be responsible for the various tasks. →

Kevin Patel will be the lead field technician responsible for the project. A copy of his résumé is included with this proposal for your review. Kevin will coordinate field activities with your job site superintendent and make sure that appropriate personnel are assigned to the job site. Overall project management will be the responsibility of Joseph Proesel. Project engineering services will be performed under the direction of Dixon O'Donnell, P.E. All field personnel assigned to the site will be familiar with and abide by the Project Site Health and Safety Plan prepared by Carlson Environmental, Inc., dated April 2020.

← The project leader's résumé is attached to the proposal, providing additional detail without cluttering up the body of the proposal.

Qualifications

The qualifications section grabs attention by mentioning compelling qualifications. →

O'Donnell & Associates has been providing quality professional services since 1972 in the areas of

- Geotechnical engineering
- Materials testing and inspection
- Pavement evaluation
- Environmental services
- Engineering and technical support (CADD) services

The company provides Phase I and Phase II environmental site assessments, preparation of LUST site closure reports, installation of groundwater monitoring wells, and testing of soil/groundwater samples for environmental contaminants. Geotechnical services include all phases of soil mechanics and foundation engineering, including foundation and lateral load analysis, slope stability analysis, site preparation recommendations, seepage analysis, pavement design, and settlement analysis.

O'Donnell & Associates materials testing laboratory is certified by AASHTO Accreditation Program for the testing of Soils, Aggregate, Hot Mix Asphalt and Portland Cement Concrete. A copy of our laboratory certification is included with this proposal. In addition to in-house training, field and laboratory technicians participate in a variety of certification programs, including those sponsored by the American Concrete Institute (ACI) and Illinois Department of Transportation (IDOT).

← Describing *certifications* (approvals by recognized industry associations or government agencies) helps build the company's credibility.

Costs

On the basis of our understanding of the scope of the work, we estimate the total cost of the two projects to be $100,260.00, as follows:

Figure 13.13 **Solicited External Proposal** (*Continued*) (presenting the main points in the order in which they appear in the text) if you're using the direct approach or *descriptive* (simply describing what the report is about, without revealing the main idea) if you're using the indirect approach. As an alternative to a synopsis or an abstract, a longer report may include an **executive summary**, a fully developed "mini" version of the report for readers who lack the time or motivation to read the entire document.

An *executive summary* is a fully developed "mini" version of the report.

For an illustration of how the various parts fit together in a formal report, see Report Writer's Notebook: Analyzing a Formal Report, beginning on page 420. To review the elements that you should consider including in formal reports and proposals, see "Checklist: Producing Formal Reports and Proposals."

DISTRIBUTING REPORTS AND PROPOSALS

For physical distribution of important printed reports or proposals, consider spending the extra money for a professional courier or package delivery service. Doing so can help you stand out in a crowd, and it lets you verify receipt. Alternatively, if you've prepared the

---

Ms. Joyce Colton, AGI Builders   Page 3   July 31, 2020

Cost Estimates

Cost Estimate: Mass Grading	Units	Rate ($)	Total Cost ($)
Field Inspection			
Labor	1,320 hours	$38.50	$ 50,820.00
Nuclear Moisture Density Meter	132 days	35.00	4,620.00
Vehicle Expense	132 days	45.00	5,940.00
Laboratory Testing			
Proctor Density Tests (ASTM D-1557)	4 tests	130.00	520.00
Engineering/Project Management			
Principal Engineer	16 hours	110.00	1,760.00
Project Manager	20 hours	80.00	1,600.00
Administrative Assistant	12 hours	50.00	600.00
Subtotal			$ 65,860.00

A clear and complete itemization of estimated costs builds confidence in the dependability of the project's financial projections.

Cost Estimate: Utility Work	Units	Rate ($)	Total Cost ($)
Field Inspection			
Labor	660 hours	$ 38.50	$ 25,410.00
Nuclear Moisture Density Meter	66 days	5.00	2,310.00
Vehicle Expense	66 days	45.00	2,970.00
Laboratory Testing			
Proctor Density Tests (ASTM D-1557)	2 tests	130.00	260.00
Engineering/Project Management			
Principal Engineer	10 hours	110.00	1,100.00
Project Manager	20 hours	80.00	1,600.00
Administrative Assistant	15 hours	50.00	750.00
Subtotal			$ 34,400.00
Total Project Costs			**$100,260.00**

This estimate assumes full-time inspection services. However, our services may also be performed on an as-requested basis, and actual charges will reflect time associated with the project. We have attached our standard fee schedule for your review. Overtime rates are for hours in excess of 8.0 hours per day, before 7:00 a.m., after 5:00 p.m., and on holidays and weekends.

To give the client some budgetary flexibility, the proposal offers an alternative to the fixed-fee approach—which may lower any resistance to accepting the bid.

Figure 13.13   Solicited External Proposal (*Continued*)

(continued)

document for a single person or small group in your office or the local area, delivering it in person will give you the chance to personally introduce the report and remind readers why they're receiving it.

For digital distribution, ask your readers what format they would like to receive the report in. The two most common formats are Microsoft Word documents and PDF files, but depending on the circumstances a different format might be more useful. With PDF files, you can select a variety of security settings that restrict who can open, edit, or print the document.[24]

If your company or client expects you to distribute your reports via cloud storage, a content management system, a shared workspace, or some other online location, double-check that you've uploaded the correct file(s) to the correct location. Verify the on-screen display of your reports after you've posted them, making sure graphics, charts, links, and other elements are in place and operational.

Whenever possible, ask your readers what digital format they would like to receive reports in.

Ms. Joyce Colton, AGI Builders   Page 4   July 31, 2020

Authorization

With a staff of over 30 personnel, including registered professional engineers, resident engineers, geologists, construction inspectors, laboratory technicians, and drillers, we are confident that O'Donnell & Associates is capable of providing the services required for a project of this magnitude.

If you would like our firm to provide the services as outlined in this proposal, please sign this letter and return it to us along with a certified check in the amount of $10,000 (our retainer) by August 14, 2020. Please call me if you have any questions regarding the terms of this proposal or our approach.

Sincerely,

Dixon O'Donnell

Dixon O'Donnell
Vice President

Enclosures

Accepted for AGI BUILDERS, INC.

By_____ Date _____

The brief close emphasizes the bidder's qualifications and asks for a decision.

The call to action clarifies the steps needed to put the project in motion.

The customer's signature will make the proposal a binding contract.

Figure 13.13 Solicited External Proposal (*Continued*)

For more information on writing and completing reports and proposals, visit **real-timeupdates.com/ebc13** and select Chapter 13.

TABLE 13.3 Production Elements to Consider for Formal Reports and Proposals

Reports	Proposals
Prefatory elements (before the introduction)	**Prefatory elements** (before the introduction)
• **Cover.** A concise title that gives readers the information they need in order to grasp the purpose and scope of the report. For a formal printed report, choose heavy, high-quality *cover stock*. • **Title fly.** Some formal reports open with a plain sheet of paper that has only the title of the report on it, although this is certainly not necessary. • **Title page.** Typically includes the report title, name(s) and title(s) of the writer(s), and date of submission; this information can be put on the cover instead. • **Letter/memo of authorization.** If you received written authorization to prepare the report, you may want to include that letter or memo in your report. • **Letter/memo of transmittal.** Cover letter that introduces the report and can include scope, methods, limitations, and highlights of the report; offers to provide follow-up information or assistance; and acknowledges help received while preparing the report. • **Table of contents.** List all section headings and major subheadings to show the location and hierarchy of the information in the report. • **List of illustrations.** Consider including if the illustrations are particularly important, and you want to call attention to them. • **Synopsis or executive summary.** See discussion on page 416.	• **Cover, title fly, title page.** Same uses as with reports; be sure to follow any instructions in the RFP, if relevant. • **Copy of or reference to the RFP.** Instead of having a letter of authorization, a solicited proposal should follow the instructions in the RFP. Some will instruct you to include the entire RFP in your proposal; others may want you to simply identify it by a name and tracking number. • **Synopsis or executive summary.** These components are less common in formal proposals than in reports. In an unsolicited proposal, your letter of transmittal will catch the reader's interest. In a solicited proposal, the introduction will provide an adequate preview of the contents. • **Letter/memo of transmittal.** If the proposal is solicited, treat the transmittal letter as a positive message, highlighting those aspects of your proposal that may give you a competitive advantage. If the proposal is unsolicited, the transmittal letter should follow the advice for persuasive messages (see Chapter 11)—the letter must persuade the reader that you have something worthwhile to offer that justifies reading the proposal.
Supplementary elements (after the close)	**Supplementary elements** (after the close)
• **Appendixes.** Additional information related to the report but not included in the main text because it is too lengthy or lacks direct relevance. List appendixes in your table of contents and refer to them as appropriate in the text. • **Bibliography.** List the secondary sources you consulted; see Appendix B. • **Index.** List names, places, and subjects mentioned in the report, along with the pages on which they occur.	• **Appendixes.** Same uses as with reports; be sure to follow any instructions in the RFP, if relevant. • **Résumés of key players.** For external proposals, résumés can convince readers that you have the talent to achieve the proposal's objectives.

CHECKLIST ✔ Producing Formal Reports and Proposals

A. Prefatory elements (before the introduction)
- ✔ Use a high-quality cover for printed reports
- ✔ Include a concise, descriptive title on the cover.
- ✔ Include a title fly only if you want an extra-formal touch.
- ✔ On the title page, typically include the report title, name(s) and title(s) of the writer(s), and date of submission; this information can be put on the cover instead.
- ✔ Include a copy of the letter of authorization, if appropriate.
- ✔ If responding to an RFP, follow its instructions for including a copy or referring to the RFP by name or tracking number.
- ✔ Include a letter or memo of transmittal that introduces the report.
- ✔ Provide a table of contents in outline form, with headings worded exactly as they appear in the body of the report.
- ✔ Include a list of illustrations if the report contains a large number of them.
- ✔ Include a synopsis (brief summary of the report) or an executive summary (a condensed, "mini" version of the report) for longer reports.

B. Supplementary elements (after the close)
- ✔ Use appendixes to provide supplementary information or supporting evidence.
- ✔ List in a bibliography any secondary sources you used.
- ✔ Provide an index if your report contains many terms or ideas and is likely to be consulted over time.

Analyzing a Formal Report

The report presented in the following pages was prepared by Linda Moreno, the cost accounting manager at Electrovision. Electrovision's main product is optical character recognition equipment, which is used by the U.S. Postal Service for sorting mail. Moreno's job is to help analyze the company's costs, and she has this to say about the background of the report:

> For the past three or four years, Electrovision has been on a roll. Our A-12 optical character reader was a real breakthrough, and the post office grabbed up as many as we could make. Our sales and profits kept climbing, and morale was fantastic. Everybody seemed to think that the good times would last forever. Unfortunately, everybody was wrong. When the Postal Service announced that it was postponing all new equipment purchases because of cuts in its budget, we woke up to the fact that we are essentially a one-product company with one customer. At that point, management started scrambling around looking for ways to cut costs until we could diversify our business a bit.
>
> The vice president of operations, Dennis McWilliams, asked me to help identify cost-cutting opportunities in travel and entertainment. On the basis of his personal observations, he felt that Electrovision was overly generous

in its travel policies and that we might be able to save a significant amount by controlling these costs more carefully. My investigation confirmed his suspicion.

> I was reasonably confident that my report would be well received. I've worked with Dennis for several years and know what he likes: plenty of facts, clearly stated conclusions, and specific recommendations for what should be done next. I also knew that my report would be passed on to other Electrovision executives, so I wanted to create a good impression. I wanted the report to be accurate and thorough, visually appealing, readable, and appropriate in tone.

When writing the analytical report that follows, Moreno based the organization on conclusions and recommendations presented in direct order. The first two sections of the report correspond to Moreno's two main conclusions: that Electrovision's travel and entertainment costs are too high and that cuts are essential. The third section presents recommendations for achieving better control over travel and entertainment expenses. As you review the report, analyze both the mechanical aspects and the way Moreno presents her ideas. Be prepared to discuss the way the various components convey and reinforce the main message.

Stockbyte/Getty Images

**Reducing Electrovision's
Travel and Entertainment Costs**

Prepared for

Dennis McWilliams,

Vice President of Operations

Electrovision, Inc.

Prepared by

Linda Moreno, Manager

Cost Accounting Services

Electrovision, Inc.

February 17, 2020

Large, bold type distinguishes the title from the other elements on the cover.

The name of the recipient, if applicable, typically comes after the title.

Generous use of white space between elements gives the cover an open feel.

Dating the report gives it a feeling of currency when it is submitted and, conversely, as time passes, signals to future readers that the material might be out of date at that point.

The "how-to" tone of Moreno's title is appropriate for an action-oriented report that emphasizes recommendations. A more neutral title, such as "An Analysis of Electrovision's Travel and Entertainment Costs," would be more suitable for an informational report.

The memo format is appropriate for this internal report; the letter format would be used for transmitting an external report.

The tone is conversational yet still businesslike and respectful.

Acknowledging help given by others is good etiquette and a way to foster positive working relationships.

<table>
<tr><td colspan="2">**MEMORANDUM**</td></tr>
<tr><td>**TO:**</td><td>Dennis McWilliams, Vice President of Operations</td></tr>
<tr><td>**FROM:**</td><td>Linda Moreno, Manager of Cost Accounting Services   *LM*</td></tr>
<tr><td>**DATE:**</td><td>February 17, 2020</td></tr>
<tr><td>**SUBJECT:**</td><td>Reducing Electrovision's Travel and Entertainment Costs</td></tr>
</table>

Here is the report you requested January 28 on Electrovision's travel and entertainment costs.

Your suspicions were right. We are spending far too much on business travel. Our unwritten policy has been "anything goes," leaving us with no real control over T&E expenses. Although this hands-off approach may have been understandable when Electrovision's profits were high, we can no longer afford the luxury of going first class.

The solutions to the problem seem rather clear. We need to have someone with centralized responsibility for travel and entertainment costs, a clear statement of policy, an effective control system, and a business-oriented travel service that can optimize our travel arrangements. We should also investigate alternatives to travel, such as videoconferencing.

Getting people to economize is not going to be easy. In the course of researching this issue, I've found that our employees are deeply attached to their generous travel privileges. I think some would almost prefer a cut in pay to a loss in travel status. We'll need a lot of top management involvement to sell people on the need for moderation.

I'm grateful to Mary Lehman and Connie McIllvain for their considerable help in rounding up and sorting through five years' worth of expense reports.

Thanks for giving me the opportunity to work on this assignment. It's been a real education. If you have any questions about the report, please give me a call.

Moreno expects a positive response, so she presents her main conclusion right away.

She closes graciously, with thanks and an offer to discuss the results.

In this report, Moreno decided to write a brief memo of transmittal and include a separate executive summary. Short reports (fewer than 10 pages) often combine the synopsis or executive summary with the memo or letter of transmittal.

The table of contents doesn't include any elements that appear before the "Contents" page.

The headings are worded exactly as they appear in the text.

Moreno lists the figures because they are all significant, and the list is fairly short.

This and other prefatory pages are numbered with Roman numerals.

CONTENTS	PAGE

LIST OF ILLUSTRATIONS

FIGURES	PAGE

TABLE

The table lists only the page number on which a section begins, not the entire range of numbers.

Moreno included only first- and second-level headings in her table of contents, even though the report contains third-level headings. She prefers a shorter table of contents that focuses attention on the main divisions of thought. She used informative titles, which are appropriate for a report to a receptive audience.

The executive summary begins by stating the purpose of the report.

Moreno presents the points in the executive summary in the same order as they appear in the report, using subheadings that summarize the content of the main sections of the report.

EXECUTIVE SUMMARY

This report analyzes Electrovision's travel and entertainment (T&E) costs and presents recommendations for reducing those costs.

Travel and Entertainment Costs Are Too High

Travel and entertainment is a large and growing expense category for Electrovision. The company spends over $16 million per year on business travel, and these costs have been increasing by 12 percent annually. Company employees make roughly 3,390 trips each year at an average cost per trip of $4,720. Airfares are the biggest expense, followed by hotels, meals, and rental cars.

The nature of Electrovision's business does require extensive travel, but the company's costs are excessive: Our employees spend more than twice the national average on travel and entertainment. Although the location of the company's facilities may partly explain this discrepancy, the main reason for our high costs is a management style that gives employees little incentive to economize.

Cuts Are Essential

Electrovision management now recognizes the need to gain more control over this element of costs. The company is currently entering a period of declining profits, prompting management to look for every opportunity to reduce spending. At the same time, rising airfares and hotel rates are making T&E expenses more significant.

Electrovision Can Save $6 Million per Year

Fortunately, Electrovision has a number of excellent opportunities for reducing T&E costs. Savings of up to $6 million per year should be achievable, judging by the experience of other companies. A sensible travel-management program can save companies as much as 35 percent a year (Gilligan 39–40), and we should be able to save even more, since we purchase many more business-class tickets than the average. Four steps will help us cut costs:

1. Hire a director of travel and entertainment to assume overall responsibility for T&E spending, policies, and technologies, including the hiring and management of a national travel agency.
2. Educate employees on the need for cost containment, both in avoiding unnecessary travel and reducing costs when travel is necessary.
3. Negotiate preferential rates with travel providers.
4. Implement technological alternatives to travel, such as virtual meetings.

As necessary as these changes are, they will likely hurt morale, at least in the short term. Management will need to make a determined effort to explain the rationale for reduced spending. By exercising moderation in their own travel arrangements, Electrovision executives can set a good example and help other employees accept the changes. On the plus side, using travel alternatives such as web conferencing will reduce the travel burden on many employees and help them balance their business and personal lives.

iv

Her audience is receptive, so the tone in the executive summary is forceful; a more neutral approach would be better for hostile or skeptical readers.

The executive summary uses the same font and paragraph treatment as the text of the report.

The page numbering in the executive summary continues with Roman numerals.

Moreno decided to include an executive summary because her report is aimed at a mixed audience, some of whom are interested in the details of her report and others who just want the "big picture." The executive summary is aimed at the second group, giving them enough information to make a decision without burdening them with the task of reading the entire report.

Her writing style matches the serious nature of the content without sounding distant or stiff. Moreno chose the formal approach because several members of her audience are considerably higher up in the organization, and she did not want to sound too familiar. In addition, her company prefers the impersonal style for formal reports.

A color bar highlights the report title and the first-level headings; a variety of other design treatments are possible as well.

REDUCING ELECTROVISION'S TRAVEL AND ENTERTAINMENT COSTS

INTRODUCTION

Electrovision has always encouraged a significant amount of business travel. To compensate employees for the stress and inconvenience of frequent trips, management has authorized generous travel and entertainment (T&E) allowances. This philosophy has been good for morale, but last year Electrovision spent $16 million on travel and entertainment—$7 million more than it spent on research and development.

This year's T&E costs will affect profits even more because of increases in airline fares and hotel rates. Also, the company anticipates that profits will be relatively weak for a variety of other reasons. Therefore, Dennis McWilliams, Vice President of Operations, has asked the accounting department to explore ways to reduce the T&E budget.

The purpose of this report is to analyze T&E expenses, evaluate the effect of recent hotel and airfare increases, and suggest ways to tighten control over T&E costs. The report outlines several steps that could reduce Electrovision's expenses, but the precise financial impact of these measures is difficult to project. The estimates presented here provide a "best guess" of what Electrovision can expect to save.

In preparing this report, the accounting department analyzed internal expense reports for the past five years to determine how much Electrovision spends on travel and entertainment. These figures were then compared with average statistics compiled by Dow Jones (publisher of the *Wall Street Journal*) and presented as the Dow Jones Travel Index. We also analyzed trends and suggestions published in a variety of business journal articles to see how other companies are coping with the high cost of business travel.

THE HIGH COST OF TRAVEL AND ENTERTAINMENT

Although many companies view travel and entertainment as an incidental cost of doing business, the dollars add up. At Electrovision the bill for airfares, hotels, rental cars, meals, and entertainment totaled $16 million last year. Our T&E budget has increased by 12 percent per year for the past five years. Compared with the average U.S. business traveler, Electrovision's expenditures are high, largely because of management's generous policy on travel benefits.

The introduction opens by establishing the need for action.

Moreno mentions her sources and methods to increase credibility and to give readers a complete picture of the study's background.

A *running footer* that contains the report title and the page number appears on every page.

In her brief introduction, Moreno counts on topic sentences and transitions to indicate that she is discussing the purpose, scope, and limitations of the study.

$16 Million per Year Spent on Travel and Entertainment

Electrovision's annual budget for T&E is only 8 percent of sales. Because this is a relatively small expense category compared with such things as salaries and commissions, it is tempting to dismiss T&E costs as insignificant. However, T&E is Electrovision's third-largest controllable expense, directly behind salaries and information systems.

Last year Electrovision personnel made about 3,390 trips at an average cost per trip of $4,720. The typical trip involved a round-trip flight of 3,000 miles, meals, hotel accommodations for two or three days, and a rental car. Roughly 80 percent of trips were made by 20 percent of the staff—top management and sales personnel traveled most, averaging 18 trips per year.

Figure 1 illustrates how the T&E budget is spent. The largest categories are airfares and lodging, which together account for $7 of every $10 that employees spend on T&E. This spending breakdown has been relatively steady for the past five years and is consistent with the distribution of expenses experienced by other companies.

Figure 1
Airfares and Lodging Account for Over
Two-Thirds of Electrovision's T&E Budget

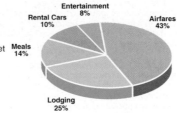

Although the composition of the T&E budget has been consistent, its size has not. As mentioned earlier, these expenditures have increased by about 12 percent per year for the past five years, roughly twice the rate of the company's sales growth (see Figure 2). This rate of growth makes T&E Electrovision's fastest-growing expense item.

Figure 2
T&E Expenses Continue to Increase as a
Percentage of Sales

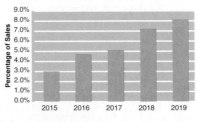

The visual is placed as close as possible to the point it illustrates.

Each visual has a title that clearly indicates what it's about; titles are consistently placed to the left of each visual.

Moreno opens the first main section of the body with a topic sentence that introduces an important fact about the subject of the section. Then she orients the reader to the three major points developed in the section.

The visuals are numbered consecutively and referred to by their numbers in the text.

Moreno introduces visuals before they appear and indicates what readers should notice about the data.

Electrovision's Travel Expenses Exceed National Averages

Much of our travel budget is justified. Two major factors contribute to Electrovision's high T&E budget:

- With our headquarters on the West Coast and our major customer on the East Coast, we naturally spend a lot of money on cross-country flights.

- A great deal of travel takes place between our headquarters here on the West Coast and the manufacturing operations in Detroit, Boston, and Dallas. Corporate managers and division personnel make frequent trips to coordinate these disparate operations.

However, even though a good portion of Electrovision's travel budget is justifiable, the company spends considerably more on T&E than the average business traveler (see Figure 3).

Figure 3
Electrovision Employees Spend Over Twice as Much as the Average Business Traveler

Source: *Wall Street Journal* and company records

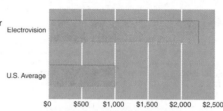

Dollars Spent per Day

The Dow Jones Travel Index calculates the average cost per day of business travel in the United States, based on average airfare, hotel rates, and rental car rates. The average fluctuates weekly as travel companies change their rates, but it has been running at about $1,000 per day for the last year or so. In contrast, Electrovision's average daily expense over the past year has been $2,250—a hefty 125 percent higher than average. This figure is based on the average trip cost of $4,720 listed earlier and an average trip length of 2.1 days.

Spending Has Been Encouraged

Although a variety of factors may contribute to this differential, Electrovision's relatively high T&E costs are at least partially attributable to the company's philosophy and management style. Since many employees do not enjoy business travel, management has tried to make the trips more pleasant by authorizing business-class airfare, luxury hotel accommodations, and full-size rental cars. The sales staff is encouraged to entertain clients at top restaurants and to invite them to cultural and sporting events.

The chart in Figure 3 is simple but effective; Moreno includes just enough data to make her point. Notice how she is as careful about the appearance of her report as she is about the quality of its content.

The cost of these privileges is easy to overlook, given the weakness of Electrovision's system for tracking T&E expenses:

A bulleted list makes it easy for readers to identify and distinguish related points.

- The monthly financial records do not contain a separate category for travel and entertainment; the information is buried under Cost of Goods Sold and under Selling, General, and Administrative Expenses.

- Each department head is given authority to approve any expense report, regardless of how large it may be.

- Receipts are not required for expenditures less than $100.

- Individuals are allowed to make their own travel arrangements.

- No one is charged with the responsibility for controlling the company's total spending on travel and entertainment.

GROWING IMPACT ON THE BOTTOM LINE

Informative headings focus reader attention on the main points. Such headings are appropriate when a report uses the direct approach and is intended for a receptive audience. However, descriptive headings are more effective when a report uses the indirect approach and readers are less receptive.

During the past three years, the company's healthy profits have resulted in relatively little pressure to push for tighter controls over all aspects of the business. However, as we all know, the situation is changing. We're projecting flat to declining profits for the next two years, a situation that has prompted all of us to search for ways to cut costs. At the same time, rising airfares and hotel rates have increased the impact of T&E expenses on the company's financial results.

Lower Profits Underscore the Need for Change

The next two years promise to be difficult for Electrovision. After several years of steady increases in spending, the Postal Service is tightening procurement policies for automated mail-handling equipment. Funding for the A-12 optical character reader has been canceled. As a consequence, the marketing department expects sales to drop by 15 percent. Although Electrovision is negotiating several other promising R&D contracts, the marketing department does not foresee any major procurements for the next two to three years.

At the same time, Electrovision is facing cost increases on several fronts. As we have known for several months, the new production facility now under construction in Salt Lake City, Utah, is behind schedule and over budget. Labor contracts in Boston and Dallas will expire within the next six months, and plant managers there anticipate that significant salary and benefits concessions may be necessary to avoid strikes.

Moreover, marketing and advertising costs are expected to increase as we attempt to strengthen these activities to better cope with competitive pressures. Given the expected decline in revenues and increase in costs, the Executive Committee's prediction that profits will fall by 12 percent in the coming fiscal year does not seem overly pessimistic.

Reducing Electrovision's Travel and Entertainment Costs   Page **4**

Moreno designed her report to include plenty of white space so even those pages that lack visuals are still attractive and easy to read.

Moreno supports her argument with objective facts and sound reasoning.

The recommendations are realistic, noting both the benefits and the risks of taking action.

Airfares and Hotel Rates Are Rising

Business travelers have grown accustomed to frequent fare wars and discounting in the travel industry in recent years. Excess capacity and aggressive price competition, particularly in the airline business, made travel a relative bargain.

However, that situation has changed as weaker competitors have been forced out and the remaining players have grown stronger and smarter. Airlines and hotels are better at managing inventory and keeping occupancy rates high, which translates into higher costs for Electrovision. Last year saw some of the steepest rate hikes in years. Business airfares (tickets most likely to be purchased by business travelers) jumped more than 40 percent in many markets. The trend is expected to continue, with rates increasing another 5 to 10 percent overall (Phillips 331; "Travel Costs Under Pressure" 30; Dahl B6).

Given the fact that air and hotel costs account for almost 70 percent of our T&E budget, the trend toward higher prices in these two categories will have serious consequences, unless management takes action to control these costs.

METHODS FOR REDUCING T&E COSTS

By implementing a number of reforms, management can expect to reduce Electrovision's T&E budget by as much as 40 percent. This estimate is based on the general assessment made by American Express (Gilligan 39) and on the fact that we have an opportunity to significantly reduce air travel costs by eliminating business-class travel. However, these measures are likely to be unpopular with employees. To gain acceptance for such changes, management will need to sell employees on the need for moderation in T&E allowances.

Four Ways to Trim Expenses

By researching what other companies are doing to curb T&E expenses, the accounting department has identified four prominent opportunities that should enable Electrovision to save about $6 million annually in travel-related costs.

Institute Tighter Spending Controls

A single individual should be appointed director of travel and entertainment to spearhead the effort to gain control of the T&E budget. More than a third of all U.S. companies now employ travel managers ("Businesses Use Savvy Managers" 4). The director should be familiar with the travel industry and should be well versed in both accounting and information technology. The director should also report to the vice president of operations. The director's first priorities should be to establish a written T&E policy and a cost-control system.

Electrovision currently has no written policy on T&E, a step that is widely recommended by air travel experts (Smith D4). Creating a policy would clarify management's position and serve as a vehicle for communicating the need for moderation.

Moreno creates a forceful tone by using action verbs in the third-level subheadings of this section. This approach is appropriate to the nature of the study and the attitude of the audience. However, in a status-conscious organization, the imperative verbs might sound a bit too presumptuous coming from a junior member of the staff.

At a minimum, the policy should include the following:

- All T&E should be strictly related to business and should be approved in advance.

- Except under special circumstances to be approved on a case-by-case basis, employees should travel by coach and stay in mid-range business hotels.

- The T&E policy should apply equally to employees at all levels.

In addition to making key points easy to find, bulleted lists help break up the text to relieve the reader's eye.

To implement the new policy, Electrovision will need to create a system for controlling T&E expenses. Each department should prepare an annual T&E budget as part of its operating plan. These budgets should be presented in detail so that management can evaluate how T&E dollars will be spent and can recommend appropriate cuts. To help management monitor performance relative to these budgets, the director of travel should prepare monthly financial statements showing actual T&E expenditures by department.

The director of travel should also be responsible for retaining a business-oriented travel service that will schedule all employee business trips and look for the best travel deals, particularly in airfares. In addition to centralizing Electrovision's reservation and ticketing activities, the agency will negotiate reduced group rates with hotels and rental car firms. The agency selected should have offices nationwide so that all Electrovision facilities can channel their reservations through the same company. This is particularly important in light of the dizzying array of often wildly different airfares available between some cities. It's not uncommon to find dozens of fares along commonly traveled routes (Rowe 30). In addition, the director can help coordinate travel across the company to secure group discounts whenever possible (Barker 31; Miller B6).

Moreno lists the steps needed to implement her recommendations.

Reduce Unnecessary Travel and Entertainment

One of the easiest ways to reduce expenses is to reduce the amount of traveling and entertaining that occurs. An analysis of last year's expenditures suggests that as much as 30 percent of Electrovision's T&E is discretionary. The professional staff spent $2.8 million attending seminars and conferences last year. Although these gatherings are undoubtedly beneficial, the company could save money by sending fewer representives to each function and perhaps by eliminating some of the less valuable seminars.

Similarly, Electrovision could economize on trips between headquarters and divisions by reducing the frequency of such visits and by sending fewer people on each trip. Although there is often no substitute for face-to-face meetings, management could try to resolve more internal issues through telephone, electronic, and written communication.

Electrovision can also reduce spending by urging employees to economize. Instead of flying business class, employees can fly coach class or take advantage of discount fares. Rather than ordering a $50 bottle of wine, employees can select a less expensive bottle or dispense with alcohol entirely. People can book rooms at moderately priced hotels and drive smaller rental cars.

Moreno takes care not to overstep the boundaries of her analysis. For instance, she doesn't analyze the value of the seminars that employees attend every year, so she avoids any absolute statements about reducing travel to seminars.

Obtain Lowest Rates from Travel Providers

Apart from urging employees to economize, Electrovision can also save money by searching for the lowest available airfares, hotel rates, and rental car fees. Currently, few employees have the time or knowledge to seek out travel bargains. When they need to travel, they make the most convenient and comfortable arrangements. A professional travel service will be able to obtain lower rates from travel providers.

Judging by the experience of other companies, Electrovision may be able to trim as much as 30 to 40 percent from the travel budget simply by looking for bargains in airfares and negotiating group rates with hotels and rental car companies. Electrovision should be able to achieve these economies by analyzing its travel patterns, identifying frequently visited locations, and selecting a few hotels that are willing to reduce rates in exchange for guaranteed business. At the same time, the company should be able to save up to 40 percent on rental car charges by negotiating a corporate rate.

The possibilities for economizing are promising; however, making the best travel arrangements often requires trade-offs such as the following:

- The best fares might not always be the lowest. Indirect flights are usually cheaper, but they take longer and may end up costing more in lost work time.

- The cheapest tickets often require booking 14 or even 30 days in advance, which is often impossible for us.

- Discount tickets are usually nonrefundable, which is a serious drawback when a trip needs to be canceled at the last minute.

Replace Travel with Technological Alternatives

Online meeting systems such as WebEx and GoTo Meeting offer a compelling alternative to many instances of business travel. With webcam video, application/screen sharing, and collaboration tools such as virtual whiteboards, they have made great strides toward replicating the in-person meeting experience.

As effective as they can be, though, they shouldn't automatically replace every in-person meeting. When establishing a business relationship, for example, meeting face to face is an important part of building trust and getting past the uncertainties of working with a new partner. Part of the new travel director's job would be to draft guidelines for choosing travel or online meeting options.

By pointing out possible difficulties and showing that she has considered all angles, Moreno builds reader confidence in her judgment.

Note how Moreno makes the transition from section to section. The first sentence under the second heading on this page refers to the subject of the previous paragraph and signals a shift in thought.

An informative title in the table is consistent with the way headings are handled throughout this report, and it is appropriate for a report to a receptive audience.

The in-text reference to the table highlights the key point the reader should get from the table.

Including financial estimates helps management envision the impact of the suggestions, even though the estimated savings are difficult to project accurately.

The Impact of Reforms

By implementing tighter controls, reducing unnecessary expenses, negotiating more favorable rates, and exploring alternatives to travel, Electrovision should be able to reduce its T&E budget significantly. As Table 1 illustrates, the combined savings should be in the neighborhood of $6 million, although the precise figures are somewhat difficult to project.

Table 1
Electrovision Can Trim Travel and Entertainment Costs by an Estimated $6 Million per Year

SOURCE OF SAVINGS	ESTIMATED SAVINGS
Switching from business-class to coach airfare	$2,300,000
Negotiating preferred hotel rates	940,000
Negotiating preferred rental car rates	460,000
Systematically searching for lower airfares	375,000
Reducing interdivisional travel	675,000
Reducing seminar and conference attendance	1,250,000
TOTAL POTENTIAL SAVINGS	**$6,000,000**

To achieve the economies outlined in the table, Electrovision will incur expenses for hiring a director of travel and for implementing a T&E cost-control system. These costs are projected at $115,000: $105,000 per year in salary and benefits for the new employee and a one-time expense of $10,000 for the cost-control system. The cost of retaining a full-service travel agency is negligible, even with the service fees that many are now passing along from airlines and other service providers.

The measures required to achieve these savings are likely to be unpopular with employees. Electrovision personnel are accustomed to generous T&E allowances, and they are likely to resent having these privileges curtailed. To alleviate their disappointment:

- Management should make a determined effort to explain why the changes are necessary.

- The director of corporate communication should be asked to develop a multi-faceted campaign that will communicate the importance of curtailing T&E costs.

- Management should set a positive example by adhering strictly to the new policies.

- The limitations should apply equally to employees at all levels in the organization.

Note how Moreno calls attention in the first paragraph to items in the table, without repeating the information in the table.

She uses a descriptive heading for the last section of the text. In informational reports, this section is often called "Summary"; in analytical reports, it is called "Conclusions" or "Conclusions and Recommendations."

Presenting the recommendations in a list gives each one emphasis.

CONCLUSIONS AND RECOMMENDATIONS

Electrovision is currently spending $16 million per year on T&E. Although much of this spending is justified, the company's costs are high relative to competitors' costs, mainly because Electrovision has been generous with its travel benefits.

Electrovision's liberal approach to T&E was understandable during years of high profitability; however, the company is facing the prospect of declining profits for the next several years. Management is therefore motivated to cut costs in all areas of the business. Reducing T&E spending is particularly important because the bottom-line impact of these costs will increase as airline fares increase.

Electrovision should be able to reduce T&E costs by as much as 40 percent by taking four important steps:

1. *Institute tighter spending controls.* Management should hire a director of travel and entertainment who will assume overall responsibility for T&E activities. Within the next six months, this director should develop a written travel policy, institute a T&E budget and a cost-control system, and retain a professional, business-oriented travel agency that will optimize arrangements with travel providers.

2. *Reduce unnecessary travel and entertainment.* Electrovision should encourage employees to economize on T&E spending. Management can accomplish this by authorizing fewer trips and by urging employees to be more conservative in their spending.

3. *Obtain lowest rates from travel providers.* Electrovision should also focus on obtaining the best rates on airline tickets, hotel rooms, and rental cars. By channeling all arrangements through a professional travel agency, the company can optimize its choices and gain clout in negotiating preferred rates.

4. *Replace some travel with technological alternatives.* Online meeting system should be adequate for most of our tactical meetings with established clients and for most internal communication as well.

Because these measures may be unpopular with employees, management should make a concerted effort to explain the importance of reducing travel costs. The director of corporate communication should be given responsibility for developing a plan to communicate the need for employee cooperation.

Moreno summarizes her conclusions in the first two paragraphs—a good approach because she organized her report around conclusions and recommendations, so readers have already been introduced to them.

Moreno doesn't introduce any new facts in this section. In a longer report she might have divided this section into subsections, labeled "Conclusions" and "Recommendations," to distinguish between the two.

MLA style lists references alphabetically by the author's last name, and when the author is unknown, by the title of the reference. (See Appendix B for additional details on preparing reference lists.)

WORKS CITED

Barker, Julie. "How to Rein in Group Travel Costs." *Successful Meetings* Feb. 2019: 31. Print.

"Businesses Use Savvy Managers to Keep Travel Costs Down." *Christian Science Monitor* 17 July 2018: 4. Print.

Dahl, Jonathan. "2000: The Year Travel Costs Took Off." *Wall Street Journal* 29 Dec. 2018: B6. Print.

Gilligan, Edward P. "Trimming Your T&E Is Easier Than You Think." *Managing Office Technology* Nov. 2017: 39–40. Print.

Miller, Lisa. "Attention, Airline Ticket Shoppers." *Wall Street Journal* 7 July 2017: B6. Print.

Phillips, Edward H. "Airlines Post Record Traffic." *Aviation Week & Space Technology* 8 Jan. 2018: 331. Print.

"Product Overview: Cisco WebEx Meeting Center," *Webex.com*. Web Ex, 2 Feb. 2019. Web.

Rowe, Irene Vlitos. "Global Solution for Cutting Travel Costs." *European Business* 12 Oct. 2018: 30. Print.

Smith, Carol. "Rising, Erratic Airfares Make Company Policy Vital." *Los Angeles Times* 2 Nov. 2019: D4. Print.

Solheim, Shelley. "Web Conferencing Made Easy." *eWeek* 22 Aug. 2019: 26. Web.

"Travel Costs Under Pressure." *Purchasing* 15 Feb. 2018: 30. Print.

Moreno's list of references follows the style recommended in the *MLA Handbook*. The box below shows how these sources would be cited following American Psychological Association (APA) style.

REFERENCES

Barker, J. (2019, February). How to rein in group travel costs. *Successful Meetings*, p. 31.

Businesses use savvy managers to keep travel costs down. (2018, July 17). *Christian Science Monitor*, p. 4.

Dahl, J. (2018, December 29). 2000: The year travel costs took off. *Wall Street Journal*, p. B6.

Gilligan, E. (2017, November). Trimming your T&E is easier than you think. *Managing Office Technology*, pp. 39–40.

Miller, L. (2017, July 7). Attention, airline ticket shoppers. *Wall Street Journal*, p. B6.

Phillips, E. (2018, January 8). *Aviation Week & Space Technology*, p. 331.

Rowe, I. (2018, October 12). Global solution for cutting travel costs. *European*, p. 30.

Smith, C. (2019, November 2). Rising, erratic airfares make company policy vital. *Los Angeles Times*, D4.

Solheim, S. (2019, August 22). Web conferencing made easy. *eWeek*, p. 26.

Travel costs under pressure. (2018, February 15). *Purchasing*, p. 30.

WebEx.com. (2019). Cisco WebEx Meeting Center. Retrieved from http://www.webex.com/product-overview/index.html

ON THE JOB: SOLVING COMMUNICATION DILEMMAS AT **MCKINSEY & COMPANY**

You landed your dream job as a digital content producer for McKinsey. This role includes writing, editing, and producing a wide variety of articles and reports. Study these scenarios and decide how to respond, based on what you learned in this chapter.

1. Article and report content can display a range of writing tones, from informal and casual to formal and distant. You encounter the following section in a report you are editing, and for this particular publication, you need to revise it to create a more formal tone.

   > You want my best advice? As you move forward, keep your eyes and ears open to innovations that could affect your career and your company. Carefully consider the predictions you hear, but trust me—don't swallow any of them hook, line, and sinker. Before you make any major career decisions, ask yourself what would have to happen for those predictions to come true.

   Which of these three rewrites is respectfully formal without being stuffy?

   a. As executives move forward, they are encouraged to maintain vigilance for innovations that could affect their careers and companies. They are encouraged to carefully consider any predictions related to these innovations while maintaining a healthy skepticism. Before making any major career decisions, they should ask themselves what changes would need to transpire in order for a given prediction to come true.

   b. As executives move forward, they should keep their eyes and ears open to innovations that could affect their careers and companies. They should carefully consider predictions while maintaining a healthy skepticism. Before

   making any major career decisions, they should ask themselves what changes would need to happen for a given prediction to come true.

   c. As you move forward, keep your eyes peeled and ears open to innovations that could help or hurt your career and your company. Carefully consider predictions but be skeptical. Before making any major career decisions, ask yourself would changes would need to happen for a given prediction to come true.

2. Which of these would make the best subheading for a section about the challenges of predicting the effects of innovation in business? The section will open with the paragraph from the previous question.

   a. Funny Thing About the Future: It's Impossible to Predict

   b. My Advice: Treat Every Prediction About Innovation with Skepticism

   c. Treat Every Prediction About Innovation with Skepticism

   d. Every Prediction About Innovation Is Best Viewed with Skepticism

3. The report discusses how the number of IPOs (*initial public offerings*, when companies sell stock to the public for the first time) tend to rise and fall in sync with the stock market. To show this relationship over the past 25 years, which type of visual should you use?

   a. Table **c.** Line chart

   b. Bar chart **d.** Surface chart

4. If you wanted to give your readers a short version of the report to read when they don't have time for the full piece, which of these elements would you include near the beginning?

   a. Abstract **c.** Executive summary

   b. Preview **d.** Synopsis

END OF CHAPTER

Learning Objectives Checkup

Assess your understanding of the principles in this chapter by reading each learning objective and studying the accompanying exercises. You can check your responses against the answer key on page 613.

Objective 13.1: List the topics commonly covered in the introduction, body, and close of informational reports, analytical reports, and proposals.

1. Why is the "you" attitude particularly important with long or complex reports and proposals?

   a. The "you" attitude takes less time to write, so you'll save considerable time with long documents.

   b. Professionals are accustomed to reading long reports, so they don't require a lot of "hand holding."

   c. People simply don't read reports that don't demonstrate good business etiquette.

   d. The length and complexity of these reports put a heavy demand on readers, making it particularly important to be sensitive to their needs.

2. Which of these sentences has the most formal tone?

   a. We discuss herein the possibility of synergistic development strategies between our firm and U.S. Medical.

   b. This report explores the potential for a strategic partnership with U.S. Medical.

   c. My report is the result of a formal investigation into the possibility of a strategic partnership with U.S. Medical.

d. In this report, I address the potential for a strategic partnership with U.S. Medical.

3. Which of these is most likely to be found in the introduction of a report?
   a. An explanation of any limitations in the report
   b. Facts, statistical evidence, and trends
   c. Conclusions and recommendations
   d. An analysis of potential courses of action

4. Where would you summarize a list of action items in a report?
   a. In the introduction
   b. In the body
   c. In the close

5. How are readers likely to react if they spot several errors in a proposal you submitted?
   a. They'll become skeptical about the quality of all your work.
   b. They'll forgive you and move on without thinking any more about it; everybody makes mistakes.
   c. They'll stop reading all your reports and proposals.
   d. They'll respect the fact that you don't waste time proofreading.

6. Which of the following is *not* a recommended strategy for strengthening your proposal argument?
   a. Provide concrete examples of the value of your proposal.
   b. Demonstrate your knowledge.
   c. Identify the amount of time you've invested in the proposal.
   d. Adopt the "you" attitude.

7. If packaging and presentation are only superficial, why are they so important in proposal writing?
   a. Readers tend to prejudge the quality of your products and services based on the quality of your proposal.
   b. They show that you're more than just a "numbers" person—that you can think creatively.
   c. They show the audience that you're willing to invest time and money in getting your proposal accepted.
   d. Attractive documents almost always have high-quality information in them.

8. The primary purpose of the body of a proposal is to
   a. list a firm's qualifications for the project in question.
   b. explain why the recipient needs to address a particular problem or opportunity.
   c. communicate passion for solving the problem or addressing the opportunity.
   d. give complete details on the proposed solution and its anticipated benefits.

Objective 13.2: Identify five characteristics of effective writing in online reports, and explain how to adapt your writing approach for wikis.

9. Which of the following is the most effectively worded link to a webpage that describes a company's products and services?
   a. Click here to learn more about what we do.
   b. Learn more about our products and services.
   c. Next page
   d. You have problems? We have solutions.

10. Which of the following is a good piece of advice for wiki collaboration?
    a. Because so many writers can be involved in a wiki, managerial control of content and process is essential.
    b. Personal responsibility is paramount with wikis, so all contributors must safeguard their contributions against unwelcome editing.
    c. Conventional web security measures such as access control should never be used on wikis because they inhibit free collaboration.
    d. Wiki writers need to let go of traditional expectations of authorship, including individual recognition and control.

Objective 13.3: Discuss six principles of graphic design that can improve the quality of your visuals, and identify the major types of business visuals.

11. Why is consistency important in visual design?
    a. It shows the audience that you're not wasting precious time doing artistic designs.
    b. It reduces confusion by eliminating arbitrary changes that force people to relearn your design scheme every time they encounter another visual.
    c. It saves on ink and toner when reports are printed.
    d. It shows the audience that you're serious and businesslike.

12. Why is it important to be careful with how you aggregate data in charts and graphs?
    a. Aggregating data in a small number of large "buckets" can obscure fluctuations that may be meaningful to your audience.
    b. Aggregating data in a small number of large "buckets" can remove troublesome fluctuations that you don't want your audience to see.
    c. Aggregating data reduces the cost of producing and printing graphs.
    d. Aggregating data to eliminate the distractions of minute fluctuations shows that you know how to view the big picture.

13. Which of the following is *not* a good reason to use a visual in a report?
    a. To communicate more effectively with multilingual audiences
    b. To help unify the separate parts of a process, an organization, or another entity, such as by using a flowchart to depict the various steps in a process
    c. To simplify access to specific data points, such as by listing them in a quick-reference table
    d. To demonstrate your creative side

14. Why are pie charts sometimes less effective than bar charts or tables?
    a. Comparing percentages accurately can be difficult with pie charts, unless every slice is labeled with a data value.
    b. Pie charts rarely add up to 100 percent.
    c. You can show ascending or descending order of size with a pie chart.
    d. Colors are less effective at distinguishing component slices in a pie.

15. _____ _____ overcomes several shortcomings of conventional charts and graphs—the inability to show only a limited number of data points before becoming too cluttered to interpret, a limited ability to show complex relationships among data points, and the ability to represent only numeric data.

16. Which of these is a good reason to use a diagram instead of a photograph?
    a. Diagrams are more colorful and aren't limited to colors found in real life.
    b. Diagrams are more realistic than photographs.
    c. Diagrams allow you to control the amount of detail shown to focus reader attention on particular parts of the image.
    d. Diagrams are always cheaper to create.

17. Assume that you have a line chart with a vertical axis scaled from 0 to 100 and data points that vary within a range of roughly 10 to 90. How would you influence audience perceptions if you increased the vertical scale so that it stretched from 0 to 200 instead of 0 to 100?
    a. The scaling change would have no effect on audience perceptions.
    b. The scaling change would maximize the perceived variations in the data.
    c. The scaling change would minimize the perceived variations in the data.
    d. You have no way of predicting in advance how the scaling change would affect perceptions.

Objective 13.4: Summarize the four tasks involved in completing business reports and proposals.

18. Which of the following is _not_ one of the four major tasks involved in completing business reports?
    a. Revising the report's organization, style, tone, and readability
    b. Producing the report
    c. Choosing the organizational pattern for the content
    d. Proofreading the report

19. In what situation should you consider including a letter or memo of authorization in a formal report?
    a. If you're getting paid to write the report
    b. If you received written authorization to write the report
    c. If the audience outranks you
    d. If you outrank the audience

20. A letter or memo of _____ is a specialized form of a cover letter that introduces your report to the audience.

21. A/an _____ is a brief overview (usually one page or less) of a report's most important points.

22. A/an _____ _____ is a fully developed "mini" version of the report itself.

Key Terms

bar chart Chart that portrays quantities by the height or length of its rectangular bars

caption Brief commentary or explanation that accompanies a visual

data visualization A diverse class of displays that can show enormous sets of data in a single visual or show text and other complex information visually

executive summary A complete but summarized version of the report; may contain headings, well-developed transitions, and even visual elements

flowchart Process diagram that illustrates a sequence of events from start to finish

infographics Diagrams that contain enough visual and textual information to function as independent documents

legend A "key" that helps readers decode a visual by explaining what various colors, symbols, or other design choices mean

line chart Chart that illustrates trends over time or plots the relationship of two or more variables

pie chart Circular chart that shows how the parts of a whole are distributed

surface chart Form of line chart with a cumulative effect; all the lines add up to the top line, which represents the total

synopsis A brief preview of the most important points in your report

title Identifies the content and purpose of a visual

visual literacy The ability (as a sender) to create effective images and (as a receiver) to correctly interpret visual messages

visual symbolism The connotative (as opposed to the denotative, or literal) meaning of visuals

Apply Your Knowledge

To review chapter content related to each question, refer to the indicated Learning Objective.

13-1. Would "Power to the People" be an effective headline for the section in an analytical report that recommends relaxing a company's strict limits on employee use of social media at work? Why or why not? [LO-1]

13-2. Should the most experienced member of a department have final approval of the content for the department's wiki? Why or why not? [LO-2]

13-3. If you wanted to compare average monthly absenteeism for five divisions in your company over the course of a year, which type of visual would you use? Explain your choice. [LO-3]

13-4. If a company receives a solicited formal proposal outlining the solution to a particular problem, is it ethical for the company to adopt the proposal's recommendations without hiring the firm that submitted the proposal? Why or why not? [LO-4]

13-5. Is an executive summary a persuasive message? Explain your answer. [LO-4]

Practice Your Skills

Messages for Analysis

13-6. **Message 13.A: Revising Web Content with a "You" Attitude [LO-2]** To access this wiki exercise, visit **real-timeupdates.com/ebc13**, select Student Assignments, then select Chapter 13, Message 13.A. Follow the instructions for evaluating the existing content and revising it to make it more reader oriented.

13-7. **Message 13.B: Improving the Effectiveness of a Wiki Article [LO-2]** To access this wiki exercise, visit **real-timeupdates.com/ebc13**, select Student Assignments, then select Chapter 13, Message 13.B. Follow the instructions for evaluating the existing content and revising it to make it clear and concise.

13-8. **Message 13.C: Improving a Solicited Proposal [LO-1]** Read Figure 13.14, a solicited proposal, and (1) analyze the strengths and weaknesses of this document and (2) revise the document so that it follows this chapter's guidelines.

Exercises

Each activity is labeled according to the primary skill or skills you will need to use. To review relevant chapter content, refer to the indicated Learning Objective. In some instances, supporting information will be found in another chapter, as indicated.

13-9. **Message Strategies: Informational Reports; Collaboration: Team Projects [LO-1], Chapter 3** You and a classmate are helping Linda Moreno prepare her report on Electrovision's travel and entertainment costs (see "Report Writer's Notebook" on page 420). This time, however, the report is to be informational rather than analytical, so it will not include recommendations. Review the existing report and determine what changes would be needed to make it an informational report. Be as specific as possible. For example, if your team decides the report needs a new title, what title would you use? Draft a letter of transmittal for Moreno to use in conveying this informational report to Dennis McWilliams, Electrovision's vice president of operations.

13-10. **Message Strategies: Informational Reports [LO-1]** Find an article in a business newspaper or journal (in print or online) that recommends a solution to a problem. Identify the problem, the recommended solution(s), and the supporting evidence provided by the author to justify his or her recommendation(s). Did the author cite

---

Memco Construction
187 W. Euclid Avenue, Glenview, IL 60025
www.memco.com
April 20, 2020

Dear Mr. Estes:

PROJECT: IDOT Letting Item #83 Contract No. 79371 DuPage County

Memco Construction proposes to furnish all labor, material, equipment, and supervision to provide Engineered Fill—Class II and IV—for the following unit prices.

Engineered Fill—Class II and IV

Description	Unit	Quantity	Unit Price	Total
Mobilization*	Lump Sum	1	$4,500.00	$4,500.00
Engineered Fill Class II	Cubic Yards	1,267	$33.50	$41,811.00
Engineered Fill Class IV	Cubic Yards	1,394	$38.00	$52,972.00

* Mobilization includes one move-in. Additional move-ins to be billed at $1,100.00 each.

The following items clarify and qualify the scope of our subcontracting work:
1. All forms, earthwork, clearing, etc., to be provided and maintained by others at no cost to Memco Construction.
2. General Contractor shall provide location for staging, stockpiling material, equipment, and storage at the job site.
3. Memco Construction shall be paid strictly based upon the amount of material actually used on the job.
4. All prep work, including geotechnical fabrics, geomembrane liners, etc., to be done by others at no cost to Memco Construction.
5. Water is to be available at project site at no charge to Memco Construction.
6. Dewatering to be done by others at no cost to Memco Construction.
7. Traffic control setup, devices, maintenance, and flagmen are to be provided by others at no cost to Memco Construction.
8. Memco Construction LLC may withdraw this bid if we do not receive a written confirmation that we are the apparent low sub-bidder within 10 days of your receipt of this proposal.
9. Our F.E.I.N. is 36-4478095.
10. Bond is not included in above prices. Bond is available for an additional 1 percent.

If you have any questions, please contact me at the phone number listed below.

Sincerely

Kris Beiersdorf

Kris Beiersdorf
Memco Construction
187 W. Euclid Avenue, Glenview, IL 60025
Office: (847) 352-9742, ext. 30
Fax: (847) 352-6595
Email: Kbeiersdorf@memco.com

Figure 13.14 Solicited Proposal (for Message 13.C)

any formal or informal studies as evidence? What facts or statistics did the author include? Did the author cite any criteria for evaluating possible options? If so, what were they?

13-11. Message Strategies: Informational Reports [LO-1] Review a long article in a business magazine (print or online). Highlight examples of how the article uses headings, links (if online), transitions, previews, and reviews to help readers navigate through the content.

13-12. Applying Visual Design Principles [LO-3] Find three visual presentations of data, information, or concepts on any business subject. Which of the three presents its data or information most clearly? What design choices promote this level of clarity? What improvements would you make to the other visuals to make them clearer?

13-13. Visual Communication: Creating Visuals [LO-3] As directed by your instructor, team up with other students, making sure that at least one of you has a digital camera or camera phone capable of downloading images to your word-processing software. Find a busy location on campus or in the surrounding neighborhood, someplace with lots of signs, storefronts, pedestrians, and traffic. Scout out two different photo opportunities, one that maximizes the visual impression of crowding and clutter and one that minimizes this impression. For the first, assume that you are someone who advocates reducing the crowding and clutter, so you want to show how bad it is. For the second, assume that you are a real estate agent or someone else who is motivated to show people that even though the location offers lots of shopping, entertainment, and other attractions, it's actually a rather calm and quiet neighborhood.

Insert the two images into a word-processing document or presentation slide, and write a caption for each that emphasizes the two opposite messages just described. Finally, write a brief paragraph discussing the ethical implications of what you've just done. Have you distorted reality or just presented it in ways that work to your advantage? Have you prevented audiences from gaining the information they would need in order to make informed decisions?

13-14. Message Strategies: Analytical Reports; Communication Ethics: Resolving Ethical Dilemmas [LO-1], Chapter 1 Your boss has asked you to prepare a feasibility report to determine whether the company should advertise its custom-crafted cabinetry in the weekly neighborhood newspaper. Based on your primary research, you think it should. As you draft the introduction to your report, however, you discover that the survey administered to the neighborhood newspaper subscribers was flawed. Several of the questions were poorly written and misleading. You used the survey results, among other findings, to justify your recommendation. The report is due in three days. What actions might you want to take, if any, before you complete your report?

13-15. Drafting Online Content [LO-2] Compare the "About Us" pages on the websites of three companies in the same industry. Which page is the most reader-friendly? Which is the worst? What specific elements make each of these pages effective or ineffective?

13-16. Communication Ethics [LO-3] Using a spreadsheet app, create a bar chart or line chart using data you find online or in a business publication. Alter the horizontal and vertical scales in several ways to produce different displays of the original data. How do the alterations distort the information? How might a reader detect whether a chart's scale has been altered?

13-17. Visual Communication: Choosing the Best Visual [LO-3] You're preparing the annual report for FretCo Guitar Corporation. For each of the following types of information, select an appropriate chart or visual to illustrate the text. Explain your choices.

a. Data on annual sales for the past 20 years

b. Comparison of FretCo sales, product by product (electric guitars, bass guitars, amplifiers, acoustic guitars), for this year and last year

c. Explanation of how a FretCo acoustic guitar is manufactured

d. Explanation of how the FretCo Guitar Corporation markets its guitars

e. Data on sales of FretCo products in each of 12 countries

f. Comparison of FretCo sales figures with sales figures for three competing guitar makers over the past 10 years

13-18. Completing: Producing Formal Reports [LO-4] You are president of the Friends of the Library, a nonprofit group that raises funds and provides volunteers to support your local library. Every February, you send a report of the previous year's activities and accomplishments to the County Arts Council, which provides an annual grant of $1,000 toward your group's summer reading festival. Now it's February 6, and you've completed your formal report. Here are the highlights:

- Back-to-school book sale raised $2,000.
- Holiday craft fair raised $1,100.
- Promotion and prizes for summer reading festival cost $1,450.
- Materials for children's program featuring local author cost $125.
- New reference databases for library's career center cost $850.
- Bookmarks promoting library's website cost $200.

Write a letter of transmittal to Erica Maki, the council's director. Because she is expecting this report, you can use the direct approach. Be sure to express gratitude for the council's ongoing financial support.

Expand Your Skills

Critique the Professionals

Browse the websites of several companies to find a downloadable PDF file of a report, white paper, company backgrounder, product overview, or other document at least two pages long. Evaluate the design and production quality of this document. Does the layout enhance the message or distract your attention from it? It what ways do design elements convey the company's brand image? Does the document strike you as "underdesigned" or "overdesigned" for its intended purpose? Using whatever medium your instructor requests, write a brief summary of your analysis. Be sure to include a link to the document.

Sharpen Your Career Skills Online

Bovée and Thill's Business Communication Web Search, at websearch.businesscommunicationnetwork.com, is a unique research tool designed specifically for business communication research. Use the Web Search function to find a website, video, article, podcast, or presentation that offers advice on creating visuals for business reports. Write a brief email message to your instructor or a post on your class blog describing the item that you found and summarizing the career skills information you learned from it.

Build Your Career

Résumé formats vary widely, but all résumés should include a brief *introductory statement* that comes immediately after your name and contact information. The goal of this section is to let readers know within a matter of seconds how you can potentially contribute to an employer. As Chapter 15 points out, you have three choices for this element. A *career objective* is the traditional choice, but it is used less nowadays because it is less informative than the other choices.

A *qualifications summary* (sometimes labeled a *summary of qualifications*) offers a concise summary of your most important qualifications as they relate to an employer's needs. This is a good choice if you don't have a long employment history (and your education is still your strongest selling point) or if you have a dominant theme to your qualifications and you want to pursue opportunities where that theme would be compelling to potential employers. If you completed your *public profile* from Chapter 5's Build Your Career activity and the *headline* from Chapter 6, you have the material you need for an effective qualifications summary.

If you are further along in your career and intend to stay on the same career track, a *career summary* is probably the best choice. This option is particularly good if you have a record of increasing levels of responsibility and performance, because it can suggest that you're ready for the next challenge.

As you start to pull your résumé package together, consider which introductory statement will work best for you. Sketch out ideas and revisit your personal brand/professional promise if needed to come up with a clear, concise, and compelling statement.

Improve Your Grammar, Mechanics, and Usage

The following exercises help you improve your knowledge of and power over English grammar, mechanics, and usage. Turn to the Handbook of Grammar, Mechanics, and Usage at the end of this book and review all of Sections 2.10 (Quotation Marks), 2.11 (Parentheses), and 2.12 (Ellipses). Then look at the following 10 items and indicate the preferred choice in the following groups of sentences. (Answers to these exercises appear on page 614.)

13-19. a. Be sure to read (How to Sell by Listening) in this month's issue of Fortune.

    b. Be sure to read "How to Sell by Listening" in this month's issue of *Fortune*.

    c. Be sure to read "How to Sell by Listening . . ." in this month's issue of Fortune.

13-20. a. Her response . . . see the attached memo . . . is disturbing.

    b. Her response (see the attached memo) is disturbing.

    c. Her response "see the attached memo" is disturbing.

13-21. a. We operate with a skeleton staff during the holidays (December 21 through January 2).

    b. We operate with a skeleton staff during the holidays "December 21 through January 2".

    c. We operate with a skeleton staff during the holidays (December 21 through January 2.)

13-22. a. "The SBP's next conference . . ." the bulletin noted, ". . . will be held in Minneapolis."

    b. "The SBP's next conference," the bulletin noted, "will be held in Minneapolis."

    c. "The SBP's next conference," the bulletin noted, "will be held in Minneapolis".

13-23. a. The term "up in the air" means "undecided."

    b. The term "up in the air" means undecided.

    c. The term up in the air means "undecided."

13-24. a. Her assistant (the one who just had the baby) won't be back for four weeks.

    b. Her assistant (the one who just had the baby), won't be back for four weeks.

    c. Her assistant . . . the one who just had the baby . . . won't be back for four weeks.

13-25. a. "Ask not what your country can do for you," begins a famous John Kennedy quotation.

    b. ". . . Ask not what your country can do for you" begins a famous John Kennedy quotation.

    c. "Ask not what your country can do for you . . ." begins a famous John Kennedy quotation.

13-26. a. Do you remember who said, "And away we go?"

    b. Do you remember who said, "And away we go"?

13-27. a. Refinements may prove profitable. (More detail about this technology appears in Appendix A).

    b. Refinements may prove profitable. (More detail about this technology appears in Appendix A.)

13-28. a. The resignation letter begins, "Since I'll never regain your respect . . .," and goes on to explain why that's true.

    b. The resignation letter begins, "Since I'll never regain your respect, . . ." and goes on to explain why that's true.

    c. The resignation letter begins, "Since I'll never regain your respect . . ." and goes on to explain why that's true.

For additional exercises focusing on quotation marks, parentheses, and ellipses, visit MyLab Business Communication. Select Chapter 13, then Additional Exercises to Improve Your Grammar, Mechanics, and Usage, then 19. Punctuation D.

Cases

For all cases, feel free to use your creativity to make up any details you need in order to craft effective messages.

Short Reports

REPORT-WRITING SKILLS / PORTFOLIO BUILDER

13.29. Message Strategies: Informational Reports [LO-1], [LO-4]   Businesses that need to deal with large collections of textual information can use text mining (also known as text analytics) to reduce the work involved in reading and analyzing everything from Twitter streams to legal cases.

Your task: Research one current business application of text mining and write a report of no longer than one page that describes this use of text mining and the benefits it can offer businesses.

REPORT-WRITING SKILLS / PORTFOLIO BUILDER

13.30. Message Strategies: Informational Reports [LO-1], [LO-4]   Tesla gets a lot of media attention for its electric vehicles, but many automakers now market electric models.

Your task: Research six electric cars currently on the market and write a short informational report identifying each manufacturer and describing its electric vehicle(s). Explain how each manufacturer positions its model(s) in the market (as luxury models, family oriented, and so on), and provide a summary assessment of what the automotive press thinks of it.

REPORT-WRITING SKILLS

13.31. Message Strategies: Informational Reports [LO-1], [LO-4]   Success in any endeavor doesn't happen all at once. For example, success in college is built one quarter or semester at a time, and the way to succeed in the long term is to make sure you succeed in the short term. After all, even a single quarter or semester of college involves a significant investment of time, money, and energy.

Your task: Imagine you work for a company that has agreed to send you to college full-time, paying all your educational expenses. You are given complete freedom in choosing your courses, as long as you graduate by an agreed-upon date. All your employer asks in return is that you develop your business skills and insights as much as possible so that you can make a significant contribution to the company when you return to full-time work after graduation. To make sure that you are using your time—and your company's money—wisely, the company requires a brief personal activity report at the end of every quarter or semester (whichever your school uses). Write a brief informational report that you can email to your instructor summarizing how you spent your quarter or semester. Itemize the classes you took, how much time you spent studying and working on class projects, whether you got involved in campus activities and organizations that help you develop leadership or communication skills, and what you learned that you can apply in a business career. (For the purposes of this assignment, your time estimates don't have to be precise.)

REPORT-WRITING SKILLS

13.32. Message Strategies: Informational Reports [LO-1], [LO-4]   You've been in your new job as human resources director for only a week, and already you have a major personnel crisis on your hands. Some employees in the marketing department got their hands on a confidential salary report and learned that, on average, marketing employees earn less than engineering employees. In addition, several top performers in the engineering group make significantly more than anybody in marketing. The report was instantly passed around the company by email, and now everyone is discussing the situation. You'll deal with the data security issue later; for now, you need to address the dissatisfaction in the marketing group.

Case Table 13.1 lists the salary and employment data you were able to pull from the employee database. You also had the opportunity to interview the engineering and marketing directors to get their opinions on the pay situation; their responses are listed in Case Table 13.2.

CASE TABLE 13.1 Selected Employment Data for Engineers and Marketing Staff		
Employment Statistic	**Engineering Department**	**Marketing Department**
Average number of years of work experience	18.2	16.3
Average number of years of experience in current profession	17.8	8.6
Average number of years with company	12.4	7.9
Average number of years of college education	6.9	4.8
Average number of years between promotions	6.7	4.3
Salary range	$58–165k	$45–85k
Median salary	$77k	$62k

CASE TABLE 13.2 Summary Statements from Department Director Interviews

Question	Engineering Director	Marketing Director
1. Should engineering and marketing professionals receive roughly similar pay?	In general, yes, but we need to make allowances for the special nature of the engineering profession. In some cases, it's entirely appropriate for an engineer to earn more than a marketing person.	Yes.
2. Why or why not?	Several reasons: (1) Top engineers are extremely hard to find, and we need to offer competitive salaries; (2) the structure of the engineering department doesn't provide as many promotional opportunities, so we can't use promotions as a motivator the way marketing can; (3) many of our engineers have advanced degrees, and nearly all pursue continuous education to stay on top of the technology.	Without marketing, the products the engineers create wouldn't reach customers, and the company wouldn't have any revenue. The two teams make equal contributions to the company's success.
3. If we decide to balance pay between the two departments, how should we do it?	If we do anything to cap or reduce engineering salaries, we'll lose key people to our competitors.	If we can't increase payroll immediately to raise marketing salaries, the only fair thing to do is freeze raises in engineering and gradually raise marketing salaries over the next few years.

Your task: The CEO has asked for a short report summarizing whatever data and information you have on engineering and marketing salaries. Feel free to offer your own interpretation of the situation as well (make up any information you need), but keep in mind that because you are a new manager with almost no experience in the company, your opinion might not have a lot of influence.

REPORT-WRITING SKILLS / PORTFOLIO BUILDER / **TEAM** SKILLS

13.33. Message Strategies: Analytical Reports [LO-1], [LO-5] Anyone looking at the fragmented 21st-century landscape of media and entertainment options might be surprised to learn that poetry was once a dominant medium for not only creative literary expression but also philosophical, political, and even scientific discourse. Alas, such is no longer the case.

Your task: With a team of fellow students, your challenge is to identify opportunities to increase sales of poetry—any kind of poetry, in any medium. The following suggestions may help you get started:

- Research recent bestsellers in the poetry field and try to identify why they have been popular.
- Interview literature professors, professional poets, librarians, publishers, and bookstore personnel.
- Consider art forms and venues in which verse plays an essential role, including popular music and poetry slams.
- Conduct surveys and interviews to find out why consumers don't buy more poetry.
- Review professional journals that cover the field of poetry, including *Publishers Weekly* and *Poets & Writers,* from both business and creative standpoints.

Summarize your findings in a brief formal report; assume that your target readers are executives in the publishing industry.

Long Reports

REPORT-WRITING SKILLS / PORTFOLIO BUILDER

13.34. Message Strategies: Analytical Reports [LO-1] Like any other endeavor that combines factual analysis and creative free thinking, the task of writing business plans generates a range of opinions.

Your task: Find at least six reputable sources of advice on writing successful business plans (focus on start-up businesses that are likely to seek outside investors). Analyze the advice you find and identify points where most or all the experts agree and points where they don't agree. Wherever you find points of significant disagreement, identify which opinion you find most convincing and explain why. Summarize your findings in a brief formal report.

REPORT-WRITING SKILLS

13.35. Message Strategies: Informational Reports [LO-1], [LO-4] Your company is the largest private employer in your metropolitan area, and the 43,500 employees in your workforce have a tremendous impact on local traffic. A group of city and county transportation officials recently approached your CEO with a request to explore ways to reduce this impact. The CEO has assigned you the task of analyzing the workforce's transportation habits and attitudes as a first step toward identifying potential solutions. He's willing to consider anything from subsidized bus passes to company-owned shuttle buses to telecommuting, but the decision requires a thorough understanding of employee transportation needs. Case Tables 13.3 through 13.7 summarize data you collected in an employee survey.

Your task: Present the results of your survey in an informational report, using the data provided in the tables.

CASE TABLE 13.3   Employee Carpool Habits

Frequency of Use: Carpooling	Portion of Workforce
Every day, every week	10,138 (23%)
Certain days, every week	4,361 (10%)
Randomly	983 (2%)
Never	28,018 (64%)

CASE TABLE 13.4   Use of Public Transportation

Frequency of Use: Public Transportation	Portion of Workforce
Every day, every week	23,556 (54%)
Certain days, every week	2,029 (5%)
Randomly	5,862 (13%)
Never	12,053 (28%)

CASE TABLE 13.5   Effect of Potential Improvements to Public Transportation

Which of the Following Would Encourage You to Use Public Transportation More Frequently? (check all that apply)	Portion of Respondents
Increased perception of safety	4,932 (28%)
Improved cleanliness	852 (5%)
Reduced commute times	7,285 (41%)
Greater convenience: fewer transfers	3,278 (18%)
Greater convenience: more stops	1,155 (6%)
Lower (or subsidized) fares	5,634 (31%)
Nothing could encourage me to take public transportation	8,294 (46%)

Note: This question was asked of respondents who use public transportation randomly or never, a subgroup that represents 17,915 employees, or 41 percent of the workforce.

CASE TABLE 13.6   Distance Traveled to/from Work

Distance You Travel to Work (one way)	Portion of Workforce
Less than 1 mile	531 (1%)
1–3 miles	6,874 (16%)
4–10 miles	22,951 (53%)
11–20 miles	10,605 (24%)
More than 20 miles	2,539 (6%)

CASE TABLE 13.7   Is Telecommuting an Option?

Does the Nature of Your Work Make Telecommuting a Realistic Option?	Portion of Workforce
Yes, every day	3,460 (8%)
Yes, several days a week	8,521 (20%)
Yes, random days	12,918 (30%)
No	18,601 (43%)

WEB WRITING SKILLS / MOBILE SKILLS / PORTFOLIO BUILDER

13.36. Message Strategies: Online Content [LO-2] Adapting conventional web content to make it mobile friendly can require rethinking the site's information architecture to simplify navigation and revising the content.

Your task: Choose the website of a company that makes products you find interesting. (Make it a conventional website, not one already optimized for mobile.) Analyze the section of the website that contains information about the company's products and determine the best way to present that material on mobile device screens. Mock up at least two screens showing how you reformat the content to make it mobile friendly. Create a brief presentation with "before" and "after" views to show how your redesign would benefit mobile site visitors.

REPORT-WRITING SKILLS / PORTFOLIO BUILDER

13.37. Message Strategies: Analytical Reports [LO-1], [LO-4] As a college student and an active consumer, you may have considered one or more of the following questions at some point in the past few years:

- What criteria distinguish the top-rated MBA programs in the country? How well do these criteria correspond to the needs and expectations of business? Are the criteria fair for students, employers, and business schools?
- Which of three companies you might like to work for has the strongest corporate ethics policies?
- What will the music industry look like in the future? What's next after online stores such as Apple's iTunes and streaming services such as Spotify?
- Which industries and job categories are forecast to experience the greatest growth—and therefore the greatest demand for workers—in the next 10 years?
- What has been the impact of Starbucks's aggressive growth on small, independent coffee shops? On midsized chains or franchises? Have the effects been similar in all countries?
- How large is the "industry" of major college sports? How much do the major football or basketball programs contribute—directly or indirectly—to other parts of a typical university?
- How much have minor league sports—baseball, hockey, arena football—grown in small- and medium-market cities?

What is the local economic impact when these municipalities build stadiums and arenas?

Your task: Answer one of the preceding questions using information from secondary research sources. Be sure to document your sources using the format your instructor indicates. Give conclusions and offer recommendations where appropriate.

Proposals

PROPOSAL-WRITING SKILLS / PORTFOLIO BUILDER

13.38. Message Strategies: Analytical Reports

After 15 years in the corporate world, you're ready to strike out on your own. Rather than building a business from the ground up, however, you think that buying a franchise is a better idea. Unfortunately, some of the most lucrative franchise opportunities, such as the major fast-food chains, require significant start-up costs—some more than a half-million dollars. Fortunately, you've met several potential investors who seem willing to help you get started in exchange for a share of ownership. Between your own savings and money from these investors, you estimate that you can raise from $350,000 to $600,000, depending on how much ownership share you want to concede to the investors.

You've worked in several functional areas already, including sales and manufacturing, so you have a fairly well-rounded business résumé. You're open to just about any type of business, too, as long as it provides the opportunity to grow; you don't want to be so tied down to the first operation that you can't turn it over to a hired manager and expand into another market.

Your task: To convene a formal meeting with the investor group, you first need to draft a report that outlines the types of franchise opportunities you'd like to pursue. Write a brief report identifying five franchises you would like to explore further. (Choose five based on your own personal interests and the criteria already identified.) For each possibility, identify the nature of the business, the financial requirements, and the level of support the company provides, and write a brief statement of why you could run such a business successfully (make up any details you need). Be sure to carefully review the information you find about each franchise company to make sure you can qualify for it. For instance, McDonald's doesn't allow investment partnerships to buy franchises, so you won't be able to start up a McDonald's outlet until you have enough money to do it on your own.

PROPOSAL-WRITING SKILLS / PORTFOLIO BUILDER

13.39. Message Strategies: Proposals [LO-1], [LO-4]

Presentations can make—or break—careers and companies. A good presentation can bring in millions of dollars in new sales or fresh investment capital. A bad presentation might cause any number of troubles, from turning away potential customers to upsetting fellow employees to derailing key projects. To help business professionals plan, create, and deliver more-effective presentations, you offer a three-day workshop that covers the essentials of good presentations:

- Understanding your audience's needs and expectations
- Formulating your presentation objectives
- Choosing an organizational approach
- Writing openings that catch your audience's attention
- Creating effective graphics and slides
- Practicing and delivering your presentation
- Leaving a positive impression on your audience
- Avoiding common mistakes with presentation slides
- Making presentations online using webcasting tools
- Handling questions and arguments from the audience
- Overcoming the top 10 worries of public speaking (including *How can I overcome stage fright?* and *I'm not the performing type; can I still give an effective presentation?*)

Workshop benefits. Students will learn how to prepare better presentations in less time and deliver them more effectively.

Who should attend. Top executives, project managers, employment recruiters, sales professionals, and anyone else who gives important presentations to internal or external audiences.

Your qualifications. 18 years of business experience, including 14 years in sales and 12 years of public speaking. Experience speaking to audiences as large as 5,000 people. More than a dozen speech-related articles published in professional journals. Have conducted successful workshops for nearly 100 companies.

Workshop details. Three-day workshop (9 A.M. to 3:30 P.M.) that combines lectures, practice presentations, and both individual and group feedback. Minimum number of students: 6. Maximum number of students per workshop: 12.

Pricing. The cost is $3,500, plus $100 per student; 10 percent discount for additional workshops.

Other information. Each attendee will have the opportunity to give three practice presentations ranging in duration from 3 to 5 minutes. Everyone is encouraged to bring PowerPoint files containing slides from actual business presentations. Each attendee will also receive a workbook and a digital video recording of his or her final class presentation. You'll also be available for phone or email coaching for six months after the workshop.

Your task: Identify a company in your local area that might be a good candidate for your services. Learn more about the company by visiting its website so you can personalize your proposal. Using the information listed above, prepare a sales proposal that explains the benefits of your training and what students can expect during the workshop.

PROPOSAL-WRITING SKILLS / PORTFOLIO BUILDER / TEAM SKILLS

13.40. Message Strategies: Proposals [LO-1], [LO-4]

It seems like everybody in your firm is frustrated. On the one hand, top executives complain about the number of lower-level employees who want promotions but just don't seem to "get it" when it comes to dealing with customers and the public, recognizing when to speak out and when to be quiet, knowing how to push new ideas through the appropriate channels, and performing other essential but difficult-to-teach tasks. On the other hand, ambitious employees who'd like to learn more feel that they have nowhere to turn for career advice from people who've been there. In between, a variety of managers and midlevel executives are overwhelmed by the growing number of mentoring requests they're getting, sometimes from employees they don't even know.

You've been assigned the challenge of proposing a formal mentoring program—and a considerable challenge it is:

- The number of employees who want mentoring relationships far exceeds the number of managers and executives willing and able to be mentors; how will you select people for the program?
- The people most in demand for mentoring also tend to be some of the busiest people in the organization.

- After several years of budget cuts and staff reductions, the entire company feels overworked; few people can imagine adding another recurring task to their seemingly endless to-do lists.
- What's in it for the mentors? Why would they be motivated to help lower-level employees?
- How will you measure the success or failure of the mentoring effort?

Your task: With a team assigned by your instructor, identify potential solutions to the issues (make up any information you need) and draft a proposal to the executive committee for a formal, companywide mentoring program that would match selected employees with successful managers and executives.

MyLab Business Communication

MyLab Assisted-Grading Writing Prompts

If your instructor has assigned one or both of the following writing assignments within the MyLab, go to your Assignments to complete these writing exercises.

13.41. What is visual literacy? [LO-3]

13.42. For providing illustration in a report or proposal, when is a diagram a better choice than a photograph? [LO-3]

Endnotes

1. McKinsey Fact Sheet, 16 March 2018, www.mckinsey.com; McKinsey Global Institute, accessed 11 April 2018, www.mckinsey .com/mgi/overview; "Company Overview of McKinsey & Company, Inc.," *Bloomberg*, accessed 11 April 2018, www.bloomberg.com.

2. Philip C. Kolin, *Successful Writing at Work*, 6th ed. (Boston: Houghton Mifflin, 2001), 552–555.

3. Upland Software website, accessed 15 April 2018, uplandsoftware .com.

4. "Codex: Guidelines," WordPress website, accessed 10 February 2016, wordpress.org; Adam Pash, "Stop Repeating Yourself: Set Up a Workplace Wiki," *Lifehacker*, 13 September 2010, lifehacker.com.

5. "Codex: Guidelines."

6. Scott Nesbitt, "3 Tips for Effectively Using Wikis for Documentation," Opensource.com, 2 January 2017, opensource.com.

7. Alexis Gerard and Bob Goldstein, *Going Visual* (Hoboken, N.J.: Wiley, 2005), 18.

8. Lindy Ryan, *The Visual Imperative: Creating a Visual Culture of Data Discovery* (Cambridge, Mass.: Morgan Kaufman, 2016), 119.

9. Ryan, *The Visual Imperative: Creating a Visual Culture of Data Discovery*, 139.

10. Charles Kostelnick and Michael Hassett, *Shaping Information: The Rhetoric of Visual Conventions* (Carbondale, Ill.: Southern Illinois University Press, 2003), 177.

11. Gerard and Goldstein, *Going Visual*, 103–106.

12. Edward R. Tufte, *Visual Explanations: Images and Quantities, Evidence and Narrative* (Cheshire, Conn.: Graphics Press, 1997), 82.

13. Joshua David McClurg-Genevese, "The Principles of Design," *Digital Web Magazine*, 13 June 2005, www.digital-web.com.

14. Kostelnick and Hassett, *Shaping Information*, 17.

15. Edward R. Tufte, *The Visual Display of Quantitative Information* (Cheshire, Conn.: Graphic Press, 1983), 113.

16. Stephen Few, "Oracle—Have You No Shame?" Visual Business Intelligence blog, 29 April 2010, www.perceptualedge.com.

17. "Pyramid Perversion—More Junk Charts," Stubborn Mule blog, 12 March 2010, www.stubbornmule.com.

18. Based in part on Tufte, *Visual Explanations*, 29–37, 53; Paul Martin Lester, *Visual Communication: Images with Messages*, 4th ed. (Belmont, Calif.: Thomson Wadsworth, 2006), 95–105, 194–196.

19. Stephen Few, "Save the Pies for Dessert," *Visual Business Intelligence Newsletter*, August 2007, www.perceptualedge.com.

20. Maria Popova, "Data Visualization: Stories for the Information Age," *Businessweek*, 12 August 2009, www.businessweek.com.

21. Ryan, *The Visual Imperative*, 39.

22. "Data Visualization: Modern Approaches," *Smashing Magazine* website, 2 August 2007, www.smashingmagazine.com; "7 Things You Should Know About Data Visualization," Educause Learning Initiative, accessed 15 March 2008, www.educause.edu; TagCrowd website, accessed 15 March 2008, www.tagcrowd.com.

23. Based in part on Tufte, *Visual Explanations*, 29–37, 53; Lester, *Visual Communication*, 95–105, 194–196.

24. "Protect PDF Files with Permissions," Adobe website, accessed 23 April 2017, helpx.adobe.com.

14

Developing and Delivering Business Presentations

LEARNING OBJECTIVES

After studying this chapter, you will be able to

1 Highlight the importance of presentations in your business career, and explain how to adapt the planning step of the three-step process to presentations.

2 Describe the tasks involved in developing a presentation.

3 Describe the six major design and writing tasks required to enhance your presentation with effective visuals.

4 Outline four major tasks involved in completing a presentation.

5 Describe four important aspects of delivering a presentation in today's social media environment.

MyLab Business Communication

Improve Your Grade!

If your instructor is using MyLab Business Communication, visit **www.pearson.com/mylab/businesscommunication** for videos, simulations, and writing exercises.

ON THE JOB: COMMUNICATING AT
BARNETT INTERNATIONAL

Using Your Body as a Performance Instrument

Presentations have much in common with other business communication efforts, from analyzing the situation and defining your purpose to gathering information and crafting audience-focused messages. They have one major difference, of course: Presentations are *performances*, and a good message isn't enough. How you perform in front of an audience has a big influence on how they respond to your message.

From her years of experience in the theater, communication coach Gina Barnett knows that the performance makes or breaks the presentation. A strong performance makes any message more compelling, whereas a weak performance can undermine even the best messages.

Communication coach Gina Barnett advises speakers to learn how to read and use their body's signals to become more relaxed, open, and engaging.

Although performance is vital, it's a mistake to think that only actors or extroverts have some special performance gift. All business professionals can learn to use their voice and bodies to perform more effectively while giving speeches and making presentations. Being mindful of your physical habits and mannerisms, from how you hold your head to the way you use your feet, can make you a more effective speaker. And there's a bonus: You'll enjoy it more, too. A body-mindful approach to speaking can help you control the anxiety that every presenter feels and harness that energy for a more natural and engaging experience.

In her performance-coaching work with corporate executives, Barnett helps presenters explore the key centers in the human body that regulate how speakers feel and how they come across to others, both visually and vocally. For example, it's easy to think a smile is merely a *reaction* to a pleasant thought or experience, but smiles can also instigate positive thoughts. The physical act of smiling can trigger improvements in your own mood and in the moods of people watching you. A warm smile helps the audience connect with you and conveys your confidence in yourself and in your message. Smiling also forces you to relax your jaw and facial muscles, which helps to release pent-up stress and improve your vocal clarity and projection. With so many benefits to offer, the simple act of smiling as you step onto the stage can launch your presentation on a strong note.

Barnett tells speakers to think of their bodies as communication instruments and to use them to their full potential, in much the same way musicians use their instruments. I like a musical instrument, your body can be treated well or poorly and played with varying degrees of success.

Using your physical self to full advantage starts with understanding the signals your body is sending to you and to the people in your audience. Tune in to your body and listen to its signals. If you are anxious leading up to a presentation, you may feel this signal in your shoulders, your jaw, or wherever you tend to "collect" stress. Explore that emotion and try to determine why you feel that way. You may identify some reasons that are real and relevant to the situation and some that are noise or distractions, at least as far as the immediate situation is concerned.

A real and extremely relevant reason might be that you haven't prepared thoroughly and therefore lack confidence in your ability to present your message or respond to audience questions. Assuming you've given yourself enough time, you can address this source of anxiety by finishing your preparation. A less relevant source of stress might be a buried memory of being embarrassed in front of your class as a child. This emotional mishap might still be stuck in your memory at some deep level, but it doesn't need to be part of who you are as a professional adult.

Barnett emphasizes that by dismissing irrelevant sources of stress and proactively dismantling relevant sources of stress, your mind can then tell your body that you're ready to go. This confidence will change the way you carry and present yourself on stage, it will give your voice fresh energy, and it will spread to your audience—your confidence in yourself will make them more confident in you, too. Rather than rushing through your presentation with your mind a nervous whirl, hoping only to make it through in one piece and get off the stage, you'll enjoy being in the moment and sharing your ideas and inspiration.[1]

BARNETTINTERNATIONALCONSULTING.COM

Planning a Presentation

Wherever your career takes you, Gina Barnett (profiled in the chapter-opening On the Job) would be the first to tell you that speeches and presentations offer great opportunities to display all your communication skills, including research, planning, writing, visual design, and interpersonal and nonverbal communication. Presentations also let you demonstrate your ability to think on your feet, grasp complex business issues, and handle challenging situations—all attributes that executives look for when searching for talented employees to promote.

Planning presentations is much like planning other business messages: You analyze the situation, gather information, select the best media and channels, and organize the information. Be aware that preparing a professional-quality business presentation can take a considerable amount of time. Presentation designer and trainer Nancy Duarte offers this rule of thumb: For a formal, 1-hour presentation, allow 36 to 90 hours to research, conceive, create, and practice.[2] Not every one-hour presentation justifies a week or two of preparation, of course, but important, career-changing presentations certainly can.

ANALYZING THE SITUATION

As with written communications, analyzing the situation involves defining your purpose and developing an audience profile (see Table 14.1 on the next page). The purpose of most

1 LEARNING OBJECTIVE
Highlight the importance of presentations in your business career, and explain how to adapt the planning step of the three-step process to presentations.

Creating a high-quality presentation for an important event can take days, so be sure to allow enough time.

REAL-TIME UPDATES
LEARN MORE BY WATCHING THIS VIDEO

Body wisdom from communication coach Gina Barnett

In this talk at Google, Gina Barnett shares some essentials of using your body as an effective speaking instrument. Go to **realtimeupdates.com/ebc13** and select Learn More in the Students section.

TABLE 14.1 Analyzing Audiences for Business Presentations

Task	Actions
To determine audience size and composition	• Estimate how many people will attend (in person and online). • Identify what they have in common and how they differ. • Analyze the mix of organizational positions, professions, language fluencies, and other demographic factors that could influence your content and delivery choices.
To predict the audience's probable reaction	• Analyze why audience members are attending the presentation. • Determine the audience's general attitude toward the topic: interested, moderately interested, unconcerned, open-minded, or hostile. • Analyze your audience's likely mood when you speak to them. • Find out what kind of supporting information will help the audience accept and respond to your message: technical data, historical information, financial data, demonstrations, samples, and so on. • Consider whether the audience has any biases that might work against you. • Anticipate possible objections or questions.
To gauge the audience's experience	• Analyze whether everybody has the same background and level of understanding. • Determine what the audience already knows about the subject. • Consider whether the audience is familiar with the vocabulary you intend to use. • Analyze what the audience expects from you. • Think about the mix of general concepts and specific details you will need to present.

Check out the "Five-Minute Guide to Planning Presentations" at the end of the chapter.

Learn as much as you can about the setting and circumstances of your presentation, from the audience's expectations to the seating arrangements.

of your presentations will be to inform or to persuade, although you may occasionally need to make a collaborative presentation, such as when you're leading a problem-solving or brainstorming session.

In addition to following the audience analysis advice in Chapter 5, try to anticipate the likely emotional state of your audience members. Figure 14.1 offers tips for dealing with a variety of audience mindsets.

As you analyze the situation, also consider the circumstances. If some or all of the audience members will be in the same room with you, how will they be seated? Can you control the environment to minimize distractions? What equipment will you need? If you're

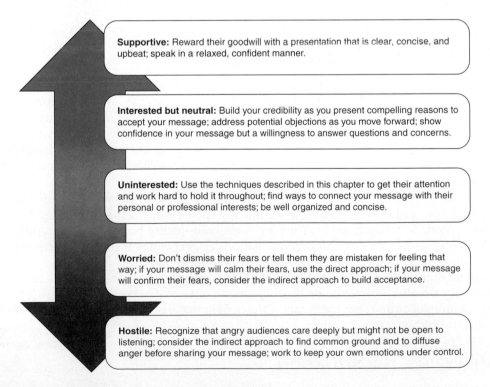

Supportive: Reward their goodwill with a presentation that is clear, concise, and upbeat; speak in a relaxed, confident manner.

Interested but neutral: Build your credibility as you present compelling reasons to accept your message; address potential objections as you move forward; show confidence in your message but a willingness to answer questions and concerns.

Uninterested: Use the techniques described in this chapter to get their attention and work hard to hold it throughout; find ways to connect your message with their personal or professional interests; be well organized and concise.

Worried: Don't dismiss their fears or tell them they are mistaken for feeling that way; if your message will calm their fears, use the direct approach; if your message will confirm their fears, consider the indirect approach to build acceptance.

Hostile: Recognize that angry audiences care deeply but might not be open to listening; consider the indirect approach to find common ground and to diffuse anger before sharing your message; work to keep your own emotions under control.

Figure 14.1 Planning for Various Audience Mindsets
Try to assess the emotional state of your audience ahead of time so you can plan your presentation approach accordingly.

presenting online, how will the meeting system you're using affect the audience's ability to see you and your presentation materials? Such variables can influence not only the style of your presentation but the content itself.

SELECTING THE BEST MEDIA AND CHANNELS

For some presentations, you'll be expected to use whatever media and channels your audience, your boss, or the circumstances require. For example, you might be required to use specific presentation software and a conference room's built-in display system or your company's online meeting software.

For other presentations, though, you might be able to choose from an array of presentation modes, from live, in-person presentations to *webcasts* (online presentations that people either view live or download later from the web), screencasts (recordings of activity on computer displays with audio voiceover), or *twebinars* (the use of Twitter as a *backchannel*—see page 469—for real-time conversation during a web-based seminar[3]).

ORGANIZING A PRESENTATION

The possibilities for organizing a business presentation fall into two basic categories, *linear* or *nonlinear*. Linear presentations are like printed documents in the sense that they are outlined like conventional messages and follow a predefined flow from start to finish. The linear model is appropriate for speeches, status updates, technical and financial presentations, and other presentations in which you want to convey your message point by point or build up to a conclusion following logical steps.

> Linear presentations generally follow a fixed path from start to finish.

In contrast, a nonlinear presentation doesn't flow in any particular direction but rather gives the presenter the option to move back and forth between topics and up and down in terms of level of detail. Nonlinear presentations can be useful when you want to be able to show complicated relationships between multiple ideas or elements, to zoom in and out between the "big picture" and specific details, to explore complex visuals, or to have the flexibility to move from topic to topic in any order.

> Nonlinear presentations can move back and forth between topics and up and down in levels of detail.

The difference between the two styles can be seen in the type of software typically used to create and deliver a presentation. Microsoft PowerPoint, Apple Keynote, Google Slides, and similar packages use sequences of individual slides, often referred to as a *slide deck*. The slides don't necessarily need to be presented in a strict linear order, because the presenter does have the option of jumping out of the predefined order, but in most presentations using slides, the speaker moves from start to finish in that order.

REAL-TIME UPDATES

LEARN MORE BY WATCHING THIS VIDEO

Get started with Prezi

Watch this tutorial to see how to create effective Prezi presentations. Go to **real-timeupdates.com/ebc13** and select Learn More in the Students section.

Prezi is the best-known nonlinear presentation software and doesn't use the concept of individual slides. Instead, you start from a main screen, or canvas, which often presents the big-picture overview of your topic (see Figure 14.2 on the next page). From there, you add individual objects (including blocks of text, photos, or videos) that convey specific information points. When you present, you can zoom in and out, discussing the individual objects and their relationship to the big picture and to each other. You can also establish a narrative flow by defining a path from one object to the next, which also lets people view the presentation on their own[4] (and effectively turns a Prezi presentation into a linear presentation).

Prezi is sometimes viewed as a more dynamic and engaging way to present, and it certainly has that potential. However, keep several points in mind if you have a choice of which approach to take and which software to use. First, match the tool to the task, not the other way around. A detailed technical discussion might need a linear presentation, whereas a free-form brainstorming session might benefit from a nonlinear approach. Second, if they are used well, software features can help you tell your story, but your story is what matters—not the software. If they are used poorly, software features only get in the way. (Overuse of zooming in Prezi is a good example.[5]) Third, despite their reputation, PowerPoint and other slide programs aren't limited to creating boring, linear flows of bullet points (see "Choosing Structured or Free-Form Slides" on page 457).

> Remember that presentations are not about flash and dazzle; they are about sharing ideas, information, and emotions with your audience.

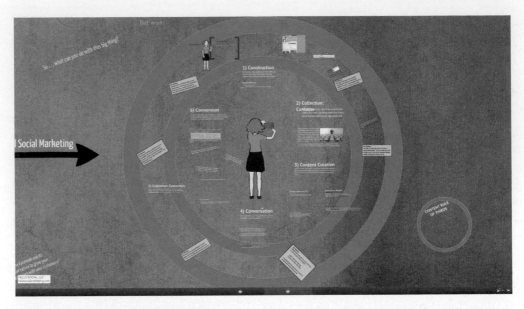

Figure 14.2   Nonlinear Presentations
Nonlinear presentations, particularly those using the cloud-based Prezi system, give the presenter more freedom to zoom in and out from the big picture to the details and to cover topics in any order.

Defining Your Main Idea

If you can't express your main idea in a single sentence, you probably haven't defined it clearly enough.

Regardless of which overall approach you take, a successful presentation starts with a clear statement of the main idea you want to share with your audience. Start by composing a one-sentence summary that links your subject and purpose to your audience's frame of reference. Here are some examples:

> Convince management that reorganizing the technical support department will improve customer service and reduce employee turnover.
>
> Convince the board of directors that we should build a new plant in Texas to eliminate manufacturing bottlenecks and improve production quality.
>
> Address employee concerns regarding a new health-care plan by showing how the plan will reduce costs and improve the quality of their care.

Each of these statements puts a particular slant on the subject, one that directly relates to the audience's interests. By focusing on your audience's needs and using the "you" attitude, you help keep their attention and convince them your points are relevant.

Limiting Your Scope

Even if you don't have strict time limits, keep your presentations as short as possible to maintain audience interest.

The only sure way to measure the length of your presentation is to complete a practice run.

Limiting your scope is important with any message, but it's particularly vital with presentations, for two reasons. First, for many presentations, you're expected to work within strict time limits. Second, the longer you speak, the more difficult it is to hold the audience's attention, and the more difficult it is for your listeners to retain your key points.[6]

The only sure way to know how much material you can cover in a given time is to practice your presentation after you complete it. As an alternative, if you're using conventional structured slides (see page 457), you can figure on three or four minutes per slide as a rough guide.[7] Of course, be sure to factor in time for introductions, coffee breaks, demonstrations, question-and-answer sessions, and anything else that takes away from your speaking time.

Approaching time constraints as a creative challenge can actually help you develop more-effective presentations. Limitations can force you to focus on the essential message points that are important to your audience.[8]

Choosing Your Approach

With a well-defined main idea to guide you and a clear notion of the scope of your presentation, you can begin to arrange your message. If you have 10 minutes or less, consider organizing your presentation much as you would a letter or other brief message: Use the direct approach if the subject involves routine information or good news, and use the indirect approach if the subject involves bad news or persuasion. Plan your introduction to arouse interest and to give a preview of what's to come. For the body of the presentation, be prepared to explain the who, what, when, where, why, and how of your topic. In the final section, review the points you've made and close with a statement that will help your audience remember the subject of your speech (see Figure 14.3).

Longer presentations are often organized more like reports. If the purpose is to motivate or inform, you'll typically use the direct approach and a structure imposed naturally by the subject: comparison, importance, sequence, chronology, geography, or category (as discussed in Chapter 12). If your purpose is to analyze, persuade, or collaborate, organize your material around conclusions and recommendations or around a logical argument. Use the direct approach if the audience is receptive and the indirect approach if you expect resistance.

No matter what the length, look for opportunities to integrate storytelling into the structure of your presentation. The dramatic tension (not knowing what will happen to the "hero") at the heart of effective storytelling is a great way to capture and keep the audience's attention.

> Organize short presentations the same way you would a letter or other brief written message; organize long presentations as you would a report or proposal.

> **REAL-TIME UPDATES**
> LEARN MORE BY VISITING THIS WEBSITE
> **The latest tools and trends in presentations**
> From design trends to new software tools, this blog covers the newest ideas in presentations. Go to **real-timeupdates.com/ebc13** and select Learn More in the Students section.

> Using a storytelling model can be a great way to catch and hold the audience's attention.

Preparing Your Outline

An outline helps you organize your message, and it serves as the foundation for delivering your speech. Prepare your outline in several stages:[9]

- State your purpose and main idea, and then use these elements to guide the rest of your planning.

> In addition to planning your speech, a presentation outline helps you plan your speaking notes.

Progress Update: August 2020

Purpose: To update the Executive Committee on our product development schedule.

I. Review goals and progress.
  A. Mechanical design:
    1. Goal: 100%
    2. Actual: 80%
    3. Reason for delay: Unanticipated problems with case durability
  B. Software development:
    1. Goal: 50%
    2. Actual: 60%
  C. Material sourcing:
    1. Goal: 100%
    2. Actual: 45% (and materials identified are at 140% of anticipated costs)
    3. Reason for delay: Purchasing is understaffed and hasn't been able to research sources adequately.
II. Discuss schedule options.
  A. Option 1: Reschedule product launch date.
  B. Option 2: Launch on schedule with more expensive materials.
III. Suggest goals for next month.
IV. Q&A

Figure 14.3 **Effective Outline for a 10-Minute Presentation**
Here is an outline of a short presentation that updates management on the status of a key project. The presenter has some bad news to deliver, so she opted for an indirect approach to lay out the reasons for the delay before sharing the news of the schedule slip.

A clear statement of purpose helps the presenter stay focused on her message while she develops her outline.

OUR TRAVEL AND ENTERTAINMENT COSTS ARE OUT OF CONTROL

Purpose: To explain why Electrovision's travel and entertainment (T&E) costs are so high and to propose a series of changes to bring them under control.

INTRODUCTION

I. Our T&E costs are way above average, and they pose a threat to the company's financial health; fortunately, we can fix the problem in four straightforward steps that could save as much as $6 million a year.

II. How we approached the investigation
   A. We analyzed internal expense reports.
   B. We compared our cost data with nationwide averages.
   C. We analyzed published information on trends and cost-control suggestions.

(Transition: This presentation reviews Electrovision's spending patterns, analyzes the impact on company profits, and recommends four steps for reducing the budget.)

BODY

I. Analysis of spending patterns
   A. The amount we've been spending on T&E:
      1. Airfares, hotels, rental cars, restaurants, and entertainment totaled $16 million last year.
      2. T&E budget increased by 12 percent per year for the past five years.
   B. Where the money goes:
      1. We took 3,390 trips last year at an average cost per trip of $4,725.
      2. Airfares and lodging represent 70 percent of T&E expenses.
   C. How our spending compares with national averages:
      1. Facilities and customers spread from coast to coast force us to spend a lot on travel.
      2. However, we spend 125 percent more than the national average for every day of travel. (Source: Dow Jones)
   D. Why do we spend so much?
      1. First-class travel has been viewed as compensation for the demands of extensive travel.
      2. The sales staff is encouraged to entertain clients.
      3. T&E costs are hard for managers to view and study.
      4. No one has central responsibility for controlling costs.

(Transition: We need to control spending for two reasons: (1) profits are projected to be flat or declining over the next two years, and (2) hotel rates and airfares continue to rise sharply.)

(Continued)

The introduction starts by highlighting the problem she will address.

The introduction continues with a description of the investigation she undertook; this will enhance her credibility by showing that the research was thorough and objective.

Part I of the body identifies the nature, scope, and causes of the problem.

The organization of the body is clear and logical, moving from one key point to the next.

Figure 14.4 Effective Outline for a 30-Minute Presentation
This outline clearly identifies the purpose and the distinct points to be made in the introduction, body, and close. Notice also how the speaker has written her major transitions in full-sentence form to be sure she can clearly phrase these critical passages when it's time to speak.

- Organize your major points and subpoints in logical order, expressing each major point as a single, complete sentence.
- Identify major points in the body first, then outline the introduction and close.
- Identify transitions between major points or sections, then write these transitions in full-sentence form.
- Prepare your bibliography or source notes; highlight those sources you want to identify by name during your talk.
- Choose a compelling title. Make it brief, action-oriented, and focused on what you can do for the audience.[10]

You may find it helpful to create a simpler speaking outline from your planning outline.

Many speakers like to prepare both a detailed *planning outline* (see Figure 14.4) and a simpler *speaking outline* that provides all the cues and reminders they need in order to present their material. Follow these steps to prepare an effective speaking outline:[11]

- Start with the planning outline and then strip away anything you don't plan to say directly to your audience.
- Condense points and transitions to key words or phrases.

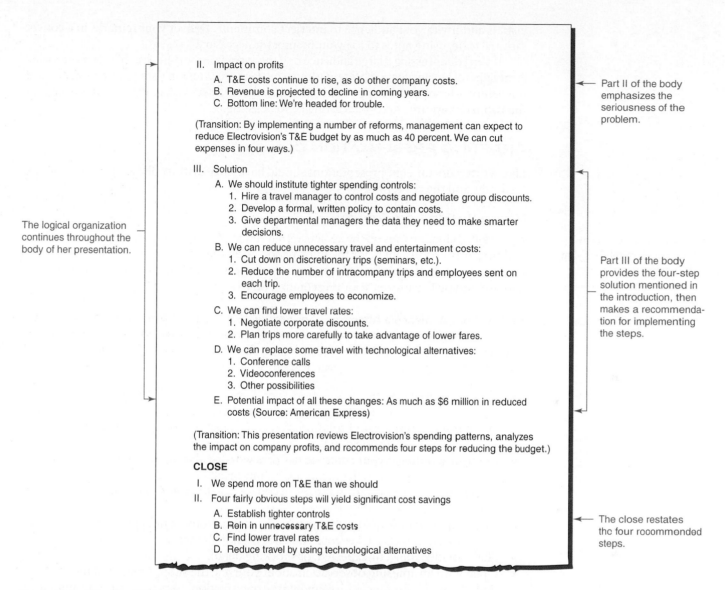

The logical organization continues throughout the body of her presentation.

Part II of the body emphasizes the seriousness of the problem.

Part III of the body provides the four-step solution mentioned in the introduction, then makes a recommendation for implementing the steps.

The close restates the four recommended steps.

Figure 14.4   Effective Outline for a 30-Minute Presentation (Continued)

- Add delivery cues, such as places where you plan to pause for emphasis or use visuals.
- Arrange your notes on numbered cards or use the notes capability in your presentation software.

Developing a Presentation

Although you don't usually write out a presentation word for word, you still engage in the writing process—developing your ideas, structuring support points, phrasing your transitions, and so on. Depending on the situation and your personal style, the eventual presentation might follow your initial words closely, or you might express your thoughts in fresh, spontaneous language.

2   LEARNING OBJECTIVE
Describe the tasks involved in developing a presentation.

ADAPTING TO YOUR AUDIENCE

The size of your audience, the venue (in person, online, or a combination of the two), your subject, your purpose, your budget, and the time available for preparation all influence the style of your presentation. If you're speaking to a small group, particularly people you already know, you can use a casual style that encourages audience participation. A small conference room, with your audience seated around a table, may be appropriate. Use simple

Adapting to your audience involves a number of issues, from speaking style to technology choices.

visuals and invite your audience to interject comments. Deliver your remarks in a conversational tone, using notes to jog your memory if necessary.

If you're addressing a large audience or if the event is important, establish a more formal atmosphere. During formal presentations, speakers are often on a stage or platform, standing behind a lectern and using a microphone so that their remarks can be heard throughout the room or captured for broadcasting or webcasting.

CRAFTING PRESENTATION CONTENT

Like written documents, presentations should have three distinct phases: the introduction, the body, and the close.

Presentation Introduction

An effective introduction fires up the audience, establishes your credibility, and prepares the audience for the body of your presentation.

A good introduction fires up the audience's interest in your topic, establishes your credibility, and prepares your listeners for the information and insights you have to share. That's a lot to accomplish in the first few minutes, so give yourself plenty of time to develop the words and visuals you'll use to get your presentation off to a great start.

Think about creative ways to capture the audience's attention and interest with your opening remarks.

Getting Your Audience's Attention   Some subjects are naturally more interesting to some audiences than others. If your presentation involves the health, wealth, or happiness of your listeners, most of them will be interested, regardless of how you begin. Other subjects call for more imagination. Here are seven ways to arouse audience interest:[12]

- If it's appropriate for the presentation, encourage your listeners to unite around a meaningful business objective. For example, if the company is struggling and your presentation offers a turnaround solution, you could start by urging your listeners to come together for the common good.
- Describe a problem your audience has or is worried about having.
- Tell a compelling story that illustrates an important and relevant point. If your entire presentation is structured as a story, of course, you'll want to keep the interest high by not giving away the ending yet.
- Pass around a sample of something you're discussing or otherwise appeal to listeners' senses.
- Ask a question that will get your audience thinking about your message.
- Share an intriguing, unexpected, or shocking detail.
- Open with an amusing observation about yourself, the subject matter of the presentation, or the circumstances surrounding the presentation—but make sure any humorous remarks are relevant, appropriate, and not offensive to anyone in the audience.

Regardless of which technique you choose, make sure you can give audience members a reason to care and to believe that the time they're about to spend listening to you will be worth their while.[13] The more you can make your opening about your listeners and their concerns, the more likely they will be to lock into your message and stay tuned.

If someone else will be introducing you, ask this person to present your credentials in a way that relates to the audience's interest in your presentation.

Building Your Credibility   Audiences tend to decide within a few minutes whether you're worth listening to, so establishing your credibility quickly is vital.[14] If you're not a well-known expert or haven't already earned your audience's trust in other situations, you'll need to build credibility in your introduction. If someone else will introduce you, he or she can present your credentials. If you will be introducing yourself, keep your comments brief, but don't be afraid to mention your accomplishments. Your listeners will be curious about your qualifications, so tell them briefly who you are, why you're there, and how they'll benefit from listening to you. You might say something like this:

I'm Karen Whitney, a market research analyst with Information Resources Corporation. For the past five years, I've specialized in studying high-technology markets. Your director of engineering, John LaBarre, asked me to talk about recent trends in computer-aided design so that you'll have a better idea of how to direct your development efforts.

This speaker establishes credibility by tying her credentials to the purpose of her presentation. By mentioning her company's name, her specialization and position, and the name of the audience's boss, she lets her listeners know immediately that she is qualified to tell them something they need to know.

Previewing Your Message   In addition to getting the audience's attention and establishing your credibility, a good introduction gives your audience a preview of what's ahead. Your preview should summarize the main idea of your presentation, identify major supporting points, and indicate the order in which you'll develop those points. By giving listeners the framework of your message, you help them process the information you'll be sharing. Of course, if you're using the indirect approach, you'll have to decide how much of your main idea to give away in the introduction.

> Offer a preview to help your audience understand the importance, the structure, and the content of your message.

Presentation Body

The bulk of your presentation is devoted to a discussion of the main points in your outline. No matter what organizational pattern you're using, your goals are to make sure that the organization is clear and that you hold the audience's attention.

Connecting Your Ideas   In written documents, you can show how ideas are related with a variety of design clues: headings, paragraph indentions, white space, and lists. However, with oral communication—particularly when you aren't using visuals for support—you have to rely primarily on spoken words to link various parts and ideas.

For the links between sentences and paragraphs, use one or two transitional words: *therefore, because, in addition, in contrast, moreover, for example, consequently, nevertheless,* or *finally.* To link major sections of a presentation, use complete sentences or paragraphs, such as "Now that we've reviewed the problem, let's take a look at some solutions." Every time you shift topics, be sure to stress the connection between ideas by summarizing what's been said and previewing what's to come. The longer your presentation, the more important your transitions. Your listeners need clear transitions to guide them to the most important points. Furthermore, they'll appreciate brief interim summaries to pick up any ideas they may have missed.

> Use transitions to help your audience move from one idea to the next, particularly in longer presentations.

Holding Your Audience's Attention   A successful introduction will have grabbed your audience's attention; now the body of your presentation needs to hold that attention. Here are some helpful tips for keeping the audience tuned in to your message:

- Keep relating your subject to your audience's needs.
- Don't overwhelm the audience with details, either in your slides or in your spoken message, particularly if you're presenting a complicated topic to people learning it for the first time.[15]
- Anticipate—and answer—likely questions as you move along so people don't get confused or distracted.
- Use clear, vivid language and throw in some variety; repeating the same words and phrases over and over puts people to sleep.
- Show how your subject is related to ideas that audience members already understand, and give people a way to categorize and remember your points.[16]
- Illustrate your ideas with visuals, which enliven your message, help you connect with audience members, and help them remember your message more effectively (see "Enhancing Your Presentation with Effective Visuals," pages 456–463).
- Invite questions. Don't assume that you need to hold off on questions until a formal question-and-answer (Q&A) session at the end of your talk. In fact, today's audiences tend to expect a more interactive give-and-take, so involve your audience members along the way.[17]

> The most important way to hold an audience's attention is to show how your message relates to their individual needs and concerns.

> Your close has two tasks: making sure your listeners leave with your key points clear in their minds and putting your audience in the appropriate emotional state.

Presentation Close

The close of a speech or presentation has two critical tasks to accomplish: making sure your listeners leave with the key points from your talk clear in their minds and putting your audience in the appropriate emotional state. For example, if the purpose of your presentation is to warn managers that their out-of-control spending threatens the company's survival, you want them to leave with that message ringing in their ears—and with enough concern for the problem to stimulate changes in their behavior.

When you repeat your main idea in the close, emphasize what you want your audience to do or to think.

Restating Your Main Points   Use the close to succinctly restate your main points, emphasizing what you want your listeners to do or to think. For example, to close a presentation on your company's executive compensation program, you could repeat your specific recommendations and then conclude with a memorable statement to motivate your audience to take action:

We can all be proud of the way our company has grown. However, if we want to continue that growth, we need to take four steps to ensure that our best people don't start looking for opportunities elsewhere:

- First, increase the overall level of compensation
- Second, establish a cash bonus program
- Third, offer a variety of stock-based incentives
- Fourth, improve our health insurance and pension benefits

By taking these steps, we can ensure that our company retains the management talent it needs in order to face our industry's largest competitors.

By summarizing the key ideas, you improve the chance that your audience will leave with your message clearly in mind.

Plan your final statement carefully so you can end on a strong, positive note.

Ending with Clarity and Confidence   If you've been successful with the introduction and body of your presentation, your listeners have the information they need, and they're in the right frame of mind to put that information to good use. Now you're ready to end on a strong note that confirms expectations about any actions or decisions that will follow the presentation—and to bolster the audience's confidence in you and your message one final time.

Some presentations require the audience to reach a decision or agree to take specific action, in which case the close should provide a clear wrap-up. If the audience reached agreement on an issue covered in the presentation, briefly review the consensus. If they didn't agree, make the lack of consensus clear by saying something like "We seem to have some fundamental disagreement on this question." Then be ready to suggest a method of resolving the differences.

If you expect any action to occur as a result of your speech, be sure to identify who is responsible for doing what. List the action items and, if possible within the time you have available, establish due dates and assign responsibility for each task.

Make sure your final remarks are memorable and have the right emotional tone.

Make sure your final remarks are memorable and expressed in a tone that is appropriate to the situation. For example, if your presentation is a persuasive request for project funding, you might emphasize the importance of this project and your team's ability to complete it on schedule and within budget. Expressing confident optimism sends the message that you believe in your ability to perform. Conversely, if your purpose is to alert the audience to a problem or risk, false optimism undermines your message.

Whatever final message is appropriate, think through your closing remarks carefully before stepping in front of the audience. You don't want to wind up on stage with nothing to say but "Well, I guess that's it."

3 LEARNING OBJECTIVE
Describe the six major design and writing tasks required to enhance your presentation with effective visuals.

Enhancing Your Presentation with Effective Visuals

Slides and other visuals can improve the quality and impact of your presentation by creating interest, illustrating points that are difficult to explain through words alone, adding variety, and increasing the audience's ability to absorb and remember information.

You can select from a variety of visuals to enhance presentations. Don't overlook "old-school" technologies such as overhead transparencies, chalkboards, whiteboards, and flipcharts—they can all have value in the right circumstances. However, most business presentation visuals are created using Microsoft PowerPoint, Apple Keynote, or Google Slides for linear presentations and Prezi for nonlinear presentations. Presentation slides and "Prezis" are easy to edit and update; you can add sound, photos, video, and animation; they can be incorporated into online meetings, webcasts, and *webinars* (a common term for web-based seminars); and you can record self-running presentations for trade shows, websites, and other uses.

Thoughtfully designed visuals create interest, illustrate complex points in your message, add variety, and help the audience absorb and remember information.

Presentation slides are practically universal in business today, but their widespread use is not always welcome. You may have already heard the expression "death by PowerPoint," which refers to the agonizing experience of sitting through too many poorly conceived and poorly delivered slide shows. However, presentations don't have to be dull. In fact, they can be satisfying, educational, and invigorating for presenters and audiences alike. Keep the audience's needs in mind, and focus on the satisfaction of sharing information and motivating people whose fortunes and futures you care about.

Focusing on making your presentations simple and authentic will help you avoid the "death by PowerPoint" stigma that presentations have in the minds of many professionals.

CHOOSING STRUCTURED OR FREE-FORM SLIDES

For linear presentations, the most important design choice you face when creating slides is whether to use conventional, bullet point–intensive **structured slides** or the looser, visually oriented **free-form slides** that many presentation specialists now advocate. Compare the two rows of slides in Figure 14.5 on the next page. The structured slides in the top row follow the same basic format throughout the presentation. In fact, they're based directly on the templates built into PowerPoint, which tend to feature lots of bullet points.

Structured slides are usually based on templates that give all the slides in a presentation the same general look (which usually involves many bullet points); free-form slides are much less rigid and emphasize visual appeal.

The free-form slides in the bottom row don't follow a rigid structure. However, free-form designs should not change randomly from one slide to the next. Even without the rigid pattern of a template, they should be unified by design elements such as color and font selections, as can be seen in Figures 14.5c and 14.5d. Also, note how Figure 14.5d combines visual and textual messages to convey the point about listening without criticizing. This complementary approach of pictures and words is a highlight of free-form design.

Free-form slides often have far less content per slide than structured designs, which requires many more slides to cover a presentation of equal length.

Advantages and Disadvantages of Structured Slides

Structured slides have the advantage of being easy to create. You simply choose a design theme for the presentation, select a template for a new slide, and start typing. If you're in a schedule crunch, going the structured route might save the day because at least you'll have *something* ready to show. Given the speed and ease of creating them, structured slides can be a more practical choice for routine presentations such as project status updates.

Structured slides are often the best choice for project updates and other routine information presentations, particularly if the slides are intended to be used only once.

Also, because more information can usually be packed on each slide, carefully designed structured slides can be more effective at conveying complex ideas or sets of interrelated data to the right audiences. For example, if you are talking to a group of executives who must decide where to make budget cuts across the company's eight divisions, at some point in the presentation they will probably want to see summary data for all eight divisions on a single slide for easy comparison. Such a slide would be overcrowded by the usual definition, but this might be the only practical way to get a big-picture view of the situation. (The best solution is probably some high-level summary slides supported by a detailed handout, as "Creating Effective Handouts" on page 464 explains.)

The primary disadvantage of structured design is the mind-numbing effect that can be caused by too many text-heavy slides that all look alike. Slide after slide of dense, highly structured bullet points with no visual relief can put an audience to sleep.

Advantages and Disadvantages of Free-Form Slides

Free-form slide designs can overcome the drawbacks of text-heavy structured design by providing complementary visual and textual information and limiting the amount of information delivered on each slide. (Of course, well-designed structured slides can also meet these criteria, but the constraints of prebuilt templates make doing so more of a challenge).

Well-designed free-form slides help viewers understand, process, and remember the speaker's message.

With appropriate imagery, free-form designs can also create a more dynamic and engaging experience for the audience. Given their ability to excite and engage, free-form

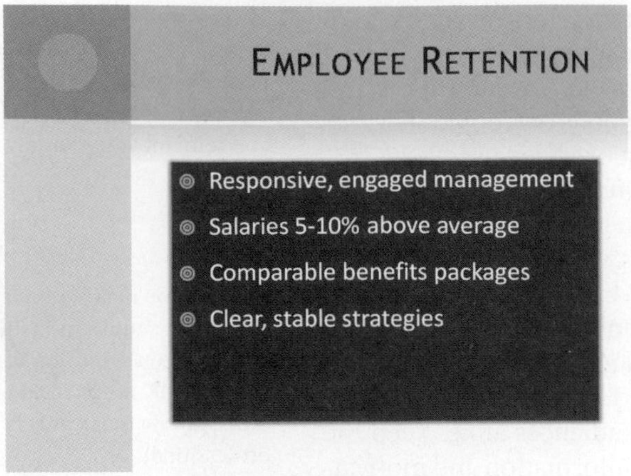

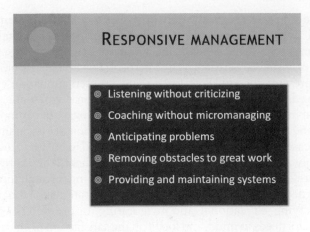

Figure 14.5a

Figure 14.5b

Figure 14.5c

Figure 14.5d

Figure 14.5 **Structured Versus Free-Form Slide Design**
Compare the rigid, predictable design of the two slides in the top row with the more dynamic free-form designs in the bottom row. Although the two free-form slides don't follow the same design structure, they are visually linked by color and font choices. (Note that Figure 14.5d is a humorous way of conveying the first bullet point in Figure 14.5b.)

designs are particularly good for motivational, educational, and persuasive presentations—particularly when the slides will be used multiple times and therefore compensate for the extra time and effort required to create them.

> Free-form slides can require more skill and time to create, and they put more demands on the speaker during the presentation.

Free-form slides have several potential disadvantages, however. First, effectively designing slides with both visual and textual elements is more creatively demanding and more time-consuming than simply typing text into preformatted templates. The emphasis on visual content also requires more images, which take time to find.

Second, because far less textual information tends to be displayed on-screen, the speaker is responsible for conveying more of the content. Ideally, of course, this is how a presentation *should* work, but presenters sometimes find themselves in less-than-ideal circumstances, such as being asked to deliver a presentation that someone else created.

Third, if not handled carefully, the division of information into smaller chunks can make it difficult to present complex subjects in a cohesive, integrated manner. For instance, if you're discussing a business problem that has five interrelated causes, it might be helpful to insert a conventional bullet-point slide as a summary and reminder after discussing each problem on its own.

DESIGNING EFFECTIVE SLIDES

Despite complaints about "death by PowerPoint," the problem is not with the software itself (or with Apple Keynote or any other presentation program). It is just a tool and, like other tools, can be used well or poorly. Unfortunately, lack of design awareness, inadequate training, schedule pressures, and the instinctive response of doing things the way they've always been done can lead to ineffective slides and lost opportunities to really connect with audiences. And although Prezi is sometimes promoted as the antidote to PowerPoint, using Prezi does not guarantee you'll end up with an effective presentation; it, too, can be misused and wind up creating a barrier between the speaker and the audience.

This section offers helpful tips for creating slides that engage audiences without overwhelming them with too much information or poorly designed layouts.

Designing Slides Around a Key Visual

Rather than structuring slide content as headlines and bullet points, a more effective and more appealing approach is to structure around a key visual that helps organize and explain the points you are trying to make. For example, a pyramid suggests a hierarchical relationship, while a circular flow diagram emphasizes that the final stage in a process loops back to the beginning of the process. Figure 14.6 on the next page shows six of the many types of visual designs you can use to organize information on a slide.

Structuring a slide around a key visual helps organize and explain the points you are trying to make.

Writing Readable Content

One of the most common mistakes beginners make—and one of the chief criticisms leveled at structured slide designs in general—is stuffing slides with too much text. Doing so overloads the audience with too much information too fast, takes attention away from the speaker by forcing people to read more, and requires the presenter to use smaller type.

Effective text slides supplement your words and help the audience follow the flow of ideas (see Figure 14.7 on page 461). Use text to highlight key points, summarize and preview your message, signal major shifts in thought, illustrate concepts, or help create interest in your spoken message.

Use slide text sparingly and only to emphasize key points, not to convey your entire message.

Creating Charts and Tables for Slides

Charts and tables for presentations need to be simpler than visuals for printed documents. Detailed images that look fine on the printed page can be too dense and too complicated for presentations. Remember that your audience will view your slides from across the room—not from a foot or two away, as you do while you create them. Keep the level of detail to a minimum, eliminating anything that is not essential. If necessary, break information into more than one chart or table. It may also be useful to provide detailed versions of charts and tables in a handout.

Charts and tables for presentations need to be simpler than visuals for printed documents.

Selecting Design Elements

As you create slides, pay close attention to the interaction of color, background and foreground designs, artwork, typefaces, and type styles:

- **Color.** Color is an expressive and powerful element of design, so take some time to choose the best colors for your slides. As Table 14.2 on page 461 indicates, colors can evoke specific moods and connotations. Color has important functional uses as well, including improving the readability of text and highlighting important visual elements.
- **Background designs and artwork.** All visuals have two layers of design: the *background* and the *foreground*. The background is the equivalent of paper in a printed document, and the elements in the foreground are the essential content of your slides. If you use a design theme or template in your presentation software, it will apply the same background treatment to every slide. Whichever design theme you choose, make sure the background stays in the background and doesn't distract viewers or compete with the foreground. Some of the template designs in presentation software have backgrounds that are too distracting for serious business use.
- **Foreground designs and artwork.** The foreground contains the unique text and graphic elements that make up each individual slide. Foreground elements can be either functional or decorative. *Functional artwork* includes photos, technical drawings, charts, and other visual elements containing information that's part of your message. In contrast, *decorative artwork* simply enhances the look of your slides and should be used sparingly, if at all.

Color is more than just decoration; colors themselves have meanings, based on both cultural experience and the relationships that you have established between the colors in your designs.

Make sure the background of your slides stays in the background; it should never get in the way of the informational elements in the foreground.

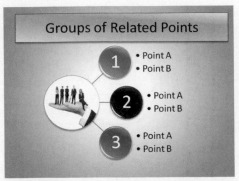

Figure 14.6a

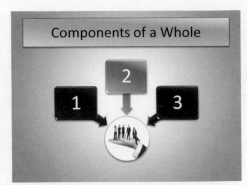

Figure 14.6b

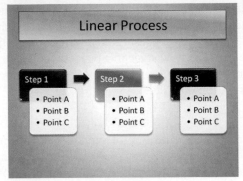

Figure 14.6c

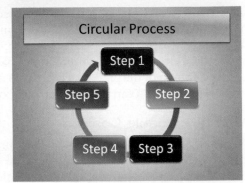

Figure 14.6d

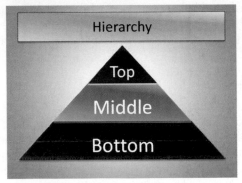

Figure 14.6e

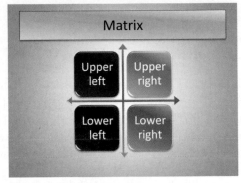

Figure 14.6f

Figure 14.6   Using a Key Visual to Organize Points on a Slide
Simple graphical elements such as these "SmartArt" images in Microsoft PowerPoint make it easy to organize slide content using a key visual. Whether you're trying to convey the relationship of ideas in a hierarchy, a linear process, a circular process, or just about any other configuration, a key visual can work in tandem with your written and spoken messages to help audiences get your main idea.

Many of the typefaces available on your computer are difficult to read on-screen, so they aren't good choices for presentation slides.

- **Typefaces and type styles.** Type is harder to read on a screen than on a printed page, so you need to choose fonts and type styles with care. Sans serif fonts are usually easier to read than serif fonts. Avoid all-caps, use generous space between lines of text, and limit the number of fonts to one or two per slide. Choose type sizes that are easy to read from anywhere in the room, usually between 28 and 36 points, and test them in the room if possible. A clever way to test readability at your computer is to stand back as many feet from the screen as your screen size in inches (17 feet for a 17-inch screen, for example). If the slides are readable at this distance, you're probably in good shape.[18]

Design inconsistencies confuse and annoy audiences; don't change colors and other design elements randomly throughout your presentation.

Maintaining design consistency is critical because audiences start to assign meaning to visual elements beginning with the first slide. For instance, if yellow is used to call attention to the first major point in your presentation, viewers will expect the next occurrence of yellow to also signal an important point. The design theme and the *slide master* features make consistency easy to achieve because they apply consistent design choices to every slide in a presentation.

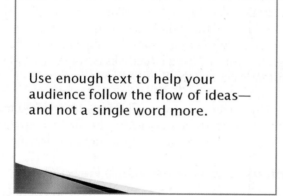

Figure 14.7a

Figure 14.7b

Figure 14.7c

Figure 14.7d

Figure 14.7 Writing Text for Slides

Effective text slides are clear, simple guides that help the audience understand and remember the speaker's message. Notice the progression toward simplicity in these slides: Figure 14.7a is a paragraph that would distract the audience for an extended period of time. Figure 14.7b offers concise, readable bullets, although too many slides in a row in this structured design would become tedious. Figure 14.7c distills the message down to a single thought that is complete on its own but doesn't convey all the information from the original and would need embellishment from the speaker. Figure 14.7d pushes this to the extreme, with only the core piece of the message to serve as an "exclamation point" for the spoken message. Figure 14.7c and especially Figure 14.7d could be even more powerful with a well-chosen visual that illustrates the notion of following a flow of ideas.

	TABLE 14.2	**Color and Emotion**	
Color	**Emotional Associations (for U.S. audiences)**	**Potential Uses**	
Blue	Peaceful, soothing, tranquil, cool, trusting	Background for presentations (usually dark blue); a safe and conservative choice	
White	Neutral, innocent, pure, wise, simple	Good choice for text displayed on a dark background	
Yellow	Warm, bright, cheerful, enthusiastic	Primarily as a highlight color, such as text bullets and subheadings with a dark background	
Red	Passionate, dangerous, active, painful	For promoting action or stimulating the audience; seldom used as a background ("in the red" specifically refers to financial losses)	
Green	Assertive, prosperous, envious, relaxed, natural	Highlight and accent color (note that green symbolizes money in the United States but not in other countries)	
Orange	Warm, dramatic	Useful to suggest energy and action	
Gray	Dignified, serious, somber, practical	Providing a visually "quiet" background, enhancing contrast with brighter colors	
Black	Serious, technical, formal	As either a functional or artistic color, depending on overall slide style	

Sources: Based in part on "Choosing Colors for Your Presentation Slides," Think Outside the Slide, accessed 15 May 2017, www.thinkoutsidetheslide.com; Claudyne Wilder and David Fine, *Point, Click & Wow* (San Francisco: Jossey-Bass Pfeiffer, 1996), 63, 527.

Adding Animation and Multimedia

You can animate just about everything in an electronic presentation, but resist the temptation to do so; make sure an animation has a purpose.

Presentation software offers many options for livening up your slides, including sound, animation, video clips, transition effects, hyperlinks, and zooming. These special effects need to be used sparingly, and always with a focus on helping viewers grasp your message.

Functional animation involves motion that is directly related to your message, such as a highlight arrow that moves around the screen to emphasize specific points in a technical diagram. Such animation is also a great way to demonstrate sequences and procedures. In contrast, *decorative animation*, such as having a block of text cartwheel in from off screen or using the zooming and panning capabilities in Prezi in ways that don't enhance audience understanding, needs to be incorporated with great care. These effects don't add any functional value, and they easily distract audiences.

Slide transitions control how one slide replaces another; *slide builds* control the reveal of individual elements on a slide.

Slide transitions control how one slide replaces another, such as having the current slide gently fade out before the next slide fades in. Such subtle transitions can ease your viewers' gaze from one slide to the next, but many transition effects are too busy and therefore are best avoided. **Slide builds** control the release of text, graphics, and other elements on individual slides. With builds, you can make key points appear on a slide one at a time, rather than all at once, thereby making it easier for you and the audience to focus on each new message point.

Hyperlinks let you build flexibility into your presentations.

A *hyperlink* instructs your software to jump to another slide in your presentation, to a website, or to another program entirely. Using hyperlinks is also a great way to build in flexibility so that you can instantly change the flow of your presentation in response to audience feedback.

Multimedia elements offer the ultimate in active presentations. Using audio and video clips can be a great way to complement your textual message. Just be sure to keep these elements brief and relevant, as supporting points for your presentation, not as replacements for it.

Using Presentation Software to Create Visual Reports

Visual reports are documents made using presentation software, but they are intended to be read like documents, not projected as presentation slides.

With its easy ability to combine text and graphics, presentation software is sometimes used to create *visual reports* that are something of a hybrid between conventional reports and presentation slides (see Figure 14.8). These are sometimes referred to as "slideuments" (*slide + document*) or "slide docs" as well. If you have a lot of diagrams or other visual material, creating a report in PowerPoint or similar software can be easier than doing so in word-processing software.

If they are intended to be read like documents, these visual reports can be an effective and appealing communication tool. As you can see from the amount of text in the example in Figure 14.8, however, these reports do not function well as slides and should not be used for presentations. Avoid the temptation to use these slide-report hybrids for presentation slides *and* as handouts (or as reading material for people who can't attend your presentation).

As "Creating Effective Handouts" on page 464 explains, the ideal solution is to create an effective slide set and a separate handout document (either a visual report or a conventional report) that provides additional details and supporting information. This way, you can optimize each piece to do the job it is really meant to do.

INTEGRATING MOBILE DEVICES IN PRESENTATIONS

Mobile devices can enhance presentations for presenters as well as audience members.

Smartphones and tablets offer a variety of ways to enhance presentations for presenters as well as audience members (see Figure 14.9). For example, you can get around the issue of everyone in the audience having a clear view of the screen with systems that broadcast your slides to tablets and smartphones. In fact, these systems can eliminate a conventional projection system entirely; everyone in the audience can view your slides on their mobile devices. You can also broadcast a live presentation to mobile users anywhere in the world. Each time you advance to a new slide, it is sent to the phone or tablet of everyone who is subscribed to your presentation.[19]

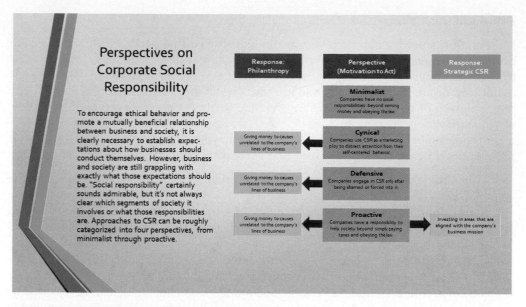

Figure 14.8 Visual Reports Using Presentation Software
Presentation software can be used to create visual reports that are designed to be read as other documents, rather than being projected as presentation slides.
Source: Courtland L. Bovée and John V. Thill, *Business in Action*, 8th ed. (Boston: Pearson, 2017), 80–81.

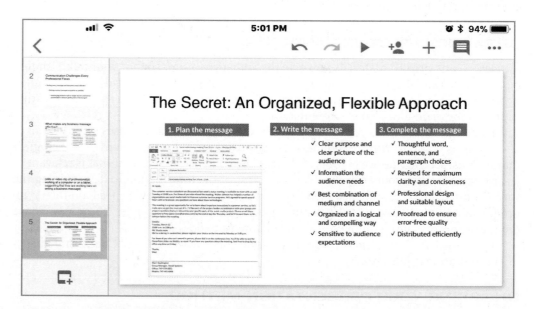

Figure 14.9 Using Mobile Devices in Presentations
Mobile presentation apps let you create and edit slides on the go, as well as control presentations directly from your device.

Completing a Presentation

The completion step for presentations involves a wider range of tasks than most other communication projects. Make sure you allow enough time to test your presentation slides, verify equipment operation, practice your speech, and create handout materials. With a first draft of your presentation in hand, revise your slides to make sure they are readable, concise, consistent, and fully operational (including transitions, builds, animation, and multimedia). Complete your production efforts by finalizing your slides, creating handouts, choosing your presentation method, and practicing your delivery.

4 LEARNING OBJECTIVE
Outline four major tasks involved in completing a presentation.

FINALIZING YOUR SLIDES

Presentation software can help you throughout the editing and revision process. For example, the *slide sorter* view (different programs have different names for this feature) lets you see some or all of the slides in your presentation on a single screen. Use this view to add and delete slides, reposition slides, check slides for design consistency, and verify the operation of any effects. Moreover, the slide sorter is a great way to review the flow of your story.[20]

In addition to using content slides, you can help your audience follow the flow of your presentation by creating slides for your title, agenda and program details, and navigation:

- **Title slide(s).** You can make a good first impression with one or two title slides, the equivalent of a report's cover and title page.
- **Agenda and program details.** These slides communicate the agenda for your presentation and any additional information the audience might need, such as hashtags and Wi-Fi log-in information.
- **Navigation slides.** To help the audience follow along, you can use a series of *navigation slides*. A simple way to do so is to repeat your agenda slide at the beginning of each major section in your presentation, with the upcoming section highlighted in some way. (The two navigation slides in Figure 14.10 show a more stylized way of showing the audience where you are in the presentation.)

Navigation slides help your audience keep track of what you've covered already and what you plan to cover next.

Figure 14.10 illustrates some of the many options you have for presenting various types of information. Note that although these slides don't follow a rigid structure of text-heavy bullet points, they are unified by the color scheme (silver background and bold color accents) and typeface selections.

CREATING EFFECTIVE HANDOUTS

Handouts—any printed materials you give the audience to supplement your talk—should be considered an integral part of your presentation strategy. Handouts can include detailed charts and tables, case studies, research results, magazine articles, and anything else that supports the main idea of your presentation.

Use handout materials to support the points made in your presentation and to offer the audience additional information on your topic.

Plan your handouts as you develop your presentation so that you use each medium as effectively as possible. Your presentation should paint the big picture, convey and connect major ideas, set the emotional tone, and rouse the audience to action (if that is relevant to your talk). Your handouts can then carry the rest of the information load, providing the supporting details that audience members can consume at their own speed, on their own time. You won't need to worry about stuffing every detail into your slides, because you have the more appropriate medium of printed documents to do that.

For a quick review of the key steps in creating effective visuals, see "Checklist: Enhancing Presentations with Visuals."

CHOOSING YOUR PRESENTATION METHOD

With all your materials ready, your next step is to decide which method of speaking you want to use. Speaking from notes (rather than from a fully written script) is nearly always the most effective and easiest delivery mode. This approach gives you something to refer to as you progress while still allowing for plenty of eye contact, a natural flow, interaction with the audience, and improvisation in response to audience feedback.

In nearly all instances, speaking from notes (rather than a full script) is the most effective delivery mode.

In contrast, reciting your speech from memory is nearly always a bad idea. Even if you can memorize the entire presentation, you will sound stiff and overly formal because you are "delivering lines," rather than talking to your audience. However, memorizing a quotation, an opening statement, or a few concluding remarks can bolster your confidence and strengthen your delivery.

Reading a speech is necessary in rare instances, such as when delivering legal information, policy statements, or other messages that must be conveyed in an exact

Left: This introductory slide is a blunt attention-getter, something that would have to be used with caution and only in special circumstances.

Right: This simple math equation gets the point across about how expensive high employee turnover is.

Left: This stylized bar graph sends a stark visual message about how bad the company's turnover really is.

Right: This slide is essentially a bullet list, with three groups of two bullets each. Repeating the photo element from the introductory slide emphasizes the message about employee turnover.

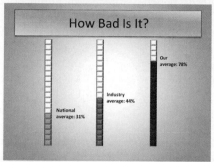

These two *navigation slides* show one way to introduce each of the four subtopics in this particular section. As the highlight moves around the central circle, the audience is reminded of which subtopics have been covered and which subtopic is going to be covered next. And each time it is shown, the message is repeated that all these problems are the "true cost of chaos" in the company's employment practices.

Left: This slide introduces three key points the speaker wants to emphasize in this particular section.

Right: This slide shows a linear flow of ideas, each with bulleted sub-points. This slide could be revealed one section at a time to help the speaker keep the audience's attention focused on a single topic.

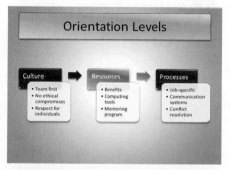

Left: This flowchart packs a lot of information onto one slide, but seeing the sequence of events in one place is essential.

Right: This simple visual highlights the presenter's spoken message about being careful to choose the right tasks to focus on and then completing them quickly.

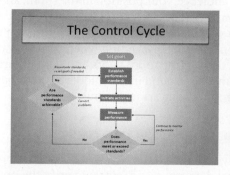

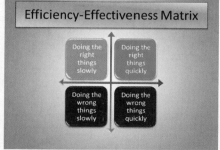

Figure 14.10   Designing Effective Visuals: Selected Slides

These slides, from a presentation that addresses a company's high employee turnover rate, illustrate the wide variety of design options you have for creating effective, appealing slides. (All the slides were created using features in PowerPoint.)

CHECKLIST ✔ Enhancing Presentations with Visuals

A. Plan your presentation visuals.
- ✔ Make sure you and your message, not your visuals, remain the focus of your presentation.
- ✔ Follow effective design principles, with an emphasis on simplicity and authenticity.

B. Choose structured or free-form slides.
- ✔ Structured slides using bullet-point templates are easy to create, require little design time or skill, and can be completed in a hurry. Best uses: routine, internal presentations
- ✔ Free-form slides make it easier to combine textual and visual information, to create a more dynamic and engaging experience, and to maintain a conversational connection with the audience. Best uses: motivational, educational, and persuasive presentations

C. Design effective slides.
- ✔ Use a key visual to organize related ideas in a clear and meaningful way.
- ✔ Write text that will be readable from everywhere in the room.
- ✔ Write short, active, parallel phrases that support, not replace, your spoken message.
- ✔ Limit the amount of text so that your audience can focus on listening, not reading.
- ✔ Use color to emphasize important ideas, create contrast, isolate visual elements, and convey intended nonverbal signals.
- ✔ Limit color to a few compatible choices and use them consistently.

- ✔ Make sure your slide background doesn't compete with the foreground.
- ✔ Use decorative artwork sparingly and only to support your message.
- ✔ Emphasize functional artwork—photos, technical drawings, charts, and other visual elements containing information that is part of your message.
- ✔ Choose typefaces that are easy to read on screen; limit the number of typefaces and use them consistently.
- ✔ Use slide masters to maintain consistency throughout your presentation.
- ✔ Use functional animation when it can support your message.
- ✔ Make sure slide transitions are subtle, if used at all.
- ✔ Use builds carefully to control the release of information.
- ✔ Use hyperlinks and action buttons to add flexibility to your presentation.
- ✔ Incorporate multimedia elements that can help engage your audience and deliver your message.

D. Complete slides and support materials.
- ✔ Review every slide carefully to ensure accuracy, consistency, and clarity.
- ✔ Make sure that all slides are fully operational.
- ✔ Use the slide sorter to verify and adjust the sequence of slides, if needed.
- ✔ Create navigation and support slides.
- ✔ Have a backup plan for all your equipment.
- ✔ Create handouts to complement and support your presentation message.

manner. However, for all other business presentations, reading is a poor choice because it limits your interaction with the audience and lacks the fresh, dynamic feel of natural talking.

Another important decision at this point is preparing the venue where you will speak. Whenever you have the opportunity to arrange the setting, think carefully about the seating for the audience, your position in the room, and the lighting. For instance, for a formal presentation where you're standing on a stage and the audience is in theater-style seating, it's often a good idea to dim the room lights so people can see the screen more clearly. However, in a less-formal setting where you to want to interact with audience members, you might turn up the room lights and perhaps arrange chairs and tables in a U shape so that you can walk around in the middle of the group. Review Figure 3.4 on page 79 for the most common seating arrangements.

PRACTICING YOUR DELIVERY

The more you practice, the more confidence you'll have.

Practicing your presentation is essential. Practice boosts your confidence, gives you a more professional demeanor, and lets you verify the operation of your visuals and equipment. A test audience can tell you if your slides are understandable and whether your delivery is effective. A day or two before you're ready to step on stage for an important talk, make sure you and your presentation are ready:

- Can you present your material naturally, without reading your slides?
- Could you still make a compelling and complete presentation if you experience an equipment failure and have to proceed without using your slides at all?
- Is the equipment working, and do you know how to operate it?
- Is your timing on track?
- Can you easily pronounce all the words you plan to use?
- Have you anticipated likely questions and objections?

If you're addressing an audience that doesn't speak your language, consider using an interpreter. Send your interpreter a copy of your speech and visuals as far in advance of your presentation as possible. If your audience is likely to include persons with hearing impairments, be sure to team up with a sign language interpreter as well. Alternatively, you can try automated translation tools available in your presentation software, such as the Presentation Translator add-in for PowerPoint.[21]

When you deliver a presentation to people from other cultures, you may need to adapt the content of your presentation. It is also important to take into account any cultural differences in appearance, mannerisms, and other customs. Your interpreter or host will be able to suggest appropriate changes for a specific audience or occasion.

> Make sure you're comfortable with the equipment you'll be expected to use; you don't want to be fumbling with controls while the audience is watching and waiting.

> **MOBILE APP**
> The **Microsoft PowerPoint** app lets you create slides, edit slide decks created on other devices, and control presentations with your smartphone or a smartwatch.

Delivering a Presentation

It's show time. This section offers practical advice on four important aspects of delivery: overcoming anxiety, handling questions responsively, embracing the backchannel, and giving presentations online.

> **5 LEARNING OBJECTIVE**
> Describe four important aspects of delivering a presentation in today's social media environment.

OVERCOMING ANXIETY

Even seasoned pros get a little nervous before a big presentation. These techniques will help you convert anxiety into positive energy:[22]

> Nervousness before a presentation is perfectly natural; use the energy to your advantage.

- **Acknowledge your nervousness.** Don't try to bury that feeling. In fact, remind yourself that it's not only normal but healthy to have your senses on high alert—nervousness is an indication that you care about your audience, your topic, and the occasion. Use this energy to your advantage.
- **Stop worrying about being perfect.** Successful speakers focus on making an authentic connection with their listeners rather than on trying to deliver a note-perfect presentation.
- **Know your material and practice until you're comfortable with it.** The more familiar you are with your material, the less panic you'll feel. And the more you rehearse, the more confident you will be.
- **Be ready with your opening line.** Have your first sentence memorized so you don't have to improvise your opening.
- **Remember to breathe.** Tension can lead people to breathe in a rapid and shallow fashion, which can create a lightheaded feeling. Breathe slowly and deeply to maintain a sense of calm and confidence.
- **Be comfortable.** Dress appropriately but as comfortably as possible. Drink plenty of water ahead of time to hydrate your voice (bring a bottle of water with you, too).
- **"Make friends with the stage."** If possible, take a tip from actors and spend some time alone on the stage (or at the front of the room) before your presentation. Get comfortable with the space, figure out where you'll stand, remind yourself how satisfying it will be to share your information with the audience, and visualize a successful outcome. Remember that your audience wants you to succeed, too.
- **Take a three-second break if you need to.** If you sense that you're starting to race, pause and arrange your notes

> **REAL-TIME UPDATES**
> LEARN MORE BY VISITING THIS WEBSITE
> **Advice from the pros on every aspect of presenting**
> Dozens of articles from the presentation specialists at Duarte cover every aspect of contemporary business presentations. Go to **real-timeupdates.com/ebc13** and select Learn More in the Students section.

or perform some other small task while taking several deep breaths. Then start again at your normal pace.

- **Concentrate on your message and your audience, not on yourself.** When you're busy thinking about your subject and observing your audience's response, you tend to forget your fears.
- **Maintain eye contact with friendly audience members.** Eye contact not only makes you appear sincere, confident, and trustworthy but can give you positive feedback as well.
- **Keep going.** Things usually get better as you move along, with each successful minute giving you more and more confidence.

HANDLING QUESTIONS RESPONSIVELY

Don't leave the question-and-answer period to chance: Anticipate potential questions and think through your answers.

Questions from the audience are often one of the most important parts of a presentation. They give you a chance to obtain important information, emphasize your main idea and supporting points, and build enthusiasm for your point of view.

Whether or not you can establish ground rules for questions depends on the audience and the situation. If you're presenting to a small group of upper managers or potential investors, for example, you will probably have no say in the matter: Audience members will likely ask as many questions as they want, whenever they want, to get the information they need. On the other hand, if you are presenting to your peers or a large public audience, you might

---

DEVELOPING AS A PROFESSIONAL

Recovering from Disasters

You've researched your topic, analyzed your audience, prepared a compelling message, crafted eye-catching visuals, and practiced until you're running like a smooth machine. You're ready to go.

Then you wake up with a sore throat and half a voice. You grab a few lozenges, hope for the best, and drive to the conference facility in plenty of time to set up your equipment. Oops, somebody forgot to tell you that your presentation has been moved up by an hour, and your audience is already in the room waiting for you. You scramble to turn on your laptop and get it connected to the projector, only to discover you forgot the power cord and your battery is dead. Feeling smart, you pull out the USB flash drive with a backup copy of your Power-Point slides and ask to use one of the several laptops you see scattered among the audience. Nice idea, but you're told these are all secured, company-issued units with USB disabled. The audience is getting restless; a few people get up to leave. You keep hoping you'll wake up from this bad dream so that your great day can really start. Sorry. This *is* your day.

Ask any business speaker with a few years of experience, and you'll hear all these horror stories and a few more: people who have driven to the wrong conference center, hit themselves in the head with a microphone, tripped over wires, started with a sure-fire joke that generated nothing but cold stares, lost their train of thought mid-sentence, watched a key decision-maker in the audience fall asleep, or been rendered speechless by tough questions. Hoping you'll be spared isn't an effective response. You must be prepared for *when*—not *if*—something goes wrong.

If you assume that something will go wrong, you can make peace with the possibility and focus on backup planning. For

technical and logistical issues, make a list of every major problem you might encounter and work out a contingency plan. For the content of your presentation, know it well enough that you can adjust on the fly, such as delivering your presentation in half the time you had planned or speaking without your slides. For performance issues, remember that you are human and so is everyone in the audience. If you lose your train of thought, have a sip of water and regroup or simply ask out loud, "Where was I?" If you can't answer a question, say, "Sorry, I don't have an answer for you right now. Can I get back to you?" If you trip getting on stage, make a joke about your upcoming appearance on *Dancing with the Stars*.

With a careful contingency plan and a dose of humility and humor, you can avoid most problems and survive the rest.

CAREER APPLICATIONS

1. If you detect trouble ahead in your presentation, such as noticing that your laptop battery is about to go dead or that you somehow have an old copy of the presentation file, should you tell your audience what's wrong? Or should you try to "wing it"? Explain your answer.
2. What steps can you take to make absolutely sure you have a usable backup copy of your presentation slides outside your office? Why is this important?

Sources: Based in part on Joby Blum, "Presentation Disasters: How to Recover," BrightCarbon blog, 11 November 2013, www.brightcarbon.com; C. Peter Guiliano and Frank J. Currilo, "Going Blank in the Boardroom," *Public Relations Quarterly*, Winter 2003, 35+; Jennifer Rotondo and Mike Rotondo Jr., *Presentation Skills for Managers* (New York: McGraw-Hill, 2002), 160–162; Mark Merritt, "No More Nightmares," *Presentations*, April 2001, 44+.

want to establish some guidelines, such as the number of questions allowed per person and the overall time limit for questions.

Don't assume you can handle whatever comes up without some preparation.[23] Learn enough about your audience members to get an idea of their concerns, and think through answers to potential questions.

When people ask questions, pay attention to nonverbal signals to help determine what each person really means. Repeat the question to confirm your understanding and to ensure that the entire audience has heard it. If the question is vague or confusing, ask for clarification; then give a simple, direct answer.

If you are asked a difficult or complex question, avoid the temptation to sidestep it. Offer to meet with the questioner afterward if the issue isn't relevant to the rest of the audience or if giving an adequate answer would take too long. If you don't know the answer, don't pretend you do. Instead, offer to get a complete answer as soon as possible.

> If you don't have the complete answer to an important question, offer to provide it after the presentation.

Be on guard for audience members who use questions to make impromptu speeches or to take control of your presentation. Without offending anyone, find a way to stay in control. You might admit that you and the questioner have differing opinions and offer to get back to the questioner after you've done more research.[24]

If a question ever puts you on the hot seat, respond honestly but keep your cool. Look the person in the eye, answer the question as well as you can, and keep your emotions under control. Defuse hostility by paraphrasing the question and asking the questioner to confirm that you've understood it correctly. Maintain a businesslike tone of voice and a pleasant expression.[25]

> If you ever face hostile questions, respond honestly and directly while keeping your cool.

EMBRACING THE BACKCHANNEL

Many business presentations these days involve more than just the conversation between the speaker and his or her audience. Using Twitter and other electronic media, audience members often carry on their own parallel communication during a presentation via the **backchannel**, which presentation expert Cliff Atkinson defines as "a line of communication created by people in an audience to connect with others inside or outside the room, with or without the knowledge of the speaker."[26] Chances are you've participated in a backchannel already, such as when texting with your classmates or live-blogging during a lecture.

> Twitter and other social media are changing business presentations by making it easy for all audience members to participate in the *backchannel*.

The backchannel presents both risks and rewards for business presenters. On the negative side, for example, listeners can research your claims the instant you make them and spread the word quickly if they think your information is shaky. The backchannel also gives contrary audience members more leverage, which can lead to presentations spinning out of control. On the plus side, listeners who are excited about your message can build support for it, expand on it, and spread it to a much larger audience in a matter of seconds. You can also get valuable feedback during and after presentations.[27]

By embracing the backchannel, rather than trying to fight it or ignore it, presenters can use this powerful force to their advantage. Follow these tips to make the backchannel work for you:[28]

> Resist the urge to ignore or fight the backchannel; instead, learn how to use it to your advantage.

- **Integrate social media into the presentation process.** For example, you can create a website for the presentation so that people can access relevant resources during or after the presentation, create a Twitter hashtag that everyone can use when sending tweets, or display the Twitter stream during Q&A so that everyone can see the questions and comments on the backchannel.
- **Monitor and ask for feedback.** Using a free service such as TweetDeck, which organizes tweets by hashtag and other variables, you can monitor comments from people in the audience. To avoid trying to monitor the backchannel while speaking, you can schedule "Twitter breaks," during which you review comments and respond as needed.
- **Review comments afterward to improve your presentation.** After a presentation is over, review comments on audience members' Twitter accounts and blogs to see which parts confused them, which parts excited them, and which parts seemed to have little effect (based on few or no comments).

- **Automatically tweet key points from your presentation while you speak.** Add-ons for presentation software can send out prewritten tweets as you show specific slides during a presentation. By making your key points readily available, you make it easy for listeners to retweet and comment on your presentation.
- **Establish expectations with the audience.** Explain that you welcome audience participation but that to ensure a positive experience for everyone, comments should be civil, relevant, and productive.

GIVING PRESENTATIONS ONLINE

Online presentations give you a way to reach more people in less time, but they require special preparation and skills.

Online presentations offer many benefits, including the opportunity to communicate with a geographically dispersed audience at a fraction of the cost of travel and the ability for a project team or an entire organization to meet at a moment's notice. However, this format also presents some challenges for the presenter, thanks to that layer of technology between you and your audience. Many of those "human moments" that guide and encourage you through an in-person presentation won't travel across the digital divide. For instance, it's often difficult to tell whether audience members are bored or confused, because your view of them is usually confined to small video images (and sometimes not even that).

To ensure successful online presentations, keep the following advice in mind:

- **Make sure everyone has time to download and configure any required apps.** If participants need to do anything to prepare their PCs or mobile devices, send a message well in advance of the presentation with the information they need.
- **Consider sending preview study materials ahead of time.** Doing so allows audience members to familiarize themselves with any important background information.
- **Allow plenty of time for everyone to get connected and familiar with the screen they're viewing.** Build extra time into your schedule to ensure that everyone is connected and ready to start.
- **Keep your presentation as simple as possible.** Break complicated slides down into multiple slides if necessary, and keep the direction of your discussion clear so that no one gets lost.
- **Ask for feedback frequently.** You won't have as much of the visual feedback that alerts you when audience members are confused, and many online viewers will be reluctant to call attention to themselves by interrupting you to ask for clarification. Setting up a backchannel via Twitter or as part of your online meeting system will help in this regard.

Last but not least, don't get lost in the technology. Use these tools whenever they'll help, but remember that the most important aspect of any presentation is getting the audience to receive, understand, and embrace your message.

ENSURING SUCCESSFUL TEAM PRESENTATIONS

Teams and other work groups are occasionally called on to give presentations together. These collaborative presentations help distribute the workload, encourage diverse points of view, allow members to present information in their individual areas of expertise, and provide opportunities for everyone on the team to receive recognition from the audience. Another potential advantage is the ability to have one or more team members operating or demonstrating equipment or systems while another team member speaks to the audience.

For audiences, team presentations give the benefit of multiple viewpoints and speaking voices, which can relieve the potential tedium of listening to a single person. Having the entire team available during question-and-answer periods is a big plus, too.

Planning a Team Presentation

In order to deliver a seamless performance, team presentations require careful planning. Follow these tips:

- Outline the presentation together so that everyone has input and agrees to the flow of topics.

- Divide the presentation into manageable sections and assign each to one team member, with each person responsible for developing his or her visuals and speaking notes. Naturally, if some team members have expertise in particular topics, make sure they are assigned those parts of the presentation.
- If one team member is a particularly dynamic speaker, consider having him or her present first in order to launch the presentation with a good energy level.
- If you are using presentation software, finalize a template before anyone starts and make sure everyone uses it so that all the slides have a consistent look.
- Merge all the slides into a single slide deck, rather than trying to switch from one file to the next during the presentation. Assign one person to edit and finalize the entire slide deck to ensure consistency and eliminate any overlaps.

Importantly, schedule even more development and rehearsal time than you would with an individual presentation. Presentations almost always take longer to develop than you might think, and with the extra coordination they require, team presentations can take considerable time to get right. To be safe, schedule double the amount of development and practice time than you first think you'll need.

Rehearsing and Delivering a Team Presentation

Follow these tips for rehearsing beforehand and coordinating everyone's activities during the presentation:

- Schedule your first rehearsal at least a week before the presentation to give everyone time to adjust timing or fix other aspects that may need attention.
- Practice exactly as if you were giving the live presentation, including switching over microphones, controlling the presentation software, moving on and off stage, and so on.
- Make sure the hand-offs from one speaker to the next are smooth and that each speaker can stay within his or her allotted time—one person running long can be a disaster in a group presentation. Don't leave anything to chance.
- Map out where everyone will stand or sit during the presentation. Don't leave anyone just hanging out on the stage while someone else is speaking. For example, arrange to have chairs set off to the side so that people can wait unobtrusively before and after their sections.
- Arrange for the first speaker to introduce the entire presentation, have each speaker introduce the next speaker, and have the final speaker present the overall conclusion to the presentation. Alternatively, you can have the first speaker take the stage again to deliver the conclusion.
- Decide how you will field questions from the audience. One good approach is to have one person, such as the first speaker, serve as team captain to take questions from the audience and direct each one to the team member best positioned to answer it.[29]
- During the presentation, make sure everyone on the team stays engaged and present. Don't mentally wander off or start checking messages on your mobile device, for example.[30] Support the person speaking and be ready with a comforting smile if the speaker makes eye contact and needs a quick boost of reassurance.

Team presentations can be the culmination of weeks or months of hard work on a project, so view them as an opportunity to celebrate your successful collaboration. Keep the attention on the audience, of course, but use the spirit of teamwork to give your presentation a lively and positive sense of energy.

For more insights into presentations, visit **real-timeupdates.com/ebc13** and select Chapter 14.

ON THE JOB: SOLVING COMMUNICATION DILEMMAS AT **BARNETT INTERNATIONAL**

You've joined Gina Barnett at Barnett International as a presentation coach, helping executives, professionals, and entrepreneurs improve their presentation skills. You are currently assisting two entrepreneurs, Aaliyah and William, in getting ready to pitch their business idea to investors. Their company sells an app that helps homeowners take care of all those home-management tasks people tend to put off, such as taking an insurance inventory, scheduling maintenance to avoid problems down the road, and keeping an eye out for refinancing opportunities. The company faces strong competition, but it is off to a good start. Now they're trying to get $2 million from venture capitalists (VCs) so they can increase marketing and pursue strategic partnerships with various financial services firms. Coach them through these four scenarios.

1. Aaliyah and William appreciate how important it is to start any presentation with an attention-getting opening, and they have brainstormed four possibilities. Which one would you advise them to use?
   a. "Imagine how silly all those people who passed on the opportunity to invest in Facebook or Google back in the beginning must feel now."
   b. "Let's be honest. Who here keeps accurate track of all those nagging home-management chores we're all supposed to do?"
   c. "Imagine how much better we'd all sleep at night if we knew all those home-management chores we are *supposed* to take care of were in fact being taken care of."
   d. "We would like to present an investment opportunity that concerns a new and promising app for handling home-management issues."

2. The closing statement of a presentation can be as crucial as the opening. Which of the following should Aaliyah and William use?
   a. "And just to close here, we are beyond thrilled to have the opportunity to talk with you today."
   b. "As you've seen, with the right level of funding and advice from experienced investors like you, this business has the potential to yield a handsome payoff for everyone involved. Thank you."
   c. "As you've seen, with the right level of funding and advice from experienced investors like you, this business is a guaranteed winner and a wise move for any investor. Thank you."
   d. "Thank you for the opportunity to make this presentation."

3. You know from sitting in on lots of investor pitches that experienced VCs can be disarmingly blunt when it comes to asking questions or challenging what they hear. Having seen thousands of pitches and worked with companies that sounded great on paper but failed in reality, most have a sharp eye for problems lurking in the plans. You want Aaliyah and William to be able to respond professionally when they get hit with tough questions, so during a rehearsal of their presentation, you've prearranged for Barnett to interrupt with "You're never going to see the rate of revenue growth you're projecting." How should Aaliyah and William respond to such unexpected criticism?
   a. "We appreciate the insight. Could we talk you through how we came up with the forecast?"
   b. "Well, we are entrepreneurs after all! We need to think optimistically."
   c. "I think if you'll let us talk you through how we came up with the forecast, you'll see the numbers are pretty solid."
   d. "You don't think so? Well, that throws a bit of a wrench into our planning, for sure."

4. Aaliyah and William are insisting on giving the presentation together, as in both being at the front of the room at the same time. She is the technical expert, and he is the business and financial expert, and they believe it will be safer to have both standing and ready to answer any question that might come up. Their plan is to alternate discussing each of the slides in their presentation, with each covering one slide in turn. How would you advise them?
   a. Tell them to go ahead with this plan.
   b. Tell them that in a fairly short presentation such as this, there isn't enough time to switch speakers constantly, so they should flip a coin and decide who gives the talk. The other person can sit nearby and be ready to answer questions.
   c. Have them both give the entire presentation to you, Barnett, and another colleague, then the three of you will vote on who should give the presentation.
   d. Advise them to divide the presentation into the business issues for William to cover and the technical issues for Aaliyah to cover and have each one present his or her area of expertise. While one is talking, the other can be sitting nearby.

END OF CHAPTER

Learning Objectives Checkup

Assess your understanding of the principles in this chapter by reading each learning objective and studying the accompanying exercises. You can check your responses against the answer key on page 613.

Objective 14.1: Highlight the importance of presentations in your business career, and explain how to adapt the planning step of the three-step process to presentations.

1. _____ presentations are outlined like conventional messages and follow a predefined flow from start to finish; _____ presentations don't flow in any particularly direction but rather give the presenter the option to move back and forth between topics and up and down in terms of level of detail.

2. Which of the following is the best way to know how much material you can cover in a given amount of time?
   a. Divide the amount of time you have for your presentation by 20 to figure out how many slides you can show.

b. Figure on one or two slides per main heading in your planning outline.

c. For the equivalent of 100 words of written speech, plan to create one slide.

d. Complete a dry run in front of a live audience after you've developed your speaking notes, slides, and other materials.

3. If you are facing an audience that is apprehensive about what you might have to say in a presentation, which of the following approaches is best?

a. Even if your presentation will confirm their worst fears, use the direct approach to confront the negative emotions head-on.

b. If your message will calm their fears, use the direct approach; if your message will confirm their fears, consider the indirect approach to build acceptance.

c. Ignore the emotional undercurrents and focus on the practical content of your message.

d. Defuse the situation with a humorous story that dismisses the audience members' fears.

Objective 14.2: Describe the tasks involved in developing a presentation.

4. Which of the following is the best way to arouse interest in a presentation to a group of fellow employees on the importance of taking ownership of the problem whenever a customer calls in with a complaint?

a. "If customers leave, so do our jobs."

b. "Everything we want as employees of this company—from stable jobs to pay raises to promotional opportunities—depends on one thing: satisfied customers."

c. "How are customers supposed to get their problems solved if we keep passing the buck from one person to the next without ever doing anything?"

d. "The company's profit margins depend on satisfied customers, and it's up to us to make sure those customers are satisfied."

5. If you suspect that your audience doesn't really care about the topic you plan to discuss, how can you generate interest in your presentation?

a. Look for ways to help them relate to the information on a personal level, such as helping the company ensure better job security.

b. Speak louder and, if possible, use lots of sound effects and visual special effects in your presentation.

c. Show your passion for the material by speaking faster than normal and pacing the room in an excited fashion.

d. Show that you empathize with their feelings by saying up front that you don't really care about the topic either, but you've been assigned to talk about it.

6. If you're giving a presentation to an internal audience in a subject area you've researched thoroughly but in which you don't have any hands-on experience (suppose your topic is coordinating a major facility relocation or hiring a tax attorney, for instance), which of these steps should you take to build credibility?

a. During your introduction, explain that your presentation is the result of research that you've done and briefly explain the extent of the research.

b. Explain that you don't have any experience in the subject area, but you've done some research.

c. Emphasize that you know a great deal about the subject matter.

d. Sidestep the issue of credibility entirely in the introduction and let your knowledge shine through during the body of your presentation.

7. Which of the following would do the best job of holding an audience's attention during a presentation on the growing importance of social networking in corporate communication? In this particular case, the audience members are all managers of the same company, but they represent a half-dozen countries and speak four different native languages (although they all have basic English skills).

a. "Social networks are now an important feature in the corporate communication landscape."

b. "Successful managers around the world now view social networks as an essential tool in their communication efforts."

c. "Millions of customers and employees are now hip to the latest wave to blow through corporate communication, the clumsily named but nevertheless vital social network."

d. "I personally get dozens of interesting social networking updates every day, which is solid evidence of how important social networks have become."

8. Your company recently relocated from another state, and the owners are eager to begin building a positive relationship with the local community. You've been asked to speak to employees about volunteering in various community organizations. Which of the following statements does the best job of communicating the owners' wishes while appealing to employees' personal interests?

a. "Becoming involved in community organizations is a great way for you and your families to meet new people and feel more at home in your new city."

b. "Becoming involved in community organizations shows our new neighbors that we're an organization of positive, caring people—and it's a great way for you and your families to meet new people and feel more at home in your new city."

c. "We really owe it to our new community to give back by volunteering."

d. "The owners feel it is vital for us to become more involved in the community."

9. Which of these techniques is mentioned in the chapter as a way to hold an audience's attention during a presentation?

a. Speak louder than average.

b. Tell people that management expects them to pay attention.

c. Use clear and vivid language.

d. Repeat each major point three times and each minor point twice.

Objective 14.3: Describe the six major design and writing tasks required to enhance your presentation with effective visuals.

10. Which of the following is an advantage of structured slide designs over free-form designs?

a. Structured designs are more colorful and therefore keep audience attention better.

b. People are accustomed to structured designs, so they are more comfortable with them.

c. Structured slides are generally easier to create than free-form slides.

d. Structured slides are cheaper.

11. Which of the following is a benefit of organizing a slide around a key visual such as a pyramid or a circular flow diagram?

a. Slides without key visuals are always boring and repetitive.

b. The key visual shows how the various ideas are related, making it easier for viewers to grasp your message.

c. With a key visual to rely on, the speaker doesn't have to know the subject matter quite as thoroughly.

d. You can use the key visual for every slide, making your presentation more consistent.

12. Which of these describes the optimum amount of text to put on presentation slides?

a. As much as the speaker needs in order to remember the key points that relate to each slide

b. None

c. Between 20 and 40 words, depending on type size

d. Only as much as the audience needs in order to follow along and remember key points

13. Charts and tables used for presentations should be

a. simpler than charts and tables used for printed documents.

b. more complex than charts and tables used for printed documents.

c. exactly the same as charts and tables used for printed documents.

14. Slide _____ control how one slide replaces another, whereas slide _____ control how text and graphical elements are revealed on an individual slide.

15. Why is consistent use of colors, typefaces and type treatments, size, and other design elements important in presentations?

a. Consistency is not important; in fact, it's a sign of a dull presentation.

b. Consistency shows that you're a smart businessperson who doesn't waste time on trivial details.

c. Consistency simplifies the viewing and listening process for your audience and enables them to pay closer attention to your message rather than spending time trying to figure out your visuals.

d. Consistency shows that you're a team player who can follow instructions.

Objective 14.4: Outline four major tasks involved in completing a presentation.

16. How does the completion stage of the three-step writing process differ between reports and presentations?

a. Completion is the same for reports and presentations.

b. Presentations are never proofread or tested ahead of time; doing so would destroy the spontaneity of your delivery.

c. You never revise presentation slides, because they're locked in place once you create them.

d. The completion state for presentations involves a wider range of tasks, including testing your presentation slides, verifying equipment operation, practicing your speech, and creating handout materials.

17. What advice would you give to a novice presenter regarding practicing before a big presentation?

a. Don't practice; it destroys the spontaneity you need to give an upbeat presentation.

b. Make multiple practice runs, a half-dozen if needed, to make sure you can deliver the material smoothly and confidently.

c. Write out a script and memorize it word for word; you can't risk forgetting any key points.

d. One practice session is adequate; use the extra time to polish your presentation slides instead.

18. What is the best approach to developing handout materials?

a. Create them after you've planned, developed, and tested your presentation so that you can see which points are confusing and could benefit from additional support.

b. Wait until you give the presentation and then ask your viewers what they would like to see in terms of additional information.

c. Always follow the lead of whatever the more experienced presenters in your department do; they've already set audience expectations.

d. Plan your handouts as you plan and create your slides so that you maintain an effective balance between information that you'll cover during the presentation and information that is better suited to a printed handout.

Objective 14.5: Describe four important aspects of delivering a presentation in today's social media environment.

19. Which of the following is the most effective way to respond if you feel nervous right before giving a presentation?

a. Think up a short joke to begin your presentation; the audience's laughter will help you relax.

b. Begin your presentation by telling people that you're nervous and asking them to be sympathetic if you make any mistakes.

c. Begin your presentation by telling the audience how much you dislike speaking in public; most of them dislike public speaking, too, so they'll be more sympathetic toward you.

d. Remind yourself that everybody gets nervous and that being nervous simply means you care about doing well; use the nervousness to be more energetic when you begin speaking.

20. If you receive a question that is important and relevant to the topic you're presenting but you lack the information needed to answer it, which of the following would be the best response?

a. "I'm sorry; I don't know the answer."

b. "You've asked an important question, but I don't have the information needed to answer it properly. I'll research the issue after we're finished here today and then send everyone an email message with the answer."

c. "Let me get back to you on that."

d. "I'd really like to stay focused on the material that I prepared for this presentation."

21. What is the best strategy for using the Twitter-enabled backchannel in a presentation?

a. Build automated Twitter feeds into your presentation slides that send out capsule points as you move through the presentation, but ignore whatever audience members

might be doing on Twitter and stay focused on your presentation.
   b. Announce up front that the use of Twitter and other messaging tools is forbidden during the presentation; the audience's job is to pay attention to you, the speaker.
   c. Embrace the backchannel fully, including building in automated feeds from your presentation, providing a hashtag for everyone to use so they can easily follow tweets related to the presentation, and taking occasional Twitter breaks to check for feedback and questions from the audience.
   d. Ignore it; you can't stop people from tweeting during a presentation, so you might as well just accept that they are going to do so.
22. Which of the following is a disadvantage of conducting presentations online?
   a. The lack of audio communication
   b. The inability of most people to participate, since businesses have different internet connection speeds
   c. The inability to use PowerPoint slides online
   d. Less ability to rely on nonverbal signals such as posture, which can provide vital feedback during a presentation
23. Which of the following is an advantage of online presentations?
   a. Lower costs as a result of less travel
   b. More opportunities for employees to meet customers in person
   c. The ability to multitask during meetings
   d. All of the above
24. Which of the following is good advice for preparing team presentations?
   a. Outline the presentation together, then script out what you're going to say and create all the slides together.
   b. Outline the presentation together, then divide the sections among team members to prepare their own slides and speaking notes.
   c. Have one person outline it, another person design the slides, a third person develop the speaking notes, and everyone else proofread the slides prior to the presentation.

Key Terms

backchannel A social media conversation that takes place during a presentation, in parallel with the speaker's presentation
free-form slides Presentation slides that are not based on a template, often with each slide having a unique look but unified by typeface, color, and other design choices; tend to be much more visually oriented than structured slides
slide builds Similar to slide transitions, these effects control the release of text, graphics, and other elements on individual slides
slide transitions Software effects that control how one slide replaces another on-screen
structured slides Presentation slides that follow the same design templates throughout and give all the slides in a presentation the same general look; they emphasize textual information in bullet-point form

Apply Your Knowledge

To review chapter content related to each question, refer to the indicated Learning Objective.

14-1. How do linear and nonlinear presentations differ? [LO-1]
14-2. You just gave an in-depth presentation on the company's new marketing programs, intended for the specialists in the marketing department. The marketing manager then asked you to give a shorter version of the presentation to the company's top executives. Generally speaking, how should you modify the scope of your presentation for this new audience? [LO-1]
14-3. Is it ethical to use design elements and special effects to persuade an audience? Why or why not? [LO-3]
14-4. If you're worried about forgetting your key message points, should you write them out and read them during your presentation? Why or why not? [LO-4]
14-5. Why is speaking from notes usually the best method of delivery? [LO-4]

Practice Your Skills

Messages for Analysis

14-6. **Message 14.A: Improving a Presentation Slide [LO-3]** To access this presentation, visit **real-timeupdates .com/ebc13**, select Student Assignments, then select Chapter 14, Message 14.A. Revise the text on these slides to make them more effective for presentation use.
14-7. **Message 14.B: Analyzing Animation [LO-3]** To access this presentation, visit **real-timeupdates.com/ebc13**, select Student Assignments, then select Chapter 14, Message 14.B. Download and watch the presentation in slide show mode. After you've watched the presentation, identify at least three ways in which various animations, builds, and transitions either enhanced or impeded your understanding of the subject matter.

Exercises

Each activity is labeled according to the primary skill or skills you will need to use. To review relevant chapter content, you can refer to the indicated Learning Objective. In some instances, supporting information will be found in another chapter, as indicated.

14-8. **Presentations: Planning a Presentation [LO-1]** Select one of the following topics; then research and prepare a brief presentation (5–10 minutes) to be given to your class:
   a. What I expect to learn in this course
   b. Past public speaking experiences: the good, the bad, and the ugly
   c. I would be good at teaching _____
   d. I am afraid of _____

e. It's easy for me to _____
_____

f. I get angry when _____
_____

g. I am happiest when I _____
_____

h. People would be surprised if they knew that I _____
_____

i. My favorite older person

j. My favorite charity

k. My favorite place

l. My favorite sport

m. My favorite store

n. My favorite television show

o. The town you live in suffers from a great deal of juvenile vandalism. Explain to a group of community members why juvenile recreational facilities should be built instead of a juvenile detention complex.

p. You are speaking to the Humane Society. Support or oppose the use of animals for medical research purposes.

q. You are talking to civic leaders of your community. Try to convince them to build an art gallery.

r. You are speaking to a first-grade class at an elementary school. Explain why they should brush their teeth after meals.

s. You are speaking to a group of traveling salespeople. Convince them that they should wear seat belts while driving.

t. You are speaking to a group of elderly people. Convince them to adopt an exercise program.

u. Energy issues (such as supply, conservation, alternative sources, national security, climate change, or pollution)

v. Financial issues (such as banking, investing, or family finances)

w. Government (such as domestic policy, foreign policy, Social Security taxes, or welfare)

x. Interesting new technologies (such as artificial intelligence, nanotechnology, or bioengineering)

y. Politics (such as political parties, elections, legislative bodies and legislation, or the presidency)

z. Sports (such as baseball, football, golf, hang gliding, hockey, rock climbing, or tennis)

14-9. Presentations: Planning, Developing, and Delivering [LO-1], [LO-2], [LO-3] Identify a company whose prospects look bright over the next few years because of highly competitive products, strong leadership, fundamental changes in the market, or any other significant reason. Prepare a 5-minute speech, without visuals, explaining why you think this company is going to do well in the near future.

14-10. Presentations: Developing a Presentation; Collaboration: Team Projects [LO-2], Chapter 3 You've been asked to give an informative 10-minute talk on vacation opportunities in your home state. Draft your introduction, which should last no more than 2 minutes. Then pair up with a classmate and analyze each other's introductions. How well do these two introductions arouse the audience's interest, build credibility, and preview the presentation? Suggest how these introductions might be improved.

14-11. Presentations: Developing a Presentation [LO-2] Locate the transcript of a speech. TED talks are a good source, and many corporate websites also have archives of executives' speeches; look in the "investor relations" section. Examine the introduction and the close of the speech you've chosen and then analyze how these two sections work together to emphasize the main idea. What action does the speaker want the audience to take? Next, identify the transitional sentences or phrases that clarify the speech's structure for the listener, especially those that help the speaker shift between supporting points. Using these transitions as clues, list the main message and supporting points; then indicate how each transitional phrase links the current supporting point to the succeeding one. Prepare a 2- to 3-minute presentation summarizing your analysis for your class.

14-12. Presentations: Designing Presentation Visuals [LO-4] Look through recent issues (print or online) of *Bloomberg Businessweek*, *Fortune*, or other business publications for articles discussing challenges that a specific company or industry is facing. Using the articles and the guidelines discussed in this chapter, create a short Prezi or three to five slides summarizing these issues.

14-13. Presentations: Designing Presentation Visuals [LO-4] Find a business-related slide presentation online and analyze the design. Do you consider it structured or free form? Does the design help the audience understand and remember the message? Why or why not? What improvements would you suggest to the design?

14-14. Presentations: Mastering Delivery; Nonverbal Communication: Analyzing Nonverbal Signals [LO-5], Chapter 2 Observe and analyze the delivery of a speaker in a school, work, or other setting. What type of delivery did the speaker use? Was this delivery appropriate for the occasion? What nonverbal signals did the speaker use to emphasize key points? Were these signals effective? Which nonverbal signals would you suggest to further enhance the delivery of this oral presentation? Why?

14-15. Presentations: Delivering a Presentation; Collaboration: Team Projects; Media Skills: Microblogging [LO-5], Chapter 3, Chapter 8 In a team of six students, develop a 10-minute Prezi or slide presentation on any topic that interests you. Nominate one person to give the presentation; the other five will participate via a Twitter backchannel. Create a webpage that holds at least one downloadable file that will be discussed during the presentation. Practice using the backchannel, including using a hashtag for the meeting and having the presenter ask for audience feedback during a "Twitter break." Be ready to discuss your experience with the entire class.

Expand Your Skills

Critique the Professionals

Visit the TED website at www.ted.com/talks and listen to any presentation that interests you. Compare the speaker's delivery and visual support materials with the concepts presented in this chapter. What works? What doesn't work? Using whatever medium your instructor requests, write a brief summary of your analysis.

Sharpen Your Career Skills Online

Bovée and Thill's Business Communication Web Search, at websearch.businesscommunicationnetwork.com, is a unique research tool designed specifically for business communication research. Use the Web Search function to find a website, video, article, podcast, or presentation that offers advice on creating and delivering business presentations. Write a brief email message to your instructor or a post for your class blog describing the item that you found and summarizing the career skills information you learned from it.

Build Your Career

A key part of your employment communication package is a list of people who will agree to serve as references. As you'll read in Chapter 15, there are three types of references to think about: *professional references* (people who are willing to vouch for your qualifications), *personal references* (people who are willing to vouch for your character), and *LinkedIn recommendations* (people willing to endorse you on LinkedIn).[31]

In the weeks ahead, start thinking about the people who might serve as positive references for you. Allow plenty of time to contact everyone, and always ask before using anyone as a personal or professional reference. Not only is this good manners (not everyone is willing or able to serve as a reference), but it can help you avoid the embarrassing scenario of giving employers the name of someone who winds up speaking negatively about you. Chapter 15 has more on compiling and using your list of references.

Improve Your Grammar, Mechanics, and Usage

The following exercises help you improve your knowledge of and power over English grammar, mechanics, and usage. Turn to the Handbook of Grammar, Mechanics, and Usage at the end of this book and review all of Sections 3.1 (Capitalization), 3.2 (Underscores and Italics), and 3.3 (Abbreviations). Then indicate the preferred choice in the following groups of sentences. (Answers to these exercises appear on page 615.)

14-16. **a.** Send this report to Mister H. K. Danforth, RR 1, Albany, NY 12885.

b. Send this report to Mister H. K. Danforth, Rural Route 1, Albany, New York 12885.

c. Send this report to Mr. H. K. Danforth, RR 1, Albany, NY 12885.

14-17. **a.** She received her MBA degree from the University of Michigan.

b. She received her Master of Business Administration degree from the university of Michigan.

14-18. **a.** Sara O'Rourke (a reporter from The Wall Street Journal) will be here Thursday.

b. Sara O'Rourke (a reporter from the Wall Street Journal) will be here Thursday.

c. Sara O'Rourke (a reporter from the *Wall Street Journal*) will be here Thursday.

14-19. **a.** The building is located on the corner of Madison and Center streets.

b. The building is located on the corner of Madison and Center Streets.

14-20. **a.** Call me at 8 a.m. tomorrow morning, PST, and I'll have the information you need.

b. Call me at 8 tomorrow morning, PST, and I'll have the information you need.

c. Call me tomorrow at 8 a.m. PST, and I'll have the information you need.

14-21. **a.** Whom do you think *Time* magazine will select as its Person of the Year?

b. Whom do you think *Time magazine* will select as its *Person of the Year*?

c. Whom do you think *Time magazine* will select as its Person of the Year?

14-22. **a.** The art department will begin work on Feb. 2, just one wk. from today.

b. The art department will begin work on February 2, just one week from today.

c. The art department will begin work on Feb. 2, just one week from today.

14-23. **a.** You are to meet him on friday at the UN building in NYC.

b. You are to meet him on Friday at the UN building in NYC.

c. You are to meet him on Friday at the un building in New York city.

14-24. **a.** You must help her distinguish between i.e. (which means "that is") and e.g. (which means "for example").

b. You must help her distinguish between i.e. (which means "that is") and *e.g.* (which means "for example").

c. You must help her distinguish between *i.e.* (which means that is) and *e.g.* (which means for example).

14-25. **a.** We plan to establish a sales office on the West coast.

b. We plan to establish a sales office on the west coast.

c. We plan to establish a sales office on the West Coast.

For additional exercises focusing on mechanics, visit MyLab Business Communication. Select Chapter 14, then Additional Exercises to Improve Your Grammar, Mechanics and Usage, then 20. Capitals or 21. Word division.

Cases

For all cases, feel free to use your creativity to make up any details you need in order to craft effective messages.

PRESENTATION SKILLS

14-26. Planning, Designing, and Creating Presentation Slides [LO-1], [LO-2], [LO-3], [LO-4]   Learning to play a musical instrument offers children multiple benefits, beyond the joys of creating and appreciating music.

Your task: Research the benefits of learning and playing an instrument, then prepare a brief presentation that conveys these benefits in a way that most parents would find compelling.

PRESENTATION SKILLS / PORTFOLIO BUILDER

14-27. Planning, Designing, and Creating Presentation Slides [LO-1], [LO-2], [LO-3], [LO-4]   Consumers who want to eat fresh, local produce and small farmers looking for more predictable revenue have found a match in *community-supported agriculture (CSA)*. CSA is essentially a subscription service in which consumers sign up for regular allotments of fruits and vegetables from a local farm. At regular intervals during the growing season, each subscriber gets a box of whatever produce is ripe and ready at that time.

Your task: Research CSA options in your area, and prepare a brief presentation on how these programs work and how they benefit farmers and consumers. If you can't find any local programs, choose any location in the United States where CSA is available.

PRESENTATION SKILLS / PORTFOLIO BUILDER

14-28. Planning, Designing, and Creating Presentation Slides [LO-1], [LO-2], [LO-3], [LO-4]   One could argue that sleep is the single most important element of healthy living. Not only is adequate sleep essential for the body on its own, but getting enough sleep enables other activities that are essential for health, including getting exercise and taking the time to eat a healthy diet. Unfortunately, millions of people who recognize the value of sleep and want nothing more than to get enough sleep every night are frequently unable to do so.

Your task: Research the types and causes of insomnia and the cures most often recommended by sleep specialists. Using Prezi or slide software, prepare a 10- to 15-minute presentation on why insomnia affects so many people and the steps people can take to reduce or eliminate it.

PRESENTATION SKILLS / TEAM SKILLS

14-29. Planning, Designing, and Creating Presentation Slides [LO-1], [LO-2], [LO-3], [LO-4]   Screencasting is a great way to demonstrate how to use software or to review a website or online service. Screencast-O-Matic lets you create free screencasts up to 15 minutes long. (Your college or university may have a site license to use the service; check with your instructor.)

Your task: Visit screencast-o-matic.com and watch the introductory tutorials and the scripted recording tutorials. Next, choose a software program (Mac or PC) or a website that interests you. Choose something substantial enough that you can talk about it for 5 to 10 minutes, as either a demo or a review. Write the script for your screencast, then record it using the Screencast-O-Matic system. Format and deliver the video as your instructor requests.

PRESENTATION SKILLS / TEAM SKILLS

14-30. Planning, Designing, and Creating Presentation Slides [LO-1], [LO-2], [LO-3], [LO-4]   Not long ago, snowboarding seemed to be on pace to pass skiing as the country's favorite way to zoom down snowy mountains, but the sport's growth has cooled off in recent years.[32]

Your task: Research and prepare a 10-minute presentation on participation trends in snowboarding and skiing, including explanations for the relative popularity of both sports. Include at least three quotations to emphasize key points in your presentation. Use either structured or free-form slides.

PRESENTATION SKILLS / PORTFOLIO BUILDER

14-31. Presentations: Designing Presentation Visuals [LO-4]   Depending on the sequence your instructor chose for this course, you've probably covered 10 to 12 chapters at this point and learned or improved many valuable skills. Think through your progress and identify five business communication skills that you've either learned for the first time or developed during this course.

Your task: Create a Prezi or slide presentation that describes each of the five skills you've identified. Be sure to explain how each skill could help you in your career. Use any visual style that you feel is appropriate for the assignment.

PRESENTATION SKILLS / MOBILE SKILLS

14-32. Presentations: Designing Presentation Visuals; Mobile Media [LO-4]   On SlideShare or any other source, find a business presentation on any topic that interests you.

Your task: Re-create the first five slides in the presentation in a manner that will make them more mobile-friendly. Create as many additional slides as you need.

PRESENTATION SKILLS / **TEAM** SKILLS

14-33. Planning, Designing, and Creating Presentation Slides; Collaboration: Team Projects [LO-1], [LO-2], [LO-3], [LO-4], Chapter 2   Changing a nation's eating habits is a Herculean task, but the physical and financial health of the United States depends on it. You work for the USDA Center for Nutrition Policy and Promotion, and it's your job to educate people on the dangers of unhealthy eating and the changes they can make to eat more balanced and healthful diets.

Your task: Visit **real-timeupdates.com/ebc13**, select Student Assignments, and download Chapter 14 Case (*Dietary Guidelines for Americans*). With a team assigned by your instructor, develop a 10- to 15-minute presentation that conveys the key points from Chapter 3 of the *Guidelines*, "Food and Food Components to Reduce." The objectives of your presentation are to alert people to the dangers of excessive consumption of the five components discussed in the chapter and to let them know what healthy levels of consumption are. This chapter has a lot of information, but you don't need to pack it all into your presentation; you can assume that the chapter will be available as a handout to anyone who attends your presentation. Draft speaking notes that someone outside your team could use to give the presentation. You can use images from the *Guidelines* PDF, the websites of the U.S. Department of Agriculture and the U.S. Department of Health and Human Services, or a nongovernment source such as Creative Commons. Cite all your image sources, and make sure you follow the usage and attribution guidelines for any photos you find on nongovernment sites.

MyLab Business Communication

MyLab Assisted-Grading Writing Prompts

If your instructor has assigned one or both of the following writing assignments within the MyLab, go to your Assignments to complete these writing exercises.

14-34. How can visually oriented free-form slides help keep an audience engaged in a presentation? [LO-3]

14-35. How does embracing the backchannel reflect the "you" attitude? [LO-5]

Endnotes

1. Barnett International, accessed 14 April 2018, barnettinternationalconsulting.com; Kate Torgovnick May and Emily Ludolph, "A TED Speaker Coach Shares 11 Tips for Right Before You Go on Stage," TED blog, 14 February 2016, blog.ted.com; Laura Montini, "Steal This TED Coach's Top 3 Public Speaking Tricks," *Inc.*, 4 June 2015, www.inc.com; Gina Barnett, "Play the Part: Master Body Signals to Connect and Communicate for Business Success," Talks at Google, video, 24 June 2015, www.youtube.com/watch?v=q3nxsdQt7Rg; "TED Conference Coach Gina Barnett Offers Public Speaking Tips," CBC News, 19 March 2015, www.cbc.ca; Gina Barnett, "Like, Totally Don't Talk Like This to Get Ahead in Business?" *Fortune*, 6 July 2015, www.fortune.com; Gina Barnett, *Play the Part: Master Body Signals to Connect and Communicate for Business Success* (New York: McGraw-Hill, 2015).
2. Nancy Duarte, *Slide:ology: The Art and Science of Creating Great Presentations* (Sebastopol, Calif.: O'Reilly Media, 2008), 13.
3. Amber Naslund, "Twebinar: GE's Tweetsquad," 4 August 2009, www.radian6.com/blog.
4. "Get Started with Prezi," Prezi website, accessed 2 May 2014, https://prezi.com.
5. Adam Noar, "PowerPoint vs. Prezi: What's the Difference?" Presentation Panda blog, 21 February 2012, presentationpanda.com.
6. Carmine Gallo, "How to Deliver a Presentation Under Pressure," *Businessweek* online, 18 September 2008, www.businessweek.com.
7. Sarah Lary and Karen Pruente, "Powerless Point: Common PowerPoint Mistakes to Avoid," *Public Relations Tactics*, February 2004, 28.
8. Garr Reynolds, *Presentation Zen: Simple Ideas on Presentation Design and Delivery* (Berkeley, Calif.: New Riders, 2008), 39–42.

9. Sherwyn P. Morreale and Courtland L. Bovée, *Excellence in Public Speaking* (Fort Worth, Tex.: Harcourt Brace College Publishers, 1998), 234–237.
10. John Windsor, "Presenting Smart: Keeping the Goal in Sight," *Presentations*, 6 March 2008, www.presentations.com.
11. Morreale and Bovée, *Excellence in Public Speaking*, 241–243.
12. Josh Bersin, "Good Presentations Need to Make People Uncomfortable," *Harvard Business Review*, 9 September 2016, https://hbr.org; Eric J. Adams, "Management Focus: User-Friendly Presentation Software," *World Trade*, March 1995, 92.
13. Carmine Gallo, "Grab Your Audience Fast," *BusinessWeek*, 13 September 2006, 19.
14. Walter Kiechel III, "How to Give a Speech," *Fortune*, 8 June 1987, 180.
15. Nancy Duarte, "How Experts Can Help a General Audience Understand Their Ideas," *Harvard Business Review*, 12 September 2016, http://hbr.org.
16. *Communication and Leadership Program* (Santa Ana, Calif.: Toastmasters International, 1980), 44, 45.
17. Kathryn Dill, "Never Give a Boring Presentation Again," *Forbes*, 27 April 2016, www.forbes.com.
18. Duarte, *Slide:ology*, 152.
19. Greg Anderson, "Presefy Syncs and Controls Presentations over Your Phone," Arctic Startup, 14 March 2013, www.arcticstartup.com; Kanda Software website, accessed 2 May 2014, www.kandasoft.com; Heather Clancy, "Broadcast Your Mobile Presentations to Remote Attendees," ZDNet, 27 March 2013, www.zdnet.com.

20. Reynolds, *Presentation Zen*, 85.

21. "Presentation Translator," Microsoft, accessed 14 April 2018, www.microsoft.com.

22. Patricia Fripp, "9 Timely Tips for Pre-Presentation Preparation," *American Salesman*, April 2016, 27–30; Richard Zeoli, "The Seven Things You Must Know About Public Speaking," *Forbes*, 3 June 2009, www .forbes.com; Morreale and Bovée, *Excellence in Public Speaking*, 24–25.

23. Jennifer Rotondo and Mike Rotondo Jr., *Presentation Skills for Managers* (New York: McGraw-Hill, 2002), 151.

24. Teresa Brady, "Fielding Abrasive Questions During Presentations," *Supervisory Management*, February 1993, 6.

25. Robert L. Montgomery, "Listening on Your Feet," *Toastmaster*, July 1987, 14–15.

26. Cliff Atkinson, *The Backchannel* (Berkeley, Calif.: New Riders, 2010), 17.

27. Atkinson, *The Backchannel*, 51, 68–73.

28. Olivia Mitchell, "10 Tools for Presenting with Twitter," Speaking About Presenting blog, 3 November 2009, www.speakingaboutpresenting.com; Atkinson, *The Backchannel*, 51, 68–73, 99.

29. "9 Tips for Better Team Presentations," Whole-Brain Presenting, accessed 14 April 2018, www.speaklikeapro.co.uk; "Team Presentations," West Side Toastmasters, accessed 14 April 2018, westsidetoastmasters.com.

30. Kelci Lynn Lucier, "How to Give a Great Group Presentation," ThoughtCo., 6 March 2017, www.thoughtco.com.

31. Alison Doyle, "How to Select and Use Job References," *The Balance*, 31 January 2018, www.thebalance.com.

32. Hugo Martin, "Snowboarding Craze Fades, Skiing Becomes Cool Again," *Seattle Times*, 7 February 2013, seattletimes.com.

Five-Minute Guide to Planning Presentations

Before you start to work on your next major presentation, review these helpful tips.

 Plan the presentation

1. Leave yourself enough time! High-quality presentations can take days to create and rehearse.
2. Learn as much as you can about the setting and circumstances of your presentation, from the audience's expectations to the seating arrangements.
3. Make sure you can express your goal for the presentation in a single sentence.
4. Decide whether your goal would be best met with a *linear* (following an outline) or a *nonlinear* (zooming in and out and moving around from topic to topic) presentation.
5. Consider preparing a detailed planning outline and a simpler speaking outline that can serve as your notes.

 Develop the presentation

1. Remember to adapt your content, materials, and speaking style to the situation and the audience.
2. Develop your presentation content:
   - The *introduction* needs to get the audience's attention and interest, establish your credibility, and preview your message.
   - The *body* needs to lay out your ideas and information—with smooth transitions from section to section—and maintain the audience's interest.
   - The *close* should restate your main points and summarize any action items; be sure you can end with clarity and confidence.

 Design and create your visuals

1. Remember that your slides are *not* your presentation; you and what you have to say are. Slides and other visual aids are only there to support your spoken message.
2. *Structured slides* (usually based on templates):
   - Are easy to create (just pick a template and start typing)
   - Are a practical choice for routine presentations such as project updates
   - Can be mind numbing if you have slide after slide of bullet points and text blocks
3. *Free form slides* (no fixed design from slide to slide, usually with lots of visuals and very little text):
   - Can create a more engaging and dynamic experience for you and the audience
   - Are usually more creatively demanding and time-consuming to create
   - Put more burden on you, the speaker, because you can't rely on displayed text
4. General design tips:
   - Design each slide around a *key visual* when you can to unify the points you are making.
   - Limit the number of words on any slide, and make sure everyone in the room can read them.
   - Use color strategically to direct and focus the audience's gaze.
   - Simple is always better—with backgrounds, artwork, animation, transitions, and builds.

 Complete your materials and practice your delivery

1. Create additional slides to help the audience follow the flow: title slide, agenda slide, and navigation slides that show where you are in the presentation.
2. Create effective handouts that work in concert with your presentation.
3. Leave plenty of time to practice until you are comfortable with the material and your equipment.

00:05 **Be ready to present with confidence**

1. Take steps to overcome anxiety: use your nervousness as positive energy, don't worry about being perfect, know your material, be ready with an opening line, remember to breathe, make friends with the stage, and concentrate on your message and your audience, not on yourself.
2. Anticipate likely questions and be ready with answers.

CHAPTER **15** Building Careers and Writing Résumés

CHAPTER **16** Applying and Interviewing for Employment

The same techniques you use to succeed in your career can also help you launch and manage that career. Understand the employer's perspective on the hiring process so that you can adapt your approach and find the best job in the shortest possible time. Learn the best ways to craft a résumé and the other elements in your job-search portfolio. Understand the interviewing process to make sure you're prepared for every stage and every type of interview.

Aleksandr Davydov/Alamy Stock Photo

15

Building Careers and Writing Résumés

LEARNING OBJECTIVES

After studying this chapter, you will be able to

1 List eight key steps to finding the ideal opportunity in today's job market.

2 Explain the process of planning your résumé, including how to choose the best résumé organization.

3 Describe the tasks involved in writing your résumé, and list the sections to consider including in your résumé.

4 Characterize the completing step for résumés, including the six most common formats in which you can produce a résumé.

5 Identify nine tips for creating a successful LinkedIn profile.

MyLab Business Communication

Improve Your Grade!

If your instructor is using MyLab Business Communication, visit **www.pearson.com/mylab/business-communication** for videos, simulations, and writing exercises.

ON THE JOB: COMMUNICATING AT
PATREON

Breaking the Hiring Templates That Limit Opportunities

When companies prepare to hire employees, it makes sense for them to establish criteria for the skills, experience, education, and other attributes that candidates should possess. Together, all these criteria create a sort of "template" that hiring managers can use to evaluate applicants, which helps ensure that all candidates get measured against the same criteria.

While this sounds sensible in theory, it is often flawed in practice, with negative consequences for companies and aspiring employees alike. Hiring templates have three potential problems. First, they can be unrealistic, with companies setting standards that few candidates can meet—and that are sometimes far in excess of what positions really require. This became a common complaint with the advent of *applicant tracking systems*, which filter out anyone who doesn't meet whatever criteria are programmed into the system (see "Make Friends with the Résumé Bots" on page 497). Companies sometimes say they can't find anybody to fill openings, but qualified applicants are standing right outside the gates, so to speak, waving their arms and saying, "We're here, but your systems won't let us in."

A second and more difficult problem to solve with hiring templates is that they are both explicit and implicit. The *explicit* parts of the template are all the written criteria in the job description and in any tests or assignments that candidates

Patreon's Erica Joy Baker is a leading voice for change in how high-tech companies hire and manage employees.

are asked to complete. The *implicit* parts are the qualitative, "gut feel" decisions, sometimes unspoken, that recruiters and interviewers make about candidates. While these criteria don't show up in job descriptions, they can be even more difficult for candidates to get past. For example, interviewers frequently try to assess whether a candidate is "one of us," somebody who can fit into the organization's work culture. This practice can be a good thing, but it can be problematic if that culture is toxic or exclusionary.

The first two problems can contribute to a third problem, which is the tendency for companies to recruit more of the same—people from the same universities, with the same degrees, from the same companies, in the same social networks, and so on. For example, Silicon Valley's most prominent companies have tended to select graduates from a small handful of universities—and not surprisingly, it's often the same schools that their founders and leaders graduated from.

When companies succumb to these hiring practices, they can end up with monocultures in which most of the workforce looks alike, talks alike, and acts alike. People who don't fit the template often don't make it through the hiring process, and those who do can feel like outsiders even if they do make it inside. In Silicon Valley, that sometimes means young white and Asian males from elite universities on the inside, and everybody else on the outside. The industry has made headlines in recent years with reports of gender bias, pay disparity, and sexual harassment.

When companies take a different approach, the results can expose the flaws in the conventional approach. For example, when firms use *blind auditions* or *blind assessments* (see page 534) to screen applicants, in which candidates' qualifications are assessed anonymously, more women and graduates of community colleges get past the initial screening stage than they do in traditional interviewing processes. Open-source software projects, in which anyone can contribute sections of program code, subject to approval of a governing body, provide more evidence of exclusionary bias. When the gender of contributors is known to the gatekeepers, women's contributions are accepted less often than men's contributions are. However, if the process is anonymized so gatekeepers don't know contributors' gender, the situation is reversed.

A growing chorus is calling for hiring and workplace reform, and one of the voices leading this discussion is Erica Joy Baker. From being the only black woman among hundreds of students in her first computer science course to a decade of working her way up the technical ranks at Google, she knows firsthand the challenges faced by people who don't fit the prevailing template. She started out questioning whether she belonged in computer science at all during her first year in college, but she is now a senior engineering manager at the crowdfunding company Patreon.

Baker uses her leadership influence within her own company to create positive change, and she has established a broad reach across the tech industry. She speaks and writes regularly on the topic and is one of the founding members of Project Include (**projectinclude.org**). This nonprofit organization works to help tech companies build comprehensive hiring practices and equitable management systems that embrace and support the entire spectrum of available talent.

If you don't fit the stereotypical template in your chosen profession, take heart. Smart companies are beginning to realize that talent comes in a lot of different packages and travels a lot of different paths. For example, Google has expanded the number of colleges where it recruits, more companies are using blind auditions, and some companies now peg executive compensation to how well leaders avoid monocultural hiring practices. Organizations such as Project Include and Code 2040 (**www.code2040.org**) are educating investors and executives on the moral imperatives and financial benefits of inclusive hiring.

Baker is often lauded for her tenacity and resilience at forging a path through the tech industry, but she and many others would like to see a business world where you don't need superhero grit to overcome odds because the odds aren't stacked against anyone in the first place.[1]

WWW.PATREON.COM

Finding the Ideal Opportunity in Today's Job Market

1 LEARNING OBJECTIVE
List eight key steps to finding the ideal opportunity in today's job market.

As Erica Joy Baker (profiled in the chapter-opening On the Job) could surely attest, identifying and landing the ideal job can be a long and challenging process. Fortunately, the skills you're developing in this course will give you a competitive advantage. This section offers a general job-search strategy with advice that applies to just about any career path you might want to pursue. As you craft your personal strategy, keep these three guidelines in mind:

- **Get organized.** Your job search could last many months and involve multiple contacts with dozens of companies. You need to keep all the details straight to ensure that you don't miss opportunities or make mistakes such as losing someone's email address or forgetting an appointment.

If you haven't already, read the Prologue, "Building a Career with Your Communication Skills," before studying this chapter.

- **Start now and stick to it.** Even if you are a year or more away from graduation, now is not too early to get started with some of the essential research and planning tasks. If you wait until the last minute, you might miss opportunities and you won't be as prepared as other candidates.
- **Look for stepping-stone opportunities.** If you can't find the opportunity you're looking for right away, you might need to take a job that doesn't meet your expectations while you keep looking to get on the right track. But view every job as an opportunity to learn workplace skills, observe effective and ineffective business practices, and fine-tune your sense of how you'd like to spend your career.

WRITING THE STORY OF YOU

What's your story? Thinking about where you've been and where you want to go will help focus your job search.

Writing or updating your résumé is a great opportunity to step back and think about where you've been and where you'd like to go. Do you like the path you're on, or is it time for a change? Are you focused on a particular field, or do you need some time to explore?

You might find it helpful to think about the "story of you"—the things you are passionate about, your skills, your ability to help an organization reach its goals, the path you've been on so far, and the path you want to follow in the future (see Figure 15.1). Think in terms of an image or a theme you'd like to project. Are you academically gifted? An effective leader? A well-rounded professional with wide-ranging talents? A creative problem solver? A technical wizard? Writing your story is a valuable planning exercise that helps you think about where you want to go and how to present yourself to target employers.

MOBILE APP

The **Good&Co** app aims to help professionals find jobs that bring more meaning to their careers.

LEARNING TO THINK LIKE AN EMPLOYER

Employers judge their recruiting success by *quality of hire*, so take steps to present yourself as a high-quality hire.

Now switch sides and look at the hiring process from an employer's perspective. Recognize that companies take risks with every hiring decision—the risk that the person hired won't meet expectations and the risk that a better candidate slipped through their fingers. Many companies judge the success of their recruiting efforts by *quality of hire*, a measure of how closely new employees meet the company's needs.[2] Given this perspective, what steps can you take to present yourself as the low-risk, high-reward choice?

In addition to your skills, employers want to know if you are reliable and motivated—if you're somebody who "gets it" when it comes to being a professional.

Of course, your perceived ability to perform the job is an essential part of your potential quality as a new hire. However, hiring managers consider more than just your ability to handle the job. They want to know if you'll be reliable and motivated—if you're somebody who "gets it" when it comes to being a professional in today's workplace. Table 15.1 lists the attributes companies list most frequently when looking for new employees. You'll recognize many of these from the discussions of professionalism and career skills in Chapter 1.

TABLE 15.1 **Attributes That Will Help You Stand Out in the Job Market**	
Core Business Skills	**Personal Qualities**
• Oral and written communication	• Committed to excellence; dissatisfied with mediocrity
• Communication with diverse audiences	• Dependable and accountable
• Information technology skills	• Committed to something greater than oneself
• Data literacy	• Confident but not brash
• Collaboration	• Curious, driven to learn
• Situation analysis and problem solving	• Flexible, adaptable, and open to change
• Time and resource management	• Respectful and inclusive
• Project management	• Ethical; lives and works with integrity
• Leadership	• Positive, resilient, able to roll with the punches and recover from setbacks
• Critical thinking	• Sensitive to expectations of etiquette
	• Self-reliant
	• Proactive; taking initiative without waiting to be told
	• Ambitious and goal-oriented

Sources: Based in part on Alison Doyle, "The Top Skills Employers Seek in College Grads," *The Balance*, 17 April 2018, www.thebalance .com; "Career Readiness Defined," National Association of Colleges and Employers, accessed 19 April 2018, www.naceweb.org; Penny Loretto, "The Top 10 Work Values Employers Look For," *The Balance Careers*, 15 March 2018, www.thebalance.com; Liz Ryan, "12 Qualities Employers Look For When They're Hiring," *Forbes*, 2 March 2016, www.forbes.com.

My Story

Where I Have Been

- Honor student and all around big shot in high school (but discovered that college is full of big shots!)

- Have worked several part-time jobs; only thing that really appealed to me in any of them was making improvements, making things work better

Where I Am Now

- Junior; on track to graduate in 2021

- Enjoy designing creative solutions to challenging problems

- Not a high-end techie in an engineering sense, but I figure most things out eventually

- Not afraid to work hard, whatever it takes to get the job done

- I can tolerate some routine, as long as I have the opportunity to make improvements if needed

- Tend to lead quietly by example, rather than by visibly and vocally taking charge

- Knowing that I do good work is more important than getting approval from others

- I tend not to follow fads and crowds; sometimes I'm ahead of the curve, sometimes I'm behind the curve

Where I Want to Be

- Get an advanced degree; not sure what subject area yet, though

- Haven't really settled on one industry or profession yet; working with systems of any kind is more appealing than any particular profession that I've learned about so far

- Develop my leadership and communication skills to become a more "obvious" leader

- Collaborate with others while still having the freedom to work independently (maybe become an independent contractor or consultant at some point?)

- Have the opportunity to work internationally, at least for a few years

- Like the big bucks that corporate executives earn but don't want to live in the public eye like that or have to "play the game" to get ahead

- Believe I would be good manager, but not sure I want to spend all my time just managing people

- Want to be known as an independent thinker and creative problem solver, as somebody who can analyze tough situations and figure out solutions that others might not consider

- Are there jobs where I could focus on troubleshooting, improving processes, or designing new systems?

Annotations (right margin):

→ What experiences from your past give you insight into where you would like to go in the future?

→ Where do you stand now in terms of your education and career, and what do you know about yourself?

→ What would you like your future to be? What do you like and dislike? What would you like to explore? If you haven't figured everything out yet, that's fine—as long as you've started to think about the future.

Figure 15.1   Writing the Story of You
Writing the "story of you" is a helpful way to think through where you've been in your life and career so far, where you are now, and where you would like to go from here. Remember that this is a private document designed to help you clarify your thoughts and plans, although you will probably find ways to adapt some of what you've written to various job-search documents, including your résumé.

RESEARCHING INDUSTRIES AND COMPANIES OF INTEREST

Learning more about professions, industries, and individual companies is a vital step in your job search. It also impresses employers, particularly when you go beyond the easily available sources such as a company's own website. Table 15.2 on the next page lists some of the many websites where you can learn more about companies and find job openings. Your college's career center placement office probably maintains an up-to-date list as well.

To learn more about contemporary business topics, scan leading business periodicals and newspapers with significant business sections. In addition, thousands of bloggers, Twitter users, and podcasters offer news and commentary on the business world. AllTop (**alltop.com/business**) is another good resource for finding people who write about topics that interest you. In addition to learning more about professions and opportunities, this research will help you get comfortable with the jargon and buzzwords currently in use in a particular field, including essential *keywords* to use in your résumé (see page 496).

Employers expect you to be familiar with important developments in their industries.

TABLE 15.2	Selected Job-Search Websites	
Website*	**URL**	**Highlights**
CollegeRecruiter	www.collegerecruiter.com	Focused on opportunities for graduates with fewer than three years of work experience
Monster	www.monster.com	One of the most popular job sites, with hundreds of thousands of openings, many from hard-to-find small companies; extensive collection of advice on the job-search process
MonsterCollege	college.monster.com	Focused on job searches for new college grads; your school's career center site probably links here
CareerBuilder	www.careerbuilder.com	One of the largest job boards; affiliated with several hundred newspapers and job-related websites
USAJOBS	www.usajobs.gov	Official job-search site for the U.S. government, featuring openings for everything from economists to astronauts to border patrol agents
IMDiversity	imdiversity.com	Good resource on diversity in the workplace, with job postings from companies that have made a special commitment to promoting diversity
Dice.com	www.dice.com	One of the best sites for high-technology jobs
TopTechJobs.com	toptechjobs.com	Concentrates on jobs for IT specialists and engineers; also incorporates NetTemps.com for contractors and freelancers looking for short-term assignments
Internship Programs	internshipprograms.com	Posts listings from companies looking for interns in a wide variety of professions
SimplyHired	www.simplyhired.com	Two specialized search engines that look for job postings on hundreds of websites worldwide; they find many postings that aren't listed on job board sites such as Monster
Indeed	www.indeed.com	

* *Note:* This list represents only a small fraction of the hundreds of job-posting sites and other resources available online; be sure to check with your college's career center for the latest information.

Sources: Individual websites, accessed 19 April 2018.

REAL-TIME UPDATES

LEARN MORE BY VISITING THIS WEBSITE

Advice for every phase of the job-search process

From an introduction to job-search strategies to details on résumé writing, this site offers advice from career counseling professionals. Go to **real-timeupdates.com/ebc13** and select Learn More in the Students section.

Take advantage of job-search apps as well, including those offered by job-posting websites and major employers (see Figure 15.2). You can use them to learn more about the company as well as about specific jobs. In addition to researching companies and applying for openings, integrating a mobile device into your job-search strategy can help with networking and staying on top of your active job applications. For instance, some companies don't wait long after extending an offer. If they don't hear from the top candidate in a short amount of time, they'll move on to their next choice. By staying plugged in via your mobile device, you won't let any opportunities pass you by.

TRANSLATING YOUR GENERAL POTENTIAL INTO A SPECIFIC SOLUTION FOR EACH EMPLOYER

An essential task in your job search is presenting your skills and accomplishments in a way that is relevant to the employer's business challenges.

An important aspect of any employer's quality-of-hire challenge is trying to determine how well a candidate's attributes and experience will translate into the demands of a specific position. As a job candidate, customizing your résumé to each job opening is an important step in showing employers that you will be a good fit. Keep in mind that employers care about *your* past only to the extent that it will help you contribute to *their* future.

Customizing your résumé is not difficult if you have done your research. From your initial contact all the way through the interviewing process, in fact, you will have opportunities to impress recruiters by explaining how your general potential translates to the specific needs of the position.

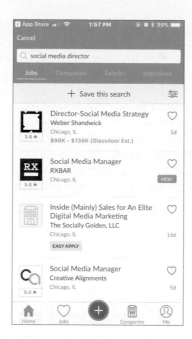

Figure 15.2 Mobile Job-Search Tools
Put your mobile phone or tablet to work in your job search, using some of the many employment apps now available.

TAKING THE INITIATIVE TO FIND OPPORTUNITIES

When it comes to finding the right opportunities for you, the easiest ways are not always the most productive ways. The major job boards such as Monster and classified services such as Craigslist have thousands of openings, but thousands of job seekers are looking at and applying for these same openings. Moreover, posting job openings on these sites is often a company's last resort, after it has exhausted other possibilities.

To maximize your chances, take the initiative and go find opportunities. Identify the companies you want to work for and focus your efforts on them. Get in touch with their human resources departments (or individual managers, if possible), describe what you can offer the company, and ask to be considered if any opportunities come up.[3] Reach out to company representatives on social networks. Your message might appear right when a company is starting to look for someone but hasn't yet advertised the opening to the outside world.

MOBILE APP
The **Indeed.com** app lets you search for jobs and apply from your phone.

Don't hesitate to contact interesting companies even if they haven't advertised job openings to the public yet—they might be looking for somebody just like you.

BUILDING YOUR NETWORK

Networking is the process of making informal connections with mutually beneficial business contacts. Networking takes place wherever and whenever people talk: at industry functions, at social gatherings, at alumni reunions—and all over the internet, from LinkedIn to Twitter to Facebook. In addition to making connections through social media tools, you might get yourself noticed by company recruiters.

Networking is more essential than ever because the vast majority of job openings are never advertised to the public. To avoid the time and expense of sifting through thousands of applications and the risk of hiring complete strangers, many companies start by asking their employees for recommendations—and these referrals are one of the most important sources of new employees.[4] The more people who know you, the better chance you have of being recommended for one of these hidden job openings.

Networking is the process of making informal connections with mutually beneficial business contacts.

Creative Ways to Build Your Network

Start building your network now. Your classmates could end up being some of your most valuable contacts, if not right away then possibly later in your career. Then branch out by identifying people with similar interests in your target professions, industries, and companies. Read news sites, blogs, and other online sources. Follow industry leaders on Twitter.

Start building your network now—your classmates could turn out to be some of your most important business contacts.

You can also follow individual executives at your target companies to learn about their interests and concerns.[5] Be on the lookout for career-oriented *Tweetups*, in which people who've connected on Twitter get together for in-person networking events. Connect with people on LinkedIn and Facebook, particularly in groups dedicated to your career interests. Depending on the system and the settings on individual users' accounts, you may be able to introduce yourself via public or private messages.[6]

Participate in student business organizations, especially those with ties to professional organizations. Visit *trade shows* to learn about various industries and rub shoulders with people who work in those industries.[7] Don't overlook volunteering; you not only meet people but also demonstrate your ability to solve problems, manage projects, and lead others. You can do some good while creating a network for yourself.

Keys to Being a Valued Networker

Remember that networking is about people helping each other, not just about other people helping you. Pay close attention to networking etiquette:[8]

- Be polite in every exchange. Not only is this the professional way to behave, but people are more inclined to help those who are positive and respectful.
- Don't speak poorly of your current employer or any past employers. Doing so is off-putting to other people, and it harms your reputation.
- Respect other people's time. Don't inundate people with messages, questions, or requests for help.
- Stay away from politics and other volatile topics. Remember that you're building a business network, not a circle of friends.
- Follow through on your promises. If you agree to make an introduction or provide information, make sure you do so.
- Follow up after meeting people. If you meet someone with shared interests, send a brief message within a day or two to solidify the connection you've made.

Networking is a mutually beneficial activity, so look for opportunities to help others.

To become a valued network member, you need to be able to help others in some way. You may not have any influential contacts yet, but because you're researching industries and trends as part of your own job search, you probably have valuable information you can share via your online and offline networks. Or you might simply be able to connect one person with another who can help. The more you network, the more valuable you become in your network—and the more valuable your network becomes to you.

Finally, be aware that your online network reflects on who you are in the eyes of potential employers, so exercise some judgment in making connections and giving recommendations on LinkedIn.

SEEKING CAREER COUNSELING

Don't overlook the many resources available through your college's career center.

Your college's career center probably offers a wide variety of services, including individual counseling, interview practice, résumé help, job fairs, on-campus interviews, and job listings. You can also find career planning advice online. Many of the websites listed in Table 15.2 offer articles and online tests to help you choose a career path, identify essential skills, and prepare to enter the job market.

AVOIDING CAREER-SEARCH MISTAKES

Don't let a careless mistake knock you out of contention for a great job.

While you're making all these positive moves to show employers you will be a quality hire, take care to avoid simple blunders such as these that can derail a job search:

- Not catching mistakes in your résumé
- Misspelling the name of a manager you're writing to
- Showing up late for an interview
- Posting something unprofessional on social media
- Failing to complete application forms correctly
- Asking for information that you can easily find yourself on a company's website

Busy recruiters will seize on these errors to narrow the list of candidates they need to spend time on, so don't give them a reason to pass on your résumé.

Striving to Excel

Pros are good at what they do, and they never stop improving. No matter what your job might be at any given time—even if it is far from where you aspire to be—strive to perform at the highest possible level. Not only do you have an ethical obligation to give your employer and your customers your best effort, but excelling at each level in your career is also the best way to keep climbing up to new positions of responsibility. Plus, being good at what you do delivers a sense of satisfaction that is hard to beat.

In many jobs and in many industries, performing at a high level requires a commitment to continuous learning and improvement. The nature of the work often changes as markets and technologies evolve, and expectations of quality tend to increase over time as well. View this constant change as a positive thing, as a way to avoid stagnation and boredom.

Striving to excel can be a challenge when there is a mismatch between the job's requirements and your skills and knowledge. If you are underqualified for a job, you need to identify your weaknesses quickly and come up with a plan to address them. A supportive manager will help you identify these areas and encourage improvement through training

or mentoring. Don't wait for a boss to tell you your work is subpar, however. If you know you're floundering, don't wait until you've failed to get help.

If you are overqualified for a job, it's easy to slip into a rut and eventually underperform simply because you aren't being challenged. However, current and future bosses aren't going to judge you on how well you performed relative to *your* needs and expectations; they're going to judge you on how well you performed relative to *the job's* requirements. Work with your boss to find ways to make your job more challenging if possible, or start looking for a better job if necessary, but be sure to maintain your level of performance until you can bring your responsibilities and talents into closer alignment.

CAREER APPLICATIONS

1. Should you ever try to sell yourself into a job for which you are not yet 100 percent qualified? Explain your answer.
2. Do you agree that you have an ethical obligation to excel at your job? Why or why not?

Also, assume that every employer will conduct an online search on you, because most companies now do so.[9] They want to know what your LinkedIn profile looks like and whether you've posted anything unprofessional on social media. If they don't like what they see or if what they see doesn't match what they read on your résumé, you probably won't be invited for an interview.[10]

Planning Your Résumé

Although you will create many messages during your career search, your résumé will be the most important document in this process. You will be able to use it directly in many instances, adapt it to a variety of uses such as an e-portfolio, and reuse pieces of it in social networking profiles and online application forms. Even if you apply to a company that doesn't request résumés, the process of developing your résumé will prepare you for interviewing and preemployment testing.

Developing a résumé is one of those projects that really benefits from multiple sessions spread out over several days or weeks. You are trying to summarize a complex subject (yourself!) and present a compelling story to strangers in a brief document. Follow the three-step writing process (see Figure 15.3 on the next page), and give yourself plenty of time.

Before you dive into your résumé, be aware that you will find a wide range of opinions regarding appropriate length, content, design, distribution methods, acceptable degrees of creativity, and whether writing a traditional résumé even makes sense in this age of online applications. For example, you may encounter a prospective employer that wants you to tweet your résumé or submit all the links that make up your online presence, rather than submit a conventional résumé.[11] You may run across examples of effective résumés that were produced as infographics, interactive videos, simulated search engine results, puzzles, games, graphic novels—you name it, somebody has probably tried it.

When you hear conflicting advice or see trendy concepts that you might be tempted to try, remember the most important question in business communication: What is the most effective way to adapt your message to the individual needs of each member of your audience? An approach that is wildly successful with one company or in one industry could be a complete disaster in another industry. To forge your own successful path through this maze of information, get inside the heads of the people you are trying to reach—try to think the way they think—and then apply the principles of effective communication you are learning in this course.

2 LEARNING OBJECTIVE
Explain the process of planning your résumé, including how to choose the best résumé organization.

Check out the "Five-Minute Guide to Planning Your Résumé" at the end of the chapter.

You will see lots of ideas and some conflicting advice about résumés; use what you know about effective business communication to decide what is right for your résumé.

1 Plan →	2 Write →	3 Complete
Analyze the Situation Recognize that the purpose of your résumé is to get an interview, not to get a job. **Gather Information** Research target industries and companies so that you know what they're looking for in new hires; learn about various jobs and what to expect; learn about the hiring manager, if possible. **Choose Media and Channels** Start with a traditional paper résumé and develop scannable, plain text, PDF, and social/online versions, as needed. Consider other formats as supplements. **Organize the Information** Choose an organizational model that highlights your strengths and downplays your shortcomings; use the chronological approach unless you have a strong reason not to.	**Adapt to Your Audience** Plan your wording carefully so that you can catch a recruiter's eye within seconds; translate your education and experience into attributes that target employers find valuable. **Compose the Message** Write clearly and succinctly, using active, powerful language that is appropriate to the industries and companies you're targeting; use a professional tone in all communications.	**Revise the Message** Evaluate content and review readability, then edit and rewrite for conciseness and clarity. **Produce the Message** Use effective design elements and a suitable layout for a clean, professional appearance; seamlessly combine text and graphical elements. When printing, use quality paper and a good printer. **Proofread the Message** Review for errors in layout, spelling, and mechanics; mistakes can cost you interview opportunities. **Distribute the Message** Deliver your résumé, carefully following the specific instructions of each employer or job board website.

Figure 15.3   Three-Step Writing Process for Résumés
Following the three-step writing process will help you create a successful résumé in a short time. Remember to pay attention to the "you" attitude and presentation quality; your résumé will not get far into the recruiting process if it doesn't speak to audience needs or contains multiple mistakes.

ANALYZING YOUR PURPOSE AND AUDIENCE

Once you view your résumé as a persuasive business message, it's easier to decide what should and shouldn't be in it.

Planning an effective résumé starts with understanding its true function—as a brief, persuasive business message intended to stimulate an employer's interest in meeting you and learning more about you (see Table 15.3). In other words, the purpose of a résumé is not to get you a job but rather to get you an interview.[12]

TABLE 15.3   Fallacies and Facts About Résumés

Fallacy	Fact
The purpose of a résumé is to list all your skills and abilities.	The purpose of a résumé is to pique employer interest and generate an interview.
A good résumé will get you the job you want.	All a résumé can do is get you in the door.
Your résumé will always be read carefully and thoroughly.	In most cases, your résumé needs to make a positive impression within a few seconds; only then will someone read it in detail. Moreover, it will likely be screened by a computer looking for keywords first—and if it doesn't contain the right keywords, a human being may never see it.
The more good information you present about yourself in your résumé, the better, so stuff your résumé with every positive detail.	Recruiters don't need that much information about you at the initial screening stage, and they probably won't read it.

As you conduct your research on various professions, industries, companies, and individual managers, you will have a better perspective on your target readers and their information needs. Learn as much as you can about the individuals who may be reading your résumé. Many professionals and managers are bloggers and Twitter users, and most are LinkedIn members, so you can learn more about them online even if you've never met them. Any bit of information can help you craft a more effective message.

By the way, if employers ask to see your "CV," they're referring to your *curriculum vitae*, the term used instead of *résumé* in academic professions and in many countries outside the United States. Résumés and CVs are essentially the same, although CVs can be much more detailed and contain personal information that is not included in a résumé.

Thanks to Twitter, LinkedIn, and other social media, you can often learn valuable details about individual managers in various companies.

> **REAL-TIME UPDATES**
> LEARN MORE BY READING THIS ARTICLE
> **Converting your résumé to a CV**
>
> Find everything you need to know to convert your U.S.-style résumé to the *curriculum vitae* format used in many other countries (and in many academic positions in the United States). Go to **real-timeupdates .com/ebc13** and select Learn More in the Students section.

GATHERING PERTINENT INFORMATION

If you haven't been building an employment portfolio thus far, you may need to do some research on yourself at this point. Gather all your pertinent work history, including the specific dates, duties, and accomplishments from any previous jobs you've held. Compile all your educational accomplishments, including formal degrees, training certificates, professional and technical certifications, academic awards, and scholarships. Also, gather information about school or volunteer activities that might be relevant to your job search, including offices you have held in any club or professional organization, presentations given, and online or print publications. You probably won't use every piece of information you come up with, but you'll want to have it at your fingertips.

SELECTING THE BEST MEDIA AND CHANNELS

You should expect to produce your résumé in several media and formats. "Producing Your Résumé" on page 500 discusses your options.

ORGANIZING YOUR RÉSUMÉ AROUND YOUR STRENGTHS

Although a résumé can be organized in a number of ways, most are some variation of chronological organization, functional organization, or a combination of the two. The right choice depends on your background and your goals.

The Chronological Résumé

In a **chronological résumé**, the work experience section dominates and is placed immediately after your contact information and introductory statement (see Figure 15.6 on page 503 for an example). The chronological approach is the most common way to organize a résumé, and many employers prefer this format because it presents your professional history in a clear, easy-to-follow arrangement.[13] With its emphasis on your work history, however, it may not be the best choice if you have limited experience in the field you are pursuing or if your work history doesn't show a linear career with a steady progression of increasing responsibility.[14]

The chronological résumé, which highlights your work history, is the most common format, but it might not be right for you at this stage in your career.

The Functional Résumé

A **functional résumé**, sometimes called a *skills résumé*, emphasizes your skills and capabilities, identifying employers and academic experience in subordinate sections. This arrangement stresses individual areas of competence rather than job history. The functional approach has three benefits: (1) Without having to read through job descriptions, employers can get an idea of what you can do for them; (2) you can emphasize earlier job experience through the skills you gained in those positions; and (3) you can deemphasize any lengthy unemployment or lack of career progress. However, you should be aware that because the functional résumé can obscure your work history, some employment professionals are suspicious of it.[15] If you don't believe the chronological format will work for you, consider the combination résumé instead.

The functional résumé highlights your skills more than your work experience, but many employers are suspicious of this format because it can obscure gaps in your work history.

The Combination Résumé

If you don't have a lot of work history to show, consider a *combination résumé* to highlight your skills while still providing a chronological history of your employment.

A **combination résumé** meshes the skills focus of the functional format with the job history focus of the chronological format. Figures 15.4 (page 501) and 15.5 (page 502) show examples of combination résumés. The chief advantage of this format is that it allows you to highlight your capabilities and education when you don't have a long or steady employment history, without raising concerns that you might be hiding something about your past.

As you look at sample résumés, you'll probably notice many variations on the three basic formats presented here. Study these other options in light of the effective communication principles you've learned in this course and the unique circumstances of your job search. If you find one that seems like the best fit for your unique situation, by all means, use it.

ADDRESSING AREAS OF CONCERN

Here are some common issues that people have regarding their professional and personal histories, with suggestions for handling them in a résumé, in your accompanying cover letter, or during an interview:

- **Slow career growth.** If you stayed in one position for many years, highlight ways in which you took on increasing responsibility, such as training new hires or filling in for your supervisor during vacations.
- **Frequent job changes.** If you've had several short-term jobs of a similar type, such as independent contracting and temporary assignments, you can group them under a single heading.[16] If past job positions were eliminated as a result of layoffs or mergers, find a subtle way to convey that information. Reasonable employers understand that many professionals have been forced to job hop by circumstances beyond their control. For both slow career growth and frequent job changes, bear in mind that these are relative perceptions that can vary by region and industry. For instance, a career history that would be viewed as stable in some fields and regions could be seen as stagnant in tech jobs in Silicon Valley, where job hopping is more common and sometimes viewed as a sign of growth.[17]
- **Gaps in work history.** Mention any relevant experience and education you gained during employment gaps, such as volunteer or community work. Also, consider the combination résumé format to emphasize your skills.
- **Inexperience.** Include related volunteer work, membership in professional groups, relevant coursework, and internships. Write a strong introductory statement that summarizes the value you can bring to an employer.
- **Overqualification.** Tone down your résumé by focusing on the experience and skills that relate most directly to the target position. If you are deeper into your career and are concerned about your age working against you, steer clear of phrases such as "decades of experience" and focus your presentation on your most recent and current accomplishments.
- **Job termination for cause.** Your résumé doesn't need to disclose that you were fired from a previous position, but if you are asked that on an application form or in an interview, you need to answer truthfully. Be prepared with an answer that illustrates how you learned from the experience and will be a positive asset to your next employer.[18]
- **Criminal record.** Employment laws related to criminal history vary by state, industry, and profession. If this affects you, you may want to consult your state's department of labor or advocacy organizations such as the National Employment Law Project (**www.nelp.org**). You don't necessarily need to disclose on your résumé if you have a criminal record, but most employers run background checks and at some point in the application process are likely to ask whether you have been convicted of a crime. Be prepared to discuss new skills you acquired and other positive changes you have made.[19]

3 LEARNING OBJECTIVE
Describe the tasks involved in writing your résumé, and list the sections to consider including in your résumé.

Writing Your Résumé

With the necessary information and a good plan in hand, you're ready to begin writing. If you feel uncomfortable writing about yourself, you're not alone. Many people, even accomplished writers, can find it difficult to write their own résumés. If you get stuck, imagine you are somebody else, writing a résumé for this person called you. By "being your own client," you might find that the words and ideas flow more easily. You could also pair up with a classmate or friend who is writing a résumé and swap projects for a while. Working on each other's résumés might speed up the process for both of you.

If you're uncomfortable writing your own résumé, you might try to trade with a classmate and write each other's résumé.

KEEPING YOUR RÉSUMÉ HONEST

Your résumé is a promotional message, so you naturally want to portray yourself in the best possible light. However, you must avoid any temptation to stretch the truth. Not only is this the right thing to do, but résumé fraud has become so widespread that many employers are stepping up their efforts to confirm the information that candidates supply. These efforts include running background checks, verifying employment details, designing interview questions specifically to expose shaky information on résumés, and using standardized application forms that require candidates to provide specific details that might be missing from a résumé.[20] Chances are good that false information on a résumé will be exposed somewhere during the application and interview process. Even if a deceptive candidate makes it past these checks, he or she must then live with the fear of being caught somewhere down the line—people have been fired years into their jobs for falsifying their résumés.[21]

To combat résumé fraud, employers now use a variety of screening techniques to expose false or exaggerated information.

By all means, express your talents and experience clearly and confidently, but don't inflate your accomplishments or do anything else to mislead employers. Stand out as a candidate with integrity.

REAL-TIME UPDATES
LEARN MORE BY VISITING THIS WEBSITE
Tune up your résumé with these practical tips
Get advice and inspiration to make your résumé the best that it can be. Go to **real-timeupdates.com/ebc13** and select Learn More in the Students section.

ADAPTING YOUR RÉSUMÉ TO YOUR AUDIENCE

Plan to adapt your résumé to each job opening in order to show how your capabilities meet the demands and expectations of the position. For example, an in-house public relations (PR) department and an independent PR agency perform many of the same tasks, but the outside agency must also sell its services to multiple clients. Consequently, it needs employees who are skilled at attracting and keeping paying customers, in addition to being skilled at PR. If you are applying for both in-house and agency PR jobs, you need to adapt your résumé for each of these audiences.

Plan to adapt your résumé to each job opening in order to show how your capabilities meet the demands and expectations of the position.

Pay close attention to any application instructions that an employer posts online. Companies may request that you include a specific detail on your résumé or other document, and they will check to see if you have demonstrated this attention to detail.

An essential step in adapting your résumé is using the same terminology as the employer uses to describe job responsibilities and professional accomplishments. In Figures 15.4 through 15.6 starting on page 501, you can see how the sample résumés do this, echoing key terms and phrases from the job postings. With the widespread use of automated **applicant tracking systems (ATSs)**, matching your language to the employer's will help you get past the filters and algorithms these systems use to rank incoming résumés.

Applicant tracking systems help employers process incoming applications by applying automated filtering and ranking rules.

If you are applying for business positions after military service or moving from one industry to another, you may need to "translate" your experience into the language of your target employers. For instance, military experience can help you develop many skills that are valuable in business, but military terminology can sound like a foreign language to people who aren't familiar with it. Isolate the important general concepts and present them in the business language your target employers use.

Military service and other specialized experiences may need to be "translated" into terms more readily understandable by your target readers.

COMPOSING YOUR RÉSUMÉ

Write your résumé using a simple and direct style. Use short, crisp phrases instead of whole sentences, and focus on what your reader needs to know. Avoid using the word *I*, which can sound both self-involved and repetitive by the time you outline all your skills and accomplishments. Instead, start your phrases with strong action verbs such as these:[22]

Draft your résumé using short, crisp phrases built around strong verbs and nouns.

accomplished	coordinated	initiated	participated	set up
achieved	created	installed	performed	simplified
administered	demonstrated	introduced	planned	sparked
approved	developed	investigated	presented	streamlined
arranged	directed	launched	proposed	strengthened
assisted	established	maintained	raised	succeeded
assumed	explored	managed	recommended	supervised
budgeted	forecasted	motivated	reduced	systematized
chaired	generated	negotiated	reorganized	targeted
changed	identified	operated	resolved	trained
compiled	implemented	organized	saved	transformed
completed	improved	oversaw	served	upgraded

Whenever you can, quantify the results with carefully selected evidence that confirms your abilities:

Instead of This	Write an Active Statement That Shows Results
Responsible for developing a new system for tracking online service requests	Developed a new service-request system that reduced scheduling errors by 90 percent and improved customer satisfaction by 22 percent
Performed various social media functions	As community manager, directed all aspects of the company's social media program
Have a solid record of acquiring new customers	Led the department in customer acquisition three years in a row
Member of special campus task force to resolve student problems with existing cafeteria assignments	Assisted in implementing new campus dining program that balances student needs with cafeteria capacity

Job-Specific Keywords

Include relevant *keywords* from job descriptions throughout your résumé and cover letter.

In addition to clear writing with specific examples, the words and phrases used throughout your résumé are critically important. Most résumés are now subjected to *keyword searches* in an applicant tracking system, in which a recruiter searches for résumés most likely to match the requirements of a particular job. Résumés that don't closely match the requirements may never be seen by a human reader, so it is essential to use the words and phrases that a recruiter is most likely to search on.

Identifying these keywords requires some research, but you can uncover many of them while you are researching various industries and companies. In particular, study job descriptions carefully. In contrast to the action verbs that catch a human reader's attention, keywords that catch a computer's attention are usually nouns that describe the specific skills, attributes, and experiences an employer is looking for in a candidate. Keywords can include the business and technical terms associated with a specific profession, industry-specific jargon, names or types of products or systems used in a profession, job titles, and college degrees.[23] See "Make Friends with the Résumé Bots" for specific tips on using keywords in your employment communication.

REAL-TIME UPDATES

LEARN MORE BY VISITING THIS WEBSITE

Find the keywords that will light up your résumé

These tips and tools will help you find the right keywords to customize your résumé for every opportunity. Go to **real-timeupdates.com/ebc13** and select Learn More in the Students section.

Name and Contact Information

Be sure to provide complete and accurate contact information; mistakes in this section of the résumé are surprisingly common.

Your name and contact information constitute the heading of your résumé; include the following:

- Name
- Address (both permanent and temporary, if you're likely to move during the job-search process)
- Email address
- Phone number(s)
- The URL of your LinkedIn profile

If the only email address you have is through your current employer, get a free personal email address from Gmail or a similar service. It's not fair to your current employer to use

INTELLIGENT COMMUNICATION TECHNOLOGY

Make Friends with the Résumé Bots

When you apply for jobs at most large companies and an increasing number of midsize and small companies, your application materials will usually be assessed by an applicant tracking system before a human ever puts eyes on it. Much of this automated filtering focuses on keywords, so follow these tips for using keywords in your résumé and cover letter:

- Use the specific terminology that each employer uses in its job descriptions. This is another good reason for adapting your résumé to each job opening; various employers can use different terms to describe the same function or quality.
- Integrate keywords naturally. Work them into your introductory statement, your education section, your employment history, and any activities and achievements that you include.
- Without going overboard in a way that makes the writing awkward or unnatural, use as many relevant keywords as you can throughout your résumé and cover letter. Don't resort to "keyword stuffing"—trying to game the system by cramming every conceivable keyword into your résumé. Advanced AI systems such as Burning Glass (see page 520) analyze whether keywords are used naturally and in context.
- Be sure to cover the full range of hard and soft skills each employer is looking for. *Hard skills* are measurable, specific abilities, such as using spreadsheets, operating equipment, speaking a second language, designing websites, and so on. *Soft skills* are the less-tangible, interpersonal side of things—including communication, teamwork, leadership, and conflict resolution. Hard skills are easier to describe because they are specific, such as saying you are fluent in Spanish or have four years of experience designing mobile apps. Soft skills are more challenging to express in a convincing way, so look for ways to quantify them with details, such as "nominated for the company's leadership development program."

Getting assessed by a bot before you get the chance to make your case with a human can be unsettling, but follow these tips and you can make the bots your friends rather than your enemies.

WHAT'S YOUR TAKE?

1. What is a company likely to conclude about applicants if it believes they are trying to game the keyword analysis process?
2. Is it ethical for companies to use AI to evaluate job applicants? Why or why not?

Sources: Burning Glass Technologies, accessed 24 April 2018, www.burningglass.com; Alison Doyle, "Resume Keywords and Tips for Using Them," *The Balance Careers*, 4 August 2017, www.thebalancecareers.com; Lily Martis, "Resume 101: How to Use Keywords," Monster, accessed 24 April 2018, www.monster.com.

company resources for a job search, and doing so sends a bad signal to potential employers. Choose a straightforward address that includes your first and last names, along with any additional numbers you might need in order to make it unique.

Use a professional-sounding email address for business correspondence, such as firstname.lastname@gmail.com.

Introductory Statement

You have three options for a brief introductory statement that follows your name and contact information:[24]

- **Career objective.** A career objective identifies either a specific job you want to land or a general career track you would like to pursue. Some experts advise against including a career objective because it can categorize you so narrowly that you miss out on interesting opportunities, and it is essentially about fulfilling your desires, not about meeting the employer's needs. In the past, most résumés included a career objective, but in recent years, more job seekers are using a qualifications summary or a career summary. However, if you have little or no work experience in your target profession, a career objective might be your best option. If you do opt for an objective, word it in a way that relates your aspirations to employer needs.

  You can choose to open with a career objective, a qualifications summary, or a career summary.

- **Qualifications summary.** A qualifications summary offers a brief view of your key qualifications. The goal is to let a reader know within a few seconds what you can deliver. You can title this section generically as "Qualifications Summary" or "Summary of Qualifications," or, if you have one dominant qualification, you can use that as the title. Consider using a qualifications summary if you have one or more important qualifications but don't yet have a long career history. Also, if you haven't been working long but your college education has given you a dominant professional "theme," such as multimedia design or statistical analysis, you can craft a qualifications summary that highlights your educational preparedness.

  If you have a focused skill set but don't yet have a long career history, a qualifications summary is probably the best type of introductory statement for you.

- **Career summary.** A career summary offers a brief recap of your career with the goal of presenting increasing levels of responsibility and performance (see Figure 15.6 on page 503 for an example). A career summary is particularly good for people who have demonstrated the ability to take on increasing levels of responsibility in their chosen field and who want to continue in that field.

Whichever option you choose, make sure it includes the most essential keywords you identified in your research—and adapt these words and phrases to each job opportunity as needed.

Education

If you are early in your career, your education is probably your strongest selling point.

If you're still in college or have recently graduated, education is probably your strongest selling point. Present your educational background in depth, choosing facts that support your professional theme. Give this section a heading such as "Education," "Technical Training," or "Academic Preparation," as appropriate. Then, starting with the most recent, list the name and location of each school you have attended, the month and year of your graduation (say "anticipated graduation: _____" if you haven't graduated yet), your major and minor fields of study, significant skills and abilities you've developed in your coursework, and the degrees or certificates you've earned. Fine-tune your message by listing courses that are most relevant to each job opening, and indicate any scholarships, awards, or academic honors you've received.

The education section should also include relevant training sponsored by business or government organizations. Include high school education only if you are still in college and searching for your first job, and include military training only if is pertinent to your career goals.

Whether you list your grade point average (GPA) depends on where you are in your career and on the quality of your grades. Including it can work to your advantage if it is relatively high (3.5 or above on a 4.0 scale) and you have little or no professional experience. Note that whatever it is, you don't have to include your GPA unless a job posting asks for it. And after you've been working for a year or two, employers will be more interested in how you performed on the job than in college, so you should think about removing your GPA at that point.[25]

Work Experience, Skills, and Accomplishments

When you describe past job responsibilities, identify the skills and knowledge that you can apply to a future job.

This section can be called "Work Experience," "Professional Experience," or "Work and Volunteer Experience," if you have limited work experience and want to bolster that with volunteer experience. Like the education section, the work experience section should focus on your overall theme in a way that shows how your past can contribute to an employer's future. Use keywords to call attention to the skills you've developed on the job and to your ability to handle responsibility. Emphasize what you accomplished in each position, not just the generic responsibilities of the job.

List your jobs in reverse chronological order, starting with the most recent. Include military service and any internships and part-time or temporary jobs related to your career objective. Include the name and location of the employer, and if readers are unlikely to recognize the organization, briefly describe what it does. When you want to keep the name of your current employer confidential, you can identify the firm by industry only ("a large video game developer"). If an organization's name or location has changed since you worked there, state the current name and location and include the old information preceded by "formerly . . ." Before or after each job listing, state your job title and give the years you worked in the job; use the phrase "to present" to denote current employment. Indicate whether a job was part-time.

Devote the most space to jobs that are most recent and most closely related to your target position.

Devote the most space to the jobs that are most recent or most closely related to your target position. If you were personally responsible for something significant, be sure to mention it. Facts about your skills and accomplishments are the most important information you can give a prospective employer, so quantify them whenever possible.

As a general rule, employers will view any experience that occurred more than 10 or 15 years ago as less relevant, although there are certainly exceptions. Not including your earliest positions keeps your résumé from getting too cluttered and avoids emphasizing your age. However many years you do go back, be sure to include every job within that timeframe so that you can show continuous work history (unless of course you were out of the workforce for part of that time).[26]

One helpful exercise is to write a 30-second "commercial" for each major skill you want to highlight. The commercial should offer proof that you really do possess the skill. For your résumé, distill the commercials down to brief phrases; you can use the more detailed proof statements in cover letters and as answers to interview questions.[27]

If you have several part-time, temporary, or entry-level jobs that don't relate to your career objective, you have to use your best judgment when it comes to including or excluding them. Too many minor and irrelevant work details can clutter your résumé, particularly if you've been in the professional workforce for a few years. However, if you don't have a long employment history, including these jobs shows your ability and willingness to keep working.

REAL-TIME UPDATES

LEARN MORE BY VISITING THIS INTERACTIVE WEBSITE

See how well your résumé matches a target job description

Increase your chances of getting past a company's résumé filters. Go to **real-timeupdates.com/ebc13** and select Learn More in the Students section.

Activities and Achievements

You can use this optional section to highlight activities and achievements outside of a work or educational context—but only if they make you a more attractive job candidate. For example, traveling, studying, or working abroad and fluency in multiple languages could weigh in your favor with employers that do business internationally.

Because many employers are involved in their local communities, they tend to look positively on applicants who are active and concerned members of their communities as well. Consider including community service activities that suggest leadership, teamwork, communication skills, technical aptitude, or other valuable attributes.

You should generally avoid indicating membership or significant activity in religious or political organizations (unless, of course, you're applying to such an organization) because doing so might raise concerns among people with differing beliefs or affiliations. However, if you want to highlight skills you developed while involved with such a group, you can refer to it generically as a "not-for-profit organization."

Finally, if you have little or no job experience and not much to discuss outside of your education, you can indicate involvement in athletics or other organized student activities. Also consider mentioning publications, projects, and other accomplishments that required relevant business skills.

Include personal accomplishments only if they suggest special skills or qualities that are relevant to the jobs you're seeking.

Personal Data

In most cases, your résumé should not include any personal data beyond the information described in the previous sections. When applying to U.S. companies, never include any of the following: physical characteristics, age, gender, marital status, sexual orientation, religious or political affiliations, race, national origin, salary history, reasons for leaving jobs, names of previous supervisors, names of references, Social Security number, or student ID number. Expectations differ in other countries, so research the job application process in specific countries if you need more information.

When applying to U.S. companies, your résumé should not include any personal data such as age, marital status, physical description, or Social Security number.

References

For professional and managerial positions, nearly all employers ask for and check references, so you need to be prepared with a list of people who are willing to speak on your behalf.[28] (The availability of references is assumed, so you don't need to put "References available upon request" at the end of your résumé.)

Plan to gather three types of references as you begin your job search:[29]

- *Professional references* are people who have had the opportunity to evaluate the knowledge and skills that you can bring to the jobs you are applying for. Professors and instructors, supervisors, colleagues, and even customers are all good candidates to approach for serving as professional references.
- Some employers may ask for *personal references*, people who are willing to vouch for your character. Good candidates here include people outside your family who have interacted with you in meaningful ways, including coaches, volunteer coordinators, and religious leaders. As appropriate, you may also ask any of your professional references to serve as personal references.
- To complete your LinkedIn profile, you will also need *LinkedIn recommendations* (see page 507).

Gather three types of references: professional references, personal references, and LinkedIn recommendations.

For professional and personal references, you must ask permission before offering anyone's name as a reference. This conversation also gives you the chance to describe the opportunities you are pursuing, which helps your references frame what they have to say about you and lets you verify that each person is a good choice for you. If someone seems hesitant, think twice about including him or her in your list, because you might get a lukewarm recommendation when an employer calls.

Reach out to the people you would like to use as references well before you need them. Describe the opportunities you are pursuing, include links to specific job postings if you have identified any, and provide any information (such as résumé) that people might need to refresh their memories about you and your qualifications.

Prepare your reference sheet with your name and contact information at the top, using the same design and layout you use for your résumé. Then list the strongest three or four references you were able to get. Include each person's name, job title, organization, work address, preferred telephone number, and email address.

Figures 15.4 through 15.6 show how a job applicant can put these guidelines to work in three job-search scenarios.

Completing Your Résumé

4 **LEARNING OBJECTIVE** Characterize the completing step for résumés, including the six most common formats in which you can produce a résumé.

Completing your résumé involves revising it for optimum quality, producing it in the various forms and media you'll need, and proofreading it for any errors before distributing it or publishing it online.

REVISING YOUR RÉSUMÉ

Revise your résumé until it is as concise and clear as possible.

Revising your résumé for clarity and conciseness is essential. Recruiters and hiring managers want to find key pieces of information about you, including your top skills, your current job, and your education, in a matter of seconds. Don't make them work to find or decode this information. Weed out minor details until your résumé is tight, clear, and focused.

If your employment history is brief, keep your printable résumé to one page; you can expand on this in your LinkedIn profile and other online platforms.

The ideal length of your résumé depends on the depth of your experience and the level of the positions for which you are applying. As a general guideline, if you have fewer than five years of professional experience, keep your conventional résumé to one page. For online résumé formats such as LinkedIn, you can always provide links to additional information. If you have more experience and are applying for a higher-level position, you may need to prepare a somewhat longer résumé.[30] For highly technical positions, longer résumés are often the norm as well because the qualifications for such jobs can require more description.

PRODUCING YOUR RÉSUMÉ

Producing your résumé starts with choosing a design strategy and then creating your résumé in as many formats as you'll need.

Choosing a Design Strategy for Your Résumé

The most important consideration in résumé design is that it be easy to read and easy to skim quickly.

Don't pick a résumé style just because it's trendy or different; make sure it works for your specific needs.

You'll find a wide range of résumé designs in use today, from text-only documents that follow a conventional layout to full-color infographics with unique designs. As with every type of business message, keep your audience, your goals, and your resources in mind. Above all else, your résumé must be easy to read and easy for recruiters to skim quickly.[31]

Don't choose a style just because it seems trendy or flashy or different. For example, you can find some eye-catching infographic résumés online, but many of those are created by graphic designers applying for visually oriented jobs in advertising, fashion, web design, and other areas in which graphic design skills are a must. In other words, the intended audience expects an applicant to have design skills, and the résumé is a good opportunity to demonstrate those. In contrast, a colorful, graphically intense résumé might just look odd to recruiters in finance, engineering, or other professions—and it's almost guaranteed to get rejected by an ATS.

REAL-TIME UPDATES
LEARN MORE BY EXPLORING THIS INTERACTIVE WEBSITE
Design inspiration and easy-to-use templates
Canva is one of many online services that let you create a nicely designed résumé. Go to **real-timeupdates.com/ebc13** and select Learn More in the Students section.

The Scenario

You are about to graduate and have found a job opening that is in your chosen field. You don't have any experience in this field, but the courses you've taken in pursuit of your degree have given you a solid academic foundation for this position.

The Opportunity

The job opening is for an associate market analyst with Living Social, the rapidly growing advertising and social commerce service that describes itself as "the online source for discovering valuable local experiences." (A market analyst researches markets to find potentially profitable business opportunities.)

The Communication Challenge

You don't have directly relevant experience as a market analyst, and you might be competing against people who do. Your education is your strongest selling point, so you need to show how your coursework relates to the position.

Don't let your lack of experience hold you back; the job posting makes it clear that this is an entry-level position. For example, the first bullet point in the job description says "Become an expert in market data . . .," and the required skills and experience section says that "Up to 2 years of experience with similar research and analysis is preferred." The important clues here are *become* (the company doesn't expect you to be an expert already) and *preferred* (experience would be great if you have it, but it's not required).

Keywords and Key Phrases

You study the job posting and highlight the following elements:

1. Working in a team environment
2. Research, including identifying trendy new businesses
3. Analyzing data using Microsoft Excel
4. Managing projects
5. Collaborating with technical experts and sales staff
6. Creating new tools to help maximize revenue and minimize risks
7. Bachelor's degree is required
8. Natural curiosity and desire to learn
9. Detail oriented
10. Hands-on experience with social media

Emma Gomes
(847) 555–2153
emma.gomes@mailsystem.net
emmawrites.blogspot.com

Address: **Permanent Address:**
860 North 8th Street, Terre Haute, IN 47809   993 Church Street, Barrington, IL 60010

Summary of Qualifications

- ② • In-depth academic preparation in marketing analysis techniques
- ③ • Intermediate skills with a variety of analytical tools, including Microsoft Excel and Google Analytics
- • Front-line experience with consumers and business owners
- ② ⑩ • Multiple research and communication projects involving the business applications of social media

Education

⑦ B.S. in Marketing (Marketing Management Track), Indiana State University, Terre Haute, IN, anticipated graduation: May 2020

Program coursework

- ⑥ • 45 credits of core business courses, including Business Information Tools, Business Statistics, Principles of Accounting, and Business Finance
- ② • 27 credits of marketing and marketing management courses, including Buyer Behavior, Marketing Research, Product and Pricing Strategy, and seminars in e-commerce and social media

Special projects

- ② • "Handcrafting a Global Marketplace: The Etsy Phenomenon," in-depth analysis of how Etsy transformed the market for handmade craft items by bringing e-commerce capabilities to individual craftspeople
- ① ② ④ ⑥ • "Hybrid Communication Platforms for Small Businesses," team service project for five small businesses in Terre Haute, recommending best practices for combining traditional and social-media methods of customer engagement and providing a customized measurement spreadsheet for each company

Work and Volunteer Experience

⑨ **Independent math tutor, 2015-present.** Assist students with a variety of math courses at the elementary, middle, and high school level; all clients have achieved combined test and homework score improvements of at least one full letter grade, with an average improvement of 38 percent.

⑩ **LeafSpring Food Bank, Terre Haute, IN, 2018-present (weekends during college terms), Volunteer.** Stock food and supply pantries; prepare emergency baskets for new clients; assist director with public relations activities, including website updates and social media news releases.

⑤ ④ ⑩ **Owings Ford, Barrington, IL, 2017–2019 (summers), Customer care agent.** Assisted the service and sales managers of this locally owned car dealership with a variety of customer-service tasks; scheduled service appointments; designed and implemented improvements to service-center waiting room to increase guest comfort; convinced dealership owners to begin using Twitter and Facebook to interact with current and potential customers.

Professional Engagement

⑧ • Collegiate member, American Marketing Association; helped establish the AMA Collegiate Chapter at Indiana State
- • Participated in AMA International Collegiate Case Competition, 2017–2018

Awards

⑧ • Dean's List: 2018, 2019
- • Forward Youth award, Barrington Chamber of Commerce, 2016

Gomes includes phone and email contacts, along with a blog that features academic-oriented writing.

Using a summary of qualifications for her opening statement lets her target the résumé and highlight her most compelling attributes.

Her education is a much stronger selling point than her work experience, so she goes into some detail—carefully selecting course names and project descriptions to echo the language of the job description.

She adjusts the descriptions and accomplishments of each role to highlight the aspects of her work and volunteer experience that are relevant to the position.

The final sections highlight activities and awards that reflect her interest in marketing and her desire to improve her skills.

Notice how Gomes adapts her résumé to "mirror" the keywords and phrases from the job posting:

① Offers concrete evidence of teamwork (rather than just calling herself a "team player," for example)

② Emphasizes research skills and experience in multiple instances

③ Calls out Microsoft Excel, as well as Google Analytics, a key online tool for measuring activity on websites

④ Indicates the ability to plan and carry out projects, even if she doesn't have formal project management experience

⑤ Indicates some experience working in a supportive or collaborative role with technical experts and sales specialists (the content of the work doesn't translate to the new job, but the concept does)

⑥ Suggests the ability to work with new analytical tools

⑦ Displays her B.S. degree prominently

⑧ Demonstrates a desire to learn and to expand her skills

⑨ Tracking the progress of her tutoring clients is strong evidence of a detail-oriented worker—not to mention someone who cares about results and the quality of her work

⑩ Lists business-oriented experience with Facebook, Twitter, and other social media

Figure 15.4   Crafting Your Résumé, Scenario 1: Positioning Yourself for an Ideal Opportunity
Even for an ideal job-search scenario, where your academic and professional experiences and interests closely match the parameters of the job opening, you still need to adapt your résumé content carefully to "echo" the specific language of the job description.[32]

The sample résumés in Figures 15.4 through 15.6 use a classic, conservative design that will serve you well for most business opportunities. Notice how they feature simplicity, an easy-to-read layout, effective use of white space, and clear typefaces. Recruiters can pick out the key pieces of information in a matter of seconds.

The Scenario

You are about to graduate but can't find job openings in the field you'd like to enter. However, you have found an opening that is in a related field, and it would give you the chance to get some valuable work experience.

The Opportunity

The job opening is for a seller support associate with Amazon, the online retail giant. Employees in this position work with merchants that sell products through the Amazon e-commerce system to make sure merchants are successful. In essence, it is a customer service job, but directed at these merchants, not the consumers who buy on Amazon.

The Communication Challenge

This isn't the job you ultimately want, but it is a great opportunity with a well-known company. You note that the position does not require a college degree, so in that sense you might be a bit overqualified. However, you also see a strong overlap between your education and the responsibilities and required skills of the job, so be sure to highlight those.

Keywords and Key Phrases

You study the job posting and highlight the following elements:

1. Be able to predict and respond to merchant needs; good business sense with the ability to appreciate the needs of a wide variety of companies

2. Strong written and oral communication skills

3. High degree of professionalism

4. Self-starter with good time management skills

5. Logically analyze problems and devise solutions

6. Comfortable with computer-based tools, including Microsoft Excel

7. Desire to expand business and technical skills

8. Customer service experience

9. Collaborate with fellow team members to resolve difficult situations

10. Record of high performance regarding quality of work and personal productivity

---

Emma Gomes
(847) 555–2153
emma.gomes@mailsystem.net
emmawrites.blogspot.com

Address:
860 North 8th Street, Terre Haute, IN 47809

Permanent Address:
993 Church Street, Barrington, IL 60010

Summary of Qualifications

⑧ • Front-line customer service experience with consumers and business owners
   • Strong business sense based on work experience and academic preparation
⑥ • Intermediate skills with a variety of software tools, including Microsoft Excel and Google Analytics
⑩ • Record of quality work in both business and academic settings

Education

B.S. in Marketing (Marketing Management Track), Indiana State University, Terre Haute, IN, expected graduation May 2020

Program coursework

⑥ • 45 credits of core business courses, including Business Information Tools, Business Statistics, Principles of Accounting, and Business Finance
① • 27 credits of marketing and marketing management courses, including Marketing Fundamentals, Buyer Behavior, Marketing Research, Retail Strategies, and seminars in e–commerce and social media

Special projects

①② • "Handcrafting a Global Marketplace: The Etsy Phenomenon," in-depth analysis of how the Etsy e-commerce platform helps craftspeople and artisans become more successful merchants
①②⑨ • "Hybrid Communication Platforms for Small Businesses," team service project for five small businesses in Terre Haute, recommending best practices for combining traditional and social–media methods of customer engagement and providing a customized measurement spreadsheet for each company

Work and Volunteer Experience

③④⑩ **Independent math tutor, 2015-present.** Assist students with a variety of math courses at the elementary, middle, and high school level; all clients have achieved combined test and homework score improvements of at least one full letter grade, with an average improvement of 38 percent.

② **LeafSpring Food Bank, Terre Haute, IN, 2018-present (weekends during college terms), Volunteer.** Stock food and supply pantries; prepare emergency baskets for new clients; assist director with public relations activities, including website updates and social media news releases.

⑧ **Owings Ford, Barrington, IL, 2017–2019 (summers), Customer care agent.** Assisted the service and sales managers of this locally owned car dealership with a variety of customer-service tasks; scheduled service appointments; designed and implemented improvements to service-center waiting room to increase ⑤ guest comfort; convinced dealership owners to begin using Twitter and Facebook to interact with current and potential customers.

Professional Engagement

⑦ • Collegiate member, American Marketing Association; helped establish the AMA Collegiate Chapter at Indiana State
   • Participated in AMA International Collegiate Case Competition, 2017–2018

Awards

③④⑩ • Dean's List: 2018, 2019
① • Forward Youth award, Barrington Chamber of Commerce, 2016

Gomes modified her summary of qualifications to increase emphasis on customer service.

She adjusts the selection of highlighted courses to reflect the retail and e-commerce aspects of this particular job opening.

She adjusts the wording of this Etsy project description to closely mirror what Amazon is—an e-commerce platform serving a multitude of independent merchants.

She provides more detail regarding her customer support experience.

The final sections are still relevant to this job opening, so she leaves them unchanged.

Notice how Gomes adapts her résumé to "mirror" the keywords and phrases from the job posting:

① Suggests strong awareness of the needs of various businesses

② Examples of experience with written business communication; she can demonstrate oral communication skills during phone, video, or in-person interviews

③ Results-oriented approach to tutoring business suggests high degree of professionalism, as do the two awards

④ The ability to work successfully as an independent tutor while attending high school and college is strong evidence of self-motivation and good time management

⑤ Indicates ability to understand problems and design solutions

⑥ Suggests the ability to work with a variety of software tools

⑦ Demonstrates a desire to learn and to expand her skills

⑧ Highlights customer service experience

⑨ Offers concrete evidence of teamwork (rather than just calling herself a "team player," for example)

⑩ Tracking the progress of her tutoring clients is strong evidence of someone who cares about results and the quality of her work; Dean's List awards also suggest quality of work; record of working while attending high school and college suggests strong productivity

Figure 15.5 **Crafting Your Résumé, Scenario 2: Repositioning Yourself for Available Opportunities**
If you can't find an ideal job opening, you'll need to adjust your plans and adapt your résumé to the openings that are available. Look for opportunities that meet your near-term financial needs while giving you the chance to expand your skill set so that you'll be even more prepared when an ideal opportunity does come along.[33]

With any résumé design, make sure that readers can find essential information in a matter of seconds.

You can certainly enhance your résumé beyond this style, but do so carefully and always with an eye on what will help the reader and avoid confusing an applicant tracking system. Make subheadings easy to find and easy to read. Avoid dense blocks of text, and use lists to itemize your most important qualifications. Color is not necessary by any means, but if you add color, make it subtle and sophisticated. Above all, don't make the reader work. Your résumé should be a high-efficiency information-delivery system, not a treasure hunt.

The Scenario

Moving forward from Figures 15.4 and 15.5, let's assume you have worked in both those positions, first for two years as a seller support associate at Amazon and since then as an associate market analyst at LivingSocial. You believe you are now ready for a bigger challenge, and the question is how to adapt your résumé for a higher-level position now that you have some experience in your chosen field. (Some of the details from the earlier résumés have been modified to accommodate this example.)

The Opportunity

The job opening is for a senior strategy analyst for Nordstrom. The position is similar in concept to the position at LivingSocial, but at a higher level and with more responsibility.

The Communication Challenge

This job is an important step up; a senior strategy analyst is expected to conduct in-depth financial analysis of business opportunities and make recommendations regarding strategy changes, merchandising partnerships with other companies, and important decisions.

You worked with a wide variety of retailers in your Amazon and Living-Social jobs, including a number of fashion retailers, but you haven't worked directly in fashion retailing yourself.

Bottom line: You can bring a good set of skills to this position, but your financial analysis skills and retailing insights might not be readily apparent, so you'll need to play those up.

Keywords and Key Phrases

You study the job posting and highlight the following elements:

1. Provide research and analysis to guide major business strategy decisions
2. Communicate across business units and departments within Nordstrom
3. Familiar with retail analytics
4. Knowledge of fashion retailing
5. Qualitative and quantitative analysis
6. Project management
7. Strong communication skills
8. Bachelor's required; MBA preferred
9. Advanced skills in financial and statistical modeling
10. Proficient in PowerPoint and Excel

Emma Gomes
(847) 555–2153
emma.gomes@mailsystem.net
Twitter: www.twitter.com/emmagomes
1605 Queen Anne Avenue North, Seattle, WA 98109

Market and Strategy Analyst

❶❸ • Five years of experience in local and online retailing, with three years of focus on market opportunity analysis

❹ • Strong business sense developed through more than 60 marketing programs across a range of retail sectors, including hospitality, entertainment, and fashion

❶❺ • Recognized by senior management for ability to make sound judgment calls in situations with incomplete or conflicting data

❷❻ • Adept at coordinating research projects and marketing initiatives across organizational boundaries and balancing the interests of multiple stakeholders

❾❿ • Advanced skills with leading analysis and communication tools, including Excel, PowerPoint, and Google Analytics

Professional Experience

LivingSocial, Seattle, WA (July 2017–present), Associate market analyst. Analyzed assigned markets for such factors as consumer demand, merchandising opportunities, and seller performance; designed, launched, and managed marketing initiatives in 27 retailing categories, including fashions and accessories; met or exceeded profit targets on 90 percent of all marketing initiatives; appointed team lead/trainer in recognition of strong quantitative and qualitative analysis skills; utilized both established and emerging social media tools and helped business partners use these communication platforms to increase consumer engagement in local markets.

Amazon, Seattle WA (July 2015–June 2017), Seller support associate. Worked with more than 300 product vendors, including many in the fashion and accessories sectors, to assure profitable retailing activities on the Amazon e-commerce platform; resolved vendor issues related to e-commerce operations, pricing, and consumer communication; anticipated potential vendor challenges and assisted in the development of more than a dozen new selling tools that improved vendor profitability while reducing Amazon's vendor support costs by nearly 15 percent.

Education

Evening MBA program, University of Washington, Seattle, WA; anticipated graduation: May 2021. Broad-based program combining financial reporting, marketing strategy, competitive strategy, and supply chain management with individual emphasis on quantitative methods, financial analysis, and marketing decision models.

B.S. in Marketing (Marketing Management Track), Indiana State University, Terre Haute, IN, May 2015. Comprehensive coursework in business fundamentals, accounting and finance, marketing fundamentals, retailing, and consumer communications.

Professional Engagement

• Member, American Marketing Association
• Member, International Social Media Association
• Active in National Retail Federation and Retail Advertising & Marketing Association

Awards

• LivingSocial Top Ten Deals (monthly employee achievement award for designing the most profitable couponing deals); awarded seven times, 2017–2019
• Social Commerce Network's Social Commerce Innovators: 30 Under 30; 2018

Gomes stays with a summary of qualifications as her opening statement but gives it a new title to reflect her experience and to focus on her career path as a market analyst.

Work experience is now her key selling point, so she shifts to a conventional chronological résumé that puts employment ahead of education. She also removes the part-time jobs she had during high school and college.

She updates the education section with a listing for the MBA program she has started (selecting points of emphasis relevant to the job opening) and reduces the amount of detail about her undergraduate degree.

She updates the professional engagement and awards sections with timely and relevant information.

Notice how Gomes adapts her résumé to "mirror" the keywords and phrases from the job posting:

❶ Highlights her experience in market and business analysis and her continuing education in this area

❷ Mentions skill at coordinating cross-functional projects

❸ Lists experiences that relate to the collection and analysis of retail data

❹ Emphasizes the work she has done with fashion-related retailing and retailing in general

❺ Identifies experience and education that relates to quantitative and qualitative analysis (this point overlaps #1 and #3 to a degree)

❻ Mentions project management experience

❼ Lists areas that suggest effective communication skills

❽ Lists education, with emphasis on coursework that relates most directly to the job posting

❾ Mentions work experience and educational background related to these topics

❿ Includes these programs in the list of software tools she uses

Figure 15.6 Crafting Your Résumé, Scenario 3: Positioning Yourself for More Responsibility
When you have a few years of experience under your belt, your résumé strategy should shift to emphasize work history and accomplishments. Here is how Emma Gomes might reshape her résumé if she had held the two jobs described in Figures 15.4 and 15.5 and is now ready for a bigger challenge. For an application letter that could accompany this résumé, see Figure 16.3 on page 525.[34]

Depending on the companies you apply to, you might want to produce your résumé in as many as six formats (all are explained in the following sections):

• Conventional résumé
• Scannable résumé
• Plain-text file
• Microsoft Word file

Be prepared to produce versions of your résumé in multiple formats.

- Online résumé
- PDF file

Unfortunately, no single format or medium will work for all situations, and employer expectations continue to change as technology evolves. Find out what each employer or job website expects, and provide your résumé in that specific format.

Considering Photos, Videos, Presentations, and Infographics

As you produce your résumé in various formats, you will encounter the question of whether to include a photograph of yourself on or with your résumé. For print or digital documents that you will be submitting to employers or job websites, the safest advice is to avoid photos. The reason is that seeing visual cues of the age, ethnicity, and gender of candidates early in the selection process exposes employers to complaints of discriminatory hiring practices. In fact, some employers won't even look at résumés that include photos, and some applicant tracking systems automatically discard résumés with any extra files.[35] However, photographs are acceptable and expected for LinkedIn and other online formats where you are not actively submitting a résumé to an employer.

Some applicants create PowerPoint or Prezi presentations, videos, or infographics to supplement a conventional résumé. These other formats have the appealing options of flexibility and multimedia capabilities. For instance, you can present a menu of choices on the opening screen and allow viewers to click through to sections of interest. (Note that most of the things you can accomplish with a presentation can be done with an online résumé, which is probably more convenient for most readers.)

A video résumé can be a compelling supplement as well, but be aware that some employment law experts advise employers not to view videos, at least not until after candidates have been evaluated solely on their credentials. The reason for this caution is the same as with photographs. In addition, videos are more cumbersome to evaluate than paper or electronic résumés, and some recruiters refuse to watch them.[36] However, not all companies share this concern over videos, so you'll have to research their individual preferences. In fact, the online retailer Zappos encourages "video cover letters" from interested candidates.[37]

An infographic résumé attempts to convey a person's career development and skill set graphically through a visual metaphor such as a timeline or subway map or as a poster with an array of individual elements. A well-designed infographic could be an intriguing element of the job-search package for candidates in certain situations and professions because it can definitely stand out from traditional résumés and can show a high level of skill in visual communication. However, infographics are likely to be incompatible with applicant tracking systems and with the screening habits of most recruiters, so don't submit an infographic when a company expects a conventional résumé. In virtually every situation, an infographic should complement a conventional résumé, not replace it. In addition, custom infographics require skills in graphic design, and if you lack those skills, you'll need to hire a designer. For a simpler, template-based approach, you might try an online service such as Visualize.me (**visualize.me**).

> **In most cases, it's best not to include photos with résumés that you send to employers or post on job websites.**

REAL-TIME UPDATES

LEARN MORE BY READING THIS ARTICLE

Points to ponder if you are considering an infographic résumé

Infographic résumés can seem like an inviting option, but consider these points carefully. Go to **real-timeupdates.com/ebc13** and select Learn More in the Students section.

Producing a Conventional Printed Résumé

Even though most of your application activity will take place online, having a copy of a conventional printed résumé is important for taking to job fairs, interviews, and other events. Many employers expect you to bring a printed résumé to the interview, even if you applied online. The résumé can serve as a note-taking form or discussion guide, and it is tangible evidence of your attention to professionalism and detail.[38] When printing a résumé, choose a heavier, higher-quality paper designed specifically for résumés and other important documents. White or slightly off-white is the best color choice. Avoid papers with borders or backgrounds.

> **Use high-quality paper when printing your résumé.**

Printing a Scannable Résumé

You might encounter a company that prefers *scannable résumés*, a type of printed résumé that is specially formatted to be compatible with optical scanning systems that convert

> **You may encounter an employer that prefers printed résumés in scannable format, but most now want online submissions.**

printed documents to digital text. These systems were once quite common, but their use has declined as more employers prefer email delivery or website application forms.[39] A scannable résumé can contain the same information as your conventional résumé, but it needs to have a simple format without underlining, bullet points, and other elements that can confuse the scanning system. If you need to produce a scannable résumé, search online for "formatting a scannable résumé" to get detailed instructions.

Creating a Plain-Text File of Your Résumé

A *plain-text file* (sometimes known as an ASCII text file) is a digital version of your résumé that has no font formatting, no bullet symbols, no colors, no lines or boxes, and no other special formatting. The plain-text version can be used in two ways. First, you can include it in the body of an email message, for employers who want email delivery but don't want file attachments. Second, you can copy and paste the sections into the application forms on an employer's website.

A plain-text version is easy to create with your word processor. Start with the file you used to create your résumé, select the "Save As" choice to save it as "plain text" or whichever similarly labeled option your software has, and verify the result using a basic text editor (such as Microsoft Notepad). If necessary, reformat the page manually, moving text and inserting space as needed. For simplicity's sake, left-justify all your headings rather than trying to center them manually.

> A plain-text version of your résumé is simply a computer file without any of the formatting that you typically apply using word-processing software.

> Verify the plain-text file that you create with word-processing apps; it might need a few manual adjustments using a text editor such as Notepad.

Creating a Word File of Your Résumé

Some employers and job websites will ask you to upload a Microsoft Word file or attach it to an email message. This method of transferring information preserves the design and layout of your résumé and saves you the trouble of creating a plain-text version. However, before you submit a file to anyone, make sure your computer is free of viruses. Infecting a potential employer's computer will not make a good first impression.

> Some employers and websites want your résumé in Microsoft Word format; make sure your computer is free from viruses before you upload the file.

Creating a PDF Version of Your Résumé

Creating a PDF file is a simple procedure, depending on the software you have. In newer versions of Microsoft Word, for example, you can save a document directly as a PDF file. The advantages of creating PDFs are that you preserve the formatting of your résumé (unlike pasting plain text into an email message) and that you create a file type that is less vulnerable to viruses than word-processor files.

Creating an Online Résumé

A variety of online résumé formats, variously referred to as *e-portfolios*, *interactive résumés*, or *social media résumés*, provide the opportunity to create a dynamic multimedia presentation of your qualifications. You can expand on the information contained in your basic résumé with links to projects, publications, screencasts, online videos, course lists, blogs, social networking profiles, and other elements that give employers a more complete picture of who you are and what you can offer. For most job hunters, though, the most important online résumé you can create is your LinkedIn profile (see page 507).

> You have various options for posting a résumé online, but your LinkedIn profile is the most important of these.

PROOFREADING YOUR RÉSUMÉ

Employers view your résumé as a concrete example of your attention to quality and detail. Your résumé doesn't need to be good or pretty good—it needs to be *perfect*. A human reader will view errors as signs of carelessness, and an applicant tracking system can be programmed to automatically reject résumés with spelling and grammatical errors.[40]

Your résumé is one of the most important documents you'll ever write, so don't rush or cut corners when it comes to proofreading. Check all headings and lists for clarity and parallelism, and be sure your grammar, spelling, and punctuation are correct. Double-check all dates, phone numbers, email addresses, and other essential data. Ask at least three other people to read it, too. As the creator of the material, you could stare at a mistake for weeks and not see it.

> Your résumé needs to be *perfect*, so proofread it thoroughly and ask several other people to verify it, too.

DISTRIBUTING YOUR RÉSUMÉ

When distributing your résumé, pay close attention to the specific instructions provided by each employer, job website, or other recipient.

How you distribute your résumé depends on the number of employers you target and their preferences for receiving résumés. Employers usually list their requirements on their websites, so verify this information and follow it carefully. Beyond that, here are some general distribution tips:

- **Mailing printed résumés.** Take some care with the packaging. Spend a few extra cents to mail your documents in a flat 9 × 12 envelope, or better yet, use a Priority Mail flat-rate envelope, which gives you a sturdy cardboard mailer and faster delivery for just a few more dollars.

- **Emailing your résumé.** Some employers want applicants to include the text of their résumés in the body of an email message; others prefer an attached Microsoft Word or PDF file. If you have a reference number or a job ad number, include it in the subject line of your email message.

- **Submitting your résumé to an employer's website.** Many employers, including most large companies, now prefer or require applicants to submit their résumés online. In some instances, you will be asked to upload a complete file. In others, you will need to copy and paste sections of your résumé into individual boxes in an online application form.

Don't post a résumé on any public website unless you understand its privacy and security policies.

- **Posting your résumé on job websites.** Before you upload your résumé to any site, learn about its privacy protection. Some sites allow you to specify levels of confidentiality, such as letting employers search your qualifications without seeing your personal contact information or preventing your current employer from seeing your résumé. You can also set your résumé to *private* on sites such as Monster so that you can use it to apply for jobs you find there but it won't be viewable or searchable by anyone.[41] To protect yourself from identity thieves and spammers, don't post your résumé to any website that doesn't give you the option of restricting the display of your personal information.

For a quick summary of the steps to take when planning, writing, and completing your résumé, refer to "Checklist: Writing an Effective Résumé." For the latest information on résumé writing and distribution, visit **http://real-timeupdates.com/ebc13** and select Chapter 15.

CHECKLIST ✔ Writing an Effective Résumé

A. Plan your résumé.
- ✔ Analyze your purpose and audience carefully to make sure your message meets employers' needs.
- ✔ Gather pertinent information about your target companies.
- ✔ Select the required media types by researching the preferences of each employer.
- ✔ Organize your résumé around your strengths, choosing the chronological, functional, or combination structure. (Be careful about using the functional structure.)

B. Write your résumé.
- ✔ Keep your résumé honest.
- ✔ Adapt your résumé to your audience to highlight the qualifications each employer is looking for.
- ✔ Choose a career objective, qualifications summary,

or career summary as your introductory statement—and make it concise, concrete, and reader-focused.
- ✔ Use powerful language to convey your name and contact information, introductory statement, education, work experience, skills, work or school accomplishments, and activities and achievements.

C. Complete your résumé.
- ✔ Revise your résumé until it is clear, concise, compelling—and perfect.
- ✔ Produce your résumé in all the formats you might need: traditional printed résumé, scannable, plain-text file, Microsoft Word file, PDF, or online.
- ✔ Proofread your résumé to make sure it is absolutely perfect.
- ✔ Distribute your résumé using the means that each employer prefers.

Building an Effective LinkedIn Profile

LinkedIn (www.linkedin.com) is the most important website to incorporate in your job search. Employment recruiters search LinkedIn for candidates far more than any other social network, many employers now want to see your LinkedIn profile rather than a conventional résumé, and companies doing background checks on you are almost certain to look for your LinkedIn profile.[42]

You can think of LinkedIn as a "socially networked multimedia résumé." An effective LinkedIn profile includes all the information from your conventional résumé, plus some additional features that help you present yourself in a compelling way to potential employers. Here are nine tips for building an effective profile:[43]

1. **Photo.** Add a photo that says "professional" without being overly formal. You don't need to hire a professional photographer, but the photo needs to be clear and lit well enough so that your face isn't in shadow. Stand against a visually "quiet" background that won't distract viewers, dress appropriately for the jobs you are pursuing, and remember to smile.

2. **Headline.** Write a headline that expresses who you are or aspire to be as a professional, such as "Data science major ready to make data come alive through leading-edge techniques in data mining, visualization, and AI." Include keywords that target employers are likely to be searching for. As with other text fields on LinkedIn, you have a limited number of characters to work with here, so focus on your most valuable attributes. Erica Baker, for instance, establishes herself as a technically astute, creative problem-solver with her LinkedIn headline: "I like to slay big problems and puzzles. My weapons of choice are logic, data, curiosity, and code."[44]

3. **Summary.** Write a summary that captures where you are and where you are going. Imagine that you are talking to a hiring manager in a personal and conversational tone, telling the story of where you've been and where you would like to go—but expressed in terms of meeting an employer's business needs. Highlight your job experience, education, skills, accomplishments, target industry, and career direction. Unlike the introductory statement on your conventional résumé, which you can fine-tune for every job opportunity, your LinkedIn summary offers a more general picture of who you are as a professional. Be sure to work in as many of the keywords from your research as you can, while keeping the style natural. Employers can use a variety of search tools to find candidates, and they'll look for these keywords.

4. **Experience.** Fill out the experience section using the material from your conventional résumé. Make sure the details of your employment match your résumé, as employers are likely to cross-check. However, you can expand beyond those basics, including linking to photos and videos of work-related accomplishments.

5. **Recommendations.** Ask for recommendations from people you know on LinkedIn. You may have a limited number of connections as you start out, but as your network expands you'll have more people to ask. A great way to get recommendations is to give them to the people in your network.

6. **Featured skills.** List your top skills and areas of expertise. As you expand your network, endorse the skills of people you know; many users will endorse your skills in return.

7. **Education.** Make sure your educational listing is complete and matches the information on your conventional résumé.

8. **Accomplishments.** LinkedIn offers a variety of categories that let you highlight academic achievements, special projects, publications, professional certifications, important coursework, honors, patents, and more. If you don't have an extensive work history, use this section to feature academic projects and other accomplishments that demonstrate your skills.

9. **Volunteer experience and causes.** Add volunteering activities and charitable organizations that you support.

---

5 LEARNING OBJECTIVE
Identify nine tips for creating a successful LinkedIn profile.

MOBILE APP
Stay in touch with your professional network with the **LinkedIn** app.

Your LinkedIn profile is a great opportunity to showcase projects, awards, and multimedia elements.

Figure 15.7 offers a helpful summary of these tips, and Figure 15.8 shows an example of an effective profile. For the most current instructions on performing these tasks, visit the LinkedIn Help center at **www.linkedin.com/help/linkedin**. Remember that the more robust you make your profile, the better your chances are of catching the eye of company recruiters.

In addition to completing your profile, search for and join groups that focus on your professional interests. This is a great way to expand your network and learn from leaders in your field. Be sure to review the privacy and communication settings as well. The options are fairly extensive, so take time to consider each one carefully.

For more information on résumé writing, visit **real-timeupdates.com/ebc13** and select Chapter 15.

> LinkedIn groups are an opportunity to expand your network and learn from experienced professionals.

Profile photo

- Strike a friendly pose that's not too formal or too casual.
- Make sure your face isn't in shadow.
- Stand against a visually quiet background that doesn't compete with your image.
- Don't wear dark glasses.
- Dress appropriately for target jobs in your chosen profession.

Flashon Studio/123RF

Headline

- Express who you are or aspire to be as a professional.
- Include keywords that target employers are likely to be searching for.
- Focus on your most valuable attributes to make best use of the limited space available.

Summary

- Capture where you are and where you are going—in terms of how you can contribute to a company.
- Imagine you are talking to a hiring manager in a company you want to work for; use a personal, conversational voice.
- Include top-level highlights of your job experience, education, skills, accomplishments, target industry, and career direction.
- Use keywords from target job descriptions.

Experience

- Start with the material from your résumé.
- Make sure the basic details of your employment (years, job titles, company names) match your résumé.
- Expand beyond those basics as appropriate, including linking to photos and videos of work-related accomplishments.

Recommendations

- Ask for recommendations from people you know on LinkedIn.
- As your network expands you'll have more people to ask.
- A great way to get recommendations is to give them to the people in your network.

Skills

- List your top skills and areas of expertise.
- As you expand your network, endorse the skills of people you know.
- Many users will endorse your skills in return.

Education

- Make sure your educational listing is complete.
- Include relevant military or company training and independent coursework.
- Verify that it matches the information on your conventional résumé.

Accomplishments

- Explore all the categories available to find opportunities to highlight academic successes, leadership qualities, creative thinking, industry certifications, and so on.
- Note that you need to manually add these categories to your profile.
- If you don't have extensive work history, use this section to feature academic projects and awards.

Volunteering

- Add volunteer work you've done, particularly activities that developed professional skills such as project management or team leadership.

Figure 15.7 **Quick Tips for a Compelling LinkedIn Profile**
Follow these tips to get started on building or expanding your LinkedIn profile.

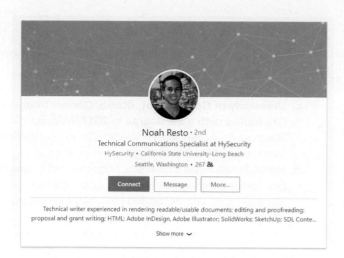

Noah Resto · 2nd
Technical Communications Specialist at HySecurity
HySecurity • California State University-Long Beach
Seattle, Washington • 267 🔗

[Connect] [Message] [More...]

Technical writer experienced in rendering readable/usable documents; editing and proofreading; proposal and grant writing; HTML; Adobe InDesign; Adobe Illustrator; SolidWorks; SketchUp; SDL Conte...

Show more ⌄

Experience

Technical Communications Specialist
HySecurity
Sep 2017 – Present • 9 mos
Kent, Washington

Author, edit, review, and update current HySecurity documentation with interfacing and collaboration with engineering, technical training staff, field service technicians and managers, technical support, marketing, and production line. Improve HySecurity documentation to better serve customer base with new manual, instruction, field service bulletin, and addendum layouts and designs that better effectively convey intended purposes and provide end users much more clarity and easier time installing and maintaining products.

Technical Writer/Editor
General Atomics Aeronautical Systems
Aug 2016 – Aug 2017 • 1 yr 1 mo
San Diego, CA

Author, edit, and peer review unmanned aircraft technical documentation for the continuous development of Interactive Electronic Technical Manuals (IETM) for MQ-9 Aircraft platforms in accordance with S1000D standards and customers requirements. Initiates collaborative discussions with writers, illustrators, leads, and supervisors to solve complex project issues. Utilizes Microsoft Office Suite, SnagIt, SDL Contenta, Data Module Requirements List (DMRL), DevTrackClient, PTC ArborText Editor, IsoView, IsoDraw, and XML-based writing to present information accurately according to source material from engineers, released drawings, schematics, software documentation, and design specifications.

Technical Writer/Illustrator
Multiquip Inc.
Jul 2014 – Aug 2016 • 2 yrs 2 mos
Carson, CA

Responsible for updating and creating user manuals for construction equipment, power generation, lighting, and parts provided by vendors and product managers. Works with Adobe InDesign, Illustrator, Photoshop CS6 and CC; SolidWorks; CorelDraw; and SketchUp to create lay outs of texts and illustrations to create Installation Instructions or Service Bulletins for power and construction equipment.

Copywriter
Smarthome
Nov 2013 – Jun 2014 • 8 mos
Irvine, CA

Responsible for writing detailed, SEO friendly Webpages for new products, updating existing Webpages for current products, researching and testing products, and other tasks.

Proposal Writer
Sullivan International Group
Aug 2013 – Nov 2013 • 4 mos
Long Beach, CA

Proposal writing internship assisting and learning Sullivan International Group's proposal writing strategies via research, outlining, advertising, preparation, and responding to RFPs and CFPs.

Show more ⌄

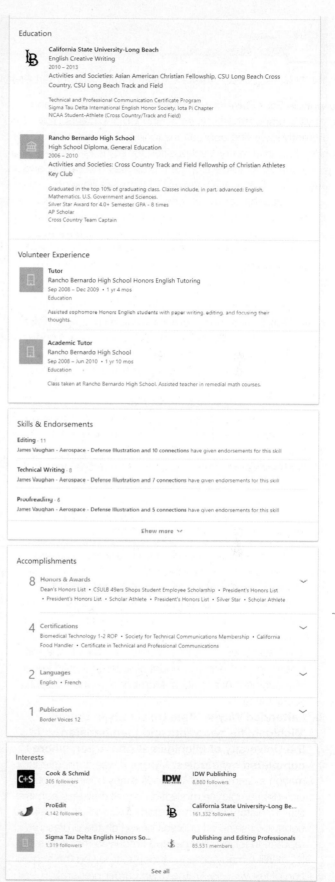

Education

California State University-Long Beach
English Creative Writing
2010 – 2013
Activities and Societies: Asian American Christian Fellowship, CSU Long Beach Cross Country, CSU Long Beach Track and Field

Technical and Professional Communication Certificate Program
Sigma Tau Delta International English Honor Society, Iota Pi Chapter
NCAA Student-Athlete (Cross Country/Track and Field)

Rancho Bernardo High School
High School Diploma, General Education
2006 – 2010
Activities and Societies: Cross Country Track and Field Fellowship of Christian Athletes Key Club

Graduated in the top 10% of graduating class. Classes include, in part, advanced: English, Mathematics, U.S. Government and Sciences.
Silver Star Award for 4.0+ Semester GPA - 8 times
AP Scholar
Cross Country Team Captain

Volunteer Experience

Tutor
Rancho Bernardo High School Honors English Tutoring
Sep 2008 – Dec 2009 • 1 yr 4 mos
Education

Assisted sophomore Honors English students with paper writing, editing, and focusing their thoughts.

Academic Tutor
Rancho Bernardo High School
Sep 2008 – Jun 2010 • 1 yr 10 mos
Education

Class taken at Rancho Bernardo High School. Assisted teacher in remedial math courses.

Skills & Endorsements

Editing · 11
James Vaughan - Aerospace - Defense Illustration and 10 connections have given endorsements for this skill

Technical Writing · 8
James Vaughan - Aerospace - Defense Illustration and 7 connections have given endorsements for this skill

Proofreading · 8
James Vaughan - Aerospace - Defense Illustration and 5 connections have given endorsements for this skill

Show more ⌄

Accomplishments

8 Honors & Awards
Dean's Honors List • CSULB 49ers Shops Student Employee Scholarship • President's Honors List • President's Honors List • Scholar Athlete • President's Honors List • Silver Star • Scholar Athlete

4 Certifications
Biomedical Technology 1-2 ROP • Society for Technical Communications Membership • California Food Handler • Certificate in Technical and Professional Communications

2 Languages
English • French

1 Publication
Border Voices 12

Interests

Cook & Schmid — 305 followers
IDW Publishing — 8,880 followers
ProEdit — 4,142 followers
California State University-Long Be... — 161,332 followers
Sigma Tau Delta English Honors So... — 1,319 followers
Publishing and Editing Professionals — 85,531 members

See all

Figure 15.8   Effective LinkedIn Profile
Noah Resto effectively communicates his capabilities and professional personality through his LinkedIn profile.

ON THE JOB: SOLVING COMMUNICATION DILEMMAS AT **PATREON**

You work in Erica Baker's engineering group at Patreon, and one of your responsibilities is screening job applicants. You are currently reviewing applications to fill a project coordinator opening. This is an entry-level position for someone who helps a project manager keep development projects on schedule and on budget. Some technical awareness of software development is a plus, because the coordinator needs to interact with software architects and coders, but the job is primarily a business role. The applicant pool is a mix of recent college graduates and people with a few years of business experience. Solve these challenges by using what you've learned about presenting oneself effectively on a résumé.

1. You've learned to pay close attention to the introductory statement on résumés in order to match applicants' interests with appropriate job openings. Which of the following is the most compelling statement for this position?

   a. Career objective: A fulfilling project-management career in a high-tech company

   b. Qualifications summary: Proven track record of keeping every project ahead of schedule and under budget while shepherding companies toward explosive growth

   c. Qualifications summary: Broad academic preparation in business principles and business management, with additional coursework in computer science.

   d. Career objective: To learn all I can about project management in an exciting environment with a company whose reputation is as outstanding as Patreon's.

2. Of the education sections included in the résumés, which of the following is the most effective?

   a. **Morehouse College, Atlanta, GA, 2013–2017.** Received BA degree with a major in Business Administration and a minor in Information Systems. Graduated with a 3.65 grade point average. Played varsity football and basketball. Worked 15 hours per week in the library. Coordinated the local student chapter of the American Management Association. Member of Alpha Phi Alpha social fraternity.

   b. **I attended Wayne State University in Detroit, Michigan, for two years and then transferred to the University of Michigan at Ann Arbor, where I completed my studies.** My major was computer information systems, but I also took many business courses, including employee motivation, small business administration, history of business start-ups, and organizational behavior. I selected courses based on the professors' reputation for excellence, and I received mostly A's and B's. Unlike many college students, I viewed the acquisition of knowledge—rather than career preparation—as my primary goal. I believe I have received a well-rounded education that has prepared me to approach technical situations as problem-solving exercises.

   c. **University of Connecticut, Storrs, Connecticut. Graduated with a BA degree in 2017.** Majored in Business Administration. Minored in Computer Science. Graduated with a 2.85 average.

   d. **North Texas State University.** I first majored in general business studies but switched to financial management. Received a scholarship offered by Rotary International recognizing academic achievement in business courses. I also won the MEGA award in 2015. Dean's List.

3. Which of these résumé sections does the best job of portraying each candidate's part-time work experience?

   a. **McDonald's, Peoria, IL, 2013–2014.** Part-time cook. Worked 15 hours per week while attending high school. Prepared all menu items. Received employee-of-the-month award for outstanding work habits.
   University Grill, Ames, IA, 2015–2016. Part-time cook. Worked 20 hours per week while attending college. Prepared hot and cold sandwiches. Helped manager purchase ingredients. Trained new kitchen workers. Prepared work schedules for kitchen staff.

   b. Although I have never held a full-time job, I have worked part-time and during summer vacations throughout my high school and college years. During my freshman and sophomore years in high school, I bagged groceries at the A&P store three afternoons a week, where I was generally acknowledged as one of the hardest-working employees. During my junior and senior years, I worked at the YMCA as an after-school counselor for elementary school children. I know I made a positive difference in their lives because I still get letters from some of them. During summer vacations while I was in college, I did construction work for a local homebuilder. The job paid well, and I also learned a lot about carpentry. I also worked part-time in college in the student cafeteria.

   c. **Macy's Department Store, Sherman Oaks, CA, Summers, 2011–2014. Sales Consultant, Furniture Department.** Interacted with a diverse group of customers to satisfy their individual needs and make their shopping experience efficient and enjoyable. Under the direction of the sales manager, prepared employee schedules and completed departmental reports. Demonstrated computer skills and attention to detail while assisting with inventory management and handling a variety of special orders and customer requests. Received the CEO Award (for best monthly sales performance) three times.

   d. **Athens, GA, Civilian Member of Public Safety Committee, January–December 2017.**
   • Organized and promoted a lecture series on vacation safety and home security for the residents of Athens, GA; recruited and trained seven committee members

to help plan and produce the lectures; persuaded local businesses to finance the program; designed, printed, and distributed flyers; wrote and distributed press releases; attracted an average of 120 people to each of three lectures

- Developed a questionnaire to determine local residents' home security needs; directed the efforts of 10 volunteers working on the survey; prepared written report for city council and delivered oral summary of findings at town meeting; helped persuade city to fund new home security program
- Initiated the Business Security Forum as an annual meeting at which local business leaders could meet to discuss safety and security issues; created promotional flyers for the first forum; convinced 19 business owners to fund a business security survey; arranged press coverage of the first forum

4. While you are analyzing four résumés suggested by your applicant tracking system, a fellow employee hands you the following résumé and says this person would be great for the project coordinator opening. What action will you take?

Darius Jaidee
809 N. Perkins Rd, Stillwater, OK 74075
Phone: (405) 555-0098
Email: dariusj@okustate.edu

Career Objective: To build a successful career in business management

Summary of Qualifications: As a student at the University of Oklahoma, Stillwater, completed a wide variety of assignments that demonstrate skills related to business and management. For example:

Planning skills: As president of the university's foreign affairs forum, organized six lectures and workshops featuring 36 speakers from 16 foreign countries within a nine-month period. Identified and recruited the speakers, handled their travel arrangements, and scheduled the facilities.

Communication skills: Wrote more than 25 essays and term papers on various academic topics, including at least 10 dealing with business and finance. As a senior, wrote a 20-page analysis of financial trends in the petroleum industry, interviewing five high-ranking executives in accounting and finance positions at ConocoPhillips's refinery in Ponca City, Oklahoma, and company headquarters in Houston, Texas.

Business and computer skills: Competent in all areas of Microsoft Office, including Excel spreadsheets and Access databases. Assisted with accounting activities in parents' small business, including the conversion from paper-based to computer-based accounting (Peachtree software). Have taken courses in accounting, financial planning, database design, web design, and computer networking.

For more information, including employment history, please access my e-portfolio at **http://dariusjaidee.com**.

- **a.** Definitely recommend that Patreon take a look at this outstanding candidate.
- **b.** Reject the application. He doesn't give enough information about when he attended college, what he majored in, or where he has worked.
- **c.** Review the candidate's web-based e-portfolio, in which he has posted many of his school projects. If the assessment contains the missing information and the candidate sounds promising, recommend him for a closer look. If vital information is still missing, send the candidate an email requesting additional information. Make the decision once you receive all necessary information.
- **d.** Consider the candidate's qualifications relative to those of other applicants. Recommend him if you cannot find three or four other applicants with more directly relevant qualifications.

END OF CHAPTER

Learning Objectives Checkup

Assess your understanding of the principles in this chapter by reading each learning objective and studying the accompanying exercises. You can check your responses against the answer key on page 613.

Objective 15.1: List eight key steps to finding the ideal opportunity in today's job market.

1. How does writing the "story of you" help you plan your job search and craft your résumé?
   - **a.** It helps you focus your résumé on your needs, rather than on the employer's.
   - **b.** It helps you think about where you want to go and how to present yourself to target employers.
   - **c.** It allows you to avoid writing a traditional structured résumé.
   - **d.** It helps you plan the speech you should make at the beginning of every job interview.

2. _____ of _____ is a measure of how closely new employees meet a company's needs.

3. Which of the following best describes the process of networking as it applies to your career?
   - **a.** Making sure you are plugged into the online scene so that you don't miss out on any new internet developments

b. Making informal connections with a broad sphere of mutually beneficial business contacts

c. Asking as many people as possible to alert you to interesting job opportunities

d. Making sure you get to know everyone in your company shortly after accepting a new position

4. If you don't yet have significant work experience but still want to become a valued network member, which of the following tactics should you consider?

   a. Limit your networking to people whose work experience is similar to yours so that you can share similar information.

   b. Create a convenient, foldable, business-card-size version of your résumé that you can give to everyone you meet so they don't have to carry around a full-size copy.

   c. Avoid networking until you have enough work experience to be able to offer insider tips on the job market in your industry.

   d. Research recent trends in the business world in order to have interesting and useful information at your fingertips whenever you encounter people in your network.

Objective 15.2: Explain the process of planning your résumé, including how to choose the best résumé organization.

5. What is the purpose of a résumé?

   a. To provide a complete catalog of your skills and knowledge

   b. To secure invitations to interviews

   c. To land you a job

   d. To fill in gaps and overcome weaknesses in your online application material

6. A _____ résumé highlights employment experience, listing jobs in reverse order from most recent to earliest.

7. A _____ résumé focuses on a person's particular skills and competencies, without itemizing his or her job history.

8. A _____ résumé uses elements of both the chronological and functional formats.

9. Which of the following is a key advantage of the chronological résumé?

   a. Employers prefer it because this format makes it easy for them to see your work history.

   b. Employers prefer it because it is more compatible with today's applicant tracking systems.

   c. It is much easier to write than other formats.

   d. Once you've created it, you rarely need to update it.

10. Why are many employers suspicious of the functional résumé?

    a. It allows applicants to hide or downplay lengthy periods of unemployment or a lack of career progress.

    b. It doesn't scan into computer databases as effectively as other résumé formats.

    c. It doesn't provide any information about education.

    d. It encourages applicants to include accomplishments that were the result of teamwork rather than individual efforts.

11. Which of the following is a disadvantage of the combination résumé?

    a. It is impossible to convert to scannable format.

    b. It tends to be longer than other formats and can be repetitive.

    c. It doesn't work for people who have extensive job experience.

    d. The combination résumé has no disadvantages.

Objective 15.3: Describe the tasks involved in writing your résumé, and list the sections to consider including in your résumé.

12. Which of the following sections should be included in any résumé, regardless of the format you've chosen?

    a. Contact information, education, and work experience

    b. Contact information, education, and personal references

    c. Personal data, contact information, and education

    d. Education, personal references, and career objectives

13. Why do some experts recommend against using a career objective as the introductory statement on your résumé?

    a. It can limit your possibilities as a candidate, particularly if you want to be considered for a variety of positions.

    b. It shows that you're selfish and thinking only about your own success.

    c. It shows that you're unrealistic because no one can plan a career that might last for 40 or 50 years.

    d. It helps focus you as a candidate in the minds of potential employers.

14. How does a qualifications summary differ from a career summary?

    a. They are identical.

    b. A qualifications summary offers a brief view of your most important skills and attributes, whereas a career summary is a recap of your career progress.

    c. No one uses a qualifications summary anymore, whereas a career summary is still popular.

    d. The career summary is best for recent graduates, whereas the qualifications summary is best for people with a decade or two of experience.

15. Which should come first on your résumé, your education or your work experience?

    a. Education should come first.

    b. Work experience should come first.

    c. It depends on which is more meaningful to an employer, given where you are in your career at this moment.

    d. The best résumés today use a two-column format in which education and work experience are listed side by side.

16. How much personal data should you put on a résumé aimed at U.S. employers?

    a. You should list your age, marital status, and physical handicaps that might require special accommodation.

    b. You should list your age, marital status, a general assessment of your health (without mentioning any specific problems), and religious affiliation.

    c. You should not list any personal data on your résumé.

    d. You should not list anything related to health or nationality, but you should list age, gender, and salary history (assuming you've had at least one full-time job).

Objective 15.4: Characterize the completing step for résumés, including the six most common formats in which you can produce a résumé.

17. Which of these is the best general design strategy to take with your résumé?
    a. Study what is currently trendy and mimic that style so employers know you are in touch with the shifting marketplace.
    b. Unless an employer specifically requests a traditional résumé, go with a video or infographic résumé.
    c. Choose the best design for your audience, your goals, and your resources—and make sure your résumé is easy to read.
    d. Use plenty of color to stand out from traditional black-and-white résumés.

18. Which of the following best describes the level of quality you should achieve when producing your résumé?
    a. With the advent of email and social networking, most companies are much more relaxed about grammar, spelling, and other old-school concerns, so don't sweat the details.
    b. The typical recruiter in a major corporation sees so many résumés on any given day that most errors pass by unnoticed.
    c. Your résumé needs to be perfect.
    d. Your résumé should reflect your work habits, so if you're more of a strategic thinker and don't worry about insignificant details, make sure your résumé reflects that.

19. A/an _____ file of your résumé is a digital version that has the same content as a traditional résumé but has had all the formatting removed so that it can be easily emailed or copied into online forms.

20. Which of these is a significant advantage of an online résumé?
    a. You can expand on the information contained in your basic résumé with links to projects, publications, screencasts, online videos, course lists, social networking profiles, and other elements.
    b. You can build up your résumé over time and don't have to worry about having every little detail in place when you launch your job search.
    c. You can use lots of color.
    d. You can use the flexibility of the web to provide extensive details on your life history.

Objective 15.5: Identify nine tips for creating a successful LinkedIn profile.

21. Which of these best characterizes the role LinkedIn should play in your career-management efforts?
    a. LinkedIn is the most important website to incorporate in your job search because many recruiters search it for candidates and include it in background checks.
    b. LinkedIn is only truly useful for professionals and managers with at least 5 years of experience.
    c. You should consider LinkedIn for your career communication if you don't think Facebook or Twitter can give you the means to present your qualifications.
    d. The best use of LinkedIn is to provide only a short summary of your job history, but it should not be used as the online equivalent of a résumé.

22. How should you use the headline field in your LinkedIn profile?
    a. Update it regularly with breaking news from the business world.
    b. Use it to briefly express who you are or aspire to be as a professional.
    c. Use it to summarize your education and career history.
    d. Use it for your name and college degrees.

Key Terms

applicant tracking systems Computer systems that capture and store incoming résumés and help recruiters find good prospects for current openings

chronological résumé The most common résumé format; it emphasizes work experience, with past jobs shown in reverse chronological order

combination résumé Format that includes the best features of the chronological and functional approaches

functional résumé Format that emphasizes your skills and capabilities while identifying employers and academic experience in subordinate sections; many recruiters view this format with suspicion

networking The process of making connections with mutually beneficial business contacts

Apply Your Knowledge

To review chapter content related to each question, refer to the indicated Learning Objective.

15-1. How can you "think like an employer" if you have no professional business experience? [LO-1]

15-2. If you were a team leader at a summer camp for children with special needs, should you include this information in your employment history if you are applying for work that is unrelated? Explain your answer. [LO-3]

15-3. Can you use a qualifications summary if you don't yet have extensive professional experience in your desired career? Why or why not? [LO-3]

15-4. Some people don't have a clear career path when they enter the job market. If you're in this situation, how would your uncertainty affect the way you write your résumé? [LO-3]

15-5. Should you bother creating a LinkedIn profile if you have no work experience? Why or why not? [LO-5]

Practice Your Skills

Message for Analysis

Read the following résumé information and then (1) analyze the strengths or weaknesses of the information and (2) revise the résumé so that it follows the guidelines presented in this chapter.

15-6. **Message 15.A: Writing a Résumé [LO-3]**

Sylvia Manchester

765 Belle Fleur Blvd.

New Orleans, LA 70113

(504) 312-9504

smanchester@rcnmail.com

PERSONAL: Single, excellent health, 5′7″, 136 lbs.; hobbies include cooking, dancing, and reading.

JOB OBJECTIVE: To obtain a responsible position in marketing or sales with a good company.

EDUCATION: BA degree in biology, University of Louisiana, 1998. Graduated with a 3.0 average. Member of the varsity cheerleading squad. President of Panhellenic League. Homecoming queen.

WORK EXPERIENCE

Fisher Scientific Instruments, 2017 to now, field sales representative. Responsible for calling on customers and explaining the features of Fisher's line of laboratory instruments. Also responsible for writing sales letters, attending trade shows, and preparing weekly sales reports.

Fisher Scientific Instruments, 2013–2016, customer service representative. Was responsible for handling incoming phone calls from customers who had questions about delivery, quality, or operation of Fisher's line of laboratory instruments. Also handled miscellaneous correspondence with customers.

Medical Electronics, Inc., 2010–2013, administrative assistant to the vice president of marketing. In addition to handling typical secretarial chores for the vice president of marketing, I was in charge of compiling the monthly sales reports, using figures provided by members of the field sales force. I also was given responsibility for doing various market research activities.

New Orleans Convention and Visitors Bureau, 2007–2010, summers, tour guide. During the summers of my college years, I led tours of New Orleans for tourists visiting the city. My duties included greeting conventioneers and their spouses at hotels, explaining the history and features of the city during an all-day sightseeing tour, and answering questions about New Orleans and its attractions. During my fourth summer with the bureau, I was asked to help train the new tour guides. I prepared a handbook that provided interesting facts about the various tourist attractions, as well as answers to the most commonly asked tourist questions. The Bureau was so impressed with the handbook they had it printed up so that it could be given as a gift to visitors.

University of Louisiana, 2007–2010, part-time clerk in admissions office. While I was a student in college, I worked 15 hours a week in the admissions office. My duties included filing, processing applications, and handling correspondence with high school students and administrators.

Exercises

Each activity is labeled according to the primary skill or skills you will need to use. To review relevant chapter content, refer to the indicated Learning Objective. In some instances, supporting information will be found in another chapter, as indicated.

15-7. Career Management: Researching Career Opportunities [LO-1] Based on the preferences you identified in the self-assessment in the Prologue (see page xxxiii) and the academic, professional, and personal qualities you have to offer, perform an online search for a career opportunity that matches your interests and qualifications (starting with any of the websites listed in Table 15.2). Draft a one-page report indicating how the career you select and the job openings you find match your strengths and preferences.

15-8. Message Strategies: Planning a Résumé [LO-2] Identify a position in an interesting career field that you could potentially be qualified for upon graduation. Using at least three different sources, including the description in an online job posting, create a list of 10 keywords that should be included in a résumé customized for this position.

15-9. Message Strategies: Writing a Résumé; Collaboration: Team Projects [LO-3], Chapter 3 Working with another student, change the following statements to make them more effective for a résumé by using action verbs and concrete keywords.

  a. Have some experience with database design.

  b. Assigned to a project to analyze the cost accounting methods for a large manufacturer.

  c. I was part of a team that developed a new inventory control system.

  d. Am responsible for preparing the quarterly department budget.

  e. Was a manager of a department with seven employees working for me.

  f. Was responsible for developing a spreadsheet to analyze monthly sales by department.

  g. Put in place a new program for ordering supplies.

15-10. Message Strategies: Writing a Résumé [LO-3] Using your team's answers to Exercise 15.9, make the statements stronger by quantifying them (make up any numbers you need).

15-11. Message Strategies: Writing a Résumé; Communication Ethics: Resolving Ethical Dilemmas [LO-3], Chapter 1 Assume that you achieved all the tasks shown in Exercise 15.9 not as an individual employee, but as part of a work team. In your résumé, must you mention other team members? Explain your answer.

15-12. Message Strategies: Completing a Résumé; Media Strategies: Video [LO-4] Imagine you are applying for work in a field that involves speaking in front of an audience, such as sales, consulting, management, or training. Using material you created for any of the exercises or cases in Chapter 14, record a two- to three-minute video demonstration of your speaking and presentation skills. Record yourself speaking to an audience, if one can be arranged.

15-13. Message Strategies: Social Media [LO-5] Search LinkedIn for three people in a profession that you might like to pursue and compare how they use the system's features to present themselves. Which person used LinkedIn most effectively? How can you apply what he or she has done to your own profile?

Expand Your Skills

Critique the Professionals

Locate an example of a résumé (a sample or an actual résumé). Analyze it following the guidelines presented in this chapter. Using whatever medium your instructor requests, write a brief analysis (no more than one page) of the résumé's strengths and weaknesses, citing specific elements from the résumé and support from the chapter. If you are analyzing a real résumé, do not include any personally identifiable data, such as the person's name, email address, or phone number, in your report.

Sharpen Your Career Skills Online

Bovée and Thill's Business Communication Web Search, at **websearch.businesscommunicationnetwork.com**, is a unique research tool designed specifically for business communication research. Use the Web Search function to find a website, video, article, podcast, or presentation that offers advice on creating effective online résumés. Write a brief email message to your instructor or a post for your class blog describing the item that you found and summarizing the career skills information you learned from it.

Build Your Career

In Chapter 13 you started work on your introductory statement. Now it's time for the other major section in a chronological or combination résumé, which is your work experience. Start by listing all the positions you've held; then decide how many to include. If you don't have much or any full-time work experience yet, use part-time jobs, volunteering assignments, and academic roles. If you've been in the workforce for up to 10 or 15 years, you'll generally want to list all the positions you've held since graduation. If you have more than 15 years of experience, include as much of your job history as is still relevant to the positions you are seeking.

Following the advice on page 498 under "Work Experience, Skills, and Accomplishments," describe your accomplishments in each position in a way that mirrors the job descriptions of the positions you are or will likely be applying for.

With your introductory statement and work experience sections in hand, you'll have the bulk of your résumé completed, and you will be ready to finalize with your education and contact information.

Improve Your Grammar, Mechanics, and Usage

The following exercises help you improve your knowledge of and power over English grammar, mechanics, and usage. Turn to the Handbook of Grammar, Mechanics, and Usage at the end of this book and review all of Sections 4.1 (Frequently Confused Words), 4.2 (Frequently Misused Words), and Sections 4.3 (Frequently Misspelled Words). Then review the following items and indicate the preferred choice within each set of parentheses. (Answers to these exercises appear on page 615.)

15-14. Everyone (*accept, except*) Barbara King has registered for the company competition.

15-15. We need to find a new security (*device, devise*).

15-16. The Jennings are (*loath, loathe*) to admit that they are wrong.

15-17. That decision lies with the director, (*who's, whose*) in charge of this department.

15-18. In this department, we see (*a lot, alot*) of mistakes like that.

15-19. In my (*judgement, judgment*), you'll need to redo the cover.

15-20. He decided to reveal the information, (*irregardless, regardless*) of the consequences.

15-21. Why not go along when it is so easy to (*accomodate, accommodate*) his demands?

15-22. When you say that, do you mean to (*infer, imply*) that I'm being unfair?

15-23. All we have to do is try (*and, to*) get along with him for a few more days.

For additional exercises focusing on frequently confused, misused, or misspelled words, visit MyLab Business Communication. Click on Chapter 15, click on Additional Exercises to Improve Your Grammar, Mechanics, and Usage, and then click on 21. Frequently confused words, 22. Frequently misused words, or 23. Frequently misspelled words.

Cases

For all cases, feel free to use your creativity to make up any details you need in order to craft effective messages.

CAREER SKILLS / EMAIL SKILLS

15-24. Career Planning: Researching Career Opportunities [LO-1] Knowing the jargon and "hot-button" issues in a particular profession or industry can give you a big advantage when it comes to writing your résumé and participating in job interviews. You can fine-tune your résumé for both human read-

ers and applicant tracking systems, sound more confident and informed in interviews, and present yourself as a professional with an inquiring mind.

Your task: Imagine a specific job category in a company that has an informative, comprehensive website (to facilitate the research you'll need to do). This doesn't have to be a current job opening, but a position you know exists or is likely to exist in this company, such as a business systems analyst at Apple or a brand manager at Unilever.

Explore the company's website and other online sources to find the following: (1) a brief description of what this job entails, with enough detail so that you could describe it to a fellow student; (2) some of the terminology used in the profession or industry, both formal terms that might serve as keywords on your résumé and informal terms and phrases that insiders are likely to use in publications and conversations; (3) an ongoing online conversation among people in this profession, such as a LinkedIn Group, a popular industry or professional blog that seems to get quite a few comments, or an industry or professional publication that attracts a lot of comments; and (4) at least one significant issue that will affect people in this profession or companies in this industry over the next few years. For example, if your chosen profession involves accounting in a publicly traded corporation, potential changes in financial reporting standards would be a significant issue. Similarly, for a company in the consumer electronics industry, the recycling and disposal of *e-waste* is an issue. Write a brief email message summarizing your findings and explaining how you could use this information on your résumé and during job interviews.

CAREER SKILLS / EMAIL SKILLS

15-25. Career Management: Researching Career Opportunities [LO-1] Perhaps you won't be able to land your ultimate dream job right out of college, but that doesn't mean you shouldn't start planning right now to make that dream come true.

Your task: Using online job-search tools, find a job that sounds just about perfect for you, even if you're not yet qualified for it. It might even be something that would take 10 or 20 years to reach. Don't settle for something that's not quite right—find a job that is so "you" and so exciting that you would jump out of bed every morning, eager to go to work. (Such jobs really do exist!) Start with the job description you found online and then supplement it with additional research so that you get a good picture of what this job and career path are all about. Compile a list of all the qualifications you would need in order to have a reasonable chance of landing such a job. Now compare this list with your current résumé. Write a brief email message to your instructor that identifies all the areas in which you would need to improve your skills, work experience, education, and other qualifications to land your dream job.

CAREER SKILLS / TEAM SKILLS

15-26. Planning a Résumé [LO-2] If you haven't begun your professional career yet or are pursuing a career change, the employment history section on your résumé can sometimes be a challenge to write. A brainstorming session with your wise and creative classmates could help.

Your task: In a team assigned by your instructor, help each other evaluate your employment histories and figure out the best way to present your work backgrounds on a résumé. First, each member of the team should compile his or her work history, including freelance projects and volunteer work if relevant, and share this information with the team. After allowing some time for everyone to review each other's information, meet as a team (in person if you can, or online otherwise). Discuss each person's history, pointing out strong spots and weak spots, and then brainstorm the best way to present each person's employment history.

Note: If you would rather not share aspects of your employment history with your teammates, substitute a similar experience of the same duration.

CAREER SKILLS / TEAM SKILLS

15-27. Message Strategies: Writing a Résumé [LO-3] The introductory statement of a résumé requires some careful thought, both in deciding which of the three types of introductory statement (see page 497) to use and what information to include in it. Getting another person's perspective on this communication challenge can be helpful. In this activity, in fact, someone else is going to write your introductory statement for you, and you will return the favor.

Your task: Pair off with a classmate. Provide each other with the basic facts about your qualifications, work history, education, and career objectives. Then meet in person or online for an informal interview in which you ask each other questions to flesh out the information you have on each other. Assume that each of you has chosen to use a qualifications summary for your résumé. Now write each other's qualifications summary and then trade them for review. As you read what your partner wrote about you, ask yourself whether it feels true to what you believe about yourself and your career aspirations. Do you think it introduces you effectively to potential employers? What about it might you change?

PRESENTATION SKILLS / PORTFOLIO BUILDER

15-28. Message Strategies: Completing a Résumé [LO-4] Creating presentations and other multimedia supplements can be a great way to expand on the brief overview that a résumé provides.

Your task: Starting with any version of a résumé you've created for yourself, create a presentation that expands on your résumé information to give potential employers a more complete picture of what you can contribute. Include samples of your work, testimonials from current or past employers and colleagues, videos of speeches you've made, and anything else that tells the story of the professional "you." If you have a specific job or type of job in mind, focus your presentation on that. Otherwise, present a more general picture that shows why you would be a great employee for any company to consider.

CAREER SKILLS / VIDEO SKILLS

15-29. Message Strategies: Completing a Résumé [LO-4] In the right circumstances, brief videos can be an effective complement to a traditional job-search communication package.

Your task: Find a job opening that interests you (something you are at least partially qualified for at this stage of your career) and produce a brief (30 to 60 seconds) video profile of yourself, highlighting the skills mentioned in the job description. For tips on producing effective video, visit **www.indie-film-making.com**.

15-30. Message Strategies: Building a LinkedIn Profile [LO-5] Your LinkedIn summary is a great opportunity to present a clear picture of who you are and what you can bring to a job.

Your task: Draft a summary for your LinkedIn profile, making sure to stay within the system's current length limits for this field. Review the advice in this chapter and search online for "writing a LinkedIn summary" if you need more tips.

MyLab Business Communication

MyLab Assisted-Grading Writing Prompts

If your instructor has assigned one or both of the following writing assignments within the MyLab, go to your Assignments to complete these writing exercises.

15-31. How does a chronological résumé differ from a functional résumé, and when is each appropriate? [LO-2]

15-32. Explain the difference between a qualifications summary and a career summary. [LO-3]

Endnotes

1. Liza Mundy, "Why Is Silicon Valley So Awful to Women?" *Atlantic*, April 2017, www.theatlantic.com; Project Include, accessed 23 April 2018, projectinclude.org; Ellen McGirt, "How Your Life Experience Could Help You Land a Great Job," *Fortune*, 18 January 2018, www.fortune.com; Julia Carrie Wong, "Segregated Valley: The Ugly Truth About Google and Diversity in Tech," *Guardian*, 7 August 2017, www.theguardian.com; Cyrus Farivar, "Slack Engineering Director: Google Should Do, 'Blind Assessments' for Hiring," *Ars Technica*, 14 December 2016, arstechnica.com; Mike Isaac, "Women in Tech Band Together to Track Diversity, After Hours," *New York Times*, 3 May 2016, www.nytimes.com; Leah Fessler, "Silicon Valley Engineer Erica Joy Baker Wishes People Would Stop Telling Women That They're Strong," *Quartz*, 6 February 2018, work.qz.com. Erica Baker, accessed 23 April 2018, www.ericabaker.com.

2. Courtland L. Bovée and John V. Thill, *Business in Action*, 8th ed. (Boston: Pearson, 2017), 256.

3. Eve Tahmincioglu, "Revamping Your Job-Search Strategy," MSNBC.com, 28 February 2010, www.msnbc.com.

4. Amy Segelin, "3 Steps to Cracking the Hidden Job Market," *Fortune*, 4 March 2017, fortune.com.

5. Tara Weiss, "Twitter to Find a Job," *Forbes*, 7 April 2009, www.forbes.com.

6. Miriam Saltpeter, "Using Facebook Groups for Job Hunting," Keppie Careers blog, 13 November 2008, www.keppiecareers.com.

7. Anne Fisher, "Greener Pastures in a New Field," *Fortune*, 26 January 2004, 48.

8. Richie Frieman, "Proper Networking Etiquette," QuickandDirtyTips.com, 1 May 2016, www.quickanddirtytips.com; Kevin Daum, "12 Rules of Highly Effective Networkers," *Inc.*, 10 November 2014; Debra Wheatman, "Five Keys to Networking Etiquette for Your Career," Glassdoor blog, 25 May 2011, www.glassdoor.com/blog/.

9. "Number of Employers Using Social Media to Screen Candidates Has Increased 500 Percent over the Last Decade," CareerBuilder, 28 April 2016, www.careerbuilder.com.

10. Susan P. Joyce, "What 80% of Employers Do Before Inviting You for an Interview," *Huffington Post*, 1 March 2014, www.huffingtonpost.com.

11. Rachel Emma Silverman, "No More Résumés, Say Some Firms," *Wall Street Journal*, 24 January 2012, www.wsj.com.

12. Randall S. Hansen and Katharine Hansen, "What Résumé Format Is Best for You?" QuintCareers.com, accessed 7 August 2010, www.quintcareers.com.

13. Hansen and Hansen, "What Résumé Format Is Best for You?"

14. Alison Doyle, "Chronological Resume Definition, Format, and Examples," *The Balance*, 28 March 2017, www.thebalance.com.

15. "Resume Red Flags to Watch For," Robert Half, 25 April 2017, www.roberthalf.com; Katharine Hansen, "Should You Consider a Functional Format for Your Resume?" QuintCareers.com, accessed 7 August 2010, www.quintcareers.com.

16. Kim Isaacs, "Resume Dilemma: Employment Gaps and Job-Hopping," Monster, accessed 27 April 2017, www.monster.com.

17. "The Biggest Mistakes Job Seekers Make Today," *Knowledge@Wharton*, 10 July 2017, knowledge.wharton.upenn.edu.

18. Wendell Brenner, "Explaining Previous Employment Issues During Your Job Interview," CareerBuilder, 14 February 2014, www.careerbuilder.com.

19. Lisa Guerin, "Getting Hired with an Arrest or Conviction Record," Nolo, accessed 27 April 2017, www.nolo.com; Jeffrey Stinson, "States, Cities 'Ban the Box' in Hiring," Pew Charitable Trusts, 22 May 2014, www.pewtrusts.org; Dona DeZube, "Job Hunting When You Have a Criminal Past," Monster, accessed 27 April 2017, www.monster.com.

20. Susan M. Heathfield, "Job Applications Serve Employer Needs That a Resume Doesn't Meet," *The Balance*, 29 August 2016, www.thebalance.com; Susan M. Heathfield, "Why Employers Use an Employment Application," *The Balance*, 12 March 2017, www.thebalance.com; Kim Isaacs, "Lying on Your Resume," Monster, accessed 28 April 2017, www.monster.com; Susan M. Heathfield, "Do You Know Who You're Hiring?" *The Balance*, 13 October 2016, www.thebalance.com.

21. Isaacs, "Lying on Your Resume."

22. Rockport Institute, "How to Write a Masterpiece of a Résumé," accessed 9 August 2010, www.rockportinstitute.com.

23. Katharine Hansen, "Tapping the Power of Keywords to Enhance Your Resume's Effectiveness," Quintessential, accessed 23 May 2017, www.livecareer.com/quintessential.

24. Anthony Balderrama, "Resume Blunders That Will Keep You from Getting Hired," CNN.com, 19 March 2008, www.cnn.com; Michelle Dumas, "5 Resume Writing Myths," Distinctive Documents blog, 17 July 2007, blog.distinctiveweb.com; Kim Isaacs, "Resume

Dilemma: Recent Graduate," Monster.com, accessed 26 March 2008, career-advice.monster.com.

25. Alison Doyle, "When to Include a GPA on Your Résumé," *The Balance Careers*, 8 January 2018, www.thebalancecareers.com.

26. Alison Doyle, "How Many Years of Experience to List on a Résumé," *The Balance Careers*, 22 March 2018, www.thebalancecareers.com.

27. Karl L. Smart, "Articulating Skills in the Job Search," *Business Communication Quarterly* 67, no. 2 (June 2004): 198–205.

28. Alison Doyle, "Will Employers Check Your References?" *The Balance Careers*, 21 November 2017, www.thebalancecareers.com.

29. Alison Doyle, "How to Select and Use Job References?" *The Balance*, 31 January 2018, www.thebalance.com.

30. "Résumé Length: What It Should Be and Why It Matters to Recruiters," *HR Focus*, June 2007, 9.

31. Madeleine Burry, "What Do Employers Look for in a Résumé?" *The Balance Careers*, 13 July 2017, www.thebalancecareers.com.

32. Job description keywords and key phrases quoted or adapted in part from "Associate Market Analyst" job opening posted on Living-Social website, accessed 9 July 2012, corporate.livingsocial.com.

33. Job description keywords and key phrases quoted or adapted in part from "Seller Support Associate" job opening posted on Amazon website, accessed 12 July 2012, us-amazon.icims.com/jobs.

34. Job description keywords and key phrases quoted or adapted in part from "Senior Strategy Analyst" job opening posted on Nordstrom website, accessed 17 July 2012, careers.nordstrom.com.

35. Lisa Vaas, "13 Ways Your Resume Can Say 'I'm Unprofessional,'" TheLadders, accessed 10 May 2016, www.theladders.com; "25 Things You Should Never Include on a Resume," *HR World*, 18 December 2007, www.hrworld.com.

36. Caroline M. L. Potter, "Video Resumes: Let the Applicant Beware," Monster, accessed 10 May 2016, www.monster.com; John Sullivan, "Résumés: Paper, Please," *Workforce Management*, 22 October

2007, 50; "Video Résumés Offer Both Pros and Cons During Recruiting," *HR Focus*, July 2007, 8.

37. Zappos, accessed 28 April 2017, jobs.jobvite.com/zappos.

38. Rachel Louise Ensign, "Is the Paper Résumé Dead?" *Wall Street Journal*, 24 January 2012, www.wsj.com.

39. Nancy M. Schullery, Linda Ickes, and Stephen E. Schullery, "Employer Preferences for Résumés and Cover Letters," *Business Communication Quarterly*, June 2009, 163–176.

40. Alison Doyle, "Top 10 Resume Mistakes to Avoid," *The Balance*, 7 November 2016, www.thebalance.com.

41. "Keep Your Online Resume Secure," Monster, accessed 28 April 2017, www.monster.com.

42. Kathryn Vasel, "Is the Résumé Dead?" CNNMoney, 14 August 2018, money.cnn.com; Quentin Fottrell, "How Job Recruiters Screen You on LinkedIn," *MarketWatch*, 16 June 2016, www.marketwatch.com.

43. Alison Doyle, "The Most Effective Ways to Use LinkedIn," *The Balance Careers*, 9 April 2018, www.thebalancecareers.com; Alison Doyle, "Learn How to Make a Better LinkedIn Profile," *The Balance Careers*, 13 December 2017, www.thebalancecareers.com; "How to Build the Perfect LinkedIn Profile," Link Humans, accessed 28 April 2017, linkhumans.com; Carly Okyle, "18 Tips to Create Your Perfect LinkedIn Profile," *Entrepreneur*, 4 April 2016, www.entrepreneur.com; Lindsay Kolowich, "How to Craft the Perfect LinkedIn Profile: A Comprehensive Guide," HubSpot, 25 January 2016, blog.hubspot.com; Quentin Fottrell, "How Job Recruiters Screen You on LinkedIn," *MarketWatch*, 16 June 2016, www.marketwatch.com; Ed Han, "How to Write a Good LinkedIn Summary with Examples," *The Balance Careers*, 5 April 2018, www.thebalancecareers.com.

44. Erica Baker profile on LinkedIn, accessed 22 April 2018, www.linkedin.com/ericajoy.

Five-Minute Guide to Planning Your Résumé

Your résumé is one of the most important documents you will ever write, so before you start, take five minutes to review these important tips.

00:01 **Choose the best format for your situation**

1. Chronological
   - Emphasizes your work history, with past jobs listed in reverse chronological order.
   - This is the format most employers prefer.
   - Use this format if you can, but if you have limited work experience or large gaps in your work history, consider the combination formation instead.
2. Functional
   - Showcases skill areas without requiring readers to dig through work history.
   - However, many employers are wary of it because it can obscure an uneven work history.
3. Combination
   - Combines the best of the other two while overcoming the weakness of the functional format.
   - Probably the best choice for new graduates and early-career professionals.

00:02 **Address any areas of concern**

1. If you have issues in your personal or professional history that might be a concern for employers, assess them objectively.
2. Remember that you don't need to address every issue in your résumé; some matters are better to address in your cover letter or during an interview.

00:03 **Choose the best type of introductory statement**

1. Career objective
   - This is the traditional choice but is used less these days.
   - Potential weakness is that it tends to be about the employee's needs, not how the employee can meet the employer's needs.
   - Consider it if you don't have much experience and no dominant theme to convey in a qualifications summary.
   - If you use it, word it in a way that relates your aspirations to employer needs.
2. Qualifications summary
   - Offers a brief view of your key qualifications, letting a reader know within a few seconds what you can deliver.
   - Consider using it if you have one or more important qualifications or a dominant professional "theme" but don't yet have a long career history.
3. Career summary
   - Offers a brief recap of your career with the goal of presenting increasing levels of responsibility and performance.
   - Particularly good for people who have demonstrated the ability to take on increasing levels of responsibility in their chosen field and who want to continue in that field.

00:04 **Choose a design strategy**

1. Don't choose any format or design just because it is trendy or unusual; choose it because it meets a specific communication need that is relevant to your job search.
2. Remember that many résumés get fed into applicant tracking systems, and the simpler the design, the fewer problems these systems will have analyzing your information.
3. A straightforward design that is easy to read is always better than an eye-catching design that is difficult to read.

00:05 **Produce it in multiple formats as needed**

1. Even if some employers don't request it, a conventional résumé helps you organize and summarize your key message points.
2. Plain-text and PDF versions are easy to create from your conventional résumé.
3. Your LinkedIn profile is the most beneficial type of online résumé to create.

16

Applying and Interviewing for Employment

LEARNING OBJECTIVES

After studying this chapter, you will be able to

1 Explain the purposes of application letters, and describe how to apply the AIDA organizational approach to them.

2 Describe the typical sequence of job interviews, the major types of interviews, and the attributes employers look for during an interview.

3 List six tasks you need to complete in order to prepare for a successful job interview.

4 Explain how to succeed in all three stages of an interview.

5 Identify the most common employment messages that follow an interview, and explain when you would use each one.

MyLab Business Communication
Improve Your Grade!

If your instructor is using MyLab Business Communication, visit **www.pearson.com/mylab/business-communication** for videos, simulations, and writing exercises.

ON THE JOB: COMMUNICATING AT
BURNING GLASS

Matching Millions of Job Seekers with Millions of Job Openings

Finding a job opening that matches your interests and qualifications—and then convincing employers you are the best person for the job—can be one of the most complicated, aggravating, and downright mystifying tasks you ever undertake.

   If you eventually move into management or take the entrepreneurial plunge and build your own company, you'll encounter this matchmaking challenge from the other side of the table. When a single job opening can attract dozens or hundreds of applicants, how can you sort through all the possibilities to identify the most promising candidates who warrant the time and expense of interviewing?

Aleksandr Davydov/Alamy Stock Photo

Burning Glass applies artificial intelligence to the challenges of matching employer needs with employee skill sets.

The challenge of matching the right people with the right jobs isn't limited to employees and employers, either. It's a vital issue for governments and educational institutions as well. Government bodies from the local up to the national level need to make workforce policy and investment decisions that reflect the real-world problems employees and employers encounter. And in the career-related facets of their broader educational missions, high schools, colleges, and universities need to understand what employers are looking for in order to provide the training and education that best prepare students for the job market.

In other words, matching people and job opportunities is one of society's most important challenges, and doing it well or poorly has a tremendous impact on everyone's financial well-being.

To a large degree, at every level this challenge is all about getting one's hands on the right data and using them to make smart decisions. With more than 150 million employees in the United States alone, though, the total collection of this workforce data is massive.

To extract usable insights from this ocean of data, the Boston-based firm Burning Glass applies the power of artificial intelligence in a specialty known as job market analytics. In particular, it studies millions of job postings and career transitions to figure out what employers are looking for, what employees have to offer, and where gaps exist between the two sides. (Incidentally, when it studied the most important "baseline skills" across all professions, the company identified overall communication abilities as the most important skill and writing as the third-most important skill.)

Burning Glass integrates these job market insights into a variety of software tools that are used by employers, job seekers, colleges, and other parties involved in meeting the job-match challenge. In the human resources area, this software works in conjunction with applicant tracking systems, which you are sure to encounter at some point in your job search. Before a human being reads your résumé, it will likely be "read" by such a system, designed to help company recruiters find the most promising candidates and manage communication and data collection all the way through the recruiting, hiring, and orientation stages.

It's difficult to fault the basic concept of an applicant tracking system. Software helps business professionals make all kinds of decisions, and most medium-sized and large companies get swamped with so many résumés that they have to rely on software to help recruiters manage the flow. However, the technology has developed a negative reputation in some quarters. Applicants express frustration that they can't get past a "robot" and explain their qualifications to an actual human being. Employers get frustrated when people clog their systems by applying for jobs for which they are clearly not qualified or when applicants try to game the system by loading up their résumés with stacks of keywords they think the system is looking for. And employers sometimes complain they can't find enough good applicants, even as good applicants are banging on the door but can't get in. Overly aggressive filtering can be a problem with poorly configured systems or for employers who dial up the qualification requirements to the point that only a superhero could make it over the barrier.

Companies such as Burning Glass aim to make this process work better for everybody by moving beyond simple keyword searches and résumé cataloging. For example, Burning Glass's technology analyzes how keywords are used in a résumé in order to separate candidates who describe themselves legitimately and naturally from those who are simply stuffing their résumés with keywords. The software has learned to read résumés the way human recruiters do, evaluating keywords in context to make informed judgments about the quality and currency of the skills someone has included. If the system is searching for candidates with database design experience, for instance, it can tell whether somebody took a class in the subject ten years ago or is currently applying those skills in a professional capacity.

From an applicant's perspective, the best way to "beat the robots" is to stop trying to beat them. Don't try to trick the system by including every keyword you can find or try to improve your odds by blasting your application to hundreds of openings. Instead, take the time to read job descriptions carefully so you can concentrate on the ones where you fit best and so you can understand employers' needs well enough that you can explain how your skills and experience align with those needs. Even though you may have to go through a machine to get to an actual human, using the same audience-focused skills and techniques you've been practicing throughout this course is the best way to get there.[1]

BURNING-GLASS.COM

Submitting Your Résumé

Your résumé (see Chapter 15) is the centerpiece of your job-search package, but it needs support from several other employment messages, including application letters, job-inquiry letters, application forms, and follow-up notes.

WRITING APPLICATION LETTERS

Whenever you email a résumé to a recruiter or other contact in a company, use the body of your email message as an **application letter**, also known as a *cover letter*. (Even though this message is often not a printed letter anymore, many professionals still refer to it as a letter.) Note that not all recruiters take the time to read application letters, particularly at

1 LEARNING OBJECTIVE
Explain the purposes of application letters, and describe how to apply the AIDA organizational approach to them.

Always accompany your résumé with a printed or email *application letter*, also known as a cover letter, that motivates the recipient to read the résumé.

companies that receive a high volume of applications.[2] However, if you are emailing someone directly, it's good practice to include one anyway. It might catch the recruiter's eye, and the hiring manager who eventually gets your résumé may be interested in reading it.[3] (Some online application systems allow you to upload an application message, but many don't, so when you apply online, you might not have the opportunity to include an application letter.)

An application letter has three goals: to introduce your résumé, persuade an employer to read it, and request an interview. Recognize that this message is a great opportunity, too: You can communicate in a more personal and conversational way than you can with your résumé, you can show that you understand what an employer is looking for, and you can demonstrate your writing skills. Another key opportunity here involves soft skills, such as interpersonal communication, which are difficult to quantify in a meaningful way on your résumé. In the letter, you can briefly describe a situation in which you used these skills to reach a measurable business result, for example, which is more compelling than simply listing skills.[4]

The best approach for an application letter depends on whether you are applying for an identified job opening or are *prospecting*—taking the initiative to write to companies even though they haven't announced a job opening that is right for you.[5] In many ways, the difference between the two is like the difference between solicited and unsolicited proposals (see page 380).

Figure 16.1 shows an application message written in response to a posted job opening. The writer knows exactly what qualifications the organization is seeking and can "echo" those attributes back in his letter.

Writing a prospecting letter is more challenging because you don't have the clear target you have with a solicited letter, and the message is unexpected. You will need to do more research to identify the qualities that a company would probably seek for the position you hope to occupy (see Figure 16.2 on page 524). Also, search for news items that involve the company, its customers, the profession, or the individual manager to whom you are writing. Using this information in your application letter helps you establish common ground with your reader—and it shows that you are tuned in to what is going on in the industry.

For either type of letter, follow these tips to be more effective:[6]

- Resist the temptation to stand out with gimmicky application letters; impress with knowledge and professionalism instead.
- If the name of the hiring manager is findable, address your letter to that person. (And if it is findable, make sure you find it, because other applicants will.) Search LinkedIn, the company's website, industry directories, Twitter, and anything else you can think of to locate an appropriate name. Ask the people in your network if they know a name, or call the company and ask. If you're sure a name can't be found, address your letter to "Dear Hiring Manager."
- Clearly identify the opportunity you are applying for or expressing interest in.
- Show that you understand the company and its business challenges. Incorporate relevant keywords from your research.
- If applicable, explain employment gaps or other potential negatives from your résumé. This explanation can be as simple as "After serving as a product manager at Microsoft, I took two years off for family reasons."
- Keep it short—no more than three or four brief paragraphs. Remember that all you are trying to do at this point is move the conversation forward one step.
- Show some personality while maintaining a business-appropriate tone. The letter gives you the opportunity to balance the facts-only tone of your résumé. Project confidence without being arrogant.
- Don't just repeat information from your résumé; use the conversational tone of the letter to convey additional professional and personal qualities and your reasons for wanting this particular job.
- Be sure to adapt each letter to a specific job opening (see Figure 16.3 on page 525).

> The best approach for an application letter depends on whether you are responding to an advertised job opening or *prospecting*—writing to companies to express interest even though they haven't posted an opening.

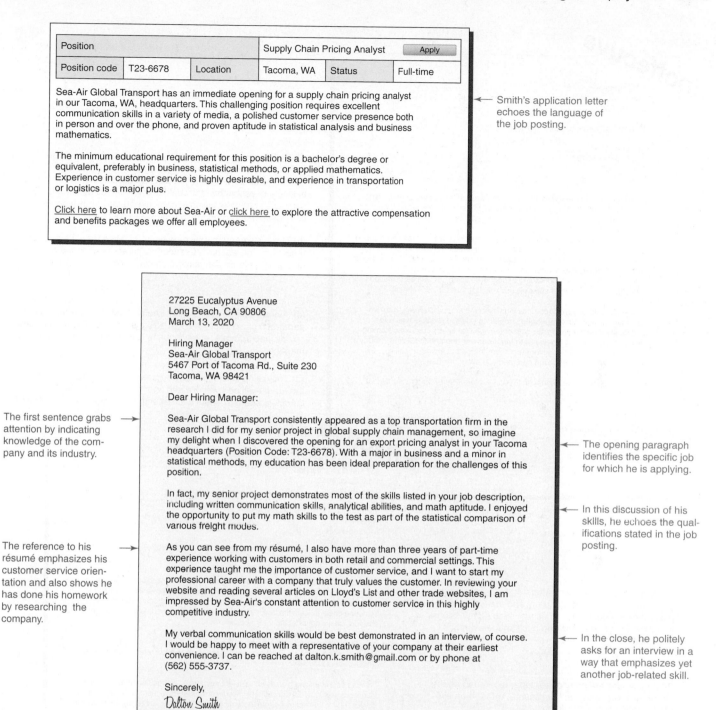

Position			Supply Chain Pricing Analyst		Apply
Position code	T23-6678	Location	Tacoma, WA	Status	Full-time

Sea-Air Global Transport has an immediate opening for a supply chain pricing analyst in our Tacoma, WA, headquarters. This challenging position requires excellent communication skills in a variety of media, a polished customer service presence both in person and over the phone, and proven aptitude in statistical analysis and business mathematics.

The minimum educational requirement for this position is a bachelor's degree or equivalent, preferably in business, statistical methods, or applied mathematics. Experience in customer service is highly desirable, and experience in transportation or logistics is a major plus.

Click here to learn more about Sea-Air or click here to explore the attractive compensation and benefits packages we offer all employees.

← Smith's application letter echoes the language of the job posting.

27225 Eucalyptus Avenue
Long Beach, CA 90806
March 13, 2020

Hiring Manager
Sea-Air Global Transport
5467 Port of Tacoma Rd., Suite 230
Tacoma, WA 98421

Dear Hiring Manager:

Sea-Air Global Transport consistently appeared as a top transportation firm in the research I did for my senior project in global supply chain management, so imagine my delight when I discovered the opening for an export pricing analyst in your Tacoma headquarters (Position Code: T23-6678). With a major in business and a minor in statistical methods, my education has been ideal preparation for the challenges of this position.

In fact, my senior project demonstrates most of the skills listed in your job description, including written communication skills, analytical abilities, and math aptitude. I enjoyed the opportunity to put my math skills to the test as part of the statistical comparison of various freight modes.

As you can see from my résumé, I also have more than three years of part-time experience working with customers in both retail and commercial settings. This experience taught me the importance of customer service, and I want to start my professional career with a company that truly values the customer. In reviewing your website and reading several articles on Lloyd's List and other trade websites, I am impressed by Sea-Air's constant attention to customer service in this highly competitive industry.

My verbal communication skills would be best demonstrated in an interview, of course. I would be happy to meet with a representative of your company at their earliest convenience. I can be reached at dalton.k.smith@gmail.com or by phone at (562) 555-3737.

Sincerely,

Dalton Smith

Dalton Smith

The first sentence grabs attention by indicating knowledge of the company and its industry.

The reference to his résumé emphasizes his customer service orientation and also shows he has done his homework by researching the company.

→ The opening paragraph identifies the specific job for which he is applying.

→ In this discussion of his skills, he echoes the qualifications stated in the job posting.

→ In the close, he politely asks for an interview in a way that emphasizes yet another job-related skill.

Figure 16.1 Solicited Application Message
In this response to an online job posting, Dalton Smith highlights his qualifications while mirroring the requirements specified in the posting. Following the AIDA model (see page 327), he grabs attention immediately by letting the reader know he is familiar with the company and the global transportation business.

Because application letters are persuasive messages, the AIDA approach you learned in Chapter 11 is ideal, as the following sections explain. However, note that this use of the AIDA model employs the direct approach, not the indirect approach used in most other persuasive messages. With an application letter, you need to let the reader know what you seek within the first sentence or two.

Ineffective

457 Mountain View Rd.
Clear Lake, IA 50428
June 16, 2020

Ms. Patricia Downing, Store Manager
Walmart
840 South Oak
Iowa Falls, IA 50126

Dear Ms. Downing:

Do you have any openings for people who want to move into store management? I am really looking for an opportunity to get a job like yours, even if it takes starting at a low level and working my way up.

Allow me to list some highlights from my enclosed résumé. First, I have a BA degree in retailing, which included such key courses as retailing, marketing, management, and business information systems. Second, I have worked as a clerk and as an assistant manager in a large department store. Third, I have experience in the customer-facing aspect of retailing, as well as operations, marketing, and personnel supervision.

Successful retailing is about more than systems and procedures. It is also about anticipating customer needs, fostering positive relationships with the community, and delivering the type of service that keeps customers coming back. Retailers that fail in any of these areas are doomed to decline in today's hypercompetitive sales environment. I am the sort of forward-thinking, customer-focused leader who can help you avoid this fate.

I will call you next Wednesday at 2:00 to explain why I would make a great addition to your team.

Sincerely,

Glenda Johns

Glenda Johns
Enclosure

(a) The writer commits three major mistakes in the first paragraph: asking a question that she could answer herself by visiting the company's website, failing to demonstrate any knowledge of the company, and making the message all about her.

(b) This paragraph merely repeats information from the enclosed résumé, which wastes the reader's time and wastes the opportunity for the writer to present a more complete picture of herself.

(c) Johns attempts to show that she understands retailing, but this paragraph comes across as an arrogant lecture. The tone is particularly inappropriate, given that she is writing to the store's top manager.

(d) The call to action is overly aggressive, and it presumes that the reader will be available and willing to take a phone call from a complete stranger about a job opening that might not even exist.

Effective

(a) Johns gets the reader's attention by demonstrating good awareness of the company and the type of people it hires, presents herself as just such a professional, and then asks to be considered for any relevant job openings.

(b) Johns uses the body of her letter to expand on the information presented in her résumé, rather than simply repeating that information.

(c) The close builds the reader's interest by demonstrating knowledge of the company's policy regarding promotion.

(d) The call to action is respectful, and it makes a response easy for the reader by providing both phone and email contact information.

457 Mountain View Rd.
Clear Lake, IA 50428
June 16, 2020

Ms. Patricia Downing, Store Manager
Walmart
840 South Oak
Iowa Falls, IA 50126

Dear Ms. Downing:

Even with its world-class supply chain, admired brand name, and competitive prices, Walmart obviously would not be the success it is without enthusiastic, service-driven associates and managers. If you have or foresee an opening for such a professional, someone eager to learn the Walmart way and eventually move into a management position, please consider me for the opportunity.

As an associate or management trainee, I can bring a passion for retailing and the perspective I've gained through academic preparation and four years of experience. (Please refer to my enclosed résumé for more information.)

Working as a clerk and then as an assistant manager in a large department store taught me how to anticipate customer needs, create effective merchandising, and deliver service that keeps customers coming back. Moreover, my recent BA degree in retailing, which encompassed such courses as retailing concepts, marketing fundamentals, management, and business information systems, prepared me with in-depth awareness of contemporary retailing issues and strategies.

I understand Walmart prefers to promote its managers from within, and I would be pleased to start out with an entry-level position until I gain the necessary experience. Could we have a brief conversation about the possibilities of joining your team? I am available by phone at 641-747-2222 or email at glendajohns@mailnet.com.

Sincerely,

Glenda Johns

Glenda Johns
Enclosure

Figure 16.2 Unsolicited Application Letter
Demonstrating knowledge of the employer's needs and presenting your qualifications accordingly are essential steps in an unsolicited application letter.

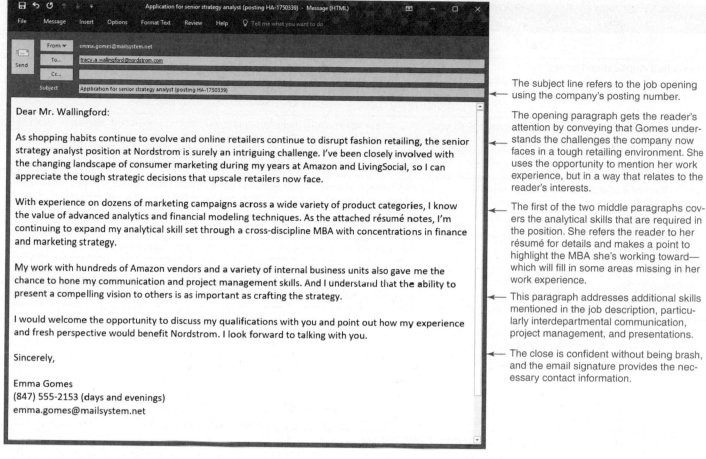

Figure 16.3 **Complementing Your Résumé with an Application Message**
When writing a letter or email message to accompany your résumé, use the opportunity to complement the information already contained in your résumé. Highlight how your qualifications match the needs of the position, without repeating the information from your résumé. Here is a message that could accompany the résumé in Figure 15.6 on page 503.

Getting Attention

The opening paragraph of your application letter must accomplish two essential tasks: (1) explain why you are writing and (2) give the recipient a reason to keep reading by showing that you have some immediate potential for meeting the company's needs. Consider this opening:

> With the recent slowdown in corporate purchasing, I can certainly appreciate the challenge of new fleet sales in this business environment. With my high energy level and 16 months of new-car sales experience, I believe I can produce the results you listed as vital in the job posting on your website.

This applicant does a smooth job of echoing the company's stated needs while highlighting personal qualifications and an understanding of the market. Notice how enthusiasm and knowledge of the industry balance the writer's relative lack of experience. Table 16.1 suggests some other ways you can spark interest and grab attention in your opening paragraph.

Building Interest and Increasing Desire

The middle section of your letter presents your strongest selling points in terms of their potential benefit to the organization, thereby building interest in you and creating a

The first paragraph of your application letter needs to clearly convey the reason you're writing and give the recipient a compelling reason to keep reading.

Use the middle section of your application letter to expand on your opening and present a more complete picture of your strengths.

TABLE 16.1 Tips for Getting Attention in Application Letters

Tip	Example
Unsolicited Application Letters	
Show how your strongest skills will benefit the organization.	If you need a regional sales specialist who consistently meets sales targets while fostering strong customer relationships, please consider my qualifications.
Describe your understanding of the job's requirements and show how well your qualifications fit them.	Your annual report stated that improving manufacturing efficiency is one of the company's top priorities for next year. Through my postgraduate research in process analysis and consulting work for several companies in the industry, I've developed reliable methods for quickly identifying ways to cut production time while reducing resource use.
Mention the name of a person known to and highly regarded by the reader.	When Janice McHugh of your franchise sales division spoke to our business communication class last week, she said you often need promising new marketing graduates at this time of year.
Refer to publicized company activities, achievements, changes, or new procedures.	Today's issue of the *Detroit News* reports that you may need software engineers with robotics experience when your Lansing tire plant automates this spring.
Use a question to demonstrate your understanding of the organization's needs.	Can your fast-growing market analytics division use a researcher with two years of field survey experience, a B.S. in math, and a strong interest in data mining? If so, please consider me for the position.
Solicited Application Letters	
Identify where you discovered the job opening; describe what you have to offer.	My eight years of experience as a social director in the travel industry have given me all the skills highlighted in the Monster.com listing for the opening in your Caribbean cruise division.

desire to interview you. Be specific and back up your assertions with convincing evidence:

> **Ineffective:** I am trained in business communication and have quite a bit of experience in dealing with customers.

> **Effective:** My business major includes coursework in business communication skills, which helped me gain a promotion to shift supervisor during my summer job at Nordstrom Rack.

In a solicited letter, be sure to discuss each major requirement listed in the job posting. If you are deficient in any of these requirements, stress other solid selling points to help strengthen your overall presentation. Don't restrict your message to just core job duties, either. Highlight personal characteristics that apply to the targeted position, such as your ability to work hard or handle responsibility:

> While attending college full-time, I worked part-time during the school year and up to 60 hours a week each summer in order to be totally self-supporting while in college. I can offer your organization the same level of effort and dedication.

Don't bring up salary in your application letter unless the recipient has asked you to include your salary requirements.

Mention your salary requirements only if the organization has asked you to state them. If you don't know the salary that's appropriate for the position and someone with your qualifications, you can find typical salary ranges at the Bureau of Labor Statistics website at **www.bls.gov** and a number of commercial websites. If you do state a target salary, tie it to the value you can offer:

> For the past two years, I have been helping a company similar to yours organize its database marketing efforts. I would therefore like to receive a salary in the same range (the mid-60s) for helping your company set up a more efficient customer database.

CHECKLIST ✔ **Writing Application Letters**

✔ Take the same care with your application letter that you took with your résumé.

✔ If you are *prospecting* using an unsolicited message, do deep research to identify the qualities the company likely wants.

✔ For solicited messages in response to a posted job opening, word your message in a way that echoes the qualifications listed in the posting.

✔ Open the letter by capturing the reader's attention in a businesslike way.

✔ Use specific language to clearly state your interests and objectives.

✔ Build interest and desire in your potential contribution by presenting your key qualifications for the job.

✔ Link your education, experience, and personal qualities to the job requirements.

✔ Outline salary requirements only if the organization has requested that you provide them.

✔ Request an interview at a time and place that is convenient for the reader.

✔ Make it easy to comply with your request by providing your complete contact information and good times to reach you.

✔ Adapt your style for cultural variations, if required.

Toward the end of the middle section, refer the reader to your résumé by citing a specific fact or general point covered there:

> As you can see in the attached résumé, I've been working part-time with a local publisher since my sophomore year. During that time, I've used client interactions as an opportunity to build strong customer service skills.

Motivating Action

The final paragraph of your application letter has two important functions: to ask the reader for a specific action (usually an interview) and to facilitate a reply. Include your email address and phone number, as well as the best times to reach you:

In the final paragraph of your application letter, respectfully ask for specific action and make it easy for the reader to respond.

> After you have reviewed my qualifications, could we discuss the possibility of putting my marketing skills to work for your company? I am available at (360) 555-7845 from 2 p.m. to 10 p.m. Monday to Friday or by email at john.wagner462@mailcom.com.

After editing and proofreading your application letter, give it a final quality check by referring to "Checklist: Writing Application Letters." Then send it along with your résumé promptly, especially if you are responding to an advertisement or online job posting.

FOLLOWING UP AFTER SUBMITTING A RÉSUMÉ

Deciding if, when, and how to follow up after submitting your résumé and application letter is one of the trickiest parts of a job search. First and foremost, keep in mind that employers continue to evaluate your communication efforts and professionalism during this phase, so don't say or do anything to leave a negative impression.

Second, follow whatever instructions the employer has provided. If a job posting says "no calls," for example, don't call. However, if the job posting doesn't say this, it's perfectly acceptable to follow up, and most hiring managers view doing so as a sign of initiative. More hiring managers prefer email than phone follow-ups, but you won't be out of line if you try to follow up via phone.[7]

Third, if the job posting lists a *close date*, don't call or write before then, because the company is still collecting applications and will not have made a decision about inviting people for interviews. Wait a week or so after the close date. If no close date is given and you have no other information to suggest a time line, you can generally contact the company starting a week or two after submitting your résumé. Some companies offer application status updates on their websites, so be sure to look for that before sending an inquiry or telephoning.[8]

When you follow up by email or telephone, you can share an additional piece of information that links your qualifications to the position (keep an eye out for late-breaking news

Think creatively about a follow-up message; show that you've continued to add to your skills or that you've learned more about the company or the industry.

about the company, too) and ask a question about the hiring process as a way to gather some information about your status. Good questions to ask include[9]

- Has a hiring decision been made yet?
- Can you tell me what to expect next in terms of the hiring process?
- What is the company's time frame for filling this position?
- Could I follow up in another week if you haven't had the chance to contact me yet?
- Can I provide any additional information regarding my qualifications for the position?

Whatever the circumstances, a follow-up message can demonstrate that you're sincerely interested in working for the organization, persistent in pursuing your goals, and committed to upgrading your skills.

If you don't land a job at your dream company on the first attempt, don't give up. You can apply again if a new opening appears, or you can send an updated résumé with a new unsolicited application letter that describes how you have gained additional work experience or completed additional coursework. Showing that you are serious about making yourself valuable to a company is a great way to impress hiring managers.

REAL-TIME UPDATES

LEARN MORE BY VISITING THIS WEBSITE

Prepare for your next interview using these Pinterest pins

The Pinterest pinboard maintained by St. Edward's University offers dozens of helpful resources. Go to **real-timeupdates.com/ebc13** and select Learn More in the Students section.

Understanding the Interviewing Process

2 **LEARNING OBJECTIVE**
Describe the typical sequence of job interviews, the major types of interviews, and the attributes employers look for during an interview.

An *employment interview* is a meeting during which you and a potential employer ask questions and exchange information.

An **employment interview** is a meeting during which you and a potential employer ask questions and exchange information. The employer's objective is to find the best talent to fill available job openings, and your objective is to find the right match for your goals and capabilities.

As you get ready to begin interviewing, keep three points in mind:

- The process takes time. Start your preparation and research early; the best job offers usually go to the best-prepared candidates.
- Don't limit your options by looking at only a few companies.
- Interviews are a two-way discovery process—the questions you ask can be as important as the questions companies ask you.

THE TYPICAL SEQUENCE OF INTERVIEWS

The interview process can vary from company to company, but most firms interview candidates in stages as they narrow down the list of possibilities.

The Screening Stage

During the screening stage of interviews, use the limited time available to confirm your fit for the position.

The process usually starts with a *screening* stage designed to filter out applicants who lack the desired qualifications or who might not be willing to accept the salary range or other parameters of the position. This first round of interviews may be conducted by an outside recruiting firm or by staff from the company's human resources (HR) department, rather than the manager you would eventually report to. Screening is often done via telephone or an online assessment system.[10] Note that in some cases you may be required to pass an assessment before you are allowed to begin the application process, so be prepared to do some online testing.[11]

During a screening interview, the company wants to know whether you meet the minimum requirements for the job. Study the job description carefully and be ready to respond to questions about the major qualifications of the position, using key points from your résumé. Screening interviews are usually rather brief, and screeners often have many candidates to interview, so keep your answers short and on topic.[12] Bear in mind that you're not going to win the job at this point; your goal is to make it past the filter and on to the next stage.

The Selection Stage

During the selection stage, continue to show how your skills and attributes can help the company.

Candidates who make it past screening are invited to more in-depth interviews that help the company select the person who is most likely to succeed in the position. Feel free to ask the recruiter or your company contact what to expect in the upcoming interviews, including what interviewing formats will be used and which managers are likely to interview you.[13]

INTELLIGENT COMMUNICATION TECHNOLOGY

Getting Comfortable with AI-Assisted Recruiting and Interviewing

Chances are you will interact with some form of artificial intelligence during your job interviews, beginning with your first contact at a company.

To manage the logistics of gathering information and scheduling interviews, many companies now use chatbots to interact with candidates, at least through the initial stages. These chatbots (which can be either standalone apps or integrated into other apps such as Facebook Messenger) typically ask routine screening questions and provide answers you may have about the application process. High-quality systems are designed to transfer the conversation to a human agent if the bot is unable to answer a question. These bots can make the process more efficient for applicants, too, because they tend to be less overloaded and therefore more responsive than the average human recruiter.

AI tools may also be used to evaluate application materials such as writing samples. The Japanese technology conglomerate Softbank, for instance, uses IBM's Watson AI to grade answers to the questions it asks college students who submit applications.

You may encounter AI during video interviews as well. Recall from Chapter 1's On the Job that companies such as Affectiva use AI to evaluate facial expression and speaking tone, and some systems process speech as well.

The advice for interacting with all these bots might seem a bit counterintuitive, but the best approach is to act naturally and try to forget that you are interacting with pieces of software, not human beings. Stay alert and respectful, the same way you would in a conversation with a manager sitting across the desk interviewing you.

By the way, you don't have to be solely on the receiving end of all this bot activity—you can flip the scheme and put bots to work for you. Jobo (**www.jobbot.me**) is a bot-based system you can use to find openings that fit your talents and interests. You can even create your own bot to interact with recruiters on your behalf—search online for "Estherbot" for one way to do it.

WHAT'S YOUR TAKE?

1. Would you use a bot-based approach such as Jobo to find job openings? Why or why not?
2. Would you resist applying to a company that forced you to take assessments and interact with bots before making connections with a human recruiter? Why or why not?

Sources: Jobo, accessed 25 April 2018, www.jobbot.me; Mya, accessed 25 April 2018, www.hiremya.com; Shinya Tokushima, "Softbank Uses AI to Assess Students' Job Applications," Asahi Shimbun, 30 May 2017, www.asahi.com; Ben Dickson, "How Artificial Intelligence Optimizes Recruitment," The Next Web, 3 June 2017, thenextweb.com.

Employers take various approaches to the selection stage, but a typical next step is a telephone interview with the hiring manager. The manager will want to dig a little deeper into your qualifications and start to determine your fit with the company's culture. This conversation also gives you the opportunity to see whether you can build rapport with your future boss. During these interviews, show keen interest in the job, relate your skills and experience to the organization's needs, listen attentively, and ask questions that show you've done your research.

The most promising applicants are usually invited to visit the company for in-person interviews with a variety of staff and managers. For some positions, you might spend most of a day on-site, meeting a variety of managers and professional staff. If you begin to emerge as a favored candidate, the company will start selling you on the advantages of joining the organization. If the interviewers agree that you're the best candidate, you may receive a job offer, either on the spot or within a few days.

COMMON TYPES OF INTERVIEWS AND INTERVIEW QUESTIONS

Be prepared to encounter a variety of interviewing approaches, often within the same interview or set of interviews. These approaches can be distinguished by the way they are structured, the number of people involved, and the purpose of the interview.

> Be prepared to encounter a variety of interviewing approaches, often within the same interview or set of interviews.

Structured Versus Unstructured Interviews

The overall format of an interview is based on whether it is structured or unstructured. In a **structured interview**, the interviewer (or an app or online system) asks a set series of questions in a fixed order. By asking every candidate the same set of questions, the structured format helps ensure fair interviews and makes it easier for an employer to compare and rank candidates.[14]

You can usually sense that you're in a structured interview if the interviewer is reading questions from a list and recording your answers. Answer each question thoughtfully and completely; your responses will be compared with those from other candidates, and you might not have the chance to revise previous answers as the interview moves along.

> A *structured interview* follows a set sequence of questions, allowing the interview team to compare answers from all candidates.

In an *unstructured interview*, the interviewer adapts the line of questioning based on your responses and questions.

In contrast, an **unstructured interview** doesn't follow a predetermined sequence. It is likely to feel more conversational and personal, as the interviewer adapts the line of questioning based on your answers. You might encounter an unstructured interview after one or more structured interviews, perhaps with a potential colleague or a higher-level manager who wants to get a sense of what you would be like to work with. Take this as good news, that the company believes you can do the job and now wants to see whether you fit the culture.

Even though it may feel like a conversation, remember that it's still an interview, so keep your answers focused and professional. If you sense that the interviewer is circling back to revisit a topic, particularly an answer that you gave in an earlier interview, chances are he or she is probing an area of concern. Use this opportunity to correct or expand on your earlier answer.

Panel and Group Interviews

Interviews can also vary by the number of people involved. Most of your interviews are likely to be one-on-one conversations, although if you are invited to visit a company you'll probably meet with a series of interviewers.

In a *panel interview*, you meet with several interviewers at once.

Some employers use panel or group interviews as well. In a **panel interview**, you answer questions from two or more interviewers in the same session. Panel interviews save time for employers and let them see how candidates perform under pressure. Facing several interviewers at once can feel intimidating, but you can minimize the "firing squad" feeling by treating it as a series of one-on-one interactions. Focus on each interviewer as you answer his or her question, then make eye contact with the others on the panel so everyone feels included.[15]

The interviewers typically come from different parts of the organization and will have different concerns, so frame each answer in that context.[16] For example, an upper-level manager is likely to be interested in your overall business sense and strategic perspective, whereas a potential colleague might be more interested in your technical skills and ability to work in a team.

Use a panel interview as an opportunity to see how people in the company work together. Are they collegial with one another or cold and distant? Does the boss interrupt and overrule or show respect to everyone regardless of rank?

In a *group interview*, you and several other candidates meet with one or more interviewers at once.

In a **group interview**, one or more interviewers meet with several candidates simultaneously. These sessions can involve group discussions and problem-solving activities. In addition to being an efficient way to interview a number of candidates, group interviews let employers see how individuals function in a group or team setting.[17] Whatever the activity, be sure to treat your fellow candidates with respect and encouragement, while looking for opportunities to show leadership and demonstrate the depth of knowledge you have about the company and its needs.

Major Categories of Interview Questions

Interviewing techniques also vary based on the types of questions you are asked. You might encounter two or more types of questions within a single interview, so be prepared to shift your answering approach if you determine that the interviewer is using different types of questions.

Behavioral interview questions ask you to describe how you handled situations from your past.

Behavioral Interview Questions In contrast to generic questions that can often be answered with "canned" responses, **behavioral interview questions** require candidates to craft answers based on their own experiences and attributes.[18] Because they measure actual behavior, behavioral questions are a better predictor of success on the job than traditional interview questions.[19] Regardless of the overall style of an interview, you should expect at least a few behavioral questions.

These questions often deal with teamwork, communication, leadership, conflict resolution, problem solving, mistakes, job commitment, and other soft-skill areas that are difficult to measure other than by someone's actual on-the-job performance.[20] To give you an idea of what these questions are like, here are some typical behavioral questions:[21]

- Tell me about a time you had to deal with a teammate who refused to do his or her share of the work.
- Describe your last high-stress project and how you dealt with the pressure.

- Explain how you resolved a communication breakdown with a boss, professor, or coworker.
- Tell me about a mistake you made on the job and how you resolved the situation and learned from the error.
- Tell me about an important goal you set for yourself and how you achieved it.

Effective answers to behavioral questions have three parts: (1) a brief summary of the situation or task, (2) the approach you took to solve the problem or meet the challenge, and (3) the results you achieved. The acronym STAR can help you remember the sequence: **S/T** for situation or task, **A** for approach, and **R** for results.[22] You are essentially telling a mini-story with a beginning, a middle, and an end. If you don't have a work-related scenario to share in response to a question, consider using something appropriate from your personal or social experience that demonstrates the skill the interviewer is asking about.

To prepare for behavioral questions, study the job description for qualities the company is looking for; then review your work and college experiences to recall several instances in which you demonstrated these qualities. Practice your answers so that you can quickly summarize the situation, the actions you took, and the outcome of those actions.[23]

Use the STAR approach to craft answers to behavioral questions:

- **S/T:** The situation you faced or the task you were given
- **A:** The approach you took
- **R:** The results you achieved

Situational Interview Questions   **Situational interview questions** are similar to behavioral questions except they focus on how you would handle various situations that could arise on the job. The situations will relate closely to the job you're applying for, so the more you know about the position and the company, the better prepared you'll be.

The interviewer might not expect you to have detailed, polished responses to all these hypothetical situations, but he or she will be judging how you go about assessing situations and formulating responses. Even if you aren't familiar with the business details of a particular scenario, use common sense to imagine how experienced people in that situation would respond.

Situational interview questions ask you to explain how you would handle various hypothetical situations.

Case Interviews and Take-Home Assessments   If you are interviewing at investment banks or management consulting firms, you are likely to encounter the **case interview**.[24] Rather than a series of questions, the case interview presents you with one or more problems or questions to solve. If you are pursuing jobs in these fields, you are probably already familiar with the case-based methodology.

In these interviews, you will be given information about a scenario and will be asked to make a forecast, solve a strategic dilemma, or come up with some other sort of answer. A particular case might have multiple viable answers or no right answer at all; what interviewers are really watching is how you approach the problem with limited time and limited resources. Do you assess the situation using all the information you were given? Do you make reasonable guesses about facts and figures you don't have in hand? Does your inquiry follow a logical progression?[25] Some management consulting firms and other organizations offer practice cases and interview preparation tips online; search for "case interviews."

In a case interview, you are asked to solve a business challenge with limited time and information.

Stress Interviews   The most unnerving type of interview is the **stress interview**, during which you might be asked questions designed to unsettle you or might be subjected to long periods of silence, criticism, interruptions, or even hostile reactions by the interviewer. The theory behind this approach is that you'll reveal how well you handle stressful situations, although some experts question whether the technique is valuable or even ethical.[26] If you find yourself in a stress interview, recognize what is happening and collect your thoughts for a few seconds before you respond. Keep in mind that the perceived attacks aren't personal but simply a way to test your responses.

Stress interviews are intended to let recruiters see how you handle yourself under pressure; recognize what is happening, and don't take it personally.

INTERVIEW MEDIA

To reduce travel costs and the demands on employee time, many employers now conduct at least some stages of interviews via telephone or video. Depending on the position, you might also encounter online interviews that range from simple structured questionnaires and tests to realistic job simulations (see Figure 16.4).

Figure 16.4 Job Task Simulations
Computer-based job simulations are an increasingly popular approach to testing job-related skills.

Interviewing by Phone

Treat a telephone interview as seriously as you would an in-person interview.

Chances are good that the screening interview and at least one interview after that will be conducted over the phone. Employers treat telephone interviews as seriously as in-person interviews, so you need to as well. Follow the advice in Table 16.2.

Interviewing by Video

MOBILE APP

Add the **Skype** app to your phone to be ready for video interviews.

To get ready for a video interview, prepare the space you will be in, set up and verify the technology you'll be using, and dress as you would for an in-person interview.

Many employers use video chat for interviews as well. This method can involve live video using Skype or similar video services or some form of video conferencing. You may also encounter video interviewing systems, in which you respond to prerecorded questions online. Everything in Table 16.2 applies to video calls, plus you need to consider the following points:[27]

- Make sure your interviewing space is clean and uncluttered. Remove anything from the walls behind you and the area around you that doesn't look professional.
- Don't sit in front of a window or other strong light source. Adjust the room lighting so that light is directed toward you, without making it glaring. You can use software to control your webcam settings to make you look great on camera.
- Make sure your video setup is ready to go. If the company asks you to use Skype or another public service, test your connection with a friend beforehand and get comfortable using it. If the company emails a link for a videoconferencing service, make sure you download and install any software that might be required well before the scheduled interview time.
- Dress and groom as you would for an in-person interview. Unlike phone interviews, where you do this to boost your mood, with a video call it's essential to look like the sort of person the company wants to hire. Choose solid colors and avoid hues that are too bright or too dark (both of which can throw off the webcam's auto-exposure).
- Maintain frequent "eye contact," which means looking at the camera on your device, not at the person's face on your screen. You'll have the natural urge to look at the person's face, but on the other end it will look like you're staring off at an angle. Move the on-screen window that shows the other person's image as close as you can to the camera on your computer or device. This way you can look into the camera while still feeling like you're looking at the interviewer.
- Don't fidget or move around too much. This is distracting to the interviewer, and your microphone will pick up all the extraneous noise.

REAL-TIME UPDATES

LEARN MORE BY READING THIS ARTICLE

In-depth advice on successful video interviews

This comprehensive article covers everything from positioning your webcam to calming your nerves. Go to **real-timeupdates.com/ebc13** and select Learn More in the Students section.

TABLE 16.2 Tips for a Successful Phone Interview

Tip	Details
Prepare your material.	Have these materials on hand: • Your résumé • Any correspondence you've had with the employer • Your research notes about the company • The job description • Note cards with key message points you'd like to make and questions you'd like to ask
Prepare your space.	Arrange a clean and quiet space to be during the interview. As much as possible, avoid distractions from pets, other people, television, music, and other audio and visual interruptions.
Practice your answers.	Call a friend and rehearse your answers to potential questions to make sure you're comfortable saying them over the phone.
Talk on a landline if possible.	If your mobile service isn't clear and reliable, try to arrange to talk on a landline.
Schedule the interview.	As much as possible, schedule a time when you can be in your prepared space, safe from interruptions.
Dress for a business meeting.	You don't need to go full out, but don't wear sweat pants and a T-shirt. Dressing up sends a signal to your mind and body to be attentive and professional.
Answer your phone professionally.	Say "Hi, this is —" to let callers know they've reached the right person. While your job search is active, answer every call from an unknown caller as if it's a potential employer.
Maintain good posture.	Whether you sit or stand during the interview, good posture will keep you alert and keep your voice strong.
Compensate for the lack of visual nonverbal signals.	You can't use facial expressions or hand gestures for emphasis, so make sure your voice is warm, friendly, and dynamic. Smile frequently—it changes the sound of your voice and lifts your mood.
Finish each answer in a definitive way.	Don't trail off and leave the interviewer wondering whether you're finished.
Speak clearly.	Remember that the interviewer can't see you; your spoken words have to carry the entire message.
Write down essential information you get during the interview.	Don't rely on your memory for important details such as arrangements for a follow-up interview. It's fine to pause and ask, "May I take a moment to write this down?"
End on a positive note.	No matter how you think the call went, thank the interviewer for the opportunity and say you look forward to hearing from the company.

Sources: Based in part on Jon Simmons, "5 Steps to Mastering Phone Interviews," Monster, accessed 25 May 2018, www.monster.com; Larry Kim, "17 Phone Interview Tips to Guarantee a Follow-Up," *Inc.*, 24 March 2015, www.inc.com; Kate Finley, "How to Nail the Dreaded Phone Interview," *Fast Company*, 6 February 2015, www.fastcompany.com.

WHAT EMPLOYERS LOOK FOR IN AN INTERVIEW

Interviews give employers the chance to go beyond the basic data of your résumé to get to know you better and to answer two essential questions. First, can you handle the responsibilities of the position? Naturally, the more you know about the demands of the position, and the more you've thought about how your skills match those demands, the better you'll be able to respond.

The first major question employers try to answer is whether you are qualified for the position.

Second, will you be a good fit with the organization and the target position? All good employers want people who are confident, dedicated, positive, curious, courteous, ethical, and willing to commit to something larger than their own individual goals. Companies also look for fit with their individual cultures. Just like people, companies have different personalities. Some are intense; others are more laid back. Some emphasize teamwork; others expect employees to forge their own way and even compete with one another. Expectations also vary from job to job within a company and from industry to industry. An outgoing personality is essential for sales but less so for research, for instance.

The second major question employers try to answer is whether you would be a good fit in terms of personality and organizational culture.

Improving Fairness and Finding Better Talent with Blind Auditions

Most people like to think they are unbiased and capable of making fair, objective decisions when it comes to judging or assessing others. Unfortunately, that is far from reality. Decades of research suggests that *unconscious* or *implicit bias* is universal and that attitudes and stereotypes affect decision-making in ways that people aren't aware of. Even people who consciously go out of their way to avoid biased assumptions can be influenced by unconscious biases that have been accumulating since childhood.

Implicit bias has been a longstanding concern in job interviews and hiring decisions. A case that opened many eyes to the problem involved classical musicians auditioning for symphony orchestras. In the 1970s, women made up only 5 percent of professional symphony musicians. Orchestras gradually moved to *blind auditions*, where performers are hidden behind a curtain so the people evaluating them can hear but not see them—meaning evaluators can't make judgments based on gender, age, appearances, or anything other than how well the musicians play. Within a decade, the ratio of women had risen to 25 percent.

The concept, sometimes called *blind assessment* or *blind hiring*, is now applied across a range of industries and professions. The GapJumpers system, for example, enables job applicants to take skill auditions anonymously. The employers sponsoring the auditions have no personal information about the applicants when they judge the scores—it is strictly about talent. Applicants who do well on blind auditions are then invited to participate in a more conventional interviewing process, at which point the employers learn who they are. GapJumpers' analysis indicates that more women and more community college graduates make it through to the second stage of interviewing than they do in a traditional selection process.

Blind auditions aren't a cure-all for biased hiring, and they obviously work only during the screening stages. However, if used as part of a comprehensive effort to ensure fair hiring, they can help ensure that a broad and worthy pool of talent has more opportunities to compete for jobs.

WHAT'S YOUR TAKE?

1. How might blind auditions help companies find better talent?
2. Do you think blind auditions can reduce employment discrimination? Why or why not?

Sources: "Understanding Implicit Bias," Kirwan Institute for the Study of Race and Ethnicity, accessed 24 April 2018, kirwaninstitute.osu.edu; Sarah Fister Gale, "Turning a Blind Eye to Hiring a Good Idea," *Workforce*, 30 September 2016, www.workforce.com; GapJumpers, accessed 3 May 2017, www.gapjumpers.me; Jacquelyn Smith, "Why Companies Are Using 'Blind Auditions' to Hire Top Talent," *Business Insider*, 31 May 2015, www.businessinsider.com.

REAL-TIME UPDATES
LEARN MORE BY WATCHING THESE VIDEOS

Five TED talks that will help you prepare for interviews

MIT career advisor Lily Zhang handpicked these talks for the insights they can give all job hunters. Go to **real-timeupdates .com/ebc13** and select Learn More in the Students section.

Beyond these two general questions, most employers look for the qualities of professionalism described in Chapter 1 (see page 5). Throughout the interview process, look for opportunities to show your commitment to excellence, dependability, teamwork, etiquette, ethics, and positive attitude.

PREEMPLOYMENT TESTING AND BACKGROUND CHECKS

Preemployment tests attempt to provide objective, quantitative information about a candidate's skills, attitudes, and habits.

In an effort to improve the predictability of the selection process, many employers now conduct a variety of preemployment evaluations and investigations. Here are the types of assessments you are likely to encounter during your job search:

- **Integrity, personality, and cognitive ability tests.** Most midsize and large companies screen candidates with tests designed to ensure compatibility with the job and with the company's values. These tests can cover such areas as emotional intelligence, ethics, and problem solving.[28]
- **Job knowledge and job skills tests.** These assessments measure the knowledge and skills required to succeed in a particular position. An accounting candidate, for example, might be tested on accounting principles and legal matters (knowledge) and asked to create a simple balance sheet or income statement (skills).
- **Substance tests.** Many companies perform some level of drug and alcohol testing. If you take prescription painkillers or other medications that trigger an alert, you will need to show proof of the prescription.[29]
- **Background checks.** In addition to testing, most companies conduct some level of background checks, including reviewing your credit record, reviewing your driving record, checking to see whether you have a criminal history, confirming your identity, and verifying your education. Note that you must consent to a background check, and

if a company finds something negative, it must report that information to you and give you the opportunity to explain.[30]

- **Online searches.** Finally, you should assume that every employer will conduct a general online search on you. To help prevent a background check from tripping you up, verify that your college transcripts are current, look for any mistakes or outdated information in your credit record, plug your name into multiple search engines to see whether anything embarrassing shows up, and scour your social network profiles and connections for potential problems. Some companies have asked applicants for the passwords to their social media accounts, but a number of states have begun to outlaw this practice.[31]

Google yourself before employers do; you need to know what they are likely to find when they study your online presence.

If you're concerned about any preemployment test, ask the employer for more information or ask your college career center for advice. You can also get more information from the U.S. Equal Employment Opportunity Commission (EEOC) at **www.eeoc.gov**.

REAL-TIME UPDATES
LEARN MORE BY READING THIS ARTICLE
Know your privacy rights

Find out what employers can and cannot ask about you during the recruiting process. Go to **real-timeupdates.com/ebc13** and select Learn More in the Students section.

Preparing for a Job Interview

Now that you're armed with insights into the interviewing and assessment process, you're ready to begin preparing for your interviews. Preparation will help you feel more confident and perform better under pressure, and it starts with learning about the organization.

3 **LEARNING OBJECTIVE**
List six tasks you need to complete in order to prepare for a successful job interview.

LEARNING ABOUT THE ORGANIZATION

You've already done some initial research to identify companies of interest, but when you're invited to an interview, it's time to dig a little deeper (see Table 16.3). Making this effort demonstrates your interest in the company, and it identifies you as a business professional who knows the importance of investigation and analysis.

In addition to learning about the company and the job opening, try to find out as much as you can about the managers who will be interviewing you, if you can get their names. Search LinkedIn in particular. As noted earlier, it's also perfectly acceptable to ask your recruiting contact at the company for the names and titles of the people who will be interviewing you. Think about ways to use whatever information you find during your interview. For example, if an interviewer lists membership in a particular professional organization, you might ask whether the organization is a good forum for people to learn about vital issues in the profession or industry. This question gives the interviewer an opportunity to talk about his or her own interests and experiences for a moment, which builds rapport and might reveal vital insights into the career path you are considering. Just make sure your questions are sincere and not uncomfortably personal.

Interviewers expect you to know some basic information about the company and its industry.

Check out the "Five-Minute Guide to Preparing for Job Interviews" at the end of the chapter.

THINKING AHEAD ABOUT QUESTIONS

Planning ahead for the interviewer's questions will help you handle them more confidently and successfully. In addition, you will want to prepare insightful questions of your own.

Planning for the Employer's Questions

Many general interview questions are "stock" queries you can expect to hear again and again during your interviews. Get ready to face variations of these six at the very least:

- **What is the hardest decision you've ever had to make?** Be prepared with a good example (that isn't too personal), explaining why the decision was difficult, how you made the choice you made, and what you learned from the experience. The STAR approach is perfect for this.

You can expect to face a number of common questions in your interviews, so be sure to prepare for them.

MOBILE APP
The **CareerBuilder** app lets you search and apply for jobs from your phone or tablet.

TABLE 16.3 **Investigating an Organization and a Job Opportunity**

Where to Look and What You Can Learn

- *Company website, blogs, and social media accounts:* Overall information about the company, including key executives, products and services, locations and divisions, employee benefits, job descriptions
- *Competitors' websites, blogs, and social media accounts:* Similar information from competitors, including the strengths these companies claim to have
- *Industry-related websites and blogs:* Objective analysis and criticism of the company, its products, its reputation, and its management
- *Marketing materials (print and online):* The company's marketing strategy and customer communication style
- *Company publications (print and online):* Key events, stories about employees, new products
- *Your social network contacts:* Names and job titles of potential contacts within a company
- *Periodicals (newspapers and trade journals, both print and online):* In-depth stories about the company and its strategies, products, successes, and failures; you may find profiles of top executives
- *Career center at your college:* Often provides a wide array of information about companies that hire graduates
- *Current and former employees:* Insights into the work environment

Points to Learn About the Organization

- Full name
- Location (headquarters and divisions, branches, subsidiaries, or other units)
- Ownership (public or private; whether it is owned by another company)
- Brief history
- Products and services
- Industry position (whether the company is a leader or a minor player; whether it is an innovator or more of a follower)
- Key financial points (such as stock price and trends, if a public company)
- Growth prospects (whether the company is investing in its future through research and development; whether it is in a thriving industry)

Points to Learn About the Position

- Title
- Functions and responsibilities
- Qualifications and expectations
- Possible career paths
- Salary range
- Travel expectations and opportunities
- Relocation expectations and opportunities

- **What is your greatest weakness?** This question seems to be a favorite of some interviewers, although it probably rarely yields definitive information as it's unlikely that many candidates will answer with a weakness that ruins their chances. Two effective approaches are answering with something that is minor and unrelated to the core responsibilities of the job or mentioning a shortcoming that you had in the past but took steps to remedy.[32] You can also mention a skill you plan to develop, without characterizing it as a weakness.

- **Where do you want to be five years from now?** This question tests (1) whether you've given thought to your long-term goals and (2) whether you're merely using this job as a stopover until something better comes along. While being truthful, frame your answer in a way that expresses your enthusiasm for the position and your desire to build a career with the company.[33]

- **What didn't you like about previous jobs you've held?** Answer this one carefully: The interviewer is trying to predict whether you'll be an unhappy or difficult employee.[34] Describe something that you didn't like in a way that puts you in a positive light, such as having limited opportunities to apply your skills or education. Avoid making negative comments about former employers or colleagues.

- **Tell me something about yourself.** One good strategy is to briefly share the "story of you" (see page 486)—quickly summarizing where you have been and where you would like to go—in a way that aligns your interests with the company's. Alternatively, you can focus on a specific skill you know is valuable to the company, share something relevant to the business that you are passionate about, or offer a short summary of what colleagues or customers think about you.[35] Whatever tactic you choose, this is not the time to be shy or indecisive, so be ready with a confident, memorable answer.

- **How do you spend your free time?** This question can pop up late in an interview, after the interviewer has covered the major work-related questions and wants to get a better idea of what sort of person you are.[36] Prepare an answer that is honest and that puts you in a positive light, without revealing more than you are comfortable revealing or suggesting that you might not fit in the corporate culture. Sports, hobbies, reading, spending time with family, and volunteer work are all "safe" answers.

Continue your preparation by planning a brief answer to each question in Table 16.4. Use the STAR approach (page 531) to frame your responses as mini-stories.

Look for ways to frame your responses as brief stories rather than as dry facts or statements.

Planning Questions of Your Own

Remember that an interview is a two-way conversation. By asking insightful questions, you can demonstrate your understanding of the organization, steer the discussion into areas that allow you to present your qualifications to best advantage, and verify for yourself whether this is a good opportunity. Plus, you can use questions to demonstrate your ability to assess and explore important business issues.[37] Interviewers also expect you to ask questions, and they tend to look negatively on candidates who don't have any questions to ask. For good questions that you can use as a starting point, see Table 16.5. Put your questions in the context of what you have learned about the company and the position, and avoid asking questions that can be easily answered on the company's website or in the job posting.

Preparing questions of your own helps you understand the company and the position, and it sends an important signal that you are truly interested.

TABLE 16.4 Twenty-Five Common Interview Questions

Questions About College

1. What courses in college did you like most? Least? Why?
2. Do you think your extracurricular activities in college were worth the time you spent on them? Why or why not?
3. When did you choose your college major? Did you ever change your major? If so, why?
4. Do you feel you did the best scholastic work you are capable of?
5. How has your college education prepared you for this position?

Questions About Employers and Jobs

6. Why did you leave your last job?
7. Why did you apply for this job opening?
8. Why did you choose your particular field of work?
9. What are the disadvantages of your chosen field?
10. What do you know about our company?
11. What do you think about how this industry operates today?
12. Why do you think you would like this particular type of job?

Questions About Work Experiences and Expectations

13. What was your biggest failure?
14. What is your biggest weakness?
15. Describe an experience in which you learned from one of your mistakes.
16. What motivates you? Why?
17. What would past managers or colleagues say about you?
18. What have you done that shows initiative and willingness to work?
19. Why should we hire you?

Questions About Work Habits

20. Do you prefer working with others or by yourself?
21. What type of boss do you prefer?
22. Have you ever had any difficulty getting along with colleagues or supervisors? With instructors? With other students?
23. What would you do if you were given an unrealistic deadline for a task or project?
24. How do you feel about overtime work?
25. How do you handle stress or pressure on the job?

Sources: "50 Most Common Interview Questions," Glassdoor, 25 March 2016, www.glassdoor.com; Liz Ryan, "How to Answer Ten Common Interview Questions—with Confidence," *Forbes*, 9 December 2017, www.forbes.com; Carole Martin, "Answers to 10 Most Common Interview Questions," Monster, accessed 25 April 2018, www.monster.com.

TABLE 16.5 Ten Questions to Consider Asking an Interviewer

Question	Reason for Asking
1. How does this job fit in the overall department or organization?	A vague answer could mean that the responsibilities have not been clearly defined, which is almost guaranteed to cause frustration if you take the job.
2. What have past employees done to excel in this position?	This will help you go beyond the job description to understand what the company really wants.
3. How do you measure success for someone in this position?	A vague or incomplete answer could mean that the expectations you will face are unrealistic or ill defined.
4. What is the first problem that needs the attention of the person you hire?	Not only will this help you prepare, but it can also signal whether you're about to jump into a problematic situation.
5. How well do my qualifications align with the current and future needs of this position?	This gives you the opportunity to address any unspoken concerns the interviewer might have.
6. Why is this job now vacant?	If the previous employee got promoted, that's a good sign. If the person quit, that might not be such a good sign.
7. What makes your organization different from others in the industry?	The answer will help you assess whether the company has a clear strategy to succeed in its industry and whether top managers communicate this to lower-level employees.
8. How would you define your organization's managerial philosophy?	You want to know whether the managerial philosophy is consistent with your own working values.
9. What is a typical workday like for you?	The interviewer's response can give you clues about daily life at the company.
10. What are the next steps in the selection process? What's the best way to follow up with you?	Knowing where the company is in the hiring process will give you clues about following up after the interview and possibly give you hints about where you stand.

Sources: Courtney Connley, "5 Things You Should Ask During Every Job Interview," *Black Enterprise*, June 2016, 29; Jacquelyn Smith and Natalie Walters, "The 29 Smartest Questions to Ask at the End of Every Job Interview," *Business Insider*, 28 January 2016, www.businessinsider.com; Heather Huhman, "5 Must-Ask Questions at Job Interviews," Glassdoor blog, 7 February 2012, www.glassdoor.com.

BOOSTING YOUR CONFIDENCE

The best way to build your confidence is to prepare thoroughly and address shortcomings as best you can.

Interviewing is stressful for everyone, so some nervousness is natural. However, you can take steps to feel more confident. Start by reminding yourself that you have value to offer the employer and that the employer already thinks highly enough of you to invite you to an interview.

If some aspect of your appearance or background makes you uneasy, correct it if possible or offset it by emphasizing positive traits such as warmth, wit, intelligence, or charm. Instead of dwelling on your weaknesses, focus on your strengths. Instead of worrying about how you will perform in the interview, focus on how you can help the organization succeed. As with public speaking, the more prepared you are, the more confident you'll be.

> **REAL-TIME UPDATES**
> LEARN MORE BY READING THIS ARTICLE
>
> ### Details that can make or break a job interview
>
> You can't control every variable, but it helps to be aware of the factors that can influence who gets hired and who doesn't. Go to **real-timeupdates.com/ebc13** and select Learn More in the Students section.

POLISHING YOUR INTERVIEW STYLE

Staging mock interviews is a good way to hone your style and boost your confidence.

Competence and confidence are the foundation of your interviewing style, and you can enhance them by giving the interviewer an impression of poise, good manners, and good judgment. You can develop a smooth style by staging mock interviews with a friend or using an interview simulator (see Figure 16.5). Record these mock interviews so you can evaluate yourself. Your college's career center may have computer-based systems for practicing interviews as well.

After each practice session, evaluate the length and clarity of your answers, your nonverbal behavior, and the quality of your voice.

After each practice session, look for opportunities to improve. Make sure your answers are clear, concise, and on-topic. Have your mock interview partner critique your performance, or critique yourself if you're able to record your practice interviews, using the list of warning signs shown in Table 16.6.

TABLE 16.6   Warning Signs: 25 Attributes Interviewers Don't Like to See

1. Poor personal appearance
2. Overbearing, overaggressive, or conceited demeanor; a "superiority complex"; a know-it-all attitude
3. Inability to express ideas clearly; poor voice, diction, or grammar
4. Lack of knowledge or experience
5. Poor preparation for the interview
6. Lack of interest in the job
7. Lack of planning for career; lack of purpose or goals
8. Lack of enthusiasm; passive and indifferent demeanor
9. Lack of confidence and poise; appearance of being nervous and ill at ease
10. Insufficient evidence of achievement
11. Failure to participate in extracurricular activities
12. Overemphasis on money or discussing salary and benefits too early in the process
13. Poor scholastic record
14. Unwillingness to start at the bottom; expecting too much too soon
15. Tendency to make excuses
16. Evasive answers; hedging on unfavorable factors in record
17. Lack of tact
18. Lack of maturity
19. Lack of courtesy and common sense, including answering mobile phones, texting, or chewing gum during the interview
20. Being critical of past or present employers
21. Lack of social skills
22. Marked dislike for schoolwork
23. Lack of vitality
24. Failure to maintain comfortable eye contact
25. Weak or overly aggressive handshake

Sources: Danial Bortz, "7 Rookie Job Interview Mistakes You Need to Avoid," Monster, accessed 25 April 2018, www.monster.com; Donna Fuscaldo, "Seven Deadly Interview Sins," Glassdoor blog, 4 April 2012, www.glassdoor.com; "CareerBuilder Releases Annual List of Strangest Interview and Body Language Mistakes," CareerBuilder.com, 12 January 2017, www.careerbuilder.com; *The Northwestern Endicott Report* (Evanston, Ill.: Northwestern University Placement Center).

In addition to reviewing your answers, evaluate your nonverbal behavior, including your posture, eye contact, facial expressions, and hand gestures and movements. Do you come across as alert and upbeat or passive and withdrawn? Pay close attention to your speaking voice as well. If you tend to speak in a monotone, for instance, practice speaking in a livelier style, with more inflection and emphasis. And watch out for fillers such as *uh*

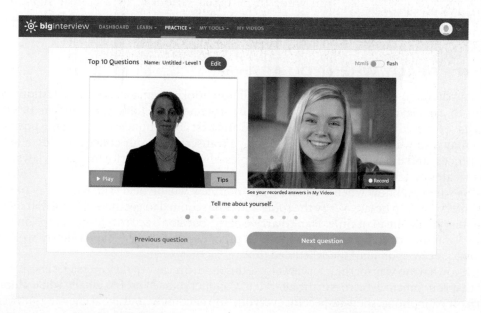

Figure 16.5   Interview Simulators
Job interview simulators can help you practice your responses to common interview questions and fine-tune your interviewing skills.

and *um*. Many people start sentences with a filler without being conscious of doing so. Train yourself to pause silently for a moment instead as you gather your thoughts and plan what to say.

PRESENTING A PROFESSIONAL IMAGE

Dress in a way that shows you understand the company's norms; a safe approach is to dress just a bit more formally than employees do.

Clothing and grooming are important elements of preparation because they reveal something about a candidate's personality, professionalism, and ability to sense the unspoken rules of a situation. Your research into various industries and professions should give you insight into expectations for business attire. If you're not sure what to wear, ask someone who works in the same industry, call the company's receptionist, or even visit the company at the end of the day and see what employees are wearing as they leave the office. However, if they are dressed extremely casually, plan to dress a notch or two above that. You don't need to spend a fortune on interview clothes, but your clothes must be clean, ironed, and appropriate. The following look will serve you well in just about any interview situation:[38]

- Hairstyle appropriate for the industry and the profession
- For more formal environments and for many professional or managerial positions, a conservative business suit (for women, that means no exposed midriffs, short skirts, or plunging necklines) in a dark solid color or a subtle pattern such as pinstripes; understated tie for men; coordinated blouse for women
- For less formal environments, smart-looking "business casual," including a pressed shirt or blouse and nice slacks or a skirt

Use style and grooming choices to send the signal that you are a serious professional.

- Stylish but professional-looking shoes (no extreme high heels, exposed toes, or casual shoes)
- Clean hands and nicely trimmed fingernails
- Little or no perfume or cologne (some people are allergic, and many people are put off by strong smells)
- Limited accessories
- Subtle makeup
- Exemplary personal hygiene

REAL-TIME UPDATES

LEARN MORE BY WATCHING THIS PRESENTATION

Simple tips for a professional interview look

Not sure how to get the right look? Follow this advice. Go to **realtimeupdates.com/ebc13** and select Learn More in the Students section.

If you're not sure how formal a company is, bring a blazer that you can wear to dress up or carry to dress down. Whatever the style, remember that an interview is not the place to express your individuality or to let your inner rebel run wild. To be taken seriously, send a clear signal that you understand the business world and know how to adapt to it.

BEING READY WHEN YOU ARRIVE

Be ready to go as soon as you arrive at the interviewing site; don't fumble around for your résumé or your list of questions.

When you go to your interview, take a small notebook, a pen, a list of the questions you want to ask, several copies of your résumé (protected in a folder), an outline of what you have learned about the organization, and any past correspondence about the position. You may also want to take a small calendar, a transcript of your college grades, a list of references, and a portfolio containing samples of your work, performance reviews, and certificates of achievement.[39]

Be sure you know when and where the interview will be held. The worst way to start any interview is to be late. Verify the route and time required to get there, even if that means traveling there ahead of time. Plan to arrive early, but don't approach the reception desk until 5 minutes or so before your appointed time.[40] Chances are the interviewer won't be ready to receive you until the scheduled time.

If you have to wait for the interviewer, use this time to review the key messages about yourself that you want to get across in the interview. Conduct yourself professionally while waiting. Turn off your phone, show respect for everyone you encounter, and avoid chewing gum, eating, or drinking. Anything you do or say at this stage may get back to the interviewer, so make sure your best qualities show from the moment you enter the premises. To review the steps for planning a successful interview, see "Checklist: Planning for a Successful Job Interview."

> **CHECKLIST** ✔ Planning for a Successful Job Interview
>
> ✔ Learn about the organization, including its operations, markets, and challenges.
> ✔ Learn as much as you can about the people who will be interviewing you if you can find their names.
> ✔ Plan for the employer's questions, including questions about tough decisions you've made, your perceived shortcomings, what you didn't like about previous jobs, and your career plans.
> ✔ Plan questions of your own to find out whether this is really the job and the organization for you and to show that you've done your research.
> ✔ Bolster your confidence by removing as many sources of apprehension as you can.
>
> ✔ Polish your interview style by staging mock interviews.
> ✔ Present a professional appearance with appropriate dress and grooming.
> ✔ Be ready when you arrive and bring along a pen, paper, a list of questions, copies of your résumé, an outline of your research on the company, and any correspondence you've had regarding the position.
> ✔ Double-check the location and time of the interview, and map out the route beforehand.
> ✔ Relax and be flexible; the schedule and interview arrangements may change when you arrive.

Interviewing for Success

At this point, you have a good sense of the overall process and know how to prepare for your interviews. The next step is to get familiar with the three stages of every interview: the warm-up, the question-and-answer session, and the close.

4 LEARNING OBJECTIVE
Explain how to succeed in all three stages of an interview.

THE WARM-UP

The warm-up stage doesn't have any official time boundary, but generally speaking, it is the first few minutes of the interview, as you meet the interviewer and settle into place. It might occur while you're walking from the lobby to a conference room or the interviewer's office and continue while you take your seats and move into a more formal conversation. Don't let your guard down if the interviewer engages in what feels like small talk; these exchanges are every bit as important as structured questions.

Show positive body language and a warm smile to create a positive first impression. When the interviewer extends a hand, respond with a firm but not overpowering handshake. Repeat the interviewer's name when you're introduced ("It's a pleasure to meet you, Ms. Litton"). Wait until you're asked to be seated or the interviewer has taken a seat. Let the interviewer start the discussion, and be ready to answer one or two substantial questions right away. Here are some questions that you might hear during the warm-up stage:[41]

The first few minutes of the interview might feel like small talk, but the interviewer is forming an impression of you, so respond with positive body language, a warm smile, and thoughtful answers.

- Why do you want this job?
- Why do you want to work here?
- What do you know about us?
- Tell me a little about yourself.
- Why should we hire you?

You'll probably feel nervous and have the urge to race through your answers, but remember to breathe slowly and take a second to respond. After you move through the first couple of questions, you should start to feel more comfortable.

You might face substantial questions as soon as your interview starts, so make sure you are prepared and ready to go.

THE QUESTION-AND-ANSWER STAGE

The bulk of the interview is likely to be a series of questions in which the interviewer asks about your qualifications, discusses some of the points mentioned in your résumé, and asks how you have handled particular situations in the past (behavioral questions) or would handle them in the future (situational questions). You'll also be asking questions of your own.

Answering and Asking Questions

Let the interviewer lead the conversation, and never answer a question before he or she has finished asking it. Not only is this type of interruption rude, but the last few words of

Listen carefully to questions before you answer.

the question might alter how you respond. As much as possible, avoid one-word yes-or-no answers. Look for opportunities to expand on an earlier positive response or explain a negative response. If you're asked a difficult or offbeat question, pause before responding. Think through the implications of the question. For instance, the recruiter may know that you can't answer a question and only wants to see whether you can construct a logical approach to solving a problem.

Whenever you're asked whether you have any questions, or whenever doing so naturally fits the flow of the conversation, ask a question from the list you've prepared. Probe for what the company is looking for in its new employees so that you can show how you meet the firm's needs. Also try to zero in on any reservations that you sense the interviewer might have about you so that you can dispel them.

Listening to the Interviewer

Paying attention to both verbal and nonverbal messages can help you turn the question-and-answer stage to your advantage.

Active listening (see Chapter 2) can help you gauge the interviewer's mood and uncover any unspoken concerns. Facial expressions, eye movements, gestures, and posture may tell you the real meaning of what is being said. Be especially aware of how your answers are received. Does the interviewer nod in agreement or smile to show approval? If so, you're making progress. If not, you might want to expand an answer or ask if you've understood the question correctly.

Handling Potentially Discriminatory Questions

Federal, state, and local laws prohibit employment discrimination based on a variety of factors, and well-trained interviewers know to avoid questions that could be used to discriminate in the hiring process.

Think about how you might respond if you are asked a potentially unlawful question.

Although it's less likely to happen in a firm with well-trained interviewers, you might encounter a question you consider discriminatory. A variety of federal, state, and local laws prohibit employment discrimination on the basis of race, ethnicity, gender, age (at least if you're between 40 and 70), marital status, religion, national origin, or disability. Interview questions designed to elicit information on these topics are potentially illegal.[42] Table 16.7 compares some specific questions that employers are and are not allowed to ask during an employment interview.

If an interviewer asks a potentially unlawful question, consider your options before you respond. You can refuse to answer it, you can answer it and move on, or you can try to identify why the interviewer might have asked it.[43] For example, if an interviewer

TABLE 16.7 Acceptable Versus Potentially Discriminatory Interview Questions

Interviewers May Ask This . . .	But Not This
What is your name?	What was your maiden name?
Are you over 18?	When were you born?
Did you graduate from high school?	When did you graduate from high school?
[Questions about race are not allowed.]	What is your race?
Can you perform [specific tasks]?	Do you have physical or mental disabilities?
[Questions about alcohol use are not allowed.]	Do you drink alcoholic beverages?
Are you currently using illegal drugs?	Have you ever been addicted to drugs in the past?
Would you be able to meet the job's requirement to frequently work weekends (or evenings)?	Would working on weekends conflict with your religion?
[Questions about marital status are not allowed.]	Are you married?
Do you have the legal right to work in the United States?	What country are you a citizen of?
Have you ever been convicted of a felony?	Have you ever been arrested?
This job requires that you speak Spanish. Do you?	What language did you speak in your home when you were growing up?
What is your current address and how long have you lived there?	Do you own or rent your home?

Sources: "Illegal Interview Questions," Betterteam, 7 January 2018, www.betterteam.com; Dave Johnson, "Illegal Job Interview Questions," *CBS Money Watch*, 27 February 2012, www.cbsnews.com; "5 Illegal Interview Questions and How to Dodge Them," *Forbes*, 20 April 2012, www.forbes.com; Vivian Giang, "11 Common Interview Questions That Are Actually Illegal," *Business Insider*, 5 July 2013, www.businessinsider.com.

inappropriately asks whether you are married or have strong family ties in the area, he or she might be trying to figure out if you're willing to travel or relocate—both of which are acceptable questions. You could respond by asking whether there are concerns about travel or relocation.

Even if you do answer the question as it was asked, think hard before accepting a job offer from this company if you have alternatives. Was the off-limits question possibly accidental (it happens, particularly during casual exchanges over meals) and therefore not really a major concern? If you think it was intentional, would you want to work for an organization that condones illegal or discriminatory questions or that doesn't train its employees to avoid them?

If you believe an interviewer's questions to be unreasonable, unrelated to the job, or an attempt to discriminate, you have the option of filing a complaint with the EEOC or with the agency in your state that regulates fair employment practices.

THE CLOSE

Like the warm-up, the end of the interview is more important than its brief duration would indicate. These last few minutes are your final opportunity to emphasize your value to the organization and to correct any misconceptions the interviewer might have. Be aware that many interviewers will ask whether you have any more questions at this point, so save one or two from your list.

> **MOBILE APP**
> The **Monster** app offers helpful tips to help you prepare for your next job interviews.

Concluding Gracefully

You can usually tell when the interviewer is moving to end to the interview. He or she may ask whether you have any more questions, check the time, summarize the discussion, or simply tell you that the allotted time for the interview is up. When you get the signal, be sure to thank the interviewer for the opportunity and express your interest in the organization. If you can do so comfortably, try to pin down what will happen next, but don't press for an immediate decision.

Conclude an interview with courtesy and enthusiasm; ask questions if you're not sure about what will happen next.

If this is your second or third interview, it may end with a job offer. If you have other offers or need time to think about this offer, it's perfectly acceptable to thank the interviewer for the offer and ask for some time to consider it. If no job offer is made, the interview team may not have reached a decision yet, but you may tactfully ask when you can expect to know the decision.

Discussing Salary

Before you reach the interview stage, you should have a salary range in mind based on the research you've done into the position. If you're asked about your salary requirements and aren't ready to name a figure, you can say that you would expect compensation in line with industry norms for someone with your experience.

Research salary ranges in your job, industry, and geographic region before you try to negotiate salary.

How far you can negotiate depends on several factors, including the market demand for your skills, the strength of the job market, the company's compensation policies, the company's financial health, and any other job offers you may be considering. If you're comparing offers, be sure to consider the entire compensation and benefits package. And remember that you're negotiating a business deal, not asking for personal favors, so focus on the unique value you can bring to the job. The more information you have, the stronger your position will be.

Negotiating benefits may be one way to get more value from an employment package.

INTERVIEW NOTES

Maintain a notebook or simple database with information about each company, interviewers' answers to your questions, contact information for each interviewer, the status of follow-up communication, and upcoming interview appointments. Carefully organized notes will help you decide which company is the right fit for you when it comes time to choose from among the job offers you receive.

Keep careful notes during the job-search process so you don't miss deadlines or commit other mistakes.

To review the important tips for successful interviews, see "Checklist: Making a Positive Impression in Job Interviews."

CHECKLIST ✔ Making a Positive Impression in Job Interviews

A. Be ready to make a positive impression in the warm-up stage.
- ✔ Be alert from the moment you arrive; even initial small talk is part of the interviewing process.
- ✔ Greet the interviewer by name, with a smile and direct eye contact.
- ✔ Offer a firm (not crushing) handshake if the interviewer extends a hand.
- ✔ Take a seat only after the interviewer invites you to sit or has taken his or her own seat.
- ✔ Listen for clues about what the interviewer is trying to get you to reveal about yourself and your qualifications.
- ✔ Exhibit positive body language, including standing up straight, walking with purpose, and sitting up straight.

B. Convey your value to the organization during the question-and-answer stage.
- ✔ Let the interviewer lead the conversation.
- ✔ Never answer a question before the interviewer finishes asking it.
- ✔ Listen carefully to the interviewer and watch for nonverbal signals.

- ✔ Don't limit yourself to simple yes-or-no answers; expand on the answer to show your knowledge of the company (but don't ramble on).
- ✔ If you encounter a potentially discriminatory question, decide how you want to respond before you say anything.
- ✔ When you have the opportunity, ask questions from the list you've prepared; remember that interviewers expect you to ask questions.

C. Close on a strong note.
- ✔ Watch and listen for signs that the interview is about to end.
- ✔ Quickly evaluate how well you've done, and correct any misperceptions the interviewer might have.
- ✔ If you receive an offer and aren't ready to decide, it's entirely appropriate to ask for time to think about it.
- ✔ Don't bring up salary, but be prepared to discuss it if the interviewer raises the subject.
- ✔ End with a warm smile and a handshake, and thank the interviewer for meeting with you.

---

5 LEARNING OBJECTIVE
Identify the most common employment messages that follow an interview, and explain when you would use each one.

Following Up After an Interview

Staying in contact with a prospective employer after an interview shows that you really want the job and are motivated to get it. Doing so also gives you another chance to demonstrate your communication skills and sense of business etiquette. Following up brings your name to the interviewer's attention once again and reminds him or her that you're actively looking and waiting for the decision.

Whenever you hear from a company during the application or interview process, be sure to respond quickly, even if it's only to ask for more time. If a company doesn't hear back from you within 24 hours, it might move on to the next candidate.[44]

FOLLOW-UP MESSAGE

A follow-up message is another chance to promote yourself to an employer.

Send a follow-up message within two days of the interview, even if you feel you have little chance of getting the job. Such messages are often referred to as "thank-you notes," but they give you an important opportunity to go beyond merely expressing your appreciation (see Figure 16.6). You can use the message to reinforce the reasons you are a good choice for the position, modify any answers you gave during the interview if you realize you made a mistake or have changed your mind, and respond to any negatives that might have arisen in the interview.[45] Email is usually acceptable for follow-up messages, unless the interviewer has asked you to use other media.

MESSAGE OF INQUIRY

You can inquire about the hiring decision if you haven't heard by the promised date.

If you're not advised of the interviewer's decision by the promised date or within two weeks, you might make an inquiry. A message of inquiry (which can be handled by email if the interviewer has given you his or her email address) is particularly appropriate if you've received a job offer from a second firm and don't want to accept it before you have an answer from the first. The following example illustrates an effective approach:

Figure 16.6 Follow-Up Message: Ineffective and Effective
Use the follow-up message after an interview to express continued interest in the opportunity, to correct or expand on any information you provided in the interview, and to thank the interviewer for his or her time.

When we talked on April 7 about the fashion coordinator position in your Park Avenue showroom, you indicated that a decision would be made by May 1. I am still enthusiastic about the position and eager to know what conclusion you've reached.

To complicate matters, another firm has now offered me a position and has asked that I reply within the next two weeks.

Provides enough information to remind the reader about the previous discussion

Introduces the sense of urgency

Makes a courteous request for specific action

> Would it be possible to hear your decision by Thursday, May 12? If you need more information from me before then, please let me know.

REQUEST FOR A TIME EXTENSION

If you receive a job offer while other interviews are still pending, you can ask the employer for a time extension. Open with a strong statement of your continued interest in the job, ask for more time to consider the offer, provide specific reasons for the request, and assure the reader that you will respond by a specific date (see Figure 16.7).

LETTER OF ACCEPTANCE

Confirm important details when writing a letter of acceptance.

When you receive a job offer you want to accept, reply in writing to confirm all the important details. Begin by accepting the position and expressing thanks. Identify the job you're accepting. In the next paragraph, cover any necessary details. Conclude by saying that you look forward to reporting for work. As always, a positive letter should convey your enthusiasm and eagerness to cooperate:

Confirms the specific terms of the offer with a good-news statement at the beginning

> I'm delighted to accept the graphic design position in your advertising department at the salary of $3,875 per month.

Covers miscellaneous details in the body

> I am enclosing the health insurance forms you asked me to complete and sign. I've already given notice to my current employer and will be able to start work on Monday, January 18.

Closes with another reference to the good news and a look toward the future

> The prospect of joining your firm is exciting. Thank you for giving me this opportunity, and I look forward to making a positive contribution.

Written acceptance of a job offer can be considered a legally binding contract, so make sure you intend to take the job.

Be aware that a job offer and a written acceptance of that offer can constitute a legally binding contract, for both you and the employer. Before you send an acceptance letter, be sure you want the job.

LETTER DECLINING A JOB OFFER

If you decide to decline a job offer, do so tactfully.

As you progress through your interviews, you may find that you need to write a letter declining a job offer. Use the techniques for negative messages (see Chapter 10): Open warmly, state the reasons for refusing the offer, decline the offer explicitly, and close on a pleasant note that expresses gratitude. By taking the time to write a sincere, tactful letter, you leave the door open for future contact:

Uses a buffer in the opening paragraph

> Thank you for your hospitality during my interview at your Durham facility last month. I'm flattered that you would offer me the systems analyst position that we talked about.

Precedes the bad news with tactfully phrased reasons for the applicant's unfavorable decision

> I was fortunate to receive two job offers during my search. Because my desire to work abroad can more readily be satisfied by another company, I have accepted that job offer.

I deeply appreciate the time you spent talking with me. Thank you again for your consideration and kindness.

Lets the reader down gently with a sincere and cordial ending

LETTER OF RESIGNATION

If you get a job offer while employed, you can maintain good relations with your current employer by writing a thoughtful letter of resignation to your immediate supervisor. Follow the advice for negative messages, and make the letter sound positive, regardless of how you

Letters of resignation should always be written in a gracious and professional tone that avoids criticism of your employer or your colleagues.

Ineffective

Request for extension - Message (HTML)

MESSAGE   INSERT   OPTIONS   FORMAT TEXT   REVIEW   DEVELOPER

To... frank.lapuzo@lonestarfoods.com
Cc...
Subject Request for extension

Dear Mr. Lapuzo:

I need more time to give you a decision about your offer of the e-commerce director position at Lone Star Foods. I am thrilled to get the offer, don't get me wrong, but I have another iron the fire, as they say.

To make a long story short, I had a follow-up interview with another company on my schedule before my interview with you. Although I am truly interested in your organization because of its commitment to quality and team-based management style, this other job bears looking into.

I am so sorry to hold you up, but you certainly understand my need to verify and compare this other opportunity. I'll let you know by January 25, possibly earlier if I can.

Sincerely,

(a) "I need" is a blunt and fairly offensive way to start any message, and particularly so when one is asking the reader to make an accommodation.

(b) "To make a long story short" only makes the story longer, and saying "this other job bears looking into" sounds self-centered.

(c) Apologizing isn't necessary under the circumstances, but the writer then commits a serious blunder by failing to ask for the extension to January 25.

Effective

Request for extension - Message (HTML)

MESSAGE   INSERT   OPTIONS   FORMAT TEXT   REVIEW   DEVELOPER

To... frank.lapuzo@lonestarfoods.com
Cc...
Subject Request for extension

Dear Mr. Lapuzo:

The e-commerce director position at Lone Star Foods is an exciting challenge, and I am thrilled that you offered me the position.

Because of another commitment, I would appreciate your giving me until January 25 to make a decision. Before our interview, I scheduled a follow-up interview with another company. I'm interested in your organization because of its commitment to quality and team-based management style, but I do feel obligated to keep my appointment.

If you need my decision immediately, I certainly understand. However, if you can allow me the added time to fulfill this earlier commitment, I would be grateful. Please let me know at your earliest convenience.

Sincerely,

Chang Li
1448 Solsbury Avenue
Thunderhawk, SD 57655
(605) 555-6897

(a) This positive opener confirms the writer's interest in the job and serves as a buffer before the upcoming request.

(b) Phrasing this as the need to meet a prior commitment is a graceful way to communicate the idea of wanting to explore the other opportunity, without coming right out and saying so.

(c) The respectful close acknowledges that it might not be possible for the reader to accommodate the request for an extension. The conditional phrasing ("if you can") is a good way to make the request without coming across as demanding.

Figure 16.7   Request for a Time Extension: Ineffective and Effective
Needing more time to decide on a job offer is not uncommon, particularly for candidates with desirable credentials. However, make the request in a respectful and subtle way. The reader understands you are comparing opportunities and looking for the best offer, so you don't need to belabor this point.

feel. Say something favorable about the organization, the people you work with, or what you've learned on the job. Then state your intention to leave and give the date of your last day on the job. Be sure you give your current employer at least two weeks' notice:

Uses an appreciative opening to serve as a buffer

> My sincere thanks to you and to all the other Emblem Corporation employees for helping me learn so much about serving the public these past two years. You have given me untold help and encouragement.

States reasons before the bad news itself, using tactful phrasing to help keep the relationship friendly, should the writer later want letters of recommendation

> You may recall that when you first interviewed me, my goal was to become a customer relations supervisor. Because that opportunity has been offered to me by another organization, I am submitting my resignation. I will miss my friends and colleagues at Emblem, but I want to take advantage of this opportunity.

Discusses necessary details in an extra paragraph

> I would like to terminate my work here two weeks from today (June 13) but can arrange to work an additional week if you want me to train a replacement.

Tempers the disappointment with a cordial close

> My sincere thanks and best wishes to all of you.

To verify the content and style of your follow-up messages, consult the tips in "Checklist: Communicating After an Interview." For more on interviewing and associated messages, visit **real-timeupdates.com/ebc13** and select Chapter 16.

CHECKLIST ✔ Communicating After an Interview

A. Follow-up messages
- ✔ Write a brief follow-up message to say thank you within two days of the interview.
- ✔ Acknowledge the interviewer's time and courtesy.
- ✔ Restate the specific job you're applying for.
- ✔ Express your enthusiasm about the organization and the job.
- ✔ Add any new information that may help your chances.

B. Messages of inquiry
- ✔ If you haven't heard from the interviewer by the promised date or within two weeks, write a brief message of inquiry.
- ✔ Use the direct approach: main idea, necessary details, and specific request.

C. Requests for a time extension
- ✔ Request an extension if you have other interviews scheduled and need time to decide about an offer.
- ✔ Open on a positive note that reiterates your interest in the job.
- ✔ Explain why you need more time.
- ✔ In the close, promise a decision by a specific date.

D. Letters of acceptance
- ✔ State clearly that you accept the offer, identify the job you're accepting, and confirm vital details such as salary and start date.
- ✔ Make sure you want the job; an acceptance letter can be treated as a legally binding contract.

E. Letters declining a job offer
- ✔ Use the indirect approach for negative messages.
- ✔ Open on a warm and appreciative note, and then explain why you are refusing the offer.
- ✔ End on a sincere, positive note.

F. Letters of resignation
- ✔ Send a letter of resignation to your current employer as soon as possible.
- ✔ Begin with an appreciative buffer.
- ✔ Say something favorable about your experience with the organization.
- ✔ State your intention to leave, and give the date of your last day on the job.
- ✔ Close cordially.

ON THE JOB: SOLVING COMMUNICATION DILEMMAS AT **BURNING GLASS**

You recently joined the recruiting team at Burning Glass. Using what you know about job applications and interviewing, address these challenges.

1. Because written communication skills are such an important part of virtually every job at Burning Glass, you pay close attention to how people present themselves in writing. Based on the following openings in unsolicited application letters, which of these candidates has done the best job of capturing your attention and interest?
   a. Having had difficulty myself finding a job that is up to my potential, I appreciate the importance of the work Burning Glass is doing.
   b. I am about to graduate with dual degrees in data science and organizational psychology, which I think you will agree makes me the ideal candidate to push Burning Glass's analytics capabilities to the next level.
   c. With your work at the intersection of human resources and big data analytics, could you use the contributions of someone with dual degrees in data science and organizational psychology?

2. During interviews, you like to put applicants at ease right away, so you usually start by asking an offbeat question to break the tension while also prompting the candidate to reveal something about his or her personality and knowledge. Which of these questions would you choose to start an interview?
   a. What would you be doing right now if you weren't in this job interview?
   b. How long should this interview last?
   c. Ever have one of those days when life seems like one endless job interview?
   d. So . . . buying that weekly lottery ticket still hasn't worked out, eh?

3. The work that Burning Glass does frequently requires employees to tackle complex problems and find answers to questions that are neither simple nor straightforward. Which of these questions would you use to judge a candidate's ability to grasp a problem and begin developing a solution?
   a. You're testifying before a congressional committee on live TV, and a senator wants to know how many mobile phone batteries will be thrown away in the next 10 years. Without access to any additional information, how would you start to construct an estimate of this number?
   b. Based on our conversation so far and my general appearance, guess how old I am.
   c. Why do telephone numbers in movies and TV shows always start with 555? Why don't movie and TV studios just use the numbers of their own offices?
   d. How would you explain the concept of a human family to a creature from another planet?

4. At the end of each interview, you make a point to ask candidates if they have any questions for you. Which of the following responses impresses you the most?
   a. No, thanks. I think I'm all set. You've done a wonderful job of answering whatever questions I might've come in with.
   b. Oh, I don't need to take any more of your time. I'm a pretty good independent thinker. If I have any questions, I'll just look you up online when I get back home.
   c. We've covered the details of the job. Can you tell me what it's like working here? Do you have any fun, or is it work, work, work all the time?
   d. Yes, thanks, I do. Will the recent controversies regarding data privacy violations in social media affect Burning Glass's business plans moving forward?

END OF CHAPTER

Learning Objectives Checkup

Assess your understanding of the principles in this chapter by reading each learning objective and studying the accompanying exercises. You can check your responses against the answer key on page 613.

Objective 16.1: Explain the purposes of application letters, and describe how to apply the AIDA organizational approach to them.

1. Which of these is *not* one of the goals of sending an application letter?

a. To introduce your résumé
b. To ask for a job
c. To persuade an employer to read your résumé
d. To request an interview

2. Why are unsolicited application letters more challenging to write than solicited application letters?
a. Nobody wants to receive unsolicited application letters.
b. With an unsolicited letter, you have to do the research to identify the qualities the company would likely be looking for and convince someone to consider you for a job that might not even be open yet.

c. Solicited application letters are shorter, making it more likely that recruiters will bother to read them.

d. Unsolicited letters do not lend themselves to the AIDA model.

3. Which of the following is a good technique to gain attention in the opening paragraph of any application letter?

a. Make sure you "jump off the page" with an eye-catching design.

b. Explain how you have some immediate potential to meet the company's needs.

c. Invoke a sense of dramatic mystery by withholding either the job you are applying for or some key facts about yourself.

d. Go deep; structure your letter more along the lines of a comprehensive informational report.

4. What are the two vital functions of the final paragraph of an application letter?

a. To ask the reader for an interview (or other appropriate action) and to express how happy would you be to work for the company

b. To ask the reader for an interview (or other appropriate action) and to make it easy for the reader to reply

c. To ask the reader for an interview (or other appropriate action) and to state your salary expectations

d. To encourage the reader to read your résumé and to highlight at least three key points from your résumé

Objective 16.2: Describe the typical sequence of job interviews, the major types of interviews, and the attributes employers look for during an interview.

5. Which of these interview stages happens first?

a. The selection stage

b. The screening stage

c. The filtering stage

d. The sorting stage

6. What is a company's primary goal during the screening stage?

a. To determine which candidates meet the minimum requirements of the job

b. To decide which candidates deserve a job offer

c. To test the market for available talent

d. To compare in-house talent with available talent

7. How do behavioral interview questions differ from situational questions?

a. Behavioral questions ask you to relate incidents and experiences from your past, whereas situational questions put you in actual work situations and ask you to perform some task, such as leading a brainstorming session.

b. They are essentially the same thing, although behavioral questions are generally conducted by computer rather than by a live interviewer.

c. Situational questions ask you to relate incidents and experiences from your past, whereas behavioral questions ask how you would respond to various hypothetical situations in the future.

d. A behavioral interview asks you to relate incidents and experiences from your past, whereas a situational interview asks how you would respond to various hypothetical situations in the future.

8. What are the two most important factors employers look for during interviews?

a. Fit with the organization and motivation

b. Motivation and ability to perform the job

c. Motivation and years of experience

d. Ability to perform the job and compatibility with the organization

Objective 16.3: List six tasks you need to complete in order to prepare for a successful job interview.

9. If an interviewer asks you to describe your biggest weakness, which of the following is a good strategy for your response?

a. The interviewer is just trying to rattle you, so what you say is less important than staying cool and calm while you say it.

b. Frame your response in terms of skills you plan to develop in the future, specifically a skill that will benefit the company.

c. Respectfully explain to the interviewer that the question is illegal.

d. Explain that you don't have any major weaknesses.

10. Which of these is a good strategy for calming your nerves before an interview?

a. Review your three greatest weaknesses and remind yourself that many candidates have weaknesses.

b. Remind yourself that you have value to offer the employer and that the employer already thinks highly enough of you to invite you to an interview.

c. Prepare a clever one-liner about your weaknesses that you can use during the interview to relieve your anxieties.

11. If you believe that you have a particular disadvantage related to some aspect of your appearance, interviewing skills, job skills, or work experience, how should you handle the situation when preparing for an interview?

a. Open the interview by discussing this weakness so you can get it out of the way and move on to more positive topics.

b. Compensate by focusing on your strengths, both while you're preparing and during the interview.

c. Correct the perceived shortcoming if possible; if not, focus on your positive attributes.

d. Ignore the situation; there's nothing you can do about a weakness at this point.

12. Which of these is a good response to the question "So tell me about yourself"?

a. Quickly summarize where you have been in your career and where you would like to go—in a way that aligns your interests with the company's.

b. Work through your top 10 or 12 qualifications from your résumé.

c. Explain that your résumé does a good job of summarizing what you can offer.

13. If you're not sure what style of clothing to wear to a particular interview and you're not able to ask someone at the company for advice, what should you do?

a. Dress in a fairly conservative style; it's better to be a little too dressy than too casual.

b. Dress as you would like to dress on the job.

c. Dress in an eye-catching style that will make a lasting impression on the interviewer.

d. Arrive early with several different changes of clothes; try to see what people there are wearing, then find a place to change into whichever outfit you have that most closely matches.

Objective 16.4: Explain how to succeed in all three stages of an interview.

14. Which of these is the best advice for handling the warm-up stage of the interview?
    a. Stay on your toes, even if it seems like friendly chitchat; the interviewer is forming a vital first impression of you at this point.
    b. Ask as many of your prepared questions as possible, in case you don't have time later.
    c. Aim to convey your top five strengths during the first two minutes of the interview.
    d. Keep it casual; employers want to know what you're like outside the artificial environment of a job interview.

15. Which of the following is an advisable response to an interviewer who asks you about your marital status, how many children you have, and what their ages are?
    a. Answer the questions; it is perfectly within the interviewer's right to ask you such personal questions, even if they are not directly related to the job you are applying for.
    b. Tell the interviewer that such questions are illegal and threaten to sue for invasion of privacy.
    c. Sidestep the questions by asking if the interviewer has some specific concerns about your commitment to the job, your willingness to travel, or some other factor.
    d. If you want the job, refuse to answer the questions but promise that you won't report the illegal questioning to the EEOC.

16. Which of these factors affects the amount of flexibility you have in negotiating salary?
    a. The number of previous positions you've held
    b. The college or university you attended
    c. The market demand for your skills
    d. The number of years since you graduated

Objective 16.5: Identify the most common employment messages that follow an interview, and explain when you would use each one.

17. After a job interview, you should send a follow-up message
    a. within two days after the interview.
    b. only if you think you got the job.
    c. that follows the AIDA organizational model.
    d. that does all of the above.

18. A letter declining a job offer should follow which of these models?
    a. The direct approach
    b. The AIDA model
    c. A negative news approach
    d. The polite plan

Key Terms

application letter Message that accompanies a résumé to let readers know what you're sending, why you're sending it, and how they can benefit from reading it

behavioral interview questions Questions in which you are asked to relate specific incidents and experiences from your past

case interview Interview that presents candidates with one or more problems or questions to solve

employment interview Formal meeting during which you and an employer ask questions and exchange information

group interview Interview in which one or more interviewers meet with several candidates simultaneously

panel interview Interview in which you meet with several interviewers at once

situational interview questions Similar to behavioral interview questions, except they focus on how you would handle various hypothetical situations on the job

stress interview Interview in which you might be asked questions designed to unsettle you or subject you to long periods of silence, criticism, interruptions, and or hostile reactions by the interviewer

structured interview Interview in which the interviewer (or a computer) asks a series of prepared questions in a set order

unstructured interview Interview that doesn't follow a predetermined sequence; it is likely to feel more conversational and personal, as the interviewer adapts the line of questioning based on the candidate's answers

Apply Your Knowledge

To review chapter content related to each question, refer to the indicated Learning Objective.

16-1. How can you distinguish yourself from other candidates in a screening interview and still keep your responses short and to the point? Explain. [LO-2]

16-2. How could you use the group interview format to distinguish yourself as a team player? [LO-2]

16-3. If you lack one important qualification for a job but have made it past the screening stage, how should you prepare to handle this issue during the next round of interviews? [LO-3]

16-4. What is an interviewer likely to conclude about you if you don't have any questions to ask during the interview? [LO-3]

16-5. Why is it important to distinguish unethical or illegal interview questions from acceptable questions? [LO-4]

Practice Your Skills

Message for Analysis

Read the following messages and then (1) analyze the strengths or weaknesses of each document and (2) revise each document so that it follows this chapter's guidelines.

16-6. **Message 16.A Writing an Application Letter [LO-1]**

I'm writing to let you know about my availability for the brand manager job you advertised. As you can see from my enclosed résumé, my background is perfect for the position. Even though I don't have any real job experience, my grades have been outstanding considering that I went to a top-ranked business school.

I did many things during my undergraduate years to prepare me for this job:

- Earned a 3.4 out of a 4.0 with a 3.8 in my business courses
- Elected representative to the student governing association
- Selected to receive the Lamar Franklin Award
- Worked to earn a portion of my tuition

I am sending my résumé to all the top firms, but I like yours better than any of the rest. Your reputation is tops in the industry, and I want to be associated with a business that can pridefully say it's the best.

If you wish for me to come in for an interview, I can come on a Friday afternoon or anytime on weekends when I don't have classes. Again, thanks for considering me for your brand manager position.

16-7. Message 16.B Writing an Application Follow-Up Message [LO-1]

Did you receive my résumé? I sent it to you at least two months ago and haven't heard anything. I know you keep résumés on file, but I just want to be sure that you keep me in mind. I heard you are hiring health-care managers and certainly would like to be considered for one of those positions.

Since I last wrote you, I've worked in a variety of positions that have helped prepare me for management. To wit, I've become lunch manager at the restaurant where I work, which involved a raise in pay. I now manage a waitstaff of 12 and take the lunch receipts to the bank every day.

Of course, I'd much rather be working at a real job, and that's why I'm writing again. Is there anything else you would like to know about me or my background? I would really like to know more about your company. Is there any literature you could send me? If so, I would really appreciate it.

I think one reason I haven't been hired yet is that I don't want to leave Atlanta. So I hope when you think of me, it's for a position that wouldn't require moving. Thanks again for considering my application.

16-8. Message 16.C Writing a Thank-You Message [LO-5]

Thank you for the really marvelous opportunity to meet you and your colleagues at Starret Engine Company. I really enjoyed touring your facilities and talking with all the people there. You have quite a crew! Some of the other companies I have visited have been so rigid and uptight that I can't imagine how I would fit in. It's a relief to run into a group of people who seem to enjoy their work as much as all of you do.

I know that you must be looking at many other candidates for this job, and I know that some of them will probably be more experienced than I am. But I do want to emphasize that my two-year hitch in the Navy involved a good deal of engineering work. I don't think I mentioned all my shipboard responsibilities during the interview.

Please give me a call within the next week to let me know your decision. You can usually find me at my dormitory in the evening after dinner (phone: 877-9080).

16-9. Message 16.D Writing a Message of Inquiry [LO-5]

I have recently received a very attractive job offer from the Warrington Company. But before I let them know one way or another, I would like to consider any offer that your firm may extend. I was quite impressed with your company during my recent interview, and I am still very interested in a career there.

I don't mean to pressure you, but Warrington has asked for my decision within 10 days. Could you let me know by Tuesday whether you plan to offer me a position? That would give me enough time to compare the two offers.

16-10. Message 16.E Writing a Message to Decline a Job Offer [LO-5]

I'm writing to say that I must decline your job offer. Another company has made me a more generous offer, and I have decided to accept. However, if things don't work out for me there, I will let you know. I sincerely appreciate your interest in me.

Exercises

Each activity is labeled according to the primary skill or skills you will need to use. To review relevant chapter content, refer to the indicated Learning Objective. In some instances, supporting information will be found in another chapter, as indicated.

16-11. **Career Management: Preparing for Interviews [LO-3]** Google yourself, scour your social networking profiles, review your Twitter messages, and explore every other possible online source you can think of that might have something about you. If you find anything potentially embarrassing, remove it if possible. Write a summary of your search-and-destroy mission. (You can skip any embarrassing details in your report to your instructor!)

16-12. **Career Management: Researching Target Employers [LO-3]** Select a large company (one on which you can easily find information) where you might like to work. Use online sources to gather some preliminary research on the company; don't limit your search to the company's own website.

- What did you learn about this organization that would help you during an interview there?
- What sources did you use to obtain this information?
- Armed with this information, what aspects of your background do you think might appeal to this company's recruiters?
- If you choose to apply for a job with this company, what keywords would you include on your résumé? Why?

16-13. **Career Management: Interviewing [LO-3]** Prepare written answers to 10 of the questions listed in Table 16.4 on page 537.

16-14. **Career Management: Interviewing [LO-4]** Write a short email to your instructor discussing what you believe are your greatest strengths and weaknesses from an employment perspective. Next, explain how these strengths and weaknesses might be viewed by interviewers evaluating your qualifications.

16-15. **Career Management: Interviewing; Collaboration: Team Projects [LO-4], Chapter 3** Divide the class into two groups. Half the class will be recruiters for a large department store chain that is looking to fill 15 manager-trainee positions. The other half of the class will be candidates for the job. The company is specifically looking for candidates who demonstrate these three qualities: initiative, dependability, and willingness to assume responsibility.

- Have each recruiter select and interview an applicant for 10 minutes.
- Have all the recruiters discuss how they assessed the applicant in each of the three desired qualities. What questions did they ask, or what did they use as an indicator to determine whether the candidate possessed the quality?
- Have all the applicants discuss what they said to convince the recruiters that they possessed each of the three desired qualities.

16-16. Message Strategies: Employment Messages, Communication Ethics: Resolving Ethical Dilemmas [LO-5], Chapter 1 You have decided to accept a new position with a competitor of your company. Write a letter of resignation to your supervisor, announcing your decision. (Make up any information you need.) In an email message to your instructor, address the following questions:

- Will you notify your employer that you are joining a competing firm? Explain.
- Will you use the direct or indirect approach? Explain.
- Will you send your letter by email, place it on your supervisor's desk, or hand it to your supervisor personally?

Expand Your Skills

Critique the Professionals

Find an online video of a business professional being interviewed by a journalist. Using whatever medium your instructor requests, write a brief (no more than one page) assessment of the professional's performance and any tips you picked up that you could use in job interviews.

Sharpen Your Career Skills Online

Bovée and Thill's Business Communication Web Search, at **websearch.businesscommunicationnetwork.com**, is a unique research tool designed specifically for business communication research. Use the Web Search function to find a website, video, article, podcast, or presentation that offers advice on successful interviewing techniques. Write a brief email message to your instructor or a post for your class blog describing the item that you found and summarizing the career skills information you learned from it.

Build Your Career

If you've followed the Build Your Career exercises through the previous 15 chapters, you should have a solid foundation in place for

your résumé. Now it's time for the other essential piece of your employment package, your application letter (or email message, as it often is). While you're working on your letter, keep these four points in mind:[46]

- **Use the direct approach.** Let the recipient know in the first or second sentence why you are writing by referring to a specific job opening (for solicited letters) or expressing your interest in particular types of openings (for unsolicited letters).
- **Complement your résumé, not repeat it.** The application letter is an opportunity to use a more conversational style and explain or expand on key points from your résumé.
- **Remember that it's a promotional message.** Don't be shy about explaining why you are a good fit for the company and the position.
- **End on a positive, grateful tone.** Be sure to include your phone number and email address so it's easy for employers to reach out to you.

Improve Your Grammar, Mechanics, and Usage

The following exercises help you improve your knowledge of and power over English grammar, mechanics, and usage. Turn to the Handbook of Grammar, Mechanics, and Usage at the end of this book and review all of Section 3.4 (Numbers). Then look at the following items and indicate the preferred choice in each group of sentences. (Answers to these exercises appear on page 615.)

16-17. a. We need to hire one office manager, four social media specialists, and 12 customer support reps.
    b. We need to hire one office manager, four social media specialists, and twelve customer support reps.
    c. We need to hire 1 office manager, 4 social media specialists, and 12 customer support reps.

16-18. a. The market for this product is nearly 6 million people in our region alone.
    b. The market for this product is nearly six million people in our region alone.
    c. The market for this product is nearly 6,000,000 million people in our region alone.

16-19. a. Make sure that all 1,835 pages are on my desk no later than 9:00 a.m.
    b. Make sure that all 1835 pages are on my desk no later than nine o'clock in the morning.
    c. Make sure that all 1,835 pages are on my desk no later than nine o'clock a.m.

16-20. a. Our deadline is 4/7, but we won't be ready before 4/11.
    b. Our deadline is April 7, but we won't be ready before April 11.
    c. Our deadline is 4/7, but we won't be ready before April 11.

16-21. a. 95 percent of our customers are men.
    b. Ninety-five percent of our customers are men.
    d. Of our customers, ninety-five percent are men.

16-22. **a.** More than half the U.S. population is female.

b. More than ½ the U.S. population is female.

c. More than one-half the U.S. population is female.

16-23. **a.** Last year, I wrote 20 15-page reports, and Michelle wrote 24 three-page reports.

b. Last year, I wrote 20 fifteen-page reports, and Michelle wrote 24 three-page reports.

c. Last year, I wrote twenty 15-page reports, and Michelle wrote 24 three-page reports.

16-24. **a.** Our blinds should measure 38 inches wide by 64 and one-half inches long by 7/16 inches deep.

b. Our blinds should measure 38 inches wide by 64-1/2 inches long by 7/16 inches deep.

c. Our blinds should measure 38 inches wide by 64-1/2" long by 7/16 inches deep.

16-25. **a.** Deliver the couch to 783 Fountain Rd., Suite 3, Procter Valley, CA 92074.

b. Deliver the couch to 783 Fountain Rd., Suite three, Procter Valley, CA 92074.

e. Deliver the couch to seven eighty-three Fountain Rd., Suite three, Procter Valley, CA 92074.

16-26. **a.** Here are the corrected figures: 42.7% agree, 23.25% disagree, 34% are undecided, and the error is 0.05%.

b. Here are the corrected figures: 42.7% agree, 23.25% disagree, 34.0% are undecided, and the error is .05%.

c. Here are the corrected figures: 42.70% agree, 23.25% disagree, 34.00% are undecided, and the error is 0.05%.

For an overall review of your grammar, mechanics, and usage skills, visit MyLab Business Communication. Select Chapter 16, then Additional Exercises to Improve Your Grammar, Mechanics, and Usage, and then 25. Grammar and Usage.

Cases

For all cases, feel free to use your creativity to make up any details you need in order to craft effective messages.

Application Letters

VIDEO SKILLS

16.27. Media Skills: Video; Message Strategies: Employment Messages [LO-1] With its encouragement of video applications and abandonment of traditional job postings, Zappos might be starting a mini-trend toward a new style of employment application.

Your task: Identify a company where you would like to work and assume that it encourages candidates to submit video introductions. Plan, record, and produce a short video (no longer than three minutes) that you might submit to this employer. Don't worry too much about fancy production quality, but make sure your content and presentation match the company's style and brand image.

EMAIL SKILLS

16.28. Message Strategies: Employment Messages [LO-1] Use one of the websites listed in Table 15.2 on page 488 to find a job opening in your target profession. If you haven't narrowed down to one career field yet, choose a business job for which you will have at least some qualifications at the time of your graduation.

Your task: Write an email message that would serve as your application letter if you were to apply for this job. Base your message on your actual qualifications for the position, and be sure to "echo" the requirements listed in the job description. Include the job description in your email message when you submit it to your instructor.

MICROBLOGGING SKILLS

16.29. Message Strategies: Employment Messages [LO-1] If you want to know whether job candidates can express themselves clearly on Twitter, why not test them as part of the application process? That's exactly what the Minneapolis advertising agency Campbell Mithun does. Rather than having intern candidates use conventional application methods, the company asks them to tweet their applications in 13 messages.[47]

Your task: Find a job opening on Twitter by searching on any of the following hashtags: #hiring, #joblisting, or #nowhiring.[48] Next, write an "application letter" comprising 13 individual tweets. If your class is set up with private Twitter accounts, go ahead and send the tweets. Otherwise, email them to your instructor or post them on your class blog, as your instructor indicates.

EMAIL SKILLS

16.30. Message Strategies: Employment Messages [LO-1] Finding job openings that align perfectly with your professional interests is wonderful, but it doesn't always happen. Sometimes you have to widen your search and go after whatever opportunities happen to be available. Even when the opportunity is not ideal, however, you still need to approach the employer with enthusiasm and a focused, audience-centric message.

Your task: Find a job opening for which you will be qualified when you graduate (or close to being qualified, for the purposes of this activity), but make it one that is outside your primary field of interest. Write an email application letter for this opening, making a compelling case that you are the right candidate for this job.

Interviewing

BLOGGING SKILLS/TEAM SKILLS

16.31. Career Management: Researching Target Employers [LO-3] Research is a critical element of the job-search process. With information in hand, you increase the chance of finding the right opportunity (and avoiding bad choices), and you impress interviewers in multiple ways by demonstrating initiative, curiosity, research and analysis skills, an appreciation for the complex challenges of running a business, and willingness to work to achieve results.

Your task: With a small team of classmates, use online job listings to identify an intriguing job opening that at least one member of the team would seriously consider pursuing as graduation approaches. (You'll find it helpful if the career is related to at least one team member's college major or on-the-job experience so that the team can benefit from some knowledge of the profession in question.) Next, research the company, its competitors, its markets, and this specific position to identify five questions that would (1) help the team member decide whether this is a good opportunity and (2) show an interviewer that you've really done your homework. Go beyond the basic and obvious questions to identify current, specific, and complex issues that only deep research can uncover. For example, is the company facing significant technical, financial, legal, or regulatory challenges that threaten its ability to grow or perhaps even survive in the long term? Or is the market evolving in a way that positions this particular company for dramatic growth? In a post for your class blog, list your five questions, identify how you uncovered the issue, and explain why each is significant.

TEAM SKILLS

16.32. Career Management: Interviewing [LO-4] Interviewing is a skill that can be improved through observation and practice.

Your task: You and all other members of your class are to write letters of application for an entry-level or management-trainee position that requires an engaging personality and intelligence but a minimum of specialized education or experience. Sign your letter with a fictitious name that conceals your identity. Next, polish (or create) a résumé that accurately identifies you and your educational and professional accomplishments.

Now, three members of the class who volunteer as interviewers divide up all the anonymously written application letters. Then each interviewer selects a candidate who seems the most convincing in his or her letter. At this time, the selected candidates identify themselves and give the interviewers their résumés.

Each interviewer then interviews his or her chosen candidate in front of the class, seeking to understand how the items on the résumé qualify the candidate for the job. At the end of the interviews, the class decides who gets the job and discusses why this candidate was successful. Afterward, retrieve your letter, sign it with the right name, and submit it to the instructor for credit.

TEAM SKILLS

16.33. Career Management: Interviewing [LO-4] Preparing answers to the most-common "stock" interviewing questions is an important step.

Your task: Working with a classmate, take turns asking each other the six questions listed on pages 535–537. With each question, the interviewer should evaluate the respondent's ability to provide a concise and coherent answer. Share your notes after the simulation, and give each other tips on where to improve.

TEAM SKILLS

16.34. Career Management: Interviewing [LO-4] Select a company in an industry in which you might like to work, and then identify an interesting position within the company. Study the company and prepare for an interview with that company.

Your task: Working with a classmate, take turns interviewing each other for your chosen positions. Interviewers should take notes during the interview. When the interview is complete, critique each other's performance. (Interviewers should critique how well candidates prepared for the interview and answered the questions; interviewees should critique the quality of the questions asked.) Write a follow-up letter thanking your interviewer, and submit the letter to your instructor.

Following Up After an Interview

LETTER-WRITING SKILLS

16.35. Message Strategies: Employment Messages [LO-5] Because of a mix-up in your job application scheduling, you accidentally applied for your third-choice job before going after the one you really wanted. What you want to do is work in retail marketing with the upscale department store Neiman Marcus in Dallas; what you have been offered is a job with Longhorn Leather and Lumber, 65 miles away in the small town of Commerce, Texas.

You review your notes. Your Longhorn interview was three weeks ago with the human resources manager, R. P. Bronson, who has just written to offer you the position. The store's address is 27 Sam Rayburn Drive, Commerce, TX 75428. Mr. Bronson notes that he can hold the position open for 10 days. You have an interview scheduled with Neiman Marcus next week, but it is unlikely that you will know the store's decision within this 10-day period.

Your task: Write to Mr. Bronson requesting a reasonable delay in your consideration of his job offer.

LETTER-WRITING SKILLS/EMAIL SKILLS

16.36. Message Strategies: Employment Messages [LO-5] Fortunately for you, your interview with Neiman Marcus (see the previous case) went well, and you've just received a job offer from the company.

Your task: Write a letter to R. P. Bronson at Longhorn Leather and Lumber declining his job offer, and write an email message to Clarissa Bartle at Neiman Marcus, accepting her job offer. Make up any information you need when accepting the Neiman Marcus offer.

LETTER-WRITING SKILLS

16.37. Message Strategies: Employment Messages (Letters of Resignation) [LO-5] Leaving a job is rarely stress free, but it's particularly difficult when you are parting ways with a mentor who played an important role in advancing your career. A half-dozen years into your career, you have benefited greatly from the advice, encouragement, and professional connections offered by your mentor, who also happens to be your current boss. She seemed to believe in your potential from the beginning and went out of her way on numerous occasions to help you. You returned the favor by becoming a stellar employee who has made important contributions to the success of the department your boss leads.

Unfortunately, you find yourself at a career impasse. You believe you are ready to move into a management position,

but your company is not growing enough to create many opportunities. Worse yet, you joined the firm during a period of rapid expansion, so there are many eager and qualified internal candidates at your career level interested in the few managerial jobs that do become available. You fear it may be years before you get the chance to move up in the company. Through your online networking activities, you found an opportunity with a firm in another industry and have decided to pursue it.

Your task: You have a close relationship with your boss, so you will announce your intention to leave the company in a private, one-on-one conversation. However, you also recognize the need to write a formal letter of resignation, which you will hand to your boss during this meeting. This letter is addressed to your boss, but as formal business correspondence that will become part of your personnel file, it should not be a "personal" letter. Making up whatever details you need, write a brief letter of resignation.

MyLab Business Communication

MyLab Assisted-Grading Writing Prompts

If your instructor has assigned one or both of the following writing assignments within the MyLab, go to your Assignments to complete these writing exercises.

16-38. How can you prepare for a situational or behavioral interview if you have no experience with the job for which you are interviewing? [LO-2]

16-39. Why are the questions you ask during an interview as important as the answers you give to the interviewer's questions? [LO-3]

Endnotes

1. Scott Bittle, "Graphic: What's the Most Important Baseline Skill? It Depends," Burning Glass, 19 November 2015, burning-glass.com; "About Us," Burning Glass, accessed 24 April 2018, burning-glass.com; James Hu, "8 Things You Need To Know About Applicant Tracking Systems," Jobscan blog, 19 July 2014, www.jobscan.co; Rob Nightingale, "How to Get Your Resume Past the Applicant Tracking System," *MakeUseOf*, 12 November 2015, www.makeuseof.com; Lisa Vaas, "Resume, Meet Technology: Making Your Resume Format Machine-Friendly," Ladders, accessed 17 May 2016, www.theladders.com; Russ Banham, "2016 Trends In Applicant Tracking Systems," *HR Today*, 2 February 2016, www.hrtoday.com; Hannah Morgan, "5 Things You Need to Know About Applicant Tracking Systems," *Career Sherpa*, 10 February 2016, careersherpa.net.

2. Stephanie Vozza, "Cover Letters Are Dead: Do This Instead," *Fast Company*, 16 February 2016, www.fastcompany.com.

3. Ambra Benjamin, "Do Recruiters Read Cover Letters?" Ladders, 14 April 2018, www.theladders.com.

4. Alison Doyle, "Interpersonal Skills List and Examples," *The Balance Careers*, 28 November 2017, www.thebalancecareers.com.

5. Allison Doyle, "Introduction to Cover Letters," About.com, accessed 13 August 2010, jobsearch.about.com.

6. Alison Doyle, "Top 10 Cover Letter Writing Tips," *The Balance*, 26 January 2017, www.thebalance.com; Alison Green, "Are You Making These 8 Mistakes on Your Cover Letter?" *U.S. News & World Report*,

18 July 2012, money.usnews.com; Alison Doyle, "Tips and Advice for Writing a Great Cover Letter," *The Balance*, 10 January 2016, www.thebalance.com.

7. Alexis Carpello, "Busy Recruiters Call on Job-Seekers to Follow Up," *Workforce*, 2 November 2017, www.workforce.com.

8. "The Job Follow Ups," Monster, accessed 1 May 2017, www.monster.com; Lisa Vaas, "How to Follow Up a Résumé Submission," The Ladders, 9 August 2010, www.theladders.com.

9. Alison Doyle, "How to Follow Up After Submitting a Resume," *The Balance*, 15 October 2016, www.thebalance.com; Vaas, "How to Follow Up a Résumé Submission."

10. Andrea Salazzaro, "Getting Through the 5 Stages of Job Interviews," Totaljobs, 5 September 2016, www.totaljobs.com; Alison Doyle, "What Is a Screening Interview?" *The Balance*, 12 April 2017, www.thebalance.com.

11. Ryan Craig, "Startups Are Making the Rejection Letter a Thing of the Past," *TechCrunch*, 9 January 2017, techcrunch.com.

12. Doyle, "What Is a Screening Interview?"

13. Hannah Morgan, "The Ultimate Interview Prep Checklist," *U.S. News & World Report*, 23 April 2014, money.usnews.com.

14. Michelle Silverstein, "Structured vs. Unstructured Interviews: The Verdict," Criteria Corp blog, accessed 2 May 2017, blog.criteriacorp.com; Alison Doyle, "What Is a Structured Job Interview?" *The Balance*, 16 July 2016, www.thebalance.com.

15. Lisa Quast, "Job Seekers: 7 Tips for a Successful Panel Interview," *Forbes*, 19 May 2014, www.forbes.com.

16. Nicole Lindsay, "The Firing Squad: How to Survive a Panel Interview," *The Muse*, accessed 2 May 2017, www.themuse.com.

17. Alison Doyle, "Group Interview Questions and Interviewing Tips," *The Balance*, 6 January 2017, www.thebalance.com; Pamela Skillings, "Acing the Group Interview," Big Interview, accessed 2 May 2017, biginterview.com.

18. Pamela Skillings, "Behavioral Interview: Tips for Crafting Your Best Answers," Big Interview, accessed 2 May 2017, biginterview.com.

19. Katherine Hansen, "Behavioral Job Interviewing Strategies for Job-Seekers," QuintCareers.com, accessed 1 May 2017, www.livecareer.com.

20. Pamela Skillings, "Behavioral Interview Questions," Big Interview, accessed 2 May 2017, biginterview.com.

21. Based in part on Alison Doyle, "Top 10 Behavioral Interview Questions and Answers," *The Balance*, 4 February 2017, www.thebalance.com; Skillings, "Behavioral Interview Questions."

22. Skillings, "Behavioral Interview: Tips for Crafting Your Best Answers."

23. "11 Ways to Prepare for (and Ace) Situational Interview Questions," *Forbes*, 25 April 2017, www.forbes.com; Hansen, "Behavioral Job Interviewing Strategies for Job-Seekers."

24. Ace the Case website, accessed 2 May 2017, www.acethecase.com.

25. Katherine Hansen, "Mastering the Case Job Interview," *Quintessential*, accessed 2 May 2017, www.livecareer.com/quintessential.

26. Liz Ryan, "Are 'Stress Interviews' Effective?" *Forbes*, 20 August 2016, www.forbes.com.

27. Dawn Dugan, "8 Tips for Acing Virtual Job Interviews," Salary.com, accessed 2 May 2017, www.salary.com; Alison Doyle, "Tips for a Successful Video Job Interview," *The Balance*, 1 May 2017, www.thebalance.com; Pamela Skillings, "The Ultimate Guide to Acing Video Interviews," Big Interview, accessed 2 May 2017, biginterview.com.

28. Tomas Chamorro-Premuzic, "Managing Yourself: Ace the Assessment," *Harvard Business Review*, July–August 2015, 118–121.

29. Suzanne Lucas, "What Happens on a Pre-employment Background Check?" *CBS MoneyWatch*, 9 December 2013, www.cbsnews.com.

30. Jeanne Sahadi, "Background Checks: What Employers Can Find Out About You," *CNN Money*, 5 January 2015, money.cnn.com; "Background Checks: What Job Applicants and Employees Should Know," U.S. Equal Employment Opportunity Commission, accessed 2 May 2017, www.eeoc.gov; Micheal Klazema, "What Information Is Revealed to an Employer When They Conduct a Background Check?" Snagajob, accessed 2 May 2017, www.snagajob.com; Lucas, "What Happens on a Pre-employment Background Check?"

31. Sahadi, "Background Checks: What Employers Can Find Out About You."

32. Jacquelyn Smith, "Here's How to Answer the Dreaded 'What's Your Greatest Weakness' Interview Question," *Business Insider*, 18 March 2014, www.businessinsider.com.

33. Pamela Skillings, "How to Answer: Where Do You See Yourself in Five Years?" Big Interview, accessed 2 May 2017, www.biginterview.com.

34. Katherine Spencer Lee, "Tackling Tough Interview Questions," *Certification Magazine*, May 2005, 35.

35. Scott Ginsberg, "10 Good Ways to 'Tell Me About Yourself,'" The Ladders, 26 June 2010, www.theladders.com.

36. Richard A. Moran, "The Number One Interview Trap Question," *Business Insider*, 23 April 2014, www.businessinsider.com.

37. "New Year, New Gig: How to Master the Modern Job Search," *Knowledge@Wharton*, 29 December 2017, knowledge.wharton.penn.edu.

38. Jacquelyn Smith, "How to Dress for Your Next Job Interview," 20 June 2013, *Forbes*, www.forbes.com; Alison Doyle, "9 Things You Shouldn't Wear to a Job Interview," *The Balance*, 23 August 2016, www.thebalance.com; Thad Peterson, "Dress Appropriately for Interviews," Monster, accessed 2 May 2017, www.monster.com.

39. William S. Frank, "Job Interview: Pre-Flight Checklist," *The Career Advisor*, accessed 28 September 2005, careerplanning.about.com.

40. Alison Green, "10 Surefire Ways to Annoy a Hiring Manager," *U.S. News & World Report*, accessed 24 July 2012, money.usnews.com.

41. Abby Roskind, "The Perfect Answers to 10 Common Job Interview Questions," CareerBuilder, 13 March 2017, www.careerbuilder.com; "20 Winning Interview Questions to Ask Candidates," RotaCloud blog, 30 September 2016, blog.rotacloud.com; Skip Freeman, "How You Answer This 'Warm-up' Question May Leave You 'Out-in-the-Cold,'" Personal Branding Blog, 30 October 2014, www.personalbrandingblog.com.

42. Steven Mitchell Sack, "The Working Woman's Legal Survival Guide: Testing," FindLaw.com, accessed 22 February 2004, www.findlaw.com.

43. Angela Smith, "5 Illegal Interview Questions and How to Dodge Them," *The Muse*, accessed 2 May 2017, www.themuse.com.

44. Lisa Vaas, "Resume, Meet Technology: Making Your Resume Format Machine-Friendly," The Ladders, accessed 13 August 2010, www.theladders.com.

45. Alison Green, "How a Thank-You Note Can Boost Your Job Chances," *U.S. News & World Report*, 27 June 2012, money.usnews.com; Joan S. Lublin, "Notes to Interviewers Should Go Beyond a Simple Thank You," *Wall Street Journal*, 5 February 2008, B1.

46. Alison Doyle, "Sample Cover Letter for a Job Application," *The Balance* Careers, 10 April 2018, www.thebalancecareers.com.

47. Tiffany Hsu, "Extreme Interviewing: Odd Quizzes, Weird Mixers, Improv Pitches. Can You Get Past the Hiring Gatekeepers?" *Los Angeles Times*, 19 February 2012, B1.

48. From Ritika Trikha, "The Best Tips for Tweeting Your Way to a Job," *U.S. News & World Report*, 24 July 2012, money.usnews.com.

Five-Minute Guide to Preparing for Job Interviews

As you begin to prepare for interviews, take five minutes to review these important tips.

00:01 **Learn about the organization**

1. Interviewers expect you to be familiar with their companies and industries.
2. Research online to get basic information about the firm, its product lines, and its competition.
3. Try to get the names of your interviewers (it's acceptable to ask your company contact) and learn about them on LinkedIn or other social media.

00:02 **Plan for the employer's questions**

1. Be ready for "stock" interview questions, including these (see Table 16.4 or research online for more):
   - What is the hardest decision you've ever had to make?
   - What is your greatest weakness?
   - Where do you want to be five years from now?
   - What didn't you like about previous jobs you've held?
   - How do you spend your free time?
2. Be ready for specific questions that will explore your readiness for the position.

00:03 **Plan questions of your own**

1. You need to prepare questions, for two important reasons:
   - This is your chance to make sure the job and the company are right for you.
   - Interviewers want to know that you are curious and serious; not having any questions can raise a red flag for interviewers.
2. Consider asking these questions, if relevant:
   - How does this job fit in the overall department or organization?
   - What have past employees done to excel in this position?
   - How do you measure success for someone in this position?
   - What is the first problem that needs the attention of the person you hire?
   - How well do my qualifications align with the current and future needs of this position?
   - Why is this job now vacant?
   - What makes your organization different from others in the industry?
   - How would you define your organization's managerial philosophy?
   - What is a typical workday like for you?
   - What are the next steps in the selection process? What's the best way to follow up with you?

00:04 **Boost your confidence and polish your style**

1. Remember that you are discussing a mutually beneficial business arrangement: You have value to offer the employer, and the employer already thinks highly enough of you to invite you to an interview.
2. Plan to offset any weaknesses you may have with positive attributes of your skill set, experience, personality, and character.
3. Conduct and record mock interviews so you can evaluate and improve your interviewing style.
4. Review the list of warning signs in Table 16.6, and make sure you don't exhibit any of these.

00:05 **Present a professional image**

1. Research the company and the industry to get a sense of what to wear to the interview.
2. As a general rule, plan to dress slightly more formally than the style most employees appear to adopt; you want to show respect for the situation while recognizing the prevailing culture at the company.

Format and Layout of Business Documents

The format and layout of business documents vary from country to country. In addition, many organizations develop their own variations of standard styles, adapting documents to the types of messages they send and the kinds of audiences they communicate with. The formats described here are the most common approaches used in U.S. business correspondence, but be sure to follow whatever practices are expected at your company.

First Impressions

Your documents tell readers a lot about you and about your company's professionalism, so all your documents must look neat, present a professional image, and be easy to read. Your audience's first impression of a document comes from the quality of its paper, the way it is customized, and its general appearance.

PAPER

To give a quality impression, businesspeople consider carefully the paper they use. Several aspects of paper contribute to the overall impression:

- **Weight.** Paper quality is judged by the weight of four reams (each a 500-sheet package) of letter-size paper. The weight most commonly used by U.S. business organizations is 20-pound paper, but 16- and 24-pound versions are also used.
- **Cotton content.** Paper quality is also judged by the percentage of cotton in the paper. Cotton doesn't yellow over time the way wood pulp does, plus it's both strong and soft. When you want to make a formal impression, you can use paper with 25 percent or even 100 percent cotton content.[1]
- **Size.** In the United States, the standard paper size for business documents is 8½ by 11 inches. Standard legal documents are 8½ by 14 inches.
- **Color.** White is the standard color for business purposes, although neutral colors such as gray and ivory are sometimes used. Memos can be produced on pastel-colored paper to distinguish them from external correspondence. In addition, memos are sometimes produced on paper of various colors for routing to separate departments. Light-colored papers are appropriate, but bright or dark colors make reading difficult and may seem too frivolous.

CUSTOMIZATION

For letters to outsiders, U.S. businesses commonly use letterhead stationery, which may be either professionally printed or designed in-house using word-processing templates and graphics. Letterhead typically contains the company name, logo, address, telephone and fax numbers, general email address, website URL, and possibly one or more social media URLs.

In the United States, businesses always use letterhead for the first page of a letter. Successive pages are usually plain sheets of paper that match the letterhead in color and quality. Some companies use a specially printed second-page letterhead that bears only the company's name.

APPEARANCE

Make sure your documents present your ideas in a positive light. Pay close attention to all the factors that affect appearance, including the following:

- **Margins.** Business letters typically use 1-inch margins at the top, bottom, and sides of the page, although these parameters are sometimes adjusted to accommodate letterhead elements.
- **Justification.** For all routine business documents, all lines (body text and headings) should be left-justified.
- **Character spacing.** Use proper spacing between characters and after punctuation. For example, U.S. conventions include leaving one space after commas, semicolons, colons, and sentence-ending periods. Each letter in a person's initials is followed by a period and a single space. However, abbreviations such as U.S.A. or MBA may or may not have periods, but they never have internal spaces.
- **Special symbols.** Take advantage of the many special symbols available with your computer's selection of fonts. In addition, see whether your company has a style guide for documents, which may include particular symbols you are expected to use.

- **Corrections.** Messy corrections are unacceptable in business documents. If you notice an error after printing a document with your word processor, correct the mistake and reprint. (With informal memos to members of your own team or department, the occasional small correction in pen or pencil is acceptable, but never in formal documents.)

Letters

All business letters have certain elements in common. Several of these elements appear in every letter; others appear only when desirable or appropriate. In addition, these letter parts are usually arranged in one of three basic formats.

STANDARD LETTER PARTS

The letter in Figure A.1 shows the placement of standard letter parts. The writer of this business letter had no letterhead available but correctly included a heading. All business letters typically include these seven elements.

Heading

The elements of the letterhead make up the heading of a letter in most cases. If letterhead stationery is not available, the heading includes a return address (but no name) and starts 13 lines from the top of the page, which leaves a 2-inch top margin.

Date

If you're using letterhead, place the date at least one blank line beneath the lowest part of the letterhead. Without letterhead, place the date immediately below the return address. The standard method of writing the date in the United States uses the full name of the month (no abbreviations), followed by the day (in numerals, without *st, nd, rd,* or *th*), a comma, and then the year: July 31, 2020 (7/31/2020). Table A.1 shows date formats commonly used in other countries.

Inside Address

The inside address identifies the recipient of the letter. For U.S. correspondence, begin the inside address at least one line below the date. Precede the addressee's name with a

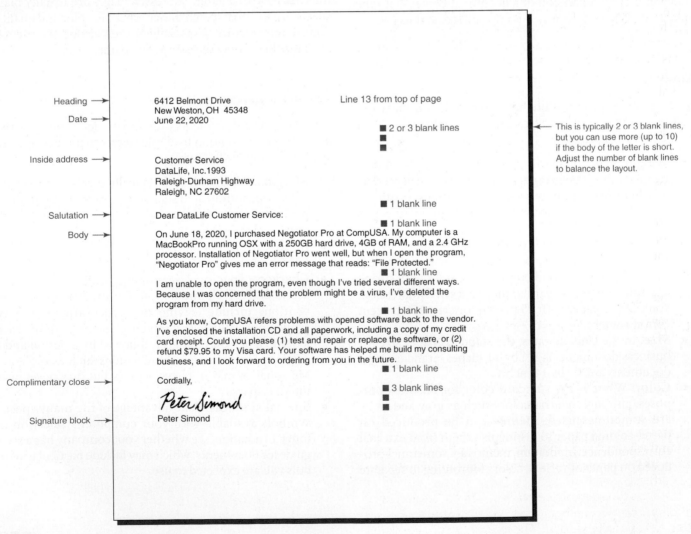

Figure A.1 Standard Letter Parts

TABLE A.1	Common Date Forms	
Convention	**Order**	**Examples**
U.S. standard	Month day year	July 31, 2020
		7/31/2020
		7-31-2020
Japan	Year month day	20/07/31
Europe (most countries)	Day month year	31 July 2020
		31/07/20
		31.07.20
International (ISO) format	Year month day	2020-07-31

courtesy title, such as *Dr.*, *Mr.*, or *Ms.* The accepted courtesy title for women in business is *Ms.*, although a woman known to prefer the title *Miss* or *Mrs.* is always accommodated. If you don't know whether a person is a man or a woman (and you have no way of finding out), omit the courtesy title. For example, *Terry Smith* could be either a man or a woman. The first line of the inside address would be just *Terry Smith*, and the salutation would be *Dear Terry Smith*. The same is true if you know only a person's initials, as in *S. J. Adams*.

Spell out and capitalize titles that precede a person's name, such as *Professor* or *General* (see Table A.2 on the next page for the proper forms of address). The person's organizational title, such as *Director*, may be included on this first line (if it is short) or on the line below; the name of a department may follow. In addresses and signature lines, don't forget to capitalize any professional title that follows a person's name:

Mr. Ray Johnson, Dean

Ms. Patricia T. Higgins

Assistant Vice President

However, professional titles not appearing in an address or signature line are capitalized only when they directly precede the name:

President Kenneth Johanson will deliver the speech.

Maria Morales, president of ABC Enterprises, will deliver the speech.

The Honorable Helen Masters, senator from Arizona, will deliver the speech.

If the name of a specific person is unavailable, you may address the letter to the department or to a specific position within the department. Also, be sure to spell out company names in full, unless the company itself uses abbreviations in its official name.

Other address information includes the treatment of buildings, house numbers, and compass directions (see Table A.3 on the next page). The following example shows all the information that may be included in the inside address and its proper order for U.S. correspondence:

Ms. Linda Coolidge, Vice President
Corporate Planning Department
Midwest Airlines
Kowalski Building, Suite 21-A
7279 Bristol Ave.
Toledo, OH 43617

Canadian addresses are similar, except that the name of the province is usually spelled out:

Dr. H. C. Armstrong
Research and Development
Commonwealth Mining Consortium
The Chelton Building, Suite 301
585 Second St. SW
Calgary, Alberta T2P 2P5

The order and layout of address information vary from country to country. So when addressing correspondence for other countries, carefully follow the format and information that appear in the company's letterhead. However, when you're sending mail from the United States, be sure that the name of the destination country appears on the last line of the address in capital letters. Use the English version of the country name so that your mail is routed from the United States to the right country. Then, to be sure your mail is routed correctly within the destination country, use the foreign spelling of the city name (using the characters and diacritical marks that would be commonly used in the region). For example, the following address uses *Köln* instead of *Cologne*:

R. Veith, Director	Addressee
Eisfieren Glaswerk	Company name
Blaubachstrasse 13	Street address
Postfach 10 80 07	Post office road
D-5000 Köln I	District, city
GERMANY	Country

TABLE A.2 Forms of Address

Person	In Address	In Salutation
Personal Titles		
Man	Mr. [first & last name]	Dear Mr. [last name]:
Woman*	Ms. [first & last name]	Dear Ms. [last name]:
Two men (or more)	Mr. [first & last name] and Mr. [first & last name]	Dear Mr. [last name] and Mr. [last name] or Messrs. [last name] and [last name]:
Two women (or more)	Ms. [first & last name] and Ms. [first & last name]	Dear Ms. [last name] and Ms. [last name] or Mses. [last name] and [last name]:
One woman and one man	Ms. [first & last name] and Mr. [first & last name]	Dear Ms. [last name] and Mr. [last name]:
Couple (married with same last name)	Mr. [husband's first name] and Mrs. [wife's first name] [couple's last name]	Dear Mr. and Mrs. [last name]:
Couple (married with different last names)	Mr. [first & last name of husband] and Ms. [first & last name of wife]	Dear Mr. [husband's last name] and Ms. [wife's last name]:
Couple (married professionals with same title and same last name)	[title in plural form] [husband's first name] and [wife's first name] [couple's last name]	Dear [title in plural form] [last name]:
Couple (married professionals with different titles and same last name)	[title] [first & last name of husband] and [title] [first & last name of wife]	Dear [title] and [title] [last name]:
Professional Titles		
President of a college or university	[title] [first & last name], President	Dear President [last name]:
Dean of a school or college	Dean [first & last name] or Dr., Mr., or Ms. [first & last name], Dean of [title]	Dear Dean [last name]: or Dear Dr., Mr., or Ms. [last name]:
Professor	Professor or Dr. [first & last name]	Dear Professor or Dr. [last name]:
Physician	[first & last name], M.D.	Dear Dr. [last name]:
Lawyer	Mr. or Ms. [first & last name], Attorney at Law	Dear Mr. or Ms. [last name]:
Military personnel	[full rank, first & last name, abbreviation of service designation] (add *Retired* if applicable)	Dear [rank] [last name]:
Company or corporation	[name of organization]	Ladies and Gentlemen: or Gentlemen and Ladies:
Governmental Titles		
President of the United States	The President	Dear Mr. or Madam President:
Senator of the United States	The Honorable [first & last name]	Dear Senator [last name]:
Cabinet member	The Honorable [first & last name]	Dear Mr. or Madam Secretary:
Attorney General	The Honorable [first & last name]	Dear Mr. or Madam Attorney General:
Mayor	The Honorable [first & last name], Mayor of [name of city]	Dear Mayor [last name]:
Judge	The Honorable [first & last name]	Dear Judge [last name]:

*Use *Mrs.* or *Miss* only if the recipient has specifically requested that you use one of these titles; otherwise *always* use *Ms.* in business correspondence. Also, never refer to a married woman by her husband's name (for example, Mrs. Robert Washington) unless she specifically requests that you do so.

TABLE A.3 Inside Address Information

Description	Example
Capitalize building names.	Empire State Building
Capitalize locations within buildings (apartments, suites, rooms).	Suite 1073
Use numerals for all house or building numbers, except the number one.	One Trinity Lane; 637 Adams Ave., Apt. 7
Spell out compass directions that fall within a street address.	1074 West Connover St.
Abbreviate compass directions that follow the street address.	783 Main St., N.E., Apt. 27

Salutation

In the salutation of your letter, follow the style of the first line of the inside address. If the first line is a person's name, the salutation is *Dear Mr.* or *Ms. Name.* The formality of the salutation depends on your relationship with the addressee. If in conversation you would say "Mary," your letter's salutation should be *Dear Mary,* followed by a colon. Otherwise, include the courtesy title and last name, followed by a colon. Presuming to write *Dear Lewis* instead of *Dear Professor Chang* demonstrates a disrespectful familiarity that the recipient will probably resent.

If the first line of the inside address is a position title such as *Director of Personnel,* then use *Dear Director.* If the addressee is unknown, use a polite description, such as *Dear Alumnus, Dear SPCA Supporter,* or *Dear Voter.* If the first line is plural (a department or company), then use *Ladies and Gentlemen* (look again at Table A.2). When you do not know whether you're writing to an individual or a group (for example, when writing a reference or a letter of recommendation), use *To whom it may concern.*

Whether your salutation is informal or formal, be especially careful that names are spelled correctly. A misspelled name is glaring evidence of carelessness, and it belies the personal interest you're trying to express.

Body

The body of the letter is your message. Almost all letters are single-spaced, with one blank line before and after the salutation, between paragraphs, and before the complimentary close. The body may include indented lists, entire paragraphs indented for emphasis, and even subheadings. If it does, all similar elements should be treated in the same way. Your department or company may select a format to use for all letters.

Complimentary Close

The complimentary close begins on the second line below the body of the letter. Alternatives for wording are available, but the current trend seems to be toward one-word closes, such as *Sincerely* and *Cordially.* In any case, the complimentary close reflects the relationship between you and the person you're writing to. Avoid cute closes, such as *Yours for bigger profits.* If your audience doesn't know you well, your sense of humor may be misunderstood.

Signature Block

Leave three blank lines for a written signature below the complimentary close, and then include the sender's name (unless it appears in the letterhead). The person's title may appear on the same line as the name or on the line below:

Cordially,

Raymond Dunnigan
Director of Personnel

Your letterhead indicates that you're representing your company. However, if your letter is on plain paper or runs to a second page, you may want to emphasize that you're speaking legally for the company. The accepted way of doing that is to place the company's name in capital letters, a double space below the complimentary close, and then include the sender's name and title four lines below that:

Sincerely,
WENTWORTH INDUSTRIES

Helen B. Taylor
President

If your name could be taken for either a man's or a woman's, a courtesy title indicating gender should be included, with or without parentheses. Also, women who prefer a particular courtesy title should include it:

Mrs. Nancy Winters
(Ms.) Juana Flores
Ms. Pat Li
(Mr.) Jamie Saunders

ADDITIONAL LETTER PARTS

Letters vary greatly in subject matter and thus in the identifying information they need and the format they adopt. The letter in Figure A.2 shows how these additional parts should be arranged. The following elements may be used in any combination, depending on the requirements of the particular letter:

- **Addressee notation.** Letters that have a restricted readership or that must be handled in a special way should include such addressee notations as *PERSONAL, CONFIDENTIAL,* or *PLEASE FORWARD.* This sort of notation appears a double space above the inside address, in all-capital letters.
- **Attention line.** If you are writing to a company and don't know the name of the person you would like to reach, you can use an attention line, such as *Attention: Customer Service.*

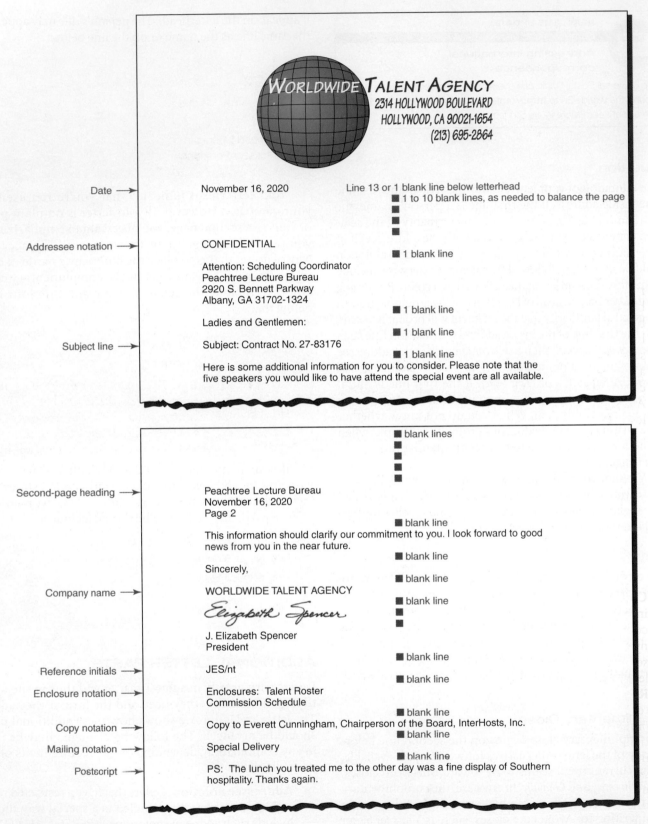

Figure A.2 Additional Letter Parts

- **Subject line.** The subject line tells recipients at a glance what the letter is about (and indicates where to file the letter for future reference). It usually appears below the salutation, either against the left margin, indented (as a paragraph in the body), or centered. It can be placed above the salutation or at the very top of the page, and it can be underscored. Some businesses omit the word *Subject*, and some organizations replace it with *Re:* or *In re:* (meaning "concerning" or "in the matter of"). The subject line may take a variety of forms, including the following:

> Subject: RainMaster Sprinklers
> Re: About your February 3, 2020, order
> In re: Fall 2020 Sales Meeting
> Reference Order No. 27920

- **Second-page heading.** Use a second-page heading whenever an additional page is required. Some companies have second-page letterhead (with the company name and address on one line and in a smaller typeface). The heading bears the name (person or organization) from the first line of the inside address, the page number, the date, and perhaps a reference number. Leave two blank lines before the body. Make sure that at least two lines of a continued paragraph appear on the first and second pages. Never allow the closing lines to appear alone on a continued page. Precede the complimentary close or signature lines with at least two lines of the body. Also, don't hyphenate the last word on a page. All the following are acceptable forms for second-page headings:

> Ms. Melissa Baker
> May 11, 2020
> Page 2
>
> Ms. Melissa Baker, May 11, 2020, Page 2
>
> Ms. Melissa Baker-2-May 11, 2020

- **Company name.** If you include the company's name in the signature block, put it a double space below the complimentary close. You usually include the company's name in the signature block only when the writer is serving as the company's official spokesperson or when letterhead has not been used.
- **Reference initials.** When one person dictates a letter and another person produces it, optional *reference initials* show who helped prepare it. Place these initials at the left margin, a double space below the signature block, using one of the following forms: *RSR/sm, RSR:sm,* or *RSR:SM* (writer/preparer). See "JES/nt" in Figure A.2 for an example. When the signature block includes the writer's name, some companies use only the preparer's initials. When the writer and the signer are different people, you can include both their initials as well as the typist's: *JFS/RSR/sm* (signer/writer/preparer).
- **Enclosure notation.** Enclosure notations appear at the bottom of a letter, one or two lines below the

reference initials. Some common forms include the following:

> Enclosure
> Enclosures (2)
> Enclosures: Résumé
> Photograph
> Brochure

- **Copy notation.** Copy notations may follow reference initials or enclosure notations. They indicate who's receiving a *courtesy copy* (*cc*). Recipients are listed in order of rank or (rank being equal) in alphabetical order. Among the forms used are the following:

> cc: David Wentworth, Vice President
>
> Copy to Hans Vogel
> 748 Chesterton Road
> Snohomish, WA 98290

- **Mailing notation.** You may place a mailing notation (such as *Special Delivery* or *Registered Mail*) at the bottom of the letter, after reference initials or enclosure notations (whichever is last) and before copy notations. Or you may place it at the top of the letter, either above the inside address on the left side or just below the date on the right side. For greater visibility, mailing notations may appear in capital letters.
- **Postscript.** A postscript is presented as an afterthought to the letter, a message that requires emphasis, or a personal note. It is usually the last thing on any letter and is usually preceded by *P.S.* A second afterthought would be designated *P.P.S.* (post postscript).

LETTER FORMATS

A letter format is the way of arranging all the basic letter parts. Sometimes a company adopts a certain format as its policy; sometimes the individual letter writer or preparer is allowed to choose the most appropriate format. In the United States, three major letter formats are commonly used:

- **Block format.** Each letter part begins at the left margin. The main advantage is quick and efficient preparation (see Figure A.3 on the next page).
- **Modified block format.** Same as block format, except that the date, complimentary close, and signature block start near the center of the page (see Figure A.4 on page 569). The modified block format does permit indentions as an option. This format mixes preparation speed with traditional placement of some letter parts. It also looks more balanced on the page than the block format does. (Note: The address and contact information

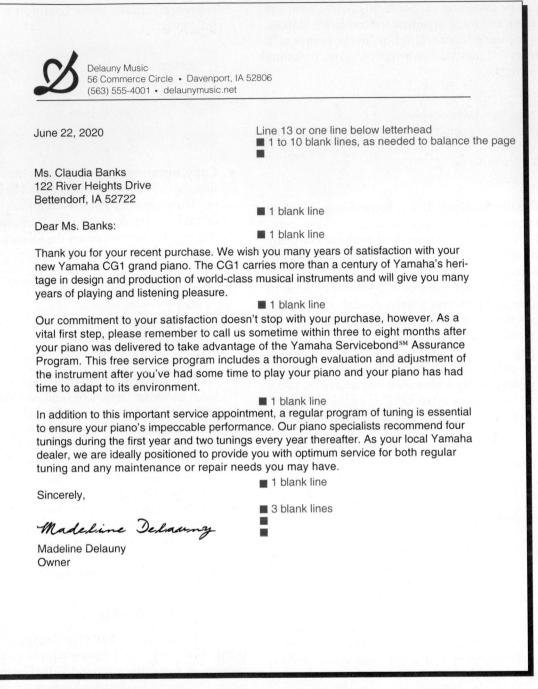

Delauny Music
56 Commerce Circle • Davenport, IA 52806
(563) 555-4001 • delaunymusic.net

June 22, 2020

Line 13 or one line below letterhead
■ 1 to 10 blank lines, as needed to balance the page
■

Ms. Claudia Banks
122 River Heights Drive
Bettendorf, IA 52722

■ 1 blank line

Dear Ms. Banks:

■ 1 blank line

Thank you for your recent purchase. We wish you many years of satisfaction with your new Yamaha CG1 grand piano. The CG1 carries more than a century of Yamaha's heritage in design and production of world-class musical instruments and will give you many years of playing and listening pleasure.

■ 1 blank line

Our commitment to your satisfaction doesn't stop with your purchase, however. As a vital first step, please remember to call us sometime within three to eight months after your piano was delivered to take advantage of the Yamaha Servicebond℠ Assurance Program. This free service program includes a thorough evaluation and adjustment of the instrument after you've had some time to play your piano and your piano has had time to adapt to its environment.

■ 1 blank line

In addition to this important service appointment, a regular program of tuning is essential to ensure your piano's impeccable performance. Our piano specialists recommend four tunings during the first year and two tunings every year thereafter. As your local Yamaha dealer, we are ideally positioned to provide you with optimum service for both regular tuning and any maintenance or repair needs you may have.

■ 1 blank line

Sincerely,

■ 3 blank lines
■
■

Madeline Delauny

Madeline Delauny
Owner

Figure A.3   Block Letter Format

in the left margin of this letter is part of this company's particular stationery design; other designs put this information at the top or bottom of the page.)

- **Simplified format.** Instead of using a salutation, this format often weaves the reader's name into the first line or two of the body and often includes a subject line in capital letters (see Figure A.5 on page 568). This format does not include a complimentary close, so your signature appears immediately below the body text. Because certain letter parts are eliminated, some line spacing is changed.

These three formats differ in the way paragraphs are indented, in the way letter parts are placed, and in some punctuation. However, the elements are always separated by at least one blank line, and the printed name is always separated from the line above by at least three blank lines to allow space for a signature. If paragraphs are indented, the indention is normally five spaces. The most common formats for intercultural business letters are the block style and the modified block style.

In addition to these three letter formats, letters may also be classified according to their style of punctuation.

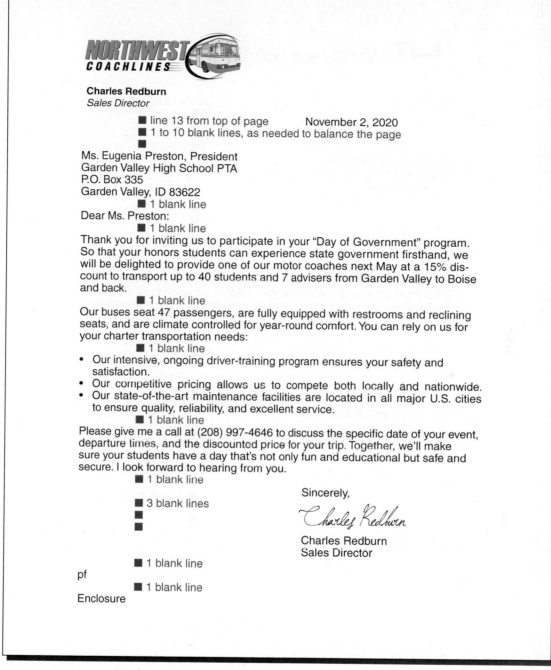

Figure A.4   Modified Block Letter Format

Standard, or *mixed, punctuation* uses a colon after the salutation (a comma if the letter is social or personal) and a comma after the complimentary close. *Open punctuation* uses no colon or comma after the salutation or the complimentary close. Although the most popular style in business communication is mixed punctuation, either style of punctuation may be used with block or modified block letter formats. Because the simplified letter format has no salutation or complimentary close, the style of punctuation is irrelevant.

Envelopes

For a first impression, the quality of the envelope is just as important as the quality of the stationery. Letterhead and envelopes should be of the same paper stock, have the same color ink, and be imprinted with the same address and logo. Most envelopes used by U.S. businesses are No. 10 envelopes 9½, which are sized for an 8½-by-11-inch piece of paper folded in thirds. Some occasions call for a

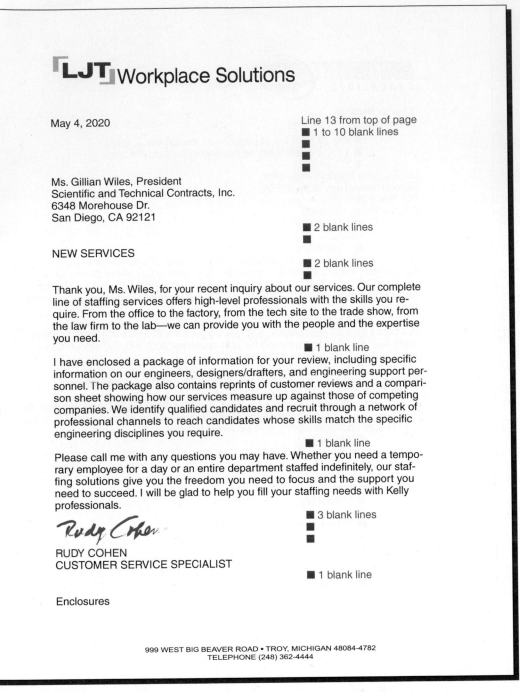

┌LJT┐Workplace Solutions

May 4, 2020   Line 13 from top of page
                                              ■ 1 to 10 blank lines
                                              ■
                                              ■
                                              ■

Ms. Gillian Wiles, President
Scientific and Technical Contracts, Inc.
6348 Morehouse Dr.
San Diego, CA 92121   ■ 2 blank lines
                                              ■

NEW SERVICES   ■ 2 blank lines
                                              ■

Thank you, Ms. Wiles, for your recent inquiry about our services. Our complete
line of staffing services offers high-level professionals with the skills you require. From the office to the factory, from the tech site to the trade show, from
the law firm to the lab—we can provide you with the people and the expertise
you need.
                                              ■ 1 blank line
I have enclosed a package of information for your review, including specific
information on our engineers, designers/drafters, and engineering support personnel. The package also contains reprints of customer reviews and a comparison sheet showing how our services measure up against those of competing
companies. We identify qualified candidates and recruit through a network of
professional channels to reach candidates whose skills match the specific
engineering disciplines you require.
                                              ■ 1 blank line
Please call me with any questions you may have. Whether you need a temporary employee for a day or an entire department staffed indefinitely, our staffing solutions give you the freedom you need to focus and the support you
need to succeed. I will be glad to help you fill your staffing needs with Kelly
professionals.
                                              ■ 3 blank lines
                                              ■
                                              ■
Rudy Cohen

RUDY COHEN
CUSTOMER SERVICE SPECIALIST
                                              ■ 1 blank line

Enclosures

999 WEST BIG BEAVER ROAD • TROY, MICHIGAN 48084-4782
TELEPHONE (248) 362-4444

Figure A.5   Simplified Letter Format

smaller No. 6¾, envelope or for envelopes proportioned to fit special stationery. Figure A.6 shows the two most common sizes.

ADDRESSING THE ENVELOPE

No matter what size the envelope, the address is always single-spaced with all lines aligned on the left. The address on the envelope is in the same style as the inside address and presents the same information. The order to follow is from the smallest division to the largest:

1. Name and title of recipient
2. Name of department or subgroup
3. Name of organization
4. Name of building
5. Street address and suite number, or post office box number
6. City, state or province, and zip code or postal code
7. Name of country (if the letter is being sent abroad)

Because the U.S. Postal Service uses optical scanners to sort mail, envelopes for quantity mailings, in particular,

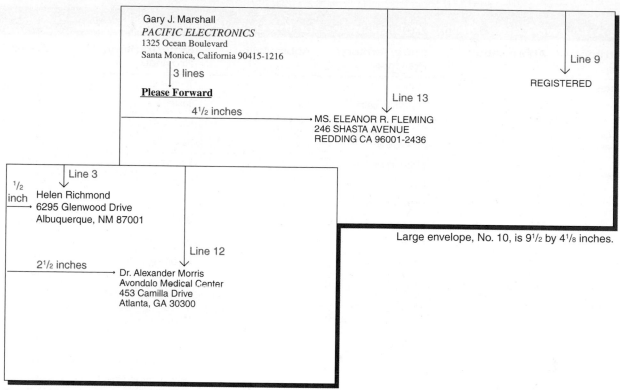

Gary J. Marshall
PACIFIC ELECTRONICS
1325 Ocean Boulevard
Santa Monica, California 90415-1216

↕ 3 lines

Please Forward

← 4½ inches →

MS. ELEANOR R. FLEMING
246 SHASTA AVENUE
REDDING CA 96001-2436

← Line 13

← Line 9

REGISTERED

Line 3
↓
½ inch →
Helen Richmond
6295 Glenwood Drive
Albuquerque, NM 87001

Line 12
↓
← 2½ inches →
Dr. Alexander Morris
Avondalo Medical Center
453 Camilla Drive
Atlanta, GA 30300

Large envelope, No. 10, is 9½ by 4⅛ inches.

Small envelope, No. 6¾, is 6½ by 3⅝ inches.

Figure A.6   Prescribed Envelope Format

should be addressed in the prescribed format. Everything is in capital letters, no punctuation is included, and all mailing instructions of interest to the post office are placed above the address area (see Figure A.6). Canada Post requires a similar format, except that only the city is all in capitals, and the postal code is placed on the line below the name of the city. The post office scanners read addresses from the bottom up, so if a letter is to be sent to a post office box rather than to a street address, the street address should appear on the line above the box number. Figure A.6 also shows the proper spacing for addresses and return addresses.

The U.S. Postal Service and the Canada Post Corporation have published lists of two-letter mailing abbreviations for states, provinces, and territories (see Table A.4 on the next page). Postal authorities prefer no punctuation with these abbreviations. Quantity mailings should always follow post office requirements. For other letters, a reasonable compromise is to use traditional punctuation, uppercase and lowercase letters for names and street addresses, but two-letter state or province abbreviations, as shown here:

Mr. Kevin Kennedy
2107 E. Packer Dr.
Amarillo, TX 79108

Canadian postal codes are alphanumeric, with a three-character "area code" and a three-character "local code" separated by a single space (K2P 5A5). Zip and postal codes

should be separated from state and province names by one space. Canadian postal codes may be treated the same or may be positioned alone on the bottom line of the address all by itself.

FOLDING TO FIT

The way a letter is folded also contributes to the recipient's overall impression of your organization's professionalism. When sending a standard-size piece of paper in a No. 10 envelope, fold it in thirds, with the bottom folded up first and the top folded down over it (see Figure A.7 on the next page); the open end should be at the top of the envelope and facing out. Fit smaller stationery neatly into the appropriate envelope simply by folding it in half or in thirds. When sending a standard-size letterhead in a No. 6¾ envelope, fold it in half from top to bottom and then in thirds from side to side.

INTERNATIONAL MAIL

Postal service differs from country to country, so it's always a good idea to investigate the quality and availability of various services before sending messages and packages internationally. Also, compare the services offered by delivery companies such as UPS and FedEx to find the best rates and options for each destination and type of shipment. No matter which service you choose, be aware that international mail requires more planning than domestic mail. For example, for anything beyond simple letters, you generally need to prepare

TABLE A.4 Two-Letter Mailing Abbreviations for the United States and Canada

State/Territory/Province	Abbreviation	State/Territory/Province	Abbreviation	State/Territory/Province	Abbreviation
United States		Maryland	MD	Tennessee	TN
Alabama	AL	Massachusetts	MA	Texas	TX
Alaska	AK	Michigan	MI	Utah	UT
American Samoa	AS	Minnesota	MN	Vermont	VT
Arizona	AZ	Mississippi	MS	Virginia	VA
Arkansas	AR	Missouri	MO	Virgin Islands	VI
California	CA	Montana	MT	Washington	WA
Canal Zone	CZ	Nebraska	NE	West Virginia	WV
Colorado	CO	Nevada	NV	Wisconsin	WI
Connecticut	CT	New Hampshire	NH	Wyoming	WY
Delaware	DE	New Jersey	NJ	**Canada**	
District of Columbia	DC	New Mexico	NM	Alberta	AB
Florida	FL	New York	NY	British Columbia	BC
Georgia	GA	North Carolina	NC	Manitoba	MB
Guam	GU	North Dakota	ND	New Brunswick	NB
Hawaii	HI	Northern Mariana	MP	Newfoundland and Labrador	NL
Idaho	ID	Ohio	OH	Northwest Territories	NT
Illinois	IL	Oklahoma	OK	Nova Scotia	NS
Indiana	IN	Oregon	OR	Nunavut	NU
Iowa	IA	Pennsylvania	PA	Ontario	ON
Kansas	KS	Puerto Rico	PR	Prince Edward Island	PE
Kentucky	KY	Rhode Island	RI	Quebec	QC
Louisiana	LA	South Carolina	SC	Saskatchewan	SK
Maine	ME	South Dakota	SD	Yukon Territory	YT

Source: U.S. Postal Service, *Publication 28—Postal Addressing Standards.*

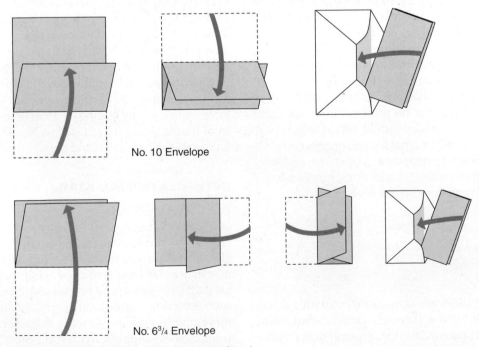

No. 10 Envelope

No. 6³/₄ Envelope

Figure A.7 Folding Standard-Size Letterhead

customs forms and possibly other documents, depending on the country of destination and the type of shipment. You are responsible for following the laws of the United States and any countries to which you send mail and packages.

To prepare your mail for international delivery, follow the instructions provided at the U.S. Postal Service website (www .usps.com). There you'll find complete information on the international services available through the USPS, along with advice on addressing and packaging mail, completing customs forms, and calculating postage rates and fees. The *International Mail Manual*, also available on this website, offers the latest information and regulations for both outbound and inbound international mail. For instance, you can select individual country names to see current information about restricted or prohibited items and materials, required customs forms, and rates for various classes of service.[2] Various countries have specific and often extensive lists of items that may not be sent by mail at all or that must be sent using particular postal service options.

Memos

Digital media have replaced most internal printed memos in many companies, but you may have occasion to send printed memos from time to time. These can be simple announcements or messages, or they can be short reports using the memo format.

On your document, include a title such as MEMO or INTEROFFICE CORRESPONDENCE (all in capitals) centered at the top of the page or aligned with the left margin. Also at the top, include the words *To, From, Date,* and *Subject*—followed by the appropriate information—with a blank line between as shown here:

MEMO

TO:
FROM:
DATE:
SUBJECT:

Sometimes the heading is organized like this:

MEMO

TO: FROM:

DATE: SUBJECT:

The following guidelines will help you effectively format specific memo elements:

- **Addressees.** When sending a memo to a long list of people, include the notation *See distribution list* or *See below* in the *To* position at the top; then list the names at the end of the memo. Arrange this list alphabetically,

except when high-ranking officials deserve more prominent placement. You can also address memos to groups of people—*All Sales Representatives, Production Group, New Product Team.*

- **Courtesy titles.** You need not use courtesy titles anywhere in a memo; first initials and last names, first names, or even initials alone are often sufficient. However, use a courtesy title if you would use one in a face-to-face encounter with the person.
- **Subject line.** The subject line of a memo helps busy colleagues quickly find out what your memo is about, so take care to make it concise and compelling.
- **Body.** Start the body of the memo on the second or third line below the heading. Like the body of a letter, it's usually single-spaced with blank lines between paragraphs. Indenting paragraphs is optional. Handle lists, important passages, and subheadings as you do in letters.
- **Second page.** If the memo carries over to a second page, head the second page just as you head the second page of a letter.
- **Writer's initials.** Unlike a letter, a memo doesn't require a complimentary close or a signature because your name is already prominent at the top. However, you may initial the memo—either beside the name appearing at the top of the memo or at the bottom of the memo.
- **Other elements.** Treat elements such as reference initials and copy notations just as you would in a letter. One difference between letters and memos is that while letters use the term *enclosure* to refer to other pieces included with the letter, memos usually use the word *attachment.*

Memos may be delivered by hand, by the post office (when the recipient works at a different location), or through interoffice mail. Interoffice mail may require the use of special reusable envelopes that have spaces for the recipient's name and department or room number; the name of the previous recipient is simply crossed out. If a regular envelope is used, the words *Interoffice Mail* appear where the stamp normally goes, so that it won't accidentally be stamped and mailed with the rest of the office correspondence.

Informal, routine, or brief reports for distribution within a company are often presented in memo form. Don't include report parts such as a table of contents and appendixes, but write the body of the memo report just as carefully as you'd write a formal report.

Reports

Enhance the effectiveness of your reports by paying careful attention to their appearance and layout. Follow whatever guidelines your organization prefers, always being neat and consistent throughout. If it's up to you to decide formatting questions, the following conventions may help you decide how to handle margins, headings, and page numbers.

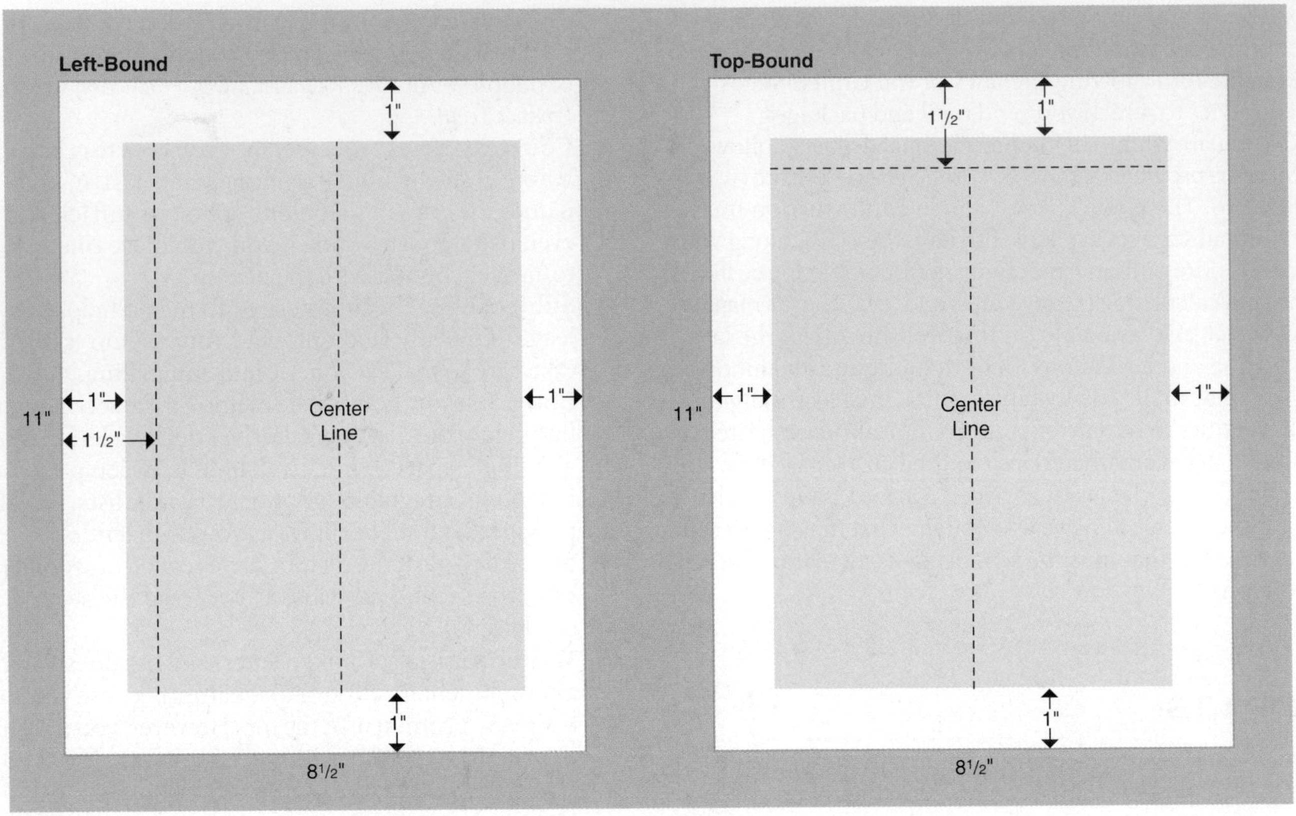

Figure A.8 **Margins for Formal Reports**

MARGINS

All margins on a report page should be at least 1 inch wide. The top, left, and right margins are usually the same, but the bottom margins can be 1½ times deeper. Some special pages also have deeper top margins. Set top margins as deep as 2 inches for pages that contain major titles: prefatory parts (such as the table of contents or the executive summary), supplementary parts (such as the reference notes or bibliography), and textual parts (such as the first page of the text or the first page of each chapter).

If you're going to bind your report at the left or at the top, add half an inch to the margin on the bound edge (see Figure A.8): The space taken by the binding on left-bound reports makes the center point of the text a quarter inch to the right of the center of the paper. Be sure to center headings between the margins, not between the edges of the paper.

HEADINGS

If you don't have a template supplied by your employer, choose a design for headings and subheadings that clearly distinguishes the various levels in the hierarchy. The first-level headings should be the most prominent, on down to the lowest-level subheading.

PAGE NUMBERS

Every page in a report is counted; however, not all pages show numbers. The first page of the report, normally the title page, is unnumbered. All other pages in the prefatory section are numbered with a lowercase roman numeral, beginning with *ii* and continuing with *iii, iv, v,* and so on. Start numbering again with arabic numerals (1, 2, and so on) starting at the first page of the body.

You have many options for placing and formatting the page numbers, although these choices are usually made for you in a template. If you're not using a standard company template, position the page number where it is easy to see as the reader flips through the report. If the report will be stapled or otherwise bound along the left side, for instance, the best place for the page number is the upper right or lower right corner.

Endnotes

1. "How to Choose Paper Content?" Southworth, accessed 21 April 2018, www.southworth.com.
2. U.S. Postal Service, *International Mail Manual,* 5 March 2018, www.usps.gov.

Documentation of Report Sources

By providing information about your sources, you improve your own credibility as well as the credibility of the facts and opinions you present. Documentation gives readers the means for checking your findings and pursuing the subject further. Also, documenting your report is the accepted way to give credit to the people whose work you have drawn from.

What style should you use to document your report? Experts recommend various forms, depending on your field or discipline. Moreover, your employer or client may use a form different from those the experts suggest. Don't let this discrepancy confuse you. If your employer specifies a form, use it; the standardized form is easier for colleagues to understand. However, if the choice of form is left to you, adopt one of the styles described here. Whatever style you choose, be consistent within any given report, using the same order, punctuation, and format from one reference citation or bibliography entry to the next.

A wide variety of style manuals provide detailed information on documentation. These publications explain the three most commonly used styles:

- American Psychological Association, *Publication Manual of the American Psychological Association*, 6th ed. (Washington, D.C.: American Psychological Association, 2013). Details the author-date system, which is preferred in the social sciences and often in the natural sciences as well.
- *The Chicago Manual of Style*, 17th ed. (Chicago: University of Chicago Press, 2017). Often referred to only as "*Chicago*" and widely used in the publishing industry; provides detailed treatment of source documentation and many other aspects of document preparation.
- *MLA Handbook*, 8th ed. (New York: Modern Language Association, 2016). Provides the citation guidelines most often used in the liberal arts and humanities.

For more information on these three guides, visit real-timeupdates.com/ebc13 and select Appendix B. Although many schemes have been proposed for organizing the information in source notes, all of them break the information into parts: (1) information about the author (name), (2) information about the work (title, edition, volume number), (3) information about the publication (place, publisher), (4) information about the date, and (5) information about location, including relevant page ranges.

The following sections summarize the major conventions for documenting sources in three styles: *The Chicago Manual of Style (Chicago)*, the *Publication Manual of the American Psychological Association (APA)*, and the *MLA Handbook (MLA)*.

Chicago Humanities Style

Chicago recommends two types of documentation systems. The *documentary-note*, or *humanities*, style gives bibliographic citations in notes—either footnotes (when printed at the bottom of a page) or endnotes (when printed at the end of the report). The humanities system is often used in literature, history, and the arts. The other system recommended by *Chicago* is the *author-date* system, which cites the author's last name and the date of publication in the text, usually in parentheses, reserving full documentation for the reference list (or bibliography). For the purpose of comparing styles, this section concentrates on the humanities system, which is described in detail in *Chicago*.

IN-TEXT CITATION—*CHICAGO* HUMANITIES STYLE

To document report sources in text, the humanities system relies on superscripts—arabic numerals placed just above the line of type at the end of the reference:

> Toward the end of his speech, Myers sounded a note of caution, saying that even though the economy is expected to grow, it could easily slow a bit.[10]

The superscript lets the reader know how to look for source information in either a footnote or an endnote (see Figure B.1 on the next page). Some readers prefer footnotes so that they can simply glance at the bottom of the page for information. Others prefer endnotes so that they can read the text without a clutter of notes on the page. Also, endnotes relieve the writer from worrying about how long each note will be and how much space it will take away from the page. Both footnotes and endnotes can be handled automatically by today's word-processing software.

For the reader's convenience, you can use footnotes for *content notes* (which may supplement your main text with asides about a particular issue or event, provide a cross-reference to another section of your report, or direct the

NOTES

Journal article with volume and issue numbers

> 1. Jonathan Clifton, "Beyond Taxonomies of Influence," *Journal of Business Communication* 46, no. 1 (2019): 57–79.

Brochure

> 2. BestTemp Staffing Services, *An Employer's Guide to Staffing Services*, 2d ed. (Denver: BestTemp Information Center, 2018), 31.

Newspaper article, no author

> 3. "Might Be Harder Than It Looks," *Los Angeles Times*, January 30 2020, sec. A, p. 22.

Annual report

> 4. The Walt Disney Company, *2018 Annual Report* (Burbank, Calif.: The Walt Disney Company, 2019), 48.

Magazine article

> 5. Kerry A. Dolan, "A Whole New Crop" *Forbes*, June 2, 2019, 72–75.

Television broadcast

> 6. Daniel Han, "Trade Wars Heating Up Around the Globe," *CNN Headline News* (Atlanta: CNN, March 5, 2019).

Website content

> 7. "Curves Fitness." *Curves*, accessed 5 May 2020. www.curves.com/fitness.

Book, component parts

> 8. Sonja Kuntz, "Moving Beyond Benefits," in *Our Changing Workforce*, ed. Randolf Jacobson, 213–27 (New York: Citadel Press, 2018).

Unpublished dissertation or thesis

> 9. George H. Morales, "The Economic Pressures on Industrialized Nations in a Global Economy" (Ph.D. diss., University of San Diego, 2017), 32–47.

Paper presented at a meeting

> 10. Charles Myers, "HMOs in Today's Environment" (paper presented at the Conference on Medical Insurance Solutions, Chicago, Ill., August 2018), 16–17.

Blog post

> 11. Seth Godin, "The Self-Healing Letter of Complaint," *Seth's Blog*, 4 May 2017, http://sethgodin.typepad.com/seths_blog/2017/05/the-self-healing-letter-of-complaint.html.

Interview

> 12. Georgia Stainer, general manager, Day Cable and Communications, interview by author, Topeka, Kan., March 2, 2020.

Newspaper article, one author

> 13. Evelyn Standish, "Global Market Crushes OPEC's Delicate Balance of Interests," *Wall Street Journal*, January 19, 2016, sec. A, p. 1.

Book, two authors

> 14. Miriam Toller and Jay Fielding, *Global Business for Smaller Companies* (Rocklin, Calif.: Prima Publishing, 2019), 102–3.

Government publication

> 15. U.S. Department of Defense, *Stretching Research Dollars: Survival Advice for Universities and Government Labs* (Washington, D.C.: GPO, 2018), 126.

Online video

> 16. Adam Grant, "The Surprising Habits of Original Thinkers," TED video, filmed February 2016; available from www.ted.com/talks/adam_grant_the_surprising_habits_of_original_thinkers.

Figure B.1   Sample Endnotes–Chicago Humanities Style

(Note: This is a collection of sample entries, not a page from an actual report; dates shown may not reflect actual sources. Also, *Chicago* doesn't specify blank lines between entries; that was done here for clarity.)

reader to a related source). Then you can use endnotes for *source notes* (which document direct quotations, paraphrased passages, and visual aids). Consider which type of note is most common in your report, and then choose whether to present these notes all as endnotes or all as footnotes. Regardless of the method you choose for referencing textual information in your report, notes for visual aids (both content notes and source notes) are placed on the same page as the visual.

BIBLIOGRAPHY—*CHICAGO* HUMANITIES STYLE

The humanities system may or may not be accompanied by a bibliography (because the notes give all the necessary bibliographic information). However, endnotes are arranged in order of appearance in the text, so an alphabetical bibliography can be valuable to your readers. The bibliography may be titled *Bibliography, Reference List, Sources, Works Cited* (if you include only those sources you actually cited in your report), or *Works Consulted* (if you include uncited sources as well). This list of sources may also serve as a reading list for those who want to pursue the subject of your report further, so you may want to annotate each entry—that is, comment on the subject matter and viewpoint of the source, as well as on its usefulness to readers. Annotations may be written in either complete or incomplete sentences. A bibliography may also be more manageable if you subdivide it into categories (a classified bibliography), either by type of reference (such as books, articles, and unpublished material) or by subject matter (such as government regulations, market forces, and so on). Following are the major conventions for

BIBLIOGRAPHY

Blog post (usually not included in *Chicago*-style bibliography unless you cite the blog frequently)

Godin, Seth. "The Self-Healing Letter of Complaint," *Seth's Blog*, May 4, 2017, http://sethgodin.typepad.com/seths_blog/2017/05/the-self-healing-letter-of-complaint.html.

Brochure

BestTemp Staffing Services. *An Employer's Guide to Staffing Services.* 2d ed. Denver: BestTemp Information Center, 2018.

Journal article with volume and issue numbers

Clifton, Jonathan. "Beyond Taxonomies of Influence." *Journal of Business Communication* 46, no. 1 (2019): 57–79.

Magazine article

Dolan, Kerry A. "A Whole New Crop," *Forbes*, June 2, 2019, 72–75.

Online video

Grant, Adam. "The Surprising Habits of Original Thinkers." Filmed February 2016. TED video, 15:25. Posted April 2016. www.ted.com/talks/adam_grant_the_surprising_habits_of_original_thinkers.

Television broadcast

Han, Daniel. "Trade Wars Heating Up Around the Globe." *CNN Headline News.* Atlanta: CNN, 5 March 2019.

Website content

"Curves Fitness." *Curves*, accessed May 5, 2020. www.curves.com/fitness.

Book, component parts

Kuntz, Sonja. "Moving Beyond Benefits." In *Our Changing Workforce*, edited by Randolf Jacobson, 52–67. New York: Citadel Press, 2018.

Newspaper article, no author

"Might Be Harder Than It Looks." *Los Angeles Times*, January 30, 2020, sec. A, p. 22.

Unpublished dissertation or thesis

Morales, George H. "The Economic Pressures on Industrialized Nations in a Global Economy." Ph.D. diss., University of San Diego, 2017.

Paper presented at a meeting

Myers, Charles. "HMOs in Today's Environment." Paper presented at the Conference on Medical Insurance Solutions, Chicago, Ill., August 2018.

Interview

Stainer, Georgia, general manager, Day Cable and Communications. Interview by author. Topeka, Kan., 2 March 2020.

Newspaper article, one author

Standish, Evelyn. "Global Market Crushes OPEC's Delicate Balance of Interests." *Wall Street Journal*, January 19, 2016, sec. A, p. 1.

Book, two authors

Toller, Miriam, and Jay Fielding. *Global Business for Smaller Companies.* Rocklin, Calif.: Prima Publishing, 2019.

Government publication

U.S. Department of Defense. *Stretching Research Dollars: Survival Advice for Universities and Government Labs.* Washington, D.C.: GPO, 2018.

Annual report

The Walt Disney Company, *2018 Annual Report*, Burbank, Calif.: The Walt Disney Company, 2019.

Figure B.2   Sample Bibliography–*Chicago* Humanities Style

(Note: This is a collection of sample entries, not a page from an actual report; dates shown may not reflect actual sources. Also, *Chicago* doesn't specify blank lines between entries; that was done here for clarity.)

developing a bibliography according to *Chicago* style (see Figure B.2):

- Exclude any page numbers that may be cited in source notes, except for journals, periodicals, newspapers, and book chapter page ranges.
- Alphabetize entries by the last name of the lead author (listing last name first). The names of second and succeeding authors are listed in normal order. Entries without an author name are alphabetized by the first important word in the title.
- Format entries as hanging indents (indent the second and succeeding lines three to five spaces).
- Arrange entries in the following general order: (1) author name, (2) title information, (3) publication information, (4) date, (5) periodical page range.

- Use quotation marks around the titles of articles from magazines, newspapers, and journals. Capitalize the first and last words, as well as all other important words (except prepositions, articles, and coordinating conjunctions).
- Use italics to set off the names of books, newspapers, journals, and other complete publications. Capitalize the first and last words, as well as all other important words.
- For journal articles, include the volume number and the issue number (if necessary). Include the year of publication inside parentheses and follow with a colon and the page range of the article: *Journal of Business Communication* 46, no. 1 (2009): 57–79. (In this source, the volume is 46, the number is 1, and the page range is 57–79.)
- Use brackets to identify all electronic references: [Online database] or [CD-ROM].

- Explain how electronic references can be reached if it's not obvious from the URL.
- Give the access date for online references: Accessed August 23, 2020.

APA Style

The American Psychological Association (APA) recommends the author-date system of documentation, which is popular in the physical, natural, and social sciences. When using this system, you simply insert the author's last name and the year of publication within parentheses following the text discussion of the material cited. Include a page number if you use a direct quotation. This approach briefly identifies the source so that readers can locate complete information in the alphabetical reference list at the end of the report. The author-date system is both brief and clear, saving readers time and effort.

IN-TEXT CITATION—APA STYLE

To document report sources in text using APA style, insert the author's surname and the date of publication at the end of a statement. Enclose this information in parentheses. If the author's name is referred to in the text itself, then the name can be omitted from parenthetical material.

> Some experts recommend both translation and back-translation when dealing with any non-English-speaking culture (Clifton, 2019).

> Toller and Fielding (2019) make a strong case for small companies succeeding in global business.

Personal communications and interviews conducted by the author would not be listed in the reference list. Such citations appear in the text only.

> Increasing the role of cable companies is high on the list of Georgia Stainer, general manager at Day Cable and Communications (personal communication, March 2, 2020).

LIST OF REFERENCES—APA STYLE

For APA style, list only those works actually cited in the text (so you would not include works for background or for further reading). Following are the major conventions for developing a reference list according to APA style (see Figure B.3):

- Format entries as hanging indents.
- List all author names in reverse order (last name first), and use only initials for the first and middle names.
- Arrange entries in the following general order: (1) author name, (2) date, (3) title information, (4) publication information, (5) periodical page range.
- Follow the author name with the date of publication in parentheses.

- List titles of articles from magazines, newspapers, and journals without underlines or quotation marks. Capitalize only the first word of the title, any proper nouns, and the first word to follow an internal colon. Italicize titles of books, capitalizing only the first word, any proper nouns, and the first word to follow a colon.
- Italicize titles of magazines, newspapers, journals, and other complete publications. Capitalize all the important words in the title.
- For journal articles, include the volume number (in italics) and, if necessary, the issue number (in parentheses). Finally, include the page range of the article: *Journal of Business Communication, 46*(1), 57–79. (In this example, the volume is 46, the number is 1, and the page range is 57–79.)
- Include personal communications (such as letters, memos, emails, and conversations) only in text, not in reference lists.
- Electronic references include author, date of publication, title of article, name of publication (if one), volume, and the URL.
- For electronic references, indicate the actual year of publication.
- For webpages with extremely long URLs, use your best judgment to determine which URL from the site to use. For example, rather than giving the long URL of a specific news release, you can provide the URL of the "Media relations" webpage.
- APA citation guidelines for social media are still evolving. For the latest information, visit the APA Style Blog (blog.apastyle.org).
- For online journals or periodicals that assign a digital object identifier (DOI), include that instead of a conventional URL. If no DOI is available, include the URL of the publication's homepage.

MLA Style

The style recommended by the Modern Language Association of America is used widely in the humanities, especially in the study of language and literature. Like APA style, MLA style uses brief parenthetical citations in the text. However, instead of including author name and year, MLA citations include author name and page reference.

IN-TEXT CITATION—MLA STYLE

To document report sources in text using MLA style, insert the author's last name and a page reference inside parentheses following the cited material: (Matthews 63). If the author's name is mentioned in the text reference, the name can be omitted from the parenthetical citation: (63). The citation indicates that the reference came from page 63 of a work by Matthews. With the author's name, readers can find complete publication information in the alphabetically arranged list of works cited that comes at the end of the report.

REFERENCES

Blog post

Godin, S. (2017, May 4). The self-healing letter of complaint. *Seth's Blog*. Retrieved from sethgodin.typepad.com/seths_blog/2017/05/the-self-healing-letter-of-complaint.html.

Brochure

BestTemp Staffing Services. (2018). *An employer's guide to staffing services* (2nd ed.) [Brochure]. Denver, CO: BestTemp Information Center.

Journal article with volume and issue numbers

Clifton, J. (2019). Beyond taxonomies of influence. *Journal of Business Communication, 46*(1), 57.

Magazine article

Dolan, K. A. (2019, June 2). A whole new crop. *Forbes*, 72–75.

Online video

Grant, A. (2016, April 26). The surprising habits of original thinkers [Video file]. Retrieved from www.ted.com/talks/adam_grant_the_surprising_habits_of_original_thinkers.

Television broadcast

Han, D. (2019, March 5). Trade wars heating up around the globe. *CNN Headline News* [Television broadcast]. Atlanta, GA: CNN.

Website content

Curves (2020). *Curves Fitness*. Retrieved from www.curves.com/fitness.

Book, component parts

Kuntz, S. (2018). Moving beyond benefits. In Randolph Jacobson (Ed.), *Our changing workforce* (pp. 213–227). New York, NY: Citadel Press.

Newspaper article, no author

Might be harder than it looks. (2020, January 30). *Los Angeles Times*, p. A22.

Unpublished dissertation or thesis

Morales, G. H. (2017). *The economic pressures on industrialized nations in a global economy*. Unpublished doctoral dissertation, University of San Diego.

Paper presented at a meeting

Myers, C. (2018, August). *HMOs in today's environment*. Paper presented at the Conference on Medical Insurance Solutions, Chicago, IL.

Interview

Cited in text only, not in the list of references.

Newspaper article, one author

Standish, E. (2016, January 19). Global market crushes OPEC's delicate balance of interests. *Wall Street Journal*, p. A1.

Book, two authors

Toller, M., & Fielding, J. (2019). *Global business for smaller companies*. Rocklin, CA: Prima Publishing.

Government publication

U.S. Department of Defense. (2018). *Stretching research dollars: Survival advice for universities and government labs*. Washington, DC: U.S. Government Printing Office.

Annual report

The Walt Disney Company. (2019). *2018 Annual report*, Burbank, CA: The Walt Disney Company.

Figure B.3   Sample References–APA Style

(Note: This is a collection of sample references, not a page from an actual report; dates shown may not reflect actual sources. Also, it is single-spaced as is the norm for business reports; APA references are double-spaced in academic reports.)

Some experts recommend both translation and back-translation when dealing with any non-English-speaking culture (Clifton 57).

Toller and Fielding make a strong case for small companies succeeding in global business (102–03).

The *MLA Handbook* offers advice on handling multiple authors, multiple works by a single author, and other details of in-text references.

LIST OF WORKS CITED—MLA STYLE

In MLA style, all the research sources that were cited are gathered in a section titled Works Cited, with that title centered at the top of the page. Alphabetize entries by the author's last name or the title of the work if there is no author.

In the 8th edition of the *MLA Handbook*, the MLA significantly changed its approach to citation guidelines. In response to the proliferation of new media formats in recent years, the handbook no longer provides specific citation guidelines for every conceivable type of media item. Instead, it offers general guidelines that you can adapt to each item you need to cite.

The MLA approach is built on three principles:

- Include the basic identifiers common to most sources, such as author name(s), the title of the work, and the date of publication or access.
- Recognize that there can be multiple "right" ways to document a source, depending on the circumstances.
- If you have any doubt about what to include, do what is best for your readers. For example, if the readers of

a report are likely to retrieve the materials to continue their own research, you'll need to provide more information than if you are simply giving credit to the authors of the materials you used.

Each entry can have up to nine parts if they are relevant to the project's and readers' needs, although most on-the-job reports won't need that many:

- **Author name(s).** Start with the lead author's name in reverse order (last name first), using either full first name or initials, followed by a period. If the source has two authors, list the second author's name in regular order. If the source has three or more authors, reverse the first name, then follow it with a comma and *et al* ("and others"). If no author name is available, such as with many corporate or governmental publications, begin the citation with the title of the work and use the organization's name as the publisher. An exception to this rule is if one organization wrote the piece and another published it, in which case list the former as the author.

- **Title of source.** Use the full title of the source, including any subtitles. Capitalize every word except articles, prepositions, coordinating conjunctions, and the *to* in infinitives, and put a period at the end of the title. If the source is one of multiple items in a *container* (see next bullet), such as an article within a magazine or on a website, put quotation marks around the title. If it is not part of a larger entity (as is the case with a book, for example), put the title in italics. This distinction applies to audio and video material as well. The title of a podcast channel, for instance, is set in italics, whereas the title of an individual podcast episode from that channel is enclosed in quotation marks. For email messages, use the subject line of the message as the title, enclosed in quotation marks and capitalized as above. For tweets, use the entire tweet, enclosed in quotation marks, and apply whatever capitalization and punctuation appear in the original.

- **Title of container.** The MLA uses *container* to refer to any entity that contains multiple sources. Books, periodicals, television series, and websites are all containers, for example. Capitalize container titles as described under source titles, and put a period at the end of them. If a source is embedded in more than one container, such as an article in a journal (container 1), which you found in an online database (container 2), include information for all the containers.

- **Other contributors.** If other named individuals were involved in the creation and production of the source, such as editors or translators, include their role(s) and name(s) next, such as "Edited by Josie Waler."

- **Version.** If a source has been released in multiple versions, such as the various editions of a book, indicate that next. The third edition of a book would be denoted as "3rd ed." followed by a comma.

- **Number.** If the source is part of a numbered sequence and this information is relevant to the project and important to readers, include that as well. Academic journals, for example, are typically identified by volume (usually corresponding to an entire year) and number (corresponding to one issue).

- **Publisher.** The publisher is the organization primarily responsible for producing the source material. This could be a book publisher, the owner of a website, or the production company behind a TV series. If you are citing an article found on Apple's website, for example, Apple is the name of the publisher.

- **Publication and access dates.** Include the date or dates most meaningful to readers in the context of the project. Use the day-month-year style, and include the time if that is relevant. You can abbreviate months to save space. Periodicals, books, tweets, and email messages all have specific publication dates. Website content and blog posts may or may not show a date. If an online source is undated, use "Accessed" followed by the date.

- **Location.** This can refer to the specific location within a source or the source's location within a container. For print sources, this usually involves page numbers, such as the pages you referenced from a book or the location of a magazine article within an issue. Use "p." to denote a single page and "pp." to denote a range of pages. For online sources, the location is usually the URL where the item can be found. How much of the URL to include is a matter of judgment, based on how long the URL is, whether your readers will want to access the source, and whether your document is print or digital. If the URL is extremely long, you might want to use the URL of the website's homepage. Many publishers now provide digital object identifiers (DOIs), which are more stable than URLs. If a DOI is available, use it instead.

If other information will help the reader or clarify the source of your information, include it as well. For example, if you used information you heard in a lecture, add "Lecture" at the end of the entry. If your source was a transcript of a podcast or video, add "Transcript."

Figure B.4 shows a variety of items in MLA citation format. Bear in mind, however, that given the flexibility the MLA now embraces, some of these entries could be configured differently for various contexts and still be correct.

WORKS CITED

Blog post

Godin, Seth. "The Self-Healing Letter of Complaint." *Seth's Blog*, 4 May 2017, sethgodin.typepad.com/seths_blog/2017/05/the-self-healing-letter-of-complaint.html.

Brochure

An Employer's Guide to Staffing Services. 2d ed. BestTemp Staffing Services, 2018.

Journal article with volume and issue numbers

Clifton, Jonathan. "Beyond Taxonomies of Influence." *Journal of Business Communication* vol. 46, no. 1, 2019, pp. 57–79.

Magazine article

Dolan, Kerry A. "A Whole New Crop." *Forbes*, 2 June 2019, 72–75.

Online video

Grant, Adam. "The Surprising Habits of Original Thinkers." TED. April 2016. Lecture.

Television broadcast

Han, Daniel. "Trade Wars Heating Up Around the Globe." *CNN Headline News*. CNN. 5 Mar. 2019.

Website content

"Curves Fitness." *Curves*, www.curves.com/fitness. Accessed 5 May 2020.

Book, component parts

Kuntz, Sonja. "Moving Beyond Benefits." *Our Changing Workforce*. Edited by Randolf Jacobson. Citadel Press, 2020, pp. 213–27.

Newspaper article, no author

"Might Be Harder Than It Looks." *Los Angeles Times,* 30 Jan. 2020, A22.

Unpublished dissertation or thesis

Morales, George H. "The Economic Pressures on Industrialized Nations in a Global Economy." Dissertation. University of San Diego, 2017.

Paper presented at a meeting

Myers, Charles. "HMOs in Today's Environment." Conference on Medical Insurance Solutions. Chicago. 13 Aug. 2018. Lecture.

Interview

Stainer, Georgia, general manager, Day Cable and Communications. Telephone interview. 2 Mar. 2020.

Tweet

@StanleyNeimeyer21. "Uber under Federal scrutiny for allegedly using Greyball software tool to deceive regulators." *Twitter*, 5 May 2017, 4:34 p.m., twitter.com/JessNeimeyer21/status/176782308736737282.

Book, two authors

Toller, Miriam, and Jay Fielding. *Global Business for Smaller Companies*. Prima Publishing, 2019.

Government publication, separate author and publisher

United States Department of Defense. *Stretching Research Dollars: Survival Advice for Universities and Government Labs*. GPO, 2018.

Annual report

Walt Disney Company, *2018 Annual Report*. Walt Disney Company, 2019.

Figure B.4   Sample Works Cited–MLA Style

(Note: This is a collection of sample references, not a page from an actual report; dates shown may not reflect actual sources. Also, it is single-spaced as is the norm for business reports; MLA works cited are double-spaced in academic reports.)

Correction Symbols

Symbol	Meaning	Symbol Used in Context	Corrected Copy
Corrections			
⌒	Close up space	self- confidence	self-confidence
ℓ	Delete	harassment ~~and abuse~~ℓ	harassment
∧	Insert	tirquoise shirts (u / and white)	turquoise and white shirts
∨	Insert apostrophe	our teams goals	our team's goals
∧	Insert comma	a, b and c	a, b, and c
⹀	Insert hyphen	third quarter sales	third-quarter sales
⊙	Insert period	Harrigan et al	Harrigan et al.
∨ ∨	Insert quotation marks	This team isn't cooperating.	This "team" isn't cooperating.
#	Insert space	real estate test case	real estate test case
≡	Capitalize	Pepsico, Inc.	PepsiCo, Inc.
/	Lowercase	TULSA, South of here	Tulsa, south of here
⬯	Spell out	(COD)	cash on delivery
(sp)	Spell out	(sp) (Assn. of Biochem. Engrs.)	Association of Biochemical Engineers
∼	Transpose	(airy, light,) casaul tone	light, airy, casual tone
(STET)	Restore	staff talked ~~openly and frankly~~ℓ (STET)	staff talked openly
Alignment and Repositioning			
═	Align horizontally	meaningful result	meaningful result
‖	Align vertically	1. Power cable 2. Keyboard	1. Power cable 2. Keyboard
⊐⊏	Center	⊐Awards Banquet⊏	Awards Banquet
(ds)	Double-space	text in first line text in second line (ds)	text in first line text in second line
⌐⌐	Move down	Sincerely,	Sincerely,
⊏	Move left	Attention: ⊏Security	Attention: Security
⊐	Move right	February 2, 2019 ⊐	February 2, 2019
⌐⌐	Move up	THIRD-QUARTER SALES	THIRD-QUARTER SALES
∫	Run lines together	Manager, Distribution	Manager, Distribution

Symbol	Meaning	Symbol Used in Context	Corrected Copy
(ss)	Single space	(ss) ⌈text in first line ⌊text in second line	text in first line text in second line
⌐	Start new line	Marla Fenton, ⌐Manager, Distri-bution	Marla Fenton, Manager, Distribution
¶	Start new paragraph	¶ The solution is easy to determine but difficult to implement in a competitive environment like the one we now face.	The solution is easy to determine but difficult to implement in a competitive environment like the one we now face.

Type Treatment

(bf)	Boldface	Recommendations (bf)	**Recommendations**
(ital)	Italics	Quarterly Report (ital)	*Quarterly Report*

Handbook of Grammar, Mechanics, and Usage

The rules of grammar, mechanics, and usage provide the guidance every professional needs in order to communicate successfully with colleagues, customers, and other audiences. These rules help you in two important ways. First, they determine how meaning is encoded and decoded in the communication process. If you don't encode your messages using the same rules your readers or listeners use to decode them, chances are your audiences will not extract your intended meaning from your messages. Without a firm grasp of the basics of grammar, mechanics, and usage, you risk being misunderstood, damaging your company's image, losing money for your company, and possibly even losing your job. In other words, if you want to get your point across, you need to follow the rules of grammar, mechanics, and usage. Second, apart from successfully transferring meaning, following the rules tells your audience that you respect the conventions and expectations of the business community.

You can think of *grammar* as the agreed-on structure of a language, the way that individual words are formed, and the manner in which those words are then combined to form meaningful sentences. *Mechanics* are style and formatting issues such as capitalization, spelling, and the use of numbers and symbols. *Usage* involves the accepted and expected way in which specific words are used by a particular community of people—in this case, the community of businesspeople who use English. This handbook can help you improve your knowledge and awareness in all three areas. It is divided into the following sections:

- **Diagnostic Test of English Skills.** Testing your current knowledge of grammar, mechanics, and usage helps you find out where your strengths and weaknesses lie. This test offers 50 items taken from the topics included in this handbook.
- **Assessment of English Skills.** After completing the diagnostic test, use the assessment form to highlight the areas you most need to review.
- **Essentials of Grammar, Mechanics, and Usage.** This section helps you quickly review the basics. You can study the things you've probably already learned but may have forgotten about grammar, punctuation, mechanics (including capitalization, abbreviation, number style, and word division), and vocabulary (including frequently confused words, frequently misused words, frequently misspelled words, and transitional words and phrases). Use this essential review not only to study and improve your English skills but also as a reference for any questions you may have during this course.

Diagnostic Test of English Skills

Use this test to determine whether you need more practice with grammar, punctuation, mechanics, or vocabulary. When you've answered all the questions, ask your instructor for an answer sheet so that you can score the test. On the Assessment of English Skills form (page 584), record the number of questions you answered incorrectly in each section.

The following choices apply to items 1–5. Write in each blank the letter of the choice that best describes the part of speech that is underlined.

A. noun
B. pronoun
C. verb
D. adjective
E. adverb
F. preposition
G. conjunction
H. article

_____ 1. The new branch location will be decided <u>by</u> next week.
_____ 2. We must hire only <u>qualified</u>, ambitious graduates.
_____ 3. After their <u>presentation</u>, I was still undecided.
_____ 4. See <u>me</u> after the meeting.
_____ 5. Margaret, pressed for time, turned in <u>unusually</u> sloppy work.

In the blanks for items 6–15, write the letter of the word or phrase that best completes each sentence.

_____ 6. (A. Russ's, B. Russ') laptop was stolen last week.
_____ 7. Speaking only for (A. me, B. myself), I think the new policy is discriminatory.
_____ 8. Of the five candidates we interviewed yesterday, (A. who, B. whom) do you believe is the best choice?
_____ 9. India has increased (A. it's, B. its) imports of corn and rice.
_____ 10. Either the New York head office or the regional offices will need to reduce (A. their, B. its) staffing costs.
_____ 11. If the IT department can't (A. lie, B. lay) the fiber-optic cable by March 1, the plant will not open on schedule.
_____ 12. Starbucks (A. is, B. are) opening five new stores in San Diego in the next year.

_____ **13.** The number of women-owned small businesses (A. has, B. have) increased sharply in the past two decades.

_____ **14.** Greg and Bernyce worked (A. good, B. well) together.

_____ **15.** They distributed the supplies (A. among, B. between) the six staff members.

The following choices apply to items 16–20. Identify the issue that best describes the problem with each sentence's structure.

A. sentence fragment
B. comma splice
C. misplaced modifier
D. fused sentence
E. lack of parallelism
F. unclear antecedent

_____ **16.** The number of employees who took the buyout offer was much higher than expected, now the entire company is understaffed.

_____ **17.** The leader in internet-only banking.

_____ **18.** Diamond doesn't actually sell financial products rather it acts as an intermediary.

_____ **19.** Helen's proposal is for not only the present but also for the future.

_____ **20.** When purchasing luxury products, quality is more important than price for consumers.

For items 21–30, circle the letter of the preferred choice in each of the following groups of sentences.

21. A. What do you think of the ad slogan "Have it your way?"
B. What do you think of the ad slogan "Have it your way"?

22. A. Send copies to Jackie Cross, Uniline, Brad Nardi, Peale & Associates, and Tom Griesbaum, MatchMakers.
B. Send copies to Jackie Cross, Uniline; Brad Nardi, Peale & Associates; and Tom Griesbaum, MatchMakers.

23. A. They've recorded 22 complaints since yesterday, all of them from long-time employees.
B. They've recorded 22 complaints since yesterday; all of them from long-time employees.

24. A. We are looking for two qualities in applicants: experience with computers and an interest in people.
B. We are looking for two qualities in applicants; experience with computers and an interest in people.

25. A. At the Center for the Blind the clients we serve have lost vision, due to a wide variety of causes.
B. At the Center for the Blind, the clients we serve have lost vision due to a wide variety of causes.

26. A. Replace your standard light bulbs with new, compact fluorescent bulbs.
B. Replace your standard light bulbs with new, compact, fluorescent bulbs.
C. Replace your standard light bulbs with new compact fluorescent bulbs.

27. A. Blue Cross of California may have changed its name to Anthem Blue Cross but the company still has the same commitment to California.
B. Blue Cross of California may have changed its name to Anthem Blue Cross, but the company still has the same commitment to California.

28. A. Only eight banks in this country—maybe nine can handle transactions of this magnitude.
B. Only eight banks in this country—maybe nine— can handle transactions of this magnitude.

29. A. Instead of focusing on high-growth companies, we targeted mature businesses with only one or two people handling the decisions.
B. Instead of focusing on high growth companies, we targeted mature businesses with only one or two people handling the decisions.

30. A. According to board president Damian Cabaza "having a crisis communication plan is a high priority."
B. According to board president Damian Cabaza, "Having a crisis communication plan is a high priority."

For items 31–40, select the best choice from among those provided.

31. A. At her previous employer, Mary-Anne worked in Marketing Communications and Human Resources.
B. At her previous employer, Mary-Anne worked in marketing communications and human resources.

32. A. By fall, we'll have a dozen locations between the Mississippi and Missouri rivers.
B. By Fall, we'll have a dozen locations between the Mississippi and Missouri Rivers.

33. A. The Board applauded President Donlan upon her reelection for a fifth term.
B. The board applauded president Donlan upon her reelection for a fifth term.
C. The board applauded President Donlan upon her reelection for a fifth term.

34. A. If you want to travel to France, you need to be au courant with the business practices.
B. If you want to travel to France, you need to be "au courant" with the business practices.

35. A. As the company's CEO, Thomas Spurgeon handles all dealings with the FDA.
B. As the company's C.E.O., Thomas Spurgeon handles all dealings with the F.D.A.

36. A. The maximum speed limit in most states is 65 mph.
B. The maximum speed limit in most states is 65 m.p.h.

37. **A.** Sales of graphic novels increased nine percent between 2016 and 2017.
    B. Sales of graphic novels increased 9 percent between 2016 and 2017.
38. **A.** Our store is open daily from nine a.m. to seven p.m.
    B. Our store is open daily from 9:00 a.m. to 7:00 p.m.
39. **A.** The organizing meeting is scheduled for July 27, and the event will be held in January 2020.
    B. The organizing meeting is scheduled for July 27th, and the event will be held in January, 2020.
40. **A.** We need six desks, eight file cabinets, and 12 trashcans.
    B. We need 6 desks, 8 file cabinets, and 12 trashcans.

For items 41–50, write in each blank the letter of the word that best completes each sentence.

_____ **41.** Will having a degree (A. affect, B. effect) my chances for promotion?

_____ **42.** Try not to (A. loose, B. lose) this key; we will charge you a fee to replace it.

_____ **43.** I don't want to discuss my (A. personal, B. personnel) problems in front of anyone.

_____ **44.** Let us help you choose the right tie to (A. complement, B. compliment) your look.

_____ **45.** The repairman's whistling (A. aggravated, B. irritated) all of us in accounting.

_____ **46.** The bank agreed to (A. loan, B. lend) the Smiths $20,000 for their start-up.

_____ **47.** The credit card company is (A. liable, B. likely) to increase your interest rate if you miss a payment.

_____ **48.** The airline tries to (A. accommodate, B. accomodate) disabled passengers.

_____ **49.** Every company needs a policy regarding sexual (A. harrassment, B. harassment).

_____ **50.** Use your best (A. judgment, B. judgement) in selecting a service provider.

Assessment of English Skills

In the space provided, record the number of questions you answered incorrectly.

Questions	Skills Area	Number of Incorrect Answers
1–5	Parts of speech	_____
6–15	Usage	_____
16–20	Sentence structure	_____
21–30	Punctuation	_____
31–40	Mechanics	_____
41–50	Vocabulary	_____

If you had more than two incorrect answers in any of the skills areas, focus on those areas in the appropriate sections of this handbook.

Essentials of Grammar, Mechanics, and Usage

The following sentence looks innocent, but is it really?

> We sell tuxedos as well as rent.

You sell tuxedos, but it's highly unlikely that you sell rent—which is what this sentence says. Whatever you're selling, some people will ignore your message because of a blunder like this. The following sentence has a similar problem:

> Vice President Eldon Neale told his chief engineer that he would no longer be with Avix, Inc., as of June 30.

Is Eldon or the engineer leaving? No matter which side the facts are on, the sentence can be read the other way. Now look at this sentence:

> The year before we budgeted more for advertising sales were up.

Confused? Perhaps this is what the writer meant:

> The year before, we budgeted more for advertising. Sales were up.

Or maybe the writer meant this:

> The year before we budgeted more for advertising, sales were up.

These examples show that even short, simple sentences can be misunderstood because of errors on the part of the writer. As you've learned in numerous courses over your schooling, an English sentence consists of the parts of speech being combined with punctuation, mechanics, and vocabulary to convey meaning. Making a point of brushing up on your grammar, punctuation, mechanics, and vocabulary skills will help ensure that you create clear, effective business messages.

1.0 Grammar

Grammar is the study of how words come together to form sentences. Categorized by meaning, form, and function, English words fall into various parts of speech: nouns, pronouns, verbs, adjectives, adverbs, prepositions, conjunctions, articles, and interjections. You will communicate more clearly if you understand how each of these parts of speech operates in a sentence.

1.1 NOUNS

A **noun** names a person, a place, a thing, or an idea. Anything you can see or detect with one of your senses has a noun to name it. Some things you can't see or sense are also nouns—ions, for example, or space. So are things that exist as ideas, such as accuracy and height. (You can see that something is accurate or that a building is tall, but you can't see the idea of accuracy or the idea of height.) These names for ideas are known as abstract nouns. The simplest nouns are the names of things you can see or touch: *car, building, cloud, brick*; these are termed concrete nouns. A few nouns, such as *algorithm, software,* and *code,* are difficult to categorize as either abstract or concrete but can reasonably be considered concrete even though they don't have a physical presence.

1.1.1 Proper Nouns and Common Nouns

So far, all the examples of nouns have been common nouns, referring to general classes of things. The word *building* refers to a whole class of structures. Common nouns such as *building* are not capitalized.

If you want to talk about one particular building, however, you might refer to the Glazier Building. The name is capitalized, indicating that *Glazier Building* is a proper noun.

Here are three sets of common and proper nouns for comparison:

Common	Proper
city	Kansas City
company	Blaisden Company
store	Books Galore

1.1.2 Nouns as Subject and Object

Nouns may be used in sentences as subjects or objects. That is, the person, place, thing, or idea that is being or doing (subject) is represented by a noun. So is the person, place, idea, or thing that is being acted on (object). In the following sentence, the nouns are underlined:

The <u>web designer</u> created the <u>homepage</u>.

The web designer (subject) is acting in a way that affects the homepage (object). The following sentence is more complicated:

The <u>installer</u> delivered the <u>carpet</u> to the <u>customer</u>.

Installer is the subject. *Carpet* is the object of the main part of the sentence (acted on by the installer), and *customer* is the

object of the phrase *to the customer*. Nevertheless, both *carpet* and *customer* are objects.

1.1.3 Plural Nouns

Nouns can be either singular or plural. The usual way to make a plural noun is to add *s* or *es* to the singular form of the word:

Singular	Plural
file	files
tax	taxes
cargo	cargoes

Many nouns have other ways of forming the plural. Some plurals involve a change in a vowel (*mouse/mice, goose/geese, woman/women*), the addition of *en* or *ren* (*ox/oxen, child/children*), the change from *y* to *ies* (*city/cities, specialty/specialties*), or the change from *f* to *v* (*knife/knives, half/halves*; some exceptions: *fifes, roofs*). Some words of Latin origin offer a choice of plurals (*phenomena/phenomenons, indexes/indices, appendixes/appendices*). It's always a good idea to consult a dictionary if you are unsure of the correct or preferred plural spelling of a word.

The plurals of compound nouns are usually formed by adding *s* or *es* to the main word of the compound (*fathers-in-law, editors-in-chief, attorneys-at-law*).

Some nouns are the same whether singular or plural (*sleep, deer, moose*). Some nouns are plural in form but singular in use (*ethics, measles*). Some nouns are used in the plural only (*scissors, trousers*).

Letters, numbers, and words used as words are sometimes made plural by adding an apostrophe and an *s* (*A's, Ph.D.'s, I's*). However, if no confusion would be created by leaving off the apostrophe, it is common practice to just add the *s* (*1990s, RFPs, DVDs*).

1.1.4 Possessive Nouns

A noun becomes possessive when it's used to show the ownership of something. Then you add *'s* to the word:

the man's car	the woman's apartment

However, ownership does not need to be legal:

the secretary's desk	the company's assets

Also, ownership may be nothing more than an automatic association:

a day's work	the job's prestige

An exception to the rule about adding *'s* to make a noun possessive occurs when the word is singular and already has two "s" sounds at the end. In cases like the following, an apostrophe is all that's needed:

crisis' dimensions	Mr. Moses' application

When the noun has only one "s" sound at the end, however, retain the 's:

Chris's book	Carolyn Nuss's office

With compound (hyphenated) nouns, add 's to the last word:

Compound Noun	Possessive Noun
mother-in-law	mother-in-law's
mayor-elect	mayor-elect's

To form the possessive of plural nouns, just begin by following the same rule as with singular nouns: add 's. However, if the plural noun already ends in an s (as most do), drop the one you've added, leaving only the apostrophe:

the clients' complaints	employees' benefits

To denote joint possession by two or more proper nouns, add the 's to the last name only (*Moody, Nation,* and *Smith's* ad agency). To denote individual possession by two or more persons, add an 's to each proper noun (*Moody's, Nation's,* and *Smith's* ad agencies).

1.1.5 Collective Nouns

Collective nouns encompass a group of people or objects: *crowd, jury, committee, team, audience, family, couple, herd, class.* They are often treated as singular nouns. (For more on collective nouns, see Section 1.3.4, Subject–Verb Agreement.)

1.2 PRONOUNS

A **pronoun** is a word that stands for a noun; it saves repeating the noun:

> Employees have some choice of weeks for vacation, but *they* must notify the HR office of *their* preference by March 1.

The pronouns *they* and *their* stand in for the noun *employees.* The noun that a pronoun stands for is called the **antecedent** of the pronoun; *employees* is the antecedent of *they* and *their.*

When the antecedent is plural, the pronoun that stands in for it has to be plural; *they* and *their* are plural pronouns because *employees* is plural. Likewise, when the antecedent is singular, the pronoun has to be singular:

> We thought the contract had expired, but we soon learned that *it* had not.

However, you should be aware that expectations are changing regarding the use of *they* (and its variants *their, them,* and *themselves*) as singular pronouns, and these evolving expectations will be a source of uncertainty for some time to come. The problem stems from the fact that English does not have a gender-neutral singular pronoun to refer to people. In the past, many writers defaulted to *he* and its variants in order to be grammatically correct, even though doing so created situations in which the language was sexist. The solutions of using *he or she* or switching back and forth between *he* and *she* in a document can be awkward, particularly in paragraphs that require multiple pronouns based on the same antecedent.

In response to this need for a gender-neutral pronoun, many linguists and some style guides now consider it grammatically acceptable to use *they* and *their* to refer to a singular noun, as in this sentence:

> Any employee seeking a promotional opportunity must check with *their* supervisor first to make sure all performance reviews are up to date.

Using *their* in this case neatly avoids the problems of sexist and awkward language and will probably become even more widely accepted in the coming years. However, some readers still continue to view it as a grammatical error and an instance of careless writing, which creates a dilemma for business communicators.

The simplest solution is often to rewrite sentences in order to make all the affected nouns and pronouns plural:

> *All employees seeking promotional opportunities* must check with *their supervisors* first to make sure all performance reviews are up to date.

If rewriting the sentence isn't feasible, you have to decide whether using *they* or one of its variants will diminish your credibility in the eyes of your readers. Using *he or she* is still perfectly acceptable, although it can feel overly formal in some contexts.

(Note that even as the usage of *they* evolves, the rule of matching singular pronouns with singular nouns and plural pronouns with plural nouns stays intact. The change taking place is that *they* is gradually becoming both a singular and plural term, depending on context, just as *you* can be singular or plural.)

1.2.1 Multiple Antecedents

Sometimes a pronoun has a double (or even a triple) antecedent:

> Kathryn Boettcher and Luis Gutierrez went beyond their sales quotas for January.

If taken alone, *Kathryn Boettcher* is a singular antecedent. So is *Luis Gutierrez.* However, when together they are the plural antecedent of a pronoun, so the pronoun has to be plural. Thus the pronoun is *their* instead of *her* or *his.*

1.2.2 Unclear Antecedents

In some sentences, the pronoun's antecedent is unclear:

> Sandy Wright sent Jane Brougham *her* production figures for the previous year. *She* thought they were too low.

To which person does the pronoun *her* refer? Someone who knew Sandy and Jane and knew their business relationship might be able to figure out the antecedent for *her.* Even with such an advantage, however, a reader might receive the wrong meaning. Also, it would be nearly impossible for any reader to know which name is the antecedent of *she.*

The best way to clarify an ambiguous pronoun is usually to rewrite the sentence, repeating nouns when needed for clarity:

> Sandy Wright sent her production figures for the previous year to Jane Brougham. Jane thought they were too low.

The noun needs to be repeated only when the antecedent is unclear.

1.2.3 Pronoun Classes

Personal pronouns consist of *I, you, we/us, he/him, she/her, it,* and *they/them.*

Compound personal pronouns are created by adding *self* or *selves* to simple personal pronouns: *myself, ourselves, yourself, yourselves, himself, herself, itself, themselves.* Compound personal pronouns are used either *intensively,* to emphasize the identity of the noun or pronoun (I *myself* have seen the demonstration), or *reflexively,* to indicate that the subject is the receiver of his or her own action (I promised *myself* I'd finish by noon). Compound personal pronouns are used incorrectly if they appear in a sentence without their antecedent:

> Walter, Virginia, and *I* (not *myself*) are the top salespeople.
>
> You need to tell *her* (not *herself*) about the mixup.

Relative pronouns refer to nouns (or groups of words used as nouns) in the main clause and are used to introduce clauses:

> Purina is the brand *that* most dog owners purchase.

The relative pronouns are *which, who, whom, whose,* and *what.* Other words used as relative pronouns include *that, whoever, whomever, whatever,* and *whichever.*

Interrogative pronouns are those used for asking questions: *who, whom, whose, which,* and *what.*

Demonstrative pronouns point out particular persons, places, or things:

> *That* is my desk.   *This* can't be correct.

The demonstrative pronouns are *this, these, that,* and *those.*

Indefinite pronouns refer to persons or things not specifically identified. They include *anyone, someone, everyone, everybody, somebody, either, neither, one, none, all, both, each, another, any, many,* and similar words.

1.2.4 Case of Pronouns

The case of a pronoun tells whether it's acting or acted upon:

> *She* sells an average of five packages each week.

In this sentence, *she* is doing the selling. Because *she* is acting, *she* is said to be in the **nominative case.** Now consider what happens when the pronoun is acted upon:

> After six months, Ms. Browning promoted *her.*

In this sentence, the pronoun *her* is acted upon and is thus said to be in the **objective case.**

Contrast the nominative and objective pronouns in this list:

Nominative	Objective
I	me
we	us
he	him
she	her
they	them
who	whom
whoever	whomever

Objective pronouns may be used as either the object of a verb (such as *promoted*) or the object of a preposition (such as *with*):

> Rob worked with *them* until the order was filled.

In this example, *them* is the object of the preposition *with* because Rob acted upon—worked with—them. Here's a sentence with three pronouns, the first one nominative, the second the object of a verb, and the third the object of a preposition:

> *He* paid *us* as soon as the check came from *them.*

He is nominative; *us* is objective because it's the object of the verb *paid; them* is objective because it's the object of the preposition *from.*

Every writer sometimes wonders whether to use *who* or *whom*:

> (*Who, Whom*) will you hire?

Because this sentence is a question, it's difficult to see that *whom* is the object of the verb *hire*. You can figure out which pronoun to use if you rearrange the question and temporarily try *she* and *her* in place of *who* and *whom*: "Will you hire *she*?" or "Will you hire *her*?" *Her* and *whom* are both objective, so the correct choice is "Whom will you hire?" Here's a different example:

> (*Who, Whom*) logged so much travel time?

Turning the question into a statement, you get:

> He logged so much travel time.

Therefore, the correct statement is:

> Who logged so much travel time?

1.2.5 Possessive Pronouns

Possessive pronouns work like possessive nouns—they show ownership or automatic association:

her job	their preferences
his account	its equipment

However, possessive pronouns are different from possessive nouns in the way they are written. Possessive pronouns never have an apostrophe:

Possessive Noun	**Possessive Pronoun**
the woman's estate	her estate
Roger Franklin's plans	his plans
the shareholders' feelings	their feelings
the vacuum cleaner's attachments	its attachments

The word *its* is the possessive of *it*. Like all other possessive pronouns, *its* has no apostrophe. Some people confuse *its* with *it's*, the contraction of *it is*. (Contractions are discussed in Section 2.9, Apostrophes.)

1.2.6 Pronoun–Antecedent Agreement

Like nouns, pronouns can be singular or plural. Pronouns must agree in number with their antecedents—a singular antecedent requires a singular pronoun:

> The president of the board tendered *his* resignation.

Multiple antecedents require a plural pronoun:

> The members of the board tendered *their* resignations.

A pronoun referring to singular antecedents connected by *or* or *nor* should be singular:

> Neither Sean nor Terry made his quota.

But a pronoun referring to a plural and a singular antecedent connected by *or* or *nor* should be plural:

> Neither Sean nor the twins made *their* quotas.

Formal English prefers the nominative case after the linking verb *to be*:

> It is *I*.   That is *he*.

However, for general usage it's perfectly acceptable to use the more natural "It's me" and "That's him."

1.3 VERBS

A **verb** describes an action or acts as a link between a subject and words that define or describe that subject:

> They all *quit* in disgust.
>
> Working conditions were substandard.

The English language is full of **action verbs**. Here are a few you'll often run across in the business world:

verify	perform	fulfill
hire	succeed	send
leave	improve	receive
accept	develop	pay

You could undoubtedly list many more.

The most common **linking verbs** are all the forms of *to be*: I *am*, *was*, or *will be*; you *are*, *were*, or *will be*. Other words that can serve as linking verbs include *seem*, *become*, *appear*, *prove*, *look*, *remain*, *feel*, *taste*, *smell*, *sound*, *resemble*, *turn*, and *grow*:

> It *seemed* a good plan at the time.
>
> She *sounds* impressive at a meeting.
>
> The time *grows* near for us to make a decision.

These verbs link what comes before them in the sentence with what comes after; no action is involved. (See Section 1.7.5 for a fuller discussion of linking verbs.)

An **auxiliary verb** is one that helps another verb and is used for showing tense, voice, and so on. A verb with its helpers is called a **verb phrase**. Verbs used as auxiliaries include *do, did, have, may, can, must, shall, might, could, would,* and *should.*

1.3.1 Verb Tenses

English has three simple verb tenses: present, past, and future.

Present:	Our branches in Hawaii *stock* other items.
Past:	We *stocked* Purquil pens for a short time.
Future:	Rotex Tire Stores *will stock* your line of tires when you begin a program of effective national advertising.

With most verbs (the regular ones), the past tense ends in *ed*, and the future tense always has *will* or *shall* in front of it. But the present tense is more complex, depending on the subject:

	First Person	Second Person	Third Person
Singular	I stock	you stock	he/she/it stocks
Plural	we stock	you stock	they stock

The basic form, *stock*, takes an additional *s* when *he, she,* or *it* precedes it. (See Section 1.3.4 for more on subject–verb agreement.)

In addition to the three simple tenses, the three **perfect tenses** are created by adding forms of the auxiliary verb *have*. The present perfect tense uses the past participle (regularly the past tense) of the main verb, *stocked*, and adds the present-tense *have* or *has* to the front of it:

(I, we, you, they) *have stocked*.

(He, she, it) *has stocked*.

The past perfect tense uses the past participle of the main verb, *stocked*, and adds the past-tense *had* to the front of it:

(I, you, he, she, it, we, they) *had* stocked.

The future perfect tense also uses the past participle of the main verb, *stocked*, but adds the future-tense *will have*:

(I, you, he, she, it, we, they) *will have* stocked.

Verbs should be kept in the same tense when the actions occur at the same time:

When the payroll checks *came in*, everyone *showed up* for work.

We *have found* that everyone *has pitched* in to help.

When the actions occur at different times, you may change tense accordingly:

The shipment *came* last Wednesday, so if another one *comes* in today, please return it.

The new employee *had been* ill at ease, but now she *has become* a full-fledged member of the team.

1.3.2 Irregular Verbs

Many verbs don't follow some of the standard patterns for verb tenses. The most irregular of these verbs is *to be*:

Tense	Singular	Plural
Present:	I *am*	we *are*
	you *are*	you *are*
	he, she, it *is*	they *are*
Past:	I *was*	we *were*
	you *were*	you *were*
	he, she, it *was*	they *were*

The future tense of *to be* is formed in the same way that the future tense of a regular verb is formed.

The perfect tenses of *to be* are also formed as they would be for a regular verb, except that the past participle is a special form, *been*, instead of just the past tense:

Present perfect:	you have been
Past perfect:	you had been
Future perfect:	you will have been

Here's a sampling of other irregular verbs:

Present	Past	Past Participle
begin	began	begun
shrink	shrank	shrunk
know	knew	known
rise	rose	risen
become	became	become
go	went	gone
do	did	done

Dictionaries list the various forms of other irregular verbs.

1.3.3 Transitive and Intransitive Verbs

Many people are confused by three particular sets of verbs:

lie/lay	sit/set	rise/raise

Using these verbs correctly is much easier when you learn the difference between transitive and intransitive verbs.

Transitive verbs require a receiver; they "transfer" their action to an object. **Intransitive verbs** do not have a receiver for their action. Some intransitive verbs are complete in themselves and need no help from other words (prices *dropped*; we *won*). Other intransitive words must be "completed" by a noun or adjective called a **complement**. Complements occur with linking verbs.

Here are some sample uses of transitive and intransitive verbs:

Intransitive	Transitive
We should include in our new offices a place to *lie* down for a nap.	The workers will be here on Monday to *lay* new carpeting.
Even the way an interviewee *sits* is important.	That crate is full of stemware, so *set* it down carefully.
Salaries at Compu-Link, Inc., *rise* swiftly.	They *raise* their level of production every year.

The workers *lay* carpeting, you *set down* the crate, they *raise* production; each action is transferred to something. In the intransitive sentences, a person *lies down*, an interviewee *sits*, and salaries *rise* without affecting anything else. Intransitive sentences are complete with only a subject and a verb; transitive sentences are not complete unless they also include an object or something to transfer the action to.

Tenses are a confusing element of the *lie/lay* problem:

Present	Past	Past Participle
I *lie*	I *lay*	I *have lain*
I *lay* (something down)	I *laid* (something down)	I *have laid* (something down)

The past tense of *lie* and the present tense of *lay* look and sound alike, even though they're different verbs.

1.3.4 Subject–Verb Agreement

Whether regular or irregular, every verb must agree with its subject, both in person (first, second, or third) and in number (singular or plural).

	First Person	**Second Person**	**Third Person**
Singular	I *am*	you *are*	he/she/it *is*
	I *write*	you *write*	he/she/it *writes*
Plural	we *are*	you *are*	they *are*
	we *write*	you *write*	they *write*

In a simple sentence, making a verb agree with its subject is a straightforward task:

Hector Ruiz *is* a strong competitor. (third-person singular)

We *write* to you every month. (first-person plural)

Confusion sometimes arises when sentences are a bit more complicated. For example, be sure to avoid agreement problems when words come between the subject and verb. In the following examples, the verb appears in italics, and its subject is underlined:

The <u>analysis</u> of existing documents *takes* a full week.

Even though *documents* is a plural, the verb is in the singular form. That's because the subject of the sentence is *analysis*, a singular noun. The phrase *of existing documents* can be disregarded. Here is another example:

The <u>answers</u> for this exercise *are* in the study guide.

Take away the phrase *for this exercise* and you are left with the plural subject *answers*. Therefore, the verb takes the plural form.

Verb agreement is also complicated when the subject is a collective noun or pronoun or when the subject may be considered either singular or plural. In such cases, you often have to analyze the surrounding sentence to determine which verb form to use:

The <u>staff</u> *is* quartered in the warehouse.

The <u>staff</u> *are* at their desks in the warehouse.

The <u>computers</u> and the <u>staff</u> *are* in the warehouse.

Neither the <u>staff</u> nor the <u>computers</u> *are* in the warehouse.

<u>Every</u> computer *is* in the warehouse.

Many a <u>computer</u> *is* in the warehouse.

Did you notice that words such as *every* use the singular verb form? In addition, when an *either/or* or a *neither/nor* phrase combines singular and plural nouns, the verb takes the form that matches the noun closest to it.

In the business world, some subjects require extra attention. Company names, for example, are considered singular and therefore take a singular verb in most cases—even if they contain plural words:

> Stater Brothers *offers* convenient grocery shopping.

In addition, quantities are sometimes considered singular and sometimes plural. If a quantity refers to a total amount, it takes a singular verb; if a quantity refers to individual, countable units, it takes a plural verb:

> Three hours *is* a long time.
>
> The eight dollars we collected for the fund are tacked on the bulletin board.

Fractions may also be singular or plural, depending on the noun that accompanies them:

> One-third of the warehouse *is* devoted to this product line.
>
> One-third of the products *are* defective.

To decide whether to use a singular or plural verb with subjects such as *number* and *variety,* follow this simple rule: If the subject is preceded by *a,* use a plural verb:

> A number of products *are* being displayed at the trade show.

If the subject is preceded by *the,* use a singular verb:

> *The* variety of products on display *is* mind-boggling.

For a related discussion, see Section 1.7.1, Longer Sentences.

1.3.5 Voice of Verbs

Verbs have two voices, active and passive. When the subject comes first, the verb is in **active voice**; when the object comes first, the verb is in **passive voice**:

> **Active:** The buyer *paid* a large amount.
>
> **Passive:** A large amount *was paid* by the buyer.

The passive voice uses a form of the verb *to be,* which adds words to a sentence. In the example, the passive-voice sentence uses eight words, whereas the active-voice sentence uses only six to say the same thing. The words *was* and *by* are unnecessary to convey the meaning of the sentence. In fact, extra words usually clog meaning. So be sure to opt for the active voice when you have a choice.

At times, however, you have no choice:

> Several items *have been taken*, but so far we don't know who took them.

The passive voice becomes necessary when you don't know (or don't want to say) who performed the action; the active voice is bolder and more direct.

1.3.6 Mood of Verbs

Verbs can express one of three moods: indicative, imperative, or subjunctive. The indicative mood is used to make a statement or to ask a question:

> The secretary mailed a letter to each supplier.
>
> Did the secretary mail a letter to each supplier?

Use the imperative mood when you wish to command or request:

> Please mail a letter to each supplier.

With the imperative mood, the subject is the understood *you.*

The subjunctive mood is used to express doubt or a wish or a condition contrary to fact:

> If I *were* you, I wouldn't send that email.

The subjunctive is also used to express a suggestion or a request:

> I asked that Rosario *be* [not *is*] present at the meeting.

1.3.7 Verbals

Verbals are verbs that are modified to function as other parts of speech. They include infinitives, gerunds, and participles.

Infinitives are formed by placing a *to* in front of the verb (*to go, to purchase, to work*). They function as nouns. Although many of us were taught that it is incorrect to split an infinitive—that is, to place an adverb between the *to* and the verb—this "rule" never had much logical linguistic basis and is no longer rigidly advocated by many contemporary language experts. In some cases, the adverb is best placed in the middle of the infinitive to avoid awkward constructions or ambiguous meaning:

> Production of steel is expected to *moderately* exceed domestic use.

Gerunds are verbals formed by adding *ing* to a verb (*going, having, working*). Like infinitives, they function as nouns. Gerunds and gerund phrases take a singular verb:

Borrowing from banks is preferable to getting venture capital.

Participles are verb forms used as adjectives. The present participle ends in *ing* and generally describes action going on at the same time as other action:

Checking the schedule, the contractor was pleased with progress on the project.

The **past participle** is usually the same form as the past tense and generally indicates completed action:

When *completed*, the project will occupy six city blocks.

The **perfect participle** is formed by adding *having* to the past participle:

Having completed the project, the contractor submitted his last invoice.

1.4 ADJECTIVES

An **adjective** modifies (tells something about) a noun or pronoun. Each of the following phrases says more about the noun or pronoun than the noun or pronoun would say alone:

an *efficient* staff   a *heavy* price
brisk trade   *light* web traffic

Adjectives modify nouns more often than they modify pronouns. When adjectives do modify pronouns, however, the sentence usually has a linking verb:

They were *attentive*.   It looked *appropriate*.
He seems *interested*.   You are *skillful*.

1.4.1 Types of Adjectives

Adjectives serve a variety of purposes. **Descriptive adjectives** express some quality belonging to the modified item (*tall, successful, green*). **Limiting** or **definitive adjectives**, on the other hand, point out the modified item or limit its meaning without expressing a quality. Types include:

- Numeral adjectives (*one, fifty, second*)
- Articles (*a, an, the*)
- Pronominal adjectives: pronouns used as adjectives (*his* desk, *each* employee)
- Demonstrative adjectives: *this, these, that, those* (*these* tires, *that* invoice)

Proper adjectives are derived from proper nouns:

Chinese customs   *Orwellian* overtones

Predicate adjectives complete the meaning of the predicate and are introduced by linking verbs:

The location is *perfect*.   Prices are *high*.

1.4.2 Comparative Degree

Most adjectives can take three forms: simple, comparative, and superlative. The simple form modifies a single noun or pronoun. Use the comparative form when comparing two items. When comparing three or more items, use the superlative form:

Simple	Comparative	Superlative
hard	harder	hardest
safe	safer	safest
dry	drier	driest

The comparative form adds *er* to the simple form, and the superlative form adds *est*. (The *y* at the end of a word changes to *i* before the *er* or *est* is added.)

A small number of adjectives are irregular, including these:

Simple	Comparative	Superlative
good	better	best
bad	worse	worst
little	less	least

When the simple form of an adjective has two or more syllables, you usually add *more* to form the comparative and *most* to form the superlative:

Simple	Comparative	Superlative
useful	more useful	most useful
exhausting	more exhausting	most exhausting
expensive	more expensive	most expensive

The most common exceptions are two-syllable adjectives that end in *y*:

Simple	Comparative	Superlative
happy	happier	happiest
costly	costlier	costliest

If you choose this option, change the *y* to *i* and tack *er* or *est* onto the end. (Note that when *more, most,* or any other adjective is used to modify another adjective, it becomes an adverb. See 1.5.2, Adverb–Adjective Confusion.)

Some adjectives cannot be used to make comparisons because they themselves indicate the extreme. For example, if something is perfect, nothing can be more perfect. If something is unique or ultimate, nothing can be more unique or more ultimate.

1.4.3 Hyphenated Adjectives

Many adjectives used in the business world are actually combinations of words: *up-to-date* report, *last-minute* effort, *fifth-floor* suite, *well-built* engine. As you can see, they are hyphenated when they come before the noun they modify. However, when such word combinations come after the noun they modify, they are not hyphenated. In the following example, the adjectives appear in italics and the nouns they modify are underlined:

> The <u>report</u> is *up to date* because of our team's *last-minute* <u>efforts</u>.

Hyphens are not used when part of the combination is a word ending in *ly* (because that word is usually not an adjective). Hyphens are also omitted from word combinations that are used so frequently that readers are used to seeing the words together and are therefore unlikely to misread them without hyphens:

> We live in a *rapidly shrinking* world.
>
> Our *highly motivated* employees will be well paid.
>
> Please consider renewing your *credit card* account.
>
> Our new intern is a *high school* student.

1.5 ADVERBS

An **adverb** modifies a verb, an adjective, or another adverb:

Modifying a verb:	Our marketing department works *efficiently*.
Modifying an adjective:	She was not dependable, although she was *highly* intelligent.
Modifying another adverb:	When signing new clients, he moved *extremely* cautiously.

An adverb can be a single word (*clearly*), a phrase (*very clearly*), or a clause (*because it was clear*).

1.5.1 Types of Adverbs

Simple adverbs are simple modifiers:

> The door opened *automatically*.
>
> The order arrived *yesterday*.
>
> Top companies were *there*.

Interrogative adverbs ask a question:

> *Where* have you been?

Conjunctive adverbs connect clauses:

> The boardroom isn't available for the meeting; *however*, the conference room should be clear.
>
> We met all our sales goals for April; *therefore*, all sales reps will get a bonus.

Words frequently used as conjunctive adverbs include *however, nevertheless, therefore, similarly, thus,* and *meanwhile.*

Negative adverbs include *not, never, seldom, rarely, scarcely, hardly,* and similar words. Negative adverbs are powerful words and therefore do not need any help in conveying a negative thought. Avoid using double negatives like these:

> I don't want no mistakes.
> (Correct: "I don't want any mistakes," or "I want no mistakes.")
>
> They couldn't hardly read the report.
> (Correct: "They could hardly read the report," or "They couldn't read the report.")
>
> They scarcely noticed neither one.
> (Correct: "They scarcely noticed either one," or "They noticed neither one.")

1.5.2 Adverb–Adjective Confusion

Many adverbs are adjectives turned into adverbs by adding *ly*: *highly, extremely, officially, closely, really.* In addition, many words can be adjectives or adverbs with no change in spelling, depending on their usage in a particular sentence:

The *early* bird gets the worm. [adjective]	We arrived *early*. [adverb]
It was a *hard* decision. [adjective]	He hit the wall *hard*. [adverb]
I enjoy *most* forms of jazz. [adjective]	My finances are my *most* important problem. [adverb]

Because of this situation, some adverbs are difficult to distinguish from adjectives. For example, in the following sentences, is the underlined word an adverb or an adjective?

> They worked <u>well</u>.
>
> The baby is <u>well</u>.

In the first sentence, *well* is an adverb modifying the verb *worked*. In the second sentence, *well* is an adjective modifying the noun *baby*. You may find it helpful to remember that a *linking verb* (such as *is* in "The baby is well") connects an adjective to the noun it modifies. In contrast, an *action verb* is modified by an adverb:

Adjective	Adverb
He is a *good* worker. (What kind of worker is he?)	He works *well*. (How does he work?)
It is a *real* computer. (What kind of computer is it?)	It *really* is a computer. (To what extent is it a computer?)
The traffic is *slow*. (What quality does the traffic have?)	The traffic moves *slowly*. (How does the traffic move?)
This food tastes *bad* without salt. (What quality does the food have?)	This food *badly* needs salt. (How much is it needed?)

1.5.3 Comparative Degree

Like adjectives, adverbs can be used to compare items. Generally, the basic adverb is combined with *more* or *most*, just as long adjectives are. However, some adverbs have one-word comparative forms:

One Item	Two Items	Three Items
quickly	more quickly	most quickly
sincerely	less sincerely	least sincerely
fast	faster	fastest
well	better	best

1.6 OTHER PARTS OF SPEECH

Nouns, pronouns, verbs, adjectives, and adverbs carry most of the meaning in a sentence. Four other parts of speech link them together in sentences: prepositions, conjunctions, articles, and interjections.

1.6.1 Prepositions

A preposition is a word or group of words that describes a relationship between other words in a sentence. A simple preposition is made up of one word: *of, in, by, above, below*. A *compound preposition* is made up of two prepositions: *out of, from among, except for, because of*.

A **prepositional phrase** is a group of words introduced by a preposition that functions as an adjective (an adjectival phrase) or as an adverb (adverbial phrase) by telling more about a pronoun, noun, or verb:

The shipment will be here *by next Friday*.

Put the mail *in the out-bin*.

Prepositional phrases should be placed as close as possible to the element they are modifying:

Shopping on the *internet* can be confusing for the uninitiated. (not Shopping can be confusing for the uninitiated on the *internet*.)

Some prepositions are closely linked with a verb. When using phrases such as *look up* and *wipe out*, keep them intact and do not insert anything between the verb and the preposition.

You may have been told that it is unacceptable to put a preposition at the end of a sentence. However, that is not a hard-and-fast rule, and trying to follow it can sometimes be a challenge. You can end a sentence with a preposition as long as the sentence sounds natural and as long as rewording the sentence would create awkward wording:

I couldn't tell what they were interested in.

What did she attribute it to?

What are you looking for?

Avoid using unnecessary prepositions. In the following examples, the prepositions in parentheses should be omitted:

All (of) the staff members were present.

I almost fell off (of) my chair with surprise.

Where was Mr. Steuben going (to)?

They couldn't help (from) wondering.

The opposite problem is failing to include a preposition when you should. Consider these two sentences:

Sales were over $100,000 for Linda and Bill.

Sales were over $100,000 for Linda and for Bill.

The first sentence indicates that Linda and Bill had combined sales over $100,000; the second, that Linda and Bill each had sales over $100,000, for a combined total in excess of $200,000. The preposition *for* is critical here.

When the same preposition can be used for two or more words in a sentence without affecting the meaning, only the last preposition is required:

We are familiar (with) and satisfied with your company's products.

But when different prepositions are normally used with the words, all the prepositions must be included:

> We are familiar with and interested in your company's products.

Some prepositions have come to be used in a particular way with certain other parts of speech. Here is a partial list of some prepositions that have come to be used with certain words:

according to	independent of
agree to (a proposal)	inferior to
agree with (a person)	plan to
buy from	prefer to
capable of	prior to
comply with	reason with
conform to	responsible for
differ from (things)	similar to
differ with (person)	talk to (without interaction)
different from	talk with (with interaction)
get from (receive)	wait for (person or thing)
get off (dismount)	wait on (like a waiter)

If you are unsure of the correct idiomatic expression, check a dictionary.

Some verb–preposition idioms vary depending on the situation: You agree *to* a proposal but *with* a person, *on* a price, or *in* principle. You argue *about* something, *with* a person, and *for* or *against* a proposition. You compare one item *to* another to show their similarities; you compare one item *with* another to show differences.

Here are some other examples of preposition usage that have given writers trouble:

among/between: *Among* is used to refer to three or more (Circulate the memo *among* the staff); *between* is used to refer to two (Put the copy machine *between* Judy and Dan).

as if/like: *As if* is used before a clause (It seems *as if* we should be doing something); *like* is used before a noun or pronoun (He seems *like* a nice guy).

have/of: *Have* is a verb used in verb phrases (They should *have* checked first); *of* is a preposition and is never used in such cases.

in/into: *In* is used to refer to a static position (The file is *in* the cabinet); *into* is used to refer to movement toward a position (Put the file *into* the cabinet).

1.6.2 Conjunctions

Conjunctions connect the parts of a sentence: words, phrases, and clauses. A **coordinating conjunction** connects two words, phrases, or clauses of equal rank. The simple coordinating conjunctions include *and, but, or, nor, for, yet,* and *so.* **Correlative conjunctions** are coordinating conjunctions used in pairs: *both/and, either/or, neither/nor, not only/but also.* Constructions with correlative conjunctions should be parallel, with the same part of speech following each element of the conjunction:

> The purchase was *not only* expensive *but also* unnecessary.
>
> The purchase *not only* was expensive *but also was* unnecessary.

Conjunctive adverbs are adverbs used to connect or show relationships between clauses. They include *however, nevertheless, consequently, moreover,* and *as a result.*

A **subordinate conjunction** connects two clauses of unequal rank; it joins a dependent (subordinate) clause to the independent clause on which it depends (for more on dependent and independent clauses, see Section 1.7.1). Subordinate conjunctions include *as, if, because, although, while, before, since, that, until, unless, when, where,* and *whether.*

1.6.3 Articles and Interjections

Only three articles exist in English: *the, a,* and *an.* These words are used, like adjectives, to specify which item you are talking about. *The* is called the *definite article* because it indicates a specific noun; *a* and *an* are called the *indefinite articles* because they are less specific about what they are referring to.

If a word begins with a vowel (soft) sound, use *an;* otherwise, use *a.* It's *a history,* not *an history, a hypothesis,* not *an hypothesis.* Use *an* with an "h" word only if it is a soft "h," as in *honor* and *hour.* Use *an* with words that are pronounced with a soft vowel sound even if they are spelled beginning with a consonant (usually in the case of abbreviations): *an SEC application, an MP3 file.* Use *a* with words that begin with vowels if they are pronounced with a hard sound: *a university, a Usenet account.*

Repeat an article if adjectives modify different nouns: *The red house and the white house are mine.* Do not repeat an article if all adjectives modify the same noun: *The red and white house is mine.*

Interjections are words that express no solid information, only emotion:

> Wow!   Well, well!
>
> Oh, no!   Good!

Such purely emotional language has its place in private life and advertising copy, but it only weakens the effect of most business writing.

1.7 SENTENCES

Sentences are constructed with the major building blocks, the parts of speech. Take, for example, this simple two-word sentence:

> Money talks.

It consists of a noun (*money*) and a verb (*talks*). When used in this way, the noun works as the first requirement for a sentence, the subject, and the verb works as the second requirement, the predicate. Without a subject (who or what does something) and a predicate (the doing of it), you have merely a collection of words, not a sentence.

1.7.1 Longer Sentences

No matter how long a sentence is, its foundation is still a subject and a predicate verb. In the following examples, the subject is underlined once, the predicate verb twice:

> <u>Marex</u> and <u>Contron</u> <u><u>enjoy</u></u> higher earnings each quarter.

Marex [and] *Contron* do something; *enjoy* is what they do.

> My <u>interview</u>, coming minutes after my freeway accident, <u><u>did</u></u> not <u><u>impress</u></u> or <u><u>move</u></u> anyone.

Interview is what did something. What did it do? It *did* [not] *impress* [or] *move*.

> In terms of usable space, a steel <u>warehouse</u>, with its extremely long span of roof unsupported by pillars, <u><u>makes</u></u> more sense.

Warehouse is what *makes*.

These three sentences demonstrate several things. First, in all three sentences, the subject and predicate verb are the "bare bones" of the sentence, the parts that carry the core idea of the sentence. When trying to find the subject and predicate verb, disregard all prepositional phrases, modifiers, conjunctions, and articles.

Second, in the third sentence, the verb is singular (*makes*) because the subject is singular (*warehouse*). Even though the plural noun *pillars* is closer to the verb, *warehouse* is the subject. So *warehouse* determines whether the verb is singular or plural. Subject and predicate must agree.

Third, the subject in the first sentence is compound (*Marex* [and] *Contron*). A compound subject, when connected by *and*, requires a plural verb (*enjoy*). Also, the second sentence shows how compound predicates can occur (*did* [not] *impress* [or] *move*).

Fourth, the second sentence incorporates a group of words—*coming minutes after my freeway accident*—containing a

form of a verb (*coming*) and a noun (*accident*). Yet, this group of words is not a complete sentence for two reasons:

- **Not all nouns are subjects:** *Accident* is not the subject of *coming*.
- **Not all verbs are predicates:** A verb that ends in *ing* can never be the predicate of a sentence (unless preceded by a form of *to be*, as in *was coming*).

Because they don't contain a subject and a predicate, the words *coming minutes after my freeway accident* (called a **phrase**) can't be written as a sentence. That is, the phrase cannot stand alone; it cannot begin with a capital letter and end with a period. So a phrase must always be just one part of a sentence.

Sometimes a sentence incorporates two or more groups of words that do contain a subject and a predicate; these word groups are called **clauses:**

> My *interview*, because it <u>came</u> minutes after my freeway accident, <u>did</u> not <u>impress</u> or <u>move</u> anyone.

The **independent clause** is the portion of the sentence that could stand alone without revision:

> My *interview* <u>did</u> not <u>impress</u> or <u>move</u> anyone.

The other part of the sentence could stand alone only by removing *because*:

> (because) *It* <u>came</u> minutes after my freeway accident.

This part of the sentence is known as a **dependent clause**; although it has a subject and a predicate (just as an independent clause does), it's linked to the main part of the sentence by a word (*because*) showing its dependence.

In summary, the two types of clauses—dependent and independent—both have a subject and a predicate. Dependent clauses, however, do not bear the main meaning of the sentence and are therefore linked to an independent clause. Nor can phrases stand alone, because they lack both a subject and a predicate. Only independent clauses can be written as sentences without revision.

1.7.2 Types of Sentences

Sentences come in four main types, depending on the extent to which they contain clauses. A **simple sentence** has one subject and one predicate; in short, it has one main independent clause:

> Boeing is the world's largest aerospace company.

A **compound sentence** consists of two independent clauses connected by a coordinating conjunction (*and, or, but,* etc.) or a semicolon:

> Airbus outsold Boeing for several years, but Boeing has recently regained the lead.

A **complex sentence** consists of an independent clause and one or more dependent clauses:

> Boeing is betting [independent clause] that airlines will begin using moderately smaller planes to fly passengers between smaller cities [dependent clause introduced by *that*].

A **compound-complex sentence** has two main clauses, at least one of which contains a subordinate (dependent clause):

> Boeing is betting [independent clause] that airlines will begin using moderately smaller planes to fly passengers between smaller cities [dependent clause], and it anticipates that new airports will be developed to meet passenger needs [independent clause].

1.7.3 Sentence Fragments

An incomplete sentence (a phrase or a dependent clause) that is written as though it were a complete sentence is called a **fragment**. Consider the following sentence fragments:

> Marilyn Sanders, having had pilferage problems in her store for the past year. Refuses to accept the results of our investigation.

This serious error can easily be corrected by putting the two fragments together:

> Marilyn Sanders, having had pilferage problems in her store for the past year, refuses to accept the results of our investigation.

The actual details of a situation will determine the best way for you to remedy a fragment problem.

The ban on fragments has one exception. Some advertising copy contains sentence fragments, written knowingly to convey a certain rhythm. However, advertising is the only area of business in which fragments are acceptable.

1.7.4 Fused Sentences and Comma Splices

Just as there can be too little in a group of words to make it a sentence, there can also be too much:

> All our mail is run through a postage meter every afternoon someone picks it up.

This example contains two sentences, not one, but the two have been blended so that it's hard to tell where one ends and the next begins. Is the mail run through a meter every afternoon? If so, the sentences should read:

> All our mail is run through a postage meter every afternoon. Someone picks it up.

Perhaps the mail is run through a meter at some other time (morning, for example) and is picked up every afternoon:

> All our mail is run through a postage meter. Every afternoon someone picks it up.

The order of words is the same in all three cases; sentence division makes all the difference. Either of the last two cases is grammatically correct. The choice depends on the facts of the situation.

Sometimes these so-called **fused sentences** have a more obvious point of separation:

> Several large orders arrived within a few days of one another, too many came in for us to process by the end of the month.

Here, the comma has been put between two independent clauses in an attempt to link them. When a lowly comma separates two complete sentences, the result is called a **comma splice**. A comma splice can be remedied in one of three ways:

- **Replace the comma with a period and capitalize the next word:** "... one another. Too many ..."
- **Replace the comma with a semicolon and do not capitalize the next word:** " ... one another; too many ... " This remedy works only when the two sentences have closely related meanings.
- **Change one of the sentences so that it becomes a phrase or a dependent clause.** This remedy often produces the best writing, but it takes more work.

The third alternative can be carried out in several ways. One is to begin the sentence with a subordinating conjunction:

> Whenever several large orders arrived within a few days of one another, too many came in for us to process by the end of the month.

Another way is to remove part of the subject or the predicate verb from one of the independent clauses, thereby creating a phrase:

> Several large orders arrived within a few days of one another, too many for us to process by the end of the month.

Finally, you can change one of the predicate verbs to its *ing* form:

> Several large orders arrived within a few days of one another, too many coming in for us to process by the end of the month.

In many cases, simply adding a coordinating conjunction can separate fused sentences or remedy a comma splice:

> You can fire them, or you can make better use of their abilities.
>
> Margaret drew up the designs, and Matt carried them out.
>
> We will have three strong months, but after that, sales will taper off.

Be careful with coordinating conjunctions: Use them only to join simple sentences that express similar ideas.

Also, because they say relatively little about the relationship between the two clauses they join, avoid using coordinating conjunctions too often: *and* is merely an addition sign; *but* is just a turn signal; *or* only points to an alternative. Subordinating conjunctions such as *because* and *whenever* tell the reader a lot more.

1.7.5 Sentences with Linking Verbs

Linking verbs were discussed briefly in the section on verbs (Section 1.3). Here, you can see more fully the way they function in a sentence. The following is a model of any sentence with a linking verb:

> A (*verb*) B.

Although words such as *seems* and *feels* can also be linking verbs, let's assume that the verb is a form of *to be*:

> A *is* B.

In such a sentence, A and B are always nouns, pronouns, or adjectives. When one is a noun and the other is a pronoun, or when both are nouns, the sentence says that one is the same as the other:

> She is president.
>
> Rachel is president.
>
> She is forceful.

Recall from Section 1.3.3 that the noun or adjective that follows the linking verb is called a *complement*. When it is a noun or noun phrase, the complement is called a *predicate nominative*; when the complement is an adjective, it is referred to as a *predicate adjective*.

1.7.6 Misplaced Modifiers

The position of a modifier in a sentence is important. The movement of *only* changes the meaning in the following sentences:

> Only we are obliged to supply those items specified in your contract.
>
> We are obliged only to supply those items specified in your contract.
>
> We are obliged to supply only those items specified in your contract.
>
> We are obliged to supply those items specified only in your contract.

In any particular set of circumstances, only one of those sentences would be accurate. The others would very likely cause problems. To prevent misunderstanding, place such modifiers as close as possible to the noun or verb they modify.

For similar reasons, whole phrases that are modifiers must be placed near the right noun or verb. Mistakes in placement create ludicrous meanings:

> Antia Information Systems bought new computer chairs for the programmers with more comfortable seats.

The anatomy of programmers is not normally a concern of business writers. Obviously, the comfort of the chairs was the issue:

> Antia Information Systems bought programmers the new computer chairs with more comfortable seats.

Here is another example:

> I asked him to file all the letters in the cabinet that had been answered.

In this ridiculous sentence, the cabinet has been answered, even though no cabinet in history is known to have asked a question. *That had been answered* is too far from *letters* and too close to *cabinet*. Here's an improvement:

> I asked him to file in the cabinet all the letters that had been answered.

The term **dangling modifier** is often used to refer to a clause or phrase that because of its position in the sentence seems to modify a word that it is not meant to modify. For instance:

> Lying motionless, coworkers rushed to Barry's aid.

Readers expect an introductory phrase to modify the subject of the main clause. But in this case it wasn't the *coworkers* who were lying motionless but rather *Barry* who was in this situation. Like this example, most instances of dangling modifiers occur at the beginning of sentences. The source of some danglers is a passive construction:

> To find the needed information, the whole book had to be read.

In such cases, switching to the active voice can usually remedy the problem:

> To find the needed information, you will need to read the whole book.

1.7.7 Parallelism

Two or more sentence elements that have the same relation to another element should be in the same form. Otherwise, the reader is forced to work harder to understand the meaning of the sentence. When a series consists of phrases or clauses, the same part of speech (preposition, gerund, etc.) should introduce them. Do not mix infinitives with participles or adjectives with nouns. Here are some examples of nonparallel elements:

> Andersen is hiring managers, programmers, and people who work in accounting. [nouns not parallel]
>
> Andersen earns income by auditing, consulting, and by bookkeeping. [prepositional phrases not parallel]
>
> Andersen's goals are to win new clients, keeping old clients happy, and finding new enterprises. [infinitive mixed with gerunds]

2.0 Punctuation

On the highway, signs tell you when to slow down or stop, where to turn, and when to merge. In similar fashion, punctuation helps readers negotiate your prose. The proper use of punctuation keeps readers from losing track of your meaning.

2.1 PERIODS

Use a period (1) to end any sentence that is not a question, (2) with certain abbreviations, and (3) as a decimal with numbers (for example, between dollars and cents in an amount of money).

2.2 QUESTION MARKS

Use a question mark after any direct question that requests an answer:

> Are you planning to enclose a check, or shall we bill you?

Don't use a question mark with commands phrased as questions for the sake of politeness:

> Will you send us a check today.

A question mark should precede quotation marks, parentheses, and brackets if it is part of the quoted or parenthetical material; otherwise, it should follow:

> This issue of *Inc.* has an article titled "What's Your Entrepreneurial IQ?"
>
> Have you read the article "Five Principles of Guerrilla Marketing"?

Do not use the question mark with indirect questions or with requests:

> Mr. Antonelli asked whether anyone had seen Nathalia lately.

Do not use a comma or a period with a question mark; the question mark takes the place of these punctuation marks.

2.3 EXCLAMATION POINTS

Use exclamation points after highly emotional language. Because business writing almost never calls for emotional language, you will seldom use exclamation points.

2.4 SEMICOLONS

Semicolons have three main uses. One is to separate two closely related independent clauses:

> The outline for the report is due within a week; the report itself is due at the end of the month.

A semicolon should also be used instead of a comma when the items in a series have commas within them:

> Our previous meetings were on November 11, 2018; February 20, 2019; and April 27, 2020.

Finally, a semicolon should be used to separate independent clauses when the second one begins with a conjunctive adverb such as *however, therefore,* or *nevertheless* or a phrase such as *for example* or *in that case:*

> Our supplier has been out of part D712 for 10 weeks; however, we have found another source that can ship the part right away.
>
> His test scores were quite low; on the other hand, he has a lot of relevant experience.

Section 4.4 provides more information on using transitional words and phrases.

Semicolons should always be placed outside parentheses:

> Events Northwest has the contract for this year's convention (August 23–28); we haven't awarded the contract for next year yet.

2.5 COLONS

Use a colon after the salutation in a business letter. You should also use a colon at the end of a sentence or phrase introducing a list or (sometimes) a quotation:

> Our study included the three most critical problems: insufficient capital, incompetent management, and inappropriate location.

A colon should not be used when the list, quotation, or idea is a direct object of the verb or preposition. This rule applies whether the list is set off or run in:

> We are able to supply
>   staples
>   wood screws
>   nails
>   toggle bolts
> This shipment includes 9 DVDs, 12 CDs, and 4 USB flash drives.

Another way you can use a colon is to separate the main clause and another sentence element when the second explains, illustrates, or amplifies the first:

> Management was unprepared for the union representatives' demands: this fact alone accounts for their arguing well into the night.

However, in contemporary usage, such clauses are frequently separated by a semicolon.

Like semicolons, colons should always be placed outside parentheses:

> He has an expensive list of new demands (none of which is covered in the purchase agreement): new carpeting, network cabling, and a new security system.

2.6 COMMAS

Commas have many uses; the most common is to separate items in a series:

> He took the job, learned it well, worked hard, and succeeded.
>
> Put paper, pencils, and paper clips on the requisition list.

Company style may dictate omitting the final comma in a series. However, if you have a choice, use the final comma; it's often necessary to prevent misunderstanding.

A second place to use a comma is between independent clauses that are joined by a coordinating conjunction (*and*, *but*, or *or*):

> She spoke to the sales staff, and he spoke to the production staff.
>
> I was advised to proceed, and I did.

A third use for the comma is to separate a dependent clause at the beginning of a sentence from an independent clause:

> Because of our lead in the market, we may be able to risk introducing a new product.

However, a dependent clause at the end of a sentence is separated from the independent clause by a comma only when the dependent clause is unnecessary to the main meaning of the sentence:

> We may be able to introduce a new product, although it may involve some risk.

A fourth use for the comma is after an introductory phrase or word:

> Starting with this amount of capital, we can survive in the red for one year.
>
> Through more careful planning, we may be able to serve more people.
>
> Yes, you may proceed as originally planned.

However, with short introductory prepositional phrases and some one-syllable words (such as *hence* and *thus*), the comma is often omitted:

> Before January 1 we must complete the inventory.
>
> Thus we may not need to hire anyone.
>
> In July we will complete the move to Tulsa.

Fifth, paired commas are used to set off nonrestrictive clauses and phrases. A **restrictive clause** is one that cannot be omitted without altering the meaning of the main clause, whereas a **nonrestrictive clause** can be:

> The *Time* magazine website, which is produced by Steve Conley, has won several design awards. [nonrestrictive: the material set off by commas could be omitted]
>
> The website that is produced by Steve Conley has won several design awards. [restrictive: no commas are used before and after *that is produced by Steve Conley* because this information is necessary to the meaning of the sentence—it specifies which website]

A sixth use for commas is to set off appositive words and phrases. (An **appositive** has the same meaning as the word it is in apposition to.) Like nonrestrictive clauses, appositives can be dropped without changing or obscuring the meaning of the sentence:

> Conley, a freelance designer, also produces the websites for several nonprofit corporations.

Seventh, commas are used between adjectives modifying the same noun (coordinate adjectives):

> She left Monday for a long, difficult recruiting trip.

To test the appropriateness of such a comma, try reversing the order of the adjectives: *a difficult, long recruiting trip.* If the order cannot be reversed, leave out the comma (*a good old friend* isn't the same as an *old good friend*). A comma should not be used when one of the adjectives is part of the noun. Compare these two phrases:

> a distinguished, well-known figure
>
> a distinguished public figure

The adjective–noun combination of *public* and *figure* has been used together so often that it has come to be considered a single thing: *public figure.* So no comma is required.

Eighth, commas are used both before and after the year in sentences that include month, day, and year:

> It will be sent by December 14, 2020, from our Cincinnati plant.

Some companies use the European style: 15 December 2018. No commas should be used in that case. Nor is a comma needed when only the month and year are present (December 2018).

Ninth, commas are used to set off a variety of parenthetical words and phrases within sentences, including state names, dates, abbreviations, transitional expressions, and contrasted elements:

> They were, in fact, prepared to submit a bid.
>
> Habermacher, Inc., went public in 1999.
>
> Our goal was increased profits, not increased market share.
>
> Service, then, is our main concern.
>
> The factory was completed in Chattanooga, Tennessee, just three weeks ago.
>
> Joanne Dubiik, M.D., has applied for a loan from First Savings.
>
> I started work here on March 1, 2003, and soon received my first promotion.

Tenth, a comma is used to separate a quotation from the rest of the sentence:

> Your warranty reads, "These conditions remain in effect for one year from date of purchase."

However, the comma is left out when the quotation as a whole is built into the structure of the sentence:

> He hurried off with an angry "Look where you're going."

Finally, a comma should be used whenever it's needed to avoid confusion or an unintended meaning. Compare the following:

> Ever since they have planned new ventures more carefully.
>
> Ever since, they have planned new ventures more carefully.

2.7 DASHES

Use dashes to surround a comment that is a sudden turn in thought:

> Membership in the IBSA—it's expensive but worth it—may be obtained by applying to our New York office.

A dash can also be used to emphasize a parenthetical word or phrase:

> Third-quarter profits—in excess of $2 million—are up sharply.

Finally, use dashes to set off a phrase that contains commas:

> All our offices—Milwaukee, New Orleans, and Phoenix—have sent representatives.

Don't confuse a dash with a hyphen. A dash separates and emphasizes words, phrases, and clauses more strongly than commas or parentheses can; a hyphen ties two words so tightly that they almost become one word.

When using a computer, use the em dash symbol. When typing a dash in email, type two hyphens with no space before, between, or after.

A second type of dash, the en dash, can be produced with computer word processing and page-layout programs. This kind of dash is shorter than the regular dash and longer than a hyphen. It is reserved almost exclusively for indicating "to" or "through" with numbers such as dates and pages: *2019–2020, pages 30–44.*

2.8 HYPHENS

Hyphens are mainly used in three ways. The first is to separate the parts of compound words beginning with such prefixes as *self-, ex-, quasi-,* and *all-*:

> self-assured   quasi-official
>
> ex-wife   all-important

However, do not use hyphens in words that have prefixes such as *pro, anti, non, re, pre, un, inter,* and *extra*:

> prolabor   nonunion
>
> antifascist   interdepartmental

Exceptions occur when (1) the prefix occurs before a proper noun or (2) the vowel at the end of the prefix is the same as the first letter of the root word:

> pro-Republican   anti-American
>
> anti-inflammatory   extra-atmospheric

When in doubt, consult your dictionary.

Hyphens are used in some types of spelled-out numbers. For instance, they are used to separate the parts of a spelled-out number from *twenty-one* to *ninety-nine* and for spelled-out fractions: *two-thirds, one-sixth* (although some style guides say not to hyphenate fractions used as nouns).

Certain compound nouns are formed by using hyphens: *secretary-treasurer, city-state.* Check your dictionary for compounds you're unsure about.

Hyphens are also used in some compound adjectives, which are adjectives made up of two or more words.

Specifically, you should use hyphens in compound adjectives that come before the noun:

> an interest-bearing account   well-informed executives

However, you need not hyphenate when the adjective follows a linking verb:

> This account is interest bearing.
>
> Their executives are well informed.

You can shorten sentences that list similar hyphenated words by dropping the common part from all but the last word:

> Check the costs of first-, second-, and third-class postage.

Finally, hyphens may be used to divide words at the end of a typed line. Such hyphenation is best avoided, but when you have to divide words at the end of a line, do so correctly (see Section 3.5). Dictionaries show how words are divided into syllables.

2.9 APOSTROPHES

Use an apostrophe in the possessive form of a noun (but not in a pronoun):

> On his desk was a reply to Bette *Ainsley's* application for the manager's position.

Apostrophes are also used in place of the missing letter(s) of a contraction:

Whole Words	Contraction
we will	we'll
do not	don't
they are	they're

2.10 QUOTATION MARKS

Use quotation marks to surround words that are repeated exactly as they were said or written:

> The collection letter ended by saying, "This is your third and final notice."

Remember: (1) When the quoted material is a complete sentence, the first word is capitalized. (2) The final comma or period goes inside the closing quotation marks.

Quotation marks are also used to set off the title of a newspaper story, magazine article, or book chapter:

> You should read "Legal Aspects of the Collection Letter" in *Today's Credit*.

Quotation marks may also be used to indicate special treatment for words or phrases, such as terms that you're using in an unusual or ironic way:

> Our management "team" spends more time squabbling than working to solve company problems.

When you are defining a word, put the definition in quotation marks:

> The abbreviation *etc.* means "and so forth."

When using quotation marks, take care to insert the closing marks as well as the opening ones.

Although periods and commas go inside any quotation marks, colons and semicolons generally go outside them. A question mark goes inside the quotation marks only if the quotation is a question:

> All that day we wondered, "Is he with us?"

If the quotation is not a question but the entire sentence is, the question mark goes outside:

> What did she mean by "You will hear from me"?

For quotes within quotes, use single quotation marks within double:

> Bonnie Schulman fired up the project team by saying, "We've all heard the doubts that this team can meet the goals outlined in '2020: The Strategic Imperative,' but I have total confidence in your ability and commitment."

Otherwise, do not use single quotation marks for anything, including titles of works—that's British style.

2.11 PARENTHESES AND BRACKETS

Use parentheses to surround comments that are entirely incidental or to supply additional information:

> Our figures do not match yours, although (if my calculations are correct) they are closer than we thought.

> Sally Wagner (no relation to our own John Wagner) was just promoted to general manager of the Detroit office.

Parentheses are used in legal documents to surround figures in arabic numerals that follow the same amount in words:

> Remittance will be one thousand two hundred dollars ($1,200).

Be careful to put punctuation marks (period, comma, and so on) outside the parentheses unless they are part of the statement in parentheses. And keep in mind that parentheses have both an opening and a closing mark; both should always be used, even when setting off listed items within text: (1), not 1).

Brackets are used for notation, comment, explanation, or correction within quoted material:

> When asked for a reason, Jackson said, "The dismissal was a carefully considered decision, with input from every member [of the board of directors]."

Brackets are also used for parenthetical material that falls within parentheses:

> Drucker's magnum opus (*Management: Tasks, Responsibilities, Practices* [Harper & Row, 1979]) has influenced generations of entrepreneurs.

2.12 ELLIPSES

Use ellipsis points, or three evenly spaced periods, to indicate that material has been left out of a direct quotation. Use them only in direct quotations and only at the point where material was left out. In the following example, the first sentence is quoted in the second:

> The Dow Jones Industrial Average fell 276.39 points, or 2.6%, during the week to 10,292.31.

> According to the *Wall Street Journal*, "The Dow Jones Industrial Average fell 276.39 points . . . to 10,292.31."

The number of dots in ellipses is not optional; always use three. Occasionally, the points of an ellipsis come at the end of a sentence, where they seem to grow a fourth dot. Don't be fooled: One of the dots is a period. Ellipsis points should always be preceded and followed by a space.

Avoid using ellipses to represent a pause in your writing; use a dash for that purpose:

> At first we had planned to leave for the conference on Wednesday—but then we changed our minds. [not *on Wednesday . . . but then*]

3.0 Mechanics

The most obvious and least tolerable mistakes that a business writer makes are probably those related to grammar and punctuation. However, a number of small details, known as writing mechanics, demonstrate the writer's polish and reflect on the company's professionalism.

When it comes to mechanics, also called *style*, many of the "rules" are not hard and fast. Publications and organizations vary in their preferred styles for capitalization, abbreviations, numbers, italics, and so on. Here, we'll try to differentiate between practices that are generally accepted and those that can vary. When you are writing materials for a specific company or organization, find out the preferred style (such as *The Chicago Manual of Style* or *Webster's Style Manual*). Otherwise, choose a respected style guide. The key to style is consistency: If you spell out the word *percent* in one part of a document, don't use the percent sign in a similar context elsewhere in the same document.

3.1 CAPITALIZATION

With capitalization, you can follow either an "up" style (when in doubt, capitalize: *Federal Government, Board of Directors*) or a "down" style (when in doubt, use lowercase: *federal government, board of directors*). The trend over the last few decades has been toward the down style. Your best bet is to get a good style manual and consult it when you have a capitalization question. Following are some rules that most style guides agree on.

Capital letters are used at the beginning of certain word groups:

- Complete sentence: Before hanging up, he said, "We'll meet here on Wednesday at noon."
- Formal statement following a colon: She has a favorite motto: Where there's a will, there's a way.
- Phrase used as sentence: Absolutely not!
- Quoted sentence embedded in another sentence: Scott said, "Nobody was here during lunch hour except me."
- List of items set off from text:

> Three preliminary steps are involved:
> Design review
> Budgeting
> Scheduling

Capitalize proper adjectives and proper nouns (the names of particular persons, places, and things):

> Darrell Greene lived in a Victorian mansion.
>
> We sent Ms. Larson an application form, informing her that not all applicants are interviewed.
>
> Let's consider opening a branch in the West, perhaps at the west end of Tucson, Arizona.
>
> As office buildings go, the Kinney Building is a pleasant setting for TDG Office Equipment.

> We are going to have to cancel our plans for hiring French and German sales reps.

Larson's name is capitalized because she is a particular applicant, whereas the general term *applicant* is left uncapitalized. Likewise, *West* is capitalized when it refers to a particular place but not when it means a direction. In the same way, *office* and *building* are not capitalized when they are general terms (common nouns), but they are capitalized when they are part of the title of a particular office or building (proper nouns). Some proper adjectives are lowercased when they are part of terms that have come into common use, such as *french fries* and *roman numerals*.

Titles within families or companies as well as professional titles may also be capitalized:

> I turned down Uncle David when he offered me a job.
>
> I wouldn't be comfortable working for one of my relatives.
>
> We've never had a president quite like President Sweeney.

People's titles are capitalized when they are used in addressing a person, especially in a formal context. They are not usually capitalized, however, when they are used merely to identify the person:

> Address the letter to Chairperson Anna Palmer.
>
> I wish to thank Chairperson Anna Palmer for her assistance.
>
> Anna Palmer, chairperson of the board, took the podium.

Also capitalize titles if they are used by themselves in addressing a person:

> Thank you, Doctor, for your donation.

Always capitalize the first word of the salutation and complimentary close of a letter:

> *Dear* Mr. Andrews: *Yours* very truly,

The names of organizations are capitalized, of course; so are the official names of their departments and divisions. However, do not use capitals when referring in general terms to a department or division, especially one in another organization:

> Route this memo to Personnel.
>
> Larry Tien was transferred to the Microchip Division.
>
> Will you be enrolled in the Psychology Department?
>
> Someone from the personnel department at EnerTech stopped by the booth.

Capitalization is unnecessary when using a word like *company, corporation,* or *university* alone:

> The corporation plans to issue 50,000 shares of common stock.

Likewise, the names of specific products are capitalized, although the names of general product types are not:

> Apple Inc.   Xerox machine
> Tide laundry detergent

When it comes to government terminology, here are some guides to capitalization: (1) Lowercase *federal* unless it is part of an agency name; (2) capitalize names of courts, departments, bureaus, offices, and agencies but lowercase such references as *the bureau* and *the department* when the full name is not used; (3) lowercase the titles of government officers unless they precede a specific person's name: *the secretary of state, the senator, the ambassador, the governor, and the mayor* but *Mayor Gonzalez* (Note: style guides vary on whether to capitalize *president* when referring to the president of the United States without including the person's name); (4) capitalize the names of laws and acts: *the Sherman Antitrust Act, the Civil Rights Act*; (5) capitalize the names of political parties but lowercase the word *party: Democratic party, Libertarian party.*

When writing about two or more geographic features of the same type, it is now accepted practice to capitalize the common noun in addition to the proper nouns, regardless of word order:

> Lakes Ontario and Huron
>
> Allegheny and Monongahela Rivers
>
> Corson and Ravenna Avenues

The names of languages, races, and ethnic groups are capitalized: Japanese, Caucasian, Hispanic. But racial terms that denote only skin color are not capitalized: black, white.

When referring to the titles of books, articles, magazines, newspapers, reports, movies, and so on, you should capitalize the first and last words and all nouns, pronouns, adjectives, verbs, and adverbs, and capitalize prepositions and conjunctions with five letters or more. Except for the first and last words, do not capitalize articles:

> *Economics During the Great War*
>
> "An Investigation into the Market for Long-Distance Services"
>
> "What Successes Are Made Of"

When *the* is part of the official name of a newspaper or magazine, it should be treated this way too:

> *The Wall Street Journal*

Style guides vary in their recommendations regarding capitalization of hyphenated words in titles. A general guide is to capitalize the second word in a temporary compound (a compound that is hyphenated for grammatical reasons and not spelling reasons), such as *Law-Abiding Citizen,* but to lowercase the word if the term is always hyphenated, such as *Son-in-law*).

References to specific pages, paragraphs, lines, and the like are not capitalized: *page 73, line 3.* However, in most other numbered or lettered references, the identifying term is capitalized:

> Chapter 4   Serial No. 382-2203   Item B-11

Finally, the names of academic degrees are capitalized when they follow a person's name but are not capitalized when used in a general sense:

> I received a bachelor of science degree.
>
> Thomas Whitelaw, Doctor of Philosophy, will attend.

Similarly, general courses of study are not capitalized, but the names of specific classes are:

> She studied accounting as an undergraduate.
>
> She is enrolled in Accounting 201.

3.2 UNDERSCORES AND ITALICS

Usually a line typed underneath a word or phrase either provides emphasis or indicates the title of a book, magazine, or newspaper. If possible, use italics instead of an underscore. Italics (or underlining) should also be used for defining terms and for discussing words as words:

> In this report, *net sales* refers to after-tax sales dollars.

Also use italics to set off foreign words, unless the words have become a common part of English:

> Top Shelf is considered the *sine qua non* of comic book publishers.
>
> Chris uses a laissez-faire [no italic] management style.

3.3 ABBREVIATIONS

Abbreviations are used heavily in tables, charts, lists, and forms. They're used sparingly in prose. Here are some abbreviation situations to watch for:

- In most cases, do not use periods with acronyms (words formed from the initial letter or letters of parts of a term): *CEO, CD-ROM, DOS, YWCA, FDA*; but *Ph.D., M.A., M. D.*
- Use periods with abbreviations such as *Mr., Ms., Sr., Jr., a.m., p.m., B.C.,* and *A.D.*
- The trend is away from using periods with such units of measure as *mph, mm,* and *lb.*
- Use periods with such Latin abbreviations as *e.g., i.e., et al.,* and *etc.* However, style guides recommend that you avoid using these Latin forms and instead use their English equivalents (*for example, that is, and others,* and *and so on,* respectively). If you must use these abbreviations, such as in parenthetical expressions or footnotes, do not put them in italics.
- Some companies have abbreviations as part of their names (*&, Co., Inc., Ltd.*). When you refer to such firms by name, be sure to double-check the preferred spelling, including spacing: *AT&T; Barnes & Noble; Carson Pirie Scott & Company; PepsiCo; Kate Spade, Inc.; National Data Corporation; Siemens Corp.; Glaxo Wellcome PLC; US Airways; U.S. Business Reporter.*
- Most style guides recommend that you spell out *United States* as a noun and reserve *U.S.* as an adjective preceding the noun modified.

One way to handle an abbreviation that you want to use throughout a document is to spell it out the first time you use it, follow it with the abbreviation in parentheses, and then use the abbreviation in the remainder of the document.

3.4 NUMBERS

Numbers may be correctly handled many ways in business writing, so follow company style. In the absence of a set style, however, generally spell out all numbers from one to nine and use arabic numerals for the rest.

There are some exceptions to this general rule. For example, never begin a sentence with a numeral:

> Twenty of us produced 641 units per week in the first 12 weeks of the year.

Use numerals for the numbers one through nine if they're in the same list as larger numbers:

> Our weekly quota rose from 9 to 15 to 27.

Use numerals for percentages, time of day (except with o'clock), dates, and (in general) dollar amounts:

> Our division is responsible for 7 percent of total sales.
>
> The meeting is scheduled for 8:30 a.m. on August 2.
>
> Add $3 for postage and handling.

When using numerals for time, be consistent: It should be *between 10:00 a.m. and 4:30 p.m.,* not *between 10 a.m. and 4:30 p.m.* Expressions such as *4:00 o'clock* and *7 a.m. in the morning* are redundant.

Use a comma in numbers expressing thousands (1,257), unless your company specifies another style. When dealing with numbers in the millions and billions, combine words and figures: 7.3 million, 2 billion.

When writing dollar amounts, use a decimal point only if cents are included. In lists of two or more dollar amounts, use the decimal point either for all or for none:

> He sent two checks, one for $67.92 and one for $90.00.

When two numbers fall next to each other in a sentence, use figures for the number that is largest, most difficult to spell, or part of a physical measurement; use words for the other:

> I have learned to manage a classroom of 30 twelve-year-olds.
>
> She won a bonus for selling 24 thirty-volume sets.
>
> You'll need twenty 3-inch bolts.

In addresses, all street numbers except One are in numerals. So are suite and room numbers and zip codes. For street names that are numbered, practice varies so widely that you should use the form specified on an organization's letterhead or in a reliable directory. All the following examples are correct:

> One Fifth Avenue   297 Ninth Street
> 1839 44th Street   11026 West 78 Place

Telephone numbers are always expressed in numerals. Parentheses may separate the area code from the rest of the number, but a slash or a hyphen may be used instead, especially if the entire phone number is enclosed in parentheses:

> 382-8329   (602/382-8329)   602-382-8329

Percentages are always expressed in numerals. The word *percent* is used in most cases, but % may be used in tables, forms, and statistical writing.

Ages are usually expressed in words—except when a parenthetical reference to age follows someone's name:

> Mrs. Margaret Sanderson is seventy-two.
>
> Mrs. Margaret Sanderson, 72, swims daily.

Also, ages expressed in years and months are treated like physical measurements that combine two units of measure: *5 years, 6 months.*

Physical measurements such as distance, weight, and volume are also often expressed in numerals: *9 kilometers, 5 feet 3 inches, 7 pounds 10 ounces.*

Decimal numbers are always written in numerals. In most cases, add a zero to the left of the decimal point if the number is less than one and does not already start with a zero:

> 1.38 .07 0.2

In a series of related decimal numbers with at least one number greater than one, make sure that all numbers smaller than one have a zero to the left of the decimal point: 1.20, 0.21, 0.09.

Simple fractions are written in words, but more complicated fractions are expressed in figures or, if easier to read, in figures and words:

> two-thirds 9/32 2 hundredths

When typing ordinal numbers, such as *3rd edition* or *21st century,* your word processing program may automatically make the letters *rd* (or *st, th,* or *nd*) into a superscript. Do yourself a favor and turn that formatting function off in your "Preferences," as superscripts should not be used in regular prose or even in bibliographies.

3.5 WORD DIVISION

In general, avoid dividing words at the end of lines. When you must do so, follow these rules:

- Don't divide one-syllable words (such as *since, walked,* and *thought*), abbreviations (*mgr.*), contractions (*isn't*), or numbers expressed in numerals (*117,500*).
- Divide words between syllables, as specified in a dictionary or word-division manual.
- Make sure that at least three letters of the divided words are moved to the second line: *sin-cerely* instead of *sincere-ly.*
- Do not end a page or more than three consecutive lines with hyphens.
- Leave syllables consisting of a single vowel at the end of the first line (*impedi-ment* instead of *imped-iment*), except when the single vowel is part of a suffix such as *-able, -ible, -ical,* or *-ity* (*re-spons-ible* instead of *re-sponsi-ble*).

- Divide between double letters (*tomor-row*), except when the root word ends in double letters (*call-ing* instead of *cal-ling*).
- Wherever possible, divide hyphenated words at the hyphen only: instead of *anti-inde-pendence,* use *anti-independence.*
- Whenever possible, do not break URLs or email addresses. If you have to break a long URL or email address, do not insert a hyphen at the end of the first line. If the break happens at an interior period (e.g., after "blogs" in http://blogs.company.com), place the period at the beginning of the second line so that it isn't misinterpreted as a sentence-ending period at the end of the first line.

4.0 Vocabulary

Using the right word in the right place is a crucial skill in business communication. However, many pitfalls await the unwary.

4.1 FREQUENTLY CONFUSED WORDS

Because the following sets of words sound similar, be careful not to use one when you mean to use the other:

Word	Meaning
accede	to comply with
exceed	to go beyond
accept	to take
except	to exclude
access	admittance
excess	too much
advice	suggestion
advise	to suggest
affect	to influence
effect	a result
allot	to distribute
a lot	much or many
all ready	completely prepared
already	completed earlier
born	given birth to
borne	carried
capital	money; chief city
capitol	a government building
cite	to quote
sight	a view
site	a location

Word	Meaning
complement	complete amount; to go well with
compliment	expression of esteem; to flatter
corespondent	party in a divorce suit
correspondent	letter writer
council	a panel of people
counsel	advice; a lawyer
defer	to put off until later
differ	to be different
device	a mechanism
devise	to plan
die	to stop living; a tool
dye	to color
discreet	careful
discrete	separate
envelop	to surround
envelope	a covering for a letter
forth	forward
fourth	number four
holey	full of holes
holy	sacred
wholly	completely
human	of people
humane	kindly
incidence	frequency
incidents	events
instance	example
instants	moments
interstate	between states
intrastate	within a state
its	indicates possession
it's	contracted form of "it is"
later	afterward
latter	the second of two
lead	a metal; to guide
led	guided
lean	to rest at an angle
lien	a claim
levee	embankment
levy	tax
loath	reluctant
loathe	to hate
loose	free; not tight
lose	to mislay

Word	Meaning
material	substance
materiel	equipment
miner	mineworker
minor	underage person
moral	virtuous; a lesson
morale	sense of well-being
ordinance	law
ordnance	weapons
overdo	to do in excess
overdue	past due
peace	lack of conflict
piece	a fragment
pedal	a foot lever
peddle	to sell
persecute	to torment
prosecute	to sue
personal	private
personnel	employees
precedence	priority
precedents	previous events
principal	sum of money; chief; main
principle	general rule
rap	to knock
wrap	to cover
residence	home
residents	inhabitants
right	correct
rite	ceremony
write	to form words on a surface
role	a part to play
roll	to tumble; a list
root	part of a plant
rout	to defeat
route	a traveler's way
shear	to cut
sheer	thin, steep
stationary	immovable
stationery	paper
than	as compared with
then	at that time
their	belonging to them
there	in that place
they're	they are

Word	Meaning
to	a preposition
too	excessively; also
two	the number
waive	to set aside
wave	a swell of water; a gesture
weather	atmospheric conditions
whether	if
who's	contraction of "who is" or "who has"
whose	possessive form of "who"

In the preceding list, only enough of each word's meaning is given to help you distinguish between the words in each group. Several meanings are left out entirely. For more complete definitions, consult a dictionary.

4.2 FREQUENTLY MISUSED WORDS

The following words tend to be misused for reasons other than their sound. Reference books (including the *Random House College Dictionary*, revised edition; Follett's *Modern American Usage*; and Fowler's *Modern English Usage*) can help you with similar questions of usage:

a lot: When the writer means "many," *a lot* is always two separate words, never one.

aggravate/irritate: *Aggravate* means "to make things worse." Sitting in the smoke-filled room *aggravated* his sinus condition. *Irritate* means "to annoy." Her constant questions *irritated* [not *aggravated*] me.

anticipate/expect: *Anticipate* means "to prepare for": Macy's *anticipated* increased demand for athletic shoes in spring by ordering in November. In formal usage, it is incorrect to use *anticipate* for *expect*: I *expected* (not *anticipated*) a better response to our presentation than we actually got.

compose/comprise: The whole comprises the parts. The following usage is incorrect:

The company's distribution division is *comprised* of four departments.

In that construction, *is composed of* or *consists of* would be preferable. It might be helpful to think of *comprise* as meaning "encompasses" or "contains."

The company's distribution division *comprises* four departments.

continual/continuous: *Continual* refers to ongoing actions that have breaks:

Her *continual* complaining will accomplish little in the long run.

Continuous refers to ongoing actions without interruptions or breaks:

A *continuous* stream of paper came out of the malfunctioning printing press.

convince/persuade: One is *convinced* of a fact or that something is true; one is *persuaded* by someone else to do something. The use of *to* with *convince* is unidiomatic—you don't convince someone to do something, you persuade them to do it.

correspond with: Use this phrase when you are talking about exchanging letters. Use *correspond to* when you mean "similar to." Use either *correspond with* or *correspond to* when you mean "relate to."

dilemma/problem: Technically, a *dilemma* is a situation in which one must choose between two undesirable alternatives. It shouldn't be used when no choice is actually involved.

disinterested: This word means "fair, unbiased, having no favorites, impartial." If you mean "bored" or "not interested," use *uninterested*.

etc.: This abbreviated form of the Latin phrase *et cetera* means "and so on" or "and so forth," so it is never correct to write *and etc.* The current tendency among business writers is to use English rather than Latin.

flaunt/flout: To *flaunt* is to be ostentatious or boastful; to *flout* is to mock or scoff at.

impact: Avoid using *impact* as a verb when *influence* or *affect* is meant.

imply/infer: Both refer to hints. Their great difference lies in who is acting. The writer *implies*, the reader *infers*, sees between the lines.

its/their: Use *its* to indicate possession by a singular entity such as a company, not *their*. "HP released its quarterly results" is correct; "HP released their quarterly results" is not. (Note that in British English, companies are treated as plural entities, so "HP released their earnings" would be correct.)

lay: This word is a transitive verb. Never use it for the intransitive *lie*. (See Section 1.3.3.)

lend/loan: *Lend* is a verb; *loan* is a noun. Usage such as "Can you loan me $5?" is therefore incorrect.

less/fewer: Use *less* for uncountable quantities (such as amounts of water, air, sugar, and oil). Use *fewer* for countable quantities (such as numbers of jars, saws, words, pages, and humans). The same distinction applies to *much* and *little* (uncountable) versus *many* and *few* (countable).

liable/likely: *Liable* means "responsible for": I will hold you *liable* if this deal doesn't go through. It is incorrect to use *liable* for "possible": Anything is *likely* (not *liable*) to happen.

literally: *Literally* means "actually" or "precisely"; it is often misused to mean "almost" or "virtually." It is usually best left out entirely or replaced with *figuratively*.

many/much: See *less/fewer.*

regardless: The *less* suffix is the negative part. No word needs two negative parts, so don't add *ir* (a negative prefix) to the beginning. There is no such word as *irregardless.*

try: Always follow with *to,* never *and.*

verbal: People in the business community who are careful with language frown on those who use *verbal* to mean "spoken" or "oral." Many others do say "verbal agreement." Strictly speaking, *verbal* means "of words" and therefore includes both spoken and written words. Follow company usage in this matter.

4.3 FREQUENTLY MISSPELLED WORDS

All of us, even the world's best spellers, sometimes have to check a dictionary for the spelling of some words. People who have never memorized the spelling of commonly used words must look up so many that they grow exasperated and give up on spelling words correctly.

Don't expect perfection and don't surrender. If you can memorize the spelling of just the words listed here, you'll need the dictionary far less often and you'll write with more confidence:

absence	clientele	endorsement	negotiable
absorption	collateral	exaggerate	newsstand
accessible	committee	exceed	noticeable
accommodate	comparative	exhaust	
accumulate	competitor	existence	occurrence
achieve	concede	extraordinary	omission
advantageous	congratulations		
affiliated	connoisseur	fallacy	parallel
analyze	consensus	familiar	pastime
apparent	convenient	flexible	peaceable
appropriate	convertible	fluctuation	permanent
argument	corroborate	forty	perseverance
asphalt	criticism		persistent
assistant		gesture	personnel
asterisk	definitely	grievous	persuade
auditor	description		possesses
	desirable	haphazard	precede
bankruptcy	dilemma	harassment	predictable
believable	disappear	holiday	preferred
brilliant	disappoint		privilege
bulletin	disbursement	illegible	procedure
	discrepancy	immigrant	proceed
calendar	dissatisfied	incidentally	pronunciation
campaign	dissipate	indelible	psychology
category		independent	pursue
ceiling	eligible	indispensable	
changeable	embarrassing	insistent	questionnaire
		intermediary	
		irresistible	receive
			recommend
		jewelry	repetition
		judgment	rescind
		judicial	rhythmical
			ridiculous
		labeling	
		legitimate	salable
		leisure	secretary
		license	seize
		litigation	separate
			sincerely
		maintenance	succeed
		mathematics	suddenness
		mediocre	superintendent
		minimum	supersede
			surprise
		necessary	
		negligence	tangible

tariff

technique

tenant

truly

unanimous

until

vacillate

vacuum

vicious

4.4 TRANSITIONAL WORDS AND PHRASES

The following sentences don't communicate as well as they could because they lack a transitional word or phrase:

> Production delays are inevitable. Our current lag time in filling orders is one month.

A semicolon between the two sentences would signal a close relationship between their meanings, but it wouldn't even hint at what that relationship is. Here are the sentences again, now linked by means of a semicolon, with a space for a transitional word or phrase:

> Production delays are inevitable; _____, our current lag time in filling orders is one month.

Now read the sentence with *nevertheless* in the blank space. Then try *therefore, incidentally, in fact,* and *at any rate* in the blank. Each substitution changes the meaning of the sentence.

Here are some transitional words (conjunctive adverbs) that will help you write more clearly:

accordingly	furthermore	moreover
anyway	however	otherwise
consequently	incidentally	still
finally	likewise	therefore
	meanwhile	

The following transitional phrases are used in the same way:

as a result	in other words
for example	in the second place
in fact	on the other hand
	to the contrary

When one of these words or phrases joins two independent clauses, it should be preceded by a semicolon and followed by a comma:

> The consultant recommended a complete reorganization; moreover, she suggested that we drop several products.absence   disappoint

Answer Keys

CHAPTER 1

1. b
2. a
3. b
4. d
5. d
6. c
7. a
8. b
9. encode, decode
10. c
11. a
12. a
13. a
14. d
15. b
16. information overload
17. b
18. b
19. b
20. d
21. dilemma, lapse
22. data literacy

CHAPTER 2

1. b
2. a
3. selective
4. d
5. active listening
6. a
7. c
8. b
9. a
10. c
11. d
12. d
13. a
14. b
15. constructive
16. destructive
17. c
18. b
19. c
20. a
21. c
22. b

CHAPTER 3

1. b
2. d

3. b
4. norms
5. d
6. d
7. d
8. a
9. constructive feedback, constructive criticism
10. c
11. c
12. b
13. c
14. parliamentary procedure
15. b
16. virtual
17. d
18. a
19. b
20. c

CHAPTER 4

1. d
2. b
3. b
4. pluralism
5. b
6. d
7. ethnocentrism
8. stereotyping
9. d
10. a
11. c
12. b
13. c
14. a
15. a
16. a
17. d
18. a
19. c
20. b

CHAPTER 5

1. b
2. c
3. a
4. general purpose
5. b
6. a
7. c
8. d
9. c

10. d
11. digital, nondigital
12. d
13. a
14. b
15. d
16. direct
17. indirect
18. a
19. a

CHAPTER 6

1. a
2. b
3. a
4. d
5. b
6. c
7. c
8. passive
9. active
10. b
11. b
12. c
13. a
14. a
15. c
16. c
17. examples
18. differences, similarities
19. a
20. b
21. inverted pyramid
22. c

CHAPTER 7

1. d
2. a
3. c
4. a
5. b
6. d
7. d
8. b
9. b
10. a
11. c
12. a
13. white space
14. c
15. a
16. c

17. d
18. a
19. c

CHAPTER 8

1. b
2. teaser
3. c
4. b
5. b
6. a
7. d
8. a
9. c
10. c
11. b
12. a
13. d
14. c
15. b
16. c
17. c
18. a
19. d
20. hashtag
21. b
22. d
23. podcast channel

CHAPTER 9

1. b
2. c
3. c
4. direct
5. a
6. a
7. b
8. b
9. d
10. b
11. b
12. c
13. tweetable
14. a

CHAPTER 10

1. direct approach
2. indirect approach
3. d
4. c
5. a
6. a
7. c
8. b
9. buffer
10. c
11. whistle-blowing
12. b
13. c
14. c
15. c
16. b

17. a
18. d

CHAPTER 11

1. b
2. d
3. d
4. b
5. c
6. c
7. d
8. emotional
9. logical
10. b
11. b
12. c
13. c
14. b
15. content marketing
16. c
17. a
18. a
19. bait and switch

CHAPTER 12

1. a
2. informational
3. analytical
4. proposals
5. d
6. a
7. primary
8. secondary
9. a
10. c
11. d
12. a
13. c
14. d
15. a
16. b
17. information architecture
18. b
19. b
20. a

CHAPTER 13

1. d
2. b
3. a
4. c
5. a
6. c
7. a
8. d
9. b
10. d
11. b
12. a
13. d
14. a
15. data visualization
16. c

17. c
18. c
19. b
20. transmittal
21. synopsis
22. executive summary

CHAPTER 14

1. linear, nonlinear
2. d
3. b
4. b
5. a
6. a
7. b
8. b
9. c
10. c
11. b
12. d
13. a
14. transitions, builds
15. c
16. d
17. b
18. d
19. d
20. b
21. c
22. d
23. a
24. b

CHAPTER 15

1. b
2. quality of hire
3. b
4. b
5. b
6. chronological
7. functional
8. combination
9. a
10. a
11. b
12. a
13. a
14. b
15. c
16. c
17. c
18. c
19. plain text
20. a
21. a
22. b

CHAPTER 16

1. b
2. b
3. b
4. b
5. b

6. a	**11.** c	**16.** c
7. d	**12.** a	**17.** a
8. d	**13.** a	**18.** c
9. b	**14.** a	
10. b	**15.** c	

ANSWER KEY FOR "IMPROVE YOUR GRAMMAR, MECHANICS, AND USAGE" EXERCISES

CHAPTER 1

1-22. boss's (1.1.4)
1-23. sheep (1.1.3)
1-24. 1990s (1.1.3)
1-25. Joneses, stopwatches (1.1.3)
1-26. attorneys (1.1.3)
1-27. copies (1.1.3)
1-28. employees' (1.1.4)
1-29. sons-in-law, businesses (1.1.3, 1.1.4)
1-30. parentheses (1.1.3)
1-31. Ness's, week's (1.1.4)

CHAPTER 2

2-13. its (1.2.5)
2-14. their (1.2.5)
2-15. its (1.2.5)
2-16. their (1.2.1)
2-17. his or her (1.2.3)
2-18. his or her (1.2.3)
2-19. a, them (1.2.3, 1.2.4)
2-20. Who (1.2.4)
2-21. whom (1.2.4)
2-22. its (1.2.5)

CHAPTER 3

3-15. b (1.3.1)
3-16. b (1.3.1)
3-17. a (1.3.1)
3-18. b (1.3.5)
3-19. a (1.3.5)
3-20. a (1.3.4)
3-21. b (1.3.4)
3-22. b (1.3.4)
3-23. a (1.3.4)
3-24. b (1.3.4)

CHAPTER 4

4-14. greater (1.4.1)
4-15. perfect (1.4.1)
4-16. most interesting (1.4.1)
4-17. hardest (1.4.1)
4-18. highly placed, last-ditch (1.4.2)
4-19. top-secret (1.4.2)
4-20. 30-year-old (1.4.2)
4-21. all-out, no-holds-barred struggle (1.4)
4-22. tiny metal (1.4)
4-23. usual cheerful, prompt service (1.4)

CHAPTER 5

5-18. good (1.5)
5-19. surely (1.5)
5-20. sick (1.5)
5-21. well (1.5)
5-22. good (1.5)
5-23. faster (1.5.2)
5-24. better (1.5.2)
5-25. any (1.5.1)
5-26. ever (1.5.1)
5-27. can, any (1.5.1)

CHAPTER 6

6-86. leading (1.6.1)
6-87. off (1.6.1)
6-88. aware of (1.6.1)
6-89. to (1.6.1)
6-90. among (1.6.1)
6-91. for (1.6.1)
6-92. to (1.6.1)
6-93. from (1.6.1)
6-94. not only in (1.6.1)
6-95. into (1.6.1)

CHAPTER 7

7-87. b (1.6.2)
7-88. b (1.6.1)
7-89. a (1.6.1)
7-90. b (1.6.1)
7-91. b (1.6.1)
7-92. a (1.6.1)
7-93. a (1.6.3)
7-94. b (1.6.2)
7-95. b (1.6.3)
7-96. b (1.6.3)

CHAPTER 8

8-20. b (1.7.3)
8-21. a (1.7.2)
8-22. b (1.7.6)
8-23. a (1.7.4)
8-24. b (1.7.4)
8-25. b (1.7.6)
8-26. a (1.7.6)
8-27. b (1.7.4)
8-28. a (1.7.3)
8-29. b (1.7.2)

CHAPTER 9

9-24. c (2.6)
9-25. a (2.6)
9-26. b (2.6)
9-27. a (2.6)
9-28. b (2.6)
9-29. c (2.6)
9-30. b (2.6)
9-31. a (2.6)
9-32. c (2.6)
9-33. b (2.6)

CHAPTER 10

10-26. a (2.4)
10-27. a (2.5)
10-28. c (2.4)
10-29. a (2.5)
10-30. b (2.5)
10-31. b (2.4)
10-32. a (2.4)
10-33. c (2.4)
10-34. b (2.4)
10-35. c (2.5)

CHAPTER 11

11-27. b (2.1)
11-28. a (2.2)
11-29. b (2.1)
11-30. a (2.1)
11-31. b (2.2, 2.3)
11-32. a (2.1)
11-33. b (2.2, 2.1)
11-34. a (2.2)
11-35. b (2.2)
11-36. a (2.2, 2.3)

CHAPTER 12

12-29. b (2.7)
12-30. a (2.8)
12-31. c (2.7)
12-32. b (2.8)
12-33. a (2.7)
12-34. b (2.7)
12-35. c (2.8)
12-36. a (2.7, 2.8)
12-37. c (2.7, 2.8)
12-38. a (2.8)

CHAPTER 13

13-19. b (2.10)
13-20. b (2.11)
13-21. a (2.11)
13-22. b (2.10)
13-23. c (2.10)
13-24. a (2.11)
13-25. c (2.10, 2.12)
13-26. b (2.10)
13-27. b (2.11)
13-28. c (2.10, 2.12)

CHAPTER 14

14-16. c (3.1, 3.3)
14-17. a (3.1, 3.3)
14-18. c (3.2)
14-19. a (3.1)
14-20. c (3.3)
14-21. a (3.1, 3.2)
14-22. b (3.1, 3.3)
14-23. b (3.1, 3.3)
14-24. a (3.2)
14-25. c (3.1)

CHAPTER 15

15-14. except (4.1)
15-15. device (4.1)
15-16. loath (4.1)
15-17. who's (4.1)
15-18. a lot (4.2)
15-19. judgment (4.3)
15-20. regardless (4.2)
15-21. accommodate (4.3)
15-22. imply (4.2)
15-23. to (4.2)

CHAPTER 16

16-17. c (3.4)
16-18. a (3.4)
16-19. a (3.4)
16-20. b (3.4)
16-21. b (3.4)
16-22. a (3.4)
16-23. b (3.4)
16-24. b (3.4)
16-25. a (3.4)
16-26. c (3.4)

Brand, Organization, and Name Index

*Indicates a fictitious company used in examples or student activities.

*Indicates a fictitious company used in examples or student activities.

Subject Index